THE AMERICAN EPHEMERIS

1951 to 1960

Compiled and Programed by
Neil F. Michelsen

Published by
Astro Computing Services
129 Secor Lane
Pelham, New York 10803

Distributed by
Para Research, Inc.
964 Washington Street
Gloucester, Massachusetts 01930

International Standard Book Number: 0-917086-04-X

Published by Astro Computing Services
129 Secor Lane
Pelham, New York 10803

Printed by Nimrod Press

Distributed by Para Research, Inc.
964 Washington Street
Gloucester, Massachusetts 01930

Manufactured in the United States of America

Fitst printing, October 1976, 4,400 copies

How This Book Was Made

The ephemeris pages in this book are exactly the same as the 1951 to 1960 ephemeris pages in *The American Ephemeris 1931 to 1980 and Book of Tables.* The larger hardcover volume includes, in addition to the fifty-year ephemeris, Placidus tables of houses, time tables, interpolation tables and a section on How to Cast a Natal Horoscope. The Book of Tables section and other ephemeris decades are available in separate paperback books like this one.

The calculations for *The American Ephemeris* were performed by Astro Computing Services (ACS) on a 64-kilobyte Interdata 7/16 computer with a 10-megabyte disk auxiliary memory. The calculation procedures used by ACS are fundamentally the same as those used in producing the *American Ephemeris and Nautical Almanac,* a basic information source used by navigators and astronomers throughout the world.

The Sun ephemeris is based on the "Tables of the Motion of the Earth on its Axis and around the Sun" by Simon Newcomb, the nineteenth-century astronomer, as they appear in the *Astronomical Papers Prepared for the Use of the American Ephemeris and Nautical Almanac* (known as the APAE), *Volume XIV, Solar Coordinates.*

The Moon ephemeris is calculated directly from E. W. Brown's theory, using the system of constants adopted in 1964 by the International Astronomical Union and technically known as j=2.

The ephemeris for the true node of the Moon is calculated according to a formulation recently provided by the United States Naval Observatory. The ephemeris for Mercury and Venus is based on the APAE, Volume VI, parts 1 and 2.

The ephemeris for Mars is based on the *Provisional Ephemeris of Mars* for 1800 to 1950 and 1950 to 2000, United States Naval Observatory Circulars 90 to 95. These ephemerides are estimated to be an order of magnitude better than any previous ones.

The ephemeris for the outer planets is based on the APAE, Volume XII. The source data for all of the planets were input to the computer in the form of heliocentric equatorial rectangular coordinates for the mean equinox and equator in 1950. They were then transformed to the mean equinox and ecliptic of date, referred to the true ecliptic of date by the addition of nutation in longitude, and corrected for light time to give the apparent position of the planet.

The ephemeris and all other tables in this and related books were "dictated" by the computer directly to a Versatec 1200A printer/plotter, an entirely new kind of printout device. Instead of selecting from a limited set of type slugs to print alphanumeric characters, the Versatec prints an array of tiny dots which can be made to form any of an open-ended set of mathematical and astrological symbols as well as the usual letters and numerals. The Versatec produces camera-ready copy for photo-offset reproduction, combining the accuracy and low cost of computer printout with the flexibility and readability of conventional printing. So far as we are aware, these books are the first ever made by this process.

KEY TO THE EPHEMERIS

Planets
- ☉ Sun
- ☽ Moon
- ☊ Moon's node
- ☿ Mercury
- ♀ Venus
- ♂ Mars
- ♃ Jupiter
- ♄ Saturn
- ♅ Uranus
- ♆ Neptune
- ♇ Pluto

D Direct
R Retrograde
SD Stationary going direct
SR Stationary going retrograde

Signs
- ♈ Aries
- ♉ Taurus
- ♊ Gemini
- ♋ Cancer
- ♌ Leo
- ♍ Virgo
- ♎ Libra
- ♏ Scorpio
- ♐ Sagittarius
- ♑ Capricorn
- ♒ Aquarius
- ♓ Pisces

☉ ♒ Sun enters Aquarius

Major Aspects
- ☌ conjunction (0°)
- ⚹ sextile (60°)
- □ square (90°)
- △ trine (120°)
- ☍ opposition (180°)

Minor Aspects
- ⚼ sesquare (135°)
- ⚻ quincunx (150°)
- ⚺ semisextile (30°)
- ∠ semisquare (45°)

Aspects in Declination
- ∥ parallel
- ∦ contraparallel

Moon Phenomena
- ● new Moon
- ☽ first quarter
- ○ full
- ☾ third quarter
- Sun eclipse
- Moon eclipse

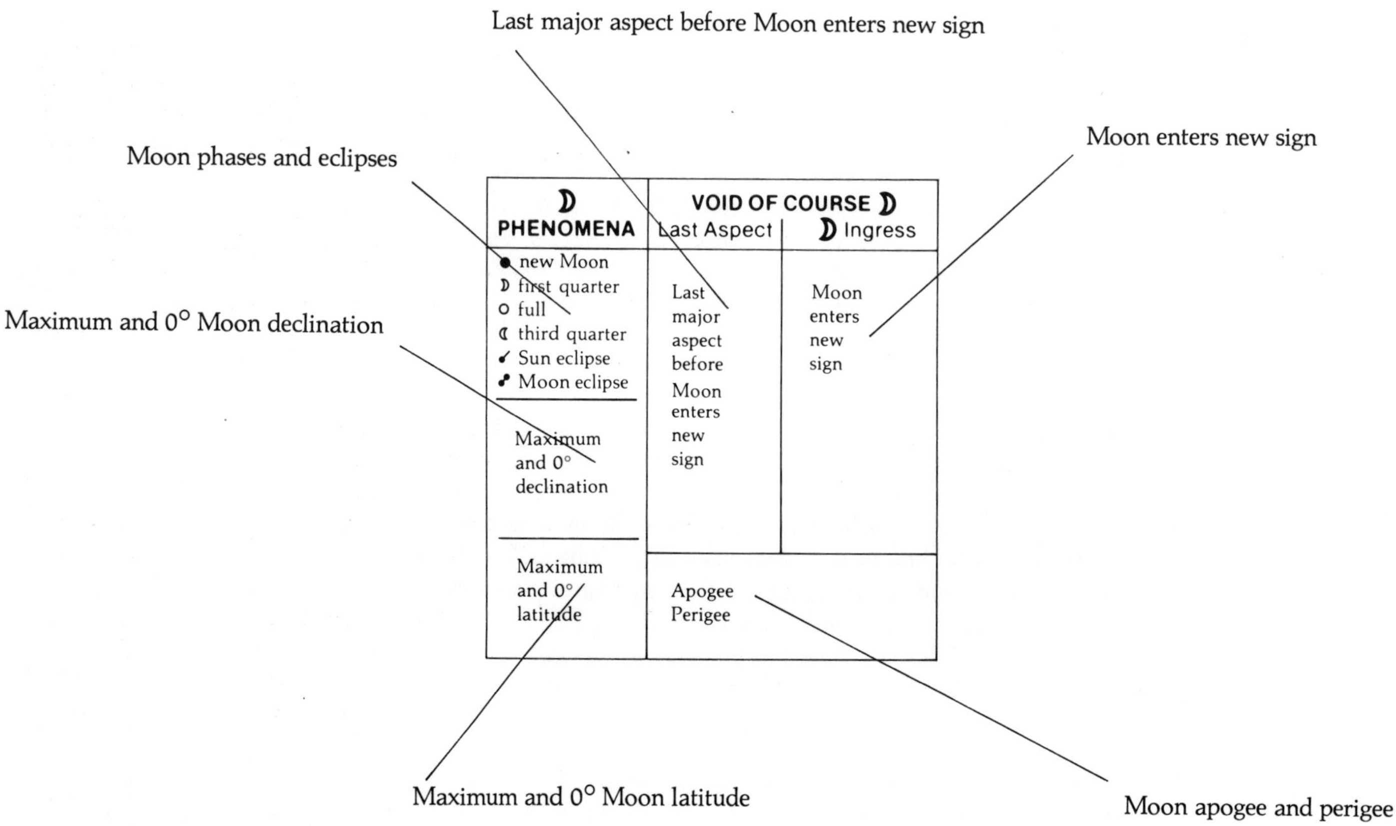

Sidereal Times are given for midnight (0h) Universal Time at 0° longitude (Greenwich).

All planetary positions are given for midnight (0h) Ephemeris Time except ☽ 12 Hour positions which are given for noon Ephemeris Time.

Aspect and Moon phenomena times are given in Ephemeris Time.

JANUARY 1951

LONGITUDE

Day	Sid. Time	☉	☽	☽ 12 Hour	Mean ☊	True ☊	☿	♀	♂	♃	♄	♅	♆	♇
	h m s	° ' "	° ' "	° ' "	° '	° '	° '	° '	° '	° '	° '	° '	° '	° '
1	6 39 21	9♑ 45 11	7♎ 3 7	13♎ 49 46	22♓ 47	21♓ 54R	11♑ 47R	21♑ 22	13♒ 2	4♓ 41	2♎ 15	7♋ 21R	19♎ 25	19♌ 29R
2	6 43 18	10 46 20	20 42 5	27 40 17	22 44	21 54	10 26	22 37	13 49	4 53	2 16	7 18	19 26	19 28
3	6 47 14	11 47 30	4♏ 44 26	11♏ 54 28	22 41	21 52	9 5	23 52	14 36	5 4	2 17	7 16	19 26	19 27
4	6 51 11	12 48 41	19 10 8	26 31 0	22 38	21 47	7 46	25 8	15 23	5 15	2 18	7 13	19 27	19 26
5	6 55 7	13 49 51	3♐ 56 25	11♐ 25 33	22 34	21 40	6 32	26 23	16 11	5 27	2 19	7 11	19 28	19 25
6	6 59 4	14 51 2	18 57 22	26 30 42	22 31	21 30	5 25	27 38	16 58	5 39	2 20	7 8	19 28	19 24
7	7 3 0	15 52 13	4♑ 4 16	11♑ 36 45	22 28	21 20	4 26	28 54	17 45	5 50	2 20	7 6	19 29	19 23
8	7 6 57	16 53 24	19 6 51	26 33 21	22 25	21 10	3 36	0♒ 9	18 32	6 2	2 21	7 3	19 29	19 22
9	7 10 53	17 54 34	3♒ 55 9	11♒ 11 20	22 22	21 1	2 57	1 24	19 20	6 14	2 21	7 1	19 30	19 21
10	7 14 50	18 55 44	18 21 11	25 24 12	22 19	20 54	2 27	2 39	20 7	6 26	2 22	6 58	19 30	19 19
11	7 18 47	19 56 54	2♓ 20 4	9♓ 8 43	22 15	20 50	2 7	3 55	20 54	6 38	2 22	6 55	19 30	19 18
12	7 22 43	20 58 3	15 50 14	22 24 51	22 12	20 48D	1 57D	5 10	21 42	6 50	2 22R	6 53	19 31	19 17
13	7 26 40	21 59 12	28 52 57	5♈ 15 1	22 9	20 48	1 56	6 25	22 29	7 3	2 22	6 51	19 31	19 16
14	7 30 36	23 0 20	11♈ 31 35	17 43 16	22 6	20 49	2 3	7 40	23 16	7 15	2 22	6 48	19 31	19 14
15	7 34 33	24 1 27	23 50 42	29 54 32	22 3	20 50R	2 18	8 56	24 3	7 27	2 21	6 46	19 31	19 13
16	7 38 29	25 2 34	5♉ 55 26	11♉ 54 2	21 59	20 49	2 39	10 11	24 51	7 40	2 21	6 43	19 32	19 12
17	7 42 26	26 3 40	17 50 57	23 46 47	21 56	20 46	3 8	11 26	25 38	7 52	2 21	6 41	19 32	19 10
18	7 46 22	27 4 45	29 42 5	5♊ 37 21	21 53	20 41	3 42	12 41	26 25	8 5	2 20	6 38	19 32	19 9
19	7 50 19	28 5 50	11♊ 33 4	17 29 39	21 50	20 34	4 22	13 56	27 12	8 18	2 19	6 36	19 32	19 8
20	7 54 16	29 6 53	23 27 26	29 26 44	21 47	20 25	5 6	15 11	28 0	8 30	2 18	6 34	19 32	19 7
21	7 58 12	0♒ 7 56	5♋ 27 51	11♋ 30 57	21 44	20 15	5 54	16 27	28 47	8 43	2 18	6 31	19 32R	19 5
22	8 2 9	1 8 59	17 36 14	23 43 49	21 40	20 5	6 47	17 42	29 34	8 56	2 17	6 29	19 32	19 4
23	8 6 5	2 10 0	29 53 43	6♌ 6 15	21 37	19 56	7 43	18 57	0♓ 21	9 9	2 15	6 27	19 32	19 2
24	8 10 2	3 11 1	12♌ 21 15	18 38 50	21 34	19 48	8 42	20 12	1 9	9 22	2 14	6 25	19 32	19 1
25	8 13 58	4 12 0	24 59 3	1♍ 21 58	21 31	19 43	9 44	21 27	1 56	9 35	2 13	6 22	19 32	19 0
26	8 17 55	5 13 0	7♍ 47 38	14 16 9	21 28	19 40D	10 49	22 42	2 43	9 49	2 11	6 20	19 32	18 58
27	8 21 52	6 13 58	20 47 38	27 22 12	21 24	19 39	11 56	23 57	3 30	10 2	2 10	6 18	19 32	18 57
28	8 25 48	7 14 56	4♎ 0 0	10♎ 41 11	21 21	19 40	13 5	25 12	4 17	10 15	2 8	6 16	19 31	18 56
29	8 29 45	8 15 53	17 25 54	24 14 20	21 18	19 41	14 16	26 27	5 5	10 29	2 6	6 14	19 31	18 54
30	8 33 41	9 16 49	1♏ 6 34	8♏ 2 41	21 15	19 42R	15 29	27 42	5 52	10 42	2 5	6 12	19 31	18 53
31	8 37 38	10♒ 17 45	15♏ 2 44	22♏ 6 37	21♓ 12	19♓ 43	16♑ 44	28♒ 57	6♓ 39	10♓ 56	2♎ 3	6♋ 10	19♎ 30	18♌ 51

DECLINATION and LATITUDE

Day	☉ Decl	☽ Decl	☽ Lat	☽ 12 Hr. Decl	☿ Decl	☿ Lat	♀ Decl	♀ Lat	♂ Decl	♂ Lat	♃ Decl	♃ Lat	♄ Decl	♄ Lat
1	23S 5	4S 1	1S20	7S12	20S33	2N22	22S53	1S 9	18S 2	1S10	10S47	1S 4	1N11	2N16
2	23 1	10 21	2 26	13 25	20 25	2 37	22 43	1 11	17 48	1 10	10 43	1 4	1 11	2 16
3	22 55	16 21	3 27	19 6	20 18	2 50	22 31	1 12	17 34	1 9	10 39	1 4	1 10	2 16
4	22 50	21 37	4 15	23 49	20 13	3 1	22 19	1 14	17 19	1 9	10 34	1 4	1 10	2 17
5	22 44	25 39	4 48	27 4	20 9	3 8	22 7	1 15	17 5	1 9	10 30	1 4	1 10	2 17
6	22 37	28 0	5 2	28 25	20 7	3 14	21 54	1 17	16 50	1 8	10 26	1 4	1 10	2 17
7	22 30	28 18	4 55	27 39	20 6	3 17	21 40	1 18	16 36	1 8	10 21	1 3	1 10	2 17
8	22 23	26 30	4 28	24 53	20 6	3 17	21 25	1 19	16 21	1 7	10 17	1 3	1 10	2 18
9	22 15	22 53	3 42	20 32	20 9	3 16	21 10	1 21	16 5	1 7	10 12	1 3	1 10	2 18
10	22 7	17 56	2 44	15 7	20 12	3 13	20 54	1 22	15 50	1 7	10 8	1 3	1 11	2 18
11	21 58	12 9	1 37	9 6	20 17	3 8	20 37	1 23	15 35	1 6	10 3	1 3	1 11	2 19
12	21 49	5 60	0 26	2 53	20 23	3 3	20 20	1 24	15 19	1 6	9 59	1 3	1 11	2 19
13	21 39	0N13	0N43	3N15	20 30	2 56	20 3	1 25	15 3	1 5	9 54	1 3	1 11	2 19
14	21 29	6 13	1 49	9 6	20 38	2 48	19 44	1 26	14 47	1 5	9 49	1 3	1 12	2 19
15	21 19	11 51	2 47	14 27	20 46	2 40	19 26	1 27	14 31	1 5	9 45	1 3	1 12	2 20
16	21 8	16 55	3 37	19 11	20 54	2 31	19 6	1 28	14 15	1 4	9 40	1 3	1 12	2 20
17	20 57	21 16	4 17	23 7	21 3	2 21	18 46	1 28	13 59	1 4	9 35	1 3	1 13	2 20
18	20 45	24 44	4 46	26 5	21 12	2 12	18 26	1 29	13 42	1 3	9 31	1 3	1 13	2 21
19	20 33	27 9	5 2	27 55	21 21	2 2	18 5	1 30	13 26	1 3	9 26	1 3	1 14	2 21
20	20 20	28 22	5 5	28 28	21 29	1 52	17 43	1 30	13 9	1 2	9 21	1 2	1 14	2 21
21	20 8	28 15	4 55	27 41	21 37	1 42	17 21	1 31	12 52	1 2	9 16	1 2	1 15	2 21
22	19 54	26 46	4 32	25 33	21 45	1 32	16 59	1 31	12 35	1 1	9 11	1 2	1 16	2 22
23	19 41	24 0	3 55	22 11	21 52	1 22	16 36	1 32	12 18	1 1	9 6	1 2	1 16	2 22
24	19 27	20 5	3 7	17 46	21 58	1 12	16 13	1 32	12 1	1 0	9 1	1 2	1 17	2 22
25	19 13	15 13	2 9	12 30	22 3	1 2	15 49	1 32	11 43	0 60	8 56	1 2	1 18	2 23
26	18 58	9 38	1 4	6 38	22 8	0 52	15 24	1 32	11 26	0 59	8 51	1 2	1 19	2 23
27	18 43	3 33	0S 6	0 25	22 12	0 43	14 60	1 32	11 8	0 59	8 46	1 2	1 20	2 23
28	18 28	2S46	1 17	5S56	22 15	0 33	14 35	1 33	10 51	0 58	8 41	1 2	1 21	2 23
29	18 12	9 4	2 25	12 8	22 17	0 24	14 9	1 32	10 33	0 58	8 36	1 2	1 21	2 24
30	17 56	15 4	3 26	17 51	22 18	0 15	13 43	1 32	10 15	0 57	8 31	1 2	1 22	2 24
31	17S40	20S25	4S16	22S44	22S18	0N 6	13S17	1S32	9S57	0S57	8S25	1S 2	1N23	2N24

Day	♅ Decl	♅ Lat	♆ Decl	♆ Lat	♇ Decl	♇ Lat
1	23N34	0N20	6S 6	1N37	23N10	8N39
5	23 35	0 20	6 7	1 37	23 12	8 39
9	23 35	0 20	6 7	1 38	23 14	8 40
13	23 36	0 20	6 8	1 38	23 17	8 41
17	23 36	0 20	6 8	1 38	23 19	8 42
21	23 37	0 20	6 8	1 38	23 21	8 43
25	23 37	0 20	6 7	1 38	23 24	8 43
29	23N38	0N20	6S 7	1N39	23N26	8N44

☽ PHENOMENA

d	h	m	
1	5	11	☾
7	20	10	●
15	0	23	☽
23	4	47	○
30	15	14	☾

d	h	° '
6	15	28S26
12	23	0
20	10	28N29
27	14	0

d	h	° '
6	4	5S 2
12	9	0
19	18	5N 6
26	22	0

VOID OF COURSE ☽

Last Aspect		☽ Ingress		
2	3am38	2	♏	3pm58
4	10am39	4	♐	5pm39
6	0am49	6	♑	5pm32
8	0am36	8	♒	5pm36
10	3am10	10	♓	7pm56
12	10am 8	13	♈	2am 6
15	0am27	15	♉	12pm11
17	6pm11	18	♊	0am36
20	9am44	20	♋	1pm 6
22	3am47	23	♌	0am12
24	4pm35	25	♍	9am26
26	6am 8	27	♎	4pm46
29	5pm28	29	♏	10pm 4

d	h	
6	13	PERIGEE
18	14	APOGEE

DAILY ASPECTARIAN

Day	Aspect	Time
1 M	☽□♅	0am32
	☉□☽	5 11
	☽□☿	7 38
	☽∥♆	7 51
	☽△♂	11 15
	☉☌☿	8pm34
	☽☌♆	9 47
	☽⚹♇	9 52
	☽⚼♃	10 33
2 T	☽∥♃	1am25
	☽□♀	3 38
	☽⚺♄	7pm51
3 W	☽△♃	0am33
	☽△♅	4 14
	☽∥♂	4 59
	☽⚹☿	6 40
	♆⚹♇	12pm12
	☉⚹☽	12 42
	☽∥☿	5 17
	☽□♂	5 25
	☽∠♄	8 56
4 Th	☽□♇	0am26
	☽⚺♆	0 28
	☽∥♀	3 33
	☽⚼♅	4 59
	☽∠☿	5 25
	☉∥☽	6 16
	☽#♇	8 26
	☽#♅	10 37
	☽⚹♀	10 39
	☿☍♅	10 43
	☉∠☽	3pm 8
	☽⚹♄	9 23
5 F	☽∠♆	0am50
	☽□♃	2 27
	☽⚺☿	3 52
	☽⚻♅	5 11
	☽∠♀	1pm 1
	☉⚺☽	4 59
	☿⚹♃	7 38
	☽⚹♂	8 40
6 S	☽△♇	0am42
	☽⚹♆	0 49
	♂⚼♄	11 16
	☽⚺♀	3pm 2
	☽□♄	9 15
	☽∠♂	9 48
7 Su	☽⚼♇	0am29
	☽☌☿	0 33
	☿⚼♇	1 26
	☽⚹♃	2 51
	☽☍♅	4 47
	☉☌☽	8pm10
	♀ ♒	9 11
	☽⚺♂	11 2
8 M	☽⚻♇	0am24
	☽□♆	0 36
	☿∠♂	1 2
	☽∠♃	3 8
	☽☌♀	7pm30
	☽#♅	8 0
	☽△♄	9 26
	☽#♇	9 59
	☽⚺☿	10 28
9 T	♂☍♇	0am23
	☉∥☽	3 30
	☽⚺♃	3 51
	♂△♆	5 3
	☽⚻♅	5 4
	☽∥♀	9 27
	☽∥☿	1pm43
	♀△♄	6 19
	☿⚺♀	9 3
	☽⚼♄	10 20
	☽∠☿	10 31
10 W	☉⚺☽	1am 3
	☽☍♇	1 38
	☽△♆	1 56
	☽☌♂	3 10
	☿□♄	5 18
	☽⚼♅	6 7
	☉⚻♇	9 4
	☽∥♂	9 25
	☉□♆	1pm31
	☽⚹☿	11 38
11 Th	☽⚻♄	0am 3
	☽⚺♀	3 2
	☽⚼♆	3 48
	☉∠☽	4 57
	☽☌♃	7 40
	☽△♅	8 2
	☽∥♃	8 23
	☿∥♀	9pm 6
	☽∥♆	11 29
12 F	♄SR	1am20
	♃△♅	4 27
	♂⚼♅	5 31
	☽⚻♇	6 15
	☽⚻♆	6 41
	☽∠♀	8 42
	☉⚹☽	10 8
	☽⚺♂	11 22
	☿SD	3pm29
	☽#♄	6 33
13 S	☉∠♃	1am38
	☽∥♄	3 49
	☽□☿	5 45
	☽☍♄	6 32
	♀⚻♅	7 49
	☽⚼♇	10 6
	♀⚺♃	2pm14
	☽□♅	2 59
	☽⚺♃	3 40
	☽⚹♀	3 48
	☽∠♂	5 20
	☽#♆	11 37
14 Su	☽#♃	2pm56
	☽△♇	2 56
	☽☍♆	3 31
	☽∠♃	9 13
15 M	☉□☽	0am23
	☽⚹♂	0 27
	☉⚺♂	3 22
	☿□♄	4 45
	☽#♂	11 40
	☽⚻♄	4pm52
	☽△☿	5 15
16 T	☽⚹♅	1am35
	☽⚹♃	3 33
	☽□♀	9 32
	☽#♀	10 44
	☉∥☿	4pm 4
	☉#☽	10 8
	☽#☿	10 39
	☽⚼♄	10 59
17 W	☽⚼☿	0am36
	☽□♇	2 41
	☽⚻♆	3 24
	☽∠♅	7 43
	☽∥♇	1pm24
	☽∥♅	3 24
	☽□♂	4 53
	☉△☽	6 11
18 Th	☽△♄	5am20
	☽⚻☿	8 34
	☽⚼♆	9 48
	☽⚺♅	2pm 1
	☿⚼♇	4 17
	☽□♃	5 17
19 F	☉⚼☽	3am25
	☽△♀	5 24
	☽⚹♇	3pm16
	☽△♆	4 7
20 S	☽△♂	9am44
	☉⚻☽	12pm23
	☽⚼♀	3 3
	☽□♄	5 42
	☉ ♒	8 53
	☽∠♇	9 16
21 Su	☽☍☿	0am57
	☽☌♅	2 6
	♆SR	5 23
	☽△♃	6 35
	♀⚼♄	4pm 4
	☿☍♅	4 19
	☽⚼♂	5 37
22 M	☽⚻♀	0am12
	☽⚺♇	2 52
	☽□♆	3 47
	☽⚼♃	12pm38
	♂ ♓	1 6
23 T	☽⚻♂	0am57
	♀☍♇	1 48
	☉△♄	2 5
	☽∥♅	2 43
	☽∥♇	4 20
	☽⚹♄	4 34
	☉☍☽	4 47
	♀△♆	11 17
	☽⚺♅	12pm37
	☽#☿	1 35
	☽⚻☿	4 23
	☽⚻♃	6 11
24 W	☉#☽	3am36
	☽∠♄	9 18
	☽☌♇	12pm41
	☽⚹♆	1 41
	☽☍♀	4 35
	☽∠♅	5 11
	☿⚹♃	7 49
	☽#♀	9 4
	♀⚼♅	10 35
	☽⚼☿	11 29
25 Th	♂⚻♄	8am22
	☽⚺♄	1pm34
	☽☍♂	1 55
	☽#♂	4 9
	☽∠♆	5 55
	☉⚻☽	6 47
	☽⚹♅	9 18
26 F	☽#♃	3am14
	☽☍♃	3 49
	☽△☿	6 8
	☽#♆	2pm 2
	☽⚺♇	8 37
	☽⚺♆	9 41
27 S	☉⚼☽	0am52
	☉⚻♅	1 32
	☽⚻♀	6 22
	☽∥♄	8 30
	☽#♄	6pm36
	☽☌♄	8 39
	☽∠♇	11 52
28 Su	☽⚻♂	0am34
	☽□♅	4 4
	☉△☽	6 19
	♂⚼♆	7 1
	☽⚻♃	11 25
	☽⚼♀	12pm16
	☽∥♆	12 40
	☽□☿	5 50
	☽∥♃	10 11
29 M	☽⚹♇	2am36
	☽☌♆	3 41
	☽⚼♂	4 58
	☽∥♂	5 28
	☽⚼♃	2pm24
	☽△♀	5 28
	☽∥♀	6 47
30 T	☽⚺♄	1am41
	☽△♂	8 44
	☽△♅	8 47
	♂△♅	9 42
	☉∥☽	11 47
	☉□☽	3pm14
	☽△♃	4 50
31 W	☽⚹☿	3am 9
	☽∠♄	3 24
	☽□♇	6 28
	☽⚺♆	7 35
	☽∥☿	9 35
	☽⚼♅	10 22
	☽#♇	4pm10
	☽#♅	5 10
	☉⚺♃	7 7
	♀ ♓	8 15

FEBRUARY 1951

LONGITUDE

Day	Sid. Time h m s	☉ ° ' "	☽ ° ' "	☽ 12 Hour ° ' "	Mean ☊ ° '	True ☊ ° '	☿ ° '	♀ ° '	♂ ° '	♃ ° '	♄ ° '	♅ ° '	♆ ° '	♇ ° '
1	8 41 34	11♒ 18 40	29♏ 14 12	6♐ 25 14	21♓ 9	19♓ 41R	18♑ 0	0♓ 12	7♓ 26	11♓ 9	2♎ 1R	6♋ 8R	19♎ 30R	18♌ 50R
2	8 45 31	12 19 35	13♐ 39 18	20 55 55	21 5	19 38	19 18	1 27	8 13	11 23	1 58	6 6	19 30	18 48
3	8 49 27	13 20 29	28 14 27	5♑ 34 10	21 2	19 34	20 37	2 41	9 0	11 36	1 56	6 4	19 29	18 47
4	8 53 24	14 21 22	12♑ 54 15	20 13 48	20 59	19 28	21 57	3 56	9 47	11 50	1 54	6 2	19 29	18 46
5	8 57 21	15 22 14	27 31 56	4♒ 47 43	20 56	19 23	23 18	5 11	10 35	12 4	1 51	6 0	19 28	18 44
6	9 1 17	16 23 4	12♒ 0 20	19 8 58	20 53	19 18	24 41	6 26	11 22	12 18	1 49	5 58	19 28	18 43
7	9 5 14	17 23 54	26 12 58	3♓ 11 48	20 50	19 15	26 5	7 41	12 9	12 31	1 46	5 57	19 27	18 41
8	9 9 10	18 24 42	10♓ 5 1	16 52 24	20 46	19 13D	27 30	8 56	12 56	12 45	1 44	5 55	19 27	18 40
9	9 13 7	19 25 29	23 33 48	0♈ 9 15	20 43	19 13	28 56	10 10	13 43	12 59	1 41	5 53	19 26	18 38
10	9 17 3	20 26 14	6♈ 38 53	13 2 57	20 40	19 14	0♒ 22	11 25	14 30	13 13	1 38	5 51	19 26	18 37
11	9 21 0	21 26 58	19 21 47	25 35 50	20 37	19 15	1 50	12 40	15 17	13 27	1 35	5 50	19 25	18 35
12	9 24 56	22 27 41	1♉ 45 35	7♉ 51 34	20 34	19 17	3 19	13 54	16 4	13 41	1 32	5 48	19 24	18 34
13	9 28 53	23 28 21	13 54 22	19 54 34	20 30	19 18R	4 48	15 9	16 51	13 55	1 29	5 47	19 23	18 32
14	9 32 50	24 29 0	25 52 48	1♊ 49 39	20 27	19 19	6 19	16 24	17 37	14 9	1 25	5 45	19 23	18 31
15	9 36 46	25 29 38	7♊ 45 45	13 41 40	20 24	19 18	7 50	17 38	18 24	14 23	1 22	5 44	19 22	18 30
16	9 40 43	26 30 14	19 38 0	25 35 15	20 21	19 16	9 23	18 53	19 11	14 38	1 19	5 43	19 21	18 28
17	9 44 39	27 30 48	1♋ 33 58	7♋ 34 34	20 18	19 14	10 56	20 7	19 58	14 52	1 15	5 41	19 20	18 27
18	9 48 36	28 31 20	13 37 30	19 43 8	20 15	19 10	12 30	21 22	20 45	15 6	1 12	5 40	19 19	18 25
19	9 52 32	29 31 51	25 51 46	2♌ 3 40	20 11	19 7	14 5	22 36	21 32	15 20	1 8	5 39	19 18	18 24
20	9 56 29	0♓ 32 20	8♌ 19 2	14 38 0	20 8	19 4	15 41	23 50	22 18	15 35	1 5	5 37	19 18	18 22
21	10 0 25	1 32 47	21 0 41	27 27 5	20 5	19 1	17 18	25 5	23 5	15 49	1 1	5 36	19 17	18 21
22	10 4 22	2 33 12	3♍ 57 12	10♍ 30 57	20 2	19 0	18 56	26 19	23 52	16 3	0 57	5 35	19 16	18 20
23	10 8 19	3 33 36	17 8 16	23 48 59	19 59	18 59D	20 35	27 33	24 38	16 18	0 53	5 34	19 15	18 18
24	10 12 15	4 33 58	0♎ 32 58	7♎ 20 1	19 56	18 59	22 14	28 48	25 25	16 32	0 49	5 33	19 14	18 17
25	10 16 12	5 34 19	14 9 57	21 2 34	19 52	19 0	23 55	0♈ 2	26 11	16 46	0 45	5 32	19 12	18 16
26	10 20 8	6 34 38	27 57 40	4♏ 55 2	19 49	19 1	25 37	1 16	26 58	17 1	0 41	5 31	19 11	18 14
27	10 24 5	7 34 56	11♏ 54 28	18 55 46	19 46	19 2	27 19	2 30	27 44	17 15	0 37	5 31	19 10	18 13
28	10 28 1	8♓ 35 12	25♏ 58 41	3♐ 3 1	19♓ 43	19♓ 3	29♒ 3	3♈ 44	28♓ 31	17♓ 30	0♎ 35	5♋ 30	19♎ 9	18♌ 11

DECLINATION and LATITUDE

Day	☉ Decl	☽ Decl	☽ Lat	☽ 12 Hr. Decl	☿ Decl	☿ Lat	♀ Decl	♀ Lat	♂ Decl	♂ Lat	♃ Decl	♃ Lat	♄ Decl	♄ Lat
1	17S23	24S43	4S51	26S21	22S16	0S 2	12S50	1S32	9S39	0S56	8S20	1S 2	1N24	2N24
2	17 6	27 33	5 9	28 18	22 14	0 11	12 23	1 32	9 21	0 56	8 15	1 2	1 26	2 25
3	16 49	28 33	5 7	28 18	22 11	0 19	11 56	1 31	9 3	0 55	8 10	1 2	1 27	2 25
4	16 32	27 33	4 45	26 19	22 6	0 27	11 29	1 31	8 45	0 55	8 5	1 2	1 28	2 25
5	16 14	24 39	4 5	22 36	22 0	0 35	11 1	1 30	8 26	0 54	7 59	1 2	1 29	2 25
6	15 56	20 13	3 9	17 34	21 53	0 42	10 33	1 30	8 8	0 54	7 54	1 2	1 30	2 26
7	15 37	14 42	2 2	11 41	21 45	0 49	10 4	1 29	7 49	0 53	7 49	1 2	1 32	2 26
8	15 19	8 33	0 50	5 23	21 35	0 56	9 35	1 28	7 31	0 52	7 43	1 2	1 33	2 26
9	14 60	2 11	0N24	0N58	21 24	1 3	9 6	1 27	7 12	0 52	7 38	1 1	1 34	2 26
10	14 41	4N 5	1 34	7 6	21 12	1 9	8 37	1 27	6 54	0 51	7 33	1 1	1 36	2 27
11	14 21	10 1	2 38	12 47	20 59	1 15	8 8	1 26	6 35	0 51	7 27	1 1	1 37	2 27
12	14 2	15 24	3 32	17 51	20 44	1 21	7 38	1 25	6 16	0 50	7 22	1 1	1 38	2 27
13	13 42	20 5	4 16	22 7	20 28	1 27	7 8	1 24	5 58	0 50	7 16	1 1	1 40	2 27
14	13 22	23 54	4 48	25 25	20 11	1 32	6 38	1 22	5 39	0 49	7 11	1 1	1 41	2 27
15	13 2	26 40	5 8	27 37	19 52	1 37	6 8	1 21	5 20	0 48	7 5	1 1	1 43	2 28
16	12 41	28 16	5 14	28 34	19 32	1 41	5 38	1 20	5 1	0 48	6 60	1 1	1 44	2 28
17	12 20	28 33	5 7	28 11	19 11	1 45	5 7	1 19	4 42	0 47	6 54	1 1	1 46	2 28
18	11 59	27 30	4 46	26 28	18 48	1 49	4 37	1 17	4 23	0 47	6 49	1 1	1 48	2 28
19	11 38	25 6	4 12	23 27	18 24	1 53	4 6	1 16	4 4	0 46	6 43	1 1	1 49	2 29
20	11 17	21 30	3 26	19 17	17 59	1 56	3 35	1 14	3 45	0 46	6 38	1 1	1 51	2 29
21	10 56	16 50	2 28	14 11	17 33	1 59	3 4	1 13	3 26	0 45	6 32	1 1	1 52	2 29
22	10 34	11 20	1 22	8 21	17 5	2 2	2 33	1 11	3 7	0 44	6 27	1 1	1 54	2 29
23	10 12	5 14	0 10	2 3	16 35	2 4	2 2	1 9	2 48	0 44	6 21	1 1	1 56	2 29
24	9 50	1S11	1S 3	4S26	16 5	2 5	1 31	1 7	2 29	0 43	6 15	1 1	1 58	2 29
25	9 28	7 39	2 15	10 49	15 33	2 7	0 59	1 6	2 10	0 43	6 10	1 1	1 59	2 30
26	9 6	13 51	3 19	16 44	14 59	2 8	0 28	1 4	1 51	0 42	6 4	1 1	2 1	2 30
27	8 44	19 25	4 13	21 50	14 25	2 8	0N 3	1 2	1 32	0 41	5 59	1 1	2 3	2 30
28	8S21	23S58	4S51	25S45	13S49	2S 8	0N34	0S60	1S13	0S41	5S53	1S 1	2N 5	2N30

Day	♅ Decl	♅ Lat	♆ Decl	♆ Lat	♇ Decl	♇ Lat
1	23N38	0N20	6S 6	1N39	23N28	8N44
5	23 38	0 20	6 6	1 39	23 30	8 44
9	23 39	0 20	6 5	1 39	23 32	8 45
13	23 39	0 20	6 3	1 40	23 34	8 45
17	23 39	0 20	6 2	1 40	23 36	8 45
21	23 39	0 20	6 0	1 40	23 38	8 45
25	23N39	0N20	5S59	1N40	23N40	8N45

☽ PHENOMENA

d	h	m	
6	7	54	●
13	20	56	☽
21	21	13	○
28	23	0	☾

d	h	° '
3	0	28S33
9	8	0
16	17	28N36
23	20	0

d	h	
2	10	5S10
8	16	0
15	23	5N14
23	3	0

VOID OF COURSE ☽

Last Aspect		☽ Ingress		
31	6am28	1	♐	1am17
2	9am38	3	♑	2am53
4	4pm20	5	♒	4am 4
6	12pm32	7	♓	6am29
9	10am57	9	♈	11am43
11	4am21	11	♉	8pm34
13	8pm56	14	♊	8am19
16	3pm 7	16	♋	8pm52
18	4pm56	19	♌	8am 1
20	8pm45	21	♍	4pm43
23	8pm34	23	♎	11pm 1
25	7pm22	26	♏	3am31
28	5am57	28	♐	6am50

d	h	
3	16	PERIGEE
15	10	APOGEE

DAILY ASPECTARIAN

1 Th	☽□♀	1am46
	☽⚹♄	4 38
	☽∠☿	6 55
	☽∠♆	8 48
	☽⚻♅	11 29
	☽□♂	2pm28
	☿⚻♇	3 10
	☽□♃	8 10
	☉⚹☽	9 38
2 F	☿□♆	3am41
	☽△♇	8 29
	☽⚹♆	9 38
	♀⚻♄	9 55
	☽⚺☿	10 13
3 S	☉∠☽	0am11
	☽□♄	6 2
	☽⚹♀	7 58
	☽⚼♇	9 4
	☽☍♅	12pm47
	☽⚹♂	6 37
	☽⚹♃	10 13
4 Su	☉⚺☽	2am33
	☽⚻♇	9 34
	♀⚼♆	10 23
	☽□♆	10 46
	☽∠♀	10 48
	☽☌☿	4pm20
	☽∠♂	8 36
	☽∠♃	11 13
5 M	☽#♅	6am12
	☽#♇	6 59
	☽△♄	7 7
	☽⚺♀	1pm51
	☽⚻♅	1 58
	♀△♅	3 19
	☽∥☿	3 33
	☽⚺♂	10 52
6 T	☽⚺♃	0am29
	☉☌☽	7 54
	☽⚼♄	8 3
	☉⚼♄	9 47
	☽☍♇	11 14
	☽△♆	12pm32
	☽⚼♅	3 3
	☉∥☽	8 0
	☽⚺☿	11 45
7 W	♂∥♃	1am27
	☽⚻♄	9 31
	☽⚼♆	2pm10
	♂☌♃	4 24
	☽△♅	4 44
	☽∥♀	7 44
	☽☌♀	9 46
8 Th	☽∥♃	3am13
	☽∥♂	4 9
	☽∠☿	4 44
	☽☌♃	4 47
	☿∠♃	5 13
	☽☌♂	5 19
	☉☍♇	5 48
	☽∥♆	9 23
	☽⚻♇	3pm10
	☉⚺☽	3 57
	☿∠♂	4 10
	☽⚻♆	4 35
9 F	☉△♆	0am17
	☽#♄	2 20
	☽⚹☿	10 57
	☽∥♄	2pm20
	☽☍♄	2 45
	☿ ♒	5 51
	☽⚼♇	6 23
	☉∠☽	9 34
	☽□♅	10 32
10 S	☽#♆	7am51
	☉⚼♅	9 43
	☽⚺♀	9 53
	☽#♂	10 37
	☽⚺♃	12pm33
	☽#♃	1 35
	☽⚺♂	3 42
	☽#♀	4 47
	☿△♄	8 1
	☽△♇	10 31
11 Su	☽☍♆	0am 6
	☉⚹☽	4 21
	☽∠♀	5pm48
	☽∠♃	5 53
	☉#☽	5 58
	♀☌♃	6 46
	☽∠♂	10 32
	☽⚻♄	11 33
12 M	☽□☿	3am28
	☽⚹♅	7 56
	♀∥♃	4pm 6
	♂∥♆	4 29
13 T	☽⚹♃	0am 2
	☽#☿	2 1
	☽⚹♀	2 46
	☽⚼♄	5 7
	☽⚹♂	6 16
	☽□♇	9 14
	☽⚻♆	10 57
	☽∠♅	1pm43
	☿⚻♅	3 16
	☉□☽	8 56
	☽∥♇	9 45
	☽∥♅	10 13
14 W	☽△♄	11am 8
	☽⚼♆	5pm 8
	☽⚺♅	7 54
15 Th	☽△☿	0am11
	♂⚻♇	2 38
	♀∥♆	4 20
	☽□♃	1pm41
	♀⚻♇	4 16
	☽⚹♇	9 39
	☽□♀	10 18
	☽□♂	11 2
	☽△♆	11 26
16 F	♂⚻♆	5am 0
	♀⚻♆	9 4
	☽⚼☿	11 0
	☉△☽	3pm 7
	♀☌♂	4 3
	☽□♄	11 23
17 S	☽∠♇	3am45
	☽☌♅	8 13
	☽⚻☿	9pm27
	☉⚼☽	11 47
18 Su	☽△♃	2am58
	☽⚺♇	9 26
	☽□♆	11 13
	☽△♂	2pm58
	☽△♀	4 56
19 M	♀∥♂	3am24
	☉⚻☽	7 45
	☽⚼♃	8 51
	☽⚹♄	10 10
	☽∥♅	10 36
	☽∥♇	10 47
	☉ ♓	11 10
	☽⚺♅	6pm51
	☽⚼♂	9 56
	☿⚺♃	10 6
20 T	☽⚼♀	1am 6
	☿⚼♄	5 36
	☉⚻♄	12pm 2
	☽⚻♃	2 3
	☽∠♄	2 39
	☽☍☿	4 1
	☽☌♇	7 1
	☽#☿	8 19
	☽⚹♆	8 45
	☽∠♅	11 14
21 W	☽⚻♂	4am 7
	☽⚻♀	8 24
	☿☍♇	3pm17
	☽⚺♄	6 30
	☉☍☽	9 13
22 Th	☽∠♆	0am34
	☽⚹♅	3 0
	☉#☽	3 20
	☿△♆	4 46
	☽#♃	7pm41
	☽#♆	9 7
	☽☍♃	10 27
	☿⚼♅	11 54
23 F	☽⚺♇	2am 6
	☽⚺♆	3 47
	♀#♄	4 23
	♅∥♇	5 9
	☽⚻☿	7 4
	☽#♂	9 40
	☽∥♄	12pm23
	☽#♀	1 7
	☽☍♂	2 18
	☉⚼♆	4 1
	☽☍♀	8 34
24 S	☽☌♄	0am29
	☽∥♀	1 6
	☽#♄	2 51
	☽∥♂	4 33
	☽∠♇	4 50
	☉⚻☽	7 41
	☽□♅	8 51
	☽⚼☿	1pm30
	☽∥♆	5 43
	☽∥♃	6 29
	☉△♅	11 12
	♀ ♈	11 27
25 Su	☽⚻♃	4am38
	☉∥☽	6 29
	☽⚹♇	7 8
	☽☌♆	8 48
	☉⚼☽	12pm 4
	♂#♄	12 17
	♀☍♄	1 20
	☽△☿	7 22
	☽⚻♂	10 11
26 M	☽∥☿	4am15
	☽⚺♄	4 41
	☽⚻♀	6 16
	☽⚼♃	7 7
	☽△♅	1pm 2
	☉△☽	4 0
27 T	☽⚼♂	1am31
	♃∥♆	4 20
	☽∠♄	6 19
	☽△♃	9 18
	☽⚼♀	10 29
	☿⚺♂	10 34
	☽□♇	10 46
	☽⚺♆	12pm24
	♀⚼♇	1 38
	☽⚼♅	2 41
	☽#♅	10 8
	☽#♇	10 19
28 W	☽△♂	4am33
	☽□☿	5 57
	☽⚹♄	7 43
	☿ ♓	1pm 5
	☽∠♆	1 51
	☽△♀	2 25
	☽⚻♅	4 8
	♀#♂	6 19
	☿⚻♄	7 47
	☉□☽	11 0

MARCH 1951

LONGITUDE

Day	Sid. Time	☉	☽	☽ 12 Hour	Mean ☊	True ☊	☿	♀	♂	♃	♄	♅	♆	♇
	h m s	° ' "	° ' "	° ' "	° '	° '	° '	° '	° '	° '	° '	° '	° '	° '
1	10 31 58	9♓ 35 27	10♐ 8 29	17♐ 14 52	19♓ 40	19♓ 3R	0♓ 48	4♈ 58	29♓ 17	17♓ 44	0♎ 29R	5♋ 29R	19♎ 8R	18♌ 10R
2	10 35 54	10 35 41	24 21 50	1♑ 29 5	19 36	19 3	2 34	6 12	0♈ 4	17 59	0 24	5 28	19 7	18 9
3	10 39 51	11 35 53	8♑ 36 15	15 43 0	19 33	19 3	4 20	7 26	0 50	18 13	0 20	5 28	19 6	18 7
4	10 43 48	12 36 3	22 48 53	29 53 29	19 30	19 2	6 8	8 40	1 36	18 28	0 16	5 27	19 4	18 6
5	10 47 44	13 36 12	6♒ 56 23	13♒ 57 8	19 27	19 1	7 57	9 54	2 23	18 42	0 11	5 27	19 3	18 5
6	10 51 41	14 36 19	20 55 17	27 50 26	19 24	19 0	9 47	11 8	3 9	18 57	0 7	5 26	19 2	18 4
7	10 55 37	15 36 25	4♓ 42 12	11♓ 30 14	19 21	19 0	11 38	12 21	3 55	19 11	0 2	5 26	19 1	18 2
8	10 59 34	16 36 29	18 14 15	24 54 2	19 17	19 0D	13 30	13 35	4 42	19 26	29♍ 58	5 25	18 59	18 1
9	11 3 30	17 36 30	1♈ 29 26	8♈ 0 21	19 14	19 0	15 23	14 49	5 28	19 40	29 53	5 25	18 58	18 0
10	11 7 27	18 36 30	14 26 48	20 48 51	19 11	19 0	17 18	16 3	6 14	19 55	29 49	5 25	18 57	17 59
11	11 11 23	19 36 28	27 6 39	3♉ 20 25	19 8	19 0R	19 13	17 16	7 0	20 9	29 44	5 24	18 55	17 57
12	11 15 20	20 36 23	9♉ 30 27	15 37 6	19 5	19 0	21 9	18 30	7 46	20 24	29 39	5 24	18 54	17 56
13	11 19 16	21 36 17	21 40 46	27 41 54	19 2	19 0	23 6	19 43	8 32	20 38	29 35	5 24	18 52	17 55
14	11 23 13	22 36 8	3♊ 41 1	9♊ 38 37	18 58	19 0	25 4	20 57	9 18	20 53	29 30	5 24D	18 51	17 54
15	11 27 10	23 35 57	15 35 17	21 31 34	18 55	19 0D	27 2	22 10	10 4	21 8	29 25	5 24	18 49	17 53
16	11 31 6	24 35 44	27 28 5	3♋ 25 23	18 52	18 59	29 1	23 23	10 50	21 22	29 21	5 24	18 48	17 52
17	11 35 3	25 35 29	9♋ 24 5	15 24 44	18 49	19 0	1♈ 0	24 37	11 36	21 37	29 16	5 24	18 47	17 51
18	11 38 59	26 35 11	21 27 55	27 34 8	18 46	19 0	3 0	25 50	12 21	21 51	29 11	5 24	18 45	17 49
19	11 42 56	27 34 52	3♌ 43 53	9♌ 57 36	18 42	19 1	4 59	27 3	13 7	22 6	29 7	5 25	18 44	17 48
20	11 46 52	28 34 30	16 15 41	22 38 26	18 39	19 2	6 59	28 16	13 53	22 20	29 2	5 25	18 42	17 47
21	11 50 49	29 34 6	29 6 6	5♍ 38 50	18 36	19 3	8 58	29 29	14 38	22 35	28 57	5 25	18 41	17 46
22	11 54 45	0♈ 33 39	12♍ 16 42	18 59 40	18 33	19 3R	10 56	0♉ 42	15 24	22 49	28 52	5 26	18 39	17 45
23	11 58 42	1 33 11	25 47 35	2♎ 40 13	18 30	19 3	12 52	1 55	16 10	23 4	28 48	5 26	18 37	17 44
24	12 2 39	2 32 40	9♎ 37 14	16 38 13	18 27	19 2	14 48	3 8	16 55	23 18	28 43	5 27	18 36	17 43
25	12 6 35	3 32 7	23 42 39	0♏ 49 57	18 23	19 1	16 41	4 21	17 41	23 32	28 38	5 27	18 34	17 42
26	12 10 32	4 31 33	7♏ 59 32	15 10 45	18 20	18 59	18 32	5 34	18 26	23 47	28 33	5 28	18 33	17 42
27	12 14 28	5 30 56	22 22 57	29 35 30	18 17	18 57	20 20	6 46	19 11	24 1	28 29	5 28	18 31	17 41
28	12 18 25	6 30 19	6♐ 47 50	13♐ 59 23	18 14	18 56	22 5	7 59	19 57	24 16	28 24	5 29	18 30	17 40
29	12 22 21	7 29 39	21 9 41	28 18 18	18 11	18 54	23 47	9 11	20 42	24 30	28 19	5 30	18 28	17 39
30	12 26 18	8 28 57	5♑ 24 53	12♑ 29 11	18 7	18 53D	25 24	10 24	21 27	24 44	28 15	5 31	18 26	17 38
31	12 30 14	9♈ 28 14	19♑ 30 57	26♑ 30 2	18♓ 4	18♓ 53	26♈ 57	11♉ 36	22♈ 13	24♓ 59	28♍ 10	5♋ 31	18♎ 25	17♌ 37

DECLINATION and LATITUDE

Day	☉ Decl	☽ Decl	☽ Lat	☽ 12 Hr. Decl	☿ Decl	☿ Lat	♀ Decl	♀ Lat	♂ Decl	♂ Lat	♃ Decl	♃ Lat	♄ Decl	♄ Lat
1	7S59	27S 8	5S13	28S 5	13S11	2S 8	1N 6	0S58	0S54	0S40	5S47	1S 1	2N 6	2N30
2	7 36	28 34	5 15	28 35	12 33	2 7	1 37	0 55	0 35	0 39	5 42	1 1	2 8	2 30
3	7 13	28 8	4 58	27 12	11 53	2 6	2 8	0 53	0 16	0 39	5 36	1 1	2 10	2 31
4	6 50	25 50	4 23	24 5	11 11	2 4	2 39	0 51	0N 3	0 38	5 30	1 1	2 12	2 31
5	6 27	21 58	3 32	19 33	10 29	2 2	3 11	0 49	0 22	0 38	5 25	1 1	2 14	2 31
6	6 4	16 53	2 29	14 1	9 45	1 59	3 42	0 46	0 41	0 37	5 19	1 1	2 16	2 31
7	5 41	11 0	1 18	7 53	8 60	1 56	4 13	0 44	1 0	0 36	5 13	1 1	2 18	2 31
8	5 17	4 43	0 4	1 32	8 13	1 53	4 44	0 41	1 19	0 36	5 8	1 1	2 20	2 31
9	4 54	1N39	1N 9	4N46	7 25	1 48	5 14	0 39	1 38	0 35	5 2	1 1	2 21	2 31
10	4 30	7 48	2 16	10 43	6 37	1 44	5 45	0 36	1 57	0 34	4 56	1 1	2 23	2 31
11	4 7	13 29	3 16	16 6	5 47	1 38	6 16	0 34	2 16	0 34	4 51	1 2	2 25	2 31
12	3 43	18 32	4 5	20 44	4 56	1 32	6 46	0 31	2 34	0 33	4 45	1 2	2 27	2 32
13	3 20	22 43	4 42	24 27	4 3	1 26	7 17	0 29	2 53	0 32	4 39	1 2	2 29	2 32
14	2 56	25 54	5 6	27 3	3 10	1 19	7 47	0 26	3 12	0 32	4 34	1 2	2 31	2 32
15	2 33	27 54	5 16	28 26	2 16	1 11	8 17	0 23	3 31	0 31	4 28	1 2	2 33	2 32
16	2 9	28 39	5 13	28 31	1 22	1 3	8 46	0 20	3 49	0 31	4 22	1 2	2 35	2 32
17	1 45	28 3	4 57	27 15	0 26	0 55	9 16	0 17	4 8	0 30	4 16	1 2	2 37	2 32
18	1 21	26 8	4 27	24 42	0N30	0 46	9 45	0 15	4 26	0 29	4 11	1 2	2 39	2 32
19	0 58	22 58	3 45	20 58	1 26	0 36	10 15	0 12	4 45	0 29	4 5	1 2	2 41	2 32
20	0 34	18 42	2 52	16 12	2 23	0 26	10 44	0 9	5 3	0 28	3 59	1 2	2 43	2 32
21	0 10	13 29	1 48	10 35	3 19	0 15	11 12	0 6	5 21	0 27	3 54	1 2	2 45	2 32
22	0N13	7 32	0 37	4 22	4 16	0 4	11 41	0 3	5 39	0 27	3 48	1 2	2 47	2 32
23	0 37	1 6	0S37	2S12	5 12	0N 7	12 9	0N 0	5 57	0 26	3 42	1 2	2 48	2 32
24	1 1	5S31	1 51	8 48	6 7	0 19	12 37	0 3	6 16	0 25	3 37	1 2	2 50	2 32
25	1 24	11 60	2 60	15 3	7 2	0 31	13 4	0 6	6 34	0 25	3 31	1 2	2 52	2 32
26	1 48	17 56	3 58	20 34	7 56	0 43	13 31	0 9	6 51	0 24	3 25	1 2	2 54	2 32
27	2 12	22 55	4 42	24 54	8 48	0 55	13 58	0 12	7 9	0 23	3 20	1 2	2 56	2 32
28	2 35	26 31	5 8	27 41	9 39	1 7	14 25	0 15	7 27	0 23	3 14	1 2	2 58	2 32
29	2 58	28 23	5 15	28 37	10 28	1 19	14 51	0 18	7 45	0 22	3 8	1 2	2 60	2 32
30	3 22	28 22	5 2	27 39	11 14	1 31	15 17	0 22	8 2	0 21	3 3	1 2	3 2	2 32
31	3N45	26S30	4S31	24S57	11N59	1N43	15N43	0N25	8N20	0S21	2S57	1S 3	3N 3	2N32

Day	♅ Decl	♅ Lat	♆ Decl	♆ Lat	♇ Decl	♇ Lat
1	23N40	0N20	5S57	1N40	23N42	8N45
5	23 40	0 20	5 55	1 40	23 43	8 45
9	23 40	0 20	5 53	1 41	23 45	8 45
13	23 40	0 20	5 50	1 41	23 46	8 45
17	23 40	0 19	5 48	1 41	23 47	8 45
21	23 40	0 19	5 46	1 41	23 48	8 44
25	23 39	0 19	5 43	1 41	23 49	8 44
29	23N39	0N19	5S41	1N41	23N50	8N43

☽ PHENOMENA

d	h	m	
7	20	51	●
15	17	40	☽
23	10	50	○
30	5	35	☾

d	h	° '
2	6	28S39
8	18	0
16	1	28N39
23	4	0
29	12	28S37

d	h	
1	15	5S16
8	1	0
15	7	5N17
22	12	0
28	20	5S15

VOID OF COURSE ☽

Last Aspect		☽ Ingress		
1	3pm10	2	♑	9am30
3	5pm41	4	♒	12pm11
5	8pm44	6	♓	3pm46
8	9pm 5	8	♈	9pm16
10	8am27	11	♉	5am33
13	3pm40	13	♊	4pm36
16	3am46	16	♋	5am 6
18	3pm 4	18	♌	4pm45
21	0am47	21	♍	1am39
23	5am13	23	♎	7am21
24	3pm18	25	♏	10am36
27	10am 6	27	♐	12pm41
29	11am58	29	♑	2pm51
31	2pm48	31	♒	6pm 3

d	h	
2	7	PERIGEE
15	6	APOGEE
27	8	PERIGEE

DAILY ASPECTARIAN

1 Th	♀□♅	9am56
	☽□♃	1pm 3
	☽△♇	1 32
	☽✶♆	3 10
	♂ ♈	10 4
2 F	♂☍♄	9am44
	☽□♄	10 8
	☽□♂	10 9
	☽⚼♇	2pm47
	♃⚻♇	3 22
	☽✶☿	3 47
	☽☍♅	6 42
	☿⚼♆	8 44
	☽□♀	9 50
3 S	♀∥♄	1am37
	☉✶☽	5 26
	☿△♅	2pm55
	☽⚻♇	4 3
	☽✶♃	4 31
	☽□♆	5 41
	☽∠☿	8 45
4 Su	☉∠☽	8am44
	☽△♄	12pm34
	☽⋕♇	2 10
	☽⋕♅	2 32
	☽✶♂	3 47
	☽∠♃	6 23
	☽⚻♅	9 27
5 M	☽⚺☿	1am59
	☽✶♀	5 32
	☉⚺☽	12pm17
	☽⚼♄	2 3
	☽∠♂	6 56
	☽☍♇	7 4
	☽⚺♃	8 32
	☽△♆	8 44
	♂⚼♇	9 14
	☽⚼♅	11 10
6 T	♃⚻♆	7am48
	☽∠♀	9 54
	☉∥♆	10 7
	☽⚻♄	3pm53
	☽⚺♂	10 33
	☽⚼♆	10 47
7 W	☽△♅	1am16
	☽∥☿	8 53
	♄ ♍	12pm 5
	☽☌☿	2 12
	☽⚺♀	2 52
	☽∥♆	7 35
	☉☌☽	8 51
	☉∥☽	9 43
	☽∥♃	10 26
	☽⚻♇	11 36
	☽⋕♀	11 58
8 Th	☽⚻♆	1am20
	☽☌♃	2 11
	☿⚺♀	3 1
	☽⋕♄	8 57
	☽⋕♂	12pm11
	☉∥♃	1 2
	☉⋕♀	2 54
	♀⋕♃	3 48
	☽☍♄	9 5
	♂□♅	10 35
	☽∥♂	11 58
9 F	☽∥♄	2am45
	☽⚼♇	2 46
	☽□♅	7 13
	☽☌♂	7 45
	☉⚻♇	9 9
	☉⋕☽	11 47
	☽⋕♃	12pm52
	☽∥♀	3 9
	☽⋕♆	4 21
	☽⋕☿	7 50
10 S	☽☌♀	3am19
	♀⋕♆	5 20
	☽⚺☿	6 18
	☽△♇	6 38
	☉⚻♆	7 50
	☽☍♆	8 27
	☿⚻♇	8 29
	☉⚺☽	8 30
	☽⚺♃	10 30
	☿⋕♀	3pm21
	☿⚻♆	8 23
	☿∥♆	9 38
11 Su	☽⚻♄	5am 0
	☉☌☿	10 11
	♀△♇	1pm15
	☿☌♃	1 24
	♂∥♄	1 43
	☉∠☽	3 44
	☽∠♃	3 50
	☽✶♅	4 0
	☽∠☿	4 14
	☉☌♃	5 24
	☽⚺♂	8 22
12 M	☿∥♃	5am33
	♀☍♆	7 42
	☽⚼♄	10 2
	☽□♇	4pm33
	☽⚻♆	6 27
	☽⚺♀	7 40
	☽∠♅	9 28
	☽✶♃	9 54
	☉✶☽	11 50
13 T	☽✶☿	3am22
	☽∠♂	3 56
	☽∥♅	6 20
	☽∥♇	7 7
	☉⋕♂	3pm 6
	☽△♄	3 40
	♀⚺♃	10 30
	☿⋕♂	11 29
14 W	☽⚼♆	0am20
	☽⚺♅	3 27
	☽∠♀	5 4
	♅SD	10 47
	☉∥☿	11 17
	☽✶♂	12pm 5
	☿⋕♄	4 53
	☉⋕♄	11 30
15 Th	☽✶♇	4am37
	☽△♆	6 32
	☽□♃	11 25
	☽✶♀	2pm49
	☉□☽	5 40
16 F	☽□☿	3am45
	☽□♄	3 46
	☿☍♄	3 50
	☽∠♇	10 51
	☿ ♈	11 54
	☽☌♅	3pm59
17 S	☽□♂	4am41
	♂⋕♃	8 43
	☽⚺♇	4pm48
	☽□♆	6 39
	☿⚼♇	9 56
18 Su	☽△♃	0am47
	☽□♀	9 33
	☉△☽	10 56
	☽✶♄	3pm 4
	☉⋕☿	3 31
	☽∥♇	6 31
	☽∥♅	7 28
19 M	☽△☿	2am54
	☽⚺♅	3 15
	☿□♅	5 5
	☽⚼♃	6 37
	☉⚼☽	6pm28
	☽△♂	7 11
	☽∠♄	7 48
20 T	☽☌♇	2am53
	☽✶♆	4 36
	☽∠♅	7 50
	☿∥♄	8 47
	☉☍♄	10 11
	☽⚻♃	11 39
	☽⚼☿	12pm44
	♀⚻♄	2 4
	☽⚺♄	11 43
21 W	☽△♀	0am47
	☉⚻☽	0 56
	☽⚼♂	1 3
	☽∠♆	8 23
	☉⚺♀	8 37
	☽∥♀	8 46
	♀ ♉	10 6
	☉ ♈	10 26
	☽✶♅	11 35
	☿⋕♃	1pm15
	☽⚻☿	9 9
22 Th	☽⚻♂	5am56
	☽⚼♀	6 45
	☽⋕♆	6 47
	☽∥♂	6 49
	♂⋕♆	7 23
	☽⚺♇	9 47
	☽∥☿	10 47
	☽⚺♆	11 22
	☽⋕♃	2pm17
	☽∥♄	5 47
	☽☍♃	7 6
23 F	☉∥☽	1am40
	☽☌♄	5 13
	☉⋕☽	6 39
	☉☍☽	10 50
	☽⚻♀	11 44
	☽∠♇	12pm 6
	☿⋕♆	1 54
	☽⋕♄	2 15
	☽□♅	4 48
	☽∥♃	5 11
24 S	☽∥♆	0am47
	☽⋕☿	2 34
	☽⋕♂	2 49
	☉⚼♇	4 15
	☿∥♂	5 15
	☽☍☿	10 15
	☽☍♂	1pm11
	☽✶♇	1 50
	☽☌♆	3 18
	☽⚻♃	11 42
25 Su	♂△♇	0am56
	☽⋕♀	4 29
	☽⚺♄	8 16
	☿△♇	1pm 5
	☉⚻☽	5 46
	☽☍♀	7 33
	☽△♅	7 46
	☿☌♂	9 44
	♀✶♅	10 2
26 M	☿☍♆	0am 8
	☽⚼♃	1 20
	♂☍♆	3 25
	☽∠♄	9 15
	☽□♇	4pm10
	☽⚺♆	5 35
	☽⚻♂	6 23
	☽⚻☿	8 7
	☉⚼☽	8 40
	☽⚼♅	8 49
	☉□♅	10 56
27 T	☽△♃	2am46
	☽⋕♅	4 14
	☽⋕♇	5 15
	☽✶♄	10 6
	☽∠♆	6pm30
	☽⚼♂	8 45
	☽⚻♅	9 49
	☉△☽	11 29
28 W	☽⚼☿	0am33
	☽⚻♀	2 9
	☽△♇	6pm 7
	☽✶♆	7 30
	☽△♂	11 11
29 Th	☉∥♄	1am25
	☽△☿	4 58
	☽⚼♀	5 33
	☽□♃	5 42
	♀∠♃	7 37
	☉⋕♃	8 13
	☽□♄	11 58
	☿⚺♃	12pm20
	☽⚼♇	7 18
30 F	☽☍♅	0am10
	♃⋕♄	3 56
	☉□☽	5 35
	☽△♀	9 15
	☽⚻♇	8pm46
	☽□♆	10 7
31 S	☽□♂	4am53
	☽✶♃	9 32
	☽□☿	2pm18
	☽△♄	2 48
	☿⚻♄	6 49
	☽⋕♇	7 11
	☽⋕♅	8 20

APRIL 1951

LONGITUDE

Day	Sid. Time	☉	☽	☽ 12 Hour	Mean ☊	True ☊	☿	♀	♂	♃	♄	♅	♆	♇
	h m s	° ′ ″	° ′ ″	° ′ ″	° ′	° ′	° ′	° ′	° ′	° ′	° ′	° ′	° ′	° ′
1	12 34 11	10♈ 27 29	3♒ 26 18	10♒ 19 41	18♓ 1	18♓ 54	28♈ 25	12♉ 49	22♈ 58	25♓ 13	28♍ 6R	5♋ 32	18♎ 23R	17♌ 36R
2	12 38 8	11 26 42	17 10 8	23 57 35	17 58	18 56	29 48	14 1	23 43	25 27	28 1	5 33	18 21	17 36
3	12 42 4	12 25 53	0♓ 42 0	7♓ 23 22	17 55	18 57	1♉ 6	15 13	24 28	25 41	27 57	5 34	18 20	17 35
4	12 46 1	13 25 2	14 1 40	20 36 50	17 52	18 58R	2 18	16 25	25 13	25 56	27 52	5 35	18 18	17 34
5	12 49 57	14 24 10	27 8 53	3♈ 37 45	17 48	18 57	3 24	17 38	25 58	26 10	27 48	5 36	18 17	17 34
6	12 53 54	15 23 15	10♈ 3 26	16 25 57	17 45	18 56	4 24	18 50	26 43	26 24	27 43	5 38	18 15	17 33
7	12 57 50	16 22 19	22 45 17	29 1 29	17 42	18 53	5 18	20 2	27 28	26 38	27 39	5 39	18 13	17 32
8	13 1 47	17 21 20	5♉ 14 37	11♉ 24 49	17 39	18 49	6 6	21 13	28 13	26 52	27 35	5 40	18 12	17 32
9	13 5 43	18 20 20	17 32 12	23 36 59	17 36	18 44	6 46	22 25	28 57	27 6	27 30	5 41	18 10	17 31
10	13 9 40	19 19 17	29 39 25	5♊ 39 46	17 33	18 39	7 21	23 37	29 42	27 20	27 26	5 43	18 8	17 30
11	13 13 37	20 18 12	11♊ 38 24	17 35 42	17 29	18 34	7 48	24 49	0♉ 27	27 34	27 22	5 44	18 7	17 30
12	13 17 33	21 17 5	23 32 5	29 28 2	17 26	18 30	8 9	26 0	1 11	27 48	27 18	5 46	18 5	17 29
13	13 21 30	22 15 56	5♋ 24 5	11♋ 20 46	17 23	18 26	8 24	27 12	1 56	28 2	27 14	5 47	18 3	17 29
14	13 25 26	23 14 44	17 18 39	23 18 21	17 20	18 25D	8 32R	28 23	2 41	28 16	27 10	5 49	18 2	17 29
15	13 29 23	24 13 30	29 20 27	5♌ 25 35	17 17	18 25	8 33	29 35	3 25	28 30	27 6	5 50	18 0	17 28
16	13 33 19	25 12 14	11♌ 34 21	17 47 20	17 13	18 26	8 29	0♊ 46	4 9	28 43	27 2	5 52	17 58	17 28
17	13 37 16	26 10 56	24 5 5	0♍ 28 6	17 10	18 27	8 18	1 57	4 54	28 57	26 58	5 54	17 57	17 27
18	13 41 12	27 9 35	6♍ 56 51	13 31 39	17 7	18 28R	8 2	3 8	5 38	29 11	26 54	5 56	17 55	17 27
19	13 45 9	28 8 12	20 12 46	27 0 21	17 4	18 29	7 41	4 19	6 22	29 24	26 51	5 57	17 54	17 27
20	13 49 6	29 6 48	3♎ 54 21	10♎ 54 37	17 1	18 28	7 15	5 30	7 7	29 38	26 47	5 59	17 52	17 26
21	13 53 2	0♉ 5 21	18 0 49	25 12 26	16 58	18 25	6 45	6 41	7 51	29 52	26 43	6 1	17 50	17 26
22	13 56 59	1 3 52	2♏ 28 48	9♏ 49 7	16 54	18 21	6 11	7 51	8 35	0♈ 5	26 40	6 3	17 49	17 26
23	14 0 55	2 2 21	17 12 27	24 37 45	16 51	18 15	5 35	9 2	9 19	0 19	26 36	6 5	17 47	17 26
24	14 4 52	3 0 48	2♐ 3 58	9♐ 30 1	16 48	18 8	4 56	10 13	10 3	0 32	26 33	6 7	17 46	17 25
25	14 8 48	3 59 14	16 54 54	24 17 40	16 45	18 1	4 16	11 23	10 47	0 45	26 30	6 9	17 44	17 25
26	14 12 45	4 57 38	1♑ 37 29	8♑ 53 40	16 42	17 56	3 35	12 33	11 31	0 58	26 27	6 11	17 42	17 25
27	14 16 41	5 56 1	16 5 42	23 13 13	16 39	17 52	2 55	13 43	12 15	1 12	26 24	6 13	17 41	17 25
28	14 20 38	6 54 22	0♒ 15 57	7♒ 13 50	16 35	17 50D	2 15	14 54	12 59	1 25	26 20	6 15	17 39	17 25
29	14 24 35	7 52 42	14 6 52	20 55 10	16 32	17 50	1 37	16 4	13 42	1 38	26 18	6 18	17 38	17 25
30	14 28 31	8♉ 50 59	27♒ 38 54	4♓ 18 18	16♓ 29	17♓ 51	1♉ 1	17♊ 13	14♉ 26	1♈ 51	26♍ 15	6♋ 20	17♎ 36	17♌ 25D

DECLINATION and LATITUDE

Day	☉	☽		☽ 12 Hr.	☿		♀		♂		♃		♄	
	Decl	Decl	Lat	Decl	Decl	Lat	Decl	Lat	Decl	Lat	Decl	Lat	Decl	Lat
1	4N 8	23S 2	3S45	20S49	12N41	1N54	16N 8	0N28	8N37	0S20	2S52	1S 3	3N 5	2N32
2	4 32	18 20	2 46	15 38	13 21	2 4	16 33	0 31	8 54	0 19	2 46	1 3	3 7	2 32
3	4 55	12 46	1 39	9 47	13 58	2 15	16 57	0 34	9 12	0 19	2 40	1 3	3 9	2 32
4	5 18	6 42	0 27	3 35	14 32	2 24	17 21	0 37	9 29	0 18	2 35	1 3	3 11	2 32
5	5 41	0 27	0N45	2N40	15 3	2 33	17 44	0 40	9 46	0 17	2 29	1 3	3 12	2 32
6	6 4	5N43	1 53	8 42	15 31	2 41	18 8	0 44	10 3	0 17	2 24	1 3	3 14	2 32
7	6 26	11 33	2 55	14 16	15 55	2 47	18 30	0 47	10 19	0 16	2 18	1 3	3 16	2 32
8	6 49	16 50	3 47	19 11	16 17	2 53	18 52	0 50	10 36	0 15	2 13	1 3	3 17	2 32
9	7 11	21 20	4 27	23 14	16 35	2 58	19 14	0 53	10 53	0 15	2 7	1 3	3 19	2 32
10	7 34	24 53	4 55	26 14	16 50	3 3	19 35	0 56	11 9	0 14	2 2	1 3	3 21	2 32
11	7 56	27 18	5 9	28 2	17 2	3 5	19 56	0 59	11 25	0 13	1 56	1 3	3 22	2 32
12	8 18	28 27	5 10	28 33	17 10	3 6	20 16	1 2	11 41	0 13	1 51	1 4	3 24	2 32
13	8 40	28 18	4 58	27 44	17 14	3 6	20 36	1 5	11 58	0 12	1 45	1 4	3 25	2 32
14	9 2	26 50	4 33	25 38	17 16	3 5	20 55	1 8	12 13	0 12	1 40	1 4	3 27	2 32
15	9 24	24 8	3 56	22 21	17 14	3 2	21 14	1 11	12 29	0 11	1 34	1 4	3 28	2 32
16	9 45	20 19	3 7	18 2	17 8	2 58	21 32	1 14	12 45	0 10	1 29	1 4	3 30	2 31
17	10 7	15 31	2 9	12 49	16 59	2 52	21 49	1 17	13 0	0 10	1 24	1 4	3 31	2 31
18	10 28	9 56	1 2	6 54	16 47	2 45	22 6	1 20	13 16	0 9	1 18	1 4	3 33	2 31
19	10 49	3 44	0S 9	0 29	16 32	2 36	22 23	1 23	13 31	0 8	1 13	1 4	3 34	2 31
20	11 10	2S49	1 23	6S 8	16 14	2 26	22 38	1 26	13 46	0 8	1 8	1 4	3 35	2 31
21	11 30	9 25	2 33	12 38	15 54	2 15	22 54	1 29	14 1	0 7	1 2	1 4	3 37	2 31
22	11 51	15 42	3 35	18 35	15 31	2 3	23 8	1 32	14 16	0 6	0 57	1 5	3 38	2 31
23	12 11	21 12	4 24	23 30	15 6	1 49	23 22	1 35	14 31	0 6	0 52	1 5	3 39	2 31
24	12 31	25 25	4 56	26 54	14 39	1 34	23 35	1 37	14 45	0 5	0 47	1 5	3 40	2 31
25	12 51	27 54	5 8	28 25	14 11	1 19	23 48	1 40	14 60	0 4	0 42	1 5	3 42	2 30
26	13 11	28 25	4 59	27 56	13 42	1 3	24 0	1 43	15 14	0 4	0 36	1 5	3 43	2 30
27	13 30	26 58	4 32	25 35	13 12	0 46	24 12	1 45	15 28	0 3	0 31	1 5	3 44	2 30
28	13 49	23 48	3 48	21 42	12 43	0 29	24 22	1 48	15 42	0 2	0 26	1 5	3 45	2 30
29	14 8	19 20	2 51	16 44	12 13	0 12	24 33	1 50	15 56	0 2	0 21	1 5	3 46	2 30
30	14N27	13S58	1S47	11S 3	11N45	0S 5	24N42	1N53	16N 9	0S 1	0S16	1S 6	3N47	2N30

Day	♅		♆		♇	
	Decl	Lat	Decl	Lat	Decl	Lat
1	23N39	0N19	5S39	1N41	23N50	8N43
5	23 39	0 19	5 36	1 41	23 51	8 42
9	23 39	0 19	5 34	1 41	23 51	8 42
13	23 38	0 19	5 31	1 41	23 51	8 41
17	23 38	0 19	5 29	1 41	23 51	8 41
21	23 38	0 19	5 26	1 41	23 51	8 40
25	23 37	0 19	5 24	1 41	23 51	8 39
29	23N37	0N19	5S22	1N41	23N50	8N39

☽ PHENOMENA

d	h	m	
6	10	52	●
14	12	56	☽
21	21	30	○
28	12	18	☾

d	h	° ′
5	2	0
12	9	28N33
19	14	0
25	18	28S29

d	h	° ′
4	9	0
11	14	5N12
18	21	0
25	2	5S 8

VOID OF COURSE ☽

Last Aspect	☽ Ingress
2 12pm15	2 ♓ 10pm45
5 1am11	5 ♈ 5am16
7 9am34	7 ♉ 1pm53
9 7pm36	10 ♊ 0am41
12 8am48	12 ♋ 1pm 5
15 0am31	15 ♌ 1am18
17 4am17	17 ♍ 11am 7
19 4pm28	19 ♎ 5pm14
20 11pm42	21 ♏ 7pm55
23 3pm 8	23 ♐ 8pm40
25 3pm32	25 ♑ 9pm20
27 5pm19	27 ♒ 11pm33
29 6am10	30 ♓ 4am13

d	h	
12	1	APOGEE
23	23	PERIGEE

DAILY ASPECTARIAN

1 Su	☽⊼♅	3am39
	♀⚼♄	5 16
	☽∠♃	12pm 1
	☉*☽	1 10
	☽⚼♄	4 45
	☽□♀	5 56
2 M	☽☍♇	0am45
	☽△♆	2 5
	☿ ♉	3 28
	☽⚼♅	5 59
	☽#♀	7 29
	☽*♂	12pm15
	☽⊻♃	2 55
	☉∠☽	5 43
	☽⊼♄	7 7
	☽#☿	7 32
3 T	☽*☿	0am48
	☽⚼♆	4 42
	☽△♅	8 45
	☽#♂	1pm40
	☽∠♂	4 41
	☉⊻☽	10 48
4 W	☽∥♆	4am12
	☽*♀	4 48
	☉#☽	5 6
	☽⊼♇	6 26
	☽∠☿	6 31
	☽⊼♆	7 46
	☽#♄	1pm30
	☽∥♃	4 4
	☉#♆	7 31
	☽⊻♂	9 41
	☽☌♃	10 9
	♀□♇	10 40
5 Th	☽☍♄	1am11
	♂⊻♃	9 16
	☽⚼♇	10 0
	☽#♃	11 10
	☽∠♀	11 11
	☽⊻☿	12pm35
	♀⊼♆	12 41
	☽∥♄	2 11
	☽□♅	3 42
	☽#♆	11 31
6 F	☉∥☽	1am27
	☉☌☽	10 52
	☽△♇	2pm 6
	☽☍♆	3 24
	☽⊻♀	6 16
	☽∥♂	6 30
7 S	♂⊼♄	5am27
	☽⊻♃	7 33
	☽⊼♄	9 18
	☽☌♂	9 34
	☿*♅	10 20
	♀∠♅	12pm40
	☽∥☿	9 10
8 Su	☽*♅	0am50
	☽☌☿	1 45
	☉△♇	4 9
	☽∥♀	11 13
	☽∠♃	1pm 8
	☽⚼♄	2 11
	☉☍♆	7 53
	☽□♇	11 58
9 M	☽⊼♆	1am14
	☉⊻☽	1 43
	☽∠♅	6 14
	☽☌♀	10 41
	☽∥♅	2pm48
	☽∥♇	4 16
	☽*♃	7 17
	☽△♄	7 36
10 T	☽⊻♂	0am 6
	☽⚼♆	6 56
	♃☍♄	7 45
	♂ ♉	9 37
	☉∠☽	10 9
	☽⊻♅	12pm 8
	☽⊻☿	4 1
11 W	☽∠♂	8am11
	☽*♇	11 48
	☽△♆	1pm 1
	☉*☽	7 3
	☽∠☿	11 13
12 Th	☽⊻♀	5am33
	☽□♄	7 34
	☽□♃	8 48
	☽*♂	4pm31
	☽∠♇	6 6
13 F	♀△♄	0am36
	☽☌♅	0 47
	☽*☿	6 8
	☽∠♀	3pm14
	♀*♃	8 56
14 S	☽⊻♇	0am20
	☽□♆	1 26
	☉□☽	12pm56
	☿SR	5 54
	☽*♄	7 34
	☽△♃	10 17
15 Su	☽*♀	0am31
	☽∥♇	2 2
	☽∥♅	3 33
	☽□♂	8 34
	♀ ♊	8 34
	☽⊻♅	12pm50
	☽∥♀	5 31
	☽□☿	6 2
16 M	☽∠♄	0am53
	☽⚼♃	4 15
	☽☌♇	11 22
	☽*♆	12pm20
	☽∥☿	4 52
	☽∠♅	5 56
17 T	☉△☽	4am17
	☽⊻♄	5 25
	☽⊼♃	9 20
	☽∥♂	10 40
	☽□♀	4pm15
	☽∠♆	4 35
	☉⊼♄	6 6
	♀⚼♆	7 45
	☽△♂	9 26
	☉∥☽	9 56
	☽*♅	10 7
18 W	☽△☿	1am57
	♂*♅	9 48
	☉⚼☽	10 17
	☽#♆	5pm29
	☽⊻♇	7 3
	☽⊻♆	7 52
19 Th	☽∥♄	0am37
	☽⚼♂	2 11
	☽⚼☿	4 15
	☽#♃	9 27
	☽☌♄	11 40
	☉⊼☽	3pm 3
	☽☍♃	4 28
	☽∥♃	5 58
	☽∠♇	9 28
20 F	☿☌♂	2am39
	☽#♄	2 48
	☽△♀	3 0
	☽□♅	3 35
	☽⊼☿	5 33
	☽⊼♂	5 49
	☽∥♆	9 30
	♀⊻♅	10 11
	☉⊻♃	4pm40
	☉ ♉	9 48
	☽*♇	11 2
	☽☌♆	11 42
21 S	☿⊻♀	0am55
	☽⚼♀	6 41
	☉#☽	8 11
	☽⊻♄	2pm27
	♃ ♈	2 57
	☽#♂	6 4
	☽⊼♃	8 0
	☉☍☽	9 30
	☽#☿	11 17
22 Su	☿*♅	5am 9
	☽☍☿	5 50
	☽△♅	5 52
	☽⊼♀	9 34
	☽☍♂	10 30
	☽∠♄	2pm57
	☽⚼♃	8 52
23 M	☽□♇	0am21
	☽⊻♆	0 56
	☽⚼♅	6 17
	☽#♀	11 56
	☽#♅	12pm46
	☽#♇	2 2
	☽*♄	3 8
	♀⊻♂	3 23
	☿∥♂	8 20
	☽△♃	9 29
24 T	☽∠♆	1am 7
	☉⊼☽	1 38
	♀∥♅	3 42
	☽⊼☿	4 26
	☽⊼♅	6 33
	☽⊼♂	1pm34
	☽☍♀	2 16
25 W	☽△♇	0am49
	☽*♆	1 19
	☉⚼☽	3 36
	☽⚼☿	3 39
	☉☌☿	4 3
	♀∥♇	4 38
	☽⚼♂	3pm11
	☽□♄	3 32
	♂⚼♄	9 49
	☽□♃	10 55
26 Th	☽⚼♇	1am18
	☽△☿	3 5
	☉△☽	5 53
	☽☍♅	7 32
	☉∥☿	3pm14
	☽△♂	5 14
	☽⊼♀	7 41
27 F	☽⊼♇	2am13
	☽□♆	2 39
	☉*♅	7 22
	☽△♄	5pm19
	☽#♀	8 33
	☽⚼♀	11 18
	☽#♇	11 48
28 S	☽#♅	1am 9
	☽*♃	2 0
	☽□☿	3 15
	☽⊼♅	10 21
	☉□☽	12pm18
	☽⚼♄	7 5
	☽□♂	11 15
	☿⊻♃	11 23
29 Su	☽△♀	3am44
	☽∠♃	4 30
	☽☍♇	5 48
	☽△♆	6 10
	☿∠♀	7 26
	☽⚼♅	12pm42
	☽#♂	2 56
	☽⊼♄	9 30
	☉#☽	10 2
30 M	♀*♇	3am55
	♇SD	5 14
	☽*☿	5 48
	☽⊻♃	7 41
	♀△♆	7 41
	☽⚼♆	8 54
	☽#☿	10 0
	☽△♅	3pm44
	☉*☽	9 53

LONGITUDE

Day	Sid. Time	☉	☽	☽ 12 Hour	Mean ☊	True ☊	☿	♀	♂	♃	♄	♅	♆	♇
	h m s	° ' "	° ' "	° ' "	° '	° '	° '	° '	° '	° '	° '	° '	° '	° '
1	14 32 28	9♉ 49 16	10♓ 53 38	17♓ 25 9	16♓ 26	17♓ 52R	0♉ 27R	18♊ 23	15♉ 10	2♈ 4	26♍ 12R	6♋ 22	17♎ 35R	17♌ 25
2	14 36 24	10 47 30	23 53 8	0♈ 17 49	16 23	17 52	29♈ 57	19 33	15 53	2 17	26 9	6 25	17 33	17 25
3	14 40 21	11 45 44	6♈ 39 27	12 58 15	16 19	17 48	29 30	20 43	16 37	2 30	26 7	6 27	17 32	17 25
4	14 44 17	12 43 55	19 14 23	25 28 1	16 16	17 46	29 8	21 52	17 20	2 42	26 4	6 29	17 30	17 25
5	14 48 14	13 42 5	1♉ 39 19	7♉ 48 22	16 13	17 40	28 49	23 1	18 4	2 55	26 2	6 32	17 29	17 25
6	14 52 10	14 40 14	13 55 19	20 0 17	16 10	17 31	28 35	24 11	18 47	3 8	25 59	6 34	17 27	17 25
7	14 56 7	15 38 21	26 3 21	2♊ 4 41	16 7	17 20	28 26	25 20	19 31	3 20	25 57	6 37	17 26	17 26
8	15 0 4	16 36 26	8♊ 4 26	14 2 48	16 4	17 9	28 21D	26 29	20 14	3 33	25 55	6 40	17 25	17 26
9	15 4 0	17 34 29	19 59 58	25 56 14	16 0	16 58	28 21	27 38	20 57	3 45	25 53	6 42	17 23	17 26
10	15 7 57	18 32 31	1♋ 51 53	7♋ 47 17	15 57	16 48	28 26	28 46	21 41	3 58	25 51	6 45	17 22	17 26
11	15 11 53	19 30 31	13 42 50	19 38 57	15 54	16 41	28 36	29 55	22 24	4 10	25 49	6 48	17 21	17 27
12	15 15 50	20 28 29	25 36 10	1♌ 34 59	15 51	16 35	28 49	1♋ 4	23 7	4 22	25 47	6 50	17 19	17 27
13	15 19 46	21 26 25	7♌ 35 59	13 39 46	15 48	16 32	29 8	2 12	23 50	4 34	25 46	6 53	17 18	17 27
14	15 23 43	22 24 20	19 46 56	25 58 9	15 45	16 31D	29 31	3 20	24 33	4 46	25 44	6 56	17 17	17 28
15	15 27 39	23 22 13	2♍ 14 2	8♍ 35 11	15 41	16 31	29 58	4 28	25 16	4 58	25 43	6 59	17 15	17 28
16	15 31 36	24 20 3	15 2 11	21 35 34	15 38	16 32R	0♉ 29	5 36	25 59	5 10	25 41	7 1	17 14	17 28
17	15 35 33	25 17 52	28 15 44	5♎ 3 2	15 35	16 31	1 5	6 44	26 42	5 22	25 40	7 4	17 13	17 29
18	15 39 29	26 15 40	11♎ 57 38	18 59 34	15 32	16 29	1 44	7 52	27 24	5 34	25 39	7 7	17 12	17 29
19	15 43 26	27 13 26	26 8 38	3♏ 24 26	15 29	16 24	2 27	8 59	28 7	5 45	25 38	7 10	17 11	17 30
20	15 47 22	28 11 10	10♏ 46 23	18 13 37	15 25	16 17	3 13	10 6	28 50	5 57	25 37	7 13	17 9	17 30
21	15 51 19	29 8 53	25 45 7	3♐ 19 41	15 22	16 8	4 3	11 14	29 32	6 8	25 36	7 16	17 8	17 31
22	15 55 15	0♊ 6 35	10♐ 55 58	18 32 38	15 19	15 57	4 57	12 21	0♊ 15	6 19	25 35	7 19	17 7	17 32
23	15 59 12	1 4 15	26 8 17	3♑ 41 37	15 16	15 47	5 54	13 27	0 58	6 31	25 34	7 22	17 6	17 32
24	16 3 8	2 1 54	11♑ 11 28	18 36 51	15 13	15 38	6 54	14 34	1 40	6 42	25 34	7 25	17 5	17 33
25	16 7 5	2 59 32	25 56 56	3♒ 11 9	15 10	15 32	7 57	15 40	2 22	6 53	25 33	7 28	17 4	17 33
26	16 11 2	3 57 9	10♒ 19 7	17 20 40	15 6	15 28	9 3	16 47	3 5	7 4	25 33	7 32	17 3	17 34
27	16 14 58	4 54 46	24 15 47	1♓ 4 37	15 3	15 26D	10 13	17 53	3 47	7 15	25 33	7 35	17 2	17 35
28	16 18 55	5 52 21	7♓ 47 25	14 24 33	15 0	15 26R	11 25	18 59	4 29	7 25	25 32	7 38	17 1	17 36
29	16 22 51	6 49 55	20 56 24	27 23 25	14 57	15 26	12 40	20 4	5 12	7 36	25 32D	7 41	17 0	17 36
30	16 26 48	7 47 28	3♈ 46 3	10♈ 4 45	14 54	15 25	13 57	21 10	5 54	7 47	25 32	7 44	16 59	17 37
31	16 30 44	8♊ 45 1	16♈ 19 58	22♈ 32 5	14♓ 51	15♓ 22	15♉ 18	22♋ 15	6♊ 36	7♈ 57	25♍ 33	7♋ 48	16♎ 58	17♌ 38

DECLINATION and LATITUDE

Day	☉ Decl	☽ Decl	☽ Lat	☽ 12 Hr. Decl	☿ Decl	☿ Lat	♀ Decl	♀ Lat	♂ Decl	♂ Lat	♃ Decl	♃ Lat	♄ Decl	♄ Lat
1	14N46	8S 4	0S37	5S 1	11N17	0S22	24N51	1N55	16N23	0S 0	0S11	1S 6	3N48	2N30
2	15 4	1 56	0N32	1N 8	10 51	0 39	24 59	1 57	16 36	0N 0	0 6	1 6	3 49	2 29
3	15 22	4N10	1 39	7 7	10 26	0 55	25 7	1 60	16 49	0 1	0 1	1 6	3 50	2 29
4	15 40	9 60	2 40	12 45	10 4	1 11	25 13	2 2	17 2	0 2	0N 4	1 6	3 51	2 29
5	15 57	15 22	3 32	17 48	9 43	1 26	25 20	2 4	17 15	0 2	0 9	1 6	3 51	2 29
6	16 15	20 3	4 14	22 5	9 25	1 40	25 25	2 6	17 28	0 3	0 14	1 6	3 52	2 29
7	16 32	23 51	4 43	25 22	9 9	1 54	25 30	2 8	17 40	0 3	0 19	1 7	3 53	2 29
8	16 48	26 35	4 60	27 30	8 55	2 6	25 34	2 10	17 52	0 4	0 23	1 7	3 54	2 28
9	17 5	28 6	5 3	28 22	8 45	2 18	25 37	2 12	18 5	0 5	0 28	1 7	3 54	2 28
10	17 21	28 19	4 53	27 56	8 36	2 29	25 40	2 14	18 16	0 5	0 33	1 7	3 55	2 28
11	17 37	27 14	4 31	26 13	8 30	2 39	25 42	2 15	18 28	0 6	0 38	1 7	3 55	2 28
12	17 52	24 54	3 56	23 19	8 27	2 48	25 43	2 17	18 40	0 7	0 42	1 7	3 56	2 28
13	18 8	21 28	3 12	19 22	8 26	2 55	25 44	2 18	18 51	0 7	0 47	1 7	3 56	2 27
14	18 23	17 3	2 17	14 33	8 27	3 2	25 44	2 20	19 2	0 8	0 52	1 8	3 57	2 27
15	18 37	11 51	1 15	9 0	8 31	3 9	25 43	2 21	19 13	0 8	0 56	1 8	3 57	2 27
16	18 52	6 1	0 8	2 55	8 37	3 14	25 42	2 22	19 24	0 9	1 1	1 8	3 58	2 27
17	19 6	0S15	1S 2	3S29	8 45	3 18	25 40	2 24	19 35	0 10	1 5	1 8	3 58	2 27
18	19 19	6 44	2 11	9 57	8 56	3 21	25 37	2 25	19 45	0 10	1 10	1 8	3 58	2 27
19	19 33	13 6	3 14	16 7	9 8	3 24	25 34	2 26	19 55	0 11	1 14	1 8	3 59	2 26
20	19 46	18 57	4 6	21 31	9 22	3 26	25 30	2 27	20 6	0 12	1 19	1 9	3 59	2 26
21	19 58	23 46	4 43	25 38	9 38	3 27	25 25	2 27	20 15	0 12	1 23	1 9	3 59	2 26
22	20 11	27 2	5 0	27 57	9 56	3 27	25 20	2 28	20 25	0 13	1 27	1 9	3 59	2 26
23	20 23	28 20	4 56	28 10	10 15	3 26	25 14	2 29	20 35	0 13	1 32	1 9	3 59	2 26
24	20 34	27 30	4 32	26 20	10 36	3 25	25 7	2 29	20 44	0 14	1 36	1 9	3 59	2 25
25	20 46	24 44	3 50	22 45	10 58	3 23	24 60	2 30	20 53	0 15	1 40	1 10	3 59	2 25
26	20 57	20 27	2 54	17 54	11 21	3 20	24 52	2 30	21 2	0 15	1 44	1 10	3 59	2 25
27	21 7	15 10	1 50	12 16	11 46	3 17	24 44	2 30	21 10	0 16	1 48	1 10	3 59	2 25
28	21 18	9 16	0 40	6 13	12 12	3 13	24 35	2 30	21 19	0 16	1 52	1 10	3 59	2 24
29	21 27	3 9	0N29	0 5	12 39	3 8	24 25	2 30	21 27	0 17	1 56	1 10	3 59	2 24
30	21 37	2N57	1 35	5N56	13 7	3 3	24 15	2 30	21 35	0 18	2 0	1 10	3 59	2 24
31	21N46	8N49	2N35	11N35	13N36	2S57	24N 4	2N29	21N43	0N18	2N 4	1S11	3N58	2N24

Day	♅ Decl	♅ Lat	♆ Decl	♆ Lat	♇ Decl	♇ Lat
1	23N37	0N19	5S21	1N41	23N50	8N38
5	23 36	0 19	5 18	1 41	23 49	8 38
9	23 36	0 19	5 16	1 41	23 48	8 37
13	23 35	0 19	5 14	1 41	23 47	8 36
17	23 34	0 19	5 13	1 41	23 46	8 36
21	23 34	0 19	5 11	1 41	23 45	8 35
25	23 33	0 19	5 9	1 41	23 43	8 34
29	23N32	0N19	5S 8	1N40	23N42	8N34

☽ PHENOMENA

d	h	m	
6	1	36	●
14	5	32	☽
21	5	45	○
27	20	17	☾

d	h	° '
2	8	0
9	16	28N24
16	23	0
23	2	28S20
29	12	0

d	h	° '
1	13	0
8	18	5N 3
16	3	0
22	8	5S 1
28	14	0

VOID OF COURSE ☽

Last Aspect		☽ Ingress		
2	4am13	2	♈	11am27
4	6pm37	4	♉	8pm47
6	11pm48	7	♊	7am51
9	5pm 4	9	♋	8pm13
12	6am38	12	♌	8am50
14	7pm30	14	♍	7pm44
16	9pm 2	17	♎	3am 5
18	9am27	19	♏	6am23
21	6am18	21	♐	6am44
22	11pm 6	23	♑	6am 8
24	11pm21	25	♒	6am42
26	12pm24	27	♓	10am 6
29	8am33	29	♈	4pm54

d	h	
9	17	APOGEE
22	4	PERIGEE

DAILY ASPECTARIAN

1 T	☽∠☿	8am 3
	☽*♂	8 18
	☽∥♆	10 43
	☽⚻♇	12pm 0
	☽⚻♆	12 16
	☽□♀	3 9
	☽#♄	4 41
	☿ ♈	9 41
2 W	☉∠☽	3am51
	☽☍♄	4 13
	☽∥♃	7 17
	☽#♃	7 51
	☉⚼♄	8 33
	☽⚺☿	10 57
	☽∠♂	1pm54
	♃⚼♇	3 8
	☽⚼♇	3 59
	☽☌♃	4 0
	☽∥♄	10 41
	☽□♅	11 36
3 Th	☽#♆	4am40
	☉⚺☽	10 30
	☽⚺♂	8pm 8
	☽△♇	8 30
	☽☍♆	8 41
4 F	☽∥☿	0am15
	♂□♇	2 33
	♂⚻♆	5 16
	☽*♀	5 34
	☽⚻♄	1pm 7
	♂∠♃	5 10
	☽☌☿	6 37
5 S	☽⚺♃	2am30
	☉∥☽	3 0
	☽*♅	9 32
	☽∥♂	9 37
	☽∠♀	1pm43
	☽⚼♄	6 15
6 Su	☉☌☽	1am36
	☽□♇	6 54
	☽⚻♆	6 57
	☽∠♃	8 27
	☽☌♂	10 12
	☽∠♅	3pm10
	☽∥♅	10 10
	☽⚺♀	10 24
	☽∥♇	11 40
	☽△♄	11 48
7 M	☽⚺☿	4am41
	♆*♇	7 51
	♀□♄	12pm33
	☽⚼♆	12 41
	☽∥♀	1 32
	☽*♃	2 47
	☽⚺♅	9 9
8 T	☽∠☿	10am36
	☿SD	11 49
	☉⚺☽	6pm41
	☽△♆	6 45
	☽*♇	6 49
	☉⚻♆	7 28
	☉□♇	8 28
9 W	☽⚺♂	2am 3
	☽□♄	11 51
	☿*♀	4pm10
	☽*☿	5 0
	☽☌♀	5 4
10 Th	☽∠♇	1am10
	♂∠♅	2 32
	☉∠☽	3 42
	☽□♃	4 19
	☽☌♅	9 56
	☽∠♂	10 23
	☉∠♃	1pm12
11 F	♀ ♋	1am42
	☽□♆	7 20
	☽⚺♇	7 33
	☉*☽	12pm45
	☽∥♀	4 49
	☽*♂	6 40
12 S	☽*♄	0am22
	☽□☿	6 38
	☽∥♇	8 36
	☽∥♅	10 3
	☽⚺♀	12pm 6
	☽△♃	5 52
	☽⚺♅	10 34
13 Su	♀∠♇	5am22
	☽∠♄	6 15
	☉∠♅	11 34
	☽∥♂	2pm11
	☉∥☽	5 38
	☽*♆	7 7
	☽☌♇	7 27
	☽∠♀	8 53
	☽⚼♃	11 59
14 M	☽∠♅	4am12
	☉□☽	5 32
	☽□♂	9 49
	☽⚺♄	11 31
	☽△☿	7pm30
15 T	☽∠♆	0am 3
	☿ ♉	1 40
	☽*♀	4 40
	☽⚻♃	5 16
	☽*♅	9 1
	♀□♃	12pm48
	☽∥☿	1 46
	♂△♄	2 28
16 W	☽⚼☿	0am52
	☽#♆	3 9
	☽⚺♆	4 2
	☽⚺♇	4 29
	☽∥♄	8 0
	☉△☽	6pm17
	☽∥♃	7 0
	☽☌♄	7 22
	☽△♂	9 2
17 Th	☽#♃	3am 9
	☽⚻☿	5 14
	☽∠♇	7 29
	♀☌♅	7 32
	☉△♄	8 57
	☽☍♃	12pm44
	☽#♄	1 47
	☽□♅	3 35
	☽□♀	4 16
	☽∥♆	6 21
	☉⚼☽	10 42
18 F	☽⚼♂	0am48
	☽#☿	8 24
	☽☌♆	8 56
	☽*♇	9 27
	☽⚺♄	11pm 8
19 S	☉⚻☽	1am55
	☽⚻♂	3 27
	☽☍☿	10 59
	☽⚻♃	4pm 3
	☽△♅	6 13
	☽△♀	10 50
	☽∠♄	11 44
20 Su	☉#☽	3am48
	☽#♂	5 20
	☽⚺♆	10 16
	☽□♇	10 51
	☽⚼♃	4pm33
	☽⚼♅	6 26
	☽#♅	10 48
	☽*♄	11 45
	☽#♇	11 49
21 M	☽⚼♀	0am49
	☉☍☽	5 45
	☽☍♂	6 18
	☽∠♆	10 6
	☽#♀	10 15
	☽⚻☿	1pm58
	♂ ♊	3 33
	☽△♃	4 38
	☽⚻♅	6 17
	☉ ♊	9 16
22 T	☽⚻♀	2am24
	☽*♆	9 44
	☽△♇	10 24
	☉☌♂	1pm20
	☽⚼☿	3 9
	☽□♄	11 6
23 W	☽⚻♂	8am 2
	☉⚻☽	8 22
	☽⚼♇	10 10
	☽△☿	4pm37
	☽□♃	4 42
	☽☍♅	5 56
	☿⚺♃	6 15
24 Th	☉⚼♆	1am15
	☽☍♀	5 53
	☽⚼♂	9 17
	☽□♆	9 30
	☉⚼☽	10 5
	☽⚻♇	10 17
	☿*♅	12pm43
	♂⚼♆	1 46
	☽#♀	10 5
	☽△♄	11 21
25 F	☽#♇	6am23
	☽#♅	7 23
	☽△♂	11 12
	☉△☽	12pm31
	☽*♃	6 26
	☽⚻♅	7 16
	☽#♂	9 13
	☉#☽	9 39
	☽□☿	9 41
26 S	☽⚼♄	0am23
	♀□♆	5 48
	☽△♆	11 29
	☽⚻♀	11 58
	☽☍♇	12pm24
	♀⚺♇	5 25
	☽∠♃	8 26
	☽⚼♅	9 3
27 Su	☽⚻♄	2am14
	☿⚼♄	6 46
	☽#☿	1pm 5
	☽⚼♆	1 41
	☽⚼♀	4 33
	☽□♂	5 45
	☉□☽	8 17
	☽⚺♃	11 20
	☽△♅	11 43
28 M	☽*☿	7am13
	☽∥♆	4pm15
	☽⚻♆	4 45
	☽⚻♇	5 51
	☉∥♂	8 32
	☽#♄	8 45
	☽△♀	10 15
29 T	♄SD	3am36
	☽#♃	4 39
	♀∠♂	7 33
	☽☍♄	8 33
	☽∠☿	1pm54
	♃□♅	4 23
	☽∥♃	8 11
	☽⚼♇	9 50
	☉⚺♅	10 38
	☉*♃	11 35
30 W	☽∥♄	4am 5
	☽*♂	4 17
	☽□♅	7 34
	☽☌♃	7 43
	☉*☽	8 16
	☽#♆	8 45
	☽⚺☿	9pm46
31 Th	☽☍♆	1am14
	☽△♇	2 31
	☽∠♂	10 48
	☽□♀	12pm33
	☉∠☽	3 34
	☽⚻♄	5 51
	☽∥☿	11 19

JUNE 1951

LONGITUDE

Day	Sid. Time	☉	☽	☽ 12 Hour	Mean ☊	True ☊	☿	♀	♂	♃	♄	♅	♆	♇
	h m s	° ' "	° ' "	° ' "	° '	° '	° '	° '	° '	° '	° '	° '	° '	° '
1	16 34 41	9♊ 42 32	28♈ 41 30	4♉ 48 33	14♓ 47	15♓ 17R	16♉ 41	23♋ 20	7♊ 18	8♈ 7	25♍ 33	7♋ 51	16♎ 57R	17♌ 39
2	16 38 37	10 40 3	10♉ 53 32	16 56 42	14 44	15 8	18 7	24 25	8 0	8 18	25 33	7 54	16 57	17 40
3	16 42 34	11 37 33	22 58 18	28 58 32	14 41	14 57	19 35	25 30	8 42	8 28	25 34	7 58	16 56	17 41
4	16 46 31	12 35 2	4♊ 57 35	10♊ 55 36	14 38	14 44	21 7	26 34	9 24	8 38	25 34	8 1	16 55	17 42
5	16 50 27	13 32 30	16 52 45	22 49 13	14 35	14 30	22 40	27 39	10 6	8 48	25 35	8 4	16 54	17 42
6	16 54 24	14 29 58	28 45 8	4♋ 40 44	14 31	14 16	24 17	28 43	10 48	8 57	25 36	8 8	16 53	17 43
7	16 58 20	15 27 24	10♋ 36 13	16 31 49	14 28	14 4	25 56	29 46	11 30	9 7	25 36	8 11	16 53	17 44
8	17 2 17	16 24 49	22 27 51	28 24 37	14 25	13 54	27 37	0♌ 50	12 12	9 17	25 37	8 14	16 52	17 45
9	17 6 13	17 22 13	4♌ 22 31	10♌ 21 58	14 22	13 46	29 21	1 53	12 53	9 26	25 38	8 18	16 51	17 47
10	17 10 10	18 19 36	16 23 25	22 27 22	14 19	13 41	1♊ 8	2 56	13 35	9 35	25 40	8 21	16 51	17 48
11	17 14 7	19 16 59	28 34 23	4♍ 45 2	14 16	13 39D	2 57	3 59	14 16	9 45	25 41	8 25	16 50	17 49
12	17 18 3	20 14 20	10♍ 59 54	17 19 35	14 12	13 39R	4 49	5 1	14 58	9 54	25 42	8 28	16 50	17 50
13	17 22 0	21 11 40	23 44 41	0♎ 15 45	14 9	13 39	6 43	6 3	15 40	10 2	25 44	8 32	16 49	17 51
14	17 25 56	22 8 59	6♎ 53 17	13 37 44	14 6	13 38	8 39	7 5	16 21	10 11	25 45	8 35	16 49	17 52
15	17 29 53	23 6 17	20 29 24	27 28 28	14 3	13 36	10 38	8 7	17 2	10 20	25 47	8 39	16 48	17 53
16	17 33 49	24 3 34	4♏ 34 57	11♏ 48 37	14 0	13 32	12 39	9 8	17 44	10 28	25 49	8 42	16 48	17 54
17	17 37 46	25 0 51	19 9 4	26 35 38	13 56	13 25	14 42	10 9	18 25	10 37	25 51	8 46	16 48	17 56
18	17 41 42	25 58 6	4♐ 7 25	11♐ 43 19	13 53	13 16	16 47	11 9	19 6	10 45	25 53	8 49	16 47	17 57
19	17 45 39	26 55 22	19 22 3	27 2 11	13 50	13 5	18 53	12 9	19 48	10 53	25 55	8 53	16 47	17 58
20	17 49 36	27 52 37	4♑ 42 16	12♑ 20 50	13 47	12 55	21 1	13 9	20 29	11 1	25 57	8 56	16 47	17 59
21	17 53 32	28 49 51	19 56 31	27 28 4	13 44	12 46	23 10	14 9	21 10	11 9	25 59	9 0	16 46	18 1
22	17 57 29	29 47 4	4♒ 54 27	12♒ 14 49	13 41	12 40	25 20	15 8	21 51	11 17	26 1	9 4	16 46	18 2
23	18 1 25	0♋ 44 18	19 28 36	26 35 25	13 37	12 35	27 31	16 6	22 32	11 24	26 4	9 7	16 46	18 3
24	18 5 22	1 41 31	3♓ 35 5	10♓ 27 40	13 34	12 34D	29 42	17 4	23 13	11 32	26 6	9 11	16 46	18 5
25	18 9 18	2 38 44	17 13 18	23 52 20	13 31	12 34	1♋ 54	18 2	23 54	11 39	26 9	9 14	16 46	18 6
26	18 13 15	3 35 57	0♈ 25 9	6♈ 52 14	13 28	12 34R	4 5	19 0	24 35	11 46	26 12	9 18	16 45	18 8
27	18 17 11	4 33 10	13 14 6	19 31 16	13 25	12 34	6 16	19 57	25 16	11 53	26 14	9 22	16 45	18 9
28	18 21 8	5 30 24	25 44 19	1♉ 53 44	13 22	12 32	8 26	20 53	25 57	12 0	26 17	9 25	16 45D	18 10
29	18 25 5	6 27 37	8♉ 0 4	14 3 47	13 18	12 28	10 36	21 49	26 37	12 6	26 20	9 29	16 45	18 12
30	18 29 1	7♋ 24 50	20♉ 5 19	26♉ 5 6	13♓ 15	12♓ 21	12♋ 44	22♌ 45	27♊ 18	12♈ 13	26♍ 23	9♋ 32	16♎ 45	18♌ 13

DECLINATION and LATITUDE

Day	☉ Decl	☽ Decl	☽ Lat	☽ 12 Hr. Decl	☿ Decl	☿ Lat	♀ Decl	♀ Lat	♂ Decl	♂ Lat	♃ Decl	♃ Lat	♄ Decl	♄ Lat
1	21N55	14N14	3N27	16N43	14N 6	2S50	23N52	2N29	21N51	0N19	2N 8	1S11	3N58	2N24
2	22 3	19 2	4 8	21 8	14 37	2 44	23 40	2 28	21 58	0 20	2 12	1 11	3 58	2 23
3	22 11	22 60	4 38	24 37	15 8	2 36	23 28	2 28	22 5	0 20	2 16	1 11	3 57	2 23
4	22 19	25 58	4 55	27 1	15 39	2 28	23 15	2 27	22 12	0 21	2 20	1 12	3 57	2 23
5	22 26	27 45	4 59	28 11	16 11	2 20	23 1	2 26	22 19	0 21	2 23	1 12	3 56	2 23
6	22 33	28 16	4 50	28 2	16 44	2 11	22 47	2 25	22 26	0 22	2 27	1 12	3 56	2 23
7	22 39	27 29	4 28	26 36	17 16	2 2	22 33	2 24	22 32	0 22	2 31	1 12	3 55	2 22
8	22 45	25 26	3 55	23 59	17 49	1 52	22 18	2 22	22 38	0 23	2 34	1 12	3 55	2 22
9	22 51	22 16	3 11	20 19	18 21	1 42	22 2	2 21	22 44	0 24	2 38	1 13	3 54	2 22
10	22 56	18 8	2 19	15 45	18 54	1 32	21 46	2 19	22 50	0 24	2 41	1 13	3 54	2 22
11	23 1	13 12	1 19	10 30	19 26	1 21	21 29	2 17	22 56	0 25	2 44	1 13	3 53	2 21
12	23 5	7 40	0 14	4 43	19 57	1 10	21 13	2 16	23 1	0 25	2 48	1 13	3 52	2 21
13	23 9	1 40	0S53	1S26	20 28	0 59	20 55	2 14	23 6	0 26	2 51	1 13	3 51	2 21
14	23 13	4S34	1 60	7 42	20 57	0 48	20 37	2 11	23 11	0 27	2 54	1 14	3 51	2 21
15	23 16	10 49	3 2	13 50	21 26	0 37	20 19	2 9	23 16	0 27	2 58	1 14	3 50	2 21
16	23 19	16 44	3 55	19 27	21 54	0 26	20 1	2 7	23 20	0 28	3 1	1 14	3 49	2 20
17	23 21	21 55	4 35	24 4	22 19	0 15	19 42	2 4	23 25	0 28	3 4	1 14	3 48	2 20
18	23 23	25 50	4 57	27 10	22 44	0 4	19 22	2 1	23 29	0 29	3 7	1 15	3 47	2 20
19	23 25	27 59	4 59	28 17	23 6	0N 7	19 3	1 58	23 32	0 29	3 10	1 15	3 46	2 20
20	23 26	28 1	4 40	27 14	23 26	0 18	18 43	1 55	23 36	0 30	3 13	1 15	3 45	2 20
21	23 26	25 56	4 1	24 11	23 44	0 28	18 22	1 52	23 39	0 30	3 15	1 15	3 44	2 19
22	23 27	22 2	3 5	19 35	24 0	0 38	18 2	1 48	23 43	0 31	3 18	1 16	3 43	2 19
23	23 27	16 52	1 59	13 58	24 13	0 48	17 41	1 45	23 46	0 32	3 21	1 16	3 41	2 19
24	23 26	10 56	0 47	7 49	24 24	0 57	17 20	1 41	23 48	0 32	3 24	1 16	3 40	2 19
25	23 25	4 40	0N25	1 31	24 31	1 5	16 58	1 37	23 51	0 33	3 26	1 16	3 39	2 19
26	23 24	1N36	1 33	4N39	24 36	1 13	16 36	1 33	23 53	0 33	3 29	1 17	3 38	2 18
27	23 22	7 37	2 35	10 28	24 38	1 20	16 14	1 29	23 55	0 34	3 31	1 17	3 36	2 18
28	23 20	13 11	3 28	15 44	24 37	1 27	15 52	1 24	23 57	0 34	3 34	1 17	3 35	2 18
29	23 17	18 7	4 10	20 18	24 34	1 33	15 30	1 20	23 59	0 35	3 36	1 17	3 34	2 18
30	23N14	22N16	4N41	23N59	24N27	1N38	15N 7	1N15	24N 0	0N35	3N38	1S18	3N32	2N18

Day	♅ Decl	♅ Lat	♆ Decl	♆ Lat	♇ Decl	♇ Lat
1	23N32	0N19	5S 7	1N40	23N40	8N33
5	23 31	0 19	5 6	1 40	23 39	8 33
9	23 30	0 19	5 5	1 40	23 37	8 32
13	23 29	0 19	5 5	1 40	23 35	8 32
17	23 28	0 19	5 4	1 40	23 33	8 31
21	23 27	0 19	5 4	1 39	23 31	8 31
25	23 27	0 19	5 4	1 39	23 29	8 30
29	23N26	0N19	5S 4	1N39	23N27	8N30

☽ PHENOMENA

d	h	m	
4	16	41	●
12	18	52	☽
19	12	36	○
26	6	22	☾

d	h	° '
5	21	28N17
13	6	0
19	12	28S17
25	18	0

d	h	° '
4	19	4N59
12	5	0
18	14	5S 1
24	16	0

VOID OF COURSE ☽

Last Aspect		☽ Ingress		
31	12pm33	1	♉	2am34
3	5am32	3	♊	2pm 3
5	5pm36	6	♋	2am32
8	12pm11	8	♌	3pm12
10	4am10	11	♍	2am47
13	3am41	13	♎	11am31
15	4am51	15	♏	4pm17
17	10am49	17	♐	5pm27
19	12pm36	19	♑	4pm38
21	9am39	21	♒	4pm 4
23	4pm 5	23	♓	5pm50
25	4pm12	25	♈	11pm14
28	0am25	28	♉	8am18
30	12pm40	30	♊	7pm52

d	h	
6	1	APOGEE
19	14	PERIGEE

DAILY ASPECTARIAN

Day	Aspect	Time
1 F	☿⊼♆	4am34
	☿□♇	4pm24
	☽⊻♂	5 57
	☽⚹♅	6 4
	☽⊻♃	6 48
	♂⊻♅	8 16
	☽⚼♄	11 20
	☉⊻☽	11 31
2 S	♀∥♇	0am57
	☽⊼♆	11 59
	♂⚹♃	1pm 8
	☽□♇	1 26
	☽☌☿	4 19
	♀∥♅	5 19
	☽∥♂	5 47
	☉∥☽	6 24
	☽∠♅	11 58
3 Su	☽∠♃	1am 0
	♀⚹♄	1 24
	☽∥♀	3 5
	☽∥♅	3 41
	☽∥♇	4 40
	☽△♄	5 10
	☽⚹♀	5 32
	☽⚼♆	5pm54
4 M	☽⊻♅	6am10
	☽⚹♃	7 29
	☽☌♂	9 29
	☽∠♀	2pm37
	☉☌☽	4 41
5 T	☽△♆	0am 3
	☽⚹♇	1 41
	☿∠♅	6 12
	☽⊻☿	1pm31
	☽□♄	5 36
	☿∠♃	6 42
	☽⊻♀	11 54
6 W	☽∠♇	8am 3
	☉∥♀	4pm37
	☽☌♅	7 4
	☿△♄	7 19
	☽□♃	8 57
7 Th	♀∥♂	0am25
	☽∠☿	0 46
	☽⊻♂	1 55
	♀ ♌	5 10
	☉⊻☽	10 41
	☽□♆	12pm42
	☽⊻♇	2 28
8 F	☽⚹♄	6am23
	☽∠♂	10 8
	☉△♆	11 17
	☽⚹☿	12pm11
	☽∥♇	2 42
	☽∥♅	3 32
	☽☌♀	6 31
	☉∠☽	7 37
	☉∥☽	8 14
	☽∥♂	8 56
9 S	☽∥♀	1am37
	☽⊻♅	7 54
	☿ ♊	8 44
	☽△♃	10 16
	☉⚹♇	10 21
	☽∠♄	12pm34
	☽⚹♂	6 4
	☽∥☿	8 21
10 Su	☽⚹♆	0am55
	☽☌♇	2 47
	☉⚹☽	4 10
	☿⚼♆	9 25
	☽∠♅	1pm50
	☽⚼♃	4 24
	☽⊻♄	6 20
11 M	☽∠♆	6am21
	☽□☿	10 1
	☽⊻♀	11 28
	☽⚹♅	7pm 8
	☽⊼♃	9 52
12 T	☿⚹♀	5am43
	☽□♂	7 59
	☽#♆	10 31
	☽⊻♆	11 3
	☽⊻♇	12pm58
	☽∥♄	3 23
	☽∠♀	6 33
	☉□☽	6 52
	☽∥♃	7 24
13 W	☽☌♄	3am41
	☿∥♀	1pm51
	☽∠♇	4 44
	☽#♃	5 36
	☽#♄	9 14
	☿⊻♅	11 6
14 Th	☽⚹♀	0am23
	☽∥♆	1 56
	☽□♅	3 3
	☽△☿	3 43
	☽☍♃	5 58
	♂△♆	3pm55
	☽☌♆	5 35
	☽△♂	5 40
	☽⚹♇	7 28
	☿⚹♃	8 3
	☉∠♀	10 13
15 F	☉∥♂	2am25
	☉△☽	4 51
	☽⊻♄	9 8
	☽⚼☿	10 20
	♀⊻♅	1pm20
	☽⚼♂	8 44
16 S	♂⚹♇	6am23
	☽△♅	6 53
	☉⚼☽	7 59
	☽□♀	8 8
	☽⊼♃	9 53
	☽∠♄	10 22
	☽#♀	1pm46
	☽⊼☿	3 33
	☽⊻♆	8 10
	☽□♇	10 1
	☽⊼♂	10 45
17 Su	☽#☿	2am21
	☽⚼♅	7 29
	☉#☽	7 51
	☽#♂	8 15
	☽#♅	8 28
	☽#♇	8 54
	☉⊼☽	10 7
	☽⚼♃	10 31
	☽⚹♄	10 49
	♀△♃	12pm56
	♀∠♄	5 10
	☽∠♆	8 17
	☉□♄	9 35
	♂∥♅	9 45
18 M	☿△♆	0am 6
	☽⊼♅	7 27
	☽△♃	10 34
	☽△♀	11 53
	☿⚹♇	1pm31
	☽⚹♆	7 57
	♂∥♇	9 32
	☽△♇	9 48
	☽☍☿	11 7
19 T	☽☍♂	0am42
	☽□♄	10 16
	☉☍☽	12pm36
	☽⚼♀	1 2
	☿☌♂	3 8
	☽⚼♇	9 19
	☉∥☿	11 7
20 W	☿∥♅	1am40
	☿∥♇	6 17
	☽☍♅	6 40
	☽□♃	10 0
	☽⊼♀	2pm12
	☿∥♂	3 26
	☽□♆	6 59
	☽⊼♇	8 56
21 Th	☽⊼♂	2am 2
	☽⊼☿	5 59
	☽△♄	9 39
	☽#☿	1pm43
	☽#♂	2 55
	☉⊼☽	3 9
	☽#♇	3 58
	☽#♅	4 17
	☉#☽	4 21
22 F	☽⚼♂	3am19
	☉ ♋	5 25
	☽⊼♅	6 48
	☿□♄	7 42
	☽⚼♄	10 1
	☽⚼☿	10 25
	☽⚹♃	10 30
	☉⚼☽	5pm20
	☽☍♀	5 58
	☽△♆	7 29
	☽#♀	8 16
	☽☍♇	9 38
23 S	☽△♂	5am23
	☽⚼♅	7 51
	☽⊼♄	11 8
	☽∠♃	11 47
	☽△☿	4pm 5
	♀⚹♆	4 15
	☉△☽	8 30
	☽⚼♆	8 51
24 Su	☿ ♋	3am14
	☽△♅	9 47
	☽⊻♃	2pm 0
	☽∥♆	10 30
	☽⊼♆	11 10
25 M	☽⊼♀	1am35
	☽⊼♇	1 35
	♀☌♇	1 38
	☽#♄	3 53
	☽#♃	4 39
	☉∠♇	11 47
	☽□♂	12pm42
	☿∠♇	1 22
	☉☌☿	2 34
	☽☍♄	4 12
	☿∠♀	10 16
26 T	☽⚼♇	5am 1
	☉□☽	6 22
	☽⚼♀	7 10
	☽∥♃	7 25
	☽∥♄	7 56
	☽□☿	8 11
	☽#♆	1pm39
	☽□♅	4 38
	☽☌♃	9 25
27 W	☽☍♆	6am42
	☽△♇	9 23
	☽△♀	1pm52
28 Th	☽⚹♂	0am25
	☽⊼♄	1 4
	♃∥♄	9 40
	☿☌♅	11 12
	☽∥♀	11 45
	♂□♄	1pm13
	☉⚹☽	8 42
	♆SD	9 51
29 F	☽⚹♅	2am56
	☽⚹☿	6 14
	☽⚼♄	6 37
	☽∠♂	7 35
	☽⊻♃	8 12
	☽⊼♆	5pm21
	☿□♃	5 52
	☽□♇	8 16
30 S	☉∠☽	5am 3
	☽□♀	5 45
	☉∥☽	6 26
	☽∥♅	7 50
	☽∥♇	7 55
	☽∠♅	8 57
	☽∥♂	12pm14
	☽△♄	12 40
	☽∠♃	2 24
	☽∥☿	2 55
	☽⊻♂	3 18
	☽∠☿	6 37
	☽⚼♆	11 24

LONGITUDE

Day	Sid. Time	☉	☽	☽ 12 Hour	Mean ☊	True ☊	☿	♀	♂	♃	♄	♅	♆	♇
	h m s	° ' "	° ' "	° ' "	° '	° '	° '	° '	° '	° '	° '	° '	° '	° '
1	18 32 58	8♋ 22 3	2♊ 3 28	8♊ 0 47	13♓ 12	12♓ 12R	14♋ 51	23♌ 40	27♊ 59	12♈ 19	26♍ 27	9♋ 36	16♎ 45	18♌ 15
2	18 36 54	9 19 17	13 57 20	19 53 22	13 9	12 1	16 57	24 34	28 39	12 25	26 30	9 40	16 45	18 16
3	18 40 51	10 16 30	25 49 8	1♋ 44 50	13 6	11 50	19 1	25 28	29 20	12 32	26 33	9 43	16 46	18 18
4	18 44 47	11 13 43	7♋ 40 40	13 36 50	13 2	11 38	21 3	26 22	0♋ 0	12 37	26 37	9 47	16 46	18 19
5	18 48 44	12 10 57	19 33 30	25 30 54	12 59	11 28	23 4	27 15	0 41	12 43	26 40	9 50	16 46	18 21
6	18 52 40	13 8 10	1♌ 29 14	7♌ 28 44	12 56	11 20	25 3	28 7	1 21	12 49	26 44	9 54	16 46	18 22
7	18 56 37	14 5 23	13 29 40	19 32 19	12 53	11 14	27 0	28 59	2 2	12 54	26 47	9 58	16 46	18 24
8	19 0 34	15 2 36	25 37 1	1♍ 44 9	12 50	11 10	28 55	29 50	2 42	12 59	26 51	10 1	16 47	18 26
9	19 4 30	15 59 49	7♍ 54 5	14 7 17	12 47	11 9D	0♌ 49	0♍ 40	3 23	13 4	26 55	10 5	16 47	18 27
10	19 8 27	16 57 2	20 24 10	26 45 13	12 43	11 9	2 40	1 30	4 3	13 9	26 59	10 9	16 47	18 29
11	19 12 23	17 54 15	3♎ 10 56	9♎ 41 45	12 40	11 10	4 29	2 19	4 43	13 14	27 3	10 12	16 48	18 30
12	19 16 20	18 51 28	16 18 8	23 0 28	12 37	11 11R	6 17	3 7	5 23	13 18	27 7	10 16	16 48	18 32
13	19 20 16	19 48 41	29 49 4	6♏ 44 8	12 34	11 11	8 2	3 54	6 3	13 23	27 11	10 19	16 48	18 34
14	19 24 13	20 45 53	13♏ 45 48	20 53 58	12 31	11 8	9 46	4 41	6 44	13 27	27 16	10 23	16 49	18 35
15	19 28 9	21 43 6	28 8 24	5♐ 28 40	12 28	11 4	11 27	5 26	7 24	13 31	27 20	10 26	16 49	18 37
16	19 32 6	22 40 19	12♐ 54 8	20 23 56	12 24	10 58	13 7	6 11	8 4	13 34	27 24	10 30	16 50	18 39
17	19 36 3	23 37 32	27 57 5	5♑ 32 23	12 21	10 52	14 44	6 55	8 44	13 38	27 29	10 34	16 51	18 41
18	19 39 59	24 34 45	13♑ 8 35	20 44 22	12 18	10 45	16 20	7 38	9 24	13 41	27 33	10 37	16 51	18 42
19	19 43 56	25 31 59	28 18 25	5♒ 49 30	12 15	10 39	17 54	8 20	10 4	13 45	27 38	10 41	16 52	18 44
20	19 47 52	26 29 13	13♒ 16 30	20 38 27	12 12	10 35	19 26	9 1	10 43	13 48	27 43	10 44	16 52	18 46
21	19 51 49	27 26 27	27 54 35	5♓ 4 20	12 8	10 33D	20 55	9 41	11 23	13 51	27 48	10 48	16 53	18 47
22	19 55 45	28 23 43	12♓ 7 19	19 3 21	12 5	10 32	22 23	10 20	12 3	13 53	27 52	10 51	16 54	18 49
23	19 59 42	29 20 58	25 52 26	2♈ 34 42	12 2	10 33	23 49	10 58	12 43	13 56	27 57	10 55	16 55	18 51
24	20 3 39	0♌ 18 15	9♈ 10 26	15 39 59	11 59	10 34	25 13	11 34	13 22	13 58	28 2	10 58	16 55	18 53
25	20 7 35	1 15 33	22 3 47	28 22 22	11 56	10 35R	26 34	12 10	14 2	14 0	28 7	11 2	16 56	18 55
26	20 11 32	2 12 51	4♉ 36 16	10♉ 46 1	11 53	10 36	27 54	12 44	14 42	14 2	28 13	11 5	16 57	18 56
27	20 15 28	3 10 11	16 52 13	22 55 23	11 49	10 34	29 11	13 17	15 21	14 4	28 18	11 9	16 58	18 58
28	20 19 25	4 7 31	28 56 6	4♊ 54 51	11 46	10 32	0♍ 27	13 48	16 1	14 5	28 23	11 12	16 59	19 0
29	20 23 21	5 4 53	10♊ 52 9	16 48 27	11 43	10 27	1 40	14 13	16 40	14 7	28 28	11 15	17 0	19 2
30	20 27 18	6 2 15	22 44 10	28 39 43	11 40	10 22	2 50	14 47	17 20	14 8	28 34	11 19	17 1	19 4
31	20 31 14	6♌ 59 39	4♋ 35 26	10♋ 31 38	11♓ 37	10♓ 16	3♍ 59	15♍ 14	17♋ 59	14♈ 9	28♍ 39	11♋ 22	17♎ 2	19♌ 5

DECLINATION and LATITUDE

Day	☉ Decl	☽ Decl	☽ Lat	☽ 12 Hr. Decl	☿ Decl	☿ Lat	♀ Decl	♀ Lat	♂ Decl	♂ Lat	♃ Decl	♃ Lat	♄ Decl	♄ Lat
1	23N11	25N27	4N58	26N37	24N18	1N42	14N44	1N10	24N 2	0N36	3N41	1S18	3N31	2N17
2	23 7	27 29	5 3	28 3	24 7	1 45	14 21	1 5	24 3	0 36	3 43	1 18	3 29	2 17
3	23 3	28 17	4 54	28 11	23 53	1 48	13 58	0 60	24 4	0 37	3 45	1 18	3 28	2 17
4	22 58	27 45	4 33	27 1	23 37	1 50	13 35	0 54	24 4	0 38	3 47	1 19	3 26	2 17
5	22 53	25 58	3 59	24 37	23 18	1 52	13 12	0 49	24 5	0 38	3 49	1 19	3 25	2 17
6	22 48	23 0	3 15	21 9	22 58	1 52	12 48	0 43	24 5	0 39	3 51	1 19	3 23	2 16
7	22 42	19 3	2 22	16 45	22 36	1 52	12 24	0 37	24 5	0 39	3 53	1 19	3 22	2 16
8	22 36	14 16	1 22	11 39	22 12	1 51	12 1	0 31	24 5	0 40	3 54	1 20	3 20	2 16
9	22 29	8 53	0 17	6 0	21 46	1 50	11 37	0 24	24 4	0 40	3 56	1 20	3 18	2 16
10	22 22	3 3	0S50	0 1	21 19	1 48	11 13	0 18	24 4	0 41	3 58	1 20	3 16	2 16
11	22 15	3S 2	1 56	6S 6	20 51	1 45	10 49	0 11	24 3	0 41	3 59	1 21	3 15	2 15
12	22 7	9 8	2 57	12 8	20 21	1 42	10 25	0 4	24 2	0 42	4 1	1 21	3 13	2 15
13	21 59	15 1	3 51	17 46	19 51	1 38	10 2	0S 3	24 1	0 42	4 2	1 21	3 11	2 15
14	21 50	20 19	4 33	22 37	19 19	1 34	9 38	0 11	23 59	0 43	4 3	1 21	3 9	2 15
15	21 42	24 37	4 60	26 14	18 47	1 29	9 14	0 18	23 58	0 43	4 5	1 22	3 7	2 15
16	21 32	27 26	5 7	28 8	18 13	1 24	8 50	0 26	23 56	0 44	4 6	1 22	3 5	2 15
17	21 23	28 20	4 54	27 59	17 39	1 18	8 27	0 34	23 54	0 44	4 7	1 22	3 3	2 14
18	21 13	27 6	4 20	25 44	17 5	1 11	8 3	0 43	23 51	0 45	4 8	1 23	3 1	2 14
19	21 2	23 54	3 28	21 40	16 30	1 5	7 39	0 51	23 49	0 45	4 9	1 23	2 59	2 14
20	20 52	19 6	2 22	16 17	15 54	0 57	7 16	0 60	23 46	0 46	4 10	1 23	2 57	2 14
21	20 41	13 16	1 8	10 7	15 19	0 50	6 53	1 8	23 44	0 46	4 11	1 23	2 55	2 14
22	20 29	6 53	0N 9	3 37	14 43	0 42	6 30	1 17	23 41	0 47	4 12	1 24	2 53	2 14
23	20 18	0 23	1 22	2N49	14 7	0 33	6 7	1 27	23 37	0 47	4 12	1 24	2 51	2 13
24	20 5	5N55	2 29	8 55	13 31	0 25	5 45	1 36	23 34	0 48	4 13	1 24	2 49	2 13
25	19 53	11 47	3 26	14 29	12 54	0 16	5 22	1 46	23 30	0 48	4 14	1 25	2 47	2 13
26	19 40	17 0	4 12	19 20	12 18	0 6	5 0	1 56	23 27	0 49	4 14	1 25	2 45	2 13
27	19 27	21 25	4 45	23 17	11 42	0S 3	4 38	2 6	23 23	0 49	4 14	1 25	2 43	2 13
28	19 14	24 52	5 4	26 11	11 7	0 13	4 17	2 16	23 18	0 50	4 15	1 25	2 40	2 13
29	19 0	27 12	5 11	27 55	10 31	0 24	3 56	2 27	23 14	0 50	4 15	1 26	2 38	2 13
30	18 46	28 18	5 4	28 21	9 56	0 34	3 35	2 37	23 10	0 51	4 15	1 26	2 36	2 12
31	18N32	28N 5	4N43	27N30	9N22	0S45	3N14	2S48	23N 5	0N51	4N15	1S26	2N33	2N12

Day	♅ Decl	♅ Lat	♆ Decl	♆ Lat	♇ Decl	♇ Lat
1	23N25	0N19	5S 4	1N39	23N26	8N30
5	23 24	0 19	5 4	1 39	23 23	8 29
9	23 23	0 19	5 5	1 38	23 21	8 29
13	23 22	0 19	5 6	1 38	23 19	8 29
17	23 21	0 19	5 7	1 38	23 16	8 29
21	23 20	0 19	5 8	1 38	23 14	8 29
25	23 19	0 19	5 9	1 38	23 12	8 29
29	23N18	0N20	5S11	1N37	23N10	8N29

☽ PHENOMENA

d	h	m	
4	7	48	●
12	4	57	☽
18	19	18	○
25	19	0	☾

d	h	° '
3	3	28N17
10	12	0
16	22	28S20
23	1	0
30	8	28N23

d	h	
1	20	5N 3
9	6	0
15	21	5S 7
21	21	0
28	23	5N11

VOID OF COURSE ☽

Last Aspect		☽ Ingress		
3	7am33	3	♋	8am28
5	2pm24	5	♌	9pm 1
7	9am46	8	♍	8am36
10	12pm30	10	♎	6pm 5
12	4am57	13	♏	0am19
14	10pm40	15	♐	3am 3
16	11pm15	17	♑	3am15
18	10pm56	19	♒	2am42
20	11am10	21	♓	3am29
23	6am40	23	♈	7am22
25	9am35	25	♉	3pm 7
27	10pm53	28	♊	2am 8
30	11am53	30	♋	2pm43

d	h	
3	4	APOGEE
17	23	PERIGEE
30	12	APOGEE

DAILY ASPECTARIAN

Day	Aspect	Time
1 Su	☉⚺☽	1pm49
	☽⚺♅	3 17
	☽*♃	8 53
	☿□♆	9 49
2 M	♀∠♅	2am29
	☽△♆	5 40
	☿∥♂	7 1
	☽⚺☿	7 20
	☽*♇	8 45
	☉☌♅	9 7
	☿⚺♇	3pm31
	♅∥♇	6 57
	☽*♀	11 15
3 T	☽□♄	1am30
	☽☌♂	7 33
	☽∠♇	3pm10
	♂ ♋	11 42
4 W	☽☌♅	4am17
	♀⚺♄	7 9
	☉☌☽	7 48
	☽∠♀	8 3
	☽□♃	10 5
	☿∥♅	4pm55
	☿∥♇	5 41
	☽□♆	6 22
	☽⚺♇	9 33
5 Th	☽☌☿	8am30
	☽*♄	2pm24
	♀⚼♃	2 32
	☉□♃	2 56
	☽∥♂	4 15
	☽⚺♀	4 42
	☉∠♀	6 33
	☽∥♅	9 17
	☽∥♇	9 24
	☽⚺♂	11 44
6 F	☽∥☿	0am18
	☉∥☽	1 29
	☉∥☿	3pm17
	☽⚺♅	4 56
	☽∠♄	8 35
	☿*♄	9 17
	☽△♃	10 48
7 S	☉⚺☽	1am17
	☽*♆	6 31
	☽∠♂	7 27
	☽☌♇	9 46
	☽∠♅	10pm49
8 Su	☽⚺♄	2am27
	☽⚼♃	4 41
	♀ ♍	4 54
	☽⚺☿	7 41
	☽☌♀	8 53
	☉∠☽	9 25
	☽∥♀	11 10
	☽∠♆	12pm 5
	☿ ♌	1 39
	☽*♂	2 42
	☿⚺♀	8 42
9 M	♂∠♇	2am52
	☽*♅	4 14
	☽⚻♃	10 3
	☽#♆	3pm46
	☉*☽	4 53
	☽⚺♆	5 6
	☽∠☿	5 53
	☉□♆	7 53
	☽⚺♇	8 20
	☽∥♃	8 20
	☽∥♄	11 4
10 T	♀∠♆	8am40
	☽☌♄	12pm30
	☽⚺♀	10 16
11 W	☽∠♇	0am36
	☽#♄	0 49
	☽*☿	2 48
	☽□♂	3 0
	☽#♃	3 45
	☿⚺♂	4 54
	☽∥♆	8 2
	☽□♅	12pm59
	☉⚺♇	3 39
	☽☍♃	6 33
12 Th	☽☌♆	0am54
	☽∠♀	3 28
	☽*♇	4 1
	☽#♀	4 48
	☉□☽	4 57
	☽⚺♄	7pm22
13 F	☽*♀	7am32
	☽△♂	11 23
	☽□☿	4pm14
	☽△♅	6 13
	☽#☿	7 39
	☽∠♄	9 26
	☽⚻♃	11 27
14 S	☽⚺♆	5am 9
	☉#☽	7 32
	☽□♇	8 9
	☿⚺♅	9 5
	☉△☽	12pm37
	☽⚼♂	2 2
	☽#♇	3 51
	☽#♅	4 12
	☽⚼♅	7 32
	☽#♂	7 51
	☽*♄	10 40
15 Su	☽⚼♃	0am37
	☽∠♆	6 3
	☽□♀	12pm35
	☿∠♄	1 15
	☉⚼☽	2 59
	☽⚻♂	3 49
	☽⚻♅	8 7
16 M	☽△☿	0am23
	☽△♃	1 5
	☽*♆	6 18
	☿△♃	7 1
	☽△♇	9 13
	☉⚻☽	4pm40
	☽□♄	11 15
17 T	☽⚼☿	3am10
	☽⚼♇	9 4
	☽△♀	2pm53
	☽☍♂	5 49
	☽☍♅	8 0
18 W	☽□♃	0am52
	☽⚻☿	5 37
	☽□♆	5 52
	☿*♆	7 57
	☽⚻♇	8 48
	☽⚼♀	3pm44
	☉☍☽	7 18
	☽△♄	10 56
19 Th	☽#♂	0am29
	☽#♅	3 12
	☽#♇	3 40
	☿☌♇	1pm18
	☉#☽	3 37
	☽⚻♀	4 49
	☽⚻♂	7 41
	☽⚻♅	7 53
	☽⚼♄	11 5
20 F	♂☌♅	0am34
	☽*♃	0 51
	☽△♆	5 51
	☽☍♇	8 57
	☽☍☿	11 10
	☽#☿	3pm 2
	☽⚼♅	8 29
	☽⚼♂	9 21
	☉⚻☽	11 10
	☽⚻♄	11 48
21 S	☽∠♃	1am34
	☽⚼♆	6 39
	☉*♄	9 40
	☽☍♀	8pm48
	☽△♅	9 49
	☽△♂	11 52
22 Su	☽#♀	1am30
	☉⚼☽	2 21
	☽⚺♃	3 3
	☽∥♆	6 26
	☽⚻♆	8 15
	☽#♃	9 53
	☽⚻♇	11 37
	☽#♄	2pm48
	☽⚻☿	7 56
	♀*♅	9 47
23 M	☽☍♄	3am44
	☉△☽	6 40
	☽∥♄	12pm 6
	☽⚼♇	2 20
	☉ ♌	4 21
	☽∥♃	5 22
	☽#♆	8 58
	☽∥♀	11 20
24 T	☽⚼☿	2am 8
	☽□♅	3 19
	☽⚻♀	4 38
	☽□♂	8 9
	☽☌♃	8 52
	☿∠♅	1pm52
	☽☍♆	2 22
	☽△♇	6 3
	♂□♃	10 51
25 W	☽∥☿	4am25
	☽△☿	9 35
	☽⚼♀	10 9
	☽⚻♄	11 36
	♀#♆	1pm52
	☉□☽	7 0
26 Th	☿⚺♄	6am 5
	☽*♅	12pm41
	☉∥☽	1 14
	☽△♀	4 36
	☽⚼♄	4 55
	☽⚺♃	6 28
	☽*♂	8 50
	☿⚼♃	9 36
27 F	☽⚻♆	0am11
	☽□♇	4 10
	☽∥♇	11 16
	☽∥♅	12pm 8
	☽∥♂	12 25
	☿ ♍	3 24
	☽∠♅	6 30
	☽△♄	10 53
28 S	☽∠♃	0am19
	♀∥♃	2 7
	☽□☿	3 22
	♂∥♅	3 25
	☽∠♂	4 25
	☽⚼♆	6 7
	☉*☽	11 19
	♀⚻♃	2pm30
29 Su	☿∠♂	0am30
	☽⚺♅	0 47
	☽*♃	6 34
	☿∠♆	6 50
	☽□♀	7 14
	♂□♆	12pm 6
	☽△♆	12 24
	☽⚺♂	12 25
	☽*♇	4 32
	☉∠☽	8 16
30 M	♂∥♇	3am30
	☽□♄	11 53
	☽*☿	10pm38
	☽∠♇	10 59
31 T	☉⚺☽	5am17
	☽☌♅	1pm46
	☽□♃	7 20
	☽*♀	10 17

AUGUST 1951

LONGITUDE

Day	Sid. Time	☉	☽	☽ 12 Hour	Mean ☊	True ☊	☿	♀	♂	♃	♄	♅	♆	♇
	h m s	° ' "	° ' "	° ' "	° '	° '	° '	° '	° '	° '	° '	° '	° '	° '
1	20 35 11	7♌ 57 3	16♋ 28 37	22♋ 26 39	11♓ 34	10♓ 10R	5♍ 4	15♍ 39	18♋ 39	14♈ 10	28♍ 45	11♋ 25	17♎ 3	19♌ 7
2	20 39 8	8 54 28	28 25 57	4♌ 26 45	11 30	10 5	6 8	16 3	19 18	14 10	28 50	11 29	17 4	19 9
3	20 43 4	9 51 55	10♌ 29 14	16 33 37	11 27	10 1	7 8	16 25	19 57	14 11	28 56	11 32	17 5	19 11
4	20 47 1	10 49 22	22 40 4	28 48 46	11 24	9 58	8 6	16 45	20 37	14 11R	29 2	11 35	17 6	19 13
5	20 50 57	11 46 50	4♍ 59 56	11♍ 13 47	11 21	9 57D	9 0	17 4	21 16	14 11	29 7	11 39	17 7	19 15
6	20 54 54	12 44 19	17 30 30	23 50 20	11 18	9 57	9 52	17 21	21 55	14 10	29 13	11 42	17 8	19 16
7	20 58 50	13 41 48	0♎ 13 33	6♎ 40 22	11 14	9 58	10 41	17 35	22 34	14 10	29 19	11 45	17 9	19 18
8	21 2 47	14 39 18	13 11 4	19 45 53	11 11	10 0	11 26	17 48	23 13	14 9	29 25	11 48	17 11	19 20
9	21 6 43	15 36 50	26 25 5	3♏ 8 52	11 8	10 1	12 7	17 59	23 52	14 9	29 31	11 51	17 12	19 22
10	21 10 40	16 34 22	9♏ 57 25	16 50 50	11 5	10 2R	12 45	18 7	24 31	14 8	29 37	11 55	17 13	19 24
11	21 14 37	17 31 55	23 49 9	0♐ 52 20	11 2	10 2	13 19	18 14	25 10	14 6	29 43	11 58	17 15	19 26
12	21 18 33	18 29 29	8♐ 0 14	15 12 32	10 59	10 1	13 49	18 18	25 49	14 5	29 49	12 1	17 16	19 28
13	21 22 30	19 27 3	22 28 49	29 48 34	10 55	9 59	14 14	18 20R	26 28	14 3	29 56	12 4	17 17	19 30
14	21 26 26	20 24 39	7♑ 11 6	14♑ 35 36	10 52	9 57	14 35	18 20	27 7	14 1	0♎ 2	12 7	17 19	19 31
15	21 30 23	21 22 16	22 1 12	29 26 56	10 49	9 54	14 51	18 17	27 46	13 59	0 8	12 10	17 20	19 33
16	21 34 19	22 19 54	6♒ 51 51	14♒ 14 56	10 46	9 52	15 2	18 12	28 25	13 57	0 15	12 13	17 21	19 35
17	21 38 16	23 17 32	21 35 16	28 51 58	10 43	9 51	15 8R	18 4	29 4	13 55	0 21	12 16	17 23	19 37
18	21 42 12	24 15 12	6♓ 4 17	13♓ 11 35	10 40	9 51D	15 9	17 54	29 42	13 52	0 27	12 19	17 24	19 39
19	21 46 9	25 12 54	20 13 21	27 9 14	10 36	9 51	15 4	17 42	0♌ 21	13 49	0 34	12 22	17 26	19 41
20	21 50 6	26 10 37	3♈ 59 1	10♈ 42 38	10 33	9 52	14 53	17 27	1 0	13 46	0 40	12 24	17 27	19 43
21	21 54 2	27 8 21	17 20 9	23 51 43	10 30	9 53	14 36	17 10	1 38	13 43	0 47	12 27	17 29	19 44
22	21 57 59	28 6 7	0♉ 17 37	6♉ 38 13	10 27	9 54	14 14	16 51	2 17	13 40	0 54	12 30	17 31	19 46
23	22 1 55	29 3 55	12 53 56	19 5 14	10 24	9 54	13 46	16 29	2 56	13 36	1 0	12 33	17 32	19 48
24	22 5 52	0♍ 1 44	25 12 39	1♊ 16 44	10 20	9 54R	13 13	16 6	3 34	13 33	1 7	12 36	17 34	19 50
25	22 9 48	0 59 36	7♊ 18 3	13 17 9	10 17	9 54	12 34	15 40	4 13	13 29	1 14	12 38	17 35	19 52
26	22 13 45	1 57 29	19 14 37	25 11 1	10 14	9 54	11 51	15 13	4 51	13 25	1 20	12 41	17 37	19 54
27	22 17 41	2 55 24	1♋ 6 51	7♋ 2 41	10 11	9 53	11 3	14 43	5 29	13 20	1 27	12 44	17 39	19 55
28	22 21 38	3 53 20	12 58 59	18 56 12	10 8	9 52	10 12	14 12	6 8	13 16	1 34	12 46	17 41	19 57
29	22 25 35	4 51 18	24 54 47	0♌ 55 6	10 5	9 52	9 18	13 40	6 46	13 11	1 41	12 49	17 42	19 59
30	22 29 31	5 49 18	6♌ 57 30	13 2 18	10 1	9 51	8 22	13 6	7 24	13 7	1 48	12 51	17 44	20 1
31	22 33 28	6♍ 47 20	19♌ 9 45	25♌ 20 6	9♓ 58	9♓ 51D	7♍ 26	12♍ 31	8♌ 3	13♈ 2	1♎ 55	12♋ 54	17♎ 46	20♌ 3

DECLINATION and LATITUDE

Day	☉	☽		☽ 12 Hr.	☿		♀		♂		♃		♄	
	Decl	Decl	Lat	Decl	Decl	Lat	Decl	Lat	Decl	Lat	Decl	Lat	Decl	Lat
1	18N17	26N35	4N11	25N22	8N48	0S56	2N54	2S59	22N60	0N52	4N15	1S27	2N31	2N12
2	18 2	23 52	3 27	22 6	8 14	1 7	2 35	3 11	22 55	0 52	4 15	1 27	2 29	2 12
3	17 47	20 5	2 34	17 51	7 41	1 18	2 15	3 22	22 50	0 53	4 15	1 27	2 26	2 12
4	17 31	15 26	1 33	12 50	7 9	1 29	1 57	3 34	22 44	0 53	4 15	1 27	2 24	2 12
5	17 16	10 6	0 27	7 15	6 38	1 41	1 39	3 45	22 39	0 53	4 15	1 28	2 22	2 12
6	16 59	4 18	0S41	1 17	6 8	1 52	1 21	3 57	22 33	0 54	4 14	1 28	2 19	2 11
7	16 43	1S45	1 49	4S49	5 39	2 4	1 5	4 9	22 27	0 54	4 14	1 28	2 17	2 11
8	16 26	7 51	2 52	10 50	5 11	2 16	0 48	4 22	22 21	0 55	4 13	1 29	2 14	2 11
9	16 10	13 44	3 48	16 31	4 45	2 27	0 33	4 34	22 15	0 55	4 13	1 29	2 12	2 11
10	15 52	19 7	4 33	21 30	4 20	2 39	0 18	4 46	22 8	0 56	4 12	1 29	2 9	2 11
11	15 35	23 36	5 2	25 24	3 56	2 50	0 4	4 59	22 2	0 56	4 11	1 29	2 7	2 11
12	15 17	26 49	5 14	27 49	3 34	3 2	0S 9	5 11	21 55	0 57	4 11	1 30	2 4	2 11
13	14 59	28 21	5 7	28 23	3 14	3 13	0 21	5 24	21 48	0 57	4 10	1 30	2 2	2 11
14	14 41	27 55	4 40	26 56	2 56	3 24	0 33	5 36	21 41	0 58	4 9	1 30	1 59	2 11
15	14 23	25 29	3 54	23 36	2 40	3 34	0 43	5 49	21 34	0 58	4 8	1 31	1 56	2 10
16	14 4	21 20	2 52	18 44	2 27	3 44	0 52	6 1	21 26	0 58	4 7	1 31	1 54	2 10
17	13 45	15 53	1 39	12 49	2 16	3 54	1 1	6 13	21 19	0 59	4 5	1 31	1 51	2 10
18	13 26	9 37	0 21	6 19	2 7	4 3	1 8	6 26	21 11	0 59	4 4	1 31	1 49	2 10
19	13 7	2 60	0N57	0N19	2 2	4 11	1 14	6 37	21 3	0 60	4 3	1 32	1 46	2 10
20	12 48	3N34	2 10	6 44	1 59	4 18	1 19	6 49	20 55	1 0	4 2	1 32	1 43	2 10
21	12 28	9 47	3 13	12 40	1 60	4 25	1 23	7 0	20 47	1 1	4 0	1 32	1 41	2 10
22	12 8	15 23	4 4	17 54	2 3	4 30	1 26	7 11	20 39	1 1	3 59	1 32	1 38	2 10
23	11 48	20 11	4 42	22 14	2 10	4 34	1 27	7 22	20 30	1 2	3 57	1 33	1 35	2 10
24	11 28	24 1	5 6	25 31	2 21	4 36	1 28	7 32	20 22	1 2	3 55	1 33	1 32	2 10
25	11 7	26 44	5 16	27 37	2 34	4 37	1 27	7 42	20 13	1 2	3 54	1 33	1 30	2 10
26	10 47	28 12	5 12	28 27	2 51	4 37	1 25	7 51	20 4	1 3	3 52	1 33	1 27	2 10
27	10 26	28 22	4 55	27 57	3 12	4 34	1 21	7 59	19 55	1 3	3 50	1 34	1 24	2 9
28	10 5	27 13	4 25	26 10	3 35	4 30	1 16	8 7	19 46	1 4	3 48	1 34	1 21	2 9
29	9 44	24 49	3 44	23 12	4 1	4 24	1 11	8 14	19 37	1 4	3 46	1 34	1 19	2 9
30	9 23	21 19	2 52	19 12	4 29	4 16	1 4	8 20	19 28	1 5	3 44	1 34	1 16	2 9
31	9N 1	16N51	1N52	14N20	4N59	4S 5	0S56	8S25	19N18	1N 5	3N42	1S34	1N13	2N 9

Day	♅		♆		♇	
	Decl	Lat	Decl	Lat	Decl	Lat
1	23N17	0N20	5S12	1N37	23N 8	8N29
5	23 16	0 20	5 14	1 37	23 6	8 29
9	23 15	0 20	5 16	1 37	23 3	8 29
13	23 14	0 20	5 18	1 37	23 1	8 29
17	23 13	0 20	5 20	1 37	22 59	8 30
21	23 12	0 20	5 23	1 36	22 57	8 30
25	23 11	0 20	5 25	1 36	22 55	8 30
29	23N10	0N20	5S28	1N36	22N53	8N31

☽ PHENOMENA

d	h	m	
2	22	40	●
10	12	23	☽
17	3	0	○
24	10	21	☾

d	h	° '
6	17	0
13	7	28S26
19	11	0
26	15	28N27

d	h	° '
5	10	0
12	3	5S15
18	6	0
25	5	5N17

VOID OF COURSE ☽

Last Aspect		☽ Ingress		
2	0am49	2	♌	3am 8
3	5pm12	4	♍	2pm19
6	10pm18	6	♎	11pm35
8	7pm11	9	♏	6am24
11	10am 7	11	♐	10am31
13	12pm17	13	♑	12pm19
15	9am42	15	♒	12pm53
17	3am 0	17	♓	1pm53
18	7pm45	19	♈	4pm59
21	7pm34	21	♉	11pm27
23	1pm26	24	♊	9am28
26	1am19	26	♋	9pm45
28	9am29	29	♌	10am10
31	1am44	31	♍	9pm 0

d	h	
15	4	PERIGEE
27	3	APOGEE

DAILY ASPECTARIAN

Day	Aspect	Time
1 W	☽□♆	1am 9
	☽☌♂	4 37
	☽⚺♇	5 20
	☽∠☿	7 57
	♂⚺♇	6pm18
2 Th	☽*♄	0am49
	☽∥♅	4 12
	☽∥♇	5 17
	☽∠♀	5 24
	☽∥♂	6 49
	♀∥♄	8 13
	☽⚺☿	4pm45
	☉☌☽	10 40
3 F	☽⚺♅	2am 5
	☽∠♄	6 52
	☽△♃	7 18
	☽⚺♀	12pm 4
	☽*♆	1 3
	☉∥☽	1 6
	☽☌♇	5 12
	☽⚺♂	7 44
4 S	♃SR	6am55
	☽∠♅	7 42
	☽⚺♄	12pm31
	☽⚼♃	12 43
	☽∠♆	6 25
	☉⚺♅	8 22
5 Su	☽∠♂	2am35
	♀⚺♆	4 41
	☽☌☿	8 19
	☽*♅	12pm51
	☉⚺☽	2 8
	☽∥☿	3 53
	☽⚻♃	5 39
	☽#♆	8 13
	☽⚺♆	11 18
	☽☌♀	11 41
6 M	☽∥♃	0am15
	☽⚺♇	3 22
	☽∥♄	7 58
	☽*♂	8 49
	☽∥♀	12pm19
	☉∠☽	8 54
	☽#♀	9 26
	☽☌♄	10 18
7 T	☽#♄	2am 2
	☽∠♇	7 38
	☽#♃	9 41
	☉△♃	11 40
	☽∥♆	1pm42
	☽#☿	2 12
	☉∠♄	5 24
	☽⚺☿	8 35
	☿#♆	8 35
	☽□♅	9 27
8 W	☽☍♃	1am47
	☉*☽	2 54
	☽☌♆	7 19
	☽⚺♀	8 33
	☽*♇	11 15
	☿*♅	1pm44
	☽□♂	7 11
9 Th	☽∠☿	1am20
	☽⚺♄	5 35
	☉#☽	9 55
	☽∠♀	11 50
10 F	☽△♅	3am26
	☽*☿	5 6
	☽⚻♃	7 16
	☿∥♃	7 44
	☽∠♄	8 12
	☉□☽	12pm23
	☽⚺♆	12 40
	☽*♀	2 20
	☽#♂	3 6
	☽□♇	4 27
	☉*♆	4 35
	☽#♇	8 36
	☽#♅	9 45
11 S	☽△♂	2am26
	☽⚼♅	5 23
	☽⚼♃	8 59
	☽*♄	10 7
	☽∠♆	2pm20
	☉⚺♀	6 57
12 Su	☽⚼♂	4am56
	☽⚻♅	6 43
	☽□☿	10 0
	☽△♃	10 7
	☿⚻♃	1pm44
	☽*♆	3 26
	☽□♀	5 10
	☉△☽	6 40
	☽△♇	7 4
13 M	☉☌♇	1am 4
	☽⚻♂	6 51
	♀SR	8 2
	☽□♄	12pm17
	♄ ♎	4 44
	☽⚼♇	7 40
	☉⚼☽	8 55
14 T	☽☍♅	8am 1
	☽□♃	11 3
	☽△☿	12pm13
	☽□♆	4 25
	☽△♀	5 59
	☽⚻♇	8 1
	☉⚻☽	10 53
15 W	☽☍♂	9am42
	☽⚼☿	12pm50
	☽△♄	1 12
	☽#♅	2 12
	☽#♇	3 24
	☽⚼♀	6 6
	☽#♂	11 29
16 Th	☽⚻♅	8am43
	☽*♃	11 29
	☽⚻☿	1pm24
	☽⚼♄	1 43
	☽△♆	5 6
	☽⚻♀	6 17
	☽☍♇	8 46
17 F	☉☍☽	3am 0
	☉#☽	8 49
	☽⚼♅	9 23
	☽∠♃	12pm 3
	☽⚻♂	12 54
	☿SR	2 7
	☽⚻♄	2 34
	☽⚼♆	5 52
18 S	☽△♅	10am33
	♂ ♌	10 56
	☽⚺♃	1pm 6
	☿∠♂	2 46
	☽☍☿	3 15
	☽⚼♂	3 16
	☽∥♆	3 30
	☽⚻♆	7 13
	☽☍♀	7 45
	☽#♃	8 12
	☽⚻♇	11 4
19 Su	☽#☿	3am33
	☽#♄	4 30
	☽∥♀	6 17
	☉⚻☽	9 16
	♂*♄	9 31
	☽#♀	3pm37
	☽∥♄	5 13
	☽☍♄	6 7
	☽∥☿	6 10
	☽△♂	6 28
	♀⚺♆	11 44
20 M	☽⚼♇	1am17
	☽∥♃	1 43
	☽#♆	6 48
	☉⚼☽	1pm50
	☽□♅	3 7
	☽☌♃	5 28
	☽⚻☿	7 9
	☽⚻♀	11 42
21 T	☽☍♆	0am16
	☽△♇	4 25
	☉∠♅	8 16
	☉∥☽	10 32
	♀∠♂	1pm20
	☉△☽	7 34
	☽⚼☿	10 4
22 W	☽⚻♄	1am 8
	☽⚼♀	2 51
	☽□♂	3 57
	☉⚼♃	1pm14
	☽*♅	11 19
23 Th	☽⚺♃	1am22
	☽△☿	1 37
	☽∥♂	1 43
	☽⚼♄	6 3
	☽△♀	6 44
	☿⚻♃	8 16
	☽⚻♆	9 0
	☽□♇	1pm26
	☽∥♇	4 25
	☽∥♅	6 8
	☉ ♍	11 17
24 F	☽∠♅	4am43
	☽∠♃	6 33
	☉□☽	10 21
	☽△♄	11 47
	☽⚼♆	2pm35
	☽*♂	5 29
	☿*♅	9 40
25 S	☉⚺♄	6am34
	☽□☿	9 58
	☽⚺♅	10 44
	☽*♃	12pm19
	☽□♀	4 11
	☽△♆	8 43
26 Su	☽∠♂	1am18
	☽*♇	1 19
	☉∠♆	4pm55
27 M	☽□♄	0am41
	☉*☽	3 59
	☽∠♇	7 44
	☽⚺♂	9 22
	☽*☿	6pm45
	☽☌♅	11 34
28 T	☽□♃	0am34
	☽*♀	2 21
	☽□♆	9 29
	☿∥♃	11 36
	☉∠☽	12pm57
	☽⚺♇	2 5
	☽∠☿	10 51
29 W	☽∠♀	7am10
	☽∥♅	12pm16
	☽*♄	1 39
	☽∥♇	2 10
	☉⚺☽	9 33
	♀⚻♃	11 20
30 Th	☽☌♂	0am56
	☽⚺☿	2 36
	♀*♅	9 25
	☽∥♂	10 56
	☽⚺♀	11 34
	☽⚺♅	11 40
	☽△♃	12pm 4
	☿⚺♂	2 41
	☽∠♄	7 33
	☽*♆	9 16
31 F	☽☌♇	1am44
	☉☌☿	8 10
	☽∠♅	5pm 0
	☽⚼♃	5 5
	☿#♆	11 51

SEPTEMBER 1951

LONGITUDE

Day	Sid. Time	☉	☽	☽ 12 Hour	Mean ☊	True ☊	☿	♀	♂	♃	♄	♅	♆	♇
	h m s	° ' "	° ' "	° ' "	° '	° '	° '	° '	° '	° '	° '	° '	° '	° '
1	22 37 24	7♍ 45 24	1♍ 33 31	7♍ 50 9	9♓ 55	9♓ 51	6♍ 30R	11♍ 55R	8♌ 41	12♈ 56R	2♎ 2	12♋ 56	17♎ 48	20♌ 5
2	22 41 21	8 43 29	14 10 7	20 33 29	9 52	9 51	5 37	11 19	9 19	12 51	2 9	12 58	17 49	20 6
3	22 45 17	9 41 35	27 0 18	3♎ 30 35	9 49	9 51R	4 46	10 42	9 57	12 46	2 16	13 1	17 51	20 8
4	22 49 14	10 39 44	10♎ 4 20	16 41 32	9 45	9 51	3 59	10 5	10 35	12 40	2 23	13 3	17 53	20 10
5	22 53 10	11 37 53	23 22 8	0♏ 6 6	9 42	9 51	3 17	9 28	11 14	12 34	2 30	13 5	17 55	20 12
6	22 57 7	12 36 5	6♏ 53 20	13 43 46	9 39	9 50	2 42	8 51	11 52	12 28	2 37	13 8	17 57	20 13
7	23 1 3	13 34 18	20 37 19	27 33 49	9 36	9 50	2 14	8 14	12 30	12 22	2 44	13 10	17 59	20 15
8	23 5 0	14 32 32	4♐ 33 10	11♐ 35 11	9 33	9 50D	1 54	7 39	13 8	12 16	2 51	13 12	18 1	20 17
9	23 8 57	15 30 48	18 39 38	25 46 19	9 30	9 49	1 42D	7 4	13 46	12 10	2 58	13 14	18 3	20 19
10	23 12 53	16 29 5	2♑ 54 55	10♑ 5 5	9 26	9 50	1 39	6 31	14 24	12 3	3 6	13 16	18 5	20 20
11	23 16 50	17 27 25	17 16 28	24 28 36	9 23	9 50	1 45	5 59	15 1	11 57	3 13	13 18	18 7	20 22
12	23 20 46	18 25 45	1♒ 41 1	8♒ 53 11	9 20	9 51	2 0	5 28	15 39	11 50	3 20	13 20	18 9	20 24
13	23 24 43	19 24 7	16 4 33	23 14 32	9 17	9 52	2 24	5 0	16 17	11 43	3 27	13 22	18 11	20 25
14	23 28 39	20 22 31	0♓ 22 33	7♓ 28 3	9 14	9 52R	2 57	4 33	16 55	11 36	3 35	13 24	18 13	20 27
15	23 32 36	21 20 56	14 30 27	21 29 16	9 11	9 52	3 38	4 8	17 32	11 29	3 42	13 26	18 15	20 29
16	23 36 33	22 19 23	28 24 3	5♈ 14 25	9 7	9 52	4 28	3 45	18 10	11 22	3 49	13 28	18 17	20 30
17	23 40 29	23 17 52	12♈ 0 4	18 40 48	9 4	9 51	5 26	3 25	18 48	11 15	3 57	13 30	18 19	20 32
18	23 44 26	24 16 23	25 16 30	1♉ 47 9	9 1	9 49	6 31	3 6	19 25	11 8	4 4	13 31	18 21	20 34
19	23 48 22	25 14 57	8♉ 12 49	14 33 41	8 58	9 47	7 42	2 50	20 3	11 0	4 11	13 33	18 23	20 35
20	23 52 19	26 13 32	20 49 59	27 2 2	8 55	9 45	9 0	2 37	20 41	10 53	4 19	13 35	18 25	20 37
21	23 56 15	27 12 10	3♊ 10 14	9♊ 15 2	8 51	9 43	10 23	2 26	21 18	10 45	4 26	13 36	18 27	20 38
22	0 0 12	28 10 49	15 16 56	21 16 28	8 48	9 41	11 51	2 17	21 56	10 38	4 33	13 38	18 29	20 40
23	0 4 8	29 9 31	27 14 11	3♋ 10 42	8 45	9 41D	13 23	2 11	22 33	10 30	4 41	13 39	18 31	20 41
24	0 8 5	0♎ 8 16	9♋ 6 35	15 2 28	8 42	9 41	14 58	2 8	23 10	10 22	4 48	13 41	18 33	20 43
25	0 12 1	1 7 2	20 58 55	26 56 33	8 39	9 42	16 37	2 6D	23 48	10 14	4 56	13 42	18 36	20 45
26	0 15 58	2 5 51	2♌ 55 55	8♌ 57 34	8 36	9 43	18 18	2 7	24 25	10 6	5 3	13 43	18 38	20 46
27	0 19 55	3 4 42	15 2 0	21 9 41	8 32	9 45	20 1	2 11	25 2	9 58	5 10	13 45	18 40	20 47
28	0 23 51	4 3 35	27 21 1	3♍ 36 21	8 29	9 47	21 46	2 16	25 40	9 50	5 18	13 46	18 42	20 49
29	0 27 48	5 2 30	9♍ 55 59	16 20 5	8 26	9 47R	23 32	2 24	26 17	9 42	5 25	13 47	18 44	20 50
30	0 31 44	6♎ 1 27	22♍ 48 47	29♍ 22 9	8♓ 23	9♓ 47	25♍ 19	2♍ 35	26♌ 54	9♈ 34	5♎ 33	13♋ 48	18♎ 46	20♌ 52

DECLINATION and LATITUDE

Day	☉ Decl	☽ Decl	☽ Lat	☽ 12 Hr. Decl	☿ Decl	☿ Lat	♀ Decl	♀ Lat	♂ Decl	♂ Lat	♃ Decl	♃ Lat	♄ Decl	♄ Lat
1	8N40	11N38	0N46	8N48	5N30	3S54	0S46	8S30	19N 9	1N 5	3N40	1S35	1N10	2N 9
2	8 18	5 52	0S24	2 50	6 3	3 40	0 36	8 34	18 59	1 6	3 37	1 35	1 7	2 9
3	7 56	0S15	1 34	3S21	6 35	3 25	0 25	8 36	18 49	1 6	3 35	1 35	1 4	2 9
4	7 34	6 26	2 40	9 29	7 7	3 9	0 13	8 38	18 39	1 7	3 33	1 35	1 2	2 9
5	7 12	12 28	3 39	15 19	7 39	2 51	0 0	8 39	18 29	1 7	3 30	1 35	0 59	2 9
6	6 50	18 0	4 26	20 29	8 8	2 33	0N13	8 39	18 19	1 7	3 28	1 36	0 56	2 9
7	6 28	22 43	4 59	24 39	8 36	2 14	0 28	8 38	18 9	1 8	3 25	1 36	0 53	2 9
8	6 5	26 13	5 15	27 24	9 1	1 55	0 42	8 36	17 58	1 8	3 23	1 36	0 50	2 9
9	5 43	28 10	5 13	28 27	9 23	1 35	0 57	8 34	17 48	1 9	3 20	1 36	0 47	2 9
10	5 20	28 16	4 52	27 37	9 42	1 16	1 13	8 30	17 37	1 9	3 17	1 36	0 44	2 9
11	4 57	26 29	4 12	24 56	9 58	0 57	1 29	8 26	17 26	1 9	3 15	1 37	0 41	2 9
12	4 35	22 58	3 16	20 40	10 10	0 39	1 44	8 20	17 16	1 10	3 12	1 37	0 39	2 9
13	4 12	18 3	2 8	15 12	10 17	0 21	2 0	8 14	17 5	1 10	3 9	1 37	0 36	2 9
14	3 49	12 10	0 52	8 59	10 21	0 5	2 16	8 8	16 54	1 11	3 6	1 37	0 33	2 9
15	3 26	5 42	0N26	2 24	10 21	0N11	2 32	8 0	16 42	1 11	3 3	1 37	0 30	2 9
16	3 3	0N54	1 41	4N10	10 16	0 26	2 47	7 52	16 31	1 11	3 0	1 37	0 27	2 9
17	2 40	7 20	2 48	10 23	10 8	0 39	3 3	7 44	16 20	1 12	2 58	1 37	0 24	2 9
18	2 17	13 16	3 45	15 59	9 56	0 52	3 17	7 35	16 9	1 12	2 55	1 37	0 21	2 9
19	1 53	18 29	4 29	20 45	9 39	1 3	3 32	7 25	15 57	1 13	2 52	1 38	0 18	2 9
20	1 30	22 46	4 58	24 29	9 20	1 13	3 46	7 15	15 45	1 13	2 49	1 38	0 15	2 9
21	1 7	25 55	5 13	27 2	8 56	1 22	3 59	7 5	15 34	1 13	2 45	1 38	0 12	2 9
22	0 43	27 50	5 14	28 18	8 30	1 29	4 12	6 55	15 22	1 14	2 42	1 38	0 9	2 9
23	0 20	28 26	5 1	28 14	8 1	1 36	4 24	6 44	15 10	1 14	2 39	1 38	0 6	2 9
24	0S 3	27 42	4 35	26 52	7 29	1 41	4 36	6 33	14 58	1 15	2 36	1 38	0 4	2 9
25	0 27	25 43	3 57	24 17	6 54	1 45	4 47	6 22	14 46	1 15	2 33	1 38	0 1	2 9
26	0 50	22 34	3 9	20 37	6 18	1 49	4 57	6 10	14 34	1 15	2 30	1 38	0S 2	2 9
27	1 13	18 26	2 12	16 2	5 39	1 51	5 7	5 59	14 22	1 16	2 27	1 38	0 5	2 9
28	1 37	13 27	1 8	10 43	4 59	1 52	5 15	5 47	14 10	1 16	2 24	1 38	0 8	2 9
29	2 0	7 50	0S 1	4 51	4 17	1 53	5 23	5 36	13 57	1 16	2 20	1 38	0 11	2 9
30	2S24	1N46	1S11	1S22	3N35	1N53	5N31	5S24	13N45	1N17	2N17	1S38	0S14	2N 9

Day	♅ Decl	♅ Lat	♆ Decl	♆ Lat	♇ Decl	♇ Lat
1	23N 9	0N20	5S30	1N36	22N52	8N31
5	23 8	0 20	5 33	1 36	22 50	8 32
9	23 8	0 20	5 36	1 36	22 48	8 33
13	23 7	0 20	5 39	1 36	22 47	8 33
17	23 6	0 21	5 42	1 36	22 45	8 34
21	23 6	0 21	5 46	1 36	22 44	8 35
25	23 5	0 21	5 49	1 36	22 43	8 36
29	23N 5	0N21	5S52	1N36	22N42	8N37

☽ PHENOMENA

d	h	m	
1	12	50	●✓
8	18	17	☽
15	12	39	○
23	4	14	☾

d	h	° '
2	23	0
9	13	28S28
15	21	0
22	23	28N26
30	7	0

d	h	
1	16	0
8	9	5S17
14	16	0
21	13	5N15
29	0	0

VOID OF COURSE ☽

Last Aspect		☽ Ingress		
1	9pm44	3	♎	5am32
4	6pm18	5	♏	11am49
6	11pm22	7	♐	4pm11
9	2am48	9	♑	7pm 7
11	1am24	11	♒	9pm12
13	7am17	13	♓	11pm22
15	12pm39	16	♈	2am48
17	3pm23	18	♉	8am42
20	11am19	20	♊	5pm47
23	4am14	23	♋	5am35
24	7pm10	25	♌	6pm 8
27	8pm34	28	♍	5am 6
30	5am21	30	♎	1pm 9

d	h	
11	21	PERIGEE
23	21	APOGEE

DAILY ASPECTARIAN

Day	Aspect	Time
1	☽⚺♄	0am55
S	♃□♅	1 11
	☽∠♆	2 22
	☽☌☿	8 50
	☉☌☽	12pm50
	☉∥☽	1 26
	☽⚺♂	2 20
	☽☌♀	6 51
	☽⚻♃	9 32
	☽⚹♅	9 44
	☽∥☿	11 20
2	☽#♆	1am24
Su	☽⚺♆	6 54
	☽∥♃	8 58
	☽⚺♇	11 11
	☽∥♄	6pm51
	☽∠♂	8 0
	☽#♀	9 22
3	☽∥♀	0am39
M	☽#♄	3 12
	☽☌♄	9 48
	☽#♃	12pm50
	☽⚺☿	1 29
	♀⚺♂	2 8
	☽∠♇	3 1
	☉☌♀	3 9
	☉⚺♂	6 56
	☽∥♆	8 29
4	☽⚺♀	0am 0
T	☽⚹♂	1 0
	☉⚺☽	1 10
	☽#☿	2 55
	☉#☽	4 10
	☽☍♃	4 41
	☽□♅	5 26
	☉∥☿	12pm 4
	☽☌♆	2 11
	☽∠☿	3 19
	☽⚹♇	6 18
5	☽∠♀	1am52
W	☉∠☽	6 17
	☿∠♆	2pm 0
	☽⚺♄	4 23
	☽⚹☿	4 54
	☉⚻♃	9 9
6	☽#♂	1am25
Th	☿⚺♄	3 13
	☽⚹♀	3 18
	☽□♂	9 9
	☽⚻♃	9 44
	☉⚹☽	10 47
	☽△♅	10 59
	☉⚹♅	1pm33
	☽∠♄	6 56
	☽⚺♆	7 24
	♂△♃	8 4
	☽□♇	11 22
7	☽#♇	0am35
F	☽#♅	2 26
	☽⚼♃	11 35
	☽⚼♅	1pm 4
	☽□☿	7 32
	☽⚹♄	9 4
	☽∠♆	9 21
8	♂⚺♅	2am57
S	☽□♀	5 5
	♀∥♄	10 31
	☽△♃	1pm 4
	☽⚻♅	2 47
	☽△♂	3 18
	☉□☽	6 17
	☽⚹♆	10 57
9	☽△♇	2am48
Su	☉#♆	6 53
	☽⚼♂	5pm49
	☿SD	8 23
	☽△☿	9 52
10	☽□♄	0am18
M	☽⚼♇	4 4
	☽△♀	5 49
	☽□♃	3pm11
	☽☍♅	5 22
	☽⚻♂	8 4
	☽⚼☿	11 6
11	☉△☽	0am20
T	☽□♆	1 24
	☽⚻♇	5 10
	☽⚼♀	5 58
	☉⚺♆	4pm39
	☽#♅	11 12
12	☽⚻☿	0am32
W	☽#♇	1 4
	☽△♄	2 46
	☉⚼☽	3 7
	☽⚻♀	6 6
	☽⚹♃	4pm47
	☽⚻♅	7 28
13	☽☍♂	0am22
Th	☽△♆	3 31
	☽⚼♄	4 1
	☽#♂	4 22
	☉⚻☽	5 58
	☽☍♇	7 17
	☽∠♃	5pm42
	☽⚼♅	8 40
14	☉⚺♇	1am57
F	☽☍☿	4 32
	☽⚼♆	4 48
	☽⚻♄	5 27
	☽☍♀	6 50
	☽#☿	6 51
	☿∠♆	10 14
	☽⚺♃	6pm53
	☽△♅	10 9
15	☽∥♆	0am 6
S	☿⚺♄	2 15
	☽⚻♂	5 27
	☽⚻♆	6 25
	☉#☽	8 46
	☽#♃	9 42
	☿☌♀	10 1
	☽⚻♇	10 17
	☽#♀	11 6
	☉☍☽	12pm39
	☽#♄	7 2
	♀⚺♄	8 35
	☽∥♄	10 21
16	☉∥♃	2am46
Su	♂⚹♆	4 20
	☽∥♀	7 12
	☉∥☽	7 26
	☽∥♃	7 40
	☽⚼♂	8 45
	☽⚻♀	9 8
	☽☍♄	9 35
	☉∥♀	9 40
	☽⚻☿	11 25
	☽⚼♇	12pm30
	♀∥♃	5 20
	☽#♆	5 48
	☽☌♃	10 40
17	☽□♅	2am40
M	♀∠♆	6 42
	♂∠♄	6 55
	☽∥☿	10 41
	☽⚼♀	11 15
	☽☍♆	11 22
	☽△♂	12pm49
	☽△♇	3 23
	☽⚼☿	4 30
	☉⚻☽	10 1
18	☽∥♂	12pm17
T	☽△♀	2 9
	☽⚻♄	4 24
	☽△☿	10 56
19	☉⚼☽	4am 9
W	☽⚺♃	5 12
	☽⚹♅	10 6
	☽⚻♆	7pm21
	☽⚼♄	9 3
	♂☌♇	9 30
	☽□♇	11 35
	☽□♂	11 41
	☽∥♇	11 52
20	☽∥♅	2am12
Th	☽∠♃	9 39
	☉△☽	11 19
	☽∠♅	3pm 2
	☽□♀	10 34
21	☽⚼♆	0am33
F	☽△♄	2 30
	☿⚻♃	5 46
	☽⚹♃	2pm50
	☽□☿	4 11
	☽⚺♅	8 42
22	☽△♆	6am25
S	☽⚹♇	10 48
	☽⚹♂	2pm 3
23	☉□☽	4am14
Su	☿⚹♅	4 17
	☽⚹♀	9 56
	☽□♄	3pm12
	☉∥♄	3 59
	☽∠♇	5 7
	☉ ♎	8 37
	☽∠♂	10 0
24	☉#♄	0am14
M	☽□♃	2 31
	☽☌♅	9 15
	☽⚹☿	1pm45
	☽∠♀	4 11
	☽□♆	7 10
	☽⚺♇	11 31
25	♀SD	1am 0
T	☽⚺♂	5 59
	☽∥♅	8pm36
	☉⚹☽	10 11
	☽⚺♀	10 23
	☽∥♇	11 7
26	☉⚺♀	0am38
W	☽∠☿	0 52
	☽⚹♄	4 16
	☿⚺♆	4 40
	☽△♃	2pm 7
	☿#♆	5 9
	☽⚺♅	9 27
	♂⚼♃	9 49
27	☉∠☽	6am30
Th	☽⚹♆	7 9
	☽∠♄	10 10
	☿⚺♇	10 43
	☽☌♇	11 18
	☽⚺☿	11 24
	☿∥♀	3pm58
	☽⚼♃	7 12
	☽☌♂	8 34
	☽∥♂	8 40
28	☽∠♅	2am44
F	☽☌♀	9 33
	☽∠♆	12pm13
	☉⚺☽	1 57
	☽⚺♄	3 22
	☽⚻♃	11 35
29	☽⚹♅	7am15
S	☽#♆	7 54
	☽∥♀	9 38
	☉☌♄	10 34
	☽∥☿	4pm 1
	☽⚺♆	4 31
	☉#♃	6 16
	☉∠♇	7 58
	☽⚺♇	8 24
	☉#☽	9 43
	☽∥♃	9 58
30	☽☌☿	5am21
Su	☽#♄	5 51
	☽∥♄	7 45
	☽⚺♂	7 52
	☽#♃	3pm24
	☉∥☽	4 59
	☽⚺♀	6 6
	☽#☿	6 21
	☽☌♄	11 24
	☽∠♇	11 48

OCTOBER 1951

LONGITUDE

Day	Sid. Time	☉	☽	☽ 12 Hour	Mean ☊	True ☊	☿	♀	♂	♃	♄	♅	♆	♇
	h m s	° ' "	° ' "	° ' "	° '	° '	° '	° '	° '	° '	° '	° '	° '	° '
1	0 35 41	7♎ 0 27	6♎ 0 6	12♎ 42 30	8♓ 20	9♓ 45R	27♍ 7	2♍ 47	27♌ 31	9♈ 26R	5♎ 40	13♋ 49	18♎ 49	20♌ 53
2	0 39 37	7 59 29	19 29 9	26 19 44	8 17	9 42	28 55	3 1	28 8	9 18	5 47	13 50	18 51	20 55
3	0 43 34	8 58 32	3♏ 13 53	10♏ 11 13	8 13	9 37	0♎ 43	3 18	28 45	9 10	5 55	13 51	18 53	20 56
4	0 47 30	9 57 37	17 11 14	24 13 30	8 10	9 33	2 31	3 36	29 22	9 2	6 2	13 52	18 55	20 57
5	0 51 27	10 56 45	1♐ 17 30	8♐ 22 47	8 7	9 28	4 19	3 56	29 59	8 54	6 10	13 53	18 57	20 59
6	0 55 24	11 55 54	15 28 53	22 35 25	8 4	9 25	6 6	4 18	0♍ 36	8 46	6 17	13 54	19 0	21 0
7	0 59 20	12 55 5	29 41 59	6♑ 48 17	8 1	9 23D	7 54	4 42	1 13	8 38	6 24	13 55	19 2	21 1
8	1 3 17	13 54 17	13♑ 54 0	20 58 55	7 57	9 22	9 40	5 8	1 50	8 30	6 32	13 55	19 4	21 2
9	1 7 13	14 53 32	28 2 48	5♒ 5 29	7 54	9 23	11 26	5 35	2 27	8 22	6 39	13 56	19 6	21 4
10	1 11 10	15 52 48	12♒ 6 48	19 6 34	7 51	9 24	13 12	6 4	3 4	8 14	6 47	13 57	19 9	21 5
11	1 15 6	16 52 6	26 4 38	3♓ 0 48	7 48	9 26R	14 56	6 34	3 41	8 6	6 54	13 57	19 11	21 6
12	1 19 3	17 51 25	9♓ 54 54	16 46 43	7 45	9 26	16 40	7 6	4 17	7 58	7 1	13 58	19 13	21 7
13	1 22 59	18 50 47	23 36 1	0♈ 22 35	7 42	9 25	18 24	7 40	4 54	7 50	7 9	13 58	19 15	21 8
14	1 26 56	19 50 11	7♈ 6 11	13 46 34	7 38	9 22	20 7	8 14	5 31	7 43	7 16	13 58	19 18	21 9
15	1 30 53	20 49 36	20 23 33	26 56 55	7 35	9 17	21 49	8 50	6 7	7 35	7 23	13 59	19 20	21 11
16	1 34 49	21 49 3	3♉ 26 33	9♉ 52 19	7 32	9 10	23 30	9 28	6 44	7 27	7 30	13 59	19 22	21 12
17	1 38 46	22 48 33	16 14 12	22 32 12	7 29	9 2	25 11	10 6	7 20	7 20	7 38	13 59	19 24	21 13
18	1 42 42	23 48 5	28 46 26	4♊ 57 2	7 26	8 54	26 51	10 46	7 57	7 13	7 45	13 59	19 26	21 14
19	1 46 39	24 47 38	11♊ 4 14	17 8 21	7 23	8 47	28 30	11 27	8 33	7 5	7 52	14 0	19 29	21 15
20	1 50 35	25 47 14	23 9 44	29 8 49	7 19	8 40	0♏ 9	12 10	9 9	6 58	7 59	14 0R	19 31	21 16
21	1 54 32	26 46 53	5♋ 6 5	11♋ 2 4	7 16	8 36	1 47	12 53	9 46	6 51	8 7	14 0	19 33	21 17
22	1 58 28	27 46 34	16 57 20	22 52 29	7 13	8 33	3 24	13 37	10 22	6 44	8 14	14 0	19 35	21 18
23	2 2 25	28 46 16	28 48 10	4♌ 45 1	7 10	8 32D	5 1	14 22	10 58	6 37	8 21	14 0	19 38	21 19
24	2 6 22	29 46 1	10♌ 43 43	16 44 54	7 7	8 33	6 37	15 9	11 34	6 30	8 28	13 59	19 40	21 19
25	2 10 18	0♏ 45 49	22 49 13	28 57 18	7 3	8 34	8 13	15 56	12 11	6 23	8 35	13 59	19 42	21 20
26	2 14 15	1 45 38	5♍ 9 42	11♍ 26 58	7 0	8 35R	9 48	16 44	12 47	6 17	8 42	13 59	19 44	21 21
27	2 18 11	2 45 30	17 49 34	24 17 50	6 57	8 34	11 23	17 33	13 23	6 10	8 49	13 59	19 46	21 22
28	2 22 8	3 45 23	0♎ 52 2	7♎ 32 19	6 54	8 32	12 57	18 23	13 59	6 4	8 56	13 58	19 49	21 23
29	2 26 4	4 45 19	14 18 42	21 11 0	6 51	8 27	14 31	19 13	14 35	5 58	9 3	13 58	19 51	21 23
30	2 30 1	5 45 18	28 8 57	5♏ 12 4	6 48	8 20	16 4	20 5	15 11	5 52	9 10	13 57	19 53	21 24
31	2 33 57	6♏ 45 17	12♏ 19 47	19♏ 31 21	6♓ 44	8♓ 11	17♏ 36	20♍ 57	15♍ 47	5♈ 46	9♎ 17	13♋ 57	19♎ 55	21♌ 25

DECLINATION and LATITUDE

Day	☉ Decl	☽ Decl	☽ Lat	☽ 12 Hr. Decl	☿ Decl	☿ Lat	♀ Decl	♀ Lat	♂ Decl	♂ Lat	♃ Decl	♃ Lat	♄ Decl	♄ Lat
1	2S47	4S30	2S19	7S38	2N51	1N52	5N37	5S13	13N33	1N17	2N14	1S38	0S17	2N 9
2	3 10	10 43	3 20	13 42	2 7	1 50	5 43	5 1	13 20	1 18	2 11	1 38	0 20	2 9
3	3 34	16 32	4 12	19 11	1 22	1 48	5 48	4 50	13 8	1 18	2 8	1 38	0 23	2 9
4	3 57	21 35	4 49	23 41	0 36	1 45	5 52	4 38	12 55	1 18	2 5	1 38	0 26	2 9
5	4 20	25 27	5 9	26 50	0S 9	1 42	5 55	4 27	12 42	1 19	2 1	1 38	0 28	2 9
6	4 43	27 47	5 10	28 17	0 55	1 38	5 58	4 15	12 30	1 19	1 58	1 38	0 31	2 9
7	5 6	28 19	4 53	27 53	1 42	1 34	5 60	4 4	12 17	1 19	1 55	1 38	0 34	2 9
8	5 29	26 59	4 17	25 39	2 28	1 29	6 1	3 53	12 4	1 20	1 52	1 38	0 37	2 9
9	5 52	23 55	3 26	21 51	3 14	1 25	6 1	3 42	11 51	1 20	1 49	1 38	0 40	2 9
10	6 15	19 27	2 23	16 49	3 59	1 20	6 1	3 31	11 38	1 21	1 46	1 38	0 43	2 9
11	6 38	13 57	1 12	10 57	4 45	1 14	5 60	3 20	11 25	1 21	1 43	1 38	0 46	2 9
12	7 0	7 49	0N 3	4 37	5 30	1 8	5 58	3 10	11 12	1 21	1 40	1 38	0 48	2 9
13	7 23	1 22	1 16	1N51	6 15	1 3	5 56	2 59	10 59	1 22	1 37	1 38	0 51	2 9
14	7 46	5N 2	2 24	8 8	6 59	0 57	5 52	2 49	10 46	1 22	1 34	1 38	0 54	2 9
15	8 8	11 6	3 23	13 56	7 43	0 50	5 48	2 39	10 33	1 22	1 31	1 38	0 57	2 10
16	8 30	16 35	4 11	19 2	8 27	0 44	5 44	2 29	10 19	1 23	1 28	1 38	0 60	2 10
17	8 52	21 14	4 44	23 10	9 10	0 38	5 38	2 19	10 6	1 23	1 25	1 37	1 2	2 10
18	9 14	24 49	5 3	26 9	9 52	0 31	5 32	2 9	9 53	1 23	1 22	1 37	1 5	2 10
19	9 36	27 11	5 7	27 52	10 34	0 24	5 25	1 60	9 40	1 24	1 20	1 37	1 8	2 10
20	9 58	28 14	4 58	28 15	11 15	0 18	5 18	1 50	9 26	1 24	1 17	1 37	1 11	2 10
21	10 20	27 56	4 36	27 18	11 55	0 11	5 10	1 41	9 13	1 24	1 14	1 37	1 14	2 10
22	10 41	26 22	4 2	25 8	12 35	0 4	5 1	1 32	8 59	1 25	1 11	1 37	1 16	2 10
23	11 2	23 37	3 17	21 51	13 14	0S 3	4 52	1 23	8 46	1 25	1 9	1 37	1 19	2 10
24	11 24	19 51	2 24	17 39	13 53	0 9	4 42	1 15	8 33	1 26	1 6	1 37	1 22	2 10
25	11 45	15 14	1 24	12 39	14 30	0 16	4 32	1 6	8 19	1 26	1 4	1 36	1 24	2 10
26	12 5	9 54	0 18	7 2	15 7	0 23	4 21	0 58	8 6	1 26	1 1	1 36	1 27	2 11
27	12 26	4 3	0S49	0 59	15 43	0 30	4 9	0 50	7 52	1 27	0 59	1 36	1 30	2 11
28	12 46	2S 8	1 57	5S16	16 18	0 36	3 57	0 42	7 38	1 27	0 57	1 36	1 32	2 11
29	13 7	8 24	2 59	11 28	16 53	0 43	3 45	0 34	7 25	1 27	0 54	1 36	1 35	2 11
30	13 27	14 26	3 53	17 16	17 26	0 50	3 32	0 26	7 11	1 28	0 52	1 35	1 38	2 11
31	13S46	19S53	4S34	22S14	17S59	0S56	3N18	0S19	6N58	1N28	0N50	1S35	1S40	2N11

Day	♅ Decl	♅ Lat	♆ Decl	♆ Lat	♇ Decl	♇ Lat
1	23N 5	0N21	5S54	1N36	22N41	8N37
5	23 4	0 21	5 57	1 36	22 40	8 38
9	23 4	0 21	6 1	1 36	22 40	8 39
13	23 4	0 21	6 4	1 36	22 39	8 40
17	23 4	0 21	6 7	1 36	22 39	8 42
21	23 4	0 22	6 11	1 36	22 39	8 43
25	23 4	0 22	6 14	1 36	22 38	8 44
29	23N 4	0N22	6S17	1N36	22N39	8N45

☽ PHENOMENA

d	h	m	
1	1	57	●
8	0	1	☽
15	0	51	○
22	23	56	☾
30	13	55	●

d	h	° '
6	19	28S22
13	5	0
20	7	28N17
27	16	0

d	h	° '
5	14	5S12
11	23	0
18	20	5N 8
26	7	0

VOID OF COURSE ☽

Last Aspect		☽ Ingress		
2	3pm52	2	♏	6pm24
4	9pm42	4	♐	9pm49
6	9am20	7	♑	0am30
8	8am47	9	♒	3am19
10	3pm25	11	♓	6am47
12	7am 4	13	♈	11am20
15	2am58	15	♉	5pm37
17	9am29	18	♊	2am22
20	5am44	20	♋	1pm43
22	11pm56	23	♌	2am25
24	9pm 5	25	♍	2pm 2
26	11pm27	27	♎	10pm26
29	12pm22	30	♏	3am10

d	h	
7	7	PERIGEE
21	17	APOGEE

DAILY ASPECTARIAN

Day	Aspect	Time
1 M	☉#☿	1am31
	☉☌☽	1 57
	☽#♀	4 19
	☽∥♆	5 19
	☽☍♃	6 6
	☿⚺♂	8 13
	☽∠♂	12pm14
	☽□♅	2 0
	☽∠♀	9 22
	☿∥♃	9 38
	☽☌♆	10 52
2 T	☽⚹♇	2am31
	☽#♂	10 10
	☿ ♎	2pm26
	☽⚹♂	3 52
	☽⚺☿	6 59
3 W	☽⚹♀	0am 7
	♂∠♅	3 48
	☉☍♃	4 8
	♄∠♇	4 17
	☽⚺♄	4 41
	☽⚻♃	10 9
	☉⚺☽	10 40
	☽△♅	6pm19
4 Th	☽∠☿	0am39
	☽⚺♆	2 58
	☿#♄	5 19
	☽#♇	6 1
	☽□♇	6 26
	☽∠♄	6 38
	☽#♅	8 18
	☽⚼♃	11 34
	☉∠☽	2pm15
	☿⚺♀	5 44
	☽⚼♅	7 55
	☽□♂	9 42
5 F	♂ ♍	0am20
	♀∠♆	1 26
	☽∠♆	4 32
	☽□♀	4 36
	☽⚹☿	5 52
	☽⚹♄	8 19
	☿∥♄	10 34
	☽△♃	12pm45
	☉⚹☽	5 33
	☽⚻♅	9 19
	☿∠♇	10 31
	♀#♆	10 56
6 S	☿☌♄	2am33
	☽⚹♆	5 57
	☽△♇	9 20
7 Su	☽△♂	2am41
	☿#♃	6 38
	☽△♀	8 42
	☿☍♃	9 16
	☽⚼♇	10 41
	☽□♄	11 26
	☽□♃	2pm57
	☽□☿	3 49
8 M	☉□☽	0am 1
	☽☍♅	0 2
	☉□♅	0 23
	☽⚼♂	5 12
	☽□♆	8 47
	☽⚼♀	10 54
	☽⚻♇	12pm 7
9 T	☽#♅	5am10
	☽#♇	7 31
	☽⚻♂	7 50
	☉∥♆	9 7
	☉#♀	9 40
	☽⚻♀	1pm17
	☽△♄	2 48
	☽⚹♃	5 25
	♀#♆	7 17
10 W	☽△☿	2am 7
	☽⚻♅	3 8
	☉△☽	6 57
	☿□♅	10 20
	☽△♆	12pm 5
	☽☍♇	3 25
	☽⚼♄	4 44
	☽∠♃	6 55
11 Th	☽⚼♅	4am58
	☽⚼☿	7 38
	☽#♂	10 31
	☉⚼☽	10 47
	☽☍♂	1pm45
	☽⚼♆	2 4
	☽☍♀	6 54
	☽⚻♄	6 55
	♀⚺♄	7 17
	☽⚺♃	8 39
	♂∠♆	9 4
12 F	☉∥☽	2am52
	☽∥♆	6 37
	☽#♀	6 58
	☽△♅	7 4
	☽∥☿	7 46
	☽⚻☿	1pm31
	☿#♀	2 14
	☉⚻☽	2 59
	☽⚻♆	4 20
	☿∥♆	5 59
	☽⚻♇	7 39
	☽#♃	11 7
13 S	☽∥♄	1am55
	♀⚻♃	6 14
	☽#♄	8 21
	☉☌♆	10 17
	☽∥♃	11 2
	☿☌♆	12pm16
	☉☌☿	2 52
	☽⚻♂	9 1
	☽⚼♇	10 18
14 Su	☽☍♄	0am18
	☽☌♃	1 5
	☽⚻♀	2 8
	☽∥♀	3 11
	☽#♆	4 2
	☽#☿	8 34
	☿∠♂	8 45
	☉#☽	11 15
	☽□♅	12pm22
	☿⚹♇	2 56
	☽∥♂	9 46
	☽☍♆	10 4
15 M	☉☍☽	0am51
	☽⚼♂	1 23
	☽△♇	1 26
	☽☍☿	2 58
	☽⚼♀	6 36
	☉⚹♇	8 37
	☉∠♂	6pm20
	♃☍♄	7 12
16 T	☉∥☿	4am 0
	☽△♂	6 25
	☽⚺♃	7 24
	☽⚻♄	7 39
	☽△♀	11 49
	☽⚹♅	7pm45
	☿∠♀	10 21
	♂⚻♃	11 55
17 W	☽⚻♆	6am 2
	☽∥♇	8 37
	☽□♇	9 29
	☽∥♅	11 21
	☽∠♃	11 30
	☽⚼♄	12pm18
	☉⚻☽	1 36
	♂⚺♄	2 25
	☽⚻☿	7 42
18 Th	☽∠♅	0am25
	☿#♂	0 25
	☽⚼♆	11 2
	☽⚹♃	4pm15
	☽△♄	5 39
	☽□♂	6 47
	☉⚼☽	9 16
19 F	☽□♀	0am48
	☉#♂	2 17
	☽⚼☿	5 33
	☽⚺♅	5 46
	☽△♆	4pm42
	☽⚹♇	8 12
	☿ ♏	9 53
20 S	☉△☽	5am44
	☽△☿	4pm14
	♅SR	8 52
21 Su	☽∠♇	2am23
	♃#♄	2 24
	☽□♃	3 30
	☽□♄	6 8
	☽⚹♂	9 56
	☽⚹♀	4pm47
	☽☌♅	6 0
22 M	☽□♆	5am21
	☽⚺♇	8 48
	♀⚹♅	11 59
	☽∠♂	5pm58
	☉□☽	11 56
23 T	☽∠♀	1am14
	☽∥♅	3 57
	☽∥♇	6 53
	☽□☿	2pm29
	☽△♃	3 36
	☽⚹♄	7 25
	☿⚻♃	10 19
24 W	☽⚺♂	1am47
	☉ ♏	5 37
	☽⚺♅	6 31
	☽⚺♀	9 25
	☽⚹♆	5pm50
	☽☌♇	9 5
	☽⚼♃	9 13
25 Th	☽∠♄	1am31
	☽#☿	3 5
	☿⚺♄	5 57
	♃⚼♇	10 14
	☽∠♅	12pm 3
	☉#☽	3 4
	☉⚹☽	4 52
	☉∠♀	8 24
	☽∠♆	11 11
26 F	☽⚻♃	2am 8
	☽⚺♄	6 50
	☽∥♂	7 57
	☽⚹☿	10 9
	☽#♆	3pm11
	☽☌♂	3 14
	☽⚹♅	4 47
	☽☌♀	11 27
	☽∥♀	11 34
	☉∠☽	11 52
27 S	☽⚺♆	3am38
	☽⚺♇	6 35
	☽#♄	9 58
	☽∥♃	12pm 6
	☽∠☿	5 59
	☽#♃	7 29
	☽∥♄	9 44
	♂⚹♅	11 39
28 Su	☉⚺☽	5am38
	☽#♀	6 46
	☽☍♃	9 18
	☽∠♇	9 56
	☽☌♄	2pm37
	☿△♅	3 38
	☽∥♆	3 52
	☽#♂	8 21
	☽□♅	11 23
29 M	☽⚺☿	0am24
	☽⚺♂	0 30
	☿⚹♂	1 45
	☽⚺♀	9 9
	☽☌♆	9 42
	☽⚹♇	12pm22
	♀⚺♆	6 22
	☉∥☽	7 40
30 T	☉⚻♃	2am26
	☽∠♂	3 37
	☽∠♀	12pm33
	☽⚻♃	1 2
	☉☌☽	1 55
	☽∥☿	2 13
	☽⚺♄	6 50
31 W	☽△♅	2am42
	☽⚹♂	6 1
	☽☌☿	9 52
	☽⚺♆	12pm41
	♀⚺♇	1 0
	☽⚼♃	1 59
	☽#♇	2 17
	☽□♇	3 9
	☽⚹♀	3 17
	☽#♅	4 44
	☽∠♄	8 3

NOVEMBER 1951

LONGITUDE

Day	Sid. Time	☉	☽	☽ 12 Hour	Mean ☊	True ☊	☿	♀	♂	♃	♄	♅	♆	♇
	h m s	° ' "	° ' "	° ' "	° '	° '	° '	° '	° '	° '	° '	° '	° '	° '
1	2 37 54	7♏45 19	26♏45 59	4♐ 2 46	6♓41	8♓ 1R	19♏ 9	21♍49	16♍22	5♈40R	9♎24	13♋56R	19♎57	21♌25
2	2 41 51	8 45 23	11♐20 48	18 39 12	6 38	7 51	20 40	22 43	16 58	5 35	9 30	13 56	19 59	21 26
3	2 45 47	9 45 28	25 57 6	3♑13 44	6 35	7 43	22 12	23 37	17 34	5 29	9 37	13 55	20 2	21 27
4	2 49 44	10 45 35	10♑28 26	17 40 40	6 32	7 37	23 43	24 32	18 10	5 24	9 44	13 54	20 4	21 27
5	2 53 40	11 45 44	24 50 0	1♒56 9	6 29	7 34	25 13	25 27	18 45	5 19	9 51	13 54	20 6	21 28
6	2 57 37	12 45 54	8♒58 56	15 58 15	6 25	7 33D	26 43	26 23	19 21	5 14	9 57	13 53	20 8	21 28
7	3 1 33	13 46 6	22 54 8	29 46 38	6 22	7 33	28 12	27 20	19 56	5 10	10 4	13 52	20 10	21 29
8	3 5 30	14 46 18	6♓35 50	13♓21 52	6 19	7 33R	29 42	28 17	20 32	5 5	10 10	13 51	20 12	21 29
9	3 9 26	15 46 33	20 4 51	26 44 55	6 16	7 33	1♐10	29 14	21 7	5 1	10 17	13 50	20 14	21 30
10	3 13 23	16 46 49	3♈22 8	9♈56 36	6 13	7 30	2 38	0♎13	21 42	4 57	10 23	13 49	20 16	21 30
11	3 17 20	17 47 6	16 28 21	22 57 24	6 9	7 25	4 6	1 11	22 18	4 53	10 30	13 48	20 18	21 31
12	3 21 16	18 47 25	29 23 45	5♉47 21	6 6	7 16	5 33	2 10	22 53	4 49	10 36	13 47	20 20	21 31
13	3 25 13	19 47 46	12♉ 8 11	18 26 13	6 3	7 5	6 59	3 10	23 28	4 45	10 43	13 45	20 22	21 31
14	3 29 9	20 48 8	24 41 25	0♊53 47	6 0	6 52	8 25	4 10	24 3	4 42	10 49	13 44	20 24	21 32
15	3 33 6	21 48 32	7♊ 3 21	13 10 11	5 57	6 38	9 51	5 11	24 38	4 39	10 55	13 43	20 26	21 32
16	3 37 2	22 48 58	19 14 24	25 16 12	5 54	6 25	11 15	6 12	25 13	4 36	11 1	13 42	20 28	21 32
17	3 40 59	23 49 25	1♋15 46	7♋13 27	5 50	6 13	12 39	7 13	25 48	4 33	11 7	13 40	20 30	21 32
18	3 44 55	24 49 54	13 9 33	19 4 31	5 47	6 4	14 2	8 15	26 23	4 30	11 13	13 39	20 32	21 32
19	3 48 52	25 50 25	24 58 47	0♌52 55	5 44	5 57	15 23	9 17	26 58	4 28	11 19	13 37	20 34	21 33
20	3 52 49	26 50 58	6♌47 27	12 43 1	5 41	5 54	16 44	10 20	27 33	4 26	11 25	13 36	20 36	21 33
21	3 56 45	27 51 32	18 40 16	24 39 52	5 38	5 52D	18 4	11 23	28 7	4 24	11 31	13 34	20 38	21 33
22	4 0 42	28 52 8	0♍42 30	6♍48 53	5 34	5 52R	19 22	12 26	28 42	4 22	11 37	13 33	20 40	21 33
23	4 4 38	29 52 46	12 59 42	19 15 35	5 31	5 52	20 38	13 30	29 17	4 20	11 43	13 31	20 42	21 33R
24	4 8 35	0♐53 26	25 37 11	2♎ 5 2	5 28	5 51	21 53	14 34	29 51	4 19	11 49	13 30	20 43	21 33
25	4 12 31	1 54 6	8♎39 35	15 21 11	5 25	5 47	23 6	15 38	0♎26	4 18	11 54	13 28	20 45	21 33
26	4 16 28	2 54 49	22 10 1	29 6 5	5 22	5 41	24 16	16 43	1 0	4 17	12 0	13 26	20 47	21 33
27	4 20 24	3 55 34	6♏ 9 15	13♏19 6	5 19	5 33	25 24	17 48	1 34	4 16	12 5	13 24	20 49	21 33
28	4 24 21	4 56 19	20 35 4	27 56 20	5 15	5 22	26 28	18 53	2 8	4 15	12 11	13 22	20 50	21 33
29	4 28 18	5 57 6	5♐21 55	12♐50 43	5 12	5 10	27 29	19 58	2 43	4 15	12 16	13 21	20 52	21 33
30	4 32 14	6♐57 55	20♐21 29	27♐52 58	5♓ 9	4♓58	28♐26	21♎ 4	3♎17	4♈15D	12♎21	13♋19	20♎54	21♌32

DECLINATION and LATITUDE

Day	☉ Decl	☽ Decl	☽ Lat	☽ 12 Hr. Decl	☿ Decl	☿ Lat	♀ Decl	♀ Lat	♂ Decl	♂ Lat	♃ Decl	♃ Lat	♄ Decl	♄ Lat
1	14S 6	24S16	4S58	25S55	18S31	1S 2	3N 4	0S12	6N44	1N28	0N48	1S35	1S43	2N11
2	14 25	27 9	5 3	27 55	19 2	1 9	2 49	0 5	6 30	1 29	0 46	1 35	1 45	2 11
3	14 44	28 12	4 49	27 59	19 32	1 15	2 34	0N 2	6 17	1 29	0 44	1 35	1 48	2 11
4	15 3	27 17	4 16	26 8	20 1	1 21	2 19	0 9	6 3	1 29	0 42	1 34	1 50	2 12
5	15 22	24 33	3 27	22 37	20 29	1 27	2 3	0 16	5 50	1 30	0 40	1 34	1 53	2 12
6	15 40	20 22	2 26	17 50	20 56	1 33	1 46	0 22	5 36	1 30	0 39	1 34	1 55	2 12
7	15 59	15 6	1 17	12 12	21 22	1 38	1 30	0 28	5 22	1 30	0 37	1 34	1 58	2 12
8	16 16	9 10	0 5	6 4	21 47	1 44	1 13	0 34	5 9	1 31	0 35	1 34	2 0	2 12
9	16 34	2 55	1N 6	0N14	22 10	1 49	0 55	0 40	4 55	1 31	0 34	1 33	2 3	2 12
10	16 51	3N22	2 12	6 26	22 33	1 54	0 37	0 46	4 41	1 31	0 32	1 33	2 5	2 12
11	17 8	9 25	3 11	12 16	22 55	1 59	0 19	0 52	4 28	1 32	0 31	1 33	2 7	2 13
12	17 25	14 58	3 58	17 30	23 15	2 3	0 0	0 57	4 14	1 32	0 30	1 33	2 10	2 13
13	17 41	19 48	4 33	21 53	23 35	2 7	0S18	1 2	4 0	1 32	0 29	1 32	2 12	2 13
14	17 58	23 41	4 54	25 13	23 53	2 11	0 38	1 7	3 47	1 33	0 28	1 32	2 14	2 13
15	18 13	26 26	5 0	27 19	24 10	2 15	0 57	1 12	3 33	1 33	0 27	1 32	2 17	2 13
16	18 29	27 53	4 53	28 6	24 25	2 19	1 17	1 17	3 20	1 33	0 26	1 31	2 19	2 13
17	18 44	27 59	4 33	27 33	24 40	2 22	1 37	1 22	3 6	1 34	0 25	1 31	2 21	2 14
18	18 59	26 47	4 1	25 44	24 53	2 24	1 57	1 26	2 52	1 34	0 24	1 31	2 23	2 14
19	19 13	24 23	3 18	22 48	25 5	2 27	2 18	1 30	2 39	1 34	0 23	1 31	2 26	2 14
20	19 27	20 57	2 27	18 54	25 15	2 29	2 39	1 34	2 25	1 35	0 23	1 30	2 28	2 14
21	19 41	16 39	1 30	14 14	25 24	2 30	2 60	1 38	2 12	1 35	0 22	1 30	2 30	2 14
22	19 55	11 39	0 27	8 56	25 32	2 31	3 21	1 42	1 58	1 35	0 22	1 30	2 32	2 15
23	20 8	6 6	0S38	3 10	25 38	2 31	3 42	1 46	1 45	1 36	0 21	1 30	2 34	2 15
24	20 21	0 10	1 42	2S53	25 43	2 31	4 4	1 49	1 32	1 36	0 21	1 29	2 36	2 15
25	20 33	5S57	2 44	9 0	25 46	2 31	4 25	1 53	1 18	1 36	0 21	1 29	2 38	2 15
26	20 45	12 1	3 39	14 55	25 48	2 29	4 47	1 56	1 5	1 37	0 21	1 29	2 40	2 15
27	20 56	17 41	4 22	20 15	25 49	2 27	5 9	1 59	0 51	1 37	0 21	1 28	2 42	2 15
28	21 8	22 34	4 50	24 32	25 48	2 24	5 31	2 2	0 38	1 37	0 21	1 28	2 44	2 16
29	21 18	26 7	4 60	27 15	25 45	2 20	5 53	2 4	0 25	1 38	0 21	1 28	2 46	2 16
30	21S29	27S54	4S49	28S 2	25S42	2S15	6S16	2N 7	0N12	1N38	0N21	1S28	2S48	2N16

Day	♅ Decl	♅ Lat	♆ Decl	♆ Lat	♇ Decl	♇ Lat
1	23N 5	0N22	6S19	1N36	22N39	8N46
5	23 5	0 22	6 23	1 36	22 39	8 47
9	23 6	0 22	6 26	1 36	22 40	8 49
13	23 6	0 22	6 29	1 36	22 40	8 50
17	23 7	0 22	6 31	1 36	22 41	8 51
21	23 7	0 22	6 34	1 36	22 42	8 53
25	23 8	0 22	6 37	1 37	22 44	8 54
29	23N 9	0N23	6S39	1N37	22N45	8N55

☽ PHENOMENA

d	h	m	
6	6	59	☽
13	15	53	○
21	20	2	☾
29	1	1	●

d	h	° '
3	1	28S12
9	11	0
16	14	28N 6
24	1	0
30	9	28S 3

d	h	° '
1	18	5S 4
8	2	0
14	23	5N 0
22	10	0
29	0	4S60

VOID OF COURSE ☽

Last Aspect	☽ Ingress
31 3pm17	1 ♐ 5am20
2 7pm54	3 ♑ 6am40
5 1am 7	5 ♒ 8am43
7 10am23	7 ♓ 12pm23
9 5pm49	9 ♈ 5pm53
11 9am19	12 ♉ 1am 8
13 10pm43	14 ♊ 10am16
16 12pm31	16 ♋ 9pm28
19 4am15	19 ♌ 10am12
21 8pm 2	21 ♍ 10pm36
23 4pm13	24 ♎ 8am 9
26 3am59	26 ♏ 1pm32
28 1am34	28 ♐ 3pm20
30 1pm42	30 ♑ 3pm23

d	h	
2	13	PERIGEE
18	13	APOGEE
30	12	PERIGEE

DAILY ASPECTARIAN

Day	Aspect	Time
1 Th	☽⚼♅	3am35
	☿⚺♆	1pm 1
	☽∠♆	1 32
	☽△♃	2 35
	☉⚺☽	7 26
	☽⚹♄	8 57
	☿⚼♃	10 38
2 F	☽⚻♅	4am14
	☽□♂	9 38
	☿□♇	12pm 5
	☽⚹♆	2 14
	☽△♇	4 35
	♂#♆	4 54
	☽⚺☿	5 6
	☽□♀	7 54
	☉⚺♄	8 16
	☉∠☽	9 53
3 S	☽□♃	3pm39
	☽⚼♇	5 20
	☽∠☿	8 44
	☽□♄	10 46
4 Su	☉⚹☽	0am31
	☽☍♅	5 42
	☽△♂	1pm22
	☽□♆	4 2
	☿∠♄	5 34
	☽⚻♇	6 20
5 M	☽⚹☿	0am43
	☽△♀	1 7
	☽#♅	9 17
	☿⚹♀	9 57
	☽#♇	11 47
	♀#♄	12pm49
	☽⚼♂	3 45
	☽⚹♃	5 39
	☽∥☿	9 22
6 T	☽△♄	1am41
	☽⚼♀	4 25
	☉□☽	6 59
	☽⚻♅	8 23
	☽⚻♂	6pm38
	☽△♆	7 14
	☽∠♃	7 16
	☉∥☽	8 27
	☽☍♇	9 32
7 W	☉△♅	2am15
	☽⚼♄	3 48
	☽⚻♀	8 17
	♂⚺♆	9 55
	☽⚼♅	10 23
	☽□☿	10 23
	☿⚼♅	10 29
	☽⚺♃	9pm21
	☽⚼♆	9 32
8 Th	☿ ♐	4am59
	☽⚻♄	6 23
	☽∥♆	10 39
	☽△♅	12pm51
	☉△☽	3 41
	☽#♂	4 7
9 F	☽⚻♆	0am17
	☽☍♂	1 57
	☽⚻♇	2 33
	☽∥♄	3 18
	☽#♀	7 58
	☽#♃	8 59
	☽∥♃	1pm12
	☽∥♀	1 56
	♂⚺♇	3 37
	☽☍♀	5 49
	♀ ♎	6 48
	☽#♄	7 2
	☉⚼☽	8 53
	☽△☿	10 30
10 S	☽☌♃	2am51
	☽∥♂	4 57
	☽⚼♇	5 43
	♀∥♃	6 47
	☿#♇	7 23
	☽#♆	12pm 3
	☽☍♄	12 55
	☽□♅	7 5
11 Su	☉⚻☽	2am38
	☽⚼☿	5 28
	☽☍♆	7 6
	☽△♇	9 19
	☽⚻♂	11 17
	☿△♃	12pm21
	☿#♅	12 47
	☿∠♆	8 26
12 M	☽⚻♀	5am39
	☽⚺♃	10 7
	☉#☽	12pm19
	☽⚻☿	1 1
	☽⚼♂	4 43
	☽⚻♄	9 16
	☉⚼♃	11 4
13 T	☽⚹♅	3am 5
	♀#♃	12pm 6
	☽⚼♀	12 29
	☉⚺♆	2 12
	☽∠♃	2 27
	☽⚻♆	3 45
	☉☍☽	3 53
	☽∥♇	5 3
	☽□♇	5 55
	☽∥♅	7 54
	☽△♂	10 43
14 W	☽#☿	1am30
	☽⚼♄	2 11
	☽∠♅	7 48
	♀☍♃	11 55
	☉□♇	5pm21
	☽⚹♃	7 19
	☽△♀	8 0
	☽⚼♆	8 50
15 Th	☽☍☿	6am10
	☽△♄	7 38
	☽⚺♅	1pm 3
	☿⚹♄	7 45
16 F	☽△♆	2am27
	☽⚹♇	4 34
	☉⚻☽	7 45
	♀∠♇	7 59
	☽□♂	12pm31
17 S	☽□♃	6am35
	☽∠♇	10 37
	☽□♀	1pm 8
	☉⚼☽	4 39
	☿⚻♅	5 30
	☽□♄	8 3
18 Su	☽☌♅	0am59
	☽⚻☿	1 59
	☽□♆	3pm 0
	☽⚺♇	5 1
	☽#☿	6 32
19 M	☉△☽	1am55
	☽⚹♂	4 15
	☽∥♅	9 41
	♀∥♄	9 52
	☽⚼☿	12pm25
	☽∥♇	12 38
	☉∠♄	12 45
	♀#♂	2 45
	☽△♃	7 13
	♂#♄	8 33
20 T	☽⚹♀	7am52
	☉#☽	8 24
	☽⚹♄	9 28
	☽∠♂	12pm15
	☽⚺♅	1 45
	☽△☿	10 38
21 W	☽⚼♃	1am27
	♀☌♄	3 32
	☽⚹♆	3 57
	☽☌♇	5 46
	☉⚹♂	2pm40
	☽∠♄	3 50
	☉⚼♅	4 33
	☽∠♀	4 54
	☽∠♅	7 44
	☽⚺♂	7 50
	☉□☽	8 2
22 Th	☽⚻♃	7am11
	☽∠♆	9 46
	☽⚺♄	9pm30
	☽#♆	9 58
23 F	♀□♅	0am30
	☽⚹♅	1 1
	☿⚹♆	1 2
	☽⚺♀	1 3
	☉ ♐	2 52
	☽#♀	9 17
	☽#♄	2pm22
	☽⚺♆	2 45
	☽□☿	4 13
	☽⚺♇	4 20
	♇SR	4 33
	☿△♇	5 28
	☽∥♂	6 25
	☽∥♃	11 18
24 S	☽#♃	2am 4
	♂ ♎	6 12
	☽#♂	6 28
	☽☌♂	8 15
	☉⚹☽	10 37
	☽∥♄	10 59
	☽☍♃	4pm 4
	☽∥♀	5 41
	☽∠♇	8 10
25 Su	☽∥♆	2am37
	☽☌♄	5 53
	☽□♅	8 37
	☽☌♀	1pm35
	☉∠☽	3 56
	☽☌♆	9 34
	☽⚹♇	10 55
26 M	☽⚹☿	3am59
	☽⚺♂	3pm54
	☉⚺☽	7 56
	☽⚻♃	8 48
27 T	☽∠☿	7am43
	☉△♃	7 55
	☽⚺♄	10 1
	☽△♅	12pm 7
	☉∥☽	4 2
	☽∠♂	6 6
	☽⚺♀	8 59
	☽⚼♃	9 49
28 W	☽⚺♆	0am25
	☽#♇	1 2
	☽□♇	1 34
	☽#♅	3 21
	☽⚺☿	10 20
	☽∠♄	10 50
	☽⚼♅	12pm41
	☽⚹♂	7 33
	☽∥☿	9 1
	☉∠♆	10 0
	☽△♃	10 12
	☽∠♀	11 19
29 Th	☽∠♆	0am49
	☉☌☽	1 1
	♂∥♃	7 20
	☽⚹♄	11 9
	☽⚻♅	12pm46
	♀☌♆	8 8
30 F	☽⚹♆	0am52
	☽⚹♀	1 14
	☽△♇	1 53
	♃SD	4 8
	♀⚹♇	10 14
	☽☌☿	1pm42
	☽□♂	9 25
	☽□♃	10 10

DECEMBER 1951

LONGITUDE

Day	Sid. Time	☉	☽	☽ 12 Hour	Mean ☊	True ☊	☿	♀	♂	♃	♄	♅	♆	♇
	h m s	° ' "	° ' "	° ' "	° '	° '	° '	° '	° '	° '	° '	° '	° '	° '
1	4 36 11	7♐ 58 45	5♑ 23 54	12♑ 53 7	5♓ 6	4♓ 48R	29♐ 19	22♎ 10	3♎ 51	4♈ 15	12♎ 27	13♋ 17R	20♎ 56	21♌ 32R
2	4 40 7	8 59 36	20 19 35	27 42 23	5 3	4 39	0♑ 6	23 17	4 25	4 15	12 32	13 15	20 57	21 32
3	4 44 4	10 0 27	5♒ 0 50	12♒ 14 24	5 0	4 34	0 48	24 23	4 58	4 16	12 37	13 13	20 59	21 32
4	4 48 0	11 1 20	19 22 45	26 25 43	4 56	4 32	1 22	25 30	5 32	4 16	12 42	13 11	21 0	21 31
5	4 51 57	12 2 13	3♓ 23 17	10♓ 15 34	4 53	4 31	1 50	26 37	6 6	4 17	12 47	13 9	21 2	21 31
6	4 55 53	13 3 7	17 2 45	23 45 6	4 50	4 31	2 9	27 44	6 39	4 18	12 52	13 6	21 4	21 31
7	4 59 50	14 4 1	0♈ 22 56	6♈ 56 34	4 47	4 31	2 19R	28 51	7 13	4 20	12 57	13 4	21 5	21 30
8	5 3 47	15 4 57	13 26 19	19 52 31	4 44	4 28	2 19	29 59	7 46	4 21	13 1	13 2	21 7	21 30
9	5 7 43	16 5 53	26 15 28	2♉ 35 25	4 40	4 23	2 8	1♏ 7	8 20	4 23	13 6	13 0	21 8	21 30
10	5 11 40	17 6 50	8♉ 52 36	15 7 13	4 37	4 14	1 46	2 15	8 53	4 25	13 10	12 58	21 9	21 29
11	5 15 36	18 7 47	21 19 27	27 29 24	4 34	4 3	1 13	3 23	9 26	4 27	13 15	12 55	21 11	21 29
12	5 19 33	19 8 46	3♊ 37 12	9♊ 42 58	4 31	3 50	0 28	4 32	9 59	4 29	13 19	12 53	21 12	21 28
13	5 23 29	20 9 45	15 46 47	21 48 45	4 28	3 36	29♐ 32	5 40	10 32	4 32	13 24	12 51	21 14	21 28
14	5 27 26	21 10 45	27 48 59	3♋ 47 37	4 25	3 22	28 27	6 49	11 5	4 35	13 28	12 48	21 15	21 27
15	5 31 23	22 11 46	9♋ 44 48	15 40 46	4 21	3 10	27 14	7 58	11 38	4 38	13 32	12 46	21 16	21 26
16	5 35 19	23 12 48	21 35 45	27 30 1	4 18	3 0	25 55	9 7	12 11	4 41	13 36	12 44	21 18	21 26
17	5 39 16	24 13 50	3♌ 23 56	9♌ 17 53	4 15	2 53	24 33	10 17	12 43	4 44	13 40	12 41	21 19	21 25
18	5 43 12	25 14 53	15 12 18	21 7 41	4 12	2 49	23 10	11 26	13 16	4 48	13 44	12 39	21 20	21 25
19	5 47 9	26 15 57	27 4 34	3♍ 3 31	4 9	2 47D	21 49	12 36	13 48	4 51	13 48	12 36	21 21	21 24
20	5 51 5	27 17 2	9♍ 5 10	15 10 9	4 6	2 47	20 34	13 45	14 21	4 55	13 51	12 34	21 22	21 23
21	5 55 2	28 18 8	21 19 8	27 32 46	4 2	2 48R	19 25	14 55	14 53	4 59	13 55	12 31	21 24	21 22
22	5 58 58	29 19 14	3♎ 51 43	10♎ 16 35	3 59	2 48	18 25	16 5	15 25	5 4	13 59	12 29	21 25	21 22
23	6 2 55	0♑ 20 21	16 47 57	23 26 17	3 56	2 46	17 35	17 16	15 57	5 8	14 2	12 26	21 26	21 21
24	6 6 52	1 21 29	0♏ 11 57	7♏ 5 13	3 53	2 43	16 56	18 26	16 29	5 13	14 5	12 24	21 27	21 20
25	6 10 48	2 22 37	14 6 6	21 14 29	3 50	2 37	16 27	19 36	17 0	5 18	14 9	12 21	21 28	21 19
26	6 14 45	3 23 46	28 30 0	5♐ 52 4	3 46	2 29	16 9	20 47	17 32	5 23	14 12	12 19	21 29	21 18
27	6 18 41	4 24 56	13♐ 19 51	20 52 19	3 43	2 20	16 2D	21 58	18 4	5 28	14 15	12 16	21 30	21 17
28	6 22 38	5 26 6	28 28 15	6♑ 6 20	3 40	2 10	16 4	23 9	18 35	5 33	14 18	12 14	21 31	21 17
29	6 26 34	6 27 17	13♑ 45 8	21 23 14	3 37	2 2	16 15	24 20	19 6	5 39	14 21	12 11	21 32	21 16
30	6 30 31	7 28 27	28 59 18	6♒ 32 7	3 34	1 56	16 34	25 31	19 38	5 45	14 23	12 9	21 32	21 15
31	6 34 27	8♑ 29 38	14♒ 0 35	21♒ 23 53	3♓ 31	1♓ 52	17♐ 1	26♏ 42	20♎ 9	5♈ 51	14♎ 26	12♋ 6	21♎ 33	21♌ 14

DECLINATION and LATITUDE

Day	☉ Decl	☽ Decl	☽ Lat	☽ 12 Hr. Decl	☿ Decl	☿ Lat	♀ Decl	♀ Lat	♂ Decl	♂ Lat	♃ Decl	♃ Lat	♄ Decl	♄ Lat
1	21S39	27S39	4S19	26S45	25S36	2S10	6S38	2N 9	0S 2	1N38	0N21	1S27	2S50	2N16
2	21 48	25 23	3 31	23 35	25 30	2 3	7 0	2 12	0 15	1 38	0 22	1 27	2 51	2 17
3	21 57	21 26	2 29	18 58	25 22	1 55	7 23	2 14	0 28	1 39	0 22	1 27	2 53	2 17
4	22 6	16 16	1 19	13 23	25 12	1 46	7 45	2 16	0 41	1 39	0 23	1 26	2 55	2 17
5	22 14	10 22	0 6	7 15	25 2	1 36	8 8	2 18	0 54	1 39	0 23	1 26	2 57	2 17
6	22 22	4 7	1N 6	0 57	24 50	1 24	8 30	2 19	1 7	1 40	0 24	1 26	2 58	2 17
7	22 30	2N10	2 12	5N14	24 36	1 11	8 52	2 21	1 20	1 40	0 25	1 26	2 60	2 18
8	22 37	8 13	3 10	11 6	24 22	0 56	9 15	2 23	1 33	1 40	0 26	1 25	3 2	2 18
9	22 43	13 49	3 57	16 23	24 6	0 40	9 37	2 24	1 46	1 41	0 27	1 25	3 3	2 18
10	22 49	18 45	4 32	20 54	23 49	0 23	9 59	2 25	1 59	1 41	0 28	1 25	3 5	2 18
11	22 55	22 48	4 53	24 27	23 31	0 5	10 21	2 26	2 11	1 41	0 29	1 24	3 6	2 19
12	23 0	25 48	5 0	26 50	23 12	0N14	10 44	2 27	2 24	1 42	0 30	1 24	3 8	2 19
13	23 5	27 33	4 54	27 56	22 52	0 34	11 5	2 28	2 37	1 42	0 31	1 24	3 9	2 19
14	23 9	27 60	4 34	27 43	22 32	0 54	11 27	2 28	2 49	1 42	0 33	1 23	3 11	2 19
15	23 13	27 7	4 2	26 12	22 11	1 14	11 49	2 29	3 2	1 42	0 34	1 23	3 12	2 20
16	23 16	25 0	3 20	23 32	21 49	1 34	12 11	2 29	3 14	1 43	0 36	1 23	3 13	2 20
17	23 19	21 49	2 30	19 53	21 28	1 52	12 32	2 30	3 27	1 43	0 37	1 23	3 15	2 20
18	23 22	17 45	1 32	15 26	21 8	2 9	12 53	2 30	3 39	1 43	0 39	1 22	3 16	2 20
19	23 24	12 58	0 30	10 22	20 49	2 23	13 14	2 30	3 51	1 44	0 41	1 22	3 17	2 21
20	23 25	7 39	0S34	4 50	20 31	2 36	13 35	2 30	4 3	1 44	0 42	1 22	3 18	2 21
21	23 26	1 57	1 37	0S59	20 16	2 45	13 56	2 30	4 16	1 44	0 44	1 21	3 19	2 21
22	23 27	3S57	2 38	6 55	20 4	2 53	14 16	2 29	4 28	1 45	0 46	1 21	3 21	2 21
23	23 27	9 52	3 33	12 46	19 54	2 58	14 36	2 29	4 40	1 45	0 48	1 21	3 22	2 22
24	23 26	15 34	4 17	18 13	19 48	3 1	14 56	2 28	4 52	1 45	0 50	1 21	3 23	2 22
25	23 25	20 40	4 49	22 53	19 44	3 2	15 16	2 28	5 4	1 45	0 53	1 20	3 24	2 22
26	23 24	24 46	5 4	26 17	19 43	3 1	15 35	2 27	5 15	1 46	0 55	1 20	3 25	2 22
27	23 22	27 21	4 59	27 56	19 45	2 59	15 54	2 26	5 27	1 46	0 57	1 20	3 26	2 23
28	23 20	27 60	4 34	27 31	19 48	2 55	16 13	2 25	5 39	1 46	0 60	1 19	3 27	2 23
29	23 17	26 31	3 48	25 1	19 54	2 51	16 31	2 24	5 50	1 47	1 2	1 19	3 27	2 23
30	23 14	23 5	2 47	20 46	20 2	2 45	16 49	2 23	6 2	1 47	1 5	1 19	3 28	2 23
31	23S10	18S 8	1S34	15S15	20S11	2N38	17S 7	2N22	6S13	1N47	1N 7	1S19	3S29	2N24

Day	♅ Decl	♅ Lat	♆ Decl	♆ Lat	♇ Decl	♇ Lat
1	23N 9	0N23	6S40	1N37	22N46	8N56
5	23 10	0 23	6 43	1 37	22 47	8 57
9	23 11	0 23	6 45	1 37	22 49	8 58
13	23 12	0 23	6 47	1 37	22 51	8 60
17	23 13	0 23	6 48	1 38	22 53	9 1
21	23 14	0 23	6 50	1 38	22 55	9 2
25	23 15	0 23	6 51	1 38	22 57	9 3
29	23N16	0N23	6S53	1N38	22N59	9N 4

☽ PHENOMENA

d	h	m	
5	16	21	☽
13	9	31	○
21	14	38	☾
28	11	44	●

d	h	° '
6	16	0
13	20	28N 1
21	8	0
27	19	28S 2

d	h	° '
5	2	0
12	0	5N 0
19	11	0
26	6	5S 5

VOID OF COURSE ☽

Last Aspect	☽ Ingress
2 5am10	2 ♒ 3pm45
4 11am18	4 ♓ 6pm 8
5 5pm 2	6 ♈ 11pm18
8 3pm 2	9 ♉ 7am 5
11 0am18	11 ♊ 1pm54
14 1am10	14 ♋ 4am23
15 11pm23	16 ♌ 5pm 5
18 10pm13	19 ♍ 5am52
21 2pm38	21 ♎ 4pm41
23 8am24	23 ♏ 11pm39
25 12pm 7	26 ♐ 2am27
27 1pm 0	28 ♑ 2am24
29 6pm 2	30 ♒ 1am36

d	h	
16	3	APOGEE
28	23	PERIGEE

DAILY ASPECTARIAN

Day	Aspect	Time
1 S	☽⚼♇	1am49
	♀∥♆	2 42
	☉⚺☽	4 26
	☽□♄	11 22
	☽☍♅	12pm36
	♂☍♃	5 13
	☿ ♑	8 42
	☽∥☿	11 3
2 Su	☽□♆	1am 1
	☽⚻♇	1 57
	☽□♀	5 10
	☉∠☽	6 23
	♂#♃	12pm50
	☽#♅	2 30
	☽⚺☿	4 44
	☽#♇	4 45
	☉∥☽	9 19
	☽⚹♃	10 45
	☽△♂	11 56
3 M	☉⚹☽	8am54
	☽△♄	12pm42
	☽⚻♅	1 36
	☽∠☿	6 44
	☽∠♃	11 49
4 T	☽⚼♂	2am 2
	☽△♆	2 46
	☽☍♇	3 38
	☽△♀	11 18
	☽⚼♄	2pm16
	☽⚼♅	2 58
	☽⚹☿	9 13
5 W	☽⚺♃	1am34
	☽⚼♆	4 37
	☽⚻♂	4 55
	☽∥♀	8 11
	☽∥♆	2pm 4
	☽⚼♀	3 40
	☉□☽	4 21
	☽⚻♄	4 33
	☽△♅	5 2
	♂∠♇	5 53
	☉⚹♄	7 9
6 Th	☉⚻♅	1am16
	☽∥♄	4 18
	☽⚻♆	7 11
	☽⚻♇	7 58
	☽∥♂	11 0
	☽#♃	2pm 6
	☽∥♃	5 13
	☽#♂	8 39
	☽⚻♀	8 58
7 F	☽#♄	3am13
	☽□☿	3 32
	☽☌♃	7 13
	☽⚼♇	11 12
	☿SR	12pm 6
	☽☍♂	1 4
	☽#♆	5 58
	☽☍♄	11 13
	☽□♅	11 15
8 S	♀ ♏	0am19
	♄□♅	2 47
	☉△☽	3 19
	☽#♀	4 30
	☽☍♆	2pm20
	☽△♇	3 2
	☉∠♀	8 20
9 Su	☉⚼☽	9am58
	☽☍♀	10 6
	☽△☿	10 51
	☽⚺♃	3pm27
	☿⚹♀	4 36
10 M	☽⚻♂	0am 1
	☉#♇	0 24
	☽⚹♅	7 49
	☽⚻♄	8 18
	☽⚼☿	2pm34
	☉⚻☽	5 16
	☽∠♃	8 21
	☽⚻♆	11 43
11 T	☽∥♇	0am 9
	☽□♇	0 18
	☉#☽	0 45
	☽∥♅	2 40
	☽#☿	4 34
	☽⚼♂	6 20
	☽∠♅	12pm48
	☽⚼♄	1 34
	☽⚻☿	6 12
	♀⚻♃	11 9
12 W	☿#♅	0am31
	☽⚹♃	1 43
	☽⚻♀	1 58
	☽⚼♆	5 5
	☿ ♐	11 32
	☉∥☿	11 59
	☽△♂	1pm 8
	☽⚺♅	6 12
	☽△♄	7 15
13 Th	☿#♇	1am58
	☉☍☽	9 31
	☽⚼♀	10 45
	☽△♆	10 51
	☽⚹♇	11 17
14 F	☽☍☿	1am10
	☉⚹♆	1 42
	☉△♇	6 21
	☽□♃	1pm38
	☽∠♇	5 20
	☽△♀	8 2
	☉#♅	10 8
15 S	☽□♂	4am 0
	☽☌♅	6 5
	☽□♄	7 42
	♂∥♄	10pm 4
	☽□♆	11 23
	☽⚺♇	11 40
16 Su	☉⚻☽	3am36
	☽⚻☿	7 53
	☉#☽	1pm46
	☽∥♅	2 22
	☽∥♇	4 50
	☿∠♀	5 6
	♂□♅	10 40
17 M	☽#☿	2am32
	☽△♃	2 44
	☉☌☿	3 9
	☽⚼☿	11 12
	☉⚼☽	12pm59
	☽□♀	3 31
	☽⚺♅	6 50
	☽⚹♂	7 52
	☽⚹♄	9 0
18 T	☽⚼♃	9am21
	☽⚹♆	12pm26
	☽☌♇	12 33
	☽△☿	2 28
	☉△☽	10 13
	☽#♀	10 47
	♂☌♄	11 38
19 W	♀△♅	0am15
	☽∠♅	1 4
	☽∠♄	3 29
	☽∠♂	3 38
	☿△♇	7 55
	☿⚹♆	8 32
	☽⚻♃	3pm40
	☽∠♆	6 36
20 Th	♀⚺♄	2am11
	☽#♆	3 32
	☽⚹♅	6 51
	♆⚹♇	9 23
	☽⚺♄	9 28
	☽⚹♀	10 12
	☽⚺♂	10 51
	☽#♂	2pm45
	☽#♄	6 20
	☽□☿	8 36
	♀⚺♂	10 19
21 F	☽⚺♇	0am 6
	☽⚺♆	0 9
	☽∥♃	4 57
	☽#♃	11 3
	☉□☽	2pm38
	☽∠♀	6 13
	☽∥♄	9 32
22 S	☽∥♂	2am 8
	☽☍♃	2 16
	☽∠♇	4 42
	☽∥♆	11 40
	☉ ♑	4pm 1
	☽□♅	4 2
	☽☌♄	6 55
	☽☌♂	10 23
23 Su	☽⚺♀	0am55
	☽⚹☿	1 21
	☿⚺♀	4 5
	☽⚹♇	8 14
	☽☌♆	8 24
	☽∥♀	9pm 7
24 M	☉⚹☽	2am12
	☽∠☿	2 55
	☽⚻♃	8 48
	☿⚹♂	10 13
	☽∥☿	7pm20
	☽△♅	9 3
25 T	☽⚺♄	0am 4
	☽⚺☿	3 52
	☽⚺♂	5 6
	☉∠☽	5 57
	☽☌♀	10 6
	☽⚼♃	10 29
	☽□♇	12pm 7
	☽⚺♆	12 23
	☽#♇	12 26
	☽#♅	2 14
	♀⚼♃	3 5
	☉∥☽	3 11
	☽⚼♅	10 3
26 W	☽∠♄	1am 9
	☽∠♂	6 50
	☉⚺☽	8 35
	♀□♇	10 29
	☽△♃	11 16
	☽∠♆	1pm 0
	♀⚺♆	2 21
	☽⚻♅	10 19
27 Th	☽⚹♄	1am28
	☽☌☿	4 18
	☿SD	6 45
	☽⚹♂	7 49
	☽△♇	12pm39
	☽⚹♆	1 0
	☽⚺♀	2 53
28 F	☉□♃	3am 7
	☽□♃	11 12
	☉☌☽	11 44
	☽⚼♇	12pm15
	☽∠♀	4 28
	☉⚼♇	7 30
	☽☍♅	9 33
29 S	☽□♄	0am56
	☽⚺☿	3 59
	☉#♅	8 20
	☽□♂	8 43
	☽⚻♇	11 47
	☽□♆	12pm14
	☽⚹♀	6 2
	☽#♅	10 56
	☉∥☽	11 9
30 Su	☽#♇	0am31
	☽∠☿	4 12
	☽⚹♃	10 49
	☉⚺☽	2pm29
	☽∥☿	3 2
	☽⚻♅	8 56
31 M	☽△♄	0am41
	☽∥♀	4 8
	☽⚹☿	5 2
	♀⚼♅	7 54
	☽△♂	10 19
	☽∠♃	11 10
	☽☍♇	11 43
	☽△♆	12pm16
	☉∠☽	4 36
	☽⚼♅	9 18
	☽□♀	10 33

JANUARY 1952

LONGITUDE

Day	Sid. Time	☉	☽	☽ 12 Hour	Mean ☊	True ☊	☿	♀	♂	♃	♄	♅	♆	♇
	h m s	° ' "	° ' "	° ' "	° '	° '	° '	° '	° '	° '	° '	° '	° '	° '
1	6 38 24	9♑ 30 49	28♒ 41 20	5♓ 52 29	3♓ 27	1♓ 50	17♐ 34	27♏ 53	20♎ 40	5♈ 57	14♎ 29	12♋ 3R	21♎ 34	21♌ 13R
2	6 42 21	10 31 59	12♓ 57 8	19 55 10	3 24	1 50	18 13	29 4	21 10	6 3	14 31	12 1	21 35	21 12
3	6 46 17	11 33 9	26 46 42	3♈ 31 56	3 21	1 51	18 58	0♐ 16	21 41	6 10	14 33	11 58	21 35	21 11
4	6 50 14	12 34 19	10♈ 11 11	16 44 48	3 18	1 52R	19 48	1 27	22 11	6 16	14 36	11 56	21 36	21 10
5	6 54 10	13 35 28	23 13 14	29 36 54	3 15	1 52	20 41	2 39	22 42	6 23	14 38	11 53	21 37	21 8
6	6 58 7	14 36 38	5♉ 56 15	12♉ 11 45	3 12	1 50	21 39	3 50	23 12	6 30	14 40	11 50	21 37	21 7
7	7 2 3	15 37 46	18 23 49	24 32 52	3 8	1 45	22 40	5 2	23 42	6 37	14 42	11 48	21 38	21 6
8	7 6 0	16 38 55	0♊ 39 15	6♊ 43 20	3 5	1 39	23 44	6 14	24 12	6 44	14 44	11 45	21 39	21 5
9	7 9 56	17 40 3	12 45 25	18 45 47	3 2	1 31	24 50	7 26	24 42	6 52	14 45	11 43	21 39	21 4
10	7 13 53	18 41 11	24 44 43	0♋ 42 25	2 59	1 22	25 59	8 38	25 11	6 59	14 47	11 40	21 40	21 3
11	7 17 50	19 42 19	6♋ 39 6	12 35 0	2 56	1 14	27 11	9 50	25 41	7 7	14 49	11 38	21 40	21 2
12	7 21 46	20 43 26	18 30 18	24 25 13	2 52	1 6	28 24	11 2	26 10	7 15	14 50	11 35	21 40	21 0
13	7 25 43	21 44 33	0♌ 19 56	6♌ 14 42	2 49	1 0	29 39	12 14	26 39	7 23	14 51	11 32	21 41	20 59
14	7 29 39	22 45 39	12 9 46	18 5 24	2 46	0 56	0♑ 55	13 27	27 8	7 31	14 52	11 30	21 41	20 58
15	7 33 36	23 46 45	24 1 55	29 59 38	2 43	0 54D	2 13	14 39	27 37	7 40	14 54	11 27	21 41	20 57
16	7 37 32	24 47 51	5♍ 58 57	12♍ 0 16	2 40	0 54	3 32	15 51	28 5	7 48	14 55	11 25	21 42	20 55
17	7 41 29	25 48 56	18 4 2	24 10 43	2 37	0 55	4 53	17 4	28 34	7 57	14 55	11 22	21 42	20 54
18	7 45 26	26 50 2	0♎ 20 49	6♎ 34 52	2 33	0 56	6 14	18 16	29 2	8 6	14 56	11 20	21 42	20 53
19	7 49 22	27 51 7	12 53 23	19 16 54	2 30	0 58	7 37	19 29	29 30	8 15	14 57	11 17	21 42	20 52
20	7 53 19	28 52 11	25 45 54	2♏ 20 51	2 27	0 59R	9 0	20 41	29 58	8 24	14 57	11 15	21 42	20 50
21	7 57 15	29 53 15	9♏ 2 10	15 50 8	2 24	0 59	10 25	21 54	0♏ 26	8 33	14 58	11 13	21 43	20 49
22	8 1 12	0♒ 54 20	22 44 58	29 46 43	2 21	0 57	11 50	23 7	0 53	8 42	14 58	11 10	21 43	20 48
23	8 5 8	1 55 23	6♐ 55 17	14♐ 10 23	2 18	0 54	13 16	24 20	1 21	8 52	14 59	11 8	21 43R	20 46
24	8 9 5	2 56 26	21 31 31	28 58 0	2 14	0 50	14 44	25 33	1 48	9 1	14 59R	11 5	21 43	20 45
25	8 13 1	3 57 29	6♑ 28 57	14♑ 3 20	2 11	0 46	16 11	26 45	2 15	9 11	14 59	11 3	21 43	20 43
26	8 16 58	4 58 31	21 39 57	29 17 31	2 8	0 43	17 40	27 58	2 41	9 21	14 59	11 1	21 43	20 42
27	8 20 55	5 59 32	6♒ 54 43	14♒ 30 17	2 5	0 40	19 9	29 11	3 8	9 31	14 58	10 58	21 43	20 41
28	8 24 51	7 0 33	22 2 58	29 31 41	2 2	0 39D	20 39	0♑ 24	3 34	9 41	14 58	10 56	21 42	20 39
29	8 28 48	8 1 32	6♓ 55 28	14♓ 13 34	1 58	0 39	22 10	1 37	4 0	9 51	14 58	10 54	21 42	20 38
30	8 32 44	9 2 30	21 25 23	28 30 33	1 55	0 39	23 41	2 51	4 26	10 1	14 57	10 52	21 42	20 36
31	8 36 41	10♒ 3 27	5♈ 28 51	12♈ 20 16	1♓ 52	0♓ 41	25♑ 13	4♑ 4	4♏ 51	10♈ 12	14♎ 57	10♋ 50	21♎ 42	20♌ 35

DECLINATION and LATITUDE

Day	☉ Decl	☽ Decl	☽ Lat	☽ 12 Hr. Decl	☿ Decl	☿ Lat	♀ Decl	♀ Lat	♂ Decl	♂ Lat	♃ Decl	♃ Lat	♄ Decl	♄ Lat
1	23S 6	12S12	0S17	9S 1	20S21	2N31	17S24	2N21	6S25	1N47	1N10	1S18	3S30	2N24
2	23 2	5 47	0N59	2 31	20 32	2 23	17 41	2 19	6 36	1 48	1 13	1 18	3 30	2 24
3	22 57	0N43	2 10	3N53	20 44	2 15	17 58	2 18	6 47	1 48	1 15	1 18	3 31	2 25
4	22 51	6 58	3 12	9 56	20 57	2 7	18 14	2 16	6 58	1 48	1 18	1 18	3 32	2 25
5	22 45	12 45	4 1	15 24	21 9	1 58	18 30	2 15	7 9	1 49	1 21	1 17	3 32	2 25
6	22 39	17 52	4 37	20 6	21 22	1 50	18 45	2 13	7 20	1 49	1 24	1 17	3 33	2 25
7	22 32	22 6	4 60	23 51	21 34	1 41	18 60	2 11	7 31	1 49	1 27	1 17	3 33	2 26
8	22 24	25 19	5 8	26 29	21 46	1 32	19 14	2 9	7 41	1 49	1 30	1 17	3 34	2 26
9	22 17	27 20	5 2	27 51	21 58	1 23	19 28	2 7	7 52	1 50	1 33	1 16	3 34	2 26
10	22 9	28 3	4 43	27 56	22 9	1 14	19 41	2 5	8 3	1 50	1 37	1 16	3 34	2 26
11	21 60	27 28	4 12	26 42	22 20	1 5	19 54	2 3	8 13	1 50	1 40	1 16	3 35	2 27
12	21 51	25 38	3 30	24 17	22 30	0 56	20 6	2 1	8 23	1 50	1 43	1 16	3 35	2 27
13	21 41	22 40	2 38	20 49	22 40	0 47	20 18	1 59	8 34	1 51	1 47	1 15	3 35	2 27
14	21 31	18 45	1 40	16 31	22 48	0 38	20 30	1 56	8 44	1 51	1 50	1 15	3 36	2 28
15	21 21	14 6	0 37	11 33	22 56	0 30	20 40	1 54	8 54	1 51	1 54	1 15	3 36	2 28
16	21 10	8 53	0S28	6 8	23 3	0 21	20 51	1 52	9 4	1 51	1 57	1 15	3 36	2 28
17	20 59	3 18	1 32	0 25	23 8	0 13	21 0	1 49	9 14	1 52	2 1	1 14	3 36	2 28
18	20 48	2S30	2 34	5S25	23 13	0 5	21 10	1 46	9 23	1 52	2 5	1 14	3 36	2 29
19	20 36	8 19	3 30	11 10	23 17	0S 3	21 18	1 44	9 33	1 52	2 8	1 14	3 36	2 29
20	20 23	13 56	4 16	16 36	23 19	0 11	21 26	1 41	9 43	1 52	2 12	1 14	3 36	2 29
21	20 11	19 6	4 51	21 24	23 21	0 19	21 34	1 39	9 52	1 53	2 16	1 13	3 36	2 30
22	19 58	23 28	5 10	25 12	23 21	0 26	21 40	1 36	10 1	1 53	2 20	1 13	3 36	2 30
23	19 44	26 35	5 12	27 33	23 20	0 33	21 47	1 33	10 11	1 53	2 24	1 13	3 36	2 30
24	19 30	28 3	4 53	28 3	23 18	0 40	21 52	1 30	10 20	1 53	2 28	1 13	3 35	2 30
25	19 16	27 32	4 15	26 30	23 15	0 47	21 57	1 27	10 29	1 53	2 32	1 12	3 35	2 31
26	19 2	24 58	3 18	22 59	23 10	0 54	22 1	1 24	10 38	1 54	2 36	1 12	3 35	2 31
27	18 47	20 36	2 7	17 53	23 4	1 0	22 5	1 21	10 47	1 54	2 40	1 12	3 34	2 31
28	18 32	14 54	0 47	11 44	22 57	1 6	22 8	1 18	10 55	1 54	2 44	1 12	3 34	2 32
29	18 16	8 26	0N35	5 4	22 48	1 12	22 11	1 15	11 4	1 54	2 48	1 12	3 34	2 32
30	18 0	1 41	1 52	1N40	22 39	1 18	22 12	1 12	11 12	1 54	2 53	1 11	3 33	2 32
31	17S44	4N56	3N 1	8N 6	22S27	1S23	22S14	1N 9	11S20	1N55	2N57	1S11	3S33	2N32

Day	♅ Decl	♅ Lat	♆ Decl	♆ Lat	♇ Decl	♇ Lat
1	23N17	0N23	6S53	1N38	23N 1	9N 5
5	23 18	0 23	6 54	1 39	23 3	9 6
9	23 19	0 23	6 55	1 39	23 5	9 7
13	23 20	0 23	6 55	1 39	23 8	9 8
17	23 21	0 23	6 55	1 39	23 10	9 8
21	23 21	0 23	6 55	1 40	23 13	9 9
25	23 22	0 23	6 55	1 40	23 15	9 10
29	23N23	0N23	6S55	1N40	23N17	9N10

☽ PHENOMENA

d	h	m	
4	4	43	☽
12	4	55	○
20	6	9	☾
26	22	27	●

d	h	° '
2	21	0
10	1	28N 4
17	14	0
24	6	28S 7
30	6	0

d	h	° '
1	5	0
8	2	5N 8
15	14	0
22	14	5S13
28	14	0

VOID OF COURSE ☽

Last Aspect		☽ Ingress		
31	10pm33	1	♓	2am11
2	9am33	3	♈	5am42
4	10pm59	5	♉	12pm44
7	5am16	7	♊	10pm43
10	2am47	10	♋	10am35
12	4pm13	12	♌	11pm20
15	7am31	15	♍	12pm 1
17	4pm34	17	♎	11pm20
20	6am 9	20	♏	7am44
21	8pm38	22	♐	12pm22
24	7am 4	24	♑	1pm39
26	0am 4	26	♒	1pm 7
27	11pm27	28	♓	12pm46
30	4am16	30	♈	2pm33

d	h	
12	6	APOGEE
26	12	PERIGEE

DAILY ASPECTARIAN

Day	Aspect	Time
1	☽⚼♄	1am19
T	☽⚼♂	12pm 4
	☽⚺♃	12 13
	☽⚼♆	1 11
	☉⚹☽	7 33
	☽∥♆	7 55
	☽∥♂	9 5
	☽△♅	10 24
2	♂⚹♇	1am 4
W	☉#♇	1 31
	☽⚻♄	2 41
	☽∥♄	8 22
	♀∠♄	9 20
	☽□☿	9 33
	☽⚻♇	2pm12
	☽⚻♂	2 43
	☽⚻♆	2 54
	☽#♃	4 45
	♀ ♐	6 45
	♂☌♆	7 38
3	☽∥♃	2am 4
Th	♃⚼♇	3 19
	☽△♀	6 46
	☉☍♅	9 26
	☽#♄	10 37
	♂∥♆	2pm52
	☽⚼♇	4 44
	☽☌♃	4 51
	☽#♆	11 43
	☽#♂	11 59
4	☽□♅	3am 9
F	☉□☽	4 43
	☽☍♄	8 4
	☽⚼♀	12pm37
	☽△☿	6 56
	☽△♇	8 8
	☽☍♆	9 0
	☽☍♂	10 59
5	☿△♇	11am17
S	☽⚻♀	7pm35
	☿⚹♆	11 23
6	☽⚺♃	1am 5
Su	☉□♄	1 19
	☽⚼☿	1 28
	☽#♀	4 52
	☽⚹♅	11 17
	☽⚻♄	4pm49
	☉△☽	6 9
	☽#☿	8 26
7	☉#☽	2am41
M	☽□♇	5 16
	☽⚻♆	6 18
	☽∠♃	6 20
	☽∥♇	6 26
	☽∥♅	8 5
	☽⚻☿	9 6
	☽⚻♂	10 47
	☽∠♅	4pm21
	☽⚼♄	10 10
8	☉⚼☽	2am 8
T	♀∠♆	8 16
	♀△♃	11 19
	☽⚼♆	11 51
	☽⚹♃	12pm10
	☽☍♀	12 15
	☽⚼♂	5 38
	☿⚹♂	6 26
	☽⚺♅	9 55
9	☽△♄	4am 0
W	☉⚻☽	10 43
	☽⚹♇	4pm35
	☽△♆	5 48
	☉∥☿	10 56
10	☽△♂	0am56
Th	☽☍☿	2 47
	☽∠♇	10pm44
11	☽□♃	0am57
F	☽⚻♀	7 9
	☽☌♅	10 1
	☽□♄	4pm32
12	♀∠♂	4am26
S	☉☍☽	4 55
	☽⚺♇	5 4
	☽□♆	6 26
	☉⚻♇	6 33
	♀⚻♅	10 34
	☽□♂	4pm13
	☽⚼♀	5 0
	☽∥♅	7 16
	☽∥♇	8 43
	☽⚻☿	10 26
	☉□♆	10 31
13	☽#☿	0am 1
Su	☿ ♑	6 45
	☉#☽	6 48
	☽#♀	2pm24
	☽△♃	2 29
	☽⚺♅	10 39
14	☽△♀	2am53
M	☽⚹♄	5 30
	☽⚼☿	8 32
	☽☌♇	5pm47
	☽⚹♆	7 16
	☽⚼♃	9 12
	☉⚻☽	11 27
15	☽∠♅	4am52
T	♀⚹♄	4 57
	☽⚹♂	7 31
	☽∠♄	11 49
	☽△☿	6pm30
	☽#♂	11 15
16	☽∠♆	1am26
W	☽⚻♃	3 41
	☉⚼☽	8 19
	☽#♆	8 36
	☽⚹♅	10 47
	☽∠♂	2pm44
	☽⚺♄	5 47
	☽□♀	9 48
	☉∥♀	10 37
	☽#♄	10 45
17	☽∥♃	5am19
Th	☽⚺♇	5 34
	☽⚺♆	7 9
	☿#♇	9 55
	☉△☽	4pm34
	☿⚼♇	5 51
	☽⚺♂	9 22
	☽#♃	10 16
18	☽∥♄	4am33
F	☽∠♇	10 38
	☽□☿	12pm44
	☽☍♃	3 4
	☽∥♆	6 14
	☽□♅	8 59
19	☽☌♄	3am53
S	☽∥♂	5 21
	☿□♃	12pm11
	☽⚹♀	1 39
	☽⚹♇	2 55
	☽☌♆	4 31
20	♂ ♏	1am34
Su	♀△♇	2 50
	☉□☽	6 9
	☽☌♂	7 58
	☽∠♀	7pm49
	♀⚹♆	8 11
	☽⚻♃	11 7
21	☉ ♒	2am39
M	☽⚹☿	2 44
	☽△♅	3 51
	☉∥☽	5 14
	☽⚺♄	10 29
	☿☍♅	1pm 2
	☽∥♀	1 11
	☽□♇	8 38
	☽⚺♆	10 13
	☽#♇	10 31
	☉□♂	11 20
	☽∥☿	11 20
	☽#♅	11 23
22	☽⚺♀	0am41
T	☽⚼♃	1 39
	☽⚼♅	5 51
	☽∠☿	7 48
	☽∠♄	12pm20
	☽⚺♂	2 20
	☉⚹☽	2 59
	☽∠♆	11 39
23	☽△♃	3am16
W	☽⚻♅	6 58
	☽⚺☿	11 41
	☽⚹♄	1pm19
	☽∠♂	4 3
	♆SR	4 19
	☉∠☽	5 44
	☽△♇	10 44
24	☽⚹♆	0am18
Th	☿□♄	4 10
	☽☌♀	7 4
	☽⚹♂	5pm 2
	♄SR	5 53
	☉⚺☽	7 41
	☿#♇	9 46
	☽⚼♇	10 48
25	☽□♃	4am20
F	☽☍♅	7 14
	☽□♄	1pm27
	☽☌☿	5 1
	☽⚻♇	10 29
26	☽□♆	0am 4
S	☽#♅	9 46
	☽#♇	10 23
	☽⚺♀	10 47
	☽∥☿	11 10
	☽∥♀	4pm47
	☽□♂	5 52
	☉☌☽	10 27
27	☽⚹♃	4am 9
Su	☽⚻♅	6 24
	☉∥☽	8 34
	☽∠♀	12pm30
	☽△♄	12 44
	♀ ♑	3 58
	☽⚺☿	9 31
	☽☍♇	9 47
	☽△♆	11 27
28	☿⚻♇	0am 4
M	☽∠♃	4 15
	☽⚼♅	6 12
	☽⚼♄	12pm42
	☽⚹♀	2 37
	☽∥♂	2 41
	☿□♆	4 46
	☽△♂	7 6
	☽⚼♆	11 38
29	☽∠☿	0am26
T	☉⚺☽	1 56
	☽⚺♃	4 51
	☽∥♆	5 27
	☽△♅	6 30
	☽⚻♄	1pm13
	☽∥♄	5 22
	☽#♃	7 49
	☽⚼♂	8 33
	☽⚻♇	10 38
30	☽⚻♆	0am28
W	☽⚹☿	4 16
	☉∠☽	4 45
	☽∥♃	4pm35
	☽#♄	6 51
	☽□♀	9 18
	☽⚻♂	10 53
31	☽⚼♇	0am11
Th	☉⚹♃	3 59
	☽#♆	7 25
	☽☌♃	8 20
	☉⚹☽	8 38
	☽□♅	9 19
	☽☍♄	4pm36
	☉⚻♅	5 31
	♀⚹♂	11 45

FEBRUARY 1952

LONGITUDE

Day	Sid. Time	☉	☽	☽ 12 Hour	Mean ☊	True ☊	☿	♀	♂	♃	♄	♅	♆	♇
	h m s	° ' "	° ' "	° ' "	° '	° '	° '	° '	° '	° '	° '	° '	° '	° '
1	8 40 37	11♒ 4 23	19♈ 4 53	25♈ 42 57	1♓ 49	0♓ 42	26♑ 46	5♑ 17	5♏ 16	10♈ 22	14♎ 56R	10♋ 47R	21♎ 42R	20♌ 34R
2	8 44 34	12 5 17	2♉ 14 47	8♉ 40 48	1 46	0 43R	28 19	6 30	5 41	10 33	14 55	10 45	21 41	20 32
3	8 48 30	13 6 11	15 1 27	21 17 15	1 43	0 44	29 54	7 43	6 6	10 44	14 54	10 43	21 41	20 31
4	8 52 27	14 7 2	27 28 42	3♊ 36 21	1 39	0 43	1♒ 28	8 56	6 31	10 55	14 53	10 41	21 41	20 29
5	8 56 24	15 7 52	9♊ 40 43	15 42 19	1 36	0 42	3 4	10 10	6 55	11 6	14 52	10 39	21 40	20 28
6	9 0 20	16 8 42	21 41 38	27 39 10	1 33	0 40	4 40	11 23	7 19	11 17	14 51	10 37	21 40	20 26
7	9 4 17	17 9 29	3♋ 35 19	9♋ 30 32	1 30	0 38	6 18	12 36	7 42	11 28	14 49	10 35	21 39	20 25
8	9 8 13	18 10 16	15 25 11	21 19 38	1 27	0 36	7 55	13 50	8 6	11 39	14 48	10 33	21 39	20 23
9	9 12 10	19 11 0	27 14 12	3♌ 9 11	1 23	0 34	9 34	15 3	8 29	11 51	14 46	10 31	21 38	20 22
10	9 16 6	20 11 44	9♌ 4 53	15 1 31	1 20	0 32	11 13	16 16	8 52	12 2	14 45	10 30	21 38	20 21
11	9 20 3	21 12 26	20 59 22	26 58 40	1 17	0 32	12 54	17 30	9 14	12 14	14 43	10 28	21 37	20 19
12	9 23 59	22 13 6	2♍ 59 37	9♍ 2 28	1 14	0 31D	14 35	18 43	9 36	12 25	14 41	10 26	21 36	20 18
13	9 27 56	23 13 46	15 7 27	21 14 48	1 11	0 32	16 17	19 57	9 58	12 37	14 39	10 24	21 36	20 16
14	9 31 53	24 14 24	27 24 45	3♎ 37 34	1 8	0 32	17 59	21 10	10 20	12 49	14 37	10 23	21 35	20 15
15	9 35 49	25 15 0	9♎ 53 32	16 12 54	1 4	0 33	19 43	22 24	10 41	13 1	14 35	10 21	21 34	20 13
16	9 39 46	26 15 36	22 35 58	29 3 2	1 1	0 33	21 27	23 37	11 2	13 13	14 33	10 19	21 34	20 12
17	9 43 42	27 16 10	5♏ 34 21	12♏ 10 14	0 58	0 34	23 13	24 51	11 22	13 25	14 30	10 18	21 33	20 10
18	9 47 39	28 16 43	18 50 53	25 36 32	0 55	0 34	24 59	26 5	11 42	13 37	14 28	10 16	21 32	20 9
19	9 51 35	29 17 15	2♐ 27 19	9♐ 23 20	0 52	0 34R	26 46	27 18	12 2	13 50	14 25	10 15	21 31	20 7
20	9 55 32	0♓ 17 46	16 24 35	23 30 56	0 49	0 34	28 34	28 32	12 21	14 2	14 23	10 13	21 30	20 6
21	9 59 28	1 18 15	0♑ 42 11	7♑ 57 58	0 45	0 34D	0♓ 23	29 46	12 40	14 14	14 20	10 12	21 29	20 5
22	10 3 25	2 18 43	15 17 48	22 41 3	0 42	0 34	2 13	0♒ 59	12 59	14 27	14 17	10 11	21 29	20 3
23	10 7 22	3 19 10	0♒ 6 59	7♒ 34 44	0 39	0 34	4 4	2 13	13 17	14 40	14 14	10 9	21 28	20 2
24	10 11 18	4 19 35	15 3 21	22 31 49	0 36	0 34R	5 55	3 27	13 35	14 52	14 11	10 8	21 27	20 0
25	10 15 15	5 19 59	29 59 6	7♓ 24 11	0 33	0 34	7 47	4 40	13 52	15 5	14 8	10 7	21 26	19 59
26	10 19 11	6 20 21	14♓ 46 6	22 3 58	0 29	0 34	9 40	5 54	14 9	15 18	14 5	10 6	21 25	19 58
27	10 23 8	7 20 41	29 17 1	6♈ 24 36	0 26	0 34	11 34	7 8	14 26	15 31	14 2	10 5	21 24	19 56
28	10 27 4	8 20 59	13♈ 26 13	20 21 33	0 23	0 33	13 28	8 21	14 42	15 44	13 59	10 4	21 22	19 55
29	10 31 1	9♓ 21 15	27♈ 10 25	3♉ 52 47	0♓ 20	0♓ 32	15♓ 22	9♒ 35	14♏ 58	15♈ 57	13♎ 55	10♋ 3	21♎ 21	19♌ 53

DECLINATION and LATITUDE

Day	☉ Decl	☽ Decl	☽ Lat	☽ 12 Hr. Decl	☿ Decl	☿ Lat	♀ Decl	♀ Lat	♂ Decl	♂ Lat	♃ Decl	♃ Lat	♄ Decl	♄ Lat
1	17S27	11N 7	3N56	13N58	22S15	1S28	22S14	1N 6	11S29	1N55	3N 1	1S11	3S32	2N33
2	17 10	16 36	4 38	19 1	22 1	1 33	22 14	1 3	11 37	1 55	3 6	1 11	3 32	2 33
3	16 53	21 11	5 4	23 6	21 46	1 37	22 13	1 0	11 45	1 55	3 10	1 11	3 31	2 33
4	16 36	24 43	5 16	26 2	21 29	1 42	22 12	0 57	11 53	1 55	3 14	1 10	3 30	2 34
5	16 18	27 3	5 12	27 44	21 11	1 46	22 10	0 54	12 0	1 55	3 19	1 10	3 30	2 34
6	16 0	28 6	4 55	28 7	20 52	1 49	22 7	0 51	12 8	1 56	3 23	1 10	3 29	2 34
7	15 42	27 49	4 26	27 12	20 31	1 52	22 3	0 48	12 15	1 56	3 28	1 10	3 28	2 34
8	15 23	26 16	3 45	25 3	20 9	1 55	21 59	0 44	12 23	1 56	3 33	1 10	3 27	2 35
9	15 4	23 34	2 54	21 49	19 45	1 58	21 55	0 41	12 30	1 56	3 37	1 9	3 26	2 35
10	14 45	19 51	1 56	17 41	19 20	2 0	21 49	0 38	12 37	1 56	3 42	1 9	3 26	2 35
11	14 26	15 20	0 53	12 50	18 54	2 2	21 43	0 35	12 44	1 56	3 46	1 9	3 25	2 35
12	14 7	10 12	0S14	7 27	18 26	2 4	21 37	0 32	12 51	1 56	3 51	1 9	3 24	2 36
13	13 47	4 38	1 20	1 45	17 57	2 5	21 29	0 29	12 58	1 56	3 56	1 9	3 23	2 36
14	13 27	1S10	2 24	4S 6	17 26	2 6	21 22	0 25	13 4	1 57	4 1	1 9	3 22	2 36
15	13 6	7 1	3 22	9 53	16 54	2 6	21 13	0 22	13 11	1 57	4 5	1 8	3 21	2 36
16	12 46	12 40	4 11	15 22	16 20	2 6	21 4	0 19	13 17	1 57	4 10	1 8	3 20	2 37
17	12 25	17 54	4 48	20 16	15 45	2 5	20 54	0 16	13 24	1 57	4 15	1 8	3 18	2 37
18	12 5	22 25	5 11	24 17	15 9	2 4	20 44	0 13	13 30	1 57	4 20	1 8	3 17	2 37
19	11 43	25 51	5 18	27 2	14 31	2 3	20 33	0 10	13 36	1 57	4 25	1 8	3 16	2 37
20	11 22	27 49	5 6	28 10	13 52	2 1	20 21	0 7	13 42	1 57	4 30	1 8	3 15	2 38
21	11 1	28 2	4 35	27 25	13 11	1 58	20 9	0 4	13 47	1 57	4 35	1 7	3 14	2 38
22	10 39	26 19	3 46	24 45	12 29	1 55	19 56	0 1	13 53	1 57	4 40	1 7	3 12	2 38
23	10 17	22 45	2 41	20 23	11 46	1 52	19 43	0S 2	13 58	1 57	4 45	1 7	3 11	2 38
24	9 56	17 41	1 25	14 43	11 1	1 48	19 29	0 5	14 4	1 57	4 50	1 7	3 10	2 38
25	9 34	11 32	0 3	8 13	10 15	1 43	19 14	0 8	14 9	1 57	4 55	1 7	3 8	2 39
26	9 11	4 48	1N18	1 22	9 28	1 38	18 59	0 11	14 14	1 57	4 60	1 7	3 7	2 39
27	8 49	2N 3	2 33	5N24	8 39	1 33	18 43	0 14	14 19	1 57	5 5	1 7	3 5	2 39
28	8 26	8 37	3 36	11 42	7 50	1 26	18 27	0 17	14 23	1 57	5 10	1 6	3 4	2 39
29	8S 4	14N35	4N25	17N15	6S59	1S19	18S10	0S20	14S28	1N57	5N15	1S 6	3S 3	2N40

Day	♅ Decl	♅ Lat	♆ Decl	♆ Lat	♇ Decl	♇ Lat
1	23N24	0N23	6S54	1N40	23N19	9N11
5	23 24	0 23	6 54	1 41	23 22	9 11
9	23 25	0 23	6 53	1 41	23 24	9 12
13	23 25	0 23	6 52	1 41	23 26	9 12
17	23 26	0 23	6 50	1 41	23 28	9 12
21	23 26	0 23	6 49	1 41	23 30	9 12
25	23 27	0 23	6 47	1 42	23 32	9 12
29	23N27	0N23	6S45	1N42	23N34	9N12

☽ PHENOMENA

d	h	m	
2	20	2	☽
11	0	29	○
18	18	2	☾
25	9	16	●

d	h	° '
6	7	28N 9
13	19	0
20	15	28S10
26	17	0
4	6	5N16
11	19	0
18	21	5S18
25	1	0

VOID OF COURSE ☽

Last Aspect		☽ Ingress		
1	3pm47	1	♉	7pm51
3	10am29	4	♊	4am55
5	11pm56	6	♋	4pm44
8	12pm38	9	♌	5am36
11	1am16	11	♍	6pm 2
13	10am31	14	♎	5am 1
16	7am24	16	♏	1pm45
18	6pm 2	18	♐	7pm43
20	8am37	20	♑	10pm50
22	10am 2	22	♒	11pm49
24	10am15	25	♓	0am 1
25	10pm59	27	♈	1am12
28	1pm46	29	♉	5am 2

d	h	
8	8	APOGEE
23	23	PERIGEE

DAILY ASPECTARIAN

Day	Aspect	Time
1 F	☽⋕♂	1am31
	☿∥♀	1 32
	☽△♇	2 39
	☽☍♆	4 42
	♀⚼♇	5 24
	☽□☿	3pm47
2 S	☉⋕☽	2am36
	☽☍♂	6 37
	☽△♀	8 45
	☽⚺♃	3pm45
	☽⚹♅	3 52
	☉□☽	8 2
	♃□♅	10 46
	☽⚻♄	11 46
3 Su	☿ ♒	1am38
	☽⋕☿	3 13
	☽⋕♀	6 14
	☽□♇	10 29
	☽⚻♆	12pm45
	☽∥♇	1 43
	☽∥♅	2 5
	☽⚼♀	4 23
	☽∠♅	8 31
	☽∠♃	8 54
4 M	☽⚼♄	4am41
	☽△☿	8 59
	☉△♄	5pm48
	☽⚼♆	6 3
	☽⚻♂	6 20
5 T	☽⚻♀	1am 4
	☽⚺♅	1 56
	☽⚹♃	2 51
	♀☍♅	9 21
	☽△♄	10 18
	☉△☽	11 51
	☽⚼☿	7pm19
	☽⚹♇	9 29
	♀□♃	9 35
	☽△♆	11 56
6 W	☽⚼♂	1am17
	☉⚼☽	8pm50
7 Th	♃⋕♄	0am50
	☽∠♇	3 42
	☽⚻☿	6 21
	☽△♂	8 38
	☽☌♅	2pm 9
	☽□♃	4 14
	☽☍♀	8 24
	☽□♄	10 44
8 F	☿□♂	3am17
	☉⚻☽	6 7
	☽⚺♇	10 5
	☽□♆	12pm38
	♀□♄	6 36
9 S	☽∥♅	1am 7
	☽∥♇	1 14
	☽⋕♀	11 42
	☿⚻♅	1pm37
	☽□♂	11 32
10 Su	☽⚺♅	2am51
	☽⋕☿	3 18
	☉☍♇	3 25
	☽☍☿	5 2
	☽△♃	6 4
	☽⚹♄	11 24
	☿⚹♃	1pm13
	☽⚻♀	4 11
	☽☌♇	10 39
11 M	☉☍☽	0am29
	☽⚹♆	1 16
	☉⋕☽	4 42
	♅∥♇	6 1
	☽∠♅	8 57
	☉△♆	9 38
	☽⋕♂	12pm10
	☽⚼♃	12 43
	☽∠♄	5 25
12 T	☿△♄	1am27
	☽⚼♀	1 37
	☽∠♆	7 10
	☽⚹♂	1pm31
	☽⋕♆	2 33
	☽⚹♅	2 43
	☽⚻♃	6 59
	☽⚺♄	11 4
13 W	☽⚻☿	2am38
	☽∥♃	2 53
	☽⋕♄	5 15
	♀⚻♇	6 11
	☽⚺♇	10 4
	☽△♀	10 31
	☽⚺♆	12pm40
	☉⚻☽	5 17
	☽∠♂	7 50
14 Th	♂△♅	3am14
	♀□♆	7 59
	☽∥♄	8 57
	☽⋕♃	11 48
	☽⚼☿	12pm30
	☽∠♇	3 5
	☉∥♂	7 58
	☽∥♆	11 20
15 F	☉⚼☽	0am45
	☽□♅	0 52
	☽⚺♂	1 32
	☉⚼♅	2 18
	☽☍♃	6 2
	☿☍♇	6 53
	☽☌♄	8 53
	☽⚹♇	7pm30
	☽△☿	9 31
	☽☌♆	10 3
16 S	☉∥☽	0am24
	☿△♆	1 24
	☽□♀	2 7
	☽∥♂	2 46
	☉△☽	7 24
	☽∥☿	2pm51
17 Su	☽△♅	8am35
	☽☌♂	10 49
	☽⚻♃	2pm29
	☽∥♀	2 49
	☽⚺♄	4 10
18 M	☽□♇	2am19
	☿⚼♅	3 50
	☽⚺♆	4 47
	☽⋕♅	6 18
	☽⋕♇	6 36
	☉∠♃	10 16
	☽⚼♅	11 23
	☽□☿	12pm32
	☽⚹♀	2 6
	☽⚼♃	5 34
	☉□☽	6 2
	☽∠♄	6 43
19 T	☉⚼♄	3am 3
	☽∠♆	7 3
	☽⚻♅	1pm27
	☽⚺♂	4 56
	☉ ♓	4 57
	☽∠♀	6 38
	☽△♃	7 54
	☽⚹♄	8 33
	☿⚺♀	10 24
20 W	☿∥♂	5am19
	☽△♇	6 14
	☿∠♃	6 57
	☽⚹♆	8 37
	☿⚼♄	10 26
	☽∠♂	6pm51
	☿ ♓	6 55
	☽⚺♀	10 17
	☽⚹☿	11 24
21 Th	☉⚹☽	1am 4
	♀ ♒	4 43
	☽⚼♇	7 14
	♃☍♄	8 37
	☽☍♅	3pm39
	☽⚹♂	8 9
	☽□♄	10 21
	☽□♃	10 36
22 F	☉☌☿	2am47
	☉∠☽	3 31
	☽∠☿	3 34
	☽⚻♇	7 43
	☽□♆	10 2
	☽⋕♇	7pm41
	☽⋕♅	8 9
23 S	☽☌♀	3am41
	☉⚺☽	5 32
	☽⚺☿	7 15
	☽∥♀	3pm49
	☽⚻♅	4 7
	☽□♂	9 35
	☽△♄	10 37
	☽⚹♃	11 42
24 Su	☿⚼♆	6am43
	☽☍♇	7 56
	☽△♆	10 15
	☽∥♂	2pm19
	☽⚼♅	4 10
	☽⚼♄	10 38
25 M	☽∠♃	0am10
	☽∥☿	5 19
	☉∥☽	7 36
	☽⚺♀	8 15
	☉☌☽	9 16
	☽⚼♆	10 24
	☽☌☿	2pm28
	☽△♅	4 23
	☽∥♆	5 3
	♂⚺♄	6 53
	☽⚻♄	10 53
	☽△♂	10 59
	☽⋕♃	11 19
26 T	☽⚺♃	0am53
	☉⚼♆	1 39
	☿△♅	5 24
	☽∥♄	5 55
	☽⚻♇	8 31
	☽⚻♆	10 54
	☽∠♀	11 0
	☉∥☿	3pm13
27 W	☽⚼♂	0am15
	☽⋕♄	3 41
	☽⚼♇	9 30
	☽∥♃	11 1
	☽⚹♀	2pm29
	☉⚺☽	2 38
	☽⋕♆	5 3
	☽□♅	6 14
	☽⋕☿	9 21
	☉⚺♀	11 5
	☉⋕☽	11 21
28 Th	☽⚺☿	0am 3
	☽☍♄	0 56
	☽⚻♂	2 13
	☽☌♃	4 1
	☿⚻♄	6 16
	☽△♇	11 12
	☽☍♆	1pm46
	☿△♂	5 58
	☉∠☽	6 37
	☽⋕♂	11 29
29 F	☿∥♆	6am26
	☽∠☿	6 39
	☿⚺♃	8 4
	♀⚻♅	8 52
	☽⋕♀	3pm31
	☉△♅	4 19
	☽⚹♅	11 11
	☉⚹☽	11 46

MARCH 1952

LONGITUDE

Day	Sid. Time	☉	☽	☽ 12 Hour	Mean ☊	True ☊	☿	♀	♂	♃	♄	♅	♆	♇
	h m s	° ' "	° ' "	° ' "	° '	° '	° '	° '	° '	° '	° '	° '	° '	° '
1	10 34 57	10♓ 21 30	10♉ 28 45	16♉ 58 31	0♓ 17	0♓ 31R	17♓ 17	10♒ 49	15♏ 13	16♈ 10	13♎ 52R	10♋ 2R	21♎ 20R	19♌ 52R
2	10 38 54	11 21 43	23 22 26	29 40 54	0 14	0 30	19 12	12 3	15 27	16 23	13 48	10 1	21 19	19 51
3	10 42 51	12 21 53	5♊ 54 23	12♊ 3 25	0 10	0 30D	21 7	13 17	15 41	16 36	13 45	10 0	21 18	19 49
4	10 46 47	13 22 1	18 8 34	24 10 24	0 7	0 30	23 2	14 30	15 55	16 49	13 41	9 59	21 17	19 48
5	10 50 44	14 22 8	0♋ 9 32	6♋ 6 33	0 4	0 30	24 56	15 44	16 8	17 3	13 37	9 59	21 15	19 47
6	10 54 40	15 22 12	12 2 2	17 56 34	0 1	0 32	26 49	16 58	16 21	17 16	13 34	9 58	21 14	19 45
7	10 58 37	16 22 14	23 50 42	29 44 57	29♒ 58	0 33	28 41	18 12	16 33	17 29	13 30	9 57	21 13	19 44
8	11 2 33	17 22 13	5♌ 39 49	11♌ 35 44	29 55	0 34	0♈ 31	19 25	16 45	17 43	13 26	9 57	21 12	19 43
9	11 6 30	18 22 11	17 33 9	23 32 25	29 51	0 35	2 19	20 39	16 56	17 56	13 22	9 56	21 10	19 42
10	11 10 26	19 22 7	29 33 53	5♍ 37 50	29 48	0 36R	4 5	21 53	17 6	18 10	13 18	9 56	21 9	19 40
11	11 14 23	20 22 1	11♍ 44 30	17 54 6	29 45	0 35	5 48	23 7	17 16	18 24	13 14	9 55	21 8	19 39
12	11 18 20	21 21 52	24 6 48	0♎ 22 43	29 42	0 34	7 27	24 21	17 25	18 37	13 10	9 55	21 6	19 38
13	11 22 16	22 21 42	6♎ 41 56	13 4 31	29 39	0 32	9 2	25 34	17 34	18 51	13 6	9 55	21 5	19 37
14	11 26 13	23 21 30	19 30 30	25 59 52	29 35	0 28	10 33	26 48	17 42	19 5	13 1	9 55	21 4	19 36
15	11 30 9	24 21 16	2♏ 32 39	9♏ 8 48	29 32	0 25	11 59	28 2	17 50	19 19	12 57	9 54	21 2	19 34
16	11 34 6	25 21 0	15 48 18	22 31 6	29 29	0 21	13 19	29 16	17 57	19 32	12 53	9 54	21 1	19 33
17	11 38 2	26 20 43	29 17 10	6♐ 6 29	29 26	0 18	14 34	0♓ 30	18 3	19 46	12 48	9 54	20 59	19 32
18	11 41 59	27 20 24	12♐ 58 57	19 54 33	29 23	0 16	15 42	1 44	18 8	20 0	12 44	9 54D	20 58	19 31
19	11 45 55	28 20 3	26 53 11	3♑ 54 45	29 20	0 15D	16 43	2 58	18 13	20 14	12 40	9 54	20 56	19 30
20	11 49 52	29 19 40	10♑ 59 7	18 6 6	29 16	0 16	17 37	4 11	18 18	20 28	12 35	9 54	20 55	19 29
21	11 53 49	0♈ 19 16	25 15 28	2♒ 26 55	29 13	0 17	18 24	5 25	18 21	20 42	12 31	9 54	20 53	19 28
22	11 57 45	1 18 51	9♒ 40 5	16 54 31	29 10	0 18	19 4	6 39	18 24	20 56	12 26	9 54	20 52	19 27
23	12 1 42	2 18 23	24 9 44	1♓ 25 8	29 7	0 19R	19 36	7 53	18 26	21 10	12 22	9 55	20 50	19 26
24	12 5 38	3 17 53	8♓ 40 4	15 53 52	29 4	0 19	19 59	9 7	18 28	21 24	12 17	9 55	20 49	19 25
25	12 9 35	4 17 21	23 5 49	0♈ 15 13	29 1	0 17	20 15	10 21	18 28R	21 39	12 12	9 55	20 47	19 24
26	12 13 31	5 16 48	7♈ 21 22	14 23 38	28 57	0 13	20 24R	11 35	18 28	21 53	12 8	9 56	20 46	19 23
27	12 17 28	6 16 12	21 21 27	28 14 21	28 54	0 8	20 24	12 48	18 28	22 7	12 3	9 56	20 44	19 22
28	12 21 24	7 15 34	5♉ 1 59	11♉ 44 4	28 51	0 2	20 18	14 2	18 26	22 21	11 58	9 57	20 42	19 21
29	12 25 21	8 14 55	18 20 31	24 51 19	28 48	29♒ 56	20 4	15 16	18 24	22 35	11 54	9 57	20 41	19 20
30	12 29 17	9 14 13	1♊ 16 35	7♊ 36 32	28 45	29 51	19 43	16 30	18 21	22 50	11 49	9 58	20 39	19 19
31	12 33 14	10♈ 13 28	13♊ 51 31	20♊ 1 56	28♒ 41	29♒ 46	19♈ 16	17♓ 44	18♏ 17	23♈ 4	11♎ 44	9♋ 58	20♎ 38	19♌ 19

DECLINATION and LATITUDE

Day	☉	☽		☽ 12 Hr.	☿		♀		♂		♃		♄	
	Decl	Decl	Lat	Decl	Decl	Lat	Decl	Lat	Decl	Lat	Decl	Lat	Decl	Lat
1	7S41	19N41	4N58	21N50	6S 7	1S12	17S33	0S23	14S33	1N57	5N20	1S 6	3S 1	2N40
2	7 18	23 42	5 15	25 15	5 15	1 4	17 35	0 25	14 37	1 56	5 26	1 6	2 59	2 40
3	6 55	26 28	5 16	27 22	4 22	0 55	17 17	0 28	14 41	1 56	5 31	1 6	2 58	2 40
4	6 32	27 56	5 2	28 9	3 28	0 46	16 59	0 31	14 45	1 56	5 36	1 6	2 56	2 40
5	6 9	28 2	4 36	27 36	2 34	0 36	16 39	0 33	14 49	1 56	5 41	1 6	2 55	2 40
6	5 46	26 51	3 58	25 47	1 39	0 25	16 20	0 36	14 53	1 56	5 46	1 6	2 53	2 41
7	5 23	24 27	3 10	22 51	0 45	0 14	15 59	0 39	14 57	1 56	5 52	1 5	2 51	2 41
8	4 59	21 1	2 14	18 58	0N10	0 3	15 39	0 41	15 0	1 55	5 57	1 5	2 50	2 41
9	4 36	16 43	1 12	14 17	1 4	0N 9	15 18	0 43	15 3	1 55	6 2	1 5	2 48	2 41
10	4 13	11 43	0 6	9 1	1 57	0 22	14 56	0 46	15 7	1 55	6 7	1 5	2 46	2 41
11	3 49	6 13	1S 1	3 20	2 50	0 34	14 35	0 48	15 10	1 54	6 13	1 5	2 45	2 41
12	3 25	0 24	2 6	2S33	3 41	0 47	14 12	0 51	15 13	1 54	6 18	1 5	2 43	2 42
13	3 2	5S30	3 6	8 26	4 30	1 0	13 50	0 53	15 15	1 54	6 23	1 5	2 41	2 42
14	2 38	11 18	3 58	14 4	5 18	1 13	13 27	0 55	15 18	1 53	6 29	1 5	2 39	2 42
15	2 15	16 42	4 38	19 10	6 4	1 26	13 3	0 57	15 20	1 53	6 34	1 5	2 38	2 42
16	1 51	21 25	5 4	23 25	6 47	1 39	12 39	0 59	15 23	1 53	6 39	1 4	2 36	2 42
17	1 27	25 6	5 14	26 27	7 28	1 52	12 15	1 1	15 25	1 52	6 45	1 4	2 34	2 42
18	1 3	27 25	5 6	27 59	8 6	2 4	11 51	1 3	15 27	1 52	6 50	1 4	2 32	2 42
19	0 40	28 5	4 41	27 45	8 40	2 16	11 26	1 5	15 29	1 51	6 55	1 4	2 31	2 42
20	0 16	26 57	3 58	25 42	9 12	2 28	11 1	1 7	15 31	1 51	7 1	1 4	2 29	2 43
21	0N 8	24 3	3 0	22 0	9 39	2 38	10 35	1 9	15 32	1 50	7 6	1 4	2 27	2 43
22	0 31	19 37	1 51	16 56	10 3	2 48	10 10	1 10	15 33	1 49	7 11	1 4	2 25	2 43
23	0 55	14 0	0 34	10 53	10 24	2 57	9 44	1 12	15 35	1 49	7 17	1 4	2 23	2 43
24	1 19	7 37	0N46	4 16	10 40	3 4	9 18	1 14	15 36	1 48	7 22	1 4	2 21	2 43
25	1 42	0 53	2 1	2N29	10 52	3 11	8 51	1 15	15 37	1 47	7 27	1 4	2 19	2 43
26	2 6	5N48	3 8	9 1	10 60	3 16	8 24	1 17	15 37	1 46	7 33	1 4	2 18	2 43
27	2 29	12 5	4 3	14 58	11 4	3 20	7 57	1 18	15 38	1 46	7 38	1 3	2 16	2 43
28	2 53	17 37	4 42	20 2	11 3	3 22	7 30	1 19	15 38	1 45	7 43	1 3	2 14	2 43
29	3 16	22 10	5 4	23 59	10 58	3 23	7 3	1 21	15 39	1 44	7 49	1 3	2 12	2 43
30	3 40	25 29	5 10	26 38	10 50	3 22	6 35	1 22	15 39	1 43	7 54	1 3	2 10	2 43
31	4N 3	27N27	5N 1	27N55	10N37	3N19	6S 7	1S23	15S39	1N42	7N59	1S 3	2S 8	2N43

Day	♅		♆		♇	
	Decl	Lat	Decl	Lat	Decl	Lat
1	23N27	0N23	6S45	1N42	23N34	9N12
5	23 27	0 23	6 43	1 42	23 36	9 12
9	23 27	0 23	6 41	1 42	23 37	9 12
13	23 27	0 23	6 39	1 42	23 39	9 12
17	23 27	0 23	6 37	1 42	23 40	9 11
21	23 27	0 23	6 34	1 43	23 41	9 11
25	23 27	0 23	6 32	1 43	23 42	9 11
29	23N27	0N23	6S29	1N43	23N43	9N10

☽ PHENOMENA

d	h	m	
3	13	44	☽
11	18	14	○
19	2	40	☾
25	20	13	●

d	h	° '
4	14	28N10
12	2	0
18	21	28S 6
25	3	0
31	22	28N 2

d	h	
2	14	5N17
10	2	0
17	2	5S14
23	10	0
29	21	5N10

VOID OF COURSE ☽

Last Aspect		☽ Ingress		
1	5pm22	2	♊	12pm37
4	11am33	4	♋	11pm41
7	11am39	7	♌	12pm31
9	7am15	10	♍	0am52
11	6pm14	12	♎	11am17
14	2pm53	14	♏	7pm21
16	6pm23	17	♐	1am16
19	2am40	19	♑	5am20
20	4pm42	21	♒	7am55
22	6pm58	23	♓	9am39
24	4pm17	25	♈	11am34
27	1am20	27	♉	3pm 6
29	1am49	29	♊	9pm36

d	h	
6	23	APOGEE
22	23	PERIGEE

DAILY ASPECTARIAN

Day	Aspect	Time
1 S	☽□♀	0am41
	☽⚻♄	6 12
	☽☍♂	8 54
	☽⚺♃	10 40
	☽⚹☿	2pm47
	☽□♇	5 22
	☿#♃	7 36
	☽⚻♆	8 8
	☽∥♅	10 19
	☽∥♇	11 13
2 Su	☽∠♅	3am 6
	☿⚻♇	7 56
	☽⚼♄	10 17
	☽∠♃	3pm32
3 M	☽⚼♆	0am46
	☿⚻♆	2 12
	☽⚺♅	7 58
	♀△♄	8 46
	☉∥♆	12pm 6
	☉□☽	1 44
	☽△♄	3 15
	☽△♀	4 0
	☽⚻♂	7 31
	☽⚹♃	9 20
4 T	☽⚹♇	3am17
	☽△♆	6 13
	☉⚻♄	7 11
	☽□☿	11 33
	☿∥♄	2pm25
5 W	☽⚼♀	1am17
	☽⚼♂	2 0
	☽∠♇	9 18
	♀□♂	9 32
	☽☌♅	7pm49
	☉#♃	11 42
6 Th	☽□♄	3am 5
	♀⚹♃	7 14
	☉△☽	7 24
	☽△♂	8 55
	☽□♃	10 50
	☽⚻♀	11 10
	☽⚺♇	3pm40
	☽□♆	6 40
7 F	☉△♂	5am22
	☽∥♇	6 32
	☽∥♅	7 44
	☽△☿	11 39
	☉⚼☽	4pm42
	☿ ♈	5 11
8 S	♀☍♇	5am36
	☽⚺♅	8 40
	☉⚺♃	10 41
	☽⚹♄	3pm37
	☿⚼♂	6 5
	☽□♂	10 43
	☽⚼☿	11 28
9 Su	☽△♃	0am48
	☉⚻☽	1 47
	☽☌♇	4 18
	☽☍♀	6 56
	☽⚹♆	7 15
	☽#♀	7 39
	☽#♂	8 11
	♀△♆	9 57
	♀∥♂	2pm 6
	☽∠♅	2 47
	☽∠♄	9 30
10 M	☉⚻♇	7am12
	☽⚼♃	7 16
	☿⚼♇	8 4
	☽⚻☿	10 26
	☽∠♆	1pm 0
	☽⚹♅	8 27
	☿#♄	9 49
	☽#♆	10 6
11 T	☽∥♃	0am 2
	☽⚺♄	2 54
	☉#☽	10 45
	☽⚹♂	10 54
	☽∥☿	12pm18
	☽⚻♃	1 12
	☽#♄	2 31
	☽⚺♇	3 22
	☉⚻♆	5 55
	☽⚺♆	6 13
	☉☍☽	6 14
	☉#☿	7 4
12 W	☽⚻♀	0am30
	♀⚼♅	11 9
	☽∥♄	12pm37
	☉∥☽	2 34
	☽∠♂	4 5
	☽#☿	7 17
	☽∠♇	8 3
13 Th	☽#♃	3am39
	☽∥♆	4 39
	☽☍☿	5 2
	☽□♅	6 4
	☽⚼♀	8 5
	☽☌♄	11 58
	☿□♅	1pm39
	☽⚺♂	8 37
	☉∥♄	10 39
	☽☍♃	11 11
14 F	☽⚹♇	0am10
	☽☌♆	2 52
	☉⚻☽	7 43
	☽∥♀	8 38
	☽△♀	2pm53
	☽∥♂	5 40
	♀⚼♄	10 26
15 S	☽△♅	1pm22
	☉⚼☽	1 23
	♃#♆	3 47
	☿☍♄	4 17
	☿#♆	6 25
	☽⚺♄	6 46
	☿∥♃	6 50
	☽⚻☿	7 3
16 Su	♃△♇	1am31
	☽☌♂	3 52
	☽□♇	6 42
	☽⚻♃	6 48
	☽⚺♆	9 18
	☽#♅	12pm17
	☽#♇	1 40
	♀ ♓	2 18
	☽⚼♅	4 14
	☉△☽	6 23
	☽∠♄	9 24
17 M	☽⚼☿	0am32
	☽□♀	2 21
	☽⚼♃	9 49
	☽∠♆	11 46
	☽⚻♅	6pm38
	☽⚹♄	11 34
18 T	♅SD	4am14
	☽△☿	5 6
	☽⚺♂	9 0
	☽△♇	11 19
	☽△♃	12pm22
	☽⚹♆	1 48
19 W	☉□☽	2am40
	☽∠♂	10 53
	☽⚹♀	11 22
	☽⚼♇	12pm59
	☽☍♅	10 10
20 Th	☽□♄	2am41
	☽□☿	11 52
	☽⚹♂	12pm23
	☽⚻♇	2 18
	☽∠♀	3 8
	☉ ♈	4 13
	☽□♃	4 14
	☽□♆	4 42
	☿⚻♂	10 6
21 F	☽#♇	2am17
	☽#♅	3 42
	♀∠♃	6 46
	♀⚼♆	8 56
	☉⚹☽	9 5
	♃☍♆	5pm15
	☽⚺♀	6 31
22 S	☽⚻♅	0am24
	☿#♀	3 14
	☽△♄	4 34
	☉∠☽	11 49
	☽□♂	2pm31
	☽☍♇	4 11
	☽⚹☿	4 11
	☿△♇	4 18
	☽∥♂	5 40
	☽△♆	6 31
	☽⚹♃	6 58
23 Su	☽⚼♅	1am14
	☽⚼♄	5 15
	☽#☿	1pm14
	☉⚺☽	2 27
	☽∥♀	5 27
	☽∠☿	5 46
	☽⚼♆	7 17
	☽∠♃	8 12
24 M	☽☌♀	0am49
	☽#♃	0 54
	☽△♅	2 4
	☽∥♆	3 53
	☉⚼♂	4 2
	☽⚻♄	5 58
	♀△♅	3pm42
	☽△♂	4 17
	☽⚻♇	5 50
	☽∥♄	6 53
	☽⚺☿	7 11
	☽⚻♆	8 9
	☉#☽	9 15
	☽⚺♃	9 32
25 T	☉⚼♇	2am36
	☉∥☽	9 46
	♂SR	11 4
	☽#♄	11 22
	☽⚼♂	5pm26
	☽⚼♇	6 58
	☉☌☽	8 13
26 W	☽#♆	2am39
	☽□♅	4 22
	☽∥♃	6 33
	☽⚺♀	7 52
	☽☍♄	8 5
	☽#♀	9 3
	♀⚻♄	10 8
	☉#♄	11 4
	☿SR	1pm55
	☽⚻♂	7 0
	☽∥☿	7 55
	☽△♇	8 34
	☽☌☿	10 21
	☽☍♆	10 55
27 Th	☽☌♃	1am20
	☽∠♀	12pm21
	♀#♃	2 18
	☽#♂	2 58
28 F	☉⚺☽	4am17
	☽⚹♅	8 47
	☽⚻♄	12pm22
	☽⚹♀	5 50
29 S	☽☍♂	0am 6
	☽□♇	1 49
	☽⚺☿	3 5
	☽⚻♆	4 17
	☽⚺♃	7 57
	☽∥♅	8 17
	☉∠☽	9 46
	☽∥♇	10 6
	☽∠♅	12pm12
	☽⚼♄	3 42
30 Su	♀∥♆	5am40
	☽∠☿	6 18
	☽⚼♆	8 16
	☽∠♃	12pm40
	☉⚹☽	4 24
	☽⚺♅	4 31
	☉□♅	5 51
	☽△♄	7 57
	☿△♇	10 11
31 M	☽□♀	8am21
	☽⚻♂	8 32
	☽⚹☿	10 6
	♀△♂	10 10
	☽⚹♇	10 35
	☽△♆	1pm 8
	☽⚹♃	6 18
	☿⚺♀	9 0

APRIL 1952

LONGITUDE

Day	Sid. Time	☉	☽	☽ 12 Hour	Mean ☊	True ☊	☿	♀	♂	♃	♄	♅	♆	♇
	h m s	° ' "	° ' "	° ' "	° '	° '	° '	° '	° '	° '	° '	° '	° '	° '
1	12 37 11	11♈ 12 42	26♊ 8 15	2♋ 11 1	28♒ 38	29♒ 43R	18♈ 44R	18♓ 58	18♏ 12R	23♈ 18	11♎ 40R	9♋ 59	20♎ 36R	19♌ 18R
2	12 41 7	12 11 53	8♋ 10 50	14 8 18	28 35	29 42D	18 7	20 12	18 7	23 33	11 35	10 0	20 34	19 17
3	12 45 4	13 11 2	20 4 3	25 58 46	28 32	29 42	17 26	21 25	18 1	23 47	11 30	10 1	20 33	19 16
4	12 49 0	14 10 8	1♌ 53 4	7♌ 47 38	28 29	29 43	16 42	22 39	17 54	24 1	11 26	10 2	20 31	19 15
5	12 52 57	15 9 12	13 43 3	19 39 57	28 26	29 44	15 56	23 53	17 47	24 16	11 21	10 3	20 30	19 15
6	12 56 53	16 8 14	25 38 54	1♍ 40 24	28 22	29 45R	15 8	25 7	17 38	24 30	11 16	10 4	20 28	19 14
7	13 0 50	17 7 14	7♍ 44 58	13 52 59	28 19	29 45	14 21	26 21	17 29	24 44	11 12	10 5	20 26	19 13
8	13 4 46	18 6 11	20 4 49	26 20 45	28 16	29 43	13 34	27 35	17 19	24 59	11 7	10 6	20 25	19 13
9	13 8 43	19 5 6	2♎ 40 58	9♎ 5 35	28 13	29 39	12 48	28 48	17 9	25 13	11 3	10 7	20 23	19 12
10	13 12 40	20 3 59	15 34 38	22 8 4	28 10	29 32	12 5	0♈ 2	16 57	25 28	10 58	10 8	20 21	19 12
11	13 16 36	21 2 51	28 45 44	5♏ 27 26	28 7	29 24	11 24	1 16	16 45	25 42	10 53	10 9	20 20	19 11
12	13 20 33	22 1 40	12♏ 12 53	19 1 46	28 3	29 15	10 48	2 30	16 32	25 57	10 49	10 10	20 18	19 10
13	13 24 29	23 0 27	25 53 42	2♐ 48 18	28 0	29 6	10 15	3 44	16 19	26 11	10 44	10 12	20 16	19 10
14	13 28 26	23 59 12	9♐ 45 10	16 43 57	27 57	28 59	9 47	4 57	16 5	26 25	10 40	10 13	20 15	19 9
15	13 32 22	24 57 56	23 44 16	0♑ 45 47	27 54	28 53	9 23	6 11	15 50	26 40	10 35	10 15	20 13	19 9
16	13 36 19	25 56 39	7♑ 48 15	14 51 24	27 51	28 49	9 5	7 25	15 34	26 54	10 31	10 16	20 11	19 9
17	13 40 15	26 55 19	21 55 2	28 58 59	27 47	28 47D	8 52	8 39	15 18	27 9	10 27	10 18	20 10	19 8
18	13 44 12	27 53 58	6♒ 3 5	13♒ 7 13	27 44	28 48	8 44	9 53	15 1	27 23	10 22	10 19	20 8	19 8
19	13 48 9	28 52 35	20 11 13	27 14 56	27 41	28 48R	8 41D	11 6	14 44	27 38	10 18	10 21	20 7	19 7
20	13 52 5	29 51 10	4♓ 18 11	11♓ 20 44	27 38	28 48	8 43	12 20	14 26	27 52	10 14	10 23	20 5	19 7
21	13 56 2	0♉ 49 44	18 22 19	25 22 37	27 35	28 47	8 50	13 34	14 7	28 7	10 9	10 24	20 3	19 7
22	13 59 58	1 48 16	2♈ 21 16	9♈ 17 54	27 32	28 43	9 2	14 48	13 48	28 21	10 5	10 26	20 2	19 7
23	14 3 55	2 46 46	16 12 6	23 3 25	27 28	28 36	9 19	16 1	13 28	28 36	10 1	10 28	20 0	19 6
24	14 7 51	3 45 15	29 51 28	6♉ 35 51	27 25	28 27	9 41	17 15	13 8	28 50	9 57	10 30	19 58	19 6
25	14 11 48	4 43 41	13♉ 16 15	19 52 22	27 22	28 16	10 7	18 29	12 48	29 4	9 53	10 32	19 57	19 6
26	14 15 44	5 42 6	26 24 0	2♊ 51 4	27 19	28 5	10 37	19 43	12 27	29 19	9 49	10 34	19 55	19 6
27	14 19 41	6 40 29	9♊ 13 32	15 31 28	27 16	27 54	11 11	20 57	12 6	29 33	9 45	10 35	19 54	19 6
28	14 23 38	7 38 50	21 45 4	27 54 34	27 12	27 44	11 50	22 10	11 44	29 48	9 41	10 38	19 52	19 6
29	14 27 34	8 37 9	4♋ 0 21	10♋ 2 48	27 9	27 37	12 32	23 24	11 23	0♉ 2	9 37	10 40	19 51	19 5
30	14 31 31	9♉ 35 26	16♋ 2 26	21♋ 59 47	27♒ 6	27♒ 32	13♈ 17	24♈ 38	11♏ 1	0♉ 16	9♎ 34	10♋ 42	19♎ 49	19♌ 5D

DECLINATION and LATITUDE

Day	☉ Decl	☽ Decl	☽ Lat	☽ 12 Hr. Decl	☿ Decl	☿ Lat	♀ Decl	♀ Lat	♂ Decl	♂ Lat	♃ Decl	♃ Lat	♄ Decl	♄ Lat
1	4N26	28N 2	4N38	27N48	10N21	3N15	5S40	1S24	15S38	1N41	8N 5	1S 3	2S 6	2N43
2	4 49	27 15	4 3	26 23	10 1	3 9	5 11	1 25	15 38	1 40	8 10	1 3	2 5	2 43
3	5 12	25 13	3 18	23 47	9 38	3 1	4 43	1 26	15 37	1 39	8 15	1 3	2 3	2 43
4	5 35	22 6	2 25	20 12	9 13	2 52	4 15	1 27	15 37	1 38	8 21	1 3	2 1	2 43
5	5 58	18 5	1 26	15 47	8 45	2 41	3 46	1 28	15 36	1 36	8 26	1 3	1 59	2 43
6	6 21	13 19	0 22	10 43	8 16	2 29	3 18	1 28	15 35	1 35	8 31	1 3	1 57	2 43
7	6 44	7 60	0S43	5 11	7 45	2 16	2 49	1 29	15 33	1 34	8 37	1 3	1 56	2 43
8	7 6	2 17	1 48	0S40	7 13	2 2	2 20	1 30	15 32	1 32	8 42	1 3	1 54	2 43
9	7 29	3S38	2 48	6 36	6 42	1 47	1 51	1 30	15 30	1 31	8 47	1 3	1 52	2 43
10	7 51	9 32	3 41	12 23	6 10	1 31	1 22	1 31	15 28	1 29	8 53	1 3	1 50	2 43
11	8 13	15 8	4 24	17 44	5 40	1 15	0 53	1 31	15 26	1 28	8 58	1 3	1 48	2 43
12	8 35	20 9	4 53	22 18	5 10	0 58	0 24	1 31	15 24	1 26	9 3	1 2	1 47	2 43
13	8 57	24 10	5 5	25 43	4 42	0 42	0N 5	1 32	15 22	1 25	9 8	1 2	1 45	2 43
14	9 19	26 52	5 0	27 37	4 16	0 25	0 34	1 32	15 20	1 23	9 14	1 2	1 43	2 43
15	9 40	27 55	4 38	27 47	3 52	0 9	1 3	1 32	15 17	1 21	9 19	1 2	1 42	2 43
16	10 1	27 11	3 58	26 9	3 30	0S 7	1 32	1 32	15 14	1 19	9 24	1 2	1 40	2 43
17	10 23	24 41	3 4	22 51	3 10	0 22	2 1	1 32	15 11	1 18	9 29	1 2	1 38	2 43
18	10 44	20 41	1 59	18 12	2 53	0 37	2 30	1 32	15 8	1 16	9 35	1 2	1 37	2 43
19	11 5	15 29	0 46	12 34	2 39	0 52	2 59	1 32	15 5	1 14	9 40	1 2	1 35	2 43
20	11 25	9 29	0N29	6 17	2 27	1 6	3 28	1 31	15 2	1 12	9 45	1 2	1 33	2 43
21	11 46	3 2	1 43	0N15	2 18	1 19	3 57	1 31	14 58	1 10	9 50	1 2	1 32	2 43
22	12 6	3N31	2 49	6 43	2 12	1 31	4 26	1 31	14 55	1 8	9 55	1 2	1 30	2 43
23	12 26	9 50	3 44	12 47	2 8	1 42	4 55	1 30	14 51	1 5	10 1	1 2	1 29	2 42
24	12 46	15 34	4 26	18 9	2 6	1 53	5 24	1 30	14 47	1 3	10 6	1 2	1 27	2 42
25	13 6	20 28	4 52	22 31	2 7	2 3	5 52	1 29	14 43	1 1	10 11	1 2	1 26	2 42
26	13 26	24 15	5 2	25 40	2 10	2 12	6 21	1 29	14 39	0 59	10 16	1 2	1 24	2 42
27	13 45	26 44	4 57	27 26	2 16	2 21	6 49	1 28	14 35	0 56	10 21	1 2	1 23	2 42
28	14 4	27 48	4 37	27 48	2 24	2 28	7 17	1 27	14 30	0 54	10 26	1 2	1 21	2 42
29	14 23	27 27	4 4	26 47	2 34	2 35	7 45	1 26	14 26	0 51	10 31	1 2	1 20	2 42
30	14N41	25N49	3N21	24N33	2N46	2S41	8N13	1S25	14S22	0N49	10N36	1S 2	1S19	2N42

Day	♅ Decl	♅ Lat	♆ Decl	♆ Lat	♇ Decl	♇ Lat
1	23N27	0N23	6S28	1N43	23N43	9N10
5	23 26	0 23	6 25	1 43	23 44	9 9
9	23 26	0 23	6 23	1 43	23 44	9 9
13	23 26	0 23	6 20	1 43	23 44	9 8
17	23 25	0 22	6 18	1 43	23 44	9 7
21	23 25	0 22	6 15	1 43	23 44	9 7
25	23 24	0 22	6 13	1 43	23 43	9 6
29	23N23	0N22	6S11	1N43	23N43	9N 5

☽ PHENOMENA

d	h	m	
2	8	49	☽
10	8	54	○
17	9	8	☾
24	7	28	●

d	h	° '
8	9	0
15	2	27S56
21	11	0
28	6	27N50

d	h	° '
6	8	0
13	6	5S 6
19	15	0
26	3	5N 3

VOID OF COURSE ☽

Last Aspect		☽ Ingress		
31	6pm18	1	♋	7am39
3	7am42	3	♌	8pm10
5	9pm40	6	♍	8am41
8	3pm53	8	♎	6pm56
10	6pm22	11	♏	2am14
12	12pm15	13	♐	7am 8
15	5am 6	15	♑	10am42
17	9am 8	17	♒	1pm44
19	3pm52	19	♓	4pm41
20	4pm53	21	♈	7pm57
23	10pm 9	24	♉	0am15
25	10am35	26	♊	6am41
28	4pm 0	28	♋	4pm 6

d	h	
3	18	APOGEE
18	9	PERIGEE

DAILY ASPECTARIAN

Day	Aspect	Time
1 T	♀⚻♇	6am26
	☉☍♄	10 11
	☽⚼♂	1pm57
	☽∠♇	4 12
	☿⚻♂	12 0
2 W	☽☌♅	3am40
	☽□♄	6 48
	♀⚻♆	7 15
	☉□☽	8 49
	☉#♀	10 21
	☽□☿	6pm58
	☽△♂	7 53
	☽⚺♇	10 23
3 Th	☽□♆	0am58
	☽△♀	3 4
	☽□♃	7 42
	☽∥♇	12pm28
	☽∥♅	2 35
4 F	☽⚼♀	1pm 5
	☽⚺♅	4 33
	☽✱♄	7 15
5 S	☉△☽	3am10
	☽△☿	4 12
	☽□♂	8 6
	♀⚺♃	9 8
	☉☌☿	10 33
	☽☌♇	11 9
	☽#♂	1pm 0
	☿∥♃	1 14
	☽✱♆	1 38
	☽△♃	9 40
	☽⚻♀	10 49
	☽∠♅	10 49
6 Su	☽∠♄	1am15
	☉#♆	3 39
	☽⚼☿	8 24
	☉⚼☽	11 54
	☽∠♆	7pm27
	☽∥♃	9 22
7 M	☽∥☿	1am11
	☽⚼♃	3 59
	☽✱♅	4 34
	☉∥☽	5 7
	☽⚺♄	6 43
	☽#♆	6 52
	☉⚻♂	7 41
	☽⚻☿	12pm 7
	☽✱♂	6 45
	☉⚻☽	7 51
	☽⚺♇	10 20
	☽#♀	11 45
8 T	☽⚺♆	0am38
	☽#♄	1 35
	☉∥☿	3 14
	☽⚻♃	9 35
	☽☍♀	3pm53
	☽∥♄	4 53
	☽∥♀	5 21
	☽∠♂	11 0
	♀∥♄	11 25
9 W	☉△♇	2am50
	☽∠♇	2 51
	☽∥♆	11 4
	☽#☿	11 22
	☽□♅	1pm55
	☿#♆	2 50
	☽☌♄	3 32
	☉#☽	4 36
	☽☍☿	5 53
	☽#♃	9 15
	♀ ♈	11 18
10 Th	☽⚺♂	2am30
	☽✱♇	6 38
	☉☍♆	6 52
	☽☌♆	8 44
	☉☍☽	8 54
	☽☍♃	6pm22
11 F	☽∥♂	1am21
	☽⚻♀	4 57
	♀⚼♂	8 8
	☽△♅	8pm23
	☽⚺♄	9 32
	☽⚻☿	9 35
	☿☍♄	11 3
12 S	☽☌♂	7am30
	☽⚼♀	10 14
	☽□♇	12pm15
	☽⚺♆	2 12
	☉⚻☽	6 35
	☽#♅	6 58
	☽#♇	8 59
	☽⚼♅	10 47
	☽⚼☿	10 55
	☽∠♄	11 44
13 Su	☽⚻♃	0am31
	☿□♅	2 26
	♀⚼♇	8 32
	☽△♀	2pm55
	☽∠♆	4 14
	☉∥♃	5 4
	☉⚼☽	10 35
14 M	☽△☿	0am 3
	☽⚻♅	0 48
	☽✱♄	1 34
	☽⚼♃	2 56
	☽⚺♂	10 41
	☽△♇	4pm 9
	☽✱♆	5 59
15 T	☉△☽	2am15
	☽△♃	5 6
	☽∠♂	11 54
	☽⚼♇	5pm46
	☽□♀	11 17
16 W	☽□☿	2am 8
	☽☍♅	4 12
	☽□♄	4 36
	♀#♄	6 2
	☽✱♂	12pm58
	☽⚻♇	7 17
	☽□♆	9 2
17 Th	☿☌♀	3am44
	☽#♇	6 33
	☉☌♃	7 21
	☽#♅	8 33
	☽□♃	9 2
	☉□☽	9 8
18 F	☽✱☿	4am31
	☽✱♀	7 7
	☽⚻♅	7 16
	☽△♄	7 18
	♀□♅	8 52
	♀☍♄	9 7
	♄□♅	12pm12
	☿∥♀	12 30
	☽□♂	2 55
	☽☍♇	10 12
	☽△♆	11 52
19 S	☿SD	1am33
	☽∥♂	1 42
	☽∠☿	5 56
	☽⚼♄	8 38
	☽⚼♅	8 47
	☽∠♀	11 1
	☽✱♃	12pm52
	☉✱☽	3 52
	☉#☽	4 53
	☽#♃	10 58
20 Su	☽⚼♆	1am19
	☉ ♉	3 37
	☽⚺☿	7 34
	☽⚻♄	10 3
	☽△♅	10 22
	☽∥♆	12pm 6
	☽∠♃	2 51
	☽⚺♀	3 0
	☽△♂	4 53
	☉∠☽	7 20
	☽#♀	8 50
21 M	☽⚻♇	1am16
	☽#☿	2 43
	☽⚻♆	2 52
	☽∥♄	5 30
	♀⚻♂	8 33
	☽#♄	4pm36
	☽⚺♃	4 59
	☽⚼♂	6 1
	☽∥☿	7 10
	☉⚺☽	10 59
22 T	☽⚼♇	3am 2
	☽∥♀	3 41
	☽#♆	10 10
	☽☌☿	11 47
	☽☍♄	1pm18
	☽□♅	2 0
	☽⚻♂	7 21
	☽☌♀	11 40
23 W	☽∥♃	0am44
	☽△♇	5 4
	☽☍♆	6 38
	☉∥☽	11 12
	☽#♂	8pm33
	☽☌♃	10 9
24 Th	☉☌☽	7am28
	☿☍♄	1pm18
	☽⚻♄	5 55
	☽⚺☿	6 6
	☽✱♅	7 2
	☽☍♂	11 10
25 F	☽⚺♀	10am26
	☽□♇	10 35
	♀△♇	12pm 0
	☽⚻♆	12 7
	♀#♆	5 2
	☽∥♅	5 51
	☽∥♇	8 7
	☽⚼♄	9 5
	☿□♅	9 8
	☽∠♅	10 26
	☽∠☿	10 30
26 S	♀☍♆	4am 0
	☽⚺♃	5 30
	☽⚼♆	3pm51
	☽∠♀	5 8
	☉⚺☽	6 47
27 Su	☽△♄	0am59
	☽⚺♅	2 36
	☽✱☿	3 55
	☽⚻♂	5 18
	☽∠♃	10 20
	☽✱♇	6pm52
	☽△♆	8 22
	☿⚻♂	9 55
28 M	☽✱♀	0am54
	☉∠☽	1 53
	☽⚼♂	9 26
	☽✱♃	4pm 0
	♃ ♉	8 51
29 T	☽∠♇	0am10
	☉#♂	3 32
	☉✱☽	9 58
	☽□♄	11 6
	☽☌♅	1pm16
	☽△♂	2 14
	☽□☿	6 6
	☉⚻♄	11 20
30 W	☽⚺♇	6am 8
	☽□♆	7 35
	☽∥♇	6pm55
	♂△♅	6 56
	☽□♀	7 20
	☽∥♅	9 25
	♇SD	11 23

MAY 1952

LONGITUDE

Day	Sid. Time	☉	☽	☽ 12 Hour	Mean ☊	True ☊	☿	♀	♂	♃	♄	♅	♆	♇
	h m s	° ' "	° ' "	° ' "	° '	° '	° '	° '	° '	° '	° '	° '	° '	° '
1	14 35 27	10♉ 33 41	27♋ 55 28	3♌ 50 6	27♒ 3	27♒ 29R	14♈ 6	25♈ 51	10♏ 39R	0♉ 31	9♎ 30R	10♋ 44	19♎ 48R	19♌ 5
2	14 39 24	11 31 54	9♌ 44 20	15 38 53	27 0	27 28D	14 59	27 5	10 17	0 45	9 26	10 46	19 46	19 5
3	14 43 20	12 30 4	21 34 24	27 31 35	26 57	27 28R	15 54	28 19	9 54	0 59	9 23	10 48	19 45	19 5
4	14 47 17	13 28 13	3♍ 31 6	9♍ 33 37	26 53	27 28	16 53	29 33	9 32	1 13	9 19	10 51	19 43	19 6
5	14 51 13	14 26 20	15 39 42	21 49 57	26 50	27 27	17 55	0♉ 46	9 10	1 28	9 16	10 53	19 42	19 6
6	14 55 10	15 24 25	28 4 50	4♎ 24 46	26 47	27 24	18 59	2 0	8 48	1 42	9 13	10 55	19 40	19 6
7	14 59 7	16 22 28	10♎ 50 4	17 20 57	26 44	27 18	20 6	3 14	8 26	1 56	9 9	10 58	19 39	19 6
8	15 3 3	17 20 29	23 57 31	0♏ 39 42	26 41	27 10	21 16	4 27	8 4	2 10	9 6	11 0	19 37	19 6
9	15 7 0	18 18 29	7♏ 27 21	14 20 9	26 38	26 59	22 28	5 41	7 43	2 24	9 3	11 3	19 36	19 6
10	15 10 56	19 16 27	21 17 40	28 19 22	26 34	26 47	23 43	6 55	7 21	2 39	9 0	11 5	19 35	19 7
11	15 14 53	20 14 23	5♐ 24 35	12♐ 32 39	26 31	26 36	25 1	8 8	7 0	2 53	8 57	11 8	19 33	19 7
12	15 18 49	21 12 18	19 42 49	26 54 21	26 28	26 25	26 20	9 22	6 39	3 7	8 54	11 10	19 32	19 7
13	15 22 46	22 10 12	4♑ 6 32	11♑ 18 43	26 25	26 17	27 43	10 36	6 19	3 21	8 52	11 13	19 30	19 7
14	15 26 42	23 8 4	18 30 19	25 40 51	26 22	26 11	29 7	11 49	5 59	3 35	8 49	11 16	19 29	19 8
15	15 30 39	24 5 55	2♒ 49 54	9♒ 57 11	26 18	26 8	0♉ 34	13 3	5 40	3 49	8 46	11 18	19 28	19 8
16	15 34 36	25 3 45	17 2 28	24 5 36	26 15	26 7D	2 3	14 17	5 20	4 3	8 44	11 21	19 27	19 9
17	15 38 32	26 1 34	1♓ 6 31	8♓ 5 10	26 12	26 7R	3 34	15 30	5 2	4 17	8 41	11 24	19 25	19 9
18	15 42 29	26 59 21	15 1 33	21 55 37	26 9	26 7	5 7	16 44	4 44	4 30	8 39	11 27	19 24	19 9
19	15 46 25	27 57 7	28 47 23	5♈ 36 49	26 6	26 5	6 43	17 58	4 26	4 44	8 37	11 29	19 23	19 10
20	15 50 22	28 54 53	12♈ 23 50	19 8 23	26 3	26 0	8 21	19 11	4 10	4 58	8 35	11 32	19 22	19 10
21	15 54 18	29 52 37	25 50 19	2♉ 29 31	25 59	25 53	10 1	20 25	3 53	5 12	8 33	11 35	19 21	19 11
22	15 58 15	0♊ 50 20	9♉ 5 50	15 39 5	25 56	25 42	11 43	21 39	3 38	5 26	8 31	11 38	19 19	19 12
23	16 2 11	1 48 1	22 9 8	28 35 49	25 53	25 30	13 28	22 52	3 23	5 39	8 29	11 41	19 18	19 12
24	16 6 8	2 45 42	4♊ 59 3	11♊ 18 44	25 50	25 17	15 14	24 6	3 9	5 53	8 27	11 44	19 17	19 13
25	16 10 5	3 43 22	17 34 53	23 47 30	25 47	25 5	17 3	25 20	2 55	6 6	8 25	11 47	19 16	19 13
26	16 14 1	4 41 0	29 56 44	6♋ 2 43	25 44	24 53	18 54	26 33	2 43	6 20	8 24	11 50	19 15	19 14
27	16 17 58	5 38 36	12♋ 5 42	18 6 0	25 40	24 45	20 47	27 47	2 31	6 33	8 22	11 53	19 14	19 15
28	16 21 54	6 36 12	24 4 0	0♌ 0 8	25 37	24 39	22 43	29 1	2 20	6 47	8 21	11 56	19 13	19 16
29	16 25 51	7 33 46	5♌ 54 53	11 48 48	25 34	24 35	24 40	0♊ 14	2 10	7 0	8 19	11 59	19 12	19 16
30	16 29 47	8 31 19	17 42 28	23 36 31	25 31	24 34D	26 40	1 28	2 0	7 14	8 18	12 3	19 11	19 17
31	16 33 44	9♊ 28 50	29♌ 31 37	5♍ 28 26	25♒ 28	24♒ 33R	28♉ 41	2♊ 42	1♏ 51	7♉ 27	8♎ 17	12♋ 6	19♎ 10	19♌ 18

DECLINATION and LATITUDE

Day	☉ Decl	☽ Decl	☽ Lat	☽ 12 Hr. Decl	☿ Decl	☿ Lat	♀ Decl	♀ Lat	♂ Decl	♂ Lat	♃ Decl	♃ Lat	♄ Decl	♄ Lat
1	14N60	23N 2	2N30	21N17	3N 0	2S47	8N41	1S25	14S17	0N46	10N41	1S 2	1S17	2N42
2	15 18	19 18	1 33	17 9	3 16	2 52	9 8	1 24	14 13	0 44	10 46	1 2	1 16	2 41
3	15 36	14 49	0 31	12 20	3 34	2 55	9 36	1 23	14 8	0 41	10 51	1 2	1 15	2 41
4	15 53	9 43	0S32	7 0	3 53	2 59	10 3	1 21	14 4	0 39	10 56	1 2	1 14	2 41
5	16 11	4 12	1 35	1 19	4 14	3 1	10 30	1 20	13 59	0 36	11 1	1 2	1 12	2 41
6	16 28	1S36	2 35	4S33	4 37	3 3	10 56	1 19	13 55	0 33	11 6	1 2	1 11	2 41
7	16 44	7 29	3 28	10 23	5 1	3 4	11 23	1 18	13 50	0 31	11 11	1 2	1 10	2 41
8	17 1	13 12	4 12	15 55	5 26	3 5	11 49	1 16	13 46	0 28	11 16	1 2	1 9	2 40
9	17 17	18 28	4 44	20 49	5 53	3 5	12 14	1 15	13 41	0 25	11 20	1 2	1 8	2 40
10	17 33	22 54	4 59	24 40	6 22	3 4	12 40	1 14	13 37	0 22	11 25	1 2	1 7	2 40
11	17 49	26 5	4 57	27 5	6 51	3 2	13 5	1 12	13 33	0 20	11 30	1 2	1 6	2 40
12	18 4	27 38	4 36	27 44	7 22	3 0	13 30	1 11	13 28	0 17	11 35	1 2	1 5	2 40
13	18 19	27 21	3 58	26 30	7 54	2 58	13 55	1 9	13 24	0 14	11 40	1 2	1 4	2 40
14	18 34	25 13	3 5	23 32	8 26	2 55	14 19	1 7	13 20	0 12	11 44	1 2	1 3	2 39
15	18 48	21 28	1 60	19 7	9 0	2 51	14 43	1 6	13 16	0 9	11 49	1 2	1 2	2 39
16	19 2	16 30	0 48	13 40	9 35	2 47	15 7	1 4	13 13	0 6	11 54	1 2	1 2	2 39
17	19 16	10 40	0N26	7 34	10 10	2 42	15 30	1 2	13 9	0 3	11 58	1 2	1 1	2 39
18	19 29	4 23	1 38	1 11	10 47	2 36	15 53	1 0	13 5	0 1	12 3	1 2	1 0	2 39
19	19 43	2N 1	2 43	5N10	11 24	2 30	16 15	0 58	13 2	0S 2	12 8	1 2	0 59	2 38
20	19 55	8 15	3 38	11 13	12 1	2 24	16 37	0 57	12 59	0 4	12 12	1 2	0 59	2 38
21	20 8	14 2	4 21	16 40	12 39	2 17	16 59	0 55	12 56	0 7	12 17	1 2	0 58	2 38
22	20 20	19 4	4 48	21 15	13 18	2 9	17 20	0 53	12 53	0 10	12 21	1 2	0 57	2 38
23	20 32	23 8	4 60	24 45	13 57	2 2	17 41	0 51	12 50	0 12	12 26	1 2	0 57	2 38
24	20 43	25 59	4 56	26 54	14 36	1 53	18 1	0 49	12 48	0 15	12 30	1 2	0 56	2 37
25	20 54	27 29	4 38	27 41	15 16	1 45	18 21	0 47	12 46	0 17	12 35	1 2	0 56	2 37
26	21 5	27 33	4 7	27 5	15 55	1 35	18 40	0 44	12 44	0 20	12 39	1 2	0 56	2 37
27	21 15	26 18	3 25	25 12	16 34	1 26	18 59	0 42	12 42	0 22	12 44	1 2	0 55	2 37
28	21 25	23 50	2 34	22 13	17 14	1 16	19 17	0 40	12 40	0 25	12 48	1 2	0 55	2 37
29	21 35	20 22	1 37	18 20	17 52	1 6	19 35	0 38	12 39	0 27	12 52	1 3	0 54	2 36
30	21 44	16 6	0 36	13 44	18 31	0 56	19 52	0 36	12 38	0 30	12 57	1 3	0 54	2 36
31	21N53	11N14	0S26	8N37	19N 8	0S45	20N 9	0S34	12S37	0S32	13N 1	1S 3	0S54	2N36

Day	♅ Decl	♅ Lat	♆ Decl	♆ Lat	♇ Decl	♇ Lat
1	23N23	0N22	6S 9	1N43	23N43	9N 5
5	23 22	0 22	6 7	1 43	23 42	9 4
9	23 21	0 22	6 5	1 43	23 41	9 3
13	23 20	0 22	6 3	1 42	23 40	9 3
17	23 20	0 22	6 1	1 42	23 39	9 2
21	23 19	0 22	5 60	1 42	23 37	9 1
25	23 17	0 22	5 58	1 42	23 36	9 0
29	23N16	0N22	5S57	1N42	23N34	8N60

☽ PHENOMENA			
d	h	m	
2	3	58	☽
9	20	16	○
16	14	40	☾
23	19	28	●
31	21	47	☽
d	h	°	'
5	17	0	
12	8	27S45	
18	16	0	
25	13	27N42	
3	12	0	
10	9	5S 1	
16	15	0	
23	6	5N 0	
30	14	0	

VOID OF COURSE ☽ Last Aspect	☽ Ingress
30 7pm20	1 ♌ 4am13
3 3pm 8	3 ♍ 4pm58
4 9pm24	6 ♎ 3am39
7 6pm39	8 ♏ 10am49
9 8pm16	10 ♐ 2pm51
12 12pm13	12 ♑ 5pm 9
14 8am18	14 ♒ 7pm15
16 2pm40	16 ♓ 10pm 6
18 10pm25	19 ♈ 2am 7
20 12pm23	21 ♉ 7am30
23 1am29	23 ♊ 2pm38
25 3am15	26 ♋ 0am 6
28 11am 9	28 ♌ 12pm 0
30 9pm56	31 ♍ 0am57

d	h	
1	14	APOGEE
13	16	PERIGEE
29	8	APOGEE

DAILY ASPECTARIAN

Day	Aspect	Time
1	⊙☍♂	1am32
Th	⊙✶♅	4 23
	☽□♃	5 21
	☽✶♄	11pm24
2	☽□♂	1am 4
F	☽⚺♅	2 6
	⊙□☽	3 58
	☽△☿	11 32
	☽☌♇	6pm59
	☽✶♆	8 18
	⊙∥☽	8 18
3	☽#♂	3am23
S	☽∠♄	5 38
	☽∠♅	8 34
	☽△♀	3pm 8
	☽∥♃	6 35
	☽△♃	7 19
	☽⚼☿	8 26
	☽∥♀	10 39
4	☽∠♆	2am23
Su	♀ ♉	8 55
	☽⚺♄	11 29
	☽✶♂	11 36
	☽✶♅	2pm35
	☽#♆	3 47
	♂⚺♄	4 27
	⊙△☽	9 24
	☽∥☿	11 51
5	☽⚼♀	0am14
M	☽⚼♃	1 36
	☽⚻☿	4 48
	☽⚺♇	6 42
	☽⚺♆	7 50
	☽#♄	12pm30
	☽∠♂	4 2
	♀☌♃	4 42
	☽∥♄	10 19
6	☿△♇	2am28
T	⊙⚼☽	4 48
	☽⚻♃	7 0
	☽⚻♀	8 15
	♀∥♃	10 52
	☽∠♇	11 24
	☽#☿	1pm 9
	☿☍♆	2 31
	☽∥♆	6 22
	☽⚺♂	7 39
	☽☌♄	8 54
7	☽□♅	0am14
W	⊙⚻☽	11 2
	☽✶♇	3pm12
	☽#♃	3 35
	☽☌♆	4 10
	☽#♀	5 32
	☽☍☿	6 39
8	☽∥♂	2am24
Th	☽☍♃	2pm56
	⊙#☽	6 1
	☽☍♀	8 35
9	☽☌♂	0am26
F	☽⚺♄	2 47
	☽△♅	6 18
	☿#♆	9 59
	⊙□♇	7pm53
	☽□♇	8 15
	⊙☍☽	8 16
	☽⚺♆	9 3
10	☽#♅	2am53
S	☽⚻☿	4 34
	☽∠♄	4 37
	☽#♇	5 0
	♀☍♂	6 43
	⊙⚻♆	7 19
	☽⚼♅	8 13
	☽⚻♃	7pm39
	☽∠♆	10 33
11	☽⚺♂	2am37
Su	☽⚻♀	5 2
	☽✶♄	5 57
	☽⚼☿	8 32
	☽⚻♅	9 39
	♀⚻♄	3pm19
	☽⚼♃	9 17
	♀#♂	10 32
	☽△♇	11 0
	☽✶♆	11 42
12	⊙⚻☽	2am40
M	☽∠♂	3 10
	☽⚼♀	8 30
	☽△☿	12pm13
	☽△♃	10 42
13	☽⚼♇	0am 2
T	☽✶♂	3 36
	⊙⚼☽	5 28
	☽□♄	7 53
	☽△♀	11 49
	☽☍♅	11 53
	♀✶♅	12pm35
14	☽⚻♇	1am 3
W	☽□♆	1 38
	⊙△☽	8 18
	☽#♇	11 9
	☽#♅	1pm12
	☿ ♉	2 44
	⊙⚼♄	4 14
	☽□☿	7 45
15	☽□♃	1am41
Th	☽□♂	4 39
	☽△♄	9 59
	⊙#☽	12pm53
	☽⚻♅	2 20
	☽□♀	6 52
16	☽☍♇	3am34
F	☽△♆	4 4
	☽#♀	5 35
	☽⚼♄	11 21
	☽∥♂	2pm 1
	⊙□☽	2 40
	☽⚼♅	3 54
	☽#♃	6 55
17	☽#☿	1am47
S	☽✶☿	4 45
	☽✶♃	5 32
	☽⚼♆	5 41
	☽△♂	6 36
	⊙∠♅	9 43
	☿☌♃	12pm55
	☽⚻♄	1 0
	☽△♅	5 47
	☽∥♆	5 53
	☿☍♂	6 57
18	☽✶♀	3am15
Su	☽⚻♇	7 11
	☽⚻♆	7 35
	☽∠♃	7 55
	☽⚼♂	8 0
	☽∠☿	10 1
	♂☍♃	10 14
	☽∥♄	12pm43
	☽#♄	8 9
	⊙✶☽	10 25
19	☽∠♀	8am 3
M	☽⚼♇	9 27
	☽⚻♂	9 44
	☽⚺♃	10 38
	☽#♆	3pm12
	☽⚺☿	3 51
	☽☍♄	5 15
	☽□♅	10 28
	♀□♇	11 42
20	⊙∠☽	2am54
T	☿⚻♄	3 14
	♀⚻♆	3 18
	☿∥♃	7 54
	☽△♇	12pm 4
	☽☍♆	12 23
	☽⚺♀	1 18
	☽∥♃	4 22
	☽∥☿	5 18
	☽#♂	7 16
21	⊙ ♊	3am 4
W	⊙⚺☽	7 50
	☿#♂	9 29
	☽☍♂	2pm15
	☽∥♀	2 34
	☽☌♃	5 12
	☿✶♅	10 46
	☽⚻♄	10 56
22	☽✶♅	4am39
Th	☽☌☿	5 31
	⊙∥☽	7 6
	☽□♇	6pm32
	☽⚻♆	6 44
23	☽∥♅	1am 9
F	☽☌♀	1 29
	☽⚼♄	2 27
	☽∥♇	3 21
	☽∠♅	8 28
	♀⚼♄	11 33
	⊙☌☽	7pm28
	☽⚻♂	8 36
	☽⚼♆	10 41
24	☽⚺♃	1am43
S	☽△♄	6 33
	⊙⚻♂	7 48
	☽⚺♅	12pm51
	☽⚺☿	10 49
25	☽⚼♂	0am39
Su	☽✶♇	3 10
	☽△♆	3 15
	☽∠♃	6 55
	⊙⚼♆	1pm23
	☽⚺♀	4 39
26	☿□♇	4am16
M	☿⚻♆	4 23
	☽△♂	5 21
	♀∠♅	5 43
	☽∠♇	8 26
	☽∠☿	9 12
	⊙⚺☽	10 7
	♆✶♇	12pm 0
	☽✶♃	12 48
	☽□♄	4 37
	♂#♃	5 47
	☽☌♅	11 35
27	☽∠♀	1am32
T	☽□♆	2pm15
	☽⚺♇	2 19
	⊙∠☽	6 36
	☽✶☿	8 45
28	☽∥♇	2am 2
W	☽∥♅	4 20
	⊙⚺♃	5 48
	☿⚼♄	7 43
	☽✶♀	11 9
	☽□♂	4pm29
	⊙∥☽	4 37
	♀ ♊	7 19
29	☽□♃	2am15
Th	⊙✶☽	3 39
	☽∥♀	4 25
	☽✶♄	4 53
	☽⚺♅	12pm25
	☽∥☿	12 39
	⊙△♄	6 40
30	☽✶♆	3am 0
F	☽☌♇	3 13
	☿∠♅	4 43
	♀⚻♂	9 20
	☽∠♄	11 22
	☽∥♃	3pm38
	☽#♂	5 23
	☽∠♅	7 3
	☽□☿	9 56
31	☽✶♂	4am39
S	☽□♀	7 8
	☽∠♆	9 22
	☿ ♊	3pm26
	☽△♃	4 16
	☽⚺♄	5 37
	⊙□☽	9 47
	☽#♆	11 52

JUNE 1952

LONGITUDE

Day	Sid. Time	☉	☽	☽ 12 Hour	Mean ☊	True ☊	☿	♀	♂	♃	♄	♅	♆	♇
	h m s	° ' "	° ' "	° ' "	° '	° '	° '	° '	° '	° '	° '	° '	° '	° '
1	16 37 41	10♊ 26 20	11♍ 27 39	17♍ 29 56	25♒ 24	24♒ 33R	0♊ 44	3♊ 55	1♏ 44R	7♉ 40	8♎ 16R	12♋ 9	19♎ 9R	19♌ 19
2	16 41 37	11 23 49	23 35 59	29 46 26	25 21	24 33	2 49	5 9	1 37	7 53	8 15	12 12	19 8	19 20
3	16 45 34	12 21 16	6♎ 1 53	12♎ 22 51	25 18	24 31	4 56	6 23	1 30	8 6	8 14	12 15	19 8	19 21
4	16 49 30	13 18 42	18 49 49	25 23 7	25 15	24 26	7 4	7 36	1 25	8 19	8 14	12 19	19 7	19 21
5	16 53 27	14 16 7	2♏ 3 0	8♏ 49 31	25 12	24 19	9 13	8 50	1 20	8 32	8 13	12 22	19 6	19 22
6	16 57 23	15 13 31	15 42 38	22 42 4	25 9	24 10	11 24	10 3	1 17	8 45	8 13	12 25	19 5	19 23
7	17 1 20	16 10 54	29 47 27	6♐ 58 10	25 5	24 0	13 35	11 17	1 14	8 58	8 12	12 29	19 4	19 24
8	17 5 16	17 8 16	14♐ 13 29	21 32 34	25 2	23 50	15 47	12 31	1 12	9 11	8 12	12 32	19 4	19 25
9	17 9 13	18 5 38	28 54 26	6♑ 18 5	24 59	23 41	17 59	13 44	1 10	9 24	8 12	12 35	19 3	19 26
10	17 13 10	19 2 58	13♑ 42 30	21 6 42	24 56	23 33	20 11	14 58	1 10D	9 36	8 12D	12 39	19 2	19 27
11	17 17 6	20 0 18	28 29 46	5♒ 50 54	24 53	23 29	22 22	16 12	1 10	9 49	8 12	12 42	19 2	19 28
12	17 21 3	20 57 37	13♒ 9 23	20 24 42	24 50	23 27D	24 34	17 25	1 11	10 2	8 12	12 46	19 1	19 30
13	17 24 59	21 54 56	27 36 24	4♓ 44 12	24 46	23 26	26 44	18 39	1 13	10 14	8 12	12 49	19 1	19 31
14	17 28 56	22 52 15	11♓ 47 55	18 47 29	24 43	23 27R	28 54	19 53	1 16	10 27	8 12	12 52	19 0	19 32
15	17 32 52	23 49 32	25 42 54	2♈ 34 14	24 40	23 27	1♋ 2	21 6	1 19	10 39	8 13	12 56	19 0	19 33
16	17 36 49	24 46 50	9♈ 21 35	16 5 5	24 37	23 26	3 9	22 20	1 23	10 51	8 13	12 59	18 59	19 34
17	17 40 45	25 44 7	22 44 52	29 21 5	24 34	23 24	5 14	23 34	1 28	11 3	8 14	13 3	18 59	19 35
18	17 44 42	26 41 25	5♉ 53 52	12♉ 23 19	24 30	23 18	7 17	24 47	1 34	11 15	8 14	13 6	18 58	19 37
19	17 48 39	27 38 41	18 49 33	25 12 40	24 27	23 11	9 19	26 1	1 40	11 28	8 15	13 10	18 58	19 38
20	17 52 35	28 35 58	1♊ 32 44	7♊ 49 50	24 24	23 2	11 19	27 15	1 48	11 39	8 16	13 14	18 58	19 39
21	17 56 32	29 33 14	14 4 1	20 15 23	24 21	22 52	13 16	28 29	1 55	11 51	8 17	13 17	18 57	19 40
22	18 0 28	0♋ 30 30	26 24 0	2♋ 30 0	24 18	22 43	15 12	29 42	2 4	12 3	8 18	13 21	18 57	19 42
23	18 4 25	1 27 46	8♋ 33 30	14 34 42	24 15	22 34	17 5	0♋ 56	2 13	12 15	8 19	13 24	18 57	19 43
24	18 8 21	2 25 1	20 33 46	26 30 58	24 11	22 28	18 57	2 10	2 23	12 26	8 21	13 28	18 57	19 44
25	18 12 18	3 22 15	2♌ 26 37	8♌ 21 1	24 8	22 24	20 46	3 23	2 34	12 38	8 22	13 31	18 56	19 46
26	18 16 14	4 19 30	14 14 36	20 7 45	24 5	22 22D	22 33	4 37	2 45	12 49	8 23	13 35	18 56	19 47
27	18 20 11	5 16 43	26 0 58	1♍ 54 47	24 2	22 22	24 17	5 51	2 57	13 1	8 25	13 39	18 56	19 49
28	18 24 8	6 13 57	7♍ 49 43	13 46 23	23 59	22 22	26 0	7 5	3 10	13 12	8 27	13 42	18 56	19 50
29	18 28 4	7 11 10	19 45 23	25 47 20	23 56	22 24	27 40	8 18	3 23	13 23	8 29	13 46	18 56	19 51
30	18 32 1	8♋ 8 22	1♎ 52 53	8♎ 2 39	23♒ 52	22♒ 25R	29♋ 18	9♋ 32	3♏ 37	13♉ 34	8♎ 30	13♋ 49	18♎ 56D	19♌ 53

DECLINATION and LATITUDE

Day	☉ Decl	☽ Decl	☽ Lat	☽ 12 Hr. Decl	☿ Decl	☿ Lat	♀ Decl	♀ Lat	♂ Decl	♂ Lat	♃ Decl	♃ Lat	♄ Decl	♄ Lat
1	22N 1	5N54	1S29	3N 7	19N45	0S35	20N26	0S31	12S37	0S34	13N 5	1S 3	0S54	2N36
2	22 9	0 17	2 28	2S36	20 20	0 24	20 41	0 29	12 36	0 37	13 9	1 3	0 54	2 35
3	22 17	5S29	3 22	8 21	20 55	0 13	20 56	0 27	12 36	0 39	13 13	1 3	0 54	2 35
4	22 24	11 11	4 7	13 56	21 28	0 2	21 11	0 25	12 37	0 41	13 18	1 3	0 54	2 35
5	22 31	16 34	4 41	19 3	21 59	0N 8	21 25	0 22	12 37	0 43	13 22	1 3	0 53	2 35
6	22 38	21 19	4 60	23 20	22 28	0 19	21 38	0 20	12 38	0 45	13 26	1 3	0 54	2 34
7	22 44	25 1	5 1	26 20	22 55	0 29	21 51	0 18	12 39	0 47	13 30	1 3	0 54	2 34
8	22 49	27 13	4 44	27 38	23 20	0 39	22 3	0 15	12 40	0 49	13 34	1 3	0 54	2 34
9	22 55	27 35	4 8	27 1	23 43	0 49	22 15	0 13	12 41	0 51	13 38	1 3	0 54	2 34
10	22 60	25 58	3 15	24 29	24 3	0 58	22 26	0 10	12 43	0 53	13 42	1 3	0 54	2 33
11	23 4	22 34	2 9	20 19	24 20	1 7	22 36	0 8	12 45	0 55	13 46	1 3	0 54	2 33
12	23 8	17 45	0 55	14 57	24 35	1 15	22 45	0 6	12 47	0 57	13 49	1 3	0 54	2 33
13	23 12	11 58	0N22	8 51	24 46	1 22	22 54	0 3	12 49	0 59	13 53	1 3	0 55	2 33
14	23 15	5 39	1 37	2 25	24 55	1 29	23 3	0 1	12 52	1 1	13 57	1 3	0 55	2 32
15	23 18	0N48	2 44	3N59	25 1	1 35	23 10	0N 2	12 55	1 2	14 1	1 4	0 55	2 32
16	23 21	7 5	3 40	10 4	25 5	1 40	23 17	0 4	12 58	1 4	14 5	1 4	0 56	2 32
17	23 23	12 55	4 23	15 36	25 5	1 45	23 24	0 6	13 1	1 6	14 8	1 4	0 56	2 32
18	23 24	18 4	4 52	20 19	25 3	1 49	23 29	0 9	13 5	1 8	14 12	1 4	0 57	2 32
19	23 25	22 18	5 5	24 0	24 59	1 52	23 34	0 11	13 8	1 9	14 16	1 4	0 57	2 31
20	23 26	25 24	5 2	26 29	24 52	1 55	23 38	0 13	13 12	1 11	14 19	1 4	0 58	2 31
21	23 27	27 13	4 45	27 36	24 43	1 56	23 42	0 16	13 17	1 12	14 23	1 4	0 59	2 31
22	23 27	27 39	4 15	27 21	24 31	1 57	23 45	0 18	13 21	1 14	14 26	1 4	0 59	2 31
23	23 26	26 43	3 33	25 47	24 18	1 57	23 47	0 20	13 26	1 15	14 30	1 4	0 60	2 30
24	23 25	24 33	2 43	23 4	24 2	1 57	23 48	0 23	13 30	1 17	14 33	1 4	1 1	2 30
25	23 24	21 20	1 45	19 23	23 45	1 56	23 49	0 25	13 35	1 18	14 37	1 4	1 1	2 30
26	23 22	17 16	0 44	14 58	23 26	1 54	23 49	0 27	13 41	1 20	14 40	1 4	1 2	2 30
27	23 20	12 32	0S20	9 60	23 5	1 51	23 48	0 29	13 46	1 21	14 43	1 5	1 3	2 29
28	23 18	7 21	1 23	4 38	22 44	1 48	23 47	0 32	13 52	1 22	14 47	1 5	1 4	2 29
29	23 15	1 52	2 23	0S57	22 20	1 44	23 45	0 34	13 57	1 24	14 50	1 5	1 5	2 29
30	23N12	3S46	3S18	6S36	21N56	1N40	23N42	0N36	14S 3	1S25	14N53	1S 5	1S 6	2N29

Day	♅ Decl	♅ Lat	♆ Decl	♆ Lat	♇ Decl	♇ Lat
1	23N15	0N22	5S56	1N42	23N33	8N59
5	23 14	0 22	5 55	1 42	23 31	8 59
9	23 13	0 22	5 54	1 41	23 29	8 58
13	23 12	0 22	5 53	1 41	23 27	8 57
17	23 10	0 22	5 53	1 41	23 25	8 57
21	23 9	0 22	5 52	1 41	23 23	8 56
25	23 8	0 22	5 52	1 41	23 21	8 56
29	23N 6	0N22	5S52	1N41	23N19	8N55

☽ PHENOMENA

d	h	m	
8	5	7	○
14	20	28	☾
22	8	46	●
30	13	12	☽

d	h	° '
2	1	0
8	16	27S41
14	21	0
21	19	27N40
29	8	0
6	14	5S 3
12	17	0
19	8	5N 5
26	17	0

VOID OF COURSE ☽

Last Aspect	☽ Ingress
1 1am23	2 ♎ 12pm26
4 0am58	4 ♏ 8pm20
6 6am20	7 ♐ 0am21
8 8am32	9 ♑ 1am47
10 8am38	11 ♒ 2am27
12 10pm17	13 ♓ 4am 1
14 8pm28	15 ♈ 7am29
17 5am50	17 ♉ 1pm11
19 1am31	19 ♊ 9pm 4
21 10am53	22 ♋ 7am 4
23 8pm45	24 ♌ 7pm 3
26 11am19	27 ♍ 8am 7
29 6pm 9	29 ♎ 8pm18

d	h	
10	7	PERIGEE
25	23	APOGEE

DAILY ASPECTARIAN

Day	Aspect	Time
1 Su	☽⚹♅	1am23
	♀⚼♆	4 30
	☽∠♂	10 22
	☿⚻♂	10 49
	☽⚺♆	3pm15
	☽⚺♇	3 36
	☽#♄	9 24
	☽⚼♃	10 35
2 M	☽∥♄	4am54
	☿⚼♆	2pm57
	☽⚺♂	3 24
	☽∠♇	8 46
	☉⚺♅	9 26
	☽△☿	9 28
3 T	☽△♀	0am44
	☽∥♆	1 50
	☿∥♀	2 4
	☽⚻♃	4 1
	☽☌♄	4 11
	☽□♅	11 49
	☉△☽	12pm55
	♃⚻♄	2 1
4 W	☽☌♆	0am31
	☽⚹♇	0 58
	☽∥♂	6 10
	☽⚼☿	7 7
	☽⚼♀	7 39
	☽#♃	9 16
	♀△♄	12pm 7
	☿△♄	12 55
	☿☌♀	2 0
	☿⚺♃	3 37
	♀⚺♃	5 6
	☉⚼☽	6 38
	☽☌♂	10 44
5 Th	☽⚺♄	10am55
	☽☍♃	11 41
	☽⚻♀	1pm12
	☽⚻☿	3 5
	☽△♅	6 16
	☉⚻☽	11 6
6 F	☽#♀	1am53
	☽⚺♆	5 49
	☽□♇	6 20
	☽#☿	7 31
	☉#☽	7 49
	☉∥☿	10 42
	☽#♅	11 23
	☿⚺♅	11 36
	☽∠♄	12pm51
	☽#♇	1 11
	☽⚼♅	8 5
7 S	☉⚼♂	1am10
	☽⚺♂	2 25
	☽∠♆	7 10
	☽⚹♄	2pm 2
	☽⚻♃	3 33
	☿∥♅	5 20
	☽☍♀	8 55
	☽⚻♅	9 12
8 Su	♀⚺♅	0am25
	☽☍☿	3 0
	☽∠♂	3 14
	☿⚼♂	4 31
	☉☍☽	5 7
	☽⚹♆	7 56
	☽△♇	8 32
	☿∥♇	9 43
	☽⚼♃	4pm33
9 M	☉☌☿	2am15
	☽⚹♂	3 41
	☽⚼♇	8 59
	☿△♆	11 39
	☽□♄	3pm 4
	☿⚹♇	4 4
	☽△♃	5 16
	☽☍♅	10 16
	☉△♆	11 46
10 T	☽⚻♀	2am14
	♂SD	2 47
	☽□♆	8 38
	☉⚻☽	9 15
	☽⚻♇	9 20
	☉⚹♇	10 25
	☽⚻☿	12pm19
	♄SD	1 23
	☽#☿	1 47
	☽#♇	6 37
	☽#♅	8 15
	☉#☽	9 8
	♀⚼♂	11 30
	☽#♀	11 52
11 W	☽□♂	4am22
	☽⚼♀	4 48
	☉⚼☽	11 22
	☽△♄	3pm51
	☽⚼☿	5 3
	☽□♃	6 47
	☽⚻♅	11 21
12 Th	☿∠♃	5am40
	☽△♀	7 42
	☽△♆	9 41
	☽☍♇	10 29
	☉△☽	1pm50
	☽#♃	4 24
	☽⚼♄	4 38
	☽∥♂	8 37
	☽△☿	10 17
	☉∥♅	10 43
13 F	☽⚼♅	0am21
	☽△♂	6 5
	♀△♆	7 0
	☽⚼♆	10 46
	♀⚹♇	5pm 5
	☽⚻♄	5 52
	☽⚹♃	9 39
	☽∥♆	11 8
14 S	☽△♅	1am51
	☽⚼♂	7 41
	☽⚻♆	12pm21
	☿ ♋	12 22
	☽⚻♇	1 18
	☽□♀	3 13
	☽∥♄	5 35
	☉□☽	8 28
	☽∠♃	11 53
15 Su	☽#♄	0am28
	♀∥♅	2 17
	☿△♂	3 21
	☽⚻♂	9 51
	☽□☿	11 0
	☽⚼♇	3pm31
	☽#♆	7 18
	☽☍♄	9 58
16 M	☽⚺♃	2am42
	☽□♅	6 30
	☿∠♇	4pm30
	☽☍♆	5 12
	☉∥♀	6 13
	☽△♇	6 17
17 T	☽#♂	0am26
	☽⚹♀	1 37
	☽∥♃	5 26
	☉⚹☽	5 50
	♀∥♇	6 8
	☉∠♃	10 13
	☽☍♂	3pm59
18 W	☽⚹☿	3am 3
	☽⚻♄	4 19
	☉∥♇	5 53
	☽∠♀	7 56
	☽☌♃	10 3
	☿□♄	11 15
	☉∠☽	11 33
	☽⚹♅	1pm24
19 Th	☽⚻♆	0am16
	☽□♇	1 31
	☽∥♅	5 48
	☽∥♇	7 30
	☉∥☽	7 43
	☽⚼♄	8 19
	☽∥♀	8 56
	♀∠♃	10 15
	☽∠☿	12pm15
	☽⚺♀	2 58
	☽∠♅	5 40
	☉⚺☽	5 57
	☽∥☿	7 17
20 F	☽⚻♂	0am29
	☽⚼♆	4 36
	☿⚹♃	4 40
	☽△♄	12pm51
	☽⚺♃	7 40
	☽⚺☿	10 11
	☽⚺♅	10 29
21 S	☿☌♅	0am 9
	☽⚼♂	5 35
	☽△♆	9 28
	☽⚹♇	10 53
	☉ ♋	11 13
22 Su	☽∠♃	1am18
	♀ ♋	5 47
	☽☌♀	7 13
	☉☌☽	8 46
	☽△♂	11 17
	☽∠♇	4pm22
	☽□♄	11 32
23 M	☽⚹♃	7am28
	☽☌♅	9 42
	☽☌☿	8pm 9
	☽□♆	8 45
	☽⚺♇	10 21
	☉△♂	11 8
	☿□♆	11 58
24 T	☽∥☿	4am52
	♀△♂	5 10
	☽∥♀	6 14
	☉∥☽	9 19
	☽∥♇	9 48
	☿⚺♇	10 35
	☽∥♅	11 30
	☿∥♀	6pm33
	☉☌♀	10 18
25 W	☽□♂	0am15
	☉⚺☽	2 3
	☽⚺♀	2 9
	☽⚹♄	12pm 4
	☽□♃	9 4
	☽⚺♅	10 39
26 Th	♀∠♇	3am20
	☉∥☿	4 35
	☿∥♇	6 53
	☽⚹♆	9 34
	☉∠☽	11 16
	☽☌♇	11 19
	☉∠♇	11 55
	☽∠♀	12pm14
	☽∥♃	1 22
	☽#♂	6 7
	☽∠♄	6 42
	☽⚺☿	7 52
	☿∥♅	10 21
27 F	☽∠♅	5am23
	☉∥♇	8 15
	☽⚹♂	2pm22
	☽∠♆	4 6
	☉⚹☽	8 29
	☽⚹♀	10 18
28 S	☽⚺♄	1am15
	☽#♆	6 36
	☽∠☿	7 28
	☽△♃	11 1
	☽⚹♅	11 55
	☽∠♂	9pm13
	☽⚺♆	10 21
29 Su	☽⚺♇	0am12
	☽#♄	3 21
	♀□♄	3 24
	☽∥♄	12pm37
	☽⚼♃	5 24
	☽⚹☿	6 9
30 M	☽⚺♂	3am28
	☽∠♇	5 52
	☽∥♆	8 54
	♆SD	9 16
	☉□♄	9 36
	☿ ♌	10 27
	☽☌♄	12pm56
	☉□☽	1 12
	☽□♀	4 31
	☽⚻♃	10 58
	☽□♅	11 13

JULY 1952

LONGITUDE

Day	Sid. Time	☉	☽	☽ 12 Hour	Mean ☊	True ☊	☿	♀	♂	♃	♄	♅	♆	♇
	h m s	° ' "	° ' "	° ' "	° '	° '	° '	° '	° '	° '	° '	° '	° '	° '
1	18 35 57	9♋ 5 34	14♎ 17 17	20♎ 37 19	23♒ 49	22♒ 25R	0♌ 54	10♋ 46	3♏ 52	13♉ 45	8♎ 32	13♋ 53	18♎ 56	19♌ 54
2	18 39 54	10 2 45	27 3 19	3♏ 35 43	23 46	22 23	2 27	12 0	4 7	13 56	8 35	13 57	18 56	19 56
3	18 43 50	10 59 57	10♏ 14 52	17 1 2	23 43	22 20	3 58	13 13	4 22	14 7	8 37	14 0	18 56	19 57
4	18 47 47	11 57 8	23 54 17	0♐ 54 34	23 40	22 16	5 27	14 27	4 39	14 18	8 39	14 4	18 56	19 59
5	18 51 43	12 54 19	8♐ 1 38	15 15 3	23 36	22 10	6 54	15 41	4 55	14 28	8 41	14 8	18 56	20 1
6	18 55 40	13 51 30	22 34 11	29 58 16	23 33	22 5	8 18	16 55	5 13	14 39	8 44	14 11	18 56	20 2
7	18 59 37	14 48 41	7♑ 26 20	14♑ 57 18	23 30	21 59	9 40	18 8	5 31	14 49	8 46	14 15	18 57	20 4
8	19 3 33	15 45 51	22 30 2	0♒ 3 21	23 27	21 56	11 0	19 22	5 49	15 0	8 49	14 18	18 57	20 5
9	19 7 30	16 43 2	7♒ 36 6	15 7 9	23 24	21 53D	12 17	20 36	6 8	15 10	8 52	14 22	18 57	20 7
10	19 11 26	17 40 13	22 35 30	0♓ 0 18	23 21	21 53	13 32	21 50	6 28	15 20	8 55	14 26	18 57	20 8
11	19 15 23	18 37 25	7♓ 20 50	14 36 30	23 17	21 53	14 44	23 4	6 48	15 30	8 57	14 29	18 58	20 10
12	19 19 19	19 34 37	21 46 55	28 51 50	23 14	21 55	15 53	24 17	7 8	15 40	9 0	14 33	18 58	20 12
13	19 23 16	20 31 49	5♈ 51 6	12♈ 44 43	23 11	21 56	17 0	25 31	7 29	15 49	9 3	14 37	18 58	20 13
14	19 27 12	21 29 2	19 32 48	26 15 29	23 8	21 56R	18 4	26 45	7 50	15 59	9 7	14 40	18 59	20 15
15	19 31 9	22 26 15	2♉ 53 0	9♉ 25 38	23 5	21 56	19 5	27 59	8 12	16 8	9 10	14 44	18 59	20 17
16	19 35 6	23 23 30	15 53 40	22 17 25	23 1	21 54	20 3	29 13	8 35	16 18	9 13	14 47	19 0	20 19
17	19 39 2	24 20 45	28 37 12	4♊ 53 19	22 58	21 51	20 58	0♌ 26	8 57	16 27	9 17	14 51	19 0	20 20
18	19 42 59	25 18 0	11♊ 6 5	17 15 48	22 55	21 47	21 50	1 40	9 21	16 36	9 20	14 55	19 1	20 22
19	19 46 55	26 15 16	23 22 43	29 27 8	22 52	21 43	22 39	2 54	9 44	16 45	9 24	14 58	19 1	20 24
20	19 50 52	27 12 33	5♋ 29 17	11♋ 29 26	22 49	21 39	23 24	4 8	10 8	16 54	9 28	15 2	19 2	20 25
21	19 54 48	28 9 51	17 27 49	23 24 41	22 46	21 35	24 5	5 22	10 33	17 3	9 31	15 5	19 3	20 27
22	19 58 45	29 7 9	29 20 17	5♌ 14 52	22 42	21 33	24 43	6 36	10 58	17 11	9 35	15 9	19 3	20 29
23	20 2 42	0♌ 4 27	11♌ 8 43	17 2 6	22 39	21 32D	25 17	7 50	11 23	17 20	9 39	15 13	19 4	20 31
24	20 6 38	1 1 47	22 55 21	28 48 47	22 36	21 31	25 47	9 4	11 49	17 28	9 43	15 16	19 5	20 33
25	20 10 35	1 59 6	4♍ 42 46	10♍ 37 41	22 33	21 32	26 12	10 18	12 15	17 36	9 47	15 20	19 6	20 34
26	20 14 31	2 56 26	16 33 57	22 32 1	22 30	21 33	26 33	11 31	12 41	17 45	9 51	15 23	19 6	20 36
27	20 18 28	3 53 47	28 32 21	4♎ 35 26	22 27	21 35	26 50	12 45	13 8	17 52	9 56	15 27	19 7	20 38
28	20 22 24	4 51 8	10♎ 41 48	16 51 57	22 23	21 36	27 1	13 59	13 35	18 0	10 0	15 30	19 8	20 40
29	20 26 21	5 48 29	23 6 25	29 25 42	22 20	21 37R	27 8R	15 13	14 3	18 8	10 4	15 34	19 9	20 42
30	20 30 17	6 45 51	5♏ 50 19	12♏ 20 42	22 17	21 37	27 10	16 27	14 31	18 15	10 9	15 37	19 10	20 43
31	20 34 14	7♌ 43 14	18♏ 57 16	25♏ 40 19	22♒ 14	21♒ 37	27♌ 7	17♌ 41	14♏ 59	18♉ 23	10♎ 13	15♋ 40	19♎ 11	20♌ 45

DECLINATION and LATITUDE

Day	☉ Decl	☽ Decl	☽ Lat	☽ 12 Hr. Decl	☿ Decl	☿ Lat	♀ Decl	♀ Lat	♂ Decl	♂ Lat	♃ Decl	♃ Lat	♄ Decl	♄ Lat
1	23N 8	9S23	4S 5	12S 8	21N30	1N35	23N39	0N38	14S 9	1S26	14N56	1S 5	1S 7	2N28
2	23 4	14 47	4 41	17 19	21 4	1 29	23 34	0 40	14 16	1 27	14 59	1 5	1 8	2 28
3	22 59	19 42	5 4	21 51	20 37	1 23	23 29	0 42	14 22	1 28	15 3	1 5	1 9	2 28
4	22 54	23 46	5 10	25 21	20 9	1 17	23 24	0 44	14 29	1 30	15 6	1 5	1 10	2 28
5	22 49	26 34	4 59	27 22	19 40	1 9	23 18	0 46	14 35	1 31	15 9	1 5	1 11	2 27
6	22 43	27 42	4 28	27 32	19 11	1 2	23 11	0 48	14 42	1 32	15 12	1 5	1 12	2 27
7	22 37	26 52	3 39	25 43	18 41	0 53	23 3	0 50	14 49	1 33	15 15	1 6	1 14	2 27
8	22 31	24 5	2 33	22 2	18 12	0 45	22 55	0 52	14 56	1 34	15 17	1 6	1 15	2 27
9	22 24	19 37	1 17	16 54	17 41	0 36	22 46	0 54	15 4	1 35	15 20	1 6	1 16	2 26
10	22 17	13 56	0N 4	10 47	17 11	0 26	22 36	0 56	15 11	1 36	15 23	1 6	1 18	2 26
11	22 9	7 31	1 24	4 12	16 41	0 16	22 26	0 58	15 19	1 37	15 26	1 6	1 19	2 26
12	22 1	0 52	2 36	2N26	16 10	0 6	22 15	0 60	15 26	1 38	15 29	1 6	1 20	2 26
13	21 53	5N39	3 38	8 46	15 40	0S 5	22 3	1 1	15 34	1 39	15 31	1 6	1 22	2 26
14	21 44	11 44	4 25	14 31	15 10	0 16	21 51	1 3	15 42	1 40	15 34	1 6	1 23	2 25
15	21 35	17 7	4 56	19 28	14 40	0 28	21 38	1 5	15 50	1 40	15 37	1 7	1 25	2 25
16	21 25	21 34	5 12	23 23	14 11	0 40	21 24	1 6	15 58	1 41	15 39	1 7	1 26	2 25
17	21 15	24 55	5 11	26 7	13 42	0 52	21 10	1 8	16 6	1 42	15 42	1 7	1 28	2 25
18	21 5	26 60	4 56	27 32	13 13	1 4	20 55	1 9	16 14	1 43	15 44	1 7	1 29	2 24
19	20 54	27 44	4 27	27 35	12 46	1 17	20 40	1 11	16 22	1 44	15 46	1 7	1 31	2 24
20	20 43	27 7	3 47	26 19	12 19	1 29	20 24	1 12	16 31	1 44	15 49	1 7	1 33	2 24
21	20 32	25 14	2 57	23 52	11 53	1 42	20 7	1 13	16 39	1 45	15 51	1 7	1 34	2 24
22	20 20	22 14	1 59	20 24	11 28	1 56	19 50	1 15	16 48	1 46	15 53	1 7	1 36	2 24
23	20 8	18 21	0 57	16 8	11 4	2 9	19 32	1 16	16 56	1 47	15 56	1 8	1 38	2 23
24	19 56	13 45	0S 8	11 16	10 42	2 22	19 14	1 17	17 5	1 47	15 58	1 8	1 39	2 23
25	19 43	8 40	1 12	5 59	10 21	2 35	18 55	1 18	17 14	1 48	16 0	1 8	1 41	2 23
26	19 30	3 15	2 14	0 28	10 1	2 49	18 36	1 19	17 22	1 49	16 2	1 8	1 43	2 23
27	19 17	2S20	3 11	5S 8	9 44	3 2	18 16	1 20	17 31	1 49	16 4	1 8	1 45	2 23
28	19 3	7 55	3 60	10 38	9 27	3 15	17 56	1 21	17 40	1 50	16 6	1 8	1 47	2 22
29	18 49	13 18	4 39	15 51	9 13	3 27	17 35	1 22	17 49	1 50	16 8	1 8	1 49	2 22
30	18 35	18 16	5 5	20 30	9 1	3 39	17 14	1 23	17 58	1 51	16 10	1 9	1 51	2 22
31	18N21	22S32	5S17	24S18	8N51	3S51	16N52	1N24	18S 7	1S51	16N12	1S 9	1S53	2N22

Day	♅ Decl	♅ Lat	♆ Decl	♆ Lat	♇ Decl	♇ Lat
1	23N 5	0N22	5S52	1N40	23N18	8N55
5	23 4	0 22	5 52	1 40	23 15	8 55
9	23 2	0 22	5 53	1 40	23 13	8 55
13	23 1	0 22	5 54	1 40	23 10	8 54
17	22 59	0 22	5 55	1 40	23 8	8 54
21	22 58	0 22	5 56	1 39	23 6	8 54
25	22 56	0 22	5 57	1 39	23 3	8 54
29	22N55	0N23	5S58	1N39	23N 1	8N54

☽ PHENOMENA				VOID OF COURSE ☽ Last Aspect		☽ Ingress		
d	h	m		1	10am40	2	♏	5am26
7	12	34	○	3	5pm11	4	♐	10am27
14	3	43	☾	5	7pm51	6	♑	12pm 3
21	23	31	●	7	6pm35	8	♒	11am55
30	1	51	☽	9	8pm 3	10	♓	12pm 0
				12	4am38	12	♈	1pm56
				14	2pm12	14	♉	6pm46
d	h	° '		16	3pm13	17	♊	2am38
6	2	27S42		18	10pm27	19	♋	1pm 5
12	3	0		21	11pm31	22	♌	1am21
19	1	27N44		24	6am 3	24	♍	2pm25
26	14	0		26	2am24	27	♎	2am54
				29	7am42	29	♏	1pm 5
				31	2pm25	31	♐	7pm38
3	21	5S10			d	h		
9	23	0			8	11	PERIGEE	
16	11	5N13			23	8	APOGEE	
23	21	0						
31	5	5S17						

DAILY ASPECTARIAN

1 T	☽☌♆	8am49
	☽✱♇	10 40
	☉∥♅	5pm 3
	☽∥♂	9 32
2 W	☽#♃	0am57
	♃✱♅	1 18
	☽□☿	11 13
	☽☌♂	1pm12
	☽⊻♄	9 4
3 Th	☉△☽	1am27
	☽#☿	4 28
	☽△♀	5 50
	☽△♅	6 43
	☽☍♃	6 59
	☿□♂	7 48
	☽⊻♆	3pm22
	♀☌♅	4 4
	☽□♇	5 11
	☉#☽	6 31
	☽#♅	7 27
	♀✱♃	8 27
	☽#♇	8 41
	☽#♀	9 38
	☽∠♄	11 33
4 F	☉⚼☽	5am38
	☽⚼♅	8 54
	☽⚼♀	10 26
	☽∠♆	5pm 8
	☽⊻♂	6 41
	☽△☿	9 54
5 S	☽✱♄	1am 6
	☉⊼☽	8 41
	♀∥♇	9 20
	☽⊼♅	10 11
	☽⊼♃	10 51
	☽⊼♀	1pm53
	☽✱♆	6 4
	☽△♇	7 51
	☽∠♂	8 5
6 Su	☽⚼☿	1am19
	☿✱♄	7 36
	☉☌♅	8 50
	☽⚼♃	11 37
	☽⚼♇	8pm11
	☽✱♂	8 51
	♀∥♅	11 23
7 M	☉✱♃	0am18
	☽□♄	2 8
	☽⊼☿	3 55
	☽☍♅	10 55
	☽△♃	11 55
	☉☍☽	12pm34
	♀□♆	3 44
	☽□♆	6 21
	☽☍♀	6 35
	☽⊼♇	8 10
8 T	☽#♇	5am21
	☽#♅	6 23
	☽#♀	7 25
	☉#☽	9 38
	♀⊻♇	2pm20
	☽□♂	9 37
9 W	☽△♄	2am 1
	☽☍☿	8 9
	☽#☿	9 28
	☽⊼♅	10 51
	☽□♃	12pm12
	☉⊼☽	3 33
	☽△♆	6 9
	☽#♃	6 15
	☽∥♂	7 7
	☽☍♇	8 3
	☽⊼♀	10 40
10 Th	☽⚼♄	2am 8
	☽⚼♅	11 7
	☉⚼☽	5pm29
	☽⚼♆	6 27
	☿⊻♅	6 55
	☽△♂	11 4
11 F	☽⚼♀	1am17
	☽⊼♄	2 39
	☽∥♆	5 55
	☉□♆	8 34
	☽△♅	11 51
	☽⊼☿	1pm16
	☽✱♃	1 38
	☿□♃	6 27
	☽⊼♆	7 16
	☉△☽	8 2
	☽⊼♇	9 20
	☽∥♄	10 18
12 S	☽⚼♂	0am36
	☽△♀	4 38
	☽#♄	8 1
	♂#♃	11 16
	☽∠♃	3pm15
	☉⊻♇	4 4
	☽⚼☿	4 48
	☽⚼♇	10 55
13 Su	☽#♆	0am54
	☽⊼♂	2 54
	☿#♂	3 44
	☽☍♄	5 35
	☿∥♃	6 17
	☽□♅	3pm21
	☽⊻♃	5 37
	☽△☿	9 9
	☽☍♆	11 0
14 M	☽△♇	1am15
	☉□☽	3 43
	☽∥☿	1pm36
	☽□♀	2 12
	☽∥♃	4 51
	☽#♂	5 46
	☿✱♆	9 44
15 T	☽☍♂	10am 2
	☽⊼♄	11 34
	☉∥♀	5pm59
	☽✱♅	9 56
	☽∥♀	11 2
	☉∥☽	11 7
16 W	☽☌♃	0am45
	☽⊼♆	5 49
	☿☌♇	6 48
	☽□♇	8 17
	☽□☿	8 24
	☽∥♅	9 13
	☽∥♇	10 14
	☉✱☽	3pm13
	♀ ♌	3 23
	☽⚼♄	3 43
17 Th	☽∠♅	2am22
	☽✱♀	3 51
	☽⚼♆	10 19
	☽⊼♂	8pm29
	☽△♄	8 34
	☉∠☽	10 19
	♂⊻♄	11 36
18 F	☽⊻♅	7am27
	☽⊻♃	10 50
	☽∠♀	12pm 3
	☽△♆	3 26
	☽✱♇	6 7
	☽✱☿	10 27
19 S	☽⚼♂	2am46
	☉⊻☽	6 9
	☽∠♃	4pm46
	☽⊻♀	9 0
	☽∠♇	11 52
20 Su	☽∠☿	6am10
	☽□♄	7 58
	☽△♂	9 37
	☽☌♅	7pm12
	☽✱♃	11 9
21 M	☽□♆	3am11
	☽⊻♇	6 2
	☽⊻☿	2pm 8
	☽∥♇	5 56
	☿∠♄	6 14
	☽∥♅	6 53
	☉☌☽	11 31
22 T	☉∥☽	12pm59
	☽☌♀	4 28
	☽∥♀	4 37
	☽✱♄	8 57
	☉ ♌	10 8
23 W	☽□♂	0am30
	☽#♂	7 29
	☽⊻♅	8 19
	☽□♃	12pm45
	☽∥♃	12 56
	☽✱♆	4 10
	☽☌♇	7 8
24 Th	☽∠♄	3am41
	☽☌☿	6 3
	♀✱♄	1pm35
	☽∠♅	3 2
	☽∥☿	3 43
	☉⊻☽	5 58
	☽∠♆	10 44
25 F	☽⊻♄	10am21
	☽#♆	12pm 9
	☽⊻♀	12 38
	☽✱♂	3 52
	☽✱♅	9 36
26 S	☽△♃	2am24
	☉∠☽	3 1
	☽⊻♆	5 7
	☽#♄	6 34
	☽⊻♇	8 9
	☽⊻☿	8pm31
	☽∥♄	9 26
	☽∠♀	10 16
	☽∠♂	11 10
27 Su	☽⚼♃	8am42
	☉✱☽	11 32
	♀□♂	11 43
	☽∠♇	2pm 5
	☽∥♆	3 34
	☽☌♄	10 38
28 M	☽∠☿	2am37
	☽⊻♂	5 52
	☽#☿	6 29
	☽✱♀	7 8
	☽□♅	9 24
	♀#♂	12pm45
	☽⊼♃	2 21
	☽☌♆	4 24
	☽✱♇	7 22
29 T	♀⊻♅	6am58
	☽✱☿	7 42
	☽#♃	1pm30
	☽#♀	7 8
	☿SR	8 31
	☽∥♂	10 26
30 W	☉#☽	1am36
	☉□☽	1 51
	☽⊻♄	8 1
	☽☌♂	4pm33
	☽△♅	6 3
	☽□♀	9 28
	☽☍♃	10 57
31 Th	☽⊻♆	0am25
	☽#♅	2 21
	☽#♇	2 58
	☽□♇	3 14
	☽∠♄	11 16
	☉#♂	2pm 5
	☽□☿	2 25
	♀□♃	3 4
	☽⚼♅	8 54

AUGUST 1952

LONGITUDE

Day	Sid. Time h m s	☉ ° ′ ″	☽ ° ′ ″	☽ 12 Hour ° ′ ″	Mean ☊ ° ′	True ☊ ° ′	☿ ° ′	♀ ° ′	♂ ° ′	♃ ° ′	♄ ° ′	♅ ° ′	♆ ° ′	♇ ° ′
1	20 38 11	8♌ 40 37	2♐ 30 6	9♐ 26 41	22♒ 11	21♒ 36R	26♌ 58R	18♌ 55	15♏ 28	18♉ 30	10♎ 18	15♋ 44	19♎ 12	20♌ 47
2	20 42 7	9 38 1	16 30 4	23 40 1	22 7	21 35	26 44	20 9	15 57	18 37	10 23	15 47	19 13	20 49
3	20 46 4	10 35 26	0♑ 56 12	8♑ 18 3	22 4	21 33	26 26	21 23	16 26	18 44	10 28	15 51	19 14	20 51
4	20 50 0	11 32 51	15 44 50	23 15 42	22 1	21 32	26 2	22 37	16 56	18 51	10 32	15 54	19 15	20 53
5	20 53 57	12 30 18	0♒ 49 36	8♒ 25 25	21 58	21 31	25 33	23 50	17 25	18 57	10 37	15 57	19 16	20 55
6	20 57 53	13 27 45	16 1 57	23 37 59	21 55	21 31D	25 0	25 4	17 56	19 4	10 42	16 1	19 17	20 56
7	21 1 50	14 25 12	1♓ 12 20	8♓ 43 51	21 52	21 31	24 22	26 18	18 26	19 10	10 47	16 4	19 18	20 58
8	21 5 46	15 22 42	16 11 33	23 34 33	21 48	21 32	23 41	27 32	18 57	19 16	10 52	16 7	19 20	21 0
9	21 9 43	16 20 12	0♈ 52 8	8♈ 3 45	21 45	21 32	22 57	28 46	19 28	19 22	10 58	16 11	19 21	21 2
10	21 13 40	17 17 44	15 9 2	22 7 45	21 42	21 32	22 10	0♍ 0	19 59	19 28	11 3	16 14	19 22	21 4
11	21 17 36	18 15 16	28 59 52	5♉ 45 27	21 39	21 33R	21 22	1 14	20 31	19 34	11 8	16 17	19 23	21 6
12	21 21 33	19 12 51	12♉ 24 40	18 57 49	21 36	21 33	20 32	2 28	21 3	19 39	11 14	16 20	19 25	21 8
13	21 25 29	20 10 27	25 25 15	1♊ 47 22	21 33	21 32	19 43	3 42	21 35	19 45	11 19	16 23	19 26	21 10
14	21 29 26	21 8 5	8♊ 4 37	14 17 29	21 29	21 32D	18 55	4 56	22 7	19 50	11 25	16 27	19 27	21 11
15	21 33 22	22 5 44	20 26 26	26 31 56	21 26	21 32	18 9	6 10	22 40	19 55	11 30	16 30	19 29	21 13
16	21 37 19	23 3 24	2♋ 34 29	8♋ 34 31	21 23	21 32	17 26	7 24	23 13	20 0	11 36	16 33	19 30	21 15
17	21 41 15	24 1 6	14 32 29	20 28 48	21 20	21 33	16 47	8 38	23 46	20 4	11 41	16 36	19 31	21 17
18	21 45 12	24 58 50	26 23 52	2♌ 18 2	21 17	21 33	16 12	9 52	24 20	20 9	11 47	16 39	19 33	21 19
19	21 49 9	25 56 35	8♌ 11 40	14 5 5	21 13	21 33	15 43	11 6	24 54	20 13	11 53	16 42	19 34	21 21
20	21 53 5	26 54 21	19 58 36	25 52 30	21 10	21 34R	15 20	12 20	25 28	20 17	11 59	16 45	19 36	21 23
21	21 57 2	27 52 9	1♍ 47 5	7♍ 42 37	21 7	21 34	15 4	13 33	26 2	20 21	12 5	16 48	19 37	21 25
22	22 0 58	28 49 58	13 39 23	19 37 39	21 4	21 33	14 55D	14 47	26 36	20 25	12 11	16 51	19 39	21 26
23	22 4 55	29 47 48	25 37 41	1♎ 39 48	21 1	21 33	14 54	16 1	27 11	20 28	12 17	16 54	19 40	21 28
24	22 8 51	0♍ 45 40	7♎ 44 16	13 51 24	20 58	21 31	15 0	17 15	27 46	20 32	12 23	16 57	19 42	21 30
25	22 12 48	1 43 34	20 1 31	26 14 58	20 54	21 30	15 14	18 29	28 21	20 35	12 29	16 59	19 44	21 32
26	22 16 44	2 41 28	2♏ 32 4	8♏ 53 11	20 51	21 29	15 36	19 43	28 56	20 38	12 35	17 2	19 45	21 34
27	22 20 41	3 39 24	15 18 39	21 48 48	20 48	21 27	16 6	20 57	29 32	20 41	12 41	17 5	19 47	21 36
28	22 24 38	4 37 21	28 23 58	5♐ 4 25	20 45	21 27D	16 44	22 11	0♐ 8	20 43	12 48	17 8	19 49	21 38
29	22 28 34	5 35 20	11♐ 50 24	18 42 6	20 42	21 27	17 29	23 25	0 44	20 46	12 54	17 10	19 50	21 39
30	22 32 31	6 33 19	25 39 35	2♑ 42 52	20 39	21 27	18 22	24 39	1 20	20 48	13 0	17 13	19 52	21 41
31	22 36 27	7♍ 31 20	9♑ 51 49	17♑ 6 11	20♒ 35	21♒ 28	19♌ 23	25♍ 53	1♐ 56	20♉ 50	13♎ 7	17♋ 16	19♎ 54	21♌ 43

DECLINATION and LATITUDE

Day	☉ Decl	☽ Decl	☽ Lat	☽ 12 Hr. Decl	☿ Decl	☿ Lat	♀ Decl	♀ Lat	♂ Decl	♂ Lat	♃ Decl	♃ Lat	♄ Decl	♄ Lat
1	18N 6	25S45	5S11	26S51	8N44	4S 2	16N30	1N24	18S16	1S52	16N14	1S 9	1S55	2N22
2	17 51	27 32	4 48	27 46	8 39	4 12	16 7	1 25	18 25	1 53	16 16	1 9	1 57	2 21
3	17 35	27 32	4 5	26 48	8 36	4 22	15 44	1 25	18 34	1 53	16 17	1 9	1 59	2 21
4	17 19	25 35	3 6	23 55	8 36	4 30	15 20	1 26	18 43	1 54	16 19	1 9	2 1	2 21
5	17 3	21 48	1 52	19 19	8 39	4 38	14 56	1 26	18 52	1 54	16 21	1 10	2 3	2 21
6	16 47	16 31	0 30	13 28	8 44	4 44	14 32	1 27	19 0	1 54	16 22	1 10	2 5	2 21
7	16 31	10 13	0N54	6 51	8 52	4 48	14 7	1 27	19 9	1 55	16 24	1 10	2 7	2 20
8	16 14	3 24	2 13	0N 2	9 3	4 51	13 42	1 27	19 18	1 55	16 26	1 10	2 9	2 20
9	15 57	3N26	3 22	6 44	9 16	4 52	13 16	1 27	19 27	1 56	16 27	1 10	2 11	2 20
10	15 39	9 54	4 16	12 54	9 31	4 52	12 50	1 28	19 36	1 56	16 28	1 10	2 14	2 20
11	15 22	15 41	4 54	18 15	9 49	4 50	12 24	1 28	19 45	1 56	16 30	1 11	2 16	2 20
12	15 4	20 32	5 14	22 33	10 8	4 45	11 58	1 28	19 54	1 57	16 31	1 11	2 18	2 20
13	14 46	24 15	5 17	25 38	10 29	4 39	11 31	1 27	20 3	1 57	16 32	1 11	2 20	2 19
14	14 27	26 40	5 5	27 22	10 51	4 31	11 4	1 27	20 12	1 57	16 34	1 11	2 23	2 19
15	14 9	27 44	4 38	27 45	11 14	4 22	10 36	1 27	20 20	1 58	16 35	1 11	2 25	2 19
16	13 50	27 25	4 0	26 47	11 38	4 11	10 8	1 27	20 29	1 58	16 36	1 11	2 27	2 19
17	13 31	25 50	3 12	24 35	12 2	3 58	9 40	1 26	20 38	1 58	16 37	1 11	2 30	2 19
18	13 12	23 6	2 15	21 21	12 25	3 44	9 12	1 26	20 46	1 59	16 38	1 12	2 32	2 19
19	12 52	19 24	1 14	17 16	12 48	3 28	8 43	1 25	20 55	1 59	16 39	1 12	2 34	2 19
20	12 33	14 58	0 9	12 31	13 11	3 12	8 15	1 25	21 3	1 59	16 40	1 12	2 37	2 18
21	12 13	9 58	0S56	7 19	13 32	2 55	7 46	1 24	21 12	1 59	16 41	1 12	2 39	2 18
22	11 53	4 35	1 60	1 49	13 51	2 38	7 17	1 24	21 20	1 59	16 42	1 12	2 42	2 18
23	11 33	0S59	2 58	3S47	14 9	2 20	6 47	1 23	21 29	1 60	16 42	1 13	2 44	2 18
24	11 12	6 35	3 49	9 19	14 24	2 2	6 18	1 22	21 37	1 60	16 43	1 13	2 47	2 18
25	10 52	12 0	4 30	14 35	14 37	1 43	5 48	1 21	21 45	2 0	16 44	1 13	2 49	2 18
26	10 31	17 2	4 60	19 20	14 48	1 25	5 18	1 20	21 53	2 0	16 44	1 13	2 52	2 18
27	10 10	21 27	5 15	23 19	14 56	1 8	4 48	1 19	22 1	2 0	16 45	1 13	2 54	2 17
28	9 49	24 55	5 14	26 12	15 1	0 51	4 18	1 18	22 9	2 0	16 45	1 13	2 57	2 17
29	9 28	27 7	4 57	27 39	15 4	0 34	3 47	1 17	22 16	2 1	16 46	1 14	2 59	2 17
30	9 6	27 45	4 22	27 23	15 3	0 18	3 17	1 16	22 24	2 1	16 46	1 14	3 2	2 17
31	8N45	26S35	3S31	25S19	14N58	0S 3	2N46	1N14	22S32	2S 1	16N47	1S14	3S 4	2N17

Day	♅ Decl	♅ Lat	♆ Decl	♆ Lat	♇ Decl	♇ Lat
1	22N53	0N23	5S60	1N39	22N59	8N54
5	22 52	0 23	6 1	1 39	22 57	8 54
9	22 50	0 23	6 3	1 38	22 54	8 54
13	22 49	0 23	6 5	1 38	22 52	8 55
17	22 48	0 23	6 8	1 38	22 50	8 55
21	22 46	0 23	6 10	1 38	22 48	8 55
25	22 45	0 23	6 12	1 38	22 46	8 56
29	22N43	0N23	6S15	1N38	22N44	8N56

☽ PHENOMENA

d	h	m	
5	19	40	○
12	13	27	☾
20	15	21	●
28	12	4	☽

d	h	° ′
2	12	27S46
8	12	0
15	6	27N47
22	20	0
29	21	27S46
6	9	0
12	17	5N18
20	3	0
27	11	5S17

VOID OF COURSE ☽

Last Aspect		☽ Ingress		
2	4pm45	2	♑	10pm28
4	5am37	4	♒	10pm41
6	3pm33	6	♓	10pm 5
8	5am 1	8	♈	10pm34
10	11am24	11	♉	1am46
12	4pm32	13	♊	8am37
15	3am32	15	♋	6pm53
17	7pm36	18	♌	7am19
20	3pm21	20	♍	8pm23
23	3am15	23	♎	8am42
25	2am56	25	♏	7pm11
27	11am38	28	♐	2am54
29	10pm 6	30	♑	7am24

d	h	
5	20	PERIGEE
19	11	APOGEE

DAILY ASPECTARIAN

1 F	☽∠♆	2am57
	♀✶♆	5 36
	☉△☽	11 28
	☽✶♄	1pm32
	♂△♅	3 11
	♀∥♃	3 18
	☽⚻♅	10 47
	☽⚺♂	11 2
2 S	☽⚻♃	3am36
	☽✶♆	4 34
	☽△♀	6 42
	☽△♇	7 16
	♀☌♇	1pm23
	☉⚼☽	2 34
	☽△☿	4 45
	☉✶♄	8 25
3 Su	☽∠♂	0am50
	☽⚼♃	4 37
	☽⚼♇	8 2
	☽⚼♀	9 41
	☽□♄	3pm34
	☽⚼☿	4 37
	☉⚻☽	4 47
4 M	☽☍♅	0am15
	☽✶♂	1 57
	☽△♃	5 0
	☽□♆	5 37
	☽⚻♇	8 13
	☽⚻♀	11 56
	☽⚻☿	3pm54
	☽#♇	5 46
	☽#♅	6 13
	☿∠♄	9 4
5 T	☽∥♂	1pm41
	☽△♄	3 33
	☉☍☽	7 40
	☉#☽	10 51
	☿☌♀	10 57
	☽⚻♅	11 58
6 W	☽#♃	0am35
	☽□♂	3 6
	☽□♃	4 49
	☽△♆	5 8
	☽☍♇	7 46
	☽#♀	8 28
	♀∠♄	1pm12
	☽☍☿	1 36
	☽⚼♄	3 22
	☽☍♀	3 33
	☽⚼♅	11 47
7 Th	☽#☿	4am43
	☽⚼♆	4 56
	☉∥♃	8 37
	☽∥♆	2pm49
	☽⚻♄	3 23
	☉⚻☽	10 36
	☽△♅	11 53
8 F	☽∥♄	4am21
	☽△♂	4 38
	☽✶♃	5 1
	☽⚻♆	5 5
	☽⚻♇	7 49
	☽⚻☿	11 36
	♃⚻♆	4pm10
	♂⚺♆	6 12
	♂☍♃	6 36
	☽#♄	7 34
	☉⚺♅	7 46
	☽⚻♀	8 13
9 S	☉⚼☽	0am50
	☽∠♃	5 52
	☽⚼♂	6 12
	☽⚼♇	8 37
	☽#♆	9 31
	☽⚼☿	11 12
	☽☍♄	4pm59
	☽∥☿	10 27
	☽⚼♀	11 43
	♀ ♍	11 58
10 Su	☽□♅	1am51
	☉△☽	3 56
	☽☍♆	7 14
	☽⚺♃	7 27
	☽⚻♂	8 38
	☽△♇	10 11
	☽∥♀	10 56
	☽△☿	11 24
	☉∥☽	10pm37
11 M	♀∠♅	1am 2
	☽∥♃	3 41
	☽△♀	4 21
	☿☌♇	7 25
	☿□♂	2pm59
	☽#♂	8 24
	☽⚻♄	9 50
12 T	♂□♇	3am50
	☉✶♆	4 59
	☽✶♅	7 12
	☉□♃	12pm 8
	☽⚻♆	12 51
	☽☌♃	1 22
	☉□☽	1 27
	☽∥♅	1 47
	☽□☿	2 1
	☽∥♇	2 8
	☽□♇	4 3
	☽☍♂	4 32
	☉☌☿	5 51
	☿□♃	11 24
13 W	☽⚼♄	1am41
	☿✶♆	8 21
	☽∠♅	11 18
	♀∠♆	2pm32
	☽⚼♆	5 3
	☽□♀	5 19
14 Th	☉☌♇	1am27
	☿∥♀	5 58
	☽△♄	6 28
	☽⚺♅	4pm15
	☽✶☿	7 47
	☽△♆	10 6
	☽⚺♃	10 57
15 F	☽✶♇	1am32
	☉✶☽	3 32
	☽⚻♂	4 35
	☽∠☿	11pm44
16 S	☽∠♃	4am51
	☽∠♇	7 22
	☉□♂	9 29
	☽✶♀	10 44
	☽⚼♂	11 50
	☉∠☽	11 55
	☽□♄	6pm13
17 Su	☽☌♅	4am10
	☽⚺☿	4 18
	☿⚺♅	6 39
	☽□♆	10 5
	☽✶♃	11 14
	☽⚺♇	1pm40
	☽△♂	7 36
	☽∠♀	8 31
	☉⚺☽	8 52
18 M	☽∥♇	2am 0
	☽∥♅	2 15
	☽#♂	3pm 9
19 T	☉∥☿	2am19
	☽⚺♀	6 36
	☽✶♄	7 35
	☽☌☿	2pm50
	☽∥♃	3 15
	♀⚺♄	4 42
	☽⚺♅	5 24
	☽✶♆	11 13
20 W	☽□♃	0am38
	☉∠♄	2 3
	☽☌♇	2 52
	☽∥☿	8 15
	☽□♂	11 43
	☉∥☽	12pm43
	☽∠♄	2 22
	☉☌☽	3 21
21 Th	☽∠♅	0am 2
	☽∠♆	5 46
	☽∥♀	10 58
	☽#♆	5pm 3
	☽⚺♄	9 0
22 F	☿⚺♀	2am21
	☽⚺☿	2 31
	☽☌♀	2 33
	☽✶♅	6 27
	☽#♄	8 9
	☽⚺♆	12pm 4
	☽△♃	1 38
	☽⚺♇	3 40
	☿SD	4 56
23 S	☽✶♂	3am15
	♂∠♄	4 53
	☉ ♍	5 3
	☽∥♄	7 32
	☽∠☿	8 32
	☉⚺☽	9 1
	♀✶♅	5pm42
	☽⚼♃	7 37
	☽∠♇	9 34
	☽∥♆	10 21
	☽#♀	10 52
24 Su	♀#♆	4am33
	☽☌♄	9 11
	☽∠♂	10 21
	☽✶☿	2pm28
	☉∠☽	5 3
	☽□♅	6 5
	☉#☽	7 10
	☽⚺♀	8 41
	☽☌♆	11 25
25 M	☽⚻♃	1am 5
	☽✶♇	2 56
	☉∠♅	6 56
	☽#☿	12pm40
	☽⚺♂	4 49
	☽#♃	10 29
26 T	☉✶☽	0am19
	♀⚺♆	0 41
	☽∠♀	4 35
	♀△♃	6pm25
	☽⚺♄	7 5
27 W	☽□☿	1am32
	☽△♅	3 18
	☽∥♂	3 36
	☽#♅	8 4
	☽#♇	8 7
	☽⚺♆	8 17
	☽☍♃	9 57
	☽✶♀	11 30
	☽□♇	11 38
	♀⚺♇	12pm52
	♂ ♐	6 54
	☽∠♄	10 53
28 Th	☽☌♂	3am16
	☉∠♆	4 48
	☽⚼♅	6 45
	☽∠♆	11 33
	☉□☽	12pm 4
	☿⚺♅	1 55
29 F	☽✶♄	1am52
	☽⚻♅	9 22
	☽△☿	10 33
	☽✶♆	2pm 0
	☽⚻♃	3 37
	☽△♇	5 9
	♅∥♇	7 20
	☽□♀	10 6
30 S	☽⚺♂	10am 5
	♀#♄	10 57
	☽⚼☿	2pm 5
	☽⚼♃	5 14
	☽⚼♇	6 44
	☉△☽	7 48
31 Su	☽□♄	5am26
	☿✶♆	11 47
	☽∠♂	12pm14
	☽☍♅	12 18
	♂⚼♅	1 49
	☽□♆	4 38
	☽⚻☿	5 1
	☽△♃	6 10
	☽⚻♇	7 37
	☉⚼☽	10 22

LONGITUDE

Day	Sid. Time	☉	☽	☽ 12 Hour	Mean ☊	True ☊	☿	♀	♂	♃	♄	♅	♆	♇
	h m s	° ' "	° ' "	° ' "	° '	° '	° '	° '	° '	° '	° '	° '	° '	° '
1	22 40 24	8♍ 29 23	24♑ 25 33	1♒ 49 23	20♒ 32	21♒ 29	20♌ 30	27♍ 7	2♐ 33	20♉ 52	13♎ 13	17♋ 18	19♎ 56	21♌ 45
2	22 44 20	9 27 27	9♒ 16 58	16 47 28	20 29	21 30R	21 43	28 21	3 10	20 53	13 20	17 21	19 57	21 47
3	22 48 17	10 25 32	24 19 54	1♓ 53 12	20 26	21 31	23 2	29 34	3 47	20 55	13 26	17 23	19 59	21 49
4	22 52 13	11 23 39	9♓ 26 15	16 57 53	20 23	21 30	24 27	0♎ 48	4 24	20 56	13 33	17 26	20 1	21 50
5	22 56 10	12 21 48	24 27 0	1♈ 52 32	20 19	21 28	25 57	2 2	5 1	20 57	13 39	17 28	20 3	21 52
6	23 0 7	13 19 58	9♈ 13 32	16 29 11	20 16	21 26	27 31	3 16	5 39	20 58	13 46	17 31	20 5	21 54
7	23 4 3	14 18 10	23 38 49	0♉ 41 58	20 13	21 23	29 9	4 30	6 16	20 59	13 53	17 33	20 7	21 56
8	23 8 0	15 16 24	7♉ 38 19	14 27 44	20 10	21 20	0♍ 51	5 44	6 54	20 59	13 59	17 35	20 8	21 57
9	23 11 56	16 14 41	21 10 16	27 46 3	20 7	21 17	2 36	6 58	7 32	20 59R	14 6	17 38	20 10	21 59
10	23 15 53	17 13 0	4♊ 15 24	10♊ 38 41	20 4	21 15	4 23	8 11	8 10	20 59	14 13	17 40	20 12	22 1
11	23 19 49	18 11 20	16 56 23	23 9 1	20 0	21 15D	6 11	9 25	8 49	20 59	14 20	17 42	20 14	22 3
12	23 23 46	19 9 43	29 17 10	5♋ 21 25	19 57	21 15	8 2	10 39	9 27	20 59	14 26	17 44	20 16	22 4
13	23 27 42	20 8 7	11♋ 22 22	17 20 38	19 54	21 16	9 53	11 53	10 6	20 58	14 33	17 47	20 18	22 6
14	23 31 39	21 6 35	23 16 48	29 11 28	19 51	21 18	11 46	13 7	10 45	20 58	14 40	17 49	20 20	22 8
15	23 35 36	22 5 3	5♌ 5 9	10♌ 58 23	19 48	21 20	13 39	14 21	11 24	20 57	14 47	17 51	20 22	22 10
16	23 39 32	23 3 34	16 51 39	22 45 25	19 45	21 21R	15 32	15 34	12 3	20 56	14 54	17 53	20 24	22 11
17	23 43 29	24 2 7	28 40 3	4♍ 35 57	19 41	21 21	17 25	16 48	12 43	20 54	15 1	17 55	20 26	22 13
18	23 47 25	25 0 43	10♍ 33 25	16 32 45	19 38	21 19	19 18	18 2	13 22	20 53	15 8	17 57	20 28	22 15
19	23 51 22	25 59 19	22 34 12	28 37 58	19 35	21 16	21 10	19 16	14 2	20 51	15 15	17 58	20 30	22 16
20	23 55 18	26 57 58	4♎ 44 14	10♎ 53 10	19 32	21 11	23 2	20 30	14 42	20 49	15 22	18 0	20 32	22 18
21	23 59 15	27 56 39	17 4 52	23 19 29	19 29	21 5	24 54	21 43	15 22	20 47	15 29	18 2	20 35	22 19
22	0 3 11	28 55 22	29 37 5	5♏ 57 47	19 25	20 58	26 45	22 57	16 2	20 44	15 37	18 4	20 37	22 21
23	0 7 8	29 54 7	12♏ 21 40	18 48 52	19 22	20 51	28 35	24 11	16 42	20 42	15 44	18 5	20 39	22 23
24	0 11 4	0♎ 52 53	25 19 27	1♐ 53 34	19 19	20 46	0♎ 24	25 25	17 23	20 39	15 51	18 7	20 41	22 24
25	0 15 1	1 51 41	8♐ 31 19	15 12 50	19 16	20 41	2 12	26 38	18 3	20 36	15 58	18 9	20 43	22 26
26	0 18 58	2 50 32	21 58 15	28 47 40	19 13	20 39D	4 0	27 52	18 44	20 33	16 5	18 10	20 45	22 27
27	0 22 54	3 49 23	5♑ 41 11	12♑ 38 52	19 10	20 39	5 46	29 6	19 25	20 30	16 13	18 12	20 47	22 29
28	0 26 51	4 48 17	19 40 42	26 46 37	19 6	20 40	7 32	0♏ 20	20 6	20 26	16 20	18 13	20 49	22 30
29	0 30 47	5 47 12	3♒ 56 30	11♒ 10 4	19 3	20 41	9 17	1 33	20 47	20 23	16 27	18 14	20 52	22 32
30	0 34 44	6♎ 46 9	18♒ 26 59	25♒ 46 44	19♒ 0	20♒ 42R	11♎ 1	2♏ 47	21♐ 28	20♉ 19	16♎ 34	18♋ 16	20♎ 54	22♌ 33

DECLINATION and LATITUDE

Day	☉ Decl	☽ Decl	☽ Lat	☽ 12 Hr. Decl	☿ Decl	☿ Lat	♀ Decl	♀ Lat	♂ Decl	♂ Lat	♃ Decl	♃ Lat	♄ Decl	♄ Lat
1	8N23	23S36	2S24	21S30	14N51	0N12	2N16	1N13	22S39	2S 1	16N47	1S14	3S 7	2N17
2	8 2	19 1	1 7	16 13	14 40	0 25	1 45	1 12	22 46	2 1	16 47	1 14	3 10	2 17
3	7 40	13 10	0N16	9 55	14 26	0 38	1 14	1 10	22 54	2 1	16 48	1 14	3 12	2 17
4	7 18	6 32	1 37	3 4	14 9	0 50	0 44	1 9	23 1	2 1	16 48	1 15	3 15	2 17
5	6 55	0N26	2 52	3N53	13 49	1 0	0 13	1 7	23 7	2 1	16 48	1 15	3 18	2 16
6	6 33	7 14	3 54	10 27	13 25	1 9	0S18	1 5	23 14	2 1	16 48	1 15	3 20	2 16
7	6 11	13 30	4 39	16 19	12 59	1 18	0 49	1 4	23 21	2 1	16 48	1 15	3 23	2 16
8	5 48	18 53	5 6	21 9	12 30	1 25	1 20	1 2	23 27	2 1	16 48	1 15	3 26	2 16
9	5 26	23 7	5 15	24 44	11 58	1 31	1 51	0 60	23 34	2 1	16 48	1 15	3 28	2 16
10	5 3	26 1	5 7	26 57	11 24	1 37	2 22	0 58	23 40	2 1	16 48	1 16	3 31	2 16
11	4 40	27 31	4 44	27 43	10 48	1 41	2 52	0 56	23 46	2 1	16 47	1 16	3 34	2 16
12	4 17	27 35	4 8	27 6	10 10	1 44	3 23	0 54	23 52	2 1	16 47	1 16	3 36	2 16
13	3 55	26 19	3 22	25 14	9 31	1 47	3 54	0 52	23 58	2 1	16 47	1 16	3 39	2 16
14	3 32	23 52	2 28	22 16	8 49	1 48	4 25	0 50	24 3	2 1	16 47	1 16	3 42	2 16
15	3 8	20 25	1 28	18 23	8 7	1 49	4 55	0 48	24 9	2 1	16 46	1 16	3 45	2 16
16	2 45	16 11	0 25	13 49	7 23	1 49	5 26	0 46	24 14	2 1	16 46	1 17	3 47	2 15
17	2 22	11 19	0S40	8 43	6 38	1 48	5 56	0 43	24 19	2 1	16 45	1 17	3 50	2 15
18	1 59	6 1	1 43	3 16	5 53	1 47	6 26	0 41	24 24	2 0	16 45	1 17	3 53	2 15
19	1 36	0 28	2 42	2S21	5 7	1 45	6 57	0 39	24 29	2 0	16 44	1 17	3 56	2 15
20	1 12	5S10	3 35	7 57	4 20	1 43	7 27	0 37	24 33	2 0	16 43	1 17	3 58	2 15
21	0 49	10 41	4 18	13 19	3 33	1 40	7 56	0 34	24 38	2 0	16 43	1 17	4 1	2 15
22	0 26	15 51	4 49	18 13	2 46	1 36	8 26	0 32	24 42	1 60	16 42	1 17	4 4	2 15
23	0 2	20 25	5 7	22 23	1 59	1 32	8 56	0 29	24 46	1 60	16 41	1 18	4 7	2 15
24	0S21	24 6	5 9	25 31	1 11	1 28	9 25	0 27	24 50	1 59	16 40	1 18	4 10	2 15
25	0 44	26 35	4 55	27 18	0 24	1 23	9 54	0 24	24 53	1 59	16 39	1 18	4 12	2 15
26	1 8	27 37	4 25	27 31	0S23	1 18	10 23	0 22	24 57	1 59	16 38	1 18	4 15	2 15
27	1 31	26 59	3 39	26 1	1 10	1 13	10 52	0 19	24 60	1 59	16 37	1 18	4 18	2 15
28	1 55	24 38	2 40	22 52	1 57	1 8	11 20	0 16	25 3	1 59	16 36	1 18	4 21	2 15
29	2 18	20 43	1 29	18 15	2 44	1 2	11 48	0 14	25 6	1 58	16 35	1 18	4 24	2 15
30	2S41	15S30	0S12	12S30	3S30	0N56	12S16	0N11	25S 8	1S58	16N34	1S18	4S26	2N15

Day	♅ Decl	♅ Lat	♆ Decl	♆ Lat	♇ Decl	♇ Lat
1	22N43	0N23	6S17	1N38	22N42	8N57
5	22 41	0 23	6 20	1 37	22 40	8 57
9	22 40	0 23	6 23	1 37	22 39	8 58
13	22 39	0 23	6 26	1 37	22 37	8 59
17	22 38	0 24	6 29	1 37	22 35	8 59
21	22 37	0 24	6 32	1 37	22 34	9 0
25	22 37	0 24	6 35	1 37	22 33	9 1
29	22N36	0N24	6S39	1N37	22N32	9N 2

☽ PHENOMENA

d	h	m	
4	3	20	○
11	2	36	☾
19	7	22	●
26	20	31	☽

d	h	° '
4	23	0
11	13	27N43
19	2	0
26	3	27S38

d	h	° '
2	20	0
9	0	5N15
16	9	0
23	16	5S10
30	4	0

VOID OF COURSE ☽

Last Aspect		☽ Ingress		
1	4am46	1	♒	9am 3
2	9pm44	3	♓	9am 0
4	6pm23	5	♈	8am58
7	10am38	7	♉	10am48
9	1am29	9	♊	4pm 6
11	9am53	12	♋	1am24
13	7pm19	14	♌	1pm39
16	10am52	17	♍	2am42
19	7am22	19	♎	2pm42
21	10am 6	22	♏	0am44
23	6pm37	24	♐	8am33
26	11am24	26	♑	2pm 6
28	1am57	28	♒	5pm25
30	6am44	30	♓	6pm53

d	h	
3	6	PERIGEE
15	19	APOGEE

DAILY ASPECTARIAN

1	☽△♀	4am46
M	☽#♅	5 22
	☽#♇	5 25
	☽∥♂	5 32
	☿□♃	7 38
	♂#♇	9 35
	♂#♅	10 58
	☽⚹♂	1pm44
2	☉⚻☽	0am18
T	☿☌♇	1 13
	☽△♄	6 31
	☽⚼♀	7 5
	☽#♃	9 39
	☽⚻♅	12pm55
	☽△♆	5 4
	☽□♃	6 33
	☽#☿	6 54
	☽☍♇	7 59
	☽☍☿	9 44
3	☽⚼♄	6am34
W	♀ ♎	8 18
	☽⚻♀	9 4
	☽⚼♅	12pm50
	☽□♂	3 39
	☽⚼♆	4 57
	☉#☽	9 10
4	☽∥♆	0am43
Th	☉☍☽	3 20
	☽⚻♄	6 35
	☽∥♄	11 17
	☽△♅	12pm47
	☽⚻♆	4 55
	☽⚹♃	6 23
	☽⚻♇	7 51
	☽#♀	9 37
	☽∥♀	11 19
5	♂∠♆	1am 7
F	☽⚻☿	2 41
	☽#♄	10 2
	☽☍♀	1pm23
	☽△♂	5 53
	☽∠♃	6 39
	☽⚼♇	8 11
	☽#♆	8 47
	☉∥☽	9 40
6	☽⚼☿	6am 6
S	☉⚻☽	7 15
	☽☍♄	7 33
	☉⚺♄	12pm 3
	☉#♆	12 54
	☽□♅	1 45
	☽☍♆	6 2
	☽⚺♃	7 30
	☿∠♄	7 39
	☽⚼♂	7 49
	☽△♇	9 6
	☽∥☿	10 4
7	☉⚼☽	10am19
Su	☽△☿	10 38
	☿ ♍	12pm 2
	☽∥♃	2 11
	☽⚻♀	8 21
	☽⚻♂	10 40
8	♀⚼♃	5am 0
M	☽⚻♄	11 15
	☉△☽	2pm29
	☽⚹♅	5 37
	☽∥♇	8 57
	☽∥♅	9 7
	☽⚻♆	10 12
	☽☌♃	11 40
9	☿∠♅	0am31
T	♀∠♇	0 32
	☽□♇	1 29
	☽⚼♀	1 34
	☽#♂	3 12
	☽⚼♄	2pm35
	♃SR	7 36
	☽∠♅	9 2
	♀⚹♂	11 20
10	☽□☿	0am15
W	☽⚼♆	1 46
	☽☍♂	7 44
	☽△♀	8 9
	☿∠♆	11 13
	☉⚹♅	11 34
	☽△♄	6pm57
11	☽⚺♅	1am28
Th	☉□☽	2 36
	☽△♆	6 22
	☽⚺♃	7 48
	☽⚹♇	9 53
12	♀∥♄	11am19
F	☽∠♃	1pm14
	☽∠♇	3 27
	☽⚹☿	8 29
	☽⚻♂	9 19
13	☉#♀	0am14
S	☽□♀	1 8
	☿□♂	4 10
	☉⚺♆	4 16
	☽□♄	6 27
	☽☌♅	12pm54
	☉#♄	2 19
	☽□♆	6 1
	☉⚹☽	7 13
	☽⚹♃	7 19
	☉△♃	8 24
	☽⚺♇	9 40
	☽#♂	10 31
14	☽⚼♂	5am18
Su	☽∠☿	8 24
	☽∥♅	9 16
	☽∥♇	9 33
15	☉⚺♇	1am54
M	☉∠☽	4 26
	♀☌♄	9 33
	☽△♂	1pm38
	☿⚺♄	3 31
	☽⚹♄	7 58
	☽⚺☿	8 46
	☽∥♃	8 55
	☽⚹♀	9 4
16	☿⚺♀	1am39
T	☽⚺♅	2 5
	☽⚹♆	7 14
	☽□♃	8 16
	☽☌♇	10 52
	☉⚺☽	1pm45
17	☽∠♄	2am46
W	☿#♆	4 45
	☿⚹♅	6 25
	☽∠♀	7 5
	☽∠♅	8 37
	☿#♀	1pm21
	☽∠♆	1 44
	☽#♆	9 54
	♀□♅	10 9
	☽#♀	10 18
18	☽∥☿	0am43
Th	♀∥♆	2 49
	☽□♂	5 59
	☽#♄	9 15
	☽⚺♄	9 16
	☽⚹♅	2pm50
	☿⚺♆	3 19
	☽⚺♀	4 41
	☉∥☽	6 48
	☽⚺♆	7 53
	☿△♃	7 55
	☽△♃	8 35
	☽☌☿	8 43
	☽⚺♇	11 24
19	☉☌☽	7am22
F	☉#☽	8 12
	☿⚺♇	2pm18
	☽∥♄	6 52
	☽#☿	8 53
20	♀☌♆	0am56
S	☽⚼♃	2 6
	☽∠♇	5 1
	☽∥♆	5 51
	♀⚻♃	6 6
	☿#♄	10 28
	☽∥♀	10 46
	☽⚹♂	8pm30
	☽☌♄	8 54
21	☽□♅	1am50
Su	♂⚹♄	5 36
	☽☌♆	6 45
	☽⚻♃	7 6
	☽☌♀	9 54
	☽⚹♇	10 6
	♀⚹♇	11 57
	☽⚺☿	5pm35
	☉⚺☽	10 34
22	☽∠♂	2am50
M	☽#♃	4 13
23	☉ ♎	2am24
T	☽∠☿	2 39
	☉∠☽	5 8
	☽⚺♄	6 20
	☽⚺♂	8 32
	☽△♅	10 41
	☽#♇	1pm 7
	☽#♅	1 31
	☽⚺♆	3 26
	☽☍♃	3 26
	♃⚻♆	3 33
	☽□♇	6 37
	☿ ♎	6 46
24	☽⚺♀	0am11
W	☽∥♂	6 2
	☽∠♄	10 12
	☽⚹☿	10 45
	☉⚹☽	10 59
	☉☌☿	2pm 3
	☽⚼♅	2 15
	☉#☿	5 4
	☽∠♆	6 55
25	♂⚻♅	3am17
Th	☽∠♀	6 10
	☽⚹♄	1pm28
	☽⚻♅	5 15
	☽☌♂	5 57
	☽⚻♃	9 30
	☽⚹♆	9 50
26	☽△♇	0am51
F	☽⚹♀	11 24
	☿⚼♃	8pm23
	☉□☽	8 31
	☽⚼♃	11 40
27	☽□☿	0am10
S	☽⚼♇	3 6
	♀ ♏	5pm37
	☽□♄	6 15
	☽∥♂	8 50
	☉∥☿	9 23
	☽☍♅	9 31
	☿∠♇	11 35
28	☽⚺♂	0am45
Su	☽△♃	1 17
	☽□♆	1 57
	☽⚻♇	4 48
	♂⚻♃	11 1
	☽#♅	1pm35
	☽#♇	2 0
	☉⚼♃	2 33
	☽□♀	7 38
29	♂⚹♆	3am 0
M	☽∠♂	3 13
	☉△☽	3 18
	☽△☿	10 5
	☽#♃	7pm26
	☽△♄	8 53
	☽⚻♅	11 41
30	☽□♃	3am 2
T	☽△♆	4 1
	☽⚹♂	5 11
	☉⚼☽	5 50
	☽☍♇	6 44
	☽∥♀	11 59
	☽⚼☿	2pm 1
	☉∠♇	7 33
	☽⚼♄	9 37

OCTOBER 1952

LONGITUDE

Day	Sid. Time	☉	☽	☽ 12 Hour	Mean ☊	True ☊	☿	♀	♂	♃	♄	♅	♆	♇
	h m s	° ' "	° ' "	° ' "	° '	° '	° '	° '	° '	° '	° '	° '	° '	° '
1	0 38 40	7♎ 45 7	3♓ 8 45	10♓ 32 16	18♒ 57	20♒ 41R	12♎ 44	4♏ 1	22♐ 9	20♉ 15R	16♎ 42	18♋ 17	20♎ 56	22♌ 34
2	0 42 37	8 44 8	17 56 28	25 20 27	18 54	20 38	14 26	5 14	22 51	20 10	16 49	18 18	20 58	22 36
3	0 46 33	9 43 10	2♈ 43 13	10♈ 3 48	18 50	20 33	16 7	6 28	23 32	20 6	16 56	18 19	21 0	22 37
4	0 50 30	10 42 15	17 21 14	24 34 38	18 47	20 26	17 48	7 42	24 14	20 1	17 3	18 20	21 3	22 39
5	0 54 27	11 41 21	1♉ 43 12	8♉ 46 16	18 44	20 18	19 27	8 55	24 56	19 56	17 11	18 22	21 5	22 40
6	0 58 23	12 40 29	15 43 19	22 34 1	18 41	20 10	21 6	10 9	25 38	19 52	17 18	18 23	21 7	22 41
7	1 2 20	13 39 40	29 18 9	5♊ 55 43	18 38	20 2	22 44	11 22	26 20	19 46	17 25	18 24	21 9	22 43
8	1 6 16	14 38 54	12♊ 26 49	18 51 43	18 35	19 55	24 21	12 36	27 2	19 41	17 33	18 24	21 11	22 44
9	1 10 13	15 38 9	25 10 48	1♋ 24 32	18 31	19 51	25 58	13 49	27 44	19 36	17 40	18 25	21 14	22 45
10	1 14 9	16 37 27	7♋ 33 27	13 38 9	18 28	19 49D	27 33	15 3	28 27	19 30	17 47	18 26	21 16	22 46
11	1 18 6	17 36 47	19 39 17	25 37 31	18 25	19 48	29 8	16 17	29 9	19 24	17 55	18 27	21 18	22 48
12	1 22 2	18 36 9	1♌ 33 32	7♌ 28 0	18 22	19 49	0♏ 43	17 30	29 52	19 18	18 2	18 28	21 20	22 49
13	1 25 59	19 35 34	13 21 37	19 15 0	18 19	19 50R	2 16	18 44	0♑ 34	19 12	18 9	18 28	21 23	22 50
14	1 29 56	20 35 1	25 8 47	1♍ 3 33	18 16	19 50	3 49	19 57	1 17	19 6	18 17	18 29	21 25	22 51
15	1 33 52	21 34 30	6♍ 59 51	12 58 9	18 12	19 48	5 22	21 11	2 0	19 0	18 24	18 29	21 27	22 52
16	1 37 49	22 34 1	18 58 54	25 2 27	18 9	19 44	6 53	22 24	2 43	18 53	18 31	18 30	21 29	22 53
17	1 41 45	23 33 35	1♎ 9 7	7♎ 19 9	18 6	19 37	8 24	23 37	3 26	18 47	18 39	18 30	21 32	22 55
18	1 45 42	24 33 10	13 32 42	19 49 51	18 3	19 28	9 54	24 51	4 9	18 40	18 46	18 31	21 34	22 56
19	1 49 38	25 32 48	26 10 39	2♏ 35 4	18 0	19 17	11 24	26 4	4 52	18 33	18 53	18 31	21 36	22 57
20	1 53 35	26 32 28	9♏ 3 0	15 34 21	17 56	19 5	12 53	27 18	5 36	18 26	19 1	18 31	21 38	22 58
21	1 57 31	27 32 10	22 8 57	28 46 36	17 53	18 53	14 21	28 31	6 19	18 19	19 8	18 32	21 41	22 59
22	2 1 28	28 31 53	5♐ 27 9	12♐ 10 23	17 50	18 42	15 49	29 45	7 3	18 12	19 15	18 32	21 43	23 0
23	2 5 25	29 31 39	18 56 11	25 44 22	17 47	18 34	17 16	0♐ 58	7 46	18 4	19 23	18 32	21 45	23 1
24	2 9 21	0♏ 31 26	2♑ 34 51	9♑ 27 33	17 44	18 29	18 42	2 11	8 30	17 57	19 30	18 32R	21 47	23 1
25	2 13 18	1 31 15	16 22 24	23 19 23	17 41	18 26	20 7	3 25	9 14	17 49	19 37	18 32	21 49	23 2
26	2 17 14	2 31 6	0♒ 18 28	7♒ 19 38	17 37	18 25D	21 32	4 38	9 58	17 42	19 44	18 32	21 52	23 3
27	2 21 11	3 30 58	14 22 49	21 27 57	17 34	18 26R	22 56	5 51	10 42	17 34	19 52	18 32	21 54	23 4
28	2 25 7	4 30 52	28 34 54	5♓ 43 27	17 31	18 25	24 19	7 5	11 26	17 26	19 59	18 32	21 56	23 5
29	2 29 4	5 30 48	12♓ 53 18	20 4 6	17 28	18 23	25 41	8 18	12 10	17 18	20 6	18 32	21 58	23 6
30	2 33 0	6 30 45	27 15 22	4♈ 26 33	17 25	18 19	27 2	9 31	12 54	17 11	20 13	18 31	22 0	23 6
31	2 36 57	7♏ 30 44	11♈ 37 1	18♈ 46 4	17♒ 22	18♒ 11	28♏ 23	10♐ 44	13♑ 39	17♉ 3	20♎ 20	18♋ 31	22♎ 3	23♌ 7

DECLINATION and LATITUDE

Day	☉ Decl	☽ Decl	☽ Lat	☽ 12 Hr. Decl	☿ Decl	☿ Lat	♀ Decl	♀ Lat	♂ Decl	♂ Lat	♃ Decl	♃ Lat	♄ Decl	♄ Lat
1	3S 5	9S19	1N 7	5S60	4S16	0N50	12S44	0N 8	25S10	1S58	16N33	1S19	4S29	2N15
2	3 28	2 36	2 22	0N50	5 1	0 44	13 11	0 5	25 13	1 58	16 32	1 19	4 32	2 15
3	3 51	4N15	3 27	7 34	5 46	0 37	13 38	0 3	25 14	1 57	16 30	1 19	4 35	2 15
4	4 14	10 47	4 18	13 48	6 31	0 31	14 5	0S 0	25 16	1 57	16 29	1 19	4 38	2 15
5	4 37	16 37	4 51	19 10	7 15	0 24	14 31	0 3	25 18	1 57	16 28	1 19	4 40	2 15
6	5 1	21 25	5 6	23 21	7 58	0 17	14 57	0 6	25 19	1 56	16 26	1 19	4 43	2 15
7	5 24	24 56	5 3	26 8	8 41	0 10	15 23	0 9	25 20	1 56	16 25	1 19	4 46	2 15
8	5 46	26 59	4 43	27 26	9 23	0 3	15 48	0 12	25 21	1 56	16 23	1 19	4 49	2 15
9	6 9	27 32	4 11	27 16	10 5	0S 3	16 13	0 14	25 21	1 55	16 22	1 19	4 52	2 15
10	6 32	26 40	3 27	25 45	10 46	0 10	16 38	0 17	25 21	1 55	16 20	1 19	4 54	2 15
11	6 55	24 33	2 35	23 5	11 27	0 17	17 2	0 20	25 21	1 55	16 19	1 19	4 57	2 15
12	7 18	21 23	1 36	19 28	12 6	0 24	17 26	0 23	25 21	1 54	16 17	1 20	4 60	2 15
13	7 40	17 22	0 35	15 6	12 45	0 31	17 49	0 26	25 21	1 54	16 15	1 20	5 3	2 15
14	8 2	12 42	0S28	10 10	13 24	0 38	18 12	0 29	25 20	1 54	16 13	1 20	5 5	2 15
15	8 25	7 33	1 31	4 50	14 1	0 45	18 34	0 32	25 19	1 53	16 12	1 20	5 8	2 15
16	8 47	2 4	2 29	0S44	14 38	0 52	18 56	0 35	25 18	1 53	16 10	1 20	5 11	2 15
17	9 9	3S33	3 22	6 21	15 14	0 59	19 18	0 38	25 16	1 52	16 8	1 20	5 14	2 15
18	9 31	9 7	4 6	11 49	15 49	1 6	19 38	0 41	25 15	1 52	16 6	1 20	5 16	2 15
19	9 53	14 26	4 38	16 54	16 24	1 12	19 59	0 43	25 13	1 52	16 4	1 20	5 19	2 15
20	10 14	19 13	4 58	21 19	16 57	1 19	20 19	0 46	25 11	1 51	16 2	1 20	5 22	2 15
21	10 36	23 10	5 2	24 44	17 30	1 25	20 38	0 49	25 8	1 51	16 0	1 20	5 25	2 15
22	10 57	25 58	4 50	26 50	18 2	1 31	20 57	0 52	25 6	1 50	15 58	1 20	5 27	2 15
23	11 19	27 19	4 21	27 24	18 33	1 38	21 15	0 55	25 3	1 50	15 56	1 20	5 30	2 15
24	11 40	27 3	3 38	26 17	19 3	1 44	21 33	0 58	24 59	1 49	15 54	1 20	5 33	2 15
25	12 0	25 7	2 41	23 33	19 32	1 49	21 50	1 1	24 56	1 49	15 52	1 20	5 35	2 15
26	12 21	21 38	1 35	19 23	20 0	1 55	22 6	1 3	24 52	1 48	15 50	1 20	5 38	2 15
27	12 41	16 52	0 21	14 6	20 27	2 1	22 22	1 6	24 48	1 48	15 48	1 20	5 41	2 15
28	13 2	11 8	0N54	8 1	20 53	2 6	22 38	1 9	24 44	1 47	15 46	1 20	5 43	2 15
29	13 22	4 47	2 6	1 30	21 18	2 11	22 52	1 11	24 40	1 47	15 44	1 20	5 46	2 15
30	13 42	1N49	3 10	5N 6	21 42	2 16	23 6	1 14	24 35	1 46	15 41	1 20	5 49	2 16
31	14S 1	8N19	4N 2	11N24	22S 5	2S20	23S20	1S17	24S30	1S46	15N39	1S20	5S51	2N16

Day	♅ Decl	♅ Lat	♆ Decl	♆ Lat	♇ Decl	♇ Lat
1	22N36	0N24	6S40	1N37	22N31	9N 3
5	22 35	0 24	6 44	1 37	22 30	9 4
9	22 35	0 24	6 47	1 37	22 29	9 5
13	22 34	0 24	6 50	1 37	22 29	9 6
17	22 34	0 24	6 54	1 37	22 28	9 7
21	22 34	0 25	6 57	1 37	22 28	9 8
25	22 34	0 25	7 0	1 37	22 28	9 9
29	22N34	0N25	7S 4	1N37	22N28	9N11

☽ PHENOMENA

d	h	m	
3	12	16	○
10	19	33	☾
18	22	43	●
26	4	4	☽

d	h	° '
2	9	0
8	21	27N33
16	9	0
23	8	27S25
29	17	0

d	h	° '
6	8	5N 7
13	13	0
20	18	5S 2
27	7	0

VOID OF COURSE ☽

Last Aspect		☽ Ingress		
2	8am21	2	♈	7pm34
4	12pm 1	4	♉	9pm 6
6	12pm14	7	♊	1am15
9	5am12	9	♋	9am16
11	3am19	11	♌	8pm50
13	7pm20	14	♍	9am51
16	7am33	16	♎	9pm45
18	10pm43	19	♏	7am10
21	12pm42	21	♐	2pm12
23	7am12	23	♑	7pm29
25	9am26	25	♒	11pm28
27	4pm 2	28	♓	2am23
29	11pm36	30	♈	4am35

d	h	
1	13	PERIGEE
13	10	APOGEE
29	6	PERIGEE

DAILY ASPECTARIAN

1	☽⚻♅	0am13
W	☽△♀	1 32
	☽⚻♆	4 32
	☿∥♄	7 32
	☉⚼☽	8 1
	☽∥♆	9 33
	♂△♇	3pm 5
	☽∥☿	4 19
	☽∥♄	5 14
	☽⚼☿	5 34
	☉∥☽	9 6
	☽⚼♄	10 10
2	☽△♅	0am35
Th	☽⚹♃	3 36
	☽⚻♀	4 4
	☽⚼♆	4 55
	☽⚼♇	7 34
	☽□♂	8 21
	☉#☽	10pm31
3	☽#♄	1am12
F	☽∠♃	3 51
	☽#☿	6 8
	☽⚼♀	6 40
	☽⚻♇	8 1
	☽#♆	8 50
	☉☍☽	12pm16
	☿☌♄	12 36
	☽☍♄	11 30
4	☽☍☿	0am49
S	☽□♅	1 38
	☽⚺♃	4 24
	☽☍♆	6 8
	☿∥♆	6 46
	☿□♅	8 0
	☽△♇	8 47
	☽△♂	12pm 1
	☽#♀	2 14
	☽∥♃	11 19
5	☉∥♄	3am30
Su	☿⚼♃	6 45
	☽☍♀	1pm26
	☽⚻♂	2 44
	☉⚼☽	6 19
6	☿☌♆	0am15
M	☽⚼♄	2 47
	☽⚹♅	4 38
	☽∥♇	6 28
	☽∥♅	7 0
	☽☌♃	7 11
	☽⚼♆	9 28
	☽⚼☿	10 42
	☽□♇	12pm14
	☽⚼♂	6 23
	♀∠♂	10 4
	☉⚻☽	10 45
	☿⚹♇	11 39
7	☽#♂	3am38
T	☽⚻♄	5 41
	☽∠♅	7 24
	☽⚻♆	12pm27
	☽⚻☿	5 29
8	☽⚼♀	0am19
W	☉△☽	4 26
	☽△♄	9 37
	☽⚺♅	11 10
	☽⚺♃	1pm27
	☽△♆	4 27
	☽⚹♇	7 22
9	☽△☿	1am43
Th	☽☍♂	5 12
	♀#♃	7 42
	☽⚻♀	7 46
	☽∠♃	6pm 4
10	☽∠♇	0am26
F	☽#♂	4pm19
	☽△♀	4 29
	☉∥♆	5 14
	☉□☽	7 33
	☽□♄	8 29
	☽☌♅	9 35
	☽⚹♃	11 30
11	☿⚹♂	0am14
S	☽□♆	3 19
	☽⚺♇	6 19
	☉☌♄	8 18
	☿ ♏	1pm 6
	☽∥♅	3 47
	☽∥♇	4 26
	☽⚼♂	8 20
	☉□♅	8 32
	☽□☿	10 1
12	♂ ♑	4am45
Su	♀⚺♄	11 38
	☉⚼♃	3pm28
	♀△♅	6 59
	☽#♀	9 43
13	☽⚻♂	4am48
M	☽∥♃	6 3
	♀☍♃	8 39
	☽⚹♄	9 53
	☽⚺♅	10 25
	☽□♃	11 48
	☽□♀	12pm12
	☉⚹☽	1 52
	☽⚹♆	4 23
	☽☌♇	7 20
	☽#☿	8 58
14	☽△♂	1pm15
T	☽∠♄	4 40
	☽∠♅	4 55
	☽⚹☿	8 12
	☉#☽	8 20
	☉☌♆	8 54
	☽∠♆	10 54
	☉∠☽	11 4
15	☽#♆	3am 1
W	♀⚺♆	5 35
	☽#♄	10 36
	♄□♅	6pm52
	☽⚹♅	11 2
	☽⚺♄	11 5
	☽△♃	11 49
16	☽⚺♆	5am 0
Th	☽∠☿	6 35
	☽⚹♀	7 33
	☉⚺☽	7 45
	☽⚺♇	7 46
	☉⚹♇	7 59
	♀□♇	9 46
	☉⚺♀	5pm17
17	☽□♂	4am44
F	☽⚻♃	5 4
	☽∥♄	7 15
	♂⚻♃	9 54
	☽∠♇	1pm10
	♃⚼♄	1 14
	☽∥♆	2 23
	☽⚺☿	4 2
	☽∠♀	4 7
18	☉∥☽	1am53
S	☽□♅	9 30
	☽⚼♃	9 41
	☽☌♄	10 5
	☿#♃	10 56
	☽☌♆	3pm20
	☽⚹♇	5 54
	☉☌☽	10 43
	☽⚺♀	11 47
19	♃⚹♅	5am46
Su	☽#♃	7 49
	☽∥☿	10 44
	☽⚹♂	5pm13
20	☽∥♀	6am39
M	☽☌☿	7 57
	☽☍♃	5pm 4
	☽△♅	5 24
	☽⚺♄	6 27
	☽#♇	7 18
	☽#♅	7 58
	☽∠♂	10 24
	☽⚺♆	11 8
21	☽□♇	1am30
T	☉⚺☽	10 33
	☽☌♀	12pm42
	☽∥♂	3 23
	☽⚻♅	8 33
	☽∠♄	9 50
22	☽∠♆	2am16
W	☽⚺♂	3 1
	♀ ♐	5 3
	☉∠☽	3pm34
	☽⚺☿	8 41
	☽⚼♃	10 29
	☽⚼♅	11 17
23	☽⚹♄	0am47
Th	☽⚹♆	4 59
	☽△♇	7 12
	♂⚻♇	7 55
	☉ ♏	11 23
	☿☍♃	12pm27
	☉⚹☽	8 7
	☿△♅	9 16
	☽⚺♀	11 15
24	☽⚻♃	0am38
F	☽∠☿	2 11
	☽⚻♇	9 31
	☽☌♂	10 55
	☿⚺♄	2pm43
	♅SR	4 42
25	☽∥♂	1am32
S	♀⚻♅	2 24
	☽△♃	2 29
	☽☍♅	3 44
	☽∠♀	3 52
	☽□♄	5 40
	☽⚹☿	7 13
	☽□♆	9 26
	☽⚼♇	11 31
	☽#♅	6pm21
	☽#♇	7 0
	☽∥♀	9 22
26	♀∠♄	2am18
Su	☉□☽	4 4
	☿⚺♆	5 44
	☽∥☿	8 3
	☽⚹♀	8 6
	☽⚺♂	5pm24
27	☿□♇	2am22
M	☽#♃	4 46
	☽□♃	5 21
	☽⚼♅	7 2
	♀#♇	8 59
	☽△♄	9 22
	☽△♆	12pm46
	☽☍♇	2 43
	☽□☿	4 2
	☉∥☽	4 49
	♀#♅	6 49
	☽∠♂	8 11
	♀∠♆	9 8
28	☽⚻♅	8am19
T	☉△☽	10 43
	☽⚻♄	10 50
	☽⚻♆	2pm 4
	☽□♀	3 36
	☽∥♆	3 36
	☽∥♄	8 25
	☽⚹♂	10 44
29	☽⚹♃	7am19
W	☽△♅	9 25
	☽⚼♄	12pm 9
	☉⚻☽	1 42
	☽⚼♆	3 13
	☽⚼♇	5 4
	☽△☿	11 36
30	☽∠♃	8am 8
Th	☽#♄	2pm44
	☉⚼☽	4 37
	☽⚻♇	6 8
	☽#♆	7 22
	☽△♀	10 23
31	☽⚻☿	3am15
F	☽□♂	3 35
	☽⚺♃	9 1
	☿∠♂	10 50
	☽□♅	11 34
	☽☍♄	2pm46
	☽☍♆	5 34
	☽△♇	7 21

NOVEMBER 1952

LONGITUDE

Day	Sid. Time	☉	☽	☽ 12 Hour	Mean ☊	True ☊	☿	♀	♂	♃	♄	♅	♆	♇
	h m s	° ' "	° ' "	° ' "	° '	° '	° '	° '	° '	° '	° '	° '	° '	° '
1	2 40 54	8♏ 30 44	25♈ 53 1	2♉ 57 6	17♒ 18	18♒ 1R	29♏ 42	11♐ 57	14♑ 23	16♉ 55R	20♎ 27	18♋ 31R	22♎ 5	23♌ 8
2	2 44 50	9 30 46	9♉ 57 40	16 54 5	17 15	17 49	1♐ 0	13 11	15 7	16 47	20 34	18 30	22 7	23 9
3	2 48 47	10 30 51	23 45 47	0♊ 32 22	17 12	17 36	2 16	14 24	15 52	16 39	20 41	18 30	22 9	23 9
4	2 52 43	11 30 57	7♊ 13 31	13 49 2	17 9	17 24	3 31	15 37	16 36	16 30	20 48	18 29	22 11	23 10
5	2 56 40	12 31 6	20 18 53	26 43 10	17 6	17 14	4 45	16 50	17 21	16 22	20 56	18 29	22 13	23 10
6	3 0 36	13 31 16	3♋ 2 6	9♋ 15 58	17 2	17 6	5 57	18 3	18 6	16 14	21 2	18 28	22 15	23 11
7	3 4 33	14 31 28	15 25 13	21 30 21	16 59	17 1	7 6	19 16	18 50	16 6	21 9	18 27	22 18	23 11
8	3 8 29	15 31 42	27 31 54	3♌ 30 32	16 56	16 58	8 14	20 29	19 35	15 58	21 16	18 27	22 20	23 12
9	3 12 26	16 31 58	9♌ 26 53	15 21 38	16 53	16 57	9 19	21 42	20 20	15 50	21 23	18 26	22 22	23 12
10	3 16 23	17 32 16	21 15 30	27 9 11	16 50	16 57	10 21	22 55	21 5	15 41	21 30	18 25	22 24	23 13
11	3 20 19	18 32 36	3♍ 3 23	8♍ 58 47	16 47	16 57	11 21	24 8	21 50	15 33	21 37	18 24	22 26	23 13
12	3 24 16	19 32 59	14 56 3	20 55 47	16 43	16 55	12 16	25 21	22 35	15 25	21 44	18 23	22 28	23 14
13	3 28 12	20 33 23	26 58 33	3♎ 4 52	16 40	16 50	13 8	26 34	23 20	15 17	21 51	18 22	22 30	23 14
14	3 32 9	21 33 48	9♎ 15 10	15 29 49	16 37	16 43	13 55	27 46	24 5	15 9	21 57	18 21	22 32	23 14
15	3 36 5	22 34 16	21 49 3	28 13 3	16 34	16 33	14 38	28 59	24 50	15 1	22 4	18 20	22 34	23 15
16	3 40 2	23 34 45	4♏ 41 53	11♏ 15 29	16 31	16 21	15 14	0♑ 12	25 36	14 53	22 11	18 19	22 36	23 15
17	3 43 58	24 35 17	17 53 43	24 36 19	16 28	16 8	15 45	1 25	26 21	14 45	22 17	18 18	22 38	23 15
18	3 47 55	25 35 49	1♐ 22 58	8♐ 13 16	16 24	15 55	16 8	2 37	27 6	14 37	22 24	18 16	22 40	23 15
19	3 51 52	26 36 24	15 6 46	22 2 58	16 21	15 44	16 24	3 50	27 52	14 29	22 30	18 15	22 42	23 16
20	3 55 48	27 37 0	29 1 23	6♑ 1 32	16 18	15 34	16 31R	5 3	28 37	14 21	22 37	18 14	22 44	23 16
21	3 59 45	28 37 37	13♑ 3 0	20 5 22	16 15	15 28	16 29	6 15	29 23	14 14	22 43	18 12	22 46	23 16
22	4 3 41	29 38 15	27 8 18	4♒ 11 31	16 12	15 24	16 17	7 28	0♒ 8	14 6	22 50	18 11	22 48	23 16
23	4 7 38	0♐ 38 54	11♒ 14 49	18 18 1	16 8	15 23D	15 54	8 40	0 54	13 59	22 56	18 9	22 49	23 16
24	4 11 34	1 39 35	25 21 0	2♓ 23 41	16 5	15 23R	15 21	9 53	1 39	13 51	23 2	18 8	22 51	23 16R
25	4 15 31	2 40 17	9♓ 25 57	16 27 45	16 2	15 23	14 37	11 5	2 25	13 44	23 8	18 6	22 53	23 16
26	4 19 27	3 40 59	23 28 56	0♈ 29 24	15 59	15 22	13 43	12 18	3 11	13 37	23 15	18 5	22 55	23 16
27	4 23 24	4 41 42	7♈ 28 58	14 27 22	15 56	15 18	12 39	13 30	3 57	13 30	23 21	18 3	22 57	23 16
28	4 27 21	5 42 27	21 24 22	28 19 38	15 53	15 11	11 27	14 42	4 42	13 23	23 27	18 1	22 59	23 16
29	4 31 17	6 43 13	5♉ 12 48	12♉ 3 30	15 49	15 2	10 9	15 55	5 28	13 16	23 33	18 0	23 0	23 16
30	4 35 14	7♐ 44 0	18♉ 51 20	25♉ 35 56	15♒ 46	14♒ 51	8♐ 48	17♑ 7	6♒ 14	13♉ 9	23♎ 39	17♋ 58	23♎ 2	23♌ 16

DECLINATION and LATITUDE

Day	☉ Decl	☽ Decl	☽ Lat	☽ 12 Hr. Decl	☿ Decl	☿ Lat	♀ Decl	♀ Lat	♂ Decl	♂ Lat	♃ Decl	♃ Lat	♄ Decl	♄ Lat
1	14S21	14N20	4N39	17N 3	22S26	2S24	23S32	1S19	24S25	1S45	15N37	1S20	5S54	2N16
2	14 40	19 30	4 58	21 41	22 47	2 28	23 44	1 22	24 19	1 45	15 35	1 20	5 56	2 16
3	14 59	23 32	4 59	25 2	23 6	2 32	23 56	1 24	24 14	1 44	15 33	1 20	5 59	2 16
4	15 17	26 10	4 43	26 55	23 24	2 35	24 7	1 27	24 8	1 44	15 30	1 20	6 2	2 16
5	15 36	27 17	4 13	27 17	23 40	2 38	24 17	1 29	24 1	1 43	15 28	1 20	6 4	2 16
6	15 54	26 55	3 30	26 12	23 56	2 40	24 26	1 32	23 55	1 42	15 26	1 19	6 7	2 16
7	16 12	25 11	2 39	23 52	24 10	2 42	24 35	1 34	23 48	1 42	15 24	1 19	6 9	2 16
8	16 30	22 19	1 41	20 31	24 22	2 43	24 42	1 36	23 41	1 41	15 21	1 19	6 12	2 16
9	16 47	18 32	0 40	16 22	24 33	2 44	24 50	1 39	23 34	1 41	15 19	1 19	6 14	2 16
10	17 4	14 4	0S23	11 37	24 42	2 44	24 56	1 41	23 26	1 40	15 17	1 19	6 17	2 16
11	17 21	9 5	1 24	6 27	24 50	2 43	25 2	1 43	23 19	1 39	15 15	1 19	6 19	2 17
12	17 37	3 45	2 22	0 60	24 57	2 42	25 7	1 45	23 11	1 39	15 12	1 19	6 21	2 17
13	17 54	1S47	3 15	4S34	25 1	2 40	25 11	1 47	23 2	1 38	15 10	1 19	6 24	2 17
14	18 10	7 20	3 59	10 4	25 4	2 37	25 15	1 49	22 54	1 38	15 8	1 19	6 26	2 17
15	18 25	12 43	4 33	15 17	25 5	2 33	25 18	1 51	22 45	1 37	15 6	1 18	6 29	2 17
16	18 40	17 42	4 54	19 57	25 4	2 27	25 20	1 53	22 36	1 36	15 3	1 18	6 31	2 17
17	18 55	21 58	5 0	23 43	25 1	2 21	25 21	1 55	22 27	1 36	15 1	1 18	6 33	2 17
18	19 10	25 10	4 50	26 15	24 56	2 14	25 21	1 56	22 18	1 35	14 59	1 18	6 36	2 17
19	19 24	26 58	4 22	27 15	24 49	2 5	25 21	1 58	22 8	1 34	14 57	1 18	6 38	2 18
20	19 38	27 6	3 39	26 31	24 40	1 55	25 20	1 60	21 58	1 34	14 55	1 18	6 40	2 18
21	19 52	25 30	2 42	24 5	24 28	1 43	25 19	2 1	21 48	1 33	14 53	1 18	6 42	2 18
22	20 5	22 18	1 35	20 10	24 14	1 30	25 16	2 2	21 38	1 32	14 51	1 17	6 45	2 18
23	20 17	17 46	0 22	15 6	23 57	1 15	25 13	2 4	21 27	1 32	14 49	1 17	6 47	2 18
24	20 30	12 15	0N53	9 14	23 37	0 59	25 9	2 5	21 16	1 31	14 47	1 17	6 49	2 18
25	20 42	6 7	2 4	2 56	23 15	0 41	25 5	2 6	21 5	1 30	14 45	1 17	6 51	2 18
26	20 54	0N17	3 8	3N29	22 49	0 23	24 59	2 7	20 54	1 29	14 43	1 17	6 53	2 19
27	21 5	6 38	3 60	9 42	22 22	0 3	24 53	2 8	20 43	1 29	14 41	1 16	6 55	2 19
28	21 16	12 38	4 37	15 23	21 52	0N18	24 46	2 9	20 31	1 28	14 39	1 16	6 57	2 19
29	21 26	17 56	4 58	20 15	21 21	0 38	24 39	2 10	20 19	1 27	14 37	1 16	6 60	2 19
30	21S36	22N16	5N 2	23N58	20S49	0N58	24S31	2S11	20S 7	1S27	14N35	1S16	7S 2	2N19

Day	♅ Decl	♅ Lat	♆ Decl	♆ Lat	♇ Decl	♇ Lat
1	22N35	0N25	7S 6	1N37	22N28	9N12
5	22 35	0 25	7 9	1 37	22 29	9 13
9	22 36	0 25	7 12	1 37	22 29	9 14
13	22 36	0 25	7 15	1 37	22 30	9 16
17	22 37	0 25	7 18	1 38	22 31	9 17
21	22 38	0 26	7 21	1 38	22 32	9 18
25	22 39	0 26	7 23	1 38	22 33	9 20
29	22N40	0N26	7S26	1N38	22N35	9N21

☽ PHENOMENA

d	h	m	
1	23	10	○
9	15	43	☾
17	12	56	●
24	11	35	☽

d	h	° '
5	6	27N20
12	16	0
19	14	27S15
25	23	0

d	h	° '
2	13	5N 0
9	15	0
16	21	5S 0
23	7	0
29	17	5N 2

VOID OF COURSE ☽

Last Aspect		☽ Ingress		
31	7pm21	1	♉	6am59
2	10pm56	3	♊	11am 2
5	5am20	5	♋	6pm13
7	1pm36	8	♌	4am57
10	3am59	10	♍	5pm47
12	11pm 5	13	♎	5am57
15	2pm49	15	♏	3pm19
17	3pm59	17	♐	9pm34
19	2pm 5	20	♑	1am41
22	4am35	22	♒	4am52
23	8pm27	24	♓	7am55
25	2pm47	26	♈	11am10
28	3am34	28	♉	2pm55
30	7am50	30	♊	7pm53

d	h	
10	6	APOGEE
23	8	PERIGEE

DAILY ASPECTARIAN

1 S	☉#☽	0am 5
	☽⚼♀	1 59
	☿#♇	2 18
	☽∥♃	5 33
	☿ ♐	5 34
	☽⚻☿	7 7
	☿#♅	9 39
	☉☍☽	11pm10
2 Su	☽⚻♀	6am 5
	☽△♂	9 25
	☽☌♃	11 40
	☽✶♅	2pm47
	☽∥♇	4 52
	☽∥♅	5 33
	☽⚻♄	6 34
	☽#☿	8 40
	☽⚻♆	9 10
	☽□♇	10 56
3 M	☽#♀	3am 4
	☽#♂	5 0
	☽⚼♂	1pm19
	☽☍☿	4 39
	☽∠♅	5 16
	♂△♃	9 20
	☽⚼♄	9 25
	☿⚼♅	11 16
	☽⚼♆	11 56
4 T	♀∥♂	1am27
	☉⚻☽	8 26
	☉#♃	2pm51
	♀⚻♃	3 52
	☽⚺♃	4 46
	☽☍♀	4 53
	☽⚻♂	6 10
	☽⚺♅	8 35
5 W	☽△♄	1am 9
	☽△♆	3 34
	☽✶♇	5 20
	☉⚼☽	2pm40
	☽∠♃	8 36
	☿∥♂	11 3
6 Th	☿∠♄	2am11
	♀⚺♂	2 17
	☽⚻☿	6 10
	♀⚻♅	8 10
	☽∠♇	9 55
	♂☍♅	11 50
	☉△☽	10pm 5
7 F	☽✶♃	1am19
	☿∠♆	4 1
	☽#♀	5 35
	☽☌♅	5 58
	☽☍♂	7 10
	☽⚻♀	8 25
	☽#☿	8 53
	☽□♄	11 25
	☽#♂	1pm 7
	☽□♆	1 36
	☽⚼☿	2 34
	☽⚺♇	3 21
	☽∥♅	9 59
	☽∥♇	10 44
8 S	☉☍♃	9am10
	♀✶♄	5pm15
	☽⚼♀	5 48
	☽△☿	11 43
9 Su	☉#☽	9am10
	☽□♃	12pm48
	♀✶♆	1 30
	☉□☽	3 43
	☽∥♃	5 42
	☽⚺♅	6 13
	☽⚻♂	11 37
10 M	☽✶♄	0am30
	☽✶♆	2 20
	☽△♀	3 45
	☽☌♇	3 59
	♀△♇	5 59
	♂□♄	3pm54
	☉△♅	8 38
11 T	☽∠♅	0am42
	☽∠♄	7 17
	☽⚼♂	8 10
	☽#♆	8 28
	☽∠♆	8 54
	☽#♄	12pm29
	☽□☿	6 12
	♂□♆	8 8
12 W	☽△♃	0am58
	☽✶♅	6 54
	☉✶☽	10 5
	☽⚺♄	1pm43
	☽⚺♆	3 6
	☽△♂	4 18
	☽⚺♇	4 35
	♂⚻♇	8 50
	☽□♀	11 5
13 Th	☽⚼♃	6am27
	☉∠☽	6pm19
	☽∥♄	8 4
	☽∠♇	10 2
	☽∥♆	11 41
14 F	☽✶☿	9am33
	☉⚺♄	10 28
	☽⚻♃	11 13
	☽□♅	5pm25
	☉⚺♆	11 54
15 S	☽☌♄	0am28
	☽☌♆	1 25
	☉⚺☽	1 33
	☽✶♇	2 41
	☽□♂	6 2
	☽#♃	11 0
	☿⚻♃	12pm 7
	☽✶♀	2 49
	☽∠☿	3 22
	☉□♇	4 7
	♀⚼♃	6 20
	♀ ♑	8 3
	♂#♅	10 59
16 Su	☉∥☽	5am21
	♂#♇	2pm30
	☽☍♃	6 23
	☽⚺☿	7 59
	☽∠♀	9 4
17 M	☽△♅	0am43
	☽∥♂	3 0
	☽#♇	3 33
	☽#♅	4 13
	☽⚺♄	7 56
	☽⚺♆	8 30
	☽□♇	9 36
	☉☌☽	12pm56
	☽✶♂	3 59
	☽∥☿	10 0
18 T	☽∥♀	1am51
	☽⚺♀	2 24
	☽⚼♅	3 19
	☽∠♄	10 39
	☽∠♆	11 3
	☽∠♂	7pm52
	☽⚻♃	10 55
19 W	☽☌☿	2am15
	☽⚻♅	5 26
	☽✶♄	12pm53
	☽✶♆	1 9
	☽△♇	2 5
	☉⚺☽	9 24
	☽⚺♂	11 16
20 Th	☽⚼♃	0am34
	☿SR	6 36
	☽☌♀	11 18
	☽⚼♇	3pm50
21 F	☉∠☽	1am 4
	☽∥♀	1 48
	☽△♃	2 0
	☽⚺☿	5 47
	☽☍♅	8 47
	☽∥☿	9 44
	♄☌♆	1pm29
	☽□♆	4 35
	☽□♄	4 36
	☽⚻♇	5 25
	♂ ♒	7 40
	☽#♅	9 53
	☽#♇	10 29
22 S	☽∥♂	4am 7
	☉✶☽	4 35
	☽☌♂	5 24
	☽∠☿	6 53
	☉ ♐	8 36
	☉∥☽	11 55
	♀⚼♇	3pm55
	☽⚺♀	7 13
23 Su	☿∠♂	0am 6
	☽□♃	4 36
	☽✶☿	7 39
	☽⚻♅	11 44
	☽#♃	1pm21
	☽△♆	7 45
	☽△♄	8 2
	☽☍♇	8 27
	☽∠♀	11 8
	☉✶♂	11 48
24 M	☽⚺♂	11am21
	☉□☽	11 35
	☽⚼♅	1pm14
	♇SR	5 8
	☽∥♆	7 11
	☽∥♄	9 14
	☽⚼♆	9 21
	☽⚼♄	9 47
25 T	☽✶♀	3am 6
	☽✶♃	7 16
	☽□☿	8 20
	☉⚼♅	10 4
	☽∠♂	2pm25
	☽△♅	2 47
	☽⚻♆	11 2
	☽⚻♄	11 35
	☽⚻♇	11 38
26 W	☉∥♂	0am30
	☿⚻♃	2 45
	♄✶♇	5 34
	☽∠♃	8 42
	☿#♅	9 23
	☿#♇	1pm59
	☿⚺♀	3 9
	☽✶♂	5 34
	☉△☽	6 50
	♀△♃	11 50
27 Th	☽#♄	1am 7
	☽⚼♇	1 21
	☽#♆	2 59
	☽△☿	8 12
	☽⚺♃	10 15
	☽□♀	11 20
	☽□♅	6pm10
	☉⚼☽	10 42
28 F	☽☍♆	2am43
	☽△♇	3 13
	☽☍♄	3 34
	☽⚼☿	8 0
	☽∥♃	8 39
	☉∥☿	9pm 1
29 S	☽□♂	0am28
	☉⚻☽	2 51
	☽⚻☿	7 53
	☽#♂	11 53
	☽☌♃	2pm 0
	☽#☿	4 14
	☉#☽	7 43
	☽△♀	8 37
	☽✶♅	10 26
30 Su	☽∥♇	2am 5
	☿∠♄	2 21
	☽∥♅	2 38
	☉∠♆	7 19
	☽⚻♆	7 26
	☽□♇	7 50
	☽⚻♄	8 35
	☉☌☿	10 37
	☿∠♆	12pm56
	☽#♀	3 38
	♀☍♅	4 38
	☉∠♄	11 59

DECEMBER 1952

LONGITUDE

Day	Sid. Time	☉	☽	☽ 12 Hour	Mean ☊	True ☊	☿	♀	♂	♃	♄	♅	♆	♇
	h m s	° ' "	° ' "	° ' "	° '	° '	° '	° '	° '	° '	° '	° '	° '	° '
1	4 39 10	8♐ 44 47	2♊ 16 56	8♊ 54 2	15♒ 43	14♒ 39R	7♐ 25R	18♑ 19	7♒ 0	13♉ 2R	23♎ 45	17♋ 56R	23♎ 4	23♌ 16R
2	4 43 7	9 45 37	15 26 59	21 55 38	15 40	14 28	6 4	19 31	7 46	12 56	23 51	17 54	23 5	23 15
3	4 47 3	10 46 27	28 19 52	4♋ 39 42	15 37	14 18	4 48	20 43	8 32	12 49	23 56	17 52	23 7	23 15
4	4 51 0	11 47 19	10♋ 55 14	17 6 38	15 34	14 11	3 38	21 55	9 18	12 43	24 2	17 51	23 9	23 15
5	4 54 56	12 48 11	23 14 9	29 18 10	15 30	14 6	2 37	23 7	10 4	12 37	24 8	17 49	23 10	23 15
6	4 58 53	13 49 5	5♌ 19 4	11♌ 17 21	15 27	14 3D	1 47	24 18	10 50	12 31	24 13	17 47	23 12	23 14
7	5 2 50	14 50 0	17 13 34	23 8 17	15 24	14 3	1 7	25 30	11 36	12 25	24 19	17 45	23 13	23 14
8	5 6 46	15 50 56	29 2 8	4♍ 55 47	15 21	14 4	0 39	26 42	12 22	12 20	24 24	17 42	23 15	23 14
9	5 10 43	16 51 54	10♍ 49 54	16 45 10	15 18	14 4R	0 22	27 53	13 8	12 14	24 30	17 40	23 16	23 13
10	5 14 39	17 52 52	22 42 16	28 41 54	15 14	14 4	0 16D	29 5	13 54	12 9	24 35	17 38	23 18	23 13
11	5 18 36	18 53 52	4♎ 44 41	10♎ 51 16	15 11	14 3	0 21	0♒ 16	14 40	12 4	24 41	17 36	23 19	23 12
12	5 22 32	19 54 53	17 2 13	23 18 1	15 8	13 59	0 35	1 28	15 26	11 59	24 46	17 34	23 21	23 12
13	5 26 29	20 55 55	29 39 7	6♏ 5 49	15 5	13 53	0 57	2 39	16 12	11 54	24 51	17 32	23 22	23 11
14	5 30 25	21 56 58	12♏ 38 23	19 16 53	15 2	13 46	1 28	3 50	16 58	11 50	24 56	17 29	23 24	23 11
15	5 34 22	22 58 2	26 1 17	2♐ 51 26	14 59	13 37	2 5	5 1	17 45	11 45	25 1	17 27	23 25	23 10
16	5 38 19	23 59 6	9♐ 47 0	16 47 32	14 55	13 28	2 49	6 12	18 31	11 41	25 6	17 25	23 26	23 10
17	5 42 15	25 0 12	23 52 30	1♑ 1 12	14 52	13 20	3 39	7 23	19 17	11 37	25 11	17 23	23 28	23 9
18	5 46 12	26 1 18	8♑ 12 56	15 26 55	14 49	13 14	4 33	8 34	20 3	11 33	25 16	17 20	23 29	23 8
19	5 50 8	27 2 25	22 42 21	29 58 29	14 46	13 10	5 32	9 45	20 49	11 30	25 20	17 18	23 30	23 8
20	5 54 5	28 3 32	7♒ 14 35	14♒ 30 0	14 43	13 8D	6 34	10 55	21 36	11 26	25 25	17 15	23 31	23 7
21	5 58 1	29 4 39	21 44 9	28 56 34	14 39	13 7	7 40	12 6	22 22	11 23	25 29	17 13	23 32	23 6
22	6 1 58	0♑ 5 47	6♓ 6 50	13♓ 14 40	14 36	13 8	8 49	13 16	23 8	11 20	25 34	17 11	23 34	23 6
23	6 5 55	1 6 54	20 19 51	27 22 13	14 33	13 10R	10 0	14 27	23 54	11 17	25 38	17 8	23 35	23 5
24	6 9 51	2 8 2	4♈ 21 39	11♈ 18 7	14 30	13 10	11 14	15 37	24 41	11 14	25 42	17 6	23 36	23 4
25	6 13 48	3 9 10	18 11 34	25 1 59	14 27	13 9	12 29	16 47	25 27	11 12	25 47	17 3	23 37	23 3
26	6 17 44	4 10 18	1♉ 49 22	8♉ 33 42	14 24	13 6	13 47	17 57	26 13	11 10	25 51	17 1	23 38	23 2
27	6 21 41	5 11 26	15 14 57	21 53 5	14 20	13 2	15 6	19 7	27 0	11 8	25 55	16 58	23 39	23 1
28	6 25 37	6 12 34	28 28 6	4♊ 59 55	14 17	12 56	16 26	20 16	27 46	11 6	25 59	16 56	23 40	23 0
29	6 29 34	7 13 41	11♊ 28 31	17 53 52	14 14	12 49	17 47	21 26	28 32	11 4	26 3	16 53	23 41	23 0
30	6 33 30	8 14 50	24 15 57	0♋ 34 44	14 11	12 43	19 10	22 35	29 18	11 3	26 6	16 50	23 42	22 59
31	6 37 27	9♑ 15 58	6♋ 50 17	13♋ 2 39	14♒ 8	12♒ 38	20♐ 33	23♒ 45	0♓ 5	11♉ 1	26♎ 10	16♋ 48	23♎ 43	22♌ 58

DECLINATION and LATITUDE

Day	☉ Decl	☽ Decl	☽ Lat	☽ 12 Hr. Decl	☿ Decl	☿ Lat	♀ Decl	♀ Lat	♂ Decl	♂ Lat	♃ Decl	♃ Lat	♄ Decl	♄ Lat
1	21S46	25N20	4N48	26N20	20S17	1N17	24S22	2S12	19S55	1S26	14N33	1S16	7S 4	2N19
2	21 55	26 57	4 20	27 12	19 45	1 36	24 12	2 12	19 42	1 25	14 32	1 15	7 6	2 20
3	22 4	27 5	3 39	26 36	19 16	1 52	24 2	2 13	19 30	1 24	14 30	1 15	7 8	2 20
4	22 12	25 46	2 47	24 39	18 49	2 6	23 51	2 13	19 17	1 24	14 28	1 15	7 9	2 20
5	22 20	23 14	1 49	21 35	18 26	2 18	23 39	2 13	19 4	1 23	14 27	1 15	7 11	2 20
6	22 28	19 42	0 47	17 38	18 6	2 28	23 27	2 13	18 50	1 22	14 25	1 14	7 13	2 20
7	22 35	15 24	0S17	13 3	17 51	2 36	23 14	2 14	18 37	1 21	14 24	1 14	7 15	2 20
8	22 42	10 34	1 20	8 0	17 40	2 41	23 0	2 14	18 23	1 21	14 22	1 14	7 17	2 21
9	22 48	5 22	2 19	2 41	17 33	2 45	22 46	2 13	18 9	1 20	14 21	1 14	7 19	2 21
10	22 54	0S 3	3 12	2S47	17 30	2 47	22 31	2 13	17 55	1 19	14 19	1 13	7 21	2 21
11	22 59	5 32	3 58	8 14	17 31	2 47	22 16	2 13	17 41	1 18	14 18	1 13	7 22	2 21
12	23 4	10 54	4 34	13 30	17 35	2 45	21 59	2 12	17 27	1 18	14 17	1 13	7 24	2 21
13	23 8	15 59	4 57	18 20	17 42	2 43	21 43	2 12	17 12	1 17	14 16	1 13	7 26	2 22
14	23 12	20 30	5 7	22 27	17 52	2 39	21 25	2 11	16 58	1 16	14 14	1 12	7 27	2 22
15	23 16	24 7	4 60	25 28	18 4	2 35	21 8	2 11	16 43	1 15	14 13	1 12	7 29	2 22
16	23 19	26 28	4 35	27 3	18 17	2 29	20 49	2 10	16 28	1 14	14 12	1 12	7 31	2 22
17	23 21	27 12	3 54	26 54	18 32	2 23	20 30	2 9	16 13	1 14	14 11	1 11	7 32	2 22
18	23 23	26 8	2 57	24 56	18 49	2 17	20 11	2 8	15 57	1 13	14 10	1 11	7 34	2 23
19	23 25	23 19	1 48	21 19	19 6	2 10	19 51	2 6	15 42	1 12	14 10	1 11	7 35	2 23
20	23 26	18 59	0 32	16 22	19 24	2 3	19 30	2 5	15 26	1 11	14 9	1 11	7 37	2 23
21	23 27	13 32	0N47	10 31	19 42	1 55	19 9	2 4	15 10	1 10	14 8	1 10	7 38	2 23
22	23 27	7 23	2 1	4 11	20 0	1 48	18 47	2 2	14 54	1 10	14 7	1 10	7 39	2 23
23	23 26	0 57	3 8	2N16	20 19	1 40	18 25	2 1	14 38	1 9	14 7	1 10	7 41	2 24
24	23 26	5N26	4 8	8 31	20 37	1 32	18 3	1 59	14 22	1 8	14 6	1 9	7 42	2 24
25	23 24	11 28	4 42	14 16	20 55	1 24	17 40	1 57	14 6	1 7	14 6	1 9	7 44	2 24
26	23 23	16 52	5 5	19 14	21 13	1 15	17 17	1 55	13 49	1 6	14 5	1 9	7 45	2 24
27	23 21	21 21	5 10	23 11	21 30	1 7	16 53	1 53	13 33	1 6	14 5	1 9	7 46	2 25
28	23 18	24 41	4 59	25 51	21 46	0 59	16 29	1 51	13 16	1 5	14 5	1 8	7 47	2 25
29	23 15	26 40	4 33	27 7	22 2	0 51	16 4	1 48	12 59	1 4	14 4	1 8	7 48	2 25
30	23 11	27 12	3 53	26 56	22 17	0 43	15 39	1 46	12 42	1 3	14 4	1 8	7 50	2 25
31	23S 7	26N19	3N 3	25N22	22S32	0N35	15S14	1S43	12S25	1S 2	14N 4	1S 7	7S51	2N26

Day	♅ Decl	♅ Lat	♆ Decl	♆ Lat	♇ Decl	♇ Lat
1	22N40	0N26	7S27	1N38	22N35	9N22
5	22 41	0 26	7 29	1 38	22 37	9 23
9	22 42	0 26	7 31	1 38	22 39	9 24
13	22 44	0 26	7 33	1 39	22 40	9 26
17	22 45	0 26	7 35	1 39	22 42	9 27
21	22 46	0 26	7 37	1 39	22 44	9 28
25	22 48	0 26	7 38	1 39	22 47	9 29
29	22N49	0N26	7S39	1N40	22N49	9N31

☽ PHENOMENA

d	h	m	
1	12	42	○
9	13	22	☾
17	2	3	●
23	19	52	☽
31	5	6	○

d	h	°
2	14	27N13
10	0	0
16	22	27S12
23	4	0
29	21	27N13
6	18	0
14	2	5S 7
20	10	0
26	20	5N11

VOID OF COURSE ☽

Last Aspect		☽ Ingress	
2	3pm42	3 ♋	3am 9
5	1am47	5 ♌	1pm23
7	2pm31	8 ♍	1am58
10	2pm10	10 ♎	2pm36
12	2pm53	13 ♏	0am39
14	6pm57	15 ♐	7am 0
17	2am13	17 ♑	10am18
19	4am22	19 ♒	12pm 3
21	1pm10	21 ♓	1pm46
22	6pm36	23 ♈	4pm30
25	1pm30	25 ♉	8pm46
27	10pm38	28 ♊	2am48
30	10am12	30 ♋	10am54

d	h	
8	3	APOGEE
19	21	PERIGEE

DAILY ASPECTARIAN

1 M	☽∠♅	1am11
	☽⚼♀	2 3
	☿✱♂	4 41
	☽☍☿	8 25
	☽△♂	9 4
	☽⚼♆	10 30
	☽⚼♄	11 48
	☉☍☽	12pm42
	☽⊻♃	7 24
2 T	☿∥♂	4am17
	☽⊻♅	4 31
	☽⚻♀	8 17
	☽△♆	2pm12
	☽⚼♂	2 25
	☽✱♇	2 29
	☿∠♀	2 57
	☽△♄	3 42
	☽∠♃	11 3
3 W	☽⚻☿	11am11
	☽∠♇	6pm52
	☽⚻♂	8 40
4 Th	☉⚻☽	1am49
	☽✱♃	3 27
	☽☌♅	1pm24
	☽⚼☿	1 48
	☿⚼♅	7 4
	☉⚻♃	8 1
	☽#♀	8 24
	☽☍♀	11 44
	☽□♆	11 52
5 F	☽⊻♇	0am 1
	♀□♆	1 15
	☽□♄	1 47
	♀⚻♇	2 39
	☽∥♅	4 9
	☽∥♇	4 41
	☉#☽	6 26
	☉⚼☽	9 51
	☽△☿	5pm21
	♀□♄	10 12
6 S	☽#♂	5am25
	☽#☿	10 1
	☽☍♂	11 50
	☽□♃	2pm22
	☉△☽	6 42
7 Su	☽⊻♅	1am 3
	☽∥♃	5 15
	♆✱♇	6 17
	☉#♇	10 20
	☽☌♇	12pm11
	☽✱♆	12 12
	☽✱♄	2 31
	☽⚻♀	6 42
	♂□♃	11 8
8 M	☉#♅	2am 1
	☽□☿	3 11
	☽∠♅	7 27
	☽#♆	2pm15
	☽#♄	3 14
	☽∠♆	6 48
	☽∠♄	9 16
	☉∥♀	9 56
9 T	☽△♃	2am50
	☽⚼♀	4 39
	☽⚻♂	4 59
	♀#♅	5 49
	♀#♇	11 48
	☉□☽	1pm22
	☽✱♅	1 49
	☉⚻♅	6 26
10 W	☽⊻♇	1am 1
	☽⊻♆	1 12
	☿SD	1 23
	☽⊻♄	3 48
	☽⚼♃	8 51
	☽⚼♂	1pm14
	☽△♀	2 10
	☽✱☿	3 11
	♀ ♒	6 31
11 Th	☿✱♀	1am40
	☽∠♇	6 48
	☽∥♄	8 11
	☽∥♆	8 53
	☿∥♂	2pm 9
	☽⚻♃	2 16
	☽△♂	8 42
	☽∠☿	9 6
12 F	☽□♅	1am 1
	☉✱☽	6 1
	☽✱♇	11 48
	☽☌♆	12pm 7
	☽☌♄	2 53
	☽#♃	3 38
13 S	☽⊻☿	2am32
	☽∥♂	5 50
	☽□♀	6 10
	☽∥☿	8 58
	☉∠☽	12pm41
	☽☍♃	10 32
14 Su	☽∥♀	5am 8
	☽□♂	8 20
	☽△♅	8 45
	☽#♇	1pm38
	☽#♅	1 58
	♂⚻♅	3 24
	☉∥☽	5 29
	☉⊻☽	6 8
	☽□♇	6 57
	☽⊻♆	7 22
	☽⊻♄	10 13
15 M	☉△♇	4am44
	☉✱♆	10 50
	☽☌☿	11 14
	☽⚼♅	11 16
	☿⚼♅	11 39
	☽✱♀	5pm14
	☽∠♆	9 41
16 T	☽∠♄	0am33
	☽⚻♃	3 15
	☽⚻♅	1pm 1
	☽✱♂	3 47
	☽∠♀	9 16
	☽△♇	10 47
	☽✱♆	11 18
17 W	☉☌☽	2am 3
	☽✱♄	2 13
	☉✱♄	4 30
	☽⚼♃	4 36
	☽⊻☿	5pm29
	☽∠♂	6 26
	☽⚼♇	11 52
18 Th	☽⊻♀	0am38
	☽△♃	5 31
	☉⚼♃	11 48
	☽☍♅	3pm 5
	☽∠☿	8 9
	☽⊻♂	8 43
	☉∥☽	11 20
19 F	☽⚻♇	0am42
	☽□♆	1 19
	☽#♅	3 32
	☽#♇	3 45
	☽□♄	4 22
	☉⊻☽	7 42
	♄∥♆	12pm23
	☽∥♀	9 15
	☽∥☿	10 5
	☽✱☿	10 49
20 S	☿∥♀	3am59
	☽☌♀	6 37
	☽□♃	6 54
	♀□♃	9 57
	☉∠☽	10 21
	☽⚻♅	4pm31
	☽∥♂	4 50
	☽#♃	9 31
21 Su	☽☌♂	1am 6
	☽☍♇	2 16
	☽△♆	3 0
	☽△♄	6 17
	☉✱☽	1pm10
	☽⚼♅	5 25
	☿∠♆	6 37
	☉ ♑	9 44
	♂☍♇	10 38
	☽∥♄	10 59
	☽∥♆	11 9
22 M	☽⚼♆	4am 7
	☽□☿	4 57
	☽⚼♄	7 31
	☽✱♃	8 44
	☽⊻♀	1pm 8
	♂△♆	1 32
	☽△♅	6 36
23 T	☽⚻♇	4am40
	☽⚻♆	5 32
	☽⊻♂	6 26
	☽⚻♄	9 5
	☽∠♃	10 6
	☿∠♄	1pm13
	☽∠♀	4 58
	☉□☽	7 52
24 W	☿⚻♃	0am 7
	☽⚼♇	6 23
	☽#♆	8 29
	☽#♄	8 49
	☽∠♂	9 44
	☽⊻♃	11 51
	☽△☿	1pm 4
	☽✱♀	9 19
	☽□♅	10 1
	♂#♃	11 56
25 Th	♀⚻♅	5am20
	☽△♇	8 [illegible]0
	☽☍♆	9 31
	☽#♂	10 42
	☽∥♃	11 13
	♂△♄	11 14
	☽☍♄	1pm23
	☽✱♂	1 30
	☽⚼☿	6 2
26 F	☽#♀	1am51
	☉△☽	4 31
	☽☌♃	4pm37
	☽⚻☿	11 41
27 S	☽#☿	0am57
	☽✱♅	3 5
	☽□♀	7 39
	☽∥♇	9 21
	☽∥♅	9 23
	☉⚼☽	9 40
	☉#☽	1pm 3
	☽□♇	2 3
	☽⚻♆	3 13
	☽⚻♄	7 26
	☽□♂	10 38
28 Su	☽∠♅	6am19
	☿⚻♅	8 34
	☉⚻☽	3pm27
	♅∥♇	6 14
	☽⚼♆	6 48
	☽⚼♄	11 12
	☽⊻♃	11 15
29 M	☽⊻♅	10am 4
	☽☍☿	1pm12
	☉⚼♇	5 45
	☽△♀	8 31
	☽✱♇	9 34
	☽△♆	10 55
30 T	☽∠♃	3am22
	☽△♄	3 31
	♀☍♇	7 59
	☽△♂	10 12
	♂ ♓	9pm35
	♀△♆	11 19
31 W	☽∠♇	2am10
	☽⚼♀	4 3
	☉☍☽	5 6
	☽✱♃	8 4
	☽⚼♂	5pm 1
	☽☌♅	7 14

JANUARY 1953

LONGITUDE

Day	Sid. Time	☉	☽	☽ 12 Hour	Mean ☊	True ☊	☿	♀	♂	♃	♄	♅	♆	♇
	h m s	° ' "	° ' "	° ' "	° '	° '	° '	° '	° '	° '	° '	° '	° '	° '
1	6 41 24	10♑ 17 6	19♋ 11 55	25♋ 18 14	14♒ 5	12♒ 34R	21♐ 58	24♒ 54	0♓ 51	11♉ 0R	26♎ 14	16♋ 45R	23♎ 43	22♌ 57R
2	6 45 20	11 18 14	1♌ 21 47	7♌ 22 49	14 1	12 31D	23 23	26 2	1 37	11 0	26 17	16 43	23 44	22 56
3	6 49 17	12 19 23	13 21 37	19 18 31	13 58	12 31	24 49	27 11	2 23	10 59	26 21	16 40	23 45	22 55
4	6 53 13	13 20 32	25 13 53	1♍ 8 11	13 55	12 31	26 15	28 20	3 10	10 59	26 24	16 38	23 46	22 54
5	6 57 10	14 21 40	7♍ 1 52	12 55 27	13 52	12 33	27 43	29 28	3 56	10 59D	26 27	16 35	23 46	22 53
6	7 1 6	15 22 49	18 49 30	24 44 34	13 49	12 35	29 11	0♓ 36	4 42	10 59	26 30	16 32	23 47	22 51
7	7 5 3	16 23 58	0♎ 41 16	6♎ 40 13	13 45	12 36	0♑ 39	1 44	5 28	10 59	26 33	16 30	23 48	22 50
8	7 8 59	17 25 7	12 42 2	18 47 22	13 42	12 37R	2 8	2 52	6 14	10 59	26 36	16 27	23 48	22 49
9	7 12 56	18 26 16	24 56 48	1♏ 10 55	13 39	12 37	3 38	4 0	7 1	11 0	26 39	16 25	23 49	22 48
10	7 16 53	19 27 25	7♏ 30 17	13 55 22	13 36	12 36	5 8	5 7	7 47	11 1	26 42	16 22	23 49	22 47
11	7 20 49	20 28 34	20 26 34	27 4 12	13 33	12 34	6 38	6 15	8 33	11 2	26 45	16 19	23 50	22 46
12	7 24 46	21 29 43	3♐ 48 28	10♐ 39 25	13 30	12 32	8 10	7 22	9 19	11 3	26 47	16 17	23 50	22 45
13	7 28 42	22 30 52	17 36 59	24 40 53	13 26	12 29	9 41	8 28	10 5	11 5	26 50	16 14	23 51	22 43
14	7 32 39	23 32 1	1♑ 50 44	9♑ 5 58	13 23	12 26	11 13	9 35	10 52	11 6	26 52	16 12	23 51	22 42
15	7 36 35	24 33 9	16 25 51	23 49 31	13 20	12 24	12 46	10 41	11 38	11 8	26 54	16 9	23 52	22 41
16	7 40 32	25 34 17	1♒ 16 3	8♒ 44 23	13 17	12 22D	14 19	11 48	12 24	11 10	26 57	16 6	23 52	22 40
17	7 44 29	26 35 25	16 13 30	23 42 20	13 14	12 22	15 53	12 53	13 10	11 13	26 59	16 4	23 52	22 38
18	7 48 25	27 36 31	1♓ 9 54	8♓ 35 16	13 11	12 23	17 27	13 59	13 56	11 15	27 1	16 1	23 52	22 37
19	7 52 22	28 37 38	15 57 39	23 16 20	13 7	12 24	19 1	15 4	14 42	11 18	27 2	15 59	23 53	22 36
20	7 56 18	29 38 43	0♈ 30 46	7♈ 40 33	13 4	12 25	20 37	16 10	15 28	11 21	27 4	15 56	23 53	22 34
21	8 0 15	0♒ 39 47	14 45 22	21 45 5	13 1	12 26	22 12	17 14	16 14	11 24	27 6	15 54	23 53	22 33
22	8 4 11	1 40 50	28 39 36	5♉ 29 0	12 58	12 26R	23 49	18 19	17 0	11 27	27 7	15 51	23 53	22 32
23	8 8 8	2 41 52	12♉ 13 20	18 52 49	12 55	12 26	25 26	19 23	17 46	11 31	27 9	15 49	23 53	22 30
24	8 12 4	3 42 53	25 27 39	1♊ 58 4	12 51	12 25	27 3	20 27	18 32	11 34	27 10	15 46	23 53	22 29
25	8 16 1	4 43 53	8♊ 24 19	14 46 42	12 48	12 25	28 41	21 30	19 18	11 38	27 11	15 44	23 53R	22 28
26	8 19 58	5 44 52	21 5 27	27 20 52	12 45	12 24	0♒ 20	22 34	20 4	11 42	27 12	15 42	23 53	22 26
27	8 23 54	6 45 51	3♋ 33 11	9♋ 42 39	12 42	12 23	1 59	23 36	20 50	11 47	27 13	15 39	23 53	22 25
28	8 27 51	7 46 48	15 49 32	21 54 2	12 39	12 22	3 39	24 39	21 36	11 51	27 14	15 37	23 53	22 23
29	8 31 47	8 47 44	27 56 24	3♌ 56 52	12 36	12 21	5 20	25 41	22 21	11 56	27 15	15 35	23 53	22 22
30	8 35 44	9 48 38	9♌ 55 38	15 52 56	12 32	12 21	7 1	26 43	23 7	12 0	27 16	15 32	23 53	22 21
31	8 39 40	10♒ 49 32	21♌ 49 2	27♌ 44 11	12♒ 29	12♒ 21D	8♒ 43	27♓ 44	23♓ 53	12♉ 5	27♎ 17	15♋ 30	23♎ 53	22♌ 19

DECLINATION and LATITUDE

Day	☉ Decl	☽ Decl	☽ Lat	☽ 12 Hr. Decl	☿ Decl	☿ Lat	♀ Decl	♀ Lat	♂ Decl	♂ Lat	♃ Decl	♃ Lat	♄ Decl	♄ Lat
1	23S 3	24N 7	2N 4	22N36	22S45	0N27	14S48	1S41	12S 8	1S 1	14N 4	1S 7	7S52	2N26
2	22 58	20 51	1 1	18 53	22 58	0 19	14 22	1 38	11 51	1 1	14 4	1 7	7 53	2 26
3	22 52	16 44	0S 5	14 27	23 9	0 11	13 56	1 35	11 33	0 60	14 4	1 7	7 54	2 26
4	22 47	12 2	1 9	9 30	23 20	0 4	13 30	1 32	11 16	0 59	14 5	1 6	7 55	2 27
5	22 40	6 54	2 11	4 15	23 29	0S 4	13 3	1 29	10 58	0 58	14 5	1 6	7 56	2 27
6	22 34	1 34	3 7	1S 9	23 38	0 11	12 35	1 25	10 41	0 57	14 5	1 6	7 57	2 27
7	22 26	3S52	3 55	6 33	23 45	0 19	12 8	1 22	10 23	0 56	14 5	1 5	7 57	2 27
8	22 19	9 13	4 33	11 48	23 51	0 26	11 40	1 18	10 5	0 56	14 6	1 5	7 58	2 28
9	22 11	14 19	5 0	16 43	23 56	0 33	11 12	1 15	9 47	0 55	14 6	1 5	7 59	2 28
10	22 2	18 58	5 14	21 2	23 60	0 39	10 44	1 11	9 29	0 54	14 7	1 4	7 60	2 28
11	21 53	22 53	5 12	24 27	24 2	0 46	10 16	1 7	9 11	0 53	14 7	1 4	8 0	2 28
12	21 44	25 44	4 54	26 38	24 4	0 52	9 47	1 3	8 53	0 52	14 8	1 4	8 1	2 29
13	21 34	27 9	4 18	27 14	24 4	0 58	9 18	0 59	8 35	0 51	14 9	1 4	8 2	2 29
14	21 24	26 52	3 26	26 1	24 2	1 4	8 49	0 55	8 17	0 51	14 10	1 3	8 2	2 29
15	21 13	24 44	2 19	22 60	23 60	1 10	8 20	0 50	7 58	0 50	14 11	1 3	8 3	2 29
16	21 2	20 53	1 1	18 24	23 55	1 15	7 51	0 46	7 40	0 49	14 12	1 3	8 4	2 30
17	20 51	15 38	0N21	12 38	23 50	1 21	7 21	0 41	7 21	0 48	14 13	1 2	8 4	2 30
18	20 39	9 28	1 42	6 11	23 43	1 26	6 52	0 37	7 3	0 47	14 14	1 2	8 4	2 30
19	20 26	2 50	2 56	0N31	23 35	1 30	6 22	0 32	6 44	0 46	14 15	1 2	8 5	2 30
20	20 14	3N49	3 56	7 2	23 26	1 35	5 52	0 27	6 26	0 46	14 16	1 1	8 5	2 31
21	20 1	10 8	4 41	13 4	23 15	1 39	5 23	0 22	6 7	0 45	14 17	1 1	8 6	2 31
22	19 47	15 48	5 8	18 18	23 2	1 43	4 53	0 17	5 48	0 44	14 18	1 1	8 6	2 31
23	19 34	20 32	5 17	22 29	22 48	1 47	4 23	0 11	5 30	0 43	14 20	1 1	8 6	2 32
24	19 20	24 8	5 9	25 26	22 33	1 50	3 53	0 6	5 11	0 42	14 21	1 0	8 6	2 32
25	19 5	26 24	4 45	27 1	22 16	1 53	3 22	0 0	4 52	0 41	14 23	1 0	8 7	2 32
26	18 50	27 16	4 8	27 10	21 58	1 56	2 52	0N 5	4 33	0 41	14 24	0 60	8 7	2 32
27	18 35	26 43	3 19	25 57	21 39	1 58	2 22	0 11	4 15	0 40	14 26	0 59	8 7	2 33
28	18 20	24 52	2 22	23 30	21 17	2 0	1 52	0 17	3 56	0 39	14 27	0 59	8 7	2 33
29	18 4	21 52	1 19	20 2	20 55	2 2	1 22	0 23	3 37	0 38	14 29	0 59	8 7	2 33
30	17 48	17 59	0 14	15 46	20 31	2 3	0 52	0 29	3 18	0 37	14 31	0 59	8 7	2 33
31	17S31	13N25	0S52	10N56	20S 5	2S 4	0S22	0N35	2S59	0S36	14N33	0S58	8S 7	2N34

Day	♅ Decl	♅ Lat	♆ Decl	♆ Lat	♇ Decl	♇ Lat
1	22N50	0N26	7S40	1N40	22N51	9N31
5	22 51	0 26	7 41	1 40	22 53	9 32
9	22 52	0 26	7 41	1 40	22 55	9 33
13	22 54	0 26	7 42	1 40	22 58	9 34
17	22 55	0 26	7 42	1 41	23 0	9 35
21	22 56	0 27	7 42	1 41	23 3	9 36
25	22 57	0 27	7 42	1 41	23 5	9 37
29	22N58	0N27	7S42	1N41	23N 8	9N37

☽ PHENOMENA

d	h	m	
8	10	9	☾
15	14	9	●
22	5	43	☽
29	23	45	○

d	h	° '
6	7	0
13	8	27S16
19	10	0
26	2	27N17

d	h	° '
2	22	0
10	10	5S15
16	18	0
23	0	5N17
30	5	0

d	h	
4	23	APOGEE
16	23	PERIGEE

VOID OF COURSE ☽

Last Aspect		☽ Ingress	
1	1pm54	1 ♌	9pm18
4	6am58	4 ♍	9am41
5	7pm22	6 ♎	10pm37
9	3am19	9 ♏	9am44
11	4am13	11 ♐	5pm15
13	3pm39	13 ♑	8pm55
15	5pm 1	15 ♒	9pm58
17	5pm18	17 ♓	10pm 7
19	10pm27	19 ♈	11pm 9
21	9pm19	22 ♉	2am21
24	3am20	24 ♊	8am21
26	11am45	26 ♋	5pm 7
28	10pm38	29 ♌	4am 6
31	11am 4	31 ♍	4pm36

DAILY ASPECTARIAN

1 Th	☽⚻☿	6am 8
	☽⚺♇	7 21
	☿#♅	8 43
	☽□♆	8 54
	☉#☽	8 55
	☽∥♇	10 12
	☽#☿	10 13
	☽∥♅	10 19
	☿#♇	10 30
	☽⚻♀	12pm21
	☽□♄	1 54
	☿△♇	4 29
	☉△♃	4 48
2 F	☉∥☿	0am 1
	☽⚻♂	0 33
	♂⚼♅	2 44
	♀△♄	5 27
	☿⚹♆	6 3
	☽⚼☿	3pm54
	♀#♃	4 35
	☽□♃	7 14
	☉⚻☽	9 43
3 S	☉#♇	2am25
	☽⚺♅	6 39
	☉#♅	7 45
	☽∥♃	1pm53
	☽#♀	4 4
	☽☌♇	7 16
	☿⚼♃	7 25
	☽⚹♆	9 1
4 Su	☽△☿	2am22
	☽⚹♄	2 23
	☉∠♀	2 25
	☿⚹♄	2 29
	☽#♂	3 54
	☉⚼☽	6 55
	☽☍♀	6 58
	☽∠♅	12pm57
	☽☍♂	5 15
	☽#♄	7 20
	☽#♆	8 28
5 M	☽∠♆	3am33
	♃SD	7 51
	☽△♃	8 2
	☽∠♄	9 3
	♀ ♓	11 11
	☉△☽	4pm20
	☽⚹♅	7 22
6 T	☽⚺♇	8am10
	☽⚺♆	10 4
	☿ ♑	1pm25
	☽⚼♃	2 30
	☽⚺♄	3 38
	♀⚼♅	7 0
	☽□☿	11 55
7 W	☉☍♅	2am11
	☽⚻♀	2 20
	☽⚻♂	10 16
	☽∠♇	2pm19
	☽∥♆	5 5
	☽∥♄	6 21
	☽⚻♃	8 36
8 Th	☽∥♂	3am47
	☽□♅	7 23
	☉□☽	10 9
	☽∥♀	10 25
	☽⚼♀	11 14
	☽⚼♂	5pm55
	☽⚹♇	7 51
	☽☌♆	9 48
	☽#♃	10 58
9 F	☽☌♄	3am19
	☽⚹☿	6pm55
	☽△♀	7 4
	☿⚹♀	11 31
10 S	☽△♂	0am33
	☽☍♃	6 35
	☽△♅	4pm28
	☉∥☽	5 37
11 Su	☉⚹☽	0am 4
	☽#♅	0 4
	☽#♇	0 29
	☽∠☿	2 28
	☽□♇	4 13
	☽⚺♆	6 10
	☽∥☿	8 42
	♂⚼♆	8 51
	☽⚺♄	11 27
	☿⚼♇	5pm31
	☽⚼♅	7 32
12 M	☉∠☽	5am 7
	☽□♀	6 48
	☽⚺☿	8 36
	☽∠♆	8 50
	☽□♂	10 15
	☽⚻♃	12pm42
	☽∠♄	2 0
	☽⚻♅	9 39
13 T	☉⚻♇	4am48
	♀⚼♆	8 4
	☽△♇	8 41
	☉⚺☽	8 59
	☽⚹♆	10 36
	☿⚹♂	12pm40
	☽⚼♃	2 23
	☽⚹♄	3 39
	☿△♃	10 10
14 W	☉□♆	7am34
	♂⚹♃	8 2
	☽⚼♇	9 41
	☽⚹♀	1pm51
	☽△♃	3 20
	☽⚹♂	3 43
	☽☌☿	5 18
	♂∥♄	6 1
	☽☍♅	11 33
15 Th	☽∥☿	5am33
	♂⚼♄	9 9
	♀⚹♃	10 1
	☽⚻♇	10 8
	☽#♇	12pm 2
	☽□♆	12 4
	☽#♅	12 32
	♀∥♄	1 51
	☉☌☽	2 9
	☽∠♀	4 13
	☽□♄	5 1
	☽∠♂	5 26
	♂∥♆	8 58
	☉∥☽	11 8
16 F	♀⚼♄	3am21
	♀∥♆	7 4
	☽□♃	3pm57
	☽⚺♀	6 14
	☽⚺♂	6 50
	☽⚺☿	11 23
	☽⚻♅	11 45
	♀∥♂	11 59
17 S	☿☍♅	2am48
	☽#♃	5 48
	☉□♄	9 24
	☽☍♇	10 16
	☽△♆	12pm16
	☽△♄	5 18
	☉⚺☽	5 51
	♀☌♂	8 7
	☽⚼♅	11 46
18 Su	☽∠☿	2am19
	☽∥♄	5 8
	☽∥♆	6 29
	☽∥♂	9 18
	☽∥♀	10 19
	☽⚼♆	12pm28
	☽⚹♃	4 23
	☽⚼♄	5 36
	☉∠☽	7 55
	☽☌♂	9 50
	☽☌♀	10 26
19 M	☽△♅	0am 2
	☽⚹☿	5 37
	☽⚻♇	10 52
	☽⚻♆	1pm 0
	☽∠♃	5 3
	☽⚻♄	6 16
	♀△♅	7 18
	☉⚹☽	10 27
20 T	☽#♀	7am 4
	☉ ♒	8 22
	☽#♂	9 15
	☽⚼♇	11 49
	♂△♅	1pm58
	☽#♆	2 32
	☽#♄	4 1
	☽⚺♃	6 16
21 W	☽□♅	1am56
	☽⚺♂	2 40
	☽⚺♀	4 36
	☿⚻♇	5 7
	☽△♇	1pm22
	☽□☿	2 27
	☽☍♆	3 41
	☽∥♃	5 19
	☽☍♄	9 19
	☿#♇	9 52
22 Th	☿□♆	1am 6
	☉□☽	5 43
	☽∠♂	6 12
	☽∠♀	8 52
	☿#♅	10 7
	☉#☽	6pm52
	☽☌♃	10 43
23 F	☽⚹♅	6am26
	☉∠♂	6 39
	☽⚹♂	10 36
	☽#☿	1pm14
	☽⚹♀	2 3
	☽∥♅	3 9
	☽∥♇	4 2
	☽□♇	6 34
	☽⚻♆	9 7
24 S	☿□♄	1am46
	☽⚻♄	3 9
	☽△☿	3 20
	☽∠♅	9 45
	☉△☽	4pm33
25 Su	♆SR	0am52
	☽⚼♆	0 54
	☽⚺♃	6 6
	☽⚼♄	7 7
	☽⚼☿	11 25
	☽⚺♅	1pm46
	☿ ♒	7 11
	♀⚻♇	9 18
	☽□♂	9 55
	☉⚼☽	11 17
26 M	☽⚹♇	2am34
	☽□♀	3 4
	☽△♆	5 21
	☽∠♃	10 49
	☽△♄	11 45
	☽⚻☿	8pm30
27 T	♀⚻♆	6am27
	☉⚻☽	6 48
	☽∠♇	7 30
	☽⚹♃	4pm 8
	☽☌♅	11 35
28 W	☽△♂	12pm 9
	☽⚺♇	12 57
	☽∥♇	2 53
	☽□♆	3 56
	☽∥♅	4 4
	☽△♀	7 5
	☽□♄	10 38
29 Th	♂⚻♇	0am22
	☽#☿	7 11
	☽☍☿	5pm12
	☽⚼♂	8 7
	☉☍☽	11 45
30 F	☉#☽	1am 7
	☽⚼♀	3 56
	☽□♃	4 13
	♀∠♃	7 34
	☽⚺♅	11 16
	♀⚻♄	1pm10
	☽∥♃	6 22
	♂⚻♆	11 53
31 S	☽☌♇	1am 1
	☿∠♂	4 4
	☽⚹♆	4 10
	☽⚻♂	4 28
	☽⚹♄	11 4
	☽⚻♀	1pm 7
	☽∠♅	5 33

FEBRUARY 1953

LONGITUDE

Day	Sid. Time	☉	☽	☽ 12 Hour	Mean ☊	True ☊	☿	♀	♂	♃	♄	♅	♆	♇
	h m s	° ' "	° ' "	° ' "	° '	° '	° '	° '	° '	° '	° '	° '	° '	° '
1	8 43 37	11♒ 50 25	3♍ 38 39	9♍ 32 44	12♒ 26	12♒ 21R	10♒ 26	28♓ 45	24♓ 39	12♉ 11	27♎ 17	15♋ 28R	23♎ 52R	22♌ 18R
2	8 47 33	12 51 17	15 26 46	21 21 4	12 23	12 21	12 9	29 45	25 24	12 16	27 17	15 25	23 52	22 16
3	8 51 30	13 52 8	27 16 3	3♎ 12 6	12 20	12 21	13 54	0♈ 45	26 10	12 21	27 18	15 23	23 52	22 15
4	8 55 27	14 52 58	9♎ 9 40	15 9 12	12 17	12 21	15 38	1 45	26 56	12 27	27 18	15 21	23 52	22 13
5	8 59 23	15 53 47	21 11 11	27 16 9	12 13	12 21	17 24	2 44	27 41	12 33	27 18R	15 19	23 51	22 12
6	9 3 20	16 54 35	3♏ 24 35	9♏ 37 3	12 10	12 20D	19 10	3 42	28 27	12 39	27 18	15 17	23 51	22 11
7	9 7 16	17 55 22	15 54 2	22 16 5	12 7	12 20	20 57	4 40	29 12	12 45	27 18	15 15	23 50	22 9
8	9 11 13	18 56 9	28 43 40	5♐ 17 12	12 4	12 21	22 45	5 38	29 58	12 52	27 17	15 13	23 50	22 8
9	9 15 9	19 56 54	11♐ 57 4	18 43 33	12 1	12 21	24 33	6 35	0♈ 43	12 58	27 17	15 11	23 49	22 6
10	9 19 6	20 57 38	25 36 49	2♑ 36 55	11 57	12 22	26 22	7 31	1 29	13 5	27 17	15 9	23 49	22 5
11	9 23 2	21 58 22	9♑ 43 45	16 57 3	11 54	12 22	28 11	8 27	2 14	13 12	27 16	15 7	23 48	22 3
12	9 26 59	22 59 4	24 16 21	1♒ 41 3	11 51	12 23	0♓ 0	9 23	3 0	13 19	27 15	15 5	23 48	22 2
13	9 30 56	23 59 45	9♒ 10 19	16 43 11	11 48	12 23R	1 50	10 17	3 45	13 26	27 15	15 3	23 47	22 0
14	9 34 52	25 0 24	24 18 33	1♓ 55 14	11 45	12 23	3 40	11 11	4 30	13 33	27 14	15 1	23 47	21 59
15	9 38 49	26 1 2	9♓ 31 57	17 7 28	11 42	12 22	5 30	12 5	5 16	13 41	27 13	14 59	23 46	21 57
16	9 42 45	27 1 39	24 40 33	2♈ 10 8	11 38	12 21	7 20	12 57	6 1	13 48	27 12	14 58	23 45	21 56
17	9 46 42	28 2 13	9♈ 35 12	16 54 56	11 35	12 19	9 9	13 49	6 46	13 56	27 10	14 56	23 44	21 54
18	9 50 38	29 2 46	24 8 43	1♉ 16 7	11 32	12 17	10 57	14 40	7 31	14 4	27 9	14 54	23 44	21 53
19	9 54 35	0♓ 3 17	8♉ 16 49	15 10 47	11 29	12 15	12 45	15 31	8 16	14 12	27 8	14 53	23 43	21 52
20	9 58 31	1 3 47	21 58 1	28 38 45	11 26	12 14D	14 31	16 20	9 2	14 20	27 6	14 51	23 42	21 50
21	10 2 28	2 4 15	5♊ 13 15	11♊ 41 53	11 23	12 14	16 16	17 9	9 47	14 29	27 5	14 49	23 41	21 49
22	10 6 25	3 4 40	18 5 6	24 23 23	11 19	12 15	17 58	17 57	10 32	14 37	27 3	14 48	23 40	21 47
23	10 10 21	4 5 4	0♋ 37 12	6♋ 47 4	11 16	12 16	19 38	18 44	11 17	14 46	27 1	14 47	23 39	21 46
24	10 14 18	5 5 26	12 53 29	18 56 57	11 13	12 18	21 14	19 30	12 2	14 54	26 59	14 45	23 39	21 44
25	10 18 14	6 5 46	24 57 54	0♌ 56 48	11 10	12 19	22 47	20 15	12 46	15 3	26 57	14 44	23 38	21 43
26	10 22 11	7 6 4	6♌ 54 3	12 50 2	11 7	12 20R	24 15	20 59	13 31	15 12	26 55	14 42	23 37	21 42
27	10 26 7	8 6 20	18 45 6	24 39 35	11 3	12 20	25 39	21 42	14 16	15 22	26 53	14 41	23 36	21 40
28	10 30 4	9♓ 6 34	0♍ 33 46	6♍ 27 55	11♒ 0	12♒ 18	26♓ 56	22♈ 23	15♈ 1	15♉ 31	26♎ 51	14♋ 40	23♎ 35	21♌ 39

DECLINATION and LATITUDE

Day	☉ Decl	☽ Decl	☽ Lat	☽ 12 Hr. Decl	☿ Decl	☿ Lat	♀ Decl	♀ Lat	♂ Decl	♂ Lat	♃ Decl	♃ Lat	♄ Decl	♄ Lat
1	17S15	8N23	1S56	5N45	19S38	2S 5	0N 8	0N41	2S40	0S36	14N34	0S58	8S 7	2N34
2	16 57	3 4	2 54	0 22	19 9	2 5	0 38	0 48	2 21	0 35	14 36	0 58	8 7	2 34
3	16 40	2S21	3 45	5S 3	18 39	2 5	1 8	0 54	2 3	0 34	14 38	0 58	8 7	2 34
4	16 22	7 42	4 26	10 19	18 7	2 4	1 37	1 1	1 44	0 33	14 40	0 57	8 6	2 35
5	16 5	12 51	4 56	15 16	17 34	2 3	2 7	1 7	1 25	0 32	14 42	0 57	8 6	2 35
6	15 46	17 34	5 14	19 42	16 59	2 1	2 37	1 14	1 6	0 31	14 44	0 57	8 6	2 35
7	15 28	21 39	5 17	23 23	16 23	1 59	3 6	1 21	0 47	0 31	14 46	0 56	8 6	2 36
8	15 9	24 50	5 5	25 59	15 46	1 56	3 35	1 28	0 28	0 30	14 49	0 56	8 5	2 36
9	14 50	26 48	4 36	27 13	15 7	1 53	4 4	1 35	0 9	0 29	14 51	0 56	8 5	2 36
10	14 31	27 14	3 52	26 49	14 26	1 49	4 33	1 42	0N 9	0 28	14 53	0 56	8 4	2 36
11	14 11	25 56	2 52	24 38	13 44	1 44	5 2	1 50	0 28	0 27	14 55	0 55	8 4	2 37
12	13 52	22 53	1 39	20 45	13 1	1 39	5 30	1 57	0 47	0 27	14 58	0 55	8 3	2 37
13	13 32	18 15	0 18	15 27	12 17	1 34	5 59	2 4	1 6	0 26	15 0	0 55	8 3	2 37
14	13 11	12 23	1N 6	9 8	11 31	1 27	6 27	2 12	1 25	0 25	15 3	0 55	8 2	2 37
15	12 51	5 46	2 25	2 19	10 45	1 21	6 55	2 19	1 43	0 24	15 5	0 54	8 2	2 38
16	12 30	1N 9	3 33	4N34	9 57	1 13	7 22	2 27	2 2	0 23	15 7	0 54	8 1	2 38
17	12 10	7 53	4 26	11 3	9 8	1 5	7 50	2 35	2 21	0 23	15 10	0 54	8 1	2 38
18	11 49	14 1	5 1	16 46	8 19	0 56	8 17	2 43	2 39	0 22	15 13	0 54	7 60	2 38
19	11 27	19 14	5 16	21 25	7 29	0 46	8 44	2 51	2 58	0 21	15 15	0 53	7 59	2 39
20	11 6	23 17	5 12	24 48	6 39	0 36	9 10	2 59	3 16	0 20	15 18	0 53	7 58	2 39
21	10 44	25 57	4 51	26 45	5 48	0 25	9 37	3 7	3 35	0 19	15 21	0 53	7 58	2 39
22	10 23	27 10	4 17	27 14	4 58	0 14	10 2	3 15	3 53	0 19	15 23	0 53	7 57	2 39
23	10 1	26 57	3 30	26 20	4 8	0 1	10 28	3 23	4 11	0 18	15 26	0 52	7 56	2 40
24	9 39	25 24	2 35	24 11	3 18	0N11	10 53	3 31	4 30	0 17	15 29	0 52	7 55	2 40
25	9 17	22 41	1 34	20 58	2 29	0 24	11 18	3 39	4 48	0 16	15 32	0 52	7 54	2 40
26	8 54	19 2	0 30	16 55	1 42	0 38	11 42	3 48	5 6	0 15	15 35	0 52	7 53	2 40
27	8 32	14 39	0S35	12 15	0 56	0 52	12 6	3 56	5 24	0 15	15 37	0 52	7 52	2 41
28	8S 9	9N44	1S39	7N 9	0S12	1N 6	12N30	4N 4	5N42	0S14	15N40	0S51	7S51	2N41

Day	♅ Decl	♅ Lat	♆ Decl	♆ Lat	♇ Decl	♇ Lat
1	22N59	0N27	7S42	1N42	23N10	9N38
5	23 0	0 26	7 41	1 42	23 12	9 38
9	23 1	0 26	7 40	1 42	23 14	9 38
13	23 2	0 26	7 39	1 42	23 17	9 39
17	23 3	0 26	7 38	1 43	23 19	9 39
21	23 3	0 26	7 36	1 43	23 21	9 39
25	23N 4	0N26	7S35	1N43	23N23	9N39

☽ PHENOMENA

d	h	m	
7	4	10	☾
14	1	11	●
20	17	45	☽
28	18	59	○

d	h	° '
2	14	0
9	18	27S17
15	20	0
22	8	27N15

d	h	
6	17	5S18
13	5	0
19	7	5N16
26	11	0

VOID OF COURSE ☽

Last Aspect		☽ Ingress		
2	9pm37	3	♎	5am32
5	12pm 3	5	♏	5pm21
7	11am46	8	♐	2am21
10	2am52	10	♑	7am32
12	4am51	12	♒	9am17
14	4am36	14	♓	8am58
15	8am36	16	♈	8am31
18	8am52	18	♉	9am51
19	11pm46	20	♊	2pm27
22	5pm 4	22	♋	10pm48
25	3am58	25	♌	10am 6
27	4pm28	27	♍	10pm51

d	h	
1	12	APOGEE
14	10	PERIGEE
28	14	APOGEE

DAILY ASPECTARIAN

1 Su	☽#♄	1am13
	☽#♆	3 9
	☉□♃	8 41
	☽∠♆	10 38
	☽⊼☿	4pm10
	☽△♃	5 29
	☽∠♄	5 35
	☉⊼☽	6 14
	☽⚹♅	11 57
2 M	☿□♃	1am34
	☽#♂	3 21
	♀ ♈	5 55
	☽∥♀	9 54
	☽⊻♇	1pm51
	☽⊻♆	5 6
	☽#♀	6 3
	☽☍♂	9 37
	☽∥♂	10 43
	☉☌☿	11 10
3 T	☽⊻♄	0am 3
	☽⚼♃	0 11
	☉⚼☽	3 33
	☽⚼☿	3 52
	☽☍♀	7 42
	☿⊼♅	8pm 6
	☽∠♇	8 7
	☽∥♆	11 54
4 W	☽∥♄	1am49
	♀#♂	3 6
	☽⊼♃	6 39
	☉⊼♅	10 41
	♂⊼♄	11 43
	☽□♅	12pm21
	☉△☽	12 31
	☽△☿	3 11
	♂∠♃	6 59
5 Th	☽⚹♇	2am 0
	♄SR	2 32
	☽☌♆	5 16
	☽#♃	9 13
	☿∠♀	10 0
	☽☌♄	12pm 3
	☽⊼♂	1 40
	☉∥☽	3 8
	☽∥☿	9 16
6 F	☽⊼♀	0am37
	☽☍♃	5pm57
	☽⚼♂	8 34
	☽△♅	10 45
7 S	☉□☽	4am10
	☽⚼♀	7 43
	☽#♅	9 19
	☽#♇	10 52
	☽□☿	11 5
	☽□♇	11 46
	☽⊻♆	2pm56
	☿☍♇	3 51
	☽⊻♄	9 21
8 Su	♂ ♈	1am 8
	☽△♂	2 25
	☽⚼♅	2 43
	☽△♀	1pm36
	☿△♆	2 26
	☽∠♆	6 24
	☉#♃	11 11
9 M	☽∠♄	0am36
	☽⊼♃	1 50
	☽⊼♅	5 43
	☿#♃	9 3
	♀⚼♇	12pm55
	☉⚹☽	3 16
	☽△♇	5 53
	☉∥☿	7 1
	☽⚹♆	8 53
10 T	☽⚹☿	1am29
	☽⚹♄	2 52
	☽⚼♃	4 17
	☽□♂	10 38
	☿△♄	12pm 4
	☉∠☽	7 1
	☽⚼♇	7 31
	☽□♀	9 43
11 W	☉☍♇	1am53
	☽△♃	5 49
	☽∠☿	6 35
	☽☍♅	8 56
	☽⊼♇	8pm21
	☽#♇	9 36
	☉⊻☽	9 45
	☽#♅	11 7
	☽□♆	11 14
	☿ ♓	11 57
12 Th	☿⚼♅	0am59
	☽□♄	4 51
	☽⊻☿	10 35
	☽⚹♂	2pm51
	☉△♆	7 6
13 F	☽⚹♀	1am53
	☽□♃	6 50
	☽⊼♅	9 20
	☽#♃	1pm43
	☽∠♂	4 1
	☽☍♇	8 20
	☉∥☽	8 46
	☽△♆	11 10
14 S	☉☌☽	1am11
	☽∠♀	3 9
	☽∥☿	3 42
	☽△♄	4 36
	☽⚼♅	8 59
	☽∥♄	3pm58
	☽☌☿	4 46
	☽⊻♂	4 55
	☽∥♆	5 22
	☿⊻♂	6 42
	☽#♀	8 12
	☽⚼♆	10 47
15 Su	☽⚼♄	4am14
	☽⊻♀	4 16
	☽⚹♃	6 36
	☽△♅	8 36
	☽#♂	1pm26
	☽⊼♇	7 38
	☽⊼♆	10 32
16 M	☽∥♂	3am13
	☉△♄	3 53
	☽⊼♄	4 1
	☉⊻☽	4 2
	☽∠♃	6 39
	♀#♆	1pm28
	☿⚼♆	6 40
	☽☌♂	7 11
	☽⚼♇	7 40
	☽#♆	11 5
	☽⊻☿	11 11
	☽∥♀	11 49
17 T	☽#♄	0am29
	♀⊻♃	3 46
	☽#☿	4 11
	♂⚼♇	4 18
	☉∠☽	6 3
	☽⊻♃	7 10
	☽☌♀	7 20
	☽□♅	8 43
	♀#♄	9 9
	☉#☽	3pm30
	☽△♇	8 14
	☽☍♆	11 18
18 W	☿#♀	0am41
	☽∠☿	3 28
	☽☍♄	5 2
	☽∥♃	5 7
	♀□♅	6 22
	☉⚹☽	8 52
	☿∥♄	9 28
	☿⚼♄	3pm46
	☉⚼♅	7 51
	☿∥♆	8 13
	☉ ♓	10 42
	☽⊻♂	11 59
19 Th	☽⚹☿	8am54
	☽☌♃	10 23
	☽⚹♅	11 27
	☽⊻♀	1pm24
	☿⚹♃	9 16
	☽∥♅	10 27
	☽□♇	11 46
20 F	☽∥♇	0am27
	☽⊼♆	3 6
	☽∠♂	3 54
	☿△♅	4 25
	☽⊼♄	9 12
	☽∠♅	2pm 9
	☉□☽	5 45
	☽∠♀	6 0
21 S	☽⚼♆	6am24
	☽⚹♂	8 56
	☉∠♀	9 15
	☽⚼♄	12pm41
	☽⊻♃	5 23
	☽⊻♅	5 49
	☿⊻♀	11 26
	☽⚹♀	11 43
	☽□☿	11 45
22 Su	☽⚹♇	7am 1
	☉#♀	10 17
	☽△♆	10 37
	☽△♄	5pm 4
	☽∠♃	10 19
	☿#♂	10 42
23 M	♃⚹♅	1am58
	☉△☽	7 20
	☽∠♇	11 56
	☽□♂	10pm11
24 T	☽☌♅	3am40
	☽⚹♃	4 2
	☿⊼♇	7 35
	☽□♀	1pm58
	☉⚼☽	3 34
	☽⊻♇	5 31
	☽∥♇	6 40
	☽△☿	7 0
	☽∥♅	9 8
	☽□♆	9 20
25 W	☽□♄	3am58
	☿⊼♆	1pm28
26 Th	☉⊼☽	0am26
	☽⚼☿	5 24
	☽△♂	2pm18
	☽⊻♅	3 46
	☽□♃	5 2
	☽∥♃	7 0
	♀△♇	11 13
27	☽☌♇	5am55
F	☽△♀	6 21
	☽⚹♆	9 49
	☉⚼♆	11 27
	☽∥♀	11 46
	♂□♅	1pm 5
	☽⊼☿	3 45
	☽⚹♄	4 28
	☽∠♅	10 11
	☿⊼♄	10 14
	☽⚼♂	10 49
28 S	☉#☽	7am56
	☽#♄	8 48
	☽#♆	10 7
	☽⚼♀	2pm44
	☽∠♆	4 16
	☽∥♂	5 34
	☉☍☽	6 59
	♂⊻♃	8 19
	☉∥♄	8 25
	☽∠♄	10 51

LONGITUDE

Day	Sid. Time	☉	☽	☽ 12 Hour	Mean ☊	True ☊	☿	♀	♂	♃	♄	♅	♆	♇
	h m s	° ' "	° ' "	° ' "	° '	° '	° '	° '	° '	° '	° '	° '	° '	° '
1	10 34 0	10♓ 6 47	12♍ 22 19	18♍ 17 11	10♒ 57	12♒ 16R	28♓ 8	23♈ 4	15♈ 46	15♉ 40	26♎ 48R	14♋ 39R	23♎ 33R	21♌ 37R
2	10 37 57	11 6 57	24 12 46	0♎ 9 17	10 54	12 11	29 13	23 43	16 30	15 50	26 46	14 38	23 32	21 36
3	10 41 54	12 7 6	6♎ 6 58	12 6 5	10 51	12 6	0♈ 10	24 22	17 15	15 59	26 43	14 37	23 31	21 35
4	10 45 50	13 7 13	18 6 52	24 9 36	10 48	12 1	1 0	24 58	18 0	16 9	26 41	14 36	23 30	21 33
5	10 49 47	14 7 19	0♏ 14 34	6♏ 22 6	10 44	11 55	1 42	25 34	18 44	16 19	26 38	14 35	23 29	21 32
6	10 53 43	15 7 23	12 32 32	18 46 13	10 41	11 50	2 15	26 8	19 29	16 29	26 35	14 34	23 28	21 31
7	10 57 40	16 7 25	25 3 34	1♐ 24 57	10 38	11 47	2 39	26 41	20 13	16 39	26 32	14 33	23 27	21 29
8	11 1 36	17 7 26	7♐ 50 47	14 21 29	10 35	11 45D	2 54	27 12	20 58	16 49	26 29	14 32	23 25	21 28
9	11 5 33	18 7 25	20 57 25	27 38 57	10 32	11 45	3 0R	27 42	21 42	17 0	26 26	14 31	23 24	21 27
10	11 9 29	19 7 23	4♑ 26 23	11♑ 19 58	10 28	11 45	2 56	28 10	22 26	17 10	26 23	14 31	23 23	21 25
11	11 13 26	20 7 19	18 19 48	25 25 56	10 25	11 47	2 45	28 36	23 11	17 21	26 20	14 30	23 22	21 24
12	11 17 23	21 7 13	2♒ 38 14	9♒ 56 23	10 22	11 48R	2 25	29 1	23 55	17 31	26 17	14 29	23 20	21 23
13	11 21 19	22 7 6	17 19 56	24 48 12	10 19	11 48	1 57	29 24	24 39	17 42	26 13	14 29	23 19	21 22
14	11 25 16	23 6 57	2♓ 20 20	9♓ 55 18	10 16	11 46	1 22	29 45	25 23	17 53	26 10	14 28	23 18	21 20
15	11 29 12	24 6 45	17 31 57	25 9 0	10 13	11 42	0 41	0♉ 4	26 7	18 4	26 7	14 28	23 16	21 19
16	11 33 9	25 6 32	2♈ 45 7	10♈ 19 0	10 9	11 37	29♓ 55	0 21	26 51	18 15	26 3	14 27	23 15	21 18
17	11 37 5	26 6 17	17 49 24	25 15 11	10 6	11 31	29 4	0 36	27 35	18 26	25 59	14 27	23 13	21 17
18	11 41 2	27 6 0	2♉ 35 23	9♉ 49 14	10 3	11 24	28 11	0 49	28 19	18 37	25 56	14 27	23 12	21 16
19	11 44 58	28 5 40	16 56 9	23 55 48	10 0	11 17	27 16	1 0	29 3	18 49	25 52	14 26	23 10	21 15
20	11 48 55	29 5 19	0♊ 48 2	7♊ 32 54	9 57	11 12	26 20	1 9	29 47	19 0	25 48	14 26	23 9	21 13
21	11 52 51	0♈ 4 56	14 10 36	20 41 48	9 54	11 9	25 26	1 15	0♉ 31	19 12	25 44	14 26	23 8	21 12
22	11 56 48	1 4 29	27 5 58	3♋ 24 37	9 50	11 7D	24 33	1 19	1 15	19 23	25 40	14 26D	23 6	21 11
23	12 0 45	2 4 1	9♋ 38 0	15 46 45	9 47	11 7	23 42	1 21R	1 59	19 35	25 36	14 26	23 5	21 10
24	12 4 41	3 3 30	21 51 30	27 52 54	9 44	11 8	22 55	1 20	2 43	19 47	25 32	14 26	23 3	21 9
25	12 8 38	4 2 57	3♌ 51 34	9♌ 48 7	9 41	11 9R	22 13	1 16	3 26	19 59	25 28	14 26	23 2	21 8
26	12 12 34	5 2 22	15 43 7	21 37 8	9 38	11 9	21 35	1 11	4 10	20 10	25 24	14 26	23 0	21 7
27	12 16 31	6 1 44	27 30 39	3♍ 24 6	9 34	11 8	21 3	1 2	4 53	20 22	25 20	14 26	22 58	21 6
28	12 20 27	7 1 5	9♍ 17 56	15 12 30	9 31	11 4	20 36	0 52	5 37	20 35	25 16	14 27	22 57	21 5
29	12 24 24	8 0 23	21 8 7	27 5 3	9 28	10 58	20 15	0 38	6 20	20 47	25 11	14 27	22 55	21 4
30	12 28 20	8 59 38	3♎ 3 32	9♎ 3 46	9 25	10 49	20 0	0 23	7 4	20 59	25 7	14 27	22 54	21 3
31	12 32 17	9♈ 58 52	15♎ 5 56	21♎ 10 9	9♒ 22	10♒ 38	19♓ 51	0♉ 4	7♉ 47	21♉ 11	25♎ 3	14♋ 28	22♎ 52	21♌ 3

DECLINATION and LATITUDE

Day	☉ Decl	☽ Decl	☽ Lat	☽ 12 Hr. Decl	☿ Decl	☿ Lat	♀ Decl	♀ Lat	♂ Decl	♂ Lat	♃ Decl	♃ Lat	♄ Decl	♄ Lat
1	7S47	4N30	2S38	1N48	0N29	1N21	12N53	4N13	6N 0	0S13	15N43	0S51	7S50	2N41
2	7 24	0S55	3 30	3S37	1 9	1 35	13 15	4 21	6 18	0 12	15 46	0 51	7 49	2 41
3	7 1	6 18	4 13	8 56	1 45	1 49	13 37	4 30	6 36	0 12	15 49	0 51	7 48	2 41
4	6 38	11 30	4 46	13 58	2 17	2 3	13 59	4 38	6 54	0 11	15 52	0 50	7 47	2 42
5	6 15	16 19	5 6	18 32	2 46	2 17	14 20	4 47	7 11	0 10	15 55	0 50	7 45	2 42
6	5 52	20 33	5 12	22 22	3 11	2 30	14 40	4 55	7 29	0 9	15 58	0 50	7 44	2 42
7	5 29	23 57	5 4	25 15	3 32	2 43	15 0	5 3	7 46	0 9	16 1	0 50	7 43	2 42
8	5 5	26 14	4 40	26 53	3 49	2 54	15 19	5 12	8 4	0 8	16 4	0 50	7 42	2 43
9	4 42	27 10	4 2	27 3	4 1	3 5	15 38	5 20	8 21	0 7	16 8	0 49	7 40	2 43
10	4 18	26 32	3 9	25 35	4 8	3 14	15 56	5 29	8 38	0 6	16 11	0 49	7 39	2 43
11	3 55	24 15	2 4	22 30	4 11	3 22	16 13	5 37	8 55	0 6	16 14	0 49	7 38	2 43
12	3 31	20 23	0 50	17 55	4 8	3 28	16 30	5 45	9 12	0 5	16 17	0 49	7 37	2 43
13	3 8	15 10	0N30	12 9	4 1	3 32	16 46	5 53	9 29	0 4	16 20	0 49	7 35	2 43
14	2 44	8 57	1 49	5 35	3 50	3 35	17 1	6 1	9 46	0 3	16 23	0 48	7 34	2 44
15	2 20	2 8	3 2	1N20	3 34	3 36	17 15	6 9	10 3	0 3	16 27	0 48	7 32	2 44
16	1 57	4N47	4 1	8 8	3 15	3 35	17 28	6 17	10 20	0 2	16 30	0 48	7 31	2 44
17	1 33	11 21	4 43	14 22	2 52	3 32	17 41	6 25	10 36	0 1	16 33	0 48	7 29	2 44
18	1 9	17 9	5 5	19 38	2 26	3 27	17 52	6 32	10 52	0 0	16 36	0 48	7 28	2 44
19	0 45	21 48	5 7	23 37	1 58	3 20	18 3	6 39	11 9	0N 0	16 40	0 47	7 26	2 44
20	0 22	25 4	4 51	26 7	1 28	3 11	18 13	6 46	11 25	0 1	16 43	0 47	7 25	2 45
21	0N 2	26 48	4 19	27 5	0 57	3 1	18 21	6 53	11 41	0 2	16 46	0 47	7 23	2 45
22	0 26	26 60	3 35	26 33	0 26	2 50	18 29	6 59	11 57	0 2	16 50	0 47	7 22	2 45
23	0 49	25 47	2 42	24 42	0S 6	2 37	18 35	7 6	12 13	0 3	16 53	0 47	7 20	2 45
24	1 13	23 21	1 42	21 45	0 37	2 23	18 40	7 11	12 28	0 4	16 56	0 47	7 19	2 45
25	1 37	19 56	0 39	17 55	1 7	2 9	18 44	7 17	12 44	0 4	16 60	0 46	7 17	2 45
26	2 0	15 44	0S25	13 25	1 36	1 54	18 46	7 22	12 60	0 5	17 3	0 46	7 16	2 45
27	2 24	10 59	1 27	8 27	2 3	1 38	18 48	7 26	13 15	0 6	17 6	0 46	7 14	2 45
28	2 47	5 51	2 25	3 11	2 28	1 22	18 47	7 30	13 30	0 7	17 10	0 46	7 12	2 46
29	3 11	0 30	3 17	2S13	2 50	1 7	18 46	7 34	13 45	0 7	17 13	0 46	7 11	2 46
30	3 34	4S54	4 1	7 34	3 11	0 51	18 43	7 36	13 60	0 8	17 17	0 45	7 9	2 46
31	3N57	10S10	4S34	12S41	3S28	0N36	18N38	7N39	14N15	0N 9	17N20	0S45	7S 7	2N46

Day	♅ Decl	♅ Lat	♆ Decl	♆ Lat	♇ Decl	♇ Lat
1	23N 5	0N26	7S33	1N43	23N25	9N39
5	23 5	0 26	7 31	1 43	23 27	9 39
9	23 5	0 26	7 29	1 43	23 28	9 39
13	23 6	0 26	7 27	1 44	23 30	9 39
17	23 6	0 26	7 25	1 44	23 31	9 38
21	23 6	0 26	7 23	1 44	23 32	9 38
25	23 6	0 26	7 21	1 44	23 33	9 38
29	23N 5	0N26	7S18	1N44	23N34	9N37

☽ PHENOMENA

d	h	m	
8	18	27	☾
15	11	5	●
22	8	11	☽
30	12	55	○

d	h	° '
1	20	0
9	3	27S10
15	7	0
21	15	27N 6
29	2	0
5	23	5S12
12	15	0
18	15	5N 9
25	15	0

VOID OF COURSE ☽

Last Aspect	☽ Ingress
2 11am 2	2 ♎ 11am41
4 4pm55	4 ♏ 11pm31
6 5pm13	7 ♐ 9am20
9 12pm31	9 ♑ 4pm10
11 5pm49	11 ♒ 7pm38
13 7pm47	13 ♓ 8pm17
15 11am 5	15 ♈ 7pm39
17 4pm38	17 ♉ 7pm45
19 8pm45	19 ♊ 10pm35
21 9pm19	22 ♋ 5am30
24 7am17	24 ♌ 4pm15
26 7pm35	27 ♍ 5am 4
28 11pm16	29 ♎ 5pm52

d	h	
14	23	PERIGEE
27	18	APOGEE

DAILY ASPECTARIAN

1 Su	☽⚹♅	4am37
	☽△♃	6 47
	☽⚻♂	7 20
	☉∥♆	2pm36
	☽∥☿	3 52
	♀☍♆	5 26
	☽⚺♇	6 43
	☽⚺♆	10 38
	☽⚻♀	10 57
2 M	☽#☿	1am 9
	☽⚺♄	5 9
	☽☍☿	11 2
	☽⚼♃	1pm33
	☉⚼♄	2 56
	☿ ♈	7 24
3 T	☽∠♇	0am55
	☽#♂	1 25
	☉∥☽	3 1
	☽∥♆	5 35
	☽∥♄	6 45
	☉⚻☽	1pm 8
	☉#♂	2 51
	☽□♅	4 59
	☽⚻♃	8 2
	☽☍♂	11 44
4 W	☿∠♃	6am 5
	☽⚹♇	6 49
	☽☌♆	10 41
	☽#♀	12pm59
	☽☍♀	2 19
	☽☌♄	4 55
	☉⚼☽	9 36
	☽#♃	9 52
5 Th	☽⚻☿	3am 0
	☉△♅	10 44
6 F	♂#♆	2am42
	☽△♅	3 54
	☉△☽	5 25
	☽☍♃	7 43
	☽⚼☿	9 24
	☽⚻♂	2pm12
	☽□♇	5 13
	☽#♅	5 13
	♀☍♄	6 17
	♂#♄	7 47
	☽#♇	8 3
	☽⚺♆	8 56
7 S	☽⚺♄	2am48
	☽⚻♀	3 12
	☽⚼♅	8 29
	☽△☿	2pm37
	☉⚹♃	3 17
	☽⚼♂	8 17
8 Su	☽∠♆	1am 4
	☽∠♄	6 43
	☽⚼♀	8 22
	☽⚻♅	12pm18
	♂△♇	4 0
	☽⚻♃	4 43
	☉□☽	6 27
9 M	☽△♇	0am53
	☽△♂	1 25
	☿SR	3 45
	☽⚹♆	4 24
	☽⚹♄	9 48
	☽△♀	12pm31
	☽⚼♃	7 57
	☽□☿	9 23
10 T	☽⚼♇	3am28
	☉#☿	9 1
	☽☍♅	5pm27
	☽△♃	10 18
11 W	♀∥♃	1am 7
	☉⚹☽	3 16
	☽⚻♇	5 12
	☽#♇	5 33
	♂☍♆	5 46
	☽#♅	8 12
	☽□♆	8 30
	☽□♂	8 39
	☽□♄	1pm28
	☽□♀	5 49
	☿∠♃	7 18
	☽⚹☿	11 38
12 Th	☉⚻♇	6am 9
	☉∠☽	6 10
	☽#♀	5pm31
	☽#♃	7 5
	☽⚻♅	7 23
	☽∠☿	11 24
13 F	☽□♃	0am36
	☽☍♇	6 28
	☉⚺☽	8 15
	☽△♆	9 36
	☽⚹♂	12pm22
	☽△♄	2 13
	☽⚼♅	7 27
	☽⚹♀	7 47
	☽#♂	9 6
	☽⚺☿	10 31
14 S	☉⚻♆	4am 9
	☽∥♄	5 0
	☽∥♆	5 25
	☽⚼♆	9 25
	☽∠♂	1pm23
	☽⚼♄	1 55
	☽#☿	6 49
	♀ ♉	6 58
	☽△♅	7 10
	☽∠♀	8 2
	☉∥☽	11 16
	♂☍♄	11 35
15 Su	☽⚹♃	0am51
	☽⚻♇	5 58
	☽⚻♆	9 1
	☉☌☽	11 5
	☽⚻♄	1pm28
	☿⚺♀	2 6
	☽⚺♂	2 13
	☉#☽	2 39
	☽∥☿	6 54
	☽☌☿	7 44
	☽⚺♀	8 8
	☿ ♓	9 2
16 M	☽∠♃	0am48
	☽⚼♇	5 37
	☽#♆	9 26
	☽#♄	9 43
	☽□♅	6pm36
	☽∥♂	9 1
	☉⚻♄	9 22
17 T	☽⚺♃	1am 0
	☽△♇	5 34
	☽☍♆	8 42
	☽☍♄	1pm 9
	☉⚺☽	2 21
	☽☌♂	4 38
	☽⚺☿	5 11
	☽☌♀	9 3
	☽∥♃	9 34
	☿⚺♂	9 54
18 W	☽∥♀	3am30
	☉☌☿	1pm37
	☽∠☿	4 35
	☉∠☽	5 1
	☽⚹♅	7 46
19 Th	☽☌♃	3am15
	☽□♇	7 21
	☽∥♅	8 18
	☽⚻♆	10 41
	☽∥♇	11 21
	☽⚻♄	3pm17
	☽⚹☿	4 41
	☉⚹☽	8 45
	☽∠♅	9 36
	☽⚺♂	10 7
20 F	☽⚺♀	0am37
	♂ ♉	6 54
	☽⚼♆	1pm 4
	☿⚻♄	3 11
	☽⚼♄	5 47
	☉ ♈	10 1
21 S	☽⚺♅	0am28
	☽∠♂	2 36
	☽∠♀	3 49
	☽⚺♃	9 22
	♄∥♆	12pm42
	☽⚹♇	12 56
	☽△♆	4 30
	☽□☿	7 30
	☽△♄	9 19
	☉∥☿	11 58
22 Su	♀☌♂	2am16
	☉⚺♀	6 5
	☽⚹♀	8 1
	☉□☽	8 11
	☽⚹♂	8 22
	☽∠♃	2pm 6
	☉⚺♂	4 6
	☽∠♇	5 19
	♅SD	9 27
23 M	♀SR	4am 3
	☽☌♅	9 22
	☽⚹♃	7pm49
	☿⚻♆	7 50
	☽∥♇	10 25
	☽⚺♇	10 36
24 T	☽△☿	2am 0
	☽∥♅	2 3
	☽□♆	2 22
	☽□♄	7 17
	☽□♀	6pm50
	☽□♂	11 6
25 W	☉△☽	0am25
	☽⚼☿	6 25
	☽∥♀	7 11
	☽∥♃	4pm58
	☽⚺♅	9 24
26 Th	☉∠♃	4am 6
	☽□♃	9 13
	☉⚼☽	9 35
	☽☌♇	10 58
	☽⚻☿	11 24
	☽∥♂	1pm26
	☽⚹♆	2 47
	☽⚹♄	7 35
	☿⚻♇	9 22
27 F	☉⚼♇	1am48
	☽∠♅	3 56
	☽△♀	7 5
	☽△♂	4pm 1
	☽#♆	5 15
	☽#♄	5 44
	☉⚻☽	6 56
	☽∠♆	9 16
	☿∠♂	11 46
28 S	☿⚹♃	1am 9
	☽∠♄	1 56
	☽⚹♅	10 27
	☉∥☽	12pm51
	☽⚼♀	1 5
	☽#☿	2 13
	☽☍☿	10 16
	☽△♃	11 16
	☽⚺♇	11 52
29 Su	☽⚼♂	0am27
	☽⚺♆	3 36
	☽⚺♄	8 8
	☽∥☿	3pm48
	☉#☽	5 34
	☽⚻♀	6 44
30 M	☽⚼♃	5am57
	☽∠♇	6 0
	♃□♇	8 17
	☽⚻♂	8 32
	☽∥♄	10 4
	☽∥♆	10 46
	☉☍☽	12pm55
	☽□♅	10 44
31 T	♀ ♈	4am50
	☽⚻☿	9 19
	☽⚹♇	11 44
	☽⚻♃	12pm15
	☽☌♆	3 19
	☽☌♄	7 30
	☽#♂	8 45

APRIL 1953

LONGITUDE

Day	Sid. Time	☉	☽	☽ 12 Hour	Mean ☊	True ☊	☿	♀	♂	♃	♄	♅	♆	♇
	h m s	° ' "	° ' "	° ' "	° '	° '	° '	° '	° '	° '	° '	° '	° '	° '
1	12 36 14	10♈ 58 4	27♎ 16 32	3♏ 25 14	9♒ 19	10♒ 27R	19♓ 47	29♈ 44R	8♉ 31	21♉ 24	24♎ 58R	14♋ 28	22♎ 51R	21♌ 2R
2	12 40 10	11 57 14	9♏ 36 20	15 49 58	9 15	10 15	19 49	29 21	9 14	21 36	24 54	14 29	22 49	21 1
3	12 44 7	12 56 22	22 6 16	28 25 23	9 12	10 5	19 56	28 56	9 57	21 49	24 49	14 29	22 47	21 0
4	12 48 3	13 55 28	4♐ 47 28	11♐ 12 45	9 9	9 57	20 9	28 29	10 40	22 1	24 45	14 30	22 46	20 59
5	12 52 0	14 54 32	17 41 27	24 13 48	9 6	9 51	20 27	28 0	11 23	22 14	24 40	14 31	22 44	20 59
6	12 55 56	15 53 35	0♑ 50 4	7♑ 30 31	9 3	9 48	20 49	27 29	12 7	22 26	24 36	14 31	22 42	20 58
7	12 59 53	16 52 36	14 15 25	21 5 1	9 0	9 47D	21 16	26 56	12 50	22 39	24 31	14 32	22 41	20 57
8	13 3 49	17 51 35	27 59 29	4♒ 58 59	8 56	9 48R	21 48	26 23	13 33	22 52	24 27	14 33	22 39	20 56
9	13 7 46	18 50 33	12♒ 3 33	19 13 7	8 53	9 48	22 23	25 47	14 16	23 5	24 22	14 34	22 38	20 56
10	13 11 43	19 49 28	26 27 28	3♓ 46 16	8 50	9 47	23 3	25 11	14 59	23 18	24 18	14 35	22 36	20 55
11	13 15 39	20 48 22	11♓ 8 58	18 34 53	8 47	9 44	23 46	24 34	15 41	23 31	24 13	14 36	22 34	20 54
12	13 19 36	21 47 14	26 3 9	3♈ 32 46	8 44	9 38	24 33	23 57	16 24	23 44	24 8	14 37	22 33	20 54
13	13 23 32	22 46 4	11♈ 2 37	18 31 31	8 40	9 29	25 23	23 19	17 7	23 57	24 4	14 38	22 31	20 53
14	13 27 29	23 44 53	25 58 17	3♉ 21 46	8 37	9 19	26 17	22 42	17 50	24 10	23 59	14 39	22 29	20 53
15	13 31 25	24 43 39	10♉ 40 54	17 54 46	8 34	9 8	27 13	22 4	18 32	24 23	23 55	14 40	22 28	20 52
16	13 35 22	25 42 23	25 2 37	2♊ 3 52	8 31	8 57	28 13	21 27	19 15	24 36	23 50	14 41	22 26	20 52
17	13 39 18	26 41 5	8♊ 58 11	15 45 24	8 28	8 48	29 15	20 50	19 58	24 50	23 45	14 43	22 24	20 51
18	13 43 15	27 39 46	22 25 32	28 58 46	8 25	8 41	0♈ 20	20 15	20 40	25 3	23 41	14 44	22 23	20 51
19	13 47 12	28 38 23	5♋ 25 26	11♋ 45 59	8 21	8 37	1 27	19 40	21 23	25 16	23 36	14 46	22 21	20 50
20	13 51 8	29 36 59	18 0 56	24 10 53	8 18	8 35	2 37	19 7	22 5	25 30	23 32	14 47	22 19	20 50
21	13 55 5	0♉ 35 33	0♌ 16 31	6♌ 18 28	8 15	8 35	3 49	18 36	22 48	25 43	23 27	14 48	22 18	20 50
22	13 59 1	1 34 4	12 17 28	18 14 10	8 12	8 35	5 4	18 6	23 30	25 57	23 22	14 50	22 16	20 49
23	14 2 58	2 32 33	24 9 15	0♍ 3 23	8 9	8 34	6 20	17 38	24 12	26 10	23 18	14 52	22 15	20 49
24	14 6 54	3 31 0	5♍ 57 11	11 51 12	8 6	8 32	7 39	17 12	24 55	26 24	23 13	14 53	22 13	20 49
25	14 10 51	4 29 25	17 45 59	23 42 1	8 2	8 27	9 0	16 48	25 37	26 38	23 9	14 55	22 11	20 49
26	14 14 47	5 27 48	29 39 43	5♎ 39 27	7 59	8 19	10 23	16 26	26 19	26 51	23 4	14 57	22 10	20 48
27	14 18 44	6 26 8	11♎ 41 32	17 46 11	7 56	8 9	11 48	16 7	27 1	27 5	23 0	14 58	22 8	20 48
28	14 22 41	7 24 27	23 53 38	0♏ 3 58	7 53	7 57	13 15	15 50	27 43	27 19	22 56	15 0	22 7	20 48
29	14 26 37	8 22 44	6♏ 17 17	12 33 37	7 50	7 43	14 44	15 35	28 25	27 32	22 51	15 2	22 5	20 48
30	14 30 34	9♉ 21 0	18♏ 52 57	25♏ 15 16	7♒ 46	7♒ 30	16♈ 15	15♈ 23	29♉ 7	27♉ 46	22♎ 47	15♋ 4	22♎ 4	20♌ 48

DECLINATION and LATITUDE

Day	☉	☽		☽ 12 Hr.	☿		♀		♂		♃		♄	
	Decl	Decl	Lat	Decl	Decl	Lat	Decl	Lat	Decl	Lat	Decl	Lat	Decl	Lat
1	4N20	15S 6	4S56	17S22	3S44	0N21	18N33	7N40	14N29	0N 9	17N23	0S45	7S 6	2N46
2	4 44	19 29	5 3	21 24	3 56	0 6	18 25	7 41	14 44	0 10	17 27	0 45	7 4	2 46
3	5 7	23 5	4 57	24 30	4 6	0S 8	18 16	7 41	14 58	0 11	17 30	0 45	7 2	2 46
4	5 30	25 37	4 36	26 25	4 14	0 22	18 6	7 41	15 12	0 11	17 33	0 45	7 1	2 46
5	5 53	26 52	4 0	26 57	4 19	0 35	17 54	7 39	15 26	0 12	17 37	0 45	6 59	2 46
6	6 15	26 38	3 12	25 57	4 22	0 47	17 40	7 37	15 40	0 13	17 40	0 44	6 57	2 46
7	6 38	24 52	2 12	23 24	4 22	0 59	17 26	7 34	15 54	0 13	17 44	0 44	6 56	2 46
8	7 1	21 35	1 2	19 26	4 20	1 10	17 10	7 30	16 8	0 14	17 47	0 44	6 54	2 46
9	7 23	16 59	0N12	14 16	4 16	1 21	16 52	7 25	16 21	0 14	17 50	0 44	6 52	2 46
10	7 45	11 20	1 27	8 12	4 9	1 31	16 34	7 20	16 34	0 15	17 54	0 44	6 50	2 46
11	8 7	4 57	2 38	1 36	4 1	1 41	16 14	7 13	16 48	0 16	17 57	0 44	6 49	2 46
12	8 30	1N47	3 39	5N 9	3 50	1 49	15 53	7 6	17 0	0 16	18 0	0 43	6 47	2 46
13	8 51	8 26	4 26	11 36	3 38	1 57	15 32	6 58	17 13	0 17	18 4	0 43	6 45	2 47
14	9 13	14 35	4 53	17 20	3 23	2 5	15 9	6 49	17 26	0 18	18 7	0 43	6 44	2 47
15	9 35	19 48	5 1	21 56	3 7	2 12	14 46	6 40	17 38	0 18	18 11	0 43	6 42	2 47
16	9 56	23 43	4 50	25 7	2 49	2 18	14 22	6 29	17 51	0 19	18 14	0 43	6 40	2 47
17	10 18	26 6	4 21	26 41	2 30	2 24	13 58	6 18	18 3	0 19	18 17	0 43	6 39	2 47
18	10 39	26 52	3 39	26 40	2 9	2 29	13 34	6 7	18 15	0 20	18 21	0 43	6 37	2 46
19	10 60	26 6	2 46	25 12	1 46	2 33	13 10	5 55	18 27	0 21	18 24	0 43	6 35	2 46
20	11 20	23 60	1 47	22 31	1 22	2 37	12 46	5 42	18 38	0 21	18 27	0 42	6 34	2 46
21	11 41	20 49	0 44	18 54	0 56	2 40	12 21	5 29	18 50	0 22	18 31	0 42	6 32	2 46
22	12 1	16 48	0S20	14 34	0 29	2 43	11 58	5 16	19 1	0 22	18 34	0 42	6 30	2 46
23	12 22	12 11	1 22	9 43	0 0	2 45	11 34	5 2	19 12	0 23	18 37	0 42	6 29	2 46
24	12 41	7 10	2 19	4 33	0N30	2 46	11 11	4 48	19 23	0 24	18 40	0 42	6 27	2 46
25	13 1	1 54	3 11	0S47	1 1	2 47	10 49	4 34	19 34	0 24	18 44	0 42	6 25	2 46
26	13 21	3S28	3 55	6 8	1 33	2 47	10 28	4 20	19 44	0 25	18 47	0 42	6 24	2 46
27	13 40	8 45	4 29	11 19	2 6	2 47	10 7	4 6	19 54	0 25	18 50	0 42	6 22	2 46
28	13 59	13 47	4 51	16 8	2 41	2 46	9 47	3 51	20 5	0 26	18 53	0 41	6 21	2 46
29	14 18	18 20	4 60	20 21	3 17	2 45	9 28	3 37	20 15	0 26	18 57	0 41	6 19	2 46
30	14N37	22S 9	4S54	23S42	3N53	2S43	9N10	3N23	20N24	0N27	18N60	0S41	6S18	2N46

Day	♅		♆		♇	
	Decl	Lat	Decl	Lat	Decl	Lat
1	23N 5	0N26	7S16	1N44	23N34	9N37
5	23 5	0 26	7 14	1 44	23 35	9 36
9	23 5	0 26	7 11	1 44	23 35	9 35
13	23 4	0 26	7 9	1 44	23 35	9 35
17	23 3	0 26	7 7	1 44	23 35	9 34
21	23 3	0 26	7 4	1 44	23 35	9 33
25	23 2	0 26	7 2	1 44	23 35	9 33
29	23N 1	0N25	6S59	1N44	23N34	9N32

☽ PHENOMENA

d	h	m	
7	4	59	☾
13	20	9	●
21	0	41	☽
29	4	21	○

d	h	° '
5	8	26S58
11	18	0
18	0	26N52
25	9	0

d	h	° '
2	1	5S 3
8	20	0
14	21	5N 1
21	17	0
29	3	4S60

VOID OF COURSE ☽

Last Aspect	☽ Ingress
1 4am40	1 ♏ 5am20
2 11pm26	3 ♐ 2pm59
5 6pm 9	5 ♑ 10pm29
7 9pm19	8 ♒ 3am28
9 9pm59	10 ♓ 5am49
11 9pm27	12 ♈ 6am19
13 8pm49	14 ♉ 6am32
16 5am49	16 ♊ 8am27
18 10am21	18 ♋ 1pm53
20 2pm51	20 ♌ 11pm27
23 4am11	23 ♍ 11am53
25 6pm15	26 ♎ 0am41
27 10pm 7	28 ♏ 11am52
30 8pm21	30 ♐ 8pm53

d	h	
12	7	PERIGEE
24	8	APOGEE

DAILY ASPECTARIAN

1 W	☿SD	3am34
	☽☍♀	4 40
	☽#♃	12pm14
	☽⚼☿	2 40
	☽#♀	6 0
	☽☍♂	11 14
2 Th	☉⚻☽	4am55
	☽△♅	9 24
	☽△☿	7pm49
	☽□♇	9 54
	☽☍♃	11 26
3 F	☽#♅	0am 4
	☽⚺♆	1 18
	☽#♇	3 59
	☽⚺♄	5 9
	☉⚼☽	12pm 1
	☽⚻♀	12 31
	☽⚼♅	2 2
4 S	☽∠♆	5am33
	☽∠♄	9 13
	☽⚻♂	11 39
	☉□♅	2pm10
	☽⚼♀	3 38
	☽⚻♅	6 7
	☉△☽	6 26
5	☽□☿	5am12
Su	☽△♇	6 2
	☽⚻♃	8 29
	☽⚹♆	9 15
	☽⚹♄	12pm44
	☽⚼♂	4 52
	☽△♀	6 9
6 M	♀∥♃	0am25
	☿⚻♇	7 55
	☽⚼♇	9 13
	☽⚼♃	12pm 4
	☽△♂	9 20
7 T	☽☍♅	0am30
	♃⚻♆	2 46
	☉□☽	4 59
	☽#♇	10 39
	☽⚻♇	11 45
	☽⚹☿	12pm48
	☽#♅	2 19
	☽□♆	2 45
	☽△♃	2 58
	☉#♄	5 20
	☽□♄	5 54
	☽□♀	9 19
8 W	☉#♆	12pm 1
	☽∠☿	3 44
	☽#♃	8 2
9 Th	☽#♀	0am35
	☽#♂	2 48
	☽□♂	3 54
	☽⚻♅	4 13
	☿⚻♆	8 34
	♂⚹♅	10 25
	☉⚹☽	12pm12
	☽☍♇	2 50
	☽△♆	5 38
	☽⚺☿	6 5
	☽□♃	6 42
	☽△♄	8 27
	☽⚹♀	9 59
	♀∥♂	11 25
10 F	☽⚼♅	5am 8
	☿⚹♃	12pm10
	☉#☽	12 56
	☉∠☽	2 42
	☽∥♆	3 50
	☽∥♄	5 9
	☽⚼♆	6 12
	☽⚼♄	8 53
	☽∠♀	9 33
11 S	☉△♇	2am27
	☽∥☿	3 26
	☽△♅	5 35
	☽⚹♂	7 43
	☿⚻♄	12pm43
	☿⚺♀	1 53
	♀☍♄	3 42
	☽⚻♇	3 44
	☉⚺☽	4 40
	☽⚻♆	6 23
	☽⚹♃	8 13
	☽⚺♀	8 46
	☽⚻♄	8 57
	☽☌☿	9 27
12 Su	♀⚺♃	6am16
	☽#☿	7 6
	☽∠♂	9 0
	☽⚼♇	3pm45
	☽#♄	5 50
	☉☍♆	6 0
	☽#♆	7 15
	☽∠♃	8 36
13 M	☉∥☽	1am38
	☽□♅	5 45
	☉☌♀	8 16
	♃⚻♄	9 20
	☽⚺♂	10 14
	☽△♇	3pm47
	☽☍♆	6 23
	☽☌♀	6 55
	☉☌☽	8 9
	☽☍♄	8 49
	☽⚺♃	9 3
14 T	☽⚺☿	0am32
	☽∥♀	2 14
	☉☍♄	5 25
	♀☍♆	8 9
	☽∥♂	12pm59
	☉⚺♃	1 15
	☽∥♃	3 52
15 W	☽∠☿	2am43
	☽⚹♅	6 37
	☽☌♂	1pm44
	☽□♇	4 57
	☽⚺♀	6 11
	☽∥♅	7 18
	☽⚻♆	7 36
	☽⚻♄	9 58
	☽∥♇	11 4
	☽☌♃	11 15
16 Th	☉⚺☽	1am13
	☽⚹☿	5 49
	☽∠♅	7 56
	☽∠♀	6pm46
	☽⚼♆	9 16
	♀△♇	11 23
	☽⚼♄	11 38
17 F	☉∠☽	5am 9
	☽⚺♅	10 10
	♀⚺♂	4pm 8
	☿ ♈	4 48
	☽⚹♀	8 14
	☽⚺♂	8 39
	☽⚹♇	9 9
	☽△♆	11 55
18 S	☽△♄	2am16
	☽⚺♃	4 52
	♂□♇	5 54
	☉⚹☽	10 21
	☽□☿	3pm52
	♂∥♃	4 29
19 Su	☽∠♇	0am47
	☽∠♂	1 54
	☽∠♃	9 20
	☽☌♅	5pm46
20 M	☽□♀	2am 3
	☽∥♇	3 33
	☽⚺♇	5 28
	♂⚻♆	7 44
	☽∥♅	7 57
	☽□♆	8 21
	☽⚹♂	8 24
	☉ ♉	9 26
	☽□♄	10 39
	☽⚹♃	2pm51
21	☉□☽	0am41
T	☽△☿	7 50
	☽∥♂	11 51
	☽∥♃	2pm 6
	♂⚻♄	8 5
	☉∥♀	9 59
22 W	☽⚺♅	5am 8
	☽△♀	11 16
	☿⚼♇	2pm20
	☽☌♇	5 14
	☽⚼☿	5 35
	☽⚹♆	8 8
	☽⚹♄	10 16
	☉∥☽	11 14
23 Th	☽□♂	0am 7
	☽∥♀	3 19
	☽□♃	4 11
	☽∠♅	11 38
	☽⚼♀	4pm37
	☉△☽	6 36
24 F	☽#♆	0am36
	☽∠♆	2 34
	☽#♄	3 20
	☽⚻☿	3 54
	☽∠♄	4 35
	☽⚹♅	6pm12
	☽⚻♀	10 6
25 S	☽∥☿	3am37
	☉⚼☽	3 48
	☽⚺♇	6 10
	☽⚺♆	8 56
	☽⚺♄	10 49
	☽#☿	2pm28
	☽△♂	4 51
	☽△♃	6 15
26 Su	☽∠♇	12pm18
	☉⚻☽	12 38
	☽∥♄	1 10
	☽∥♆	4 2
27 M	☽☍☿	0am16
	☽⚼♂	0 41
	☽⚼♃	0 47
	♂☌♃	3 3
	☿∠♃	5 25
	☽#♀	5 58
	☽□♅	6 30
	☿∠♂	6 56
	☽☍♀	8 32
	☽⚹♇	5pm57
	☽☌♆	8 31
	☽☌♄	10 7
28 T	☉#☽	1am 7
	☽⚻♃	6 47
	☽⚻♂	7 54
29 W	☽#♃	3am35
	☉☍☽	4 21
	☿□♅	4 48
	☿☌♀	11 45
	☽#♂	11 51
	☽△♅	4pm45
	☽⚻♀	5 28
	☽⚻☿	6 21
30 Th	☽□♇	3am37
	☽⚺♆	5 59
	☽#♅	6 26
	☽⚺♄	7 19
	☽#♇	10 54
	☽☍♃	5pm 1
	☽☍♂	8 21
	☽⚼♅	9 3
	☽⚼♀	9 19

LONGITUDE

Day	Sid. Time h m s	☉ ° ' "	☽ ° ' "	☽ 12 Hour ° ' "	Mean ☊ ° '	True ☊ ° '	☿ ° '	♀ ° '	♂ ° '	♃ ° '	♄ ° '	♅ ° '	♆ ° '	♇ ° '
1	14 34 30	10♉ 19 13	1♐ 40 31	8♐ 8 39	7♒ 43	7♒ 17R	17♈ 48	15♈ 13R	29♉ 49	28♉ 0	22♎ 43R	15♋ 6	22♎ 2R	20♌ 48R
2	14 38 27	11 17 25	14 39 37	21 13 23	7 40	7 7	19 23	15 6	0♊ 31	28 14	22 38	15 8	22 0	20 48D
3	14 42 23	12 15 36	27 49 56	4♑ 29 16	7 37	7 0	21 0	15 1	1 13	28 27	22 34	15 10	21 59	20 48
4	14 46 20	13 13 45	11♑ 11 27	17 56 31	7 34	6 56	22 38	14 58D	1 55	28 41	22 30	15 12	21 57	20 48
5	14 50 16	14 11 52	24 44 35	1♒ 35 42	7 31	6 54D	24 19	14 58	2 37	28 55	22 26	15 14	21 56	20 48
6	14 54 13	15 9 58	8♒ 30 0	15 27 31	7 27	6 54R	26 1	15 1	3 18	29 9	22 22	15 16	21 54	20 48
7	14 58 10	16 8 3	22 28 18	29 32 20	7 24	6 54	27 45	15 5	4 0	29 23	22 18	15 19	21 53	20 48
8	15 2 6	17 6 7	6♓ 39 30	13♓ 49 38	7 21	6 53	29 31	15 12	4 42	29 37	22 14	15 21	21 51	20 48
9	15 6 3	18 4 8	21 2 24	28 17 23	7 18	6 50	1♉ 19	15 21	5 23	29 51	22 10	15 23	21 50	20 48
10	15 9 59	19 2 9	5♈ 34 3	12♈ 51 43	7 15	6 44	3 9	15 32	6 5	0♊ 5	22 6	15 26	21 49	20 48
11	15 13 56	20 0 8	20 9 39	27 26 59	7 12	6 36	5 1	15 46	6 46	0 19	22 2	15 28	21 47	20 49
12	15 17 52	20 58 6	4♉ 42 50	11♉ 56 20	7 8	6 26	6 55	16 1	7 28	0 33	21 58	15 30	21 46	20 49
13	15 21 49	21 56 2	19 6 35	26 12 49	7 5	6 14	8 51	16 18	8 9	0 47	21 55	15 33	21 44	20 49
14	15 25 45	22 53 57	3♊ 14 19	10♊ 10 31	7 2	6 4	10 48	16 37	8 51	1 1	21 51	15 35	21 43	20 50
15	15 29 42	23 51 51	17 1 0	23 45 29	6 59	5 54	12 47	16 58	9 32	1 15	21 47	15 38	21 42	20 50
16	15 33 39	24 49 43	0♋ 23 52	6♋ 56 10	6 56	5 48	14 48	17 21	10 13	1 29	21 44	15 40	21 40	20 50
17	15 37 35	25 47 33	13 22 33	19 43 18	6 52	5 43	16 51	17 45	10 55	1 43	21 41	15 43	21 39	20 51
18	15 41 32	26 45 22	25 58 49	2♌ 9 34	6 49	5 41D	18 56	18 11	11 36	1 57	21 37	15 46	21 38	20 51
19	15 45 28	27 43 9	8♌ 16 7	14 19 4	6 46	5 41	21 2	18 39	12 17	2 11	21 34	15 48	21 37	20 51
20	15 49 25	28 40 54	20 19 2	26 16 42	6 43	5 41R	23 9	19 8	12 58	2 25	21 31	15 51	21 35	20 52
21	15 53 21	29 38 38	2♍ 12 43	8♍ 7 47	6 40	5 41	25 18	19 38	13 39	2 40	21 28	15 54	21 34	20 52
22	15 57 18	0♊ 36 20	14 2 32	19 57 38	6 37	5 40	27 28	20 10	14 20	2 54	21 25	15 57	21 33	20 53
23	16 1 14	1 34 0	25 53 40	1♎ 51 15	6 33	5 37	29 38	20 44	15 1	3 8	21 22	15 59	21 32	20 53
24	16 5 11	2 31 39	7♎ 50 52	13 53 2	6 30	5 32	1♊ 50	21 18	15 42	3 22	21 19	16 2	21 31	20 54
25	16 9 8	3 29 17	19 58 8	26 6 33	6 27	5 24	4 1	21 54	16 23	3 36	21 16	16 5	21 29	20 55
26	16 13 4	4 26 53	2♏ 18 33	8♏ 34 19	6 24	5 15	6 13	22 31	17 4	3 50	21 13	16 8	21 28	20 55
27	16 17 1	5 24 28	14 54 1	21 17 41	6 21	5 5	8 25	23 9	17 45	4 4	21 10	16 11	21 27	20 56
28	16 20 57	6 22 1	27 45 19	4♐ 16 48	6 17	4 54	10 36	23 49	18 26	4 18	21 8	16 14	21 26	20 57
29	16 24 54	7 19 34	10♐ 52 2	17 30 48	6 14	4 45	12 47	24 29	19 6	4 32	21 5	16 17	21 25	20 57
30	16 28 50	8 17 5	24 12 53	0♑ 58 2	6 11	4 37	14 56	25 11	19 47	4 46	21 3	16 20	21 24	20 58
31	16 32 47	9♊ 14 35	7♑ 46 0	14♑ 36 32	6♒ 8	4♒ 32	17♊ 5	25♈ 53	20♊ 28	5♊ 0	21♎ 1	16♋ 23	21♎ 23	20♌ 59

DECLINATION and LATITUDE

Day	☉ Decl	☽ Decl	☽ Lat	☽ 12 Hr. Decl	☿ Decl	☿ Lat	♀ Decl	♀ Lat	♂ Decl	♂ Lat	♃ Decl	♃ Lat	♄ Decl	♄ Lat
1	14N55	24S58	4S34	25S55	4N31	2S40	8N54	3N 9	20N34	0N28	19N 3	0S41	6S16	2N46
2	15 13	26 31	3 59	26 45	5 10	2 37	8 38	2 55	20 43	0 28	19 6	0 41	6 15	2 46
3	15 31	26 36	3 11	26 4	5 49	2 34	8 23	2 41	20 53	0 29	19 9	0 41	6 13	2 46
4	15 49	25 9	2 11	23 52	6 30	2 30	8 10	2 27	21 2	0 29	19 13	0 41	6 12	2 45
5	16 6	22 14	1 4	20 16	7 11	2 25	7 58	2 14	21 10	0 30	19 16	0 41	6 10	2 45
6	16 23	18 0	0N 8	15 29	7 53	2 20	7 46	2 1	21 19	0 30	19 19	0 41	6 9	2 45
7	16 40	12 45	1 21	9 49	8 35	2 14	7 36	1 48	21 27	0 31	19 22	0 40	6 8	2 45
8	16 57	6 44	2 30	3 34	9 19	2 8	7 27	1 36	21 36	0 31	19 25	0 40	6 6	2 45
9	17 13	0 19	3 31	2N56	10 2	2 1	7 20	1 23	21 44	0 32	19 28	0 40	6 5	2 45
10	17 29	6N10	4 18	9 19	10 47	1 54	7 13	1 11	21 52	0 32	19 31	0 40	6 4	2 45
11	17 45	12 20	4 49	15 11	11 31	1 47	7 7	0 60	21 59	0 33	19 34	0 40	6 2	2 45
12	18 0	17 49	5 1	20 10	12 16	1 39	7 3	0 48	22 7	0 33	19 37	0 40	6 1	2 44
13	18 15	22 13	4 54	23 54	13 2	1 30	6 59	0 37	22 14	0 34	19 40	0 40	5 60	2 44
14	18 30	25 12	4 28	26 6	13 47	1 21	6 57	0 27	22 21	0 34	19 43	0 40	5 59	2 44
15	18 45	26 36	3 48	26 41	14 32	1 12	6 55	0 16	22 28	0 35	19 46	0 40	5 57	2 44
16	18 59	26 22	2 56	25 42	15 17	1 3	6 54	0 6	22 34	0 35	19 49	0 40	5 56	2 44
17	19 13	24 41	1 56	23 23	16 2	0 53	6 55	0S 4	22 41	0 36	19 52	0 39	5 55	2 44
18	19 26	21 48	0 51	19 59	16 46	0 43	6 56	0 13	22 47	0 36	19 55	0 39	5 54	2 43
19	19 39	17 59	0S14	15 48	17 30	0 32	6 58	0 22	22 53	0 37	19 58	0 39	5 53	2 43
20	19 52	13 30	1 17	11 4	18 13	0 22	7 1	0 31	22 59	0 37	20 1	0 39	5 52	2 43
21	20 5	8 34	2 17	5 59	18 54	0 11	7 4	0 40	23 4	0 38	20 4	0 39	5 51	2 43
22	20 17	3 22	3 10	0 43	19 35	0 1	7 9	0 48	23 10	0 38	20 6	0 39	5 50	2 43
23	20 29	1S57	3 55	4S37	20 14	0N10	7 14	0 56	23 15	0 39	20 9	0 39	5 49	2 43
24	20 40	7 14	4 30	9 49	20 52	0 20	7 20	1 4	23 20	0 39	20 12	0 39	5 48	2 42
25	20 51	12 20	4 53	14 44	21 27	0 30	7 26	1 11	23 24	0 40	20 15	0 39	5 47	2 42
26	21 2	17 1	5 4	19 9	22 1	0 40	7 34	1 18	23 29	0 40	20 17	0 39	5 47	2 42
27	21 13	21 5	4 60	22 47	22 32	0 50	7 41	1 25	23 33	0 41	20 20	0 39	5 46	2 42
28	21 23	24 13	4 41	25 21	23 1	0 60	7 50	1 31	23 37	0 41	20 23	0 38	5 45	2 42
29	21 32	26 9	4 6	26 34	23 28	1 8	7 59	1 37	23 41	0 42	20 25	0 38	5 44	2 41
30	21 42	26 37	3 18	26 16	23 52	1 17	8 8	1 43	23 45	0 42	20 28	0 38	5 44	2 41
31	21N51	25S31	2S18	24S23	24N13	1N25	8N19	1S49	23N49	0N42	20N31	0S38	5S43	2N41

Day	♅ Decl	♅ Lat	♆ Decl	♆ Lat	♇ Decl	♇ Lat
1	23N 1	0N25	6S58	1N44	23N34	9N31
5	22 60	0 25	6 56	1 44	23 33	9 31
9	22 59	0 25	6 54	1 44	23 32	9 30
13	22 57	0 25	6 52	1 44	23 31	9 29
17	22 56	0 25	6 50	1 44	23 30	9 28
21	22 55	0 25	6 48	1 44	23 29	9 27
25	22 54	0 25	6 47	1 44	23 27	9 27
29	22N52	0N25	6S45	1N43	23N26	9N26

☽ PHENOMENA

d	h	m	
6	12	21	☾
13	5	6	●
20	18	21	☽
28	17	3	○

d	h	° '
2	13	26S45
9	1	0
15	9	26N42
22	15	0
29	19	26S39

d	h	° '
5	21	0
12	3	5N 1
18	19	0
26	6	5S 4

VOID OF COURSE ☽

Last Aspect		☽ Ingress		
2	2pm30	3	♑	3am55
5	7am27	5	♒	9am13
7	11am56	7	♓	12pm47
9	2pm49	9	♈	2pm49
11	3am 4	11	♉	4pm12
13	5am 6	13	♊	6pm27
15	8am27	15	♋	11pm17
18	1am37	18	♌	7am47
20	6pm21	20	♍	7pm31
22	3am52	23	♎	8am16
25	3am59	25	♏	7pm33
27	11am20	28	♐	4am 8
30	1am49	30	♑	10am17

d	h	
10	5	PERIGEE
22	2	APOGEE

DAILY ASPECTARIAN

1 F
☽⚼☿ 2am23
♂ ♊ 6 8
☽∠♆ 9 55
♂∠♅ 10 4
☽∠♄ 11 8
♀∠♂ 11 27
☉⚻☽ 5pm18
♀□♅ 5 32

2 S
☽△♀ 0am48
☽⚻♅ 0 52
☽△☿ 9 51
☽△♇ 11 13
☽⚹♆ 1pm24
☽⚹♄ 2 30
♇SD 8 31
☿△♇ 9 4
☉⚼☽ 10 53

3 Su
☽⚻♃ 1am 9
☽⚻♂ 6 27
☿#♄ 1pm52
☿☍♆ 2 15
☽⚼♇ 2 21
☿☍♄ 10 5

4 M
☉△☽ 3am55
☽⚼♃ 4 32
☽□♀ 6 44
☽☍♅ 7 10
☽⚼♂ 10 44
♀SD 12pm31
☽#♇ 2 29
☿#♆ 3 39
☽⚻♇ 5 3
☽#♅ 6 41
☽□♆ 7 4
☽□♄ 7 57
☽□☿ 11 8

5 T
☽#♂ 6am27
☽△♃ 7 27
☽△♂ 2pm30
☽#♃ 5 18
☉⚺♀ 7 55
☿∥♀ 9 10

6 W
☉⚹♅ 2am47
☉#☽ 7 25
☽⚹♀ 11 17
☽⚻♅ 11 43
☉□☽ 12pm21
☽☍♇ 9 9
☽△♆ 11 0
☽△♄ 11 42

7 Th
☽⚹☿ 10am15
☽□♃ 11 56
☽∠♀ 1pm 1
☽⚼♅ 1 20
☽#☿ 3 4
☽□♂ 8 32
☽#♀ 9 10
☽∥♆ 11 21

8 F
☽⚼♆ 0am20
☽⚼♄ 0 57
☿⚺♃ 1 26
☽∥♄ 2 26
☿ ♉ 6 24
☽⚺♀ 2pm26
☽△♅ 2 35
☽∠☿ 3 2
☉⚹☽ 6 43
☽⚻♇ 11 37

9 S
☽⚻♆ 1am19
☽⚻♄ 1 51
♀□♅ 6 7
☽⚹♃ 2pm49
♃ ♊ 3 34
☽⚺☿ 7 27
☉∠☽ 9 18
☽#♄ 11 37

10 Su
☽⚼♇ 0am24
☽⚹♂ 0 53
☽#♆ 2 44
☽∥♀ 3 54
☽∠♃ 3pm54
☽□♅ 4 16
☽☌♀ 4 39
☽∥☿ 8 14
☉⚺☽ 11 43

11 M
♂⚼♆ 0am27
☽△♇ 1 4
☽☍♆ 2 40
☽∠♂ 2 47
☽☍♄ 3 4
♂⚼♄ 8 21
☽⚺♃ 5pm 0
♃∠♅ 6 44
☉□♇ 8 11

12 T
☉∥☽ 0am57
☽☌☿ 4 12
☽⚺♂ 4 47
☽∥♃ 9 10
☿⚺♂ 10 44
☽⚹♅ 6pm 1
☽⚺♀ 7 11
☉⚻♆ 7 17
☉⚻♄ 11 28

13 W
☽∥♂ 0am 9
☽□♇ 2 53
☽⚻♆ 4 25
☽⚻♄ 4 42
☽∥♅ 5 1
☉☌☽ 5 6
☽∥♇ 9 7
☽∠♅ 7pm27
☽☌♃ 8 8
☽∠♀ 9 10

14 Th
☽⚼♆ 5am59
☽⚼♄ 6 12
☽☌♂ 10 12
☽⚺☿ 3pm18
☽⚺♅ 9 33
☽⚹♀ 11 55

15 F
☽⚹♇ 6am46
☽△♆ 8 18
☽△♄ 8 27
☉⚺☽ 1pm 8
☽∠☿ 10 44

16 S
☽⚺♃ 2am 1
☽∠♇ 9 59
☿⚹♅ 10 25
☉∠☽ 6pm46
☽⚺♂ 7 8

17 Su
☽☌♅ 4am25
☽∠♃ 6 25
☽⚹☿ 7 50
☽□♀ 8 33
☽∥♇ 11 0
☿⚺♀ 1pm 9
☽⚺♇ 2 9
☽∥♅ 3 34
☽□♆ 3 39
☽□♄ 3 40
☽∥♂ 4 59
♄☌♆ 5 22

18 M
☽∠♂ 1am16
☉⚹☽ 1 37
☽⚹♃ 11 50
☽∥♃ 12pm18
☉∥☽ 2 35
☿□♇ 10 2

19 T
☽∥☿ 2am21
☿⚻♄ 5 56
☿⚻♆ 6 31
☽⚹♂ 8 26
♂∥♅ 10 32
☽⚺♅ 3pm 2
☽△♀ 9 31

20 W
☽☌♇ 1am 6
☽⚹♄ 2 23
☽⚹♆ 2 33
☽□☿ 6 57
☉□☽ 6pm21
☉∥♃ 8 50
☽∠♅ 9 20

21 Th
☽□♃ 0am55
☽⚼♀ 5 9
☽∥♀ 6 53
☽#♆ 8 14
☽∠♄ 8 34
☽∠♆ 8 49
☉ ♊ 8 53
☽#♄ 12pm40

22 F
☽□♂ 0am38
☽⚹♅ 3 52
☉∠♅ 8 53
☽⚻♀ 1pm 2
☽⚺♇ 1 53
☽⚺♄ 2 52
☽⚺♆ 3 11
☿∥♃ 8 37

23 S
☿ ♊ 3am59
♀△♇ 6 59
☽△☿ 9 14
☉△☽ 12pm25
☉∥☿ 1 21
☽△♃ 2 51
☿∠♅ 3 11
☽∥♄ 5 26
☽∠♇ 8 6
☽∥♆ 9 55

24 Su
♀☍♄ 0am12
☽#♀ 0 25
♀☍♆ 8 1
♂⚺♅ 12pm37
☉☌☿ 1 39
☽□♅ 4 19
☽△♂ 4 32
☿☌♃ 6 50
☉⚼☽ 8 50
☽⚼♃ 9 15
☽⚼☿ 9 44

25 M
☽⚹♇ 1am51
☽☌♄ 2 32
☽☌♆ 2 59
☉☌♃ 3 39
☽☍♀ 3 59
♂∥♇ 1pm24
☽⚼♂ 11 31
☿⚼♄ 12 0

26 T
☿⚼♆ 2am45
☽⚻♃ 2 59
☉⚻☽ 4 27
☽⚻☿ 9 6
☽#♃ 7pm10
☿∠♀ 8 2

27 W
☉#☽ 0am55
☽△♅ 2 26
☽⚻♂ 5 40
☽□♇ 11 20
☽⚺♄ 11 44
☽#☿ 12pm 4
☽⚺♆ 12 17
☽#♅ 12 45
☽⚻♀ 4 18
☿∥♅ 4 29
☽#♇ 5 12
☉⚼♄ 6 20
☽#♂ 6 38

28 Th
☉⚼♆ 1am41
☽⚼♅ 6 26
☽☍♃ 12pm16
☽∠♄ 3 20
☽∠♆ 3 55
☉☍☽ 5 3
☽⚼♀ 9 22
☿∥♇ 9 48

29 F
☽☍☿ 4am 8
☽⚻♅ 9 49
☿∥♂ 3pm26
☽☍♂ 3 40
☽△♇ 6 12
☽⚹♄ 6 22
☽⚹♆ 6 59

30 S
☽△♀ 1am49
☿⚺♅ 3pm58
☽⚻♃ 7 3
☽⚼♇ 8 51

31 Su
☉⚻☽ 2am47
☽#☿ 11 56
♄⚹♇ 2pm 9
☽☍♅ 3 10
☽#♂ 4 32
♂△♄ 6 20
♂⚹♇ 6 39
☽⚻☿ 7 18
☽#♇ 8 1
☽⚼♃ 9 47
☽□♄ 11 6
☽⚻♇ 11 8
☽⚻♂ 11 22
☽□♆ 11 47

JUNE 1953

LONGITUDE

Day	Sid. Time	☉	☽	☽ 12 Hour	Mean ☊	True ☊	☿	♀	♂	♃	♄	♅	♆	♇
	h m s	° ' "	° ' "	° ' "	° '	° '	° '	° '	° '	° '	° '	° '	° '	° '
1	16 36 43	10♊ 12 5	21♑ 29 23	28♑ 24 20	6♒ 5	4♒ 29	19♊ 12	26♈ 37	21♊ 9	5♊ 14	20♎ 58R	16♋ 26	21♎ 22R	21♌ 0
2	16 40 40	11 9 34	5♒ 21 11	12♒ 19 45	6 2	4 28	21 17	27 21	21 49	5 28	20 56	16 29	21 21	21 0
3	16 44 37	12 7 1	19 19 53	26 21 28	5 58	4 29	23 21	28 6	22 30	5 42	20 54	16 32	21 20	21 1
4	16 48 33	13 4 28	3♓ 24 20	10♓ 28 22	5 55	4 30R	25 23	28 52	23 10	5 56	20 52	16 36	21 19	21 2
5	16 52 30	14 1 55	17 33 24	24 39 15	5 52	4 30	27 22	29 39	23 51	6 10	20 50	16 39	21 19	21 3
6	16 56 26	14 59 20	1♈ 45 40	8♈ 52 25	5 49	4 29	29 20	0♉ 27	24 31	6 24	20 49	16 42	21 18	21 4
7	17 0 23	15 56 45	15 59 8	23 5 26	5 46	4 26	1♋ 14	1 15	25 12	6 38	20 47	16 45	21 17	21 5
8	17 4 19	16 54 10	0♉ 10 54	7♉ 15 2	5 43	4 21	3 7	2 4	25 52	6 52	20 45	16 48	21 16	21 6
9	17 8 16	17 51 34	14 17 21	21 17 19	5 39	4 14	4 57	2 54	26 32	7 6	20 44	16 52	21 15	21 7
10	17 12 12	18 48 58	28 14 25	5♊ 8 10	5 36	4 7	6 45	3 45	27 13	7 20	20 42	16 55	21 15	21 8
11	17 16 9	19 46 20	11♊ 58 8	18 43 56	5 33	4 0	8 30	4 36	27 53	7 34	20 41	16 58	21 14	21 9
12	17 20 6	20 43 43	25 25 16	2♋ 1 54	5 30	3 54	10 13	5 28	28 33	7 48	20 40	17 2	21 13	21 10
13	17 24 2	21 41 4	8♋ 33 45	15 0 47	5 27	3 50	11 53	6 20	29 13	8 2	20 39	17 5	21 13	21 11
14	17 27 59	22 38 25	21 23 3	27 40 45	5 23	3 47D	13 31	7 13	29 54	8 16	20 38	17 8	21 12	21 12
15	17 31 55	23 35 44	3♌ 54 7	10♌ 3 29	5 20	3 47	15 6	8 7	0♋ 34	8 30	20 37	17 12	21 12	21 13
16	17 35 52	24 33 3	16 9 16	22 11 54	5 17	3 48	16 38	9 1	1 14	8 43	20 36	17 15	21 11	21 14
17	17 39 48	25 30 22	28 11 55	4♍ 9 52	5 14	3 49	18 8	9 55	1 54	8 57	20 35	17 19	21 10	21 16
18	17 43 45	26 27 39	10♍ 6 20	16 1 55	5 11	3 51	19 35	10 50	2 34	9 11	20 35	17 22	21 10	21 17
19	17 47 41	27 24 55	21 57 15	27 52 56	5 8	3 51R	20 59	11 46	3 14	9 25	20 34	17 26	21 10	21 18
20	17 51 38	28 22 11	3♎ 49 38	9♎ 47 55	5 4	3 51	22 21	12 42	3 54	9 38	20 34	17 29	21 9	21 19
21	17 55 35	29 19 26	15 48 25	21 51 39	5 1	3 50	23 40	13 38	4 34	9 52	20 33	17 33	21 9	21 21
22	17 59 31	0♋ 16 41	27 58 9	4♏ 8 24	4 58	3 47	24 56	14 35	5 14	10 6	20 33	17 36	21 8	21 22
23	18 3 28	1 13 54	10♏ 22 48	16 41 41	4 55	3 43	26 9	15 33	5 54	10 19	20 33D	17 40	21 8	21 23
24	18 7 24	2 11 8	23 5 19	29 33 52	4 52	3 38	27 20	16 30	6 33	10 33	20 33	17 43	21 8	21 25
25	18 11 21	3 8 21	6♐ 7 27	12♐ 46 0	4 49	3 33	28 27	17 28	7 13	10 46	20 33	17 47	21 7	21 26
26	18 15 17	4 5 33	19 29 27	26 17 36	4 45	3 29	29 32	18 27	7 53	11 0	20 33	17 50	21 7	21 27
27	18 19 14	5 2 45	3♑ 10 8	10♑ 6 41	4 42	3 25	0♌ 33	19 26	8 33	11 13	20 34	17 54	21 7	21 29
28	18 23 11	5 59 57	17 6 51	24 10 7	4 39	3 23	1 31	20 25	9 12	11 26	20 34	17 57	21 7	21 30
29	18 27 7	6 57 8	1♒ 15 58	8♒ 23 53	4 36	3 22D	2 25	21 25	9 52	11 40	20 34	18 1	21 7	21 31
30	18 31 4	7♋ 54 20	15♒ 33 19	22♒ 43 45	4♒ 33	3♒ 23	3♌ 17	22♉ 24	10♋ 32	11♊ 53	20♎ 35	18♋ 5	21♎ 7	21♌ 33

DECLINATION and LATITUDE

Day	☉ Decl	☽ Decl	☽ Lat	☽ 12 Hr. Decl	☿ Decl	☿ Lat	♀ Decl	♀ Lat	♂ Decl	♂ Lat	♃ Decl	♃ Lat	♄ Decl	♄ Lat
1	21N59	22S52	1S 9	21S 1	24N32	1N32	8N29	1S55	23N52	0N43	20N33	0S38	5S42	2N41
2	22 7	18 52	0N 5	16 26	24 48	1 38	8 40	1 60	23 55	0 43	20 36	0 38	5 42	2 40
3	22 15	13 47	1 19	10 56	25 1	1 44	8 52	2 5	23 58	0 44	20 38	0 38	5 41	2 40
4	22 22	7 57	2 29	4 51	25 11	1 49	9 4	2 9	24 0	0 44	20 41	0 38	5 41	2 40
5	22 29	1 41	3 30	1N30	25 19	1 54	9 16	2 14	24 3	0 45	20 43	0 38	5 40	2 40
6	22 36	4N40	4 19	7 46	25 24	1 57	9 28	2 18	24 5	0 45	20 46	0 38	5 40	2 40
7	22 42	10 47	4 52	13 39	25 27	2 0	9 41	2 22	24 7	0 46	20 48	0 38	5 39	2 39
8	22 48	16 19	5 7	18 46	25 27	2 2	9 55	2 26	24 9	0 46	20 51	0 38	5 39	2 39
9	22 53	20 57	5 3	22 49	25 25	2 4	10 8	2 30	24 10	0 46	20 53	0 38	5 39	2 39
10	22 58	24 20	4 41	25 29	25 21	2 4	10 22	2 33	24 12	0 47	20 55	0 38	5 38	2 39
11	23 3	26 15	4 3	26 36	25 14	2 4	10 36	2 36	24 13	0 47	20 58	0 37	5 38	2 38
12	23 7	26 34	3 12	26 9	25 6	2 3	10 51	2 39	24 14	0 48	21 0	0 37	5 38	2 38
13	23 11	25 22	2 12	24 15	24 56	2 2	11 5	2 42	24 15	0 48	21 2	0 37	5 38	2 38
14	23 14	22 51	1 7	21 10	24 44	1 59	11 20	2 44	24 15	0 48	21 5	0 37	5 37	2 38
15	23 17	19 16	0S 1	17 11	24 31	1 56	11 35	2 47	24 15	0 49	21 7	0 37	5 37	2 37
16	23 20	14 56	1 7	12 34	24 16	1 52	11 50	2 49	24 15	0 49	21 9	0 37	5 37	2 37
17	23 22	10 5	2 9	7 32	23 60	1 48	12 5	2 51	24 15	0 50	21 11	0 37	5 37	2 37
18	23 24	4 56	3 5	2 17	23 42	1 43	12 20	2 53	24 15	0 50	21 13	0 37	5 37	2 37
19	23 25	0S22	3 53	3S 1	23 24	1 37	12 36	2 55	24 15	0 50	21 15	0 37	5 37	2 36
20	23 26	5 39	4 30	8 15	23 5	1 30	12 51	2 56	24 14	0 51	21 18	0 37	5 37	2 36
21	23 27	10 47	4 57	13 14	22 44	1 23	13 7	2 57	24 13	0 51	21 20	0 37	5 37	2 36
22	23 27	15 35	5 10	17 47	22 23	1 15	13 22	2 59	24 12	0 51	21 22	0 37	5 38	2 36
23	23 26	19 50	5 10	21 41	22 1	1 7	13 38	2 60	24 11	0 52	21 24	0 37	5 38	2 35
24	23 26	23 18	4 54	24 38	21 39	0 58	13 54	3 0	24 9	0 52	21 26	0 37	5 38	2 35
25	23 24	25 39	4 23	26 20	21 16	0 48	14 9	3 1	24 7	0 52	21 28	0 37	5 38	2 35
26	23 23	26 38	3 37	26 33	20 53	0 38	14 25	3 2	24 5	0 53	21 30	0 37	5 39	2 34
27	23 21	26 2	2 38	25 7	20 29	0 28	14 40	3 2	24 3	0 53	21 31	0 37	5 39	2 34
28	23 19	23 48	1 28	22 7	20 6	0 17	14 56	3 2	24 1	0 54	21 33	0 37	5 39	2 34
29	23 16	20 4	0 12	17 43	19 42	0 5	15 11	3 2	23 58	0 54	21 35	0 37	5 40	2 34
30	23N13	15S 7	1N 6	12S18	19N19	0S 7	15N26	3S 2	23N56	0N54	21N37	0S36	5S40	2N33

Day	♅ Decl	♅ Lat	♆ Decl	♆ Lat	♇ Decl	♇ Lat
1	22N51	0N25	6S44	1N43	23N24	9N25
5	22 49	0 25	6 43	1 43	23 23	9 25
9	22 48	0 25	6 42	1 43	23 21	9 24
13	22 46	0 25	6 41	1 43	23 19	9 23
17	22 44	0 25	6 41	1 43	23 17	9 23
21	22 43	0 25	6 40	1 42	23 14	9 22
25	22 41	0 25	6 40	1 42	23 12	9 22
29	22N39	0N25	6S40	1N42	23N10	9N21

☽ PHENOMENA

d	h	m	
4	17	36	☾
11	14	55	●
19	12	1	☽
27	3	30	○

d	h	° '
5	6	0
11	17	26N39
18	22	0
26	3	26S39

d	h	° '
1	23	0
8	7	5N 8
15	0	0
22	11	5S12
29	4	0

VOID OF COURSE ☽

Last Aspect		☽ Ingress		
1	9am23	1	♒	2pm46
3	3pm50	3	♓	6pm12
5	7pm14	5	♈	9pm 2
7	4pm20	7	♉	11pm42
9	11am43	10	♊	3am 3
12	5am58	12	♋	8am18
13	11pm39	14	♌	4pm28
16	6pm 8	17	♍	3am37
19	12pm 1	19	♎	4pm17
21	5pm22	22	♏	3am58
24	8am38	24	♐	12pm48
26	3am29	26	♑	6pm29
28	6am49	28	♒	9pm52

d	h	
5	14	PERIGEE
18	21	APOGEE

DAILY ASPECTARIAN

1	☽#♅	0am 8
M	☉#☽	5 46
	☉⚼☽	6 56
	♂△♆	7 52
	☽□♀	9 23
	☽#♃	2pm34
	☿△♄	8 0
	☿✶♇	8 43
2	☽△♃	0am13
T	☿△♆	0 44
	☽⚼☿	1 54
	☽⚼♂	2 39
	☿☌♂	9 7
	☉△☽	10 44
	☽⚻♅	7pm12
3	☽△♄	2am41
W	☽☍♇	2 54
	☽△♆	3 26
	☽△♂	5 41
	☽△☿	8 2
	☽✶♀	3pm50
	♃⚼♄	5 41
	☽#♀	7 43
	☽⚼♅	8 54
4	☽⚼♄	4am11
Th	☽□♃	4 23
	☽∥♆	4 46
	☽⚼♆	4 57
	☽∥♄	8 50
	☉□☽	5pm36
	☽∠♀	6 48
	☽△♅	10 27
5	☽⚻♄	5am32
F	☽⚻♇	5 55
	☽⚻♆	6 20
	♀ ♉	10 34
	☽□♂	11 10
	♃⚼♆	1pm 6
	☽□☿	7 14
	☽⚺♀	9 39
6	☽#♄	3am49
S	☽⚼♇	7 16
	☽#♆	7 53
	☽✶♃	7 58
	☿ ♋	8 24
	☽∥♀	7pm26
	☉✶☽	11 56
7	☿✶♀	0am17
Su	☽□♅	1 18
	☽☍♄	8 5
	☽△♇	8 37
	☽☍♆	8 56
	☽∠♃	9 42
	☽✶♂	4pm20
	☉⚺♅	9 28
8	☉∥♅	0am45
M	☉∠☽	3 8
	☽☌♀	3 24
	☽✶☿	5 44
	☽⚺♃	11 33
	☽∠♂	7pm 4
	☽∥♃	11 37
9	☽✶♅	4am25
T	☉⚺☽	6 34
	☉∠♀	9 14
	☽⚻♄	11 1
	☽∠☿	11 9
	☽□♇	11 43
	☽∥♅	11 52
	☽⚻♆	11 56
	☉∥☽	12pm53
	☿∠♇	3 34
	☽∥♇	3 51
	☽⚺♂	10 8
	☽∥♂	10 44
10	☽∠♅	6am25
W	☿⚺♃	9 10
	☽∥☿	9 48
	☽⚺♀	10 12
	☽⚼♄	12pm59
	☽⚼♆	1 56
	☽☌♃	4 8
	☽⚺☿	5 1
11	☽⚺♅	8am54
Th	☽∠♀	2pm29
	☉☌☽	2 55
	☽△♄	3 28
	☽✶♇	4 21
	☽△♆	4 28
	☉△♄	10 27
12	☽☌♂	5am58
F	☉✶♇	11 13
	☉△♆	12pm16
	☽✶♀	7 36
	☽∠♇	7 37
	☽⚺♃	11 0
13	☽∥☿	5am37
S	☽☌☿	7 4
	☽∥♂	12pm 5
	☽☌♅	3 57
	☽∥♇	8 21
	☉∥☽	8 55
	☽□♄	10 34
	♆✶♇	10 46
	☽⚺♇	11 39
	☽□♆	11 39
14	☽∥♅	0am39
Su	☉⚺☽	2 35
	☽∠♃	3 38
	♂ ♋	3 49
	☽∥♃	12pm30
	☽⚺♂	5 11
15	☉∥♇	1am18
M	☽□♀	8 50
	☽✶♃	9 7
	☉∠☽	9 55
	♀⚺♃	1pm42
16	☽∠♂	0am10
T	☿∥♂	0 42
	☽⚺☿	1 5
	☽⚺♅	2 11
	☽✶♄	8 49
	☽✶♆	9 58
	☽☌♇	10 7
	☿☌♅	10 15
	☽∥♀	2pm49
	☉✶☽	6 8
17	☽✶♂	7am53
W	☽∠♅	8 18
	☽∠☿	11 18
	☽∠♄	2pm52
	☽#♆	3 58
	☽∠♆	4 3
	☽#♄	8 50
	☽□♃	10 6
18	☽△♀	1am37
Th	☽✶♅	2pm47
	☿□♄	4 49
	☽⚺♄	9 12
	☽✶☿	9 47
	☽⚺♆	10 23
	☉∥☿	10 32
	☽⚺♇	10 41
19	☿□♆	2am56
F	☿⚺♇	5 31
	☽⚼♀	10 34
	☿∥♇	10 58
	☉□☽	12pm 1
	☽∥♄	11 51
20	☽□♂	0am 9
S	☽∥♆	4 40
	☽∠♇	5 2
	☽△♃	11 54
	☽⚻♀	7pm19
21	☿∥♅	1am52
Su	☽□♅	3 28
	☽☌♄	9 25
	☽☌♆	10 35
	☽✶♇	11 0
	☽#♀	12pm 3
	☉ ♋	5 0
	☽□☿	5 22
	☽⚼♃	6 15
22	☿∠♃	3am42
M	☉△☽	4 53
	☽△♂	2pm54
	☽⚻♃	11 53
23	☽#♃	10am 8
T	☽☍♀	10 37
	☉⚼☽	12pm 2
	☽#☿	12 58
	☽△♅	1 53
	♄SD	5 28
	♂∠♇	6 28
	☽⚺♄	7 15
	☽#♅	7 16
	☽⚺♆	8 20
	☽□♇	8 51
	☽⚼♂	8 59
	☽#♇	11 21
24	☉#☽	1am 6
W	☽#♂	7 19
	☽△☿	8 38
	☿∥♃	12pm50
	☽⚼♅	5 52
	☉⚻☽	6 8
	☽∠♄	10 58
25	☽∠♆	0am 0
Th	☽⚻♂	2 6
	♀✶♅	8 3
	☽☍♃	8 33
	☽⚼☿	2pm24
	☽⚻♅	9 3
	☽⚻♀	10 0
26	☽✶♄	1am53
F	☽✶♆	2 53
	☽△♇	3 29
	☿ ♌	11 1
	☽⚻☿	7pm 5
27	☽⚼♀	2am21
S	☉☍☽	3 30
	☽⚼♇	5 44
	☽☍♂	9 46
	☽⚻♃	2pm 8
	☽#♂	10 16
28	☽☍♅	1am27
Su	♀⚻♄	3 41
	☉#☽	3 50
	☽#♇	4 47
	☽□♄	5 53
	☽△♀	6 3
	☽□♆	6 49
	☽⚻♇	7 29
	☽#♅	8 25
	☉∠♇	12pm57
	☽#♃	3 20
	☽⚼♃	4 6
	♀⚻♆	4 52
29	☽☍☿	2am 5
M	☽#☿	2 10
	♀□♇	2 50
	☉⚻☽	10 15
	☽⚻♂	3pm10
	☽△♃	5 45
	☽#♀	10 39
30	☽⚻♅	4am14
T	☽△♄	8 25
	☽△♆	9 18
	☽☍♇	10 3
	☽□♀	12pm19
	☉⚼☽	1 10
	☽⚼♂	5 29

LONGITUDE

Day	Sid. Time	☉	☽	☽ 12 Hour	Mean ☊	True ☊	☿	♀	♂	♃	♄	♅	♆	♇
	h m s	° ' "	° ' "	° ' "	° '	° '	° '	° '	° '	° '	° '	° '	° '	° '
1	18 35 0	8♋ 51 31	29♒ 54 41	7♓ 5 37	4♒ 29	3♒ 24	4♌ 4	23♉ 25	11♋ 11	12♊ 6	20♎ 36	18♋ 8	21♎ 7R	21♌ 34
2	18 38 57	9 48 43	14♓ 16 9	21 25 53	4 26	3 25	4 49	24 25	11 51	12 20	20 36	18 12	21 7D	21 36
3	18 42 53	10 45 55	28 34 28	5♈ 41 35	4 23	3 26R	5 29	25 26	12 30	12 33	20 37	18 16	21 6	21 37
4	18 46 50	11 43 7	12♈ 46 58	19 50 22	4 20	3 27	6 5	26 27	13 10	12 46	20 38	18 19	21 7	21 39
5	18 50 46	12 40 19	26 51 32	3♉ 50 17	4 17	3 26	6 38	27 29	13 49	12 59	20 39	18 23	21 7	21 40
6	18 54 43	13 37 32	10♉ 46 25	17 39 45	4 14	3 24	7 6	28 31	14 29	13 12	20 41	18 26	21 7	21 42
7	18 58 40	14 34 45	24 30 8	1♊ 17 23	4 10	3 22	7 30	29 33	15 8	13 25	20 42	18 30	21 7	21 43
8	19 2 36	15 31 58	8♊ 1 23	14 41 59	4 7	3 20	7 50	0♊ 35	15 48	13 38	20 43	18 34	21 7	21 45
9	19 6 33	16 29 12	21 19 5	27 52 35	4 4	3 17	8 5	1 38	16 27	13 51	20 45	18 37	21 7	21 47
10	19 10 29	17 26 26	4♋ 22 26	10♋ 48 36	4 1	3 16	8 15	2 40	17 6	14 4	20 46	18 41	21 7	21 48
11	19 14 26	18 23 41	17 11 5	23 29 58	3 58	3 15D	8 21R	3 44	17 46	14 16	20 48	18 45	21 8	21 50
12	19 18 22	19 20 55	29 45 18	5♌ 57 15	3 55	3 14	8 22	4 47	18 25	14 29	20 50	18 48	21 8	21 52
13	19 22 19	20 18 9	12♌ 6 0	18 11 46	3 51	3 14	8 19	5 50	19 4	14 42	20 51	18 52	21 8	21 53
14	19 26 15	21 15 24	24 14 51	0♍ 15 35	3 48	3 15	8 10	6 54	19 43	14 54	20 53	18 56	21 9	21 55
15	19 30 12	22 12 39	6♍ 14 18	12 11 26	3 45	3 16	7 57	7 58	20 23	15 7	20 55	18 59	21 9	21 57
16	19 34 9	23 9 54	18 7 26	24 2 47	3 42	3 17	7 39	9 2	21 2	15 19	20 58	19 3	21 9	21 58
17	19 38 5	24 7 9	29 58 0	5♎ 53 37	3 39	3 18	7 17	10 7	21 41	15 32	21 0	19 7	21 10	22 0
18	19 42 2	25 4 24	11♎ 50 10	17 48 16	3 35	3 19R	6 51	11 11	22 20	15 44	21 2	19 10	21 10	22 2
19	19 45 58	26 1 40	23 48 27	29 51 19	3 32	3 19	6 20	12 16	22 59	15 56	21 4	19 14	21 11	22 3
20	19 49 55	26 58 56	5♏ 57 26	12♏ 7 20	3 29	3 18	5 47	13 21	23 38	16 8	21 7	19 17	21 11	22 5
21	19 53 51	27 56 11	18 21 32	24 40 31	3 26	3 18	5 10	14 26	24 17	16 21	21 10	19 21	21 12	22 7
22	19 57 48	28 53 28	1♐ 4 41	7♐ 34 24	3 23	3 17	4 31	15 32	24 56	16 33	21 12	19 25	21 12	22 9
23	20 1 44	29 50 45	14 9 54	20 51 21	3 20	3 17	3 50	16 37	25 35	16 45	21 15	19 28	21 13	22 10
24	20 5 41	0♌ 48 2	27 38 49	4♑ 32 14	3 16	3 17	3 7	17 43	26 14	16 56	21 18	19 32	21 14	22 12
25	20 9 38	1 45 19	11♑ 31 23	18 35 57	3 13	3 17D	2 25	18 49	26 53	17 8	21 21	19 35	21 14	22 14
26	20 13 34	2 42 37	25 45 28	2♒ 59 21	3 10	3 17	1 42	19 55	27 32	17 20	21 24	19 39	21 15	22 16
27	20 17 31	3 39 56	10♒ 16 55	17 37 22	3 7	3 17R	1 1	21 1	28 11	17 32	21 27	19 43	21 16	22 18
28	20 21 27	4 37 15	24 59 51	2♓ 23 29	3 4	3 17	0 21	22 7	28 50	17 43	21 30	19 46	21 17	22 19
29	20 25 24	5 34 35	9♓ 47 23	17 10 39	3 1	3 17	29♋ 44	23 14	29 29	17 55	21 34	19 50	21 17	22 21
30	20 29 20	6 31 56	24 32 28	1♈ 52 6	2 57	3 16	29 11	24 21	0♌ 7	18 6	21 37	19 53	21 18	22 23
31	20 33 17	7♌ 29 19	9♈ 8 51	16♈ 22 12	2♒ 54	3♒ 16	28♋ 41	25♊ 28	0♌ 46	18♊ 18	21♎ 40	19♋ 57	21♎ 19	22♌ 25

DECLINATION and LATITUDE

Day	☉ Decl	☽ Decl	☽ Lat	☽ 12 Hr. Decl	☿ Decl	☿ Lat	♀ Decl	♀ Lat	♂ Decl	♂ Lat	♃ Decl	♃ Lat	♄ Decl	♄ Lat
1	23N 9	9S19	2N21	6S12	18N55	0S20	15N41	3S 2	23N53	0N55	21N39	0S36	5S41	2N33
2	23 5	3 1	3 26	0N11	18 32	0 33	15 56	3 2	23 50	0 55	21 41	0 36	5 41	2 33
3	23 1	3N23	4 19	6 32	18 9	0 46	16 11	3 1	23 46	0 55	21 42	0 36	5 42	2 33
4	22 56	9 34	4 55	12 29	17 47	1 0	16 26	3 1	23 43	0 56	21 44	0 36	5 42	2 32
5	22 50	15 13	5 13	17 44	17 25	1 14	16 41	3 0	23 39	0 56	21 46	0 36	5 43	2 32
6	22 45	19 60	5 12	21 59	17 4	1 29	16 55	2 59	23 35	0 56	21 47	0 36	5 44	2 32
7	22 39	23 39	4 54	24 58	16 44	1 43	17 9	2 58	23 31	0 57	21 49	0 36	5 44	2 32
8	22 32	25 55	4 19	26 29	16 25	1 58	17 23	2 57	23 27	0 57	21 51	0 36	5 45	2 31
9	22 26	26 40	3 31	26 29	16 6	2 13	17 37	2 56	23 23	0 57	21 52	0 36	5 46	2 31
10	22 18	25 55	2 33	25 1	15 49	2 28	17 50	2 55	23 18	0 58	21 54	0 36	5 47	2 31
11	22 11	23 47	1 28	22 17	15 33	2 43	18 4	2 54	23 13	0 58	21 55	0 36	5 48	2 31
12	22 3	20 31	0 19	18 33	15 19	2 58	18 17	2 52	23 8	0 58	21 57	0 36	5 49	2 30
13	21 55	16 23	0S49	14 5	15 6	3 12	18 29	2 51	23 3	0 58	21 58	0 36	5 50	2 30
14	21 46	11 39	1 54	9 8	14 54	3 26	18 42	2 49	22 58	0 59	21 60	0 36	5 50	2 30
15	21 37	6 33	2 53	3 55	14 45	3 40	18 54	2 47	22 52	0 59	22 1	0 36	5 51	2 30
16	21 27	1 16	3 44	1S24	14 37	3 53	19 5	2 45	22 47	0 59	22 3	0 36	5 53	2 29
17	21 18	4S 2	4 25	6 39	14 30	4 5	19 17	2 43	22 41	0 60	22 4	0 36	5 54	2 29
18	21 7	9 12	4 55	11 41	14 26	4 16	19 28	2 41	22 35	0 60	22 5	0 36	5 55	2 29
19	20 57	14 5	5 13	16 21	14 23	4 26	19 38	2 39	22 29	1 0	22 7	0 36	5 56	2 28
20	20 46	18 29	5 17	20 26	14 23	4 35	19 49	2 37	22 22	1 0	22 8	0 36	5 57	2 28
21	20 35	22 12	5 6	23 43	14 24	4 43	19 59	2 35	22 16	1 1	22 9	0 36	5 58	2 28
22	20 23	24 57	4 41	25 53	14 27	4 49	20 8	2 32	22 9	1 1	22 10	0 36	5 59	2 28
23	20 11	26 29	4 0	26 42	14 32	4 54	20 17	2 30	22 2	1 1	22 12	0 36	6 1	2 27
24	19 59	26 31	3 5	25 55	14 39	4 57	20 26	2 27	21 55	1 2	22 13	0 36	6 2	2 27
25	19 46	24 54	1 58	23 29	14 47	4 58	20 34	2 25	21 48	1 2	22 14	0 36	6 3	2 27
26	19 34	21 41	0 42	19 31	14 57	4 58	20 42	2 22	21 40	1 2	22 15	0 36	6 5	2 27
27	19 20	17 3	0N39	14 18	15 8	4 55	20 49	2 19	21 33	1 2	22 16	0 36	6 6	2 27
28	19 7	11 21	1 58	8 13	15 20	4 51	20 56	2 17	21 25	1 3	22 17	0 36	6 7	2 26
29	18 53	4 59	3 9	1 41	15 33	4 45	21 3	2 14	21 17	1 3	22 18	0 36	6 9	2 26
30	18 39	1N37	4 8	4N53	15 47	4 38	21 9	2 11	21 9	1 3	22 19	0 36	6 10	2 26
31	18N24	8N 4	4N50	11N 6	16N 2	4S29	21N14	2S 8	21N 1	1N 3	22N20	0S35	6S12	2N26

Day	♅ Decl	♅ Lat	♆ Decl	♆ Lat	♇ Decl	♇ Lat
1	22N38	0N25	6S40	1N42	23N 9	9N21
5	22 36	0 25	6 40	1 42	23 6	9 21
9	22 34	0 25	6 40	1 41	23 4	9 20
13	22 32	0 25	6 41	1 41	23 1	9 20
17	22 30	0 25	6 42	1 41	22 59	9 20
21	22 28	0 25	6 43	1 41	22 56	9 19
25	22 26	0 25	6 44	1 41	22 54	9 19
29	22N24	0N25	6S45	1N40	22N51	9N19

☽ PHENOMENA

d	h	m	
3	22	4	☾
11	2	29	●
19	4	48	☽
26	12	21	○

d	h	° '
2	11	0
9	0	26N40
16	6	0
23	13	26S42
29	18	0

d	h	
5	11	5N15
12	7	0
19	19	5S17
26	12	0

VOID OF COURSE ☽

Last Aspect		☽ Ingress		
30	12pm19	1	♓	0am 9
2	6pm19	3	♈	2am24
4	3pm 7	5	♉	5am24
7	9am39	7	♊	9am43
9	0am50	9	♋	3pm55
11	7am29	12	♌	0am28
13	7pm21	14	♍	11am29
16	11am 7	17	♎	0am 4
19	4am48	19	♏	12pm17
21	7pm36	21	♐	9pm59
23	2pm22	24	♑	4am 7
26	3am 6	26	♒	7am 3
27	7pm39	28	♓	8am 7
30	7am20	30	♈	8am56

d	h	
1	0	PERIGEE
16	15	APOGEE
28	14	PERIGEE

DAILY ASPECTARIAN

1 W	☉∥♇	2am37
	☽⚼♅	5 25
	☽⚻☿	7 20
	☽⚼♄	9 30
	☽∥♆	10 14
	☽⚼♆	10 21
	☽∥♄	1pm58
	☉△☽	4 1
	☽△♂	7 45
	☽□♃	8 42
2 Th	☽△♅	6am36
	☽⚼☿	9 45
	☽⚻♄	10 38
	☽⚻♆	11 28
	☽⚻♇	12pm18
	☽⚹♀	6 19
	♆SD	10 2
3 F	♂⚺♃	2am 9
	☽#♄	8 49
	☽△☿	12pm11
	☽#♆	12 32
	☽⚼♇	1 36
	☽∠♀	9 35
	☉□☽	10 4
	☽⚹♃	11 58
4 S	☽□♂	0am41
	☽□♅	9 27
	☽☍♄	1pm23
	☽☍♆	2 10
	☽△♇	3 7
5 Su	☽⚺♀	1am 9
	☽∠♃	1 57
	☽∥♀	7 12
	☽∥☿	9 45
	☉⚺♃	10 6
	☽□☿	5pm26
6 M	☽⚺♃	4am17
	☉⚹☽	5 20
	☿∥♀	6 18
	☽⚹♂	6 46
	☽∥♃	10 51
	☽⚹♅	1pm25
	☽∥♅	4 6
	☉∥☽	4 45
	☽⚻♄	5 18
	☽⚻♆	6 3
	☽□♇	7 6
	☽∥♇	7 41
	☽∥♂	11 3
7 T	☉∠♀	9am31
	☉∠☽	9 39
	☽☌♀	9 39
	☽∠♂	10 28
	♀ ♊	10 30
	☉∥♅	3pm56
	☽∠♅	4 0
	☽⚼♄	7 53
	☽⚼♆	8 35
	☽⚹☿	11 39
8 W	☽☌♃	10am14
	♀∠♂	12pm58
	☉⚺☽	2 33
	☽⚺♂	2 42
	☽⚺♅	7 5
	☉☌♂	8 59
	☽△♄	10 57
	☽△♆	11 38
9 Th	☽⚹♇	0am50
	☽∠☿	3 16
	☽⚺♀	8pm35
10 F	☽∠♇	4am32
	☽⚺☿	7 18
	☽⚺♃	6pm25
11 S	♀∠♅	0am26
	☽☌♂	1 9
	☉☌☽	2 29
	☽☌♅	2 58
	☽∠♀	3 11
	☽∥♂	4 54
	☽∥♇	6 13
	☽□♄	6 52
	☽□♆	7 29
	☽⚺♇	8 50
	☉☌♅	9 24
	☽∥♅	10 1
	☉∥☽	1pm14
	☽∥♃	2 28
	☿SR	5 27
	☽∠♃	11 28
12 Su	☽⚹♀	10am38
	☽∥♀	12pm54
	☉∥♃	3 8
	♂☌♅	3 45
	☽☌☿	4 39
13 M	♀⚼♄	0am23
	☽⚹♃	5 11
	♀⚼♆	6 43
	☽∥☿	7 6
	♂∥♇	9 38
	☽⚺♅	1pm23
	☉□♄	2 26
	☽⚺♂	2 31
	☽⚹♄	5 19
	☉⚺☽	5 33
	☽⚹♆	5 50
	☽☌♇	7 21
	☉□♆	9 5
14 T	☉⚺♇	5pm 2
	☽∠♅	7 27
	☽∠♂	10 10
	☽#♆	11 21
	☽∠♄	11 22
	☿⚹♀	11 39
	☽∠♆	11 49
15 W	☉∠☽	2am 8
	☽#♄	3 9
	☽⚺☿	3 22
	☽□♀	3 50
	☽□♃	6pm14
	♂□♄	9 14
16 Th	☽⚹♅	1am53
	♂□♆	4 39
	☽⚺♄	5 46
	☽⚺♆	6 9
	☽⚹♂	6 14
	☽⚺♇	7 49
	☽∠☿	8 55
	☉⚹☽	11 7
17 F	☽∥♄	8am32
	♂⚺♇	12pm12
	☽∥♆	12 14
	☽∠♇	2 16
	☽⚹☿	2 18
	☽△♀	10 34
18 S	☽△♃	7am59
	☽□♅	2pm49
	☽☌♄	6 32
	☽☌♆	6 45
	☽⚹♇	8 30
	♂∥♅	10 10
	☽□♂	10 16
19 Su	☽#☿	1am35
	☉□☽	4 48
	☽⚼♀	7 33
	☽⚼♃	2pm23
	☽□☿	11 40
20 M	☽#♀	8am22
	☉#☽	1pm26
	☽⚻♀	3 45
	☽⚻♃	8 4
	☽#♃	11 41
21 T	☽#♂	0am28
	☽△♅	1 54
	☽#♅	2 0
	☽⚺♄	5 21
	☽⚺♆	5 25
	☽#♇	5 36
	☽□♇	7 10
	☽△♂	11 52
	☉△☽	7pm36
	♂∥♃	7 38
22 W	♄☌♆	1am48
	☽△☿	6 3
	☽⚼♅	6 12
	☽∠♆	9 30
	☽∠♄	9 31
	☉∥♀	5pm10
	☽⚼♂	5 10
23 Th	☉⚼☽	1am19
	♀☌♃	3 19
	☉ ♌	3 53
	☽☍♃	4 43
	☽☍♀	4 49
	☽⚼☿	7 58
	☽⚻♅	9 34
	☽⚹♆	12pm39
	☽⚹♄	12 45
	☽△♇	2 22
	☽⚻♂	9 24
24 F	☿∠♀	5am26
	☉⚻☽	5 55
	☽⚻☿	9 5
	☽⚼♇	4pm38
25 S	☿∠♃	7am14
	☉☌☿	9 28
	☽⚻♃	9 40
	☉∠♃	12pm 7
	☽⚻♀	1 24
	☽☍♅	1 44
	☽#♇	4 13
	☽□♆	4 27
	☽□♄	4 41
	♀⚺♅	5 58
	☽⚻♇	6 9
	☽#♅	7 19
	☽#♃	8 28
26 Su	☽#♂	0am 2
	☽☍♂	3 6
	☽#♀	5 30
	☽☍☿	9 25
	☽⚼♃	11 4
	☉☍☽	12pm21
	☉#☽	12 23
	☽⚼♀	4 25
27 M	♀△♆	5am26
	☽#☿	8 12
	♀△♄	9 52
	☽△♃	12pm 0
	☽⚻♅	3 28
	☽△♆	5 57
	☽△♄	6 18
	☽△♀	6 57
	☽☍♇	7 39
28 T	♀⚹♇	4am27
	☽⚻♂	6 30
	☽⚻☿	8 21
	☿ ♋	2pm 9
	☽⚼♅	3 55
	☉⚻☽	4 42
	☽∥♆	5 28
	☽⚼♆	6 19
	☽⚼♄	6 44
	☽∥♄	7 43
29 W	☿☌♂	5am10
	☽⚼☿	7 44
	☽⚼♂	7 57
	☽□♃	1pm22
	☽△♅	4 23
	☽⚻♆	6 43
	☉⚼☽	6 45
	☽⚻♄	7 12
	♂ ♌	7 26
	☽⚻♇	8 28
	☽□♀	11 39
30 Th	♀∥♂	1am15
	☽△☿	7 20
	☽△♂	9 34
	☽#♄	4pm54
	☽#♆	7 4
	☉△☽	9 4
	☽⚼♇	9 8
31 F	☽⚹♃	3pm25
	☽□♅	6 3
	☽☍♆	8 19
	☽☍♄	8 58
	☽△♇	10 11

AUGUST 1953

LONGITUDE

Day	Sid. Time	☉	☽	☽ 12 Hour	Mean ☊	True ☊	☿	♀	♂	♃	♄	♅	♆	♇
	h m s	° ' "	° ' "	° ' "	° '	° '	° '	° '	° '	° '	° '	° '	° '	° '
1	20 37 13	8♌ 26 42	23♈ 31 40	0♉ 36 57	2♒ 51	3♒ 15R	28♋ 16R	26♊ 35	1♌ 25	18♊ 29	21♎ 44	20♋ 0	21♎ 20	22♌ 27
2	20 41 10	9 24 6	7♉ 37 47	14 34 5	2 48	3 15D	27 56	27 42	2 4	18 40	21 48	20 4	21 21	22 29
3	20 45 7	10 21 32	21 25 46	28 12 52	2 45	3 15	27 41	28 49	2 42	18 51	21 51	20 7	21 22	22 30
4	20 49 3	11 18 59	4♊ 55 29	11♊ 33 45	2 41	3 16	27 33D	29 57	3 21	19 2	21 55	20 11	21 23	22 32
5	20 53 0	12 16 27	18 7 49	24 37 58	2 38	3 16	27 30	1♋ 4	4 0	19 13	21 59	20 14	21 24	22 34
6	20 56 56	13 13 56	1♋ 4 8	7♋ 26 48	2 35	3 17	27 34	2 12	4 38	19 24	22 3	20 18	21 25	22 36
7	21 0 53	14 11 27	13 46 4	20 2 10	2 32	3 18	27 45	3 20	5 17	19 35	22 7	20 21	21 26	22 38
8	21 4 49	15 8 59	26 15 17	2♌ 25 37	2 29	3 19R	28 2	4 28	5 56	19 45	22 11	20 25	21 27	22 40
9	21 8 46	16 6 32	8♌ 33 23	14 38 46	2 26	3 19	28 26	5 36	6 34	19 56	22 15	20 28	21 28	22 42
10	21 12 42	17 4 6	20 41 59	26 43 14	2 22	3 18	28 57	6 45	7 13	20 6	22 20	20 31	21 30	22 44
11	21 16 39	18 1 41	2♍ 42 46	8♍ 40 48	2 19	3 17	29 35	7 53	7 52	20 17	22 24	20 35	21 31	22 46
12	21 20 36	18 59 17	14 37 37	20 33 29	2 16	3 15	0♌ 19	9 2	8 30	20 27	22 28	20 38	21 32	22 47
13	21 24 32	19 56 54	26 28 43	2♎ 23 41	2 13	3 12	1 10	10 10	9 9	20 37	22 33	20 41	21 33	22 49
14	21 28 29	20 54 32	8♎ 18 43	14 14 14	2 10	3 10	2 8	11 19	9 47	20 47	22 37	20 45	21 35	22 51
15	21 32 25	21 52 11	20 10 41	26 8 30	2 6	3 7	3 12	12 28	10 26	20 57	22 42	20 48	21 36	22 53
16	21 36 22	22 49 52	2♏ 8 12	8♏ 10 18	2 3	3 5	4 22	13 37	11 4	21 7	22 47	20 51	21 37	22 55
17	21 40 18	23 47 33	14 15 18	20 23 46	2 0	3 4D	5 37	14 46	11 42	21 16	22 52	20 54	21 38	22 57
18	21 44 15	24 45 15	26 36 14	2♐ 53 14	1 57	3 3	6 59	15 56	12 21	21 26	22 56	20 57	21 40	22 59
19	21 48 11	25 42 59	9♐ 15 18	15 42 54	1 54	3 4	8 25	17 5	12 59	21 35	23 1	21 1	21 41	23 1
20	21 52 8	26 40 43	22 16 29	28 56 23	1 51	3 5	9 57	18 14	13 38	21 45	23 6	21 4	21 43	23 3
21	21 56 5	27 38 29	5♑ 42 53	12♑ 36 8	1 47	3 6	11 32	19 24	14 16	21 54	23 11	21 7	21 44	23 5
22	22 0 1	28 36 16	19 36 9	26 42 48	1 44	3 8	13 12	20 34	14 54	22 3	23 17	21 10	21 46	23 6
23	22 3 58	29 34 4	3♒ 55 46	11♒ 14 35	1 41	3 8R	14 56	21 44	15 33	22 12	23 22	21 13	21 47	23 8
24	22 7 54	0♍ 31 54	18 38 33	26 6 52	1 38	3 8	16 43	22 54	16 11	22 21	23 27	21 16	21 49	23 10
25	22 11 51	1 29 44	3♓ 38 30	11♓ 12 20	1 35	3 6	18 32	24 4	16 49	22 30	23 32	21 19	21 50	23 12
26	22 15 47	2 27 36	18 47 10	26 21 45	1 32	3 2	20 24	25 14	17 27	22 38	23 38	21 22	21 52	23 14
27	22 19 44	3 25 30	3♈ 54 53	11♈ 25 23	1 28	2 58	22 18	26 24	18 6	22 47	23 43	21 25	21 53	23 16
28	22 23 40	4 23 26	18 52 13	26 14 29	1 25	2 54	24 14	27 34	18 44	22 55	23 49	21 28	21 55	23 18
29	22 27 37	5 21 23	3♉ 31 28	10♉ 42 38	1 22	2 51	26 10	28 45	19 22	23 3	23 54	21 31	21 57	23 20
30	22 31 34	6 19 22	17 47 36	24 46 13	1 19	2 48	28 7	29 55	20 0	23 11	24 0	21 34	21 58	23 22
31	22 35 30	7♍ 17 23	1♊ 38 28	8♊ 24 26	1♒ 16	2♒ 46D	0♍ 5	1♌ 6	20♌ 39	23♊ 19	24♎ 6	21♋ 36	22♎ 0	23♌ 23

DECLINATION and LATITUDE

Day	☉ Decl	☽ Decl	☽ Lat	☽ 12 Hr. Decl	☿ Decl	☿ Lat	♀ Decl	♀ Lat	♂ Decl	♂ Lat	♃ Decl	♃ Lat	♄ Decl	♄ Lat
1	18N 9	13N58	5N13	16N38	16N17	4S19	21N19	2S 5	20N53	1N 4	22N21	0S35	6S13	2N25
2	17 54	19 2	5 16	21 9	16 32	4 7	21 24	2 2	20 45	1 4	22 22	0 35	6 15	2 25
3	17 39	22 58	5 1	24 26	16 48	3 55	21 28	1 59	20 36	1 4	22 23	0 35	6 17	2 25
4	17 23	25 33	4 30	26 17	17 3	3 41	21 31	1 56	20 27	1 4	22 24	0 35	6 18	2 25
5	17 7	26 39	3 45	26 38	17 17	3 26	21 34	1 52	20 18	1 5	22 25	0 35	6 20	2 24
6	16 51	26 16	2 49	25 32	17 32	3 11	21 36	1 49	20 9	1 5	22 26	0 35	6 22	2 24
7	16 35	24 30	1 46	23 9	17 45	2 55	21 38	1 46	20 0	1 5	22 27	0 35	6 23	2 24
8	16 18	21 33	0 39	19 42	17 58	2 39	21 40	1 43	19 51	1 5	22 28	0 35	6 25	2 24
9	16 1	17 40	0S29	15 27	18 9	2 23	21 40	1 39	19 42	1 6	22 29	0 35	6 27	2 24
10	15 43	13 6	1 35	10 38	18 19	2 6	21 41	1 36	19 32	1 6	22 29	0 35	6 29	2 23
11	15 26	8 5	2 35	5 29	18 28	1 49	21 40	1 33	19 22	1 6	22 30	0 35	6 30	2 23
12	15 8	2 51	3 29	0 11	18 35	1 33	21 39	1 29	19 12	1 6	22 31	0 35	6 32	2 23
13	14 50	2S28	4 13	5S 6	18 40	1 16	21 38	1 26	19 2	1 6	22 32	0 35	6 34	2 23
14	14 32	7 41	4 46	10 11	18 43	1 0	21 36	1 22	18 52	1 7	22 32	0 35	6 36	2 22
15	14 13	12 37	5 7	14 57	18 43	0 45	21 33	1 19	18 42	1 7	22 33	0 35	6 38	2 22
16	13 55	17 8	5 15	19 11	18 42	0 29	21 30	1 15	18 32	1 7	22 34	0 35	6 40	2 22
17	13 36	21 2	5 9	22 41	18 38	0 15	21 26	1 12	18 21	1 7	22 34	0 35	6 42	2 22
18	13 16	24 5	4 49	25 13	18 31	0 1	21 22	1 8	18 11	1 7	22 35	0 35	6 44	2 22
19	12 57	26 2	4 14	26 31	18 22	0N13	21 17	1 5	18 0	1 8	22 36	0 35	6 46	2 21
20	12 37	26 39	3 26	26 24	18 10	0 25	21 11	1 1	17 49	1 8	22 36	0 35	6 48	2 21
21	12 18	25 44	2 25	24 41	17 55	0 37	21 5	0 58	17 38	1 8	22 37	0 35	6 50	2 21
22	11 58	23 14	1 14	21 24	17 37	0 48	20 59	0 54	17 27	1 8	22 37	0 35	6 52	2 21
23	11 38	19 12	0N 4	16 42	17 17	0 58	20 51	0 51	17 16	1 8	22 38	0 35	6 54	2 21
24	11 17	13 55	1 24	10 54	16 54	1 7	20 44	0 47	17 5	1 9	22 38	0 35	6 56	2 20
25	10 57	7 42	2 39	4 23	16 28	1 15	20 35	0 44	16 54	1 9	22 39	0 35	6 58	2 20
26	10 36	0 60	3 44	2N24	15 59	1 22	20 26	0 40	16 42	1 9	22 39	0 35	7 0	2 20
27	10 15	5N44	4 33	8 58	15 28	1 28	20 17	0 37	16 30	1 9	22 40	0 35	7 2	2 20
28	9 54	12 4	5 3	14 57	14 55	1 33	20 7	0 33	16 19	1 9	22 40	0 35	7 5	2 20
29	9 33	17 35	5 12	19 56	14 20	1 38	19 56	0 30	16 7	1 10	22 41	0 35	7 7	2 20
30	9 12	21 58	5 2	23 39	13 43	1 41	19 45	0 26	15 55	1 10	22 41	0 35	7 9	2 19
31	8N50	24N58	4N34	25N54	13N 4	1N44	19N33	0S23	15N43	1N10	22N41	0S35	7S11	2N19

Day	♅ Decl	♅ Lat	♆ Decl	♆ Lat	♇ Decl	♇ Lat
1	22N22	0N25	6S46	1N40	22N49	9N19
5	22 20	0 26	6 48	1 40	22 47	9 19
9	22 18	0 26	6 50	1 40	22 45	9 19
13	22 16	0 26	6 52	1 40	22 42	9 20
17	22 15	0 26	6 54	1 40	22 40	9 20
21	22 13	0 26	6 56	1 39	22 38	9 20
25	22 11	0 26	6 59	1 39	22 35	9 21
29	22N 9	0N26	7S 1	1N39	22N33	9N21

☽ PHENOMENA

d	h	m	
2	3	17	☾
9	16	10	●
17	20	8	☽
24	20	21	○
31	10	47	☾

d	h	° '
5	6	26N42
12	13	0
19	22	26S39
26	4	0

1	17	5N17
8	14	0
16	2	5S15
22	23	0
28	23	5N12

VOID OF COURSE ☽

Last Aspect		☽ Ingress		
1	7am48	1	♉	10am57
3	10am55	3	♊	3pm11
5	8am12	5	♋	10pm 0
8	3am33	8	♌	7am16
10	4am 3	10	♍	6pm34
12	12pm13	13	♎	7am 9
15	5am28	15	♏	7pm44
17	8pm 8	18	♐	6am30
20	8am34	20	♑	1pm53
22	6am15	22	♒	5pm29
24	7am47	24	♓	6pm12
26	11am 3	26	♈	5pm46
28	3pm25	28	♉	6pm11
30	8pm48	30	♊	9pm 7

d	h	
13	7	APOGEE
25	18	PERIGEE

DAILY ASPECTARIAN

Day	Aspect	Time
1 S	☽✶♀	5am35
	☽□☿	7 48
	☽∥☿	10 55
	☽□♂	2pm 0
	♃∥♅	4 25
	☽∠♃	5 7
	☉∥☽	6 30
2 Su	☉□☽	3am17
	☿⊻♀	3 58
	☽∥♂	9 12
	☽∠♀	9 32
	☽∥♀	1pm43
	☽⊻♃	7 25
	☽∥♅	7 43
	☽∥♃	7 55
	☽✶♅	9 42
	☽∥♇	10 50
	☽⚻♆	11 53
3 M	☽⚻♄	0am45
	☽□♇	1 54
	☽✶☿	10 55
	☽⊻♀	2pm16
	☽✶♂	9 2
4 T	☽∠♅	0am28
	♀ ♋	1 9
	☽⚼♆	2 38
	☽⚼♄	3 36
	☉✶☽	12pm27
	☽∠☿	1 43
	☉∥☿	4 4
	☿SD	9 21
5 W	☽∠♂	1am41
	☽☌♃	2 2
	☽⊻♅	3 54
	☽△♆	6 2
	☽△♄	7 8
	☽✶♇	8 12
	♂∠♃	11 29
	☽⊻☿	5pm24
	☉∠☽	6 16
6 Th	☽☌♀	2am20
	☽⊻♂	7 4
	☽∠♇	12pm19
7 F	☉⊻☽	0am52
	☽⊻♃	11 17
	☽☌♅	12pm40
	☽□♆	2 43
	☽∥♇	3 8
	☽□♄	4 6
	☽⊻♇	5 3
	☽∥♃	5 24
	☽∥♅	6 27
	☽∥♀	11 12
8 S	☽☌☿	3am33
	☽∥♂	11 34
	☽∠♃	4pm47
	☽⊻♀	5 37
	☽☌♂	7 54
	☽∥☿	9 21
9 Su	☉∥☽	9am39
	☉☌☽	4pm10
	☽✶♃	10 48
	☽⊻♅	11 39
10 M	☽✶♆	1am35
	☽∠♀	2 18
	☽✶♄	3 15
	☽☌♇	4 3
	☽⊻☿	5pm21
	♀∠♇	9 16
	♀⊻♂	10 42
11 T	☽#♆	5am45
	☽∠♅	5 47
	☽#♄	7 17
	☽∠♆	7 39
	☽∠♄	9 29
	☽⊻♂	10 56
	☽✶♀	11 30
	☿ ♌	2pm 4
12 W	☽∠☿	1am30
	☉⊻☽	9 36
	☽□♃	11 57
	☽✶♅	12pm13
	☽⊻♆	2 0
	☽⊻♄	3 59
	☽⊻♇	4 34
	☽∠♂	7 0
13 Th	☽✶☿	10am20
	♃⊻♅	3pm15
	☉∠☽	6 42
	☽∥♄	6 56
	☉⊻♅	7 35
	☉✶♃	8 12
	☽∥♆	8 14
	☽∠♇	11 4
14 F	☽✶♂	3am 9
	☽□♀	6 45
	☉✶♆	5pm 2
	☿∥♂	9 0
15 S	☽□♅	1am15
	☽△♃	1 34
	☽☌♆	2 52
	☉✶☽	3 43
	☽☌♄	5 7
	☽✶♇	5 28
	☉#☽	7 40
	☉✶♄	10pm36
16 Su	☉☌♇	2am14
	☽□☿	4 56
	☽#♂	7 45
	☽⚼♃	8 1
	☽#☿	8 58
	☽□♂	6pm43
17 M	☽△♀	1am 7
	☽#♀	2 45
	☽#♅	8 39
	☽#♃	11 13
	☽#♇	11 51
	☽△♅	1pm 3
	☿∠♃	1 18
	☽⚻♃	1 53
	☽⊻♆	2 27
	☽⊻♄	4 53
	☽□♇	5 0
	☉□☽	8 8
18 T	☽⚼♀	9am 6
	☽⚼♅	5pm53
	☽∠♆	7 10
	♄✶♇	7 22
	☽∠♄	9 41
	☽△☿	10 14
19 W	☽△♂	7am19
	☽⚻♀	3pm56
	♃△♆	5 51
	☽⚻♅	9 47
	☽✶♆	10 59
	☽☍♃	11 2
20 Th	☽△♇	1am24
	☽✶♄	1 31
	☽⚼☿	5 28
	☉△☽	8 34
	☽⚼♂	12pm 1
21 F	☽⚼♇	4am 9
	☽⚻☿	11 32
	☉⚼☽	12pm58
	☽⚻♂	3 35
	♃∥♇	6 45
22 S	☽☍♀	1am47
	☽☍♅	2 40
	☽□♆	3 40
	☽⚻♃	4 12
	☽#♃	4 14
	☽#♇	4 17
	☽⚻♇	5 57
	☽□♄	6 15
	☽#♅	7 0
	♀☌♅	1pm 1
	☽#♀	2 51
	☉⚻☽	4 15
23 Su	♀□♆	1am16
	☿∥♂	1 30
	☽⚼♃	5 26
	☽#♂	9 43
	☽#☿	10 3
	☉ ♍	10 46
	♀⊻♃	11 12
	☿☌♂	12pm58
	☽☍♂	7 51
	☽☍☿	8 27
24 M	☽⚻♅	4am14
	☽△♆	5 7
	♀⊻♇	5 54
	☽△♃	6 1
	☽☍♇	7 18
	☽⚻♀	7 25
	☽△♄	7 47
	☉#☽	11 5
	♀□♄	12pm25
	☉☍☽	8 21
25 T	☽∥♆	2am38
	☽∥♄	2 39
	☽⚼♅	4 16
	☽⚼♆	5 5
	♄∥♆	7 23
	☽⚼♄	7 49
	☽⚼♀	9 19
	☽⚻♂	9pm48
26 W	☽⚻☿	2am56
	☽△♅	4 6
	☽⚻♆	4 53
	☽□♃	6 9
	☽⚻♇	7 3
	☽⚻♄	7 43
	☽△♀	11 3
	☿⊻♅	12pm31
	☿✶♆	6 44
	☽⚼♂	10 38
	☉⚻☽	11 10
27 Th	☽#♆	4am38
	☽#♄	4 49
	☽⚼☿	6 12
	☿✶♃	6 26
	☽⚼♇	6 57
	☿☌♇	12pm14
	☉∥☽	4 0
	☿✶♄	6 35
	☽△♂	11 46
28 F	☉⚼☽	0am54
	☽□♅	4 13
	☽☍♆	4 57
	☽✶♃	6 38
	☽△♇	7 12
	☽☍♄	8 5
	☽△☿	10 2
	☽∥☿	10 47
	☽□♀	3pm25
	☽∥♂	5 26
29 S	☉△☽	3am16
	☽∠♃	7 37
	☽∥♀	11 32
30 Su	☽∥♅	1am12
	♀ ♌	1 35
	☽∥♇	3 53
	☽□♂	3 58
	☽∥♃	4 52
	☉∠♅	6 11
	☽✶♅	6 29
	☽⚻♆	7 11
	☽⊻♃	9 21
	☽□♇	9 35
	☽⚻♄	10 44
	☉∠♆	4pm38
	☽□☿	8 48
	☽✶♀	10 58
	☿ ♍	10 59
31 M	☽∠♅	8am49
	☽⚼♆	9 31
	☉□☽	10 47
	☽⚼♄	1pm19
	♃✶♇	4 7

SEPTEMBER 1953

LONGITUDE

Day	Sid. Time	☉	☽	☽ 12 Hour	Mean ☊	True ☊	☿	♀	♂	♃	♄	♅	♆	♇
	h m s	° ' "	° ' "	° ' "	° '	° '	° '	° '	° '	° '	° '	° '	° '	° '
1	22 39 27	8♍ 15 27	15♊ 4 22	21♊ 38 35	1♒ 12	2♒ 47	2♍ 3	2♌ 17	21♌ 17	23♊ 27	24♎ 11	21♋ 39	22♎ 2	23♌ 25
2	22 43 23	9 13 32	28 7 27	4♋ 31 23	1 9	2 48	4 1	3 28	21 55	23 35	24 17	21 42	22 4	23 27
3	22 47 20	10 11 39	10♋ 50 51	17 6 17	1 6	2 49	5 58	4 39	22 33	23 42	24 23	21 45	22 5	23 29
4	22 51 16	11 9 48	23 18 8	29 26 50	1 3	2 51R	7 55	5 50	23 11	23 50	24 29	21 47	22 7	23 31
5	22 55 13	12 7 59	5♌ 32 47	11♌ 36 23	1 0	2 51	9 52	7 1	23 49	23 57	24 35	21 50	22 9	23 33
6	22 59 9	13 6 11	17 37 58	23 37 52	0 57	2 50	11 47	8 12	24 27	24 4	24 41	21 53	22 11	23 34
7	23 3 6	14 4 25	29 36 23	5♍ 33 46	0 53	2 47	13 42	9 23	25 5	24 11	24 47	21 55	22 13	23 36
8	23 7 3	15 2 42	11♍ 30 16	17 26 7	0 50	2 42	15 36	10 35	25 43	24 18	24 53	21 58	22 14	23 38
9	23 10 59	16 1 0	23 21 32	29 16 44	0 47	2 35	17 29	11 46	26 22	24 25	24 59	22 0	22 16	23 40
10	23 14 56	16 59 20	5♎ 11 56	11♎ 7 21	0 44	2 26	19 21	12 58	27 0	24 31	25 5	22 3	22 18	23 42
11	23 18 52	17 57 41	17 3 13	22 59 48	0 41	2 17	21 12	14 10	27 38	24 37	25 12	22 5	22 20	23 43
12	23 22 49	18 56 4	28 57 24	4♏ 56 19	0 38	2 9	23 2	15 21	28 16	24 44	25 18	22 7	22 22	23 45
13	23 26 45	19 54 29	10♏ 56 53	16 59 31	0 34	2 1	24 50	16 33	28 54	24 50	25 24	22 10	22 24	23 47
14	23 30 42	20 52 56	23 4 38	29 12 39	0 31	1 56	26 38	17 45	29 32	24 55	25 31	22 12	22 26	23 49
15	23 34 38	21 51 24	5♐ 24 4	11♐ 39 23	0 28	1 52	28 24	18 57	0♍ 9	25 1	25 37	22 14	22 28	23 50
16	23 38 35	22 49 54	17 59 8	24 23 48	0 25	1 51D	0♎ 10	20 9	0 47	25 7	25 43	22 17	22 30	23 52
17	23 42 32	23 48 26	0♑ 53 54	7♑ 29 54	0 22	1 51	1 54	21 21	1 25	25 12	25 50	22 19	22 32	23 54
18	23 46 28	24 46 59	14 12 14	21 1 15	0 18	1 52	3 38	22 34	2 3	25 17	25 57	22 21	22 34	23 55
19	23 50 25	25 45 33	27 57 10	5♒ 0 6	0 15	1 53R	5 20	23 46	2 41	25 22	26 3	22 23	22 36	23 57
20	23 54 21	26 44 10	12♒ 9 59	19 26 36	0 12	1 52	7 1	24 58	3 19	25 27	26 10	22 25	22 38	23 59
21	23 58 18	27 42 48	26 49 29	4♓ 17 57	0 9	1 50	8 41	26 11	3 57	25 32	26 16	22 27	22 40	24 0
22	0 2 14	28 41 28	11♓ 51 7	19 27 53	0 6	1 45	10 21	27 23	4 35	25 36	26 23	22 29	22 42	24 2
23	0 6 11	29 40 9	27 7 0	4♈ 47 4	0 3	1 38	11 59	28 36	5 13	25 41	26 30	22 31	22 44	24 4
24	0 10 7	0♎ 38 53	12♈ 26 40	20 4 20	29♑ 59	1 30	13 36	29 48	5 50	25 45	26 37	22 33	22 46	24 5
25	0 14 4	1 37 39	27 38 44	5♉ 8 37	29 56	1 21	15 12	1♍ 1	6 28	25 49	26 43	22 34	22 48	24 7
26	0 18 1	2 36 27	12♉ 32 58	19 50 57	29 53	1 12	16 48	2 14	7 6	25 53	26 50	22 36	22 50	24 8
27	0 21 57	3 35 17	27 1 57	4♊ 5 39	29 50	1 5	18 22	3 27	7 44	25 56	26 57	22 38	22 53	24 10
28	0 25 54	4 34 9	11♊ 1 52	17 50 41	29 47	1 1	19 56	4 40	8 22	26 0	27 4	22 40	22 55	24 12
29	0 29 50	5 33 4	24 32 18	1♋ 7 4	29 44	0 58D	21 29	5 53	8 59	26 3	27 11	22 41	22 57	24 13
30	0 33 47	6♎ 32 1	7♋ 35 27	13♋ 57 59	29♑ 40	0♒ 58	23♎ 1	7♍ 6	9♍ 37	26♊ 6	27♎ 18	22♋ 43	22♎ 59	24♌ 15

DECLINATION and LATITUDE

Day	☉ Decl	☽ Decl	☽ Lat	☽ 12 Hr. Decl	☿ Decl	☿ Lat	♀ Decl	♀ Lat	♂ Decl	♂ Lat	♃ Decl	♃ Lat	♄ Decl	♄ Lat
1	8N29	26N26	3N51	26N36	12N23	1N46	19N21	0S19	15N31	1N10	22N42	0S35	7S14	2N19
2	8 7	26 24	2 58	25 50	11 42	1 47	19 8	0 16	15 19	1 10	22 42	0 35	7 16	2 19
3	7 45	24 57	1 57	23 45	10 59	1 47	18 54	0 13	15 7	1 10	22 43	0 35	7 18	2 19
4	7 23	22 17	0 52	20 34	10 15	1 46	18 40	0 9	14 54	1 11	22 43	0 35	7 20	2 19
5	7 1	18 39	0S15	16 33	9 30	1 45	18 26	0 6	14 42	1 11	22 43	0 35	7 23	2 18
6	6 38	14 17	1 19	11 55	8 44	1 44	18 11	0 3	14 29	1 11	22 44	0 35	7 25	2 18
7	6 16	9 26	2 20	6 52	7 58	1 41	17 55	0N 1	14 17	1 11	22 44	0 35	7 27	2 18
8	5 54	4 16	3 14	1 37	7 12	1 39	17 39	0 4	14 4	1 11	22 44	0 35	7 30	2 18
9	5 31	1S 1	3 59	3S39	6 25	1 35	17 23	0 7	13 51	1 11	22 44	0 35	7 32	2 18
10	5 8	6 15	4 34	8 48	5 37	1 32	17 6	0 10	13 38	1 11	22 45	0 35	7 34	2 18
11	4 46	11 16	4 57	13 38	4 50	1 28	16 48	0 14	13 25	1 12	22 45	0 35	7 37	2 18
12	4 23	15 53	5 7	17 59	4 3	1 23	16 30	0 17	13 12	1 12	22 45	0 35	7 39	2 17
13	3 60	19 55	5 4	21 39	3 15	1 18	16 12	0 20	12 59	1 12	22 45	0 35	7 42	2 17
14	3 37	23 10	4 47	24 26	2 28	1 13	15 53	0 23	12 46	1 12	22 46	0 35	7 44	2 17
15	3 14	25 25	4 17	26 6	1 40	1 8	15 33	0 26	12 33	1 12	22 46	0 35	7 47	2 17
16	2 51	26 27	3 33	26 27	0 53	1 2	15 13	0 29	12 19	1 12	22 46	0 35	7 49	2 17
17	2 28	26 5	2 39	25 21	0 6	0 56	14 53	0 32	12 6	1 12	22 46	0 35	7 52	2 17
18	2 4	24 14	1 34	22 45	0S41	0 50	14 32	0 34	11 52	1 12	22 47	0 35	7 54	2 17
19	1 41	20 55	0 21	18 45	1 27	0 44	14 11	0 37	11 39	1 13	22 47	0 35	7 56	2 17
20	1 18	16 16	0N55	13 31	2 13	0 37	13 50	0 40	11 25	1 13	22 47	0 35	7 59	2 17
21	0 55	10 33	2 9	7 23	2 59	0 31	13 28	0 43	11 12	1 13	22 47	0 35	8 1	2 16
22	0 31	4 5	3 17	0 42	3 44	0 24	13 5	0 45	10 58	1 13	22 47	0 35	8 4	2 16
23	0 8	2N42	4 11	6N 4	4 29	0 17	12 43	0 48	10 44	1 13	22 47	0 35	8 6	2 16
24	0S15	9 20	4 48	12 26	5 13	0 10	12 20	0 50	10 30	1 13	22 47	0 35	8 9	2 16
25	0 39	15 21	5 4	17 60	5 57	0 3	11 56	0 53	10 17	1 13	22 48	0 35	8 12	2 16
26	1 2	20 20	4 58	22 20	6 40	0S 4	11 32	0 55	10 3	1 13	22 48	0 35	8 14	2 16
27	1 26	23 56	4 34	25 9	7 23	0 12	11 8	0 57	9 49	1 14	22 48	0 35	8 17	2 16
28	1 49	25 57	3 54	26 21	8 5	0 19	10 44	0 60	9 35	1 14	22 48	0 35	8 19	2 16
29	2 12	26 21	3 1	25 59	8 47	0 26	10 19	1 2	9 20	1 14	22 48	0 35	8 22	2 16
30	2S36	25N15	2N 1	24N12	9S28	0S34	9N54	1N 4	9N 6	1N14	22N48	0S35	8S24	2N16

Day	♅ Decl	♅ Lat	♆ Decl	♆ Lat	♇ Decl	♇ Lat
1	22N 8	0N26	7S 3	1N39	22N32	9N22
5	22 6	0 26	7 6	1 39	22 30	9 22
9	22 5	0 26	7 9	1 39	22 28	9 23
13	22 3	0 26	7 12	1 39	22 26	9 23
17	22 2	0 26	7 15	1 39	22 25	9 24
21	22 1	0 27	7 18	1 38	22 23	9 25
25	21 60	0 27	7 21	1 38	22 22	9 26
29	21N59	0N27	7S24	1N38	22N20	9N27

☽ PHENOMENA

d	h	m	
8	7	48	●
16	9	50	☽
23	4	16	○
29	21	52	☾

d	h	° '
1	11	26N36
8	19	0
16	6	26S30
22	14	0
28	18	26N24

d	h	° '
4	19	0
12	6	5S 7
19	7	0
25	6	5N 4

VOID OF COURSE ☽

Last Aspect		☽ Ingress		
1	4pm49	2	♋	3am30
4	2am19	4	♌	1pm 5
6	2pm25	7	♍	0am48
9	2am 9	9	♎	1pm28
11	10pm31	12	♏	2am 6
14	1pm18	14	♐	1pm32
16	2pm35	16	♑	10pm21
18	8pm42	19	♒	3am30
20	11pm 6	21	♓	5am 7
23	4am16	23	♈	4am31
24	10pm31	25	♉	3am45
26	7pm11	27	♊	5am 1
29	4am50	29	♋	9am57

d	h	
9	16	APOGEE
23	4	PERIGEE

DAILY ASPECTARIAN

Day	Aspect	Time
1 T	☽∠♀	4am24
	☿⚺♀	7 7
	☽∗♂	11 55
	☽⚺♅	12pm 4
	☽△♆	12 44
	♂⚺♅	3 13
	☽∗♇	3 19
	☽☌♃	3 29
	☽△♄	4 49
2 W	☉∠♄	1am37
	♂∗♆	5 43
	☽⚺♀	11 1
	☽∗☿	1pm 3
	☽∠♂	5 24
	☽∠♇	7 29
	☉∗☽	10 39
3 Th	☿∠♅	9am45
	☿∠♆	1pm59
	☽∥♃	8 41
	☽☌♅	9 3
	☽□♆	9 42
	☽∥♇	10 19
	☽∠☿	11 7
	☽⚺♂	11 46
4 F	☽⚺♇	0am25
	☽⚺♃	1 2
	☽∥♅	1 17
	☽□♄	2 19
	☉#♄	2 25
	☉∠☽	6 3
	♂☌♇	12pm58
	☉#♆	6 34
	☿∠♄	8 21
5 S	☽∥♀	1am24
	☽☌♀	3 13
	♂∗♃	6 3
	☽∠♃	6 48
	☽⚺☿	10 9
	☉⚺☽	2pm11
	☽∥♂	10 56
6 Su	☽⚺♅	8am31
	☽∗♆	9 7
	♂∗♄	10 3
	☽☌♇	11 55
	☽∗♃	1pm 0
	☽∗♄	2 13
	☽☌♂	2 25
	♀∠♃	7 26
7 M	☽∥☿	8am 5
	☽#♄	9 12
	☉☌☿	9 36
	☽#♆	10 49
	☽∠♅	2pm47
	☿#♄	3 10
	☽∠♆	3 22
	☉∥☽	3 56
	☽∠♄	8 42
	☽⚺♀	9 55
8 T	☿#♆	1am51
	☉☌☽	7 48
	☽☌☿	9 51
	☽∗♅	9pm15
	☽⚺♆	9 47
9 W	☽⚺♇	0am37
	☽□♃	2 9
	☽⚺♄	3 19
	☽⚺♂	6 26
	☽∠♀	7 42
	☉#☽	7pm11
	☽#☿	9 28
10 Th	☽∥♆	4am15
	☽∥♄	6 15
	☽∠♇	7 6
	☽∠♂	2pm32
	☽∗♀	5 30
11 F	☉⚺☽	2am 0
	☉∥☿	4 18
	☽⚺☿	9 53
	☽□♅	10 12
	☽#♂	10 25
	☽☌♆	10 42
	☿∗♅	11 53
	☽∗♇	1pm30
	☿⚺♆	3 11
	☽△♃	3 25
	☽☌♄	4 34
	☽∗♂	10 31
12 S	☽#♀	3am13
	☿⚺♇	9 46
	☉∠☽	10 52
	☽∠☿	9pm24
	☽⚼♃	9 45
	☿□♃	11 51
13 Su	☿⚺♄	8am 1
	☽□♀	12pm21
	☽#♅	2 59
	☽#♇	5 55
	☉∗☽	7 18
	☽#♃	8 35
	☽△♅	10 16
	☽⚺♆	10 44
14 M	☽□♇	1am27
	☽⚻♃	3 39
	☽⚺♄	4 49
	☽∗☿	8 9
	☽□♂	1pm18
	♂ ♍	6 0
15 T	☽⚼♅	3am33
	☽∠♆	3 59
	☉∗♅	9 46
	☽∠♄	10 6
	☉⚺♆	3pm29
	☿ ♎	9 45
16 W	☽△♀	4am30
	☽⚻♅	8 4
	☽∗♆	8 29
	☉□☽	9 50
	☽△♇	11 2
	☽☍♃	1pm25
	☿⚺♂	1 32
	☽∗♄	2 35
17 Th	☽△♂	1am 1
	☽□☿	2 7
	☉⚺♇	2 15
	☽⚼♀	10 55
	☽⚼♇	2pm33
	♀⚺♅	7 39
18 F	♀∗♆	0am 7
	☽⚼♂	5 17
	☽#♃	11 50
	☉□♃	1pm34
	☽☍♅	2 21
	☽#♇	2 31
	☽□♆	2 43
	☽⚻♀	4 5
	☽#♅	5 3
	☽⚻♇	5 5
	☽⚻♃	7 32
	☉△☽	7 56
	☽□♄	8 42
19 S	♀☌♇	3am50
	☉#☿	4 54
	☉⚺♄	8 7
	☽⚻♂	8 27
	☽△☿	2pm15
	☽⚼♃	9 8
	☉⚼☽	11 14
20 Su	♀∗♃	10am15
	☽#♀	11 27
	☽⚻♅	4pm53
	☽△♆	5 15
	☽⚼☿	6 16
	☽☍♇	7 26
	☽#♂	9 21
	☽△♃	9 54
	☽☍♀	10 52
	☽△♄	11 6
21 M	☉⚻☽	1am32
	♀∗♄	2 6
	☿∠♇	4 42
	☽∥♄	9 33
	☽☍♂	11 56
	☽∥♆	12pm17
	☽⚼♅	5 3
	☽⚼♆	5 24
	☽⚻☿	9 19
	☽⚼♄	11 15
22 T	☽∥☿	1am 8
	☉#☽	1pm25
	☉∥☽	3 26
	☽△♅	4 46
	☽⚻♆	5 7
	☽⚻♇	7 12
	☽□♃	9 44
	☽⚻♄	11 1
23 W	☽⚻♀	2am31
	☉☍☽	4 16
	☽#☿	7 7
	☉ ♎	8 7
	☽⚻♂	1pm12
	☽#♆	4 37
	☽⚼♇	6 44
	☽#♄	7 35
24 Th	☽☍☿	2am 2
	♀ ♍	3 48
	☽⚼♀	4 2
	☽∥♂	4 18
	☽∥♀	10 50
	☽⚼♂	1pm47
	☽□♅	3 56
	☽☍♆	4 18
	☽△♇	6 23
	☽∗♃	9 4
	☽☍♄	10 31
25 F	☽△♀	5am52
	☉⚻☽	6 48
	☽△♂	2pm46
	☽∠♃	9 16
26 S	☽⚻☿	7am49
	☉⚼☽	8 54
	☽∥♅	9 49
	☽∥♇	12pm12
	☽∥♃	3 14
	☽∗♅	4 37
	☽⚻♆	5 1
	☽□♇	7 11
	♂∠♅	8 10
	☽⚺♃	10 9
	☿∥♆	11 42
	☽⚻♄	11 52
27 Su	☿∠♀	5am14
	♂∠♆	5 59
	☽□♀	11 56
	☉△☽	11 58
	☽⚼☿	12pm 7
	☉⚺♀	2 12
	☽∠♅	6 8
	☽⚼♆	6 34
	☽□♂	7 8
28 M	☽⚼♄	1am49
	☿∥♄	8 28
	☽△☿	5pm46
	☽⚺♅	8 39
	☽△♆	9 7
	☽∗♇	11 25
29 T	☽☌♃	2am45
	☽△♄	4 50
	☿#♂	2pm33
	☿□♅	7 17
	☉□☽	9 52
	☽∗♀	10 59
	☿☌♆	11 36
30 W	☽∠♇	3am 6
	☽∗♂	3 59
	☿#♀	9 25
	♀∠♅	12pm20
	♀∠♆	5 55
	☿∗♇	7 50

OCTOBER 1953

LONGITUDE

Day	Sid. Time	☉	☽	☽ 12 Hour	Mean ☊	True ☊	☿	♀	♂	♃	♄	♅	♆	♇
	h m s	° ' "	° ' "	° ' "	° '	° '	° '	° '	° '	° '	° '	° '	° '	° '
1	0 37 43	7♎ 31 1	20♋ 15 14	26♋ 27 49	29♑ 37	0♒ 58R	24♎ 31	8♍ 19	10♍ 15	26♊ 9	27♎ 25	22♋ 44	23♎ 1	24♌ 16
2	0 41 40	8 30 2	2♌ 36 20	8♌ 41 23	29 34	0 59	26 2	9 32	10 52	26 12	27 32	22 46	23 3	24 17
3	0 45 36	9 29 6	14 43 32	20 43 22	29 31	0 58	27 31	10 46	11 30	26 14	27 39	22 47	23 6	24 19
4	0 49 33	10 28 12	26 41 22	2♍ 38 0	29 28	0 55	28 59	11 59	12 8	26 16	27 46	22 49	23 8	24 20
5	0 53 30	11 27 20	8♍ 33 43	14 28 52	29 24	0 49	0♏ 27	13 13	12 46	26 18	27 53	22 50	23 10	24 22
6	0 57 26	12 26 31	20 23 47	26 18 45	29 21	0 40	1 53	14 26	13 23	26 20	28 0	22 51	23 12	24 23
7	1 1 23	13 25 44	2♎ 14 2	8♎ 9 50	29 18	0 29	3 19	15 40	14 1	26 22	28 7	22 53	23 14	24 25
8	1 5 19	14 24 58	14 6 21	20 3 44	29 15	0 16	4 43	16 53	14 39	26 24	28 14	22 54	23 17	24 26
9	1 9 16	15 24 15	26 2 9	2♏ 1 45	29 12	0 2	6 7	18 7	15 16	26 25	28 21	22 55	23 19	24 27
10	1 13 12	16 23 34	8♏ 2 42	14 5 9	29 9	29♑ 48	7 30	19 21	15 54	26 26	28 29	22 56	23 21	24 29
11	1 17 9	17 22 54	20 9 18	26 15 23	29 5	29 36	8 52	20 34	16 31	26 27	28 36	22 57	23 23	24 30
12	1 21 5	18 22 17	2♐ 23 38	8♐ 34 22	29 2	29 26	10 12	21 48	17 9	26 28	28 43	22 58	23 26	24 31
13	1 25 2	19 21 41	14 47 52	21 4 32	28 59	29 19	11 32	23 2	17 47	26 28	28 50	22 59	23 28	24 32
14	1 28 58	20 21 8	27 24 45	3♑ 48 57	28 56	29 16	12 50	24 16	18 24	26 29	28 57	23 0	23 30	24 34
15	1 32 55	21 20 36	10♑ 17 34	16 51 3	28 53	29 14D	14 7	25 30	19 2	26 29R	29 5	23 1	23 32	24 35
16	1 36 52	22 20 6	23 29 50	0♒ 14 17	28 49	29 14R	15 23	26 44	19 39	26 29	29 12	23 1	23 34	24 36
17	1 40 48	23 19 38	7♒ 4 47	14 1 33	28 46	29 14	16 37	27 58	20 17	26 28	29 19	23 2	23 37	24 37
18	1 44 45	24 19 11	21 4 43	28 14 17	28 43	29 13	17 50	29 12	20 54	26 28	29 26	23 3	23 39	24 38
19	1 48 41	25 18 46	5♓ 30 2	12♓ 51 34	28 40	29 9	19 1	0♎ 26	21 32	26 27	29 33	23 3	23 41	24 39
20	1 52 38	26 18 23	20 18 18	27 49 23	28 37	29 3	20 11	1 41	22 9	26 26	29 41	23 4	23 43	24 40
21	1 56 34	27 18 1	5♈ 23 47	13♈ 0 19	28 34	28 54	21 18	2 55	22 47	26 25	29 48	23 4	23 46	24 41
22	2 0 31	28 17 42	20 37 37	28 14 18	28 30	28 43	22 23	4 9	23 24	26 24	29 55	23 5	23 48	24 42
23	2 4 27	29 17 24	5♉ 48 58	13♉ 20 15	28 27	28 31	23 25	5 23	24 1	26 22	0♏ 3	23 5	23 50	24 43
24	2 8 24	0♏ 17 9	20 46 56	28 8 0	28 24	28 20	24 25	6 38	24 39	26 21	0 10	23 5	23 52	24 44
25	2 12 21	1 16 55	5♊ 22 37	12♊ 30 11	28 21	28 11	25 22	7 52	25 16	26 19	0 17	23 6	23 55	24 45
26	2 16 17	2 16 44	19 30 21	26 22 56	28 18	28 4	26 16	9 7	25 54	26 17	0 24	23 6	23 57	24 46
27	2 20 14	3 16 35	3♋ 8 2	9♋ 45 51	28 15	28 0	27 6	10 21	26 31	26 14	0 32	23 6	23 59	24 47
28	2 24 10	4 16 28	16 16 46	22 41 16	28 11	27 58D	27 53	11 36	27 8	26 12	0 39	23 6	24 1	24 48
29	2 28 7	5 16 23	28 59 54	5♌ 13 18	28 8	27 58R	28 34	12 50	27 46	26 9	0 46	23 6R	24 3	24 49
30	2 32 3	6 16 21	11♌ 22 7	17 27 2	28 5	27 58	29 11	14 5	28 23	26 6	0 53	23 6	24 6	24 50
31	2 36 0	7♏ 16 21	23♌ 28 42	29♌ 27 47	28♑ 2	27♑ 57	29♏ 43	15♎ 20	29♍ 0	26♊ 3	1♏ 1	23♋ 6	24♎ 8	24♌ 50

DECLINATION and LATITUDE

Day	☉ Decl	☽ Decl	☽ Lat	☽ 12 Hr. Decl	☿ Decl	☿ Lat	♀ Decl	♀ Lat	♂ Decl	♂ Lat	♃ Decl	♃ Lat	♄ Decl	♄ Lat
1	2S59	22N51	0N57	21N16	10S 8	0S41	9N28	1N 6	8N52	1N14	22N48	0S35	8S27	2N15
2	3 22	19 27	0S 9	17 26	10 48	0 48	9 3	1 8	8 38	1 14	22 48	0 35	8 29	2 15
3	3 46	15 16	1 12	12 58	11 27	0 55	8 37	1 10	8 24	1 14	22 48	0 35	8 32	2 15
4	4 9	10 33	2 12	8 3	12 5	1 3	8 11	1 12	8 9	1 14	22 48	0 35	8 35	2 15
5	4 32	5 30	3 5	2 54	12 43	1 10	7 44	1 14	7 55	1 14	22 48	0 35	8 37	2 15
6	4 55	0 17	3 50	2S21	13 20	1 17	7 17	1 15	7 41	1 14	22 49	0 35	8 40	2 15
7	5 18	4S57	4 25	7 30	13 56	1 24	6 50	1 17	7 26	1 14	22 49	0 35	8 42	2 15
8	5 41	9 60	4 49	12 24	14 31	1 31	6 23	1 19	7 12	1 14	22 49	0 35	8 45	2 15
9	6 4	14 42	4 59	16 52	15 6	1 38	5 56	1 20	6 57	1 15	22 49	0 35	8 47	2 15
10	6 27	18 52	4 57	20 42	15 40	1 44	5 28	1 22	6 43	1 15	22 49	0 35	8 50	2 15
11	6 50	22 18	4 42	23 40	16 12	1 51	5 1	1 23	6 28	1 15	22 49	0 35	8 53	2 15
12	7 12	24 46	4 13	25 35	16 44	1 57	4 33	1 24	6 13	1 15	22 49	0 35	8 55	2 15
13	7 35	26 5	3 32	26 15	17 15	2 3	4 5	1 26	5 59	1 15	22 49	0 35	8 58	2 15
14	7 57	26 5	2 40	25 33	17 45	2 9	3 36	1 27	5 44	1 15	22 49	0 35	9 0	2 15
15	8 20	24 41	1 38	23 27	18 14	2 15	3 8	1 28	5 30	1 15	22 49	0 35	9 3	2 15
16	8 42	21 54	0 30	20 1	18 42	2 21	2 40	1 29	5 15	1 15	22 49	0 35	9 5	2 15
17	9 4	17 50	0N41	15 23	19 9	2 26	2 11	1 30	5 0	1 15	22 49	0 35	9 8	2 15
18	9 26	12 42	1 53	9 48	19 34	2 31	1 42	1 31	4 45	1 15	22 49	0 35	9 11	2 15
19	9 48	6 43	2 59	3 31	19 59	2 36	1 13	1 32	4 31	1 15	22 49	0 35	9 13	2 15
20	10 9	0 15	3 55	3N 4	20 22	2 41	0 45	1 32	4 16	1 15	22 49	0 35	9 16	2 15
21	10 31	6N21	4 35	9 34	20 44	2 45	0 16	1 33	4 1	1 15	22 49	0 35	9 18	2 15
22	10 52	12 38	4 57	15 31	21 5	2 48	0S13	1 33	3 46	1 15	22 49	0 35	9 21	2 15
23	11 13	18 8	4 58	20 27	21 24	2 52	0 42	1 34	3 32	1 15	22 49	0 35	9 23	2 15
24	11 35	22 25	4 38	23 59	21 42	2 54	1 11	1 34	3 17	1 15	22 49	0 35	9 26	2 15
25	11 55	25 8	3 60	25 52	21 58	2 56	1 40	1 35	3 2	1 15	22 49	0 35	9 28	2 15
26	12 16	26 9	3 8	26 2	22 12	2 58	2 9	1 35	2 47	1 15	22 49	0 35	9 31	2 15
27	12 37	25 32	2 7	24 40	22 25	2 59	2 38	1 35	2 32	1 15	22 49	0 35	9 33	2 15
28	12 57	23 28	1 1	21 60	22 36	2 59	3 7	1 35	2 17	1 15	22 49	0 35	9 36	2 15
29	13 17	20 17	0S 5	18 21	22 45	2 59	3 36	1 35	2 3	1 15	22 49	0 35	9 39	2 15
30	13 37	16 15	1 10	14 0	22 52	2 57	4 5	1 35	1 48	1 15	22 49	0 35	9 41	2 15
31	13S57	11N38	2S11	9N11	22S57	2S55	4S34	1N35	1N33	1N15	22N48	0S35	9S43	2N15

Day	♅ Decl	♅ Lat	♆ Decl	♆ Lat	♇ Decl	♇ Lat
1	21N58	0N27	7S26	1N38	22N20	9N27
5	21 57	0 27	7 29	1 38	22 19	9 29
9	21 57	0 27	7 32	1 38	22 18	9 30
13	21 56	0 27	7 36	1 38	22 17	9 31
17	21 56	0 27	7 39	1 38	22 17	9 32
21	21 55	0 28	7 42	1 38	22 16	9 33
25	21 55	0 28	7 45	1 38	22 16	9 34
29	21N55	0N28	7S49	1N38	22N16	9N36

☽ PHENOMENA

d	h	m	
8	0	41	●
15	21	45	☽
22	12	56	○
29	13	10	☾

d	h	° '
6	1	0
13	12	26S15
20	1	0
26	2	26N10

d	h	° '
1	21	0
9	8	5S 0
16	10	0
22	13	4N60
28	22	0

VOID OF COURSE ☽

Last Aspect		☽ Ingress		
1	1pm59	1	♌	6pm54
4	5am17	4	♍	6am41
6	12pm 5	6	♎	7pm28
9	4am42	9	♏	7am56
11	8am34	11	♐	7pm20
14	2am56	14	♑	4am52
16	10am15	16	♒	11am35
18	2pm 7	18	♓	2pm56
20	9am47	20	♈	3pm27
22	2pm47	22	♉	2pm47
24	6am34	24	♊	3pm 5
26	11am47	26	♋	6pm24
28	11pm 8	29	♌	1am55
31	12pm59	31	♍	1pm 5

d	h	
6	18	APOGEE
21	16	PERIGEE

DAILY ASPECTARIAN

Day	Aspect	Time
1	☽∥♃	0am25
Th	☽∥♇	4 9
	☽☌♅	4 48
	☽□♆	5 21
	☽∠♀	6 33
	☽∥♅	6 53
	☽⚺♇	7 45
	☽□☿	9 23
	☽∠♂	10 9
	☽⚺♃	11 26
	☽□♄	1pm59
	☿∠♂	7 48
2	☿△♃	2am45
F	♂#♄	12pm 6
	☉⚹☽	12 39
	☽⚺♀	3 14
	☽∠♃	5 1
	☽⚺♂	5 14
	☉∠♇	7 46
3	☿☌♄	2am21
S	♀#♄	4 1
	☽⚺♅	4pm11
	☽⚹♆	4 49
	☽#☿	5 17
	☽☌♇	7 16
	☉∠☽	9 19
	☽⚹♃	11 9
4	☽⚹♄	2am11
Su	♀∥♂	2 30
	☽⚹☿	5 17
	♀☌♂	5 52
	☽#♄	9 27
	☽∥♂	12pm 6
	☽∥♀	12 31
	☽#♆	2 43
	☿ ♏	4 41
	♀∠♄	4 53
	☽∠♅	10 31
	☽∠♆	11 12
5	☉#☽	4am 9
M	♂∠♄	5 45
	☉⚺☽	6 24
	☽∠♄	8 51
	☽☌♂	8 59
	☽☌♀	10 31
	♀#♆	1pm 7
	☽∠☿	3 54
6	☽⚹♅	5am 0
T	☽⚺♆	5 43
	☽⚺♇	8 7
	☽□♃	12pm 5
	☽⚺♄	3 35
	♂#♆	4 48
7	☉∥☽	1am48
W	☽⚺☿	2 29
	☽#♀	8 9
	☽#♂	11 9
	☽∥♆	12pm 5
	☽∠♇	2 33
	☽∥♄	5 54
8	☉☌☽	0am41
Th	☽⚺♂	1 9
	☽⚺♀	6 15
	☉⚺♂	3pm 2
	☽□♅	5 43
	☽☌♆	6 31
	☉#♀	8 7
	☽⚹♇	8 49
9	☽△♃	0am46
F	☽∥☿	2 27
	☽☌♄	4 42
	☽∠♂	8 57
	☽∠♀	3pm47
	☽☌☿	10 47
10	☽⚼♃	6am45
S	☉#♂	10 8
	☽⚹♂	4pm26
	☉⚺☽	6 2
	☽#♅	9 8
	☽#♇	11 56
11	☽⚹♀	0am55
Su	☽#♃	4 13
	☽△♅	5 31
	☽⚺♆	6 23
	☽□♇	8 34
	☽⚻♃	12pm23
	☽⚺♄	4 45
12	☉∠☽	2am 4
M	☽⚼♅	10 50
	☽∠♆	11 45
	☽⚺☿	4pm58
	☽∠♄	10 8
	☿⚼♃	10 51
	♀⚹♅	10 56
13	☉∥♆	0am54
T	☽□♂	6 0
	♀⚺♆	8 34
	☉⚹☽	9 29
	☽⚻♅	3pm38
	☽⚹♆	4 35
	☽□♀	5 25
	☽△♇	6 36
	☽☍♃	10 14
14	☽∠☿	0am54
W	☽⚹♄	2 56
	♀⚺♇	5 46
	☽⚼♇	10pm41
15	♃SR	2am54
Th	☽⚹☿	7 47
	☽△♂	4pm44
	☽#♃	5 15
	♀□♃	7 0
	☽#♇	9 15
	☉□☽	9 45
	☽☍♅	11 9
	☽#♅	11 46
16	☽□♆	0am 8
F	☽⚻♇	1 58
	☽⚻♃	5 19
	☽△♀	6 22
	☽□♄	10 15
	☉□♅	4pm49
	☽∥☿	5 38
	☽⚼♂	8 42
17	☉∥♄	5am 6
S	☉☌♆	7 9
	☽⚼♃	7 36
	☽⚼♀	11 10
	☽□☿	6pm 0
	☽⚻♂	11 41
18	☽⚻♅	3am19
Su	☽△♆	4 20
	♀⚺♄	5 1
	☉△☽	5 52
	☽☍♇	5 59
	☉⚹♇	7 47
	☽△♃	9 2
	☉∥☽	12pm41
	☽△♄	2 7
	☽∥♄	2 21
	☽⚻♀	2 53
	♀ ♎	3 27
	☽∥♆	8 20
19	☽⚼♅	4am11
M	☽⚼♆	5 14
	☉⚼☽	8 26
	☽#♂	8 40
	☽⚼♄	2pm52
	☽#♀	10 2
	☽△☿	11 47
20	☽☍♂	3am 5
T	☉△♃	3 7
	☽∥♀	3 20
	☽△♅	4 25
	☽⚻♆	5 29
	☽⚻♇	6 59
	☽□♃	9 47
	☉⚻☽	10 16
	☽⚻♄	3pm 4
	☽∥♂	3 45
	☽☍♀	7 43
21	☽⚼☿	1am32
W	☽#♆	4 59
	☽⚼♇	6 47
	☽#♄	11 4
	♂⚹♅	11 30
	☉#☽	4pm35
22	☽⚻☿	2am58
Th	☽□♅	3 52
	☽⚻♂	4 33
	☽☍♆	5 0
	☽△♇	6 26
	☽⚹♃	9 5
	☉☍☽	12pm56
	☽☍♄	2 47
	♄ ♏	3 38
	☿△♅	4 4
	♂⚺♆	4 16
	☽⚻♀	11 16
23	☽⚼♂	5am20
F	☽∠♃	8 51
	☿⚺♆	10 7
	☉ ♏	5pm 7
	☽#☿	6 59
	☉☌♄	8 38
	☽∥♅	8 48
	☽∥♇	11 4
24	☽⚼♀	1am30
S	☽∥♃	2 48
	♂⚺♇	3 38
	☽⚹♅	3 45
	☽⚻♆	5 2
	☽☍☿	6 21
	☽□♇	6 27
	☽△♂	6 34
	☿□♇	7 58
	☽⚺♃	9 3
	☽⚻♄	3pm29
	☿⚹♂	4 1
	☉⚻☽	4 42
	☿#♅	8 6
25	☽∠♅	4am33
Su	☽△♀	4 34
	☽⚼♆	5 56
	☽⚼♄	4pm53
	☉⚼☽	7 52
26	☿⚻♃	0am14
M	☽⚺♅	6 15
	☿#♇	6 53
	☽△♆	7 45
	☽⚹♇	9 11
	☽□♂	11 41
	☽☌♃	11 47
	☽⚻☿	12pm36
	♀∠♇	12 53
	♂□♃	2 0
	☽△♄	7 18
	♀#♂	8 38
27	☉△☽	0am17
T	☽∠♇	12pm 3
	☽□♀	2 27
	☽⚼☿	5 20
28	☽∥♃	5am38
W	☽#☿	6 57
	☽∥♇	9 55
	☽∥♅	12pm33
	☽☌♅	12 47
	☽□♆	2 34
	☽⚺♇	4 1
	☽⚺♃	6 36
	☽⚹♂	9 31
	☽△☿	11 8
29	☽□♄	3am26
Th	☿#♃	11 8
	☉□☽	1pm10
	♅SR	2 21
	☽∠♃	11 29
30	☿∠♀	3am38
F	☽∠♂	4 11
	☽⚹♀	5 57
	☉#☽	1pm 5
	☽⚺♅	11 15
31	☽⚹♆	1am19
S	☽☌♇	2 44
	☽⚹♃	5 8
	☽#♄	9 20
	☽⚺♂	11 42
	☽□☿	12pm59
	☽⚹♄	3 16
	☽∠♀	3 21
	☿ ♐	3 51
	☽#♆	6 26

NOVEMBER 1953

LONGITUDE

Day	Sid. Time	☉	☽	☽ 12 Hour	Mean ☊	True ☊	☿	♀	♂	♃	♄	♅	♆	♇
	h m s	° ' "	° ' "	° ' "	° '	° '	° '	° '	° '	° '	° '	° '	° '	° '
1	2 39 56	8♏ 16 22	5♍ 24 54	11♍ 20 40	27♑ 59	27♑ 54R	0♐ 8	16♎ 34	29♍ 38	26♊ 0R	1♏ 8	23♋ 6R	24♎ 10	24♌ 51
2	2 43 53	9 16 26	17 15 37	23 10 16	27 55	27 49	0 27	17 49	0♎ 15	25 57	1 15	23 6	24 12	24 52
3	2 47 50	10 16 32	29 5 4	5♎ 0 25	27 52	27 40	0 38R	19 4	0 52	25 53	1 22	23 6	24 14	24 53
4	2 51 46	11 16 40	10♎ 56 40	16 54 7	27 49	27 29	0 41	20 19	1 30	25 49	1 30	23 6	24 17	24 53
5	2 55 43	12 16 50	22 53 1	28 53 33	27 46	27 17	0 36	21 34	2 7	25 45	1 37	23 5	24 19	24 54
6	2 59 39	13 17 1	4♏ 55 54	11♏ 0 10	27 43	27 3	0 22	22 48	2 44	25 41	1 44	23 5	24 21	24 55
7	3 3 36	14 17 15	17 6 27	23 14 51	27 40	26 49	29♏ 58	24 3	3 21	25 37	1 51	23 4	24 23	24 55
8	3 7 32	15 17 31	29 25 25	5♐ 38 14	27 36	26 37	29 24	25 18	3 59	25 32	1 58	23 4	24 25	24 56
9	3 11 29	16 17 48	11♐ 53 23	18 10 58	27 33	26 27	28 41	26 33	4 36	25 27	2 5	23 3	24 27	24 56
10	3 15 25	17 18 6	24 31 6	0♑ 53 56	27 30	26 20	27 47	27 48	5 13	25 22	2 12	23 3	24 29	24 57
11	3 19 22	18 18 27	7♑ 19 41	13 48 33	27 27	26 16	26 46	29 3	5 50	25 17	2 20	23 2	24 31	24 57
12	3 23 19	19 18 49	20 20 47	26 56 39	27 24	26 14D	25 36	0♏ 18	6 27	25 12	2 27	23 1	24 34	24 58
13	3 27 15	20 19 12	3♒ 36 26	10♒ 20 24	27 21	26 14	24 20	1 33	7 4	25 7	2 34	23 1	24 36	24 58
14	3 31 12	21 19 37	17 8 49	24 1 52	27 17	26 15R	23 1	2 48	7 41	25 1	2 41	23 0	24 38	24 59
15	3 35 8	22 20 3	0♓ 59 43	8♓ 2 25	27 14	26 15	21 40	4 3	8 18	24 55	2 48	22 59	24 40	24 59
16	3 39 5	23 20 30	15 9 54	22 21 59	27 11	26 12	20 21	5 18	8 55	24 49	2 55	22 58	24 42	24 59
17	3 43 1	24 20 58	29 38 17	6♈ 58 19	27 8	26 8	19 6	6 33	9 33	24 43	3 2	22 57	24 44	25 0
18	3 46 58	25 21 28	14♈ 21 24	21 46 42	27 5	26 1	17 56	7 49	10 10	24 37	3 9	22 56	24 46	25 0
19	3 50 54	26 21 59	29 13 13	6♉ 39 56	27 1	25 53	16 56	9 4	10 47	24 31	3 16	22 55	24 48	25 0
20	3 54 51	27 22 32	14♉ 5 43	21 29 26	26 58	25 43	16 5	10 19	11 24	24 25	3 22	22 54	24 50	25 0
21	3 58 48	28 23 6	28 50 0	6♊ 6 26	26 55	25 34	15 25	11 34	12 0	24 18	3 29	22 53	24 52	25 1
22	4 2 44	29 23 41	13♊ 17 54	20 23 40	26 52	25 26	14 57	12 49	12 37	24 11	3 36	22 52	24 54	25 1
23	4 6 41	0♐ 24 18	27 23 14	4♋ 16 15	26 49	25 20	14 40D	14 5	13 14	24 4	3 43	22 50	24 55	25 1
24	4 10 37	1 24 57	11♋ 2 35	17 42 13	26 46	25 17	14 35	15 20	13 51	23 57	3 50	22 49	24 57	25 1
25	4 14 34	2 25 37	24 15 20	0♌ 42 13	26 42	25 16D	14 41	16 35	14 28	23 50	3 56	22 48	24 59	25 1
26	4 18 30	3 26 18	7♌ 3 16	13 18 59	26 39	25 16	14 57	17 50	15 5	23 43	4 3	22 46	25 1	25 1R
27	4 22 27	4 27 2	19 29 56	25 36 42	26 36	25 17	15 22	19 6	15 42	23 36	4 10	22 45	25 3	25 1
28	4 26 24	5 27 47	1♍ 39 56	7♍ 40 17	26 33	25 18R	15 56	20 21	16 19	23 28	4 16	22 43	25 5	25 1
29	4 30 20	6 28 33	13 38 24	19 34 56	26 30	25 18	16 37	21 36	16 56	23 21	4 23	22 42	25 7	25 1
30	4 34 17	7♐ 29 20	25♍ 30 31	1♎ 25 45	26♑ 27	25♑ 16	17♏ 25	22♏ 52	17♎ 32	23♊ 13	4♏ 29	22♋ 40	25♎ 8	25♌ 1

DECLINATION and LATITUDE

Day	☉ Decl	☽ Decl	☽ Lat	☽ 12 Hr. Decl	☿ Decl	☿ Lat	♀ Decl	♀ Lat	♂ Decl	♂ Lat	♃ Decl	♃ Lat	♄ Decl	♄ Lat
1	14S16	6N40	3S 4	4N 6	22S59	2S52	5S 3	1N35	1N18	1N16	22N48	0S35	9S46	2N15
2	14 35	1 31	3 49	1S 5	22 58	2 47	5 32	1 35	1 3	1 16	22 48	0 35	9 48	2 15
3	14 54	3S41	4 24	6 14	22 55	2 41	6 1	1 35	0 48	1 16	22 48	0 35	9 51	2 15
4	15 13	8 45	4 48	11 11	22 49	2 34	6 29	1 34	0 34	1 16	22 48	0 35	9 53	2 15
5	15 32	13 32	4 59	15 45	22 39	2 26	6 57	1 34	0 19	1 16	22 48	0 35	9 56	2 15
6	15 50	17 50	4 58	19 45	22 26	2 15	7 26	1 33	0 4	1 16	22 48	0 34	9 58	2 15
7	16 8	21 27	4 42	22 56	22 10	2 4	7 54	1 33	0S11	1 16	22 48	0 34	10 1	2 15
8	16 26	24 9	4 13	25 6	21 49	1 50	8 22	1 32	0 26	1 16	22 48	0 34	10 3	2 15
9	16 43	25 43	3 32	26 2	21 25	1 35	8 50	1 31	0 40	1 16	22 48	0 34	10 6	2 15
10	17 0	25 60	2 40	25 37	20 57	1 18	9 17	1 30	0 55	1 15	22 48	0 34	10 8	2 15
11	17 17	24 53	1 39	23 49	20 25	1 0	9 45	1 30	1 10	1 15	22 47	0 34	10 10	2 15
12	17 34	22 25	0 31	20 43	19 50	0 41	10 12	1 29	1 24	1 15	22 47	0 34	10 13	2 15
13	17 50	18 43	0N39	16 28	19 12	0 21	10 39	1 28	1 39	1 15	22 47	0 34	10 15	2 15
14	18 6	13 58	1 49	11 16	18 32	0 0	11 5	1 27	1 54	1 15	22 47	0 34	10 17	2 15
15	18 21	8 25	2 54	5 25	17 52	0N20	11 32	1 25	2 8	1 15	22 47	0 34	10 20	2 15
16	18 37	2 19	3 50	0N51	17 11	0 40	11 58	1 24	2 23	1 15	22 47	0 34	10 22	2 15
17	18 52	4N 1	4 32	7 10	16 33	0 60	12 24	1 23	2 38	1 15	22 47	0 34	10 24	2 15
18	19 6	10 14	4 58	13 10	15 57	1 17	12 50	1 22	2 52	1 15	22 46	0 34	10 27	2 15
19	19 21	15 55	5 3	18 26	15 24	1 34	13 15	1 20	3 7	1 15	22 46	0 34	10 29	2 15
20	19 35	20 40	4 49	22 33	14 56	1 48	13 40	1 19	3 21	1 15	22 46	0 34	10 31	2 16
21	19 48	24 3	4 15	25 8	14 33	1 60	14 5	1 18	3 36	1 15	22 46	0 34	10 33	2 16
22	20 2	25 47	3 25	26 1	14 15	2 10	14 29	1 16	3 50	1 15	22 46	0 33	10 35	2 16
23	20 14	25 49	2 24	25 13	14 3	2 18	14 53	1 14	4 5	1 15	22 45	0 33	10 38	2 16
24	20 27	24 15	1 16	22 57	13 55	2 24	15 16	1 13	4 19	1 15	22 45	0 33	10 40	2 16
25	20 39	21 22	0 5	19 32	13 53	2 29	15 40	1 11	4 33	1 15	22 45	0 33	10 42	2 16
26	20 51	17 30	1S 3	15 18	13 55	2 31	16 2	1 9	4 48	1 15	22 45	0 33	10 44	2 16
27	21 2	12 58	2 7	10 32	14 1	2 32	16 25	1 8	5 2	1 15	22 44	0 33	10 46	2 16
28	21 13	8 2	3 3	5 28	14 11	2 32	16 47	1 6	5 16	1 15	22 44	0 33	10 48	2 16
29	21 24	2 53	3 51	0 17	14 24	2 31	17 8	1 4	5 30	1 15	22 44	0 33	10 51	2 16
30	21S34	2S19	4S28	4S53	14S40	2N29	17S29	1N 2	5S44	1N15	22N44	0S33	10S53	2N16

Day	♅ Decl	♅ Lat	♆ Decl	♆ Lat	♇ Decl	♇ Lat
1	21N56	0N28	7S51	1N38	22N16	9N37
5	21 56	0 28	7 54	1 38	22 17	9 38
9	21 56	0 28	7 57	1 39	22 17	9 40
13	21 57	0 28	8 0	1 39	22 18	9 41
17	21 58	0 28	8 3	1 39	22 19	9 42
21	21 58	0 29	8 6	1 39	22 20	9 44
25	21 59	0 29	8 8	1 39	22 21	9 45
29	22N 0	0N29	8S11	1N39	22N22	9N47

☽ PHENOMENA

d	h	m	
6	17	58	●
14	7	53	☽
20	23	13	○
28	8	17	☾

d	h	° '
2	7	0
9	17	26S 3
16	9	0
22	12	26N 1
29	13	0

d	h	° '
5	9	5S 0
12	11	0
18	19	5N 4
25	2	0

VOID OF COURSE ☽

Last Aspect		☽ Ingress		
2	5pm32	3	♎	1am51
5	5am42	5	♏	2pm12
7	11pm58	8	♐	1am 7
10	6am51	10	♑	10am19
12	8am45	12	♒	5pm31
14	1pm39	14	♓	10pm18
16	3pm57	17	♈	0am36
18	5pm12	19	♉	1am15
20	11pm13	21	♊	1am55
22	7pm55	23	♋	4am32
25	1am21	25	♌	10am41
27	10am55	27	♍	8pm41
29	7pm25	30	♎	9am 6

d	h	
3	2	APOGEE
18	23	PERIGEE
30	18	APOGEE

DAILY ASPECTARIAN

Day	Aspect	Time
1 Su	☽∠♅	5am26
	☉✶☽	6 19
	☽#♀	6 57
	☽∠♆	7 37
	♂ ♎	2pm19
	☽∠♄	9 56
2 M	☽⚺♀	1am16
	☽∥♂	2 13
	☽#♂	11 18
	☿✶♂	11 33
	☽✶♅	11 51
	☽⚺♆	2pm 8
	☽⚺♇	3 27
	☉∠☽	3 33
	☽□♃	5 32
3 T	☽✶☿	3am10
	☽☌♂	3 50
	☽⚺♄	4 41
	☽∥♀	12pm 3
	☉⚼♃	1 43
	☽∥♆	7 51
	☿SR	9 47
	☽∠♇	9 52
	♂⚺♄	11 57
4 W	☉⚺☽	0am44
	☿#♃	1 41
	☽∥♄	5 37
	☽∠☿	9 32
	☽☌♀	9pm 2
5 Th	☽□♅	0am24
	☽☌♆	2 52
	☽✶♇	4 2
	☽△♃	5 42
	☉∥☽	11 32
	☽⚺☿	3pm 8
	☽☌♄	5 35
	☽⚺♂	7 24
6 F	♀□♅	5am14
	☽⚼♃	11 18
	☿#♇	2pm11
	☉☌☽	5 58
	☿ ♏	9 36
7 S	♀∥♆	1am31
	☽∠♂	2 34
	☽#♅	3 42
	☽∥☿	4 59
	☽#♇	6 30
	♀☌♆	6 31
	☽#♃	10 50
	☽△♅	11 39
	☽⚺♆	2pm15
	☽⚺♀	3 6
	☽□♇	3 16
	☿#♅	4 24
	☽⚻♃	4 30
	♀✶♇	4 47
	☽☌☿	11 58
8 Su	♀△♃	4am12
	☽⚺♄	4 59
	☽✶♂	9 15
	☽⚼♅	4pm39
	☽∠♆	7 19
	☽∠♀	11 17
9 M	☉⚺☽	9am 8
	☽∠♄	10 1
	☽⚻♅	9pm13
	☿⚺♀	11 53
	☽✶♆	11 57
10 T	☽△♇	0am49
	☽☍♃	1 36
	☽⚺☿	5 44
	☽✶♀	6 51
	☽✶♄	2pm35
	☉∠☽	3 52
	☽□♂	9 5
11 W	☽⚼♇	4am53
	☽∠☿	7 34
	♀ ♏	6pm12
	☽#♃	9 4
	☉✶☽	9 57
12 Th	♀∥♄	0am47
	☽#♇	0 57
	☽#♅	3 33
	☽☍♅	4 53
	☽□♆	7 42
	☿⚻♃	8 20
	☽⚻♇	8 25
	☽✶☿	8 45
	☽⚻♃	8 47
	☿□♇	12pm13
	☿⚺♆	7 24
	☽□♀	7 56
	☽∥☿	8 44
	☽□♄	10 7
13 F	☉∥☽	4am35
	☽△♂	6 29
	☽⚼♃	11 31
	♀☌♄	9pm23
14 S	☿△♅	0am21
	☿∠♂	4 1
	☉□☽	7 53
	☽□☿	9 20
	♃✶♇	9 43
	☽⚼♂	10 7
	☽⚻♅	10 12
	☉∥☿	11 16
	☽∥♀	11 51
	☽△♆	1pm 4
	☽△♃	1 37
	☽☍♇	1 39
	☽∥♄	4 5
	☉☌☿	5 15
15 Su	☽∥♆	1am34
	☽△♄	3 6
	☽△♀	5 44
	☽⚼♅	11 53
	☽⚻♂	1pm 1
	☽⚼♆	2 47
	☉△♅	3 15
	☽∥♂	11 44
16 M	☽⚼♄	4am38
	☽△☿	7 57
	☽⚼♀	9 24
	☽△♅	12pm59
	☉△☽	2 38
	☽⚻♆	3 54
	☽□♃	3 57
	☽⚻♇	4 21
	☽#♂	6 31
	♃△♆	11 5
17 T	☽⚻♄	5am36
	☽⚼☿	6 45
	☉⚻♃	8 6
	☉⚺♆	9 21
	☉∠♂	11 48
	☽⚻♀	12pm23
	☉□♇	3 25
	☽#♆	3 26
	☽☍♂	4 53
	☽⚼♇	4 55
	☉⚼☽	5 2
	♂∠♇	5 43
18 W	☽#♄	0am50
	☽⚻☿	5 25
	☽#♀	11 24
	☽□♅	1pm51
	☽✶♃	4 28
	☽☍♆	4 51
	☽△♇	5 12
	☉⚻☽	7 4
	☽#☿	9 51
19 Th	☽☍♄	6am33
	♀⚼♃	8 0
	☽∠♃	4pm29
	☽☍♀	5 20
	☉#☽	5 37
	☽⚻♂	7 26
20 F	☽☍☿	3am 4
	☽∥♅	8 7
	☽∥♇	10 30
	☽∥♃	1pm37
	☽✶♅	2 17
	☽⚺♃	4 38
	☽⚻♆	5 29
	☽□♇	5 44
	☽⚼♂	8 53
	☉☍☽	11 13
21 S	☽⚻♄	7am43
	☽∠♅	2pm56
	☿∥♀	3 47
	♀⚺♂	4 32
	☽⚼♆	6 17
	☽△♂	10 49
	☽⚻♀	11 7
22 Su	☽⚻☿	2am43
	☽⚼♄	9 1
	☉ ♐	2pm23
	☽⚺♅	4 11
	☽☌♃	6 20
	☽△♆	7 45
	☽✶♇	7 55
23 M	☽⚼♀	3am13
	☽⚼☿	3 55
	☉⚻☽	5 39
	☿☌♀	10 19
	☽△♄	11 7
	☽∠♇	10pm10
	☿SD	10 51
24 T	☽□♂	5am17
	☽△☿	6 23
	☽△♀	8 30
	☉⚼☽	10 28
	☽∥♃	1pm34
	☽∥♇	4 46
	☽∥♅	7 28
	☽☌♅	9 19
	☽⚺♃	11 14
25 W	☽□♆	1am21
	☽⚺♇	1 25
	☉#☽	4 34
	☿⚺♂	1pm40
	☉△☽	4 33
	☽□♄	6 15
	♆✶♇	11 25
26 Th	☽∠♃	3am 9
	☽#♀	7 25
	☽□☿	3pm40
	☽✶♂	4 13
	☉⚺♄	4 15
	☽#☿	6 49
	♇SR	8 45
	☽□♀	11 7
27 F	☽⚺♅	6am21
	☽✶♃	7 57
	☽#♄	10 48
	☽☌♇	10 50
	☽✶♆	10 55
	☽∠♂	11pm16
	☽#♆	11 21
28 S	☽✶♄	5am14
	☉□☽	8 17
	☽∠♅	12pm 5
	☽#♂	12 24
	☽∠♆	4 53
29 Su	☽✶☿	6am25
	☽⚺♂	6 59
	☽∠♄	11 42
	☽✶♀	6pm 0
	☽✶♅	6 16
	☽□♃	7 25
	♀△♅	8 31
	☽⚺♇	11 0
	☽⚺♆	11 15
30 M	☉⚼♅	4am15
	♀⚻♃	6 20
	☿⚺♂	11 7
	☽∠☿	3pm 8
	☽∥♂	4 50
	☽⚺♄	6 22

DECEMBER 1953

LONGITUDE

Day	Sid. Time	☉	☽	☽ 12 Hour	Mean ☊	True ☊	☿	♀	♂	♃	♄	♅	♆	♇
	h m s	° ' "	° ' "	° ' "	° '	° '	° '	° '	° '	° '	° '	° '	° '	° '
1	4 38 13	8♐ 30 10	7♎ 21 12	13♎ 17 23	26♑ 23	25♑ 12R	18♏ 19	24♏ 7	18♎ 9	23♊ 6R	4♏ 36	22♋ 39R	25♎ 10	25♌ 1R
2	4 42 10	9 31 0	19 14 49	25 13 54	26 20	25 6	19 18	25 22	18 46	22 58	4 42	22 37	25 12	25 1
3	4 46 6	10 31 52	1♏ 15 2	7♏ 18 32	26 17	24 59	20 21	26 38	19 23	22 50	4 48	22 35	25 14	25 1
4	4 50 3	11 32 45	13 24 40	19 33 37	26 14	24 51	21 28	27 53	19 59	22 42	4 55	22 34	25 15	25 0
5	4 53 59	12 33 40	25 45 34	2♐ 0 36	26 11	24 42	22 39	29 8	20 36	22 34	5 1	22 32	25 17	25 0
6	4 57 56	13 34 36	8♐ 18 46	14 40 6	26 7	24 35	23 53	0♐ 24	21 13	22 26	5 7	22 30	25 19	25 0
7	5 1 53	14 35 33	21 4 33	27 32 5	26 4	24 29	25 9	1 39	21 49	22 18	5 14	22 28	25 20	25 0
8	5 5 49	15 36 30	4♑ 2 38	10♑ 36 10	26 1	24 25	26 27	2 55	22 26	22 10	5 20	22 26	25 22	24 59
9	5 9 46	16 37 29	17 12 34	23 51 49	25 58	24 23D	27 47	4 10	23 2	22 2	5 26	22 24	25 23	24 59
10	5 13 42	17 38 29	0♒ 33 52	7♒ 18 40	25 55	24 22	29 9	5 26	23 39	21 54	5 32	22 22	25 25	24 59
11	5 17 39	18 39 28	14 6 13	20 56 29	25 52	24 23	0♐ 32	6 41	24 15	21 46	5 38	22 20	25 26	24 58
12	5 21 35	19 40 29	27 49 29	4♓ 45 11	25 48	24 25	1 56	7 56	24 52	21 38	5 44	22 18	25 28	24 58
13	5 25 32	20 41 30	11♓ 43 34	18 44 33	25 45	24 26R	3 22	9 12	25 28	21 30	5 50	22 16	25 29	24 57
14	5 29 28	21 42 32	25 48 1	2♈ 53 49	25 42	24 26	4 48	10 27	26 5	21 21	5 55	22 14	25 31	24 57
15	5 33 25	22 43 33	10♈ 1 43	17 11 22	25 39	24 25	6 15	11 43	26 41	21 13	6 1	22 12	25 32	24 56
16	5 37 22	23 44 36	24 22 24	1♉ 34 21	25 36	24 22	7 42	12 58	27 18	21 5	6 7	22 10	25 34	24 56
17	5 41 18	24 45 39	8♉ 46 37	15 58 38	25 33	24 19	9 11	14 14	27 54	20 57	6 12	22 8	25 35	24 55
18	5 45 15	25 46 42	23 9 44	0♊ 19 13	25 29	24 14	10 39	15 29	28 30	20 49	6 18	22 5	25 36	24 55
19	5 49 11	26 47 46	7♊ 26 25	14 30 39	25 26	24 10	12 9	16 45	29 7	20 41	6 23	22 3	25 38	24 54
20	5 53 8	27 48 50	21 31 20	28 27 56	25 23	24 7	13 38	18 0	29 43	20 33	6 29	22 1	25 39	24 53
21	5 57 4	28 49 55	5♋ 19 59	12♋ 7 7	25 20	24 4	15 8	19 16	0♏ 19	20 25	6 34	21 59	25 40	24 53
22	6 1 1	29 51 0	18 49 8	25 25 53	25 17	24 3D	16 39	20 31	0 55	20 17	6 40	21 56	25 41	24 52
23	6 4 57	0♑ 52 6	1♌ 57 21	8♌ 23 37	25 13	24 3	18 9	21 47	1 31	20 9	6 45	21 54	25 43	24 51
24	6 8 54	1 53 12	14 44 54	21 1 27	25 10	24 4	19 41	23 2	2 8	20 1	6 50	21 51	25 44	24 50
25	6 12 51	2 54 19	27 13 38	3♍ 21 53	25 7	24 6	21 12	24 17	2 44	19 53	6 55	21 49	25 45	24 50
26	6 16 47	3 55 26	9♍ 26 40	15 28 32	25 4	24 7	22 44	25 33	3 20	19 46	7 0	21 47	25 46	24 49
27	6 20 44	4 56 34	21 28 1	27 25 44	25 1	24 8	24 16	26 48	3 56	19 38	7 5	21 44	25 47	24 48
28	6 24 40	5 57 42	3♎ 22 16	9♎ 18 14	24 58	24 9R	25 48	28 4	4 32	19 30	7 10	21 42	25 48	24 47
29	6 28 37	6 58 51	15 14 14	21 10 52	24 54	24 9	27 20	29 19	5 8	19 23	7 15	21 39	25 49	24 46
30	6 32 33	8 0 1	27 8 44	3♏ 8 23	24 51	24 8	28 53	0♑ 35	5 44	19 15	7 20	21 37	25 50	24 45
31	6 36 30	9♑ 1 11	9♏ 10 19	15♏ 15 2	24♑ 48	24♑ 7	0♑ 26	1♑ 50	6♏ 19	19♊ 8	7♏ 24	21♋ 34	25♎ 51	24♌ 45

DECLINATION and LATITUDE

Day	☉ Decl	☽ Decl	☽ Lat	☽ 12 Hr. Decl	☿ Decl	☿ Lat	♀ Decl	♀ Lat	♂ Decl	♂ Lat	♃ Decl	♃ Lat	♄ Decl	♄ Lat
1	21S44	7S24	4S53	9S52	14S58	2N25	17S50	1N 0	5S58	1N14	22N43	0S33	10S55	2N17
2	21 53	12 15	5 6	14 32	15 17	2 21	18 10	0 58	6 12	1 14	22 43	0 32	10 57	2 17
3	22 2	16 41	5 6	18 41	15 39	2 17	18 30	0 56	6 26	1 14	22 43	0 32	10 59	2 17
4	22 10	20 30	4 52	22 7	16 1	2 11	18 49	0 54	6 40	1 14	22 42	0 32	11 1	2 17
5	22 18	23 29	4 24	24 35	16 25	2 6	19 7	0 52	6 54	1 14	22 42	0 32	11 3	2 17
6	22 26	25 22	3 43	25 51	16 49	1 59	19 25	0 50	7 8	1 14	22 42	0 32	11 5	2 17
7	22 33	25 59	2 51	25 46	17 14	1 53	19 43	0 48	7 22	1 14	22 41	0 32	11 7	2 17
8	22 40	25 11	1 48	24 15	17 39	1 46	19 60	0 46	7 35	1 14	22 41	0 32	11 8	2 17
9	22 46	22 59	0 39	21 23	18 4	1 39	20 16	0 43	7 49	1 14	22 41	0 32	11 10	2 18
10	22 52	19 29	0N34	17 19	18 28	1 32	20 32	0 41	8 3	1 14	22 40	0 32	11 12	2 18
11	22 58	14 55	1 45	12 19	18 53	1 25	20 47	0 39	8 16	1 13	22 40	0 31	11 14	2 18
12	23 3	9 32	2 52	6 38	19 17	1 17	21 2	0 37	8 30	1 13	22 40	0 31	11 16	2 18
13	23 7	3 37	3 50	0 34	19 41	1 10	21 16	0 34	8 43	1 13	22 39	0 31	11 18	2 18
14	23 11	2N32	4 34	5N36	20 5	1 2	21 30	0 32	8 56	1 13	22 39	0 31	11 19	2 18
15	23 15	8 36	5 3	11 31	20 27	0 55	21 42	0 30	9 10	1 13	22 39	0 31	11 21	2 18
16	23 18	14 17	5 12	16 52	20 49	0 47	21 54	0 27	9 23	1 13	22 38	0 31	11 23	2 19
17	23 20	19 12	5 3	21 15	21 11	0 40	22 6	0 25	9 36	1 13	22 38	0 31	11 25	2 19
18	23 23	22 59	4 34	24 20	21 31	0 32	22 17	0 23	9 49	1 12	22 37	0 30	11 26	2 19
19	23 24	25 18	3 48	25 51	21 51	0 25	22 27	0 20	10 2	1 12	22 37	0 30	11 28	2 19
20	23 26	25 59	2 49	25 42	22 10	0 17	22 36	0 18	10 15	1 12	22 36	0 30	11 29	2 19
21	23 26	25 1	1 41	23 58	22 27	0 10	22 45	0 15	10 28	1 12	22 36	0 30	11 31	2 19
22	23 27	22 36	0 29	20 56	22 44	0 3	22 53	0 13	10 41	1 12	22 36	0 30	11 33	2 20
23	23 27	19 1	0S43	16 55	22 60	0S 5	23 1	0 11	10 53	1 12	22 35	0 30	11 34	2 20
24	23 26	14 38	1 52	12 14	23 14	0 12	23 8	0 8	11 6	1 11	22 35	0 29	11 36	2 20
25	23 25	9 44	2 53	7 10	23 28	0 19	23 14	0 6	11 18	1 11	22 34	0 29	11 37	2 20
26	23 23	4 34	3 45	1 56	23 40	0 25	23 19	0 3	11 31	1 11	22 34	0 29	11 39	2 20
27	23 21	0S41	4 26	3S17	23 51	0 32	23 24	0 1	11 43	1 11	22 34	0 29	11 40	2 20
28	23 19	5 51	4 55	8 22	24 1	0 39	23 28	0S 2	11 55	1 11	22 33	0 29	11 41	2 21
29	23 16	10 48	5 12	13 8	24 10	0 45	23 31	0 4	12 8	1 10	22 33	0 29	11 43	2 21
30	23 12	15 21	5 15	17 26	24 18	0 51	23 33	0 7	12 20	1 10	22 32	0 28	11 44	2 21
31	23S 8	19S22	5S 5	21S 6	24S24	0S57	23S35	0S 9	12S32	1N10	22N32	0S28	11S45	2N21

Day	♅ Decl	♅ Lat	♆ Decl	♆ Lat	♇ Decl	♇ Lat
1	22N 1	0N29	8S12	1N39	22N23	9N47
5	22 2	0 29	8 14	1 39	22 25	9 49
9	22 4	0 29	8 17	1 40	22 26	9 50
13	22 5	0 29	8 19	1 40	22 28	9 51
17	22 6	0 29	8 20	1 40	22 30	9 53
21	22 8	0 29	8 22	1 40	22 32	9 54
25	22 10	0 29	8 24	1 40	22 34	9 55
29	22N11	0N29	8S25	1N41	22N37	9N57

☽ PHENOMENA

d	h	m	
6	10	48	●
13	16	31	☽
20	11	44	○
28	5	44	☾

d	h	° '
6	23	25S59
13	14	0
19	22	25N60
26	21	0

2	12	5S 8
9	13	0
16	0	5N12
22	9	0
29	18	5S16

VOID OF COURSE ☽

Last Aspect		☽ Ingress		
2	11am58	2	♏	9pm31
5	7am14	5	♐	8am 9
7	7am57	7	♑	4pm33
9	9pm11	9	♒	11pm 0
11	7pm53	12	♓	3am47
13	5pm58	14	♈	7am 6
16	5am 5	16	♉	9am23
18	2am55	18	♊	11am28
20	11am44	20	♋	2pm40
22	12pm30	22	♌	8pm23
24	9pm 7	25	♍	5am24
27	12pm 1	27	♎	5pm11
30	4am 1	30	♏	5am43

d	h	
16	14	PERIGEE
28	15	APOGEE

DAILY ASPECTARIAN

Day	Aspect	Time
1 T	☉⚹☽	2am33
	☽∥♆	3 50
	☽∠♀	3 59
	☽∠♇	5 23
	♀□♇	5pm 9
	☽∥♄	5 18
	♀⚺♆	8 36
	☽☌♂	10 59
2 W	☽⚺☿	0am 7
	☽□♅	6 45
	☽△♃	7 23
	☉∠☽	11 33
	☽⚹♇	11 33
	☽☌♆	11 58
	☽⚺♀	1pm43
	☉∠♆	4 35
	☽∥☿	5 33
	☉#♅	11 10
3 Th	☽☌♄	7am 7
	☽∥♀	11 46
	☽⚼♃	12pm54
	☉⚺☽	8 1
4 F	☽#♅	11am23
	☉∥☽	1pm 6
	☽⚺♂	1 30
	☽#♇	2 24
	☽#♃	4 55
	☽☌☿	5 21
	☽△♅	5 47
	☽⚻♃	5 55
	☿△♅	9 39
	☽□♇	10 32
	☿⚻♃	10 36
	☽⚺♆	11 5
5 S	☽☌♀	7am14
	♃⚺♅	9 58
	♀ ♐	4pm24
	☽⚺♄	5 53
	☽∠♂	7 48
	☉#♇	7 59
	☽⚼♅	10 28
6 Su	☽∠♆	3am47
	☉☌☽	10 48
	☿□♇	9pm 8
	☽∠♄	10 24
7 M	☽⚹♂	1am28
	☽☍♃	2 16
	☽⚻♅	2 36
	☿⚺♆	3 37
	☽△♇	7 17
	☽⚹♆	7 57
	☽⚺☿	8 25
	♂△♃	3pm41
	☽⚺♀	9 42
8 T	♂□♅	0am18
	☽⚹♄	2 22
	☉#♃	3 41
	☽⚼♇	10 52
	☽∠☿	3pm 4
	☉⚺☽	10 51
9 W	☉∥☽	1am38
	☽#♃	2 27
	☽∠♀	3 55
	☽#♇	4 20
	☽#♅	7 10
	☽⚻♃	8 38
	☽☍♅	9 21
	☽□♂	11 1
	☽⚻♇	2pm 0
	☽□♆	2 46
	☽∥♀	5 59
	☽⚹☿	9 11
10 Th	♀⚺♄	2am10
	☉∠☽	4 0
	☽∥☿	5 17
	☽□♄	8 54
	☽⚹♀	9 33
	☽⚼♃	11 10
	☿ ♐	2pm49
11 F	♂∥♆	2am34
	☉⚹☽	8 39
	♀⚼♅	12pm12
	☽△♃	1 19
	☽⚻♅	2 25
	☽∥♄	4 39
	☽△♂	6 37
	☽☍♇	7 1
	☽△♆	7 53
12 S	♂⚹♇	3am45
	☽∥♂	4 11
	☽∥♆	5 8
	☽□☿	7 57
	☽△♄	1pm47
	☽⚼♅	4 22
	☽□♀	7 14
	☽⚼♂	9 45
	☽⚼♆	9 52
13 Su	♂☌♆	0am39
	☉∠♄	3 30
	☽⚼♄	3pm39
	☉□☽	4 31
	☽□♃	4 32
	☉☍♃	4 42
	☽△♅	5 58
	☽⚻♇	10 33
	☽⚻♆	11 31
14 M	☽⚻♂	0am30
	♀∠♆	1 8
	☉⚻♅	12pm 1
	☽△☿	4 55
	☽⚻♄	5 13
	☿⚺♄	8 0
	☽#♆	10 51
	♀∠♂	11 3
	☽⚼♇	11 51
15 T	☽#♂	2am20
	☽△♀	3 6
	☽#♄	11 21
	☿⚼♅	3pm20
	☽⚹♃	6 34
	☽□♅	8 19
	☽⚼☿	8 54
	♃⚼♄	9 6
	☉△☽	10 52
16 W	☽△♇	0am56
	☽☍♆	1 59
	☽☍♂	5 5
	☽⚼♀	6 34
	☽∠♃	7pm20
	☽☍♄	7 41
17 Th	☽⚻☿	0am44
	♀#♅	1 13
	☉⚼☽	1 46
	☉△♇	3 42
	☽⚻♀	9 57
	☽#☿	12pm42
	☽∥♅	5 41
	☽#♀	6 34
	☉⚹♆	7 50
	☽⚺♃	8 7
	☽∥♇	8 28
	☽∥♃	9 19
	☽⚹♅	10 13
	☿∠♆	11 11
18 F	☽□♇	2am55
	☉#☽	3 14
	☽⚻♆	4 6
	☉⚻☽	4 43
	☽⚻♂	9 21
	☽⚻♄	10pm13
	☽∠♅	11 21
19 S	☽⚼♆	5am24
	☽☍☿	8 55
	♀#♇	10 44
	☽⚼♂	11 49
	☽☍♀	5pm22
	☿#♅	9 26
	☽☌♃	10 20
	☽⚼♄	11 56
20 Su	♀#♃	0am 0
	☽⚺♅	0 51
	☽⚹♇	5 48
	☽△♆	7 8
	♂ ♏	11 23
	☉☍☽	11 44
	☽△♂	2pm49
21 M	☽△♄	2am12
	☿∠♂	4 45
	☿#♇	7 1
	☽∠♇	8 1
	☿#♃	12pm 7
	☉#☽	4 56
	☽⚻☿	7 36
	♀☍♃	7 54
	☽#♀	9 45
	☽#☿	11 1
22 T	☽∥♃	0am 2
	☽∥♇	0 25
	☽⚺♃	2 37
	☽⚻♀	3 23
	☽∥♅	3 29
	☉ ♑	3 32
	☽☌♅	5 37
	☽⚺♇	10 57
	☽□♆	12pm30
	☉⚻☽	9 49
	☽□♂	11 10
	♀∠♄	11 26
23 W	♀⚻♅	2am16
	☽⚼☿	2 32
	☿∥♀	3 36
	☽∠♃	5 52
	☽□♄	8 59
	☽⚼♀	9 57
24 Th	☉⚼☽	4am26
	☿☍♃	4 57
	☽⚹♃	9 58
	☽△☿	10 43
	☽⚺♅	1pm34
	☉⚹♂	1 45
	☽#♄	3 1
	☽#♂	4 48
	☽△♀	5 40
	☉∥☿	6 59
	☽☌♇	7 21
	☽⚹♆	9 7
25 F	♃∥♇	1am40
	☽#♆	6 17
	☿⚻♅	9 29
	♀△♇	10 8
	☽⚹♂	11 18
	☿∠♄	11 59
	☉△☽	12pm 6
	☽∠♅	6 44
	☽⚹♄	7 8
26 S	☽∠♆	2am38
	♀⚹♆	4 12
	☉∥♀	3pm 3
	♂∥♄	5 5
	☽∠♂	6 38
	☽□♃	8 21
27 Su	☽⚹♅	0am32
	☽∠♄	1 15
	☽□☿	6 27
	☽⚺♇	6 42
	☿△♇	8 24
	☽⚺♆	8 42
	☽□♀	12pm 1
	♂⚼♃	11 14
28 M	☿⚹♆	0am 5
	☽⚺♂	2 28
	☉□☽	5 44
	☽⚺♄	7 44
	☽∥♆	12pm15
	☽∠♇	12 58
29 T	☽∥♄	4am41
	☉⚹♄	6 47
	☽∥♂	7 6
	☽△♃	8 17
	♀ ♑	12pm54
	☽□♅	12 54
	☽⚹♇	7 12
	☽☌♆	9 22
30 W	☽⚹☿	4am 1
	☽⚹♀	7 42
	☽⚼♃	2pm 5
	☿ ♑	5 14
	☽☌♂	6 3
	☽☌♄	8 28
	☉⚹☽	11 40
31 Th	☽∠☿	2pm10
	☉⚼♇	4 45
	☽∠♀	4 51
	☽⚻♃	7 26
	☽#♅	8 32
	☽#♃	11 10

LONGITUDE

Day	Sid. Time	☉	☽	☽ 12 Hour	Mean ☊	True ☊	☿	♀	♂	♃	♄	♅	♆	♇
	h m s	° ' "	° ' "	° ' "	° '	° '	° '	° '	° '	° '	° '	° '	° '	° '
1	6 40 26	10♑ 2 21	21♏ 22 59	27♏ 34 31	24♑ 45	24♑ 5R	2♑ 0	3♑ 6	6♏ 55	19♊ 1R	7♏ 29	21♋ 32R	25♎ 52	24♌ 44R
2	6 44 23	11 3 31	3♐ 49 58	10♐ 9 35	24 42	24 3	3 33	4 21	7 31	18 54	7 33	21 29	25 53	24 43
3	6 48 20	12 4 42	16 33 32	23 1 55	24 38	24 1	5 8	5 37	8 7	18 47	7 38	21 27	25 54	24 42
4	6 52 16	13 5 53	29 34 46	6♑ 12 0	24 35	23 59	6 42	6 52	8 43	18 40	7 42	21 24	25 54	24 41
5	6 56 13	14 7 4	12♑ 53 31	19 39 7	24 32	23 59	8 17	8 8	9 18	18 33	7 46	21 21	25 55	24 40
6	7 0 9	15 8 15	26 28 31	3♒ 21 25	24 29	23 58D	9 52	9 23	9 54	18 27	7 50	21 19	25 56	24 39
7	7 4 6	16 9 25	10♒ 17 27	17 16 14	24 26	23 58	11 27	10 39	10 30	18 20	7 55	21 16	25 57	24 37
8	7 8 2	17 10 35	24 17 21	1♓ 20 25	24 23	23 59	13 3	11 54	11 5	18 14	7 59	21 14	25 57	24 36
9	7 11 59	18 11 45	8♓ 24 59	15 30 39	24 19	23 59	14 40	13 10	11 41	18 8	8 3	21 11	25 58	24 35
10	7 15 56	19 12 55	22 37 3	29 43 49	24 16	24 0	16 17	14 25	12 16	18 2	8 6	21 8	25 59	24 34
11	7 19 52	20 14 4	6♈ 50 35	13♈ 57 3	24 13	24 0	17 54	15 41	12 51	17 56	8 10	21 6	25 59	24 33
12	7 23 49	21 15 12	21 2 56	28 7 56	24 10	24 0R	19 31	16 56	13 27	17 50	8 14	21 3	26 0	24 32
13	7 27 45	22 16 19	5♉ 11 48	12♉ 14 17	24 7	24 0	21 9	18 12	14 2	17 45	8 17	21 1	26 0	24 31
14	7 31 42	23 17 26	19 15 9	26 14 9	24 4	24 0	22 48	19 27	14 37	17 40	8 21	20 58	26 1	24 29
15	7 35 38	24 18 33	3♊ 11 2	10♊ 5 36	24 0	24 0D	24 27	20 43	15 13	17 34	8 24	20 55	26 1	24 28
16	7 39 35	25 19 38	16 57 37	23 46 50	23 57	24 0	26 7	21 58	15 48	17 29	8 27	20 53	26 2	24 27
17	7 43 31	26 20 43	0♋ 33 3	7♋ 16 5	23 54	24 0	27 47	23 14	16 23	17 24	8 31	20 50	26 2	24 26
18	7 47 28	27 21 47	13 55 44	20 31 50	23 51	24 0R	29 27	24 29	16 58	17 20	8 34	20 48	26 2	24 24
19	7 51 25	28 22 51	27 4 18	3♌ 33 2	23 48	24 0	1♒ 9	25 44	17 33	17 15	8 37	20 45	26 3	24 23
20	7 55 21	29 23 54	9♌ 57 59	16 19 11	23 44	24 0	2 50	27 0	18 8	17 11	8 40	20 43	26 3	24 22
21	7 59 18	0♒ 24 56	22 36 42	28 50 38	23 41	24 0	4 32	28 15	18 43	17 7	8 43	20 40	26 3	24 21
22	8 3 14	1 25 58	5♍ 1 11	11♍ 8 35	23 38	23 59	6 15	29 31	19 17	17 3	8 45	20 37	26 3	24 19
23	8 7 11	2 26 59	17 13 6	23 15 5	23 35	23 58	7 58	0♒ 46	19 52	16 59	8 48	20 35	26 4	24 18
24	8 11 7	3 28 0	29 14 56	5♎ 13 5	23 32	23 56	9 42	2 1	20 27	16 55	8 51	20 32	26 4	24 17
25	8 15 4	4 28 59	11♎ 10 0	17 6 12	23 29	23 55	11 25	3 17	21 2	16 52	8 53	20 30	26 4	24 15
26	8 19 0	5 29 59	23 2 13	28 58 38	23 25	23 55	13 10	4 32	21 36	16 49	8 55	20 27	26 4	24 14
27	8 22 57	6 30 58	4♏ 56 1	10♏ 54 59	23 22	23 54D	14 54	5 48	22 11	16 46	8 58	20 25	26 4R	24 12
28	8 26 54	7 31 56	16 56 7	23 0 0	23 19	23 55	16 39	7 3	22 45	16 43	9 0	20 22	26 4	24 11
29	8 30 50	8 32 54	29 7 13	5♐ 18 19	23 16	23 55	18 24	8 18	23 20	16 40	9 2	20 20	26 4	24 10
30	8 34 47	9 33 51	11♐ 33 48	17 54 8	23 13	23 57	20 8	9 34	23 54	16 38	9 4	20 17	26 4	24 8
31	8 38 43	10♒ 34 47	24♐ 19 42	0♑ 50 49	23♑ 10	23♑ 58	21♒ 53	10♒ 49	24♏ 28	16♊ 36	9♏ 6	20♋ 15	26♎ 4	24♌ 7

DECLINATION and LATITUDE

Day	☉ Decl	☽ Decl	☽ Lat	☽ 12 Hr. Decl	☿ Decl	☿ Lat	♀ Decl	♀ Lat	♂ Decl	♂ Lat	♃ Decl	♃ Lat	♄ Decl	♄ Lat
1	23S 4	22S37	4S41	23S54	24S29	1S 3	23S36	0S11	12S44	1N10	22N31	0S28	11S47	2N21
2	22 59	24 54	4 3	25 36	24 32	1 9	23 36	0 14	12 56	1 10	22 31	0 28	11 48	2 22
3	22 54	25 58	3 13	25 58	24 35	1 14	23 36	0 16	13 7	1 9	22 31	0 28	11 49	2 22
4	22 48	25 38	2 11	24 55	24 36	1 19	23 34	0 18	13 19	1 9	22 30	0 28	11 50	2 22
5	22 42	23 50	1 1	22 24	24 35	1 24	23 32	0 21	13 31	1 9	22 30	0 27	11 52	2 22
6	22 35	20 38	0N14	18 34	24 34	1 29	23 30	0 23	13 42	1 9	22 29	0 27	11 53	2 22
7	22 28	16 14	1 29	13 40	24 30	1 34	23 26	0 25	13 53	1 8	22 29	0 27	11 54	2 23
8	22 20	10 54	2 40	7 60	24 26	1 38	23 22	0 28	14 5	1 8	22 29	0 27	11 55	2 23
9	22 13	4 59	3 42	1 54	24 20	1 42	23 17	0 30	14 16	1 8	22 28	0 27	11 56	2 23
10	22 4	1N13	4 31	4N19	24 12	1 46	23 12	0 32	14 27	1 7	22 28	0 26	11 57	2 23
11	21 55	7 21	5 3	10 18	24 3	1 49	23 6	0 34	14 38	1 7	22 28	0 26	11 58	2 24
12	21 46	13 6	5 17	15 44	23 53	1 52	22 59	0 37	14 49	1 7	22 27	0 26	11 59	2 24
13	21 36	18 8	5 11	20 17	23 41	1 55	22 51	0 39	14 60	1 7	22 27	0 26	11 60	2 24
14	21 26	22 8	4 47	23 40	23 27	1 58	22 42	0 41	15 10	1 6	22 27	0 26	12 1	2 24
15	21 16	24 49	4 6	25 36	23 12	1 60	22 33	0 43	15 21	1 6	22 26	0 25	12 2	2 24
16	21 5	25 59	3 11	25 58	22 56	2 2	22 24	0 45	15 31	1 6	22 26	0 25	12 3	2 25
17	20 53	25 33	2 7	24 46	22 37	2 3	22 13	0 47	15 42	1 5	22 26	0 25	12 3	2 25
18	20 42	23 38	0 56	22 12	22 18	2 4	22 2	0 49	15 52	1 5	22 26	0 25	12 4	2 25
19	20 29	20 28	0S17	18 31	21 57	2 5	21 50	0 51	16 2	1 5	22 25	0 25	12 5	2 25
20	20 17	16 21	1 27	14 2	21 34	2 6	21 38	0 53	16 12	1 4	22 25	0 25	12 6	2 26
21	20 4	11 35	2 32	9 3	21 10	2 5	21 25	0 55	16 22	1 4	22 25	0 24	12 6	2 26
22	19 51	6 27	3 28	3 48	20 44	2 5	21 11	0 56	16 32	1 4	22 25	0 24	12 7	2 26
23	19 37	1 9	4 14	1S29	20 16	2 4	20 56	0 58	16 42	1 3	22 25	0 24	12 8	2 26
24	19 23	4S 6	4 48	6 39	19 48	2 2	20 41	1 0	16 51	1 3	22 25	0 24	12 8	2 26
25	19 9	9 9	5 9	11 33	19 17	2 0	20 26	1 2	17 1	1 2	22 24	0 24	12 9	2 27
26	18 54	13 51	5 16	16 1	18 45	1 58	20 9	1 3	17 10	1 2	22 24	0 23	12 9	2 27
27	18 39	18 2	5 11	19 53	18 12	1 55	19 53	1 5	17 20	1 2	22 24	0 23	12 10	2 27
28	18 24	21 33	4 51	22 59	17 37	1 51	19 35	1 6	17 29	1 1	22 24	0 23	12 10	2 27
29	18 8	24 10	4 19	25 5	17 0	1 47	19 17	1 8	17 38	1 1	22 24	0 23	12 11	2 28
30	17 52	25 42	3 33	25 59	16 23	1 42	18 59	1 9	17 47	1 0	22 24	0 23	12 11	2 28
31	17S35	25S56	2S37	25S31	15S44	1S36	18S40	1S11	17S56	0N60	22N24	0S22	12S11	2N28

Day	♅ Decl	♅ Lat	♆ Decl	♆ Lat	♇ Decl	♇ Lat
1	22N12	0N30	8S26	1N41	22N38	9N57
5	22 14	0 30	8 27	1 41	22 41	9 58
9	22 16	0 30	8 28	1 41	22 43	9 60
13	22 17	0 30	8 28	1 42	22 46	10 1
17	22 19	0 30	8 28	1 42	22 48	10 1
21	22 21	0 30	8 29	1 42	22 51	10 2
25	22 22	0 30	8 29	1 42	22 53	10 3
29	22N24	0N30	8S28	1N43	22N56	10N 4

☽ PHENOMENA

d	h	m	
5	2	22	●
12	0	22	☽
19	2	37	○
27	3	28	☾

d	h	°	'
3	7	26S	1
9	19	0	
16	5	26N	1
23	5	0	
30	16	26S	1

d	h	
5	20	0
12	5	5N17
18	18	0
26	2	5S16

VOID OF COURSE ☽

Last Aspect		☽ Ingress		
1	6am29	1	♐	4pm40
3	5pm17	4	♑	0am46
5	11pm 3	6	♒	6am 9
8	2am51	8	♓	9am43
9	9pm31	10	♈	12pm27
12	8am23	12	♉	3pm10
14	8am59	14	♊	6pm30
16	3pm59	16	♋	11pm 1
19	2am37	19	♌	5am25
21	6am37	21	♍	2pm14
23	6am39	24	♎	1am30
26	6am 7	26	♏	2pm 4
28	2pm18	29	♐	1am43
31	3am12	31	♑	10am27

d	h	
10	10	PERIGEE
25	12	APOGEE

DAILY ASPECTARIAN

Day	Aspect	Time
1 F	☽#♇	0am 8
	☽△♅	0 17
	☉∥☽	3 47
	☽□♇	6 29
	☉∠☽	7 44
	☽⚺♆	8 42
	☽∥♀	8 58
	☽∥☿	7pm11
	☽⚺☿	11 24
2 S	☽⚺♀	1am 7
	♂☌♄	1 38
	☽⚼♅	5 2
	☽⚺♄	7 7
	☽⚺♂	7 21
	☽∠♆	1pm22
	☉⚺☽	2 53
3 Su	☽☍♃	4am 6
	☽⚻♅	9 2
	☽∠♄	11 19
	☽∠♂	12pm44
	☽△♇	3 2
	☽⚹♆	5 17
4 M	☿☌♀	1pm 3
	☽☌♀	2 35
	☽☌☿	2 38
	☽⚹♄	2 47
	☿⚹♄	3 56
	☽∥☿	3 57
	♀⚹♄	4 43
	☽⚹♂	5 17
	☽⚼♇	6 14
5 T	☉☌☽	2am22
	☽∥♀	2 43
	☉#♇	3 28
	☽#♇	9 49
	☽⚻♃	9 59
	☉∥☽	10 4
	☽#♃	11 16
	☽#♅	1pm10
	☽☍♅	2 58
	☿⚼♇	8 40
	☽⚻♇	8 47
	☽□♆	11 3
6 W	☿⚹♂	0am49
	♀⚼♇	4 44
	☽⚼♃	12pm 4
	♀⚹♂	6 23
	☽□♄	7 52
	☉#♃	8 15
7 Th	☽□♂	0am22
	☽⚺♀	0 41
	☽⚺☿	2 16
	☽∥♂	10 36
	☉⚺☽	10 53
	☽△♃	1pm44
	☽⚻♅	6 47
	☽∥♄	7 42
8 F	☽☍♇	0am32
	☽△♆	2 51
	☽∠♀	4 54
	☽∠☿	7 14
	☽∥♆	10 8
	☉∠☽	2pm28
	☉#♅	2 40
	☽⚼♅	8 14
	☉⚻♃	10 40
	☽△♄	11 22
9 S	☽⚼♆	4am19
	☽△♂	5 45
	☽⚹♀	8 49
	☽⚹☿	11 55
	☽□♃	4pm19
	☉⚹☽	5 49
	☽△♅	9 31
10 Su	☽⚼♄	0am50
	☽⚻♇	3 17
	☽⚻♆	5 40
	☽⚼♂	8 11
11 M	☿⚻♃	0am34
	☽⚻♄	2 15
	☽#♆	4 28
	☽⚼♇	4 34
	☽⚻♂	10 36
	☽□♀	4pm22
	☽⚹♃	6 37
	☽#♄	7 7
	☉☍♅	7 31
	☽□☿	9 5
12 T	☽□♅	0am 1
	☉□☽	0 22
	☽△♇	5 53
	☽#♂	8 0
	☽☍♆	8 23
	♀⚻♃	4pm 3
	☽∠♃	7 52
	☿☍♅	9 54
13 W	☽☍♄	5am17
	♀#♇	1pm39
	☽☍♂	3 44
	☉#☽	7 25
	☽⚺♃	9 17
14 Th	☽△♀	0am23
	☽∥♅	1 8
	☽∥♃	2 13
	☽⚹♅	2 56
	☽#♀	3 59
	☽∥♇	4 42
	☽△☿	6 54
	☉△☽	7 29
	☽□♇	8 59
	☽#☿	9 23
	☽⚻♆	11 37
	☉☌☿	6pm33
15 F	☿⚻♇	0am14
	☉⚻♇	3 43
	♀☍♅	3 56
	☽∠♅	4 44
	☽⚼♀	4 49
	☽⚻♄	9 6
	☉⚼☽	11 29
	☽⚼☿	12pm22
	☽⚼♆	1 37
	♀#♃	5 26
	☽⚻♂	9 52
	☿□♆	10 45
16 S	☽☌♃	0am55
	☽⚺♅	6 52
	☽⚻♀	9 42
	☿#♇	10 21
	♀#♅	10 53
	☽⚼♄	11 29
	☽⚹♇	1pm10
	☉⚻☽	3 56
	☽△♆	3 59
	☉□♆	4 36
	☽⚻☿	6 23
17 Su	☽⚼♂	1am33
	☽△♄	2pm17
	☿#♃	2 32
	☽∠♇	3 51
	☿#♅	10 7
	♀⚻♇	10 34
18 M	☽△♂	5am45
	☽⚺♃	6 8
	☽∥♇	7 6
	☿ ♒	7 44
	☽∥♃	10 13
	☽∥♅	10 59
	☽☌♅	12pm27
	☽#☿	12 35
	♂⚻♃	1 21
	☽#♀	2 3
	☽⚺♇	7 4
	☽☍♀	9 17
	☽□♆	10 6
	☉#☽	11 52
19 T	☉☍☽	2am37
	♀□♆	5 49
	☽☍☿	8 40
	☽∠♃	9 32
	☿⚼♃	3pm 7
	☿∥♀	3 40
	☽□♄	9 33
20 W	☽#♂	0am45
	☽⚹♃	1pm34
	☉ ♒	2 11
	☽□♂	4 11
	☽⚺♅	8 17
	☽#♄	9 30
21 Th	☽☌♇	3am19
	☽⚹♆	6 37
	☽⚻♀	12pm 5
	☽#♆	2 38
	☉⚻☽	4 24
22 F	☽∠♅	1am10
	☽⚻☿	2 48
	☽⚹♄	7 20
	♀ ♒	9 21
	☽∠♆	11 50
	☉⚼♃	1pm40
	☽⚼♀	8 48
	☽□♃	11 32
23 S	☉⚼☽	0am30
	☽⚹♂	5 32
	☽⚹♅	6 39
	☿□♄	11 54
	☽∠♄	1pm 9
	☽⚼☿	1 21
	☽⚺♇	2 4
	☽⚺♆	5 37
	♀⚼♃	10 12
24 Su	♂△♅	3am30
	☽△♀	6 14
	☉△☽	9 16
	☽∠♂	1pm 6
	☽⚺♄	7 22
	☽∠♇	8 9
	☽∥♆	8 44
25 M	☽△☿	0am37
	☽△♃	11 28
	☉∥☿	11 49
	☽∥♄	3pm 4
	☽□♅	6 48
	☽⚺♂	8 57
26 T	☽⚹♇	2am24
	☽☌♆	6 7
	☽⚼♃	5pm39
	☽∥♂	7 29
27 W	☽∥☿	0am50
	☽□♀	1 56
	☉□☽	3 28
	☉∥☽	3 35
	☽☌♄	8 6
	♆SR	10 49
	☽∥♀	11 0
	☽□☿	11pm20
	☽⚻♃	11 34
28 Th	☿△♃	0am57
	☿∥♂	4 18
	☽△♅	6 47
	☽#♅	6 48
	☽#♃	6 53
	☽#♇	11 29
	☽☌♂	12pm 5
	☽□♇	2 18
	☽⚺♆	6 1
29 F	☉□♄	11am46
	☽⚼♅	12pm 1
	♀□♄	2 13
	♃∥♅	5 59
	☽⚺♄	7 13
	☽⚹♀	7 45
	☉⚹☽	7 51
	☽∠♆	11 3
30 S	☉☌♀	0am19
	☿⚻♅	2 4
	☉∥♂	4 48
	☽☍♃	9 35
	♂□♇	9 36
	☽⚻♅	4pm26
	☽⚹☿	6 44
	☽∠♄	11 34
	☽△♇	11 36
31 Su	☽⚺♂	0am16
	☉∠☽	2 31
	☽∠♀	3 3
	☽⚹♆	3 12

FEBRUARY 1954

LONGITUDE

Day	Sid. Time	☉	☽	☽ 12 Hour	Mean ☊	True ☊	☿	♀	♂	♃	♄	♅	♆	♇
	h m s	° ' "	° ' "	° ' "	° '	° '	° '	° '	° '	° '	° '	° '	° '	° '
1	8 42 40	11♒ 35 43	7♑ 27 41	14♑ 10 25	23♑ 6	23♑ 59	23♒ 37	12♒ 4	25♏ 2	16♊ 34R	9♏ 7	20♋ 13R	26♎ 3R	24♌ 5R
2	8 46 36	12 36 37	20 59 0	27 53 18	23 3	24 0R	25 20	13 20	25 36	16 32	9 9	20 10	26 3	24 4
3	8 50 33	13 37 31	4♒ 53 2	11♒ 57 47	23 0	23 59	27 3	14 35	26 11	16 30	9 11	20 8	26 3	24 2
4	8 54 29	14 38 23	19 7 0	26 20 3	22 57	23 58	28 45	15 50	26 44	16 29	9 12	20 6	26 3	24 1
5	8 58 26	15 39 15	3♓ 36 9	10♓ 54 30	22 54	23 56	0♓ 25	17 6	27 18	16 28	9 13	20 3	26 3	24 0
6	9 2 23	16 40 4	18 14 12	25 34 23	22 50	23 53	2 3	18 21	27 52	16 27	9 15	20 1	26 2	23 58
7	9 6 19	17 40 53	2♈ 54 12	10♈ 12 51	22 47	23 49	3 38	19 36	28 26	16 26	9 16	19 59	26 2	23 57
8	9 10 16	18 41 40	17 29 36	24 43 50	22 44	23 46	5 11	20 52	29 0	16 25	9 17	19 57	26 2	23 55
9	9 14 12	19 42 26	1♉ 55 2	9♉ 2 47	22 41	23 44	6 41	22 7	29 33	16 25	9 18	19 55	26 1	23 54
10	9 18 9	20 43 10	16 6 49	23 6 57	22 38	23 43D	8 6	23 22	0♐ 7	16 25D	9 18	19 52	26 1	23 52
11	9 22 5	21 43 52	0♊ 3 6	6♊ 55 14	22 35	23 43	9 27	24 37	0 40	16 25	9 19	19 50	26 0	23 51
12	9 26 2	22 44 33	13 43 26	20 27 46	22 31	23 44	10 42	25 52	1 13	16 25	9 20	19 48	26 0	23 49
13	9 29 58	23 45 12	27 8 24	3♋ 45 27	22 28	23 46	11 51	27 8	1 46	16 25	9 20	19 46	25 59	23 48
14	9 33 55	24 45 49	10♋ 19 5	16 49 28	22 25	23 47R	12 53	28 23	2 20	16 26	9 21	19 44	25 59	23 46
15	9 37 52	25 46 25	23 16 43	29 40 59	22 22	23 48	13 48	29 38	2 53	16 27	9 21	19 42	25 58	23 45
16	9 41 48	26 47 0	6♌ 2 23	12♌ 21 1	22 19	23 47	14 34	0♓ 53	3 25	16 28	9 21	19 40	25 57	23 43
17	9 45 45	27 47 32	18 36 59	24 50 23	22 16	23 44	15 12	2 8	3 58	16 29	9 21R	19 38	25 57	23 42
18	9 49 41	28 48 3	1♍ 1 17	7♍ 9 48	22 12	23 40	15 40	3 23	4 31	16 31	9 21	19 37	25 56	23 40
19	9 53 38	29 48 32	13 16 4	19 20 10	22 9	23 34	15 59	4 38	5 4	16 32	9 21	19 35	25 55	23 39
20	9 57 34	0♓ 49 0	25 22 19	1♎ 22 40	22 6	23 27	16 7R	5 54	5 36	16 34	9 21	19 33	25 55	23 37
21	10 1 31	1 49 27	7♎ 21 29	13 19 1	22 3	23 20	16 5	7 9	6 9	16 36	9 20	19 31	25 54	23 36
22	10 5 27	2 49 51	19 15 35	25 11 33	22 0	23 13	15 53	8 24	6 41	16 38	9 20	19 29	25 53	23 35
23	10 9 24	3 50 15	1♏ 7 19	7♏ 3 20	21 56	23 7	15 32	9 39	7 13	16 41	9 19	19 28	25 52	23 33
24	10 13 21	4 50 37	13 0 6	18 58 8	21 53	23 3	15 1	10 54	7 45	16 43	9 19	19 26	25 51	23 32
25	10 17 17	5 50 58	24 58 0	1♐ 0 18	21 50	23 0	14 21	12 9	8 17	16 46	9 18	19 25	25 50	23 30
26	10 21 14	6 51 17	7♐ 5 37	13 14 35	21 47	23 0D	13 34	13 24	8 49	16 49	9 17	19 23	25 50	23 29
27	10 25 10	7 51 35	19 27 49	25 45 55	21 44	23 0	12 41	14 39	9 21	16 52	9 16	19 22	25 49	23 27
28	10 29 7	8♓ 51 52	2♑ 9 26	8♑ 38 54	21♑ 41	23♑ 1	11♓ 44	15♓ 54	9♐ 52	16♊ 56	9♏ 15	19♋ 20	25♎ 48	23♌ 26

DECLINATION and LATITUDE

Day	☉ Decl	☽ Decl	☽ Lat	☽ 12 Hr. Decl	☿ Decl	☿ Lat	♀ Decl	♀ Lat	♂ Decl	♂ Lat	♃ Decl	♃ Lat	♄ Decl	♄ Lat
1	17S19	24S44	1S30	23S35	15S 4	1S30	18S20	1S12	18S 4	0N59	22N24	0S22	12S12	2N28
2	17 2	22 5	0 17	20 14	14 22	1 23	17 60	1 13	18 13	0 59	22 24	0 22	12 12	2 29
3	16 44	18 5	0N60	15 39	13 40	1 15	17 39	1 15	18 21	0 58	22 24	0 22	12 12	2 29
4	16 27	12 58	2 14	10 6	12 57	1 7	17 18	1 16	18 30	0 58	22 24	0 22	12 12	2 29
5	16 9	7 4	3 21	3 56	12 13	0 57	16 56	1 17	18 38	0 57	22 24	0 21	12 13	2 29
6	15 51	0 44	4 15	2N28	11 29	0 47	16 34	1 18	18 46	0 57	22 24	0 21	12 13	2 30
7	15 32	5N38	4 53	8 43	10 45	0 37	16 12	1 19	18 54	0 56	22 24	0 21	12 13	2 30
8	15 14	11 40	5 12	14 26	10 0	0 25	15 49	1 20	19 2	0 56	22 24	0 21	12 13	2 30
9	14 55	16 60	5 11	19 17	9 16	0 13	15 25	1 21	19 9	0 55	22 25	0 21	12 13	2 30
10	14 35	21 17	4 50	22 58	8 32	0N 0	15 1	1 22	19 17	0 55	22 25	0 20	12 13	2 31
11	14 16	24 17	4 13	25 14	7 49	0 14	14 37	1 22	19 25	0 54	22 25	0 20	12 13	2 31
12	13 56	25 48	3 22	25 58	7 7	0 28	14 12	1 23	19 32	0 54	22 25	0 20	12 13	2 31
13	13 36	25 46	2 21	25 11	6 28	0 43	13 47	1 24	19 39	0 53	22 25	0 20	12 13	2 31
14	13 16	24 16	1 13	23 1	5 50	0 58	13 22	1 24	19 46	0 52	22 26	0 20	12 13	2 32
15	12 56	21 29	0 3	19 42	5 14	1 14	12 56	1 25	19 53	0 52	22 26	0 19	12 13	2 32
16	12 35	17 42	1S 6	15 30	4 42	1 29	12 30	1 25	20 0	0 51	22 26	0 19	12 12	2 32
17	12 15	13 10	2 11	10 43	4 13	1 45	12 3	1 26	20 7	0 51	22 27	0 19	12 12	2 32
18	11 54	8 10	3 9	5 34	3 48	2 1	11 36	1 26	20 14	0 50	22 27	0 19	12 12	2 33
19	11 33	2 56	3 57	0 17	3 26	2 16	11 9	1 26	20 20	0 49	22 27	0 19	12 12	2 33
20	11 11	2S21	4 33	4S56	3 9	2 31	10 42	1 27	20 27	0 49	22 28	0 19	12 11	2 33
21	10 50	7 28	4 58	9 56	2 57	2 45	10 14	1 27	20 33	0 48	22 28	0 18	12 11	2 33
22	10 28	12 18	5 9	14 32	2 50	2 58	9 46	1 27	20 39	0 47	22 28	0 18	12 11	2 34
23	10 6	16 39	5 6	18 36	2 47	3 10	9 18	1 27	20 45	0 47	22 29	0 18	12 10	2 34
24	9 44	20 22	4 51	21 56	2 50	3 20	8 49	1 27	20 51	0 46	22 29	0 18	12 10	2 34
25	9 22	23 16	4 23	24 21	2 57	3 29	8 21	1 27	20 57	0 45	22 30	0 18	12 9	2 34
26	8 60	25 9	3 43	25 40	3 9	3 35	7 52	1 27	21 3	0 44	22 30	0 17	12 9	2 34
27	8 37	25 52	2 51	25 45	3 25	3 40	7 22	1 26	21 8	0 44	22 31	0 17	12 8	2 35
28	8S15	25S16	1S50	24S27	3S44	3N42	6S53	1S26	21S14	0N43	22N31	0S17	12S 8	2N35

Day	♅ Decl	♅ Lat	♆ Decl	♆ Lat	♇ Decl	♇ Lat
1	22N25	0N30	8S28	1N43	22N58	10N 4
5	22 26	0 30	8 28	1 43	23 0	10 5
9	22 27	0 30	8 27	1 43	23 3	10 5
13	22 29	0 30	8 26	1 43	23 5	10 5
17	22 30	0 30	8 25	1 44	23 7	10 6
21	22 31	0 30	8 24	1 44	23 10	10 6
25	22N32	0N30	8S22	1N44	23N12	10N 6

☽ PHENOMENA

d	h	m	
3	15	56	●
10	8	30	☽
17	19	18	○
25	23	29	☾

d	h	° '
6	3	0
12	11	25N58
19	13	0
27	1	25S53

d	h	° '
2	5	0
8	10	5N14
15	1	0
22	8	5S 9

VOID OF COURSE ☽

Last Aspect		☽ Ingress		
2	8am50	2	♒	3pm38
4	6pm 4	4	♓	6pm 4
6	4pm23	6	♈	7pm15
8	2pm 9	8	♉	8pm47
10	1pm40	10	♊	11pm55
12	11pm59	13	♋	5am10
15	5am 1	15	♌	12pm36
17	7pm18	17	♍	10pm 1
19	12pm27	20	♎	9am15
22	1pm23	22	♏	9pm44
24	9pm 5	25	♐	10am 1
27	12pm 4	27	♑	7pm58

d	h	
6	6	PERIGEE
22	7	APOGEE

DAILY ASPECTARIAN

Day	Aspect	Time
1 M	☽∠☿	2am23
	☽⚼♇	2 55
	☽*♄	2 59
	☽∠♂	4 50
	☿☍♇	6 29
	☉⚺☽	8 1
	☽⚺♀	9 7
	♀∥♂	1pm11
	☽⚻♃	4 12
	☽#♇	5 13
	☽#♅	9 32
	☽#♃	9 40
	☽☍♅	10 35
2 T	☽⚻♇	5am22
	☿□♂	5 35
	☽*♂	8 24
	☽⚺☿	8 40
	☽□♆	8 50
	☿△♆	9 58
	☽⚼♃	6pm14
	♂⚺♆	6 48
	☽∥♂	10 37
3 W	☽∥♀	2am24
	☉∥☽	7 12
	☽□♄	7 18
	☉☌☽	3pm56
	☽☌♀	5 59
	☽△♃	7 36
4 Th	☽∥☿	0am 5
	☽⚻♅	1 38
	☽∥♄	3 16
	☽☍♇	8 9
	☽△♆	11 31
	♀△♃	12pm 6
	☽□♂	1 11
	☿ ♓	6 4
	☽☌☿	6 4
	☽∥♆	6 32
5 F	☿∥♄	0am27
	☽⚼♅	2 23
	☽△♄	9 15
	☽⚼♆	12pm13
	☉△♃	6 49
	☽□♃	9 4
	☉⚺☽	9 15
6 S	☽⚺♀	0am12
	☽△♅	2 55
	☽⚻♇	9 22
	☽⚼♄	9 50
	☽⚻♆	12pm45
	☽△♂	4 23
	☉∠☽	11 37
7 Su	☽⚺☿	1am21
	☽∠♀	3 3
	♀⚻♅	7 1
	☽⚼♇	9 54
	☽⚻♄	10 27
	☽#♆	10 57
	☽#☿	3pm54
	☽⚼♂	5 59
	☿⚼♅	8 18
	☽*♃	10 14
8 M	☉*☽	2am 8
	☽#♄	2 18
	☽□♅	4 3
	☽∠☿	4 59
	☽*♀	6 6
	☽△♇	10 38
	☽☍♆	2pm 9
	☉#☽	2 41
	☽#♀	5 0
	☽⚻♂	7 53
	☽∠♃	11 10
9 T	☉⚻♅	4am37
	☽*☿	8 54
	☽#♂	11 37
	☽☍♄	12pm26
	♂ ♐	7 18
10 W	☽⚺♃	0am31
	☿∥♆	2 55
	☽*♅	6 25
	☽∥♃	7 47
	☽∥♅	8 9
	☉□☽	8 30
	♀☍♇	9 27
	♃SD	9 32
	☽∥♇	12pm48
	☽□♇	1 17
	☽□♀	1 40
	☽⚻♆	4 59
	☿△♄	9 41
11 Th	☽☍♂	1am 7
	☽∠♅	8 20
	☽⚻♄	4pm14
	☽□☿	6 7
	☽⚼♆	7 11
12 F	♀△♆	2am19
	☽☌♃	4 47
	☿⚼♆	5 58
	☽⚺♅	10 48
	☉△☽	5pm24
	☽*♇	5 59
	☽⚼♄	6 57
	☽△♆	9 55
	☽△♀	11 59
13 S	☉☍♇	1am 0
	☽⚻♂	8 45
	☽∠♇	9pm10
	☽△♄	10 13
	☉⚼☽	10 54
14 Su	☽△☿	5am 6
	☽⚼♀	6 14
	☽∥♇	11 16
	☽⚺♃	11 17
	☽⚼♂	1pm30
	☽∥♅	4 24
	☽∥♃	4 50
	☽☌♅	5 21
	☉∥♀	11 23
15 M	☽⚺♇	0am52
	☉△♆	4 34
	☽□♆	5 1
	☉⚻☽	5 4
	♀ ♓	7 2
	☽#♂	10 28
	☽⚼☿	11 3
	☽⚻♀	1pm12
	☽∠♃	3 21
	☽△♂	6 50
16 T	☽□♄	6am17
	♀∥♄	3pm39
	☽⚻☿	5 8
	☽*♃	7 54
17 W	☽⚺♅	1am58
	☉∥♄	2 42
	☽#♄	4 47
	☉#☽	4 56
	☽#♀	6 5
	♄SR	6 18
	☽☌♇	9 46
	☽*♆	2pm 8
	☉☍☽	7 18
	☽#♆	10 53
18 Th	♂⚼♅	3am50
	☽☍♀	5 9
	☽∠♅	6 59
	☽□♂	7 8
	☽*♄	4pm18
	☽∠♆	7 23
	☽#☿	9 33
	♀⚼♅	10 49
19 F	☉ ♓	4am33
	☽☍☿	5 27
	☽□♃	6 28
	☽*♅	12pm27
	♀□♂	2 12
	☽⚺♇	8 32
	☽∠♄	9 57
20 S	☽⚺♆	1am 4
	☽∥☿	3 34
	☿SR	7 38
	☉⚻☽	11 53
	☽*♂	9pm27
	☽⚻♀	11 31
21 Su	☽∠♇	2am30
	☽⚺♄	3 59
	☽∥♆	4 26
	☽∥♀	12pm18
	☉∥☽	3 19
	☽⚻☿	5 20
	☽△♃	6 41
	☉⚼☽	8 51
	☽∥♄	11 24
22 M	☽□♅	0am28
	☽∠♂	5 8
	☽*♇	8 43
	☽⚼♀	9 21
	☽☌♆	1pm23
	♀△♄	5 53
	☽⚼☿	10 50
23 T	☽⚼♃	1am 8
	☉△☽	6 0
	☽⚺♂	12pm55
	☉⚼♅	2 32
	☽☌♄	4 34
	☽△♀	7 15
	♀⚼♆	11 14
24 W	☽∥♂	3am44
	☽△☿	3 51
	☽⚻♃	7 31
	☽△♅	12pm55
	☽#♃	4 50
	☽#♅	5 8
	☽□♇	9 5
	♀∥♆	10 34
	☽#♇	11 21
25 Th	☽⚺♆	1am44
	☽⚼♅	6pm41
	☉□☽	11 29
26 F	☿☌♀	2am 2
	☽☌♂	3 32
	☽⚺♄	4 17
	☽∠♆	7 17
	☽□☿	11 49
	☽□♀	1pm41
	☽☍♃	7 0
	♂⚺♄	8 38
	☽⚻♅	11 48
27 S	☽△♇	7am36
	☽∠♄	9 9
	☽*♆	12pm 4
	☉∥♆	5 21
28 Su	☉△♄	9am 8
	☽⚼♇	11 35
	☽*♄	1pm 5
	☉*☽	1 25
	☽⚺♂	2 50
	☽*☿	4 22
	♀□♃	8 47
	☿⚼♆	10 23

MARCH 1954

LONGITUDE

Day	Sid. Time	☉	☽	☽ 12 Hour	Mean ☊	True ☊	☿	♀	♂	♃	♄	♅	♆	♇
	h m s	° ' "	° ' "	° ' "	° '	° '	° '	° '	° '	° '	° '	° '	° '	° '
1	10 33 3	9♓52 7	15♑14 44	21♑57 19	21♑37	23♑ 3R	10♓42R	17♓ 9	10♐24	16♊59	9♏14R	19♋19R	25♎47R	23♌25R
2	10 37 0	10 52 20	28 46 50	5♒43 23	21 34	23 3	9 40	18 24	10 55	17 3	9 13	19 17	25 46	23 23
3	10 40 56	11 52 32	12♒46 51	19 56 59	21 31	23 1	8 37	19 38	11 27	17 7	9 11	19 16	25 45	23 22
4	10 44 53	12 52 42	27 13 15	4♓35 0	21 28	22 57	7 35	20 53	11 58	17 11	9 10	19 15	25 43	23 20
5	10 48 50	13 52 50	12♓ 1 20	19 31 13	21 25	22 51	6 36	22 8	12 29	17 15	9 8	19 14	25 42	23 19
6	10 52 46	14 52 57	27 3 27	4♈36 48	21 22	22 43	5 40	23 23	12 59	17 19	9 7	19 12	25 41	23 18
7	10 56 43	15 53 1	12♈ 9 57	19 41 40	21 18	22 35	4 49	24 38	13 30	17 24	9 5	19 11	25 40	23 16
8	11 0 39	16 53 4	27 10 47	4♉36 16	21 15	22 27	4 4	25 53	14 1	17 29	9 3	19 10	25 39	23 15
9	11 4 36	17 53 4	11♉57 15	19 13 5	21 12	22 20	3 24	27 8	14 31	17 34	9 1	19 9	25 38	23 14
10	11 8 32	18 53 2	26 23 17	3♊27 33	21 9	22 16	2 51	28 22	15 1	17 39	8 59	19 8	25 36	23 12
11	11 12 29	19 52 59	10♊25 49	17 18 5	21 6	22 14D	2 24	29 37	15 31	17 44	8 57	19 7	25 35	23 11
12	11 16 25	20 52 53	24 4 33	0♋45 28	21 2	22 13	2 4	0♈52	16 1	17 50	8 55	19 7	25 34	23 10
13	11 20 22	21 52 44	7♋21 11	13 52 5	20 59	22 14	1 51	2 6	16 31	17 55	8 53	19 6	25 33	23 8
14	11 24 19	22 52 34	20 18 34	26 41 2	20 56	22 14R	1 44D	3 21	17 0	18 1	8 50	19 5	25 31	23 7
15	11 28 15	23 52 21	2♌59 56	9♌15 36	20 53	22 14	1 43	4 36	17 30	18 7	8 48	19 4	25 30	23 6
16	11 32 12	24 52 6	15 28 26	21 38 44	20 50	22 11	1 48	5 50	17 59	18 13	8 45	19 4	25 29	23 5
17	11 36 8	25 51 49	27 46 47	3♍52 52	20 47	22 6	1 59	7 5	18 28	18 20	8 42	19 3	25 27	23 4
18	11 40 5	26 51 30	9♍57 10	15 59 54	20 43	21 58	2 15	8 20	18 57	18 26	8 40	19 2	25 26	23 2
19	11 44 1	27 51 8	22 1 14	28 1 18	20 40	21 47	2 37	9 34	19 26	18 33	8 37	19 2	25 25	23 1
20	11 47 58	28 50 45	4♎ 0 17	9♎58 18	20 37	21 35	3 3	10 49	19 54	18 39	8 34	19 2	25 23	23 0
21	11 51 54	29 50 20	15 55 31	21 52 6	20 34	21 22	3 34	12 3	20 22	18 46	8 31	19 1	25 22	22 59
22	11 55 51	0♈49 52	27 48 15	3♏44 12	20 31	21 9	4 10	13 17	20 51	18 53	8 28	19 1	25 20	22 58
23	11 59 47	1 49 23	9♏40 14	15 36 38	20 27	20 58	4 49	14 32	21 18	19 1	8 25	19 1	25 19	22 57
24	12 3 44	2 48 52	21 33 47	27 32 3	20 24	20 48	5 33	15 46	21 46	19 8	8 22	19 0	25 17	22 56
25	12 7 41	3 48 19	3♐31 54	9♐33 50	20 21	20 42	6 19	17 1	22 14	19 15	8 18	19 0	25 16	22 55
26	12 11 37	4 47 44	15 38 23	21 46 5	20 18	20 38	7 10	18 15	22 41	19 23	8 15	19 0	25 14	22 53
27	12 15 34	5 47 8	27 57 34	4♑13 25	20 15	20 37D	8 3	19 29	23 8	19 31	8 12	19 0D	25 13	22 52
28	12 19 30	6 46 30	10♑34 15	17 0 40	20 12	20 36R	9 0	20 44	23 35	19 39	8 8	19 0	25 11	22 51
29	12 23 27	7 45 50	23 33 13	0♒12 25	20 8	20 37	9 59	21 58	24 1	19 47	8 4	19 0	25 10	22 50
30	12 27 23	8 45 8	6♒58 38	13 52 11	20 5	20 36	11 1	23 12	24 28	19 55	8 1	19 0	25 8	22 50
31	12 31 20	9♈44 25	20♒53 11	28♒ 1 35	20♑ 2	20♑33	12♓ 6	24♈26	24♐54	20♊ 3	7♏57	19♋ 0	25♎ 7	22♌49

DECLINATION and LATITUDE

Day	☉	☽		☽ 12 Hr.	☿		♀		♂		♃		♄	
	Decl	Decl	Lat	Decl	Decl	Lat	Decl	Lat	Decl	Lat	Decl	Lat	Decl	Lat
1	7S52	23S16	0S42	21S45	4S 7	3N43	6S24	1S26	21S19	0N42	22N32	0S17	12S 7	2N35
2	7 29	19 54	0N31	17 45	4 32	3 41	5 54	1 25	21 25	0 41	22 32	0 17	12 7	2 35
3	7 7	15 19	1 44	12 37	4 60	3 37	5 24	1 25	21 30	0 40	22 33	0 17	12 6	2 36
4	6 44	9 44	2 53	6 40	5 28	3 31	4 54	1 24	21 35	0 39	22 33	0 16	12 5	2 36
5	6 21	3 29	3 52	0 13	5 57	3 23	4 24	1 23	21 40	0 39	22 34	0 16	12 5	2 36
6	5 57	3N 3	4 36	6N17	6 26	3 13	3 54	1 23	21 44	0 38	22 34	0 16	12 4	2 36
7	5 34	9 25	5 1	12 25	6 55	3 3	3 23	1 22	21 49	0 37	22 35	0 16	12 3	2 37
8	5 11	15 12	5 5	17 45	7 22	2 51	2 53	1 21	21 54	0 36	22 36	0 16	12 2	2 37
9	4 47	19 59	4 48	21 54	7 49	2 38	2 22	1 20	21 58	0 35	22 36	0 16	12 2	2 37
10	4 24	23 27	4 13	24 37	8 13	2 24	1 52	1 19	22 3	0 34	22 37	0 15	12 1	2 37
11	4 0	25 23	3 24	25 45	8 36	2 10	1 21	1 18	22 7	0 33	22 38	0 15	11 60	2 37
12	3 37	25 43	2 25	25 19	8 56	1 56	0 50	1 17	22 11	0 32	22 38	0 15	11 59	2 38
13	3 13	24 33	1 19	23 28	9 15	1 41	0 20	1 16	22 15	0 31	22 39	0 15	11 58	2 38
14	2 50	22 5	0 10	20 26	9 31	1 27	0N11	1 15	22 19	0 30	22 40	0 15	11 57	2 38
15	2 26	18 34	0S57	16 30	9 45	1 12	0 42	1 14	22 23	0 29	22 40	0 15	11 56	2 38
16	2 2	14 17	2 1	11 56	9 56	0 58	1 13	1 12	22 27	0 28	22 41	0 14	11 55	2 38
17	1 39	9 28	2 57	6 56	10 5	0 44	1 43	1 11	22 30	0 26	22 42	0 14	11 54	2 39
18	1 15	4 22	3 45	1 45	10 12	0 30	2 14	1 10	22 34	0 25	22 42	0 14	11 53	2 39
19	0 51	0S51	4 22	3S26	10 17	0 17	2 45	1 8	22 37	0 24	22 43	0 14	11 52	2 39
20	0 28	5 59	4 48	8 28	10 20	0 4	3 15	1 7	22 41	0 23	22 44	0 14	11 51	2 39
21	0 4	10 53	4 60	13 11	10 20	0S 9	3 46	1 5	22 44	0 22	22 45	0 14	11 50	2 39
22	0N20	15 21	4 59	17 22	10 18	0 20	4 16	1 3	22 47	0 21	22 45	0 14	11 49	2 39
23	0 44	19 13	4 46	20 53	10 14	0 32	4 47	1 2	22 50	0 19	22 46	0 13	11 48	2 40
24	1 7	22 20	4 20	23 33	10 9	0 43	5 17	1 0	22 53	0 18	22 47	0 13	11 46	2 40
25	1 31	24 30	3 42	25 10	10 1	0 53	5 47	0 58	22 56	0 17	22 48	0 13	11 45	2 40
26	1 54	25 33	2 54	25 38	9 52	1 3	6 17	0 56	22 59	0 15	22 48	0 13	11 44	2 40
27	2 18	25 23	1 57	24 48	9 41	1 13	6 47	0 55	23 2	0 14	22 49	0 13	11 43	2 40
28	2 41	23 54	0 53	22 41	9 28	1 22	7 17	0 53	23 5	0 13	22 50	0 13	11 42	2 40
29	3 5	21 8	0N16	19 17	9 13	1 30	7 47	0 51	23 7	0 11	22 51	0 12	11 40	2 40
30	3 28	17 9	1 26	14 45	8 57	1 38	8 16	0 49	23 10	0 10	22 51	0 12	11 39	2 41
31	3N52	12S 7	2N33	9S17	8S39	1S45	8N45	0S47	23S13	0N 8	22N52	0S12	11S38	2N41

Day	♅		♆		♇	
	Decl	Lat	Decl	Lat	Decl	Lat
1	22N32	0N29	8S21	1N44	23N14	10N 6
5	22 33	0 29	8 19	1 44	23 15	10 6
9	22 34	0 29	8 17	1 45	23 17	10 6
13	22 34	0 29	8 15	1 45	23 19	10 6
17	22 34	0 29	8 13	1 45	23 20	10 5
21	22 35	0 29	8 11	1 45	23 21	10 5
25	22 35	0 29	8 9	1 45	23 22	10 4
29	22N35	0N29	8S 6	1N45	23N23	10N 4

☽ PHENOMENA			
d	h	m	
5	3	12	●
11	17	52	☽
19	12	43	○
27	16	14	☾
d	h	°	
5	13	0	
11	17	25N47	
18	20	0	
26	9	25S38	
1	14	0	
7	16	5N 6	
14	4	0	
21	11	5S 1	
28	19	0	

VOID OF COURSE ☽ Last Aspect		☽ Ingress		
1	6pm43	2	♒	2am 7
3	9pm33	4	♓	4am33
5	5pm38	6	♈	4am41
7	9pm32	8	♉	4am33
10	3am40	10	♊	6am 7
12	2am39	12	♋	10am38
14	9am47	14	♌	6pm17
16	7pm27	17	♍	4am22
19	12pm43	19	♎	3pm58
21	7pm 1	22	♏	4am26
24	2am44	24	♐	4pm56
26	6pm42	27	♑	3am55
29	2am55	29	♒	11am38
31	7am 7	31	♓	3pm17

d	h	
6	10	PERIGEE
21	18	APOGEE

DAILY ASPECTARIAN

Day	Aspect	Time
1 M	☽#♇	0am22
	☽⚻♃	3 9
	☽⚹♀	3 46
	☿□♂	4 44
	☽#♅	6 5
	☽#♃	6 11
	☽☍♅	7 17
	☉☌☿	9 51
	☽⚻♇	2pm33
	☽∥♂	2 37
	♂∠♆	4 44
	☽∠☿	5 18
	☉∠☽	6 30
	☽□♆	6 43
	☽∠♂	6 48
	☉⚼♆	9 21
2 T	☉□♂	2am30
	☽⚼♃	5 42
	☽∠♀	8 47
	☿△♄	10 26
	♀△♅	4pm57
	☽⚺☿	5 25
	☽□♄	5 56
	☽⚹♂	9 39
	☉⚺☽	10 21
3 W	♃∥♅	5am 2
	☽△♃	7 18
	☿∥♀	10 4
	☽⚻♅	10 51
	☽⚺♀	12pm34
	☽∥♄	2 15
	☽☍♇	5 37
	☽△♆	9 33
4 Th	☽∥♆	5am34
	☽⚼♅	11 26
	☉∥☽	12pm31
	☽∥☿	3 22
	☽☌☿	3 47
	☽△♄	7 22
	☽∥♀	8 16
	☽⚼♆	9 53
5 F	☽□♂	0am45
	☉☌☽	3 12
	☽□♃	8 25
	☉∥☿	10 44
	☽△♅	11 31
	☽☌♀	5pm38
	☽⚻♇	6 1
	☽⚼♄	7 20
	☽⚻♆	9 49
	♀⚻♇	10 16
6 S	☽#♀	2am53
	☉#☽	10 10
	☽⚺☿	12pm56
	☽#☿	1 37
	♀⚼♄	1 41
	☽⚼♇	5 49
	☽⚻♄	7 7
	☽#♆	7 40
7 Su	☽△♂	2am12
	☉⚺☽	6 20
	☽⚹♃	8 23
	☽#♄	10 31
	☽□♅	11 11
	☽∠☿	11 36
	☽△♇	5pm42
	♀⚻♆	7 37
	☿⚼♅	8 10
	☽☍♆	9 32
	☽⚺♀	9 43
8 M	☽⚼♂	3am 3
	☉∠☽	8 9
	☽∠♃	8 36
	☽⚹☿	10 37
	☉□♃	3pm37
	☽☍♄	7 12
9 T	☽∠♀	0am18
	☽⚻♂	4 22
	☽⚺♃	9 19
	☉⚹☽	10 31
	☽⚹♅	11 53
	☽#♂	12pm45
	☽∥♅	4 46
	☽∥♃	5 8
	☽□♇	6 40
	☽∥♇	10 36
	☽⚻♆	10 41
10 W	☿∥♆	3am25
	☽⚹♀	3 40
	☉△♅	6 2
	☽□☿	10 36
	☽∠♅	1pm 9
	☽⚻♄	9 27
11 Th	☽⚼♆	0am16
	♀ ♈	7 22
	☽☍♂	9 13
	☽☌♃	12pm51
	☽⚺♅	3 12
	☉□☽	5 52
	☽⚹♇	10 22
	☽⚼♄	11 43
12 F	☽△♆	2am39
	☽□♀	1pm27
	☽△☿	2 7
	☿⚺♀	7 32
13 S	☽∠♇	1am26
	☽△♄	2 47
	☽∥♇	1pm24
	☽⚼☿	5 21
	☽⚻♂	5 35
	☽∥♃	7 16
	☽⚺♃	7 41
	☽∥♅	8 1
	☽☌♅	9 43
	☽#♂	10 8
14 Su	☉△☽	5am14
	☽⚺♇	5 16
	☉⚻♇	5 45
	☽□♆	9 47
	☿SD	3pm 9
	☽⚻☿	9 32
	☉⚼♄	10 12
	☽⚼♂	11 0
15 M	☽∠♃	0am14
	☽△♀	3 23
	☽□♄	11 4
	☉⚼☽	12pm14
16 T	☽△♂	5am 4
	☽⚹♃	5 23
	☽⚺♅	6 58
	☽⚼♀	11 36
	☽#♄	12pm 5
	☉⚻♆	2 23
	☽☌♇	2 46
	♂☍♃	3 4
	☽⚹♆	7 27
	☉⚻☽	7 55
	☽#☿	9 6
	☉#♀	9 54
17 W	☽#♆	6am 0
	☽☍☿	8 26
	☽∠♅	12pm20
	♀⚼♇	6 33
	☽⚻♀	8 25
	☽⚹♄	9 27
18 Th	☽∠♆	0am57
	♂#♅	4 13
	♂⚻♅	4 33
	♀⚻♄	6 16
	☽∥♀	8 55
	☉#☽	3pm30
	☽□♃	5 0
	☽⚹♅	6 3
	☽□♂	6 37
19 F	☉∥☽	0am 1
	☽⚺♇	1 59
	☽∠♄	3 10
	☽⚺♆	6 45
	☽#♀	9 44
	☉☍☽	12pm43
	☽⚻☿	10 1
20 S	☽∠♇	8am 1
	☽⚺♄	9 8
	☽∥♆	10 35
	☽☍♀	3pm17
	☽∥☿	9 14
21 Su	☉ ♈	3am54
	☽∥♄	4 53
	♂#♃	5 26
	☽⚼☿	5 37
	☽△♃	5 48
	☽□♅	6 15
	☽⚹♂	9 21
	☽⚹♇	2pm14
	☿⚼♅	6 16
	☽☌♆	7 1
22 M	☉⚻☽	6am41
	☽⚼♃	12pm26
	☽△☿	1 36
	☽∠♂	4 55
	☽☌♄	9 28
	♃⚺♅	11 57
23 T	☽⚻♀	10am58
	☉⚼☽	3pm46
	☽△♅	6 51
	☽⚻♃	7 3
24 W	☽⚺♂	0am26
	☽#♅	2 15
	☽□♇	2 44
	☽#♃	4 11
	☽∥♂	5 20
	☽⚺♆	7 29
	☽#♇	10 8
	☽⚼♀	8pm37
25 Th	☉△☽	0am36
	☽⚼♅	0 56
	☽□☿	5 58
	☽⚺♄	9 28
	☽∠♆	1pm22
26 F	☽△♀	5am42
	☽⚻♅	6 36
	☽☍♃	7 25
	♂△♇	10 46
	☽△♇	2pm10
	☽☌♂	2 18
	♀□♅	2 30
	☽∠♄	2 49
	☽⚹♆	6 42
27 S	♀⚹♃	0am29
	♂∠♄	2 53
	☿△♄	3 26
	☉□☽	4pm14
	♅SD	5 34
	☽⚼♇	6 54
	☽⚹♄	7 26
	☽⚹☿	8 47
28 Su	☽#♇	5am27
	☽∥♂	8 14
	☽#♃	10 35
	☽#♅	12pm51
	☽☍♅	3 40
	☽⚻♃	5 2
	☽□♀	8 48
	☽⚻♇	10 42
29 M	☽⚺♂	0am53
	☉⚼♇	1 51
	☽∠☿	2 48
	☽□♆	2 55
	☿⚼♆	4 9
	☉⚻♄	7 7
	♀#♆	3pm47
	♀△♇	4 44
	☽⚼♃	8 20
30 T	☽□♄	1am49
	☉⚹☽	3 21
	☽∠♂	4 29
	☽⚺☿	7 39
	☽⚻♅	8pm48
	☿#♀	8 50
	☽△♃	10 34
31 W	☽∥♄	2am 9
	☽☍♇	3 15
	☽⚹♀	6 34
	☽⚹♂	6 58
	☉∠☽	6 59
	☽△♆	7 7
	♂⚹♆	11 18
	♀☍♆	12pm42
	☽#♀	1 5
	♀△♂	1 30
	☽∥☿	3 24
	☽∥♆	4 52
	☽⚼♅	9 54

APRIL 1954

LONGITUDE

Day	Sid. Time	☉	☽	☽ 12 Hour	Mean ☊	True ☊	☿	♀	♂	♃	♄	♅	♆	♇
	h m s	° ' "	° ' "	° ' "	° '	° '	° '	° '	° '	° '	° '	° '	° '	° '
1	12 35 16	10♈ 43 40	5♓ 17 8	12♓ 39 19	19♑ 59	20♑ 27R	13♓ 13	25♈ 41	25♐ 20	20♊ 12	7♏ 53R	19♋ 0	25♎ 5R	22♌ 48R
2	12 39 13	11 42 53	20 7 24	27 40 26	19 56	20 19	14 22	26 55	25 45	20 20	7 50	19 1	25 3	22 47
3	12 43 10	12 42 3	5♈ 17 13	12♈ 56 25	19 53	20 9	15 33	28 9	26 10	20 29	7 46	19 1	25 2	22 46
4	12 47 6	13 41 12	20 36 34	28 16 10	19 49	19 58	16 47	29 23	26 35	20 38	7 42	19 1	25 0	22 45
5	12 51 3	14 40 19	5♉ 53 47	13♉ 28 3	19 46	19 47	18 3	0♉ 37	27 0	20 47	7 38	19 2	24 59	22 44
6	12 54 59	15 39 24	20 57 46	28 21 57	19 43	19 38	19 21	1 51	27 25	20 56	7 34	19 2	24 57	22 43
7	12 58 56	16 38 26	5♊ 39 52	12♊ 50 59	19 40	19 31	20 40	3 5	27 49	21 5	7 30	19 3	24 55	22 43
8	13 2 52	17 37 27	19 55 0	26 51 52	19 37	19 26	22 2	4 19	28 12	21 14	7 26	19 3	24 54	22 42
9	13 6 49	18 36 25	3♋ 41 40	10♋ 24 40	19 33	19 25D	23 25	5 33	28 36	21 23	7 21	19 4	24 52	22 41
10	13 10 45	19 35 20	17 1 13	23 31 47	19 30	19 24R	24 50	6 47	28 59	21 33	7 17	19 5	24 51	22 41
11	13 14 42	20 34 14	29 56 53	6♌ 17 2	19 27	19 24	26 17	8 1	29 22	21 43	7 13	19 5	24 49	22 40
12	13 18 39	21 33 5	12♌ 32 48	18 44 44	19 24	19 23	27 46	9 15	29 45	21 52	7 9	19 6	24 47	22 39
13	13 22 35	22 31 54	24 53 21	0♍ 59 9	19 21	19 20	29 16	10 29	0♑ 7	22 2	7 4	19 7	24 46	22 39
14	13 26 32	23 30 40	7♍ 2 36	13 4 7	19 18	19 15	0♈ 48	11 43	0 29	22 12	7 0	19 8	24 44	22 38
15	13 30 28	24 29 24	19 4 3	25 2 47	19 14	19 6	2 21	12 57	0 50	22 22	6 56	19 9	24 42	22 37
16	13 34 25	25 28 7	1♎ 0 34	6♎ 57 40	19 11	18 55	3 57	14 10	1 12	22 32	6 51	19 10	24 41	22 37
17	13 38 21	26 26 47	12 54 18	18 50 40	19 8	18 41	5 33	15 24	1 32	22 43	6 47	19 11	24 39	22 36
18	13 42 18	27 25 25	24 46 56	0♏ 43 17	19 5	18 27	7 12	16 38	1 53	22 53	6 42	19 12	24 37	22 36
19	13 46 14	28 24 1	6♏ 39 53	12 36 53	19 2	18 13	8 52	17 51	2 13	23 3	6 38	19 13	24 36	22 35
20	13 50 11	29 22 36	18 34 28	24 32 52	18 59	18 0	10 34	19 5	2 33	23 14	6 33	19 14	24 34	22 35
21	13 54 8	0♉ 21 8	0♐ 32 17	6♐ 33 1	18 55	17 50	12 17	20 18	2 52	23 25	6 29	19 16	24 32	22 35
22	13 58 4	1 19 39	12 35 22	13 39 41	18 52	17 42	14 2	21 32	3 11	23 35	6 24	19 17	24 31	22 34
23	14 2 1	2 18 8	24 46 21	0♑ 55 49	18 49	17 38	15 49	22 46	3 29	23 46	6 20	19 18	24 29	22 34
24	14 5 57	3 16 36	7♑ 8 32	13 25 0	18 46	17 36D	17 37	23 59	3 47	23 57	6 15	19 20	24 28	22 34
25	14 9 54	4 15 2	19 45 45	26 11 18	18 43	17 35	19 27	25 12	4 5	24 8	6 11	19 21	24 26	22 33
26	14 13 50	5 13 26	2♒ 42 9	9♒ 18 49	18 39	17 36R	21 19	26 26	4 22	24 19	6 6	19 23	24 24	22 33
27	14 17 47	6 11 48	16 1 42	22 51 10	18 36	17 36	23 13	27 39	4 39	24 30	6 2	19 24	24 23	22 33
28	14 21 43	7 10 10	29 47 27	6♓ 50 40	18 33	17 34	25 8	28 53	4 55	24 41	5 57	19 26	24 21	22 33
29	14 25 40	8 8 29	14♓ 0 44	21 17 22	18 30	17 30	27 5	0♊ 6	5 10	24 53	5 52	19 28	24 20	22 32
30	14 29 37	9♉ 6 47	28♓ 40 6	6♈ 8 12	18♑ 27	17♑ 23	29♈ 3	1♊ 19	5♑ 26	25♊ 4	5♏ 48	19♋ 29	24♎ 18	22♌ 32

DECLINATION and LATITUDE

Day	☉ Decl	☽ Decl	☽ Lat	☽ 12 Hr. Decl	☿ Decl	☿ Lat	♀ Decl	♀ Lat	♂ Decl	♂ Lat	♃ Decl	♃ Lat	♄ Decl	♄ Lat
1	4N15	6S17	3N33	3S 8	8S20	1S52	9N14	0S44	23S15	0N 7	22N53	0S12	11S36	2N41
2	4 38	0N 4	4 20	3N19	7 59	1 58	9 43	0 42	23 17	0 5	22 54	0 12	11 35	2 41
3	5 1	6 32	4 50	9 41	7 36	2 4	10 12	0 40	23 20	0 4	22 54	0 12	11 34	2 41
4	5 24	12 41	5 0	15 29	7 12	2 9	10 40	0 38	23 22	0 2	22 55	0 12	11 32	2 41
5	5 47	18 1	4 49	20 15	6 47	2 14	11 8	0 36	23 24	0 1	22 56	0 12	11 31	2 41
6	6 10	22 8	4 17	23 37	6 20	2 18	11 36	0 33	23 26	0S 1	22 57	0 11	11 30	2 41
7	6 33	24 41	3 29	25 19	5 53	2 22	12 4	0 31	23 28	0 3	22 58	0 11	11 28	2 41
8	6 55	25 32	2 29	25 21	5 23	2 25	12 31	0 29	23 31	0 5	22 58	0 11	11 27	2 42
9	7 18	24 46	1 22	23 49	4 53	2 28	12 58	0 26	23 33	0 6	22 59	0 11	11 25	2 42
10	7 40	22 34	0 13	21 2	4 21	2 30	13 24	0 24	23 35	0 8	22 60	0 11	11 24	2 42
11	8 2	19 16	0S55	17 17	3 48	2 32	13 51	0 21	23 37	0 10	23 0	0 11	11 22	2 42
12	8 24	15 9	1 59	12 52	3 14	2 33	14 17	0 19	23 39	0 12	23 1	0 11	11 21	2 42
13	8 46	10 28	2 56	7 60	2 39	2 34	14 42	0 17	23 40	0 14	23 2	0 10	11 20	2 42
14	9 8	5 28	3 43	2 55	2 2	2 34	15 8	0 14	23 42	0 16	23 3	0 10	11 18	2 42
15	9 30	0 20	4 20	2S14	1 25	2 33	15 33	0 12	23 44	0 18	23 3	0 10	11 17	2 42
16	9 51	4S46	4 45	7 15	0 46	2 33	15 57	0 9	23 46	0 20	23 4	0 10	11 15	2 42
17	10 12	9 40	4 58	11 60	0 6	2 31	16 21	0 6	23 48	0 22	23 5	0 10	11 14	2 42
18	10 34	14 13	4 58	16 18	0N34	2 29	16 45	0 4	23 50	0 24	23 5	0 10	11 12	2 42
19	10 55	18 13	4 44	19 58	1 16	2 27	17 8	0 1	23 52	0 26	23 6	0 10	11 11	2 42
20	11 15	21 30	4 19	22 49	1 59	2 24	17 31	0N 1	23 53	0 28	23 7	0 10	11 9	2 42
21	11 36	23 53	3 41	24 40	2 42	2 20	17 54	0 4	23 55	0 30	23 7	0 9	11 8	2 42
22	11 56	25 11	2 54	25 24	3 27	2 16	18 15	0 7	23 57	0 33	23 8	0 9	11 6	2 42
23	12 17	25 18	1 58	24 54	4 12	2 12	18 37	0 9	23 59	0 35	23 9	0 9	11 5	2 42
24	12 37	24 10	0 55	23 8	4 58	2 7	18 58	0 12	24 1	0 37	23 9	0 9	11 3	2 42
25	12 56	21 48	0N11	20 10	5 45	2 1	19 18	0 15	24 3	0 40	23 10	0 9	11 2	2 42
26	13 16	18 16	1 19	16 7	6 32	1 55	19 38	0 17	24 5	0 42	23 11	0 9	11 0	2 42
27	13 35	13 44	2 25	11 8	7 20	1 49	19 58	0 20	24 6	0 45	23 11	0 9	10 59	2 42
28	13 55	8 22	3 24	5 26	8 9	1 42	20 17	0 23	24 8	0 47	23 12	0 9	10 57	2 42
29	14 13	2 24	4 13	0N43	8 58	1 34	20 35	0 25	24 10	0 50	23 12	0 8	10 56	2 42
30	14N32	3N51	4N47	6N59	9N48	1S26	20N53	0N28	24S12	0S52	23N13	0S 8	10S54	2N42

Day	♅ Decl	♅ Lat	♆ Decl	♆ Lat	♇ Decl	♇ Lat
1	22N35	0N29	8S 5	1N45	23N24	10N 3
5	22 34	0 29	8 2	1 45	23 24	10 3
9	22 34	0 29	7 60	1 45	23 25	10 2
13	22 33	0 29	7 57	1 46	23 25	10 2
17	22 33	0 29	7 55	1 46	23 25	10 1
21	22 32	0 29	7 53	1 46	23 25	10 0
25	22 31	0 29	7 50	1 46	23 25	9 59
29	22N30	0N28	7S48	1N45	23N24	9N58

☽ PHENOMENA

d	h	m	
3	12	25	●
10	5	6	☽
18	5	49	○
26	4	58	☾

d	h	° '
2	0	0
8	0	25N32
15	2	0
22	14	25S24
29	9	0

d	h	° '
3	23	5N 0
10	4	0
17	11	4S60
24	20	0

VOID OF COURSE ☽

Last Aspect		☽ Ingress		
2	9am13	2	♈	3pm40
4	9am38	4	♉	2pm43
6	2am50	6	♊	2pm40
8	2pm46	8	♋	5pm29
10	4pm15	11	♌	0am 6
12	11pm45	13	♍	10am 3
15	6am43	15	♎	9pm58
18	5am49	18	♏	10am33
20	8am 3	20	♐	10pm55
22	11pm27	23	♑	10am12
25	11am15	25	♒	7pm 3
27	10pm17	28	♓	0am21
29	6pm 5	30	♈	2am 9

d	h	
3	20	PERIGEE
17	20	APOGEE

DAILY ASPECTARIAN

Day	Aspect	Time
1 Th	☽△♄	4am14
	☉#☽	7 21
	☽⚼♆	7 49
	☉⚺☽	9 31
	☽∠♀	9 36
	☽☌☿	1pm58
	☿∥♆	5 47
	☽△♅	10 13
2 F	☽□♃	0am21
	☽⚻♇	4 14
	☽⚼♄	4 17
	☽⚻♆	7 50
	☽□♂	9 13
	☽⚺♀	11 45
	☉∥☽	5pm56
3 S	☽#☿	3am47
	☽⚻♄	3 52
	☽⚼♇	3 53
	☽#♆	5 44
	☉☌☽	12pm25
	☽∥♀	3 11
	☽⚺☿	5 30
	☽#♄	7 22
	☽□♅	9 31
4 Su	☽⚹♃	0am 2
	☽△♇	3 21
	☽☍♆	6 52
	☽△♂	9 38
	♀ ♉	11 56
	☽☌♀	2pm58
	☽∠☿	7 6
	☽∠♃	11 48
5 M	☽☍♄	2am44
	♂#♇	3 21
	☽⚼♂	9 56
	☉⚺☽	2pm54
	☿△♅	6 20
	♀#♄	6 43
	☽⚹♅	8 54
	☽⚹☿	9 9
	☽⚺♃	11 56
6 T	☽□♇	2am50
	☽∥♅	3 15
	☉#☿	5 5
	☽∥♃	6 15
	☽⚻♆	6 26
	☽∥♇	10 11
	☽#♂	10 35
	☽⚻♂	10 44
	☉∠☽	4pm53
	☽⚺♀	7 21
	☽∠♅	9 19
7 W	☽⚻♄	3am 2
	☽⚼♆	7 5
	☿□♃	8 11
	☉⚹☽	7pm48
	☽⚺♅	10 32
	☽∠♀	10 53
8 Th	☽☌♃	2am17
	☽□☿	4 2
	☽⚼♄	4 17
	☽⚹♇	4 47
	☿⚼♄	6 35
	☽△♆	8 34
	☿⚻♇	11 31
	☽☍♂	2pm46
9 F	☽⚹♀	3am38
	☽△♄	6 29
	☽∠♇	7 6
	☉□♅	11 22
	☽#♂	2pm44
	☽∥♇	4 14
	♀∠♃	6 39
	☽∥♃	8 15
10 S	☽∥♅	0am 4
	☿⚻♆	0 5
	☽☌♅	3 47
	☉□☽	5 6
	☽⚺♃	8 26
	♀☍♄	9 12
	☽⚺♇	10 24
	☽□♆	2pm25
	☽△☿	4 15
	☉#♆	8 12
	☽⚻♂	10 53
11 Su	☽∠♃	12pm59
	☽□♄	1 42
	☽□♀	4 59
12 M	☽⚼☿	0am28
	☽∥♀	4 13
	☽⚼♂	4 22
	☉⚹♃	9 26
	☽⚺♅	12pm43
	♂ ♑	4 28
	☽⚹♃	6 20
	☉△☽	6 59
	☽☌♇	7 36
	☽#♄	7 44
	☽⚹♆	11 45
13 T	☉△♇	2am43
	♃⚼♄	3 47
	☉∥☽	7 44
	☽⚻☿	9 50
	☽△♂	10 36
	☿ ♈	11 35
	☽#♆	12pm14
	☿□♂	5 35
	☽∠♅	6 13
	☽⚹♄	11 55
14 W	☉⚼☽	3am11
	☽∠♆	5 20
	☽△♀	10 21
	☽#☿	6pm18
15 Th	☽⚹♅	0am10
	☉☍♆	5 9
	☽∠♄	5 42
	☽□♃	6 43
	☽⚺♇	7 8
	☽∥☿	7 16
	☽⚺♆	11 17
	☉⚻☽	11 51
	☽⚼♀	7pm52
16 F	☽□♂	0am23
	☽☍☿	6 50
	♃⚹♇	10 18
	☽⚺♄	11 43
	☽∠♇	1pm19
	☽∥♆	3 16
17 S	☉#☽	2am57
	☽⚻♀	5 37
	☽∥♄	7 56
	☽□♅	12pm42
	☿⚻♄	5 11
	☽⚹♇	7 35
	☽△♃	8 6
	☽☌♆	11 41
18 Su	☿⚼♇	5am47
	☉☍☽	5 49
	♀⚼♂	6 51
	☽⚹♂	2pm46
	☽#♀	4 23
	☽☌♄	11 56
19 M	☽⚼♃	2am51
	☽⚻☿	5 10
	☉#♄	5pm24
	☽∠♂	9 52
20 T	☽☍♀	1am 8
	☽△♅	1 21
	♀⚹♅	3 10
	☽□♇	8 3
	☽#♅	9 18
	☽⚻♃	9 30
	☽⚺♆	12pm 1
	☽#♃	3 13
	☉ ♉	3 20
	☽⚼☿	4 23
	☽#♇	6 29
	☉⚻☽	11 36
21 W	☽∥♂	0am35
	☽⚺♂	4 47
	☽⚼♅	7 27
	☽⚺♄	11 47
	☽∠♆	5pm55
22 Th	☽△☿	3am21
	☉⚼☽	8 2
	☽⚻♅	1pm15
	☽∠♄	5 18
	☽⚻♀	7 37
	☽△♇	7 41
	♀□♇	8 14
	☽☍♃	10 0
	☽⚹♆	11 27
23 F	☉△☽	3pm55
	☽☌♂	5 23
	☽⚹♄	10 18
	♀⚺♃	11 13
24 S	☽⚼♇	0am48
	☽∥♂	2 3
	☽⚼♀	3 55
	☽#♇	9 6
	♀⚻♆	9 9
	☽#♃	11 44
	☽#♅	5pm52
	☉△♂	6 3
	☿□♅	10 39
	☽☍♅	11 14
	☽□☿	11 20
25 Su	☽⚻♇	5am14
	☽⚻♃	8 18
	☽□♆	8 43
	☽△♀	11 15
	☽#♀	4pm14
26 M	☽⚺♂	3am 6
	☉□☽	4 58
	☽□♄	6 9
	♃△♆	10 8
	☽⚼♃	12pm10
	☿△♇	3 38
	☉☍♄	8 7
27 T	☉#☽	0am38
	☽⚻♅	5 58
	☽∠♂	6 31
	☽☍♇	11 28
	☽∥♄	12pm45
	☿#♆	1 59
	☿☍♆	2 28
	☽△♆	2 38
	☽⚹☿	2 39
	☽△♃	3 5
	☿⚹♃	5 57
	☽□♀	10 17
28 W	☽#☿	0am46
	☽∥♆	2 19
	☽⚼♅	7 56
	☽⚹♂	8 54
	☽△♄	10 26
	☉⚹☽	1pm28
	☽⚼♆	4 11
	☽∠☿	8 16
	♀ ♊	10 4
29 Th	☽△♅	9am 1
	☽⚼♄	11 16
	☽⚻♇	2pm 2
	☉∠☽	4 5
	☽⚻♆	4 56
	☽□♃	6 5
30 F	☽⚺☿	0am43
	☽⚹♀	4 39
	☽□♂	11 3
	☽⚻♄	11 24
	☿ ♉	11 26
	☽⚼♇	2pm14
	☽#♆	3 7
	☉⚺☽	5 54

MAY 1954

LONGITUDE

Day	Sid. Time h m s	☉ ° ' "	☽ ° ' "	☽ 12 Hour ° ' "	Mean ☊ ° '	True ☊ ° '	☿ ° '	♀ ° '	♂ ° '	♃ ° '	♄ ° '	♅ ° '	♆ ° '	♇ ° '
1	14 33 33	10♉ 5 4	13♈ 40 45	21♈ 16 36	18♑ 24	17♑ 14R	1♉ 3	2♊ 32	5♑ 40	25♊ 16	5♏ 43R	19♋ 31	24♎ 16R	22♌ 32R
2	14 37 30	11 3 19	28 54 28	6♉ 32 59	18 20	17 5	3 5	3 46	5 54	25 27	5 39	19 33	24 15	22 32
3	14 41 26	12 1 32	14♉ 10 41	21 46 13	18 17	16 55	5 8	4 59	6 8	25 39	5 34	19 35	24 13	22 32
4	14 45 23	12 59 43	29 18 14	6♊ 45 37	18 14	16 47	7 12	6 12	6 21	25 50	5 30	19 36	24 12	22 32D
5	14 49 19	13 57 53	14♊ 7 24	21 22 49	18 11	16 41	9 18	7 25	6 34	26 2	5 25	19 38	24 10	22 32
6	14 53 16	14 56 1	28 31 22	5♋ 32 45	18 8	16 37	11 26	8 38	6 45	26 14	5 21	19 40	24 9	22 32
7	14 57 12	15 54 7	12♋ 26 53	19 13 50	18 5	16 36D	13 34	9 51	6 57	26 26	5 16	19 42	24 7	22 32
8	15 1 9	16 52 11	25 53 50	2♌ 27 16	18 1	16 36	15 43	11 4	7 8	26 38	5 12	19 44	24 6	22 32
9	15 5 6	17 50 14	8♌ 54 33	15 16 14	17 58	16 37R	17 53	12 17	7 18	26 50	5 8	19 47	24 4	22 32
10	15 9 2	18 48 14	21 32 52	27 45 1	17 55	16 37	20 3	13 30	7 27	27 2	5 3	19 49	24 3	22 32
11	15 12 59	19 46 13	3♍ 53 18	9♍ 58 17	17 52	16 36	22 14	14 43	7 36	27 14	4 59	19 51	24 1	22 32
12	15 16 55	20 44 9	16 0 33	22 0 36	17 49	16 33	24 25	15 56	7 45	27 27	4 55	19 53	24 0	22 33
13	15 20 52	21 42 4	27 58 58	3♎ 56 6	17 45	16 28	26 35	17 9	7 52	27 39	4 50	19 55	23 58	22 33
14	15 24 48	22 39 57	9♎ 52 26	15 48 21	17 42	16 20	28 45	18 22	7 59	27 51	4 46	19 58	23 57	22 33
15	15 28 45	23 37 48	21 44 12	27 40 16	17 39	16 11	0♊ 54	19 34	8 6	28 4	4 42	20 0	23 56	22 33
16	15 32 41	24 35 38	3♏ 36 50	9♏ 34 8	17 36	16 1	3 2	20 47	8 11	28 16	4 38	20 2	23 54	22 34
17	15 36 38	25 33 26	15 32 22	21 31 44	17 33	15 51	5 8	22 0	8 16	28 29	4 34	20 5	23 53	22 34
18	15 40 35	26 31 13	27 32 25	3♐ 34 35	17 30	15 42	7 13	23 12	8 21	28 41	4 29	20 7	23 52	22 34
19	15 44 31	27 28 59	9♐ 38 24	15 44 4	17 26	15 35	9 15	24 25	8 24	28 54	4 25	20 10	23 50	22 35
20	15 48 28	28 26 43	21 51 44	28 1 39	17 23	15 30	11 16	25 37	8 27	29 6	4 21	20 12	23 49	22 35
21	15 52 24	29 24 25	4♑ 14 2	10♑ 29 9	17 20	15 28D	13 15	26 50	8 30	29 19	4 18	20 15	23 48	22 36
22	15 56 21	0♊ 22 7	16 47 17	23 8 44	17 17	15 27	15 11	28 2	8 31	29 32	4 14	20 18	23 47	22 36
23	16 0 17	1 19 48	29 33 51	6♒ 2 56	17 14	15 28	17 4	29 15	8 32R	29 45	4 10	20 20	23 45	22 37
24	16 4 14	2 17 27	12♒ 36 22	19 14 26	17 11	15 29	18 55	0♋ 27	8 32	29 57	4 6	20 23	23 44	22 37
25	16 8 10	3 15 6	25 57 28	2♓ 45 42	17 7	15 30R	20 43	1 39	8 31	0♋ 10	4 2	20 26	23 43	22 38
26	16 12 7	4 12 43	9♓ 39 18	16 38 24	17 4	15 31	22 28	2 51	8 30	0 23	3 59	20 28	23 42	22 38
27	16 16 4	5 10 20	23 42 55	0♈ 52 45	17 1	15 29	24 10	4 4	8 27	0 36	3 55	20 31	23 41	22 39
28	16 20 0	6 7 56	8♈ 7 33	15 26 51	16 58	15 26	25 49	5 16	8 24	0 49	3 52	20 34	23 39	22 40
29	16 23 57	7 5 31	22 50 1	0♉ 16 15	16 55	15 22	27 25	6 28	8 21	1 2	3 48	20 37	23 38	22 40
30	16 27 53	8 3 5	7♉ 44 37	15 14 5	16 51	15 16	28 59	7 40	8 16	1 15	3 45	20 40	23 37	22 41
31	16 31 50	9♊ 0 38	22♉ 43 31	0♊ 11 49	16♑ 48	15♑ 11	0♋ 29	8♋ 52	8♑ 11	1♋ 29	3♏ 42	20♋ 43	23♎ 36	22♌ 42

DECLINATION and LATITUDE

Day	☉ Decl	☽ Decl	☽ Lat	☽ 12 Hr. Decl	☿ Decl	☿ Lat	♀ Decl	♀ Lat	♂ Decl	♂ Lat	♃ Decl	♃ Lat	♄ Decl	♄ Lat
1	14N51	10N 2	5N 2	12N58	10N38	1S18	21N10	0N30	24S14	0S55	23N13	0S 8	10S53	2N42
2	15 9	15 42	4 56	18 11	11 27	1 9	21 27	0 33	24 17	0 58	23 14	0 8	10 51	2 42
3	15 27	20 23	4 29	22 13	12 18	1 0	21 43	0 36	24 19	1 1	23 14	0 8	10 50	2 42
4	15 45	23 39	3 44	24 39	13 7	0 51	21 59	0 38	24 21	1 3	23 15	0 8	10 49	2 42
5	16 2	25 13	2 44	25 20	13 57	0 41	22 14	0 41	24 23	1 6	23 15	0 8	10 47	2 42
6	16 19	25 1	1 35	24 18	14 47	0 31	22 28	0 43	24 26	1 9	23 16	0 8	10 46	2 42
7	16 36	23 14	0 22	21 50	15 35	0 21	22 41	0 46	24 28	1 12	23 16	0 7	10 44	2 42
8	16 53	20 10	0S49	18 15	16 23	0 10	22 55	0 49	24 30	1 15	23 17	0 7	10 43	2 42
9	17 9	16 10	1 56	13 55	17 10	0N 0	23 7	0 51	24 33	1 18	23 17	0 7	10 42	2 42
10	17 25	11 33	2 56	9 6	17 56	0 11	23 19	0 54	24 36	1 22	23 18	0 7	10 40	2 42
11	17 41	6 35	3 45	4 2	18 41	0 22	23 30	0 56	24 38	1 25	23 18	0 7	10 39	2 41
12	17 56	1 28	4 23	1S 5	19 24	0 32	23 40	0 58	24 41	1 28	23 18	0 7	10 38	2 41
13	18 12	3S38	4 50	6 7	20 5	0 42	23 50	1 1	24 44	1 31	23 19	0 7	10 36	2 41
14	18 27	8 34	5 3	10 55	20 44	0 52	23 59	1 3	24 47	1 35	23 19	0 7	10 35	2 41
15	18 41	13 10	5 4	15 18	21 21	1 2	24 7	1 6	24 50	1 38	23 19	0 7	10 34	2 41
16	18 55	17 17	4 51	19 6	21 56	1 11	24 15	1 8	24 53	1 42	23 20	0 6	10 32	2 41
17	19 9	20 44	4 26	22 9	22 28	1 20	24 22	1 10	24 56	1 45	23 20	0 6	10 31	2 41
18	19 23	23 19	3 49	24 14	22 58	1 28	24 28	1 12	24 59	1 49	23 20	0 6	10 30	2 41
19	19 36	24 53	3 1	25 13	23 25	1 36	24 34	1 15	25 3	1 52	23 20	0 6	10 29	2 41
20	19 49	25 15	2 4	24 59	23 50	1 43	24 39	1 17	25 6	1 56	23 20	0 6	10 27	2 40
21	20 2	24 23	1 0	23 29	24 12	1 49	24 43	1 19	25 10	1 60	23 21	0 6	10 26	2 40
22	20 14	22 16	0N 7	20 47	24 32	1 55	24 47	1 21	25 13	2 3	23 21	0 6	10 25	2 40
23	20 26	19 1	1 16	17 0	24 48	2 0	24 49	1 23	25 17	2 7	23 21	0 6	10 24	2 40
24	20 37	14 46	2 22	12 19	25 3	2 4	24 52	1 25	25 21	2 11	23 21	0 6	10 23	2 40
25	20 49	9 42	3 22	6 57	25 15	2 8	24 53	1 27	25 25	2 15	23 21	0 6	10 22	2 40
26	20 60	4 4	4 12	1 6	25 24	2 10	24 53	1 29	25 29	2 19	23 21	0 5	10 21	2 40
27	21 10	1N55	4 48	4N56	25 31	2 12	24 53	1 30	25 33	2 23	23 21	0 5	10 20	2 39
28	21 20	7 56	5 8	10 51	25 36	2 13	24 53	1 32	25 37	2 27	23 21	0 5	10 19	2 39
29	21 30	13 38	5 7	16 14	25 39	2 13	24 51	1 34	25 41	2 31	23 21	0 5	10 18	2 39
30	21 39	18 37	4 47	20 41	25 39	2 13	24 49	1 36	25 46	2 35	23 21	0 5	10 17	2 39
31	21N48	22N26	4N 6	23N47	25N38	2N11	24N46	1N37	25S50	2S39	23N21	0S 5	10S16	2N39

Day	♅ Decl	♅ Lat	♆ Decl	♆ Lat	♇ Decl	♇ Lat
1	22N30	0N28	7S47	1N45	23N24	9N58
5	22 29	0 28	7 45	1 45	23 23	9 57
9	22 27	0 28	7 42	1 45	23 22	9 56
13	22 26	0 28	7 40	1 45	23 21	9 55
17	22 24	0 28	7 38	1 45	23 20	9 55
21	22 23	0 28	7 37	1 45	23 19	9 54
25	22 21	0 28	7 35	1 45	23 17	9 53
29	22N20	0N28	7S33	1N45	23N16	9N52

☽ PHENOMENA

d	h	m	
2	20	23	●
9	18	18	☽
17	21	47	○
25	13	50	☾

d	h	° '
5	9	25N21
12	7	0
19	19	25S17
26	16	0

d	h	° '
1	6	5N 3
7	7	0
14	13	5S 5
21	21	0
28	12	5N10

d	h	
2	7	PERIGEE
15	1	APOGEE
30	14	PERIGEE

VOID OF COURSE ☽

Last Aspect		☽ Ingress		
1	6pm30	2	♉	1am43
3	1pm13	4	♊	1am 7
5	8pm 5	6	♋	2am30
7	8pm45	8	♌	7am29
10	10am47	10	♍	4pm23
12	11pm19	13	♎	4am 4
15	1pm 1	15	♏	4pm42
17	9pm47	18	♐	4am54
20	2pm20	20	♑	3pm49
22	1pm10	22	♒	0am49
24	8pm 1	25	♓	7am 9
27	0am52	27	♈	10am32
29	8am17	29	♉	11am34
30	11pm57	31	♊	11am41

DAILY ASPECTARIAN

Day	Aspect	Time
1 S	☽∥☿	2am46
	☽#♄	3 24
	♂⚹♄	3 54
	☉∠♃	5 25
	☽∠♀	6 38
	☿#♄	7 12
	☽□♅	9 15
	☽△♇	1pm59
	☽☍♆	4 41
	☽⚹♃	6 30
	☉∥☽	9 22
2 Su	☽☌☿	7am34
	☽⚺♀	8 17
	☽☍♄	10 32
	☽△♂	11 10
	♀∠♅	3pm50
	☽∠♃	6 22
	☿⚺♀	7 44
	☉☌☽	8 23
3 M	☿☍♄	4am56
	☽⚹♅	8 33
	☽∥♀	9 13
	♀⚻♄	10 57
	☽⚼♂	11 9
	☿△♂	1pm 0
	☽□♇	1 13
	☽∥♅	2 3
	☽⚻♆	3 52
	☽⚺♃	6 24
	☽∥♃	8 18
	☽∥♇	9 35
4 T	♀⚻♂	3am36
	☽#♂	8 0
	☽∠♅	8 32
	☽⚻♄	9 54
	☽⚻♂	11 30
	☽☌♀	12pm 5
	☽⚺☿	2 50
	☽⚼♆	3 56
	♇SD	5 59
	☉⚺☽	11 43
5 W	☽⚺♅	9am 8
	☽⚼♄	10 21
	☽⚹♇	1pm55
	☽△♆	4 38
	☽∠☿	7 50
	☽☌♃	8 5
	☿∠♃	9 36
6 Th	♀∥♅	0am39
	☉∠☽	2 34
	♀⚼♆	9 48
	☽#♂	10 6
	☽△♄	11 36
	☽☍♂	2pm18
	☽∠♇	3 26
	☽⚺♀	7 2
	☽∥♇	10 31
	☽∥♃	11 35
7 F	☽⚹☿	2am20
	☽∥♀	4 34
	☉⚹☽	6 33
	☽∥♅	6 54
	☽☌♅	12pm53
	☽⚺♇	5 55
	☽□♆	8 45
8 S	☽∠♀	0am21
	☽⚺♃	1 22
	☽□♄	4pm59
	☉∥☽	6 48
	☽∥☿	7 13
	☽⚻♂	8 57
	☉∥☿	11 2
	☉☌☿	11 2
9 Su	☽∠♃	5am35
	☽⚹♀	7 1
	☉□☽	6pm18
	☽□☿	8 32
	☽⚺♅	8 39
	☿⚹♅	9 14
	♀∥♃	9 35
10 M	☽⚼♂	1am46
	☽☌♇	1 54
	☽#♄	4 23
	☽⚹♆	4 48
	♀∥♇	7 6
	☽⚹♃	10 47
	♂⚼♇	1pm29
	☽#♆	6 46
11 T	☽∠♅	1am54
	☉⚹♅	2 1
	☽⚹♄	2 8
	☿□♇	3 22
	☿⚼♂	4 21
	☽△♂	7 24
	☽∠♆	10 6
	☿⚻♆	7pm29
	☽□♀	11 50
12 W	☽∠♄	7am45
	☽⚹♅	7 46
	☉△☽	10 16
	☽⚺♇	1pm 5
	☽⚺♆	3 57
	☽△☿	8 34
	☽□♃	11 19
13 Th	☿⚺♃	1pm 0
	☽⚺♄	1 44
	☉⚼☽	7 8
	☽∠♇	7 18
	☽∥♆	7 33
	☽□♂	8 9
	☉□♇	9 10
14 F	☉⚼♂	9am 2
	☽⚼☿	9 34
	☽∥♄	10 14
	☿ ♊	1pm58
	☽△♀	7 7
	☽□♅	8 29
15 S	☽⚹♇	1am40
	♀⚼♄	2 21
	☉⚻☽	4 10
	☽☌♆	4 25
	☉⚻♆	7 15
	♀⚺♅	8 48
	☽△♃	1pm 1
	☽⚻☿	10 33
16 Su	☽☌♄	2am 2
	☽⚼♀	4 52
	☽⚹♂	9 17
	☉#☽	11 31
	☿⚻♄	5pm39
	☽⚼♃	7 47
	☿∥♅	9 7
	☿∠♅	11 25
17 M	☽△♅	9am 8
	♀⚹♇	11 27
	♃∥♇	12pm58
	☽□♇	2 5
	☽⚻♀	2 23
	☽#♅	2 25
	☽∠♂	3 35
	☽⚺♆	4 40
	☽#☿	7 4
	☉☍☽	9 47
18 T	☽#♇	0am 4
	☽#♃	0 7
	☽⚻♃	2 19
	♀△♆	12pm49
	☿⚻♂	1 41
	☽⚺♄	1 44
	☽⚼♅	3 7
	☽#♀	5 2
	☿∥♇	6 36
	☿⚼♆	7 7
	☿∥♃	7 14
	☽⚺♂	9 33
	☽∠♆	10 25
	☽☍☿	11 5
19 W	☽∥♂	4am58
	☽∠♄	7pm 8
	☽⚻♅	8 45
20 Th	☽△♇	1am25
	☽⚹♆	3 48
	☽∥♂	7 22
	☽☍♀	8 7
	☉⚻☽	1pm53
	☽☍♃	2 20
	☽#♀	6 15
	☉⚺♃	9 8
21 F	☽⚹♄	0am 7
	☽#☿	2 15
	☽⚼♇	6 28
	☽☌♂	8 12
	☽#♃	1pm27
	☽#♇	1 51
	☉ ♊	2 48
	☽⚻☿	8 24
	☉⚼☽	9 5
	☽#♅	11 4
22 S	☽☍♅	6am39
	☽⚻♇	10 59
	☽□♆	1pm10
	☉#☽	3 1
	☽⚻♀	11 20
23 Su	☽⚻♃	0am20
	☿∥♀	1 51
	☉△☽	3 33
	☽⚼☿	5 25
	☽□♄	8 29
	♀☌♃	12pm 7
	♂SR	12 46
	♀ ♋	3 4
	☽⚺♂	4 34
24 M	☿⚼♄	2am26
	☽⚼♃	4 20
	♃ ♋	4 44
	☽⚼♀	5 40
	☽△☿	1pm12
	☽⚻♅	2 6
	☽☍♇	6 4
	☽∠♂	7 40
	☽△♆	8 1
	☿⚺♅	8 6
	☽∥♄	9 3
25 T	☽△♃	7am34
	☽∥♆	9 17
	☽△♀	11 2
	☉□☽	1pm50
	☽△♄	2 10
	☽⚼♅	4 43
	☉⚻♄	6 33
	☽⚹♂	10 0
	☽⚼♆	10 20
26 W	☿⚹♇	2am28
	☽⚼♄	3pm55
	☿△♆	5 7
	☽△♅	6 35
	♀△♄	9 19
	☽⚻♇	10 12
	☽⚻♆	11 56
27 Th	☽□☿	0am52
	☉∠♅	9 9
	☽□♃	11 43
	☽⚻♄	4pm59
	☽□♀	6 51
	☉⚹☽	8 29
	☽#♆	10 31
	☽⚼♇	11 14
28 F	☽□♂	0am28
	☽#♄	9 44
	☽□♅	8pm24
	☉∠☽	10 43
	☽△♇	11 44
29 S	☽☍♆	1am18
	☽⚹☿	8 17
	☽⚹♃	1pm26
	☽☍♄	5 37
	☽⚹♀	11 52
30 Su	♀∠♇	0am15
	☉⚺☽	0 32
	☽△♂	0 50
	☉⚻♂	4 58
	☽∠☿	11 7
	♀☍♂	11 10
	☽∠♃	1pm50
	☉⚼♆	2 0
	☿ ♋	4 13
	☉∥☽	7 13
	☽⚹♅	8 46
	☽∥♅	11 7
	☽□♇	11 57
31 M	☽⚼♂	0am43
	☽⚻♆	1 24
	☽∠♀	2 0
	☽∥♇	6 52
	☽∥♃	7 53
	☽⚺☿	1pm49
	☉⚺♀	1 58
	☽⚺♃	2 16
	☽⚻♄	5 34
	☿☌♃	7 16
	☽∠♅	8 58
	☽∥♀	11 58

JUNE 1954

LONGITUDE

Day	Sid. Time	☉	☽	☽ 12 Hour	Mean ☊	True ☊	☿	♀	♂	♃	♄	♅	♆	♇
	h m s	° ' "	° ' "	° ' "	° '	° '	° '	° '	° '	° '	° '	° '	° '	° '
1	16 35 46	9♊ 58 10	7♊ 37 51	15♊ 0 34	16♑ 45	15♑ 7R	1♋ 56	10♋ 4	8♑ 5R	1♋ 42	3♏ 38R	20♋ 46	23♎ 35R	22♌ 42
2	16 39 43	10 55 41	22 19 3	29 32 29	16 42	15 4	3 20	11 16	7 58	1 55	3 35	20 49	23 34	22 43
3	16 43 39	11 53 12	6♋ 40 16	13♋ 41 56	16 39	15 2D	4 41	12 28	7 50	2 8	3 32	20 52	23 33	22 44
4	16 47 36	12 50 41	20 37 10	27 25 52	16 36	15 2	5 58	13 40	7 42	2 21	3 29	20 55	23 32	22 45
5	16 51 33	13 48 9	4♌ 8 3	10♌ 43 54	16 32	15 3	7 13	14 52	7 33	2 35	3 26	20 58	23 31	22 46
6	16 55 29	14 45 35	17 13 40	23 37 43	16 29	15 5	8 24	16 4	7 23	2 48	3 23	21 1	23 30	22 47
7	16 59 26	15 43 1	29 56 32	6♍ 10 34	16 26	15 6	9 31	17 15	7 13	3 1	3 21	21 4	23 30	22 47
8	17 3 22	16 40 25	12♍ 20 24	18 26 34	16 23	15 7R	10 36	18 27	7 2	3 15	3 18	21 7	23 29	22 48
9	17 7 19	17 37 48	24 29 40	0♎ 30 15	16 20	15 7	11 36	19 39	6 50	3 28	3 15	21 10	23 28	22 49
10	17 11 15	18 35 10	6♎ 28 55	12 26 11	16 16	15 5	12 33	20 50	6 37	3 41	3 13	21 14	23 27	22 50
11	17 15 12	19 32 32	18 22 36	24 18 39	16 13	15 3	13 27	22 2	6 24	3 55	3 10	21 17	23 26	22 51
12	17 19 8	20 29 52	0♏ 14 50	6♏ 11 33	16 10	14 59	14 17	23 13	6 11	4 8	3 8	21 20	23 26	22 52
13	17 23 5	21 27 11	12 9 13	18 8 11	16 7	14 56	15 3	24 24	5 57	4 22	3 6	21 23	23 25	22 53
14	17 27 2	22 24 29	24 8 47	0♐ 11 17	16 4	14 52	15 44	25 36	5 42	4 35	3 3	21 27	23 24	22 54
15	17 30 58	23 21 47	6♐ 15 55	12 22 56	16 1	14 48	16 22	26 47	5 27	4 49	3 1	21 30	23 24	22 56
16	17 34 55	24 19 4	18 32 30	24 44 45	15 57	14 46	16 56	27 58	5 11	5 2	2 59	21 33	23 23	22 57
17	17 38 51	25 16 21	0♑ 59 51	7♑ 17 54	15 54	14 44	17 26	29 9	4 55	5 16	2 57	21 37	23 22	22 58
18	17 42 48	26 13 36	13 38 59	20 3 13	15 51	14 44D	17 51	0♌ 20	4 38	5 29	2 56	21 40	23 22	22 59
19	17 46 44	27 10 52	26 30 41	3♒ 1 27	15 48	14 44	18 12	1 31	4 21	5 43	2 54	21 43	23 21	23 0
20	17 50 41	28 8 7	9♒ 35 36	16 13 12	15 45	14 45	18 28	2 42	4 4	5 56	2 52	21 47	23 21	23 1
21	17 54 37	29 5 22	22 54 19	29 39 0	15 42	14 47	18 40	3 53	3 46	6 10	2 51	21 50	23 20	23 3
22	17 58 34	0♋ 2 36	6♓ 27 18	13♓ 19 13	15 38	14 48	18 47	5 4	3 28	6 24	2 49	21 54	23 20	23 4
23	18 2 31	0 59 50	20 14 43	27 13 45	15 35	14 48R	18 50R	6 15	3 10	6 37	2 48	21 57	23 20	23 5
24	18 6 27	1 57 5	4♈ 16 12	11♈ 21 52	15 32	14 48	18 48	7 26	2 52	6 51	2 46	22 1	23 19	23 6
25	18 10 24	2 54 19	18 30 30	25 41 46	15 29	14 48	18 42	8 36	2 33	7 4	2 45	22 4	23 19	23 8
26	18 14 20	3 51 33	2♉ 55 14	10♉ 10 24	15 26	14 47	18 31	9 47	2 15	7 18	2 44	22 8	23 19	23 9
27	18 18 17	4 48 47	17 26 42	24 43 29	15 22	14 46	18 16	10 57	1 56	7 32	2 43	22 11	23 18	23 10
28	18 22 13	5 46 2	2♊ 0 4	9♊ 15 43	15 19	14 45	17 57	12 8	1 37	7 45	2 42	22 15	23 18	23 12
29	18 26 10	6 43 16	16 29 43	23 41 20	15 16	14 44	17 34	13 18	1 19	7 59	2 41	22 18	23 18	23 13
30	18 30 7	7♋ 40 30	0♋ 49 54	7♋ 54 48	15♑ 13	14♑ 44D	17♋ 8	14♌ 28	1♑ 0	8♋ 13	2♏ 41	22♋ 22	23♎ 18	23♌ 15

DECLINATION and LATITUDE

Day	☉ Decl	☽ Decl	☽ Lat	☽ 12 Hr. Decl	☿ Decl	☿ Lat	♀ Decl	♀ Lat	♂ Decl	♂ Lat	♃ Decl	♃ Lat	♄ Decl	♄ Lat
1	21N57	24N42	3N10	25N11	25N35	2N 9	24N42	1N39	25S54	2S43	23N21	0S 5	10S15	2N38
2	22 5	25 14	2 1	24 50	25 30	2 6	24 38	1 40	25 59	2 47	23 21	0 5	10 14	2 38
3	22 13	24 2	0 46	22 52	25 24	2 2	24 33	1 42	26 4	2 51	23 21	0 5	10 13	2 38
4	22 21	21 22	0S30	19 35	25 16	1 58	24 27	1 43	26 8	2 55	23 21	0 4	10 12	2 38
5	22 28	17 34	1 43	15 22	25 7	1 52	24 20	1 44	26 13	2 59	23 21	0 4	10 11	2 38
6	22 34	13 1	2 47	10 34	24 57	1 46	24 13	1 45	26 18	3 4	23 21	0 4	10 11	2 37
7	22 41	8 2	3 41	5 28	24 45	1 39	24 5	1 46	26 22	3 8	23 20	0 4	10 10	2 37
8	22 47	2 52	4 24	0 16	24 32	1 31	23 57	1 47	26 27	3 12	23 20	0 4	10 9	2 37
9	22 52	2S18	4 53	4S50	24 19	1 23	23 48	1 48	26 32	3 16	23 20	0 4	10 9	2 37
10	22 57	7 19	5 10	9 43	24 4	1 14	23 38	1 49	26 37	3 20	23 20	0 4	10 8	2 37
11	23 2	12 1	5 13	14 13	23 49	1 4	23 27	1 50	26 41	3 24	23 19	0 4	10 7	2 36
12	23 6	16 17	5 2	18 11	23 34	0 53	23 16	1 51	26 46	3 28	23 19	0 4	10 7	2 36
13	23 10	19 54	4 39	21 26	23 17	0 42	23 4	1 52	26 51	3 32	23 19	0 4	10 6	2 36
14	23 14	22 44	4 3	23 48	23 1	0 30	22 52	1 52	26 56	3 37	23 18	0 3	10 6	2 36
15	23 17	24 35	3 16	25 4	22 43	0 17	22 39	1 53	27 0	3 40	23 18	0 3	10 5	2 35
16	23 19	25 16	2 19	25 8	22 26	0 4	22 25	1 53	27 5	3 44	23 18	0 3	10 5	2 35
17	23 22	24 42	1 15	23 56	22 9	0S10	22 11	1 53	27 9	3 48	23 17	0 3	10 4	2 35
18	23 23	22 51	0 6	21 28	21 51	0 24	21 56	1 54	27 14	3 52	23 17	0 3	10 4	2 35
19	23 25	19 48	1N 5	17 53	21 34	0 39	21 41	1 54	27 18	3 56	23 16	0 3	10 4	2 34
20	23 26	15 43	2 13	13 21	21 16	0 55	21 25	1 54	27 22	3 60	23 16	0 3	10 3	2 34
21	23 27	10 48	3 15	8 7	20 59	1 10	21 8	1 54	27 27	4 3	23 15	0 3	10 3	2 34
22	23 27	5 18	4 8	2 24	20 42	1 26	20 51	1 54	27 31	4 7	23 15	0 3	10 3	2 34
23	23 26	0N33	4 48	3N30	20 26	1 42	20 33	1 54	27 34	4 10	23 14	0 3	10 2	2 33
24	23 26	6 27	5 11	9 20	20 10	1 59	20 15	1 54	27 38	4 13	23 14	0 3	10 2	2 33
25	23 25	12 7	5 15	14 45	19 55	2 15	19 56	1 53	27 42	4 17	23 13	0 2	10 2	2 33
26	23 23	17 11	5 1	19 23	19 40	2 31	19 37	1 53	27 45	4 20	23 12	0 2	10 2	2 33
27	23 21	21 18	4 26	22 52	19 26	2 47	19 17	1 52	27 49	4 23	23 12	0 2	10 2	2 32
28	23 19	24 5	3 35	24 52	19 13	3 3	18 57	1 52	27 52	4 26	23 11	0 2	10 2	2 32
29	23 16	25 15	2 30	25 11	19 1	3 18	18 36	1 51	27 55	4 29	23 10	0 2	10 2	2 32
30	23N13	24N43	1N16	23N50	18N50	3S32	18N15	1N50	27S58	4S31	23N10	0S 2	10S 2	2N32

Day	♅ Decl	♅ Lat	♆ Decl	♆ Lat	♇ Decl	♇ Lat
1	22N18	0N28	7S32	1N45	23N14	9N51
5	22 16	0 28	7 31	1 44	23 13	9 51
9	22 14	0 28	7 30	1 44	23 11	9 50
13	22 12	0 28	7 29	1 44	23 9	9 49
17	22 10	0 28	7 28	1 44	23 6	9 49
21	22 8	0 28	7 28	1 44	23 4	9 48
25	22 6	0 28	7 27	1 44	23 2	9 47
29	22N 3	0N28	7S27	1N43	22N59	9N47

☽ PHENOMENA

d	h	m	
1	4	3	●
8	9	14	☽
16	12	6	○
23	19	46	☾
30	12	26	● (eclipse)

d	h	° '
1	19	25N16
8	13	0
16	i	25S16
22	22	0
29	4	25N17

d	h	
3	14	0
10	17	5S13
18	2	0
24	18	5N16

VOID OF COURSE ☽

Last Aspect		☽ Ingress		
2	2am 4	2	♋	12pm46
4	5am 7	4	♌	4pm35
6	11am46	7	♍	0am 7
8	5pm22	9	♎	10am59
11	10am14	11	♏	11pm30
14	3am12	14	♐	11am38
16	12pm 6	16	♑	10pm 5
18	6pm 9	19	♒	6am26
21	11am50	21	♓	12pm37
23	2am57	23	♈	4pm44
25	8am 2	25	♉	7pm 9
27	9am28	27	♊	8pm42
29	11am20	29	♋	10pm36

d	h	
11	15	APOGEE
27	10	PERIGEE

DAILY ASPECTARIAN

Day	Aspect	Time
1	☽⚻♂	0am43
T	☽⚼♆	1 33
	☉☌☽	4 3
	☽⚺♀	4 18
	☽⚼♄	5pm53
	☽⚺♅	9 30
2	☽⚹♇	0am40
W	☽△♆	2 4
	☿△♄	4 17
	☽☌♃	4pm14
	☽∥♀	4 36
	☽△♄	6 43
	☽☌☿	8 17
3	☽∠♇	1am48
Th	☽☍♂	1 58
	☽∥♃	7 24
	☽∥♇	8 39
	☉⚺☽	9 33
	☽☌♀	10 49
	☉∥♅	12pm13
	☉∥☽	4 43
	♂⚼♇	4 46
	☽∥♅	4 55
4	☽☌♅	0am31
F	☽⚺♇	3 44
	☽□♆	5 7
	☉∠☽	1pm43
	☽⚺♃	9 9
	☽□♄	10 45
5	☿☍♂	5am57
S	☽⚻♂	6 7
	☽⚺☿	6 8
	☿∠♇	11 8
	☉⚹☽	7pm 3
	☽⚺♀	9 37
6	☽∠♃	1am 5
Su	☽⚺♅	7 6
	☽⚼♂	9 32
	☽☌♇	10 24
	☽⚹♆	11 46
	☽∠☿	12pm42
	☽#♄	1 55
7	☽#♆	2am29
M	☽∠♀	4 54
	☽⚹♃	6 1
	☽⚹♄	6 30
	☽∠♅	11 50
	☽△♂	1pm48
	☽∠♆	4 29
	☽⚹☿	8 16
8	♃△♄	4am48
T	☉□☽	9 14
	☽∠♄	11 40
	☽⚹♀	1pm19
	☽⚹♅	5 22
	☽⚺♇	8 40
	☽⚺♆	9 57
9	☉⚼♄	2pm59
W	☽⚺♄	5 27
	☽□♃	6 17
10	☽□♂	0am17
Th	☽∥♆	0 54
	☽∠♇	2 44
	♀☌♅	8 12
	☽□☿	1pm15
	☽∥♄	2 6
11	☉△☽	2am34
F	☽□♅	5 54
	☽□♀	8 12
	☽⚹♇	9 4
	☽☌♆	10 14
	♀⚺♇	4pm55
	♀∥♃	5 33
12	♀□♆	4am11
S	☽☌♄	5 48
	☽△♃	8 0
	☉⚼☽	11 31
	☽⚹♂	11 45
	☉∥♇	2pm50
	☉∥♀	3 10
	♀∥♇	3 17
	☿∥♃	9 44
	☉⚺♅	10 15
13	☽△☿	6am10
Su	☉∥☿	8 26
	☿∥♇	1pm 1
	☽⚼♃	2 44
	☽∠♂	5 16
	☽△♅	6 35
	☽#♅	6 46
	☉⚻☽	8 14
	☽□♇	9 32
	☽⚺♆	10 31
14	☽#♀	1am12
M	☽#☿	2 31
	☽△♀	3 12
	☽#♇	4 9
	☉#☽	5 21
	☽#♃	6 6
	☉⚹♇	12pm47
	☽⚼☿	1 50
	☽⚺♄	5 37
	☽⚻♃	9 5
	☽⚺♂	10 25
15	☽⚼♅	0am28
T	☉△♆	0 47
	☽∠♆	4 11
	☉∥♃	10 9
	☽⚼♀	11 59
	☽⚻☿	8pm44
	☽∠♄	10 56
16	☽⚻♅	5am52
W	☿∥♀	6 25
	♂☍♃	7 9
	☽△♇	8 32
	☽⚹♆	9 22
	☉☍☽	12pm 6
	☽⚻♀	8 6
	☿∥♅	9 47
17	♀∥♅	1am15
Th	☽⚹♄	3 44
	☽☌♂	7 19
	☽☍♃	8 17
	☽⚼♇	1pm17
	♀ ♌	5 5
	☉#☽	6 25
	☽#♃	7 32
	☽#♇	9 28
18	☽#♅	6am16
F	☽☍☿	8 7
	☽#♀	8 58
	☽#☿	9 51
	☽☍♅	3pm 4
	☽⚻♇	5 29
	☽□♆	6 9
19	☉⚻☽	1am20
S	☽☍♀	10 10
	☽□♄	11 44
	☽⚺♂	2pm 8
	☽⚻♃	5 13
20	♀□♄	3am12
Su	☉⚼☽	6 55
	☽⚻☿	4pm18
	☽∠♂	4 45
	☽⚼♃	8 50
	☽⚻♅	10 5
	♀⚻♂	10 6
21	☽☍♇	0am15
M	☽△♆	0 47
	☽∥♄	3 26
	☉△☽	11 50
	☽∥♆	2pm48
	☽△♄	5 37
	☽⚹♂	6 52
	☽⚼☿	7 17
	☽⚻♀	9 20
	☉ ♋	10 55
	☽△♃	11 53
22	☽⚼♅	0am46
T	☽⚼♆	3 17
	☽⚼♄	7pm46
	☽△☿	9 34
23	☽⚼♀	1am53
W	☿SR	2 9
	☽△♅	2 57
	☽⚻♇	4 54
	☽⚻♆	5 18
	♀⚺♃	9 22
	☉□☽	7pm46
	☽⚻♄	9 28
	☽□♂	9 40
24	☽#♆	4am 9
Th	☽□♃	4 26
	☽△♀	5 50
	☽⚼♇	6 31
	♂⚹♄	7 32
	☽#♄	2pm59
	☉☍♂	5 21
	☉△♄	8 16
25	☽□☿	0am19
F	☽□♅	5 58
	☽△♇	7 44
	☿∥♀	8 1
	☽☍♆	8 2
	☽△♂	10pm54
	☽☍♄	11 42
26	☉⚹☽	1am40
S	☽⚹♃	7 22
	☽□♀	12pm21
	☽∥♀	12 21
	☽∥☿	12 55
	☽⚼♂	11 10
27	☽⚹☿	1am20
Su	☉∠☽	4 11
	☽∥♅	5 36
	☽⚹♅	7 51
	☽∠♃	8 31
	☽□♇	9 28
	☽⚻♆	9 39
	☽∥♇	1pm10
	☽∥♃	2 48
	☉∥☽	4 9
	☽⚻♂	11 23
28	☽⚻♄	1am10
M	☽∠☿	1 32
	☉⚺☽	6 39
	☽∠♅	8 42
	☽⚺♃	9 39
	☽⚼♆	10 24
	☽⚹♀	6pm14
29	☽⚺☿	1am44
T	☽⚼♄	1 59
	☽⚺♅	9 43
	☽⚹♇	11 14
	☽△♆	11 20
	☽∠♀	9pm30
30	☽☍♂	0am17
W	☽△♄	3 7
	♃∠♇	4 5
	☉☌☽	12pm26
	☽∠♇	12 35
	☽☌♃	12 43
	☉∠♇	2 41
	☉☌♃	5 39
	☉∥☽	6 45
	☽∥♃	7 1
	☽∥♇	8 39

LONGITUDE

Day	Sid. Time	☉	☽	☽ 12 Hour	Mean ☊	True ☊	☿	♀	♂	♃	♄	♅	♆	♇
	h m s	° ' "	° ' "	° ' "	° '	° '	° '	° '	° '	° '	° '	° '	° '	° '
1	18 34 3	8♋ 37 45	14♋ 55 28	21♋ 51 29	15♑ 10	14♑ 44	16♋ 39R	15♌ 39	0♑ 42R	8♋ 26	2♏ 40R	22♋ 25	23♎ 17R	23♌ 16
2	18 38 0	9 34 59	28 42 28	5♌ 28 13	15 7	14 44	16 7	16 49	0 23	8 40	2 40	22 29	23 17	23 18
3	18 41 56	10 32 12	12♌ 8 34	18 43 32	15 3	14 44	15 32	17 59	0 5	8 53	2 39	22 33	23 17	23 19
4	18 45 53	11 29 25	25 13 10	1♍ 37 39	15 0	14 45	14 57	19 9	29♐ 48	9 7	2 39	22 36	23 17	23 21
5	18 49 49	12 26 39	7♍ 57 16	14 12 21	14 57	14 45	14 20	20 19	29 30	9 21	2 39	22 40	23 17D	23 22
6	18 53 46	13 23 52	20 23 18	26 30 33	14 54	14 45R	13 43	21 29	29 13	9 34	2 39D	22 43	23 17	23 24
7	18 57 42	14 21 4	2♎ 34 38	8♎ 36 3	14 51	14 45	13 6	22 38	28 57	9 48	2 39	22 47	23 17	23 25
8	19 1 39	15 18 17	14 35 23	20 33 10	14 48	14 45	12 30	23 48	28 41	10 1	2 39	22 51	23 17	23 27
9	19 5 36	16 15 30	26 30 0	2♏ 26 26	14 44	14 45D	11 55	24 58	28 25	10 15	2 39	22 54	23 17	23 28
10	19 9 32	17 12 42	8♏ 23 3	14 20 22	14 41	14 45	11 23	26 7	28 10	10 29	2 39	22 58	23 18	23 30
11	19 13 29	18 9 54	20 18 56	26 19 14	14 38	14 45	10 53	27 16	27 55	10 42	2 40	23 2	23 18	23 31
12	19 17 25	19 7 6	2♐ 21 44	8♐ 26 51	14 35	14 45	10 26	28 26	27 41	10 56	2 40	23 5	23 18	23 33
13	19 21 22	20 4 19	14 34 58	20 46 24	14 32	14 46	10 4	29 35	27 28	11 9	2 41	23 9	23 18	23 35
14	19 25 18	21 1 32	27 1 26	3♑ 20 17	14 23	14 46	9 45	0♍ 44	27 15	11 23	2 41	23 13	23 18	23 36
15	19 29 15	21 58 44	9♑ 43 7	16 10 0	14 25	14 47R	9 31	1 53	27 3	11 36	2 42	23 16	23 19	23 38
16	19 33 11	22 55 57	22 41 1	29 16 6	14 22	14 47	9 21	3 2	26 52	11 50	2 43	23 20	23 19	23 40
17	19 37 8	23 53 10	5♒ 55 11	12♒ 38 7	14 19	14 47	9 17D	4 11	26 42	12 3	2 44	23 24	23 19	23 41
18	19 41 5	24 50 24	19 24 42	26 14 44	14 16	14 46	9 18	5 19	26 32	12 17	2 45	23 27	23 20	23 43
19	19 45 1	25 47 38	3♓ 7 55	10♓ 3 57	14 13	14 45	9 25	6 28	26 23	12 30	2 46	23 31	23 20	23 45
20	19 48 58	26 44 53	17 2 32	24 3 20	14 9	14 43	9 37	7 36	26 14	12 43	2 47	23 34	23 21	23 47
21	19 52 54	27 42 9	1♈ 6 0	8♈ 10 12	14 6	14 42	9 55	8 45	26 7	12 57	2 49	23 38	23 21	23 48
22	19 56 51	28 39 25	15 15 37	22 21 54	14 3	14 41	10 19	9 53	26 0	13 10	2 50	23 42	23 22	23 50
23	20 0 47	29 36 42	29 28 44	6♉ 35 50	14 0	14 40D	10 48	11 1	25 54	13 23	2 52	23 45	23 22	23 52
24	20 4 44	0♌ 34 0	13♉ 42 52	20 49 32	13 57	14 41	11 24	12 9	25 49	13 37	2 53	23 49	23 23	23 54
25	20 8 40	1 31 20	27 55 32	5♊ 0 33	13 54	14 41	12 5	13 17	25 44	13 50	2 55	23 53	23 23	23 55
26	20 12 37	2 28 40	12♊ 4 18	19 6 26	13 50	14 43	12 51	14 24	25 41	14 3	2 57	23 56	23 24	23 57
27	20 16 34	3 26 1	26 6 38	3♋ 4 36	13 47	14 44	13 43	15 32	25 38	14 16	2 59	24 0	23 25	23 59
28	20 20 30	4 23 22	9♋ 59 58	16 52 28	13 44	14 45R	14 41	16 40	25 37	14 30	3 1	24 4	23 25	24 1
29	20 24 27	5 20 45	23 41 45	0♌ 27 34	13 41	14 44	15 44	17 47	25 36D	14 43	3 3	24 7	23 26	24 3
30	20 28 23	6 18 9	7♌ 9 41	13 47 52	13 38	14 43	16 53	18 54	25 35	14 56	3 5	24 11	23 27	24 5
31	20 32 20	7♌ 15 33	20♌ 21 59	26♌ 51 57	13♑ 34	14♑ 41	18♋ 7	20♍ 1	25♐ 36	15♋ 9	3♏ 7	24♋ 14	23♎ 28	24♌ 6

DECLINATION and LATITUDE

Day	☉ Decl	☽ Decl	☽ Lat	☽ 12 Hr. Decl	☿ Decl	☿ Lat	♀ Decl	♀ Lat	♂ Decl	♂ Lat	♃ Decl	♃ Lat	♄ Decl	♄ Lat
1	23N10	22N36	0S 1	21N 1	18N40	3S46	17N53	1N49	28S 1	4S34	23N 9	0S 2	10S 2	2N31
2	23 6	19 10	1 17	17 5	18 31	3 59	17 31	1 48	28 3	4 36	23 8	0 2	10 2	2 31
3	23 2	14 49	2 26	12 24	18 24	4 10	17 9	1 47	28 5	4 39	23 7	0 2	10 2	2 31
4	22 57	9 53	3 26	7 17	18 17	4 21	16 46	1 46	28 8	4 41	23 6	0 2	10 2	2 31
5	22 52	4 39	4 14	2 1	18 12	4 30	16 22	1 45	28 10	4 43	23 5	0 1	10 2	2 30
6	22 46	0S37	4 49	3S13	18 9	4 37	15 59	1 43	28 12	4 45	23 5	0 1	10 3	2 30
7	22 40	5 46	5 10	8 14	18 6	4 43	15 35	1 42	28 13	4 47	23 4	0 1	10 3	2 30
8	22 34	10 37	5 17	12 54	18 5	4 48	15 10	1 40	28 15	4 48	23 3	0 1	10 3	2 30
9	22 27	15 2	5 10	17 3	18 5	4 51	14 45	1 39	28 16	4 50	23 2	0 1	10 3	2 29
10	22 20	18 53	4 50	20 32	18 7	4 52	14 20	1 37	28 17	4 51	23 1	0 1	10 4	2 29
11	22 13	21 58	4 18	23 11	18 9	4 51	13 54	1 35	28 18	4 53	22 60	0 1	10 4	2 29
12	22 5	24 8	3 34	24 49	18 13	4 49	13 29	1 33	28 19	4 54	22 59	0 1	10 4	2 28
13	21 57	25 12	2 40	25 16	18 19	4 46	13 2	1 31	28 20	4 55	22 58	0 1	10 5	2 28
14	21 48	25 2	1 37	24 27	18 25	4 41	12 36	1 29	28 21	4 56	22 57	0 1	10 5	2 28
15	21 39	23 33	0 28	22 20	18 32	4 35	12 9	1 27	28 21	4 57	22 56	0 0	10 6	2 28
16	21 30	20 49	0N44	19 1	18 40	4 27	11 42	1 24	28 22	4 57	22 55	0 0	10 6	2 27
17	21 20	16 57	1 54	14 39	18 49	4 18	11 15	1 22	28 22	4 58	22 54	0 0	10 7	2 27
18	21 10	12 9	3 0	9 29	18 59	4 9	10 47	1 19	28 22	4 58	22 52	0 0	10 8	2 27
19	20 59	6 41	3 57	3 47	19 9	3 58	10 20	1 17	28 22	4 59	22 51	0 0	10 8	2 27
20	20 49	0 49	4 40	2N10	19 20	3 46	9 52	1 14	28 22	4 59	22 50	0 0	10 9	2 26
21	20 38	5N 8	5 7	8 3	19 31	3 34	9 24	1 11	28 22	4 59	22 49	0N 0	10 10	2 26
22	20 26	10 52	5 16	13 33	19 43	3 20	8 55	1 8	28 22	4 59	22 48	0 0	10 10	2 26
23	20 14	16 3	5 5	18 20	19 54	3 7	8 27	1 5	28 22	4 59	22 47	0 0	10 11	2 26
24	20 2	20 21	4 36	22 4	20 5	2 53	7 58	1 2	28 21	4 59	22 45	0 0	10 12	2 25
25	19 50	23 27	3 50	24 27	20 16	2 38	7 29	0 59	28 21	4 58	22 44	0 0	10 13	2 25
26	19 37	25 4	2 51	25 16	20 27	2 23	6 60	0 56	28 20	4 58	22 43	0 1	10 14	2 25
27	19 24	25 4	1 41	24 28	20 36	2 9	6 30	0 52	28 20	4 58	22 41	0 1	10 15	2 24
28	19 10	23 30	0 26	22 11	20 45	1 54	6 1	0 49	28 19	4 57	22 40	0 1	10 16	2 24
29	18 56	20 34	0S49	18 40	20 53	1 38	5 31	0 45	28 18	4 56	22 39	0 1	10 17	2 24
30	18 42	16 33	2 0	14 15	20 60	1 23	5 2	0 41	28 18	4 56	22 37	0 1	10 18	2 24
31	18N28	11N48	3S 3	9N15	21N 5	1S 9	4N32	0N38	28S17	4S55	22N36	0N 1	10S19	2N23

Day	♅ Decl	♅ Lat	♆ Decl	♆ Lat	♇ Decl	♇ Lat
1	22N 2	0N28	7S27	1N43	22N58	9N46
5	21 60	0 28	7 27	1 43	22 56	9 46
9	21 58	0 28	7 28	1 43	22 53	9 46
13	21 55	0 28	7 28	1 43	22 51	9 45
17	21 53	0 28	7 29	1 42	22 48	9 45
21	21 50	0 28	7 30	1 42	22 46	9 45
25	21 48	0 28	7 31	1 42	22 43	9 45
29	21N45	0N28	7S32	1N42	22N40	9N44

☽ PHENOMENA

d	h	m	
8	1	34	☽
16	0	29	○
23	0	14	☾
29	22	20	●

d	h	° '
5	21	0
13	9	25S17
20	3	0
26	12	25N16

d	h	° '
1	0	0
8	0	5S17
15	9	0
21	23	5N16
28	8	0

VOID OF COURSE ☽

Last Aspect		☽ Ingress		
1	2pm30	2	♌	2am17
4	8am22	4	♍	8am56
6	4pm58	6	♎	6pm54
9	3am47	9	♏	7am 4
11	3pm22	11	♐	7pm19
14	0am26	14	♑	5am40
16	1am11	16	♒	1pm20
18	12pm21	18	♓	6pm33
20	5pm48	20	♈	10pm 8
23	0am14	23	♉	0am53
24	5pm13	25	♊	3am31
26	11pm12	27	♋	6am41
29	0am45	29	♌	11am11
31	9am40	31	♍	5pm50

d	h	
9	8	APOGEE
23	19	PERIGEE

DAILY ASPECTARIAN

1 Th	♀⚼♂	0am49
	☽⊻♀	1 21
	☽☌☿	2 51
	☽∥♅	4 31
	☉∥♃	8 41
	☽☌♅	1pm 2
	☿⊻♀	2 9
	☽⊻♇	2 29
	☽□♆	2 30
	♆⚹♇	8 53
2 F	☽⊼♂	2am54
	☽∥☿	4 0
	☽□♄	7 0
	☽∥♀	10 32
	☽⊻♃	6pm 2
	☉⊻☽	8 52
3 S	☽⚼♂	5am14
	☽⊻☿	5 55
	♂ ♐	7 28
	☽☌♀	11 41
	☽⊻♅	7pm 7
	☽⚹♆	8 25
	☽☌♇	8 30
	☽∠♃	9 55
	☽#♄	11 17
4 Su	☉∠☽	2am33
	☉∥♇	2 46
	☽△♂	8 22
	☽∠☿	8 26
	☽#♆	11 15
	☽⚹♄	1pm55
	☽∠♅	11 26
5 M	☽∠♆	0am38
	☽⚹♃	2 42
	♆SD	8 26
	☉⚹☽	9 19
	☽⚹☿	11 40
	☽∠♄	6pm39
6 T	☽⊻♀	2am21
	☽⚹♅	4 35
	☉☌☿	4 48
	☽⊻♆	5 40
	☽⊻♇	5 53
	♄SD	3pm51
	☽□♂	4 58
7 W	☽⊻♄	0am 8
	♀⊻♅	3 8
	☽∥♆	8 11
	☽∠♀	11 9
	☽∠♇	11 40
	♀⚹♆	1pm24
	☽□♃	2 40
	♀☌♇	4 28
	☽□☿	8 0
	☽∥♄	9 6
8 Th	☉□☽	1am34
	☽□♅	4pm42
	☽☌♆	5 31
	☽⚹♇	5 52
	☽⚹♀	8 33
	☽#♀	10 30
9 F	☽⚹♂	3am47
	♀∠♃	7 30
	☽☌♄	12pm25
	☽#☿	6 47
10 S	☿∠♀	3am44
	☽△♃	4 18
	☽△☿	5 47
	☽∠♂	9 27
	☉△☽	7pm19
	☽#♅	11 43
11 Su	☉#☽	2am 7
	☽△♅	5 27
	☽⊻♆	5 58
	☿☌♃	6 12
	☽□♇	6 26
	☽#♇	8 37
	☽#♃	9 58
	☽⚼☿	10 43
	☽⚼♃	10 58
	♀△♂	11 13
	☽⊻♂	2pm54
	☽□♀	3 22
12 M	☽⊻♄	0am36
	☉⚼☽	3 46
	☽⚼♅	11 21
	☽∠♆	11 43
	☽⊼☿	3pm25
	☽⊼♃	5 11
13 T	☉∥♅	4am38
	☽∠♄	6 1
	♀ ♍	8 43
	☉⊼☽	11 32
	☽⊼♅	4pm39
	☽⚹♆	4 52
	☽△♇	5 26
14 W	☽☌♂	0am26
	☽△♀	7 46
	☽⚹♄	10 47
	☽⚼♇	9pm58
	☽☍☿	11 37
15 Th	☽☍♃	3am35
	☽#♃	6 35
	☽#♇	7 36
	☽⚼♀	2pm37
	☽#♅	3 47
	♀⚹♄	5 19
	♅□♆	5 54
	☉#☽	6 40
16 F	☉☍☽	0am29
	☽□♆	1 10
	☽☍♅	1 11
	☽⊼♇	1 48
	☽⊻♂	7 32
	☉□♆	9 44
	☉☌♅	10 42
	☽#☿	1pm35
	☽□♄	6 15
	☉⊻♇	6 55
	☽⊼♀	8 34
17 S	☽⊼☿	6am 2
	☿SD	6 52
	☽∠♂	10 12
	☽⊼♃	11 9
18 Su	☽#♀	6am47
	☽△♆	6 54
	☽⊼♅	7 8
	☽☍♇	7 35
	☽⚼☿	8 39
	☽∥♄	9 8
	☉⊼☽	10 15
	☽⚹♂	12pm21
	☽⚼♃	2 2
	☽∥♆	8 36
	☽△♄	11 22
19 M	☽☍♀	6am18
	☽⚼♆	9 1
	☽⚼♅	9 22
	♀#♄	9 33
	☽△☿	11 1
	☉⊼♂	12pm46
	☉⚼☽	2 14
	☽△♃	4 28
20 T	☽⚼♄	1am17
	☽⊼♆	10 47
	☽△♅	11 14
	☽⊼♇	11 33
	☽□♂	3pm35
	♀∠♆	3 42
	☉△☽	5 48
	♀∠♅	9 37
21 W	☽⊼♄	2am55
	☽#♆	9 42
	☽⚼♇	1pm 6
	☽⊼♀	2 6
	☽□☿	3 23
	☽∥♀	4 19
	☽□♃	8 24
	☽#♄	9 1
22 Th	☽☍♆	1pm41
	☽□♅	2 19
	☽△♇	2 31
	☿⚹♀	3 54
	☽⚼♀	5 39
	☽△♂	6 0
23 F	☉□☽	0am14
	☽☍♄	5 43
	☉ ♌	9 45
	☽⚼♂	7pm 8
	☽⚹☿	7 54
	☉∥☿	8 42
	☽△♀	9 8
	☉∥☽	10 7
	☽∥☿	10 16
	☽⚹♃	11 50
24 S	☽∥♅	10am 1
	☽⊼♆	4pm20
	☽⚹♅	5 8
	☽□♇	5 13
	☽∥♇	5 20
	☽∥♃	5 31
	☽⊼♂	8 19
	☽∠☿	10 29
	♀#♆	10 31
25 Su	☽∠♃	1am34
	☉⚹☽	6 32
	☽⊼♄	8 28
	♀⚹♃	2pm38
	☽⚼♆	5 45
	☽∠♅	6 39
26 M	☽⊻☿	1am25
	☽⊻♃	3 26
	☽□♀	4 20
	☉∠☽	9 53
	☽⚼♄	10 3
	♅⊻♇	10 47
	☉□♄	12pm13
	♃∥♇	6 5
	☽△♆	7 22
	☽⚹♇	8 20
	☽⊻♅	8 22
	☽☍♂	11 12
27 T	☽△♄	11am52
	☉⊻☽	1pm33
	☿☌♃	6 7
	☽∠♇	10 17
28 W	☽∥♇	7am50
	☽☌♃	7 58
	☽∥♃	7 59
	☽☌☿	8 50
	☽⚹♀	12pm40
	☽∥♅	3 22
	☽∥☿	9 50
	☽□♆	11 32
29 Th	☽⊻♇	0am37
	☽☌♅	0 45
	☽⊼♂	3 21
	♀∠♄	5 53
	☉∥☽	11 1
	♂SD	3pm13
	☽□♄	4 40
	☽∠♀	5 37
	☉☌☽	10 20
30 F	☽⚼♂	6am11
	☽⊻♃	2pm18
	☽⊻☿	7 25
	☽⊻♀	11 19
31 S	☽⚹♆	5am42
	☽☌♇	6 54
	☽#♄	7 3
	☽⊻♅	7 10
	☽△♂	9 40
	☽∠♃	6pm25
	☽#♆	7 51
	☽⚹♄	11 45

AUGUST 1954

LONGITUDE

Day	Sid. Time	☉	☽	☽ 12 Hour	Mean ☊	True ☊	☿	♀	♂	♃	♄	♅	♆	♇
	h m s	° ' "	° ' "	° ' "	° '	° '	° '	° '	° '	° '	° '	° '	° '	° '
1	20 36 16	8♌ 12 58	3♍ 17 44	9♍ 39 21	13♑ 31	14♑ 38R	19♋ 25	21♍ 8	25♐ 38	15♋ 22	3♏ 10	24♋ 18	23♎ 29	24♌ 8
2	20 40 13	9 10 24	15 56 55	22 10 37	13 28	14 34	20 49	22 15	25 40	15 35	3 12	24 22	23 29	24 10
3	20 44 9	10 7 50	28 20 41	4♎ 27 26	13 25	14 30	22 18	23 22	25 43	15 48	3 15	24 25	23 30	24 12
4	20 48 6	11 5 17	10♎ 31 13	16 32 28	13 22	14 27	23 51	24 28	25 48	16 1	3 18	24 29	23 31	24 14
5	20 52 3	12 2 45	22 31 39	28 29 15	13 19	14 24	25 28	25 35	25 52	16 14	3 20	24 32	23 32	24 16
6	20 55 59	13 0 14	4♏ 25 51	10♏ 22 0	13 15	14 22D	27 9	26 41	25 58	16 27	3 23	24 36	23 33	24 18
7	20 59 56	13 57 43	16 18 18	22 15 20	13 12	14 22	28 54	27 47	26 5	16 39	3 26	24 39	23 34	24 19
8	21 3 52	14 55 13	28 13 44	4♐ 14 6	13 9	14 22	0♌ 42	28 53	26 12	16 52	3 29	24 43	23 35	24 21
9	21 7 49	15 52 44	10♐ 17 0	16 23 2	13 6	14 24	2 33	29 58	26 20	17 5	3 32	24 46	23 36	24 23
10	21 11 45	16 50 16	22 32 42	28 46 30	13 3	14 26	4 27	1♎ 4	26 29	17 17	3 35	24 50	23 37	24 25
11	21 15 42	17 47 49	5♑ 4 53	11♑ 28 10	13 0	14 27R	6 24	2 9	26 39	17 30	3 39	24 53	23 39	24 27
12	21 19 38	18 45 22	17 56 41	24 30 34	12 56	14 27	8 22	3 14	26 50	17 43	3 42	24 57	23 40	24 29
13	21 23 35	19 42 57	1♒ 9 56	7♒ 54 43	12 53	14 26	10 21	4 19	27 1	17 55	3 46	25 0	23 41	24 31
14	21 27 32	20 40 33	14 44 46	21 39 50	12 50	14 24	12 22	5 24	27 13	18 8	3 49	25 4	23 42	24 33
15	21 31 28	21 38 10	28 39 29	5♓ 43 14	12 47	14 19	14 23	6 29	27 25	18 20	3 53	25 7	23 43	24 35
16	21 35 25	22 35 48	12♓ 50 29	20 0 34	12 44	14 14	16 25	7 33	27 39	18 32	3 56	25 10	23 45	24 37
17	21 39 21	23 33 27	27 12 44	4♈ 26 17	12 40	14 8	18 27	8 37	27 53	18 45	4 0	25 14	23 46	24 39
18	21 43 18	24 31 8	11♈ 40 27	18 54 34	12 37	14 3	20 29	9 41	28 7	18 57	4 4	25 17	23 47	24 40
19	21 47 14	25 28 51	26 7 58	3♉ 20 6	12 34	13 58	22 31	10 44	28 23	19 9	4 8	25 20	23 49	24 42
20	21 51 11	26 26 35	10♉ 30 28	17 38 41	12 31	13 55	24 32	11 48	28 39	19 21	4 12	25 23	23 50	24 44
21	21 55 7	27 24 21	24 44 28	1♊ 47 34	12 28	13 54D	26 33	12 51	28 56	19 33	4 16	25 27	23 51	24 46
22	21 59 4	28 22 9	8♊ 47 53	15 45 18	12 25	13 55	28 32	13 54	29 13	19 45	4 20	25 30	23 53	24 48
23	22 3 1	29 19 58	22 39 48	29 31 22	12 21	13 56	0♍ 31	14 57	29 31	19 57	4 25	25 33	23 54	24 50
24	22 6 57	0♍ 17 49	6♋ 20 1	13♋ 5 46	12 18	13 57R	2 29	15 59	29 49	20 9	4 29	25 36	23 56	24 52
25	22 10 54	1 15 42	19 48 38	26 28 38	12 15	13 57	4 25	17 1	0♑ 9	20 21	4 33	25 40	23 57	24 54
26	22 14 50	2 13 37	3♌ 5 44	9♌ 39 55	12 12	13 56	6 21	18 3	0 28	20 32	4 38	25 43	23 59	24 56
27	22 18 47	3 11 33	16 11 9	22 39 23	12 9	13 52	8 15	19 5	0 49	20 44	4 42	25 46	24 0	24 58
28	22 22 43	4 9 30	29 4 35	5♍ 26 42	12 5	13 45	10 8	20 6	1 10	20 55	4 47	25 49	24 2	25 0
29	22 26 40	5 7 29	11♍ 45 43	18 1 38	12 2	13 37	11 59	21 7	1 31	21 7	4 52	25 52	24 3	25 2
30	22 30 36	6 5 30	24 14 29	0♎ 24 21	11 59	13 27	13 50	22 8	1 53	21 18	4 56	25 55	24 5	25 3
31	22 34 33	7♍ 3 33	6♎ 31 22	12♎ 35 42	11♑ 56	13♑ 18	15♍ 39	23♎ 8	2♑ 16	21♋ 30	5♏ 1	25♋ 58	24♎ 7	25♌ 5

DECLINATION and LATITUDE

Day	☉ Decl	☽ Decl	☽ Lat	☽ 12 Hr. Decl	☿ Decl	☿ Lat	♀ Decl	♀ Lat	♂ Decl	♂ Lat	♃ Decl	♃ Lat	♄ Decl	♄ Lat
1	18N13	6N38	3S56	3N59	21N 9	0S54	4N 2	0N34	28S16	4S54	22N35	0N 1	10S20	2N23
2	17 58	1 19	4 35	1S20	21 11	0 40	3 32	0 30	28 15	4 53	22 33	0 1	10 21	2 23
3	17 43	3S57	5 1	6 29	21 11	0 26	3 2	0 26	28 15	4 52	22 32	0 1	10 22	2 23
4	17 27	8 57	5 12	11 19	21 9	0 12	2 32	0 22	28 14	4 51	22 31	0 1	10 23	2 22
5	17 11	13 34	5 10	15 40	21 4	0N 1	2 2	0 18	28 13	4 50	22 29	0 2	10 24	2 22
6	16 55	17 37	4 54	19 23	20 57	0 13	1 31	0 13	28 12	4 49	22 28	0 2	10 25	2 22
7	16 39	20 58	4 26	22 19	20 48	0 25	1 1	0 9	28 11	4 48	22 26	0 2	10 27	2 22
8	16 22	23 27	3 46	24 19	20 36	0 36	0 31	0 5	28 10	4 46	22 25	0 2	10 28	2 21
9	16 5	24 54	2 56	25 12	20 21	0 47	0 1	0 0	28 9	4 45	22 23	0 2	10 29	2 21
10	15 48	25 11	1 57	24 51	20 4	0 56	0S30	0S 5	28 7	4 44	22 22	0 2	10 30	2 21
11	15 30	24 12	0 51	23 13	19 44	1 5	0 60	0 9	28 6	4 42	22 20	0 2	10 32	2 21
12	15 12	21 56	0N19	20 20	19 21	1 13	1 30	0 14	28 5	4 41	22 19	0 2	10 33	2 20
13	14 54	18 27	1 30	16 18	18 56	1 20	2 0	0 19	28 4	4 39	22 17	0 2	10 35	2 20
14	14 36	13 54	2 37	11 19	18 28	1 26	2 30	0 24	28 3	4 38	22 16	0 2	10 36	2 20
15	14 18	8 33	3 37	5 39	17 59	1 31	3 1	0 29	28 1	4 36	22 14	0 3	10 37	2 20
16	13 59	2 40	4 25	0N22	17 26	1 36	3 31	0 34	28 0	4 35	22 12	0 3	10 39	2 19
17	13 40	3N25	4 56	6 26	16 52	1 39	4 1	0 39	27 59	4 33	22 11	0 3	10 40	2 19
18	13 21	9 21	5 9	12 9	16 17	1 42	4 31	0 44	27 57	4 31	22 9	0 3	10 42	2 19
19	13 2	14 47	5 3	17 12	15 39	1 44	5 0	0 49	27 56	4 30	22 8	0 3	10 43	2 19
20	12 42	19 21	4 37	21 13	15 0	1 45	5 30	0 55	27 54	4 28	22 6	0 3	10 45	2 18
21	12 23	22 45	3 55	23 55	14 20	1 46	5 60	0 60	27 53	4 26	22 4	0 3	10 47	2 18
22	12 3	24 43	2 58	25 7	13 38	1 46	6 29	1 5	27 51	4 25	22 3	0 3	10 48	2 18
23	11 43	25 7	1 52	24 44	12 56	1 45	6 59	1 11	27 50	4 23	22 1	0 3	10 50	2 18
24	11 22	23 59	0 41	22 53	12 12	1 43	7 28	1 16	27 48	4 21	21 59	0 4	10 51	2 18
25	11 2	21 28	0S32	19 46	11 28	1 41	7 57	1 22	27 46	4 19	21 58	0 4	10 53	2 17
26	10 41	17 50	1 41	15 41	10 43	1 39	8 26	1 28	27 44	4 18	21 56	0 4	10 55	2 17
27	10 20	13 22	2 45	10 56	9 58	1 36	8 55	1 33	27 42	4 16	21 55	0 4	10 57	2 17
28	9 59	8 23	3 38	5 47	9 12	1 32	9 23	1 39	27 40	4 14	21 53	0 4	10 58	2 17
29	9 38	3 9	4 20	0 30	8 26	1 28	9 52	1 45	27 38	4 12	21 51	0 4	11 0	2 17
30	9 17	2S 8	4 48	4S43	7 39	1 24	10 20	1 51	27 36	4 10	21 50	0 4	11 2	2 16
31	8N55	7S14	5S 3	9S39	6N53	1N19	10S48	1S57	27S34	4S 8	21N48	0N 4	11S 4	2N16

Day	♅ Decl	♅ Lat	♆ Decl	♆ Lat	♇ Decl	♇ Lat
1	21N43	0N28	7S33	1N42	22N38	9N44
5	21 41	0 28	7 34	1 41	22 36	9 44
9	21 38	0 28	7 36	1 41	22 33	9 44
13	21 36	0 28	7 38	1 41	22 31	9 45
17	21 34	0 28	7 40	1 41	22 28	9 45
21	21 31	0 29	7 42	1 41	22 26	9 45
25	21 29	0 29	7 44	1 40	22 24	9 46
29	21N27	0N29	7S47	1N40	22N21	9N46

☽ PHENOMENA

d	h	m	
6	18	51	☽
14	11	3	○
21	4	51	☾
28	10	21	●

d	h	° '
2	6	0
9	18	25S14
16	11	0
22	18	25N10
29	14	0

d	h	° '
4	8	5S13
11	18	0
18	4	5N 9
24	14	0
31	13	5S 5

VOID OF COURSE ☽

Last Aspect		☽ Ingress		
2	6pm52	3	♎	3am14
5	6am52	5	♏	3pm 3
8	1am26	8	♐	3am33
10	7am43	10	♑	2pm21
12	12pm51	12	♒	9pm55
14	9pm51	15	♓	2am17
17	1am 8	17	♈	4am38
19	3am49	19	♉	6am26
21	4am51	21	♊	8am57
23	12pm33	23	♋	12pm50
25	10am34	25	♌	6pm23
27	4pm20	28	♍	1am44
30	3am16	30	♎	11am12

d	h	
6	3	APOGEE
18	6	PERIGEE

DAILY ASPECTARIAN

1 Su	☽∠☿	2am22
	☽∠♆	9 47
	☉⊻☽	10 2
	☽∠♅	11 23
	☽∥♀	12pm58
	☽⚹♃	11 17
2 M	☽∠♄	4am21
	☽⚹☿	10 37
	☽☌♀	1pm21
	☽⊻♆	2 34
	☽⊻♇	3 54
	☽⚹♅	4 19
	☉∠☽	5 12
	☽□♂	6 52
	☽#♀	8 9
3 T	♀⊻♆	3am 7
	☽⊻♄	9 39
	☉⚼♂	3pm59
	☽∥♆	5 11
	♀⊻♇	6 37
	☿□♆	7 3
	☽∠♇	9 26
4 W	♀⚹♅	0am11
	☉⚹☽	1 14
	☿⊻♇	5 57
	☽∥♄	7 14
	☿☌♅	9 55
	☽□♃	11 9
5 Th	☽☌♆	2am 2
	☽⚹♇	3 30
	☽□♅	4 4
	☿⚹♀	4 55
	☿⊼♂	6 17
	☽⊻♀	6 46
	☽⚹♂	6 47
	☽□☿	6 52
	♀□♂	7 2
	☉#☽	7pm52
	☽☌♄	9 53
6 F	☽∠♂	1pm20
	☽∠♀	4 9
	☉□☽	6 51
	☽#☿	10 44
7 S	☽△♃	0am43
	☽#♅	5 54
	☽#♃	12pm59
	☽#♇	2 27
	☽⊻♆	2 40
	☿ ♌	2 44
	☽□♇	4 12
	☽△♅	4 55
	☽⊻♂	7 54
8 Su	☽⚹♀	1am26
	☽△☿	5 51
	☽⚼♃	7 25
	☽⊻♄	10 33
	☽∠♆	8pm40
	☽⚼♅	10 59
9 M	♀ ♎	0am34
	☉△☽	11 57
	☿□♄	12pm49
	☽⊼♃	1 36
	☽∠♄	4 17
	☽⚼☿	4 54
10 T	☽⚹♆	2am 5
	☽△♇	3 38
	☽⊼♅	4 26
	☽☌♂	7 43
	☉⊻♃	2pm32
	☽□♀	5 56
	☉⚼☽	7 19
	☽⚹♄	9 16
11 W	☽⊼☿	2am55
	☽⚼♇	8 15
	☽#♇	6pm48
	☽#♃	8 42
	☽☍♃	11 34
12 Th	☉⊼☽	1am37
	☽#♅	2 34
	☽□♆	10 28
	♀⊻♄	10 50
	☽⊼♇	11 59
	☽☍♅	12pm51
	☽⊻♂	4 25
	☽#☿	8 41
13 F	☽□♄	4am39
	☽△♀	6 7
	☽☍☿	7pm 7
	☽∠♂	7 30
	☉#☽	8 22
	☿⚼♂	9 59
14 S	☽⊼♃	5am58
	☽⚼♀	10 38
	☉☍☽	11 3
	☽∥♄	3pm 6
	☽△♆	3 32
	☽☍♇	5 0
	☽⊼♅	5 55
	☽⚹♂	9 51
15 Su	☽∥♆	3am47
	☽⚼♃	8 4
	☽△♄	8 55
	☽⊼♀	2pm22
	☽⚼♆	5 6
	☽⚼♅	7 30
	☽∥♀	8 53
16 M	☽⊼☿	7am 0
	☽△♃	9 41
	☽⚼♄	10 16
	☉∠♀	10 59
	☉⊼☽	5pm29
	☽⊼♆	6 15
	☽⊼♇	7 43
	☽△♅	8 41
17 T	☽□♂	1am 8
	☽#♀	2 33
	☿⊻♃	3 46
	☉⚹♆	5 17
	☽⊼♄	11 20
	☽⚼☿	12pm 4
	☽#♆	5 2
	☉⚼☽	8 10
	☽☍♀	8 26
	☽⚼♇	8 41
	♀∠♇	11 53
18 W	☉☌♇	4am 1
	☽#♄	5 42
	☽□♃	12pm14
	☉∥☽	4 21
	☽△☿	5 1
	☽☍♆	8 8
	☉⊻♅	8 11
	☽△♇	9 37
	☽□♅	10 40
	☉△☽	10 50
19 Th	☽∥☿	3am42
	☽△♂	3 49
	☽☍♄	1pm24
	☿⚹♆	3 30
20 F	☽⊼♀	2am20
	☿☌♇	2 27
	☽⚼♂	5 23
	☿⊻♅	10 29
	☽∥♅	2pm15
	☽⚹♃	3 6
	☽∥♃	6 26
	☽∥♇	9 19
	☽⊼♆	10 30
21 S	☽□♇	0am 3
	☽⚹♅	1 12
	☽□☿	3 34
	☉□☽	4 51
	☽⚼♀	5 42
	☽⊼♂	7 16
	☽⊼♄	4pm19
	☽∠♃	4 57
	☉☌☿	8 1
22 Su	☽⚼♆	0am 8
	☽∠♅	2 56
	☿∠♀	9 13
	☽△♀	9 30
	☿△♂	9 37
	☿ ♍	5pm42
	☽⚼♄	6 18
	☽⊻♃	7 12
23 M	☽△♆	2am10
	☽⚹♇	3 48
	☽⊻♅	5 4
	☉△♂	6 36
	☽☍♂	12pm16
	☉⚹☽	12 33
	☽⚹☿	4 4
	☉ ♍	4 36
	☽△♄	8 43
24 T	☽∠♇	6am16
	♀∥♆	1pm21
	♂ ♑	1 24
	☽∥♇	4 21
	☉∠☽	5 9
	☽□♀	6 35
	☽∥♃	7 59
	☽∠☿	11 11
	☽∥♅	11 49
25 W	☽☌♃	0am58
	☿⚹♄	1 44
	☽□♆	7 28
	☽⊻♇	9 10
	☉#♄	9 18
	☽☌♅	10 34
	☿∠♃	12pm47
	☿#♄	5 55
	☽⊼♂	7 7
	☉⊻☽	10 18
26 Th	☉∥☿	1am50
	☽□♄	2 49
	☽⊻☿	6 56
	☽⚼♂	11pm17
27 F	☽⚹♀	5am49
	☽⊻♃	8 33
	☿∠♆	9 46
	☽#♄	11 52
	☽⚹♆	2pm32
	☉∥☽	3 56
	☽☌♇	4 20
	☽⊻♅	5 52
	☽∥☿	7 34
	☽#♀	7 43
	☿#♀	8 16
28 S	☽#♆	2am52
	☽△♂	4 2
	☿∠♅	9 4
	☉☌☽	10 21
	☽⚹♄	10 49
	☽∠♀	12pm20
	☽∠♃	1 6
	☉⚹♄	4 50
	☉#♀	5 25
	☽∠♆	6 50
	☽∠♅	10 17
	♀□♃	11 56
29 Su	☽☌☿	0am30
	☽∠♄	3pm38
	☽⚹♃	6 14
	☽⊻♀	7 33
	☿#♆	7 47
	☽⊻♆	11 42
30 M	☽⊻♇	1am35
	☽⚹♅	3 16
	☉∠♃	6 37
	☽□♂	3pm22
	☽⊻♄	9 1
	☽#☿	10 32
31 T	☉⊻☽	1am 9
	☽∥♆	2 48
	☽∠♇	7 3
	☉#☽	7 45
	♀∥♄	2pm28
	☽∥♄	7 18
	☽∥♀	7 48
	☽⊻☿	9 14
	♀☌♆	11 58

SEPTEMBER 1954

LONGITUDE

Day	Sid. Time	☉	☽	☽ 12 Hour	Mean ☊	True ☊	☿	♀	♂	♃	♄	♅	♆	♇
	h m s	° ' "	° ' "	° ' "	° '	° '	° '	° '	° '	° '	° '	° '	° '	° '
1	22 38 30	8♍ 1 36	18♎ 37 35	24♎ 37 19	11♑ 53	13♑ 8R	17♍ 27	24♎ 8	2♑ 39	21♋ 41	5♏ 6	26♋ 1	24♎ 8	25♌ 7
2	22 42 26	8 59 41	0♏ 35 14	6♏ 31 45	11 50	13 0	19 13	25 8	3 2	21 52	5 11	26 4	24 10	25 9
3	22 46 23	9 57 48	12 27 19	18 22 26	11 46	12 54	20 58	26 7	3 27	22 3	5 16	26 7	24 12	25 11
4	22 50 19	10 55 56	24 17 39	0♐ 13 33	11 43	12 51	22 43	27 6	3 51	22 14	5 21	26 9	24 13	25 13
5	22 54 16	11 54 6	6♐ 10 45	12 9 54	11 40	12 49D	24 25	28 5	4 16	22 25	5 26	26 12	24 15	25 15
6	22 58 12	12 52 17	18 11 38	24 16 38	11 37	12 49	26 7	29 3	4 42	22 36	5 32	26 15	24 17	25 17
7	23 2 9	13 50 30	0♑ 25 32	6♑ 38 58	11 34	12 49R	27 48	0♏ 1	5 8	22 47	5 37	26 18	24 19	25 18
8	23 6 5	14 48 44	12 57 31	19 21 43	11 31	12 50	29 27	0 59	5 34	22 57	5 42	26 21	24 21	25 20
9	23 10 2	15 47 0	25 52 1	2♒ 28 46	11 27	12 49	1♎ 5	1 56	6 1	23 8	5 48	26 23	24 22	25 22
10	23 13 59	16 45 17	9♒ 12 13	16 2 26	11 24	12 46	2 42	2 52	6 29	23 18	5 53	26 26	24 24	25 24
11	23 17 55	17 43 35	22 59 21	0♓ 2 42	11 21	12 41	4 18	3 48	6 56	23 29	5 59	26 29	24 26	25 26
12	23 21 52	18 41 56	7♓ 12 3	14 26 47	11 18	12 33	5 52	4 44	7 25	23 39	6 4	26 31	24 28	25 27
13	23 25 48	19 40 13	21 46 5	29 9 2	11 15	12 24	7 26	5 39	7 53	23 49	6 10	26 34	24 30	25 29
14	23 29 45	20 38 42	6♈ 34 32	14♈ 1 30	11 11	12 14	8 58	6 33	8 22	23 59	6 16	26 36	24 32	25 31
15	23 33 41	21 37 8	21 28 48	28 55 18	11 8	12 4	10 30	7 27	8 51	24 9	6 21	26 39	24 34	25 33
16	23 37 38	22 35 36	6♉ 19 59	13♉ 41 59	11 5	11 55	12 0	8 21	9 21	24 19	6 27	26 41	24 36	25 35
17	23 41 34	23 34 6	21 0 31	28 15 1	11 2	11 49	13 29	9 14	9 51	24 29	6 33	26 43	24 38	25 36
18	23 45 31	24 32 38	5♊ 25 3	12♊ 30 21	10 59	11 46	14 57	10 6	10 22	24 39	6 39	26 46	24 40	25 38
19	23 49 27	25 31 13	19 30 48	26 26 25	10 56	11 45D	16 24	10 58	10 52	24 48	6 45	26 48	24 42	25 40
20	23 53 24	26 29 50	3♋ 17 18	10♋ 3 38	10 52	11 45R	17 50	11 49	11 23	24 58	6 51	26 50	24 44	25 41
21	23 57 21	27 28 29	16 45 38	23 23 34	10 49	11 45	19 15	12 39	11 55	25 7	6 57	26 53	24 46	25 43
22	0 1 17	28 27 10	29 57 42	6♌ 28 19	10 46	11 44	20 38	13 29	12 26	25 16	7 3	26 55	24 48	25 45
23	0 5 14	29 25 54	12♌ 55 40	19 19 57	10 43	11 41	22 1	14 18	12 59	25 25	7 9	26 57	24 50	25 47
24	0 9 10	0♎ 24 39	25 41 23	2♍ 0 7	10 40	11 34	23 22	15 6	13 31	25 34	7 16	26 59	24 52	25 48
25	0 13 7	1 23 27	8♍ 16 18	14 30 2	10 37	11 25	24 42	15 53	14 4	25 43	7 22	27 1	24 54	25 50
26	0 17 3	2 22 17	20 41 24	26 50 30	10 33	11 13	26 0	16 40	14 37	25 52	7 28	27 3	24 56	25 51
27	0 21 0	3 21 8	2♎ 57 24	9♎ 2 10	10 30	11 0	27 17	17 26	15 10	26 1	7 34	27 5	24 58	25 53
28	0 24 56	4 20 2	15 4 54	21 5 44	10 27	10 46	28 33	18 11	15 43	26 9	7 41	27 7	25 0	25 55
29	0 28 53	5 18 58	27 4 50	3♏ 2 21	10 24	10 32	29 47	18 55	16 17	26 17	7 47	27 9	25 2	25 56
30	0 32 50	6♎ 17 56	8♏ 58 34	14♏ 53 44	10♑ 21	10♑ 20	1♏ 0	19♏ 38	16♑ 51	26♋ 26	7♏ 54	27♋ 11	25♎ 4	25♌ 58

DECLINATION and LATITUDE

Day	☉ Decl	☽ Decl	☽ Lat	☽ 12 Hr. Decl	☿ Decl	☿ Lat	♀ Decl	♀ Lat	♂ Decl	♂ Lat	♃ Decl	♃ Lat	♄ Decl	♄ Lat
1	8N34	11S59	5S 4	14S10	6N 6	1N14	11S16	2S 2	27S32	4S 6	21N46	0N 4	11S 5	2N16
2	8 12	16 13	4 51	18 6	5 19	1 9	11 43	2 8	27 29	4 5	21 45	0 4	11 7	2 16
3	7 50	19 48	4 26	21 17	4 32	1 3	12 11	2 14	27 27	4 3	21 43	0 5	11 9	2 16
4	7 28	22 33	3 49	23 35	3 46	0 57	12 38	2 20	27 24	4 1	21 41	0 5	11 11	2 15
5	7 6	24 21	3 3	24 50	2 59	0 51	13 4	2 26	27 21	3 59	21 40	0 5	11 13	2 15
6	6 44	25 2	2 8	24 57	2 13	0 44	13 31	2 33	27 18	3 57	21 38	0 5	11 15	2 15
7	6 21	24 33	1 6	23 50	1 27	0 38	13 57	2 39	27 16	3 55	21 36	0 5	11 17	2 15
8	5 59	22 48	0N 1	21 28	0 41	0 31	14 23	2 45	27 13	3 53	21 35	0 5	11 19	2 15
9	5 36	19 51	1 9	17 57	0S 4	0 24	14 49	2 51	27 9	3 51	21 33	0 5	11 21	2 14
10	5 14	15 47	2 16	13 22	0 49	0 17	15 14	2 57	27 6	3 49	21 31	0 5	11 23	2 14
11	4 51	10 46	3 17	7 58	1 34	0 9	15 40	3 3	27 3	3 47	21 30	0 5	11 25	2 14
12	4 28	5 3	4 7	2 1	2 18	0 2	16 4	3 9	26 59	3 45	21 28	0 6	11 27	2 14
13	4 5	1N 4	4 43	4N10	3 2	0S 6	16 29	3 16	26 56	3 43	21 26	0 6	11 29	2 14
14	3 42	7 13	5 1	10 10	3 46	0 13	16 53	3 22	26 52	3 41	21 25	0 6	11 31	2 13
15	3 19	12 59	4 58	15 36	4 29	0 21	17 17	3 28	26 48	3 39	21 23	0 6	11 33	2 13
16	2 56	17 58	4 35	20 2	5 11	0 29	17 40	3 34	26 44	3 37	21 21	0 6	11 35	2 13
17	2 33	21 47	3 55	23 10	5 53	0 36	18 3	3 40	26 40	3 36	21 20	0 6	11 37	2 13
18	2 10	24 10	2 60	24 45	6 34	0 44	18 26	3 46	26 35	3 34	21 18	0 6	11 39	2 13
19	1 47	24 57	1 55	24 44	7 15	0 52	18 48	3 52	26 31	3 32	21 17	0 6	11 41	2 13
20	1 24	24 9	0 45	23 13	7 55	0 60	19 10	3 59	26 26	3 30	21 15	0 7	11 43	2 13
21	1 0	21 57	0S27	20 25	8 35	1 7	19 31	4 5	26 22	3 28	21 14	0 7	11 45	2 12
22	0 37	18 37	1 35	16 37	9 13	1 15	19 52	4 11	26 17	3 26	21 12	0 7	11 47	2 12
23	0 14	14 26	2 37	12 6	9 51	1 23	20 13	4 17	26 12	3 24	21 10	0 7	11 49	2 12
24	0S10	9 40	3 30	7 9	10 29	1 31	20 33	4 23	26 6	3 22	21 9	0 7	11 52	2 12
25	0 33	4 35	4 12	1 59	11 5	1 38	20 53	4 28	26 1	3 20	21 7	0 7	11 54	2 12
26	0 57	0S37	4 41	3S11	11 41	1 46	21 12	4 34	25 55	3 18	21 6	0 7	11 56	2 12
27	1 20	5 43	4 57	8 10	12 16	1 53	21 31	4 40	25 50	3 16	21 4	0 7	11 58	2 11
28	1 43	10 32	4 59	12 47	12 50	2 0	21 49	4 46	25 44	3 14	21 3	0 8	12 0	2 11
29	2 7	14 54	4 48	16 52	13 23	2 7	22 7	4 51	25 38	3 12	21 1	0 8	12 2	2 11
30	2S30	18S39	4S24	20S15	13S55	2S14	22S24	4S57	25S31	3S10	21N 0	0N 8	12S 5	2N11

Day	♅ Decl	♅ Lat	♆ Decl	♆ Lat	♇ Decl	♇ Lat
1	21N25	0N29	7S49	1N40	22N20	9N46
5	21 23	0 29	7 51	1 40	22 18	9 47
9	21 21	0 29	7 54	1 40	22 16	9 48
13	21 19	0 29	7 57	1 40	22 14	9 48
17	21 18	0 29	7 60	1 40	22 12	9 49
21	21 16	0 29	8 3	1 40	22 11	9 50
25	21 14	0 29	8 6	1 40	22 9	9 51
29	21N13	0N30	8S 9	1N39	22N 8	9N52

☽ PHENOMENA

d	h	m	
5	12	29	☽
12	20	20	○
19	11	12	☾
27	0	51	●

d	h	° '
6	2	25S 3
12	20	0
19	0	24N57
25	21	0

d	h	° '
8	0	0
14	9	5N 2
20	15	0
27	16	4S60

VOID OF COURSE ☽

Last Aspect		☽ Ingress		
1	2pm51	1	♏	10pm49
4	3am47	4	♐	11am33
6	11pm 9	6	♑	11pm10
9	0am57	9	♒	7am31
11	4am11	11	♓	11am55
13	7am49	13	♈	1pm23
15	8am21	15	♉	1pm45
17	9am29	17	♊	2pm55
19	11am12	19	♋	6pm13
21	9pm 1	22	♌	0am 4
24	0am13	24	♍	8am11
26	12pm27	26	♎	6pm11
29	0am 8	29	♏	5am52

d	h	
2	22	APOGEE
14	20	PERIGEE
30	14	APOGEE

DAILY ASPECTARIAN

1 W	☽□♃	6am12
	☉∠☽	9 35
	☽☌♆	11 3
	☽☌♀	12pm 2
	☽✶♇	1 2
	☽□♅	2 51
2 Th	♀✶♇	0am25
	☉∠♆	4 22
	☽✶♂	5 7
	☽∠☿	8 36
	☽☌♄	9 21
	☿∠♄	1pm49
	☉✶☽	6 30
	♀□♅	11 38
3 F	☉#♆	0am 8
	☽∠♂	12pm34
	☽#♅	12 59
	☽#♃	3 39
	☿✶♃	4 40
	☽△♃	7 46
	☽✶☿	8 15
	☽#♇	9 28
	☽⚺♆	11 51
4 S	☽□♇	1am52
	☽△♅	3 47
	☉∠♅	5 52
	☽⚺♀	6 13
	☽⚺♂	8pm 1
	☿⚺♆	9 33
	☽⚺♄	10 30
5 Su	☽⚼♃	2am32
	☽∠♆	6 11
	☽⚼♅	10 7
	☿⚺♇	11 49
	☉□☽	12pm29
	☽∠♀	3 3
6 M	☿✶♅	1am58
	☽∠♄	4 39
	☽⚻♃	8 50
	☽✶♆	12pm 2
	☽△♇	2 0
	☽⚻♅	3 56
	☽□☿	6 4
	☽✶♀	11 9
	♀ ♏	11 29
7 T	☽☌♂	9am25
	☽✶♄	10 5
	☽⚼♇	7pm 1
8 W	☉△☽	3am47
	☽#♇	5 8
	☿ ♎	8 6
	♂✶♄	8 50
	☽#♃	11 15
	☽#♅	12pm55
	☽☍♃	6 55
	☽□♆	9 15
	☽⚻♇	11 5
9 Th	☽☍♅	0am57
	☉⚼☽	9 39
	☽△☿	10 48
	☽□♀	11 51
	☽□♄	6pm 4
	☽⚺♂	6 59
10 F	☽∥♀	2am33
	☿⚺♀	6 10
	☉⚻☽	2pm15
	☽⚼☿	4 49
	☽∥♄	9 7
	☽∠♂	10 8
11 S	☽⚻♃	0am51
	☽△♆	2 29
	☽☍♇	4 11
	☽⚻♅	5 58
	☽∥♆	12pm10
	☽△♀	7 35
	☽⚻☿	9 31
	☽△♄	10 6
12 Su	☽✶♂	0am22
	☉#☽	2 26
	☽⚼♃	2 26
	☿⚺♄	3 13
	☽⚼♆	3 46
	☽⚼♅	7 11
	☽∥☿	9 41
	☉☍☽	8pm20
	☽⚼♀	10 3
	☽⚼♄	11 1
13 M	☽△♃	3am23
	☽⚻♆	4 27
	☽⚻♇	6 4
	☽△♅	7 49
	☽#☿	8 38
	☿□♂	10 11
	☉∥☽	11 2
	♀☌♄	3pm14
	☉#☿	10 52
	☽⚻♄	11 29
	☽⚻♀	11 58
14 T	☽□♂	2am59
	☽#♆	3 0
	☽☍☿	4 19
	☽⚼♇	6 22
	☉∠♄	4pm49
	☽#♄	5 45
15 W	☉⚻☽	0am14
	☿∠♇	0 48
	☽□♃	4 21
	☽☍♆	4 59
	☽△♇	6 34
	☽□♅	8 21
	☽#♀	10pm16
16 Th	☽☍♄	0am12
	☉⚼☽	2 12
	☽☍♀	3 29
	☽△♂	5 5
	☽⚻☿	10 16
	☽∥♅	8pm22
	☽∥♃	8 39
17 F	☽∥♇	3am18
	☉△☽	4 32
	☽✶♃	5 48
	☽⚻♆	6 0
	☽⚼♂	6 35
	☽□♇	7 37
	☽✶♅	9 29
	☽⚼☿	1pm49
18 S	☽⚻♄	2am 5
	☉✶♃	2 55
	☉⚺♆	2 56
	♃□♆	3 8
	☽⚼♆	7 11
	☽∠♃	7 13
	☽⚻♀	8 26
	☽⚻♂	8 40
	☽∠♅	10 46
	♂⚼♇	1pm43
	♀✶♂	5 47
	☽△☿	6 3
	♃∥♅	9 34
19 Su	☉⚺♇	3am37
	☽⚼♄	3 53
	☽△♆	8 59
	☽⚺♃	9 15
	☽✶♇	10 40
	☉□☽	11 12
	☽⚼♀	11 54
	☽⚺♅	12pm40
20 M	☿∥♆	4am17
	☽△♄	6 20
	☉✶♅	8 43
	☽∠♇	1pm 9
	☽☍♂	2 57
	☽△♀	4 8
	☽∥♇	10 5
21 T	☽□☿	5am 1
	☽∥♅	5 38
	☽∥♃	5 59
	☽□♆	2pm32
	☽☌♃	3 19
	☽⚺♇	4 16
	☽#♀	4 32
	☽☌♅	6 24
	☉✶☽	9 1
22 W	☉∠♀	3am41
	☽□♄	1pm11
23 Th	☽⚻♂	0am 6
	☽□♀	2 43
	☉∠☽	3 2
	☽#♄	1pm18
	☉ ♎	1 56
	☽✶☿	7 5
	☽#☿	8 29
	☽✶♆	10 26
	☽⚺♃	11 46
24 F	☽☌♇	0am13
	☽⚺♅	2 27
	☽⚼♂	5 36
	☽#♆	7 32
	☉⚺☽	9 43
	☽✶♄	10pm15
25 S	☽∠☿	3am 4
	☽∠♆	3 8
	☿☌♆	3 46
	☽∠♃	4 46
	☽∠♅	7 14
	☽△♂	11 40
	☽✶♀	3pm40
	♀#♃	4 58
	☉#☽	5 17
	☿□♃	9 5
	☿✶♇	9 13
	♃⚺♇	10 29
26 Su	☉∥☽	1am38
	♀#♅	2 42
	☽∠♄	3 29
	☽⚺♆	8 17
	☽⚺♇	10 6
	☽✶♃	10 13
	☿∥♄	10 46
	☽⚺☿	11 35
	☽✶♅	12pm27
	☿□♅	7 59
	☽∠♀	10 53
27 M	☉☌☽	0am51
	☽⚺♄	9 11
	☽∥♆	11 49
	☽∠♇	3pm42
28 T	☽□♂	1am21
	☽⚺♀	6 34
	☽∥♄	7 50
	☽∥☿	2pm 5
	☽☌♆	7 53
	☽✶♇	9 42
	☽□♃	10 24
29 W	☽□♅	0am 8
	♀#♇	1 1
	☿ ♏	4 7
	☽☌☿	6 4
	☉⚺☽	6pm 6
	☽☌♄	9 48
30 Th	☽✶♂	4pm48
	☽#♃	6 8
	☽#♅	8 7
	☽☌♀	10 59

OCTOBER 1954

LONGITUDE

Day	Sid. Time	☉	☽	☽ 12 Hour	Mean ☊	True ☊	☿	♀	♂	♃	♄	♅	♆	♇
	h m s	° ' "	° ' "	° ' "	° '	° '	° '	° '	° '	° '	° '	° '	° '	° '
1	0 36 46	7♎ 16 55	20♏ 48 13	26♏ 42 24	10♑ 17	10♑ 11R	2♏ 11	20♏ 20	17♑ 26	26♋ 34	8♏ 0	27♋ 12	25♎ 7	25♌ 59
2	0 40 43	8 15 57	2♐ 36 44	8♐ 31 42	10 14	10 4	3 20	21 1	18 1	26 42	8 7	27 14	25 9	26 1
3	0 44 39	9 15 0	14 27 51	20 25 46	10 11	10 0	4 27	21 41	18 35	26 50	8 13	27 16	25 11	26 2
4	0 48 36	10 14 5	26 26 4	2♑ 29 25	10 8	9 59	5 32	22 20	19 11	26 57	8 20	27 17	25 13	26 4
5	0 52 32	11 13 12	8♑ 36 28	14 47 55	10 5	9 58	6 35	22 57	19 46	27 5	8 27	27 19	25 15	26 5
6	0 56 29	12 12 21	21 4 24	27 26 34	10 2	9 58	7 36	23 34	20 22	27 12	8 33	27 21	25 17	26 7
7	1 0 25	13 11 31	3♒ 55 1	10♒ 30 15	9 58	9 57	8 33	24 9	20 58	27 20	8 40	27 22	25 20	26 8
8	1 4 22	14 10 43	17 12 40	24 2 34	9 55	9 54	9 28	24 43	21 34	27 27	8 47	27 23	25 22	26 10
9	1 8 19	15 9 57	1♓ 0 2	8♓ 5 1	9 52	9 48	10 20	25 16	22 10	27 34	8 54	27 25	25 24	26 11
10	1 12 15	16 9 13	15 17 13	22 36 6	9 49	9 40	11 8	25 47	22 46	27 41	9 0	27 26	25 26	26 12
11	1 16 12	17 8 31	0♈ 0 55	7♈ 30 43	9 46	9 30	11 53	26 16	23 23	27 47	9 7	27 27	25 28	26 14
12	1 20 8	18 7 50	15 4 19	22 40 26	9 43	9 18	12 33	26 44	24 0	27 54	9 14	27 29	25 31	26 15
13	1 24 5	19 7 12	0♉ 17 40	7♉ 54 38	9 39	9 7	13 9	27 11	24 37	28 0	9 21	27 30	25 33	26 16
14	1 28 1	20 6 35	15 29 58	23 2 25	9 36	8 58	13 40	27 36	25 15	28 7	9 28	27 31	25 35	26 17
15	1 31 58	21 6 1	0♊ 30 54	7♊ 54 33	9 33	8 51	14 6	27 59	25 52	28 13	9 35	27 32	25 37	26 19
16	1 35 54	22 5 29	15 12 38	22 24 44	9 30	8 46	14 26	28 20	26 30	28 19	9 42	27 33	25 40	26 20
17	1 39 51	23 5 0	29 30 33	6♋ 30 1	9 27	8 44D	14 39	28 40	27 8	28 24	9 49	27 34	25 42	26 21
18	1 43 48	24 4 33	13♋ 23 12	20 10 18	9 23	8 44	14 45R	28 58	27 46	28 30	9 56	27 35	25 44	26 22
19	1 47 44	25 4 8	26 51 37	3♌ 27 30	9 20	8 44R	14 44	29 13	28 24	28 36	10 3	27 36	25 46	26 24
20	1 51 41	26 3 45	9♌ 58 23	16 24 39	9 17	8 44	14 35	29 27	29 2	28 41	10 10	27 37	25 49	26 25
21	1 55 37	27 3 25	22 46 47	29 5 9	9 14	8 41	14 17	29 38	29 41	28 46	10 17	27 37	25 51	26 26
22	1 59 34	28 3 7	5♍ 20 12	11♍ 32 15	9 11	8 36	13 51	29 48	0♒ 19	28 51	10 24	27 38	25 53	26 27
23	2 3 30	29 2 51	17 41 40	23 48 44	9 8	8 28	13 16	29 55	0 58	28 56	10 31	27 39	25 55	26 28
24	2 7 27	0♏ 2 37	29 53 42	5♎ 56 50	9 4	8 17	12 32	0♐ 0	1 37	29 0	10 38	27 39	25 58	26 29
25	2 11 23	1 2 25	11♎ 58 18	17 58 17	9 1	8 5	11 39	0 3R	2 16	29 5	10 46	27 40	26 0	26 30
26	2 15 20	2 2 16	23 56 58	29 54 29	8 58	7 52	10 39	0 4	2 55	29 9	10 53	27 40	26 2	26 31
27	2 19 17	3 2 8	5♏ 51 1	11♏ 46 44	8 55	7 40	9 32	0 2	3 35	29 13	11 0	27 41	26 4	26 32
28	2 23 13	4 2 2	17 41 48	23 36 26	8 52	7 29	8 19	29♏ 57	4 14	29 17	11 7	27 41	26 6	26 33
29	2 27 10	5 1 58	29 30 54	5♐ 25 27	8 49	7 20	7 3	29 51	4 54	29 21	11 14	27 42	26 9	26 34
30	2 31 6	6 1 57	11♐ 20 26	17 16 11	8 45	7 14	5 46	29 41	5 34	29 25	11 21	27 42	26 11	26 35
31	2 35 3	7♏ 1 56	23♐ 13 9	29♐ 11 45	8♑ 42	7♑ 10	4♏ 30	29♏ 30	6♒ 14	29♋ 28	11♏ 29	27♋ 42	26♎ 13	26♌ 36

DECLINATION and LATITUDE

Day	☉ Decl	☽ Decl	☽ Lat	☽ 12 Hr. Decl	☿ Decl	☿ Lat	♀ Decl	♀ Lat	♂ Decl	♂ Lat	♃ Decl	♃ Lat	♄ Decl	♄ Lat
1	2S53	21S38	3S49	22S47	14S26	2S21	22S41	5S 3	25S25	3S 8	20N59	0N 8	12S 7	2N11
2	3 17	23 41	3 4	24 20	14 56	2 28	22 58	5 8	25 19	3 6	20 57	0 8	12 9	2 11
3	3 40	24 42	2 10	24 47	15 25	2 34	23 13	5 13	25 12	3 4	20 56	0 8	12 11	2 11
4	4 3	24 35	1 11	24 5	15 53	2 40	23 29	5 18	25 5	3 2	20 54	0 8	12 13	2 11
5	4 26	23 17	0 7	22 12	16 20	2 46	23 44	5 23	24 58	3 0	20 53	0 8	12 16	2 11
6	4 50	20 50	0N58	19 11	16 45	2 51	23 58	5 28	24 51	2 58	20 52	0 9	12 18	2 10
7	5 13	17 17	2 3	15 8	17 8	2 56	24 11	5 33	24 43	2 57	20 51	0 9	12 20	2 10
8	5 36	12 46	3 3	10 12	17 31	3 1	24 24	5 38	24 35	2 55	20 49	0 9	12 22	2 10
9	5 58	7 27	3 55	4 34	17 51	3 5	24 37	5 42	24 28	2 53	20 48	0 9	12 25	2 10
10	6 21	1 35	4 34	1N28	18 10	3 9	24 49	5 47	24 20	2 51	20 47	0 9	12 27	2 10
11	6 44	4N32	4 57	7 35	18 27	3 12	24 60	5 51	24 12	2 49	20 46	0 9	12 29	2 10
12	7 7	10 32	4 59	13 21	18 42	3 15	25 10	5 55	24 3	2 47	20 44	0 9	12 31	2 10
13	7 29	15 57	4 41	18 18	18 55	3 17	25 20	5 58	23 55	2 45	20 43	0 10	12 34	2 10
14	7 52	20 21	4 2	22 2	19 5	3 18	25 30	6 2	23 46	2 43	20 42	0 10	12 36	2 10
15	8 14	23 19	3 8	24 11	19 13	3 18	25 38	6 5	23 37	2 41	20 41	0 10	12 38	2 10
16	8 36	24 38	2 1	24 39	19 19	3 18	25 46	6 8	23 28	2 39	20 40	0 10	12 41	2 9
17	8 58	24 15	0 49	23 29	19 21	3 16	25 53	6 10	23 19	2 38	20 39	0 10	12 43	2 9
18	9 20	22 22	0S25	20 56	19 20	3 13	25 59	6 13	23 9	2 36	20 38	0 10	12 45	2 9
19	9 42	19 15	1 34	17 20	19 16	3 9	26 5	6 15	22 60	2 34	20 37	0 10	12 47	2 9
20	10 4	15 13	2 37	12 58	19 8	3 3	26 9	6 16	22 50	2 32	20 36	0 11	12 50	2 9
21	10 26	10 36	3 31	8 9	18 56	2 56	26 13	6 18	22 40	2 30	20 35	0 11	12 52	2 9
22	10 47	5 38	4 13	3 5	18 40	2 47	26 16	6 19	22 30	2 28	20 34	0 11	12 54	2 9
23	11 8	0 32	4 43	2S 1	18 19	2 37	26 18	6 19	22 20	2 26	20 33	0 11	12 56	2 9
24	11 29	4S31	4 59	6 59	17 54	2 25	26 20	6 19	22 9	2 25	20 33	0 11	12 59	2 9
25	11 50	9 21	5 1	11 38	17 24	2 11	26 20	6 19	21 59	2 23	20 32	0 11	13 1	2 9
26	12 11	13 47	4 50	15 48	16 51	1 55	26 19	6 18	21 48	2 21	20 31	0 11	13 3	2 9
27	12 32	17 40	4 27	19 21	16 13	1 38	26 17	6 16	21 37	2 19	20 30	0 12	13 5	2 9
28	12 52	20 49	3 52	22 4	15 32	1 19	26 14	6 14	21 25	2 17	20 30	0 12	13 8	2 9
29	13 12	23 5	3 7	23 51	14 49	0 60	26 10	6 12	21 14	2 15	20 29	0 12	13 10	2 9
30	13 32	24 21	2 13	24 34	14 4	0 39	26 5	6 9	21 3	2 14	20 29	0 12	13 12	2 9
31	13S52	24S30	1S14	24S 9	13S19	0S18	25S59	6S 5	20S51	2S12	20N28	0N12	13S14	2N 9

Day	♅ Decl	♅ Lat	♆ Decl	♆ Lat	♇ Decl	♇ Lat
1	21N12	0N30	8S11	1N39	22N 7	9N52
5	21 11	0 30	8 14	1 39	22 6	9 53
9	21 10	0 30	8 17	1 39	22 5	9 54
13	21 9	0 30	8 20	1 39	22 4	9 56
17	21 9	0 30	8 24	1 39	22 4	9 57
21	21 8	0 30	8 27	1 39	22 3	9 58
25	21 8	0 30	8 30	1 39	22 3	9 59
29	21N 8	0N31	8S33	1N39	22N 3	10N 1

☽ PHENOMENA

d	h	m	
5	5	31	☽
12	5	10	○
18	20	31	☾
26	17	47	●

d	h	° '
3	10	24S48
10	6	0
16	6	24N42
23	2	0
30	15	24S35

5	3	0
11	15	5N 1
17	16	0
24	16	5S 2

VOID OF COURSE ☽

Last Aspect		☽ Ingress		
1	1pm 3	1	♐	6pm42
3	11pm16	4	♑	7am 5
6	11am50	6	♒	4pm46
8	3pm42	8	♓	10pm17
10	8pm23	10	♈	11pm59
12	8pm22	12	♉	11pm32
14	8pm16	14	♊	11pm10
16	6pm38	17	♋	0am50
19	4am21	19	♌	5am41
21	1pm14	21	♍	1pm45
23	10pm14	24	♎	0am12
26	10am32	26	♏	12pm11
29	0am40	29	♐	0am59
31	6am47	31	♑	1pm37

d	h	
13	2	PERIGEE
27	23	APOGEE

DAILY ASPECTARIAN

1 F	☉∠☽	3am17
	☽#♇	4 47
	☽⚺♆	8 47
	☽□♇	10 34
	☽△♃	11 50
	☽∥♀	12pm34
	☽△♅	1 3
	☉⚺♄	7 49
2 S	☽∠♂	0am51
	☽⚺☿	1 37
	☽⚺♄	11 16
	☉⚹☽	12pm30
	☽∠♆	3 19
	☽⚼♃	6 37
	☽⚼♅	7 33
3 Su	☽⚺♂	8am44
	☽∠☿	11 3
	☽⚺♀	3pm21
	☽∠♄	5 45
	☽⚹♆	9 34
	☽△♇	11 16
4 M	☽⚻♃	1am 3
	☽⚻♅	1 42
	☽∥♀	6pm42
	☽⚹☿	7 41
	☉∠♇	8 42
	☽∠♀	10 40
	☽⚹♄	11 41
5 T	☽⚼♇	4am50
	☉□☽	5 31
	☽#♇	12pm59
	☽#♅	9 8
	☽☌♂	10 35
	☽#♃	11 44
6 W	☽⚹♀	4am57
	☽□♆	7 59
	☽⚻♇	9 31
	☽☍♃	11 40
	☽☍♅	11 50
7 Th	☽∥☿	0am47
	☿☌♄	3 16
	☽□♄	8 45
	☽□☿	9 7
	♃☌♅	9 58
	☉△☽	6pm10
8 F	☽∥♄	1am53
	☽⚺♂	8 1
	♀∥♂	1pm 0
	☽□♀	1 43
	☽△♆	2 20
	☽☍♇	3 42
	☽⚻♅	5 50
	☽⚻♃	6 3
	☽∥♆	8 27
	☉⚼☽	10 28
9 S	☉∥☽	5am50
	♀⚺♆	6 51
	☽∠♂	10 55
	☽△♄	1pm28
	☽⚼♆	3 55
	☽△☿	4 43
	☽⚼♅	7 16
	☽⚼♃	7 38
10 Su	☉⚻☽	1am32
	☽⚹♂	12pm49
	☽⚼♄	2 24
	☽⚻♆	4 39
	☽△♀	5 45
	☽⚻♇	5 53
	☽⚼☿	6 41
	☽△♅	7 52
	☽△♃	8 23
	♀□♇	9 35
11 M	☉#☽	9am13
	☽⚻♄	2pm40
	☽#♆	2 58
	☽⚼♇	5 56
	☽⚼♀	6 34
	☽⚻☿	7 50
12 T	☉☍☽	5am10
	☽#♄	8 29
	☽□♂	2pm41
	☽☍♆	4 31
	☽△♇	5 39
	☽⚻♀	6 58
	☽□♅	7 36
	☽□♃	8 22
13 W	☽☍♄	2pm23
	☽#☿	4 6
	♀△♅	6 58
	☽☍☿	9 1
14 Th	☽∥♃	2am20
	☽∥♅	5 27
	☉⚻☽	7 51
	☽∥♇	12pm21
	♂□♆	2 2
	☽⚻♆	4 7
	☽△♂	4 12
	☽□♇	5 14
	☽⚹♅	7 12
	☽☍♀	7 49
	☽⚹♃	8 16
15 F	☽#♂	3am18
	☉∥♆	8 44
	☉⚼☽	9 42
	☽⚻♄	2pm51
	☽⚼♆	4 29
	☽⚼♂	5 36
	♂⚻♇	5 36
	☽∠♅	7 37
	☽∠♃	8 51
	♀△♃	9 20
	☽⚻☿	10 41
16 S	☉△☽	12pm19
	☽⚼♄	3 59
	☽△♆	5 31
	☽⚹♇	6 38
	☽⚻♂	7 46
	☽⚺♅	8 42
	☽⚺♃	10 7
	☽⚻♀	10 32
17 Su	☽⚼☿	0am14
	☽#♂	3pm13
	♂☍♅	5 12
	☽△♄	5 54
	☽∠♇	8 28
18 M	☽⚼♀	1am 2
	☽△☿	2 24
	☽∥♇	2 47
	☿SR	8 30
	☽∥♅	10 25
	☽∥♃	2pm22
	☉□☽	8 31
	☽□♆	10 2
	☽⚺♇	11 9
	☽#☿	11 51
19 T	☽☌♅	1am20
	☽☍♂	2 55
	☽☌♃	3 10
	☽△♀	4 21
	♂☍♃	8 39
	☉☌♆	5pm39
20 W	☽□♄	0am22
	☽□☿	8 25
	☉⚹♇	8 35
	☽#♄	12pm39
	♀⚹♂	10 11
21 Th	☉#☽	0am48
	☽⚹♆	5 50
	☽☌♇	6 57
	☉⚹☽	8 49
	☽⚺♅	9 13
	☽#♆	10 31
	☽⚺♃	11 28
	♂ ♒	12pm 3
	☽□♀	1 14
	☽⚻♂	1 50
	☉□♅	1 52
22 F	☽⚹♄	9am54
	☽∠♆	10 46
	☽∠♅	2pm 9
	☽⚹☿	3 47
	☉∠☽	4 15
	☽∠♃	4 36
	☽⚼♂	8 26
	☉□♃	8 57
23 S	☽∠♄	3pm31
	☽⚺♆	4 12
	☽⚺♇	5 15
	☽⚹♅	7 34
	☽∠☿	7 37
	♀ ♐	10 7
	☽⚹♃	10 14
	☉ ♏	10 57
	☉⚺♀	11 1
24 Su	☽⚹♀	0am13
	☉⚺☽	0 19
	☽△♂	3 36
	♂#♇	1pm56
	☽∥♆	7 38
	☽⚺♄	9 33
	☽∠♇	11 3
	☽⚺☿	11 25
25 M	☽∠♀	6am10
	☉∥☽	2pm16
	♀SR	4 30
	☿☌♄	7 16
	☽∥♄	7 48
26 T	☽☌♆	4am12
	☽⚹♇	5 10
	☽□♅	7 30
	☽□♃	10 32
	☽⚺♀	12pm17
	☽∥☿	3 56
	☉☌☽	5 47
	☽□♂	7 9
27 W	☽☌☿	6am46
	♀ ♏	7 28
	☽☌♄	10 31
	☽#♃	9pm15
28 Th	☽#♅	2am47
	☽∥♂	5 9
	☽#♇	11 45
	☉□♂	2pm46
	☽⚺♆	5 8
	☽□♇	6 0
	☽△♅	8 18
	☉∥♄	8 58
	☽△♃	11 40
29 F	☽☌♀	0am40
	☽⚹♂	11 36
	☉⚺☽	12pm14
	♂#♅	1 27
	☽⚺☿	1 49
	☉☌☿	9 15
	☽∠♆	11 41
30 S	☽⚺♄	0am 2
	☿□♂	2 30
	☽⚼♅	2 45
	☽⚼♃	6 15
	☉∥☿	11 43
	☽∠☿	5pm13
	☽∠♂	7 46
	☉∠☽	9 23
31 Su	☿∥♄	2am16
	♀△♃	2 46
	☽⚹♆	6 3
	☽∠♄	6 37
	☽△♇	6 47
	☽⚻♅	9 1
	☽⚺♀	12pm22
	☽⚻♃	12 36
	☽⚹☿	8 31

NOVEMBER 1954

LONGITUDE

Day	Sid. Time	☉	☽	☽ 12 Hour	Mean ☊	True ☊	☿	♀	♂	♃	♄	♅	♆	♇
	h m s	° ' "	° ' "	° ' "	° '	° '	° '	° '	° '	° '	° '	° '	° '	° '
1	2 38 59	8♏ 1 58	5♑ 12 31	11♑ 15 57	8♑ 39	7♑ 9	3♏ 18R	29♏ 16R	6♒ 54	29♋ 31	11♏ 36	27♋ 42	26♎ 15	26♌ 36
2	2 42 56	9 2 1	17 22 39	23 33 12	8 36	7 10	2 11	28 59	7 34	29 34	11 43	27 42	26 18	26 37
3	2 46 52	10 2 6	29 48 13	6♒ 8 17	8 33	7 11R	1 12	28 41	8 15	29 37	11 50	27 42R	26 20	26 38
4	2 50 49	11 2 12	12♒ 34 1	19 5 57	8 29	7 11	0 22	28 20	8 55	29 40	11 57	27 42	26 22	26 39
5	2 54 46	12 2 20	25 44 34	2♓ 30 17	8 26	7 10	29♎ 43	27 56	9 36	29 42	12 5	27 42	26 24	26 39
6	2 58 42	13 2 29	9♓ 23 20	16 23 52	8 23	7 7	29 15	27 31	10 16	29 44	12 12	27 42	26 26	26 40
7	3 2 39	14 2 40	23 31 48	0♈ 46 52	8 20	7 1	28 59D	27 4	10 57	29 46	12 19	27 42	26 28	26 41
8	3 6 35	15 2 52	8♈ 8 35	15 36 13	8 17	6 55	28 55	26 35	11 38	29 48	12 26	27 42	26 31	26 41
9	3 10 32	16 3 6	23 8 48	0♉ 45 13	8 14	6 47	29 1	26 4	12 19	29 50	12 33	27 42	26 33	26 42
10	3 14 28	17 3 22	8♉ 24 9	16 4 12	8 10	6 39	29 18	25 32	13 0	29 52	12 41	27 41	26 35	26 43
11	3 18 25	18 3 39	23 43 56	1♊ 21 57	8 7	6 32	29 45	24 58	13 41	29 53	12 48	27 41	26 37	26 43
12	3 22 21	19 3 58	8♊ 56 56	16 27 43	8 4	6 27	0♏ 21	24 23	14 22	29 54	12 55	27 40	26 39	26 44
13	3 26 18	20 4 19	23 53 20	1♋ 12 59	8 1	6 24	1 5	23 48	15 3	29 55	13 2	27 40	26 41	26 44
14	3 30 15	21 4 42	8♋ 26 8	15 32 27	7 58	6 24D	1 57	23 12	15 45	29 56	13 9	27 39	26 43	26 45
15	3 34 11	22 5 7	22 31 45	29 24 4	7 54	6 24	2 54	22 35	16 26	29 56	13 17	27 39	26 45	26 45
16	3 38 8	23 5 33	6♌ 9 36	12♌ 48 36	7 51	6 25	3 57	21 59	17 8	29 56	13 24	27 38	26 47	26 46
17	3 42 4	24 6 2	19 21 29	25 48 39	7 48	6 26R	5 5	21 22	17 49	29 57R	13 31	27 37	26 49	26 46
18	3 46 1	25 6 32	2♍ 10 37	8♍ 27 53	7 45	6 26	6 16	20 46	18 31	29 56	13 38	27 37	26 52	26 46
19	3 49 57	26 7 4	14 40 58	20 50 22	7 42	6 25	7 32	20 11	19 13	29 56	13 45	27 36	26 54	26 46
20	3 53 54	27 7 38	26 56 36	3♎ 0 7	7 39	6 21	8 50	19 37	19 55	29 56	13 52	27 35	26 56	26 47
21	3 57 50	28 8 13	9♎ 1 21	15 0 44	7 35	6 16	10 11	19 3	20 36	29 55	13 59	27 34	26 58	26 47
22	4 1 47	29 8 50	20 58 37	26 55 21	7 32	6 9	11 34	18 31	21 18	29 54	14 6	27 33	27 0	26 47
23	4 5 44	0♐ 9 29	2♏ 51 15	8♏ 46 36	7 29	6 2	12 59	18 1	22 0	29 53	14 13	27 32	27 1	26 47
24	4 9 40	1 10 9	14 41 39	20 36 37	7 26	5 55	14 25	17 32	22 42	29 52	14 20	27 31	27 3	26 48
25	4 13 37	2 10 51	26 31 46	2♐ 27 16	7 23	5 49	15 53	17 6	23 25	29 50	14 27	27 30	27 5	26 48
26	4 17 33	3 11 35	8♐ 23 23	14 20 18	7 20	5 45	17 22	16 41	24 7	29 49	14 34	27 29	27 7	26 48
27	4 21 30	4 12 19	20 18 16	26 17 31	7 16	5 42	18 51	16 18	24 49	29 47	14 41	27 28	27 9	26 48
28	4 25 26	5 13 5	2♑ 18 20	8♑ 21 0	7 13	5 40D	20 22	15 58	25 31	29 45	14 48	27 26	27 11	26 48R
29	4 29 23	6 13 52	14 25 51	20 33 14	7 10	5 40	21 53	15 39	26 14	29 42	14 55	27 25	27 13	26 48
30	4 33 19	7♐ 14 40	26♑ 43 31	2♒ 57 7	7♑ 7	5♑ 42	23♏ 24	15♏ 24	26♒ 56	29♋ 40	15♏ 2	27♋ 24	27♎ 15	26♌ 48

DECLINATION and LATITUDE

Day	☉ Decl	☽ Decl	☽ Lat	☽ 12 Hr. Decl	☿ Decl	☿ Lat	♀ Decl	♀ Lat	♂ Decl	♂ Lat	♃ Decl	♃ Lat	♄ Decl	♄ Lat
1	14S11	23S31	0S10	22S36	12S35	0N 2	25S52	6S 1	20S39	2S10	20N27	0N12	13S17	2N 9
2	14 31	21 25	0N55	19 58	11 53	0 22	25 43	5 56	20 27	2 8	20 27	0 13	13 19	2 8
3	14 50	18 16	1 58	16 20	11 15	0 41	25 33	5 50	20 15	2 6	20 27	0 13	13 21	2 8
4	15 9	14 11	2 58	11 51	10 41	0 59	25 22	5 43	20 2	2 5	20 26	0 13	13 23	2 8
5	15 27	9 19	3 51	6 39	10 12	1 15	25 10	5 36	19 50	2 3	20 26	0 13	13 26	2 8
6	15 45	3 51	4 32	0 57	9 49	1 29	24 56	5 28	19 37	2 1	20 25	0 13	13 28	2 8
7	16 3	1N60	4 58	4N58	9 32	1 41	24 41	5 20	19 24	1 59	20 25	0 13	13 30	2 8
8	16 21	7 55	5 7	10 48	9 21	1 52	24 25	5 11	19 11	1 58	20 25	0 13	13 32	2 8
9	16 39	13 33	4 54	16 7	9 15	2 1	24 8	5 1	18 58	1 56	20 25	0 14	13 34	2 8
10	16 56	18 26	4 21	20 26	9 14	2 8	23 50	4 50	18 45	1 54	20 25	0 14	13 36	2 8
11	17 13	22 5	3 29	23 20	9 19	2 13	23 31	4 39	18 31	1 53	20 24	0 14	13 39	2 8
12	17 30	24 9	2 23	24 30	9 28	2 17	23 11	4 27	18 17	1 51	20 24	0 14	13 41	2 8
13	17 46	24 25	1 7	23 54	9 41	2 19	22 49	4 14	18 4	1 49	20 24	0 14	13 43	2 8
14	18 2	22 60	0S11	21 43	9 58	2 20	22 28	4 1	17 50	1 47	20 24	0 14	13 45	2 8
15	18 18	20 9	1 26	18 18	10 17	2 20	22 5	3 47	17 36	1 46	20 24	0 15	13 47	2 8
16	18 33	16 15	2 34	14 1	10 40	2 19	21 42	3 33	17 22	1 44	20 25	0 15	13 49	2 8
17	18 48	11 40	3 32	9 13	11 4	2 17	21 18	3 19	17 7	1 42	20 25	0 15	13 51	2 8
18	19 3	6 42	4 17	4 9	11 30	2 14	20 54	3 4	16 53	1 41	20 25	0 15	13 54	2 8
19	19 17	1 36	4 48	0S57	11 58	2 10	20 30	2 49	16 38	1 39	20 25	0 15	13 56	2 8
20	19 31	3S28	5 6	5 56	12 27	2 6	20 6	2 33	16 23	1 38	20 25	0 15	13 58	2 8
21	19 45	8 19	5 10	10 37	12 57	2 2	19 42	2 18	16 8	1 36	20 26	0 16	13 60	2 8
22	19 58	12 49	5 0	14 53	13 28	1 57	19 18	2 2	15 53	1 34	20 26	0 16	14 2	2 8
23	20 11	16 48	4 37	18 33	13 59	1 51	18 55	1 47	15 38	1 33	20 26	0 16	14 4	2 9
24	20 24	20 7	4 3	21 28	14 30	1 45	18 32	1 31	15 23	1 31	20 27	0 16	14 6	2 9
25	20 36	22 35	3 18	23 28	15 1	1 39	18 9	1 16	15 8	1 29	20 27	0 16	14 8	2 9
26	20 48	24 4	2 24	24 25	15 32	1 33	17 48	1 1	14 52	1 28	20 28	0 17	14 10	2 9
27	20 59	24 28	1 23	24 15	16 3	1 26	17 27	0 46	14 36	1 26	20 28	0 17	14 12	2 9
28	21 11	23 44	0 18	22 56	16 34	1 19	17 7	0 31	14 21	1 25	20 29	0 17	14 14	2 9
29	21 21	21 52	0N48	20 32	17 4	1 12	16 48	0 16	14 5	1 23	20 30	0 17	14 16	2 9
30	21S31	18S58	1N53	17S10	17S34	1N 6	16S29	0S 2	13S49	1S22	20N30	0N17	14S18	2N 9

Day	♅ Decl	♅ Lat	♆ Decl	♆ Lat	♇ Decl	♇ Lat
1	21N 8	0N31	8S36	1N39	22N 3	10N 2
5	21 8	0 31	8 39	1 40	22 3	10 3
9	21 8	0 31	8 42	1 40	22 4	10 5
13	21 8	0 31	8 45	1 40	22 5	10 6
17	21 9	0 31	8 47	1 40	22 5	10 7
21	21 10	0 31	8 50	1 40	22 6	10 9
25	21 11	0 32	8 53	1 40	22 7	10 10
29	21N12	0N32	8S55	1N40	22N 8	10N12

☽ PHENOMENA

d	h	m	
3	20	55	☽
10	14	30	○
17	9	33	☾
25	12	31	●

d	h	° '
6	16	0
12	16	24N32
19	8	0
26	20	24S29

d	h	° '
1	4	0
7	22	5N 7
13	21	0
20	19	5S10
28	7	0

VOID OF COURSE ☽

Last Aspect	☽ Ingress
2 11pm39	3 ♒ 0am22
5 6am48	5 ♓ 7am35
7 10am22	7 ♈ 10am43
9 10am34	9 ♉ 10am49
11 9am40	11 ♊ 9am51
13 4am39	13 ♋ 10am 0
15 12pm57	15 ♌ 1pm 3
17 1pm56	17 ♍ 7pm53
20 5am54	20 ♎ 6am 3
22 6pm 0	22 ♏ 6pm13
25 6am41	25 ♐ 7am 2
27 1pm45	27 ♑ 7pm24
30 5am40	30 ♒ 6am20

d	h	
10	13	PERIGEE
23	23	APOGEE

DAILY ASPECTARIAN

1 M	☽⊻♂	3am34
	☉⚹☽	6 7
	☽⚼♇	12pm41
	☽⚹♄	12 47
	☽∠♀	5 31
	☽⋕♇	5 54
	♂⋕♃	11 44
2 T	☽⋕♅	2am33
	☽⋕♃	8 13
	☽∥♂	8 49
	☽□♆	5pm20
	☽⚻♇	5 55
	☽☍♅	8 0
	☽⚹♀	9 54
	☽☍♃	11 39
3 W	☽□☿	2am28
	♅SR	10 56
	☽☌♂	4pm50
	☉∥☽	7 9
	☉□☽	8 55
	☽□♄	10 52
4 Th	☽∥♄	4am10
	☿ ♎	2pm18
	☽∥☿	7 28
5 F	☿□♃	0am30
	☉☌♄	1 3
	☽△♆	1 11
	☽☍♇	1 38
	☽∥♆	3 6
	☽⚻♅	3 30
	☽□♀	3 48
	☽△☿	6 48
	☽⚻♃	7 4
	♀△♅	1pm40
6 S	☽⊻♂	1am36
	☽⚼♆	3 32
	☽△♄	4 52
	☽⚼♅	5 42
	☉△☽	6 46
	☽⚼☿	8 9
	☽⚼♃	9 12
7 Su	☽∠♂	4am13
	☽⚻♆	4 54
	☽⚻♇	5 14
	☽△♀	5 41
	☽⚼♄	6 21
	☽△♅	6 55
	☽⚻☿	8 58
	☉⚼☽	9 49
	☽△♃	10 22
	♀□♇	6pm42
	☿SD	9 41
8 M	♀⊻♆	3am 2
	☽⋕♆	3 8
	☽⚼♀	5 22
	☽⚼♇	5 44
	☽⋕☿	5 44
	☽⚹♂	5 54
	☽⚻♄	6 59
	☉⚻☽	11 54
9 T	☽⋕♄	0am 6
	☽⚻♀	4 27
	☽☍♆	5 23
	☽△♇	5 37
	☽□♅	7 11
	☽☍☿	9 25
	♂□♄	10 23
	☽□♃	10 34
	☉⋕☽	3pm35
10 W	☽⋕♂	1am41
	☽☍♄	6 45
	☽□♂	7 32
	☽∥♃	11 50
	☉☍☽	2pm30
	☽∥♅	4 46
	☽∥♇	11 49
11 Th	☽☍♀	1am52
	☽⚻♆	4 32
	☽□♇	4 41
	☿□♃	5 35
	☽⚹♅	6 12
	☽⚹♃	9 40
	☽⚻☿	9 50
	☿ ♏	10 23
	☽⋕♀	12pm11
12 F	☽⚼♆	4am19
	☽∠♅	5 56
	☽⚻♄	6 22
	☽△♂	9 4
	☽∠♃	9 30
	☽⚼☿	10 44
	☉⚻☽	5pm22
	☽⚻♀	11 51
13 S	☽△♆	4am34
	☽⚹♇	4 39
	☽⊻♅	6 10
	☽⚼♄	6 50
	☽⊻♃	9 52
	☽⚼♂	10 36
	☽△☿	12pm30
	☉∥♂	2 16
	☉⚼☽	7 46
	☽⚼♀	11 37
14 Su	☽∠♇	5am34
	☽⋕♀	6 22
	☽△♄	8 1
	☽∥♇	8 58
	☽⚻♂	12pm59
	☽∥♅	4 39
	♆⚹♇	7 4
	☽∥♃	10 8
	☉△☽	11 10
15 M	☽△♀	0am 6
	♀⋕♇	0 22
	☽⊻♇	7 21
	☽□♆	7 23
	☉☌♀	7 27
	☽☌♅	8 55
	☉⋕☽	11 19
	☽☌♃	12pm57
	☽⋕♂	5 16
	☽□☿	7 43
16 T	☽⋕♄	12pm57
	☽□♄	1 11
	☽☍♂	9 1
17 W	☽⋕☿	2am44
	♃SR	3 6
	☽□♀	3 34
	♀⋕♅	9 4
	☉□☽	9 33
	☽☌♇	1pm48
	☽⚹♆	1 56
	☽⋕♆	2 1
	☽⊻♅	3 23
	☽⊻♃	7 46
18 Th	☽⚹☿	8am39
	☽∠♆	6pm35
	☽∠♅	7 58
	☽⚹♄	10 11
19 F	☽∠♃	0am30
	♀⋕♃	5 4
	☽⚻♂	9 21
	☽⚹♀	10 14
	☉□♇	3pm41
	☽∠☿	5 8
	♀□♂	6 20
	☉⊻♆	7 3
	☽⊻♇	11 41
	☽⊻♆	11 58
20 S	☉⚹☽	0am24
	☽⚹♅	1 16
	☽∠♄	3 51
	☽⚹♃	5 54
	☉△♅	10 42
	☽∠♀	2pm32
	☽⚼♂	4 46
	☉∥♀	10 8
21 Su	☽⊻☿	2am37
	☽∥♆	2 39
	☽∠♇	5 32
	☉∠☽	9 0
	☽⊻♄	10 2
	☽⊻♀	7pm16
22 M	☽△♂	0am42
	☽∥☿	4 9
	☽∥♄	7 0
	☽⚹♇	11 44
	☽☌♆	12pm10
	☽□♅	1 15
	☽∥♂	5 3
	☉△♃	5 39
	☽□♃	6 0
	☉⊻☽	6 2
	☉ ♐	8 15
23 T	☿∥♄	4am23
	☽∥♀	1pm 7
	☿☌♄	10 28
	☽☌♄	11 16
	☽☌☿	11 23
24 W	☉∥☽	2am36
	☽⋕♃	2 49
	☽☌♀	5 33
	☉⋕♃	5 51
	☽⋕♅	9 19
	☽□♂	5pm17
	☽⋕♇	6 42
25 Th	☽□♇	0am32
	☽⊻♆	1 8
	☽△♅	1 58
	☿∥♂	3 21
	☽△♃	6 41
	☉☌☽	12pm31
	☿☌♀	3 17
26 F	☽∠♆	7am33
	☽⚼♅	8 15
	☽⊻♄	12pm36
	☽⚼♃	12 55
	☽⊻♀	4 11
	☽⊻☿	8 41
27 S	☽⚹♂	9am37
	☽△♇	1pm 1
	☽⚹♆	1 45
	☽⚻♅	2 19
	☽⚻♃	6 55
	☽∠♄	6 58
	☽∠♀	9 23
28 Su	☉⋕♅	2am32
	☉⊻☽	6 19
	☽∠☿	6 57
	♂∥♄	9 11
	☿∥♀	3pm45
	☽∠♂	5 18
	☽⚼♇	6 49
	☽⋕♇	9 14
	♇SR	11 36
29 M	☽⚹♄	0am58
	☽⚹♀	2 21
	☉∥☽	4 37
	☽⋕♅	6 19
	☽⋕♃	12pm20
	☉∠☽	2 31
	☽⚹☿	4 38
	♂☍♇	7 20
30 T	☽⚻♇	0am 9
	☽⊻♂	0 26
	☽□♆	1 0
	☽☍♅	1 18
	☽☍♃	5 40
	☽∥☿	8 18
	♂△♆	10 55
	♂⚻♅	3pm 2
	☽∥♀	5 24
	☉⚹☽	9 58

DECEMBER 1954

LONGITUDE

Day	Sid. Time	☉	☽	☽ 12 Hour	Mean ☊	True ☊	☿	♀	♂	♃	♄	♅	♆	♇
	h m s	° ' "	° ' "	° ' "	° '	° '	° '	° '	° '	° '	° '	° '	° '	° '
1	4 37 16	8♐ 15 29	9♒ 14 26	15♒ 35 56	7♑ 4	5♑ 43	24♏ 56	15♏ 10R	27♒ 39	29♋ 37R	15♏ 9	27♋ 22R	27♎ 16	26♌ 48R
2	4 41 13	9 16 19	22 2 0	28 33 6	7 0	5 45	26 28	14 59	28 21	29 35	15 16	27 21	27 18	26 48
3	4 45 9	10 17 10	5♓ 9 36	11♓ 51 50	6 57	5 46R	28 0	14 51	29 4	29 31	15 22	27 19	27 20	26 48
4	4 49 6	11 18 2	18 40 6	25 34 33	6 54	5 46	29 33	14 45	29 46	29 28	15 29	27 18	27 22	26 48
5	4 53 2	12 18 54	2♈ 35 17	9♈ 42 12	6 51	5 44	1♐ 5	14 41D	0♓ 29	29 25	15 36	27 16	27 23	26 47
6	4 56 59	13 19 47	16 55 6	24 13 32	6 48	5 42	2 38	14 40	1 12	29 21	15 43	27 15	27 25	26 47
7	5 0 55	14 20 41	1♉ 36 58	9♉ 4 37	6 45	5 40	4 11	14 41	1 54	29 17	15 49	27 13	27 27	26 47
8	5 4 52	15 21 37	16 35 34	24 8 46	6 41	5 37	5 44	14 45	2 37	29 13	15 56	27 11	27 29	26 47
9	5 8 48	16 22 32	1♊ 43 4	9♊ 17 15	6 38	5 34	7 17	14 51	3 20	29 9	16 2	27 9	27 30	26 46
10	5 12 45	17 23 29	16 50 7	24 20 28	6 35	5 33	8 51	15 0	4 3	29 5	16 9	27 8	27 32	26 46
11	5 16 42	18 24 26	1♋ 47 14	9♋ 9 28	6 32	5 32D	10 24	15 10	4 45	29 0	16 15	27 6	27 33	26 46
12	5 20 38	19 25 25	16 26 21	23 37 14	6 29	5 32	11 57	15 23	5 28	28 56	16 22	27 4	27 35	26 45
13	5 24 35	20 26 25	0♌ 41 42	7♌ 39 27	6 26	5 33	13 31	15 38	6 11	28 51	16 28	27 2	27 36	26 45
14	5 28 31	21 27 25	14 30 23	21 14 32	6 22	5 34	15 4	15 56	6 54	28 46	16 35	27 0	27 38	26 45
15	5 32 28	22 28 26	27 52 5	4♍ 23 19	6 19	5 35	16 38	16 15	7 37	28 41	16 41	26 58	27 39	26 44
16	5 36 24	23 29 28	10♍ 48 36	17 8 24	6 16	5 36	18 12	16 36	8 20	28 35	16 47	26 56	27 41	26 44
17	5 40 21	24 30 32	23 23 14	29 33 36	6 13	5 36R	19 46	16 59	9 3	28 30	16 53	26 54	27 42	26 43
18	5 44 17	25 31 36	5♎ 40 5	11♎ 43 15	6 10	5 36	21 20	17 24	9 46	28 24	17 0	26 52	27 44	26 43
19	5 48 14	26 32 41	17 43 39	23 41 51	6 6	5 36	22 54	17 50	10 29	28 18	17 6	26 50	27 45	26 42
20	5 52 11	27 33 47	29 38 23	5♏ 33 46	6 3	5 35	24 28	18 19	11 12	28 13	17 12	26 48	27 46	26 41
21	5 56 7	28 34 53	11♏ 28 28	17 22 57	6 0	5 34	26 2	18 49	11 55	28 6	17 18	26 46	27 48	26 41
22	6 0 4	29 36 1	23 17 38	29 12 54	5 57	5 33	27 37	19 20	12 38	28 0	17 24	26 43	27 49	26 40
23	6 4 0	0♑ 37 9	5♐ 9 6	11♐ 6 32	5 54	5 32	29 12	19 53	13 21	27 54	17 30	26 41	27 50	26 39
24	6 7 57	1 38 18	17 5 30	23 6 16	5 51	5 32	0♑ 47	20 28	14 4	27 47	17 36	26 39	27 52	26 39
25	6 11 53	2 39 27	29 9 2	5♑ 14 1	5 47	5 31	2 22	21 4	14 47	27 41	17 41	26 36	27 53	26 38
26	6 15 50	3 40 36	11♑ 21 24	17 31 22	5 44	5 31	3 58	21 41	15 30	27 34	17 47	26 34	27 54	26 37
27	6 19 47	4 41 46	23 44 3	29 59 37	5 41	5 31	5 33	22 20	16 13	27 27	17 53	26 32	27 55	26 37
28	6 23 43	5 42 56	6♒ 18 13	12♒ 39 59	5 38	5 31	7 9	23 0	16 56	27 20	17 59	26 29	27 56	26 36
29	6 27 40	6 44 6	19 5 5	25 33 40	5 35	5 31	8 46	23 41	17 39	27 13	18 4	26 27	27 57	26 35
30	6 31 36	7 45 16	2♓ 5 52	8♓ 41 49	5 32	5 31	10 22	24 23	18 22	27 6	18 10	26 25	27 58	26 34
31	6 35 33	8♑ 46 26	15♓ 21 41	22♓ 5 35	5♑ 28	5♑ 30	11♑ 59	25♏ 6	19♓ 6	26♋ 58	18♏ 15	26♋ 22	27♎ 59	26♌ 33

DECLINATION and LATITUDE

Day	☉ Decl	☽ Decl	☽ Lat	☽ 12 Hr. Decl	☿ Decl	☿ Lat	♀ Decl	♀ Lat	♂ Decl	♂ Lat	♃ Decl	♃ Lat	♄ Decl	♄ Lat
1	21S41	15S 9	2N54	12S57	18S 4	0N58	16S12	0N12	13S33	1S20	20N31	0N17	14S20	2N 9
2	21 51	10 34	3 48	8 3	18 32	0 51	15 56	0 25	13 17	1 18	20 32	0 18	14 22	2 9
3	21 60	5 25	4 31	2 40	19 0	0 44	15 41	0 38	13 0	1 17	20 33	0 18	14 23	2 9
4	22 8	0N 8	5 1	2N59	19 27	0 37	15 27	0 51	12 44	1 15	20 33	0 18	14 25	2 9
5	22 17	5 50	5 15	8 39	19 54	0 30	15 15	1 3	12 27	1 14	20 34	0 18	14 27	2 9
6	22 24	11 24	5 9	14 1	20 19	0 23	15 3	1 15	12 11	1 12	20 35	0 18	14 29	2 9
7	22 32	16 28	4 43	18 41	20 44	0 16	14 53	1 26	11 54	1 11	20 36	0 18	14 31	2 9
8	22 38	20 36	3 58	22 11	21 8	0 9	14 43	1 37	11 37	1 9	20 37	0 19	14 33	2 9
9	22 45	23 23	2 56	24 9	21 30	0 2	14 35	1 47	11 21	1 8	20 38	0 19	14 35	2 9
10	22 51	24 29	1 42	24 21	21 52	0S 5	14 28	1 57	11 4	1 6	20 39	0 19	14 36	2 10
11	22 56	23 47	0 21	22 48	22 13	0 12	14 22	2 7	10 47	1 5	20 40	0 19	14 38	2 10
12	23 1	21 26	0S60	19 46	22 32	0 19	14 17	2 16	10 30	1 4	20 42	0 19	14 40	2 10
13	23 6	17 49	2 15	15 38	22 51	0 26	14 13	2 24	10 12	1 2	20 43	0 19	14 42	2 10
14	23 10	13 18	3 19	10 50	23 8	0 32	14 10	2 33	9 55	1 1	20 44	0 20	14 43	2 10
15	23 14	8 17	4 11	5 41	23 25	0 39	14 9	2 40	9 38	0 59	20 45	0 20	14 45	2 10
16	23 17	3 4	4 48	0 28	23 40	0 45	14 7	2 48	9 21	0 58	20 46	0 20	14 47	2 10
17	23 20	2S 7	5 10	4S39	23 54	0 51	14 7	2 54	9 3	0 57	20 48	0 20	14 48	2 10
18	23 22	7 6	5 17	9 28	24 6	0 57	14 8	3 1	8 46	0 55	20 49	0 20	14 50	2 10
19	23 24	11 44	5 10	13 52	24 18	1 3	14 10	3 7	8 28	0 54	20 50	0 20	14 52	2 10
20	23 25	15 52	4 50	17 42	24 28	1 8	14 12	3 13	8 11	0 52	20 52	0 21	14 53	2 10
21	23 26	19 21	4 17	20 48	24 37	1 14	14 15	3 18	7 53	0 51	20 53	0 21	14 55	2 11
22	23 27	22 3	3 34	23 3	24 44	1 19	14 18	3 23	7 35	0 50	20 55	0 21	14 56	2 11
23	23 27	23 48	2 41	24 17	24 51	1 24	14 23	3 28	7 17	0 48	20 56	0 21	14 58	2 11
24	23 26	24 29	1 41	24 24	24 55	1 29	14 28	3 32	6 60	0 47	20 57	0 21	14 59	2 11
25	23 25	24 2	0 35	23 22	24 59	1 34	14 33	3 36	6 42	0 46	20 59	0 22	15 1	2 11
26	23 24	22 25	0N32	21 12	25 1	1 38	14 39	3 40	6 24	0 44	21 0	0 22	15 2	2 11
27	23 22	19 44	1 39	18 1	25 2	1 42	14 46	3 43	6 6	0 43	21 2	0 22	15 4	2 11
28	23 19	16 4	2 43	13 56	25 1	1 46	14 53	3 46	5 48	0 42	21 3	0 22	15 5	2 11
29	23 16	11 38	3 39	9 11	24 59	1 50	14 60	3 49	5 30	0 40	21 5	0 22	15 7	2 12
30	23 13	6 36	4 25	3 56	24 55	1 53	15 8	3 51	5 12	0 39	21 7	0 22	15 8	2 12
31	23S 9	1S11	4N58	1N36	24S50	1S56	15S16	3N54	4S54	0S38	21N 8	0N22	15S 9	2N12

Day	♅ Decl	♅ Lat	♆ Decl	♆ Lat	♇ Decl	♇ Lat
1	21N13	0N32	8S57	1N40	22N 9	10N13
5	21 14	0 32	8 59	1 40	22 11	10 14
9	21 15	0 32	9 1	1 41	22 12	10 16
13	21 17	0 32	9 3	1 41	22 14	10 17
17	21 18	0 32	9 5	1 41	22 16	10 18
21	21 20	0 32	9 7	1 41	22 18	10 20
25	21 22	0 32	9 9	1 41	22 20	10 21
29	21N24	0N32	9S10	1N42	22N23	10N22

☽ PHENOMENA

d	h	m	
3	9	56	☽
10	0	57	○
17	2	22	☾
25	7	34	● ecl.

d	h	° '
3	23	0
10	3	24N29
16	14	0
24	3	24S30
31	5	0

d	h	° '
5	5	5N15
11	6	0
18	0	5S17
25	13	0

VOID OF COURSE ☽

Last Aspect	☽ Ingress
2 12pm18	2 ♓ 2pm39
4 6pm37	4 ♈ 7pm35
6 8pm15	6 ♉ 9pm23
8 7pm57	8 ♊ 9pm17
10 5pm 9	10 ♋ 9pm 7
12 8pm52	12 ♌ 10pm49
14 11pm37	15 ♍ 3am54
17 9am51	17 ♎ 12pm52
19 9pm 8	20 ♏ 0am44
22 9am28	22 ♐ 1pm35
24 9pm29	25 ♑ 1am41
27 8am 3	27 ♒ 12pm 1
29 4pm26	29 ♓ 8pm10

d	h	
9	2	PERIGEE
21	9	APOGEE

DAILY ASPECTARIAN

1 W	♀☌♄	1am37
	☽∥♄	4 33
	☽∥♂	9 23
	☽□♀	11 2
	☽□♄	11 15
2 Th	☿□♇	5am11
	☽∥♆	7 45
	☽☍♇	8 47
	☽□☿	9 16
	☽△♆	9 44
	☽⚻♅	9 47
	☽☌♂	12pm18
	☿⚺♆	1 21
	☿△♅	1 33
	☽⚻♃	1 49
	♅□♆	6 53
3 F	☉□☽	9am56
	☽⚼♅	12pm47
	☽⚼♆	12 52
	♂⚻♃	2 32
	☽⚼♃	4 39
	☽△♀	5 9
	☽△♄	6 22
	☿△♃	10 52
4 S	☉⋕♇	5am32
	☿□♂	6 30
	☿ ♐	7 3
	♂ ♓	7 41
	☽⚻♇	2pm 5
	☽△♅	2 56
	☽⚻♆	3 6
	☽△♃	6 37
	☽⚼♀	7 4
	☽⚺♂	8 14
	☽⚼♄	8 35
	☽△☿	9 8
	☉⚼♅	10 58
5 Su	☉∠♆	1am52
	☽⋕♆	1pm26
	☽⚼♇	3 29
	☉△☽	5 36
	☽⚻♀	8 16
	☽⚻♄	9 59
	♀SD	10 39
	☽∠♂	10 44
6 M	☽⚼☿	1am20
	☽⋕♂	3 19
	☽⋕♄	2pm17
	☿⋕♃	4 8
	☽△♇	4 10
	☽⋕♀	4 21
	☽□♅	4 53
	☽☍♆	5 14
	☉⚼☽	8 3
	☽□♃	8 15
	☉⚼♃	10 48
7 T	☽⚹♂	0am29
	☽⚻☿	4 38
	☉⚺♀	8 35
	☽☍♀	9pm 3
	☉⚻☽	9 54
	☽☍♄	10 56
8 W	☽∥♃	0am 7
	☽⋕☿	4 11
	☽∥♅	4 35
	☿⋕♅	7 41
	☽∥♇	12pm 9
	☉⚺♄	3 6
	☽□♇	4 10
	☽⚹♅	4 47
	☉⋕☽	4 50
	☽⚻♆	5 19
	☽⚹♃	7 57
9 Th	♀∥♄	1am39
	☽□♂	2 41
	☽☍☿	9 51
	☽∠♅	4pm32
	☽⚼♆	5 8
	☽∠♃	7 38
	☽⚻♀	9 2
	☽⚻♄	10 54
10 F	☉☍☽	0am57
	☽⚹♇	3pm54
	☽⚺♅	4 27
	☽△♆	5 9
	☽⚺♃	7 32
	☽⚼♀	9 21
	☽⚼♄	11 8
11 S	☿⋕♇	0am26
	☽△♂	5 4
	☉⋕☽	10 5
	☽⋕☿	3pm33
	☽⚻☿	3 43
	☽∠♇	4 16
	☽∥♇	5 25
	☽△♀	10 14
	☽△♄	11 53
12 Su	☽∥♅	1am18
	☿⚼♅	1 40
	☉⚻☽	5 21
	☽∥♃	5 35
	☽⚼♂	7 4
	☿∠♆	9 49
	☽⚺♇	5pm17
	☽☌♅	5 47
	☽□♆	6 44
	☽⚼☿	7 49
	☽☌♃	8 52
13 M	☿⚼♃	4am55
	☉⚼☽	8 48
	☽⚻♂	9 58
	☽⋕♄	4pm51
	☽⋕♀	7 34
14 T	☽△☿	1am 8
	☽□♀	2 34
	☉∥☿	3 11
	☽□♄	3 42
	☉△☽	1pm25
	☿⚺♀	4 27
	☽⋕♂	5 20
	☽⋕♆	8 21
	☽☌♇	9 56
	☽⚺♅	10 22
	☽⚹♆	11 37
15 W	☿⚺♄	0am49
	☽⚺♃	1 28
	☽☍♂	7pm 4
16 Th	☽∠♅	2am 7
	☽∠♆	3 32
	☽∠♃	5 13
	☽⚹♀	11 18
	☽⚹♄	11 25
	☽□☿	4pm 1
	♀☌♄	4 28
	♂∥♆	9 12
17 F	☉□☽	2am22
	☽⚺♇	6 27
	☽⚹♅	6 48
	☽⚺♆	8 24
	☽⚹♃	9 51
	☽∠♄	4pm42
	☽∠♀	5 20
18 S	☽∥♂	7am53
	☽⚻♂	8 37
	☽∥♆	10 5
	☽∠♇	11 58
	☽⚺♄	10pm43
19 Su	☽⚺♀	0am14
	☉△♇	3 39
	☉⚻♅	6 32
	☽⚹☿	11 57
	☽∥♀	1pm49
	☽⚼♂	4 35
	☽∥♄	5 59
	☽⚹♇	6 3
	☽□♅	6 16
	☉⚹☽	7 24
	☽☌♆	8 13
	☽□♃	9 8
20 M	☉⚹♆	5am 5
	☉⚻♃	1pm50
	♂⚼♅	7 9
	☽∠☿	10 59
21 T	☽△♂	0am57
	☉∠☽	4 41
	☿△♇	9 41
	☿⚻♅	10 42
	☽☌♄	11 56
	☽⋕♃	12pm49
	☽☌♀	3 36
	☽⋕♅	4 56
22 W	☽⋕♇	2am56
	☿⚹♆	3 5
	☿⚻♃	5 30
	♂⚼♆	6 30
	☽□♇	6 50
	☽△♅	6 56
	☽⚺♆	9 11
	☉ ♑	9 25
	☽△♃	9 28
	☽⚺☿	10 7
	♂⚼♃	10 55
	☉⚺☽	1pm59
	☉∥☽	5 48
23 Th	♃□♆	10am52
	☿ ♑	12pm10
	☽⚼♅	1 7
	☽⚼♃	3 27
	☽∠♆	3 30
	☽□♂	5 33
24 F	♅⚺♇	0am 3
	☽⚺♄	1 1
	☽⚺♀	7 6
	☽⚻♅	6pm59
	☽△♇	7 1
	☽⚻♃	9 7
	☽⚹♆	9 29
25 S	☉∠♄	0am52
	☿∠♄	5 11
	☽∠♄	7 3
	☽☌☿	7 19
	☉☌☽	7 34
	☉∥☽	11 23
	☉☌☿	12pm 8
	☽∠♀	2 22
26 Su	☽⚼♇	0am31
	☽⋕♇	0 48
	☽⚹♂	8 34
	☽⋕♅	10 25
	☽⚹♄	12pm37
	☽⋕♃	1 35
	☽⚹♀	9 9
27 M	☽☍♅	5am21
	☽⚻♇	5 31
	☽☍♃	7 4
	☽□♆	8 3
	☽∠♂	3pm12
	☉⚺☽	10 47
28 T	☽⚺☿	1am51
	☽∥♄	5 38
	☽∥♀	6 40
	☽⚺♂	9pm11
	☿∠♀	9 45
	☽□♄	10 6
29 W	☉∠☽	5am21
	☽□♀	9 0
	☽∠☿	9 54
	☽∥♆	12pm 2
	☽⚻♅	1 36
	☽☍♇	1 52
	☽⚻♃	2 55
	♂△♄	3 50
	☽△♆	4 26
30 Th	♀∥♄	0am54
	☽∥♂	6 42
	☉⚹☽	11 9
	☽⚼♅	4pm51
	☽⚹☿	5 6
	☿⚼♇	5 37
	☽⚼♃	5 58
	☽⚼♆	7 44
31 F	☽△♄	5am12
	☽☌♂	7 2
	☽△♀	6pm19
	☽△♅	7 30
	☽⚻♇	7 52
	☽△♃	8 26
	☽⚻♆	10 26

JANUARY 1955

LONGITUDE

Day	Sid. Time	☉	☽	☽ 12 Hour	Mean ☊	True ☊	☿	♀	♂	♃	♄	♅	♆	♇
	h m s	° ' "	° ' "	° ' "	° '	° '	° '	° '	° '	° '	° '	° '	° '	° '
1	6 39 29	9♑ 47 36	28♓ 53 35	5♈ 45 47	5♑ 25	5♑ 30	13♑ 36	25♏ 50	19♓ 49	26♋ 51R	18♏ 20	26♋ 20R	28♎ 0	26♌ 32R
2	6 43 26	10 48 45	12♈ 42 11	19 42 44	5 22	5 30	15 14	26 35	20 32	26 44	18 26	26 17	28 1	26 31
3	6 47 22	11 49 54	26 47 19	3♉ 55 46	5 19	5 30	16 52	27 22	21 15	26 36	18 31	26 15	28 2	26 30
4	6 51 19	12 51 3	11♉ 7 45	18 22 54	5 16	5 31	18 30	28 9	21 58	26 28	18 36	26 12	28 3	26 29
5	6 55 16	13 52 13	25 40 44	3♊ 0 38	5 12	5 32	20 8	28 57	22 41	26 21	18 41	26 10	28 4	26 28
6	6 59 12	14 53 21	10♊ 21 56	17 43 53	5 9	5 32	21 47	29 46	23 24	26 13	18 46	26 7	28 5	26 27
7	7 3 9	15 54 29	25 5 38	2♋ 26 20	5 6	5 33R	23 26	0♐ 36	24 7	26 5	18 51	26 5	28 6	26 26
8	7 7 5	16 55 37	9♋ 45 8	17 1 12	5 3	5 33	25 5	1 26	24 50	25 57	18 56	26 2	28 6	26 25
9	7 11 2	17 56 45	24 13 43	1♌ 22 0	5 0	5 32	26 44	2 18	25 34	25 49	19 1	26 0	28 7	26 24
10	7 14 58	18 57 53	8♌ 25 26	15 23 30	4 57	5 31	28 24	3 10	26 17	25 41	19 6	25 57	28 8	26 23
11	7 18 55	19 59 0	22 15 52	29 2 16	4 53	5 29	0♒ 4	4 3	27 0	25 33	19 10	25 54	28 8	26 22
12	7 22 51	21 0 7	5♍ 42 38	12♍ 16 59	4 50	5 27	1 44	4 56	27 43	25 25	19 15	25 52	28 9	26 21
13	7 26 48	22 1 15	18 45 28	25 8 20	4 47	5 25	3 23	5 50	28 26	25 17	19 20	25 49	28 10	26 20
14	7 30 45	23 2 22	1♎ 25 56	7♎ 38 41	4 44	5 23	5 3	6 45	29 9	25 9	19 24	25 47	28 10	26 19
15	7 34 41	24 3 28	13 47 6	19 51 43	4 41	5 22D	6 42	7 41	29 52	25 1	19 28	25 44	28 11	26 17
16	7 38 38	25 4 35	25 53 6	1♏ 51 52	4 38	5 22	8 21	8 37	0♈ 35	24 53	19 33	25 41	28 11	26 16
17	7 42 34	26 5 41	7♏ 48 38	13 44 0	4 34	5 22	9 59	9 33	1 18	24 45	19 37	25 39	28 12	26 15
18	7 46 31	27 6 48	19 38 36	25 33 3	4 31	5 24	11 36	10 31	2 1	24 37	19 41	25 36	28 12	26 14
19	7 50 27	28 7 54	1♐ 27 54	7♐ 23 44	4 28	5 25	13 13	11 28	2 44	24 29	19 45	25 33	28 12	26 12
20	7 54 24	29 8 59	13 21 3	19 20 20	4 25	5 27	14 48	12 27	3 27	24 21	19 49	25 31	28 13	26 11
21	7 58 20	0♒ 10 4	25 22 2	1♑ 26 31	4 22	5 28R	16 21	13 25	4 10	24 13	19 53	25 28	28 13	26 10
22	8 2 17	1 11 9	7♑ 34 8	13 45 8	4 18	5 29	17 52	14 24	4 53	24 5	19 57	25 26	28 13	26 9
23	8 6 14	2 12 13	19 59 45	26 18 7	4 15	5 28	19 20	15 24	5 36	23 57	20 0	25 23	28 14	26 7
24	8 10 10	3 13 17	2♒ 40 19	9♒ 6 22	4 12	5 25	20 46	16 24	6 19	23 49	20 4	25 20	28 14	26 6
25	8 14 7	4 14 19	15 36 16	22 9 53	4 9	5 22	22 7	17 24	7 1	23 41	20 8	25 18	28 14	26 5
26	8 18 3	5 15 21	28 47 7	5♓ 27 48	4 6	5 17	23 25	18 25	7 44	23 33	20 11	25 15	28 14	26 3
27	8 22 0	6 16 22	12♓ 11 43	18 58 39	4 3	5 12	24 37	19 26	8 27	23 26	20 14	25 13	28 14	26 2
28	8 25 56	7 17 21	25 48 23	2♈ 40 42	3 59	5 7	25 43	20 28	9 10	23 18	20 18	25 10	28 14	26 0
29	8 29 53	8 18 20	9♈ 35 21	16 32 8	3 56	5 3	26 43	21 30	9 53	23 10	20 21	25 8	28 14R	25 59
30	8 33 49	9 19 17	23 30 51	0♉ 31 19	3 53	5 0	27 36	22 32	10 36	23 3	20 24	25 5	28 14	25 58
31	8 37 46	10♒ 20 13	7♉ 33 22	14♉ 36 49	3♑ 50	4♑ 59D	28♒ 20	23♐ 35	11♈ 18	22♋ 56	20♏ 27	25♋ 3	28♎ 14	25♌ 56

DECLINATION and LATITUDE

Day	☉	☽		☽ 12 Hr.	☿		♀		♂		♃		♄	
	Decl	Decl	Lat	Decl	Decl	Lat	Decl	Lat	Decl	Lat	Decl	Lat	Decl	Lat
1	23S 5	4N23	5N15	7N 9	24S43	1S59	15S24	3N55	4S36	0S37	21N10	0N23	15S11	2N12
2	23 0	9 51	5 15	12 27	24 35	2 1	15 33	3 57	4 18	0 35	21 11	0 23	15 12	2 12
3	22 55	14 56	4 56	17 12	24 25	2 3	15 42	3 59	3 60	0 34	21 13	0 23	15 13	2 12
4	22 49	19 16	4 18	21 2	24 14	2 5	15 51	3 60	3 42	0 33	21 15	0 23	15 15	2 12
5	22 43	22 29	3 24	23 34	24 1	2 6	16 1	4 1	3 23	0 32	21 16	0 23	15 16	2 13
6	22 37	24 14	2 15	24 30	23 46	2 7	16 10	4 1	3 5	0 31	21 18	0 23	15 17	2 13
7	22 30	24 19	0 58	23 43	23 30	2 8	16 20	4 2	2 47	0 29	21 19	0 24	15 18	2 13
8	22 22	22 42	0S23	21 19	23 13	2 8	16 30	4 2	2 29	0 28	21 21	0 24	15 19	2 13
9	22 14	19 36	1 42	17 37	22 54	2 7	16 40	4 2	2 11	0 27	21 23	0 24	15 21	2 13
10	22 6	15 23	2 52	12 59	22 33	2 7	16 50	4 2	1 53	0 26	21 24	0 24	15 22	2 13
11	21 57	10 27	3 51	7 50	22 11	2 5	17 0	4 2	1 34	0 25	21 26	0 24	15 23	2 13
12	21 48	5 10	4 35	2 28	21 47	2 3	17 10	4 1	1 16	0 23	21 27	0 24	15 24	2 14
13	21 39	0S12	5 3	2S50	21 22	2 1	17 20	4 0	0 58	0 22	21 29	0 24	15 25	2 14
14	21 29	5 23	5 15	7 52	20 55	1 58	17 31	3 59	0 40	0 21	21 31	0 25	15 26	2 14
15	21 18	10 14	5 13	12 29	20 27	1 54	17 41	3 58	0 22	0 20	21 32	0 25	15 27	2 14
16	21 7	14 36	4 56	16 33	19 57	1 50	17 50	3 57	0 4	0 19	21 34	0 25	15 28	2 14
17	20 56	18 19	4 27	19 54	19 26	1 45	18 0	3 56	0N15	0 18	21 35	0 25	15 29	2 15
18	20 44	21 17	3 47	22 26	18 54	1 39	18 10	3 54	0 33	0 17	21 37	0 25	15 30	2 15
19	20 32	23 21	2 57	23 60	18 21	1 33	18 19	3 52	0 51	0 16	21 39	0 25	15 31	2 15
20	20 20	24 23	1 59	24 29	17 46	1 26	18 29	3 51	1 9	0 15	21 40	0 25	15 32	2 15
21	20 7	24 17	0 55	23 48	17 11	1 18	18 38	3 49	1 27	0 14	21 42	0 25	15 33	2 15
22	19 54	23 2	0N11	21 59	16 35	1 9	18 47	3 47	1 45	0 12	21 43	0 26	15 33	2 15
23	19 40	20 39	1 19	19 4	15 58	0 59	18 56	3 44	2 3	0 11	21 45	0 26	15 34	2 16
24	19 26	17 14	2 24	15 11	15 21	0 49	19 4	3 42	2 21	0 10	21 46	0 26	15 35	2 16
25	19 12	12 56	3 22	10 31	14 44	0 38	19 12	3 39	2 39	0 9	21 48	0 26	15 36	2 16
26	18 58	7 58	4 11	5 18	14 7	0 25	19 20	3 37	2 57	0 8	21 49	0 26	15 36	2 16
27	18 43	2 33	4 47	0N14	13 31	0 12	19 28	3 34	3 14	0 7	21 51	0 26	15 37	2 16
28	18 27	3N 3	5 8	5 50	12 55	0N 2	19 35	3 31	3 32	0 6	21 52	0 26	15 38	2 17
29	18 12	8 34	5 11	11 12	12 21	0 17	19 42	3 28	3 50	0 5	21 53	0 26	15 38	2 17
30	17 56	13 43	4 56	16 3	11 48	0 32	19 49	3 25	4 8	0 4	21 55	0 26	15 39	2 17
31	17S39	18N11	4N23	20N 3	11S18	0N48	19S55	3N22	4N25	0S 3	21N56	0N27	15S40	2N17

Day	♅		♆		♇	
	Decl	Lat	Decl	Lat	Decl	Lat
1	21N25	0N32	9S11	1N42	22N24	10N23
5	21 27	0 33	9 12	1 42	22 27	10 24
9	21 29	0 33	9 13	1 42	22 29	10 26
13	21 31	0 33	9 14	1 43	22 32	10 27
17	21 33	0 33	9 14	1 43	22 35	10 28
21	21 35	0 33	9 14	1 43	22 37	10 28
25	21 37	0 33	9 14	1 43	22 40	10 29
29	21N39	0N33	9S14	1N44	22N43	10N30

☽ PHENOMENA	VOID OF COURSE ☽ Last Aspect	☽ Ingress
d h m	31 8pm26	1 ♈ 1am56
1 20 29 ☽	3 2am 6	3 ♉ 5am25
8 12 45 ○	5 5am40	5 ♊ 7am 5
15 22 14 ☾	7 4am54	7 ♋ 8am 1
24 1 7 ●	9 6am32	9 ♌ 9am42
31 5 6 ☽	11 10am24	11 ♍ 1pm43
	13 7pm22	13 ♎ 9pm15
d h ° '	16 4am37	16 ♏ 8am15
6 13 24N30	18 4pm36	18 ♐ 9pm 2
12 23 0	21 5am39	21 ♑ 9am10
20 10 24S29	23 3pm39	23 ♒ 6pm59
27 11 0	25 11pm 1	26 ♓ 2am11
	27 10pm53	28 ♈ 7am20
	30 8am 6	30 ♉ 11am 6
1 12 5N18		
7 17 0	d h	
14 8 5S16	6 9 PERIGEE	
21 20 0	18 3 APOGEE	
28 16 5N12		

DAILY ASPECTARIAN

1 S	☽#♂	0am53
	☽⚼♄	7 50
	♀△♅	2pm55
	☉□☽	8 29
	☽#♆	9 1
	♀□♇	9 53
	☽⚼♇	9 58
	☽⚼♀	9 58
2 Su	♀△♃	3am38
	☽□☿	4 55
	☽⊼♄	9 52
	☽⊻♂	2pm 7
	☉⚼♇	4 27
	☽□♅	11 5
	☽△♇	11 31
	☽□♃	11 41
3 M	☽⊼♀	1am 1
	☽#♄	1 30
	☽☍♆	2 6
	☽#♀	4 6
	☽∠♂	4pm43
	♃⊻♇	8 16
	♀⊻♆	8 59
4 T	☿⚹♄	1am39
	☉△☽	3 4
	☽☍♄	12pm26
	☽∥♃	1 42
	☽△☿	1 44
	☽∥♅	3 12
	☽⚹♂	6 50
	☽∥♇	11 42
5 W	☽⚹♅	0am47
	☽⚹♃	1 5
	☽□♇	1 18
	☉#☽	2 16
	☽⊼♆	3 55
	☉⚼☽	5 37
	☽☍♀	5 40
	☉∠♀	9 15
	☽#☿	4pm23
	☽⚼☿	5 25
6 Th	☽∠♅	1am14
	☽∠♃	1 22
	☽⚼♆	4 26
	♀ ♐	6 48
	☉⊼☽	7 55
	☽⊼♄	1pm46
	☽⊼☿	8 57
	☽□♂	10 20
7 F	☽⊻♃	1am36
	☽⊻♅	1 36
	♃☌♅	1 59
	☽⚹♇	2 12
	☉#♇	4 54
	☽△♆	4 54
	☽⊼♀	9 32
	☽⚼♄	2pm24
	☽#☿	5 26
	☿⚹♂	5 45
8 S	☽∥♇	2am 7
	☽∠♇	2 45
	☉#☽	3 17
	☽∥♅	10 41
	☽∥♃	11 38
	☿☍♃	11 40
	☽⚼♀	11 44
	☉☍☽	12pm45
	☿☍♅	1 25
	☽△♄	3 16
	☿⊼♇	7 10
9 Su	☽△♂	2am21
	☽☌♃	2 39
	☽☌♅	2 57
	☽⊻♇	3 38
	☽☍☿	4 46
	☽□♆	6 32
	♂△♃	7 26
	♂△♅	1pm40
	☽△♀	2 27
	☽#♀	4 36
	☿□♆	8 2
10 M	☽#♄	0am 8
	☿#♇	3 17
	☉⚹♄	3 22
	♂⊼♇	3 33
	☽⚼♂	5 10
	☽□♄	6pm33
	☉⊼☽	7 41
	☿ ♒	11 5
11 T	☽#♆	5am41
	☽⊻♃	5 45
	☽⊻♅	6 25
	☽☌♇	7 14
	☽⊼♂	8 50
	☽⚹♆	10 24
	☽⊼☿	3pm48
	☉∥☿	10 11
	☽□♀	10 30
12 W	☉⚼☽	0am34
	☽∠♃	8 30
	☽∠♅	9 22
	☽∠♆	1pm37
	♂⊼♆	2 52
	☿#♅	3 23
	☿#♃	5 40
	☽#♂	6 26
	☽⚼☿	11 12
13 Th	☽⚹♄	1am 4
	☽∥♂	3 18
	☉△☽	6 39
	☽⚹♃	12pm 9
	☽⚹♅	1 15
	☽⊻♇	2 14
	☉#♅	4 59
	☽⊻♆	5 45
	☽☍♂	7 22
	☉#♃	7 52
14 F	☽∠♄	5am45
	☽△☿	8 2
	☽⚹♀	11 6
	☽∥♆	6pm50
	☽∠♇	7 7
	♃∥♅	11 42
15 S	♂ ♈	4am34
	☽⊻♄	11 18
	☽∠♀	7pm 5
	☉☍♃	8 1
	☽□♃	10 1
	☉□☽	10 14
	☽□♅	11 37
16 Su	☽⚹♇	0am46
	☽☌♆	4 37
	☽∥♄	5 16
	☿⚹♀	9 8
	☽⊼♂	10 1
	☉☍♅	1pm51
	☽∥♀	9 39
17 M	☉⊼♇	3am33
	☽⊻♀	3 51
	♀⚼♃	4 16
	☽□☿	5 6
	☽∥☿	7 5
	☽⚼♂	6pm19
	☉∥☽	7 23
18 T	☽☌♄	0am 5
	♀⚼♅	2 11
	☽#♅	2 43
	☽#♃	3 17
	☽△♃	9 59
	☽△♅	12pm 4
	☽□♇	1 21
	☽#♇	1 55
	☉⚹☽	4 36
	☽⊻♆	5 23
19 W	☿∥♀	0am38
	☉□♆	1 48
	☽△♂	2 44
	☽⚼♃	4pm 2
	☽⚼♅	6 19
	☽☌♀	10 1
	☽∠♆	11 43
20 Th	☉∠☽	1am45
	☽⚹☿	3 20
	☽⊻♄	1pm 2
	♀∠♆	7 4
	☉ ♒	8 3
	☽⊼♃	9 44
21 F	☽⊼♅	0am12
	☽△♇	1 35
	☽⚹♆	5 39
	☉⊻☽	10 21
	☽∠☿	1pm30
	☽□♂	6 25
	☽∠♄	6 51
22 S	♂⚼♄	2am30
	☽#♇	4 58
	☽⚼♇	6 56
	☽⊻♀	2pm25
	☽#♃	2 26
	☽#♅	3 42
	☽⊻☿	10 35
23 Su	☽⚹♄	0am 1
	☽☍♃	7 27
	☉∥☽	8 11
	☽☍♅	10 14
	☽⊼♇	11 38
	☿□♄	11 38
	☽∥♀	12pm26
	☿∥♄	3 7
	☽□♆	3 39
	☽∠♀	9 24
24 M	☉☌☽	1am 7
	☽⚹♂	7 12
	☽∥♄	9 43
	☽∥☿	12pm55
	☿∠♂	8 7
	☉∥♀	11 46
25 T	☽⚹♀	3am35
	☽□♄	8 19
	☽∠♂	12pm25
	☽☌☿	1 14
	☽⊼♃	2 37
	☽⊼♅	5 38
	☽∥♆	6 5
	☽☍♇	7 4
	☽△♆	11 1
26 W	☿⊼♃	2am32
	☉⊻☽	12pm35
	☽⊻♂	4 58
	☽⚼♃	5 22
	☽⚼♅	8 29
	☽#♂	9 11
27 Th	☽⚼♆	1am51
	☿⊼♅	12pm11
	☽□♀	1 51
	☽△♄	2 17
	☉∠☽	5 20
	☽△♃	7 39
	♀⊻♄	7 47
	☽△♅	10 53
	☽⊻☿	11 51
28 F	☽⊼♇	0am21
	☽∥♂	2 14
	☽⊼♆	4 16
	☿☍♇	6 23
	☽⚼♄	4pm37
	☉⚹☽	9 36
29 S	☽☌♂	0am32
	☽⚼♇	2 25
	☽#♆	3 1
	☽∠☿	3 57
	☽#☿	3pm41
	☽⊼♄	6 38
	♆SR	7 24
	☽△♀	10 11
	☽□♃	11 13
30 Su	☽□♅	2am41
	☽△♇	4 11
	☽⚹☿	7 24
	☽☍♆	8 6
	☽#♄	9 54
	♀⊼♃	10 34
	♂⚼♇	11 55
	☿△♆	8pm52
	☉#☽	9 6
31 M	☽⚼♀	1am53
	☉□☽	5 6
	☽⊻♂	6 43
	☽#♀	11 26
	☽☍♄	9pm58

FEBRUARY 1955

LONGITUDE

Day	Sid. Time	☉	☽	☽ 12 Hour	Mean ☊	True ☊	☿	♀	♂	♃	♄	♅	♆	♇
	h m s	° ' "	° ' "	° ' "	° '	° '	° '	° '	° '	° '	° '	° '	° '	° '
1	8 41 43	11♒ 21 8	21♉ 41 30	28♉ 47 13	3♑ 47	5♑ 0	28♒ 55	24♐ 38	12♈ 1	22♋ 48R	20♏ 30	25♋ 0R	28♎ 14R	25♌ 55R
2	8 45 39	12 22 2	5♊ 53 47	13♊ 0 56	3 43	5 1	29 20	25 41	12 44	22 41	20 33	24 58	28 14	25 53
3	8 49 36	13 22 54	20 8 23	27 15 50	3 40	5 2R	29 35R	26 44	13 27	22 34	20 35	24 55	28 14	25 52
4	8 53 32	14 23 45	4♋ 22 54	11♋ 29 10	3 37	5 3	29 39	27 48	14 9	22 27	20 38	24 53	28 14	25 50
5	8 57 29	15 24 34	18 34 9	25 37 22	3 34	5 2	29 32	28 52	14 52	22 20	20 40	24 50	28 14	25 49
6	9 1 25	16 25 22	2♌ 38 19	9♌ 36 28	3 31	4 59	29 14	29 57	15 35	22 13	20 43	24 48	28 14	25 48
7	9 5 22	17 26 9	16 31 20	23 22 26	3 28	4 54	28 45	1♑ 1	16 17	22 6	20 45	24 46	28 13	25 46
8	9 9 18	18 26 55	0♍ 9 22	6♍ 51 48	3 24	4 47	28 6	2 6	17 0	22 0	20 47	24 43	28 13	25 45
9	9 13 15	19 27 39	13 29 28	20 2 14	3 21	4 39	27 18	3 11	17 42	21 53	20 49	24 41	28 13	25 43
10	9 17 12	20 28 22	26 30 1	2♎ 52 53	3 18	4 31	26 23	4 17	18 25	21 47	20 52	24 39	28 12	25 42
11	9 21 8	21 29 4	9♎ 10 58	15 24 31	3 15	4 23	25 20	5 22	19 7	21 41	20 53	24 37	28 12	25 40
12	9 25 5	22 29 45	21 33 51	27 39 23	3 12	4 17	24 14	6 28	19 50	21 35	20 55	24 34	28 12	25 39
13	9 29 1	23 30 24	3♏ 41 36	9♏ 41 2	3 9	4 13	23 4	7 34	20 32	21 29	20 57	24 32	28 11	25 37
14	9 32 58	24 31 3	15 38 16	21 33 55	3 5	4 11D	21 54	8 40	21 15	21 23	20 59	24 30	28 11	25 36
15	9 36 54	25 31 41	27 28 38	3♐ 23 5	3 2	4 10	20 45	9 47	21 57	21 18	21 0	24 28	28 10	25 34
16	9 40 51	26 32 17	9♐ 17 56	15 13 52	2 59	4 11	19 39	10 53	22 40	21 12	21 2	24 26	28 10	25 33
17	9 44 47	27 32 52	21 11 32	27 11 35	2 56	4 12	18 37	12 0	23 22	21 7	21 3	24 24	28 9	25 31
18	9 48 44	28 33 26	3♑ 14 35	9♑ 21 6	2 53	4 13R	17 41	13 7	24 4	21 2	21 4	24 22	28 8	25 30
19	9 52 41	29 33 58	15 31 39	21 46 38	2 49	4 12	16 50	14 15	24 47	20 57	21 5	24 20	28 8	25 28
20	9 56 37	0♓ 34 29	28 6 26	4♒ 31 15	2 46	4 9	16 7	15 22	25 29	20 52	21 6	24 18	28 7	25 27
21	10 0 34	1 34 59	11♒ 1 17	17 36 33	2 43	4 4	15 31	16 29	26 11	20 48	21 7	24 16	28 6	25 25
22	10 4 30	2 35 27	24 16 58	1♓ 2 20	2 40	3 56	15 3	17 37	26 53	20 43	21 8	24 14	28 6	25 24
23	10 8 27	3 35 54	7♓ 52 21	14 46 36	2 37	3 47	14 42	18 45	27 35	20 39	21 9	24 12	28 5	25 22
24	10 12 23	4 36 18	21 44 35	28 45 44	2 34	3 36	14 28	19 53	28 18	20 35	21 9	24 10	28 4	25 21
25	10 16 20	5 36 41	5♈ 49 26	12♈ 55 4	2 30	3 26	14 22D	21 1	29 0	20 31	21 10	24 8	28 3	25 19
26	10 20 16	6 37 2	20 1 59	27 9 38	2 27	3 17	14 22	22 9	29 42	20 27	21 10	24 7	28 2	25 18
27	10 24 13	7 37 22	4♉ 17 27	11♉ 25 0	2 24	3 11	14 29	23 18	0♉ 24	20 24	21 10	24 5	28 1	25 17
28	10 28 10	8♓ 37 39	18♉ 31 52	25♉ 37 45	2♑ 21	3♑ 7	14♒ 43	24♑ 26	1♉ 6	20♋ 20	21♏ 11	24♋ 3	28♎ 1	25♌ 15

DECLINATION and LATITUDE

Day	☉ Decl	☽ Decl	☽ Lat	☽ 12 Hr. Decl	☿ Decl	☿ Lat	♀ Decl	♀ Lat	♂ Decl	♂ Lat	♃ Decl	♃ Lat	♄ Decl	♄ Lat
1	17S23	21N38	3N34	22N54	10S50	1N 5	20S 1	3N19	4N43	0S 2	21N57	0N27	15S40	2N17
2	17 6	23 47	2 32	24 18	10 25	1 22	20 7	3 16	5 1	0 1	21 59	0 27	15 41	2 18
3	16 48	24 25	1 20	24 7	10 4	1 39	20 12	3 12	5 18	0 1	21 60	0 27	15 41	2 18
4	16 31	23 26	0 4	22 22	9 47	1 57	20 17	3 9	5 35	0N 0	22 1	0 27	15 42	2 18
5	16 13	20 57	1S13	19 14	9 33	2 13	20 21	3 5	5 53	0 1	22 2	0 27	15 42	2 18
6	15 55	17 14	2 24	15 1	9 24	2 30	20 25	3 2	6 10	0 2	22 4	0 27	15 43	2 18
7	15 37	12 37	3 26	10 5	9 20	2 45	20 29	2 58	6 27	0 3	22 5	0 27	15 43	2 19
8	15 18	7 27	4 14	4 46	9 20	2 59	20 32	2 54	6 45	0 4	22 6	0 27	15 43	2 19
9	14 59	2 4	4 48	0S38	9 25	3 11	20 34	2 50	7 2	0 5	22 7	0 27	15 44	2 19
10	14 40	3S17	5 5	5 51	9 33	3 22	20 36	2 46	7 19	0 6	22 8	0 27	15 44	2 19
11	14 21	8 20	5 7	10 43	9 46	3 31	20 38	2 43	7 36	0 7	22 9	0 28	15 44	2 19
12	14 1	12 57	4 54	15 2	10 2	3 37	20 39	2 39	7 53	0 8	22 10	0 28	15 45	2 20
13	13 41	16 57	4 29	18 41	10 21	3 41	20 39	2 35	8 9	0 8	22 11	0 28	15 45	2 20
14	13 21	20 13	3 51	21 31	10 42	3 43	20 40	2 30	8 26	0 9	22 12	0 28	15 45	2 20
15	13 1	22 36	3 5	23 26	11 4	3 42	20 39	2 26	8 43	0 10	22 13	0 28	15 45	2 20
16	12 40	23 60	2 10	24 17	11 27	3 39	20 38	2 22	8 59	0 11	22 14	0 28	15 46	2 20
17	12 20	24 19	1 10	24 3	11 51	3 34	20 37	2 18	9 16	0 12	22 15	0 28	15 46	2 21
18	11 59	23 30	0 5	22 39	12 15	3 27	20 35	2 14	9 32	0 13	22 16	0 28	15 46	2 21
19	11 38	21 32	1N 0	20 9	12 38	3 19	20 32	2 10	9 48	0 14	22 17	0 28	15 46	2 21
20	11 16	18 31	2 5	16 38	12 60	3 9	20 29	2 5	10 5	0 14	22 17	0 28	15 46	2 21
21	10 55	14 31	3 4	12 13	13 21	2 58	20 26	2 1	10 21	0 15	22 18	0 28	15 46	2 22
22	10 33	9 44	3 55	7 7	13 40	2 47	20 21	1 57	10 37	0 16	22 19	0 28	15 46	2 22
23	10 11	4 23	4 34	1 34	13 58	2 34	20 17	1 52	10 53	0 17	22 20	0 28	15 46	2 22
24	9 49	1N17	4 57	4N 8	14 14	2 21	20 11	1 48	11 9	0 17	22 20	0 28	15 46	2 22
25	9 27	6 57	5 3	9 42	14 29	2 8	20 6	1 44	11 24	0 18	22 21	0 28	15 46	2 22
26	9 5	12 19	4 51	14 47	14 41	1 55	19 59	1 39	11 40	0 19	22 21	0 29	15 46	2 23
27	8 43	17 2	4 20	19 3	14 52	1 42	19 53	1 35	11 55	0 20	22 22	0 29	15 46	2 23
28	8S20	20N46	3N34	22N10	15S 1	1N28	19S45	1N31	12N11	0N20	22N23	0N29	15S45	2N23

Day	♅ Decl	♅ Lat	♆ Decl	♆ Lat	♇ Decl	♇ Lat
1	21N40	0N33	9S14	1N44	22N44	10N30
5	21 42	0 33	9 14	1 44	22 47	10 31
9	21 44	0 33	9 13	1 44	22 50	10 32
13	21 45	0 33	9 12	1 44	22 52	10 32
17	21 47	0 33	9 11	1 45	22 54	10 32
21	21 48	0 33	9 10	1 45	22 57	10 32
25	21N49	0N33	9S 9	1N45	22N59	10N33

☽ PHENOMENA

d	h	m	
7	1	43	○
14	19	40	☾
22	15	55	●

d	h	° '
2	21	24N25
9	9	0
16	19	24S20
23	19	0

d	h	° '
4	1	0
10	15	5S 8
18	2	0
24	20	5N 4

VOID OF COURSE ☽

Last Aspect		☽ Ingress		
1	12pm37	1	♊	2pm 3
3	4pm 1	3	♋	4pm37
5	4pm27	5	♌	7pm29
7	8pm34	7	♍	11pm43
9	8pm33	10	♎	6am34
12	1pm 3	12	♏	4pm39
14	8pm 8	15	♐	5am 7
17	1pm54	17	♑	5pm35
20	0am 1	20	♒	3am33
22	6am47	22	♓	10am10
24	4am 9	24	♈	2pm 6
26	1pm28	26	♉	4pm47
28	11am21	28	♊	7pm24

d	h	
2	20	PERIGEE
15	0	APOGEE
27	13	PERIGEE

DAILY ASPECTARIAN

1 T	☽∥♅	0am17
	☽⚹♃	1 52
	☽∥♃	2 46
	☽⚻♀	5 22
	☽⚹♅	5 35
	☽□♇	7 8
	♀⚻♅	8 16
	☽∠♂	9 29
	☽∥♇	10 24
	☽⚻♆	11 4
	☽□☿	12pm37
2 W	☽∠♃	2am59
	♀△♇	4 38
	☽∠♅	6 50
	☉△☽	11 45
	☽⚹♂	12pm 8
	☽⚼♆	12 22
3 Th	☽⚻♄	0am45
	☽⚺♃	4 3
	☉⚹♂	5 0
	☽⚺♅	8 2
	☽⚹♇	9 38
	☽☍♀	12pm 1
	☽△♆	1 38
	☉⚼☽	2 57
	☽△☿	4 1
	☿SR	9 5
4 F	☽⚼♄	2am 7
	☽∥♇	7 50
	♀⚹♆	9 40
	☽∠♇	10 53
	☿∠♂	3pm 3
	☽∥♃	3 6
	☽⚼☿	5 15
	☽□♂	5 23
	☽∥♅	6 1
	☉⚻☽	6 14
5 S	☽△♄	3am35
	☽#♀	4 20
	☽☌♃	6 21
	☽☌♅	10 38
	☿⚹♀	12pm 2
	☽⚺♇	12 19
	☽□♆	4 27
	☽⚻☿	6 19
	☽⚻♀	7 0
6 Su	♀ ♑	1am16
	☉#☽	7 47
	☽#♄	8 21
	☉∥♄	3pm56
	☽⚼♀	11 3
	☽△♂	11 34
7 M	☉☍☽	1am43
	☽□♄	7 25
	☽⚺♃	9 42
	☽⚺♅	2pm24
	☽#☿	3 30
	☽#♆	3 58
	☽☌♇	4 12
	☿△♆	8 20
	☽☍☿	8 33
	☽⚹♆	8 34
8 T	☽∥♂	3am 2
	☽⚼♂	3 28
	☽△♀	3 46
	☽∠♃	12pm 9
	☽∠♅	5 7
	☽∠♆	11 30
9 W	☽⚻♂	8am 9
	☉⚻☽	11 52
	☽⚹♄	1pm29
	☽⚹♃	3 18
	☽⚹♅	8 33
	☽⚺♇	10 30
	☽⚻☿	11 47
10 Th	☽⚺♆	3am12
	☉□♄	9 27
	☽□♀	4pm 2
	☿☍♇	4 25
	☽∠♄	5 42
	☉⚼☽	6 24
	☽#♂	8 7
11 F	☽⚼☿	2am 3
	☽∠♇	2 51
	☉⚻♃	4 17
	☽∥♆	4 20
	☽∥☿	7 31
	♀∠♄	11 43
	☿⚻♅	4pm28
	☽☍♂	8 24
	☽⚺♄	10 44
12 S	☽□♃	0am 2
	☉△☽	2 0
	☽△☿	4 47
	☉∥☽	5 34
	☽□♅	5 54
	☽⚹♇	8 1
	☽☌♆	1pm 3
	☽∥♄	4 18
	☉☌☿	7 13
13 Su	☿∠♀	5am20
	☽⚹♀	8 32
	♂⚻♄	2pm29
	☉⚻♅	11 35
14 M	☽∥♀	3am51
	♂□♃	4 16
	☿⚹♂	8 28
	☽☌♄	10 50
	☽△♃	11 33
	☽□☿	11 33
	☿⚻♃	11 38
	☽⚻♂	12pm 5
	☽#♅	2 30
	☽△♅	5 54
	☽∠♀	5 57
	☿□♄	6 54
	☽#♃	7 25
	☉□☽	7 40
	☽□♇	8 8
15 T	☉☍♇	1am 0
	☽⚺♆	1 24
	☽#♇	3 49
	♀⚼♇	4pm43
	☽⚼♃	5 46
	☽⚼♂	8 28
16 W	☽⚼♅	0am16
	☽⚺♀	3 34
	☽∠♆	7 48
	♂#♆	5pm41
	☽⚹☿	7 14
	☽⚺♄	11 43
	☽⚻♃	11 51
17 Th	☽△♂	4am38
	☽⚻♅	6 24
	☽△♇	8 39
	☉⚹☽	1pm52
	☽⚹♆	1 54
	☉△♆	2 10
	☉∥☿	3 21
	♃△♄	3 53
	☽∠☿	10 58
18 F	☽∠♄	5am34
	☽#♇	8 37
	♂□♅	9 24
	☽⚼♇	2pm12
	☽#♃	4 28
	☽☌♀	9 16
	☽#♅	9 33
	☉∠☽	9 59
19 S	☽⚺☿	2am23
	☽∥♀	9 3
	☉ ♓	10 19
	☽☍♃	10 21
	☽⚹♄	10 42
	☽☍♅	4pm48
	☽□♂	6 45
	☽⚻♇	6 59
	♂△♇	10 55
20 Su	☽□♆	0am 1
	☉⚺☽	5 2
	☿⚺♀	10 18
	☽∥♄	5pm 2
21 M	☽∥☿	5am48
	☽☌☿	7 54
	☽⚺♀	10 54
	☽⚻♃	5pm39
	☽□♄	6 21
	☉∠♀	6 30
	☉∥☽	7 49
	☽#♂	8 3
	☉#♂	9 44
	☽⚻♅	11 54
22 T	☽☍♇	1am59
	☽∥♆	2 40
	☽⚹♂	4 54
	☽△♆	6 47
	☉☌☽	3pm55
	☽∠♀	4 7
	☽⚼♃	8 8
23 W	☽⚼♅	2am19
	☽∠♂	8 39
	☽⚼♆	9 3
	☽⚺☿	11 39
	♂☍♆	4pm26
	☽⚹♀	8 31
	☽△♃	10 1
	☽△♄	10 59
24 Th	☽△♅	4am 9
	☽⚻♇	6 10
	☽⚻♆	10 48
	☽⚺♂	11 47
	☽∠☿	1pm 5
	♀☍♃	1 59
	☉⚼♃	9 52
	☉⚺☽	11 37
25 F	☽⚼♄	0am34
	♀⚹♄	3 4
	☽⚼♇	7 36
	☽#♆	9 33
	☉#☽	10 14
	☿SD	10 20
	☽⚹☿	2pm26
	☉∥♆	8 14
	☽∥♂	8 46
26 S	☽□♃	0am42
	☽⚻♄	1 55
	☉∠☽	2 52
	☽□♀	3 53
	☽□♅	6 51
	☽△♇	8 51
	♂ ♉	10 23
	☽#☿	12pm 1
	☽☍♆	1 28
	☽#♄	5 4
	☽☌♂	5 7
27 Su	☉⚹☽	6am 2
	♀☍♅	4pm 9
	☽#♀	4 56
	☽□☿	5 26
28 M	☽⚹♃	3am 3
	☽☍♄	4 28
	☽∥♅	8 54
	☽⚹♅	9 19
	☉⚼♅	9 55
	☽△♀	10 51
	☽□♇	11 21
	☽∥♃	2pm 7
	☽⚻♆	4 1
	♀⚻♇	4 46
	☽∥♇	9 13
	☽⚺♂	10 23

MARCH 1955

LONGITUDE

Day	Sid. Time h m s	☉ ° ' "	☽ ° ' "	☽ 12 Hour ° ' "	Mean ☊ ° '	True ☊ ° '	☿ ° '	♀ ° '	♂ ° '	♃ ° '	♄ ° '	♅ ° '	♆ ° '	♇ ° '
1	10 32 6	9♓ 37 54	2♊ 42 25	9♊ 45 43	2♑ 18	3♑ 5	15♒ 1	25♑ 35	1♉ 48	20♋ 17R	21♏ 11R	24♋ 2R	28♎ 0R	25♌ 14R
2	10 36 3	10 38 8	16 47 31	23 47 45	2 15	3 5	15 26	26 44	2 30	20 14	21 11	24 0	27 59	25 12
3	10 39 59	11 38 19	0♋ 46 22	7♋ 43 20	2 11	3 5R	15 55	27 52	3 12	20 11	21 10	23 59	27 58	25 11
4	10 43 56	12 38 28	14 38 35	21 32 4	2 8	3 5	16 29	29 1	3 54	20 9	21 10	23 57	27 57	25 9
5	10 47 52	13 38 35	28 23 41	5♌ 13 17	2 5	3 2	17 7	0♒ 10	4 36	20 7	21 10	23 56	27 56	25 8
6	10 51 49	14 38 40	12♌ 0 42	18 45 45	2 2	2 57	17 49	1 20	5 17	20 4	21 9	23 54	27 55	25 7
7	10 55 45	15 38 43	25 28 12	2♍ 7 49	1 59	2 49	18 35	2 29	5 59	20 2	21 9	23 53	27 53	25 5
8	10 59 42	16 38 43	8♍ 44 20	15 17 34	1 55	2 38	19 25	3 38	6 41	20 0	21 8	23 52	27 52	25 4
9	11 3 39	17 38 42	21 47 17	28 13 19	1 52	2 26	20 17	4 48	7 23	19 59	21 8	23 50	27 51	25 3
10	11 7 35	18 38 39	4♎ 35 36	10♎ 54 3	1 49	2 12	21 13	5 57	8 4	19 57	21 7	23 49	27 50	25 1
11	11 11 32	19 38 35	17 8 43	23 19 42	1 46	2 0	22 12	7 7	8 46	19 56	21 6	23 48	27 49	25 0
12	11 15 28	20 38 28	29 27 12	5♏ 31 27	1 43	1 49	23 13	8 17	9 28	19 55	21 5	23 47	27 48	24 59
13	11 19 25	21 38 19	11♏ 32 47	17 31 38	1 40	1 40	24 17	9 27	10 9	19 54	21 4	23 46	27 46	24 57
14	11 23 21	22 38 9	23 28 27	29 23 46	1 36	1 34	25 24	10 37	10 51	19 54	21 2	23 45	27 45	24 56
15	11 27 18	23 37 58	5♐ 18 9	11♐ 12 15	1 33	1 31	26 32	11 47	11 32	19 53	21 1	23 44	27 44	24 55
16	11 31 14	24 37 44	17 6 41	23 2 10	1 30	1 30	27 43	12 57	12 14	19 53D	21 0	23 43	27 43	24 53
17	11 35 11	25 37 29	28 59 22	4♑ 59 0	1 27	1 30	28 55	14 7	12 55	19 53	20 58	23 42	27 41	24 52
18	11 39 8	26 37 12	11♑ 1 45	17 8 17	1 24	1 29	0♓ 10	15 17	13 37	19 53	20 56	23 41	27 40	24 51
19	11 43 4	27 36 53	23 19 15	29 35 13	1 21	1 28	1 26	16 28	14 18	19 53	20 55	23 41	27 39	24 50
20	11 47 1	28 36 33	5♒ 56 42	12♒ 24 8	1 17	1 25	2 45	17 38	15 0	19 54	20 53	23 40	27 37	24 48
21	11 50 57	29 36 10	18 57 49	25 37 55	1 14	1 19	4 5	18 49	15 41	19 54	20 51	23 39	27 36	24 47
22	11 54 54	0♈ 35 46	2♓ 24 29	9♓ 17 23	1 11	1 10	5 26	19 59	16 22	19 55	20 49	23 39	27 34	24 46
23	11 58 50	1 35 20	16 16 18	23 20 48	1 8	0 59	6 49	21 10	17 4	19 56	20 47	23 38	27 33	24 45
24	12 2 47	2 34 52	0♈ 30 14	7♈ 43 50	1 5	0 47	8 14	22 21	17 45	19 58	20 45	23 38	27 32	24 44
25	12 6 43	3 34 22	15 0 43	22 19 57	1 1	0 35	9 40	23 31	18 26	19 59	20 42	23 37	27 30	24 43
26	12 10 40	4 33 50	29 40 33	7♉ 1 32	0 58	0 24	11 8	24 42	19 7	20 1	20 40	23 37	27 29	24 42
27	12 14 36	5 33 16	14♉ 22 0	21 41 7	0 55	0 16	12 38	25 53	19 48	20 3	20 38	23 36	27 27	24 41
28	12 18 33	6 32 39	28 58 11	6♊ 12 35	0 52	0 10	14 8	27 4	20 29	20 5	20 35	23 36	27 26	24 40
29	12 22 30	7 32 1	13♊ 23 55	20 31 49	0 49	0 8	15 40	28 15	21 11	20 7	20 33	23 36	27 24	24 39
30	12 26 26	8 31 20	27 36 9	4♋ 36 47	0 46	0 7D	17 14	29 26	21 52	20 9	20 30	23 36	27 23	24 38
31	12 30 23	9♈ 30 37	11♋ 33 44	18♋ 27 3	0♑ 42	0♑ 7R	18♓ 49	0♓ 37	22♉ 33	20♋ 12	20♏ 27	23♋ 36	27♎ 21	24♌ 37

DECLINATION and LATITUDE

Day	☉ Decl	☽ Decl	☽ Lat	☽ 12 Hr. Decl	☿ Decl	☿ Lat	♀ Decl	♀ Lat	♂ Decl	♂ Lat	♃ Decl	♃ Lat	♄ Decl	♄ Lat
1	7S58	23N14	2N34	23N55	15S 8	1N15	19S37	1N26	12N26	0N21	22N23	0N29	15S45	2N23
2	7 35	24 13	1 26	24 7	15 13	1 2	19 29	1 22	12 41	0 22	22 24	0 29	15 45	2 23
3	7 12	23 39	0 12	22 49	15 17	0 50	19 20	1 17	12 56	0 23	22 24	0 29	15 45	2 24
4	6 49	21 38	1S 1	20 8	15 19	0 37	19 10	1 13	13 11	0 23	22 24	0 29	15 45	2 24
5	6 26	18 22	2 10	16 21	15 19	0 25	18 60	1 9	13 26	0 24	22 25	0 29	15 44	2 24
6	6 3	14 8	3 11	11 46	15 17	0 13	18 49	1 4	13 41	0 25	22 25	0 29	15 44	2 24
7	5 40	9 16	4 0	6 40	15 14	0 2	18 38	1 0	13 55	0 25	22 26	0 29	15 44	2 24
8	5 16	4 2	4 36	1 22	15 9	0S 9	18 26	0 56	14 10	0 26	22 26	0 29	15 43	2 25
9	4 53	1S16	4 56	3S53	15 2	0 19	18 14	0 52	14 24	0 27	22 26	0 29	15 43	2 25
10	4 30	6 25	5 1	8 52	14 54	0 30	18 1	0 47	14 38	0 27	22 26	0 29	15 42	2 25
11	4 6	11 12	4 51	13 24	14 44	0 39	17 48	0 43	14 52	0 28	22 27	0 29	15 42	2 25
12	3 43	15 27	4 27	17 18	14 33	0 49	17 34	0 39	15 6	0 29	22 27	0 29	15 42	2 25
13	3 19	18 58	3 52	20 26	14 20	0 58	17 20	0 35	15 20	0 29	22 27	0 29	15 41	2 26
14	2 55	21 40	3 7	22 39	14 6	1 6	17 5	0 31	15 34	0 30	22 27	0 29	15 41	2 26
15	2 32	23 23	2 14	23 52	13 50	1 14	16 50	0 26	15 47	0 31	22 27	0 29	15 40	2 26
16	2 8	24 4	1 16	24 0	13 33	1 22	16 34	0 22	16 1	0 31	22 27	0 29	15 39	2 26
17	1 44	23 40	0 13	23 3	13 14	1 29	16 18	0 18	16 14	0 32	22 27	0 29	15 39	2 26
18	1 21	22 9	0N50	20 60	12 55	1 36	16 1	0 14	16 27	0 33	22 27	0 29	15 38	2 27
19	0 57	19 35	1 53	17 55	12 33	1 42	15 44	0 10	16 40	0 33	22 27	0 29	15 38	2 27
20	0 33	16 1	2 51	13 55	12 11	1 48	15 27	0 7	16 53	0 34	22 27	0 29	15 37	2 27
21	0 9	11 36	3 43	9 8	11 47	1 53	15 9	0 3	17 5	0 34	22 27	0 29	15 36	2 27
22	0N14	6 31	4 24	3 46	11 21	1 58	14 50	0S 1	17 18	0 35	22 27	0 29	15 36	2 27
23	0 38	0 57	4 51	1N55	10 55	2 3	14 31	0 5	17 30	0 36	22 27	0 29	15 35	2 27
24	1 2	4N47	5 0	7 38	10 27	2 7	14 12	0 9	17 42	0 36	22 27	0 29	15 34	2 28
25	1 25	10 23	4 51	13 1	9 58	2 11	13 52	0 12	17 54	0 37	22 27	0 29	15 33	2 28
26	1 49	15 27	4 23	17 40	9 27	2 14	13 32	0 16	18 6	0 37	22 26	0 29	15 33	2 28
27	2 12	19 36	3 37	21 13	8 56	2 17	13 12	0 19	18 18	0 38	22 26	0 29	15 32	2 28
28	2 36	22 29	2 37	23 22	8 23	2 19	12 51	0 23	18 30	0 38	22 26	0 30	15 31	2 28
29	2 59	23 51	1 27	23 57	7 49	2 21	12 30	0 26	18 41	0 39	22 25	0 30	15 30	2 28
30	3 23	23 39	0 13	22 58	7 14	2 22	12 8	0 30	18 52	0 39	22 25	0 30	15 29	2 29
31	3N46	21N57	1S 0	20N36	6S37	2S23	11S46	0S33	19N 3	0N40	22N25	0N30	15S29	2N29

Day	♅ Decl	♅ Lat	♆ Decl	♆ Lat	♇ Decl	♇ Lat
1	21N51	0N33	9S 7	1N45	23N 1	10N33
5	21 52	0 32	9 6	1 45	23 3	10 33
9	21 52	0 32	9 4	1 46	23 5	10 32
13	21 53	0 32	9 2	1 46	23 6	10 32
17	21 54	0 32	9 0	1 46	23 8	10 32
21	21 54	0 32	8 58	1 46	23 9	10 32
25	21 54	0 32	8 56	1 46	23 10	10 31
29	21N54	0N32	8S54	1N46	23N11	10N31

☽ PHENOMENA

d	h	m	
1	12	41	☽
8	15	42	○
16	16	36	☾
24	3	43	●
30	20	10	☽

d	h	° '
2	3	24N13
8	18	0
16	3	24S 5
23	4	0
29	9	23N58

d	h	° '
3	4	0
9	20	5S 1
17	5	0
24	0	5N 0
30	4	0

VOID OF COURSE ☽

Last Aspect		☽ Ingress		
2	7pm10	2	♋	10pm40
4	11pm11	5	♌	2am49
7	4am21	7	♍	8am 9
9	3am48	9	♎	3pm20
11	8pm45	12	♏	1am 5
14	4am17	14	♐	1pm14
16	11pm51	17	♑	2am 2
19	8am57	19	♒	12pm47
21	3pm28	21	♓	7pm45
23	12pm29	23	♈	11pm10
25	8pm25	26	♉	0am32
27	8pm35	28	♊	1am42
30	3am25	30	♋	4am 6

d	h	
14	21	APOGEE
26	15	PERIGEE

DAILY ASPECTARIAN

1	☽∠♃	4am22
T	♄SR	6 19
	☽∠♅	10 44
	☉□☽	12pm41
	☽⚼♀	2 35
	☽⚼♆	5 30
	☽△☿	9 35
2	☽∠♂	1am16
W	☽⚺♃	5 53
	☽⚻♄	7 30
	☽⚺♅	12pm20
	☽*♇	2 24
	☽⚻♀	6 34
	☽△♆	7 10
3	☽⚼☿	0am15
Th	♀□♆	1 49
	☽*♂	4 24
	☽∥♇	9 12
	☽⚼♄	9 19
	☽∠♇	4pm14
	☽∥♃	4 28
	☉△☽	8 15
	☽∥♅	9 56
4	☽⚻☿	3am20
F	☉⚼♆	7 8
	☽☌♃	9 33
	☽△♄	11 22
	☽☌♅	4pm11
	☽⚺♇	6 18
	☽#♀	7 41
	♀ ♒	8 22
	☽□♆	11 11
5	☉⚼☽	0am28
S	☽☍♀	3 25
	☽□♂	11 29
	☽#♄	3pm27
	☽#☿	5 52
6	☽∥♂	2am16
Su	☉⚻☽	5 3
	☽☍☿	10 56
	☽⚺♃	2pm18
	☽□♄	4 16
	☽⚺♅	9 9
	☽☌♇	11 19
7	☽#♆	0am50
M	☽*♆	4 21
	☽⚻♀	1pm51
	☽∠♃	5 14
	☉#☽	5 57
	☽△♂	8 3
8	☽∠♅	0am13
T	☽∠♆	7 33
	☉☍☽	3pm42
	☿⚻♃	3 56
	☽⚼♀	7 57
	☽*♃	8 39
	☽⚻☿	9 1
	☽*♄	10 46
9	☽⚼♂	1am10
W	☽*♅	3 48
	☽⚺♇	6 3
	☽⚺♆	11 18
	☉∥☽	3pm30
	☿□♄	9 16
10	☽△♀	2am51
Th	☽∠♄	2 52
	☽⚼☿	3 20
	☽⚻♂	7 0
	☽∠♇	10 18
	☽∥♆	12pm56
	☿#♂	3 54
11	☉⚻☽	5am15
F	☽□♃	5 24
	☉△♃	6 55
	☽⚺♄	7 39
	☽△☿	10 41
	☽□♅	12pm54
	☽*♇	3 14
	☽∥☿	6 52
	☽☌♆	8 45
	☽#♂	9 48
12	☽∥♄	1am33
S	☉△♄	10 21
	☿⚻♅	12pm30
	☽∥♀	12 58
	☉⚼☽	1 20
	☽□♀	7 21
	☽☍♂	9 3
13	☿☍♇	2pm17
Su	☽△♃	4 46
	☽☌♄	7 5
	☉△☽	10 9
14	☽△♅	0am33
M	☽#♅	2 31
	☽□♇	2 57
	☽□☿	4 17
	☽⚺♆	8 39
	☽#♃	9 21
	♂#♄	11 52
	♀□♂	11 54
	☽#♇	7pm 3
	☽⚼♃	11 9
15	☉△♅	2am21
T	☽⚼♅	6 58
	☽⚻♂	1pm28
	☽*♀	2 37
	☽∠♆	3 5
	☿△♆	11 58
16	☽⚻♃	5am37
W	☉⚻♇	6 9
	☽⚺♄	7 51
	☽⚻♅	1pm22
	☽△♇	3 43
	☉□☽	4 36
	♃SD	8 40
	☽*♆	9 23
	☽⚼♂	9 43
	☽*☿	11 51
17	☽∠♀	0am17
Th	♀#♂	3 35
	☽#♇	10 34
	☽∠♄	1pm56
	☽#♃	8 18
	☿ ♓	8 49
	☽⚼♇	9 40
18	☽#♅	2am53
F	☽△♂	5 24
	☽∠☿	9 5
	☽⚺♀	9 16
	☽☍♃	5pm21
	☽*♄	7 21
19	☉⚻♆	0am40
S	☽☍♅	0 41
	☽⚻♇	2 54
	☽□♆	8 17
	☉*☽	8 57
	♀∥♄	9 31
	☽⚺☿	5pm17
	☽#♂	7 1
20	☽∥♄	2am23
Su	☽∥♀	3 38
	☉∠☽	3pm23
	☽□♂	5 41
	☽∥☿	11 4
	☽☌♀	11 42
21	☽⚻♃	1am43
M	☽□♄	3 24
	☽⚻♅	8 27
	☉ ♈	9 35
	☽☍♇	10 29
	☽∥♆	12pm46
	☿⚼♃	2 53
	☽△♆	3 28
	☉⚺☽	8 33
	♀⚻♃	10 39
22	☽⚼♃	4am25
T	☽☌☿	5 53
	☽⚼♅	10 52
	♀□♄	4pm25
	☽⚼♆	5 38
23	☉#☽	1am15
W	☽*♂	1 25
	☽△♃	6 15
	☉∥☽	7 8
	☽△♄	7 39
	☽⚺♀	9 4
	☽△♅	12pm29
	☽⚻♇	2 21
	☽⚻♆	7 2
24	☉☌☽	3am43
Th	☽∠♂	3 55
	☿⚼♅	6 32
	☽⚼♄	8 41
	☽∠♀	12pm22
	☉∠♂	1 0
	☽⚺☿	2 14
	☽⚼♇	3 17
	☽#♆	5 38
	☽#☿	10 17
25	♀⚻♅	1am57
F	☽⚺♂	5 53
	☽□♃	8 11
	☽⚻♄	9 19
	☽□♅	2pm 6
	☽#♀	3 7
	☽*♀	3 10
	☽△♇	3 52
	☽∠☿	5 35
	☽☍♆	8 25
	♀☍♇	11 49
26	☽#♄	0am29
S	☉⚺☽	8 33
	☽∥♂	3pm20
	☽*☿	8 50
	☿⚼♆	9 16
27	☿∥♆	0am33
Su	☉⚼♄	1 42
	♂*♃	8 50
	☽*♃	9 20
	☽☌♂	9 21
	☽☍♄	10 14
	☉∠☽	10 53
	☽*♅	3pm 9
	☽□♇	4 54
	☽∥♅	6 8
	☽□♀	8 35
	☽⚻♆	9 28
	☽∥♃	11 26
28	♂☍♄	3am 8
M	♀△♆	7 11
	☽∥♇	9 5
	☽∠♃	10 9
	☉*☽	1pm29
	☽∠♅	3 59
	☽⚼♆	10 20
29	☽□☿	4am17
T	☽⚺♃	11 20
	☽⚻♄	11 59
	☽⚺♂	1pm45
	☽⚺♅	5 12
	☽*♇	6 57
	☽△♆	11 37
30	☽△♀	3am25
W	☽∥♇	8 40
	♀ ♓	11 31
	☽⚼♄	1pm29
	☽∠♂	4 41
	☽∥♃	6 57
	☉□☽	8 10
	☽∠♇	8 37
31	☽∥♅	0am21
Th	☉⚼♇	2 22
	☽⚼♀	7 43
	☽△☿	2pm19
	☽☌♃	3 7
	☽△♄	3 27
	☽*♂	8 11
	☽☌♅	9 2
	☿△♃	9 16
	☽∥♂	10 16
	☽⚺♇	10 47
	☿△♄	11 41

APRIL 1955

LONGITUDE

Day	Sid. Time	☉	☽	☽ 12 Hour	Mean ☊	True ☊	☿	♀	♂	♃	♄	♅	♆	♇
	h m s	° ' "	° ' "	° ' "	° '	° '	° '	° '	° '	° '	° '	° '	° '	° '
1	12 34 19	10♈ 29 51	25♋ 16 51	2♌ 3 16	0♑ 39	0♑ 7R	20♓ 26	1♓ 48	23♉ 14	20♋ 15	20♏ 24R	23♋ 36	27♎ 20R	24♌ 36R
2	12 38 16	11 29 2	8♌ 46 25	15 26 27	0 36	0 5	22 3	2 59	23 55	20 18	20 21	23 36	27 18	24 35
3	12 42 12	12 28 12	22 3 27	28 37 32	0 33	0 0	23 43	4 10	24 35	20 21	20 18	23 36	27 16	24 34
4	12 46 9	13 27 19	5♍ 8 44	11♍ 37 6	0 30	29♐ 52	25 23	5 22	25 16	20 24	20 15	23 36	27 15	24 33
5	12 50 5	14 26 24	18 2 38	24 25 21	0 27	29 41	27 5	6 33	25 57	20 28	20 12	23 36	27 13	24 32
6	12 54 2	15 25 27	0♎ 45 13	7♎ 2 14	0 23	29 29	28 49	7 44	26 38	20 31	20 9	23 36	27 12	24 31
7	12 57 59	16 24 28	13 16 25	19 27 46	0 20	29 16	0♈ 34	8 56	27 19	20 35	20 5	23 36	27 10	24 30
8	13 1 55	17 23 27	25 36 20	1♏ 42 12	0 17	29 3	2 21	10 7	27 59	20 39	20 2	23 37	27 8	24 30
9	13 5 52	18 22 23	7♏ 45 31	13 46 28	0 14	28 52	4 8	11 18	28 40	20 43	19 59	23 37	27 7	24 29
10	13 9 48	19 21 18	19 45 17	25 42 15	0 11	28 43	5 58	12 30	29 21	20 48	19 55	23 38	27 5	24 28
11	13 13 45	20 20 11	1♐ 37 44	7♐ 32 7	0 7	28 37	7 49	13 41	0♊ 1	20 52	19 52	23 38	27 4	24 27
12	13 17 41	21 19 2	13 25 53	19 19 32	0 4	28 33	9 41	14 53	0 42	20 57	19 48	23 39	27 2	24 27
13	13 21 38	22 17 51	25 13 37	1♑ 8 44	0 1	28 32D	11 35	16 5	1 23	21 2	19 44	23 39	27 0	24 26
14	13 25 34	23 16 39	7♑ 5 31	13 4 36	29♐ 58	28 32	13 31	17 16	2 3	21 7	19 40	23 40	26 59	24 25
15	13 29 31	24 15 25	19 6 41	25 12 25	29 55	28 33R	15 28	18 28	2 44	21 12	19 37	23 41	26 57	24 25
16	13 33 28	25 14 9	1♒ 22 30	7♒ 37 32	29 52	28 33	17 26	19 40	3 24	21 17	19 33	23 41	26 55	24 24
17	13 37 24	26 12 51	13 58 9	20 24 53	29 48	28 31	19 26	20 51	4 5	21 23	19 29	23 42	26 54	24 23
18	13 41 21	27 11 32	26 58 10	3♓ 38 22	29 45	28 28	21 27	22 3	4 45	21 28	19 25	23 43	26 52	24 23
19	13 45 17	28 10 11	10♓ 25 41	17 20 9	29 42	28 22	23 30	23 15	5 25	21 34	19 21	23 44	26 50	24 22
20	13 49 14	29 8 48	24 21 39	1♈ 29 51	29 39	28 14	25 33	24 27	6 6	21 40	19 17	23 45	26 49	24 22
21	13 53 10	0♉ 7 24	8♈ 44 13	16 4 2	29 36	28 5	27 38	25 39	6 46	21 46	19 13	23 46	26 47	24 21
22	13 57 7	1 5 57	23 28 25	0♉ 56 20	29 32	27 56	29 44	26 51	7 26	21 53	19 9	23 47	26 46	24 21
23	14 1 3	2 4 29	8♉ 26 37	15 58 5	29 29	27 48	1♉ 51	28 2	8 7	21 59	19 4	23 48	26 44	24 21
24	14 5 0	3 2 59	23 29 32	0♊ 59 51	29 26	27 42	3 59	29 14	8 47	22 6	19 0	23 49	26 42	24 20
25	14 8 57	4 1 27	8♊ 27 57	15 52 56	29 23	27 38	6 7	0♈ 26	9 27	22 12	18 56	23 50	26 41	24 20
26	14 12 53	4 59 53	23 14 2	0♋ 30 39	29 20	27 37D	8 16	1 38	10 7	22 19	18 52	23 52	26 39	24 20
27	14 16 50	5 58 17	7♋ 42 22	14 48 55	29 17	27 37	10 24	2 50	10 47	22 26	18 47	23 53	26 37	24 19
28	14 20 46	6 56 39	21 50 8	28 46 3	29 13	27 38	12 33	4 2	11 27	22 33	18 43	23 54	26 36	24 19
29	14 24 43	7 54 59	5♌ 36 44	12♌ 22 22	29 10	27 39R	14 41	5 14	12 8	22 40	18 39	23 56	26 34	24 19
30	14 28 39	8♉ 53 16	19♌ 3 9	25♌ 39 20	29♐ 7	27♐ 38	16♉ 48	6♈ 26	12♊ 48	22♋ 48	18♏ 34	23♋ 57	26♎ 33	24♌ 19

DECLINATION and LATITUDE

Day	☉	☽		☽ 12 Hr.	☿		♀		♂		♃		♄	
	Decl	Decl	Lat	Decl	Decl	Lat	Decl	Lat	Decl	Lat	Decl	Lat	Decl	Lat
1	4N 9	18N58	2S 9	17N 6	5S60	2S24	11S24	0S36	19N14	0N40	22N24	0N30	15S28	2N29
2	4 33	15 1	3 9	12 47	5 21	2 24	11 1	0 39	19 25	0 41	22 24	0 30	15 27	2 29
3	4 56	10 24	3 58	7 55	4 41	2 23	10 38	0 42	19 36	0 41	22 23	0 30	15 26	2 29
4	5 19	5 22	4 34	2 47	4 0	2 22	10 15	0 45	19 46	0 42	22 23	0 30	15 25	2 29
5	5 42	0 12	4 55	2S22	3 18	2 20	9 52	0 48	19 56	0 42	22 23	0 30	15 24	2 29
6	6 4	4S54	5 1	7 22	2 35	2 18	9 28	0 51	20 6	0 43	22 22	0 30	15 23	2 30
7	6 27	9 44	4 52	11 59	1 51	2 16	9 4	0 54	20 16	0 43	22 21	0 30	15 22	2 30
8	6 50	14 5	4 30	16 2	1 6	2 13	8 39	0 57	20 26	0 44	22 21	0 30	15 21	2 30
9	7 12	17 49	3 56	19 23	0 20	2 9	8 15	0 60	20 35	0 44	22 20	0 30	15 20	2 30
10	7 35	20 44	3 11	21 52	0N27	2 5	7 50	1 2	20 45	0 45	22 20	0 30	15 19	2 30
11	7 57	22 45	2 18	23 22	1 15	2 1	7 25	1 5	20 54	0 45	22 19	0 30	15 18	2 30
12	8 19	23 44	1 20	23 50	2 4	1 56	6 59	1 7	21 3	0 46	22 18	0 30	15 17	2 30
13	8 41	23 39	0 18	23 13	2 53	1 50	6 34	1 10	21 12	0 46	22 17	0 30	15 16	2 30
14	9 3	22 30	0N45	21 32	3 44	1 44	6 8	1 12	21 20	0 47	22 17	0 30	15 15	2 30
15	9 24	20 18	1 48	18 51	4 35	1 38	5 42	1 14	21 29	0 47	22 16	0 30	15 13	2 30
16	9 46	17 9	2 46	15 15	5 27	1 31	5 16	1 16	21 37	0 48	22 15	0 30	15 12	2 31
17	10 7	13 9	3 38	10 53	6 19	1 23	4 50	1 18	21 45	0 48	22 14	0 30	15 11	2 31
18	10 29	8 26	4 21	5 52	7 12	1 15	4 23	1 20	21 53	0 48	22 13	0 30	15 10	2 31
19	10 50	3 11	4 50	0 24	8 5	1 7	3 56	1 22	22 1	0 49	22 12	0 30	15 9	2 31
20	11 10	2N25	5 4	5N15	8 59	0 58	3 30	1 24	22 8	0 49	22 12	0 30	15 8	2 31
21	11 31	8 3	4 60	10 47	9 52	0 49	3 3	1 26	22 16	0 50	22 11	0 30	15 7	2 31
22	11 52	13 23	4 36	15 48	10 46	0 39	2 36	1 28	22 23	0 50	22 10	0 30	15 5	2 31
23	12 12	17 59	3 52	19 53	11 40	0 29	2 9	1 29	22 30	0 50	22 9	0 30	15 4	2 31
24	12 32	21 26	2 53	22 37	12 33	0 19	1 41	1 31	22 36	0 51	22 8	0 30	15 3	2 31
25	12 52	23 23	1 41	23 44	13 26	0 9	1 14	1 32	22 43	0 51	22 6	0 30	15 2	2 31
26	13 11	23 40	0 24	23 11	14 18	0N 2	0 47	1 33	22 49	0 52	22 5	0 30	15 1	2 31
27	13 31	22 19	0S54	21 7	15 9	0 12	0 19	1 35	22 56	0 52	22 4	0 30	14 60	2 31
28	13 50	19 35	2 7	17 48	15 59	0 23	0N 8	1 36	23 2	0 52	22 3	0 30	14 58	2 31
29	14 9	15 48	3 10	13 37	16 47	0 34	0 36	1 37	23 7	0 53	22 2	0 30	14 57	2 31
30	14N28	11N17	4S 1	8N52	17N34	0N44	1N 3	1S38	23N13	0N53	22N 1	0N30	14S56	2N31

Day	♅		♆		♇	
	Decl	Lat	Decl	Lat	Decl	Lat
1	21N54	0N32	8S52	1N46	23N12	10N30
5	21 54	0 32	8 50	1 46	23 12	10 30
9	21 54	0 32	8 47	1 47	23 13	10 29
13	21 54	0 32	8 45	1 47	23 13	10 28
17	21 53	0 32	8 43	1 47	23 13	10 27
21	21 52	0 32	8 40	1 47	23 13	10 27
25	21 51	0 31	8 38	1 47	23 13	10 26
29	21N50	0N31	8S36	1N47	23N13	10N25

☽ PHENOMENA			
d	h	m	
7	6	35	○
15	11	1	☾
22	13	7	●
29	4	23	☽
d	h	° '	
5	1	0	
12	10	23S50	
19	14	0	
25	16	23N46	
5	22	5S 1	
13	7	0	
20	6	5N 5	
26	7	0	

VOID OF COURSE ☽ Last Aspect		☽ Ingress		
1	3am36	1	♌	8am21
3	9am30	3	♍	2pm31
5	7pm44	5	♎	10pm34
8	3am 0	8	♏	8am38
10	8pm33	10	♐	8pm42
13	3am36	13	♑	9am41
15	3pm22	15	♒	9pm20
18	0am26	18	♓	5am29
20	0am 9	20	♈	9am30
22	5am17	22	♉	10am30
24	9am59	24	♊	10am24
26	5am37	26	♋	11am 9
28	8am13	28	♌	2pm 9
30	1pm36	30	♍	7pm58

d	h	
11	14	APOGEE
23	19	PERIGEE

DAILY ASPECTARIAN

1 F	☽□♆	3am36
	☽⊼♀	12pm40
	♅SD	12 52
	♂*♅	12 56
	☽⚼☿	8 30
	☽#♄	9 38
2 S	☉△☽	5am15
	♃△♄	1pm42
	☉#☿	6 29
	☽□♄	8 49
	☽⊻♃	8 53
	☿△♅	10 20
	☽#♀	10 43
	♂□♇	11 2
3 Su	☽⊻♅	2am48
	☽⊼☿	3 27
	☽☌♇	4 34
	☽□♂	4 52
	☽#♆	7 34
	☽*♆	9 30
	☉⚼☽	10 41
	☿⊼♇	12pm 7
	☿*♂	9 12
4 M	☉∥☽	0am16
	☽☍♀	0 26
	☽∠♃	0 29
	♀⚼♃	0 55
	☽∠♅	6 23
	☽#☿	7 22
	☽∠♆	1pm 9
	☉⊼☽	4 42
5 T	☿⊼♆	1am47
	☽*♄	4 2
	☽*♃	4 34
	☽*♅	10 27
	☽⊻♇	12pm12
	☽∥☿	2 23
	☽△♂	3 44
	☽⊻♆	5 15
	☽☍☿	7 44
6 W	☉#☽	6am 9
	☽∠♄	8 21
	☽⊼♀	2pm45
	☿ ♈	4 15
	☽∠♇	4 45
	♀⚼♅	5 32
	♂⊼♆	7 6
	☽∥♆	7 18
	☽∥♀	8 51
	☽⚼♂	10 2
7 Th	☉☍☽	6am35
	☽⊻♄	1pm10
	☽□♃	2 16
	♀∥♆	3 14
	☽□♅	8 6
	☽*♇	9 49
	☽⚼♀	10 56
8 F	☽☌♆	3am 0
	☽⊼♂	4 58
	☽∥♄	7 36
	☽⊼☿	3pm34
9 S	☽△♀	7am51
	☿⚼♄	10 41
	♀⚼♆	3pm53
	☉⊼☽	11 7
10 Su	☽#♂	0am 3
	☽☌♄	0 20
	☽△♃	2 7
	☽⚼☿	2 53
	☉#♀	7 40
	☽△♅	7 48
	☽□♇	9 29
	☽#♅	12pm24
	☉⊼♄	1 0
	☽⊻♆	2 46
	☽#♃	5 43
	☽☍♂	8 33
	♂ ♊	11 9
11 M	☉⚼☽	8am13
	☽#♇	8 33
	☽⚼♃	8 40
	☉□♃	2pm13
	☽⚼♅	2 15
	☽△☿	2 56
	☿⚼♇	8 54
	☽∠♆	9 10
12 T	☽□♀	3am17
	☽⊻♄	12pm54
	☽⊼♃	3 25
	☉△☽	5 30
	☽⊼♅	8 48
	☽△♇	10 23
13 W	☽*♆	3am36
	☉#♆	4 22
	☽#♇	11 43
	☽⊼♂	1pm13
	☽∠♄	7 9
14 Th	☽#♃	3am 3
	☽⚼♇	4 41
	☽#♅	7 52
	☉□♅	9 35
	☽#♂	1pm11
	☽□☿	3 21
	☽⚼♂	9 6
	☽*♀	10 35
15 F	☽*♄	0am59
	☉△♇	3 44
	☽☍♃	4 9
	☽☍♅	9 0
	☽⊼♇	10 26
	☉□☽	11 1
	☽□♆	3pm22
	☿#♀	8 38
	♀△♄	9 50
16 S	☽△♂	4am 8
	☽∠♀	7 0
	☽∥♄	12pm21
	☿∠♂	5 38
17 Su	☿⊼♄	0am36
	☽□♄	10 13
	♀△♃	11 25
	☽*☿	12pm 3
	☽⊼♃	1 53
	☽⊻♀	2 7
	☉#☽	2 43
	☉☍♆	4 17
	☽⊼♅	6 4
	☽☍♇	7 17
	☽∥♆	10 45
	♂∥♅	11 21
	☽△♆	11 49
18 M	☿□♃	0am19
	☉*☽	0 26
	☽#☿	4 59
	☽□♂	2pm43
	☽⚼♃	5 10
	☿⊻♀	5 11
	☽∠☿	8 0
	☽∥♀	8 20
	☽⚼♅	9 1
19 T	☽⚼♆	2am28
	☿□♅	2 49
	☉∠☽	5 9
	♀△♅	9 47
	☿△♇	10 15
	☽△♄	3pm23
	☿#♆	4 3
	☽△♃	7 24
	♀⊼♇	10 23
	☽△♅	10 57
20 W	☽⊼♇	0am 0
	☽☌♀	0 9
	☽⊻☿	2 22
	☽⊼♆	4 8
	☽#♀	4 13
	☉⊻☽	8 39
	♂∥♃	9 11
	☿☍♆	2pm20
	☽⚼♄	4 33
	☽*♂	8 36
	☉ ♉	8 58
21 Th	♂∠♃	0am12
	☽⚼♇	1 1
	☽#♆	2 40
	☽∥☿	9 31
	☉∥☽	4pm23
	☽⊼♄	5 2
	☽□♃	9 24
	☽∠♂	10 15
	♀⊼♆	10 23
22 F	☽□♅	0am30
	☽△♇	1 25
	☿ ♉	2 58
	☽☍♆	5 17
	☽⊻♀	5 54
	☽#♄	8 20
	☽☌☿	11 44
	☉☌☽	1pm 7
	☽⊻♂	11 27
23 S	☉☌☿	4am35
	☽∠♀	7 58
	☽☍♄	4pm52
	☽*♃	9 45
	☉∥☿	11 19
24 Su	☽*♅	0am31
	☽□♇	1 21
	♂∠♅	1 25
	☽∥♅	3 55
	☽⊼♆	5 7
	☽∥♃	6 31
	☽*♀	9 59
	☽∥♂	12pm43
	♀ ♈	3 14
	☉⊻☽	4 21
	☽⊻☿	7 36
	☽∥♇	8 48
	☽∠♃	9 57
25 M	☽∠♅	0am36
	☽☌♂	1 40
	☽⚼♆	5 11
	☽⊼♄	4pm53
	☉∠☽	6 20
	☽⊻♃	10 29
26 T	☽∠☿	0am 3
	☽⊻♅	1 2
	☽*♇	1 48
	☽△♆	5 37
	☽∥♇	11 23
	☽□♀	3pm 8
	☽∥♂	4 36
	☽⚼♄	5 29
	☿#♄	7 48
	☉*☽	8 53
27 W	☽∠♇	2am43
	☽∥♃	2 48
	☽∥♅	5 4
	☽*☿	5 21
	☽⊻♂	5 27
	☿⊻♂	6 13
	♀⚼♄	5pm55
	☽△♄	6 41
28 Th	☽☌♃	1am15
	☽☌♅	3 34
	☽⊻♇	4 17
	♂⚼♆	4 48
	☽□♆	8 13
	☽∠♂	8 23
	☽∥☿	7pm12
	☽△♀	11 17
29 F	☉□☽	4am23
	☽#♄	4 47
	☉∥☽	8 31
	☽*♂	12pm10
	☽□☿	7 10
	♂∥♇	10 24
	☽□♄	11 8
30 S	☽⚼♀	4am45
	☽⊻♃	6 51
	☽⊻♅	8 55
	☽☌♇	9 32
	☽#♆	1pm22
	☽*♆	1 36
	☿☍♄	7 31

LONGITUDE

Day	Sid. Time	☉	☽	☽ 12 Hour	Mean ☊	True ☊	☿	♀	♂	♃	♄	♅	♆	♇
	h m s	° ' "	° ' "	° ' "	° '	° '	° '	° '	° '	° '	° '	° '	° '	° '
1	14 32 36	9♉ 51 32	2♍ 11 13	8♍ 39 5	29♐ 4	27♐ 36R	18♉ 54	7♈ 38	13♊ 28	22♋ 55	18♏ 30R	23♋ 59	26♎ 31R	24♌ 18R
2	14 36 32	10 49 45	15 3 11	21 23 49	29 1	27 32	20 59	8 51	14 8	23 3	18 25	24 0	26 29	24 18
3	14 40 29	11 47 56	27 41 12	3♎ 55 35	28 58	27 25	23 2	10 3	14 48	23 11	18 21	24 2	26 28	24 18
4	14 44 26	12 46 6	10♎ 7 11	16 16 11	28 54	27 18	25 3	11 15	15 27	23 19	18 16	24 4	26 26	24 18
5	14 48 22	13 44 13	22 22 47	28 27 8	28 51	27 10	27 1	12 27	16 7	23 27	18 12	24 5	26 25	24 18
6	14 52 19	14 42 19	4♏ 29 26	10♏ 29 52	28 48	27 2	28 58	13 39	16 47	23 35	18 7	24 7	26 23	24 18D
7	14 56 15	15 40 23	16 28 35	22 25 49	28 45	26 55	0♊ 51	14 51	17 27	23 43	18 3	24 9	26 22	24 18
8	15 0 12	16 38 26	28 21 47	4♐ 16 44	28 42	26 49	2 42	16 3	18 7	23 52	17 58	24 11	26 20	24 18
9	15 4 8	17 36 27	10♐ 10 56	16 4 43	28 38	26 46	4 30	17 16	18 47	24 0	17 54	24 13	26 19	24 18
10	15 8 5	18 34 26	21 58 26	27 52 27	28 35	26 45D	6 14	18 28	19 26	24 9	17 49	24 14	26 17	24 18
11	15 12 1	19 32 24	3♑ 47 13	9♑ 43 11	28 32	26 45	7 55	19 40	20 6	24 17	17 45	24 16	26 16	24 18
12	15 15 58	20 30 21	15 40 51	21 40 45	28 29	26 46	9 33	20 52	20 46	24 26	17 40	24 18	26 14	24 18
13	15 19 55	21 28 16	27 43 25	3♒ 49 27	28 26	26 48	11 7	22 5	21 25	24 35	17 36	24 21	26 13	24 18
14	15 23 51	22 26 10	9♒ 59 25	16 13 55	28 23	26 49	12 38	23 17	22 5	24 44	17 31	24 23	26 11	24 19
15	15 27 48	23 24 3	22 33 30	28 58 43	28 19	26 50R	14 5	24 29	22 45	24 53	17 27	24 25	26 10	24 19
16	15 31 44	24 21 54	5♓ 30 2	12♓ 7 52	28 16	26 49	15 28	25 42	23 24	25 3	17 22	24 27	26 8	24 19
17	15 35 41	25 19 44	18 52 32	25 44 15	28 13	26 48	16 48	26 54	24 4	25 12	17 18	24 29	26 7	24 19
18	15 39 37	26 17 33	2♈ 43 3	9♈ 48 48	28 10	26 44	18 3	28 7	24 43	25 22	17 13	24 32	26 6	24 20
19	15 43 34	27 15 21	17 1 15	24 19 52	28 7	26 41	19 15	29 19	25 23	25 31	17 9	24 34	26 4	24 20
20	15 47 30	28 13 8	1♉ 43 59	9♉ 12 45	28 4	26 37	20 23	0♉ 31	26 2	25 41	17 5	24 36	26 3	24 20
21	15 51 27	29 10 53	16 45 7	24 19 58	28 0	26 33	21 27	1 44	26 42	25 51	17 0	24 39	26 2	24 21
22	15 55 24	0♊ 8 38	1♊ 56 4	9♊ 32 10	27 57	26 31	22 27	2 56	27 21	26 1	16 56	24 41	26 0	24 21
23	15 59 20	1 6 21	17 7 3	24 39 32	27 54	26 29D	23 23	4 9	28 1	26 11	16 52	24 44	25 59	24 22
24	16 3 17	2 4 2	2♋ 8 36	9♋ 33 21	27 51	26 29	24 15	5 21	28 40	26 21	16 47	24 46	25 58	24 22
25	16 7 13	3 1 43	16 53 1	24 7 3	27 48	26 30	25 3	6 34	29 19	26 31	16 43	24 49	25 57	24 23
26	16 11 10	3 59 22	1♌ 15 4	8♌ 16 50	27 44	26 31	25 46	7 46	29 59	26 41	16 39	24 51	25 55	24 23
27	16 15 6	4 56 59	15 12 16	22 1 24	27 41	26 33	26 25	8 59	0♋ 38	26 52	16 35	24 54	25 54	24 24
28	16 19 3	5 54 34	28 44 26	5♍ 21 35	27 38	26 34R	26 59	10 11	1 17	27 2	16 30	24 56	25 53	24 24
29	16 22 59	6 52 9	11♍ 53 10	18 19 34	27 35	26 34	27 29	11 24	1 56	27 13	16 26	24 59	25 52	24 25
30	16 26 56	7 49 42	24 41 9	0♎ 58 21	27 32	26 33	27 54	12 36	2 36	27 23	16 22	25 2	25 51	24 26
31	16 30 53	8♊ 47 13	7♎ 11 35	13♎ 21 16	27♐ 29	26♐ 31	28♊ 15	13♉ 49	3♋ 15	27♋ 34	16♏ 18	25♋ 5	25♎ 50	24♌ 26

DECLINATION and LATITUDE

Day	☉ Decl	☽ Decl	☽ Lat	☽ 12 Hr. Decl	☿ Decl	☿ Lat	♀ Decl	♀ Lat	♂ Decl	♂ Lat	♃ Decl	♃ Lat	♄ Decl	♄ Lat
1	14N46	6N21	4S39	3N49	18N20	0N55	1N31	1S39	23N18	0N53	21N59	0N30	14S55	2N31
2	15 5	1 16	5 1	1S17	19 3	1 5	1 59	1 40	23 23	0 54	21 58	0 30	14 53	2 31
3	15 23	3S48	5 8	6 15	19 44	1 15	2 26	1 41	23 28	0 54	21 57	0 30	14 52	2 31
4	15 40	8 37	5 1	10 53	20 24	1 24	2 54	1 41	23 33	0 54	21 56	0 30	14 51	2 31
5	15 58	13 2	4 39	15 2	21 0	1 33	3 21	1 42	23 38	0 55	21 54	0 30	14 50	2 31
6	16 15	16 52	4 6	18 31	21 35	1 41	3 49	1 43	23 42	0 55	21 53	0 30	14 49	2 31
7	16 32	19 59	3 21	21 13	22 7	1 49	4 16	1 43	23 46	0 55	21 51	0 30	14 47	2 31
8	16 49	22 13	2 28	22 57	22 36	1 56	4 44	1 43	23 50	0 56	21 50	0 30	14 46	2 31
9	17 5	23 27	1 29	23 41	23 3	2 3	5 11	1 44	23 54	0 56	21 49	0 30	14 45	2 31
10	17 21	23 38	0 26	23 20	23 27	2 8	5 38	1 44	23 58	0 56	21 47	0 30	14 44	2 31
11	17 37	22 45	0N38	21 55	23 49	2 13	6 5	1 44	24 1	0 57	21 45	0 30	14 42	2 31
12	17 53	20 51	1 42	19 32	24 9	2 17	6 33	1 44	24 4	0 57	21 44	0 30	14 41	2 31
13	18 8	17 59	2 41	16 14	24 26	2 20	6 59	1 44	24 7	0 57	21 42	0 30	14 40	2 31
14	18 23	14 18	3 35	12 11	24 41	2 23	7 26	1 44	24 10	0 58	21 41	0 30	14 39	2 31
15	18 38	9 55	4 19	7 30	24 53	2 24	7 53	1 44	24 13	0 58	21 39	0 30	14 38	2 31
16	18 52	4 58	4 52	2 20	25 3	2 25	8 20	1 44	24 15	0 58	21 37	0 30	14 37	2 31
17	19 6	0N21	5 10	3N 6	25 11	2 25	8 46	1 43	24 17	0 58	21 36	0 30	14 35	2 31
18	19 20	5 51	5 12	8 34	25 17	2 24	9 12	1 43	24 19	0 59	21 34	0 30	14 34	2 31
19	19 33	11 12	4 54	13 44	25 22	2 21	9 38	1 42	24 21	0 59	21 32	0 30	14 33	2 31
20	19 46	16 5	4 17	18 13	25 24	2 18	10 4	1 42	24 22	0 59	21 31	0 30	14 32	2 31
21	19 59	20 4	3 21	21 34	25 24	2 15	10 30	1 41	24 24	0 60	21 29	0 30	14 31	2 30
22	20 11	22 42	2 11	23 24	25 23	2 10	10 55	1 41	24 25	0 60	21 27	0 30	14 30	2 30
23	20 23	23 40	0 51	23 30	25 21	2 4	11 20	1 40	24 26	1 0	21 25	0 30	14 29	2 30
24	20 35	22 55	0S31	21 55	25 16	1 57	11 45	1 39	24 27	1 0	21 23	0 30	14 27	2 30
25	20 46	20 33	1 50	18 53	25 11	1 50	12 10	1 38	24 27	1 1	21 21	0 30	14 26	2 30
26	20 57	16 57	3 0	14 49	25 4	1 41	12 34	1 37	24 28	1 1	21 19	0 31	14 25	2 30
27	21 8	12 30	3 57	10 4	24 56	1 32	12 58	1 36	24 28	1 1	21 17	0 31	14 24	2 30
28	21 18	7 33	4 39	4 59	24 46	1 22	13 22	1 35	24 28	1 1	21 15	0 31	14 23	2 30
29	21 28	2 24	5 6	0S11	24 36	1 10	13 46	1 34	24 27	1 2	21 13	0 31	14 22	2 30
30	21 37	2S43	5 16	5 12	24 24	0 58	14 9	1 33	24 27	1 2	21 11	0 31	14 21	2 29
31	21N46	7S36	5S10	9S55	24N11	0N45	14N32	1S31	24N26	1N 2	21N 9	0N31	14S20	2N29

Day	♅ Decl	♅ Lat	♆ Decl	♆ Lat	♇ Decl	♇ Lat
1	21N50	0N31	8S35	1N47	23N12	10N24
5	21 49	0 31	8 32	1 47	23 12	10 24
9	21 47	0 31	8 30	1 46	23 11	10 23
13	21 46	0 31	8 28	1 46	23 10	10 22
17	21 44	0 31	8 26	1 46	23 9	10 21
21	21 42	0 31	8 24	1 46	23 7	10 20
25	21 41	0 31	8 23	1 46	23 6	10 19
29	21N39	0N31	8S21	1N46	23N 4	10N18

☽ PHENOMENA

d	h	m	
6	22	15	○
15	1	43	☾
21	20	59	●
28	14	2	☽

d	h	° '
2	6	0
9	16	23S42
16	22	0
23	1	23N41
29	11	0

d	h	
3	0	5S 8
10	10	0
17	14	5N13
23	15	0
30	4	5S16

VOID OF COURSE ☽

Last Aspect		☽ Ingress		
2	5pm 0	3	♎	4am26
5	7am57	5	♏	3pm 4
7	3pm47	8	♐	3am19
10	8am45	10	♑	4pm19
12	9pm 1	13	♒	4am29
15	6am45	15	♓	1pm54
17	12pm 8	17	♈	7pm21
19	2pm49	19	♉	9pm12
21	2pm33	21	♊	8pm57
23	6pm 9	23	♋	8pm33
25	4pm13	25	♌	9pm53
27	8pm42	28	♍	2am16
30	6am18	30	♎	10am 8

d	h	
9	0	APOGEE
22	4	PERIGEE

DAILY ASPECTARIAN

1 Su	☉#♄	10am 8
	☽∠♃	10 45
	☽⚻♀	11 9
	☽∠♅	12pm38
	☉△☽	3 25
	☽∠♆	5 19
	☽∥♀	8 55
	☽□♂	10 10
2 M	☽⚹♄	6am19
	♀⚼♇	9 13
	☽△☿	1pm23
	☽⚹♃	3 18
	☽#♀	4 50
	☽⚹♅	5 0
	☽⚺♇	5 32
	☽⚺♆	9 40
	☉⚼☽	10 9
3 T	☿⚹♃	1am54
	☽∠♄	10 49
	☿⚹♅	12pm 3
	☿□♇	3 6
	☽∠♇	10 24
	☽∥♆	11 39
	☽⚼☿	11 49
4 W	☽☍♀	2am26
	☉⚻☽	5 36
	☽△♂	11 0
	☽⚺♄	3pm50
	☿⚻♆	4 38
5 Th	☽□♃	2am 7
	☽□♅	3 22
	☽⚹♇	3 47
	☽☌♆	7 57
	☽∥♄	10 42
	☽⚻☿	10 56
	☿∠♀	1pm41
	☽⚼♂	6 18
	☉#☽	7 30
6 F	☿∥♅	9am50
	☿∥♃	12pm44
	☿ ♊	1 6
	♇SD	6 30
	☽⚻♀	8 22
	☉☍☽	10 15
7 S	☽⚻♂	2am 5
	☽☌♄	3 8
	☽△♃	2pm47
	☽△♅	3 30
	☽□♇	3 47
	☽#♅	6 41
	☽#♃	7 12
	♂⚻♄	7 24
	☽⚺♆	7 54
8 Su	☽⚼♀	6am 5
	☽#☿	8 33
	☽☍☿	10 23
	☽#♇	4pm43
	☽⚼♃	9 34
	☽⚼♅	10 1
9 M	☽∠♆	2am17
	☉☍♄	6 40
	☿∥♇	7 16
	♀⚻♄	11 56
	☽⚺♄	3pm36
	☽△♀	4 3
	☉⚻☽	4 28
	☽☍♂	6 32
10 T	♃∥♅	1am26
	☽⚻♃	4 28
	☽⚻♅	4 38
	☽△♇	4 44
	☽#☿	5 2
	☽⚹♆	8 45
	☉⚺♀	10 57
	☽#♇	3pm46
	♃☌♅	8 40
	☽∠♄	9 54
11 W	☉⚼☽	1am40
	♃⚺♇	2 10
	☽⚻☿	9 43
	☽⚼♇	11 10
	☽#♅	1pm49
	☽#♃	2 11
	☿∥♂	4 58
	♀⚹♂	7 2
	☿∠♅	8 20
	♅⚺♇	10 4
	☿∠♃	10 11
12 Th	☽⚹♄	3am58
	☉△☽	10 30
	☽⚻♂	10 46
	☽□♀	11 33
	☽⚻♇	5pm14
	☽☍♅	5 17
	☽☍♃	5 42
	☉⚺♂	8 12
	☽⚼☿	8 22
	☽□♆	9 1
	☉#☽	11 0
13 F	☿⚼♆	1am26
	☽⚼♂	6pm 2
	☽∥♄	9 55
14 S	☽△☿	5am46
	☽□♄	2pm22
	♀△♇	8 30
	♀□♅	10 25
15 Su	☽△♂	0am22
	☉□☽	1 43
	☽☍♇	3 18
	☽⚻♅	3 30
	☽⚹♀	4 0
	☽⚻♃	4 26
	☽△♆	6 45
	☽∥♆	7 21
	♀□♃	9 9
	☽#♀	9 17
	☉□♇	10pm51
16 M	☉⚹♅	2am12
	♀#♆	6 19
	☽⚼♅	7 11
	☽⚼♃	8 21
	♀☍♆	8 41
	☽⚼♆	10 12
	☽∠♀	10 21
	☽□☿	7pm56
	☉⚹♃	8 15
	☽△♄	9 14
17 T	☿⚻♄	8am54
	☽⚻♇	9 33
	☽□♂	9 33
	♂⚹♇	9 36
	☽△♅	9 51
	☽△♃	11 12
	☉⚹☽	12pm 8
	☽⚻♆	12 38
	☽⚺♀	3 21
	♂⚺♅	4 25
	☉⚻♆	7 11
	☽⚼♄	11 10
18 W	☽⚼♇	11am11
	☽#♆	11 23
	☉∠☽	3pm31
	☽∥♀	4 11
19 Th	☽⚻♄	0am13
	☽⚹☿	4 0
	♂⚺♃	6 51
	☽△♇	12pm 1
	☽□♅	12 25
	♀ ♉	1 36
	☽□♃	2 6
	☽⚹♂	2 21
	☽☍♆	2 49
	☽#♄	3 59
	☉⚺☽	5 55
	☽☌♀	9 52
20 F	♂△♆	0am26
	☽∠☿	6 21
	☽∠♂	3pm36
	☉∥☽	11 24
21 S	☽☍♄	0am24
	☽⚺☿	7 59
	☽∥♃	11 8
	☽□♇	12pm 2
	☽⚹♅	12 31
	☽∥♅	1 18
	☽⚹♃	2 33
	☽⚻♆	2 39
	☽⚺♂	4 27
	☉ ♊	8 25
	☉☌☽	8 59
	♃□♆	11 15
22 Su	☽⚺♀	1am43
	☽∥♇	6 18
	☽∠♅	12pm16
	☽⚼♆	2 18
	☽∠♃	2 30
	☽⚻♄	11 36
23 M	☽∠♀	3am30
	☽☌☿	10 36
	☽⚹♇	11 32
	☽⚺♅	12pm 8
	☽△♆	2 6
	☽⚺♃	2 36
	☽☌♂	6 9
	☽∥♇	8 51
	☽⚼♄	11 26
	☉⚺☽	11 52
24 T	☿⚹♇	3am30
	☽⚹♀	5 39
	☽∠♇	11 42
	☽∥♅	2pm16
	☿⚺♅	4 17
	☽∥♃	5 13
	☉∥☽	10 24
	☽△♄	11 44
25 W	☉∠☽	2am 1
	☽⚺♇	12pm27
	☽☌♅	1 12
	☽⚺☿	2 17
	☽□♆	3 2
	☽☌♃	4 13
	☽⚺♂	9 44
26 Th	♂ ♋	0am50
	☉⚹☽	5 0
	☿△♆	5 31
	☽□♀	12pm11
	☽#♄	2 8
	☽∠☿	5 6
	☽∥♀	9 46
27 F	☽∠♂	0am47
	☽□♄	2 23
	☽☌♇	4pm14
	☽⚺♅	5 10
	☽⚹♆	6 53
	☉∥♃	7 0
	☽#♆	8 9
	☽⚹☿	8 42
	☽⚺♃	8 54
28 S	☿⚺♃	3am34
	☽⚹♂	4 50
	♂⚼♄	7 21
	☉□☽	2pm 2
	☽∠♅	8 29
	☽∠♆	10 7
	☽△♀	11 0
29 Su	☽∠♃	0am37
	☽⚹♄	8 26
	☿∥♂	5pm52
	☽⚺♇	11 31
30 M	☽⚹♅	0am40
	☽⚺♆	2 12
	☉∥♅	2 21
	☽⚹♃	5 13
	☽⚼♀	6 9
	☽□☿	6 18
	☿∠♀	8 22
	♀#♄	11 58
	☽∠♄	12pm42
	☽□♂	3 57
31 T	☉△☽	3am21
	☽∥♆	3 45
	☽∠♇	4 22
	☽⚻♀	2pm19
	☽⚺♄	5 41

JUNE 1955

LONGITUDE

Day	Sid. Time	☉	☽	☽ 12 Hour	Mean ☊	True ☊	☿	♀	♂	♃	♄	♅	♆	♇
	h m s	° ' "	° ' "	° ' "	° '	° '	° '	° '	° '	° '	° '	° '	° '	° '
1	16 34 49	9♊ 44 43	19♎ 27 50	25♎ 31 38	27♐ 25	26♐ 29R	28♊ 31	15♉ 2	3♋ 54	27♋ 45	16♏ 14R	25♋ 7	25♎ 49R	24♌ 27
2	16 38 46	10 42 12	1♏ 33 5	7♏ 32 32	27 22	26 26	28 42	16 14	4 33	27 56	16 10	25 10	25 47	24 28
3	16 42 42	11 39 40	13 30 18	19 26 44	27 19	26 24	28 49R	17 27	5 12	28 7	16 7	25 13	25 46	24 28
4	16 46 39	12 37 6	25 22 8	1♐ 16 47	27 16	26 22	28 51	18 39	5 51	28 18	16 3	25 16	25 45	24 29
5	16 50 35	13 34 32	7♐ 10 59	13 5 0	27 13	26 21	28 48	19 52	6 31	28 29	15 59	25 19	25 44	24 30
6	16 54 32	14 31 57	18 59 7	24 53 36	27 10	26 20D	28 41	21 5	7 10	28 40	15 55	25 22	25 43	24 31
7	16 58 28	15 29 21	0♑ 48 45	6♑ 44 52	27 6	26 20	28 30	22 17	7 49	28 51	15 52	25 25	25 43	24 32
8	17 2 25	16 26 43	12 42 15	18 41 15	27 3	26 21	28 15	23 30	8 28	29 2	15 48	25 28	25 42	24 33
9	17 6 22	17 24 5	24 42 11	0♒ 45 25	27 0	26 21	27 56	24 43	9 7	29 14	15 45	25 31	25 41	24 34
10	17 10 18	18 21 27	6♒ 51 22	13 0 24	26 57	26 22	27 33	25 56	9 46	29 25	15 41	25 34	25 40	24 35
11	17 14 15	19 18 48	19 12 57	25 29 26	26 54	26 23	27 8	27 8	10 25	29 37	15 38	25 37	25 39	24 35
12	17 18 11	20 16 9	1♓ 50 16	8♓ 15 51	26 50	26 24	26 40	28 21	11 3	29 48	15 35	25 40	25 38	24 36
13	17 22 8	21 13 28	14 46 35	21 22 50	26 47	26 24R	26 9	29 34	11 42	0♌ 0	15 31	25 44	25 37	24 37
14	17 26 4	22 10 48	28 4 52	4♈ 52 57	26 44	26 24	25 37	0♊ 47	12 21	0 12	15 28	25 47	25 37	24 39
15	17 30 1	23 8 7	11♈ 47 12	18 47 40	26 41	26 23	25 4	1 59	13 0	0 23	15 25	25 50	25 36	24 40
16	17 33 57	24 5 26	25 54 14	3♉ 6 41	26 38	26 23	24 30	3 12	13 39	0 35	15 22	25 53	25 35	24 41
17	17 37 54	25 2 44	10♉ 24 36	17 47 25	26 35	26 23	23 56	4 25	14 18	0 47	15 19	25 56	25 35	24 42
18	17 41 51	26 0 2	25 14 28	2♊ 44 50	26 31	26 23D	23 23	5 38	14 57	0 59	15 16	26 0	25 34	24 43
19	17 45 47	26 57 20	10♊ 17 35	17 51 35	26 28	26 23	22 50	6 51	15 35	1 11	15 13	26 3	25 33	24 44
20	17 49 44	27 54 38	25 25 44	2♋ 58 52	26 25	26 23R	22 20	8 4	16 14	1 23	15 11	26 6	25 33	24 45
21	17 53 40	28 51 55	10♋ 29 51	17 57 38	26 22	26 23	21 52	9 17	16 53	1 35	15 8	26 10	25 32	24 46
22	17 57 37	29 49 11	25 21 14	2♌ 39 50	26 19	26 23	21 26	10 30	17 32	1 47	15 5	26 13	25 32	24 48
23	18 1 33	0♋ 46 27	9♌ 52 46	16 59 32	26 16	26 22	21 3	11 43	18 11	2 0	15 3	26 16	25 31	24 49
24	18 5 30	1 43 42	23 59 48	0♍ 53 23	26 12	26 22	20 44	12 56	18 49	2 12	15 1	26 20	25 31	24 50
25	18 9 26	2 40 57	7♍ 40 15	14 20 32	26 9	26 21	20 29	14 9	19 28	2 24	14 58	26 23	25 30	24 51
26	18 13 23	3 38 11	20 54 27	27 22 19	26 6	26 21	20 18	15 22	20 7	2 37	14 56	26 27	25 30	24 53
27	18 17 20	4 35 25	3♎ 44 34	10♎ 1 37	26 3	26 21D	20 11D	16 35	20 45	2 49	14 54	26 30	25 30	24 54
28	18 21 16	5 32 37	16 14 0	22 22 14	26 0	26 21	20 9	17 48	21 24	3 1	14 52	26 34	25 29	24 55
29	18 25 13	6 29 50	28 26 52	4♏ 28 26	25 56	26 21	20 12	19 1	22 3	3 14	14 50	26 37	25 29	24 57
30	18 29 9	7♋ 27 2	10♏ 27 28	16♏ 24 30	25♐ 53	26♐ 22	20♊ 19	20♊ 14	22♋ 41	3♌ 26	14♏ 48	26♋ 41	25♎ 29	24♌ 58

DECLINATION and LATITUDE

Day	☉ Decl	☽ Decl	☽ Lat	☽ 12 Hr. Decl	☿ Decl	☿ Lat	♀ Decl	♀ Lat	♂ Decl	♂ Lat	♃ Decl	♃ Lat	♄ Decl	♄ Lat
1	21N55	12S 6	4S51	14S 9	23N58	0N32	14N55	1S30	24N25	1N 2	21N 7	0N31	14S19	2N29
2	22 3	16 3	4 19	17 47	23 44	0 17	15 17	1 29	24 24	1 2	21 5	0 31	14 18	2 29
3	22 11	19 19	3 36	20 39	23 29	0 2	15 39	1 27	24 23	1 3	21 3	0 31	14 17	2 29
4	22 19	21 45	2 43	22 37	23 13	0S13	16 0	1 26	24 22	1 3	21 1	0 31	14 16	2 29
5	22 26	23 14	1 44	23 35	22 57	0 29	16 21	1 24	24 20	1 3	20 58	0 31	14 15	2 28
6	22 33	23 40	0 41	23 29	22 40	0 46	16 42	1 23	24 18	1 3	20 56	0 31	14 14	2 28
7	22 39	23 2	0N25	22 19	22 23	1 3	17 2	1 21	24 16	1 3	20 54	0 31	14 14	2 28
8	22 45	21 21	1 30	20 9	22 6	1 20	17 22	1 19	24 14	1 4	20 52	0 31	14 13	2 28
9	22 51	18 43	2 31	17 4	21 48	1 37	17 42	1 18	24 12	1 4	20 49	0 31	14 12	2 28
10	22 56	15 14	3 27	13 13	21 31	1 54	18 1	1 16	24 9	1 4	20 47	0 31	14 11	2 28
11	23 1	11 3	4 13	8 44	21 13	2 11	18 19	1 14	24 6	1 4	20 45	0 31	14 10	2 27
12	23 5	6 19	4 49	3 48	20 56	2 28	18 38	1 12	24 3	1 4	20 42	0 31	14 9	2 27
13	23 9	1 13	5 11	1N26	20 39	2 44	18 55	1 10	24 0	1 5	20 40	0 31	14 9	2 27
14	23 13	4N 6	5 18	6 45	20 23	2 60	19 12	1 8	23 57	1 5	20 37	0 31	14 8	2 27
15	23 16	9 22	5 6	11 53	20 7	3 14	19 29	1 6	23 53	1 5	20 35	0 31	14 7	2 27
16	23 19	14 18	4 37	16 33	19 52	3 28	19 45	1 4	23 49	1 5	20 32	0 31	14 7	2 26
17	23 21	18 34	3 49	20 19	19 38	3 41	20 1	1 2	23 45	1 5	20 30	0 31	14 6	2 26
18	23 23	21 45	2 45	22 48	19 25	3 52	20 16	0 60	23 41	1 5	20 27	0 31	14 5	2 26
19	23 25	23 27	1 28	23 41	19 13	4 2	20 31	0 58	23 37	1 5	20 25	0 31	14 5	2 26
20	23 26	23 27	0 5	22 48	19 3	4 11	20 45	0 55	23 33	1 6	20 22	0 31	14 4	2 26
21	23 26	21 44	1S18	20 18	18 54	4 18	20 58	0 53	23 28	1 6	20 19	0 31	14 4	2 25
22	23 27	18 33	2 34	16 31	18 46	4 24	21 11	0 51	23 23	1 6	20 17	0 31	14 3	2 25
23	23 27	14 16	3 39	11 50	18 40	4 29	21 24	0 49	23 18	1 6	20 14	0 31	14 3	2 25
24	23 26	9 18	4 28	6 41	18 36	4 32	21 35	0 46	23 13	1 6	20 11	0 31	14 2	2 25
25	23 25	4 2	5 1	1 23	18 33	4 34	21 47	0 44	23 8	1 6	20 8	0 32	14 2	2 25
26	23 24	1S14	5 16	3S49	18 32	4 34	21 57	0 42	23 2	1 6	20 6	0 32	14 1	2 24
27	23 22	6 18	5 15	8 42	18 33	4 33	22 7	0 39	22 56	1 7	20 3	0 32	14 1	2 24
28	23 20	10 59	4 59	13 7	18 35	4 31	22 16	0 37	22 50	1 7	20 0	0 32	14 0	2 24
29	23 17	15 7	4 29	16 56	18 39	4 27	22 25	0 34	22 44	1 7	19 57	0 32	14 0	2 24
30	23N14	18S34	3S48	20S 0	18N44	4S22	22N33	0S32	22N38	1N 7	19N54	0N32	13S60	2N23

Day	♅ Decl	♅ Lat	♆ Decl	♆ Lat	♇ Decl	♇ Lat
1	21N37	0N31	8S20	1N46	23N 3	10N17
5	21 35	0 31	8 19	1 46	23 1	10 17
9	21 33	0 31	8 17	1 45	22 59	10 16
13	21 30	0 31	8 16	1 45	22 57	10 15
17	21 28	0 31	8 16	1 45	22 55	10 14
21	21 25	0 31	8 15	1 45	22 52	10 14
25	21 23	0 31	8 14	1 45	22 50	10 13
29	21N20	0N31	8S14	1N44	22N48	10N12

☽ PHENOMENA

d	h	m	
5	14	9	○
13	12	37	☾
20	4	12	●
27	1	44	☽

d	h	° '
5	22	23S40
13	6	0
19	12	23N40
25	18	0

d	h	
6	15	0
13	21	5N18
20	2	0
26	10	5S18

VOID OF COURSE ☽

Last Aspect		☽ Ingress		
1	6pm14	1	♏	8pm54
4	6am 2	4	♐	9am24
6	7pm24	6	♑	10pm21
9	9am 7	9	♒	10am30
11	4pm44	11	♓	8pm32
13	7pm53	14	♈	3am24
15	11pm58	16	♉	6am50
18	1am13	18	♊	7am37
20	4am12	20	♋	7am15
22	1am25	22	♌	7am37
24	2am38	24	♍	10am26
26	10am19	26	♎	4pm56
28	8pm22	29	♏	3am 5

d	h	
5	3	APOGEE
19	14	PERIGEE

DAILY ASPECTARIAN

1 W	☽⚹♇	9am52
	☉∠♅	10 0
	☽□♅	11 15
	☉⚼☽	11 21
	☽☌♆	12pm32
	☽∥♄	12 56
	☽□♃	4 40
	☽△☿	6 14
	☽#♀	6 26
	♀☍♄	10 51
2 Th	☉⚼♆	2am 9
	☽△♂	6 21
	☉⚻☽	7pm58
3 F	☽⚼☿	0am37
	☽☌♄	5 14
	☽☍♀	8 52
	☽⚼♂	2pm20
	☽#♃	3 48
	☽#♅	10 6
	☽□♇	10 13
	☿SR	10 47
	☽△♅	11 48
4 S	☽⚺♆	0am47
	☽△♃	6 2
	☽⚻☿	7 3
	☉#☽	8 2
	☿∥♇	5pm58
	☽#☿	7 4
	☽#♇	7 18
	☉∠♃	8 58
	☽⚻♂	10 33
5 Su	☽⚼♅	6am24
	☽∠♆	7 14
	☽⚼♃	1pm 0
	☉☍☽	2 9
	☽⚺♄	5 48
6 M	☿⚺♃	1am38
	☽⚻♀	4 44
	☉∥☿	7 37
	☽△♇	11 15
	☽⚻♅	1pm 1
	☽⚹♆	1 40
	☽☍☿	7 24
	☽⚻♃	7 58
7 T	☽∠♄	0am 6
	☽#♇	0 36
	☉#☽	6 23
	☉⚻♄	8 49
	☽#☿	1pm13
	☽⚼♀	2 35
	☽☍♂	2 58
	☽⚼♇	5 38
	☽#♅	9 41
	♀∠♂	10 16
8 W	☽#♃	5am16
	☽⚹♄	6 12
	☉⚻☽	8 10
	♀□♇	8pm56
	☽⚻♇	11 43
9 Th	☽△♀	0am 1
	☽☍♅	1 38
	☽□♆	1 56
	☽⚻☿	6 14
	☽#♀	6 54
	☽☍♃	9 7
	☉⚼☽	4pm33
	♀⚹♅	4 38
	♂∠♇	5 0
	♀⚻♆	6 55
	☿∥♅	10 17
10 F	☽⚻♂	6am 0
	☽∥♄	6 23
	☉∥♇	10 40
	☽⚼☿	10 46
	☽□♄	5pm 7
	☿⚺♀	11 56
11 S	☉△☽	0am12
	☽☍♇	10 18
	♅□♆	11 20
	☽⚻♅	12pm18
	☽△♆	12 18
	☽⚼♂	12 29
	☽∥♆	2 20
	☽△☿	2 35
	☽□♀	4 44
	☽⚻♃	8 7
12 Su	☽⚼♆	4pm23
	☽⚼♅	4 31
	☽△♂	6 4
	☿∥♃	11 22
13 M	♃ ♌	0am 8
	☽⚼♃	0 25
	☽△♄	1 21
	♀ ♊	8 38
	♀⚹♃	10 16
	☉□☽	12pm37
	☿⚺♅	5 37
	☽⚻♇	5 51
	☽⚻♆	7 36
	☽□☿	7 47
	☽△♅	7 53
14 T	☿△♆	0am19
	☽△♃	3 48
	☽⚼♄	4 13
	☽⚹♀	5 15
	☽#♆	6pm57
	☽⚼♇	8 19
15 W	☽□♂	2am12
	☽⚻♄	6 13
	☽∠♀	9 46
	☿⚹♇	4pm42
	☉⚹☽	8 44
	☽⚹☿	9 44
	☽△♇	9 56
	☽#♄	11 1
	☽☍♆	11 28
	☽□♅	11 58
16 Th	☿∥♀	5am20
	☉☌☿	6 27
	☽□♃	7 55
	☽⚺♀	1pm16
	☉⚹♇	3 2
	☽∠☿	9 40
	☉∠☽	11 22
17 F	☽⚹♂	6am38
	☽∥☿	6 40
	☽☍♄	7 58
	☽∥♀	10 38
	☽∥♃	1pm12
	☉△♆	1 14
	☽⚺☿	9 7
	☽∥♅	9 21
	☽□♇	11 9
	☉⚺♅	11 50
18 S	☽⚻♆	0am31
	☽⚹♅	1 13
	☉⚺☽	1 18
	☽∠♂	7 52
	☽⚹♃	9 19
	♂△♄	11 13
	☽∥♇	1pm26
	♀∥♃	3 13
	☽☌♀	6 3
	☉∥☽	10 50
19 Su	☽⚼♆	0am25
	☽∠♅	1 12
	☽⚻♄	7 48
	☽⚺♂	8 47
	☽∠♃	9 28
	☽☌☿	7pm15
	☽⚹♇	10 56
20 M	☽△♆	0am11
	☉∥☽	0 41
	☽⚺♅	1 5
	☉☌☽	4 12
	☽⚼♄	7 31
	☽⚺♃	9 35
	☽∥♇	10 50
	☽⚺♀	9pm53
	☽∠♇	10 50
21	☽∥♅	2am55
T	☽∥♀	6 18
	☉∥♂	7 2
	☽△♄	7 25
	☽☌♂	10 44
	☽∥♃	12pm 2
	☽⚺☿	5 48
	☽∥☿	10 32
	☽⚺♇	11 5
22 W	☽∠♀	0am15
	☽□♆	0 17
	♀⚼♆	0 42
	☽☌♅	1 25
	☉ ♋	4 32
	☉⚼♄	6 31
	☉⚺☽	7 50
	☽☌♃	10 43
	♀∠♅	2pm57
	☽∠☿	5 47
23 Th	☽#♄	1am 6
	♀∥♅	1 6
	☽⚹♀	3 22
	☽□♄	8 41
	☉∠☽	10 39
	☽⚺♂	2pm41
	☽⚹☿	6 31
24 F	☽☌♇	1am27
	☽⚹♆	2 38
	☽⚺♅	4 3
	☽#♆	4 54
	☉⚹☽	2pm29
	☽⚺♃	2 31
	☉⚺♃	3 2
	☽∠♂	6 1
25 S	☽∠♆	5am 5
	☽∠♅	6 41
	☽□♀	12pm49
	☽⚹♄	1 6
	♀⚻♄	3 49
	☽∠♃	5 51
	☽⚹♂	10 28
	☽□☿	10 54
26 Su	☿⚺♂	5am50
	☽⚺♇	7 22
	☽⚺♆	8 30
	☽⚹♅	10 19
	☽∠♄	4pm46
	☽⚹♃	10 13
27 M	☉□☽	1am44
	☽∥♆	9 39
	☽∠♇	11 47
	☽⚺♄	9pm21
	☿SD	11 11
28	☽△♀	3am23
T	♀∠♃	5 24
	☽△☿	7 40
	♂∥♇	9 37
	☽□♂	10 39
	☽⚹♇	5pm 4
	☽∥♄	5 11
	☽☌♆	6 8
	☽□♅	8 22
29 W	☽□♃	9am41
	☽⚼♀	12pm20
	☽⚼☿	1 34
	☉△☽	5 26
30 Th	☽#☿	1am16
	☿☌♀	1 59
	♀∥♂	8 24
	☽☌♄	8 44
	☽#♃	10 54
	☽⚻☿	8pm15
	☽⚻♀	10 0
	☽□♄	11 8

JULY 1955

LONGITUDE

Day	Sid. Time	☉	☽	☽ 12 Hour	Mean ☊	True ☊	☿	♀	♂	♃	♄	♅	♆	♇
	h m s	° ' "	° ' "	° ' "	° '	° '	° '	° '	° '	° '	° '	° '	° '	° '
1	18 33 6	8♋ 24 14	22♏ 20 1	28♏ 14 32	25♐ 50	26♐ 23	20♊ 31	21♊ 27	23♋ 20	3♌ 39	14♏ 46R	26♋ 44	25♎ 29R	25♌ 0
2	18 37 2	9 21 25	4♐ 8 27	10♐ 2 14	25 47	26 24	20 48	22 40	23 58	3 52	14 45	26 48	25 28	25 1
3	18 40 59	10 18 36	15 56 16	21 50 54	25 44	26 25	21 10	23 53	24 37	4 4	14 43	26 51	25 28	25 3
4	18 44 55	11 15 47	27 46 29	3♑ 43 18	25 41	26 25R	21 37	25 6	25 16	4 17	14 41	26 55	25 28	25 4
5	18 48 52	12 12 58	9♑ 41 40	15 41 50	25 37	26 25	22 9	26 20	25 54	4 30	14 40	26 58	25 28	25 5
6	18 52 49	13 10 9	21 44 1	27 48 28	25 34	26 24	22 46	27 33	26 33	4 42	14 39	27 2	25 28	25 7
7	18 56 45	14 7 20	3♒ 55 24	10♒ 4 59	25 31	26 22	23 27	28 46	27 11	4 55	14 37	27 6	25 28D	25 8
8	19 0 42	15 4 31	16 17 27	22 32 59	25 28	26 20	24 14	29 59	27 50	5 8	14 36	27 9	25 28	25 10
9	19 4 38	16 1 42	28 51 46	5♓ 14 0	25 25	26 17	25 5	1♋ 12	28 28	5 21	14 35	27 13	25 28	25 12
10	19 8 35	16 58 54	11♓ 39 53	18 9 37	25 21	26 14	26 1	2 26	29 7	5 34	14 34	27 16	25 28	25 13
11	19 12 31	17 56 5	24 43 23	1♈ 21 21	25 18	26 11	27 1	3 39	29 45	5 46	14 33	27 20	25 28	25 15
12	19 16 28	18 53 18	8♈ 3 42	14 50 34	25 15	26 10D	28 6	4 52	0♌ 23	5 59	14 33	27 24	25 28	25 16
13	19 20 24	19 50 31	21 42 3	28 38 12	25 12	26 10	29 15	6 6	1 2	6 12	14 32	27 27	25 28	25 18
14	19 24 21	20 47 44	5♉ 39 1	12♉ 44 25	25 9	26 10	0♋ 29	7 19	1 40	6 25	14 31	27 31	25 29	25 20
15	19 28 18	21 44 58	19 54 13	27 8 9	25 6	26 11	1 47	8 33	2 19	6 38	14 31	27 35	25 29	25 21
16	19 32 14	22 42 13	4♊ 25 48	11♊ 46 40	25 2	26 13	3 10	9 46	2 57	6 51	14 31	27 38	25 29	25 23
17	19 36 11	23 39 29	19 10 6	26 35 23	24 59	26 14R	4 36	10 59	3 36	7 4	14 30	27 42	25 29	25 25
18	19 40 7	24 36 45	4♋ 1 39	11♋ 27 59	24 56	26 14	6 7	12 13	4 14	7 17	14 30	27 46	25 30	25 26
19	19 44 4	25 34 1	18 53 26	26 17 0	24 53	26 12	7 42	13 26	4 52	7 31	14 30D	27 49	25 30	25 28
20	19 48 0	26 31 18	3♌ 37 45	10♌ 54 45	24 50	26 9	9 20	14 40	5 31	7 44	14 30	27 53	25 30	25 30
21	19 51 57	27 28 36	18 7 14	25 14 28	24 47	26 6	11 3	15 54	6 9	7 57	14 30	27 57	25 31	25 32
22	19 55 54	28 25 53	2♍ 15 55	9♍ 11 12	24 43	26 1	12 48	17 7	6 47	8 10	14 30	28 0	25 31	25 33
23	19 59 50	29 23 11	16 0 4	22 42 25	24 40	25 56	14 37	18 21	7 26	8 23	14 31	28 4	25 32	25 35
24	20 3 47	0♌ 20 30	29 18 19	5♎ 47 58	24 37	25 52	16 29	19 34	8 4	8 36	14 31	28 8	25 32	25 37
25	20 7 43	1 17 48	12♎ 11 40	18 29 48	24 34	25 49	18 24	20 48	8 42	8 49	14 32	28 11	25 33	25 39
26	20 11 40	2 15 7	24 42 52	0♏ 51 23	24 31	25 47D	20 22	22 2	9 21	9 3	14 32	28 15	25 33	25 40
27	20 15 36	3 12 27	6♏ 55 57	12 57 10	24 27	25 47	22 21	23 15	9 59	9 16	14 33	28 19	25 34	25 42
28	20 19 33	4 9 47	18 55 41	24 52 5	24 24	25 48	24 23	24 29	10 37	9 29	14 34	28 22	25 34	25 44
29	20 23 29	5 7 8	0♐ 47 3	6♐ 41 9	24 21	25 49	26 25	25 43	11 16	9 42	14 35	28 26	25 35	25 46
30	20 27 26	6 4 29	12 34 59	18 29 7	24 18	25 51	28 30	26 56	11 54	9 55	14 36	28 30	25 36	25 48
31	20 31 23	7♌ 1 50	24♐ 24 4	0♑ 20 20	24♐ 15	25♐ 52R	0♌ 35	28♋ 10	12♌ 32	10♌ 9	14♏ 37	28♋ 33	25♎ 37	25♌ 50

DECLINATION and LATITUDE

Day	☉ Decl	☽ Decl	☽ Lat	☽ 12 Hr. Decl	☿ Decl	☿ Lat	♀ Decl	♀ Lat	♂ Decl	♂ Lat	♃ Decl	♃ Lat	♄ Decl	♄ Lat
1	23N11	21S13	2S58	22S13	18N50	4S17	22N41	0S30	22N32	1N 7	19N51	0N32	13S59	2N23
2	23 7	22 57	2 1	23 26	18 58	4 10	22 48	0 27	22 25	1 7	19 49	0 32	13 59	2 23
3	23 3	23 40	0 58	23 37	19 7	4 2	22 54	0 25	22 18	1 7	19 46	0 32	13 59	2 23
4	22 58	23 18	0N 7	22 43	19 18	3 54	22 59	0 22	22 12	1 7	19 43	0 32	13 59	2 22
5	22 53	21 53	1 13	20 47	19 29	3 44	23 4	0 20	22 5	1 7	19 40	0 32	13 59	2 22
6	22 48	19 28	2 15	17 55	19 41	3 34	23 8	0 17	21 57	1 8	19 37	0 32	13 58	2 22
7	22 42	16 9	3 13	14 13	19 54	3 24	23 12	0 15	21 50	1 8	19 34	0 32	13 58	2 22
8	22 36	12 7	4 2	9 52	20 7	3 12	23 15	0 12	21 42	1 8	19 31	0 32	13 58	2 21
9	22 29	7 30	4 40	5 2	20 21	3 0	23 17	0 10	21 35	1 8	19 27	0 32	13 58	2 21
10	22 22	2 29	5 5	0N 6	20 35	2 48	23 18	0 7	21 27	1 8	19 24	0 32	13 58	2 21
11	22 15	2N43	5 15	5 20	20 49	2 36	23 19	0 5	21 19	1 8	19 21	0 32	13 58	2 21
12	22 7	7 55	5 8	10 26	21 3	2 23	23 19	0 2	21 11	1 8	19 18	0 32	13 58	2 20
13	21 59	12 51	4 44	15 8	21 17	2 10	23 19	0N 0	21 2	1 8	19 15	0 32	13 58	2 20
14	21 50	17 14	4 3	19 6	21 30	1 56	23 17	0 3	20 54	1 8	19 12	0 33	13 58	2 20
15	21 41	20 43	3 7	22 1	21 43	1 43	23 15	0 5	20 45	1 8	19 9	0 33	13 58	2 20
16	21 32	22 57	1 57	23 30	21 55	1 29	23 13	0 8	20 37	1 8	19 5	0 33	13 59	2 19
17	21 22	23 39	0 39	23 22	22 6	1 16	23 10	0 10	20 28	1 8	19 2	0 33	13 59	2 19
18	21 12	22 40	0S43	21 35	22 16	1 2	23 6	0 13	20 19	1 8	18 59	0 33	13 59	2 19
19	21 2	20 7	2 1	18 19	22 25	0 49	23 1	0 15	20 10	1 8	18 56	0 33	13 59	2 19
20	20 51	16 15	3 11	13 57	22 32	0 35	22 56	0 17	20 0	1 9	18 52	0 33	13 59	2 18
21	20 40	11 29	4 7	8 53	22 37	0 22	22 50	0 20	19 51	1 9	18 49	0 33	13 60	2 18
22	20 29	6 13	4 46	3 30	22 40	0 10	22 43	0 22	19 41	1 9	18 46	0 33	14 0	2 18
23	20 17	0 48	5 8	1S53	22 41	0N 2	22 36	0 24	19 31	1 9	18 42	0 33	14 0	2 17
24	20 5	4S29	5 12	7 1	22 40	0 14	22 28	0 27	19 22	1 9	18 39	0 33	14 1	2 17
25	19 53	9 25	4 60	11 41	22 36	0 25	22 19	0 29	19 12	1 9	18 35	0 33	14 1	2 17
26	19 40	13 49	4 34	15 46	22 30	0 36	22 9	0 31	19 2	1 9	18 32	0 33	14 2	2 17
27	19 27	17 32	3 56	19 6	22 21	0 46	21 60	0 34	18 51	1 9	18 29	0 33	14 2	2 16
28	19 13	20 28	3 8	21 35	22 9	0 55	21 49	0 36	18 41	1 9	18 25	0 33	14 2	2 16
29	18 60	22 29	2 12	23 7	21 55	1 4	21 38	0 38	18 30	1 9	18 22	0 33	14 3	2 16
30	18 46	23 30	1 12	23 37	21 38	1 12	21 26	0 40	18 20	1 9	18 18	0 34	14 4	2 16
31	18N31	23S28	0S 8	23S 2	21N19	1N19	21N13	0N42	18N 9	1N 9	18N15	0N34	14S 4	2N15

Day	♅ Decl	♅ Lat	♆ Decl	♆ Lat	♇ Decl	♇ Lat
1	21N19	0N31	8S14	1N44	22N46	10N12
5	21 16	0 31	8 14	1 44	22 44	10 11
9	21 13	0 31	8 14	1 44	22 41	10 11
13	21 10	0 31	8 15	1 44	22 39	10 10
17	21 8	0 31	8 15	1 44	22 36	10 10
21	21 5	0 31	8 16	1 43	22 33	10 10
25	21 2	0 31	8 17	1 43	22 31	10 10
29	20N59	0N31	8S18	1N43	22N28	10N 9

☽ PHENOMENA

d	h	m	
5	5	29	○
12	20	31	☾
19	11	35	●
26	16	0	☽

d	h	° '
3	4	23S41
10	12	0
16	22	23N39
23	4	0
30	11	23S37

d	h	° '
3	21	0
11	3	5N15
17	11	0
23	18	5S12
31	3	0

VOID OF COURSE ☽

Last Aspect	☽ Ingress
1 8am59	1 ♐ 3pm34
3 7pm20	4 ♑ 4am30
6 10am31	6 ♒ 4pm19
8 5pm33	9 ♓ 2am 9
11 4am46	11 ♈ 9am33
13 2pm18	13 ♉ 2pm21
15 12pm47	15 ♊ 4pm43
17 10am13	17 ♋ 5pm30
19 2pm34	19 ♌ 6pm 4
21 12pm31	21 ♍ 8pm 7
23 9pm50	24 ♎ 1am16
26 6am56	26 ♏ 10am19
28 7pm12	28 ♐ 10pm24
31 2am53	31 ♑ 11am19

d	h	
2	9	APOGEE
17	21	PERIGEE
29	22	APOGEE

DAILY ASPECTARIAN

1 F	☽#♅	0am58
	☽△♂	2 8
	☉⚼☽	2 22
	☽□♇	5 25
	☽⚺♆	6 23
	☽△♅	8 59
	☽#♂	3pm36
	♀∥♇	6 10
	☽#♇	8 33
	☽#♀	8 46
	☽△♃	11 25
2 S	☉#☽	3am11
	☽⚼♂	10 24
	☉⚻☽	11 33
	☽∠♆	12pm53
	☽⚼♅	3 39
	☉∠♇	5 4
	☽⚺♄	9 31
3 Su	☽⚼♃	6am29
	☽☍☿	11 2
	♂⚺♇	4pm32
	☽☍♀	5 59
	☽△♇	6 31
	☽⚻♂	6 37
	☽*♆	7 20
	☉∥♀	9 15
	☽⚻♅	10 15
	♀*♇	11 12
4 M	☽∠♄	3am52
	♀⚺♂	6 21
	☽#♀	6 42
	♀△♆	7 8
	♂□♆	7 50
	☉#☽	8 4
	☽#♇	11 44
	☽⚻♃	1pm22
	☽#♂	9 20
5 T	☽⚼♇	0am48
	☉☍☽	5 29
	☽#♅	7 5
	☽*♄	9 55
	♀⚺♅	1pm24
	☿∥♃	5 16
	☽#☿	10 15
	☽#♃	10 43
6 W	☽⚻☿	2am10
	☽⚻♇	6 42
	☽□♆	7 23
	☽☍♂	10 2
	☽☍♅	10 31
	☽⚻♀	12pm46
	♂☌♅	8 13
	☉∥♇	8 25
7 Th	☽☍♃	1am59
	☽⚼☿	9 25
	☉△♄	12pm23
	☽∥♄	1 26
	♀⚼♄	4 36
	♆SD	7 40
	☽□♄	8 45
	☽⚼♀	9 13
	☉⚻☽	9 28
8 F	♀ ♋	0am16
	☽△☿	4pm17
	☽☍♇	5 1
	☽△♆	5 33
	☽∥♆	8 18
	☽⚻♅	8 52
	☽⚻♂	11 13
9 S	☿*♇	3am 7
	☉⚼☽	4 25
	☽△♀	4 54
	☿△♆	10 12
	☽⚻♃	12pm25
	☽⚼♆	9 46
10 Su	☽⚼♅	1am 8
	☽⚼♂	4 46
	☽△♄	5 23
	☉△☽	10 36
	☽⚼♃	4pm41
11 M	☽⚻♇	0am57
	☽⚻♆	1 21
	☽□☿	4 31
	☽△♅	4 46
	☿⚺♅	7 42
	☽⚼♄	8 45
	♂ ♌	9 23
	☽△♂	9 34
	☽□♀	5pm44
	☽△♃	8 15
	♂∥♅	10 40
12 T	☽#♆	1am31
	☽⚼♇	3 56
	☿∥♂	8 15
	☽⚻♄	11 28
	☿∥♅	1pm12
	☉□☽	8 31
13 W	♀⚺♃	2am37
	☿⚼♄	5 33
	☽#♄	5 47
	☽△♇	6 15
	☽☍♆	6 33
	☽□♅	10 1
	☽*☿	2pm18
	☿ ♋	2 45
	☽□♂	4 53
14 Th	☽□♃	1am20
	☽*♀	3 6
	☽∥♃	12pm25
	☽☍♄	2 59
	☽∠☿	6 16
	☉∥☿	9 46
15 F	☽∥♂	0am20
	☉*☽	3 17
	☽∥♅	3 42
	☽∠♀	6 37
	☉∥☽	8 13
	☽□♇	9 4
	☽⚻♆	9 16
	☽∥☿	9 54
	☽*♅	12pm47
	☿⚺♂	5 25
	☽∥♇	7 8
	☽*♂	9 28
	☽⚺☿	9 42
16 S	☽*♃	4am 2
	☽∥♀	4 32
	☉∠☽	5 44
	☽⚺♀	9 31
	☽⚼♆	9 54
	♀∠♇	12pm22
	☽∠♅	1 27
	☽⚻♄	4 26
	☽∠♂	11 1
17 Su	☽∠♃	4am46
	☉⚺☽	7 46
	☽*♇	10 7
	☽△♆	10 13
	☽⚺♅	1pm51
	☽⚼♄	4 42
	☽∥♀	5 13
18 M	☽⚺♂	0am21
	☽∥♇	1 6
	☽☌☿	3 46
	☽∥☿	4 34
	☽⚺♃	5 21
	☽∠♇	10 22
	☉∥♅	1pm47
	☽☌♀	2 24
	☽∥♅	4 10
	☉∥☽	4 18
	☽△♄	4 54
	☿⚺♃	8 46
	☉⚺♇	9 26
	☉□♆	10 16
	☽∥♂	11 39
19 T	♄SD	7am36
	☽∥♃	8 17
	☽⚺♇	10 42
	☽□♆	10 44
	☉☌☽	11 35
	☽☌♅	2pm34
	♀△♄	8 46
20 W	☽☌♂	3am14
	☽☌♃	6 51
	☿∥♇	8 55
	♆*♇	9 14
	☽⚺☿	10 38
	☽#♄	11 50
	☿∠♇	4pm41
	☽□♄	5 58
	☽⚺♀	7 56
21 Th	☽*♆	12pm28
	☽☌♇	12 31
	☉☌♅	12 34
	☽#♆	2 50
	☽∠☿	3 15
	☽⚺♅	4 40
	☉⚺☽	4 57
	☽∠♀	11 43
22 F	☿∥♀	8am 7
	☽⚺♂	8 12
	☽⚺♃	10 23
	☽∠♆	2pm20
	☽∠♅	6 47
	☉∠☽	8 55
	☽*☿	9 10
	☽*♄	9 22
	☿△♄	10 33
23 S	☽*♀	4am35
	♀∥♇	11 56
	☽∠♂	12pm 5
	☽∠♃	1 27
	☉ ♌	3 25
	☽⚺♆	5 7
	☽⚺♇	5 15
	☽*♅	9 50
24 Su	☽∠♄	0am23
	☉*☽	2 3
	☽*♂	5pm 5
	☽*♃	5 33
	☽∥♆	6 15
	☽∠♇	9 4
25 M	☽⚺♄	4am25
	♂☌♃	6 46
	☽□☿	2pm 0
	☽□♀	6 13
	☿∥♇	11 3
26 T	☽∥♄	1am15
	☽☌♆	1 38
	☽*♇	1 52
	☽□♅	6 56
	☉□☽	4pm 0
27 W	☽□♃	4am43
	☽□♂	6 24
	☽#♃	6 53
	☽#♂	9 25
	☉#☽	1pm45
	☽☌♄	3 13
28 Th	☿☌♀	3am10
	☽#♅	5 19
	☽△♀	12pm31
	☽△☿	1 18
	☽⚺♆	1 27
	☽#♀	1 28
	☽□♇	1 47
	☿□♆	2 9
	☿⚺♇	4 10
	☽#☿	5 2
	☽△♅	7 12
	♀□♆	9 31
	☽#♇	11 48
29 F	♀⚺♇	1am 3
	☉△☽	9 35
	☽△♃	6pm29
	☽∠♆	7 57
	☽△♂	10 31
	☽⚼♀	10 32
30 S	☿☌♅	0am 2
	☽⚼♅	1 52
	☽⚼☿	2 15
	☽⚺♄	4 6
	♂∥♃	4 53
	☿ ♌	5pm23
	☉⚼☽	6 46
31 Su	☽⚼♃	1am32
	☽*♆	2 27
	☽△♇	2 53
	☽⚼♂	6 42
	♀☌♅	7 56
	☽⚻♅	8 27
	☽⚻♀	8 30
	☽∠♄	10 33
	☽⚻☿	3pm 8
	☿∥♀	3 30
	☽#♇	10 50

AUGUST 1955

LONGITUDE

Day	Sid. Time	☉	☽	☽ 12 Hour	Mean ☊	True ☊	☿	♀	♂	♃	♄	♅	♆	♇
	h m s	° ' "	° ' "	° ' "	° '	° '	° '	° '	° '	° '	° '	° '	° '	° '
1	20 35 19	7♌ 59 13	6♑ 18 20	12♑ 18 29	24♐ 12	25♐ 51R	2♌ 40	29♋ 24	13♌ 10	10♌ 22	14♏ 38	28♋ 37	25♎ 37	25♌ 51
2	20 39 16	8 56 36	18 21 6	24 26 29	24 8	25 49	4 46	0♌ 38	13 49	10 35	14 39	28 41	25 38	25 53
3	20 43 12	9 53 59	0♒ 34 52	6♒ 46 26	24 5	25 45	6 51	1 52	14 27	10 48	14 41	28 44	25 39	25 55
4	20 47 9	10 51 24	13 1 18	19 19 33	24 2	25 39	8 57	3 5	15 5	11 2	14 42	28 48	25 40	25 57
5	20 51 5	11 48 50	25 41 14	2♓ 6 20	23 59	25 31	11 2	4 19	15 43	11 15	14 44	28 52	25 41	25 59
6	20 55 2	12 46 16	8♓ 34 50	15 6 38	23 56	25 23	13 6	5 33	16 22	11 28	14 45	28 55	25 42	26 1
7	20 58 58	13 43 44	21 41 42	28 19 57	23 53	25 15	15 9	6 47	17 0	11 41	14 47	28 59	25 42	26 3
8	21 2 55	14 41 12	5♈ 1 16	11♈ 45 36	23 49	25 8	17 11	8 1	17 38	11 54	14 49	29 2	25 43	26 5
9	21 6 52	15 38 43	18 32 53	25 23 3	23 46	25 3	19 12	9 15	18 16	12 8	14 51	29 6	25 44	26 6
10	21 10 48	16 36 14	2♉ 16 4	9♉ 11 51	23 43	25 0	21 12	10 29	18 54	12 21	14 53	29 9	25 45	26 8
11	21 14 45	17 33 47	16 10 24	23 11 37	23 40	24 59D	23 11	11 43	19 33	12 34	14 55	29 13	25 46	26 10
12	21 18 41	18 31 21	0♊ 15 26	7♊ 21 44	23 37	25 0	25 8	12 57	20 11	12 47	14 57	29 16	25 48	26 12
13	21 22 38	19 28 57	14 30 19	21 40 58	23 33	25 1R	27 4	14 11	20 49	13 0	15 0	29 20	25 49	26 14
14	21 26 34	20 26 35	28 53 20	6♋ 7 3	23 30	25 1	28 58	15 25	21 27	13 14	15 2	29 23	25 50	26 16
15	21 30 31	21 24 14	13♋ 21 35	20 36 23	23 27	25 0	0♍ 51	16 39	22 5	13 27	15 4	29 27	25 51	26 18
16	21 34 27	22 21 54	27 50 47	5♌ 4 5	23 24	24 56	2 42	17 53	22 44	13 40	15 7	29 30	25 52	26 20
17	21 38 24	23 19 36	12♌ 15 33	19 24 25	23 21	24 50	4 32	19 8	23 22	13 53	15 10	29 34	25 53	26 22
18	21 42 21	24 17 19	26 29 57	3♍ 31 30	23 18	24 42	6 21	20 22	24 0	14 6	15 13	29 37	25 55	26 24
19	21 46 17	25 15 3	10♍ 28 28	17 20 20	23 14	24 32	8 8	21 36	24 38	14 19	15 15	29 41	25 56	26 26
20	21 50 14	26 12 48	24 6 45	0♎ 47 29	23 11	24 22	9 54	22 50	25 16	14 32	15 18	29 44	25 57	26 28
21	21 54 10	27 10 35	7♎ 22 25	13 51 34	23 8	24 13	11 38	24 4	25 55	14 45	15 21	29 48	25 59	26 30
22	21 58 7	28 8 23	20 15 6	26 33 18	23 5	24 6	13 21	25 19	26 33	14 59	15 24	29 51	26 0	26 32
23	22 2 3	29 6 12	2♏ 46 31	8♏ 55 12	23 2	24 0	15 3	26 33	27 11	15 12	15 28	29 54	26 1	26 34
24	22 6 0	0♍ 4 2	14 59 54	21 1 12	22 59	23 57	16 43	27 47	27 49	15 25	15 31	29 58	26 3	26 35
25	22 9 56	1 1 54	26 59 42	2♐ 56 6	22 55	23 56D	18 22	29 2	28 27	15 38	15 34	0♌ 1	26 4	26 37
26	22 13 53	1 59 47	8♐ 51 3	14 45 14	22 52	23 56	19 59	0♍ 16	29 6	15 50	15 38	0 4	26 6	26 39
27	22 17 49	2 57 41	20 39 20	26 34 1	22 49	23 56R	21 35	1 30	29 44	16 3	15 41	0 7	26 7	26 41
28	22 21 46	3 55 36	2♑ 29 55	8♑ 27 38	22 46	23 56	23 10	2 45	0♍ 22	16 16	15 45	0 11	26 9	26 43
29	22 25 43	4 53 33	14 27 45	20 30 46	22 43	23 54	24 43	3 59	1 0	16 29	15 49	0 14	26 10	26 45
30	22 29 39	5 51 31	26 37 8	2♒ 47 15	22 39	23 49	26 15	5 13	1 38	16 42	15 52	0 17	26 12	26 47
31	22 33 36	6♍ 49 30	9♒ 1 24	15♒ 19 49	22♐ 36	23♐ 43	27♍ 46	6♍ 28	2♍ 16	16♌ 55	15♏ 56	0♌ 20	26♎ 13	26♌ 49

DECLINATION and LATITUDE

Day	☉ Decl	☽ Decl	☽ Lat	☽ 12 Hr. Decl	☿ Decl	☿ Lat	♀ Decl	♀ Lat	♂ Decl	♂ Lat	♃ Decl	♃ Lat	♄ Decl	♄ Lat
1	18N17	22S21	0N56	21S25	20N57	1N25	21N 0	0N44	17N58	1N 9	18N11	0N34	14S 5	2N15
2	18 2	20 13	1 59	18 48	20 32	1 30	20 46	0 46	17 47	1 9	18 8	0 34	14 5	2 15
3	17 46	17 9	2 57	15 18	20 6	1 35	20 32	0 48	17 36	1 9	18 4	0 34	14 6	2 15
4	17 31	13 17	3 47	11 5	19 37	1 39	20 17	0 50	17 25	1 9	18 1	0 34	14 7	2 14
5	17 15	8 46	4 27	6 19	19 6	1 42	20 2	0 52	17 13	1 9	17 57	0 34	14 7	2 14
6	16 59	3 48	4 55	1 13	18 33	1 44	19 45	0 54	17 2	1 9	17 54	0 34	14 8	2 14
7	16 43	1N24	5 7	4N 2	17 58	1 45	19 29	0 56	16 50	1 9	17 50	0 34	14 9	2 14
8	16 26	6 38	5 3	9 10	17 22	1 46	19 12	0 57	16 39	1 9	17 46	0 34	14 10	2 13
9	16 9	11 37	4 42	13 56	16 45	1 46	18 54	0 59	16 27	1 9	17 43	0 34	14 10	2 13
10	15 52	16 6	4 5	18 3	16 6	1 45	18 35	1 1	16 15	1 9	17 39	0 34	14 11	2 13
11	15 34	19 46	3 13	21 12	15 26	1 44	18 17	1 2	16 3	1 9	17 35	0 35	14 12	2 13
12	15 17	22 19	2 9	23 5	14 45	1 42	17 57	1 4	15 51	1 9	17 32	0 35	14 13	2 12
13	14 59	23 29	0 56	23 29	14 4	1 40	17 37	1 6	15 39	1 9	17 28	0 35	14 14	2 12
14	14 41	23 6	0S21	22 19	13 21	1 37	17 17	1 7	15 27	1 9	17 24	0 35	14 15	2 12
15	14 22	21 10	1 37	19 41	12 38	1 34	16 56	1 8	15 14	1 9	17 21	0 35	14 16	2 11
16	14 4	17 53	2 46	15 49	11 54	1 30	16 35	1 10	15 2	1 9	17 17	0 35	14 17	2 11
17	13 45	13 31	3 45	11 4	11 10	1 25	16 13	1 11	14 49	1 9	17 13	0 35	14 18	2 11
18	13 26	8 28	4 29	5 48	10 26	1 21	15 51	1 12	14 36	1 9	17 10	0 35	14 19	2 11
19	13 6	3 5	4 55	0 22	9 41	1 16	15 28	1 14	14 24	1 9	17 6	0 35	14 20	2 10
20	12 47	2S19	5 4	4S56	8 57	1 10	15 5	1 15	14 11	1 9	17 2	0 35	14 21	2 10
21	12 27	7 28	4 56	9 52	8 12	1 4	14 41	1 16	13 58	1 9	16 59	0 35	14 22	2 10
22	12 7	12 8	4 34	14 14	7 27	0 58	14 18	1 17	13 45	1 9	16 55	0 36	14 23	2 10
23	11 47	16 10	3 58	17 53	6 42	0 52	13 53	1 18	13 32	1 9	16 51	0 36	14 25	2 10
24	11 27	19 24	3 12	20 41	5 57	0 45	13 29	1 19	13 18	1 9	16 47	0 36	14 26	2 9
25	11 7	21 44	2 19	22 33	5 12	0 38	13 3	1 20	13 5	1 8	16 44	0 36	14 27	2 9
26	10 46	23 6	1 20	23 23	4 27	0 31	12 38	1 20	12 52	1 8	16 40	0 36	14 28	2 9
27	10 25	23 24	0 17	23 10	3 42	0 24	12 12	1 21	12 38	1 8	16 36	0 36	14 29	2 9
28	10 4	22 40	0N46	21 54	2 58	0 17	11 46	1 22	12 25	1 8	16 32	0 36	14 31	2 8
29	9 43	20 53	1 47	19 38	2 14	0 9	11 20	1 22	12 11	1 8	16 29	0 36	14 32	2 8
30	9 22	18 9	2 45	16 26	1 30	0 1	10 53	1 23	11 57	1 8	16 25	0 36	14 33	2 8
31	9N 1	14S32	3N35	12S28	0N47	0S 7	10N26	1N23	11N44	1N 8	16N21	0N36	14S35	2N 8

Day	♅ Decl	♅ Lat	♆ Decl	♆ Lat	♇ Decl	♇ Lat
1	20N57	0N31	8S19	1N43	22N26	10N 9
5	20 54	0 31	8 20	1 42	22 23	10 9
9	20 51	0 31	8 22	1 42	22 21	10 9
13	20 48	0 31	8 23	1 42	22 18	10 9
17	20 45	0 31	8 25	1 42	22 15	10 10
21	20 42	0 31	8 27	1 42	22 13	10 10
25	20 40	0 31	8 30	1 42	22 11	10 10
29	20N37	0N31	8S32	1N41	22N 8	10N11

☽ PHENOMENA	VOID OF COURSE ☽ Last Aspect	☽ Ingress
d h m	2 8pm23	2 ♒ 10pm52
3 19 31 ○	5 0am33	5 ♓ 8am 4
11 2 33 ☾	7 1pm13	7 ♈ 3pm 0
17 19 58 ●	9 6pm34	9 ♉ 8pm 3
25 8 52 ☽	11 10pm20	11 ♊ 11pm34
	14 0am 9	14 ♋ 1am51
	16 2am46	16 ♌ 3am34
d h ° '	17 11pm50	18 ♍ 5am58
6 18 0	20 10am 8	20 ♎ 10am34
13 6 23N32	22 6pm25	22 ♏ 6pm38
19 14 0	25 4am34	25 ♐ 6am 4
26 19 23S26	27 12pm17	27 ♑ 6pm57
	29 11pm11	30 ♒ 6am36
7 6 5N 7		
13 18 0	d h	
20 0 5S 4	14 18 PERIGEE	
27 7 0	26 15 APOGEF	

DAILY ASPECTARIAN

1	☿∥♅	0am 4
M	☉⊼☽	3 40
	♀∥♅	6 25
	☽⊼♃	8 16
	☽⚼♇	9 8
	☉∥♃	11 4
	♀ ♌	11 43
	☽⊼♂	2pm29
	☽⚹♄	4 39
	☽#♅	5 6
	☽#♀	6 11
	☽#☿	8 26
2	☽□♆	2pm21
T	☽⊼♇	2 52
	☽#♃	5 22
	☉#☽	7 17
	☽☍♅	8 23
	☽#♂	8 41
3	☽☍♀	2am46
W	♂□♄	8 58
	☽☍☿	2pm37
	☽∥♄	7 12
	☉☍☽	7 31
	☽☍♃	8 7
4	☽□♄	3am13
Th	☽☍♂	4 9
	☉☌♃	5 32
	☽△♆	11pm59
5	☽☍♇	0am33
F	☽∥♆	2 8
	☿☌♃	2 50
	☽⊼♅	5 58
	☉∥♂	7 58
	☉☌☿	4pm58
	☽⊼♀	5 49
6	☽⚼♆	3am54
S	☽⊼♃	5 24
	☉⊼☽	8 19
	☽⊼☿	9 51
	☽⚼♅	9 52
	☽△♄	11 22
	☽⊼♂	3pm 1
	☿□♄	7 39
7	☽⚼♀	0am11
Su	☿∥♃	6 15
	☽⊼♆	7 16
	☽⊼♇	7 54
	☽⚼♃	9 11
	☽△♅	1pm13
	☉⚼☽	1 42
	☽⚼♄	2 39
	☽⚼☿	6 1
	☽⚼♂	7 31
8	☉□♄	3am19
M	☽△♀	5 53
	☿☌♂	7 43
	☽#♆	8 7
	☽⚼♇	10 49
	☽△♃	12pm28
	☽⊼♄	5 27
	☉△☽	6 29
	☽△♂	11 29
9	☽△☿	1am21
T	☽☍♆	12pm38
	☽#♄	1 18
	☽△♇	1 18
	☿∥♂	3 54
	☽□♅	6 34
	☉∥☽	10 44
10	☽∥☿	0am 1
W	☽∥♂	0 52
	☽∥♃	9 17
	☽∥♀	2pm20
	☉∥☿	3 10
	☽□♀	3 36
	☽□♃	5 42
	☽☍♄	9 50
11	☉□☽	2am33
Th	☽□♂	6 3
	☽∥♅	8 36
	☽□☿	1pm54
	☽⊼♆	4 25
	☽□♇	5 6
	♀☌♃	8 9
	☽⚹♅	10 20
	☽∥♇	11 59
12	☿⚹♆	8am17
F	☿☌♇	1pm32
	☽⚼♆	5 48
	☿#♄	6 8
	☽⚹♃	9 27
	☽⚹♀	11 25
	☽∠♅	11 43
13	☽⊼♄	0am49
S	☉⚹☽	8 55
	☽⚹♂	11 3
	♀∥♃	1pm19
	♀□♄	4 13
	☽△♆	6 54
	☽⚹♇	7 38
	☽∠♃	10 53
14	☽⚹☿	0am 9
Su	☽⊻♅	0 50
	☽⚼♄	1 54
	☽∠♀	2 47
	☿⊻♅	5 34
	☉∠☽	11 39
	☽∥♇	12pm22
	☽∠♂	1 8
	☿ ♍	1 8
	☽∠♇	8 35
15	☽⊻♃	0am 9
M	☽△♄	2 51
	☽∥♅	3 26
	☽∠☿	4 44
	☽⊻♀	5 58
	☉#♄	7 49
	☉⊻☽	2pm16
	☽⊻♂	3 7
	☽□♆	8 43
	☽⊻♇	9 29
16	☽☌♅	2am46
T	☽∥♃	3 38
	☽∥♀	8 24
	☽⊻☿	9 15
	☽∥♂	5pm 1
	☽#♄	8 3
	☉∥☽	10 47
17	☽☌♃	2am46
W	☉☌♂	2 48
	☽□♄	4 53
	☽☌♀	12pm37
	☽∥☿	1 25
	☽☌♂	7 34
	☉☌☽	7 58
	☽⚹♆	11 0
	☽☌♇	11 50
18	☽#♆	0am11
Th	☽⊻♅	5 20
	☽☌☿	7pm21
19	☽∠♆	0am48
F	♂#♄	6 4
	☽⊻♃	6 49
	☽∠♅	7 22
	☽⚹♄	8 22
	☉⚹♆	5pm24
	☽⊻♀	9 30
20	☽⊻♂	2am11
S	☽⊻♆	3 18
	☉⊻☽	4 3
	☽⊻♇	4 13
	☉☌♇	6 25
	☽∠♃	9 54
	☽⚹♅	10 8
	☽∠♄	11 10
	☿∠♆	2pm44
	☿#♆	3 40
21	♂⚹♆	2am35
Su	☽#☿	3 6
	☽∠♀	3 27
	☽∥♆	4 53
	☽∠♂	6 52
	☽∠♇	7 37
	☽⊻☿	9 5
	☉∠☽	9 35
	☽⚹♃	1pm55
	☽⊻♄	2 51
	♀#♄	6 30
	♂☌♇	11 11
	☉#☽	11 57
22	☽#♂	8am39
M	☽⚹♀	10 40
	☽☌♆	10 57
	☽#♀	11 13
	☽⚹♇	11 59
	☽⚹♂	12pm38
	☽∥♄	12 59
	♀⚹♆	1 35
	☉⚹☽	4 18
	☽∠☿	5 53
	☽□♅	6 25
	☿∠♅	9 56
23	♀☌♇	0am12
T	☿⊻♃	2 27
	☽#♃	4 34
	☿⚹♄	6 10
	☉⊻♅	9pm 8
	☉ ♍	10 20
24	☽□♃	0am50
W	☽☌♄	1 2
	♀☌♂	1 18
	☽⚹☿	3 57
	☽#♅	11 47
	♃□♄	4pm 3
	♅ ♌	6 7
	♀∥♂	8 52
	☽⊻♆	10 8
	☽□♇	11 15
25	☽□♂	3am 7
Th	☽□♀	4 34
	☽#♇	6 2
	☽△♅	6 7
	☉□☽	8 52
	♀ ♍	6pm53
	♀⊻♅	8 1
26	☽∠♆	4am34
F	☽⚼♅	12pm42
	☽⊻♄	1 51
	☽△♃	2 29
27	☽□☿	2am11
S	♂ ♍	10 14
	☽⚹♆	11 7
	☽△♇	12pm17
	♂⊻♅	4 12
	☽⊼♅	7 17
	☽△♂	7 27
	☽∠♄	8 27
	☽⚼♃	9 29
28	☽△♀	0am33
Su	☉△☽	3 8
	☽#♇	8 35
	☽⚼♇	6pm35
29	☽⚹♄	2am42
M	☽#♅	2 48
	☽⚼♂	3 14
	☽⊼♃	4 6
	☽⚼♀	10 0
	☉⚼☽	11 42
	☿⊻♆	11pm 4
	☽□♆	11 10
	☽△☿	11 11
30	☽⊼♇	0am19
T	☽☍♅	7 10
	☿⊻♇	8 33
	☽⊼♂	10 18
	☽#♃	12pm24
	☽⊼♀	6 33
	☉⊼☽	7 26
	☽∥♄	11 47
31	☽⚼☿	8am 6
W	☽□♄	1pm13
	☽☍♃	3 15
	☽#♂	4 53

LONGITUDE

Day	Sid. Time	☉	☽	☽ 12 Hour	Mean ☊	True ☊	☿	♀	♂	♃	♄	♅	♆	♇
	h m s	° ' "	° ' "	° ' "	° '	° '	° '	° '	° '	° '	° '	° '	° '	° '
1	22 37 32	7♍ 47 31	21♒ 42 38	28♒ 9 54	22♐ 33	23♐ 33R	29♍ 15	7♍ 42	2♍ 55	17♌ 8	16♏ 0	0♌ 23	26♎ 15	26♌ 51
2	22 41 29	8 45 33	4♓ 41 33	11♓ 17 28	22 30	23 22	0♎ 43	8 57	3 33	17 20	16 4	0 26	26 17	26 53
3	22 45 25	9 43 38	17 57 26	24 41 10	22 27	23 10	2 10	10 11	4 11	17 33	16 8	0 29	26 18	26 55
4	22 49 22	10 41 43	1♈ 28 20	8♈ 18 34	22 24	22 58	3 36	11 25	4 49	17 46	16 13	0 32	26 20	26 57
5	22 53 18	11 39 51	15 11 28	22 6 39	22 20	22 47	4 59	12 40	5 27	17 58	16 17	0 35	26 22	26 58
6	22 57 15	12 38 0	29 3 44	6♉ 2 24	22 17	22 39	6 22	13 54	6 6	18 11	16 21	0 38	26 23	27 0
7	23 1 12	13 36 12	13♉ 2 19	20 3 14	22 14	22 34	7 43	15 9	6 44	18 23	16 26	0 41	26 25	27 2
8	23 5 8	14 34 25	27 4 56	4♊ 7 17	22 11	22 32	9 3	16 23	7 22	18 36	16 30	0 44	26 27	27 4
9	23 9 5	15 32 41	11♊ 10 6	18 13 19	22 8	22 31D	10 21	17 38	8 0	18 48	16 35	0 47	26 29	27 6
10	23 13 1	16 30 58	25 16 49	2♋ 20 29	22 5	22 31R	11 37	18 52	8 38	19 1	16 39	0 50	26 30	27 8
11	23 16 58	17 29 18	9♋ 24 13	16 27 49	22 1	22 31	12 52	20 7	9 17	19 13	16 44	0 53	26 32	27 10
12	23 20 54	18 27 40	23 31 6	0♌ 33 48	21 58	22 28	14 6	21 22	9 55	19 26	16 49	0 55	26 34	27 12
13	23 24 51	19 26 4	7♌ 35 35	14 36 5	21 55	22 23	15 17	22 36	10 33	19 38	16 54	0 58	26 36	27 13
14	23 28 47	20 24 30	21 34 52	28 31 30	21 52	22 15	16 27	23 51	11 11	19 50	16 58	1 1	26 38	27 15
15	23 32 44	21 22 58	5♍ 25 29	12♍ 16 21	21 49	22 5	17 34	25 5	11 49	20 2	17 3	1 3	26 40	27 17
16	23 36 41	22 21 28	19 3 40	25 47 1	21 45	21 52	18 40	26 20	12 28	20 14	17 8	1 6	26 42	27 19
17	23 40 37	23 20 0	2♎ 26 5	9♎ 0 36	21 42	21 39	19 43	27 35	13 6	20 27	17 14	1 9	26 43	27 21
18	23 44 34	24 18 33	15 30 25	21 55 26	21 39	21 27	20 44	28 49	13 44	20 39	17 19	1 11	26 45	27 22
19	23 48 30	25 17 9	28 15 44	4♏ 31 26	21 36	21 17	21 42	0♎ 4	14 22	20 51	17 24	1 14	26 47	27 24
20	23 52 27	26 15 46	10♏ 42 47	16 50 6	21 33	21 9	22 38	1 19	15 1	21 2	17 29	1 16	26 49	27 26
21	23 56 23	27 14 25	22 53 48	28 54 22	21 30	21 4	23 31	2 33	15 39	21 14	17 35	1 19	26 51	27 28
22	0 0 20	28 13 6	4♐ 52 21	10♐ 48 20	21 26	21 2	24 20	3 48	16 17	21 26	17 40	1 21	26 53	27 29
23	0 4 16	29 11 48	16 42 57	22 36 53	21 23	21 1	25 7	5 3	16 55	21 38	17 45	1 23	26 55	27 31
24	0 8 13	0♎ 10 33	28 30 48	4♑ 25 24	21 20	21 1	25 49	6 18	17 34	21 49	17 51	1 26	26 57	27 33
25	0 12 10	1 9 18	10♑ 21 23	16 19 27	21 17	21 0	26 28	7 32	18 12	22 1	17 57	1 28	26 59	27 34
26	0 16 6	2 8 6	22 20 13	28 24 21	21 14	20 59	27 2	8 47	18 50	22 13	18 2	1 30	27 2	27 36
27	0 20 3	3 6 56	4♒ 32 25	10♒ 44 55	21 10	20 55	27 32	10 2	19 28	22 24	18 8	1 32	27 4	27 38
28	0 23 59	4 5 47	17 2 18	23 24 55	21 7	20 49	27 57	11 16	20 7	22 35	18 14	1 35	27 6	27 39
29	0 27 56	5 4 40	29 53 0	6♓ 26 40	21 4	20 40	28 16	12 31	20 45	22 47	18 19	1 37	27 8	27 41
30	0 31 52	6♎ 3 34	13♓ 5 58	19♓ 50 43	21♐ 1	20♐ 29	28♎ 30	13♎ 46	21♍ 23	22♌ 58	18♏ 25	1♌ 39	27♎ 10	27♌ 43

DECLINATION and LATITUDE

Day	☉ Decl	☽ Decl	☽ Lat	☽ 12 Hr. Decl	☿ Decl	☿ Lat	♀ Decl	♀ Lat	♂ Decl	♂ Lat	♃ Decl	♃ Lat	♄ Decl	♄ Lat
1	8N39	10S13	4N17	7S51	0N 4	0S15	9N59	1N24	11N30	1N 8	16N17	0N37	14S36	2N 7
2	8 17	5 21	4 46	2 47	0S39	0 23	9 31	1 24	11 16	1 8	16 13	0 37	14 37	2 7
3	7 55	0 9	4 60	2N30	1 21	0 31	9 3	1 24	11 2	1 8	16 10	0 37	14 39	2 7
4	7 33	5N 8	4 58	7 45	2 2	0 40	8 35	1 25	10 48	1 8	16 6	0 37	14 40	2 7
5	7 11	10 16	4 39	12 41	2 43	0 48	8 7	1 25	10 34	1 8	16 2	0 37	14 41	2 7
6	6 49	14 56	4 3	16 59	3 24	0 57	7 38	1 25	10 20	1 8	15 58	0 37	14 43	2 6
7	6 27	18 49	3 13	20 22	4 4	1 5	7 9	1 25	10 5	1 8	15 55	0 37	14 44	2 6
8	6 5	21 37	2 10	22 33	4 43	1 14	6 40	1 25	9 51	1 7	15 51	0 37	14 46	2 6
9	5 42	23 6	0 60	23 18	5 21	1 22	6 11	1 25	9 37	1 7	15 47	0 38	14 47	2 6
10	5 19	23 7	0S15	22 34	5 59	1 31	5 42	1 25	9 22	1 7	15 43	0 38	14 49	2 5
11	4 57	21 39	1 28	20 24	6 36	1 39	5 12	1 24	9 8	1 7	15 40	0 38	14 50	2 5
12	4 34	18 50	2 36	16 60	7 13	1 48	4 43	1 24	8 53	1 7	15 36	0 38	14 52	2 5
13	4 11	14 55	3 34	12 39	7 48	1 56	4 13	1 24	8 39	1 7	15 32	0 38	14 53	2 5
14	3 48	10 13	4 19	7 41	8 23	2 4	3 43	1 23	8 24	1 7	15 28	0 38	14 55	2 5
15	3 25	5 3	4 48	2 24	8 56	2 12	3 13	1 23	8 10	1 7	15 25	0 38	14 57	2 4
16	3 2	0S16	5 0	2S54	9 28	2 20	2 43	1 22	7 55	1 7	15 21	0 38	14 58	2 4
17	2 39	5 29	4 55	7 58	9 60	2 28	2 13	1 22	7 40	1 7	15 17	0 39	14 60	2 4
18	2 16	10 20	4 35	12 33	10 30	2 36	1 42	1 21	7 25	1 6	15 14	0 39	15 1	2 4
19	1 52	14 36	4 1	16 29	10 59	2 43	1 12	1 20	7 10	1 6	15 10	0 39	15 3	2 4
20	1 29	18 9	3 16	19 36	11 27	2 50	0 41	1 19	6 55	1 6	15 6	0 39	15 5	2 3
21	1 6	20 48	2 23	21 47	11 53	2 57	0 11	1 18	6 41	1 6	15 2	0 39	15 6	2 3
22	0 43	22 30	1 25	22 58	12 17	3 4	0S20	1 17	6 26	1 6	14 59	0 39	15 8	2 3
23	0 19	23 10	0 23	23 6	12 40	3 10	0 50	1 16	6 11	1 6	14 55	0 39	15 10	2 3
24	0S 4	22 46	0N40	22 12	13 1	3 16	1 21	1 15	5 55	1 6	14 52	0 40	15 11	2 3
25	0 28	21 22	1 41	20 18	13 21	3 21	1 51	1 14	5 40	1 6	14 48	0 40	15 13	2 3
26	0 51	18 60	2 38	17 28	13 38	3 26	2 22	1 13	5 25	1 5	14 44	0 40	15 15	2 2
27	1 14	15 45	3 29	13 49	13 52	3 31	2 52	1 12	5 10	1 5	14 41	0 40	15 17	2 2
28	1 38	11 44	4 12	9 29	14 5	3 34	3 23	1 11	4 55	1 5	14 37	0 40	15 18	2 2
29	2 1	7 6	4 42	4 37	14 14	3 37	3 53	1 9	4 40	1 5	14 34	0 40	15 20	2 2
30	2S24	2S 2	4N59	0N36	14S21	3S39	4S23	1N 8	4N25	1N 5	14N30	0N40	15S22	2N 2

Day	♅ Decl	♅ Lat	♆ Decl	♆ Lat	♇ Decl	♇ Lat
1	20N35	0N31	8S34	1N41	22N 6	10N11
5	20 32	0 31	8 36	1 41	22 4	10 12
9	20 30	0 31	8 39	1 41	22 2	10 12
13	20 28	0 32	8 42	1 41	22 0	10 13
17	20 25	0 32	8 44	1 41	21 58	10 14
21	20 23	0 32	8 47	1 41	21 57	10 14
25	20 21	0 32	8 50	1 41	21 55	10 15
29	20N20	0N32	8S53	1N40	21N54	10N16

☽ PHENOMENA

d	h	m	
2	8	0	○
9	8	0	☾
16	6	20	●
24	3	41	☽

d	h	° '
3	1	0
9	12	23N18
15	23	0
23	3	23S10
30	9	0

d	h	° '
3	9	5N 1
9	19	0
16	5	5S 0
23	9	0
30	13	5N 2

VOID OF COURSE ☽

Last Aspect	☽ Ingress
1 9am35	1 ♓ 3pm23
2 8pm43	3 ♈ 9pm24
5 8pm27	6 ♉ 1am37
7 11pm39	8 ♊ 4am59
10 3am 9	10 ♋ 8am 1
12 5am12	12 ♌ 11am 2
14 9am49	14 ♍ 2pm34
16 2pm20	16 ♎ 7pm36
18 10pm22	19 ♏ 3am19
21 9am26	21 ♐ 2pm12
23 10pm 2	24 ♑ 3am 1
26 9am44	26 ♒ 3pm 8
28 8pm58	29 ♓ 0am13

d	h	
10	1	PERIGEE
23	11	APOGEE

DAILY ASPECTARIAN

1 Th	☽#♀	1am23
	☉#♆	5 40
	☉☌♀	7 59
	☽∥♆	8 25
	☽△♆	8 28
	☉#☽	8 39
	☽☍♇	9 35
	☿ ♎	12pm 7
	☽⊼☿	3 48
	☽⊼♅	4 10
	☿⚹♅	7 6
	☽☍♂	9 48
2 F	☿∠♄	6am 1
	☉☍☽	8 0
	☽☍♀	8 33
	☽⚼♆	12pm 0
	☽∥☿	7 14
	☽⚼♅	7 33
	☽△♄	8 43
	☽⊼♃	11 16
3 S	☿∠♃	7am30
	☽#☿	7 49
	☽⊼♆	2pm54
	☽⊼♇	3 59
	♀∠♆	10 11
	☽△♅	10 21
	☽⚼♄	11 32
	♀#♆	11 37
4 Su	☽⚼♃	2am18
	☽☍☿	4 10
	☽⊼♂	6 10
	☉∥☽	10 24
	☽∥♀	2pm36
	☽#♆	4 1
	☉∠♆	4 14
	☉⊼☽	5 24
	☽⚼♇	6 23
	☽⊼♀	7 10
5 M	☽∥♂	1am23
	☽⊼♄	1 54
	☽△♃	4 54
	☽⚼♂	9 34
	☿⊻♂	2pm58
	☽☍♆	7 23
	☽△♇	8 27
	☉⚼☽	9 21
	☽#♄	10 49
	☽⚼♀	11 42
6 T	☽□♅	2am43
	☽∥♃	5 51
	☽△♂	12pm40
	☽⊼☿	1 55
7 W	☉△☽	1am 2
	☽△♀	3 58
	☽☍♄	5 50
	☽□♃	9 18
	♀∠♅	10 50
	☽∥♅	1pm15
	☽⚼☿	6 17
	☽⊼♆	10 55
	☽□♇	11 59
8 Th	♀⚹♄	2am18
	☽∥♇	4 57
	☽⚹♅	6 15
	☽□♂	6pm21
	☽△☿	10 28
9 F	☽⚼♆	0am32
	☉∠♅	6 10
	☽∠♅	7 53
	☉□☽	8 0
	☉#☿	8 7
	☽⊼♄	9 15
	☽□♀	12pm 3
	☽⚹♃	1 11
	☿#♀	5 47
10 S	☽△♆	2am 5
	☽⚹♇	3 9
	♀⊻♃	3 15
	☉⚹♄	3 42
	☽⊻♅	9 28
	☿∠♇	9 55
	☽⚼♄	10 53
	☽∠♃	3pm 4
	☽∥♇	7 36
	☽⚹♂	11 46
11 Su	☽∠♇	4am42
	☽□☿	6 28
	☽∥♅	11 17
	☽△♄	12pm32
	☉⚹☽	2 46
	☽⊻♃	4 56
	☽⚹♀	7 58
12 M	☽∠♂	2am29
	☽□♆	5 12
	☽⊻♇	6 16
	☽☌♅	12pm39
	☉∠☽	6 12
	♂#♆	7 36
	☽∥♃	8 32
13 T	☽∠♀	0am 1
	☽#♄	0 11
	☽⊻♂	5 18
	☉⊻♃	6 8
	☉∥♀	6 40
	☽⚹☿	2pm22
	☽□♄	4 2
	☽☌♃	8 57
	☉⊻☽	9 50
14 W	☿#♂	0am50
	☽⊻♀	4 18
	☽#♆	7 12
	☽#☿	7 53
	☽⚹♆	8 44
	☽∥♂	9 3
	☽☌♇	9 49
	☿⊻♄	12pm 6
	☿∥♆	2 24
	☽⊻♅	4 22
	♂∠♆	5 34
	☽∠☿	6 35
15 Th	☉∥☽	7am58
	☽∥♀	9 10
	☽∠♆	10 57
	☽☌♂	11 46
	☽∠♅	6pm44
	☽⚹♄	8 34
	☽⊻☿	11 14
16 F	☽⊻♃	2am 8
	☉☌☽	6 20
	♀⊻♆	7 5
	☽#♀	10 8
	☉#☽	11 43
	☽⊻♆	1pm40
	☽☌♀	2 20
	☽⊻♇	2 47
	♀⊻♇	7 20
	☽⚹♅	9 39
	☽∠♄	11 37
17 S	☽∠♃	5am33
	☽#♂	10 2
	☽∥♆	3pm55
	☽∠♇	6 11
	☽⊻♂	8 33
	☿⚹♃	9 18
18 Su	☽∥☿	1am 1
	☽⊻♄	3 23
	☽⚹♃	9 45
	☽☌☿	10 35
	☉⊻☽	5pm53
	☽☌♆	9 12
	☽⚹♇	10 22
	♀ ♎	10 41
19 M	☽∠♂	2am14
	☽∥♄	2 46
	☽#♃	3 24
	☽⊻♀	3 49
	☽□♅	5 41
	♀⚹♅	11pm10
20 T	☉∠☽	1am10
	♃#♄	6 31
	☽⚹♂	8 52
	☽∠♀	12pm13
	☽☌♄	1 23
	☉⊻♆	2 14
	☽#♅	7 37
	☽□♃	8 39
21 W	♀∠♄	0am24
	☽⊻☿	1 19
	☉⊻♇	5 34
	☽⊻♆	7 55
	☽□♇	9 8
	☉⚹☽	9 26
	☽#♇	2pm21
	☽△♅	4 53
	☽⚹♀	9 35
22 Th	♂∠♅	2am39
	☽∠☿	9 41
	☉#♀	10 13
	☽∠♆	2pm14
	☽⚼♅	11 20
23 F	☽□♂	0am27
	☽⊻♄	2 8
	☽△♃	10 10
	☽⚹☿	6pm12
	☉ ♎	7 41
	☽⚹♆	8 50
	☽△♇	10 2
24 S	☉□☽	3am41
	☽⊼♅	5 57
	☽∠♄	8 53
	♀∠♃	12pm 8
	♂⚹♄	12 45
	☽#♇	4 24
	☽⚼♃	5 9
	☽□♀	5 38
25 Su	☽⚼♇	4am29
	☉⚹♅	7 57
	☽#♅	11 24
	☽⚹♄	3pm22
	☽△♂	4 38
	☿☌♆	11 18
	☽⊼♃	11 45
26 M	☽□♆	9am18
	☽□☿	9 44
	☽⊼♇	10 26
	☽☍♅	6pm 8
	☉△☽	8 59
	☽⚼♂	11 52
27 T	☉∠♄	0am27
	☽∥♄	3 0
	☿⚹♇	5 17
	☽#♃	6 54
	☽∥☿	11 7
	☽△♀	11 47
28 W	☽□♄	2am16
	☉⚼☽	4 13
	☽⊼♂	6 7
	☽☍♃	10 37
	☽∥♆	3pm 4
	☽△♆	6 54
	☽⚼♀	7 10
	☽☍♇	7 56
	☽△☿	8 58
29 Th	☽⊼♅	3am11
	♀∠♇	3 14
	☉⊼☽	10 17
	☽#♂	12pm22
	☽∥♀	2 2
	☽⚼♆	10 19
	☉∥☽	10 23
30 F	♀#♂	0am38
	☽⚼☿	0 43
	☽⊼♀	1 19
	☽⚼♅	6 21
	☽△♄	9 33
	☽☍♂	3pm27
	☽⊼♃	5 44
	☉#☽	9 43

OCTOBER 1955

LONGITUDE

Day	Sid. Time	☉	☽	☽ 12 Hour	Mean ☊	True ☊	☿	♀	♂	♃	♄	♅	♆	♇
	h m s	° ' "	° ' "	° ' "	° '	° '	° '	° '	° '	° '	° '	° '	° '	° '
1	0 35 49	7♎ 2 31	26♓ 40 42	3♈ 35 30	20♐ 58	20♐ 17R	28♎ 37R	15♎ 1	22♍ 2	23♌ 9	18♏ 31	1♌ 41	27♎ 12	27♌ 44
2	0 39 45	8 1 30	10♈ 34 39	17 37 34	20 55	20 6	28 38	16 15	22 40	23 20	18 37	1 43	27 14	27 46
3	0 43 42	9 0 30	24 43 35	1♉ 52 0	20 51	19 56	28 31	17 30	23 18	23 31	18 43	1 45	27 16	27 47
4	0 47 38	9 59 33	9♉ 2 8	16 13 18	20 48	19 48	28 17	18 45	23 57	23 42	18 49	1 46	27 18	27 49
5	0 51 35	10 58 38	23 24 50	0♊ 36 11	20 45	19 42	27 55	20 0	24 35	23 53	18 55	1 48	27 21	27 50
6	0 55 32	11 57 45	7♊ 46 50	14 56 23	20 42	19 40D	27 26	21 14	25 13	24 4	19 2	1 50	27 23	27 52
7	0 59 28	12 56 55	22 4 30	29 10 56	20 39	19 39	26 48	22 29	25 52	24 14	19 8	1 52	27 25	27 53
8	1 3 25	13 56 7	6♋ 15 30	13♋ 18 4	20 36	19 40R	26 3	23 44	26 30	24 25	19 14	1 54	27 27	27 55
9	1 7 21	14 55 22	20 18 35	27 16 57	20 32	19 40	25 11	24 59	27 8	24 36	19 20	1 55	27 29	27 56
10	1 11 18	15 54 38	4♌ 13 9	11♌ 7 7	20 29	19 38	24 12	26 14	27 47	24 46	19 27	1 57	27 32	27 58
11	1 15 14	16 53 57	17 58 47	24 48 4	20 26	19 35	23 7	27 28	28 25	24 56	19 33	1 58	27 34	27 59
12	1 19 11	17 53 18	1♍ 34 51	8♍ 19 1	20 23	19 29	21 58	28 43	29 3	25 7	19 39	2 0	27 36	28 0
13	1 23 7	18 52 42	15 0 23	21 38 49	20 20	19 20	20 46	29 58	29 42	25 17	19 46	2 1	27 38	28 2
14	1 27 4	19 52 7	28 14 7	4♎ 46 8	20 16	19 10	19 34	1♏ 13	0♎ 20	25 27	19 52	2 3	27 40	28 3
15	1 31 1	20 51 35	11♎ 14 43	17 39 45	20 13	18 59	18 23	2 28	0 59	25 37	19 59	2 4	27 43	28 4
16	1 34 57	21 51 5	24 1 9	0♏ 18 54	20 10	18 49	17 15	3 42	1 37	25 47	20 6	2 5	27 45	28 6
17	1 38 54	22 50 37	6♏ 33 1	12 43 36	20 7	18 41	16 13	4 57	2 16	25 56	20 12	2 6	27 47	28 7
18	1 42 50	23 50 11	18 50 49	24 54 52	20 4	18 34	15 17	6 12	2 54	26 6	20 19	2 8	27 49	28 8
19	1 46 47	24 49 47	0♐ 56 3	6♐ 54 43	20 1	18 30	14 31	7 27	3 32	26 16	20 25	2 9	27 52	28 9
20	1 50 43	25 49 25	12 51 18	18 46 14	19 57	18 28D	13 54	8 42	4 11	26 25	20 32	2 10	27 54	28 11
21	1 54 40	26 49 4	24 40 4	0♑ 33 21	19 54	18 28	13 28	9 57	4 49	26 34	20 39	2 11	27 56	28 12
22	1 58 36	27 48 45	6♑ 26 41	12 20 43	19 51	18 29	13 13D	11 11	5 28	26 44	20 46	2 12	27 58	28 13
23	2 2 33	28 48 28	18 16 5	24 13 27	19 48	18 30R	13 10	12 26	6 6	26 53	20 52	2 13	28 1	28 14
24	2 6 30	29 48 13	0♒ 13 30	6♒ 16 53	19 45	18 31	13 18	13 41	6 45	27 2	20 59	2 14	28 3	28 15
25	2 10 26	0♏ 48 0	12 24 16	18 36 15	19 42	18 30	13 36	14 56	7 23	27 11	21 6	2 14	28 5	28 16
26	2 14 23	1 47 48	24 53 23	1♓ 16 10	19 38	18 27	14 4	16 11	8 2	27 19	21 13	2 15	28 7	28 17
27	2 18 19	2 47 38	7♓ 45 0	14 20 11	19 35	18 23	14 42	17 26	8 40	27 28	21 20	2 16	28 10	28 18
28	2 22 16	3 47 29	21 1 54	27 50 11	19 32	18 17	15 28	18 40	9 19	27 37	21 27	2 17	28 12	28 19
29	2 26 12	4 47 23	4♈ 44 55	11♈ 45 48	19 29	18 10	16 22	19 55	9 57	27 45	21 34	2 17	28 14	28 20
30	2 30 9	5 47 18	18 52 25	26 4 11	19 26	18 3	17 22	21 10	10 36	27 53	21 41	2 18	28 16	28 21
31	2 34 5	6♏ 47 14	3♉ 20 20	10♉ 40 2	19♐ 22	17♐ 57	18♎ 28	22♏ 25	11♎ 15	28♌ 1	21♏ 48	2♌ 18	28♎ 18	28♌ 22

DECLINATION and LATITUDE

Day	☉ Decl	☽ Decl	☽ Lat	☽ 12 Hr. Decl	☿ Decl	☿ Lat	♀ Decl	♀ Lat	♂ Decl	♂ Lat	♃ Decl	♃ Lat	♄ Decl	♄ Lat
1	2S48	3N16	4N60	5N55	14S24	3S40	4S54	1N 6	4N 9	1N 5	14N27	0N41	15S24	2N 2
2	3 11	8 32	4 43	11 3	14 25	3 40	5 24	1 5	3 54	1 5	14 23	0 41	15 25	2 1
3	3 34	13 26	4 9	15 39	14 21	3 38	5 54	1 3	3 39	1 4	14 20	0 41	15 27	2 1
4	3 58	17 38	3 18	19 22	14 13	3 36	6 24	1 2	3 23	1 4	14 16	0 41	15 29	2 1
5	4 21	20 48	2 15	21 54	14 2	3 32	6 53	1 0	3 8	1 4	14 13	0 41	15 31	2 1
6	4 44	22 39	1 3	23 1	13 46	3 26	7 23	0 58	2 53	1 4	14 9	0 41	15 33	2 1
7	5 7	22 60	0S13	22 36	13 25	3 19	7 53	0 57	2 37	1 4	14 6	0 42	15 34	2 1
8	5 30	21 51	1 27	20 45	13 0	3 9	8 22	0 55	2 22	1 4	14 2	0 42	15 36	2 1
9	5 53	19 20	2 36	17 40	12 30	2 58	8 51	0 53	2 6	1 3	13 59	0 42	15 38	2 0
10	6 16	15 44	3 34	13 37	11 57	2 45	9 20	0 51	1 51	1 3	13 56	0 42	15 40	2 0
11	6 38	11 19	4 20	8 54	11 19	2 30	9 49	0 49	1 36	1 3	13 52	0 42	15 42	2 0
12	7 1	6 24	4 50	3 50	10 38	2 14	10 17	0 47	1 20	1 3	13 49	0 42	15 44	1 60
13	7 24	1 14	5 3	1S21	9 54	1 56	10 45	0 45	1 5	1 3	13 46	0 43	15 45	1 60
14	7 46	3S54	5 1	6 23	9 9	1 37	11 13	0 43	0 49	1 2	13 43	0 43	15 47	1 60
15	8 9	8 46	4 42	11 3	8 23	1 17	11 41	0 41	0 34	1 2	13 39	0 43	15 49	1 60
16	8 31	13 11	4 10	15 9	7 39	0 56	12 9	0 39	0 18	1 2	13 36	0 43	15 51	1 59
17	8 53	16 56	3 25	18 31	6 55	0 36	12 36	0 37	0 3	1 2	13 33	0 43	15 53	1 59
18	9 15	19 52	2 32	20 60	6 15	0 15	13 3	0 35	0S13	1 2	13 30	0 43	15 55	1 59
19	9 37	21 52	1 33	22 29	5 39	0N 4	13 29	0 32	0 28	1 1	13 27	0 44	15 57	1 59
20	9 59	22 51	0 30	22 57	5 8	0 23	13 56	0 30	0 44	1 1	13 24	0 44	15 59	1 59
21	10 20	22 47	0N33	22 22	4 42	0 41	14 22	0 28	0 59	1 1	13 21	0 44	16 0	1 59
22	10 42	21 42	1 36	20 47	4 21	0 57	14 47	0 25	1 14	1 1	13 18	0 44	16 2	1 59
23	11 3	19 39	2 34	18 18	4 7	1 11	15 12	0 23	1 30	1 1	13 15	0 44	16 4	1 59
24	11 24	16 45	3 26	14 60	3 58	1 24	15 37	0 21	1 45	1 0	13 12	0 45	16 6	1 59
25	11 45	13 5	4 10	10 60	3 55	1 35	16 2	0 18	2 1	1 0	13 9	0 45	16 8	1 58
26	12 6	8 46	4 44	6 25	3 57	1 44	16 26	0 16	2 16	0 60	13 6	0 45	16 10	1 58
27	12 27	3 57	5 4	1 25	4 4	1 52	16 49	0 13	2 31	0 60	13 4	0 45	16 12	1 58
28	12 47	1N11	5 9	3N48	4 16	1 58	17 12	0 11	2 47	0 60	13 1	0 45	16 14	1 58
29	13 7	6 25	4 57	9 0	4 33	2 3	17 35	0 9	3 2	0 59	12 58	0 45	16 15	1 58
30	13 27	11 30	4 26	13 51	4 52	2 6	17 57	0 6	3 18	0 59	12 56	0 46	16 17	1 58
31	13S47	16N 3	3N38	18N 0	5S16	2N 9	18S19	0N 4	3S33	0N59	12N53	0N46	16S19	1N58

Day	♅ Decl	♅ Lat	♆ Decl	♆ Lat	♇ Decl	♇ Lat
1	20N19	0N32	8S55	1N40	21N53	10N17
5	20 17	0 32	8 58	1 40	21 52	10 18
9	20 16	0 32	9 1	1 40	21 51	10 19
13	20 15	0 33	9 4	1 40	21 50	10 20
17	20 14	0 33	9 8	1 40	21 49	10 21
21	20 13	0 33	9 11	1 40	21 49	10 23
25	20 12	0 33	9 14	1 40	21 48	10 24
29	20N12	0N33	9S17	1N40	21N48	10N25

☽ PHENOMENA

d	h	m	
1	19	18	○
8	14	4	☾
15	19	33	●
23	23	5	☽
31	6	4	○

d	h	° '
6	17	23N 3
13	6	0
20	10	22S57
27	19	0

d	h	° '
6	20	0
13	8	5S 4
20	11	0
27	19	5N 9

VOID OF COURSE ☽

Last Aspect		☽ Ingress		
30	3pm27	1	♈	5am47
3	6am18	3	♉	8am52
5	7am24	5	♊	11am 0
7	9am50	7	♋	1pm23
9	12pm23	9	♌	4pm42
11	6pm25	11	♍	9pm12
13	8am40	14	♎	3am14
16	7am46	16	♏	11am24
18	6pm27	18	♐	10pm 8
21	7am12	21	♑	10am52
23	11pm 5	23	♒	11pm33
26	6am26	26	♓	9am38
28	0am45	28	♈	3pm47
30	3pm48	30	♉	6pm30

d	h	
5	11	PERIGEE
21	6	APOGEE

DAILY ASPECTARIAN

1 S	☽⚻♆	0am55
	☽⚻♇	1 51
	☽⚻☿	3 23
	☽∥♂	3 49
	☽#♀	8 6
	☽△♅	8 43
	☿#♃	11 18
	☽⚼♄	11 58
	☿SR	2pm 2
	☉☍☽	7 18
	☽⚼♃	8 7
2 Su	☽#♆	1am54
	☽⚼♇	3 44
	☉∠♃	9 22
	☽☍♀	10 37
	☽⚻♄	1pm47
	☽⚻♂	9 29
	☽△♃	9 56
3 M	☉#♂	2am44
	☽☍♆	4 18
	☽∥♃	4 40
	☽#☿	4 44
	☽△♇	5 10
	☽☍☿	6 18
	☽#♄	11 0
	☿#♃	11 8
	♂⚺♃	11 25
	☽□♅	11 49
	☽⚼♂	11pm50
4 T	♀⚺♄	1am33
	☉⚻☽	1 43
	☽☍♄	4pm27
	☽⚻♀	5 45
	☽∥♅	7 21
5 W	☽□♃	0am48
	☽△♂	2 2
	☿⚹♇	4 16
	☉⚼☽	4 36
	☽⚻♆	6 35
	☽⚻☿	7 18
	☽□♇	7 24
	☽∥♇	11 26
	☽⚹♅	2pm 2
	☽⚼♀	9 11
6 Th	☿☌♆	2am 1
	☽⚼☿	7 29
	☉△☽	7 31
	☽⚼♆	7 44
	☽∠♅	3pm13
	☽⚻♄	7 0
	☉∠♇	10 31
7 F	☽△♀	0am46
	☽⚹♃	3 42
	☽□♂	6 41
	☽△☿	7 36
	☽△♆	9 2
	☽⚹♇	9 50
	☿⚺♂	4pm34
	☽⚺♅	4 35
	☽⚼♄	8 32
	☽∥♇	11 57
8 S	☽∠♃	5am27
	☽∠♇	11 21
	☉□☽	2pm 4
	♀⚹♃	3 22
	☽∥♅	4 24
	☽△♄	10 19
9 Su	☿☌♀	2am11
	☽⚺♃	7 27
	☽□☿	7 50
	♀∥♆	8 46
	☽□♀	8 49
	☽⚹♂	12pm19
	☿⚹♃	12 22
	☽□♆	12 23
	☽⚺♇	1 9
	♂⚺♆	1 59
	☽☌♅	8 3
10 M	☽#♄	0am25
	♂⚺♇	7 9
	☽∥♃	10 24
	☽∠♂	3pm37
	☉⚹☽	9 57
11 T	☽#☿	0am 3
	♀☌♆	1 48
	☽□♄	2 47
	☽#♀	6 54
	☽⚹☿	8 20
	♀⚹♇	10 3
	☽#♆	11 17
	☽☌♃	12pm24
	☽⚹♆	4 56
	☽☌♇	5 39
	☽⚹♀	6 25
	☽⚺♂	7 18
	☉#☽	9 16
12 W	☽⚺♅	0am44
	☉∠☽	2 30
	☿∥♀	6 58
	☽∠☿	8 49
	♀⚺♂	1pm24
	☽∠♆	7 44
	☽∠♀	11 55
13 Th	♀ ♏	0am39
	☽∥♂	0 47
	☽∠♅	3 38
	☉⚺☽	7 33
	☽⚹♄	8 40
	☽⚺☿	9 33
	☽#♂	10 15
	♂ ♎	11 20
	☿⚺♄	6pm23
	☽⚺♃	6 51
	☉☌☿	8 41
	☽⚺♆	10 58
	☽⚺♇	11 40
14 F	☉⚺♄	0am 8
	☿∥♆	1 59
	☽☌♂	4 3
	☽⚺♀	6 2
	☽⚹♅	7 0
	☽∠♄	12pm18
	♀□♅	4 17
	☉∥☽	8 32
	☽∥☿	10 19
	☽∠♃	10 49
15 S	☽∥♆	1am42
	☽∠♇	3 25
	☉∥☿	5 14
	☽☌☿	12pm15
	☽⚺♄	4 30
	☽∥♀	5 21
	☉☌☽	7 33
16 Su	☽#♃	2am27
	☽⚹♃	3 23
	☽☌♆	7 7
	☽⚹♇	7 46
	☽⚺♂	3pm17
	☽□♅	3 26
	☽∥♄	4 41
	♂⚹♅	6 9
	☽☌♀	8 34
17 M	☉∥♆	4pm23
	☽⚺☿	5 29
	☽∠♂	10 2
18 T	☽☌♄	2am55
	☽#♅	3 29
	☉⚺☽	10 45
	☽□♃	2pm33
	☽⚺♆	5 51
	☽□♇	6 27
	☽∠☿	9 19
	♀#♃	10 1
	☽#♇	11 8
19 W	☽△♅	2am26
	☽⚹♂	5 31
	☽⚺♀	2pm37
	☉∠☽	7 31
20 Th	☽∠♆	0am 5
	☽⚹☿	2 2
	☽⚼♅	8 45
	☽⚺♄	3pm44
	☉⚹♃	5 1
21 F	☽∠♀	0am38
	☽△♃	3 56
	☉⚹☽	4 47
	☽⚹♆	6 41
	☽△♇	7 12
	☽⚻♅	3pm20
	☽□♂	9 53
	☽#♇	10 17
	☽∠♄	10 36
22 S	☿∠♇	0am ♋
	☉☌♆	4 0
	☉⚹♇	9 57
	☽⚹♀	10 48
	☽⚼♃	10 53
	♂∠♄	1pm26
	☽□☿	1 40
	☽⚼♇	1 48
	☽#♅	6 28
	☿SD	7 16
23 Su	☽⚹♄	5am19
	☿⚺♀	3pm10
	☽⚻♃	5 32
	☽□♆	7 39
	☽⚻♇	8 4
	☿∠♇	8 8
	☉□☽	11 5
24 M	☽☍♅	3am59
	☽∥♄	4 33
	☉ ♏	4 44
	☽∥♀	7 3
	☽△♂	1pm38
	☽#♃	11 32
25 T	☽△☿	2am24
	☽□♀	5 27
	♀∥♄	6 44
	☉∥☽	7 7
	☽□♄	4pm57
	☽⚼♂	8 17
	☽∥♆	9 29
26 W	☽☍♃	4am39
	☽△♆	6 7
	☽☍♇	6 26
	☽⚼☿	8 15
	☉□♅	11 9
	☽⚻♅	1pm51
	☉△☽	2 4
	☽∥☿	11 28
27 Th	☽⚻♂	1am47
	☽∥♂	6 29
	☽⚼♆	9 54
	☽⚻☿	1pm24
	☽⚼♅	5 17
	☽△♀	7 22
	☉⚼☽	7 41
28 F	☽△♄	0am45
	☽#♂	7 42
	☽⚻♃	11 43
	☽⚻♆	12pm40
	☽⚻♇	12 52
	☉#♃	2 27
	☽#☿	2 52
	☽△♅	7 45
29 S	☉⚻☽	0am 5
	☽⚼♀	0 19
	☽⚼♄	3 9
	☽☍♂	9 21
	☽#♆	1pm23
	☽⚼♃	1 48
	☽⚼♇	2 41
	☽☍☿	9 16
30 Su	☽⚻♀	4am12
	☽⚻♄	4 44
	☽∥♃	7 6
	☉#☽	10 39
	♀☌♄	10 53
	☽△♃	3pm 9
	☽☍♆	3 41
	☽△♇	3 48
	☽□♅	10 18
31 M	☽#♄	1am37
	☉☍☽	6 4
	☽⚻♂	1pm32
	☽#♀	3 43

LONGITUDE

Day	Sid. Time	☉	☽	☽ 12 Hour	Mean ☊	True ☊	☿	♀	♂	♃	♄	♅	♆	♇
	h m s	° ' "	° ' "	° ' "	° '	° '	° '	° '	° '	° '	° '	° '	° '	° '
1	2 38 2	7♏ 47 13	18♉ 2 22	25♉ 26 22	19♐ 19	17♐ 52R	19♎ 40	23♏ 40	11♎ 53	28♌ 9	21♏ 55	2♌ 19	28♎ 21	28♌ 23
2	2 41 59	8 47 14	2♊ 51 2	10♊ 15 28	19 16	17 49	20 56	24 54	12 32	28 17	22 2	2 19	28 23	28 24
3	2 45 55	9 47 17	17 38 45	25 0 6	19 13	17 48D	22 16	26 9	13 10	28 25	22 9	2 19	28 25	28 25
4	2 49 52	10 47 22	2♋ 18 52	9♋ 34 28	19 10	17 48	23 39	27 24	13 49	28 33	22 16	2 20	28 27	28 26
5	2 53 48	11 47 29	16 46 28	23 54 33	19 7	17 49	25 4	28 39	14 28	28 40	22 23	2 20	28 29	28 26
6	2 57 45	12 47 38	0♌ 58 31	7♌ 58 14	19 3	17 51R	26 32	29 54	15 6	28 48	22 30	2 20	28 32	28 27
7	3 1 41	13 47 49	14 53 40	21 44 51	19 0	17 51	28 2	1♐ 8	15 45	28 55	22 37	2 20	28 34	28 28
8	3 5 38	14 48 2	28 31 51	5♍ 14 45	18 57	17 50	29 33	2 23	16 23	29 2	22 44	2 20R	28 36	28 29
9	3 9 34	15 48 18	11♍ 53 43	18 28 51	18 54	17 48	1♏ 6	3 38	17 2	29 9	22 51	2 20	28 38	28 29
10	3 13 31	16 48 35	25 0 19	1♎ 28 14	18 51	17 44	2 39	4 53	17 41	29 16	22 58	2 20	28 40	28 30
11	3 17 28	17 48 54	7♎ 52 45	14 13 59	18 48	17 40	4 14	6 8	18 19	29 22	23 6	2 20	28 43	28 31
12	3 21 24	18 49 15	20 32 3	26 47 5	18 44	17 35	5 48	7 22	18 58	29 29	23 13	2 20	28 45	28 31
13	3 25 21	19 49 38	2♏ 59 12	9♏ 8 31	18 41	17 30	7 24	8 37	19 37	29 35	23 20	2 20	28 47	28 32
14	3 29 17	20 50 3	15 15 11	21 19 21	18 38	17 26	8 59	9 52	20 16	29 41	23 27	2 19	28 49	28 32
15	3 33 14	21 50 29	27 21 11	3♐ 20 54	18 35	17 23	10 35	11 7	20 54	29 47	23 34	2 19	28 51	28 33
16	3 37 10	22 50 57	9♐ 18 43	15 14 54	18 32	17 21D	12 11	12 22	21 33	29 53	23 41	2 19	28 53	28 33
17	3 41 7	23 51 27	21 9 45	27 3 37	18 28	17 21	13 47	13 37	22 12	29 59	23 48	2 18	28 55	28 34
18	3 45 3	24 51 58	2♑ 56 51	8♑ 49 53	18 25	17 22	15 23	14 51	22 51	0♍ 5	23 56	2 18	28 57	28 34
19	3 49 0	25 52 30	14 43 11	20 37 12	18 22	17 23	16 59	16 6	23 29	0 10	24 3	2 17	28 59	28 34
20	3 52 57	26 53 4	26 32 28	2♒ 29 33	18 19	17 25	18 35	17 21	24 8	0 15	24 10	2 17	29 1	28 35
21	3 56 53	27 53 39	8♒ 29 1	14 31 26	18 16	17 26	20 10	18 36	24 47	0 20	24 17	2 16	29 3	28 35
22	4 0 50	28 54 16	20 37 25	26 47 34	18 13	17 27R	21 46	19 51	25 26	0 25	24 24	2 15	29 5	28 35
23	4 4 46	29 54 53	3♓ 2 27	9♓ 22 38	18 9	17 28	23 21	21 5	26 4	0 30	24 31	2 14	29 7	28 36
24	4 8 43	0♐ 55 31	15 48 37	22 20 50	18 6	17 27	24 57	22 20	26 43	0 35	24 39	2 14	29 9	28 36
25	4 12 39	1 56 11	28 59 40	5♈ 45 21	18 3	17 26	26 32	23 35	27 22	0 39	24 46	2 13	29 11	28 36
26	4 16 36	2 56 52	12♈ 38 0	19 37 38	18 0	17 24	28 7	24 50	28 1	0 43	24 53	2 12	29 13	28 36
27	4 20 32	3 57 33	26 44 1	3♉ 56 50	17 57	17 22	29 42	26 4	28 40	0 47	25 0	2 11	29 15	28 36
28	4 24 29	4 58 16	11♉ 15 31	18 39 23	17 54	17 21	1♐ 17	27 19	29 19	0 51	25 7	2 10	29 17	28 37
29	4 28 26	5 59 1	26 7 31	3♊ 38 57	17 50	17 20	2 51	28 34	29 57	0 55	25 14	2 9	29 19	28 37
30	4 32 22	6♐ 59 46	11♊ 12 33	18♊ 47 9	17♐ 47	17♐ 19D	4♐ 26	29♐ 48	0♏ 36	0♍ 58	25♏ 21	2♌ 8	29♎ 21	28♌ 37

DECLINATION and LATITUDE

Day	☉ Decl	☽ Decl	☽ Lat	☽ 12 Hr. Decl	☿ Decl	☿ Lat	♀ Decl	♀ Lat	♂ Decl	♂ Lat	♃ Decl	♃ Lat	♄ Decl	♄ Lat
1	14S 7	19N41	2N35	21N 3	5S42	2N10	18S41	0N 1	3S48	0N59	12N50	0N46	16S21	1N58
2	14 26	22 3	1 21	22 40	6 10	2 10	19 1	0S 1	4 3	0 58	12 48	0 46	16 23	1 58
3	14 45	22 53	0 1	22 42	6 40	2 9	19 22	0 4	4 19	0 58	12 45	0 47	16 25	1 58
4	15 4	22 7	1S18	21 10	7 13	2 7	19 41	0 7	4 34	0 58	12 43	0 47	16 27	1 58
5	15 23	19 53	2 32	18 18	7 46	2 5	20 1	0 9	4 49	0 58	12 40	0 47	16 28	1 58
6	15 41	16 28	3 34	14 24	8 21	2 2	20 19	0 12	5 4	0 57	12 38	0 47	16 30	1 58
7	15 59	12 11	4 23	9 49	8 56	1 58	20 37	0 14	5 19	0 57	12 36	0 47	16 32	1 57
8	16 17	7 22	4 55	4 51	9 32	1 54	20 55	0 17	5 34	0 57	12 33	0 48	16 34	1 57
9	16 34	2 18	5 11	0S15	10 9	1 50	21 12	0 19	5 49	0 56	12 31	0 48	16 36	1 57
10	16 52	2S46	5 10	5 14	10 46	1 45	21 28	0 22	6 4	0 56	12 29	0 48	16 38	1 57
11	17 9	7 37	4 54	9 55	11 22	1 39	21 44	0 24	6 19	0 56	12 27	0 48	16 40	1 57
12	17 26	12 5	4 23	14 6	11 59	1 34	21 59	0 27	6 34	0 56	12 25	0 48	16 41	1 57
13	17 42	15 57	3 40	17 37	12 36	1 28	22 14	0 29	6 49	0 55	12 23	0 49	16 43	1 57
14	17 58	19 5	2 48	20 19	13 12	1 22	22 28	0 32	7 4	0 55	12 21	0 49	16 45	1 57
15	18 14	21 20	1 48	22 5	13 49	1 15	22 41	0 34	7 19	0 55	12 19	0 49	16 47	1 57
16	18 29	22 35	0 44	22 49	14 24	1 9	22 53	0 37	7 34	0 54	12 17	0 49	16 49	1 57
17	18 44	22 48	0N21	22 31	14 59	1 2	23 5	0 39	7 48	0 54	12 15	0 50	16 50	1 57
18	18 59	21 60	1 25	21 13	15 34	0 56	23 17	0 42	8 3	0 54	12 13	0 50	16 52	1 57
19	19 14	20 13	2 26	18 60	16 8	0 49	23 27	0 44	8 18	0 54	12 12	0 50	16 54	1 57
20	19 28	17 35	3 20	15 58	16 41	0 42	23 37	0 47	8 32	0 53	12 10	0 50	16 56	1 57
21	19 42	14 11	4 7	12 14	17 14	0 35	23 46	0 49	8 47	0 53	12 9	0 51	16 57	1 57
22	19 55	10 9	4 43	7 56	17 45	0 28	23 54	0 51	9 1	0 53	12 7	0 51	16 59	1 57
23	20 8	5 37	5 7	3 12	18 16	0 21	24 2	0 54	9 16	0 52	12 6	0 51	17 1	1 57
24	20 21	0 44	5 17	1N48	18 47	0 14	24 9	0 56	9 30	0 52	12 4	0 51	17 3	1 57
25	20 33	4N21	5 10	6 53	19 16	0 8	24 15	0 58	9 44	0 52	12 3	0 51	17 4	1 57
26	20 45	9 23	4 47	11 49	19 44	0 1	24 21	1 0	9 58	0 51	12 2	0 52	17 6	1 57
27	20 57	14 7	4 5	16 15	20 11	0S 6	24 26	1 3	10 13	0 51	12 0	0 52	17 8	1 57
28	21 8	18 10	3 7	19 49	20 38	0 13	24 30	1 5	10 27	0 51	11 59	0 52	17 10	1 57
29	21 19	21 9	1 55	22 7	21 3	0 19	24 33	1 7	10 41	0 50	11 58	0 52	17 11	1 57
30	21S29	22N41	0N34	22N50	21S28	0S26	24S36	1S 9	10S55	0N50	11N57	0N53	17S13	1N57

Day	♅ Decl	♅ Lat	♆ Decl	♆ Lat	♇ Decl	♇ Lat
1	20N11	0N33	9S19	1N40	21N48	10N26
5	20 11	0 33	9 23	1 40	21 48	10 28
9	20 11	0 34	9 26	1 40	21 48	10 29
13	20 12	0 34	9 29	1 41	21 49	10 31
17	20 12	0 34	9 31	1 41	21 50	10 32
21	20 13	0 34	9 34	1 41	21 51	10 34
25	20 14	0 34	9 37	1 41	21 52	10 35
29	20N15	0N34	9S39	1N41	21N53	10N37

☽ PHENOMENA

d	h	m	
6	21	56	☾
14	12	2	●
22	17	29	☽
29	16	50	○

d	h	° '
3	0	22N53
9	11	0
16	17	22S51
24	3	0
30	10	22N50

d	h	
3	0	0
9	11	5S13
16	16	0
24	3	5N17
30	10	0

VOID OF COURSE ☽

Last Aspect		☽ Ingress		
1	4pm47	1	♊	7pm23
3	5pm45	3	♋	8pm12
5	9pm59	5	♌	10pm20
8	2am 3	8	♍	2am37
9	8pm13	10	♎	9am16
12	5pm21	12	♏	6pm13
15	4am55	15	♐	5am17
17	3pm50	17	♑	5pm59
20	5am 2	20	♒	6am59
22	5pm29	22	♓	6pm11
24	6pm59	25	♈	1am48
27	4am13	27	♉	5am27
29	3am58	29	♊	6am11

d	h	
2	3	PERIGEE
17	23	APOGEE
30	11	PERIGEE

DAILY ASPECTARIAN

1 T	☽⚻☿	2am53
	☽∥♅	4 7
	☽☍♄	6 20
	☽☍♀	9 57
	☽⚼♂	3pm 0
	☽□♃	4 33
	☽⚻♆	4 45
	☽□♇	4 47
	☽∥♇	8 33
	☽⚹♅	11 8
2 W	☽⚼☿	5am28
	☉⚻☽	10 19
	☽△♂	4pm24
	☽⚼♆	5 7
	♆⚹♇	8 10
	☿⚺♄	9 47
	♃☌♇	11 2
	☽∠♅	11 28
	♃⚹♆	11 55
3 Th	☽⚻♄	7am24
	☽△☿	8 18
	♂∠♇	9 15
	♂∠♃	11 29
	☉⚼☽	12pm30
	☽⚻♀	3 11
	☽⚹♇	5 36
	☽△♆	5 39
	☽⚹♃	5 45
4 F	☽⚺♅	0am 1
	☽∥♇	4 31
	☽⚼♄	8 14
	☉△☽	3pm 4
	☽⚼♀	6 17
	☽∠♇	6 26
	☽∠♃	6 46
	☽□♂	7 57
	♀□♇	7 59
	♀⚺♆	8 55
	☽∥♅	9 25
	☽#♀	11 3
5 S	♀□♃	0am31
	☽△♄	9 30
	♀#♅	1pm33
	☽□☿	3 34
	☽⚺♇	7 42
	☽□♆	7 49
	☽⚺♃	8 15
	☽△♀	9 59
	☽#♄	11 44
6 Su	♀ ♐	2am 3
	☽☌♅	2 19
	☉#☽	4 22
	♀∠♂	8 18
	☽∥♃	9pm49
	☉□☽	9 56
7 M	☽⚹♂	1am33
	☿⚹♇	6 55
	☿☌♆	8 38
	☽□♄	1pm39
	☽#♆	2 3
	☽#☿	2 35
	☿⚹♃	3 7
	☿∥♆	7 0
	♀△♅	11 1
	☽☌♇	11 54
8 T	☽⚹♆	0am 7
	☽☌♃	0 54
	☽⚹☿	2 3
	☽∠♂	5 21
	☽⚺♅	6 47
	☿ ♏	6 58
	☽□♀	7 35
	☽#♂	8 10
	♅SR	9 35
9 W	☉∥♄	2am10
	☽∠♆	3 10
	☉⚹☽	7 42
	☽∠☿	8 40
	☽⚺♂	9 50
	☽∠♅	9 54
	☿□♅	7pm 6
	☽⚹♄	8 13
10 Th	☽⚺♇	6am29
	☽⚺♆	6 49
	☽⚺♃	7 57
	☽⚹♅	1pm37
	☉∠☽	1 42
	☽⚺☿	4 11
	☽∥♂	5 4
	☽⚹♀	8 21
11 F	☽∠♄	0am24
	♀#♇	7 17
	☽∥♆	9 34
	☽∠♇	10 38
	☽∠♃	12pm22
	☉⚺☽	8 27
	☽☌♂	8 51
	☽∥☿	11 24
12 S	☽#♃	1am54
	☽∠♀	3 55
	☽⚺♄	5 11
	☉⚺♂	9 53
	☽⚹♇	3pm21
	☿#♃	3 46
	☽☌♆	3 50
	☽⚹♃	5 21
	☽□♅	10 43
13 Su	☽∥♄	5am23
	☽☌☿	9 52
	☽⚺♀	12pm14
	☉∥☽	1 48
14 M	☽⚺♂	10am27
	☽#♅	10 41
	☉☌☽	12pm 2
	☽☌♄	4 23
15 T	☽□♇	2am23
	☽⚺♆	3 0
	☽□♃	4 55
	☽#♇	7 27
	☽△♅	9 56
	☽∠♂	6pm 7
16 W	☽⚺☿	6am42
	☽☌♀	6 53
	☽∠♆	9 16
	☿⚺♀	12pm18
	☽⚼♅	4 10
	☉☌♄	10 40
17 Th	☽⚹♂	2am13
	♃ ♍	4 1
	☽⚺♄	5 26
	☉⚺☽	6 0
	♀∠♆	6 9
	☽△♇	3pm 4
	☽⚹♆	3 50
	☽∠☿	5 57
	☽△♃	6 6
	☽⚻♅	10 40
18 F	☽#♇	2am51
	☽∠♄	12pm19
	☉∠☽	3 26
	☽⚼♇	9 40
19 S	☽#♅	0am 9
	☽⚼♃	0 55
	☽⚺♀	3 9
	☽⚹☿	5 19
	☉∥☽	9 3
	☽□♂	6pm51
	☽⚹♄	7 9
	♀⚼♅	10 35
20 Su	☉⚹☽	0am46
	♂⚺♄	1 25
	☽⚻♇	4 7
	☽∥♄	4 56
	☽□♆	5 2
	☽∥☿	5 48
	☽⚻♃	7 33
	☿∥♄	11 18
	☽☍♅	11 33
	☽∠♀	1pm 5
21 M	☽#♃	12pm36
	☉□♇	4 30
	☽⚹♀	10 18
22 T	☽□☿	2am34
	☽∥♆	3 7
	☉⚺♆	4 35
	☽∥♂	5 52
	☽□♄	7 27
	☽△♂	9 52
	☽☍♇	3pm28
	☽△♆	4 29
	☉□☽	5 29
	☽☍♃	7 7
	☽⚻♅	10 28
23 W	☉ ♐	2am 1
	☉#♅	9 22
	☉□♃	3pm 4
	☽⚼♂	3 59
	☿☌♄	7 3
	☽⚼♆	8 56
24 Th	☽⚼♅	2am37
	♂∥♆	11 6
	☽□♀	1pm13
	☽△♄	4 19
	☽△☿	6 59
	☽⚻♂	8 56
	☽⚻♇	11 18
25 F	☽⚻♆	0am21
	☽⚻♃	2 58
	☉△☽	5 40
	☽△♅	5 44
	☉△♅	6 26
	☽⚼♄	7pm11
	☿⚺♂	9 25
26 S	☽⚼☿	0am56
	☽#♆	1 9
	♀⚺♄	1 10
	☽⚼♇	1 41
	☽#♂	2 59
	☽⚼♃	5 21
	☿□♇	7 25
	☉⚼☽	9 51
	☽∥♃	1pm 0
	☿⚺♆	5 7
	☽⚻♄	9 4
	♂⚹♇	9 56
	☽△♀	10 47
27 Su	☿#♅	2am25
	☽△♇	3 8
	☽☍♂	3 23
	☽☍♆	4 13
	☿ ♐	4 35
	☽⚻☿	5 34
	☽△♃	6 48
	☽□♅	9 4
	☉⚻☽	12pm55
	☿□♃	5 17
	☽#♄	5 25
	♂☌♆	11 3
28 M	☽⚼♀	1am53
	☿△♅	1pm19
	☽∥♅	3 29
	☽☍♄	10 34
	☽#☿	10 46
29 T	♀△♇	0am55
	♂ ♏	1 34
	☉#☽	1 50
	☽□♇	3 58
	☽⚻♀	4 15
	☽⚻♆	5 7
	☽⚻♂	6 24
	☽□♃	7 41
	☽∥♇	8 40
	☽⚹♅	9 36
	☽☍☿	11 59
	♀⚹♆	2pm56
	☉☍☽	4 50
30 W	☉∥☿	2am32
	♀ ♑	3 43
	☽⚼♆	4 59
	☽⚼♂	7 17
	☽∠♅	9 22
	♂⚹♃	2pm58
	☽⚻♄	10 35
	♀△♃	11 34

DECEMBER 1955

LONGITUDE

Day	Sid. Time	☉	☽	☽ 12 Hour	Mean ☊	True ☊	☿	♀	♂	♃	♄	♅	♆	♇
	h m s	° ' "	° ' "	° ' "	° '	° '	° '	° '	° '	° '	° '	° '	° '	° '
1	4 36 19	8♐ 0 33	26♊ 21 35	3♋ 54 40	17♐ 44	17♐ 19	6♐ 0	1♑ 3	1♏ 15	1♍ 2	25♏ 28	2♌ 6R	29♎ 23	28♌ 37R
2	4 40 15	9 1 21	11♋ 25 20	18 52 36	17 41	17 19	7 35	2 18	1 54	1 5	25 35	2 5	29 25	28 37
3	4 44 12	10 2 11	26 15 38	3♌ 33 44	17 38	17 20	9 9	3 33	2 33	1 8	25 42	2 4	29 26	28 37
4	4 48 8	11 3 1	10♌ 46 24	17 53 14	17 34	17 21	10 43	4 47	3 12	1 11	25 49	2 3	29 28	28 37
5	4 52 5	12 3 53	24 54 2	1♍ 48 45	17 31	17 21	12 18	6 2	3 51	1 13	25 56	2 1	29 30	28 36
6	4 56 1	13 4 47	8♍ 37 25	15 20 11	17 28	17 21R	13 52	7 17	4 30	1 16	26 3	2 0	29 32	28 36
7	4 59 58	14 5 41	21 57 17	28 29 2	17 25	17 21	15 26	8 31	5 9	1 18	26 10	1 58	29 33	28 36
8	5 3 55	15 6 38	4♎ 55 45	11♎ 17 49	17 22	17 21	17 0	9 46	5 48	1 20	26 17	1 57	29 35	28 36
9	5 7 51	16 7 35	17 35 38	23 49 35	17 19	17 21D	18 34	11 0	6 27	1 22	26 24	1 55	29 37	28 36
10	5 11 48	17 8 33	0♏ 0 3	6♏ 7 26	17 15	17 21	20 9	12 15	7 6	1 24	26 31	1 54	29 39	28 35
11	5 15 44	18 9 33	12 12 4	18 14 18	17 12	17 21	21 43	13 30	7 45	1 25	26 38	1 52	29 40	28 35
12	5 19 41	19 10 34	24 14 28	0♐ 12 53	17 9	17 21	23 17	14 44	8 24	1 27	26 45	1 50	29 42	28 35
13	5 23 37	20 11 35	6♐ 9 49	12 5 34	17 6	17 21R	24 52	15 59	9 3	1 28	26 51	1 49	29 43	28 35
14	5 27 34	21 12 37	18 0 24	23 54 33	17 3	17 21	26 26	17 14	9 42	1 29	26 58	1 47	29 45	28 34
15	5 31 30	22 13 41	29 48 18	5♑ 41 55	16 59	17 21	28 1	18 28	10 21	1 29	27 5	1 45	29 47	28 34
16	5 35 27	23 14 45	11♑ 35 39	17 29 48	16 56	17 21	29 36	19 43	11 0	1 30	27 12	1 43	29 48	28 33
17	5 39 24	24 15 50	23 24 39	29 20 31	16 53	17 20	1♑ 11	20 57	11 39	1 30	27 18	1 41	29 50	28 33
18	5 43 20	25 16 55	5♒ 17 46	11♒ 16 44	16 50	17 18	2 46	22 12	12 18	1 30R	27 25	1 39	29 51	28 32
19	5 47 17	26 18 0	17 17 50	23 21 28	16 47	17 17	4 21	23 26	12 57	1 30	27 31	1 38	29 52	28 32
20	5 51 13	27 19 6	29 28 5	5♓ 38 7	16 44	17 16	5 56	24 41	13 36	1 30	27 38	1 36	29 54	28 31
21	5 55 10	28 20 12	11♓ 52 3	18 10 22	16 40	17 15	7 31	25 55	14 15	1 30	27 44	1 34	29 55	28 31
22	5 59 6	29 21 19	24 33 31	1♈ 1 57	16 37	17 15D	9 6	27 10	14 54	1 29	27 51	1 31	29 57	28 30
23	6 3 3	0♑ 22 25	7♈ 36 6	14 16 20	16 34	17 15	10 42	28 24	15 33	1 28	27 57	1 29	29 58	28 30
24	6 7 0	1 23 32	21 2 57	27 56 10	16 31	17 15	12 17	29 39	16 13	1 27	28 4	1 27	29 59	28 29
25	6 10 56	2 24 39	4♉ 56 4	12♉ 2 36	16 28	17 17	13 52	0♒ 53	16 52	1 26	28 10	1 25	0♏ 0	28 28
26	6 14 53	3 25 46	19 15 36	26 34 40	16 25	17 18	15 28	2 7	17 31	1 24	28 16	1 23	0 2	28 28
27	6 18 49	4 26 54	3♊ 59 17	11♊ 28 41	16 21	17 19R	17 3	3 22	18 10	1 23	28 23	1 21	0 3	28 27
28	6 22 46	5 28 1	19 1 59	26 38 6	16 18	17 19	18 38	4 36	18 49	1 21	28 29	1 18	0 4	28 26
29	6 26 42	6 29 9	4♋ 15 52	11♋ 53 59	16 15	17 18	20 12	5 50	19 28	1 19	28 35	1 16	0 5	28 25
30	6 30 39	7 30 16	19 31 10	27 6 9	16 12	17 17	21 46	7 5	20 7	1 17	28 41	1 14	0 6	28 24
31	6 34 35	8♑ 31 24	4♌ 37 44	12♌ 4 48	16♐ 9	17♐ 14	23♑ 20	8♒ 19	20♏ 47	1♍ 14	28♏ 47	1♌ 11	0♏ 7	28♌ 24

DECLINATION and LATITUDE

Day	☉ Decl	☽ Decl	☽ Lat	☽ 12 Hr. Decl	☿ Decl	☿ Lat	♀ Decl	♀ Lat	♂ Decl	♂ Lat	♃ Decl	♃ Lat	♄ Decl	♄ Lat
1	21S39	22N34	0S50	21N52	21S51	0S32	24S37	1S11	11S 8	0N49	11N56	0N53	17S15	1N37
2	21 48	20 48	2 10	19 22	22 13	0 39	24 38	1 13	11 22	0 49	11 55	0 53	17 16	1 57
3	21 58	17 38	3 20	15 38	22 34	0 45	24 39	1 15	11 36	0 49	11 54	0 53	17 18	1 57
4	22 6	13 26	4 16	11 4	22 54	0 51	24 38	1 17	11 50	0 48	11 54	0 54	17 20	1 57
5	22 15	8 36	4 54	6 3	23 13	0 57	24 37	1 19	12 3	0 48	11 53	0 54	17 21	1 57
6	22 22	3 29	5 14	0 54	23 31	1 3	24 35	1 21	12 17	0 48	11 52	0 54	17 23	1 57
7	22 30	1S40	5 17	4S10	23 47	1 9	24 32	1 22	12 30	0 47	11 52	0 54	17 24	1 57
8	22 37	6 36	5 3	8 56	24 3	1 14	24 29	1 24	12 43	0 47	11 51	0 55	17 26	1 57
9	22 43	11 8	4 35	13 13	24 17	1 20	24 25	1 26	12 56	0 46	11 51	0 55	17 28	1 57
10	22 49	15 8	3 54	16 52	24 29	1 25	24 20	1 27	13 10	0 46	11 50	0 55	17 29	1 57
11	22 55	18 25	3 4	19 45	24 41	1 30	24 14	1 29	13 23	0 46	11 50	0 55	17 31	1 57
12	23 0	20 51	2 5	21 44	24 51	1 35	24 8	1 30	13 36	0 45	11 50	0 56	17 32	1 57
13	23 5	22 21	1 2	22 44	24 60	1 39	24 0	1 32	13 48	0 45	11 50	0 56	17 34	1 57
14	23 9	22 51	0N 4	22 42	25 7	1 43	23 52	1 33	14 1	0 44	11 50	0 56	17 35	1 57
15	23 13	22 18	1 9	21 39	25 13	1 47	23 44	1 34	14 14	0 44	11 50	0 57	17 37	1 57
16	23 16	20 46	2 11	19 39	25 18	1 51	23 34	1 36	14 26	0 44	11 50	0 57	17 38	1 57
17	23 19	18 20	3 7	16 49	25 21	1 55	23 24	1 37	14 39	0 43	11 50	0 57	17 40	1 57
18	23 22	15 8	3 56	13 17	25 23	1 58	23 14	1 38	14 51	0 43	11 50	0 57	17 41	1 57
19	23 24	11 17	4 35	9 10	25 23	2 1	23 2	1 39	15 4	0 42	11 50	0 58	17 42	1 57
20	23 25	6 56	5 2	4 37	25 22	2 4	22 50	1 40	15 16	0 42	11 51	0 58	17 44	1 57
21	23 26	2 14	5 16	0N12	25 20	2 6	22 37	1 41	15 28	0 41	11 51	0 58	17 45	1 57
22	23 27	2N39	5 15	5 7	25 16	2 8	22 24	1 42	15 40	0 41	11 52	0 58	17 47	1 57
23	23 27	7 34	4 58	9 58	25 10	2 9	22 10	1 43	15 52	0 40	11 52	0 59	17 48	1 57
24	23 26	12 17	4 24	14 29	25 3	2 11	21 55	1 43	16 3	0 40	11 53	0 59	17 49	1 58
25	23 25	16 32	3 34	18 22	24 54	2 11	21 39	1 44	16 15	0 39	11 53	0 59	17 51	1 58
26	23 24	19 56	2 29	21 13	24 44	2 12	21 23	1 44	16 26	0 39	11 54	0 59	17 52	1 58
27	23 22	22 9	1 13	22 42	24 32	2 12	21 7	1 45	16 38	0 38	11 55	0 60	17 53	1 58
28	23 20	22 50	0S 9	22 33	24 19	2 11	20 49	1 45	16 49	0 38	11 56	0 60	17 55	1 58
29	23 17	21 50	1 32	20 43	24 4	2 10	20 31	1 46	17 0	0 37	11 57	1 0	17 56	1 58
30	23 14	19 14	2 49	17 26	23 47	2 8	20 13	1 46	17 11	0 37	11 58	1 0	17 57	1 58
31	23S10	15N21	3S53	13N 2	23S30	2S 6	19S54	1S46	17S22	0N36	11N59	1N 1	17S58	1N58

Day	♅ Decl	♅ Lat	♆ Decl	♆ Lat	♇ Decl	♇ Lat
1	20N15	0N34	9S41	1N41	21N54	10N38
5	20 16	0 34	9 43	1 41	21 55	10 39
9	20 18	0 35	9 45	1 41	21 57	10 41
13	20 20	0 35	9 47	1 42	21 59	10 42
17	20 21	0 35	9 49	1 42	22 1	10 44
21	20 23	0 35	9 51	1 42	22 3	10 45
25	20 25	0 35	9 53	1 42	22 5	10 47
29	20N27	0N35	9S54	1N42	22N 7	10N48

☽ PHENOMENA

d	h	m	
6	8	36	☾
14	7	8	●
22	9	40	☽
29	3	44	○

d	h	° '
6	16	0
13	23	22S51
21	11	0
27	22	22N50

d	h	° '
6	16	5S18
13	23	0
21	10	5N17
27	21	0

d	h	
15	7	APOGEE
29	0	PERIGEE

VOID OF COURSE ☽

Last Aspect		☽ Ingress	
1	4am48	1 ♋	5am47
3	5am13	3 ♌	6am 8
5	7am59	5 ♍	8am50
7	7am48	7 ♎	2pm49
9	11pm18	9 ♏	12pm 0
12	8am43	12 ♐	11am34
14	11pm56	15 ♑	0am24
17	1pm 0	17 ♒	1pm20
20	0am50	20 ♓	1am 2
22	9am40	22 ♈	10am 6
24	12pm56	24 ♉	3pm33
26	3pm 3	26 ♊	5pm33
28	2pm49	28 ♋	5pm18
30	2pm37	30 ♌	4pm36

DAILY ASPECTARIAN

1 Th	☿#♇	2am58
	☽⚹♇	3 34
	♇SR	4 30
	☽△♆	4 48
	☽⚹♃	7 27
	♀⚹♂	8 5
	☽☍♀	8 7
	☽△♂	8 7
	☽⚺♅	9 7
	☽#☿	10 4
	☽∥♇	11 36
	☉#☽	1pm40
	☽⚻☿	5 8
	☉⚻☽	7 53
	♀⚻♅	8 0
	☽⚼♄	10 39
2 F	☽∠♇	3am31
	☽∥♅	4 48
	♂□♅	6 37
	☽∠♃	7 31
	☉#♇	2pm58
	☽⚼☿	8 9
	☉⚼☽	9 51
	☽△♄	11 5
3 S	☽#♄	2am 4
	☽⚺♇	3 51
	☽□♆	5 13
	☽⚺♃	8 1
	☽☌♅	9 31
	☽□♂	10 49
	☽⚻♀	1pm 6
	☽△☿	11 54
4 Su	☉△☽	0am30
	♂#♃	6 54
	☽#♂	7 53
	☽∥♃	7 56
	☉☌☿	2pm10
	☽⚼♀	4 43
	☽#♆	6 39
5 M	☽□♄	1am48
	☽☌♇	6 25
	☽⚹♆	7 59
	☽☌♃	11 0
	☽⚺♅	12pm21
	☽⚹♂	4 21
	☽△♀	9 22
6 T	☉□☽	8am36
	☿∠♆	10 23
	☽∠♆	10 34
	☽□☿	10 36
	☽∠♅	2pm58
	☽∠♂	8 32
7 W	☽⚹♄	7am48
	☉∠♆	11 16
	☽⚺♇	12pm13
	☽⚺♆	2 1
	☽⚺♃	5 17
	☽⚹♅	6 27
	☿⚼♅	11 11
8 Th	☽⚺♂	1am43
	☽□♀	10 5
	☽∠♄	12pm 5
	☽∠♇	4 22
	☽∥♆	4 24
	☉⚹☽	8 57
	☽∠♃	9 39
9 F	☽⚹☿	2am 9
	☽#♃	4 0
	♀∠♄	8 19
	☿∥♀	10 55
	☽∥♂	10 59
	☽⚺♄	5pm 9
	☉⚼♅	6 19
	☽⚹♇	9 15
	☽☌♆	11 18
10 S	☽⚹♃	2am44
	☽□♅	3 42
	☉∠☽	4 34
	☽∠☿	11 34
	☽☌♂	2pm42
	☽∥♄	4 46
11 Su	♀⚼♇	1am44
	☽⚹♀	2 52
	☉⚺☽	12pm56
	☽#♅	5 51
	☽⚺☿	9 48
12 M	☿∠♂	2am45
	☽☌♄	5 4
	☽□♇	8 43
	☽⚺♆	10 59
	☽∠♀	12pm20
	☽□♃	2 30
	☽△♅	3 14
	☽#♇	4 7
13 T	☽⚺♂	6am10
	♀⚼♃	9 23
	☽∠♆	5pm22
	☽⚼♅	9 31
	☽⚺♀	10 14
14 W	☉☌☽	7am 8
	☿⚺♄	8 38
	☽∠♂	2pm24
	☽⚺♄	6 24
	☽☌☿	7 48
	☽△♇	9 28
	☽⚹♆	11 56
15 Th	☽△♃	3am26
	☽⚻♅	3 57
	☽#♇	6 12
	☿△♇	8 15
	☽⚹♂	10pm43
16 F	☽∠♄	1am14
	☿⚹♆	3 9
	☽⚼♇	3 59
	☽#♅	4 48
	☿ ♑	6 7
	☽⚼♃	9 59
	☽☌♀	6pm26
17 S	☉⚺☽	1am53
	☿△♃	4 58
	☽∥♄	5 30
	☿⚻♅	7 37
	☽⚹♄	7 57
	☉∥♀	9 24
	☽⚻♇	10 23
	☽□♆	1pm 0
	☽⚻♃	4 22
	☽☍♅	4 42
	☽⚺☿	6 7
18 Su	☽∥♂	1am45
	♃SR	4 34
	☉∠☽	10 56
	☽□♂	2pm51
	☽#♃	8 44
19 M	☽∠☿	4am41
	☽∥♆	8 13
	☽⚺♀	1pm33
	☉⚹☽	7 25
	☽□♄	8 22
	☽☍♇	10 9
20 T	☽△♆	0am50
	☽☍♃	3 58
	☽⚻♅	4 8
	☉⚺♄	8 17
	☽⚹☿	2pm25
	☽∠♀	9 59
21 W	☉△♇	4am 7
	☽△♂	4 48
	☽⚼♆	5 50
	☽⚼♅	8 55
22 Th	☽⚹♀	5am22
	☽△♄	6 10
	☽⚻♇	7 19
	☉□☽	9 40
	☽⚻♆	10 1
	☽⚼♂	10 27
	☽⚻♃	12pm49
	☽△♅	12 52
	☉⚹♆	2 10
	♀⚹♄	2 31
	☉ ♑	3 12
23 F	♀⚻♇	1am42
	☽□☿	6 21
	♀#♇	9 10
	☽⚼♄	9 43
	☽⚼♇	10 36
	☽#♆	11 29
	☉∠♂	12pm 0
	☽⚻♂	3 1
	☽⚼♃	3 53
	☽∥♃	9 49
24 S	☉△♃	1am22
	☉⚻♅	1 24
	♃⚺♅	3 26
	♀□♆	6 45
	♀ ♒	6 53
	☽⚻♄	12pm19
	☿∠♄	12 35
	☽△♇	12 56
	♆ ♏	2 40
	☽☍♆	3 34
	☽□♀	4 24
	☿⚼♇	5 57
	☽□♅	6 1
	☽△♃	6 2
	☉△☽	7 21
	☽#♂	10 12
25 Su	☽#♄	8am32
	♀☍♅	10 2
	♀⚻♃	10 24
	☽△☿	4pm56
	☽☍♂	8 58
	☉⚼☽	10 31
26 M	☽∥♅	4am16
	☽#♀	12pm20
	☿⚼♃	2 5
	☽☍♄	2 52
	☽□♇	3 3
	☽⚻♆	5 38
	☽⚹♅	7 45
	☽□♃	7 48
	☽⚼☿	8 30
	☽△♀	10 54
	☽∥♇	11 13
27 T	☉⚻☽	0am48
	♄□♇	2pm10
	☽⚼♆	5 42
	☽∠♅	7 41
	☽⚻☿	11 17
	☽⚻♂	11 39
28 W	☽⚼♀	0am59
	☿⚹♂	4 54
	☽⚹♇	2pm49
	☽⚻♄	3 0
	☽△♆	5 26
	☽⚺♅	7 18
	☽⚹♃	7 23
	☽∥♇	7 59
29 Th	☽⚼♂	0am20
	☽⚻♀	2 42
	☉☍☽	3 44
	♀#♅	5 22
	☽∥♅	2pm20
	☽∠♇	2 23
	☽⚼♄	2 45
	☽#♀	3 29
	☽∠♃	6 54
30 F	☽△♂	1am 0
	☽☍☿	3 58
	☽#♄	8 40
	☽#♂	12pm54
	☽⚺♇	2 4
	☽△♄	2 37
	☽□♆	4 48
	☽☌♅	6 31
	☽⚺♃	6 36
31 S	☽☍♀	6am27
	☉⚻☽	6 43
	☽∥♃	5pm10
	☉⚺♀	11 5

JANUARY 1956

LONGITUDE

Day	Sid. Time	☉	☽	☽ 12 Hour	Mean ☊	True ☊	☿	♀	♂	♃	♄	♅	♆	♇
	h m s	° ' "	° ' "	° ' "	° '	° '	° '	° '	° '	° '	° '	° '	° '	° '
1	6 38 32	9♑ 32 33	19♌ 26 28	26♌ 41 58	16♐ 5	17♐ 11R	24♑ 53	9♒ 33	21♏ 26	1♍ 12R	28♏ 53	1♌ 9R	0♏ 9	28♌ 23R
2	6 42 29	10 33 41	3♍ 50 46	10♍ 52 32	16 2	17 8	26 25	10 47	22 5	1 9	28 59	1 7	0 10	28 22
3	6 46 25	11 34 50	17 47 6	24 34 29	15 59	17 5	27 56	12 1	22 44	1 6	29 5	1 4	0 11	28 21
4	6 50 22	12 35 59	1♎ 14 51	7♎ 48 31	15 56	17 4D	29 26	13 15	23 23	1 3	29 11	1 2	0 12	28 20
5	6 54 18	13 37 8	14 15 52	20 37 23	15 53	17 3	0♒ 54	14 30	24 3	1 0	29 17	0 59	0 12	28 19
6	6 58 15	14 38 18	26 53 35	3♏ 5 3	15 50	17 4	2 20	15 44	24 42	0 56	29 23	0 57	0 13	28 18
7	7 2 11	15 39 28	9♏ 12 21	15 16 3	15 46	17 5	3 43	16 58	25 21	0 52	29 28	0 55	0 14	28 17
8	7 6 8	16 40 38	21 16 45	27 15 0	15 43	17 7	5 4	18 12	26 0	0 49	29 34	0 52	0 15	28 16
9	7 10 4	17 41 48	3♐ 11 19	9♐ 6 12	15 40	17 9	6 21	19 26	26 40	0 45	29 39	0 49	0 16	28 15
10	7 14 1	18 42 58	15 0 6	20 53 28	15 37	17 10R	7 34	20 40	27 19	0 40	29 45	0 47	0 17	28 14
11	7 17 58	19 44 8	26 46 40	2♑ 40 3	15 34	17 9	8 43	21 53	27 58	0 36	29 50	0 44	0 17	28 13
12	7 21 54	20 45 18	8♑ 33 57	14 28 36	15 31	17 7	9 46	23 7	28 37	0 31	29 56	0 42	0 18	28 12
13	7 25 51	21 46 27	20 24 18	26 21 15	15 27	17 3	10 43	24 21	29 17	0 27	0♐ 1	0 39	0 19	28 11
14	7 29 47	22 47 36	2♒ 19 39	8♒ 19 43	15 24	16 57	11 33	25 35	29 56	0 22	0 6	0 37	0 19	28 10
15	7 33 44	23 48 45	14 21 36	20 25 31	15 21	16 50	12 15	26 49	0♐ 35	0 17	0 12	0 34	0 20	28 8
16	7 37 40	24 49 53	26 31 39	2♓ 40 11	15 18	16 43	12 48	28 2	1 15	0 11	0 17	0 32	0 21	28 7
17	7 41 37	25 51 1	8♓ 51 21	15 5 22	15 15	16 36	13 11	29 16	1 54	0 6	0 22	0 29	0 21	28 6
18	7 45 33	26 52 7	21 22 30	27 43 1	15 11	16 30	13 24R	0♓ 29	2 33	0 0	0 27	0 26	0 22	28 5
19	7 49 30	27 53 13	4♈ 7 14	10♈ 35 26	15 8	16 25	13 26	1 43	3 12	29♌ 55	0 32	0 24	0 22	28 3
20	7 53 27	28 54 18	17 7 58	23 45 7	15 5	16 23D	13 16	2 57	3 52	29 49	0 37	0 21	0 23	28 2
21	7 57 23	29 55 23	0♉ 27 13	7♉ 14 31	15 2	16 22	12 55	4 10	4 31	29 43	0 41	0 18	0 23	28 1
22	8 1 20	0♒ 56 26	14 7 15	21 5 34	14 59	16 23	12 22	5 23	5 10	29 37	0 46	0 16	0 23	28 0
23	8 5 16	1 57 28	28 9 32	5♊ 19 4	14 56	16 24	11 38	6 37	5 50	29 31	0 51	0 13	0 24	27 58
24	8 9 13	2 58 30	12♊ 34 0	19 53 57	14 52	16 25R	10 45	7 50	6 29	29 24	0 55	0 11	0 24	27 57
25	8 13 9	3 59 31	27 18 23	4♋ 46 37	14 49	16 24	9 43	9 3	7 8	29 18	1 0	0 8	0 24	27 56
26	8 17 6	5 0 30	12♋ 17 45	19 50 46	14 46	16 21	8 34	10 16	7 48	29 11	1 4	0 5	0 25	27 54
27	8 21 2	6 1 28	27 24 30	4♌ 57 45	14 43	16 16	7 21	11 29	8 27	29 5	1 8	0 3	0 25	27 53
28	8 24 59	7 2 26	12♌ 29 15	19 57 45	14 40	16 9	6 5	12 42	9 6	28 58	1 13	0 0	0 25	27 52
29	8 28 56	8 3 23	27 22 9	4♍ 41 24	14 37	16 1	4 50	13 55	9 46	28 51	1 17	29♋ 58	0 25	27 50
30	8 32 52	9 4 19	11♍ 54 40	19 1 18	14 33	15 53	3 36	15 8	10 25	28 44	1 21	29 55	0 25	27 49
31	8 36 49	10♒ 5 13	26♍ 0 52	2♎ 53 7	14♐ 30	15♐ 45	2♒ 27	16♓ 21	11♐ 4	28♌ 37	1♐ 25	29♋ 52	0♏ 25	27♌ 48

DECLINATION and LATITUDE

Day	☉ Decl	☽ Decl	☽ Lat	☽ 12 Hr. Decl	☿ Decl	☿ Lat	♀ Decl	♀ Lat	♂ Decl	♂ Lat	♃ Decl	♃ Lat	♄ Decl	♄ Lat
1	23S 6	10N34	4S39	7N59	23S10	2S 3	19S34	1S46	17S33	0N36	12N 0	1N 1	17S60	1N58
2	23 1	5 20	5 7	2 39	22 50	1 59	19 14	1 46	17 43	0 35	12 1	1 1	18 1	1 58
3	22 56	0S 1	5 15	2S38	22 28	1 55	18 53	1 46	17 54	0 35	12 3	1 1	18 2	1 58
4	22 51	5 10	5 6	7 37	22 4	1 50	18 32	1 46	18 4	0 34	12 4	1 2	18 3	1 58
5	22 45	9 56	4 41	12 7	21 40	1 44	18 11	1 46	18 14	0 34	12 5	1 2	18 4	1 58
6	22 38	14 8	4 2	15 58	21 14	1 38	17 48	1 46	18 25	0 33	12 7	1 2	18 5	1 59
7	22 32	17 38	3 14	19 4	20 47	1 30	17 26	1 45	18 35	0 33	12 8	1 2	18 7	1 59
8	22 24	20 18	2 18	21 17	20 20	1 22	17 2	1 45	18 44	0 32	12 10	1 3	18 8	1 59
9	22 16	22 3	1 16	22 33	19 52	1 13	16 39	1 44	18 54	0 32	12 12	1 3	18 9	1 59
10	22 8	22 48	0 12	22 48	19 23	1 2	16 15	1 44	19 4	0 31	12 13	1 3	18 10	1 59
11	21 60	22 32	0N52	22 1	18 54	0 51	15 50	1 43	19 13	0 30	12 15	1 3	18 11	1 59
12	21 51	21 16	1 54	20 16	18 26	0 39	15 25	1 42	19 22	0 30	12 17	1 4	18 12	1 59
13	21 41	19 4	2 52	17 39	17 58	0 26	14 60	1 41	19 31	0 29	12 19	1 4	18 13	1 59
14	21 31	16 3	3 42	14 16	17 30	0 11	14 34	1 40	19 40	0 29	12 21	1 4	18 14	1 59
15	21 21	12 20	4 22	10 17	17 4	0N 4	14 8	1 39	19 49	0 28	12 23	1 4	18 15	1 60
16	21 10	8 6	4 51	5 50	16 39	0 20	13 41	1 38	19 58	0 27	12 25	1 5	18 16	1 60
17	20 59	3 30	5 7	1 7	16 16	0 37	13 15	1 37	20 6	0 27	12 27	1 5	18 17	1 60
18	20 47	1N19	5 9	3N45	15 55	0 55	12 47	1 36	20 15	0 26	12 29	1 5	18 18	1 60
19	20 35	6 9	4 56	8 32	15 38	1 13	12 20	1 34	20 23	0 26	12 31	1 5	18 19	1 60
20	20 23	10 50	4 27	13 2	15 23	1 31	11 52	1 33	20 31	0 25	12 34	1 5	18 19	2 0
21	20 10	15 7	3 43	17 1	15 11	1 50	11 24	1 31	20 39	0 24	12 36	1 6	18 20	2 0
22	19 57	18 43	2 46	20 10	15 3	2 8	10 56	1 30	20 47	0 24	12 38	1 6	18 21	2 0
23	19 44	21 20	1 37	22 10	14 59	2 25	10 27	1 28	20 54	0 23	12 41	1 6	18 22	2 0
24	19 30	22 39	0 21	22 45	14 58	2 41	9 58	1 26	21 2	0 22	12 43	1 6	18 23	2 1
25	19 16	22 27	0S59	21 44	14 60	2 56	9 29	1 24	21 9	0 22	12 45	1 6	18 24	2 1
26	19 1	20 38	2 15	19 10	15 6	3 8	8 59	1 22	21 16	0 21	12 48	1 7	18 24	2 1
27	18 46	17 22	3 23	15 17	15 14	3 19	8 30	1 20	21 23	0 20	12 51	1 7	18 25	2 1
28	18 31	12 58	4 16	10 28	15 25	3 27	7 60	1 18	21 30	0 20	12 53	1 7	18 26	2 1
29	18 15	7 50	4 51	5 7	15 37	3 33	7 30	1 16	21 37	0 19	12 56	1 7	18 26	2 1
30	17 60	2 23	5 6	0S21	15 51	3 36	6 59	1 14	21 43	0 18	12 58	1 7	18 27	2 1
31	17S43	3S 2	5S 2	5S38	16S 6	3N37	6S29	1S11	21S49	0N17	13N 1	1N 8	18S28	2N 2

Day	♅ Decl	♅ Lat	♆ Decl	♆ Lat	♇ Decl	♇ Lat
1	20N29	0N35	9S55	1N43	22N 9	10N49
5	20 31	0 35	9 57	1 43	22 11	10 50
9	20 33	0 35	9 57	1 43	22 14	10 51
13	20 35	0 35	9 58	1 43	22 17	10 52
17	20 38	0 35	9 59	1 44	22 19	10 53
21	20 40	0 36	9 59	1 44	22 22	10 54
25	20 42	0 36	9 59	1 44	22 25	10 55
29	20N45	0N36	9S60	1N44	22N27	10N56

☽ PHENOMENA

d	h	m	
4	22	41	☾
13	3	1	●
20	22	59	☽
27	14	41	○

d	h	° '
3	0	0
10	6	22S50
17	18	0
24	9	22N46
30	10	0

d	h	° '
2	23	5S15
10	4	0
17	15	5N10
24	6	0
30	7	5S 7

VOID OF COURSE ☽

Last Aspect		☽ Ingress		
1	3pm46	1	♍	5pm31
3	8pm18	3	♎	9pm44
6	2am43	6	♏	6am 0
8	4pm48	8	♐	5pm33
11	2am55	11	♑	6am34
13	6pm55	13	♒	7pm20
16	3am17	16	♓	6am48
18	11am18	18	♈	4pm18
20	10pm59	20	♉	11pm12
23	2am16	23	♊	3am 6
25	3am11	25	♋	4am20
25	8pm29	27	♌	4am 7
29	2am24	29	♍	4am18
31	6am42	31	♎	6am56

d	h	
11	8	APOGEE
26	13	PERIGEE

DAILY ASPECTARIAN

1 Su	☽#♆	3am 2
	☽□♂	3 25
	☉∥☿	6 27
	☉⚼☽	9 3
	☽⊼☿	10 3
	☽☌♇	2pm47
	☽□♄	3 46
	☽*♆	5 47
	☽⊻♅	7 24
	☽☌♃	7 28
2 M	☉△☽	12pm22
	☽⊼♀	1 0
	☽⚼☿	2 32
	☽∠♆	7 26
	☽∠♅	9 1
3 T	☿⊼♇	6am32
	☽*♂	9 10
	☿#♇	5pm26
	☽⚼♀	6 3
	☽⊻♇	6 45
	☿*♄	7 44
	☽*♄	8 14
	☽△☿	8 18
	♂∥♄	9 19
	☽⊻♆	10 5
	☽*♅	11 37
	☽⊻♃	11 39
4 W	☿ ♒	9am17
	☿□♆	12pm34
	☽∠♂	1 46
	☉⚼♇	5 1
	♀∥♂	9 2
	☽∠♇	10 14
	☉□☽	10 41
5 Th	☽∠♄	0am 2
	☽∥♆	0 3
	☽△♀	0 28
	☿☍♅	1 32
	☿⊼♃	1 34
	☽∠♃	3 14
	♃⊻♅	3 40
	♀∥♄	6 22
	☽#♃	11 56
	☉∠♄	5pm11
	☽⊻♂	7 33
6 F	☽*♇	2am43
	☽⊻♄	4 50
	☽☌♆	6 27
	☽*♃	7 47
	☽□♅	7 49
	☽□☿	11 53
	☽∥♀	10pm38
7 S	☽∥♄	3am52
	☉⚼♃	4 48
	☽∥♂	8 10
	☿#♅	1pm 4
	☉*☽	1 57
	☽□♀	5 8
8 Su	☽∥☿	0am18
	☽#♅	2 46
	☽☌♂	10 3
	☽□♇	2pm 2
	☽☌♄	4 48
	☽⊻♆	6 5
	☽□♃	7 5
	☽△♅	7 14
	☉∠☽	10 55
9 M	☽#♇	3am56
	☉∥☽	4 16
	☉#♇	6 42
	☽*☿	7 10
10 T	☽∠♆	0am34
	☽⚼♅	1 35
	☉⊻☽	8 17
	☿∥♂	12pm17
	☽*♀	12 52
	☽∠☿	5 6
11 W	☽⊻♂	2am34
	☽△♇	2 55
	☽⊻♄	6 17
	☽#♇	7 5
	☽*♆	7 10
	☽△♃	7 44
	☽⊼♅	8 3
	♂□♇	8 48
	☉∥☽	2pm 4
	☽∠♀	10 59
12 Th	☽⊻☿	2am40
	☽#♅	8 30
	☽⚼♇	9 23
	☽∠♂	10 52
	☿∥♄	11 21
	☽∠♄	1pm 1
	☽⚼♃	2 2
	♄ ♐	6 47
	☽∥♂	7 56
13 F	☉☌☽	3am 1
	☽∥♄	7 21
	☽⊻♀	8 53
	☽∥☿	11 14
	☽⊼♇	3pm39
	☽*♂	6 55
	☽*♄	7 31
	☽□♆	7 59
	☽⊼♃	8 5
	☽☍♅	8 34
14 S	♂ ♐	2am28
	♂☌♄	7 22
	♃*♆	9 23
	☽∥♀	11 24
	♂□♃	1pm56
	♂⊻♆	2 35
	☽☌☿	7 34
	♂△♅	11 22
	☽#♃	11 46
15 Su	♃□♄	11am40
	☽∥♆	1pm42
	☉⊻☽	8 22
16 M	♀☍♇	1am34
	☽☍♇	3 7
	☽☌♀	3 17
	☽☍♃	7 7
	☽□♄	7 23
	☽△♆	7 28
	☽⊼♅	7 48
	☽□♂	9 44
	♄⊻♆	8pm53
17 T	☉∠☽	4am12
	☽⊻☿	8 32
	☽⚼♆	12pm31
	☽⚼♅	12 43
	♀ ♓	2 23
	♀☍♃	3 12
	♀△♆	9 27
	♄△♅	10 36
	♀⊼♅	11 0
	♀□♄	11 3
18 W	♃ ♌	1am59
	☉*☽	11 18
	☽⊼♇	12pm40
	☽∠☿	1 22
	♀#♃	2 47
	☿SR	3 43
	☽⊼♃	4 11
	☽⊼♆	4 59
	☽△♅	5 3
	☉#♅	5 13
	☽△♄	5 14
	☽⊻♀	7 2
	☽△♂	10 12
19 Th	☉⊼♇	3am58
	♅□♆	11 57
	☉∥♂	2pm29
	☽⚼♇	4 31
	☽*☿	5 4
	☽#♆	7 31
	☽⚼♃	7 48
	☽⚼♄	9 12
20 F	☽∠♀	1am38
	☽⚼♂	3 19
	☽#♀	5 0
	☽∥♃	9 24
	☉⊼♃	7pm35
	☽△♇	7 40
	☽△♃	10 42
	☉□☽	10 59
	☽□♅	11 44
	☽☍♆	11 53
21 S	☽#☿	0am24
	☽⊼♄	0 25
	☉ ♒	1 49
	♂#♅	3 23
	☽*♀	7 14
	☽⊼♂	7 34
	☉☍♅	8 42
	☉□♆	10 56
	♀□♂	2pm52
	☉*♄	7 33
	☽□☿	9 6
	☽#♄	9 16
22 Su	☉#☽	9am18
	☽∥♅	4pm55
	☽#♂	6 56
	☽□♇	11 41
23 M	☽□♃	2am16
	☽*♅	3 28
	☽⊼♆	3 46
	☽☍♄	4 32
	☉△☽	6 52
	☽☍♂	1pm28
	☽□♀	3 27
	☽∥♇	4 33
	☽△☿	9 11
	♀∥♆	10 41
24 T	☽∠♅	4am16
	☽⚼♆	4 39
	☉⚼☽	9 31
	☽⚼☿	8pm 6
25 W	☽∥♇	0am41
	☽*♇	1 0
	☽*♃	3 11
	☽⊻♅	4 32
	☽△♆	4 59
	☽⊼♄	5 58
	☿⊻♀	6 49
	☉⊼☽	11 31
	☽⊼♂	4pm30
	☽#♂	5 52
	☽⊼☿	6 29
	☽△♀	8 29
	☽∥♅	11 14
26 Th	☽∠♇	0am58
	☽∠♃	2 59
	☽⚼♄	6 2
	☿*♂	9 59
	☉#☽	2pm 5
	☽#♄	5 16
	☽⚼♂	5 26
	☽⚼♀	10 25
27 F	☽⊻♇	0am45
	☽⊻♃	2 38
	☽☌♅	4 11
	☽□♆	4 46
	☽△♄	5 57
	☽#☿	11 50
	☉☌☿	2pm 0
	☽☍☿	2 35
	☉☍☽	2 41
	☽△♂	6 21
28 S	☽⊼♀	0am23
	☽∥♃	0 24
	♅ ♋	1 51
	☉∥♄	7 45
	☽#♆	2pm12
29 Su	☽☌♇	0am46
	☽#♀	1 40
	☽☌♃	2 24
	☽⊻♅	4 13
	☽*♆	4 59
	☽□♄	6 25
	☽⊼☿	11 17
	☉⊼☽	6pm54
	♀⚼♅	7 51
	☽□♂	9 23
30 M	☽∠♅	5am 2
	♀⚼♆	5 37
	☽∠♆	5 54
	☽☍♀	5 55
	☽⚼☿	10 26
	☉⚼☽	10pm16
31 T	☽⊻♇	3am 5
	☽⊻♃	4 28
	☽*♅	6 42
	☽⊻♆	7 40
	☽*♄	9 27
	☽△☿	10 24
	☿∠♀	11 29
	☽∥♀	2pm35
	☿*♄	9 58

FEBRUARY 1956

LONGITUDE

Day	Sid. Time	☉	☽	☽ 12 Hour	Mean ☊	True ☊	☿	♀	♂	♃	♄	♅	♆	♇
	h m s	° ' "	° ' "	° ' "	° '	° '	° '	° '	° '	° '	° '	° '	° '	° '
1	8 40 45	11♒ 6 8	9♎ 38 1	16♎ 15 41	14♐ 27	15♐ 38R	1♒ 23R	17♓ 34	11♐ 44	28♌ 29R	1♐ 29	29♋ 50R	0♏ 25R	27♌ 46R
2	8 44 42	12 7 1	22 46 24	29 10 34	14 24	15 34	0 26	18 46	12 23	28 22	1 33	29 47	0 25	27 45
3	8 48 38	13 7 54	5♏ 28 44	11♏ 41 26	14 21	15 32D	29♑ 37	19 59	13 3	28 15	1 36	29 45	0 25	27 43
4	8 52 35	14 8 45	17 49 20	23 53 5	14 17	15 32	28 56	21 11	13 42	28 7	1 40	29 42	0 25	27 42
5	8 56 31	15 9 37	29 53 23	5♐ 50 54	14 14	15 32	28 23	22 24	14 21	28 0	1 43	29 40	0 25	27 40
6	9 0 28	16 10 27	11♐ 46 19	17 40 18	14 11	15 33R	28 0	23 36	15 1	27 52	1 47	29 37	0 25	27 39
7	9 4 25	17 11 16	23 33 26	29 26 18	14 8	15 33	27 44	24 48	15 40	27 44	1 50	29 35	0 25	27 37
8	9 8 21	18 12 4	5♑ 19 28	11♑ 13 23	14 5	15 31	27 36D	26 1	16 20	27 37	1 54	29 32	0 24	27 36
9	9 12 18	19 12 51	17 8 31	23 5 13	14 2	15 26	27 36	27 13	16 59	27 29	1 57	29 30	0 24	27 35
10	9 16 14	20 13 37	29 3 50	5♒ 4 37	13 58	15 18	27 43	28 25	17 38	27 21	2 0	29 28	0 24	27 33
11	9 20 11	21 14 22	11♒ 7 47	17 13 30	13 55	15 8	27 57	29 37	18 18	27 13	2 3	29 25	0 24	27 32
12	9 24 7	22 15 5	23 21 52	29 32 59	13 52	14 56	28 17	0♈ 49	18 57	27 6	2 6	29 23	0 23	27 30
13	9 28 4	23 15 47	5♓ 46 53	12♓ 3 34	13 49	14 44	28 43	2 0	19 37	26 58	2 9	29 20	0 23	27 29
14	9 32 0	24 16 28	18 23 4	24 45 23	13 46	14 31	29 14	3 12	20 16	26 50	2 12	29 18	0 22	27 27
15	9 35 57	25 17 7	1♈ 10 30	7♈ 38 28	13 43	14 20	29 49	4 24	20 55	26 42	2 14	29 16	0 22	27 26
16	9 39 54	26 17 44	14 9 18	20 43 5	13 39	14 11	0♒ 30	5 35	21 35	26 34	2 17	29 14	0 22	27 24
17	9 43 50	27 18 20	27 19 55	3♉ 59 54	13 36	14 5	1 14	6 46	22 14	26 26	2 19	29 11	0 21	27 23
18	9 47 47	28 18 54	10♉ 43 12	17 29 58	13 33	14 1	2 2	7 58	22 53	26 18	2 22	29 9	0 21	27 21
19	9 51 43	29 19 26	24 20 21	1♊ 14 30	13 30	14 0D	2 54	9 9	23 33	26 10	2 24	29 7	0 20	27 20
20	9 55 40	0♓ 19 56	8♊ 12 31	15 14 27	13 27	14 0R	3 49	10 20	24 12	26 2	2 26	29 5	0 19	27 18
21	9 59 36	1 20 25	22 20 18	29 29 57	13 23	14 0	4 47	11 31	24 52	25 54	2 28	29 3	0 19	27 17
22	10 3 33	2 20 52	6♋ 43 8	13♋ 59 31	13 20	13 59	5 47	12 41	25 31	25 46	2 30	29 1	0 18	27 15
23	10 7 29	3 21 16	21 18 34	28 39 39	13 17	13 54	6 50	13 52	26 10	25 39	2 32	28 59	0 17	27 14
24	10 11 26	4 21 39	6♌ 1 58	13♌ 24 39	13 14	13 47	7 56	15 3	26 50	25 31	2 34	28 57	0 17	27 12
25	10 15 23	5 22 0	20 46 41	28 7 5	13 11	13 38	9 4	16 13	27 29	25 23	2 36	28 55	0 16	27 11
26	10 19 19	6 22 20	5♍ 24 48	12♍ 38 54	13 8	13 26	10 13	17 23	28 8	25 15	2 37	28 53	0 15	27 9
27	10 23 16	7 22 37	19 48 29	26 52 48	13 4	13 14	11 25	18 33	28 48	25 8	2 39	28 51	0 14	27 8
28	10 27 12	8 22 52	3♎ 51 15	10♎ 43 24	13 1	13 2	12 39	19 44	29 27	25 0	2 40	28 49	0 13	27 6
29	10 31 9	9♓ 23 7	17♎ 29 1	24♎ 7 59	12♐ 58	12♐ 52	13♒ 54	20♈ 53	0♑ 6	24♌ 53	2♐ 41	28♋ 47	0♏ 13	27♌ 5

DECLINATION and LATITUDE

Day	☉ Decl	☽ Decl	☽ Lat	☽ 12 Hr. Decl	☿ Decl	☿ Lat	♀ Decl	♀ Lat	♂ Decl	♂ Lat	♃ Decl	♃ Lat	♄ Decl	♄ Lat
1	17S27	8S 7	4S40	10S28	16S22	3N35	5S58	1S 9	21S55	0N17	13N 4	1N 8	18S28	2N 2
2	17 10	12 39	4 5	14 39	16 37	3 31	5 28	1 6	22 1	0 16	13 6	1 8	18 29	2 2
3	16 53	16 28	3 18	18 4	16 53	3 26	4 57	1 4	22 7	0 15	13 9	1 8	18 30	2 2
4	16 35	19 26	2 23	20 35	17 8	3 19	4 26	1 1	22 13	0 14	13 12	1 8	18 30	2 2
5	16 18	21 29	1 23	22 8	17 23	3 10	3 55	0 58	22 18	0 14	13 15	1 8	18 31	2 2
6	15 60	22 32	0 20	22 41	17 37	3 1	3 24	0 56	22 23	0 13	13 17	1 8	18 31	2 2
7	15 41	22 35	0N43	22 13	17 50	2 51	2 52	0 53	22 28	0 12	13 20	1 9	18 32	2 3
8	15 23	21 37	1 44	20 46	18 2	2 40	2 21	0 50	22 33	0 11	13 23	1 9	18 32	2 3
9	15 4	19 42	2 40	18 25	18 13	2 29	1 49	0 47	22 38	0 11	13 26	1 9	18 33	2 3
10	14 45	16 55	3 30	15 15	18 23	2 17	1 18	0 44	22 43	0 10	13 28	1 9	18 33	2 3
11	14 25	13 25	4 11	11 25	18 32	2 5	0 47	0 41	22 47	0 9	13 31	1 9	18 34	2 3
12	14 6	9 18	4 41	7 5	18 40	1 53	0 15	0 37	22 51	0 8	13 34	1 9	18 34	2 3
13	13 46	4 46	4 58	2 23	18 47	1 41	0N17	0 34	22 55	0 7	13 37	1 9	18 35	2 4
14	13 26	0N 2	5 1	2N28	18 52	1 29	0 48	0 31	22 59	0 6	13 40	1 9	18 35	2 4
15	13 6	4 53	4 49	7 17	18 56	1 17	1 20	0 27	23 2	0 6	13 43	1 10	18 35	2 4
16	12 45	9 36	4 22	11 51	18 59	1 6	1 51	0 24	23 6	0 5	13 45	1 10	18 36	2 4
17	12 25	13 57	3 41	15 55	19 1	0 54	2 23	0 20	23 9	0 4	13 48	1 10	18 36	2 4
18	12 4	17 41	2 47	19 14	19 1	0 43	2 54	0 17	23 12	0 3	13 51	1 10	18 36	2 4
19	11 43	20 31	1 42	21 31	18 60	0 32	3 25	0 13	23 15	0 2	13 54	1 10	18 37	2 5
20	11 21	22 11	0 31	22 31	18 58	0 21	3 57	0 10	23 18	0 1	13 56	1 10	18 37	2 5
21	11 0	22 29	0S44	22 5	18 54	0 11	4 28	0 6	23 20	0 0	13 59	1 10	18 37	2 5
22	10 38	21 19	1 57	20 12	18 49	0 1	4 59	0 2	23 23	0S 1	14 2	1 10	18 37	2 5
23	10 17	18 44	3 4	16 58	18 43	0S 9	5 30	0N 2	23 25	0 2	14 5	1 10	18 38	2 5
24	9 55	14 55	3 58	12 38	18 35	0 19	6 1	0 6	23 27	0 3	14 7	1 10	18 38	2 5
25	9 33	10 11	4 37	7 36	18 26	0 28	6 32	0 9	23 29	0 3	14 10	1 10	18 38	2 6
26	9 11	4 55	4 58	2 11	18 16	0 37	7 2	0 13	23 30	0 4	14 13	1 10	18 38	2 6
27	8 48	0S32	4 59	3S14	18 5	0 45	7 33	0 17	23 32	0 5	14 15	1 10	18 38	2 6
28	8 26	5 50	4 41	8 20	17 52	0 53	8 3	0 21	23 33	0 6	14 18	1 10	18 38	2 6
29	8S 3	10S41	4S 8	12S52	17S38	1S 1	8N33	0N26	23S34	0S 7	14N20	1N10	18S38	2N 6

Day	♅ Decl	♅ Lat	♆ Decl	♆ Lat	♇ Decl	♇ Lat
1	20N46	0N36	9S59	1N45	22N29	10N57
5	20 48	0 36	9 59	1 45	22 32	10 57
9	20 50	0 36	9 59	1 45	22 35	10 58
13	20 52	0 36	9 58	1 45	22 37	10 58
17	20 54	0 35	9 57	1 45	22 40	10 59
21	20 56	0 35	9 56	1 46	22 42	10 59
25	20 58	0 35	9 55	1 46	22 44	10 59
29	20N59	0N35	9S54	1N46	22N46	10N59

☽ PHENOMENA

d	h	m	
3	16	8	☾
11	21	38	●
19	9	22	☽
26	1	42	○

d	h	° '
6	13	22S41
14	0	0
20	17	22N33
26	22	0

d	h	° '
6	8	0
13	17	5N 2
20	10	0
26	13	5S 1

VOID OF COURSE ☽

Last Aspect	☽ Ingress
2 1pm29	2 ♏ 1pm34
4 11pm33	5 ♐ 0am13
7 8am27	7 ♑ 1pm 9
10 0am47	10 ♒ 1am52
12 8am 1	12 ♓ 12pm52
14 9pm21	14 ♈ 9pm49
17 3am21	17 ♉ 4am49
19 9am22	19 ♊ 9am51
21 8am16	21 ♋ 12pm50
23 12pm29	23 ♌ 2pm11
25 11am28	25 ♍ 3pm 5
27 4pm 2	27 ♎ 5pm21
29 8pm28	29 ♏ 10pm45

d	h	
7	19	APOGEE
23	18	PERIGEE

DAILY ASPECTARIAN

1 W	☉△☽	2am51
	☽⚹♂	3 58
	☽∠♇	5 38
	♆SR	6 36
	☽∠♃	6 54
	☽∥♆	9 33
	☽∠♄	12pm28
	☽⚻♀	3 51
2 Th	☿□♆	0am29
	☽#♃	2 41
	☽∠♂	9 6
	☽⚹♇	9 17
	☽⚹♃	10 23
	☽□♅	1pm 7
	☿ ♑	1 17
	☽□☿	1 29
	☽☌♆	2 21
	☽⚺♄	4 34
	☉⚹♂	6 6
	☿☍♅	7 41
	☽⚼♀	10 57
	☉∥☿	11 59
3 F	☉∥☽	2am45
	☽∥☿	3 15
	☽⚺♂	3pm28
	☽∥♄	3 38
	☉□☽	4 8
4 S	☿∠♂	4am27
	☽△♀	7 23
	☽#♅	2pm39
	☽□♇	7 34
	☽□♃	8 15
	☽⚹☿	9 7
	☽△♅	11 33
5 Su	☽⚺♆	1am 3
	☽☌♄	3 42
	♂⚼♅	10 33
	☽∥♂	5pm54
6 M	☽#♇	0am13
	☽∠☿	2 25
	☽⚼♅	5 46
	☽☌♂	6 59
	☽∠♆	7 24
	☉⚹☽	9 48
	♂∠♆	2pm35
	☿⚻♃	8 58
7 T	☽#♇	1am 3
	☽□♀	2 50
	☽∥♂	3 55
	☽△♇	8 17
	☽⚺☿	8 24
	☽△♃	8 27
	☽⚻♅	12pm15
	☽⚹♆	1 59
	☽⚺♄	4 59
	☉∠☽	7 16
8 W	☿⚻♃	2am56
	♃☌♇	3 4
	♂#♇	3 59
	☽#♅	11 8
	☿SD	12pm14
	☽⚼♃	2 40
	☽⚼♇	2 46
	☽∠♄	11 36
	☽⚺♂	11 40
9 Th	☉⚺☽	4am35
	♀⚻♃	4 54
	♀⚻♇	7 7
	☿⚹♀	8 19
	☽∥♄	10 45
	☽∥☿	12pm50
	☽⚻♃	8 37
	☽⚻♇	8 58
	☽☌☿	9 16
	☽⚹♀	10 33
10 F	☽☍♅	0am47
	☽□♆	2 40
	☽⚹♄	5 54
	☽∠♂	7 33
	☉∥☽	4pm53
	♀△♅	8 17
	☽#♃	11 18
11 S	☿∥♄	5am 0
	☽∠♀	7 37
	♀ ♈	7 47
	☽⚹♂	2pm54
	♀⚻♆	3 36
	☽∥♆	8 18
	☉☌☽	9 38
12 Su	☽☍♃	7am10
	☽☍♇	8 1
	☽⚺☿	9 52
	☽⚻♅	11 38
	☽△♆	1pm37
	☽⚺♀	3 58
	☽□♄	4 59
13 M	♀△♄	2am58
	☉#♃	9 38
	☽∠☿	3pm46
	☽⚼♅	4 17
	☽⚼♆	6 18
	☽#♀	8 18
14 T	☿☍♅	3am 4
	☽□♂	3 45
	☽∥♀	4 17
	☉⚺☽	12pm 3
	☽⚻♃	3 43
	☽⚻♇	5 1
	☽△♅	8 27
	☽⚹☿	9 21
	☽⚻♆	10 30
15 W	☽△♄	1am59
	☿ ♒	6 34
	☽☌♀	6 35
	☉∠☽	6pm18
	☽⚼♃	7 17
	☿□♆	7 25
	☽⚼♇	8 47
16 Th	☽#♆	1am50
	☉☍♃	5 38
	☽⚼♄	5 45
	☽△♂	2pm17
	☉#☽	3 48
	☽△♃	10 23
	☽∥♃	11 5
	☉⚹☽	11 57
17 F	☽△♇	0am 5
	☉☍♇	1 39
	☽□♅	3 21
	☽☍♆	5 27
	☽□☿	7 28
	☽⚻♄	9 1
	☽⚺♀	6pm37
	☽⚼♂	6 42
18 S	☽#♄	6am58
	☿⚹♄	9 36
	☽#☿	10 13
	☉⚻♅	7pm15
	☽⚻♂	10 33
	☽∠♀	11 38
19 Su	☽□♃	3am10
	☽∥♅	4 30
	☽□♇	5 12
	☽⚹♅	8 18
	☉□☽	9 22
	☽⚻♆	10 25
	☽☍♄	2pm 2
	☽△☿	3 54
	☉ ♓	4 5
	☉△♆	11 46
20 M	☽⚹♀	3am58
	☽∠♅	10 0
	☽⚼♆	12pm 8
	♀⚼♃	12 54
	☽⚼☿	7 22
21 T	☽☍♂	4am26
	☽⚹♃	5 56
	☽⚹♇	8 16
	☽⚺♅	11 13
	☽△♆	1pm21
	♀⚼♇	3 15
	☉△☽	4 12
	☽⚻♄	4 59
	☽⚻☿	10 20
22 W	☉□♄	3am49
	☽∥♅	4 29
	☽∠♃	6 38
	♂△♃	7 53
	☽∠♇	9 7
	☽□♀	10 43
	☽⚼♄	5pm48
	☉⚼☽	6 48
23 Th	☽#☿	0am 7
	☽#♄	0 46
	☽⚺♃	7 1
	☽⚻♂	8 19
	☽⚺♇	9 39
	☽☌♅	12pm29
	☽□♆	2 38
	☿∥♄	5 7
	☽△♄	6 21
	☉⚻☽	9 5
	☉∥♆	11 36
24 F	☽☍☿	3am20
	☽∥♃	4 16
	☽⚼♂	9 52
	♂△♇	1pm13
	☽△♀	3 56
25 S	☽#♆	1am17
	☉#☽	3 15
	☽☌♃	7 28
	☽☌♇	10 27
	☽△♂	11 28
	☽⚺♅	1pm16
	☽∥♀	3 20
	☽⚹♆	3 31
	☽⚼♀	6 35
	☽□♄	7 23
26 Su	☉☍☽	1am42
	♀⚼♄	4 48
	☽⚻☿	8 41
	☽∠♅	2pm 1
	☽∠♆	4 20
	☽⚻♀	9 43
27 M	♂⚻♅	1am52
	☽⚺♃	8 56
	☽⚼☿	12pm17
	☽⚺♇	12 24
	☽⚹♅	3 20
	☽□♂	4 2
	☽⚺♆	5 44
	☽⚹♄	9 56
28 T	☉⚻☽	8am31
	☉#♀	10 24
	☽∠♃	10 38
	☉∥☽	11 36
	☽#♀	11 51
	☽∠♇	2pm25
	☽△☿	4 57
	☽∥♆	7 53
	♂ ♑	8 5
29 W	☽∠♄	0am22
	♂⚹♆	3 41
	☽☍♀	6 43
	☽⚹♃	1pm14
	☉⚼☽	1 29
	☽⚹♇	5 21
	☽□♅	8 28
	☽#♃	8 55
	☽☌♆	11 7

MARCH 1956

LONGITUDE

Day	Sid. Time	☉	☽	☽ 12 Hour	Mean ☊	True ☊	☿	♀	♂	♃	♄	♅	♆	♇
	h m s	° ' "	° ' "	° ' "	° '	° '	° '	° '	° '	° '	° '	° '	° '	° '
1	10 35 5	10♓ 23 20	0♏ 40 25	7♏ 6 32	12♐ 55	12♐ 45R	15♒ 11	22♈ 3	0♑ 46	24♌ 45R	2♐ 42	28♋ 45R	0♏ 12R	27♌ 3R
2	10 39 2	11 23 30	13 26 42	19 41 21	12 52	12 40	16 30	23 13	1 25	24 38	2 44	28 44	0 11	27 2
3	10 42 58	12 23 40	25 51 3	1♐ 56 24	12 48	12 38	17 50	24 22	2 4	24 31	2 45	28 42	0 10	27 0
4	10 46 55	13 23 48	7♐ 58 4	13 56 43	12 45	12 37	19 11	25 31	2 44	24 24	2 45	28 40	0 9	26 59
5	10 50 52	14 23 54	19 53 5	25 47 52	12 42	12 37	20 34	26 41	3 23	24 16	2 46	28 39	0 8	26 58
6	10 54 48	15 23 59	1♑ 41 44	7♑ 35 23	12 39	12 36	21 59	27 50	4 2	24 9	2 47	28 37	0 7	26 56
7	10 58 45	16 24 2	13 29 28	19 24 35	12 36	12 34	23 24	28 58	4 42	24 3	2 47	28 36	0 6	26 55
8	11 2 41	17 24 4	25 21 17	1♒ 20 6	12 33	12 29	24 51	0♉ 7	5 21	23 56	2 48	28 34	0 5	26 53
9	11 6 38	18 24 4	7♒ 21 29	13 25 47	12 29	12 22	26 20	1 16	6 0	23 49	2 48	28 33	0 4	26 52
10	11 10 34	19 24 2	19 33 21	25 44 24	12 26	12 11	27 49	2 24	6 40	23 43	2 49	28 31	0 2	26 51
11	11 14 31	20 23 58	1♓ 59 6	8♓ 17 31	12 23	11 59	29 20	3 32	7 19	23 36	2 49	28 30	0 1	26 49
12	11 18 27	21 23 53	14 39 42	21 5 33	12 20	11 46	0♓ 52	4 40	7 58	23 30	2 49R	28 29	0 0	26 48
13	11 22 24	22 23 45	27 34 59	4♈ 7 50	12 17	11 32	2 25	5 48	8 37	23 24	2 49	28 28	29♎ 59	26 47
14	11 26 20	23 23 35	10♈ 43 54	17 22 59	12 14	11 20	4 0	6 55	9 17	23 18	2 49	28 26	29 58	26 45
15	11 30 17	24 23 24	24 4 51	0♉ 49 18	12 10	11 10	5 35	8 3	9 56	23 12	2 48	28 25	29 56	26 44
16	11 34 14	25 23 10	7♉ 36 9	14 25 12	12 7	11 3	7 12	9 10	10 35	23 6	2 48	28 24	29 55	26 43
17	11 38 10	26 22 55	21 16 21	28 9 30	12 4	11 0	8 50	10 17	11 14	23 0	2 48	28 23	29 54	26 41
18	11 42 7	27 22 36	5♊ 4 35	12♊ 1 32	12 1	10 58D	10 30	11 24	11 53	22 55	2 47	28 22	29 53	26 40
19	11 46 3	28 22 16	19 0 21	26 1 0	11 58	10 59R	12 10	12 30	12 32	22 49	2 46	28 21	29 51	26 39
20	11 50 0	29 21 54	3♋ 3 26	10♋ 7 33	11 54	10 59	13 52	13 37	13 12	22 44	2 46	28 20	29 50	26 38
21	11 53 56	0♈ 21 29	17 13 15	24 20 20	11 51	10 58	15 35	14 43	13 51	22 39	2 45	28 19	29 49	26 37
22	11 57 53	1 21 1	1♌ 28 31	8♌ 37 26	11 48	10 55	17 20	15 49	14 30	22 34	2 44	28 19	29 47	26 35
23	12 1 49	2 20 32	15 46 41	22 55 42	11 45	10 49	19 5	16 55	15 9	22 30	2 43	28 18	29 46	26 34
24	12 5 46	3 20 0	0♍ 3 56	7♍ 10 44	11 42	10 40	20 52	18 0	15 48	22 25	2 42	28 17	29 44	26 33
25	12 9 43	4 19 26	14 15 25	21 17 21	11 39	10 30	22 40	19 5	16 27	22 21	2 41	28 17	29 43	26 32
26	12 13 39	5 18 49	28 15 53	5♎ 10 27	11 35	10 19	24 30	20 10	17 6	22 16	2 39	28 16	29 42	26 31
27	12 17 36	6 18 11	12♎ 0 33	18 45 47	11 32	10 9	26 21	21 15	17 45	22 12	2 38	28 15	29 40	26 30
28	12 21 32	7 17 30	25 25 52	2♏ 0 38	11 29	10 0	28 13	22 19	18 24	22 9	2 36	28 15	29 39	26 29
29	12 25 29	8 16 48	8♏ 30 2	14 54 10	11 26	9 53	0♈ 6	23 23	19 3	22 5	2 35	28 14	29 37	26 28
30	12 29 25	9 16 4	21 13 12	27 27 26	11 23	9 49	2 1	24 27	19 42	22 1	2 33	28 14	29 36	26 26
31	12 33 22	10♈ 15 18	3♐ 37 16	9♐ 43 8	11♐ 20	9♐ 47D	3♈ 57	25♉ 30	20♑ 21	21♌ 58	2♐ 31	28♋ 14	29♎ 34	26♌ 25

DECLINATION and LATITUDE

Day	☉	☽		☽ 12 Hr.	☿		♀		♂		♃		♄	
	Decl	Decl	Lat	Decl	Decl	Lat	Decl	Lat	Decl	Lat	Decl	Lat	Decl	Lat
1	7S40	14S52	3S23	16S40	17S22	1S 8	9N 3	0N30	23S35	0S 8	14N23	1N10	18S38	2N 6
2	7 18	18 14	2 28	19 34	17 6	1 15	9 33	0 34	23 36	0 9	14 25	1 11	18 38	2 7
3	6 55	20 39	1 28	21 28	16 48	1 22	10 2	0 38	23 36	0 10	14 28	1 11	18 38	2 7
4	6 32	22 3	0 25	22 22	16 28	1 28	10 32	0 42	23 36	0 11	14 30	1 11	18 38	2 7
5	6 9	22 25	0N38	22 14	16 8	1 34	11 1	0 46	23 37	0 12	14 33	1 11	18 38	2 7
6	5 45	21 47	1 39	21 6	15 46	1 40	11 29	0 51	23 37	0 14	14 35	1 11	18 38	2 7
7	5 22	20 11	2 36	19 3	15 22	1 45	11 58	0 55	23 36	0 15	14 37	1 11	18 38	2 7
8	4 59	17 42	3 26	16 10	14 58	1 50	12 26	0 59	23 36	0 16	14 39	1 11	18 38	2 8
9	4 35	14 27	4 7	12 35	14 32	1 54	12 54	1 4	23 35	0 17	14 42	1 11	18 38	2 8
10	4 12	10 34	4 38	8 25	14 5	1 58	13 22	1 8	23 35	0 18	14 44	1 10	18 38	2 8
11	3 48	6 10	4 56	3 49	13 37	2 2	13 50	1 12	23 34	0 19	14 46	1 10	18 38	2 8
12	3 25	1 26	4 60	1N 1	13 7	2 5	14 17	1 16	23 32	0 20	14 48	1 10	18 38	2 8
13	3 1	3N27	4 49	5 53	12 36	2 8	14 44	1 21	23 31	0 21	14 50	1 10	18 38	2 8
14	2 37	8 16	4 22	10 34	12 4	2 10	15 10	1 25	23 30	0 22	14 52	1 10	18 37	2 9
15	2 14	12 46	3 41	14 49	11 31	2 12	15 36	1 30	23 28	0 24	14 54	1 10	18 37	2 9
16	1 50	16 41	2 47	18 20	10 56	2 14	16 2	1 34	23 26	0 25	14 56	1 10	18 37	2 9
17	1 26	19 44	1 42	20 51	10 21	2 15	16 28	1 38	23 24	0 26	14 57	1 10	18 37	2 9
18	1 3	21 40	0 31	22 9	9 44	2 16	16 53	1 43	23 22	0 27	14 59	1 10	18 36	2 9
19	0 39	22 17	0S43	22 4	9 5	2 16	17 18	1 47	23 19	0 28	15 1	1 10	18 36	2 9
20	0 15	21 30	1 54	20 36	8 26	2 16	17 42	1 51	23 17	0 30	15 3	1 10	18 36	2 10
21	0N 9	19 22	2 60	17 50	7 46	2 15	18 6	1 56	23 14	0 31	15 4	1 10	18 36	2 10
22	0 32	16 1	3 55	13 59	7 4	2 14	18 29	1 60	23 11	0 32	15 6	1 10	18 35	2 10
23	0 56	11 44	4 35	9 20	6 21	2 12	18 52	2 4	23 8	0 33	15 7	1 10	18 35	2 10
24	1 20	6 48	4 58	4 12	5 37	2 10	19 15	2 8	23 5	0 35	15 9	1 10	18 35	2 10
25	1 43	1 33	5 2	1S 6	4 52	2 8	19 37	2 13	23 2	0 36	15 10	1 10	18 34	2 10
26	2 7	3S43	4 48	6 16	4 6	2 5	19 59	2 17	22 58	0 37	15 11	1 10	18 34	2 11
27	2 30	8 42	4 18	11 0	3 18	2 1	20 21	2 21	22 54	0 38	15 12	1 10	18 33	2 11
28	2 54	13 9	3 34	15 6	2 30	1 57	20 41	2 25	22 50	0 40	15 14	1 9	18 33	2 11
29	3 17	16 51	2 39	18 22	1 40	1 52	21 2	2 29	22 46	0 41	15 15	1 9	18 32	2 11
30	3 40	19 38	1 38	20 40	0 50	1 47	21 22	2 33	22 42	0 43	15 16	1 9	18 32	2 11
31	4N 4	21S25	0S33	21S55	0N 1	1S41	21N41	2N37	22S38	0S44	15N17	1N 9	18S31	2N11

Day	♅		♆		♇	
	Decl	Lat	Decl	Lat	Decl	Lat
1	20N59	0N35	9S53	1N46	22N47	10N59
5	21 1	0 35	9 52	1 46	22 49	10 59
9	21 2	0 35	9 50	1 47	22 51	10 59
13	21 3	0 35	9 48	1 47	22 53	10 59
17	21 4	0 35	9 46	1 47	22 54	10 58
21	21 4	0 35	9 44	1 47	22 55	10 58
25	21 5	0 35	9 42	1 47	22 57	10 58
29	21N 5	0N35	9S40	1N47	22N58	10N57

☽ PHENOMENA

d	h	m	
4	11	54	☾
12	13	37	●
19	17	14	☽
26	13	12	○

d	h	° '
4	21	22S26
12	7	0
18	23	22N17
25	7	0

4	9	0
11	19	5N 0
18	10	0
24	18	5S 3
31	12	0

VOID OF COURSE ☽

Last Aspect		☽ Ingress		
3	5am35	3	♐	8am10
5	3pm16	5	♑	8pm33
8	6am27	8	♒	9am20
10	6pm13	10	♓	8pm12
13	1am37	13	♈	4am26
15	10am25	15	♉	10am32
17	12pm23	17	♊	3pm12
19	6pm31	19	♋	6pm48
21	9pm10	21	♌	9pm31
23	11pm27	23	♍	11pm53
26	0am 0	26	♎	3am 0
28	7am39	28	♏	8am19
30	1pm30	30	♐	4pm56

d	h	
6	13	APOGEE
22	0	PERIGEE

DAILY ASPECTARIAN

1	☽⚹♂	0am10
Th	☽⚺♄	3 47
	☽∥☿	3pm52
	☉△☽	7 45
	☿∠♂	9 18
2	☽∥♄	3am29
F	☽∠♂	6 1
	☽□☿	6 32
	♀#♆	4pm 5
	☽⚻♀	8 48
	☽□♃	9 24
3	☽□♇	2am16
S	♀△♃	2 42
	☽#♅	4 45
	☽△♅	5 35
	☽⚺♆	8 28
	☽⚺♂	12pm58
	☽☌♄	1 36
4	♂⚺♄	1am 1
Su	☽⚼♀	5 40
	☉⚼♅	6 27
	☽⚼♅	11 26
	☉□☽	11 54
	☽∠♆	2pm24
5	☽⚹☿	1am35
M	♀△♇	5 48
	☽△♃	8 49
	☽△♇	2pm20
	☽△♀	3 16
	☉⚼♆	5 15
	☽⚻♅	5 45
	☽⚹♆	8 47
6	☽⚺♄	2am13
T	☽☌♂	5 3
	☽∠☿	12pm14
	☽#♅	1 7
	☽⚼♃	3 3
	♀□♅	4 16
	☽⚼♇	8 48
7	☉⚹☽	6am27
W	☽∠♄	8 44
	☿☍♃	9 49
	☽∥♄	3pm50
	☽⚻♃	9 9
	♀ ♉	9 32
	☽⚺☿	10 51
	♀☍♆	11 11
8	☽⚻♇	3am 5
Th	☽☍♅	6 27
	☽□♆	9 28
	☽□♀	10 34
	☽⚹♄	2pm56
	☉∠☽	3 25
	☿#♃	3 58
	☽⚺♂	9 9
	☽#♃	10 24
	☽∥☿	11 23
9	☿☍♇	8am35
F	☽#♀	8 53
	☉⚺☽	11pm40
10	☽∥♆	4am11
S	☽∠♂	4 19
	☽☍♃	8 0
	♀⚻♄	8 43
	☿⚻♅	11 2
	☽☍♇	2pm 6
	☽⚻♅	5 20
	☽☌☿	6 13
	☿#♀	6 28
	☽△♆	8 15
11	☽□♄	1am35
Su	☽⚹♀	3 15
	☿ ♓	10 28
	☿△♆	10 40
	☽⚹♂	10 42
	☉∥☽	1pm11
	☽⚼♅	9 47
12	☽⚼♆	0am38
M	♆ ♎	2 14
	♄SR	3 29
	☽∠♀	10 15
	☉☌☽	1pm37
	☽⚻♃	4 20
	♂⚼♃	4 45
	☉#☽	10 0
	☽⚻♇	10 31
13	☽△♅	1am37
T	☽⚻♆	4 24
	☿□♄	5 59
	♀∥♃	6 6
	☽△♄	9 36
	☽⚺☿	10 5
	☽⚺♀	4pm27
	☽⚼♃	7 37
	☽□♂	9 13
	☉⚻♃	9 48
14	☽⚼♇	1am51
W	☽#♆	7 52
	☽⚼♄	12pm46
	☽∠☿	4 54
	☽#☿	5 51
	☽△♃	10 26
15	☉⚺☽	0am36
Th	☽△♇	4 43
	☽□♅	7 43
	☽☍♆	10 25
	☽∥♃	12pm37
	☽⚻♄	3 31
	☽∥♀	7 9
	☽⚹☿	11 12
16	☽☌♀	3am 0
F	☉∠☽	5 18
	☽△♂	5 31
	☽#♄	2pm16
17	☽□♃	3am 0
S	☉⚻♇	7 17
	☽⚼♂	9 5
	☽□♇	9 26
	☉⚹☽	9 36
	☽⚹♅	12pm23
	☽∥♅	2 45
	☽⚻♆	3 0
	♂⚼♇	4 13
	☽☍♄	8 2
	☿∥♆	10 37
18	☽□☿	10am38
Su	☽⚺♀	11 52
	☽⚻♂	12pm20
	☽∠♅	2 18
	☽⚼♆	4 53
	☉△♅	11 33
19	♀△♂	1am41
M	☽⚹♃	6 30
	☿⚹♂	8 30
	☽⚹♇	1pm 4
	☿⚹♀	1 46
	☽∠♀	3 47
	☽⚺♅	3 58
	☿⚼♅	4 34
	☉□☽	5 14
	☽△♆	6 31
	☽⚻♄	11 30
20	☽∥♅	6am14
T	☽∠♃	7 54
	☉⚻♆	11 3
	☿⚼♆	1pm19
	☽∠♇	2 31
	☉ ♈	3 20
	☽☍♂	6 1
	☽⚹♀	7 25
	☽△☿	8 51
21	☽⚼♄	0am53
W	☽#♄	6 18
	☽∥♀	8 57
	☽⚺[illegible]	9 7
	☽⚺♇	3pm48
	☽☌♅	6 41
	☽□♆	9 10
	☉△☽	11 46
22	☽⚼☿	1am38
Th	☽△♄	2 7
	☽∥♃	5 34
	♀#♄	6 0
	☽⚻♂	10pm53
23	☽□♀	2am 3
F	☉⚼☽	2 49
	☽⚻☿	6 20
	☉△♄	8 52
	☽#♆	10 7
	☽☌♃	11 13
	☽☌♇	6pm 6
	☽⚺♅	9 0
	☽⚹♆	11 27
24	☽⚼♂	1am17
S	☽□♄	4 26
	☉⚻☽	5 55
	☽#☿	6 25
	☿⚻♃	7pm51
	☽∠♅	10 20
	☉∥☽	11 17
25	☽∠♆	0am47
Su	☽△♂	3 55
	☽△♀	8 55
	☽⚺♃	1pm44
	☉#☽	4 1
	☽☍☿	4 31
	☽⚺♇	8 59
26	☽⚹♅	0am 0
M	☽∥☿	1 31
	☽⚺♆	2 28
	♂#♇	6 23
	☽⚹♄	7 36
	☽⚼♀	1pm 0
	☉☍☽	1 12
	☽∠♃	3 36
	♂∠♄	7 49
	☽∠♇	11 6
27	☿⚻♇	1am56
T	☽∥♆	5 1
	☽∠♄	9 58
	☽□♂	10 42
	☉#☿	4pm 5
	☉∠♀	5 7
	☽⚻♀	5 53
	☽⚹♃	6 6
	♀□♃	8 21
	☉⚼♃	8 36
28	☿△♅	0am28
W	☽⚹♇	1 54
	☽□♅	5 7
	☽⚻☿	5 54
	☽☌♆	7 39
	☽#♃	12pm53
	☽⚺♄	1 4
	☿⚻♆	5 57
	☿ ♈	10 41
	☉⚻☽	11 33
29	♀∥♅	4am 1
Th	☽∥♄	1pm29
	☽⚼☿	2 34
	☽⚹♂	8 56
30	☽□♃	1am32
F	☉⚼☽	6 21
	☿△♄	6 32
	☽☍♀	6 46
	☽□♇	10 1
	☽△♅	1pm30
	☽⚺♆	4 7
	☽#♅	6 14
	☽☌♄	9 51
31	☽△☿	0am46
S	☽∠♂	3 34
	☽#♀	8 27
	☉△☽	2pm13
	☽⚼♅	6 57
	♀□♇	8 41
	☽∠♆	9 35

APRIL 1956

LONGITUDE

Day	Sid. Time	☉	☽	☽ 12 Hour	Mean ☊	True ☊	☿	♀	♂	♃	♄	♅	♆	♇
	h m s	° ' "	° ' "	° ' "	° '	° '	° '	° '	° '	° '	° '	° '	° '	° '
1	12 37 18	11♈ 14 30	15♐ 45 34	21♐ 45 10	11♐ 16	9♐ 47	5♈ 55	26♉ 33	20♑ 59	21♌ 55R	2♐ 29R	28♋ 14R	29♎ 33R	26♌ 25R
2	12 41 15	12 13 40	27 42 31	3♑ 38 18	11 13	9 48	7 53	27 36	21 38	21 52	2 27	28 13	29 31	26 24
3	12 45 12	13 12 49	9♑ 33 9	15 27 44	11 10	9 48R	9 53	28 39	22 17	21 49	2 25	28 13	29 29	26 23
4	12 49 8	14 11 55	21 22 45	27 18 50	11 7	9 48	11 54	29 41	22 56	21 46	2 23	28 13	29 28	26 22
5	12 53 5	15 11 0	3♒ 16 37	9♒ 16 43	11 4	9 46	13 56	0♊ 43	23 35	21 44	2 21	28 13D	29 26	26 21
6	12 57 1	16 10 4	15 19 41	21 26 1	11 0	9 42	16 0	1 44	24 14	21 42	2 18	28 13	29 25	26 20
7	13 0 58	17 9 5	27 36 10	3♓ 50 30	10 57	9 36	18 3	2 45	24 52	21 40	2 16	28 13	29 23	26 19
8	13 4 54	18 8 4	10♓ 9 19	16 32 49	10 54	9 28	20 8	3 46	25 31	21 38	2 14	28 13	29 22	26 18
9	13 8 51	19 7 2	23 1 6	29 34 10	10 51	9 20	22 13	4 47	26 10	21 36	2 11	28 13	29 20	26 17
10	13 12 47	20 5 58	6♈ 11 58	12♈ 54 17	10 48	9 11	24 19	5 47	26 48	21 34	2 8	28 14	29 18	26 17
11	13 16 44	21 4 51	19 40 52	26 31 22	10 45	9 3	26 25	6 46	27 27	21 33	2 6	28 14	29 17	26 16
12	13 20 41	22 3 43	3♉ 25 25	10♉ 22 32	10 41	8 56	28 30	7 45	28 5	21 32	2 3	28 14	29 15	26 15
13	13 24 37	23 2 33	17 22 17	24 24 11	10 38	8 52	0♉ 36	8 44	28 44	21 31	2 0	28 15	29 13	26 14
14	13 28 34	24 1 21	1♊ 27 47	8♊ 32 39	10 35	8 50D	2 40	9 43	29 22	21 30	1 57	28 15	29 12	26 14
15	13 32 30	25 0 6	15 38 23	22 44 37	10 32	8 50	4 43	10 40	0♒ 1	21 30	1 54	28 15	29 10	26 13
16	13 36 27	25 58 49	29 51 2	6♋ 57 22	10 29	8 51	6 45	11 38	0 39	21 29	1 51	28 16	29 9	26 12
17	13 40 23	26 57 31	14♋ 3 21	21 8 48	10 26	8 53	8 46	12 35	1 17	21 29D	1 47	28 17	29 7	26 12
18	13 44 20	27 56 9	28 13 29	5♌ 17 14	10 22	8 53R	10 44	13 31	1 55	21 29	1 44	28 17	29 5	26 11
19	13 48 16	28 54 46	12♌ 19 51	19 21 7	10 19	8 53	12 40	14 27	2 34	21 29	1 41	28 18	29 4	26 11
20	13 52 13	29 53 20	26 20 49	3♍ 18 43	10 16	8 50	14 33	15 22	3 12	21 30	1 37	28 19	29 2	26 10
21	13 56 10	0♉ 51 52	10♍ 14 34	17 8 6	10 13	8 46	16 23	16 17	3 50	21 30	1 34	28 20	29 0	26 10
22	14 0 6	1 50 22	23 59 1	0♎ 47 3	10 10	8 41	18 10	17 11	4 28	21 31	1 30	28 20	28 59	26 9
23	14 4 3	2 48 50	7♎ 31 56	14 13 24	10 6	8 35	19 53	18 4	5 6	21 32	1 27	28 21	28 57	26 9
24	14 7 59	3 47 15	20 51 14	27 25 15	10 3	8 29	21 33	18 57	5 44	21 33	1 23	28 22	28 55	26 8
25	14 11 56	4 45 39	3♏ 55 19	10♏ 21 23	10 0	8 24	23 8	19 49	6 22	21 34	1 19	28 23	28 54	26 8
26	14 15 52	5 44 1	16 43 25	23 1 28	9 57	8 21	24 40	20 41	7 0	21 36	1 16	28 24	28 52	26 8
27	14 19 49	6 42 22	29 15 40	5♐ 26 13	9 54	8 19D	26 8	21 32	7 37	21 37	1 12	28 25	28 51	26 7
28	14 23 45	7 40 40	11♐ 33 21	17 37 24	9 51	8 19	27 31	22 22	8 15	21 39	1 8	28 27	28 49	26 7
29	14 27 42	8 38 57	23 38 45	29 37 48	9 47	8 20	28 50	23 11	8 53	21 41	1 4	28 28	28 47	26 7
30	14 31 38	9♉ 37 13	5♑ 35 2	11♑ 30 58	9♐ 44	8♐ 22	0♊ 4	24♊ 0	9♒ 30	21♌ 43	1♐ 0	28♋ 29	28♎ 46	26♌ 7

DECLINATION and LATITUDE

Day	☉ Decl	☽ Decl	☽ Lat	☽ 12 Hr. Decl	☿ Decl	☿ Lat	♀ Decl	♀ Lat	♂ Decl	♂ Lat	♃ Decl	♃ Lat	♄ Decl	♄ Lat
1	4N27	22S 9	0N32	22S 8	0N53	1S35	22N 0	2N41	22S33	0S45	15N18	1N 9	18S31	2N11
2	4 50	21 51	1 35	21 19	1 46	1 29	22 19	2 45	22 28	0 47	15 19	1 9	18 30	2 12
3	5 13	20 34	2 33	19 35	2 40	1 21	22 37	2 49	22 24	0 48	15 19	1 9	18 30	2 12
4	5 36	18 23	3 24	16 60	3 35	1 14	22 54	2 53	22 18	0 49	15 20	1 9	18 29	2 12
5	5 59	15 25	4 7	13 41	4 30	1 6	23 11	2 57	22 13	0 51	15 21	1 9	18 29	2 12
6	6 22	11 47	4 40	9 45	5 25	0 57	23 27	3 0	22 8	0 52	15 22	1 9	18 28	2 12
7	6 44	7 36	5 0	5 21	6 21	0 48	23 43	3 4	22 3	0 54	15 22	1 8	18 28	2 12
8	7 7	3 2	5 7	0 38	7 17	0 38	23 59	3 8	21 57	0 55	15 23	1 8	18 27	2 12
9	7 29	1N48	4 58	4N14	8 13	0 28	24 14	3 11	21 51	0 57	15 23	1 8	18 26	2 12
10	7 52	6 39	4 34	9 1	9 9	0 18	24 28	3 14	21 45	0 58	15 23	1 8	18 26	2 13
11	8 14	11 18	3 54	13 28	10 5	0 8	24 42	3 18	21 39	0 60	15 24	1 8	18 25	2 13
12	8 36	15 28	2 59	17 16	10 60	0N 3	24 55	3 21	21 33	1 1	15 24	1 8	18 24	2 13
13	8 58	18 50	1 54	20 8	11 54	0 14	25 7	3 24	21 27	1 3	15 24	1 8	18 24	2 13
14	9 19	21 7	0 40	21 46	12 48	0 25	25 20	3 27	21 20	1 5	15 24	1 8	18 23	2 13
15	9 41	22 4	0S37	22 0	13 40	0 36	25 31	3 30	21 14	1 6	15 24	1 8	18 22	2 13
16	10 2	21 35	1 51	20 49	14 31	0 47	25 42	3 33	21 7	1 8	15 24	1 7	18 22	2 13
17	10 23	19 44	2 59	18 20	15 21	0 58	25 53	3 36	21 0	1 9	15 24	1 7	18 21	2 13
18	10 45	16 40	3 56	14 46	16 8	1 9	26 2	3 38	20 53	1 11	15 24	1 7	18 20	2 13
19	11 5	12 39	4 38	10 23	16 54	1 19	26 12	3 41	20 46	1 13	15 24	1 7	18 19	2 13
20	11 26	7 59	5 3	5 29	17 38	1 29	26 21	3 43	20 39	1 14	15 24	1 7	18 19	2 13
21	11 47	2 56	5 10	0 22	18 19	1 39	26 29	3 46	20 32	1 16	15 24	1 7	18 18	2 14
22	12 7	2S12	4 60	4S43	18 59	1 48	26 36	3 48	20 24	1 18	15 23	1 7	18 17	2 14
23	12 27	7 9	4 32	9 29	19 35	1 57	26 44	3 50	20 17	1 19	15 23	1 7	18 16	2 14
24	12 47	11 42	3 50	13 44	20 10	2 5	26 50	3 52	20 9	1 21	15 22	1 6	18 16	2 14
25	13 7	15 36	2 57	17 15	20 41	2 12	26 56	3 54	20 1	1 23	15 22	1 6	18 15	2 14
26	13 26	18 41	1 55	19 52	21 11	2 18	27 2	3 55	19 54	1 25	15 21	1 6	18 14	2 14
27	13 45	20 48	0 49	21 28	21 37	2 24	27 7	3 57	19 46	1 26	15 21	1 6	18 13	2 14
28	14 4	21 53	0N18	22 2	22 2	2 29	27 11	3 58	19 38	1 28	15 20	1 6	18 12	2 14
29	14 23	21 55	1 23	21 32	22 23	2 33	27 15	3 59	19 29	1 30	15 19	1 6	18 11	2 14
30	14N42	20S56	2N24	20S 5	22N42	2N36	27N19	4N 0	19S21	1S32	15N18	1N 6	18S11	2N14

Day	♅ Decl	♅ Lat	♆ Decl	♆ Lat	♇ Decl	♇ Lat
1	21N 5	0N35	9S38	1N47	22N58	10N57
5	21 5	0 35	9 36	1 47	22 59	10 56
9	21 5	0 35	9 34	1 47	22 60	10 55
13	21 5	0 34	9 31	1 48	22 60	10 54
17	21 4	0 34	9 29	1 48	23 0	10 54
21	21 4	0 34	9 27	1 48	22 60	10 53
25	21 3	0 34	9 24	1 48	22 60	10 52
29	21N 2	0N34	9S22	1N48	22N59	10N51

☽ PHENOMENA

d	h	m	
3	8	7	☾
11	2	39	●
17	23	28	☽
25	1	41	○

d	h	° '
1	5	22S10
8	15	0
15	4	22N 5
21	14	0
28	13	22S 2

7	23	5N 7
14	13	0
20	21	5S11
27	18	0

VOID OF COURSE ☽

Last Aspect		☽ Ingress		
2	3am39	2	♑	4am38
4	4pm18	4	♒	5pm25
7	3am26	7	♓	4am38
9	9am33	9	♈	12pm47
11	4pm46	11	♉	6pm 4
13	8pm17	13	♊	9pm31
15	10pm48	16	♋	0am15
18	1am28	18	♌	3am 1
20	4am37	20	♍	6am17
22	7am41	22	♎	10am37
24	2pm44	24	♏	4pm45
26	10pm23	27	♐	1am26
29	10am17	29	♑	12pm45

d	h	
3	10	APOGEE
15	21	PERIGEE

DAILY ASPECTARIAN

1 Su	☉⚼♇	3am59
	☽#♀	10 45
	☽⚺♂	11 4
	☿⚼♃	11 55
	☽△♃	12pm16
	☽△♇	9 21
	☽⚻♀	11 46
2 M	☽⚻♅	1am 2
	☽✶♆	3 39
	♂⚻♃	7 46
	☽⚺♄	9 34
	♀#♂	10 9
	♀✶♅	2pm12
	☽#♅	4 6
	☽⚼♃	6 28
3 T	☽□☿	0am49
	☽⚼♇	3 42
	☉□☽	8 7
	☽⚼♀	9 7
	☽∠♄	3pm56
	☿⚼♇	5 37
	♀⚻♆	7 5
	☽∥♄	11 1
4 W	☽⚻♃	0am48
	☽☌♂	3 20
	♀∥♇	6 46
	♀ ♊	7 23
	☽⚻♇	10 4
	☽☍♅	1pm49
	☽□♆	4 18
	☽△♀	6 22
	☽✶♄	10 8
5 Th	☽#♃	0am31
	♅SD	11 19
6 F	☽✶☿	1am35
	☉✶☽	1 48
	☉☌☿	3 55
	☽☍♃	12pm28
	♀☍♄	12 54
	☽∥♆	12 58
	☿⚼♄	3 1
	☿∠♀	5 9
	☽⚺♂	6 25
	☽☍♇	9 31
7 S	☽⚻♅	1am11
	☉⚼♄	2 44
	☽△♆	3 26
	☉#☽	4 20
	☽#☿	5 37
	☽□♄	8 57
	☉∠☽	9 30
	☽□♀	10 48
	☽∠☿	12pm35
	☉∥☿	4 48
8 Su	☽∠♂	0am43
	☽⚼♅	5 46
	☽⚼♆	7 54
	☉⚺☽	4pm11
	☿△♃	4 55
	☽⚻♃	9 23
	☽⚺☿	10 15
9 M	♂⚻♇	4am47
	☽⚻♇	6 0
	☽✶♂	6 4
	☽△♅	9 33
	☽⚻♆	11 33
	☽△♄	4pm41
	☽✶♀	11 11
10 T	☽⚼♃	0am40
	☉∥☽	6 36
	☽⚼♇	9 5
	☿#♆	10 21
	☽#♆	2pm44
	☽∥☿	3 50
	☽⚼♄	7 27
	☿△♇	10 18
11 W	☉☌☽	2am39
	☽△♃	3 17
	☽∠♀	3 58
	☉△♃	11 19
	☽△♇	11 32
	☽☌☿	1pm56
	☽□♂	2 17
	☽□♅	2 59
	☽☍♆	4 46
	☿□♂	5 3
	☿□♅	8 53
	☽⚻♄	9 37
	☽∥♃	11 35
12 Th	♂☍♅	5am37
	☽⚺♀	8 4
	☿☍♆	8 27
	☿ ♉	5pm10
	☽#♄	8 26
13 F	☽□♃	7am 5
	☉⚺☽	10 24
	☽□♇	3pm 7
	☿⚻♄	3 51
	♂□♆	5 50
	☽✶♅	6 32
	☽⚻♆	8 10
	☽△♂	8 17
	☽∥♅	11 33
14 S	☽☍♄	0am49
	☽⚺☿	2 23
	☽#♂	3 21
	☉#♆	12pm32
	☉∠☽	1 46
	☽☌♀	3 0
	☽∠♅	7 58
	☽⚼♆	9 31
	☽⚼♂	10 53
	♂ ♒	11 40
15 Su	☽∠☿	8am 3
	☽✶♃	9 53
	☉✶☽	4pm59
	☽✶♇	5 51
	☽⚺♅	9 19
	☽△♆	10 48
16 M	☽⚻♂	1am25
	☽⚻♄	3 21
	☉△♇	5 32
	☽#♂	8 32
	☽∥♅	8 36
	♂#♅	9 36
	☽∠♃	11 13
	☽✶☿	1pm35
	☽∠♇	7 10
	☽⚺♀	9 19
17 T	☿∥♃	1am54
	☽⚼♄	4 37
	☽#♄	11 57
	☽⚺♃	12pm34
	♃SD	12 59
	♂✶♄	5 32
	♀∠♅	6 3
	☽⚺♇	8 33
	☉□☽	11 28
18 W	☽☌♅	0am 6
	☽∠♀	0 32
	☽□♆	1 28
	☽∥☿	2 53
	☽△♄	5 56
	☽☍♂	6 35
	☽∥♃	8 7
	☉□♅	8 44
	♀⚼♆	2pm18
19 Th	☽□☿	0am39
	☉☍♆	3 33
	☽✶♀	3 52
	☉∥☽	7 45
	☽☌♃	3pm40
	☽#♆	4 40
	☽☌♇	11 42
20 F	☉ ♉	2am44
	☽⚺♅	3 23
	☽✶♆	4 37
	☉△☽	6 33
	☽□♄	9 3
	☽⚻♂	12pm22
	☿⚺♀	9 19
	☿#♄	11 10
21 S	☽∠♅	5am22
	☽∠♆	6 32
	☉⚼☽	10 32
	☽□♀	11 15
	☽△☿	12pm17
	☽⚼♂	3 41
	☉⚻♄	4 18
	☽⚺♃	7 40
22 Su	☽⚺♇	3am49
	☽✶♅	7 41
	☽⚺♆	8 47
	☽✶♄	1pm13
	☉⚻☽	2 57
	☽⚼☿	6 36
	☽△♂	7 27
	☽∠♃	10 13
23 M	☽∠♇	6am28
	☽∥♆	11 38
	☽∠♄	3pm56
	☽△♀	8 18
	☿#♂	11 45
24 T	☿□♃	0am 5
	☽✶♃	1 16
	☽⚻☿	1 26
	☉#☽	6 49
	☽✶♇	9 39
	☽□♅	1pm46
	☽☌♆	2 44
	☽⚺♄	7 13
	☽#♃	10 25
25 W	☉☍☽	1am41
	☽⚼♀	1 48
	☽□♂	4 46
	☉∠♀	1pm15
	☿∥♅	5 10
	☽∥♄	8 2
26 Th	☽⚻♀	8am 4
	☽□♃	9 17
	☽∥♂	11 35
	☽☍☿	5pm10
	☽□♇	5 57
	☽△♅	10 23
	☽⚺♆	11 12
	☿□♇	11 55
27 F	♀✶♃	2am50
	☽#♅	3 43
	☽☌♄	3 44
	☉⚻☽	3pm44
	☽✶♂	5 9
28 S	☽⚼♅	3am44
	☽∠♆	4 27
	☿✶♅	5pm 7
	☽△♃	8 5
	☽☍♀	11 1
	☿⚻♆	11 17
29 Su	☉⚼☽	0am 0
	☽∠♂	0 29
	☽△♇	4 56
	☽⚻♅	9 40
	☽✶♆	10 17
	☽⚻☿	11 37
	☽⚺♄	2pm49
	☉□♂	3 55
	☽#♅	10 23
	☿ ♊	10 42
30 M	☽⚼♃	2am19
	☽⚺♂	8 22
	☉△☽	8 53
	☽⚼♇	11 10
	☿☍♄	6pm11
	☽∠♄	8 59
	☽⚼☿	9 17
	☽∥♂	9 56
	☿∥♇	11 46

LONGITUDE

Day	Sid. Time h m s	☉ ° ' "	☽ ° ' "	☽ 12 Hour ° ' "	Mean ☊ ° '	True ☊ ° '	☿ ° '	♀ ° '	♂ ° '	♃ ° '	♄ ° '	♅ ° '	♆ ° '	♇ ° '
1	14 35 35	10♉ 35 26	17♑ 26 9	23♑ 21 9	9♐ 41	8♐ 23	1♊ 14	24♊ 47	10♒ 8	21♌ 46	0♐ 56R	28♋ 30	28♎ 44R	26♌ 6R
2	14 39 32	11 33 38	29 16 34	5♒ 13 0	9 38	8 25	2 18	25 34	10 45	21 48	0 52	28 32	28 43	26 6
3	14 43 28	12 31 49	11♒ 11 5	17 11 24	9 35	8 25R	3 19	26 20	11 23	21 51	0 48	28 33	28 41	26 6
4	14 47 25	13 29 59	23 14 34	29 21 9	9 32	8 25	4 14	27 5	12 0	21 54	0 44	28 35	28 39	26 6
5	14 51 21	14 28 6	5♓ 31 41	11♓ 46 40	9 28	8 23	5 5	27 50	12 37	21 57	0 40	28 36	28 38	26 6
6	14 55 18	15 26 12	18 6 31	24 31 37	9 25	8 21	5 50	28 33	13 14	22 0	0 35	28 38	28 36	26 6
7	14 59 14	16 24 17	1♈ 2 14	7♈ 38 32	9 22	8 18	6 31	29 15	13 51	22 4	0 31	28 39	28 35	26 6D
8	15 3 11	17 22 21	14 20 35	21 8 21	9 19	8 15	7 6	29 56	14 28	22 7	0 27	28 41	28 33	26 6
9	15 7 7	18 20 23	28 1 39	5♉ 0 12	9 16	8 12	7 37	0♋ 36	15 5	22 11	0 23	28 43	28 32	26 6
10	15 11 4	19 18 23	12♉ 3 35	19 11 16	9 12	8 10	8 2	1 15	15 42	22 15	0 18	28 45	28 30	26 6
11	15 15 1	20 16 22	26 22 40	3♊ 37 5	9 9	8 9D	8 22	1 53	16 19	22 19	0 14	28 46	28 29	26 6
12	15 18 57	21 14 20	10♊ 53 47	18 11 59	9 6	8 9	8 37	2 30	16 55	22 23	0 10	28 48	28 27	26 6
13	15 22 54	22 12 16	25 30 56	2♋ 49 54	9 3	8 9	8 47	3 5	17 32	22 28	0 5	28 50	28 26	26 6
14	15 26 50	23 10 10	10♋ 8 8	17 25 2	9 0	8 10	8 52R	3 39	18 8	22 32	0 1	28 52	28 24	26 6
15	15 30 47	24 8 3	24 40 0	1♌ 52 33	8 57	8 11	8 52	4 12	18 44	22 37	29♏ 56	28 54	28 23	26 6
16	15 34 43	25 5 53	9♌ 2 16	16 8 48	8 53	8 12	8 47	4 43	19 20	22 42	29 52	28 56	28 21	26 7
17	15 38 40	26 3 42	23 11 56	0♍ 11 26	8 50	8 13R	8 38	5 12	19 57	22 47	29 47	28 58	28 20	26 7
18	15 42 37	27 1 29	7♍ 7 13	13 59 12	8 47	8 12	8 24	5 41	20 32	22 52	29 43	29 0	28 18	26 7
19	15 46 33	27 59 14	20 47 21	27 31 40	8 44	8 12	8 7	6 7	21 8	22 57	29 38	29 2	28 17	26 8
20	15 50 30	28 56 58	4♎ 12 12	10♎ 48 59	8 41	8 11	7 45	6 32	21 44	23 3	29 34	29 5	28 16	26 8
21	15 54 26	29 54 40	17 22 6	23 51 37	8 37	8 9	7 20	6 55	22 19	23 8	29 29	29 7	28 14	26 8
22	15 58 23	0♊ 52 21	0♏ 17 39	6♏ 40 16	8 34	8 8	6 53	7 17	22 55	23 14	29 25	29 9	28 13	26 9
23	16 2 19	1 50 0	12 59 36	19 15 45	8 31	8 8	6 23	7 37	23 30	23 20	29 20	29 11	28 12	26 9
24	16 6 16	2 47 38	25 28 52	1♐ 39 6	8 28	8 7D	5 51	7 54	24 5	23 26	29 16	29 14	28 10	26 10
25	16 10 12	3 45 15	7♐ 46 37	13 51 36	8 25	8 7	5 18	8 10	24 40	23 32	29 12	29 16	28 9	26 10
26	16 14 9	4 42 50	19 54 16	25 54 53	8 22	8 8	4 44	8 24	25 15	23 39	29 7	29 19	28 8	26 11
27	16 18 5	5 40 24	1♑ 53 41	7♑ 51 1	8 18	8 8	4 10	8 35	25 50	23 45	29 3	29 21	28 7	26 11
28	16 22 2	6 37 58	13 47 12	19 42 36	8 15	8 8	3 36	8 45	26 25	23 52	28 58	29 24	28 6	26 12
29	16 25 59	7 35 30	25 37 37	1♒ 32 41	8 12	8 8R	3 3	8 52	26 59	23 59	28 54	29 26	28 4	26 12
30	16 29 55	8 33 1	7♒ 28 17	13 24 53	8 9	8 8	2 33	8 58	27 33	24 5	28 49	29 29	28 3	26 13
31	16 33 52	9♊ 30 32	19♒ 23 1	25♒ 23 12	8♐ 6	8♐ 8	2♊ 4	9♋ 0R	28♒ 8	24♌ 13	28♏ 45	29♋ 32	28♎ 2	26♌ 14

DECLINATION and LATITUDE

Day	☉ Decl	☽ Decl	☽ Lat	☽ 12 Hr. Decl	☿ Decl	☿ Lat	♀ Decl	♀ Lat	♂ Decl	♂ Lat	♃ Decl	♃ Lat	♄ Decl	♄ Lat
1	15N 0	19S 2	3N18	17S46	22N59	2N38	27N22	4N 1	19S13	1S34	15N17	1N 6	18S10	2N14
2	15 18	16 19	4 4	14 42	23 14	2 39	27 24	4 2	19 4	1 35	15 16	1 5	18 9	2 14
3	15 36	12 56	4 40	11 1	23 26	2 39	27 26	4 2	18 56	1 37	15 15	1 5	18 8	2 14
4	15 54	8 59	5 4	6 51	23 35	2 38	27 27	4 3	18 47	1 39	15 14	1 5	18 7	2 14
5	16 11	4 37	5 14	2 18	23 43	2 36	27 28	4 3	18 38	1 41	15 13	1 5	18 6	2 14
6	16 28	0N 3	5 10	2N27	23 48	2 33	27 29	4 2	18 30	1 43	15 12	1 5	18 5	2 14
7	16 45	4 51	4 50	7 14	23 51	2 29	27 29	4 2	18 21	1 45	15 11	1 5	18 4	2 14
8	17 1	9 34	4 15	11 49	23 52	2 24	27 28	4 2	18 12	1 47	15 10	1 5	18 4	2 14
9	17 18	13 57	3 24	15 54	23 51	2 18	27 27	4 1	18 3	1 49	15 8	1 5	18 3	2 14
10	17 33	17 40	2 19	19 10	23 48	2 10	27 26	3 60	17 54	1 51	15 7	1 4	18 2	2 14
11	17 49	20 24	1 5	21 17	23 42	2 2	27 24	3 58	17 45	1 53	15 5	1 4	18 1	2 14
12	18 4	21 50	0S15	22 0	23 35	1 52	27 22	3 57	17 36	1 55	15 4	1 4	18 0	2 14
13	18 19	21 48	1 35	21 13	23 26	1 41	27 20	3 55	17 26	1 57	15 2	1 4	17 59	2 14
14	18 34	20 16	2 48	18 60	23 15	1 30	27 17	3 53	17 17	1 59	15 1	1 4	17 58	2 14
15	18 49	17 25	3 50	15 36	23 3	1 17	27 13	3 51	17 8	2 1	14 59	1 4	17 57	2 14
16	19 3	13 33	4 37	11 19	22 49	1 3	27 10	3 48	16 59	2 3	14 57	1 4	17 56	2 14
17	19 16	8 58	5 6	6 31	22 33	0 49	27 6	3 45	16 49	2 5	14 56	1 4	17 55	2 14
18	19 30	3 60	5 17	1 27	22 16	0 33	27 1	3 42	16 40	2 8	14 54	1 3	17 55	2 14
19	19 43	1S 5	5 9	3S35	21 57	0 17	26 56	3 38	16 30	2 10	14 52	1 3	17 54	2 14
20	19 56	6 2	4 45	8 22	21 37	0 1	26 51	3 34	16 21	2 12	14 50	1 3	17 53	2 14
21	20 8	10 36	4 6	12 42	21 16	0S17	26 46	3 30	16 11	2 14	14 48	1 3	17 52	2 14
22	20 20	14 37	3 15	16 21	20 54	0 34	26 40	3 26	16 2	2 16	14 46	1 3	17 51	2 14
23	20 32	17 53	2 15	19 12	20 32	0 51	26 34	3 21	15 52	2 19	14 44	1 3	17 50	2 14
24	20 43	20 16	1 10	21 5	20 9	1 9	26 28	3 15	15 42	2 21	14 42	1 3	17 49	2 14
25	20 54	21 39	0 2	21 57	19 46	1 26	26 21	3 10	15 33	2 23	14 40	1 3	17 48	2 14
26	21 5	21 59	1N 5	21 46	19 23	1 44	26 14	3 4	15 23	2 25	14 37	1 2	17 47	2 14
27	21 15	21 18	2 8	20 35	19 1	2 0	26 7	2 57	15 13	2 28	14 35	1 2	17 47	2 14
28	21 25	19 39	3 5	18 31	18 39	2 16	25 59	2 50	15 4	2 30	14 33	1 2	17 46	2 14
29	21 35	17 11	3 54	15 40	18 18	2 31	25 51	2 43	14 54	2 32	14 31	1 2	17 45	2 13
30	21 44	14 0	4 33	12 11	17 58	2 46	25 43	2 35	14 45	2 35	14 28	1 2	17 44	2 13
31	21N53	10S15	5N 1	8S12	17N39	2S59	25N35	2N27	14S35	2S37	14N26	1N 2	17S43	2N13

Day	♅ Decl	♅ Lat	♆ Decl	♆ Lat	♇ Decl	♇ Lat
1	21N 1	0N34	9S21	1N48	22N59	10N50
5	20 60	0 34	9 19	1 47	22 58	10 50
9	20 58	0 34	9 17	1 47	22 57	10 49
13	20 57	0 34	9 15	1 47	22 56	10 48
17	20 55	0 34	9 13	1 47	22 55	10 47
21	20 53	0 34	9 11	1 47	22 54	10 46
25	20 51	0 33	9 9	1 47	22 52	10 45
29	20N49	0N33	9S 8	1N47	22N51	10N44

☽ PHENOMENA

d	h	m	
3	2	56	☾
10	13	5	●
17	5	16	☽
24	15	26	○

d	h	° '
6	0	0
12	11	22N 0
18	19	0
25	20	21S60

d	h	° '
5	6	5N15
11	19	0
18	2	5S17
25	1	0

VOID OF COURSE ☽

Last Aspect	☽ Ingress
1 10pm51	2 ♒ 1am28
4 10am37	4 ♓ 1pm16
6 8pm32	6 ♈ 10pm 6
9 1am11	9 ♉ 3am24
11 3am59	11 ♊ 6am 1
13 4am46	13 ♋ 7am21
15 8am43	15 ♌ 8am52
17 11am15	17 ♍ 11am40
19 3pm42	19 ♎ 4pm26
21 9pm51	21 ♏ 11pm27
24 7am18	24 ♐ 8am47
26 4pm25	26 ♑ 8pm12
29 7am45	29 ♒ 8am52
31 6pm35	31 ♓ 9pm10

d	h	
1	5	APOGEE
13	1	PERIGEE
28	21	APOGEE

DAILY ASPECTARIAN

1 T	☽∥♄	8am29
	☽⚻♃	8 48
	☽⚻♀	3pm58
	☽⚻♇	5 35
	☉∥♃	9 38
	☽☍♅	10 29
	☽□♆	10 51
2 W	☽✶♄	3am12
	☽△☿	6 43
	☉#☽	7 3
	☽#♃	7 57
	♀✶♇	4pm36
3 Th	☽⚼♀	0am20
	☽☌♂	0 24
	☉□☽	2 56
	♀⚼♂	7 8
	☽☍♃	9pm20
	☽∥♆	10 3
4 F	☽☍♇	5am37
	☽△♀	8 3
	☽⚻♅	10 30
	☽△♆	10 37
	☽□♄	2pm36
	☽□☿	11 4
5 S	♅□♆	12pm 7
	☽⚺♂	2 18
	☽⚼♆	3 30
	☽⚼♅	3 31
	☉✶☽	6 32
6 Su	♀△♆	1am54
	♀⚺♅	2 57
	☽⚻♃	7 20
	☽⚻♇	2pm54
	☽⚻♆	7 30
	☽△♅	7 37
	☽∠♂	7 48
	☽□♀	8 32
	☽△♄	11 3
7 M	☉∠☽	0am44
	☽✶☿	10 26
	☽⚼♃	11 0
	☽⚼♇	6pm12
	♇SD	7 48
	☽#♆	10 33
8 T	☽✶♂	0am14
	☽⚼♄	1 57
	♀ ♋	2 18
	☉⚺☽	5 47
	☽△♃	1pm47
	☽∠☿	2 14
	♀⚻♄	4 34
	☽△♇	8 39
9 W	♂∥♄	0am48
	☽☍♆	0 52
	☽□♅	1 11
	☽⚻♄	4 2
	☽✶♀	4 40
	☽∥♃	7 7
	☽⚺☿	4pm58
	☉∥☽	11 9
10 Th	☽#♂	1am40
	☽#♄	2 43
	☽□♂	6 25
	☽∠♀	7 24
	☉☌☽	1pm 5
	☽□♃	5 12
	☉#♂	7 51
	☽□♇	11 32
11 F	☽⚻♆	3am29
	☽✶♅	3 59
	☽☍♄	6 22
	☽∥♅	7 3
	☽⚺♀	9 32
	☉#♄	5pm25
	☽☌☿	8 11
12 S	☽⚼♆	4am12
	☽∠♅	4 47
	☽△♂	10 20
	☉⚺☽	6pm11
	☽✶♃	6 58
13 Su	☽✶♇	0am58
	☽△♆	4 46
	☽⚺♅	5 27
	☉□♃	6 51
	☽⚻♄	7 27
	☽⚼♂	12pm 0
	☽☌♀	12 55
	☽∥♅	3 49
	☽∠♃	7 42
	☉∠☽	8 32
	☽⚺☿	9 54
14 M	☽∠♇	1am36
	♄ ♏	3 39
	☽⚼♄	7 59
	☿SR	12pm11
	☽⚻♂	1 46
	☉∥☽	2 18
	☽#♄	8 9
	☽⚺♃	8 35
	☽∠☿	10 41
	☉✶☽	11 3
15 T	☽#♂	2am 7
	☽⚺♇	2 24
	☽□♆	6 10
	☽☌♅	7 3
	☽△♄	8 43
	☿∥♇	12pm28
	☽∥♃	3 49
	☽⚺♀	4 29
	☽✶☿	11 35
16 W	☽☍♂	6pm12
	☽∠♀	6 43
	☽#♆	10 46
	☽☌♃	11 17
17 Th	☉□♇	1am22
	☽☌♇	5 0
	☉□☽	5 16
	☽✶♆	8 47
	☽⚺♅	9 55
	☽□♄	11 15
	☽✶♀	9pm24
18 F	☽□☿	2am12
	☽∠♆	10 47
	☽∠♅	12pm 4
	♀⚼♂	9 39
19 S	☽⚻♂	0am39
	☽⚺♃	3 52
	☉⚻♆	7 15
	☽⚺♇	9 30
	☽⚺♆	1pm20
	☉△☽	1 49
	☽✶♅	2 45
	☽✶♄	3 42
20 Su	☉✶♅	3am19
	☽□♀	4 21
	☽⚼♂	4 47
	☽△☿	6 14
	☽∠♃	7 0
	☽∠♇	12pm35
	☉☍♄	2 16
	☽∥♆	4 17
	☽∠♄	6 45
	☉⚼☽	7 8
21 M	☉ ♊	2am13
	☽⚼☿	8 52
	☽△♂	9 35
	☽✶♃	10 44
	☿⚺♀	12pm13
	☽✶♇	4 15
	☽☌♆	8 7
	☽□♅	9 51
	☽⚺♄	10 22
22 T	☽#♃	0am59
	☉⚻☽	1 10
	☿∥♅	1 48
	☽∥♂	9 12
	☽⚻☿	11 56
	☽△♀	1pm31
	♂☍♃	3 39
	☽∥♄	11 34
23 W	☉∥☿	0am 1
	☽⚼♀	6pm54
	☽□♃	8 1
	☽□♂	9 10
	☽#☿	10 52
24 Th	☽□♇	1am19
	☽⚺♆	5 13
	☉#☽	7 7
	☽☌♄	7 18
	☽△♅	7 18
	♄△♅	7 36
	☽#♅	8 22
	☉☍☽	3pm26
	☉∥♅	5 21
	☽☍☿	7 20
25 F	☽⚻♀	0am47
	☽∠♆	10 35
	☽⚼♅	12pm51
26 S	☉☌☿	0am12
	☽△♃	7 32
	☽✶♂	11 14
	☽△♇	12pm32
	☽✶♆	4 25
	☽⚺♄	6 19
	☽⚻♅	6 53
27 Su	☉#☽	0am40
	☽⚻☿	4 21
	☽#♅	8 15
	☉⚻☽	8 17
	☽☍♀	1pm41
	☽⚼♃	1 57
	♂☍♇	2 46
	☽⚼♇	6 45
	☽∠♂	6 57
28 M	☽∠♄	0am22
	☽⚼☿	9 19
	☽#☿	12pm31
	☉⚼☽	5 18
	☽∥♄	7 6
	☽⚻♃	8 37
29 T	☽⚻♇	1am10
	☽⚺♂	2 54
	☽□♆	4 57
	☽✶♄	6 36
	☽☍♅	7 45
	☽△☿	2pm26
	☽∥♂	6 33
	☽#♃	8 42
30 W	☉△☽	2am22
	☽⚻♀	3 1
	☉⚺♀	10 54
	☿#♄	6pm24
	♂△♆	8 11
31 Th	☽∥♆	6am42
	☽⚼♀	9 16
	☽☍♃	9 45
	☽☍♇	1pm41
	☽△♆	5 14
	♀SR	5 58
	☽☌♂	6 19
	☽□♄	6 35
	☽⚻♅	8 18
	♂□♄	11 28

JUNE 1956

LONGITUDE

Day	Sid. Time	☉	☽	☽ 12 Hour	Mean ☊	True ☊	☿	♀	♂	♃	♄	♅	♆	♇
	h m s	° ′ ″	° ′ ″	° ′ ″	° ′	° ′	° ′	° ′	° ′	° ′	° ′	° ′	° ′	° ′
1	16 37 48	10♊ 28 1	1♓ 25 59	7♓ 31 55	8♐ 3	8♐ 8R	1♊ 38R	9♋ 1R	28♒ 42	24♌ 20	28♏ 41R	29♋ 34	28♎ 1R	26♌ 14
2	16 41 45	11 25 30	13 41 34	19 55 27	7 59	8 8D	1 14	8 59	29 15	24 27	28 36	29 37	28 0	26 15
3	16 45 41	12 22 58	26 14 5	2♈ 37 56	7 56	8 8	0 55	8 55	29 49	24 34	28 32	29 40	27 59	26 16
4	16 49 38	13 20 25	9♈ 7 26	15 42 56	7 53	8 8	0 38	8 49	0♓ 22	24 42	28 28	29 42	27 58	26 16
5	16 53 34	14 17 52	22 24 42	29 12 54	7 50	8 9	0 26	8 40	0 56	24 50	28 24	29 45	27 57	26 17
6	16 57 31	15 15 18	6♉ 7 33	13♉ 8 34	7 47	8 9	0 18	8 28	1 29	24 57	28 19	29 48	27 56	26 18
7	17 1 28	16 12 44	20 15 42	27 28 33	7 43	8 10	0 14D	8 15	2 2	25 5	28 15	29 51	27 55	26 19
8	17 5 24	17 10 8	4♊ 46 32	12♊ 8 57	7 40	8 10R	0 15	7 59	2 34	25 13	28 11	29 54	27 54	26 20
9	17 9 21	18 7 33	19 34 57	27 3 34	7 37	8 10	0 20	7 40	3 7	25 22	28 7	29 57	27 53	26 21
10	17 13 17	19 4 56	4♋ 33 46	12♋ 4 28	7 34	8 10	0 30	7 20	3 39	25 30	28 3	0♌ 0	27 52	26 22
11	17 17 14	20 2 18	19 34 35	27 3 4	7 31	8 9	0 44	6 57	4 11	25 38	27 59	0 3	27 51	26 22
12	17 21 10	20 59 39	4♌ 28 57	11♌ 51 21	7 28	8 7	1 3	6 32	4 42	25 47	27 55	0 6	27 50	26 23
13	17 25 7	21 57 0	19 9 34	26 22 59	7 24	8 6	1 26	6 5	5 14	25 55	27 51	0 9	27 49	26 24
14	17 29 4	22 54 19	3♍ 31 10	10♍ 33 50	7 21	8 4	1 53	5 36	5 45	26 4	27 47	0 12	27 49	26 25
15	17 33 0	23 51 38	17 30 50	24 22 8	7 18	8 4D	2 25	5 5	6 16	26 13	27 44	0 15	27 48	26 26
16	17 36 57	24 48 55	1♎ 7 50	7♎ 48 5	7 15	8 4	3 1	4 33	6 47	26 22	27 40	0 18	27 47	26 28
17	17 40 53	25 46 12	14 23 9	20 53 19	7 12	8 4	3 42	3 59	7 17	26 31	27 36	0 21	27 46	26 29
18	17 44 50	26 43 28	27 18 55	3♏ 40 17	7 9	8 5	4 26	3 24	7 47	26 40	27 33	0 25	27 46	26 30
19	17 48 46	27 40 43	9♏ 57 47	16 11 46	7 5	8 7	5 15	2 48	8 17	26 49	27 29	0 28	27 45	26 31
20	17 52 43	28 37 58	22 22 36	28 30 36	7 2	8 8	6 8	2 12	8 47	26 59	27 25	0 31	27 45	26 32
21	17 56 39	29 35 12	4♐ 36 5	10♐ 39 23	6 59	8 9R	7 4	1 34	9 16	27 8	27 22	0 34	27 44	26 33
22	18 0 36	0♋ 32 25	16 40 45	22 40 29	6 56	8 9	8 5	0 57	9 45	27 18	27 19	0 38	27 43	26 34
23	18 4 33	1 29 38	28 38 49	4♑ 36 1	6 53	8 7	9 9	0 19	10 14	27 27	27 15	0 41	27 43	26 36
24	18 8 29	2 26 51	10♑ 32 19	16 27 59	6 49	8 5	10 17	29♊ 42	10 42	27 37	27 12	0 44	27 42	26 37
25	18 12 26	3 24 3	22 23 15	28 18 23	6 46	8 1	11 29	29 5	11 10	27 47	27 9	0 48	27 42	26 38
26	18 16 22	4 21 15	4♒ 13 39	10♒ 9 23	6 43	7 57	12 45	28 28	11 38	27 57	27 6	0 51	27 41	26 40
27	18 20 19	5 18 27	16 5 52	22 3 27	6 40	7 53	14 4	27 53	12 5	28 7	27 3	0 54	27 41	26 41
28	18 24 15	6 15 39	28 2 31	4♓ 3 28	6 37	7 48	15 26	27 18	12 32	28 17	27 0	0 58	27 41	26 42
29	18 28 12	7 12 51	10♓ 6 43	16 12 43	6 34	7 44	16 53	26 45	12 59	28 27	26 57	1 1	27 40	26 44
30	18 32 8	8♋ 10 2	22♓ 21 56	28♓ 34 53	6♐ 30	7♐ 42	18♊ 22	26♊ 13	13♓ 25	28♌ 37	26♏ 54	1♌ 5	27♎ 40	26♌ 45

DECLINATION and LATITUDE

Day	☉ Decl	☽ Decl	☽ Lat	☽ 12 Hr. Decl	☿ Decl	☿ Lat	♀ Decl	♀ Lat	♂ Decl	♂ Lat	♃ Decl	♃ Lat	♄ Decl	♄ Lat
1	22N 1	6S 3	5N15	3S50	17N22	3S12	25N26	2N18	14S25	2S39	14N23	1N 2	17S42	2N13
2	22 9	1 33	5 16	0N46	17 6	3 23	25 17	2 9	14 16	2 42	14 21	1 2	17 41	2 13
3	22 17	3N 7	5 2	5 28	16 52	3 33	25 8	1 60	14 6	2 44	14 18	1 2	17 41	2 13
4	22 24	7 47	4 32	10 3	16 41	3 42	24 59	1 50	13 56	2 47	14 15	1 1	17 40	2 13
5	22 31	12 15	3 48	14 19	16 31	3 49	24 49	1 39	13 47	2 49	14 13	1 1	17 39	2 13
6	22 38	16 13	2 49	17 55	16 23	3 55	24 39	1 28	13 37	2 52	14 10	1 1	17 38	2 13
7	22 44	19 23	1 38	20 34	16 17	4 0	24 28	1 17	13 28	2 54	14 7	1 1	17 37	2 13
8	22 50	21 24	0 19	21 53	16 14	4 4	24 18	1 5	13 18	2 57	14 5	1 1	17 37	2 12
9	22 55	21 59	1S 3	21 42	16 12	4 7	24 7	0 53	13 9	2 59	14 2	1 1	17 36	2 12
10	22 60	21 1	2 21	19 57	16 13	4 8	23 55	0 41	12 60	3 2	13 59	1 1	17 35	2 12
11	23 4	18 33	3 30	16 51	16 15	4 9	23 44	0 28	12 50	3 4	13 56	1 1	17 34	2 12
12	23 8	14 52	4 24	12 41	16 20	4 8	23 32	0 15	12 41	3 7	13 53	1 1	17 34	2 12
13	23 12	10 20	4 59	7 52	16 26	4 6	23 20	0 1	12 32	3 10	13 50	1 1	17 33	2 12
14	23 15	5 19	5 15	2 44	16 34	4 3	23 7	0S12	12 23	3 12	13 47	1 1	17 32	2 12
15	23 18	0 9	5 12	2S25	16 44	3 60	22 55	0 26	12 14	3 15	13 44	1 0	17 31	2 11
16	23 21	4S54	4 51	7 18	16 55	3 55	22 42	0 40	12 5	3 18	13 41	1 0	17 31	2 11
17	23 23	9 35	4 15	11 44	17 8	3 50	22 29	0 54	11 56	3 20	13 37	1 0	17 30	2 11
18	23 24	13 44	3 27	15 33	17 22	3 44	22 16	1 8	11 47	3 23	13 34	1 0	17 29	2 11
19	23 25	17 10	2 29	18 34	17 37	3 37	22 2	1 23	11 39	3 26	13 31	1 0	17 29	2 11
20	23 26	19 45	1 26	20 42	17 54	3 29	21 49	1 37	11 30	3 28	13 28	0 60	17 28	2 11
21	23 27	21 23	0 20	21 49	18 11	3 21	21 35	1 51	11 21	3 31	13 24	0 60	17 28	2 10
22	23 27	22 0	0N47	21 55	18 30	3 12	21 22	2 5	11 13	3 34	13 21	0 60	17 27	2 10
23	23 26	21 36	1 51	21 1	18 49	3 3	21 8	2 18	11 5	3 37	13 18	0 60	17 26	2 10
24	23 25	20 13	2 49	19 12	19 8	2 53	20 55	2 32	10 56	3 40	13 14	0 60	17 26	2 10
25	23 24	17 58	3 40	16 34	19 28	2 43	20 42	2 45	10 48	3 42	13 11	0 60	17 25	2 10
26	23 22	14 59	4 21	13 15	19 49	2 32	20 29	2 57	10 40	3 45	13 7	0 60	17 25	2 9
27	23 20	11 23	4 51	9 24	20 9	2 21	20 16	3 10	10 32	3 48	13 4	0 59	17 24	2 9
28	23 18	7 20	5 8	5 10	20 30	2 10	20 4	3 21	10 25	3 51	13 0	0 59	17 24	2 9
29	23 15	2 57	5 13	0 41	20 51	1 58	19 52	3 33	10 17	3 54	12 57	0 59	17 23	2 9
30	23N12	1N36	5N 3	3N54	21N11	1S46	19N40	3S43	10S 9	3S57	12N53	0N59	17S23	2N 9

Day	♅ Decl	♅ Lat	♆ Decl	♆ Lat	♇ Decl	♇ Lat
1	20N47	0N33	9S 6	1N47	22N49	10N43
5	20 45	0 33	9 5	1 47	22 47	10 42
9	20 42	0 33	9 4	1 46	22 45	10 41
13	20 40	0 33	9 3	1 46	22 43	10 40
17	20 37	0 33	9 2	1 46	22 41	10 40
21	20 34	0 33	9 1	1 46	22 39	10 39
25	20 31	0 33	9 1	1 46	22 36	10 38
29	20N28	0N33	9S 0	1N45	22N34	10N37

☽ PHENOMENA

d	h	m	
1	19	14	☾
8	21	30	●
15	11	57	☽
23	6	14	○

d	h	°	′
2	8	0	
8	21	22N	0
15	1	0	
22	2	22S	0
29	16	0	

d	h	
1	13	5N17
8	6	0
14	8	5S16
21	7	0
28	19	5N13

VOID OF COURSE ☽

Last Aspect		☽ Ingress		
3	6am28	3	♈	7am 5
5	12pm59	5	♉	1pm22
7	3pm58	7	♊	4pm10
9	1pm18	9	♋	4pm42
11	1pm27	11	♌	4pm45
13	2pm24	13	♍	6pm 4
15	5pm51	15	♎	9pm59
18	0am50	18	♏	5am 3
20	9am49	20	♐	2pm56
22	10pm 8	23	♑	2am43
25	10am46	25	♒	3pm26
28	0am29	28	♓	3am55
30	8am44	30	♈	2pm43

d	h	
10	3	PERIGEE
25	8	APOGEE

DAILY ASPECTARIAN

1 F	☽□☿	0am22
	♂#♃	6 53
	☽△♀	2pm53
	☉□☽	7 14
	☽⚼♆	10 39
2 S	☽⚼♅	1am47
	♂⚻♅	4pm41
	☽⚻♃	8 49
3 Su	☽⚻♇	0am 3
	☽⚻♆	3 17
	☽△♄	4 19
	☽△♅	6 28
	☽⚺♂	7 3
	♂ ♓	7 52
	☽⚹☿	8 35
	☉⚼♆	2pm41
	☽□♀	11 26
4 M	☽⚼♃	1am 4
	☽⚼♇	3 56
	☽#♆	6 50
	☽⚼♄	7 53
	☿□♂	8 9
	☉⚹☽	8 18
	☽∠☿	11 40
	☽∠♂	11 53
5 T	☽△♃	4am19
	☽△♇	6 52
	☽#♂	8 31
	☽☍♆	9 46
	☽⚻♄	10 30
	☽∥♃	11 17
	☉∠♅	12pm 1
	☽□♅	12 59
	☉∠☽	1 3
	☽⚺☿	1 59
	☽⚹♂	3 37
6 W	☽∥☿	1am 4
	☽⚹♀	3 58
	☽#♄	9 49
	☉⚺☽	4pm42
7 Th	☽∠♀	4am54
	☽□♃	8 7
	☿SD	8 34
	☉∥♇	9 48
	☽□♇	10 5
	☽⚻♆	12pm42
	☽☍♄	1 13
	☽∥♅	2 2
	☽⚹♅	3 58
	☽☌☿	4 33
	☽□♂	8 15
8 F	☽⚺♀	5am 7
	☽⚼♆	1pm12
	☽∠♅	4 30
	☉☌☽	9 30
9 S	☽⚹♃	9am22
	☽⚹♇	10 52
	☽△♆	1pm18
	☽⚻♄	1 38
	☽⚺♅	4 41
	☽⚺☿	5 25
	☽△♂	10 29
10 Su	♅ ♌	1am52
	☽∥♅	4 4
	☽☌♀	4 19
	☽∠♃	9 34
	☽∠♇	10 52
	☽⚼♄	1pm30
	☽∠☿	5 44
	☽⚼♂	11 20
11 M	☉⚺☽	0am47
	☽#♄	7 10
	☽⚺♃	9 49
	☽⚺♇	10 55
	☽□♆	1pm17
	☽△♄	1 27
	☽∥☿	3 29
	☽☌♅	4 53
	☽⚹☿	6 18
12 T	☽⚻♂	0am22
	☉∠☽	2 37
	☽⚺♀	3 14
	☽∥♃	5 39
	☽#♂	12pm25
13 W	☽∠♀	3am 5
	☉⚹☽	4 57
	☽#♆	6 19
	☽☌♃	11 21
	☉∥♀	11 53
	☽☌♇	12pm 3
	♄⚺♆	2 14
	☽□♄	2 24
	☽⚹♆	2 24
	☽⚺♅	6 23
	♀△♂	8 26
	☽□☿	9 9
14 Th	☽⚹♀	3am24
	☽☍♂	3 56
	☽∠♆	3pm51
	☽∠♅	8 4
15 F	☉□☽	11am57
	☽⚺♃	3pm26
	☽⚺♇	3 41
	☽⚹♄	5 51
	☽⚺♆	6 3
	☽⚹♅	10 31
16 S	♀∥♇	0am42
	☽△☿	3 33
	☽□♀	5 53
	☽⚻♂	10 33
	♃☌♇	5pm28
	☽∠♇	6 40
	☽∠♃	6 41
	☽∠♄	8 45
	☽∥♆	9 1
17 Su	☿⚺♀	5am25
	☽⚼☿	8 24
	☽∥♂	12pm41
	☽⚼♂	3 11
	☉⚹♇	6 9
	☉⚹♃	10 16
	☽⚹♇	10 28
	☽⚹♃	10 46
	☉△☽	10 48
	☽#♃	11 0
18 M	☽⚺♄	0am26
	☽☌♆	0 50
	☽□♅	5 51
	☽△♀	10 59
	☿#♄	11 24
	☽⚻☿	2pm22
	☉⚻♄	7 22
	☽△♂	8 39
19 T	☉△♆	1am51
	☽∥♄	2 30
	☽#☿	4 4
	☉⚼☽	5 39
	☽⚼♀	2pm24
20 W	☽□♇	8am 8
	☽□♃	9 7
	☽☌♄	9 49
	☽#♅	10 22
	☽⚺♆	10 29
	☉⚻☽	1pm17
	☽△♅	4 1
	☽⚻♀	6 19
21 Th	☽#♀	3am53
	☽☍☿	5 19
	☽□♂	9 38
	☉ ♋	10 24
	☽∠♆	4pm 7
	☽⚼♅	9 53
22 F	♃□♄	2am 3
	☉⚺♅	2 18
	☉☌♀	6 10
	♀⚺♅	11 13
	☽△♇	7pm52
	☽⚺♄	9 13
	☽△♃	9 34
	☽⚹♆	10 8
23 S	☽☍♀	3am12
	☽⚻♅	4 7
	☉☍☽	6 14
	☽#♀	11 54
	♀ ♊	12pm14
	☽#♅	7 39
	☽⚻☿	11 26
24 Su	☽⚹♂	0am21
	☽⚼♇	2 11
	☽∠♄	3 21
	☽⚼♃	4 16
	☽#☿	10 59
	♃⚹♆	12pm45
	☿□♂	1 54
25 M	☽∥♄	4am52
	☽∠♂	7 59
	☽⚻♇	8 38
	☽⚼☿	9 17
	☽⚹♄	9 37
	☽□♆	10 46
	☽⚻♃	11 5
	☽⚻♀	12pm54
	☽☍♅	5 7
	♀∥♅	8 26
	☿⚼♆	11 3
26 T	☉⚻☽	0am17
	☽#♃	1pm 3
	☽⚺♂	3 35
	♀⚹♃	4 30
	☽⚼♀	5 48
	☽△☿	7 22
27 W	☿∥♀	4am50
	☽∥♂	5 23
	♀△♆	7 59
	☉⚼☽	9 13
	☽∥♆	2pm20
	☽☍♇	9 19
	☽□♄	9 55
	☽△♀	10 35
	☿∥♅	10 59
	☽△♆	11 16
28 Th	☽☍♃	0am29
	☽⚻♅	5 52
	♂⚼♆	7 23
	☿∠♅	9 13
	♀⚻♄	2pm22
	☉△☽	5 47
29 F	♀⚹♇	1am 1
	☽⚼♆	5 3
	☽☌♂	5 53
	☽⚼♅	11 41
	☽□☿	3pm 8
30 S	☽□♀	7am10
	☽⚻♇	8 30
	☽△♄	8 44
	☽⚻♆	10 14
	☽⚻♃	12pm15
	☽△♅	4 52

JULY 1956

LONGITUDE

Day	Sid. Time h m s	☉ ° ' "	☽ ° ' "	☽ 12 Hour ° ' "	Mean ☊ ° '	True ☊ ° '	☿ ° '	♀ ° '	♂ ° '	♃ ° '	♄ ° '	♅ ° '	♆ ° '	♇ ° '
1	18 36 5	9♋ 7 14	4♈ 52 3	11♈ 13 55	6♐ 27	7♐ 40	19♊ 56	25♊ 43R	13♓ 51	28♌ 48	26♏ 51R	1♌ 8	27♎ 40R	26♌ 46
2	18 40 2	10 4 26	17 40 57	24 13 39	6 24	7 40	21 32	25 15	14 17	28 58	26 49	1 12	27 40	26 48
3	18 43 58	11 1 39	0♉ 52 22	7♉ 37 27	6 21	7 41	23 12	24 49	14 42	29 9	26 46	1 15	27 39	26 49
4	18 47 55	11 58 51	14 29 10	21 27 36	6 18	7 43	24 55	24 25	15 7	29 19	26 44	1 19	27 39	26 51
5	18 51 51	12 56 4	28 32 47	5♊ 44 30	6 15	7 44R	26 42	24 3	15 31	29 30	26 41	1 22	27 39	26 52
6	18 55 48	13 53 18	13♊ 2 26	20 26 1	6 11	7 44	28 31	23 43	15 55	29 41	26 39	1 26	27 39	26 54
7	18 59 44	14 50 31	27 54 31	5♋ 27 0	6 8	7 43	0♋ 23	23 26	16 18	29 51	26 37	1 29	27 39	26 55
8	19 3 41	15 47 45	13♋ 2 23	20 39 26	6 5	7 40	2 18	23 11	16 41	0♍ 2	26 35	1 33	27 39	26 57
9	19 7 37	16 44 59	28 16 53	5♌ 53 23	6 2	7 36	4 16	22 58	17 3	0 13	26 32	1 36	27 39D	26 58
10	19 11 34	17 42 13	13♌ 27 38	20 58 26	5 59	7 30	6 16	22 48	17 25	0 24	26 30	1 40	27 39	27 0
11	19 15 31	18 39 26	28 24 43	5♍ 45 35	5 55	7 25	8 18	22 40	17 47	0 35	26 29	1 44	27 39	27 1
12	19 19 27	19 36 40	13♍ 0 19	20 8 26	5 52	7 19	10 22	22 34	18 8	0 47	26 27	1 47	27 39	27 3
13	19 23 24	20 33 54	27 9 38	4♎ 3 50	5 49	7 16	12 27	22 31D	18 28	0 58	26 25	1 51	27 39	27 5
14	19 27 20	21 31 8	10♎ 51 4	17 31 35	5 46	7 13D	14 34	22 30	18 48	1 9	26 23	1 55	27 39	27 6
15	19 31 17	22 28 22	24 5 41	0♏ 33 47	5 43	7 13	16 42	22 32	19 7	1 21	26 22	1 58	27 39	27 8
16	19 35 13	23 25 36	6♏ 56 23	13 13 59	5 40	7 14	18 50	22 35	19 26	1 32	26 20	2 2	27 39	27 10
17	19 39 10	24 22 50	19 27 8	25 36 22	5 36	7 15	20 58	22 41	19 44	1 43	26 19	2 6	27 40	27 11
18	19 43 6	25 20 4	1♐ 42 15	7♐ 45 18	5 33	7 16R	23 7	22 49	20 2	1 55	26 18	2 9	27 40	27 13
19	19 47 3	26 17 19	13 45 59	19 44 47	5 30	7 16	25 15	22 59	20 19	2 7	26 17	2 13	27 40	27 15
20	19 51 0	27 14 33	25 42 7	1♑ 38 23	5 27	7 14	27 23	23 12	20 35	2 18	26 16	2 17	27 41	27 16
21	19 54 56	28 11 49	7♑ 33 55	13 29 3	5 24	7 10	29 30	23 26	20 51	2 30	26 15	2 20	27 41	27 18
22	19 58 53	29 9 4	19 24 4	25 19 13	5 21	7 4	1♌ 37	23 42	21 6	2 42	26 14	2 24	27 41	27 20
23	20 2 49	0♌ 6 21	1♒ 14 43	7♒ 10 48	5 17	6 55	3 42	24 0	21 21	2 54	26 13	2 28	27 42	27 22
24	20 6 46	1 3 37	13 7 39	19 5 29	5 14	6 46	5 46	24 20	21 35	3 6	26 12	2 31	27 42	27 24
25	20 10 42	2 0 55	25 4 29	1♓ 4 52	5 11	6 35	7 49	24 42	21 48	3 18	26 12	2 35	27 43	27 25
26	20 14 39	2 58 13	7♓ 6 50	13 10 40	5 8	6 25	9 50	25 5	22 1	3 30	26 11	2 39	27 43	27 27
27	20 18 35	3 55 32	19 16 37	25 25 0	5 5	6 16	11 50	25 31	22 13	3 42	26 11	2 42	27 44	27 29
28	20 22 32	4 52 52	1♈ 36 7	7♈ 50 22	5 1	6 9	13 48	25 57	22 24	3 54	26 10	2 46	27 44	27 31
29	20 26 29	5 50 13	14 8 6	20 29 46	4 58	6 5	15 45	26 26	22 34	4 6	26 10	2 50	27 45	27 33
30	20 30 25	6 47 35	26 55 46	3♉ 26 32	4 55	6 3D	17 40	26 55	22 44	4 18	26 10D	2 53	27 46	27 34
31	20 34 22	7♌ 44 58	10♉ 2 30	16♉ 44 3	4♐ 52	6♐ 2	19♌ 34	27♊ 27	22♓ 53	4♍ 30	26♏ 10	2♌ 57	27♎ 46	27♌ 36

DECLINATION and LATITUDE

Day	☉ Decl	☽ Decl	☽ Lat	☽ 12 Hr. Decl	☿ Decl	☿ Lat	♀ Decl	♀ Lat	♂ Decl	♂ Lat	♃ Decl	♃ Lat	♄ Decl	♄ Lat
1	23N 8	6N12	4N39	8N27	21N30	1S34	19N29	3S54	10S 2	3S60	12N49	0N59	17S23	2N 8
2	23 4	10 38	4 0	12 44	21 49	1 21	19 18	4 3	9 55	4 3	12 46	0 59	17 22	2 8
3	22 59	14 43	3 8	16 32	22 7	1 9	19 8	4 12	9 48	4 5	12 42	0 59	17 22	2 8
4	22 54	18 9	2 4	19 33	22 24	0 57	18 59	4 21	9 41	4 8	12 38	0 59	17 21	2 8
5	22 49	20 39	0 50	21 27	22 40	0 44	18 50	4 29	9 34	4 11	12 34	0 59	17 21	2 8
6	22 43	21 54	0S29	21 58	22 54	0 32	18 42	4 36	9 28	4 14	12 30	0 59	17 21	2 7
7	22 37	21 38	1 48	20 55	23 7	0 20	18 34	4 43	9 21	4 17	12 27	0 59	17 20	2 7
8	22 31	19 49	3 0	18 22	23 18	0 8	18 27	4 49	9 15	4 20	12 23	0 59	17 20	2 7
9	22 24	16 35	4 0	14 32	23 26	0N 4	18 21	4 55	9 9	4 23	12 19	0 59	17 20	2 7
10	22 16	12 15	4 43	9 49	23 33	0 15	18 16	4 60	9 3	4 26	12 15	0 59	17 20	2 6
11	22 9	7 14	5 6	4 36	23 37	0 26	18 11	5 4	8 58	4 29	12 11	0 59	17 19	2 6
12	22 1	1 56	5 8	0S44	23 38	0 36	18 6	5 8	8 52	4 32	12 7	0 59	17 19	2 6
13	21 52	3S20	4 51	5 51	23 37	0 46	18 3	5 12	8 47	4 35	12 3	0 59	17 19	2 6
14	21 43	8 15	4 18	10 31	23 33	0 55	17 60	5 15	8 42	4 38	11 59	0 58	17 19	2 6
15	21 34	12 38	3 32	14 34	23 27	1 3	17 57	5 17	8 37	4 41	11 55	0 58	17 19	2 5
16	21 25	16 18	2 37	17 49	23 18	1 11	17 55	5 19	8 33	4 44	11 50	0 58	17 19	2 5
17	21 15	19 7	1 35	20 11	23 6	1 18	17 54	5 21	8 28	4 47	11 46	0 58	17 19	2 5
18	21 5	20 60	0 30	21 34	22 51	1 25	17 53	5 22	8 24	4 50	11 42	0 58	17 19	2 5
19	20 54	21 53	0N35	21 56	22 34	1 30	17 53	5 23	8 20	4 53	11 38	0 58	17 18	2 4
20	20 43	21 45	1 38	21 19	22 14	1 35	17 53	5 24	8 16	4 56	11 34	0 58	17 18	2 4
21	20 32	20 38	2 36	19 44	21 52	1 39	17 53	5 24	8 13	4 59	11 29	0 58	17 18	2 4
22	20 20	18 38	3 27	17 20	21 28	1 42	17 54	5 24	8 9	5 2	11 25	0 58	17 19	2 4
23	20 8	15 51	4 9	14 12	21 1	1 44	17 56	5 23	8 6	5 5	11 21	0 58	17 19	2 3
24	19 56	12 24	4 40	10 29	20 33	1 46	17 57	5 22	8 4	5 8	11 17	0 58	17 19	2 3
25	19 43	8 28	4 59	6 22	20 3	1 47	17 59	5 21	8 1	5 11	11 12	0 58	17 19	2 3
26	19 30	4 11	5 5	1 57	19 31	1 47	18 1	5 20	7 59	5 14	11 8	0 58	17 19	2 3
27	19 17	0N19	4 57	2N35	18 57	1 47	18 4	5 18	7 57	5 17	11 3	0 58	17 19	2 2
28	19 3	4 51	4 36	7 5	18 23	1 46	18 7	5 16	7 55	5 20	10 59	0 58	17 19	2 2
29	18 49	9 16	4 1	11 23	17 47	1 44	18 10	5 14	7 53	5 23	10 55	0 58	17 19	2 2
30	18 35	13 23	3 13	15 15	17 10	1 42	18 13	5 12	7 52	5 26	10 50	0 58	17 20	2 2
31	18N20	16N57	2N14	18N28	16N32	1N39	18N16	5S10	7S51	5S28	10N46	0N58	17S20	2N 1

Day	♅ Decl	♅ Lat	♆ Decl	♆ Lat	♇ Decl	♇ Lat
1	20N27	0N33	9S 0	1N45	22N32	10N37
5	20 24	0 33	9 0	1 45	22 30	10 36
9	20 21	0 33	9 0	1 45	22 27	10 36
13	20 17	0 33	9 1	1 45	22 24	10 35
17	20 14	0 33	9 1	1 44	22 22	10 35
21	20 11	0 33	9 2	1 44	22 19	10 35
25	20 7	0 33	9 3	1 44	22 16	10 34
29	20N 4	0N33	9S 4	1N44	22N13	10N34

☽ PHENOMENA

d	h	m	
1	8	41	☾
8	4	38	●
14	20	47	☽
22	21	29	○
30	19	32	☾

d	h	° '
6	8	21N59
12	9	0
19	9	21S57
26	22	0

d	h	° '
5	15	0
11	15	5S10
18	11	0
25	23	5N 5

VOID OF COURSE ☽

Last Aspect		☽ Ingress		
2	8pm51	2	♉	10pm26
5	1am37	5	♊	2am26
7	3am 9	7	♋	3am20
8	11pm 0	9	♌	2am42
10	10pm45	11	♍	2am35
12	10pm43	13	♎	4am55
15	6am35	15	♏	10am57
17	3pm 8	17	♐	8pm38
20	3am59	20	♑	8am41
22	9pm29	22	♒	9pm29
25	5am17	25	♓	9am51
27	1pm28	27	♈	8pm54
30	1am32	30	♉	5am41

d	h	
8	11	PERIGEE
22	11	APOGEE

DAILY ASPECTARIAN

1 Su	☉□☽	8am41
	☽⚼♇	1pm 2
	☽⚼♄	1 7
	☽⋕♆	3 1
	☽⚼♃	5 1
	☽⚺♂	5 29
	☽⋕♂	8 7
2 M	♄□♇	5am46
	☽⚹☿	8 6
	☽∥♃	11 57
	☽⚹♀	1pm25
	☽⚻♄	4 38
	☽△♇	4 41
	☽☍♆	6 13
	☽△♃	8 51
	☽∠♂	9 50
3 T	☽□♅	0am41
	☽∠☿	2pm53
	☽∠♀	3 24
	☽⋕♄	5 54
	☉⚼♄	5 54
	☿☌♀	6 19
	☉⚹☽	7 19
	☉∠♇	8 29
4 W	☽⚹♂	1am 7
	☽∥♀	6 31
	☿∥♇	8 52
	☽⚺♀	4pm36
	☽⚺☿	8 26
	☽☍♄	8 53
	☽∥♅	8 55
	☽□♇	9 10
	☽⚻♆	10 30
	☉∠☽	10 54
	☿⚻♄	11 54
5 Th	☽□♃	1am37
	☿⚹♇	2 21
	☽⚹♅	4 45
	☉∥☿	10 37
	☿△♆	12pm38
	☽⚼♆	11 21
6 F	☉⚺☽	1am29
	☽□♂	4 48
	☽∠♅	5 32
	☿⚹♃	4pm29
	☽☌♀	4 58
	☿ ♋	7 2
	☽⚻♄	9 56
	☽⚹♇	10 25
	☽△♆	11 35
7 S	☉∠♃	0am26
	☽⚹♃	3 9
	☽☌☿	4 32
	☽⚺♅	5 44
	♂⚼♅	1pm51
	☿⚺♅	2 15
	☽∥♅	6 32
	♃ ♍	7 3
	☽⚼♄	9 42
	☽∠♇	10 16
8 Su	☽∠♃	3am11
	☉☌☽	4 38
	☽△♂	5 53
	☉∥♇	10 56
	☽∥♀	11 38
	☽⚺♀	3pm45
	☽⋕♄	7 11
	☽△♄	9 16
	☽⚺♇	9 56
	☽□♆	11 0
9 M	☽⚺♃	3am 6
	☽☌♅	5 16
	☽⚼♂	6 6
	♆SD	6 18
	☽⚺☿	10 52
	☉△♂	12pm34
	☽∠♀	3 7
10 T	☽∥♃	0am 4
	☽⚻♂	6 28
	☉⚺☽	7 13
	♂∥♆	12pm29
	☽∠☿	2 26
	☽⚹♀	2 48
	☽⋕♆	3 48
	☽⋕♂	3 52
	☽□♄	8 52
	☽☌♇	9 45
	☽⚹♆	10 45
11 W	☽☌♃	3am35
	☽⚺♅	5 25
	☉∠☽	9 9
	☽⚹☿	6pm53
	☽∠♆	11 24
12 Th	☽∠♅	6am22
	☽☍♂	8 49
	☉⚹☽	11 54
	☿⚼♄	12pm15
	☽□♀	4 4
	☿∠♇	7 37
	☽⚹♄	10 43
	☽⚺♇	11 51
13 F	☽⚺♆	0am50
	☽⚺♃	6 41
	☽⚹♅	8 10
	♀SD	9pm22
14 S	☽∠♄	0am58
	☽∠♇	2 15
	☽∥♂	2 16
	☽∥♆	3 55
	☽□☿	7 55
	☽∠♃	9 39
	☽⚻♂	2pm40
	☿∠♃	7 38
	☽⋕♃	7 51
	☉□☽	8 47
	☽△♀	9 7
15 Su	☉⚺♀	1am29
	☽⚺♄	4 11
	☽⚹♇	5 38
	☽☌♆	6 35
	☽⚹♃	1pm40
	☽□♅	2 42
	☽⚼♂	7 9
16 M	☽⚼♀	1am14
	☽∥♄	7 47
	☿△♂	7 52
	☽⋕♀	12pm45
17 T	☽△♂	0am34
	☽△☿	3 35
	☽⚻♀	6 21
	☉△☽	10 25
	☽⋕♅	12pm38
	☽☌♄	1 22
	☽□♇	3 8
	☽⚺♆	4 2
	☿⚺♀	8 26
18 W	☽□♃	0am26
	☽△♅	0 54
	☉⋕☽	1 14
	☽⚼☿	3pm28
	☉⚼☽	6 37
	☽∠♆	9 48
	☉△♄	11 42
19 Th	☽⚼♅	6am57
	☿△♄	11 22
	☽□♂	1pm27
	☿∥♇	5 31
	♃⚺♅	6 44
	☽☍♀	6 51
	☉☌☿	9 1
	☿⚺♇	10 42
20 F	☉⚺♇	0am50
	☽⚺♄	1 7
	☽△♇	3 11
	☿□♆	3 15
	☉⚻☽	3 23
	☽⚹♆	3 59
	☽⚻☿	4 9
	☉□♆	10 58
	☽⚻♅	1pm21
	☽△♃	1 34
21 S	☉⋕☽	1am52
	☿ ♌	5 36
	☽⋕♅	6 32
	☽∠♄	7 27
	☽⚼♇	9 38
	☽⚼♃	8pm29
22 Su	☽⚹♂	3am32
	☽⋕♀	6 50
	☽⚻♀	8 56
	☿☌♅	9 17
	☽∥♄	12pm 9
	☿⚺♃	1 44
	☽⚹♄	1 49
	☽⚻♇	4 7
	☽□♆	4 48
	☉ ♌	9 20
	☉∥♅	9 28
	☉☍☽	9 29
23 M	☽☍♅	2am28
	☽⚻♃	3 24
	☽☍☿	6 1
	☽∠♂	10 32
	☽⚼♀	4pm 8
24 T	☽⋕♃	7am19
	☿⚼♂	10 40
	☽⚺♂	5pm19
	☿∥♅	8 11
	☽∥♆	8 40
	☽△♀	11 13
25 W	☽□♄	2am14
	☽∥♂	2 38
	☽☍♇	4 42
	☽△♆	5 17
	☉⚻☽	3pm 3
	☽⚻♅	3 4
	☉☌♅	3 14
	☽☍♃	4 41
26 Th	☉∥☿	1am 5
	☿∠♀	3 48
	☽⚻☿	6 28
	☽⚼♆	11 6
	☉⚺♃	4pm35
	☽⚼♅	8 54
	☉⚼☽	11 15
27 F	☽☌♂	5am50
	☽□♀	12pm38
	☽△♄	1 28
	☽⚻♇	4 3
	☽⚻♆	4 31
	☽⚼☿	5 34
28 S	☽△♅	2am16
	☽⚻♃	4 30
	☉△☽	6 51
	☿∥♀	10 3
	♀⚻♄	11 9
	☽⋕♂	4pm24
	☽⚼♄	6 22
	☽⚼♇	8 58
	☽⋕♆	10 49
29 Su	☽△☿	3am37
	☽∥♃	9 7
	☽⚼♃	9 31
	☽⚺♂	4pm 5
	☿⋕♄	5 44
	☽⚻♄	10 35
	☽⚹♀	11 59
30 M	☽△♇	1am12
	☽☍♆	1 32
	☽□♅	11 2
	☽△♃	1pm47
	♄SD	6 35
	☉□☽	7 32
	☽∠♂	8 3
	☽∥☿	9 23
31 T	☽⋕♄	2am51
	☉⚼♂	3 55
	☽∠♀	4 30
	☉∥♀	5 57
	♀⚹♇	7 44
	☉∥☽	10 5
	☽∥♀	10 31
	♀△♆	2pm59
	☽□☿	7 44
	☽⚹♂	11 6

AUGUST 1956

LONGITUDE

Day	Sid. Time	☉	☽	☽ 12 Hour	Mean ☊	True ☊	☿	♀	♂	♃	♄	♅	♆	♇
	h m s	° ′ ″	° ′ ″	° ′ ″	° ′	° ′	° ′	° ′	° ′	° ′	° ′	° ′	° ′	° ′
1	20 38 18	8♌ 42 22	23♉ 31 32	0♊ 25 12	4♐ 49	6♐ 3R	21♌ 26	27♊ 59	23♓ 1	4♍ 42	26♏ 10	3♌ 1	27♎ 47	27♌ 38
2	20 42 15	9 39 47	7♊ 25 14	14 31 40	4 46	6 3	23 16	28 33	23 9	4 55	26 10	3 4	27 48	27 40
3	20 46 11	10 37 14	21 44 23	29 3 5	4 42	6 2	25 5	29 8	23 15	5 7	26 10	3 8	27 48	27 42
4	20 50 8	11 34 42	6♋ 27 16	13♋ 56 13	4 39	5 59	26 52	29 45	23 21	5 19	26 11	3 12	27 49	27 44
5	20 54 4	12 32 11	21 29 2	29 4 37	4 36	5 54	28 37	0♋ 22	23 26	5 32	26 11	3 15	27 50	27 46
6	20 58 1	13 29 41	6♌ 41 43	14♌ 19 1	4 33	5 46	0♍ 21	1 1	23 30	5 44	26 12	3 19	27 51	27 48
7	21 1 58	14 27 12	21 55 6	29 28 37	4 30	5 36	2 3	1 41	23 34	5 57	26 12	3 23	27 52	27 49
8	21 5 54	15 24 44	6♍ 58 18	14♍ 23 2	4 26	5 26	3 44	2 22	23 36	6 9	26 13	3 26	27 53	27 51
9	21 9 51	16 22 17	21 41 52	28 54 4	4 23	5 17	5 23	3 4	23 38	6 22	26 14	3 30	27 54	27 53
10	21 13 47	17 19 51	5♎ 59 9	12♎ 56 50	4 20	5 10	7 1	3 47	23 39R	6 35	26 15	3 34	27 55	27 55
11	21 17 44	18 17 26	19 47 3	26 29 55	4 17	5 4	8 36	4 31	23 39	6 47	26 16	3 37	27 56	27 57
12	21 21 40	19 15 2	3♏ 5 42	9♏ 34 49	4 14	5 2	10 11	5 15	23 39	7 0	26 17	3 41	27 57	27 59
13	21 25 37	20 12 38	15 57 46	22 15 7	4 11	5 1D	11 44	6 1	23 37	7 13	26 18	3 44	27 58	28 1
14	21 29 33	21 10 16	28 27 28	4♐ 35 29	4 7	5 1R	13 15	6 48	23 35	7 25	26 20	3 48	27 59	28 3
15	21 33 30	22 7 55	10♐ 39 49	16 41 5	4 4	5 1	14 45	7 35	23 32	7 38	26 21	3 52	28 0	28 5
16	21 37 27	23 5 34	22 39 56	28 36 56	4 1	5 0	16 13	8 23	23 28	7 51	26 23	3 55	28 1	28 7
17	21 41 23	24 3 15	4♑ 32 39	10♑ 27 35	3 58	4 56	17 39	9 12	23 23	8 4	26 24	3 59	28 2	28 9
18	21 45 20	25 0 57	16 22 14	22 17 0	3 55	4 51	19 4	10 1	23 18	8 16	26 26	4 2	28 4	28 11
19	21 49 16	25 58 40	28 12 14	4♒ 8 17	3 52	4 42	20 28	10 52	23 12	8 29	26 28	4 6	28 5	28 13
20	21 53 13	26 56 24	10♒ 5 24	16 3 49	3 48	4 30	21 49	11 43	23 5	8 42	26 30	4 9	28 6	28 15
21	21 57 9	27 54 10	22 3 45	28 5 19	3 45	4 17	23 9	12 34	22 57	8 55	26 32	4 13	28 7	28 17
22	22 1 6	28 51 56	4♓ 8 41	10♓ 13 57	3 42	4 3	24 27	13 26	22 48	9 8	26 34	4 16	28 9	28 19
23	22 5 2	29 49 45	16 21 14	22 30 38	3 39	3 50	25 44	14 19	22 39	9 21	26 36	4 19	28 10	28 21
24	22 8 59	0♍ 47 35	28 42 16	4♈ 56 16	3 36	3 38	26 58	15 13	22 29	9 34	26 38	4 23	28 11	28 23
25	22 12 56	1 45 26	11♈ 12 47	17 32 0	3 32	3 28	28 11	16 7	22 19	9 47	26 41	4 26	28 13	28 25
26	22 16 52	2 43 19	23 54 8	0♉ 19 26	3 29	3 22	29 21	17 2	22 7	9 59	26 43	4 30	28 14	28 26
27	22 20 49	3 41 14	6♉ 48 10	13 20 38	3 26	3 18	0♎ 30	17 57	21 56	10 12	26 46	4 33	28 16	28 28
28	22 24 45	4 39 11	19 57 8	26 37 59	3 23	3 17D	1 36	18 53	21 43	10 25	26 48	4 36	28 17	28 30
29	22 28 42	5 37 9	3♊ 23 30	10♊ 13 56	3 20	3 16R	2 40	19 49	21 30	10 38	26 51	4 40	28 19	28 32
30	22 32 38	6 35 10	17 9 28	24 10 16	3 17	3 16	3 42	20 46	21 17	10 51	26 54	4 43	28 20	28 34
31	22 36 35	7♍ 33 12	1♋ 16 18	8♋ 27 29	3♐ 13	3♐ 15	4♎ 41	21♋ 43	21♓ 3	11♍ 4	26♏ 57	4♌ 46	28♎ 22	28♌ 36

DECLINATION and LATITUDE

Day	☉ Decl	☽ Decl	☽ Lat	☽ 12 Hr. Decl	☿ Decl	☿ Lat	♀ Decl	♀ Lat	♂ Decl	♂ Lat	♃ Decl	♃ Lat	♄ Decl	♄ Lat
1	18N 5	19N44	1N 6	20N44	15N53	1N36	18N19	5S 7	7S50	5S31	10N41	0N58	17S20	2N 1
2	17 50	21 26	0S 7	21 48	15 13	1 32	18 22	5 4	7 50	5 34	10 37	0 58	17 20	2 1
3	17 35	21 49	1 23	21 27	14 33	1 28	18 26	5 1	7 50	5 36	10 32	0 58	17 21	2 1
4	17 19	20 43	2 34	19 37	13 52	1 23	18 29	4 58	7 50	5 39	10 27	0 58	17 21	2 0
5	17 3	18 9	3 37	16 23	13 11	1 18	18 32	4 54	7 50	5 42	10 23	0 58	17 21	2 0
6	16 47	14 20	4 25	12 2	12 29	1 13	18 36	4 51	7 51	5 44	10 18	0 58	17 22	1 60
7	16 30	9 34	4 54	6 57	11 47	1 7	18 39	4 47	7 51	5 47	10 14	0 58	17 22	1 60
8	16 13	4 16	5 2	1 33	11 5	1 0	18 42	4 43	7 53	5 49	10 9	0 58	17 23	1 59
9	15 56	1S 9	4 50	3S48	10 22	0 54	18 45	4 39	7 54	5 51	10 4	0 58	17 23	1 59
10	15 39	6 22	4 20	8 47	9 40	0 47	18 48	4 35	7 56	5 53	9 60	0 58	17 23	1 59
11	15 21	11 4	3 36	13 10	8 58	0 40	18 51	4 31	7 57	5 56	9 55	0 58	17 24	1 59
12	15 3	15 4	2 41	16 45	8 15	0 32	18 54	4 27	7 60	5 58	9 50	0 58	17 24	1 58
13	14 45	18 12	1 39	19 25	7 33	0 25	18 56	4 22	8 2	5 60	9 46	0 58	17 25	1 58
14	14 27	20 23	0 35	21 6	6 50	0 17	18 59	4 18	8 5	6 1	9 41	0 58	17 25	1 58
15	14 8	21 33	0N30	21 45	6 8	0 8	19 1	4 13	8 7	6 3	9 36	0 58	17 26	1 58
16	13 49	21 42	1 32	21 25	5 26	0 0	19 2	4 9	8 10	6 5	9 31	0 58	17 27	1 57
17	13 30	20 52	2 30	20 7	4 45	0S 9	19 4	4 4	8 14	6 6	9 27	0 58	17 27	1 57
18	13 11	19 8	3 20	17 57	4 4	0 17	19 5	3 59	8 17	6 8	9 22	0 58	17 28	1 57
19	12 52	16 34	4 2	15 2	3 23	0 26	19 6	3 54	8 21	6 9	9 17	0 58	17 29	1 57
20	12 32	13 20	4 34	11 29	2 42	0 35	19 7	3 50	8 25	6 10	9 12	0 58	17 29	1 57
21	12 12	9 32	4 53	7 28	2 3	0 44	19 7	3 45	8 29	6 11	9 7	0 58	17 30	1 56
22	11 52	5 20	4 60	3 8	1 23	0 53	19 7	3 40	8 33	6 12	9 3	0 58	17 31	1 56
23	11 32	0 53	4 53	1N23	0 44	1 3	19 7	3 35	8 37	6 13	8 58	0 58	17 31	1 56
24	11 12	3N39	4 32	5 53	0 6	1 12	19 6	3 29	8 42	6 13	8 53	0 58	17 32	1 56
25	10 51	8 5	3 58	10 13	0S31	1 22	19 5	3 24	8 46	6 14	8 48	0 58	17 33	1 55
26	10 30	12 15	3 12	14 9	1 8	1 31	19 4	3 19	8 51	6 14	8 43	0 58	17 34	1 55
27	10 9	15 55	2 15	17 29	1 44	1 41	19 2	3 14	8 56	6 14	8 38	0 58	17 34	1 55
28	9 48	18 51	1 10	19 59	2 19	1 50	19 0	3 9	9 1	6 14	8 33	0 58	17 35	1 55
29	9 27	20 50	0S 1	21 23	2 53	1 60	18 57	3 3	9 6	6 14	8 29	0 58	17 36	1 54
30	9 6	21 37	1 13	21 31	3 27	2 9	18 54	2 58	9 11	6 14	8 24	0 58	17 37	1 54
31	8N44	21N 4	2S22	20N16	3S59	2S18	18N51	2S53	9S16	6S13	8N19	0N58	17S38	1N54

Day	♅ Decl	♅ Lat	♆ Decl	♆ Lat	♇ Decl	♇ Lat
1	20N 2	0N33	9S 4	1N44	22N11	10N34
5	19 58	0 33	9 6	1 43	22 8	10 34
9	19 55	0 33	9 7	1 43	22 6	10 34
13	19 52	0 33	9 9	1 43	22 3	10 34
17	19 48	0 33	9 11	1 43	22 0	10 34
21	19 45	0 33	9 13	1 43	21 58	10 35
25	19 42	0 34	9 15	1 42	21 55	10 35
29	19N39	0N34	9S17	1N42	21N53	10N35

☽ PHENOMENA

d	h	m	
6	11	25	●
13	8	45	☽
21	12	38	○
29	4	13	☾

d	h	° ′
2	18	21N51
8	19	0
15	16	21S46
23	5	0
30	2	21N37

d	h	
1	22	0
7	22	5S 2
14	13	0
22	0	4N60
29	0	0

VOID OF COURSE ☽

Last Aspect		☽ Ingress		
1	7am11	1	♊	11am16
3	12pm39	3	♋	1pm33
5	10am 3	5	♌	1pm27
7	9am27	7	♍	12pm50
9	7am33	9	♎	1pm51
11	2pm40	11	♏	6pm21
13	11pm12	14	♐	3am 0
16	11am 1	16	♑	2pm48
18	11pm45	19	♒	3am38
21	12pm38	21	♓	3pm48
23	8pm16	24	♈	2am30
26	8am31	26	♉	11am24
28	3pm23	28	♊	6pm 0
30	7pm30	30	♋	9pm52

d	h	
5	21	PERIGEE
18	16	APOGEE

DAILY ASPECTARIAN

1 W	☽∥♅	3am12
	☽☍♄	4 37
	☽□♇	7 11
	☽⚻♆	7 26
	☽⚺♀	8 7
	☽⚹♅	4pm32
	☽□♃	7 39
	☿⚻♂	10 16
2 Th	☉⚹☽	4am 5
	☽⚼♆	9 6
	☽∠♅	6pm 0
3 F	☽□♂	2am31
	☽⚹☿	6 16
	☉∠☽	6 50
	☽⚻♄	7 18
	☽⚹♇	9 49
	☽△♆	9 59
	☽☌♀	12pm39
	☿□♄	2 45
	☽⚺♅	6 43
	☉#♄	8 56
	☽⚹♃	10 9
4 S	☽⚼♄	7am36
	☽∥♅	8 22
	☉⚺☽	8 47
	♀ ♋	9 49
	☽∠☿	9 50
	☽∠♇	10 5
	☿☌♇	12pm 1
	☿⚹♆	1 9
	☽∥♀	9 8
	☽∠♃	10 28
5 Su	☽△♂	3am 6
	☽#♄	5 39
	☽△♄	7 27
	☉∥☽	8 20
	☽⚺♇	9 57
	☽□♆	10 3
	☽⚺☿	12pm44
	☽⚺♀	2 40
	☽☌♅	6 40
	☿ ♍	7 7
	☽⚺♃	10 29
6 M	☽⚼♂	2am52
	☽∥☿	11 25
	☉☌☽	11 25
	☿⚹♀	3pm20
	☽∠♀	3 21
	☽∥♃	8 48
7 T	☽#♆	2am 8
	☽⚻♂	2 37
	☽□♄	6 48
	☽#♂	7 53
	☽☌♇	9 23
	☽⚹♆	9 27
	☽⚹♀	4pm16
	☽☌☿	6 9
	☽⚺♅	6 18
	☿⚺♅	7 38
	☽☌♃	10 40
8 W	☽∠♆	9am34
	☉⚺☽	2pm38
	☽∠♅	6 43
9 Th	☽☍♂	3am13
	☽⚹♄	7 33
	☽⚺♆	10 20
	☽⚺♇	10 20
	♆⚹♇	10 20
	☿∥♃	11 29
	♀⚺♅	4pm 0
	☿☌♃	4 38
	☉∠☽	5 20
	☽⚹♅	7 51
	☽□♀	8 3
10 F	☽⚺♃	1am 2
	☽⚺☿	1 59
	☽∥♂	7 43
	☽∠♄	9 4
	☽∠♇	11 59
	☽∥♆	1pm45
	☽#☿	2 20
	♂SR	4 20
	☽#♃	5 57
	☿#♆	6 6
	☉⚹☽	9 10
11 S	☽∠♃	3am37
	☽⚻♂	6 53
	☽∠☿	7 43
	☽⚺♄	11 36
	☽☌♆	2pm36
	☽⚹♇	2 40
	☉#☽	11 55
12 Su	☽□♅	1am 5
	☽△♀	4 13
	☽⚹♃	7 19
	☿#♂	8 16
	☽⚼♂	10 14
	☽⚹☿	2pm56
	☽∥♄	5 14
13 M	☽#♀	7am 5
	☉□☽	8 45
	☽⚼♀	10 16
	☽△♂	2pm35
	☽#♅	4 59
	☿∠♆	7 42
	☽☌♄	7 52
	☽⚺♆	11 4
	☽□♇	11 12
14 T	☽△♅	10am30
	☽⚻♀	5pm28
	☽□♃	5 54
15 W	♀⚹♃	2am13
	☽∠♆	4 39
	☽□☿	9 16
	☽⚼♅	4pm26
16 Th	☉△☽	0am56
	☽□♂	1 36
	☽⚺♄	7 30
	☉⚻♂	8 38
	☽⚹♆	10 49
	☽△♇	11 1
	☽⚻♅	10pm51
17 F	☽△♃	7am16
	☉⚼☽	9 57
	☽☍♀	10 8
	☽∠♄	1pm57
	☽#♅	4 7
	☽⚼♇	5 30
	☿∠♅	11 21
18 S	☽#♀	0am26
	☉∠♀	1 5
	☽△☿	6 13
	☽⚹♂	1pm56
	☽⚼♃	2 16
	☽∥♄	4 18
	☉⚻☽	7 5
	☽⚹♄	8 28
	☽□♆	11 45
19 Su	☽⚻♇	0am 1
	☽☍♅	11 58
	☉□♄	12pm34
	☽⚼☿	4 34
	♀⚼♄	5 48
	☽∠♂	7 59
	☽⚻♃	9 9
20 M	♃#♆	0am23
	☽⚻♀	3 31
	☉#☽	5 47
	☿☍♂	8pm38
21 T	☽⚺♂	1am45
	☽∥♆	1 54
	☽⚻☿	2 26
	☽#♃	2 28
	☉⚹♆	5 39
	☽∥♂	6 6
	☽□♄	8 56
	☉☌♇	9 41
	☽⚼♀	11 49
	☽△♆	12pm 6
	☽☍♇	12 25
	☉☍☽	12 38
	♀∠♇	8 18
22 W	☽⚻♅	0am15
	☽☍♃	10 1
	☽⚼♆	5pm45
	☽△♀	7 43
23 Th	☽#☿	0am55
	☉ ♍	4 15
	☽⚼♅	5 49
	☽∥☿	7 33
	☽☌♂	12pm 7
	☿⚹♄	5 24
	☽△♄	8 0
	☽☍☿	8 16
	☽⚻♆	11 0
	☽⚻♇	11 22
24 F	☉⚻☽	4am22
	☽△♅	10 59
	☽⚻♃	9pm13
25 S	☿⚺♆	0am47
	☽⚼♄	0 53
	☽#♂	3 53
	☽∥♃	3 54
	☽⚼♇	4 11
	♂#♃	4 27
	☿⚺♇	4 49
	☽#♆	6 29
	☽□♀	10 2
	☉⚼☽	11 24
	☉∥☽	2pm29
	☽⚺♂	8 43
26 Su	☽⚼♃	2am 5
	☽⚻♄	5 18
	☽☍♆	8 8
	☽△♇	8 31
	☽⚻☿	11 12
	☿ ♎	1pm30
	☉△☽	5 47
	☽□♅	7 49
27 M	☽∠♂	0am14
	☽△♃	6 22
	☽#♄	12pm46
	☽⚼☿	5 23
	☽⚹♀	9 54
	☉⚺♅	10 43
28 T	☽∥♀	1am25
	☽⚹♂	3 8
	☽∥♅	8 17
	☽☍♄	12pm21
	☽⚻♆	2 59
	☽□♇	3 23
	☽△☿	10 37
29 W	☽⚹♅	2am15
	☽∠♀	2 42
	☉□☽	4 13
	☉#♆	11 8
	☽□♃	12pm55
	☽⚼♆	5 23
	☉#♂	7 31
30 Th	☽∠♅	4am24
	☽⚺♀	6 38
	☽□♂	6 57
	♀△♂	10 29
	☽⚻♄	4pm41
	☽△♆	7 6
	☽⚹♇	7 30
31 F	☿⚹♅	2am15
	☽⚺♅	5 53
	☽□☿	6 7
	☉⚹☽	11 15
	♂∥♆	12pm43
	☽⚹♃	4 35
	☽⚼♄	5 50
	☽∥♅	7 24
	☽∠♇	8 33

SEPTEMBER 1956

LONGITUDE

Day	Sid. Time	☉	☽	☽ 12 Hour	Mean ☊	True ☊	☿	♀	♂	♃	♄	♅	♆	♇
	h m s	° ' "	° ' "	° ' "	° '	° '	° '	° '	° '	° '	° '	° '	° '	° '
1	22 40 31	8♍ 31 17	15♋ 43 31	23♋ 3 58	3♐ 10	3♐ 12R	5♎ 37	22♋ 41	20♓ 48R	11♍ 17	27♏ 0	4♌ 49	28♎ 23	28♌ 38
2	22 44 28	9 29 23	0♌ 28 11	7♌ 55 23	3 7	3 5	6 31	23 39	20 33	11 30	27 3	4 53	28 25	28 40
3	22 48 25	10 27 31	15 24 34	22 54 39	3 4	2 57	7 22	24 37	20 18	11 43	27 6	4 56	28 27	28 42
4	22 52 21	11 25 41	0♍ 24 28	7♍ 52 46	3 1	2 46	8 9	25 36	20 2	11 56	27 9	4 59	28 28	28 44
5	22 56 18	12 23 53	15 18 22	22 40 10	2 58	2 35	8 53	26 36	19 46	12 9	27 13	5 2	28 30	28 46
6	23 0 14	13 22 6	29 57 8	7♎ 8 27	2 54	2 24	9 34	27 35	19 30	12 22	27 16	5 5	28 32	28 48
7	23 4 11	14 20 21	14♎ 13 28	21 11 45	2 51	2 16	10 10	28 36	19 14	12 35	27 19	5 8	28 33	28 50
8	23 8 7	15 18 38	28 3 4	4♏ 47 20	2 48	2 9	10 42	29 36	18 57	12 48	27 23	5 11	28 35	28 52
9	23 12 4	16 16 56	11♏ 24 41	17 55 23	2 45	2 6	11 10	0♌ 37	18 41	13 1	27 27	5 14	28 37	28 53
10	23 16 0	17 15 16	24 19 50	0♐ 38 30	2 42	2 4D	11 33	1 38	18 24	13 14	27 30	5 17	28 39	28 55
11	23 19 57	18 13 38	6♐ 51 58	13 0 52	2 38	2 4R	11 51	2 40	18 7	13 27	27 34	5 20	28 40	28 57
12	23 23 54	19 12 1	19 5 49	25 7 30	2 35	2 4	12 3	3 42	17 51	13 40	27 38	5 23	28 42	28 59
13	23 27 50	20 10 26	1♑ 6 35	7♑ 3 44	2 32	2 4	12 10R	4 44	17 34	13 53	27 42	5 26	28 44	29 1
14	23 31 47	21 8 52	12 59 35	18 54 45	2 29	2 1	12 11	5 47	17 18	14 6	27 46	5 29	28 46	29 3
15	23 35 43	22 7 19	24 49 48	0♒ 45 15	2 26	1 57	12 5	6 50	17 2	14 19	27 50	5 32	28 48	29 5
16	23 39 40	23 5 49	6♒ 41 35	12 39 15	2 23	1 49	11 52	7 53	16 46	14 32	27 55	5 34	28 50	29 6
17	23 43 36	24 4 20	18 38 35	24 39 56	2 19	1 40	11 33	8 56	16 31	14 45	27 59	5 37	28 51	29 8
18	23 47 33	25 2 53	0♓ 43 32	6♓ 49 36	2 16	1 29	11 6	10 0	16 16	14 58	28 3	5 40	28 53	29 10
19	23 51 29	26 1 27	12 58 17	19 9 41	2 13	1 17	10 33	11 4	16 1	15 11	28 8	5 42	28 55	29 12
20	23 55 26	27 0 4	25 23 51	1♈ 40 50	2 10	1 5	9 53	12 8	15 46	15 24	28 12	5 45	28 57	29 14
21	23 59 22	27 58 43	8♈ 0 37	14 23 12	2 7	0 54	9 6	13 13	15 33	15 37	28 17	5 48	28 59	29 15
22	0 3 19	28 57 23	20 48 33	27 16 41	2 4	0 46	8 14	14 18	15 19	15 50	28 21	5 50	29 1	29 17
23	0 7 16	29 56 6	3♉ 47 35	10♉ 21 15	2 0	0 40	7 16	15 23	15 6	16 2	28 26	5 53	29 3	29 19
24	0 11 12	0♎ 54 50	16 57 46	23 37 9	1 57	0 37	6 14	16 28	14 54	16 15	28 31	5 55	29 5	29 21
25	0 15 9	1 53 38	0♊ 19 31	7♊ 4 57	1 54	0 36D	5 9	17 34	14 42	16 28	28 36	5 58	29 7	29 22
26	0 19 5	2 52 27	13 53 33	20 45 26	1 51	0 37	4 2	18 40	14 31	16 41	28 41	6 0	29 9	29 24
27	0 23 2	3 51 18	27 40 41	4♋ 39 20	1 48	0 37R	2 56	19 46	14 20	16 53	28 46	6 3	29 11	29 26
28	0 26 58	4 50 12	11♋ 41 23	18 46 45	1 44	0 37	1 51	20 52	14 10	17 6	28 51	6 5	29 13	29 27
29	0 30 55	5 49 9	25 55 14	3♌ 6 35	1 41	0 36	0 50	21 59	14 1	17 19	28 56	6 7	29 16	29 29
30	0 34 51	6♎ 48 7	10♌ 20 23	17♌ 36 8	1♐ 38	0♐ 32	29♍ 54	23♌ 6	13♓ 53	17♍ 31	29♏ 1	6♌ 9	29♎ 18	29♌ 31

DECLINATION and LATITUDE

Day	☉ Decl	☽ Decl	☽ Lat	☽ 12 Hr. Decl	☿ Decl	☿ Lat	♀ Decl	♀ Lat	♂ Decl	♂ Lat	♃ Decl	♃ Lat	♄ Decl	♄ Lat
1	8N23	19N 8	3S24	17N41	4S30	2S28	18N47	2S47	9S21	6S12	8N14	0N58	17S39	1N54
2	8 1	15 55	4 14	13 54	4 59	2 37	18 43	2 42	9 26	6 12	8 9	0 58	17 40	1 53
3	7 39	11 39	4 47	9 13	5 27	2 46	18 38	2 37	9 31	6 10	8 4	0 58	17 41	1 53
4	7 17	6 38	5 0	3 59	5 54	2 54	18 33	2 31	9 36	6 9	7 59	0 58	17 42	1 53
5	6 55	1 17	4 53	1S25	6 20	3 3	18 27	2 26	9 41	6 8	7 54	0 58	17 43	1 53
6	6 32	4S 4	4 27	6 37	6 43	3 11	18 21	2 21	9 46	6 6	7 49	0 58	17 44	1 53
7	6 10	9 4	3 45	11 20	7 5	3 19	18 14	2 15	9 51	6 4	7 44	0 59	17 45	1 52
8	5 47	13 25	2 50	15 18	7 24	3 27	18 7	2 10	9 55	6 2	7 39	0 59	17 46	1 52
9	5 25	16 57	1 47	18 22	7 42	3 34	17 60	2 5	9 60	6 0	7 34	0 59	17 47	1 52
10	5 2	19 31	0 41	20 25	7 57	3 40	17 52	1 59	10 4	5 58	7 29	0 59	17 48	1 52
11	4 39	21 3	0N25	21 25	8 9	3 46	17 43	1 54	10 8	5 55	7 24	0 59	17 49	1 51
12	4 17	21 31	1 29	21 22	8 19	3 51	17 34	1 49	10 12	5 52	7 20	0 59	17 50	1 51
13	3 54	20 59	2 28	20 21	8 26	3 56	17 25	1 43	10 16	5 50	7 15	0 59	17 51	1 51
14	3 31	19 30	3 19	18 27	8 29	3 59	17 15	1 38	10 20	5 47	7 10	0 59	17 52	1 51
15	3 8	17 12	4 2	15 46	8 29	4 2	17 4	1 33	10 23	5 43	7 5	0 59	17 53	1 51
16	2 44	14 11	4 34	12 26	8 25	4 3	16 53	1 28	10 26	5 40	6 60	0 59	17 54	1 50
17	2 21	10 34	4 55	8 35	8 18	4 3	16 42	1 23	10 29	5 37	6 55	0 59	17 56	1 50
18	1 58	6 30	5 2	4 21	8 6	4 2	16 30	1 17	10 32	5 33	6 50	0 59	17 57	1 50
19	1 35	2 8	4 56	0N 8	7 50	3 59	16 18	1 12	10 34	5 29	6 45	0 59	17 58	1 50
20	1 12	2N24	4 36	4 39	7 30	3 54	16 5	1 7	10 36	5 25	6 40	0 59	17 59	1 50
21	0 48	6 53	4 2	9 3	7 6	3 48	15 52	1 2	10 38	5 21	6 35	0 59	18 0	1 49
22	0 25	11 9	3 16	13 7	6 37	3 39	15 38	0 57	10 39	5 17	6 30	0 59	18 1	1 49
23	0 2	14 57	2 18	16 36	6 5	3 29	15 24	0 52	10 41	5 13	6 25	0 60	18 3	1 49
24	0S22	18 4	1 12	19 17	5 29	3 17	15 9	0 47	10 42	5 9	6 20	0 60	18 4	1 49
25	0 45	20 15	0 2	20 56	4 51	3 3	14 54	0 43	10 42	5 4	6 16	0 60	18 5	1 49
26	1 9	21 18	1S11	21 22	4 10	2 47	14 38	0 38	10 42	4 60	6 11	0 60	18 6	1 48
27	1 32	21 6	2 20	20 30	3 28	2 30	14 22	0 33	10 42	4 55	6 6	0 60	18 8	1 48
28	1 55	19 35	3 22	18 21	2 45	2 11	14 6	0 28	10 42	4 51	6 1	0 60	18 9	1 48
29	2 19	16 50	4 12	15 3	2 3	1 52	13 49	0 24	10 41	4 46	5 56	1 0	18 10	1 48
30	2S42	13N 2	4S48	10N49	1S22	1S32	13N31	0S19	10S40	4S42	5N51	1N 0	18S12	1N48

Day	♅ Decl	♅ Lat	♆ Decl	♆ Lat	♇ Decl	♇ Lat
1	19N36	0N34	9S19	1N42	21N51	10N36
5	19 34	0 34	9 21	1 42	21 49	10 36
9	19 31	0 34	9 24	1 42	21 47	10 37
13	19 28	0 34	9 26	1 42	21 45	10 37
17	19 25	0 34	9 29	1 42	21 43	10 38
21	19 23	0 34	9 32	1 41	21 41	10 39
25	19 20	0 34	9 35	1 41	21 39	10 40
29	19N18	0N34	9S38	1N41	21N38	10N41

☽ PHENOMENA

d	h	m	
4	18	58	●
12	0	13	☽
20	3	20	○
27	11	26	☾

d	h	° '
5	6	0
11	23	21S31
19	11	0
26	8	21N23

d	h	° '
4	4	5S 1
10	15	0
18	1	5N 2
25	1	0

VOID OF COURSE ☽

Last Aspect		☽ Ingress		
1	8pm40	1	♌	11pm14
3	9pm19	3	♍	11pm21
5	7pm48	6	♎	0am 5
8	2am58	8	♏	3am27
10	8am44	10	♐	10am46
12	7pm47	12	♑	9pm46
15	8am 3	15	♒	10am28
17	8pm55	17	♓	10pm34
20	5am24	20	♈	8am48
22	3pm45	22	♉	5pm 1
24	10pm18	24	♊	11pm25
27	3am 2	27	♋	4am 0
29	5am36	29	♌	6am49

d	h	
3	4	PERIGEE
15	5	APOGEE

DAILY ASPECTARIAN

1 S	☽∥♀	3am14
	☽△♂	8 10
	☽#♄	12pm 9
	☽☌♀	12 10
	☉∥♃	12 29
	☉∠☽	1 38
	☽∠♃	5 29
	☽△♄	6 27
	☽□♆	8 40
	☽⊻♇	9 5
2 Su	☽☌♅	7am 8
	☽⚼♂	8 3
	☽⚹☿	10 20
	☉⊻☽	3pm31
	☽⊻♃	6 0
3 M	☽⊼♂	7am41
	☽#♂	10 22
	☽#♆	11 24
	☽∠☿	11 45
	☽⊻♀	3pm46
	☽∥♃	5 42
	☽□♄	6 46
	☉∥☽	8 50
	☽⚹♆	8 53
	☽☌♇	9 19
4 T	☽#☿	3am 6
	♂⚼♅	4 6
	☽⊻♅	7 22
	☽⊻☿	1pm 6
	☉☌♃	4 18
	☽∠♀	5 34
	☽☌♃	6 49
	☉☌☽	6 58
	☽∠♆	9 4
5 W	☽☍♂	7am 8
	☽∠♅	7 43
	♀△♄	3pm43
	♀∠♃	5 19
	☉#☿	6 19
	☽⚹♄	7 32
	☽⚹♀	7 48
	☽⊻♆	9 38
	☽⊻♇	10 5
6 Th	☉∠♆	4am 1
	☽⚹♅	8 35
	☉#☽	10 48
	☽∥☿	1pm27
	☽☌☿	4 49
	☽#♃	5 31
	☽∠♄	8 45
	☽⊻♃	9 10
	♀□♆	11 2
	☽∠♇	11 19
7 F	☉⊻☽	0am13
	☽∥♆	1 37
	☽∥♂	4 7
	♀⊻♇	5 46
	☽⊼♂	8 26
	☽⊻♄	10pm49
	☽∠♃	11 34
8 S	☽☌♆	0am57
	☽⚹♇	1 26
	☽□♀	2 58
	☉∠☽	4 19
	♀ ♌	9 24
	☽⚼♂	10 17
	☽□♅	12pm46
	☿#♃	3 54
	☽⊻☿	11 32
9 Su	☽⚹♃	3am 0
	☽∥♄	6 47
	☽#♀	8 13
	☉⚹☽	9 41
	☽△♂	1pm 7
	☽#♅	11 46
10 M	☽∠☿	4am19
	☽☌♄	6 3
	☽⊻♆	8 12
	☽□♇	8 44
	♀#♄	9 39
	☽△♀	3pm 9
	☽△♅	9 1
	☉☍♂	9 59
11 T	♀⚼♂	8am23
	☽⚹☿	9 54
	☽□♃	1pm 6
	☽∠♆	1 20
	☽□♂	9 35
	☽⚼♀	11 8
12 W	☉□☽	0am13
	☽⚼♅	2 34
	♃∠♆	3 46
	☽⊻♄	5pm 7
	☽⚹♆	7 13
	☽△♇	7 47
13 Th	☉∠♅	6am42
	☽⊼♀	8 0
	☽⊼♅	8 45
	☿SR	2pm11
	♀☌♅	4 47
	☽□☿	10 21
	☽∠♄	11 33
14 F	☽#♅	0am38
	☽⚼♇	2 8
	☽△♃	2 18
	☽⚹♂	8 32
	☽∥♄	5pm39
	☉△☽	6 1
15 S	☽#♀	1am13
	☽⚹♄	6 8
	☽□♆	8 3
	☽⊼♇	8 38
	☽⚼♃	9 16
	☽∠♂	2pm16
	☽☍♅	9 44
16 Su	☽☍♀	2am38
	☉⚼☽	3 5
	☽△☿	10 11
	☽⊼♃	4pm 4
	☽⊻♂	7 50
17 M	☽∥♂	0am29
	☽∥♆	6 35
	☉⊼☽	11 46
	☽∥☿	2pm18
	☽⚼☿	3 12
	☽□♄	6 41
	☽△♆	8 22
	☽☍♇	8 55
	☽#♃	10 5
18 T	☽⊼♅	9am45
	☉∠♀	12pm19
	☿⚹♀	4 32
	☽⊼☿	7 30
	☽⊼♀	7 56
19 W	☽⚼♆	1am51
	☉#☽	3 12
	☽☍♃	4 22
	☽☌♂	5 48
	☽⚼♅	3pm 2
	☉∥☽	6 9
20 Th	☉☍☽	3am20
	☽⚼♀	3 39
	☽△♄	5 24
	☽⊼♆	6 49
	☽⊼♇	7 21
	☽△♅	7pm48
	♂☍♃	8 18
	☽∥♃	10 24
21 F	☽#☿	1am 3
	☽☍☿	1 56
	☉⚹♄	8 1
	☽⚼♄	9 59
	☽△♀	10 43
	☽⚼♇	11 47
	☽⊻♂	1pm55
	☽⊼♃	2 32
	☽#♆	2 44
	☽#♂	9 8
22 S	☉⊻♆	1am38
	☿#♃	6 33
	☉⊻♇	8 21
	☽⊼♄	2pm 5
	☽☍♆	3 15
	☽△♇	3 45
	☉⊼☽	4 20
	☽∠♂	5 19
	♀⊼♂	6 48
	☽⚼♃	6 51
23 Su	☉ ♎	1am36
	☽∥♀	2 53
	☽□♅	3 50
	☽⊼☿	5 54
	♀⊻♃	5pm55
	☽⚹♂	8 19
	☉⚼☽	9 57
	☽△♃	10 42
	☽□♀	11 2
24 M	☽#♄	0am 2
	☿⚹♅	6 38
	☽⚼☿	7 8
	☽∥♅	12pm40
	☽☍♄	8 54
	☽⊼♆	9 51
	☽□♇	10 18
25 T	☉△☽	3am 1
	☽△☿	7 55
	☽⚹♅	10 3
26 W	☽⚼♆	0am28
	☽□♂	1 5
	☿∠♀	4 1
	☽□♃	4 57
	☽⚹♀	9 5
	☽∠♅	12pm28
	☉☌☿	1 21
27 Th	☽⊼♄	1am53
	☽△♆	2 37
	☽⚹♇	3 2
	☽□☿	8 23
	☉□☽	11 26
	☽∠♀	1pm14
	☽⊻♅	2 25
	♂⚼♆	5 40
28 F	☽∥♅	2am54
	☽⚼♄	3 41
	☽△♂	4 10
	☽∠♇	4 42
	☽⚹♃	9 18
	☽#♄	1pm37
	☽⊻♀	4 50
	☉∥☿	6 5
29 S	☽△♄	5am 4
	☽⚼♂	5 8
	☽□♆	5 36
	☽⊻♇	5 58
	☉⚹♅	7 37
	☽⚹☿	7 42
	☽∠♃	10 50
	☽☌♅	5pm 3
	☉⚹☽	5 42
	☽∥♀	8 59
	☿ ♍	9 40
30 Su	☽⊼♂	5am48
	☽∠☿	7 8
	☿⊻♇	10 42
	☽⊻♃	12pm 3
	☽#♂	12 49
	☿⊻♆	4 49
	☽#♆	5 56
	☉∠☽	8 17
	☽☌♀	10 48
	☿⚹♄	11 27

OCTOBER 1956

LONGITUDE

Day	Sid. Time	☉	☽	☽ 12 Hour	Mean ☊	True ☊	☿	♀	♂	♃	♄	♅	♆	♇
	h m s	° ' "	° ' "	° ' "	° '	° '	° '	° '	° '	° '	° '	° '	° '	° '
1	0 38 48	7♎ 47 8	24♌ 53 12	2♍ 10 51	1♐ 35	0♐ 25R	29♍ 5R	24♌ 13	13♓ 45R	17♍ 44	29♏ 6	6♌ 12	29♎ 20	29♌ 32
2	0 42 45	8 46 11	9♍ 28 18	16 44 40	1 32	0 18	28 24	25 20	13 38	17 57	29 12	6 14	29 22	29 34
3	0 46 41	9 45 16	23 59 6	1♎ 10 44	1 29	0 10	27 52	26 27	13 31	18 9	29 17	6 16	29 24	29 36
4	0 50 38	10 44 23	8♎ 18 46	15 22 30	1 25	0 2	27 30	27 35	13 26	18 22	29 22	6 18	29 26	29 37
5	0 54 34	11 43 32	22 21 19	29 14 46	1 22	29♏ 56	27 18D	28 43	13 21	18 34	29 28	6 20	29 28	29 39
6	0 58 31	12 42 44	6♏ 2 31	12♏ 44 22	1 19	29 51	27 17	29 51	13 17	18 47	29 34	6 22	29 30	29 40
7	1 2 27	13 41 57	19 20 18	25 50 23	1 16	29 49D	27 27	0♍ 59	13 14	18 59	29 39	6 24	29 33	29 42
8	1 6 24	14 41 12	2♐ 14 52	8♐ 34 2	1 13	29 48	27 47	2 7	13 11	19 11	29 45	6 26	29 35	29 43
9	1 10 20	15 40 29	14 48 19	20 58 11	1 10	29 49	28 17	3 16	13 10	19 24	29 51	6 28	29 37	29 45
10	1 14 17	16 39 48	27 4 11	3♑ 6 53	1 6	29 51	28 56	4 25	13 9D	19 36	29 56	6 29	29 39	29 46
11	1 18 14	17 39 9	9♑ 6 56	15 4 56	1 3	29 52R	29 43	5 33	13 9	19 48	0♐ 2	6 31	29 41	29 48
12	1 22 10	18 38 31	21 1 32	26 57 22	1 0	29 52	0♎ 39	6 42	13 10	20 0	0 8	6 33	29 44	29 49
13	1 26 7	19 37 55	2♒ 53 3	8♒ 49 13	0 57	29 51	1 42	7 52	13 12	20 12	0 14	6 34	29 46	29 50
14	1 30 3	20 37 21	14 46 24	20 45 10	0 54	29 48	2 51	9 1	13 14	20 24	0 20	6 36	29 48	29 52
15	1 34 0	21 36 49	26 46 0	2♓ 49 21	0 50	29 44	4 6	10 10	13 17	20 37	0 26	6 38	29 50	29 53
16	1 37 56	22 36 18	8♓ 55 36	15 5 5	0 47	29 38	5 25	11 20	13 22	20 48	0 32	6 39	29 52	29 54
17	1 41 53	23 35 50	21 18 4	27 34 45	0 44	29 32	6 49	12 30	13 26	21 0	0 38	6 40	29 55	29 56
18	1 45 49	24 35 23	3♈ 55 14	10♈ 19 38	0 41	29 26	8 16	13 40	13 32	21 12	0 44	6 42	29 57	29 57
19	1 49 46	25 34 58	16 47 53	23 19 59	0 38	29 20	9 46	14 50	13 38	21 24	0 51	6 43	29 59	29 58
20	1 53 42	26 34 35	29 55 46	6♉ 35 6	0 35	29 16	11 19	16 0	13 45	21 36	0 57	6 44	0♏ 1	0♍ 0
21	1 57 39	27 34 14	13♉ 17 47	20 3 37	0 31	29 13	12 53	17 10	13 53	21 48	1 3	6 46	0 4	0 1
22	2 1 36	28 33 55	26 52 20	3♊ 43 43	0 28	29 12D	14 30	18 21	14 2	21 59	1 9	6 47	0 6	0 2
23	2 5 32	29 33 39	10♊ 37 31	17 33 31	0 25	29 12	16 7	19 32	14 11	22 11	1 16	6 48	0 8	0 3
24	2 9 29	0♏ 33 25	24 31 30	1♋ 31 14	0 22	29 13	17 46	20 42	14 21	22 22	1 22	6 49	0 10	0 4
25	2 13 25	1 33 12	8♋ 32 31	15 35 11	0 19	29 14	19 25	21 53	14 31	22 34	1 29	6 50	0 13	0 5
26	2 17 22	2 33 3	22 39 1	29 43 48	0 15	29 15R	21 5	23 4	14 43	22 45	1 35	6 51	0 15	0 7
27	2 21 18	3 32 55	6♌ 49 19	13♌ 55 20	0 12	29 16	22 45	24 15	14 55	22 56	1 42	6 52	0 17	0 8
28	2 25 15	4 32 49	21 1 33	28 7 41	0 9	29 15	24 25	25 27	15 7	23 8	1 48	6 53	0 19	0 9
29	2 29 12	5 32 46	5♍ 13 22	12♍ 18 13	0 6	29 13	26 5	26 38	15 20	23 19	1 55	6 54	0 22	0 10
30	2 33 8	6 32 45	19 21 51	26 23 49	0 3	29 10	27 45	27 50	15 34	23 30	2 2	6 55	0 24	0 11
31	2 37 5	7♏ 32 46	3♎ 23 40	10♎ 21 0	0♐ 0	29♏ 7	29♎ 25	29♍ 1	15♓ 49	23♍ 41	2♐ 8	6♌ 55	0♏ 26	0♍ 12

DECLINATION and LATITUDE

Day	☉ Decl	☽ Decl	☽ Lat	☽ 12 Hr. Decl	☿ Decl	☿ Lat	♀ Decl	♀ Lat	♂ Decl	♂ Lat	♃ Decl	♃ Lat	♄ Decl	♄ Lat
1	3S 5	8N26	5S 5	5N56	0S44	1S11	13N14	0S14	10S39	4S37	5N46	1N 0	18S13	1N47
2	3 29	3 21	5 2	0 43	0 9	0 51	12 55	0 10	10 37	4 32	5 42	1 0	18 14	1 47
3	3 52	1S54	4 41	4S29	0N22	0 31	12 37	0 5	10 35	4 27	5 37	1 0	18 16	1 47
4	4 15	6 59	4 1	9 23	0 49	0 12	12 18	0 1	10 33	4 22	5 32	1 0	18 17	1 47
5	4 38	11 36	3 8	13 39	1 10	0N 6	11 58	0N 3	10 30	4 17	5 27	1 1	18 18	1 47
6	5 1	15 30	2 5	17 7	1 26	0 23	11 39	0 7	10 27	4 13	5 22	1 1	18 20	1 47
7	5 24	18 28	0 56	19 34	1 37	0 39	11 18	0 12	10 24	4 8	5 18	1 1	18 21	1 46
8	5 47	20 24	0N13	20 58	1 42	0 54	10 58	0 16	10 20	4 3	5 13	1 1	18 22	1 46
9	6 10	21 15	1 20	21 16	1 42	1 7	10 37	0 20	10 17	3 58	5 8	1 1	18 24	1 46
10	6 33	21 2	2 22	20 34	1 37	1 18	10 16	0 24	10 12	3 53	5 3	1 1	18 25	1 46
11	6 56	19 52	3 17	18 56	1 28	1 28	9 54	0 28	10 8	3 48	4 59	1 1	18 26	1 46
12	7 18	17 49	4 2	16 30	1 13	1 37	9 32	0 31	10 3	3 43	4 54	1 1	18 28	1 46
13	7 41	15 1	4 37	13 23	0 55	1 44	9 10	0 35	9 58	3 38	4 49	1 1	18 29	1 45
14	8 3	11 37	4 60	9 44	0 33	1 50	8 47	0 39	9 53	3 34	4 45	1 2	18 31	1 45
15	8 26	7 44	5 10	5 39	0 7	1 55	8 24	0 42	9 47	3 29	4 40	1 2	18 32	1 45
16	8 48	3 29	5 6	1 16	0S21	1 58	8 1	0 46	9 41	3 24	4 35	1 2	18 33	1 45
17	9 10	0N58	4 49	3N14	0 52	2 0	7 38	0 49	9 35	3 20	4 31	1 2	18 35	1 45
18	9 32	5 29	4 16	7 42	1 25	2 1	7 14	0 53	9 28	3 15	4 26	1 2	18 36	1 45
19	9 54	9 51	3 31	11 54	2 0	2 2	6 50	0 56	9 22	3 10	4 22	1 2	18 38	1 45
20	10 15	13 50	2 33	15 37	2 37	2 1	6 26	0 59	9 15	3 6	4 17	1 2	18 39	1 44
21	10 37	17 12	1 26	18 34	3 15	1 60	6 1	1 2	9 8	3 1	4 13	1 2	18 40	1 44
22	10 58	19 40	0 13	20 30	3 54	1 58	5 36	1 5	9 0	2 57	4 8	1 3	18 42	1 44
23	11 19	21 1	1S 2	21 13	4 34	1 55	5 11	1 8	8 52	2 52	4 4	1 3	18 43	1 44
24	11 40	21 6	2 14	20 38	5 15	1 52	4 46	1 11	8 45	2 48	3 59	1 3	18 45	1 44
25	12 1	19 51	3 19	18 46	5 56	1 48	4 21	1 13	8 36	2 44	3 55	1 3	18 46	1 44
26	12 22	17 23	4 12	15 45	6 37	1 44	3 55	1 16	8 28	2 39	3 51	1 3	18 47	1 44
27	12 42	13 53	4 51	11 49	7 18	1 40	3 29	1 19	8 20	2 35	3 46	1 3	18 49	1 44
28	13 2	9 35	5 11	7 13	7 60	1 35	3 3	1 21	8 11	2 31	3 42	1 3	18 50	1 43
29	13 22	4 45	5 12	2 14	8 41	1 29	2 37	1 23	8 2	2 27	3 38	1 4	18 52	1 43
30	13 42	0S19	4 55	2S51	9 22	1 24	2 10	1 26	7 53	2 23	3 33	1 4	18 53	1 43
31	14S 2	5S20	4S20	7S44	10S 3	1N18	1N44	1N28	7S44	2S19	3N29	1N 4	18S55	1N43

Day	♅ Decl	♅ Lat	♆ Decl	♆ Lat	♇ Decl	♇ Lat
1	19N17	0N35	9S40	1N41	21N37	10N41
5	19 15	0 35	9 43	1 41	21 36	10 42
9	19 13	0 35	9 46	1 41	21 34	10 44
13	19 12	0 35	9 49	1 41	21 34	10 45
17	19 10	0 35	9 52	1 41	21 33	10 46
21	19 9	0 35	9 55	1 41	21 32	10 47
25	19 8	0 35	9 58	1 41	21 32	10 49
29	19N 8	0N36	10S 1	1N41	21N32	10N50

☽ PHENOMENA

d	h	m	
4	4	25	●
11	18	45	☽
19	17	25	○
26	18	3	☾

d	h	° '
2	15	0
9	7	21S18
16	19	0
23	13	21N13
29	23	0

d	h	° '
1	9	5S 6
7	19	0
15	6	5N10
22	4	0
28	14	5S14

VOID OF COURSE ☽

Last Aspect		☽ Ingress	
1	7am40	1 ♍	8am25
3	8am53	3 ♎	10am 2
5	12pm44	5 ♏	1pm19
7	7pm16	7 ♐	7pm46
10	5am22	10 ♑	5am48
12	5pm40	12 ♒	6pm10
15	6am12	15 ♓	6am25
16	11pm26	17 ♈	4pm36
20	0am 7	20 ♉	0am 8
21	3pm17	22 ♊	5am29
23	8pm15	24 ♋	9am24
26	0am47	26 ♌	12pm27
28	6am29	28 ♍	3pm10
30	3pm48	30 ♎	6pm10

d	h	
1	2	PERIGEE
12	23	APOGEE
27	6	PERIGEE

DAILY ASPECTARIAN

1 M	☽⊻☿	6am35
	☽□♄	6 59
	☽∗♆	7 20
	☽☌♇	7 40
	☽∥♃	12pm57
	☽⊻♅	6 39
	☉⊻☽	10 46
	☉#☽	11 26
2 T	☽☍♂	6am48
	☽∠♆	8 5
	☽☌♃	2pm11
	☽∥☿	2 30
	☽#☿	4 15
	☽∠♅	7 28
3 W	☽⊻♀	4am28
	☽☌☿	6 17
	☽∗♄	8 53
	☽⊻♆	9 3
	☽⊻♇	9 22
	☉∥☽	9 49
	☽#♃	5pm 4
	☽∗♅	8 36
	☿⊻♀	10 35
4 Th	☉☌☽	4am25
	☽∠♀	7 52
	☽⊼♂	8 38
	☽∠♄	10 22
	☽∠♇	10 44
	☽∥♆	1pm43
	☽⊻♃	5 23
	☽∥♂	6 2
5 F	☽#♀	1am55
	♄⊻♆	2 23
	☽⊻☿	8 34
	☽⚼♂	10 23
	☽∗♀	12pm 4
	☽☌♆	12 26
	☽⊻♄	12 28
	☽∗♇	12 44
	☿SD	2 28
	♀∗♆	4 34
	♀□♄	5 20
	☽∠♃	7 55
	♀☌♇	8 10
6 S	☽□♅	0am35
	♀ ♍	3 13
	☽∠☿	11 17
	☉⊻☽	12pm55
	☽△♂	12 56
	☉⊼♂	1 9
	☉#♃	6 6
	☽∥♄	10 49
	☽∗♃	11 20
7 Su	☽#♅	8am 4
	♄□♇	3pm 9
	☽∗☿	3 21
	☉∠☽	6 47
	☽⊻♆	6 58
	☽□♇	7 14
	☽☌♄	7 16
	☽□♀	11 45
8 M	☉∠♇	0am51
	☉∠♄	1 37
	☽△♅	7 56
	☽□♂	8pm50
	☽∠♆	11 38
9 T	☉∗☽	1am50
	☽□♃	9 4
	☽⚼♅	12pm59
10 W	☽□☿	3am55
	♀#♂	4 49
	☽∗♆	5 8
	☽△♇	5 22
	☽⊻♄	5 44
	♂SD	10 2
	♄ ♐	3pm14
	☽△♀	4 7
	☽⊼♅	6 47
	☿⊻♆	11 0
11 Th	☿⊻♇	1am59
	♀#♆	7 22
	☿ ♎	7 29
	☽∗♂	8 7
	☽#♅	8 43
	☿∗♄	9 27
	☽⚼♇	11 27
	☽∠♄	12pm 0
	☽∥♄	5 22
	☉□☽	6 45
	♀⊻♅	8 33
	☽△♃	9 54
12 F	☽⚼♀	1am32
	☽∠♂	2pm29
	☽□♆	5 40
	☽⊼♇	5 50
	☽∗♄	6 35
	☽△☿	9 21
13 S	☽⚼♃	4am47
	☽☍♅	7 29
	☽⊼♀	11 9
	☉⊻♃	5pm28
	☽⊻♂	8 54
14 Su	☽⚼☿	6am53
	♂∥♆	11 17
	☽∥♆	11 22
	☽∥♂	11 22
	☽⊼♃	11 30
	☉△☽	12pm48
	☽#♀	7 35
	☉∥☽	8 14
	☉#♀	11 23
15 M	☽△♆	6am 7
	☽☍♇	6 12
	☽□♄	7 20
	☽⊼☿	4pm16
	☽#♃	5 48
	☽⊼♅	7 32
	☉⚼☽	9 11
16 T	☽☍♀	5am12
	☽☌♂	8 42
	☽⚼♆	11 38
	☽∥☿	3pm14
	☿∗♅	9 37
	☽#☿	11 21
	☽☍♃	11 26
17 W	☽⚼♅	0am43
	☉⊼☽	4 47
	☽⊼♆	4pm29
	☽⊼♇	4 29
	☽△♄	5 57
	☽∥♃	6 31
	♀☍♂	9 3
	☉∥♂	9 7
18 Th	♆∗♇	4am44
	☽△♅	5 14
	☽∥♀	8 41
	☽☍☿	9 13
	☽⊻♂	6pm 6
	☽⊼♀	8 0
	☽⚼♇	8 37
	☽#♂	9 20
	☽⚼♄	10 13
	☉∥♆	11 55
19 F	☽#♆	0am16
	☉#☽	0 18
	♀∠♆	3 16
	☽⊼♃	8 36
	♆ ♏	9 12
	☉☍☽	5pm25
	☽∠♂	9 51
20 S	☽△♇	0am 7
	☽☍♆	0 10
	☽⊼♄	1 51
	☽⚼♀	2 8
	♇ ♍	8 12
	☽⚼♃	12pm12
	☽□♅	12 18
	♃∠♅	7 54
	☽⊼☿	11 11
21 Su	☽∗♂	1am 4
	☽△♀	7 33
	☽#♄	1pm14
	☽△♃	3 17
	☿⊼♂	4 20
	☽∥♅	6 3
22 M	☉⊼☽	3am12
	☽⚼☿	5 13
	☽□♇	5 33
	☽⊼♆	5 40
	☽☍♄	7 34
	☿#♃	7 42
	☿∠♇	8 5
	☉⚼♂	1pm 7
	☽∗♅	5 21
23 T	☿∠♄	2am16
	☽□♂	6 14
	☉⚼☽	7 21
	☽⚼♆	7 50
	☉ ♏	10 35
	☽△☿	10 47
	☉∗♇	12pm 5
	☿#♀	1 36
	☉☌♆	2 22
	☽□♀	4 49
	☽∠♅	7 20
	☽□♃	8 15
24 W	☽∗♇	9am32
	☽△♆	9 43
	☉△☽	11 9
	☽⊼♄	11 50
	☽⊻♅	9pm 5
	☉⊻♄	9 59
	♀∠♅	10 56
25 Th	☽∥♅	8am15
	☽△♂	10 19
	☽∠♇	11 10
	☽#♄	11 52
	☽⚼♄	1pm37
	♀☌♃	4 16
	☽□☿	8 58
26 F	☽∗♃	0am10
	☽∗♀	0 47
	♀∥♃	4 44
	☽⚼♂	12pm 8
	☽⊻♇	12 39
	☽□♆	12 55
	☽△♄	3 16
	☉□☽	6 3
27 S	☽☌♅	0am 5
	☽∠♃	1 55
	☿⊻♃	3 12
	☽∠♀	4 30
	☉#☽	6 26
	☽⊼♂	1pm52
	☽#♆	9 44
28 Su	☽⊻♃	3am36
	☿∥♂	5 20
	☽∗☿	6 29
	☽#☿	7 3
	☽#♂	7 22
	☽⊻♀	8 9
	☽☌♇	3pm26
	☽∗♆	3 45
	☽□♄	6 22
29 M	☉∗☽	0am35
	♂⚼♆	2 36
	☽⊻♅	2 50
	☽∥♃	5 26
	☽∥♀	11 8
	☽∠☿	11 16
	☽∠♆	5pm14
	☽☍♂	5 26
30 T	☿⊻♀	3am42
	☉∠☽	4 0
	☽∠♅	4 20
	☽☌♃	7 8
	☽#♀	8 6
	☉□♅	8 49
	☽#♃	3pm12
	☽☌♀	3 48
	☽⊻☿	4 15
	☽⊻♇	6 30
	☽⊻♆	6 54
	☽∗♄	9 49
	☿∥♆	11 51
31 W	☽∗♅	6am 5
	☉⊻☽	7 42
	☿ ♏	8 20
	☿∗♇	11 13
	☽∥♂	11 37
	☿☌♆	2pm55
	♀ ♎	7 40
	☽∠♇	8 26
	☽⊼♂	9 53
	☿⚼♂	11 35
	♀⊻♇	11 51
	☽∠♄	11 59

NOVEMBER 1956

LONGITUDE

Day	Sid. Time	☉	☽	☽ 12 Hour	Mean ☊	True ☊	☿	♀	♂	♃	♄	♅	♆	♇
	h m s	° ' "	° ' "	° ' "	° '	° '	° '	° '	° '	° '	° '	° '	° '	° '
1	2 41 1	8♏ 32 49	17♎ 15 21	24♎ 6 20	29♏ 56	29♏ 4R	1♏ 5	0♎ 13	16♓ 4	23♍ 52	2♐ 15	6♌ 56	0♏ 28	0♍ 13
2	2 44 58	9 32 54	0♏ 53 36	7♏ 36 51	29 53	29 2	2 45	1 25	16 19	24 3	2 22	6 56	0 30	0 13
3	2 48 54	10 33 1	14 15 51	20 50 27	29 50	29 0	4 24	2 37	16 36	24 13	2 28	6 57	0 33	0 14
4	2 52 51	11 33 10	27 20 33	3♐ 46 9	29 47	29 0D	6 3	3 49	16 53	24 24	2 35	6 58	0 35	0 15
5	2 56 47	12 33 20	10♐ 7 21	16 24 17	29 44	29 0	7 42	5 1	17 10	24 35	2 42	6 58	0 37	0 16
6	3 0 44	13 33 33	22 37 11	28 46 22	29 41	29 1	9 20	6 13	17 28	24 45	2 49	6 58	0 39	0 17
7	3 4 40	14 33 47	4♑ 52 10	10♑ 55 2	29 37	29 2	10 58	7 25	17 46	24 56	2 56	6 59	0 42	0 18
8	3 8 37	15 34 2	16 55 24	22 53 48	29 34	29 3	12 36	8 38	18 6	25 6	3 3	6 59	0 44	0 18
9	3 12 34	16 34 19	28 50 47	4♒ 46 53	29 31	29 4	14 13	9 50	18 25	25 16	3 10	6 59	0 46	0 19
10	3 16 30	17 34 37	10♒ 42 42	16 38 50	29 28	29 5R	15 50	11 3	18 45	25 27	3 17	6 59	0 48	0 20
11	3 20 27	18 34 57	22 35 54	28 34 28	29 25	29 5	17 27	12 15	19 6	25 37	3 23	6 59	0 50	0 20
12	3 24 23	19 35 19	4♓ 35 7	10♓ 38 26	29 21	29 5	19 3	13 28	19 27	25 47	3 30	6 59R	0 52	0 21
13	3 28 20	20 35 41	16 44 56	22 55 7	29 18	29 4	20 39	14 41	19 48	25 57	3 37	6 59	0 55	0 22
14	3 32 16	21 36 5	29 9 24	5♈ 28 11	29 15	29 3	22 15	15 54	20 10	26 6	3 44	6 59	0 57	0 22
15	3 36 13	22 36 31	11♈ 51 45	18 20 21	29 12	29 2	23 50	17 7	20 33	26 16	3 51	6 59	0 59	0 23
16	3 40 9	23 36 58	24 54 7	1♉ 33 5	29 9	29 2	25 25	18 20	20 55	26 26	3 58	6 59	1 1	0 23
17	3 44 6	24 37 26	8♉ 17 12	15 6 19	29 6	29 1	27 0	19 33	21 19	26 35	4 6	6 59	1 3	0 24
18	3 48 3	25 37 56	22 0 10	28 58 24	29 2	29 1	28 35	20 46	21 42	26 44	4 13	6 59	1 5	0 24
19	3 51 59	26 38 27	6♊ 0 34	13♊ 6 10	28 59	29 1	0♐ 9	21 59	22 6	26 54	4 20	6 58	1 7	0 25
20	3 55 56	27 39 1	20 14 36	27 25 15	28 56	29 1	1 43	23 12	22 31	27 3	4 27	6 58	1 9	0 25
21	3 59 52	28 39 35	4♋ 37 30	11♋ 50 41	28 53	29 1	3 17	24 26	22 55	27 12	4 34	6 57	1 11	0 25
22	4 3 49	29 40 11	19 4 12	26 17 25	28 50	29 1	4 51	25 39	23 20	27 21	4 41	6 57	1 13	0 26
23	4 7 45	0♐ 40 49	3♌ 29 49	10♌ 40 54	28 47	29 1	6 24	26 53	23 46	27 30	4 48	6 56	1 15	0 26
24	4 11 42	1 41 29	17 50 15	24 57 28	28 43	29 0D	7 58	28 6	24 12	27 38	4 55	6 56	1 17	0 26
25	4 15 38	2 42 10	2♍ 2 17	9♍ 4 27	28 40	29 0	9 31	29 20	24 38	27 47	5 2	6 55	1 19	0 26
26	4 19 35	3 42 53	16 3 48	23 0 10	28 37	29 1	11 4	0♏ 34	25 4	27 55	5 9	6 54	1 21	0 27
27	4 23 32	4 43 37	29 53 28	6♎ 43 37	28 34	29 1	12 37	1 47	25 31	28 4	5 17	6 54	1 23	0 27
28	4 27 28	5 44 23	13♎ 30 35	20 14 20	28 31	29 2	14 10	3 1	25 58	28 12	5 24	6 53	1 25	0 27
29	4 31 25	6 45 11	26 54 51	3♏ 32 6	28 27	29 2	15 43	4 15	26 26	28 20	5 31	6 52	1 27	0 27
30	4 35 21	7♐ 46 0	10♏ 6 5	16♏ 36 49	28♏ 24	29♏ 3	17♐ 16	5♏ 29	26♓ 53	28♍ 28	5♐ 38	6♌ 51	1♏ 29	0♍ 27

DECLINATION and LATITUDE

Day	☉ Decl	☽ Decl	☽ Lat	☽ 12 Hr. Decl	☿ Decl	☿ Lat	♀ Decl	♀ Lat	♂ Decl	♂ Lat	♃ Decl	♃ Lat	♄ Decl	♄ Lat
1	14S21	10S 1	3S30	12S 9	10S44	1N12	1N17	1N30	7S34	2S15	3N25	1N 4	18S56	1N43
2	14 40	14 7	2 29	15 52	11 24	1 6	0 51	1 32	7 24	2 11	3 21	1 4	18 57	1 43
3	14 59	17 24	1 20	18 41	12 3	0 60	0 24	1 34	7 14	2 7	3 17	1 4	18 59	1 43
4	15 18	19 43	0 9	20 29	12 42	0 53	0S 3	1 36	7 4	2 3	3 13	1 5	19 0	1 43
5	15 37	20 58	1N 1	21 11	13 21	0 47	0 30	1 37	6 54	1 59	3 9	1 5	19 2	1 43
6	15 55	21 8	2 7	20 49	13 58	0 40	0 57	1 39	6 44	1 56	3 5	1 5	19 3	1 42
7	16 13	20 16	3 6	19 29	14 35	0 34	1 24	1 41	6 33	1 52	3 1	1 5	19 5	1 42
8	16 30	18 29	3 55	17 18	15 12	0 27	1 52	1 42	6 22	1 49	2 57	1 5	19 6	1 42
9	16 48	15 55	4 34	14 24	15 47	0 20	2 19	1 43	6 12	1 45	2 53	1 5	19 7	1 42
10	17 5	12 44	5 1	10 56	16 22	0 13	2 46	1 45	6 0	1 42	2 49	1 6	19 9	1 42
11	17 22	9 1	5 15	7 1	16 56	0 7	3 13	1 46	5 49	1 38	2 45	1 6	19 10	1 42
12	17 38	4 56	5 15	2 47	17 29	0S 0	3 41	1 47	5 38	1 35	2 41	1 6	19 12	1 42
13	17 54	0 36	5 2	1N38	18 2	0 7	4 8	1 48	5 27	1 32	2 37	1 6	19 13	1 42
14	18 10	3N52	4 34	6 5	18 33	0 14	4 35	1 49	5 15	1 28	2 34	1 6	19 14	1 42
15	18 26	8 16	3 53	10 23	19 4	0 20	5 2	1 49	5 3	1 25	2 30	1 6	19 16	1 42
16	18 41	12 24	2 58	14 18	19 33	0 27	5 29	1 50	4 51	1 22	2 26	1 7	19 17	1 42
17	18 56	16 3	1 53	17 35	20 2	0 33	5 56	1 51	4 39	1 19	2 23	1 7	19 18	1 42
18	19 10	18 54	0 39	19 56	20 30	0 40	6 23	1 51	4 27	1 16	2 19	1 7	19 20	1 41
19	19 25	20 41	0S39	21 6	20 56	0 46	6 50	1 52	4 15	1 13	2 16	1 7	19 21	1 41
20	19 38	21 10	1 55	20 54	21 22	0 52	7 17	1 52	4 3	1 10	2 12	1 7	19 23	1 41
21	19 52	20 17	3 5	19 20	21 46	0 58	7 44	1 52	3 50	1 7	2 9	1 8	19 24	1 41
22	20 5	18 4	4 4	16 31	22 10	1 4	8 10	1 52	3 38	1 4	2 6	1 8	19 25	1 41
23	20 18	14 44	4 46	12 43	22 32	1 10	8 37	1 53	3 25	1 2	2 2	1 8	19 27	1 41
24	20 30	10 33	5 11	8 14	22 53	1 16	9 3	1 53	3 12	0 59	1 59	1 8	19 28	1 41
25	20 42	5 49	5 17	3 20	23 13	1 21	9 29	1 52	2 60	0 56	1 56	1 8	19 29	1 41
26	20 54	0 50	5 3	1S40	23 32	1 27	9 55	1 52	2 47	0 54	1 53	1 9	19 31	1 41
27	21 5	4S 7	4 33	6 31	23 50	1 32	10 21	1 52	2 34	0 51	1 49	1 9	19 32	1 41
28	21 16	8 49	3 47	10 59	24 6	1 37	10 46	1 52	2 20	0 48	1 46	1 9	19 33	1 41
29	21 27	13 0	2 49	14 51	24 22	1 41	11 12	1 51	2 7	0 46	1 43	1 9	19 34	1 41
30	21S37	16S29	1S43	17S54	24S36	1S46	11S37	1N51	1S54	0S43	1N40	1N10	19S36	1N41

Day	♅ Decl	♅ Lat	♆ Decl	♆ Lat	♇ Decl	♇ Lat
1	19N 7	0N36	10S 4	1N41	21N31	10N51
5	19 7	0 36	10 7	1 41	21 32	10 53
9	19 7	0 36	10 10	1 41	21 32	10 54
13	19 7	0 36	10 13	1 41	21 32	10 56
17	19 7	0 36	10 15	1 41	21 33	10 57
21	19 8	0 36	10 18	1 42	21 34	10 59
25	19 8	0 37	10 21	1 42	21 35	11 1
29	19N 9	0N37	10S23	1N42	21N36	11N 2

☽ PHENOMENA

d	h	m	
2	16	44	●
10	15	10	☽
18	6	45	○
25	1	13	☾

d	h	°
5	16	21S11
13	3	0
19	21	21N11
26	4	0

4	3	0
11	13	5N17
18	12	0
24	19	5S17

VOID OF COURSE ☽

Last Aspect	☽ Ingress
31 6am 5	1 ♏ 10pm25
3 6pm29	4 ♐ 4am57
6 4am13	6 ♑ 2pm24
8 4pm41	9 ♒ 2am20
10 3pm10	11 ♓ 2pm51
13 6pm 4	14 ♈ 1am37
15 10am44	16 ♉ 9am13
18 12pm45	18 ♊ 1pm45
20 11am30	20 ♋ 4pm18
22 1pm54	22 ♌ 6pm10
24 6pm58	24 ♍ 8pm32
26 8pm47	27 ♎ 0am11
28 1am19	29 ♏ 5am35

d	h	
9	19	APOGEE
21	17	PERIGEE

DAILY ASPECTARIAN

1 Th	☽∥♆	0am16
	☽∥☿	4 38
	♀⊻♆	5 17
	☉∠♃	9 16
	☽⊻♃	11 44
	☿⊻♄	6pm 1
	☽⚹♇	10 49
	☽☌♆	11 19
2 F	☽⚼♂	0am47
	☽⊻♀	1 1
	☽⊻♄	2 38
	☽☌☿	3 46
	☉∥☽	4 3
	☽□♅	10 48
	☽∠♃	2pm46
	☉☌☽	4 44
	♀⚹♄	8 58
3 S	☽△♂	4am20
	☽∠♀	6 42
	☽∥♄	3pm16
	☽#♅	4 36
	☽⚹♃	6 29
4 Su	☽□♇	5am25
	☽⊻♆	6 3
	☽☌♄	9 52
	☿□♅	1pm14
	☽⚹♀	1 20
	☽△♅	6 1
	☽⊻☿	6 44
5 M	☉⊻☽	5am 2
	☽∠♆	10 31
	☽□♂	1pm48
	☽⚼♅	10 45
6 T	☽∠☿	3am51
	☽□♃	4 13
	☿∠♃	6 49
	☉∠☽	12pm37
	☽△♇	2 58
	♀⚹♅	3 7
	☽⚹♆	3 45
	☽⊻♄	8 8
7 W	☽⊼♅	4am10
	☽□♀	5 37
	☽⚹☿	2pm 0
	☽#♅	4 44
	☽∥♄	4 58
	☽⚼♇	8 45
	☉⚹☽	9 2
8 Th	☽∠♄	2am16
	☽⚹♂	2 24
	♄#♅	12pm25
	☽△♃	4 41
	☉∥☽	5 16
9 F	☽∥☿	0am55
	☽⊼♇	2 58
	☽□♆	3 53
	☽⚹♄	8 48
	☽∠♂	9 30
	☽☍♅	4pm28
	☽⚼♃	11 27
10 S	☽△♀	0am45
	♀#♃	2 12
	☽□☿	12pm 0
	☉□☽	3 10
	☽⊻♂	4 44
	☽∥♆	4 46
11 Su	☽⊼♃	6am 9
	☽⚼♀	10 25
	☽☍♇	3pm33
	☽△♆	4 35
	☉△♂	6 43
	☽∥♂	7 49
	☽□♄	9 50
12 M	☽⊼♅	4am47
	☽∥♀	6 23
	♅SR	6 54
	☿△♂	7 32
	☉∥☿	12pm39
	☽#♃	12 44
	☽⊼♀	7 30
	☉☌☿	9 37
	☽⚼♆	10 21
13 T	☽☌♂	6am 8
	☉△☽	8 10
	☽△☿	8 44
	☽⚼♅	10 12
	♀∠♇	1pm31
	☽∥♃	5 7
	☽☍♃	6 4
14 W	☽⊼♇	2am19
	☽⊼♆	3 25
	☽#♀	4 21
	☽#♂	7 11
	☽△♄	8 49
	☽△♅	2pm52
	☉⚼☽	3 21
	☽⚼☿	5 32
15 Th	♀∥♂	0am37
	☿#♅	2 30
	☽⚼♇	6 32
	☿∥♄	10 5
	☽☍♀	10 44
	☽#♆	11 11
	☽⚼♄	1pm 4
	☽⊻♂	4 31
	☉⊼☽	9 28
16 F	☽⊼☿	1am 4
	☽⊼♃	2 48
	☽△♇	9 55
	☽☍♆	11 4
	♀∠♄	2pm 6
	☽⊼♄	4 29
	☿⚹♃	4 58
	☽∠♂	8 23
	☽□♅	9 41
17 S	☽⚼♃	5am53
	☉#♅	6pm38
	☽⊼♀	9 39
	☽⚹♂	11 28
18 Su	☽∥♅	2am18
	☉#☽	3 14
	☽#♄	4 40
	☉☍☽	6 45
	☽△♃	8 16
	☽☍☿	12pm45
	☽□♇	2 27
	☽⊼♆	3 39
	♂⚼♅	4 12
	☉∥♄	5 36
	☽☍♄	9 7
	☿ ♐	9 43
19 M	☽⚹♅	1am38
	☽⚼♀	1 49
	♀⊼♂	3 25
	☿□♇	3 59
	☉⚹♃	7 8
	☿⊻♆	3pm10
	☽⚼♆	5 7
20 T	☽∠♅	2am53
	☽□♂	3 54
	☽△♀	5 26
	☽□♃	11 30
	☿#♇	11 44
	☉⊼☽	1pm19
	☽⚹♇	5 0
	☽△♆	6 16
	☽⊼☿	9 30
	☽⊼♄	11 54
21 W	☽⊻♅	3am52
	☉#☽	5 8
	☽#♄	11 7
	☽∥♅	2pm 7
	☉⚼☽	4 9
	☽∠♇	5 57
	☿☌♄	9 17
22 Th	☽⚼♄	1am 2
	☽⚼☿	1 27
	☽△♂	7 19
	☉ ♐	7 51
	☽□♀	11 58
	☽⚹♃	1pm54
	☉□♇	6 4
	☽⊻♇	6 53
	☉△☽	6 57
	☽□♆	8 15
23 F	☽△♄	2am12
	☽△☿	5 27
	☽☌♅	5 44
	☿△♅	8 10
	☽⚼♂	9 4
	♀⊻♃	1pm40
	☉⊻♆	2 7
	☽∠♃	3 11
24 S	☽#♆	1am 6
	☽#♀	7 9
	☽⊼♂	11 3
	☽⊻♃	4pm42
	☽⚹♀	6 58
	☽☌♇	9 17
	☽⚹♆	10 47
25 Su	☉□☽	1am13
	☽□♄	5 9
	☽⊻♅	8 18
	♀ ♏	1pm 2
	☽#♂	2 17
	☽□☿	2 21
	☽∥♃	6 58
	♀⚹♇	9 42
	☽∠♀	11 3
26 M	☽∠♆	0am30
	☽∠♅	10 5
	☽#♃	12pm54
	♀☌♆	3 55
	☽☍♂	4 7
	☽∥♂	4 40
	☽☌♃	8 47
27 T	☽⊻♇	0am58
	♀∥♆	1 13
	☽⊻♆	2 38
	☽⊻♀	3 39
	☉⚹☽	9 10
	☽⚹♄	9 32
	☽⚹♅	12pm17
	☉☌♄	2 43
28 W	☽⚹☿	1am19
	☽∠♇	3 27
	☽∥♆	8 37
	☽∥♀	12pm 1
	☽∠♄	12 23
	☉∠☽	1 57
	☽⊼♂	11 6
29 Th	☉△♅	2am36
	☽⊻♃	2 36
	☽⚹♇	6 24
	☽∠☿	7 47
	☽☌♆	8 14
	☿∠♆	11 42
	☽☌♀	2pm41
	☽⊻♄	3 45
	☽□♅	6 3
	☉⊻☽	7 22
	☉#♇	12 0
30 F	♀⊻♄	3am11
	☽⚼♂	3 25
	☽∠♃	6 15
	☽⊻☿	2pm59

DECEMBER 1956

LONGITUDE

Day	Sid. Time	☉	☽	☽ 12 Hour	Mean ☊	True ☊	☿	♀	♂	♃	♄	♅	♆	♇
	h m s	° ' "	° ' "	° ' "	° '	° '	° '	° '	° '	° '	° '	° '	° '	° '
1	4 39 18	8♐ 46 50	23♏ 4 16	29♏ 28 29	28♏ 21	29♏ 3R	18♐ 48	6♏ 43	27♓ 22	28♍ 36	5♐ 45	6♌ 50R	1♏ 31	0♍ 27
2	4 43 14	9 47 42	5♐ 49 29	12♐ 7 19	28 18	29 3	20 21	7 57	27 50	28 44	5 52	6 49	1 33	0 27R
3	4 47 11	10 48 34	18 22 3	24 33 48	28 15	29 3	21 53	9 11	28 18	28 51	5 59	6 48	1 35	0 27
4	4 51 8	11 49 28	0♑ 42 40	6♑ 48 50	28 12	29 1	23 25	10 25	28 47	28 59	6 6	6 47	1 36	0 27
5	4 55 4	12 50 23	12 52 31	18 53 58	28 8	28 59	24 57	11 39	29 17	29 6	6 13	6 46	1 38	0 27
6	4 59 1	13 51 19	24 53 27	0♒ 51 20	28 5	28 57	26 29	12 53	29 46	29 13	6 21	6 44	1 40	0 27
7	5 2 57	14 52 16	6♒ 47 58	12 43 48	28 2	28 54	28 1	14 8	0♈ 16	29 20	6 28	6 43	1 42	0 27
8	5 6 54	15 53 13	18 39 16	24 34 52	27 59	28 52	29 33	15 22	0 46	29 27	6 35	6 42	1 44	0 27
9	5 10 50	16 54 11	0♓ 31 9	6♓ 28 38	27 56	28 50	1♑ 4	16 36	1 16	29 34	6 42	6 40	1 45	0 27
10	5 14 47	17 55 10	12 27 55	18 29 36	27 53	28 50D	2 35	17 50	1 46	29 41	6 49	6 39	1 47	0 26
11	5 18 43	18 56 9	24 34 15	0♈ 42 29	27 49	28 50	4 5	19 5	2 17	29 47	6 56	6 37	1 49	0 26
12	5 22 40	19 57 8	6♈ 54 52	13 11 56	27 46	28 51	5 35	20 19	2 47	29 53	7 3	6 36	1 50	0 26
13	5 26 37	20 58 9	19 34 13	26 2 10	27 43	28 52	7 5	21 34	3 19	29 59	7 10	6 34	1 52	0 25
14	5 30 33	21 59 10	2♉ 36 9	9♉ 16 26	27 40	28 54	8 34	22 48	3 50	0♎ 5	7 17	6 33	1 54	0 25
15	5 34 30	23 0 11	16 3 12	22 56 29	27 37	28 55R	10 1	24 2	4 21	0 11	7 24	6 31	1 55	0 25
16	5 38 26	24 1 13	29 56 10	7♊ 1 58	27 33	28 55	11 28	25 17	4 53	0 17	7 31	6 29	1 57	0 24
17	5 42 23	25 2 16	14♊ 13 27	21 30 0	27 30	28 55	12 54	26 31	5 25	0 22	7 38	6 28	1 58	0 24
18	5 46 19	26 3 19	28 50 53	6♋ 15 10	27 27	28 52	14 18	27 46	5 57	0 28	7 45	6 26	2 0	0 23
19	5 50 16	27 4 23	13♋ 41 52	21 9 55	27 24	28 49	15 41	29 1	6 29	0 33	7 51	6 24	2 1	0 23
20	5 54 12	28 5 27	28 38 12	6♌ 5 38	27 21	28 45	17 2	0♐ 15	7 1	0 38	7 58	6 22	2 3	0 22
21	5 58 9	29 6 32	13♌ 31 13	20 54 1	27 18	28 40	18 20	1 30	7 34	0 43	8 5	6 20	2 4	0 22
22	6 2 6	0♑ 7 38	28 13 14	5♍ 28 15	27 14	28 37	19 36	2 44	8 6	0 48	8 12	6 18	2 5	0 21
23	6 6 2	1 8 44	12♍ 38 33	19 43 50	27 11	28 34	20 48	3 59	8 39	0 52	8 19	6 16	2 7	0 21
24	6 9 59	2 9 51	26 43 54	3♎ 38 42	27 8	28 32D	21 57	5 14	9 12	0 57	8 25	6 14	2 8	0 20
25	6 13 55	3 10 59	10♎ 28 18	17 12 51	27 5	28 33	23 1	6 29	9 45	1 1	8 32	6 12	2 9	0 20
26	6 17 52	4 12 8	23 52 35	0♏ 27 46	27 2	28 34	24 0	7 43	10 18	1 5	8 39	6 10	2 11	0 19
27	6 21 48	5 13 16	6♏ 58 41	13 25 41	26 59	28 35	24 54	8 58	10 52	1 9	8 45	6 8	2 12	0 18
28	6 25 45	6 14 26	19 49 3	26 9 6	26 55	28 37R	25 40	10 13	11 25	1 13	8 52	6 6	2 13	0 17
29	6 29 41	7 15 36	2♐ 26 6	8♐ 40 20	26 52	28 37	26 20	11 28	11 59	1 16	8 59	6 4	2 14	0 17
30	6 33 38	8 16 46	14 52 2	21 1 24	26 49	28 35	26 51	12 43	12 33	1 19	9 5	6 2	2 16	0 16
31	6 37 35	9♑ 17 57	27♐ 8 38	3♑ 13 54	26♏ 46	28♏ 32	27♑ 12	13♐ 57	13♈ 7	1♎ 23	9♐ 12	6♌ 0	2♏ 17	0♍ 15

DECLINATION and LATITUDE

Day	☉ Decl	☽ Decl	☽ Lat	☽ 12 Hr. Decl	☿ Decl	☿ Lat	♀ Decl	♀ Lat	♂ Decl	♂ Lat	♃ Decl	♃ Lat	♄ Decl	♄ Lat
1	21S46	19S 5	0S33	20S 0	24S48	1S50	12S 2	1N50	1S41	0S41	1N37	1N10	19S37	1N41
2	21 55	20 40	0N37	21 4	24 60	1 54	12 26	1 49	1 27	0 39	1 35	1 10	19 38	1 41
3	22 4	21 12	1 45	21 4	25 10	1 58	12 51	1 49	1 14	0 36	1 32	1 10	19 40	1 41
4	22 13	20 40	2 46	20 2	25 18	2 2	13 15	1 48	1 0	0 34	1 29	1 10	19 41	1 41
5	22 21	19 11	3 39	18 7	25 26	2 5	13 38	1 47	0 46	0 32	1 26	1 11	19 42	1 41
6	22 28	16 52	4 22	15 26	25 32	2 8	14 2	1 46	0 33	0 30	1 24	1 11	19 43	1 41
7	22 35	13 51	4 52	12 9	25 36	2 10	14 25	1 45	0 19	0 27	1 21	1 11	19 44	1 41
8	22 42	10 19	5 11	8 23	25 39	2 13	14 48	1 44	0 5	0 25	1 19	1 11	19 46	1 41
9	22 48	6 22	5 15	4 17	25 41	2 14	15 10	1 43	0N 9	0 23	1 16	1 12	19 47	1 41
10	22 54	2 10	5 7	0N 0	25 41	2 16	15 32	1 41	0 23	0 21	1 14	1 12	19 48	1 40
11	22 59	2N12	4 44	4 23	25 40	2 17	15 54	1 40	0 37	0 19	1 11	1 12	19 49	1 40
12	23 4	6 33	4 9	8 41	25 37	2 18	16 15	1 39	0 51	0 17	1 9	1 12	19 50	1 40
13	23 8	10 45	3 20	12 43	25 33	2 18	16 36	1 37	1 5	0 15	1 7	1 13	19 52	1 40
14	23 12	14 34	2 20	16 16	25 27	2 17	16 56	1 36	1 19	0 13	1 5	1 13	19 53	1 40
15	23 16	17 46	1 10	19 3	25 20	2 16	17 16	1 34	1 33	0 11	1 3	1 13	19 54	1 40
16	23 19	20 3	0S 6	20 46	25 11	2 15	17 36	1 32	1 48	0 10	1 1	1 13	19 55	1 40
17	23 21	21 8	1 23	21 10	25 1	2 12	17 55	1 31	2 2	0 8	0 59	1 14	19 56	1 40
18	23 23	20 50	2 37	20 8	24 49	2 10	18 13	1 29	2 16	0 6	0 57	1 14	19 57	1 40
19	23 25	19 4	3 41	17 42	24 37	2 6	18 32	1 27	2 31	0 4	0 55	1 14	19 58	1 40
20	23 26	16 1	4 31	14 5	24 22	2 2	18 49	1 25	2 45	0 3	0 53	1 14	19 59	1 40
21	23 27	11 57	5 2	9 38	24 7	1 57	19 6	1 23	2 59	0 1	0 51	1 15	20 0	1 40
22	23 27	7 12	5 12	4 42	23 50	1 51	19 23	1 21	3 14	0N 1	0 50	1 15	20 2	1 40
23	23 26	2 9	5 3	0S24	23 33	1 44	19 39	1 19	3 28	0 2	0 48	1 15	20 3	1 40
24	23 26	2S55	4 36	5 22	23 14	1 36	19 55	1 17	3 43	0 4	0 47	1 15	20 4	1 40
25	23 24	7 43	3 53	9 57	22 55	1 27	20 10	1 15	3 57	0 6	0 45	1 16	20 5	1 40
26	23 23	12 2	2 58	13 56	22 35	1 17	20 24	1 13	4 12	0 7	0 44	1 16	20 6	1 40
27	23 21	15 40	1 55	17 10	22 14	1 6	20 38	1 11	4 26	0 9	0 43	1 16	20 7	1 41
28	23 18	18 28	0 48	19 31	21 54	0 54	20 52	1 8	4 41	0 10	0 41	1 16	20 8	1 41
29	23 15	20 19	0N21	20 51	21 33	0 40	21 4	1 6	4 55	0 12	0 40	1 17	20 9	1 41
30	23 11	21 9	1 27	21 10	21 13	0 26	21 16	1 4	5 10	0 13	0 39	1 17	20 10	1 41
31	23S 7	20S56	2N28	20S28	20S53	0S10	21S28	1N 1	5N24	0N14	0N38	1N17	20S11	1N41

Day	♅ Decl	♅ Lat	♆ Decl	♆ Lat	♇ Decl	♇ Lat
1	19N10	0N37	10S25	1N42	21N37	11N 3
5	19 11	0 37	10 27	1 42	21 38	11 4
9	19 12	0 37	10 29	1 42	21 40	11 6
13	19 14	0 37	10 31	1 42	21 42	11 8
17	19 16	0 37	10 33	1 43	21 44	11 9
21	19 18	0 37	10 35	1 43	21 46	11 11
25	19 20	0 38	10 37	1 43	21 48	11 12
29	19N22	0N38	10S38	1N43	21N51	11N13

☽ PHENOMENA

d	h	m	
2	8	13	●
10	11	51	☽
17	19	7	○
24	10	10	☾

d	h	° '
3	0	21S12
10	12	0
17	7	21N12
23	10	0
30	7	21S11
1	11	0
8	21	5N15
15	22	0
22	1	5S12
28	17	0

VOID OF COURSE ☽

Last Aspect	☽ Ingress
1 10am28	1 ♐ 12pm59
3 8pm35	3 ♑ 10pm36
6 10am14	6 ♒ 10am17
7 5pm52	8 ♓ 10pm57
11 10am17	11 ♈ 10am37
13 2am50	13 ♉ 7pm16
15 3pm15	16 ♊ 0am 7
17 7pm 7	18 ♋ 1am52
19 3am31	20 ♌ 2am11
20 3pm 9	22 ♍ 2am56
23 3pm 4	24 ♎ 5am39
26 0am15	26 ♏ 11am 9
28 11am44	28 ♐ 7pm20
29 7pm20	31 ♑ 5am37

d	h	
7	16	APOGEE
19	13	PERIGEE

DAILY ASPECTARIAN

1 S	☽#♅	0am58
	♀□♅	2 14
	☽∥♄	6 38
	♂#♃	7 20
	☽△♂	8 20
	☽⚹♃	10 28
	☽□♇	1pm51
	☽⚺♆	3 53
2 Su	☽☌♄	0am 5
	☽△♅	1 53
	☽⚺♀	4 29
	♇SR	7 2
	☉☌☽	8 13
	☽∠♆	8pm32
	☿⚼♅	10 40
3 M	☽⚼♅	6am37
	☽☌☿	7 46
	☽∠♀	12pm31
	☽□♂	8 5
	☽□♃	8 35
	☽△♇	11 30
4 T	☽⚹♆	1am46
	☽⚺♄	10 42
	☽⚻♅	11 55
	♂☍♃	12pm35
	☽∥♄	5 13
	☽⚹♀	9 18
	☉⚺☽	11 55
5 W	☽#♅	0am 0
	☽⚼♇	5 7
	☽∠♄	4pm49
6 Th	☽⚺☿	3am41
	☉∠☽	8 43
	☽△♃	8 48
	☽⚹♂	10 14
	☽⚻♇	11 11
	♂ ♈	11 24
	☽□♆	1pm40
	☽∥♀	8 20
	☽⚹♄	11 18
	☽☍♅	11 50
7 F	♀∠♃	4am31
	♂⚻♇	9 2
	☽∠☿	2pm27
	☽⚼♃	3 24
	☽□♀	4 33
	☉⚹☽	5 52
	☽∠♂	5 53
	☿□♃	10 27
	☽∥♆	10 56
8 S	☿ ♑	7am12
	♀⚼♂	12pm52
	☿△♇	2 12
	♄△♅	7 58
	☉∠♆	8 23
	☽⚻♃	10 3
	☽☍♇	11 51
9 Su	☽⚹☿	1am16
	☽⚺♂	1 34
	☽△♆	2 30
	☿□♂	4 40
	☿⚹♆	11 8
	☽⚻♅	12pm22
	☽□♄	12 34
10 M	♂⚻♆	0am46
	☽#♃	5 13
	☉⚺♀	8 32
	☽⚼♆	8 37
	☽#♂	9 21
	☉□☽	11 51
	☽△♀	11 56
	☽∥♂	2pm50
	☽⚼♅	6 12
	☽∥♃	6 32
	☿∠♀	11 12
11 T	☽☍♃	10am17
	☽⚻♇	11 28
	☽⚻♆	2pm10
	☽☌♂	3 42
	☽⚼♀	8 35
	☽□☿	9 6
	☽△♅	11 24
12 W	☽△♄	0am15
	☿⚻♅	3pm58
	☽⚼♇	4 13
	☽#♆	10 42
13 Th	☿⚺♄	1am28
	♃ ♎	2 17
	♂∥♃	2 41
	☉△☽	2 50
	☽⚻♀	4 6
	☽⚼♄	4 53
	☉⚼♅	1pm53
	☽⚻♃	7 24
	☽△♇	8 2
	☽☍♆	10 42
14 F	☽⚺♂	2am19
	☽□♅	7 6
	☽⚻♄	8 30
	☉⚼☽	8 33
	☽△☿	12pm 2
	☽#♀	7 18
	☽⚼♃	10 28
15 S	☽∠♂	6am 0
	☉⚻☽	1pm 4
	☽∥♅	2 16
	☽☍♀	3 15
	☽⚼☿	5 24
	☽#♄	10 10
16 Su	☽△♃	0am36
	☽□♇	0 48
	☽⚻♆	3 25
	☽⚹♂	8 42
	☽⚹♅	11 4
	☽☍♄	12pm54
	☽⚻☿	9 34
17 M	☽⚼♆	4am33
	♃⚺♇	6 2
	☽∠♅	11 55
	☉☍☽	7pm 7
	☽⚻♀	10 5
18 T	☽⚹♇	2am30
	☽□♃	2 39
	☽△♆	5 7
	☽□♂	11 56
	☽⚺♅	12pm16
	☽#♄	2 4
	☽⚻♄	2 31
	☿⚼♇	6 44
	♂△♅	8 42
	☽∥♅	9 54
19 W	☽⚼♀	0am33
	☽∠♇	2 43
	☽☍☿	3 31
	☽#♀	4 34
	☽⚼♄	2pm50
	♀ ♐	7 7
	☉⚻☽	11 4
20 Th	♀□♇	2am20
	☽⚺♇	2 48
	☽△♀	2 50
	☽⚹♃	3 14
	☽□♆	5 29
	♀⚹♃	7 55
	☽☌♅	12pm25
	☽△♂	2 0
	☽△♄	3 9
21 F	☉⚼☽	1am 1
	☽∠♃	3 35
	☽#♆	7 9
	☽⚻☿	8 34
	♀⚺♆	11 13
	☽⚼♂	3pm17
	♀#♅	4 50
	☉ ♑	9 0
22 S	☉△☽	3am23
	☽☌♇	3 31
	☽⚺♃	4 16
	♂△♄	5 9
	☉△♇	5 21
	☽⚹♆	6 24
	☽□♀	8 10
	☽⚼☿	11 31
	☽⚺♅	1pm22
	☽□♄	4 41
	☽⚻♂	5 2
	☉□♃	5 2
	☽∥♂	6 4
23 Su	☽∥♃	6am21
	☽∠♆	7 34
	☉∥☿	8 31
	☽#♃	1pm50
	☽∠♅	2 36
	☽△☿	3 4
	☉⚹♆	11 19
24 M	☽#♂	4am 3
	☽⚺♇	6 14
	☽☌♃	7 20
	☽⚺♆	9 23
	☉□☽	10 10
	♀∥♄	3pm 1
	☽⚹♀	4 15
	☽⚹♅	4 30
	♀△♅	6 58
	☽⚹♄	8 33
	☽☍♂	10 41
25 T	☽∠♇	8am37
	☿∠♄	1pm56
	☽∥♆	3 48
	☽∠♀	9 42
	☽∠♄	11 35
26 W	☽□☿	0am15
	☽⚹♇	11 43
	☽⚺♃	1pm12
	☽☌♆	3 10
	♀☌♄	7 31
	☉⚹☽	8 29
	☽□♅	10 27
27 Th	☽⚺♄	3am19
	☽⚺♀	4 5
	☽⚻♂	7 33
	☽∠♃	5pm11
	☉⚻♅	8 51
28 F	☉∠☽	2am55
	☿#♇	4 10
	☽#♅	10 7
	☽⚹☿	11 44
	☽⚼♂	1pm 6
	☿∠♀	7 6
	☽□♇	7 52
	☽∥♄	9 5
	☽⚹♃	9 45
	☽⚺♆	11 38
29 S	☽△♅	6am57
	☉⚺☽	10 6
	☽☌♄	12pm42
	☽∠☿	5 55
	♀△♂	6 24
	☽△♂	7 17
	☽☌♀	7 20
	☿∥♀	9 26
30 Su	☽∥☿	
	☽∠♆	4 40
	☽⚼♅	11 59
	☉⚺♄	9pm13
31 M	☽⚺☿	0am 8
	☽∥☿	2 41
	☽△♇	6 7
	☽□♃	8 22
	☽⚹♆	10 8
	☽∥♄	5pm 9
	☽⚻♅	5 24

LONGITUDE

Day	Sid. Time	☉	☽	☽ 12 Hour	Mean ☊	True ☊	☿	♀	♂	♃	♄	♅	♆	♇
	h m s	° ' "	° ' "	° ' "	° '	° '	° '	° '	° '	° '	° '	° '	° '	° '
1	6 41 31	10♑ 19 8	9♑ 17 21	15♑ 19 8	26♏ 43	28♏ 26R	27♑ 24R	15♐ 12	13♈ 41	1♎ 26	9♐ 18	5♌ 57R	2♏ 18	0♍ 14R
2	6 45 28	11 20 19	21 19 26	27 18 22	26 39	28 18	27 25	16 27	14 15	1 28	9 25	5 55	2 19	0 13
3	6 49 24	12 21 30	3♒ 16 8	9♒ 12 56	26 36	28 9	27 14	17 42	14 50	1 31	9 31	5 53	2 20	0 12
4	6 53 21	13 22 40	15 8 59	21 4 32	26 33	28 0	26 51	18 57	15 24	1 33	9 37	5 50	2 21	0 12
5	6 57 17	14 23 50	26 59 55	2♓ 55 26	26 30	27 51	26 16	20 12	15 59	1 36	9 44	5 48	2 22	0 11
6	7 1 14	15 25 1	8♓ 51 29	14 48 30	26 27	27 44	25 31	21 27	16 33	1 38	9 50	5 46	2 23	0 10
7	7 5 10	16 26 11	20 46 56	26 47 19	26 24	27 39	24 34	22 42	17 8	1 40	9 56	5 43	2 24	0 9
8	7 9 7	17 27 20	2♈ 50 10	8♈ 56 5	26 20	27 35	23 29	23 57	17 43	1 41	10 2	5 41	2 25	0 8
9	7 13 4	18 28 29	15 5 39	21 19 29	26 17	27 34D	22 16	25 11	18 18	1 43	10 8	5 38	2 26	0 7
10	7 17 0	19 29 37	27 38 11	4♉ 2 21	26 14	27 34	20 59	26 26	18 53	1 44	10 14	5 36	2 26	0 6
11	7 20 57	20 30 45	10♉ 32 31	17 9 12	26 11	27 35	19 39	27 41	19 28	1 45	10 20	5 33	2 27	0 4
12	7 24 53	21 31 53	23 52 47	0♊ 43 35	26 8	27 36R	18 20	28 56	20 4	1 46	10 26	5 31	2 28	0 3
13	7 28 50	22 32 59	7♊ 41 46	14 47 18	26 4	27 36	17 3	0♑ 11	20 39	1 47	10 32	5 28	2 29	0 2
14	7 32 46	23 34 6	21 59 58	29 19 21	26 1	27 33	15 51	1 26	21 14	1 47	10 38	5 26	2 29	0 1
15	7 36 43	24 35 12	6♋ 44 47	14♋ 15 23	25 58	27 28	14 45	2 41	21 50	1 48	10 44	5 23	2 30	0 0
16	7 40 39	25 36 17	21 50 4	29 27 34	25 55	27 20	13 48	3 56	22 26	1 48R	10 50	5 21	2 31	29♌ 59
17	7 44 36	26 37 21	7♌ 6 31	14♌ 45 27	25 52	27 11	12 59	5 11	23 1	1 48	10 55	5 18	2 31	29 58
18	7 48 33	27 38 25	22 22 56	29 57 38	25 49	27 2	12 20	6 26	23 37	1 48	11 1	5 15	2 32	29 56
19	7 52 29	28 39 29	7♍ 28 18	14♍ 53 55	25 45	26 53	11 50	7 41	24 13	1 47	11 6	5 13	2 32	29 55
20	7 56 26	29 40 32	22 13 41	29 26 58	25 42	26 46	11 30	8 56	24 49	1 47	11 12	5 10	2 33	29 54
21	8 0 22	0♒ 41 34	6♎ 33 26	13♎ 32 55	25 39	26 41	11 18D	10 11	25 25	1 46	11 17	5 8	2 33	29 53
22	8 4 19	1 42 37	20 25 28	27 11 15	25 36	26 38D	11 16	11 26	26 1	1 45	11 23	5 5	2 34	29 51
23	8 8 15	2 43 39	3♏ 50 36	10♏ 23 55	25 33	26 37	11 21	12 41	26 37	1 44	11 28	5 2	2 34	29 50
24	8 12 12	3 44 40	16 51 41	23 14 24	25 30	26 38R	11 34	13 56	27 13	1 42	11 33	5 0	2 34	29 49
25	8 16 8	4 45 41	29 32 37	5♐ 46 51	25 26	26 38	11 53	15 11	27 49	1 41	11 39	4 57	2 35	29 48
26	8 20 5	5 46 42	11♐ 57 37	18 5 24	25 23	26 37	12 19	16 26	28 25	1 39	11 44	4 55	2 35	29 46
27	8 24 2	6 47 42	24 10 39	0♑ 13 47	25 20	26 34	12 51	17 41	29 2	1 37	11 49	4 52	2 35	29 45
28	8 27 58	7 48 41	6♑ 15 8	12 15 3	25 17	26 27	13 28	18 56	29 38	1 35	11 54	4 49	2 35	29 43
29	8 31 55	8 49 39	18 13 49	24 11 39	25 14	26 18	14 10	20 11	0♉ 15	1 33	11 59	4 47	2 36	29 42
30	8 35 51	9 50 37	0♒ 8 46	6♒ 5 22	25 10	26 6	14 56	21 26	0 51	1 30	12 4	4 44	2 36	29 41
31	8 39 48	10♒ 51 33	12♒ 1 36	17♒ 57 37	25♏ 7	25♏ 52	15♑ 46	22♑ 41	1♉ 28	1♎ 28	12♐ 8	4♌ 41	2♏ 36	29♌ 39

DECLINATION and LATITUDE

Day	☉ Decl	☽ Decl	☽ Lat	☽ 12 Hr. Decl	☿ Decl	☿ Lat	♀ Decl	♀ Lat	♂ Decl	♂ Lat	♃ Decl	♃ Lat	♄ Decl	♄ Lat
1	23S 3	19S45	3N22	18S50	20S35	0N 7	21S39	0N59	5N39	0N16	0N37	1N18	20S12	1N41
2	22 58	17 42	4 6	16 23	20 17	0 24	21 49	0 57	5 53	0 17	0 36	1 18	20 12	1 41
3	22 52	14 54	4 39	13 16	20 1	0 43	21 59	0 54	6 8	0 18	0 35	1 18	20 13	1 41
4	22 46	11 31	4 60	9 39	19 47	1 2	22 8	0 52	6 22	0 20	0 35	1 18	20 14	1 41
5	22 40	7 42	5 7	5 40	19 34	1 21	22 16	0 49	6 37	0 21	0 34	1 19	20 15	1 41
6	22 33	3 35	5 2	1 28	19 24	1 40	22 24	0 47	6 51	0 22	0 34	1 19	20 16	1 41
7	22 26	0N41	4 43	2N50	19 16	1 59	22 31	0 44	7 6	0 24	0 33	1 19	20 17	1 41
8	22 18	4 58	4 12	7 5	19 9	2 17	22 37	0 42	7 20	0 25	0 33	1 20	20 18	1 41
9	22 10	9 9	3 28	11 8	19 5	2 33	22 42	0 39	7 35	0 26	0 32	1 20	20 19	1 41
10	22 2	13 2	2 34	14 48	19 3	2 48	22 47	0 36	7 49	0 27	0 32	1 20	20 19	1 41
11	21 53	16 25	1 30	17 51	19 2	3 0	22 52	0 34	8 3	0 28	0 32	1 20	20 20	1 41
12	21 43	19 4	0 20	20 2	19 3	3 10	22 55	0 31	8 18	0 29	0 32	1 21	20 21	1 41
13	21 33	20 43	0S54	21 4	19 5	3 18	22 58	0 29	8 32	0 30	0 32	1 21	20 22	1 41
14	21 23	21 6	2 7	20 45	19 9	3 23	23 0	0 26	8 47	0 32	0 32	1 21	20 23	1 41
15	21 13	20 3	3 13	18 60	19 14	3 25	23 2	0 23	9 1	0 33	0 32	1 21	20 23	1 41
16	21 2	17 35	4 8	15 53	19 20	3 25	23 3	0 21	9 15	0 34	0 32	1 22	20 24	1 41
17	20 50	13 53	4 46	11 40	19 26	3 23	23 3	0 18	9 29	0 35	0 32	1 22	20 25	1 41
18	20 38	9 17	5 3	6 45	19 34	3 20	23 2	0 15	9 43	0 36	0 33	1 22	20 26	1 41
19	20 26	4 8	4 59	1 30	19 41	3 14	23 1	0 13	9 58	0 37	0 33	1 23	20 26	1 42
20	20 13	1S 7	4 35	3S42	19 50	3 8	22 59	0 10	10 12	0 38	0 34	1 23	20 27	1 42
21	20 0	6 11	3 54	8 33	19 58	3 0	22 56	0 7	10 26	0 39	0 34	1 23	20 28	1 42
22	19 47	10 46	3 0	12 48	20 7	2 51	22 52	0 5	10 40	0 40	0 35	1 23	20 28	1 42
23	19 33	14 39	1 58	16 18	20 16	2 42	22 48	0 2	10 54	0 40	0 36	1 24	20 29	1 42
24	19 19	17 42	0 52	18 53	20 25	2 32	22 43	0S 0	11 8	0 41	0 36	1 24	20 30	1 42
25	19 5	19 48	0N15	20 29	20 33	2 22	22 38	0 3	11 21	0 42	0 37	1 24	20 30	1 42
26	18 50	20 54	1 20	21 4	20 41	2 12	22 32	0 6	11 35	0 43	0 38	1 25	20 31	1 42
27	18 35	20 59	2 21	20 39	20 49	2 1	22 25	0 8	11 49	0 44	0 39	1 25	20 31	1 42
28	18 19	20 4	3 14	19 17	20 56	1 51	22 17	0 11	12 3	0 45	0 40	1 25	20 32	1 42
29	18 3	18 17	3 57	17 5	21 2	1 40	22 9	0 13	12 16	0 46	0 41	1 25	20 32	1 42
30	17 47	15 43	4 30	14 11	21 8	1 29	21 60	0 16	12 30	0 46	0 43	1 26	20 33	1 42
31	17S31	12S31	4N51	10S44	21S13	1N19	21S50	0S18	12N43	0N47	0N44	1N26	20S34	1N42

Day	♅ Decl	♅ Lat	♆ Decl	♆ Lat	♇ Decl	♇ Lat
1	19N24	0N38	10S39	1N43	21N52	11N14
5	19 26	0 38	10 41	1 44	21 55	11 16
9	19 29	0 38	10 42	1 44	21 58	11 17
13	19 31	0 38	10 42	1 44	22 0	11 18
17	19 34	0 38	10 43	1 44	22 3	11 19
21	19 36	0 38	10 43	1 45	22 6	11 20
25	19 39	0 38	10 44	1 45	22 8	11 21
29	19N41	0N38	10S44	1N45	22N11	11N22

☽ PHENOMENA

d	h	m	
1	2	14	●
9	7	7	☽
16	6	22	○
22	21	48	☾
30	21	25	●

d	h	°	'
6	20	0	
13	19	21N	8
19	19	0	
26	14	21S	4
5	2	5N	7
12	7	0	
18	7	5S	4
24	18	0	

VOID OF COURSE ☽

Last Aspect		☽ Ingress		
2	12pm 4	2	♒	5pm25
4	8am36	5	♓	6am 5
7	6am58	7	♈	6pm23
9	9pm30	10	♉	4am27
11	7pm30	12	♊	10am44
13	10pm42	14	♋	1pm 6
16	6am22	16	♌	12pm51
18	11am57	18	♍	12pm 4
19	6am51	20	♎	12pm55
22	4pm46	22	♏	5pm 3
25	0am29	25	♐	0am52
27	11am 1	27	♑	11am33
29	4am24	29	♒	11pm42

d	h	
4	8	APOGEE
16	22	PERIGEE
31	14	APOGEE

DAILY ASPECTARIAN

1 T	☽⚺♄	0am 1
	☉☌☽	2 14
	☽#♅	4 56
	☽□♂	9 10
	☽⚼♇	11 49
	☽⚺♀	1pm 8
	☿SR	1 34
2 W	☽∠♄	6am14
	☿∥♄	6 31
	♀#♇	10 41
	☽☌☿	12pm 4
	♀∠♆	4 50
	☽⚻♇	5 51
	☽△♃	8 27
	☽□♆	10 7
	☽∠♀	10 43
3 Th	☽☍♅	5am15
	☽⚹♄	12pm43
	♂⚼♇	3 31
	☉⚺☽	8 5
4 F	☽⚹♂	0am32
	☽⚼♃	2 51
	☽∥♆	5 31
	☽⚹♀	8 36
	☽⚺☿	10pm37
5 S	☉∠☽	5am19
	☽#♂	6 7
	☽☍♇	6 26
	☽∠♂	8 28
	☽⚻♃	9 20
	☽△♆	10 53
	♀⚼♅	11 14
	☿#♅	5pm19
	☽⚻♅	5 45
	☉⚼♇	6 4
6 Su	☽□♄	1am59
	☽∠☿	3 6
	☉⚹☽	2pm28
	☿∠♄	4 2
	☉∥♀	4 18
	☽⚺♂	4 18
	☽#♃	5 6
	☽⚼♆	5 12
	☽∥♃	11 16
	☽⚼♅	11 52
7 M	☽□♀	4am16
	☽⚹☿	6 58
	☽⚻♇	6pm39
	☿⚺♀	7 21
	☽☍♃	9 43
	☽⚻♆	11 10
8 T	☽△♅	5am35
	☽△♄	2pm16
	☽∥♂	2 16
	☉□♂	2 24
9 W	☽⚼♇	0am 2
	☽☌♂	6 30
	☉□☽	7 7
	☽#♆	9 18
	☽□☿	12pm32
	☽⚼♄	7 25
	☽△♀	9 30
10 Th	☽△♇	4am37
	☽⚻♃	7 43
	☉#♇	8 40
	☽☍♆	9 2
	☽□♅	2pm51
	☉☌☿	3 13
	☽⚻♄	11 38
11 F	☿□♂	2am15
	☽⚼♀	4 20
	☽⚼♃	11 18
	☽△☿	3pm 0
	☽⚺♂	4 54
	☉△☽	7 30
	☽#☿	11 47
12 S	☽∥♅	5am 6
	☽⚻♀	9 46
	☽□♇	10 49
	☽△♃	1pm49
	☽⚻♆	3 2
	☽⚼☿	3 6
	☽#♄	5 7
	☽⚹♅	8 12
	☽∠♂	8 21
	♀ ♑	8 24
	♀△♇	9 10
	☉⚼☽	11 44
13 Su	☽☍♄	4am52
	☽⚻☿	2pm33
	☽⚼♆	4 31
	☽∠♅	9 25
	☽⚹♂	10 42
14 M	☉⚻☽	2am47
	♀□♃	6 49
	☽⚹♇	1pm 7
	☽□♃	4 1
	☽☍♀	4 51
	☽△♆	5 9
	☿⚼♇	6 16
	☽#♄	7 1
	♀⚹♆	8 23
	☽⚺♅	9 49
15 T	♇ ♌	0am18
	☽∥♅	6 13
	☽⚻♄	6 25
	☽#☿	9 13
	☽☍☿	12pm 0
	☽∠♇	1 10
16 W	☽□♂	0am58
	☉∠♄	5 47
	☽⚼♄	6 20
	☉☍☽	6 22
	♃SR	9 20
	☽⚺♇	12pm48
	☽⚹♃	3 40
	☽□♆	4 48
	☽⚻♀	8 43
	☽☌♅	9 10
17 Th	♀⚻♅	2am 7
	☽△♄	6 1
	☽⚻☿	8 49
	☽∠♃	3pm12
	☽#♆	4 52
	☽∥♂	9 54
	☽⚼♀	10 22
18 F	☽△♂	2am 2
	☿#♅	2 54
	☽⚼☿	7 33
	☉⚻☽	8 55
	☽☌♇	11 57
	☽⚺♃	2pm55
	☽⚹♆	4 6
	☽⚺♅	8 24
	☉∥♄	11 40
19 S	☽△♀	0am23
	☽⚼♂	2 55
	☽□♄	5 54
	☽△☿	6 51
	☉⚼☽	10 43
	☽∥♃	4pm19
	☽∠♆	4 19
	☽∠♅	8 38
	☽#♃	9 24
20 Su	☽⚻♂	4am28
	☉⚻♇	5 11
	☉ ♒	7 40
	☽⚺♇	12pm44
	☉△☽	1 20
	☽☌♃	3 54
	☽⚺♆	5 13
	☽⚹♅	9 35
21 M	☿⚺♄	1am23
	☉∥☿	2 10
	☽□♀	6 49
	☽□☿	8 5
	☽⚹♄	8 9
	☽∠♇	2pm17
	☿SD	8 2
	☿☌♀	8 35
	♀⚺♄	10 52
	☽#♂	11 24
	☽∥♆	11 47
22 T	☉△♃	0am54
	♂#♆	6 34
	☽☍♂	10 22
	☽∠♄	10 38
	☉#♅	4pm45
	☽⚹♇	4 46
	♂⚼♄	5 16
	☽⚺♃	8 11
	☉□♆	8 11
	☽☌♆	9 41
	☉□☽	9 48
23 W	☽□♅	2am10
	☽⚹☿	1pm57
	☽⚺♄	2 4
	☽⚹♀	5 58
	☿⚺♄	11 35
	☽∠♃	11 43
24 Th	☿∥♄	2pm59
	☉∥☽	3 23
	♀⚼♇	4 33
	☽∠☿	6 47
	☽⚻♂	8 32
	☽#♅	9 41
25 F	☽□♇	0am29
	☽∠♀	1 22
	☽⚹♃	4 5
	☉☍♅	4 20
	☽⚺♆	5 50
	☽△♅	10 22
	☉⚹☽	10 55
	☽∥♄	12pm37
	☽∥☿	3 47
	☽☌♄	11 33
26 S	☽⚺☿	0am44
	☽⚼♂	3 0
	☽⚺♀	9 45
	☽∠♆	11 0
	☽⚼♅	3pm31
	☉∠☽	6 52
27 Su	☽∥☿	5am53
	☽△♂	10 8
	☽△♇	11 1
	☽□♃	2pm43
	☽∥♄	2 50
	☽⚹♆	4 42
	☽⚻♅	9 9
28 M	♂△♇	3am19
	☉⚺☽	3 24
	☽#♅	6 20
	☽⚺♄	11 22
	♂ ♉	2pm19
	☽☌☿	3 19
	☽⚼♇	4 56
	♀#♇	5 42
29 T	☉∥☽	2am45
	☽☌♀	4 24
	☿⚼♇	4pm36
	☽∠♄	5 44
	☽⚻♇	11 4
30 W	☽□♂	1am30
	☽△♃	2 44
	☽□♆	4 57
	☽☍♅	9 14
	☉☌☽	9pm25
	☽#♂	10 41
	♂⚻♃	11 50
31 Th	☽⚹♄	0am14
	☽⚺☿	8 9
	☽⚼♃	8 56
	☽∥♆	12pm 0

FEBRUARY 1957

LONGITUDE

Day	Sid. Time	☉	☽	☽ 12 Hour	Mean ☊	True ☊	☿	♀	♂	♃	♄	♅	♆	♇
	h m s	° ' "	° ' "	° ' "	° '	° '	° '	° '	° '	° '	° '	° '	° '	° '
1	8 43 44	11♒ 52 28	23♒ 53 35	29♒ 49 39	25♏ 4	25♏ 38R	16♑ 39	23♑ 56	2♉ 4	1♎ 25R	12♐ 13	4♌ 39R	2♏ 36	29♌ 38R
2	8 47 41	12 53 23	5♓ 46 0	11♓ 42 50	25 1	25 24	17 36	25 12	2 41	1 22	12 18	4 36	2 36R	29 36
3	8 51 37	13 54 16	17 40 23	23 38 55	24 58	25 11	18 36	26 27	3 18	1 18	12 22	4 34	2 36	29 35
4	8 55 34	14 55 8	29 38 46	5♈ 40 16	24 55	25 1	19 38	27 42	3 55	1 15	12 27	4 31	2 36	29 34
5	8 59 31	15 55 58	11♈ 43 51	17 49 56	24 51	24 54	20 43	28 57	4 31	1 11	12 31	4 29	2 36	29 32
6	9 3 27	16 56 47	23 59 2	0♉ 11 41	24 48	24 50	21 50	0♒ 12	5 8	1 8	12 36	4 26	2 36	29 31
7	9 7 24	17 57 35	6♉ 28 24	12 49 48	24 45	24 48D	22 59	1 27	5 45	1 4	12 40	4 23	2 36	29 29
8	9 11 20	18 58 21	19 16 26	25 48 50	24 42	24 48R	24 11	2 42	6 22	1 0	12 44	4 21	2 36	29 28
9	9 15 17	19 59 5	2♊ 27 32	9♊ 12 59	24 39	24 48	25 24	3 57	6 59	0 55	12 48	4 18	2 35	29 26
10	9 19 13	20 59 48	16 5 30	23 5 19	24 36	24 47	26 38	5 12	7 36	0 51	12 52	4 16	2 35	29 25
11	9 23 10	22 0 30	0♋ 12 29	7♋ 26 49	24 32	24 44	27 55	6 27	8 13	0 46	12 56	4 13	2 35	29 23
12	9 27 6	23 1 10	14 47 58	22 15 18	24 29	24 37	29 12	7 42	8 50	0 41	13 0	4 11	2 35	29 22
13	9 31 3	24 1 48	29 47 58	7♌ 24 52	24 26	24 29	0♒ 31	8 57	9 27	0 37	13 4	4 9	2 34	29 20
14	9 35 0	25 2 24	15♌ 4 42	22 46 1	24 23	24 18	1 52	10 12	10 5	0 31	13 7	4 6	2 34	29 19
15	9 38 56	26 3 0	0♍ 27 20	8♍ 7 5	24 20	24 6	3 14	11 26	10 42	0 26	13 11	4 4	2 33	29 17
16	9 42 53	27 3 34	15 43 49	23 16 14	24 16	23 55	4 37	12 41	11 19	0 21	13 14	4 1	2 33	29 16
17	9 46 49	28 4 6	0♎ 43 10	8♎ 3 44	24 13	23 45	6 1	13 56	11 56	0 15	13 18	3 59	2 33	29 14
18	9 50 46	29 4 36	15 17 17	22 23 24	24 10	23 38	7 26	15 11	12 33	0 10	13 21	3 57	2 32	29 13
19	9 54 42	0♓ 5 6	29 21 55	6♏ 12 51	24 7	23 34	8 53	16 26	13 11	0 4	13 24	3 55	2 32	29 11
20	9 58 39	1 5 34	12♏ 56 24	19 32 57	24 4	23 32D	10 20	17 41	13 48	29♍ 58	13 28	3 52	2 31	29 10
21	10 2 35	2 6 1	26 2 57	2♐ 26 55	24 1	23 32R	11 49	18 56	14 25	29 52	13 31	3 50	2 30	29 8
22	10 6 32	3 6 27	8♐ 45 28	14 59 11	23 57	23 32	13 18	20 11	15 2	29 46	13 34	3 48	2 30	29 7
23	10 10 29	4 6 51	21 8 44	27 14 42	23 54	23 31	14 49	21 26	15 40	29 39	13 37	3 46	2 29	29 5
24	10 14 25	5 7 15	3♑ 17 42	9♑ 18 17	23 51	23 28	16 21	22 41	16 17	29 33	13 39	3 44	2 28	29 4
25	10 18 22	6 7 36	15 16 58	21 14 14	23 48	23 22	17 54	23 56	16 55	29 26	13 42	3 41	2 28	29 2
26	10 22 18	7 7 56	27 10 32	3♒ 6 13	23 45	23 14	19 27	25 11	17 32	29 20	13 45	3 39	2 27	29 1
27	10 26 15	8 8 14	9♒ 1 38	14 57 5	23 42	23 3	21 2	26 26	18 10	29 13	13 47	3 37	2 26	28 59
28	10 30 11	9♓ 8 31	20♒ 52 49	26♒ 49 2	23♏ 38	22♏ 49	22♒ 38	27♒ 41	18♉ 47	29♍ 6	13♐ 50	3♌ 35	2♏ 25	28♌ 58

DECLINATION and LATITUDE

Day	☉ Decl	☽ Decl	☽ Lat	☽ 12 Hr. Decl	☿ Decl	☿ Lat	♀ Decl	♀ Lat	♂ Decl	♂ Lat	♃ Decl	♃ Lat	♄ Decl	♄ Lat
1	17S14	8S50	4N60	6S52	21S17	1N 8	21S40	0S21	12N57	0N48	0N45	1N26	20S34	1N43
2	16 57	4 49	4 55	2 44	21 20	0 58	21 29	0 23	13 10	0 49	0 47	1 26	20 35	1 43
3	16 39	0 37	4 38	1N31	21 22	0 47	21 17	0 26	13 23	0 49	0 48	1 27	20 35	1 43
4	16 22	3N39	4 8	5 45	21 23	0 37	21 5	0 28	13 37	0 50	0 50	1 27	20 36	1 43
5	16 4	7 48	3 26	9 48	21 24	0 28	20 52	0 30	13 50	0 51	0 52	1 27	20 36	1 43
6	15 46	11 42	2 35	13 31	21 23	0 18	20 39	0 33	14 3	0 52	0 53	1 27	20 36	1 43
7	15 27	15 11	1 35	16 41	21 21	0 9	20 25	0 35	14 16	0 52	0 55	1 28	20 37	1 43
8	15 8	18 1	0 29	19 8	21 17	0S 1	20 10	0 37	14 29	0 53	0 57	1 28	20 37	1 43
9	14 49	19 60	0S40	20 36	21 13	0 9	19 55	0 40	14 42	0 54	0 59	1 28	20 38	1 43
10	14 30	20 54	1 50	20 53	21 8	0 18	19 39	0 42	14 54	0 54	1 1	1 28	20 38	1 43
11	14 11	20 31	2 55	19 50	21 1	0 26	19 22	0 44	15 7	0 55	1 3	1 29	20 39	1 44
12	13 51	18 47	3 51	17 25	20 53	0 34	19 5	0 46	15 19	0 55	1 5	1 29	20 39	1 44
13	13 31	15 45	4 33	13 47	20 44	0 42	18 48	0 48	15 32	0 56	1 7	1 29	20 39	1 44
14	13 11	11 36	4 56	9 12	20 33	0 50	18 30	0 50	15 44	0 57	1 9	1 29	20 40	1 44
15	12 50	6 40	4 58	4 1	20 22	0 57	18 11	0 52	15 57	0 57	1 12	1 29	20 40	1 44
16	12 30	1 20	4 39	1S20	20 9	1 4	17 52	0 54	16 9	0 58	1 14	1 30	20 40	1 44
17	12 9	3S58	4 0	6 30	19 55	1 10	17 32	0 56	16 21	0 58	1 16	1 30	20 41	1 44
18	11 48	8 54	3 7	11 8	19 39	1 17	17 12	0 58	16 33	0 59	1 19	1 30	20 41	1 44
19	11 27	13 11	2 4	15 1	19 22	1 23	16 52	0 60	16 45	0 59	1 21	1 30	20 41	1 44
20	11 5	16 37	0 56	17 58	19 4	1 28	16 30	1 1	16 56	1 0	1 24	1 30	20 42	1 45
21	10 44	19 3	0N13	19 53	18 45	1 34	16 9	1 3	17 8	1 1	1 26	1 31	20 42	1 45
22	10 22	20 27	1 20	20 46	18 24	1 39	15 47	1 5	17 19	1 1	1 29	1 31	20 42	1 45
23	10 0	20 49	2 20	20 37	18 2	1 43	15 24	1 6	17 31	1 2	1 32	1 31	20 42	1 45
24	9 38	20 11	3 14	19 31	17 39	1 48	15 1	1 8	17 42	1 2	1 34	1 31	20 42	1 45
25	9 16	18 38	3 57	17 34	17 15	1 52	14 38	1 9	17 53	1 3	1 37	1 31	20 43	1 45
26	8 54	16 18	4 31	14 53	16 49	1 55	14 14	1 11	18 4	1 3	1 40	1 31	20 43	1 45
27	8 31	13 19	4 52	11 36	16 22	1 59	13 50	1 12	18 15	1 3	1 43	1 32	20 43	1 45
28	8S 9	9S47	5N 0	7S53	15S53	2S 2	13S26	1S13	18N26	1N 4	1N46	1N32	20S43	1N45

Day	♅ Decl	♅ Lat	♆ Decl	♆ Lat	♇ Decl	♇ Lat
1	19N43	0N38	10S44	1N45	22N13	11N23
5	19 46	0 38	10 44	1 45	22 16	11 23
9	19 48	0 38	10 43	1 46	22 19	11 24
13	19 51	0 38	10 43	1 46	22 21	11 24
17	19 53	0 38	10 42	1 46	22 24	11 25
21	19 55	0 38	10 41	1 46	22 26	11 25
25	19N57	0N38	10S40	1N47	22N29	11N25

☽ PHENOMENA

d	h	m	
7	23	24	☽
14	16	38	○
21	12	19	☾

d	h	° '
3	3	0
10	5	20N56
16	6	0
22	20	20S49

d	h	° '
1	3	4N60
8	10	0
14	14	4S60
20	19	0
28	4	5N 0

VOID OF COURSE ☽

Last Aspect		☽ Ingress		
1	11am35	1	♓	12pm21
3	7pm39	4	♈	0am42
6	10am40	6	♉	11am38
8	6pm35	8	♊	7pm35
10	10pm38	10	♋	11pm39
11	1pm51	13	♌	0am19
14	10pm11	14	♍	11pm17
15	8pm 3	16	♎	10pm50
18	11pm42	19	♏	1am 6
21	7am 5	21	♐	7am23
23	4pm37	23	♑	5pm27
26	4am19	26	♒	5am43
28	4pm18	28	♓	6pm25

d	h	
14	11	PERIGEE
27	15	APOGEE

DAILY ASPECTARIAN

1 F	☽⚺♀	0am 7
	☉⚹♄	8 49
	☽☍♇	11 35
	☽⚻♃	3pm 8
	☽∠☿	5 2
	☽⚹♂	5 26
	☽△♆	5 36
	♂☍♆	8 39
	☽⚻♅	9 40
2 S	☽∠♀	9am59
	☽□♄	1pm16
	☿∥♀	3 29
	☉⚺☽	3 43
	♆SR	4 0
	☽#♃	10 54
	☽⚼♆	11 51
3 Su	☽∠♂	1am19
	☽⚹☿	2 2
	☽⚼♅	3 47
	☽∥♃	8 1
	♀∠♄	6pm59
	☽⚹♀	7 39
	☽⚻♇	11 50
4 M	☉∠☽	0am36
	☽☍♃	3 11
	☽⚻♆	5 53
	☽⚺♂	8 57
	☽△♅	9 41
	♂□♅	10pm15
5 T	☽△♄	1am34
	☽⚼♇	5 31
	☉⚼♃	5 43
	☉⚹☽	9 1
	♀⚻♇	11 9
	☽#♆	5pm44
	☽□☿	7 24
	♀ ♒	8 17
6 W	♀∥♄	3am54
	☽⚼♄	7 2
	☽△♇	10 40
	☽□♀	1pm20
	☽⚻♃	1 43
	☽☍♆	4 36
	☽∥♂	4 50
	♀△♃	5 1
	☽□♅	8 3
	☽☌♂	10 34
7 Th	☉#☽	1am53
	☽⚻♄	11 45
	☽⚼♃	5pm57
	♀□♆	10 3
	☉□☽	11 24
8	☽△☿	9am56
F	☽□♇	6pm35
	☽∥♅	9 0
	☽△♃	9 15
	☽#♀	10 52
9 S	☽⚻♆	0am14
	☽△♀	2 56
	☽⚹♅	3 17
	☉#♂	5 51
	♀☍♅	6 45
	☽⚺♂	8 27
	♀#♅	9 36
	☽#♄	1pm 8
	☽⚼☿	3 28
	☽☍♄	6 22
10 Su	☽⚼♆	2am35
	☽∠♅	5 27
	☽⚼♀	7 45
	☉△☽	9 5
	☽∠♂	11 41
	☽⚻☿	7pm46
	☽#♄	9 0
	☽⚹♇	10 38
11 M	☿∠♄	0am29
	☽□♃	0 56
	☽△♆	3 57
	☽⚺♅	6 40
	☽⚻♀	11 19
	☽∥♅	11 56
	☉⚼☽	12pm 7
	☽⚹♂	1 51
	☽#♀	8 25
	☽⚻♄	9 4
	☽∠♇	11 18
12 T	☿⚻♇	2am51
	☉⚻☽	2pm10
	☿ ♒	2 30
	☽⚼♄	9 14
	☽⚺♇	11 16
13 W	☽☍☿	1am15
	☽⚹♃	1 16
	☽∥♂	1 19
	☿△♃	1 26
	☽□♆	4 22
	☽☌♅	6 50
	☿∥♄	10 18
	☉#☽	2pm44
	☽☍♀	3 41
	☽□♂	3 51
	♀□♂	7 32
	☽△♄	8 56
14 Th	☽∠♃	0am42
	☽#♆	4 33
	☿□♆	12pm17
	☉☍☽	4 38
	☽☌♇	10 11
	☽⚺♃	11 58
15 F	☽⚹♆	3am17
	☽⚻☿	4 46
	☽⚺♅	5 38
	☿☍♅	2pm 7
	☽△♂	4 44
	☽⚻♀	6 46
	☽□♄	8 3
16 S	☽∥♃	0am29
	☽∠♆	2 53
	☽∠♅	5 13
	☽⚼☿	6 48
	♀⚹♄	11 5
	☽#♃	11 37
	☽⚼♂	5pm37
	☉⚻☽	7 24
	☽⚼♀	8 51
	☽⚺♇	9 36
	☽☌♃	11 15
17 Su	☿#♅	2am48
	☽⚺♆	2 58
	☽⚹♅	5 18
	☽△☿	9 34
	☽⚻♂	7pm14
	☽⚹♄	8 45
	☉⚼☽	9 49
	☽∠♇	10 12
	♀⚼♃	11 29
	☽△♀	11 49
18 M	☉☍♇	3am11
	☽∥♆	9 32
	☉∥☽	2pm32
	☉ ♓	9 58
	☽∠♄	10 20
	☉⚻♃	11 33
	☽⚹♇	11 42
19 T	☽⚺♃	1am12
	☉△☽	1 21
	♀#♂	5 8
	☽☌♆	5 30
	☽□♅	7 55
	♂⚻♄	9 49
	♃ ♍	3pm27
	☽□☿	6 46
	☽∥♀	11 15
20 W	☽⚺♄	0am57
	☽☍♂	1 37
	☽#♂	2 55
	☽∠♃	3 38
	☽□♀	9 30
	☽∥☿	8pm51
21	☉∥♆	3am22
Th	☽□♇	5 46
	☽⚹♃	7 5
	☉△♆	9 35
	☽⚺♆	12pm 6
	☉□☽	12 19
	☽#♅	12 34
	☽△♅	2 35
	♂⚼♃	2 43
22 F	☿⚹♄	4am12
	☽∥♄	8 29
	☽☌♄	9 17
	☽⚹☿	9 58
	☽⚻♂	12pm45
	☉⚻♅	3 53
	☽∠♆	4 52
	☽⚼♅	7 21
	☿⚼♃	9 35
23 S	☽⚹♀	0am38
	☽∥♄	8 6
	☽△♇	3pm37
	☽□♃	4 37
	☽∠☿	7 34
	☽⚼♂	7 47
	☿#♂	9 57
	☽⚹♆	10 22
	☿□♂	10 25
24	☽⚻♅	0am51
Su	☉⚹☽	3 58
	☽#♅	4 43
	☽∠♀	9 46
	☽⚺♄	8pm49
	☽⚼♇	9 30
25 M	☽△♂	3am27
	☽⚺☿	6 3
	☽#♂	7 53
	☉∠☽	12pm52
	☽∥☿	6 21
	☽⚺♀	7 29
26 T	☽∠♄	3am11
	☽⚻♇	3 43
	☽△♃	4 19
	☽□♆	10 40
	☽☍♅	1pm 5
	☽∥♀	7 31
	☉⚺☽	10 2
27 W	☽⚹♄	9am41
	☽⚼♃	10 25
	☽∥♆	6pm26
	☽□♂	7 31
28 Th	☽☌☿	4am 6
	☉∥☽	11 28
	☽☌♀	3pm21
	☽☍♇	4 18
	☽⚻♃	4 27
	☽△♆	11 17

LONGITUDE

Day	Sid. Time	☉	☽	☽ 12 Hour	Mean ☊	True ☊	☿	♀	♂	♃	♄	♅	♆	♇
	h m s	° ' "	° ' "	° ' "	° '	° '	° '	° '	° '	° '	° '	° '	° '	° '
1	10 34 8	10♓ 8 46	2♓ 45 55	8♓ 43 38	23♏ 35	22♏ 35R	24♒ 15	28♒ 56	19♉ 24	28♍ 59R	13♐ 52	3♌ 33R	2♏ 25R	28♌ 56R
2	10 38 4	11 8 59	14 42 20	20 42 9	23 32	22 22	25 53	0♓ 10	20 2	28 52	13 54	3 31	2 24	28 55
3	10 42 1	12 9 11	26 43 15	2♈ 45 46	23 29	22 9	27 31	1 25	20 40	28 45	13 56	3 30	2 23	28 53
4	10 45 58	13 9 21	8♈ 49 54	14 55 51	23 26	21 59	29 11	2 40	21 17	28 38	13 58	3 28	2 22	28 52
5	10 49 54	14 9 28	21 3 50	27 14 10	23 22	21 52	0♓ 52	3 55	21 55	28 30	14 0	3 26	2 21	28 51
6	10 53 51	15 9 34	3♉ 27 8	9♉ 43 6	23 19	21 48	2 35	5 10	22 32	28 23	14 2	3 24	2 20	28 49
7	10 57 47	16 9 38	16 2 26	22 25 34	23 16	21 47D	4 18	6 25	23 10	28 16	14 4	3 22	2 19	28 48
8	11 1 44	17 9 39	28 52 55	5♊ 24 55	23 13	21 47	6 2	7 39	23 47	28 8	14 6	3 21	2 18	28 46
9	11 5 40	18 9 38	12♊ 1 59	18 44 32	23 10	21 47R	7 47	8 54	24 25	28 1	14 7	3 19	2 17	28 45
10	11 9 37	19 9 36	25 32 53	2♋ 27 17	23 7	21 47	9 34	10 9	25 3	27 53	14 9	3 17	2 16	28 43
11	11 13 33	20 9 31	9♋ 27 53	16 34 40	23 3	21 46	11 22	11 24	25 40	27 45	14 10	3 16	2 15	28 42
12	11 17 30	21 9 24	23 47 30	1♌ 6 1	23 0	21 42	13 10	12 39	26 18	27 38	14 11	3 14	2 14	28 41
13	11 21 27	22 9 14	8♌ 29 40	15 57 40	22 57	21 35	15 0	13 53	26 56	27 30	14 12	3 13	2 13	28 39
14	11 25 23	23 9 2	23 29 6	1♍ 2 51	22 54	21 27	16 51	15 8	27 33	27 22	14 13	3 11	2 11	28 38
15	11 29 20	24 8 49	8♍ 37 39	16 12 13	22 51	21 18	18 44	16 23	28 11	27 14	14 14	3 10	2 10	28 37
16	11 33 16	25 8 33	23 45 13	1♎ 15 22	22 48	21 10	20 37	17 37	28 48	27 7	14 15	3 9	2 9	28 35
17	11 37 13	26 8 15	8♎ 41 30	16 2 36	22 44	21 2	22 32	18 52	29 26	26 59	14 16	3 7	2 8	28 34
18	11 41 9	27 7 55	23 17 50	0♏ 26 35	22 41	20 57	24 27	20 7	0♊ 4	26 51	14 17	3 6	2 7	28 33
19	11 45 6	28 7 33	7♏ 28 25	14 23 9	22 38	20 54	26 24	21 21	0 41	26 43	14 17	3 5	2 5	28 31
20	11 49 2	29 7 10	21 10 43	27 51 17	22 35	20 53D	28 22	22 36	1 19	26 36	14 18	3 4	2 4	28 30
21	11 52 59	0♈ 6 45	4♐ 25 7	10♐ 52 38	22 32	20 53	0♈ 21	23 51	1 57	26 28	14 18	3 3	2 3	28 29
22	11 56 55	1 6 18	17 14 17	23 30 39	22 28	20 55	2 20	25 5	2 35	26 20	14 18	3 2	2 1	28 28
23	12 0 52	2 5 49	29 42 17	5♑ 49 49	22 25	20 55R	4 21	26 20	3 12	26 12	14 18	3 1	2 0	28 26
24	12 4 49	3 5 19	11♑ 53 52	17 55 4	22 22	20 55	6 22	27 35	3 50	26 5	14 18R	3 0	1 59	28 25
25	12 8 45	4 4 46	23 54 0	29 51 15	22 19	20 53	8 24	28 49	4 28	25 57	14 18	2 59	1 57	28 24
26	12 12 42	5 4 12	5♒ 47 23	11♒ 42 53	22 16	20 49	10 26	0♈ 4	5 5	25 49	14 18	2 58	1 56	28 23
27	12 16 38	6 3 36	17 38 15	23 33 53	22 13	20 42	12 28	1 18	5 43	25 42	14 18	2 57	1 54	28 22
28	12 20 35	7 2 59	29 30 11	5♓ 27 29	22 9	20 35	14 30	2 33	6 21	25 34	14 18	2 57	1 53	28 21
29	12 24 31	8 2 19	11♓ 26 5	17 26 15	22 6	20 27	16 31	3 47	6 58	25 27	14 17	2 56	1 52	28 19
30	12 28 28	9 1 37	23 28 10	29 32 2	22 3	20 18	18 32	5 2	7 36	25 19	14 17	2 55	1 50	28 18
31	12 32 24	10♈ 0 54	5♈ 38 1	11♈ 46 14	22♏ 0	20♏ 11	20♈ 32	6♈ 17	8♊ 14	25♍ 12	14♐ 16	2♌ 55	1♏ 49	28♌ 17

DECLINATION and LATITUDE

Day	☉ Decl	☽ Decl	☽ Lat	☽ 12 Hr. Decl	☿ Decl	☿ Lat	♀ Decl	♀ Lat	♂ Decl	♂ Lat	♃ Decl	♃ Lat	♄ Decl	♄ Lat
1	7S46	5S53	4N56	3S50	15S24	2S 4	13S 1	1S15	18N37	1N 4	1N49	1N32	20S43	1N46
2	7 23	1 45	4 38	0N22	14 52	2 6	12 36	1 16	18 48	1 5	1 52	1 32	20 44	1 46
3	7 0	2N30	4 8	4 36	14 20	2 8	12 10	1 17	18 58	1 5	1 54	1 32	20 44	1 46
4	6 37	6 40	3 27	8 41	13 46	2 9	11 44	1 18	19 8	1 6	1 57	1 32	20 44	1 46
5	6 14	10 37	2 35	12 27	13 12	2 10	11 18	1 19	19 19	1 6	2 0	1 32	20 44	1 46
6	5 51	14 10	1 36	15 44	12 35	2 11	10 52	1 20	19 29	1 6	2 4	1 33	20 44	1 46
7	5 28	17 8	0 30	18 19	11 58	2 11	10 25	1 21	19 39	1 7	2 7	1 33	20 44	1 46
8	5 4	19 18	0S38	20 2	11 19	2 10	9 58	1 22	19 48	1 7	2 10	1 33	20 44	1 46
9	4 41	20 29	1 46	20 40	10 39	2 9	9 30	1 22	19 58	1 7	2 13	1 33	20 44	1 47
10	4 17	20 32	2 50	20 6	9 58	2 8	9 3	1 23	20 8	1 8	2 16	1 33	20 44	1 47
11	3 54	19 21	3 46	18 17	9 15	2 6	8 35	1 24	20 17	1 8	2 19	1 33	20 44	1 47
12	3 30	16 55	4 29	15 16	8 31	2 4	8 7	1 24	20 26	1 8	2 22	1 33	20 44	1 47
13	3 7	13 22	4 57	11 14	7 46	2 1	7 39	1 25	20 35	1 9	2 25	1 33	20 44	1 47
14	2 43	8 54	5 4	6 25	7 0	1 58	7 10	1 25	20 44	1 9	2 28	1 33	20 44	1 47
15	2 20	3 50	4 51	1 12	6 13	1 54	6 42	1 26	20 53	1 9	2 31	1 33	20 44	1 47
16	1 56	1S27	4 17	4S 4	5 24	1 50	6 13	1 26	21 2	1 10	2 35	1 33	20 44	1 47
17	1 32	6 36	3 26	9 1	4 34	1 45	5 44	1 26	21 10	1 10	2 38	1 33	20 44	1 48
18	1 8	11 15	2 22	13 18	3 44	1 40	5 15	1 26	21 19	1 10	2 41	1 33	20 44	1 48
19	0 45	15 8	1 11	16 43	2 52	1 34	4 45	1 27	21 27	1 11	2 44	1 33	20 44	1 48
20	0 21	18 2	0N 2	19 5	1 59	1 27	4 16	1 27	21 35	1 11	2 47	1 33	20 44	1 48
21	0N 3	19 51	1 12	20 20	1 5	1 20	3 46	1 27	21 43	1 11	2 50	1 33	20 44	1 48
22	0 26	20 34	2 17	20 31	0 11	1 13	3 17	1 27	21 51	1 11	2 53	1 34	20 44	1 48
23	0 50	20 13	3 13	19 41	0N44	1 5	2 47	1 26	21 58	1 12	2 56	1 34	20 44	1 48
24	1 14	18 56	3 60	17 58	1 40	0 56	2 17	1 26	22 6	1 12	2 59	1 34	20 44	1 48
25	1 37	16 49	4 35	15 30	2 36	0 47	1 47	1 26	22 13	1 12	3 2	1 33	20 44	1 49
26	2 1	14 1	4 58	12 24	3 33	0 38	1 17	1 26	22 20	1 12	3 5	1 33	20 43	1 49
27	2 24	10 40	5 8	8 49	4 30	0 28	0 47	1 25	22 27	1 13	3 8	1 33	20 43	1 49
28	2 48	6 54	5 4	4 54	5 27	0 17	0 17	1 25	22 34	1 13	3 11	1 33	20 43	1 49
29	3 11	2 50	4 48	0 45	6 24	0 6	0N13	1 24	22 41	1 13	3 14	1 33	20 43	1 49
30	3 35	1N22	4 19	3N28	7 20	0N 5	0 43	1 24	22 47	1 13	3 17	1 33	20 43	1 49
31	3N58	5N34	3N37	7N36	8N16	0N16	1N13	1S23	22N54	1N14	3N20	1N33	20S43	1N49

Day	♅ Decl	♅ Lat	♆ Decl	♆ Lat	♇ Decl	♇ Lat
1	19N59	0N38	10S38	1N47	22N31	11N25
5	20 0	0 38	10 37	1 47	22 33	11 25
9	20 2	0 38	10 35	1 47	22 35	11 25
13	20 3	0 38	10 34	1 47	22 37	11 25
17	20 4	0 38	10 32	1 48	22 38	11 25
21	20 5	0 38	10 30	1 48	22 40	11 24
25	20 6	0 38	10 28	1 48	22 41	11 24
29	20N 7	0N37	10S26	1N48	22N42	11N23

☽ PHENOMENA

d	h	m	
1	16	13	●
9	11	51	☽
16	2	22	○
23	5	5	☾
31	9	19	●

d	h	° '
2	10	0
9	13	20N40
15	17	0
22	4	20S34
29	16	0

d	h	° '
7	11	0
13	21	5S 4
19	23	0
27	6	5N 8

VOID OF COURSE ☽

Last Aspect	☽ Ingress
3 4am 0	3 ♈ 6am31
5 3pm 5	5 ♉ 5pm21
7 11pm48	8 ♊ 2am 4
10 5am32	10 ♋ 7am45
12 6am16	12 ♌ 10am12
14 8am10	14 ♍ 10am20
16 8am26	16 ♎ 9am59
18 8am47	18 ♏ 11am15
20 3pm28	20 ♐ 3pm54
22 9pm33	23 ♑ 0am35
25 11am 4	25 ♒ 12pm18
27 9pm40	28 ♓ 1am 0
30 3am38	30 ♈ 12pm55

d	h	
14	22	PERIGEE
27	3	APOGEE

DAILY ASPECTARIAN

1 F	♀☍♇	0am16
	♀⚻♃	1 3
	☽⚻♅	1 35
	♃⚺♇	11 49
	☉☌☽	4pm13
	♀ ♓	8 40
	☽□♄	10 23
	☽#♃	11 21
2 S	☽⚼♆	5am23
	☽⚼♅	7 38
	☽⚹♂	11 15
	☽∥♃	8pm38
3 Su	☽⚺☿	1am51
	☽☍♃	4 0
	☽⚻♇	4 18
	☽⚺♀	10 25
	☽⚻♆	11 14
	☽△♅	1pm25
	☿⚻♃	4 28
	♀△♆	6 15
	☽∠♂	6 42
	☿☍♇	7 25
	☉#☽	11 44
4 M	☉⚺☽	9am17
	☽⚼♇	9 53
	☽△♄	10 9
	☿ ♓	11 34
	☽∠☿	12pm14
	♀⚻♅	2 54
	☽∠♀	7 20
	☉□♄	8 15
	☽#♆	11 58
5 T	☽⚺♂	1am44
	☽#♀	3 53
	☽⚻♃	2pm19
	☽#☿	2 31
	☽△♇	3 5
	☽⚼♄	3 28
	☉∠☽	5 6
	☿△♆	8 39
	☽☍♆	9 51
	☽⚹☿	10 3
	☽□♅	11 54
6 W	☽⚹♀	3am39
	☿⚻♅	11 23
	♀∥♆	1pm37
	☽⚼♃	6 47
	☽⚻♄	8 15
7 Th	☉⚹☽	0am15
	☽☌♂	2pm 4
	☽△♃	10 38
	☽□♇	11 48
8 F	☉⚼♆	3am18
	☽⚻♆	6 17
	☽⚹♅	8 12
	☽∥♂	8 59
	☽∥♅	12pm 3
	☽□☿	3 8
	☽□♀	5 45
9 S	☿∥♆	2am 7
	☉⚼♅	3 40
	☽☍♄	3 45
	☽⚼♆	9 24
	♂∥♅	9 58
	☽∠♅	11 13
	☉□☽	11 51
	☽⚺♂	11pm 4
10 Su	☽□♃	4am 2
	☽⚹♇	5 32
	☽∥♂	10 2
	☽△♆	11 39
	☽∥♅	1pm10
	☽⚺♅	1 25
11 M	☿☌♀	1am37
	☽∠♂	2 8
	☽△♀	3 35
	☽△☿	3 41
	☽∠♇	7 9
	☽⚻♄	7 58
	☉△☽	7pm19
12 T	☽⚹♂	4am19
	☽⚹♃	6 16
	☽⚼♀	6 56
	☽⚺♇	8 1
	☽⚼☿	8 14
	☽⚼♄	8 53
	☿□♄	1pm27
	☽□♆	1 49
	☽☌♅	3 28
	☉⚼☽	9 41
13 W	♀□♄	6am13
	☽∠♃	6 24
	☽△♄	9 12
	☽⚻♀	9 28
	☿∥♀	10 26
	☽⚻☿	11 56
	☽#♆	3pm33
	♂△♃	6 12
	☉⚻☽	11 26
	♂#♄	11 37
14 Th	☿⚼♆	4am15
	☽⚺♃	6 7
	☽□♂	6 44
	☽☌♇	8 10
	☽#♀	9 20
	☽#☿	10 57
	☉#♃	1pm19
	☽⚹♆	1 48
	☽⚺♅	3 22
	☿⚼♅	4 55
15 F	☽∥♃	5am56
	☉#☽	7 27
	☽□♄	8 54
	☽☍♀	1pm23
	☽∠♆	1 31
	♀⚼♆	3 2
	☽∠♅	3 6
	♂□♇	3 52
	☽☍☿	6 18
16 S	☉∥☽	2am 1
	☉☍☽	2 22
	☽#♃	5 10
	☽☌♃	5 19
	☽⚺♇	7 43
	☽△♂	8 26
	♀⚼♅	9 54
	☽⚺♆	1pm25
	☽⚹♅	3 1
	☽∥☿	3 42
	☽∥♀	8 10
17 Su	☽∠♇	7am56
	☽⚹♄	9 6
	☽⚼♂	9 47
	☉☍♃	6pm 1
	☽⚻♀	6 13
	☽∥♆	8 0
	♂ ♊	9 35
18 M	☽⚻☿	2am14
	☽⚺♃	5 54
	☉⚻☽	6 54
	☽⚹♇	8 47
	☽∠♄	10 2
	☽⚻♂	11 53
	☽☌♆	2pm48
	☽□♅	4 30
	☽⚼♀	9 54
19 T	☿#♃	3am24
	☿☍♃	3 40
	☽∠♃	7 17
	☽⚼☿	7 55
	☉⚻♇	9 23
	☉⚼☽	10 34
	☽⚺♄	11 50
20 W	☿⚻♇	1am37
	☽△♀	2 48
	☽⚹♃	9 37
	☽□♇	1pm 9
	☽△☿	3 13
	☉△☽	3 28
	☉☌☿	6 20
	☽☍♂	7 14
	☽⚺♆	7 39
	☿ ♈	7 48
	☉ ♈	9 17
	☽△♅	9 29
21 Th	♂⚻♆	3am36
	☽#♅	5 10
	☽☌♄	6pm27
	☉#☿	7 17
	☿⚻♆	8 13
	☽∠♆	11 35
22 F	☽⚼♅	1am30
	☿⚹♂	4 5
	☿△♅	8 11
	☽□♀	4pm43
	♂⚹♅	4 55
	♀#♃	5 2
	☽□♃	5 16
	☽△♇	9 33
	☉⚻♆	9 42
	♀☍♃	9 45
23 S	☽#♅	3am14
	☉∥☿	4 21
	☽⚹♆	4 28
	☉□☽	5 5
	☽⚻♅	6 27
	☽⚻♂	7 13
	☽□☿	10 53
	☉△♅	9pm50
24 Su	♄SR	0am42
	☽⚼♇	3 1
	☽⚺♄	4 48
	☿#♀	10 16
	☽⚼♂	2pm36
	♀⚻♇	4 1
25 M	☽△♃	4am 5
	☉#♀	4 22
	☽⚻♇	9 3
	☽∠♄	10 54
	☽⚹♀	11 4
	☿∥♃	11 39
	☽□♆	4pm13
	☽☍♅	6 18
	☉⚹☽	10 25
	☽△♂	10 30
	♀ ♈	10 47
26 T	☉⚹♂	1am14
	☽⚼♃	10 5
	☽⚹☿	11 20
	☽⚹♄	5pm15
	☽∠♀	8 59
27 W	☽∥♆	1am26
	☉∠☽	7 34
	☿⚼♇	10 33
	♀⚻♆	11 23
	☽⚻♃	4pm 8
	☽☍♇	9 40
	☿△♄	9 41
	☽∠☿	11 58
28 Th	☽△♆	4am47
	☽⚺♀	6 51
	☽⚻♅	6 56
	☽#☿	7 2
	♀△♅	7 33
	☽□♂	2pm33
	☉⚺☽	4 34
	☽#♃	9 42
	☉#☽	10 8
29 F	☉∥♃	3am30
	♂∥♇	5 26
	☽□♄	5 42
	☽⚼♆	10 49
	☽⚺☿	12pm13
	☽⚼♅	12 58
	☽#♀	1 25
	☽∥♀	7 50
30 S	☽☍♃	3am38
	☽⚻♇	9 34
	☽∥♃	11 4
	☉∥☽	1pm53
	☽⚻♆	4 30
	☽△♅	6 39
31 Su	☽☌♀	1am24
	☽⚹♂	5 22
	☉☌☽	9 19
	☽⚼♇	2pm56
	☽△♄	4 51
	☽∥☿	8 46

APRIL 1957

LONGITUDE

Day	Sid. Time	☉	☽	☽ 12 Hour	Mean ☊	True ☊	☿	♀	♂	♃	♄	♅	♆	♇
	h m s	° ' "	° ' "	° ' "	° '	° '	° '	° '	° '	° '	° '	° '	° '	° '
1	12 36 21	11♈ 0 8	17♈ 56 48	24♈ 9 49	21♏ 57	20♏ 5R	22♈ 30	7♈ 31	8♊ 52	25♍ 5R	14♐ 15R	2♌ 54R	1♏ 47R	28♌ 16R
2	12 40 18	11 59 20	0♉ 25 26	6♉ 43 43	21 53	20 1	24 26	8 46	9 29	24 57	14 14	2 54	1 46	28 15
3	12 44 14	12 58 31	13 4 50	19 28 53	21 50	19 59D	26 21	10 0	10 7	24 50	14 13	2 53	1 44	28 14
4	12 48 11	13 57 39	25 56 3	2♊ 26 29	21 47	19 59	28 13	11 14	10 45	24 43	14 12	2 53	1 42	28 13
5	12 52 7	14 56 45	9♊ 0 22	15 37 54	21 44	20 1	0♉ 2	12 29	11 23	24 36	14 11	2 53	1 41	28 12
6	12 56 4	15 55 48	22 19 16	29 4 37	21 41	20 2	1 47	13 43	12 0	24 29	14 10	2 52	1 39	28 11
7	13 0 0	16 54 49	5♋ 54 8	12♋ 47 53	21 38	20 4R	3 29	14 58	12 38	24 23	14 9	2 52	1 38	28 11
8	13 3 57	17 53 49	19 45 56	26 48 14	21 34	20 4	5 7	16 12	13 16	24 16	14 7	2 52	1 36	28 10
9	13 7 53	18 52 45	3♌ 54 40	11♌ 5 0	21 31	20 3	6 41	17 26	13 54	24 9	14 6	2 52	1 35	28 9
10	13 11 50	19 51 39	18 18 51	25 35 47	21 28	20 1	8 10	18 41	14 31	24 3	14 4	2 52D	1 33	28 8
11	13 15 47	20 50 31	2♍ 55 9	10♍ 16 15	21 25	19 58	9 34	19 55	15 9	23 57	14 3	2 52	1 31	28 7
12	13 19 43	21 49 21	17 38 17	25 0 21	21 22	19 54	10 53	21 9	15 47	23 51	14 1	2 52	1 30	28 6
13	13 23 40	22 48 9	2♎ 21 33	9♎ 40 56	21 19	19 50	12 7	22 24	16 24	23 44	13 59	2 52	1 28	28 6
14	13 27 36	23 46 54	16 57 37	24 10 46	21 15	19 47	13 16	23 38	17 2	23 39	13 57	2 52	1 27	28 5
15	13 31 33	24 45 37	1♏ 19 39	8♏ 23 39	21 12	19 45	14 19	24 52	17 40	23 33	13 55	2 52	1 25	28 4
16	13 35 29	25 44 19	15 22 16	22 15 9	21 9	19 44D	15 16	26 7	18 18	23 27	13 53	2 53	1 23	28 3
17	13 39 26	26 42 59	29 2 7	5♐ 43 5	21 6	19 44	16 8	27 21	18 55	23 21	13 50	2 53	1 22	28 3
18	13 43 22	27 41 37	12♐ 18 6	18 47 21	21 3	19 45	16 54	28 35	19 33	23 16	13 48	2 53	1 20	28 2
19	13 47 19	28 40 13	25 11 7	1♑ 29 46	20 59	19 47	17 33	29 49	20 11	23 11	13 46	2 54	1 19	28 2
20	13 51 15	29 38 47	7♑ 43 43	13 53 27	20 56	19 48	18 7	1♉ 3	20 48	23 6	13 43	2 54	1 17	28 1
21	13 55 12	0♉ 37 20	19 59 32	26 2 29	20 53	19 49R	18 35	2 18	21 26	23 1	13 41	2 55	1 15	28 0
22	13 59 9	1 35 51	2♒ 2 54	8♒ 1 22	20 50	19 50	18 57	3 32	22 4	22 56	13 38	2 55	1 14	28 0
23	14 3 5	2 34 20	13 58 29	19 54 48	20 47	19 49	19 13	4 46	22 41	22 51	13 35	2 56	1 12	27 59
24	14 7 2	3 32 48	25 50 54	1♓ 47 19	20 44	19 48	19 22	6 0	23 19	22 47	13 33	2 57	1 10	27 59
25	14 10 58	4 31 15	7♓ 44 33	13 43 4	20 40	19 46	19 27R	7 14	23 57	22 42	13 30	2 58	1 9	27 59
26	14 14 55	5 29 39	19 43 21	25 45 45	20 37	19 44	19 25	8 28	24 34	22 38	13 27	2 58	1 7	27 58
27	14 18 51	6 28 2	1♈ 50 38	7♈ 58 19	20 34	19 42	19 18	9 42	25 12	22 34	13 24	2 59	1 5	27 58
28	14 22 48	7 26 23	14 9 3	20 23 2	20 31	19 40	19 6	10 56	25 50	22 30	13 21	3 0	1 4	27 57
29	14 26 44	8 24 43	26 40 26	3♉ 1 20	20 28	19 38	18 49	12 11	26 27	22 27	13 17	3 1	1 2	27 57
30	14 30 41	9♉ 23 0	9♉ 25 51	15♉ 53 57	20♏ 25	19♏ 38D	18♉ 28	13♉ 25	27♊ 5	22♍ 23	13♐ 14	3♌ 2	1♏ 1	27♌ 57

DECLINATION and LATITUDE

Day	☉	☽		☽ 12 Hr.	☿		♀		♂		♃		♄	
	Decl	Decl	Lat	Decl	Decl	Lat	Decl	Lat	Decl	Lat	Decl	Lat	Decl	Lat
1	4N21	9N35	2N45	11N29	9N11	0N27	1N43	1S22	22N60	1N14	3N23	1N33	20S42	1N49
2	4 44	13 15	1 44	14 54	10 5	0 39	2 13	1 22	23 6	1 14	3 26	1 33	20 42	1 49
3	5 8	16 22	0 38	17 39	10 58	0 51	2 43	1 21	23 12	1 14	3 29	1 33	20 42	1 50
4	5 30	18 43	0S32	19 33	11 49	1 2	3 13	1 20	23 17	1 14	3 31	1 33	20 42	1 50
5	5 53	20 8	1 42	20 26	12 38	1 14	3 43	1 19	23 23	1 14	3 34	1 33	20 41	1 50
6	6 16	20 26	2 47	20 9	13 26	1 25	4 13	1 18	23 28	1 15	3 37	1 33	20 41	1 50
7	6 39	19 34	3 45	18 42	14 11	1 36	4 43	1 17	23 33	1 15	3 39	1 33	20 41	1 50
8	7 1	17 32	4 30	16 6	14 55	1 47	5 12	1 16	23 38	1 15	3 42	1 33	20 41	1 50
9	7 24	14 25	5 0	12 30	15 35	1 57	5 42	1 15	23 43	1 15	3 44	1 33	20 40	1 50
10	7 46	10 23	5 12	8 6	16 14	2 6	6 11	1 14	23 48	1 15	3 47	1 32	20 40	1 50
11	8 8	5 42	5 5	3 11	16 49	2 15	6 41	1 12	23 52	1 15	3 49	1 32	20 40	1 50
12	8 30	0 38	4 37	1S56	17 22	2 24	7 10	1 11	23 56	1 16	3 51	1 32	20 40	1 50
13	8 52	4S28	3 51	6 56	17 52	2 31	7 39	1 10	24 0	1 16	3 54	1 32	20 39	1 51
14	9 14	9 17	2 50	11 29	18 20	2 38	8 7	1 8	24 4	1 16	3 56	1 32	20 39	1 51
15	9 36	13 29	1 39	15 17	18 44	2 43	8 36	1 7	24 8	1 16	3 58	1 32	20 39	1 51
16	9 57	16 50	0 24	18 7	19 6	2 48	9 4	1 5	24 11	1 16	4 0	1 32	20 38	1 51
17	10 18	19 7	0N51	19 50	19 24	2 52	9 33	1 4	24 15	1 16	4 2	1 32	20 38	1 51
18	10 39	20 16	2 1	20 26	19 40	2 54	10 1	1 2	24 18	1 16	4 4	1 31	20 37	1 51
19	11 0	20 19	3 3	19 56	19 53	2 56	10 28	1 0	24 21	1 16	4 6	1 31	20 37	1 51
20	11 21	19 19	3 54	18 29	20 3	2 56	10 56	0 59	24 24	1 16	4 8	1 31	20 37	1 51
21	11 42	17 26	4 34	16 13	20 10	2 55	11 23	0 57	24 26	1 17	4 10	1 31	20 36	1 51
22	12 2	14 49	5 0	13 17	20 14	2 53	11 50	0 55	24 29	1 17	4 12	1 31	20 36	1 51
23	12 22	11 37	5 14	9 51	20 15	2 49	12 17	0 53	24 31	1 17	4 13	1 31	20 36	1 51
24	12 42	7 59	5 14	6 2	20 13	2 45	12 43	0 51	24 33	1 17	4 15	1 30	20 35	1 51
25	13 2	4 1	5 0	1 58	20 8	2 39	13 9	0 49	24 35	1 17	4 17	1 30	20 35	1 52
26	13 21	0N 7	4 34	2N13	20 1	2 31	13 35	0 47	24 37	1 17	4 18	1 30	20 34	1 52
27	13 41	4 19	3 54	6 23	19 50	2 22	14 0	0 45	24 38	1 17	4 20	1 30	20 34	1 52
28	13 60	8 24	3 4	10 21	19 38	2 12	14 26	0 43	24 40	1 17	4 21	1 30	20 33	1 52
29	14 19	12 13	2 4	13 57	19 22	2 1	14 50	0 41	24 41	1 17	4 22	1 30	20 33	1 52
30	14N37	15N32	0N56	16N56	19N 4	1N49	15N15	0S39	24N42	1N17	4N23	1N29	20S33	1N52

Day	♅		♆		♇	
	Decl	Lat	Decl	Lat	Decl	Lat
1	20N 7	0N37	10S24	1N48	22N43	11N23
5	20 7	0 37	10 22	1 48	22 44	11 22
9	20 8	0 37	10 20	1 48	22 44	11 22
13	20 7	0 37	10 18	1 48	22 45	11 21
17	20 7	0 37	10 15	1 48	22 45	11 20
21	20 7	0 37	10 13	1 48	22 45	11 19
25	20 6	0 37	10 11	1 48	22 45	11 18
29	20N 5	0N37	10S 9	1N48	22N45	11N17

☽ PHENOMENA

d	h	m	
7	20	33	☽
14	12	10	○
21	23	1	☾
29	23	54	●

d	h	° '
5	19	20N28
12	3	0
18	13	20S26
25	23	0

3	13	0
10	3	5S13
16	8	0
23	12	5N15
30	19	0

VOID OF COURSE ☽

Last Aspect		☽ Ingress		
1	7pm51	1	♉	11pm11
4	4am14	4	♊	7am31
6	10am25	6	♋	1pm38
8	7am38	8	♌	5pm25
10	4pm 9	10	♍	7pm13
12	10am 2	12	♎	8pm 9
14	6pm31	14	♏	9pm46
16	10pm15	17	♐	1am43
19	7am10	19	♑	9am 8
21	5am56	21	♒	7pm54
24	4am19	24	♓	8am23
26	10am10	26	♈	8pm22
29	2am25	29	♉	6am18

d	h	
12	1	PERIGEE
23	21	APOGEE

DAILY ASPECTARIAN

1 M	☽#♆	5am 7
	☽☌☿	10 26
	☽∠♂	12pm 1
	☽⚻♃	1 37
	☽△♇	7 51
	☽⚼♄	9 44
2 T	☿∠♂	0am54
	☽☍♆	2 33
	☽□♅	4 43
	☿⚻♃	6 4
	☿#♆	8 28
	☽⚺♀	5pm34
	☽⚼♃	5 57
	☽⚺♂	6 7
	☉⚺☽	11 47
3 W	☽⚻♄	2am 9
	♀✶♂	4 38
	☉⚼♇	6 18
	☽△♃	9pm46
4 Th	☿△♇	0am 8
	☽∠♀	0 38
	☽□♇	4 14
	☽⚺☿	4 54
	☉△♄	5 54
	☉∠☽	6 3
	☽⚻♆	10 38
	☽✶♅	12pm48
	☿⚼♄	12 57
	♀∥♃	3 52
	☿ ♉	11 38
	☽∥♅	11 53
5 F	☽☌♂	4am31
	☽✶♀	6 58
	☽☍♄	9 23
	☉✶☽	11 37
	☽∠☿	12pm35
	♀⚼♇	1 51
	☽⚼♆	1 52
	☽∠♅	4 2
	☿☍♆	10 13
6 S	☽□♃	3am50
	♀△♄	8 29
	☽✶♇	10 25
	☽∥♅	12pm47
	☿□♅	3 11
	☽△♆	4 31
	☽⚺♅	6 41
	☽✶☿	7 11
7 Su	☽⚺♂	12pm16
	☽∠♇	12 38
	☽⚻♄	2 18
	☽□♀	5 17
	☉□☽	8 33
8 M	☽✶♃	7am38
	☽⚺♇	2pm17
	☽∠♂	3 9
	☽⚼♄	3 54
	☽∥☿	5 10
	☽□♆	8 5
	☽☌♅	10 14
9 T	☽□☿	5am12
	♂☍♄	7 31
	☽∠♃	8 43
	☽△♄	4pm59
	☽✶♂	5 26
10 W	☽#♆	0am20
	☽△♀	0 40
	☉△☽	2 44
	♅SD	8 19
	☽⚺♃	9 23
	☉∥☽	12pm42
	☿⚼♃	1 55
	☽☌♇	4 9
	☽∥♀	7 37
	☽✶♆	9 43
	☽⚺♅	11 55
11 Th	☽⚼♀	3am34
	☉⚼☽	5 7
	☽∥♃	8 57
	☽△☿	11 57
	☽□♄	6pm 6
	☽□♂	8 50
	☽∠♆	10 9
12 F	☽∠♅	0am22
	☽⚻♀	6 15
	☉⚻☽	7 18
	☽☌♃	10 2
	☽⚼☿	2pm41
	☽⚺♇	5 2
	☽#♃	9 14
	☽⚺♆	10 33
13 S	☽✶♅	0am50
	♂⚼♆	2 21
	☽#♀	5pm19
	☽⚻☿	5 24
	☽∠♇	5 36
	☽✶♄	7 2
	☉⚻♃	8 54
	☉#☽	11 42
14 Su	☽△♂	0am 8
	♀⚻♃	0 9
	☽∥♆	5 21
	☽⚺♃	11 2
	☽☍♀	12pm 8
	☉☍☽	12 10
	☉☌♀	1 38
	☿⚻♄	2 51
	☽✶♇	6 31
	☽∠♄	7 57
15 M	☽☌♆	0am 9
	☽⚼♂	2 22
	☽□♅	2 37
	♂∠♅	8 3
	☽∠♃	12pm11
	☽⚺♄	9 26
	☽☍☿	11 49
16 T	☽⚻♂	5am19
	☽✶♃	2pm 1
	☉⚻☽	7 33
	☽⚻♀	8 42
	☉#♆	8 53
	☽□♇	10 15
17 W	☽⚺♆	4am 9
	☽#☿	5 15
	☽△♅	6 54
	♀△♇	1pm29
	☽#♅	6 45
18 Th	☉⚼☽	0am47
	☽⚼♀	2 36
	☽☌♄	2 45
	♀⚼♄	4 7
	☽∠♆	7 26
	☉△♇	8 21
	☽⚻☿	8 57
	☽⚼♅	10 20
	♀#♆	12pm 5
	☽☍♂	2 6
	☽□♃	8 15
19 F	☉⚼♄	2am10
	♀ ♉	3 29
	☽△♇	5 23
	☉△☽	7 10
	☽#♅	7 14
	☽△♀	9 46
	☽#☿	11 15
	☽✶♆	11 37
	☽⚻♅	2pm42
	☽⚼☿	2 43
20 S	♀☍♆	4am16
	☉ ♉	8 42
	☽⚼♇	10 17
	☽⚺♄	11 38
	☿∥♅	12pm 4
	☽△☿	9 7
21 Su	☽⚻♂	3am 0
	☽△♃	5 56
	♀□♅	12pm 9
	☉☍♆	3 7
	☽⚻♇	3 55
	☽∠♄	5 12
	☽□♆	10 21
	☉□☽	11 1
22 M	☽☍♅	1am45
	☽□♀	3 19
	☽⚼♂	10 38
	☽⚼♃	11 44
	☉#☽	7pm13
	☽#♀	7 55
	☽✶♄	11 13
23 T	♂□♃	5am37
	☉□♅	9 3
	☽∥♆	9 43
	☽□☿	10 45
	☽⚻♃	5pm50
	☽△♂	6 36
	☉∥♀	8 2
24 W	☽☍♇	4am19
	☽△♆	10 44
	☽⚻♅	2pm21
	☉✶☽	4 56
	☽#♃	10 30
	☽✶♀	10 52
25 Th	☿SR	5am29
	♀⚼♃	8 40
	☿∥♅	8 59
	☽□♄	11 30
	☽⚼♆	4pm49
	☽⚼♅	8 30
	☽✶☿	11 24
26 F	☉∠☽	1am40
	☽☍♃	5 46
	☽∠♀	8 18
	☽□♂	10 10
	☽⚻♇	4pm21
	☽⚻♆	10 31
27 S	☽∥♃	0am 3
	☽△♅	2 15
	☽∠☿	4 46
	☉⚺☽	9 50
	☽⚺♀	5pm 5
	♀∠♂	7 37
	☽⚼♇	9 41
	☽△♄	10 26
28 Su	☉⚼♃	1am33
	☽⚺☿	9 21
	☽#♆	10 42
	☽⚻♃	3pm59
	☽✶♂	11 34
29 M	☽△♇	2am25
	☽⚼♄	3 3
	☽☍♆	8 14
	☽□♅	12pm 1
	☉∥☽	4 15
	☽⚼♃	8 12
	♀⚻♄	8 45
	☽∥♀	9 27
	☉☌☽	11 54
30 T	☽∠♂	5am11
	☽⚻♄	7 2
	☽☌♀	8 10
	☽☌☿	4pm13
	☽△♃	11 49

MAY 1957

LONGITUDE

Day	Sid. Time h m s	☉ ° ' "	☽ ° ' "	☽ 12 Hour ° ' "	Mean ☊ ° '	True ☊ ° '	☿ ° '	♀ ° '	♂ ° '	♃ ° '	♄ ° '	♅ ° '	♆ ° '	♇ ° '
1	14 34 38	10♉ 21 16	22♉ 25 39	29♉ 0 54	20♏ 21	19♏ 38	18♉ 2R	14♉ 39	27♊ 43	22♍ 20R	13♐ 11R	3♌ 3	0♏ 59R	27♌ 56R
2	14 38 34	11 19 31	5♊ 39 37	12♊ 21 43	20 18	19 38	17 34	15 53	28 21	22 17	13 7	3 4	0 57	27 56
3	14 42 31	12 17 43	19 7 3	25 55 29	20 15	19 39	17 2	17 7	28 58	22 14	13 4	3 6	0 56	27 56
4	14 46 27	13 15 54	2♋ 46 54	9♋ 41 6	20 12	19 39	16 27	18 21	29 36	22 11	13 0	3 7	0 54	27 56
5	14 50 24	14 14 2	16 37 56	23 37 12	20 9	19 40	15 51	19 35	0♋ 14	22 8	12 57	3 8	0 53	27 56
6	14 54 20	15 12 9	0♌ 38 42	7♌ 42 13	20 5	19 40R	15 14	20 49	0 51	22 6	12 53	3 9	0 51	27 56
7	14 58 17	16 10 14	14 47 29	21 54 15	20 2	19 40	14 37	22 2	1 29	22 3	12 50	3 11	0 49	27 55
8	15 2 13	17 8 16	29 2 12	6♍ 10 59	19 59	19 40	14 0	23 16	2 7	22 1	12 46	3 12	0 48	27 55
9	15 6 10	18 6 17	13♍ 20 15	20 29 35	19 56	19 40	13 24	24 30	2 44	21 59	12 42	3 14	0 46	27 55D
10	15 10 7	19 4 16	27 38 33	4♎ 46 41	19 53	19 40	12 49	25 44	3 22	21 58	12 38	3 15	0 45	27 55
11	15 14 3	20 2 13	11♎ 53 31	18 58 33	19 50	19 40D	12 16	26 58	3 59	21 56	12 34	3 17	0 43	27 55
12	15 18 0	21 0 8	26 1 19	3♏ 1 19	19 46	19 40	11 46	28 12	4 37	21 55	12 30	3 18	0 42	27 55
13	15 21 56	21 58 1	9♏ 58 9	16 51 23	19 43	19 40	11 19	29 26	5 15	21 54	12 26	3 20	0 40	27 56
14	15 25 53	22 55 53	23 40 42	0♐ 25 48	19 40	19 40R	10 56	0♊ 40	5 52	21 53	12 22	3 22	0 39	27 56
15	15 29 49	23 53 44	7♐ 6 28	13 42 33	19 37	19 40	10 36	1 53	6 30	21 52	12 18	3 24	0 37	27 56
16	15 33 46	24 51 33	20 14 1	26 40 53	19 34	19 40	10 20	3 7	7 8	21 51	12 14	3 25	0 36	27 56
17	15 37 42	25 49 21	3♑ 3 13	9♑ 21 14	19 31	19 39	10 9	4 21	7 45	21 51	12 10	3 27	0 34	27 56
18	15 41 39	26 47 7	15 35 9	21 45 18	19 27	19 38	10 2	5 35	8 23	21 50	12 6	3 29	0 33	27 56
19	15 45 36	27 44 53	27 52 2	3♒ 55 48	19 24	19 37	9 59D	6 48	9 0	21 50D	12 2	3 31	0 31	27 57
20	15 49 32	28 42 37	9♒ 57 3	15 56 18	19 21	19 37	10 1	8 2	9 38	21 50	11 57	3 33	0 30	27 57
21	15 53 29	29 40 20	21 54 4	27 50 57	19 18	19 36	10 8	9 16	10 16	21 51	11 53	3 35	0 29	27 57
22	15 57 25	0♊ 38 2	3♓ 47 29	9♓ 44 16	19 15	19 36D	10 19	10 30	10 53	21 51	11 49	3 37	0 27	27 58
23	16 1 22	1 35 43	15 41 53	21 40 53	19 11	19 36	10 35	11 43	11 31	21 52	11 45	3 39	0 26	27 58
24	16 5 18	2 33 22	27 41 52	3♈ 45 20	19 8	19 37	10 55	12 57	12 8	21 52	11 40	3 41	0 25	27 58
25	16 9 15	3 31 1	9♈ 51 47	16 1 43	19 5	19 38	11 19	14 11	12 46	21 53	11 36	3 44	0 23	27 59
26	16 13 11	4 28 39	22 15 30	28 33 32	19 2	19 39	11 48	15 24	13 24	21 55	11 31	3 46	0 22	27 59
27	16 17 8	5 26 16	4♉ 56 5	11♉ 23 21	18 59	19 40	12 21	16 38	14 1	21 56	11 27	3 48	0 21	28 0
28	16 21 5	6 23 52	17 55 30	24 32 32	18 56	19 40R	12 58	17 52	14 39	21 57	11 23	3 51	0 19	28 0
29	16 25 1	7 21 26	1♊ 14 26	8♊ 1 2	18 52	19 40	13 38	19 5	15 16	21 59	11 18	3 53	0 18	28 1
30	16 28 58	8 19 0	14 52 7	21 47 21	18 49	19 39	14 23	20 19	15 54	22 1	11 14	3 55	0 17	28 1
31	16 32 54	9♊ 16 33	28♊ 46 20	5♋ 48 35	18♏ 46	19♏ 37	15♉ 11	21♊ 33	16♋ 32	22♍ 3	11♐ 9	3♌ 58	0♏ 16	28♌ 2

DECLINATION and LATITUDE

Day	☉ Decl	☽ Decl	☽ Lat	☽ 12 Hr. Decl	☿ Decl	☿ Lat	♀ Decl	♀ Lat	♂ Decl	♂ Lat	♃ Decl	♃ Lat	♄ Decl	♄ Lat
1	14N56	18N 8	0S15	19N 6	18N44	1N35	15N39	0S37	24N43	1N17	4N24	1N29	20S32	1N52
2	15 14	19 49	1 28	20 15	18 22	1 21	16 2	0 35	24 43	1 17	4 26	1 29	20 32	1 52
3	15 32	20 24	2 36	20 15	17 58	1 6	16 26	0 33	24 44	1 17	4 27	1 29	20 31	1 52
4	15 49	19 48	3 37	19 3	17 33	0 50	16 48	0 30	24 44	1 17	4 27	1 29	20 31	1 52
5	16 7	18 1	4 26	16 42	17 7	0 33	17 11	0 28	24 44	1 17	4 28	1 28	20 30	1 52
6	16 24	15 8	4 60	13 21	16 40	0 16	17 33	0 26	24 44	1 17	4 29	1 28	20 30	1 52
7	16 41	11 22	5 16	9 12	16 12	0S 2	17 54	0 24	24 44	1 17	4 30	1 28	20 29	1 52
8	16 57	6 55	5 13	4 32	15 44	0 19	18 15	0 21	24 43	1 17	4 30	1 28	20 29	1 52
9	17 14	2 5	4 50	0S24	15 17	0 36	18 36	0 19	24 42	1 17	4 31	1 27	20 28	1 52
10	17 30	2S53	4 10	5 20	14 50	0 54	18 56	0 17	24 42	1 17	4 32	1 27	20 28	1 52
11	17 45	7 41	3 15	9 56	14 24	1 10	19 15	0 14	24 41	1 17	4 32	1 27	20 27	1 52
12	18 1	12 2	2 7	13 57	13 60	1 26	19 34	0 12	24 39	1 17	4 32	1 27	20 27	1 52
13	18 16	15 39	0 54	17 8	13 37	1 42	19 53	0 10	24 38	1 17	4 33	1 27	20 26	1 52
14	18 31	18 20	0N22	19 17	13 15	1 57	20 11	0 7	24 36	1 17	4 33	1 26	20 26	1 52
15	18 45	19 56	1 35	20 19	12 56	2 11	20 28	0 5	24 34	1 17	4 33	1 26	20 25	1 52
16	18 59	20 24	2 41	20 13	12 39	2 24	20 45	0 2	24 33	1 17	4 33	1 26	20 25	1 52
17	19 13	19 47	3 38	19 6	12 24	2 36	21 1	0N 0	24 30	1 17	4 33	1 26	20 24	1 52
18	19 27	18 11	4 23	17 5	12 11	2 47	21 17	0 3	24 28	1 17	4 33	1 25	20 24	1 52
19	19 40	15 47	4 54	14 20	12 1	2 57	21 32	0 5	24 26	1 17	4 33	1 25	20 23	1 52
20	19 53	12 45	5 12	11 2	11 53	3 6	21 46	0 7	24 23	1 17	4 32	1 25	20 22	1 52
21	20 5	9 13	5 16	7 19	11 47	3 14	22 0	0 10	24 20	1 17	4 32	1 25	20 22	1 52
22	20 17	5 21	5 7	3 20	11 44	3 21	22 14	0 12	24 17	1 17	4 32	1 25	20 21	1 52
23	20 29	1 16	4 44	0N49	11 44	3 27	22 26	0 15	24 14	1 17	4 31	1 24	20 21	1 52
24	20 41	2N54	4 9	4 58	11 45	3 31	22 38	0 17	24 10	1 17	4 31	1 24	20 20	1 52
25	20 52	7 1	3 23	9 0	11 49	3 35	22 50	0 19	24 7	1 17	4 30	1 24	20 20	1 52
26	21 2	10 55	2 26	12 44	11 55	3 38	23 0	0 22	24 3	1 17	4 29	1 24	20 19	1 52
27	21 13	14 26	1 21	15 59	12 3	3 40	23 11	0 24	23 59	1 17	4 29	1 23	20 19	1 52
28	21 23	17 20	0 10	18 29	12 13	3 41	23 20	0 27	23 55	1 17	4 28	1 23	20 18	1 52
29	21 33	19 23	1S 3	20 1	12 25	3 41	23 29	0 29	23 51	1 17	4 27	1 23	20 17	1 52
30	21 42	20 22	2 14	20 24	12 39	3 41	23 37	0 31	23 46	1 17	4 26	1 23	20 17	1 52
31	21N51	20N 7	3S19	19N32	12N54	3S39	23N44	0N34	23N42	1N17	4N25	1N22	20S16	1N52

Day	♅ Decl	♅ Lat	♆ Decl	♆ Lat	♇ Decl	♇ Lat
1	20N 4	0N37	10S 7	1N48	22N44	11N17
5	20 3	0 36	10 5	1 48	22 44	11 16
9	20 2	0 36	10 3	1 48	22 43	11 15
13	20 0	0 36	10 1	1 48	22 42	11 14
17	19 58	0 36	9 59	1 48	22 41	11 13
21	19 56	0 36	9 57	1 48	22 39	11 12
25	19 54	0 36	9 56	1 48	22 38	11 10
29	19N52	0N36	9S54	1N48	22N36	11N 9

☽ PHENOMENA

d	h	m	
7	2	30	☽
13	22	35	○
21	17	4	☾
29	11	39	●

d	h	° '
3	0	20N24
9	10	0
15	22	20S24
23	7	0
30	8	20N25

d	h	° '
7	8	5S17
13	17	0
20	19	5N17
28	3	0

d	h	
9	4	PERIGEE
21	16	APOGEE

VOID OF COURSE ☽

Last Aspect	☽ Ingress
1 10am 3	1 ♊ 1pm47
3 6pm10	3 ♋ 7pm 9
5 9am26	5 ♌ 10pm54
7 10pm 8	8 ♍ 1am37
9 8pm30	10 ♎ 3am58
12 3am15	12 ♏ 6am49
14 7am32	14 ♐ 11am14
16 2pm21	16 ♑ 6pm14
18 11pm45	19 ♒ 4am13
21 12pm13	21 ♓ 4pm21
23 12pm22	24 ♈ 4am34
26 10am55	26 ♉ 2pm43
28 6pm14	28 ♊ 9pm47
30 10pm44	31 ♋ 2am 6

DAILY ASPECTARIAN

Day	Aspect	Time
1 W	☽∥☿	6am 1
	♂⚹♇	8 38
	☽□♇	10 3
	☽⊻♂	10 7
	☽⊼♆	3pm32
	☽⚹♅	7 20
2 Th	☽∥♅	5am55
	☉⊻☽	10 56
	☽☍♄	1pm18
	☽⚼♆	6 21
	☽⊻♀	8 5
	☽⊻☿	8 27
	☽∠♅	10 11
	☿☌♀	10 54
3 F	☽□♃	5am28
	☉∠☽	3pm30
	☽⚹♇	3 31
	☉⊼♄	6 0
	☽∥♅	6 7
	☽☌♂	6 10
	☽△♆	8 44
	☽∠☿	9 47
4 S	☽⊻♅	0am35
	☽∠♀	1 5
	♂ ♋	3pm22
	☽∠♇	5 37
	☽⊼♄	5 40
	☉⚹☽	7 33
	☿∥♀	10 6
	☽⚹☿	10 43
5 Su	☽⚹♀	5am33
	☽∥♀	6 55
	☽⚹♃	9 26
	☽∥☿	10 4
	☿∠♂	12pm13
	☉∥☽	3 16
	☽⚼♄	7 19
	☽⊻♇	7 22
	♂△♆	11 50
6 M	☽□♆	0am21
	☽⊻♂	0 22
	☉☌☿	0 34
	☽☌♅	4 17
	☉∥☿	8 31
	☽∠♃	10 56
	☽△♄	8pm42
	☽□☿	11 43
7 T	♀△♃	0am19
	☉□☽	2 30
	☽∠♂	2 59
	☽#♆	7 18
	☽⊻♃	12pm14
	☽□♀	1 23
	☉∠♂	9 56
	☽☌♇	10 8
8 W	☽⚹♆	2am57
	☽⚹♂	5 24
	☽⊻♅	7 1
	☽∥♃	12pm 6
	☽□♄	10 56
9 Th	☽△☿	0am 5
	☽∠♆	4 4
	☽∠♅	8 13
	☉△☽	8 34
	☽☌♃	2pm29
	♂⊻♅	7 36
	♇SD	7 42
	☽△♀	8 30
10 F	☽⚼☿	0am17
	☽⊻♇	0 28
	☽⊻♆	5 12
	☽#♃	8 2
	☿⊼♄	8 35
	☽⚹♅	9 27
	☽□♂	10 4
	☉⚼☽	11 36
11 S	☽⚼♀	0am 8
	☽⊼☿	0 37
	☽⚹♄	1 9
	☽∠♇	1 45
	☽∥♆	12pm33
	☉⊼☽	2 49
	☽⊻♃	5 0
	♀□♇	6 39
12 Su	☽∠♄	2am32
	☽⚹♇	3 15
	☽⊼♀	4 5
	☽☌♆	7 59
	☽#☿	11 8
	☽□♅	12pm31
	☽△♂	3 27
	☽∠♃	6 41
	☉△♃	10 12
13 M	☽☍☿	2am16
	☽⊻♄	4 16
	♀∥♅	9 40
	♀ ♊	11 8
	☽⚼♂	6pm49
	☽⚹♃	8 49
	☉☍☽	10 35
	♀⊼♆	11 43
14 T	☉#☽	2am13
	☽□♇	7 32
	☽⊻♆	12pm22
	☽☍♀	1 40
	☽△♅	5 18
	♀#♄	8 5
	☽⊼♂	10 51
15 W	☽#♅	1am13
	☽⊼☿	6 12
	☽☌♄	9 23
	☽∠♆	3pm28
	☽⚼♅	8 39
16 Th	☽□♃	3am 0
	♀⚹♅	6 4
	☉⊼☽	9 17
	☽⚼☿	9 20
	☽△♇	2pm21
	☽⚹♆	7 19
	☽#♅	7 28
17 F	☽⊼♅	0am46
	☽⊼♀	2 43
	☉#☽	8 47
	☽☍♂	9 24
	☽△☿	1pm23
	☉⚼☽	4 3
	☽⊻♄	5 18
	☽⚼♇	6 53
18 S	☽⚼♀	10am47
	☽△♃	12pm10
	☽∠♄	10 21
	☉△☽	11 45
19 Su	☽⊼♇	0am 9
	☿SD	1 4
	♃SD	2 20
	☉□♇	4 54
	☽□♆	5 14
	☽☍♅	11 13
	☽⚼♃	5pm47
	☽△♀	7 44
	☽⊼♂	11 20
20 M	☽□☿	0am 9
	☽⚹♄	3 59
	☽#☿	6 20
	☉∥♅	7 56
	☿⚹♂	5pm53
	☽∥♆	7 11
	☽⊼♃	11 53
21 T	☽⚼♂	7am 9
	☉ ♊	8 11
	☽☍♇	12pm13
	☉□☽	5 4
	☽△♆	5 16
	☉⊼♆	7 37
	☿⊻♀	7 55
	☽⊼♅	11 39
22 W	☽#♃	4am55
	☉#♄	7 48
	☽⚹☿	1pm27
	☽□♀	3 5
	☽△♂	3 7
	♀⊻♂	3 40
	☽□♄	4 5
	☽⚼♆	11 28
23 Th	♀☍♄	0am22
	☽⚼♅	5 57
	♂⊼♄	7 53
	☽☍♃	12pm22
	☽∠☿	8 21
	♀∥♇	11 29
24 F	☽⊼♇	0am33
	☽⊼♆	5 22
	☽∥♃	9 18
	☉⚹☽	10 28
	☽△♅	11 54
25 S	☽⊻☿	2am58
	☽△♄	3 22
	☉⚹♅	5 28
	☽□♂	5 58
	☽⚼♇	6 5
	♂∠♇	8 16
	☽⚹♀	9 20
	☿⊼♄	12pm16
	☽#♆	5 40
	☉∠☽	6 13
	♀⚼♆	11 14
	☽⊼♃	11 20
26 Su	☽∥☿	6am41
	☽⚼♄	8 5
	☽△♇	10 55
	☽☍♆	3pm23
	☽∠♀	5 9
	☽□♅	9 52
27 M	☉⊻☽	1am 1
	☽⚼♃	3 44
	☽⊼♄	12pm 3
	☽☌☿	2 26
	☽⚹♂	5 42
	☽⊻♀	11 52
28 T	☽△♃	7am20
	☽□♇	6pm14
	♀∠♅	7 50
	☽∠♂	10 11
	☽⊼♆	10 20
29 W	☽⚹♅	4am42
	☽∥♅	8 41
	☉☌☽	11 39
	☽☍♄	5pm40
	☽#♄	8 18
	☽⊻☿	11 6
30 Th	☽⚼♆	0am43
	☽⊻♂	1 53
	☽∠♅	7 4
	☽☌♀	10 22
	☽□♃	12pm25
	♀∥♂	6 58
	☽⚹♇	10 44
	☽#♄	28 58
31 F	☽△♆	2am33
	☽∠☿	2 34
	☽∥♅	6 22
	☽⊻♅	8 53
	♀□♃	10 14
	☉⊻☽	7pm11
	☽⊼♄	8 57

JUNE 1957

LONGITUDE

Day	Sid. Time	☉	☽	☽ 12 Hour	Mean ☊	True ☊	☿	♀	♂	♃	♄	♅	♆	♇
	h m s	° ' "	° ' "	° ' "	° '	° '	° '	° '	° '	° '	° '	° '	° '	° '
1	16 36 51	10♊ 14 4	12♋ 53 35	20♋ 0 46	18♏ 43	19♏ 35R	16♉ 3	22♊ 46	17♋ 9	22♍ 5	11♐ 5R	4♌ 0	0♏ 15R	28♌ 3
2	16 40 47	11 11 35	27 9 35	4♌ 19 27	18 40	19 32	16 58	24 0	17 47	22 8	11 0	4 3	0 13	28 3
3	16 44 44	12 9 4	11♌ 29 48	18 40 7	18 36	19 30	17 57	25 13	18 24	22 10	10 56	4 5	0 12	28 4
4	16 48 40	13 6 32	25 49 56	2♍ 58 48	18 33	19 28	18 59	26 27	19 2	22 13	10 51	4 8	0 11	28 5
5	16 52 37	14 3 58	10♍ 6 22	17 12 20	18 30	19 27D	20 5	27 40	19 39	22 16	10 47	4 11	0 10	28 5
6	16 56 34	15 1 23	24 16 24	1♎ 18 23	18 27	19 27	21 13	28 54	20 17	22 19	10 43	4 13	0 9	28 6
7	17 0 30	15 58 47	8♎ 18 6	15 15 24	18 24	19 28	22 25	0♋ 7	20 55	22 22	10 38	4 16	0 8	28 7
8	17 4 27	16 56 10	22 10 10	29 2 18	18 21	19 29	23 40	1 21	21 32	22 25	10 34	4 19	0 7	28 8
9	17 8 23	17 53 32	5♏ 51 41	12♏ 38 13	18 17	19 30	24 58	2 34	22 10	22 29	10 29	4 22	0 6	28 9
10	17 12 20	18 50 52	19 21 50	26 2 24	18 14	19 31R	26 19	3 48	22 47	22 33	10 25	4 24	0 5	28 9
11	17 16 16	19 48 13	2♐ 39 50	9♐ 14 4	18 11	19 30	27 42	5 1	23 25	22 37	10 21	4 27	0 4	28 10
12	17 20 13	20 45 32	15 45 0	22 12 34	18 8	19 28	29 9	6 15	24 3	22 41	10 16	4 30	0 3	28 11
13	17 24 9	21 42 50	28 36 46	4♑ 57 33	18 5	19 25	0♊ 39	7 28	24 40	22 45	10 12	4 33	0 2	28 12
14	17 28 6	22 40 8	11♑ 14 58	17 29 5	18 2	19 20	2 12	8 41	25 18	22 49	10 8	4 36	0 2	28 13
15	17 32 3	23 37 25	23 40 2	29 47 59	17 58	19 14	3 47	9 55	25 55	22 54	10 3	4 39	0 1	28 14
16	17 35 59	24 34 42	5♒ 53 10	11♒ 55 50	17 55	19 8	5 26	11 8	26 33	22 59	9 59	4 42	0 0	28 15
17	17 39 56	25 31 58	17 56 21	23 55 5	17 52	19 2	7 7	12 22	27 10	23 3	9 55	4 45	29♎ 59	28 16
18	17 43 52	26 29 14	29 52 28	5♓ 48 58	17 49	18 58	8 51	13 35	27 48	23 8	9 51	4 48	29 58	28 17
19	17 47 49	27 26 30	11♓ 45 6	17 41 26	17 46	18 55	10 38	14 48	28 26	23 14	9 47	4 51	29 58	28 18
20	17 51 45	28 23 45	23 38 32	29 37 0	17 42	18 53D	12 27	16 2	29 3	23 19	9 43	4 54	29 57	28 20
21	17 55 42	29 21 0	5♈ 37 27	11♈ 40 29	17 39	18 53	14 19	17 15	29 41	23 24	9 38	4 57	29 56	28 21
22	17 59 38	0♋ 18 15	17 46 44	23 56 47	17 36	18 54	16 14	18 28	0♌ 18	23 30	9 34	5 1	29 56	28 22
23	18 3 35	1 15 30	0♉ 11 12	6♉ 30 30	17 33	18 55	18 11	19 41	0 56	23 36	9 30	5 4	29 55	28 23
24	18 7 32	2 12 45	12 55 8	19 25 30	17 30	18 57R	20 11	20 55	1 33	23 41	9 27	5 7	29 55	28 24
25	18 11 28	3 9 59	26 1 53	2♊ 44 27	17 27	18 57	22 12	22 8	2 11	23 47	9 23	5 10	29 54	28 26
26	18 15 25	4 7 14	9♊ 33 13	16 28 7	17 23	18 55	24 16	23 21	2 49	23 54	9 19	5 14	29 53	28 27
27	18 19 21	5 4 28	23 28 52	0♋ 35 4	17 20	18 51	26 21	24 35	3 26	24 0	9 15	5 17	29 53	28 28
28	18 23 18	6 1 43	7♋ 46 7	15 1 19	17 17	18 46	28 29	25 48	4 4	24 6	9 11	5 20	29 53	28 29
29	18 27 14	6 58 56	22 19 50	29 40 44	17 14	18 39	0♋ 37	27 1	4 42	24 13	9 8	5 24	29 52	28 31
30	18 31 11	7♋ 56 10	7♌ 3 3	14♌ 25 47	17♏ 11	18♏ 32	2♋ 46	28♋ 14	5♌ 19	24♍ 20	9♐ 4	5♌ 27	29♎ 52	28♌ 32

DECLINATION and LATITUDE

Day	☉ Decl	☽ Decl	☽ Lat	☽ 12 Hr. Decl	☿ Decl	☿ Lat	♀ Decl	♀ Lat	♂ Decl	♂ Lat	♃ Decl	♃ Lat	♄ Decl	♄ Lat
1	21N59	18N38	4S12	17N26	13N11	3S37	23N51	0N36	23N37	1N17	4N24	1N22	20S16	1N52
2	22 7	15 59	4 51	14 16	13 29	3 34	23 57	0 38	23 32	1 17	4 23	1 22	20 15	1 52
3	22 15	12 21	5 11	10 15	13 49	3 30	24 2	0 41	23 27	1 17	4 22	1 22	20 15	1 52
4	22 23	8 0	5 12	5 39	14 10	3 26	24 7	0 43	23 21	1 17	4 20	1 22	20 14	1 52
5	22 30	3 14	4 54	0 47	14 33	3 20	24 10	0 45	23 16	1 17	4 19	1 21	20 14	1 52
6	22 36	1S41	4 18	4S 6	14 56	3 15	24 14	0 47	23 10	1 16	4 18	1 21	20 13	1 51
7	22 42	6 28	3 27	8 44	15 21	3 8	24 16	0 49	23 5	1 16	4 16	1 21	20 13	1 51
8	22 48	10 52	2 24	12 51	15 46	3 1	24 18	0 52	22 59	1 16	4 14	1 21	20 12	1 51
9	22 54	14 39	1 14	16 14	16 12	2 54	24 19	0 54	22 52	1 16	4 13	1 20	20 11	1 51
10	22 59	17 35	0 1	18 41	16 39	2 46	24 19	0 56	22 46	1 16	4 11	1 20	20 11	1 51
11	23 3	19 32	1N11	20 6	17 6	2 37	24 19	0 58	22 40	1 16	4 9	1 20	20 10	1 51
12	23 7	20 23	2 18	20 24	17 34	2 28	24 18	0 60	22 33	1 16	4 8	1 20	20 10	1 51
13	23 11	20 9	3 17	19 39	18 2	2 19	24 16	1 2	22 26	1 16	4 6	1 20	20 9	1 51
14	23 15	18 54	4 5	17 56	18 30	2 9	24 13	1 4	22 19	1 16	4 4	1 19	20 9	1 51
15	23 17	16 46	4 41	15 25	18 58	1 59	24 10	1 6	22 12	1 16	4 2	1 19	20 8	1 51
16	23 20	13 55	5 2	12 17	19 26	1 48	24 6	1 7	22 5	1 16	3 60	1 19	20 8	1 50
17	23 22	10 32	5 11	8 41	19 54	1 37	24 1	1 9	21 58	1 15	3 58	1 19	20 7	1 50
18	23 24	6 45	5 5	4 46	20 21	1 26	23 56	1 11	21 50	1 15	3 55	1 18	20 7	1 50
19	23 25	2 44	4 47	0 41	20 48	1 15	23 49	1 13	21 43	1 15	3 53	1 18	20 6	1 50
20	23 26	1N23	4 16	3N27	21 14	1 4	23 43	1 14	21 35	1 15	3 51	1 18	20 6	1 50
21	23 27	5 30	3 33	7 30	21 40	0 52	23 35	1 16	21 27	1 15	3 49	1 18	20 5	1 50
22	23 27	9 27	2 41	11 20	22 4	0 41	23 27	1 17	21 19	1 15	3 46	1 18	20 5	1 50
23	23 26	13 6	1 40	14 45	22 26	0 29	23 18	1 19	21 10	1 15	3 44	1 17	20 5	1 50
24	23 26	16 14	0 33	17 33	22 47	0 18	23 8	1 20	21 2	1 15	3 41	1 17	20 4	1 49
25	23 24	18 39	0S38	19 30	23 7	0 6	22 58	1 22	20 53	1 14	3 39	1 17	20 4	1 49
26	23 23	20 6	1 49	20 23	23 24	0N 5	22 47	1 23	20 44	1 14	3 36	1 17	20 3	1 49
27	23 21	20 22	2 55	20 1	23 39	0 16	22 36	1 24	20 36	1 14	3 33	1 17	20 3	1 49
28	23 18	19 21	3 52	18 22	23 52	0 26	22 24	1 26	20 27	1 14	3 31	1 16	20 2	1 49
29	23 16	17 4	4 35	15 29	24 3	0 36	22 11	1 27	20 17	1 14	3 28	1 16	20 2	1 49
30	23N12	13N40	5S 1	11N37	24N11	0N46	21N57	1N28	20N 8	1N14	3N25	1N16	20S 2	1N49

Day	♅ Decl	♅ Lat	♆ Decl	♆ Lat	♇ Decl	♇ Lat
1	19N50	0N36	9S53	1N48	22N35	11N 9
5	19 48	0 36	9 51	1 47	22 33	11 8
9	19 45	0 36	9 50	1 47	22 31	11 7
13	19 42	0 36	9 49	1 47	22 29	11 6
17	19 39	0 36	9 48	1 47	22 26	11 5
21	19 36	0 35	9 47	1 47	22 24	11 4
25	19 33	0 35	9 47	1 47	22 21	11 3
29	19N30	0N35	9S46	1N46	22N19	11N 3

☽ PHENOMENA

d	h	m	
5	7	10	☽
12	10	2	○
20	10	23	☾
27	20	54	●

d	h	° '
5	16	0
12	7	20S26
19	16	0
26	17	20N25

d	h	° '
3	13	5S14
10	0	0
17	2	5N11
24	11	0
30	19	5S 7

VOID OF COURSE ☽

Last Aspect	☽ Ingress
1 3pm32	2 ♌ 4am46
4 3am46	4 ♍ 7am 0
6 8am38	6 ♎ 9am46
8 10am25	8 ♏ 1pm41
10 3pm51	10 ♐ 7pm10
12 11pm14	13 ♑ 2am37
15 12pm24	15 ♒ 12pm24
18 0am12	18 ♓ 0am15
20 11am28	20 ♈ 12pm46
22 11pm29	22 ♉ 11pm39
25 4am19	25 ♊ 7am 7
27 10am49	27 ♋ 11am 1
29 12pm18	29 ♌ 12pm31

d	h	
3	5	PERIGEE
18	11	APOGEE
30	8	PERIGEE

DAILY ASPECTARIAN

Day	Aspect	Time
1	☽∠♇	0am15
S	☽⚹☿	5 41
	☽☌♂	7 31
	☽⚹♃	3pm32
	☽⚺♀	6 12
	☉☍♄	7 40
	☽⚼♄	10 5
	☉∠☽	10 16
2	☽⚺♇	1am30
Su	☽□♆	5 8
	☽☌♅	11 34
	☽∥☿	3pm39
	☽∠♃	4 44
	☽∠♀	9 40
	☽△♄	11 4
3	☉⚹☽	1am10
M	☽□☿	11 38
	☽⚺♂	12pm 5
	☽#♆	2 7
	☽⚺♃	5 55
4	☽⚹♀	1am 8
T	☿⚹♂	2 20
	☽☌♇	3 46
	☽⚹♆	7 18
	☽⚺♅	1pm59
	☽∠♂	2 24
	☽∥♃	6 40
5	☽□♄	1am 8
W	☉□☽	7 10
	♀⚹♇	8 14
	☽∠♆	8 33
	☉∥♇	10 38
	☽∠♅	3pm23
	☽⚹♂	4 54
	☽△☿	6 21
	☽☌♃	8 39
6	☉⚼♆	3am 9
Th	☽⚺♇	6 32
	☽□♀	8 38
	☽⚺♆	10 1
	☽#♃	12pm53
	☽⚹♅	5 3
	♀ ♋	9 35
	☽⚼☿	10 20
	☿△♃	11 0
7	♀△♆	0am12
F	☽⚹♄	4 0
	☽∠♇	8 18
	☉△☽	2pm14
	☽∥♆	6 8
	☽□♂	10 51
8	☽⚺♃	0am27
S	☽⚻☿	2 52
	☽∠♄	5 53
	☽⚹♇	10 25
	☽☌♆	1pm52
	☽△♀	5 38
	☉⚼☽	6 22
	☽□♅	9 21
	☉∥♂	9 42
9	☽∠♃	2am53
Su	☽⚺♄	8 9
	♂⚹♃	1pm38
	☽#☿	1 51
	☽⚼♀	10 53
	☉⚻☽	11 0
10	☽⚹♃	5am44
M	☽△♂	6 27
	♀⚺♅	12pm26
	☽☍☿	1 57
	☉∠♅	2 45
	☽□♇	3 51
	☽⚺♆	7 18
11	☽△♅	3am16
T	☽#♅	3 33
	☽⚻♀	4 44
	☿□♇	7 53
	☽⚼♂	11 2
	☽☌♄	1pm58
	☽∥♄	2 10
	☽∠♆	10 43
12	☽⚼♅	6am59
W	☉☍☽	10 2
	☽□♃	12pm57
	☿ ♊	1 40
	☿⚻♆	2 24
	♂∥♇	3 35
	☽⚻♂	4 13
	☽△♇	11 14
	☽∥♄	11 47
13	☽⚹♆	2am41
Th	☽⚻☿	4 22
	☽#♅	10 53
	☽⚻♅	11 16
	♂⚼♄	6pm16
	☽☍♀	6 35
	☽⚺♄	9 52
14	☽⚼♇	3am47
F	☉□♃	4 11
	☽#☿	4 13
	☽⚼☿	1pm 6
	☽△♃	10 30
	☉⚻☽	11 54
15	♀⚻♄	2am39
S	☽∠♄	2 42
	☽☍♂	4 38
	☽⚻♇	8 57
	☽□♆	12pm24
	☿⚹♅	1 7
	♆ ♎	8 33
	☽☍♅	9 39
	☽△☿	10 57
16	☽⚼♃	4am10
Su	☉⚼☽	7 57
	☽⚹♄	8 5
	☽⚻♀	11 36
	☿∥♅	11 40
17	☽∥♆	4am47
M	☽⚻♃	10 20
	☿#♄	11 25
	☉△☽	4pm35
	♀∠♇	6 9
	☽⚻♂	7 35
	☽☍♇	8 48
	☽⚼♀	9 6
18	☽△♆	0am12
T	☽⚻♅	9 59
	☿☍♄	1pm 3
	☽#♃	5 10
	♂⚺♇	7 19
	☽□♄	8 2
	☽□☿	9 19
19	☽⚼♂	3am34
W	☽⚼♆	6 29
	☽△♀	6 53
	☽⚼♅	4pm26
	☉⚹♇	10 13
	☽☍♃	11 20
20	☽⚻♇	9am26
Th	☉□☽	10 23
	☽△♂	11 28
	☽⚻♆	12pm39
	☽∥♃	2 11
	☿∥♂	2 36
	☽△♅	10 40
21	☿∠♂	6am45
F	☿⚼♆	7 46
	☽△♄	7 56
	♂□♆	9 48
	♂ ♌	12pm18
	☉△♆	2 39
	☽⚼♇	3 19
	☉ ♋	4 21
	☽⚹☿	8 24
22	☉⚺♂	0am 5
S	☉∥♀	0 45
	☽□♀	1 30
	☽#♆	2 3
	☽⚻♃	11 13
	☽⚼♄	1pm 9
	☿∥♇	8 16
	☽△♇	8 33
	☽☍♆	11 29
23	☽□♂	1am30
Su	☉⚹☽	2 13
	☽∠☿	6 46
	☽□♅	9 19
	☽⚼♃	4pm 3
	☽⚻♄	5 33
	☿∠♅	11 15
24	☉∠☽	8am34
M	☽⚺☿	3pm48
	☽⚹♀	4 13
	☿∥♀	5 1
	☽△♃	7 55
	☿⚺♀	9 54
25	☽□♇	4am19
T	☽⚻♆	6 56
	☽⚹♂	11 33
	☽∥♅	12pm42
	☉⚺☽	1 43
	☽⚹♅	4 22
	☿□♃	7 27
	☽∠♀	9 42
	☉∥☿	10 18
	☽#♄	11 0
	☽☍♄	11 35
26	☽⚼♆	9am16
W	♀⚹♃	11 35
	☽∠♂	2pm59
	♀⚼♄	5 56
	☽∠♅	6 31
27	☽□♃	0am53
Th	☽⚺♀	2 2
	☉⚺♅	5 30
	☽☌☿	5 44
	☽⚹♇	8 27
	☽△♆	10 49
	☽#♄	11 25
	☽⚺♂	5pm33
	☽⚺♅	7 56
	☉☌☽	8 54
	☽∥♅	9 33
28	☿⚹♇	0am10
F	☽⚻♄	2 21
	♀∥♇	8 0
	☽∠♇	9 29
	☿△♆	3pm42
	☿ ♋	5 8
29	☽⚼♄	2am56
S	☽⚹♃	3 6
	☽☌♀	8 21
	☽⚺♇	10 7
	☽□♆	12pm18
	☽⚺☿	3 50
	☽☌♂	9 4
	☽☌♅	9 23
30	☉⚺☽	1am32
Su	☽△♄	3 16
	☽∠♃	3 44
	♂☌♅	5 24
	♀⚺♇	6 0
	♂#♄	5pm29
	☽∠☿	8 26
	☽#♆	10 6

JULY 1957

LONGITUDE

Day	Sid. Time	☉	☽	☽ 12 Hour	Mean ☊	True ☊	☿	♀	♂	♃	♄	♅	♆	♇
	h m s	° ' "	° ' "	° ' "	° '	° '	° '	° '	° '	° '	° '	° '	° '	° '
1	18 35 8	8♋ 53 24	21♌ 48 0	29♌ 8 47	17♏ 8	18♏ 25R	4♋ 56	29♋ 27	5♌ 57	24♍ 26	9♐ 0R	5♌ 30	29♎ 51R	28♌ 33
2	18 39 4	9 50 37	6♍ 27 22	13♍ 43 4	17 4	18 19	7 7	0♌ 40	6 34	24 33	8 57	5 34	29 51	28 35
3	18 43 1	10 47 49	20 55 21	28 3 48	17 1	18 16	9 17	1 54	7 12	24 41	8 54	5 37	29 51	28 36
4	18 46 57	11 45 1	5♎ 8 11	12♎ 8 21	16 58	18 14D	11 28	3 7	7 50	24 48	8 50	5 41	29 51	28 38
5	18 50 54	12 42 14	19 4 14	25 55 55	16 55	18 14	13 38	4 20	8 27	24 55	8 47	5 44	29 50	28 39
6	18 54 50	13 39 26	2♏ 43 29	9♏ 27 6	16 52	18 15	15 48	5 33	9 5	25 3	8 44	5 47	29 50	28 41
7	18 58 47	14 36 37	16 6 58	22 43 15	16 48	18 16R	17 56	6 46	9 43	25 10	8 40	5 51	29 50	28 42
8	19 2 43	15 33 48	29 16 10	5♐ 45 53	16 45	18 15	20 4	7 59	10 20	25 18	8 37	5 54	29 50	28 44
9	19 6 40	16 31 0	12♐ 12 34	18 36 22	16 42	18 13	22 10	9 12	10 58	25 26	8 34	5 58	29 50	28 45
10	19 10 37	17 28 11	24 57 24	1♑ 15 46	16 39	18 8	24 15	10 25	11 36	25 34	8 31	6 2	29 50	28 47
11	19 14 33	18 25 23	7♑ 31 32	13 44 49	16 36	18 0	26 19	11 38	12 13	25 42	8 28	6 5	29 50D	28 48
12	19 18 30	19 22 34	19 55 39	26 4 7	16 33	17 51	28 21	12 51	12 51	25 50	8 26	6 9	29 50	28 50
13	19 22 26	20 19 46	2♒ 10 20	8♒ 14 23	16 29	17 39	0♌ 21	14 4	13 29	25 58	8 23	6 12	29 50	28 52
14	19 26 23	21 16 58	14 16 26	20 16 40	16 26	17 28	2 20	15 17	14 6	26 7	8 20	6 16	29 50	28 53
15	19 30 19	22 14 11	26 15 16	2♓ 12 33	16 23	17 17	4 17	16 30	14 44	26 15	8 18	6 19	29 50	28 55
16	19 34 16	23 11 24	8♓ 8 48	14 4 23	16 20	17 7	6 12	17 43	15 22	26 24	8 15	6 23	29 50	28 56
17	19 38 12	24 8 37	19 59 44	25 55 17	16 17	17 0	8 5	18 56	15 59	26 33	8 13	6 27	29 50	28 58
18	19 42 9	25 5 52	1♈ 51 35	7♈ 49 9	16 14	16 55	9 57	20 8	16 37	26 42	8 10	6 30	29 50	29 0
19	19 46 6	26 3 6	13 48 35	19 50 29	16 10	16 52	11 47	21 21	17 15	26 51	8 8	6 34	29 50	29 1
20	19 50 2	27 0 22	25 55 31	2♉ 4 19	16 7	16 52D	13 34	22 34	17 53	27 0	8 6	6 38	29 51	29 3
21	19 53 59	27 57 38	8♉ 17 31	14 35 46	16 4	16 52R	15 20	23 47	18 30	27 9	8 4	6 41	29 51	29 5
22	19 57 55	28 54 56	20 59 38	27 29 40	16 1	16 52	17 5	25 0	19 8	27 18	8 2	6 45	29 51	29 7
23	20 1 52	29 52 13	4♊ 6 18	10♊ 49 54	15 58	16 51	18 47	26 12	19 46	27 27	8 0	6 49	29 52	29 8
24	20 5 48	0♌ 49 32	17 40 39	24 38 36	15 54	16 48	20 28	27 25	20 24	27 37	7 58	6 52	29 52	29 10
25	20 9 45	1 46 52	1♋ 43 38	8♋ 55 23	15 51	16 42	22 7	28 38	21 1	27 47	7 56	6 56	29 52	29 12
26	20 13 41	2 44 13	16 13 17	23 36 36	15 48	16 34	23 44	29 50	21 39	27 56	7 55	7 0	29 53	29 14
27	20 17 38	3 41 34	1♌ 4 20	8♌ 35 23	15 45	16 24	25 19	1♍ 3	22 17	28 6	7 53	7 3	29 53	29 16
28	20 21 35	4 38 56	16 8 30	23 42 23	15 42	16 14	26 52	2 16	22 55	28 16	7 52	7 7	29 54	29 17
29	20 25 31	5 36 19	1♍ 15 42	8♍ 47 15	15 39	16 4	28 24	3 28	23 33	28 26	7 50	7 11	29 54	29 19
30	20 29 28	6 33 42	16 15 52	23 40 35	15 35	15 55	29 54	4 41	24 10	28 36	7 49	7 15	29 55	29 21
31	20 33 24	7♌ 31 6	1♎ 0 36	8♎ 15 22	15♏ 32	15♏ 49	1♍ 22	5♍ 53	24♌ 48	28♍ 46	7♐ 48	7♌ 18	29♎ 55	29♌ 23

DECLINATION and LATITUDE

Day	☉ Decl	☽ Decl	☽ Lat	☽ 12 Hr. Decl	☿ Decl	☿ Lat	♀ Decl	♀ Lat	♂ Decl	♂ Lat	♃ Decl	♃ Lat	♄ Decl	♄ Lat
1	23N 9	9N24	5S 6	7N 4	24N16	0N55	21N43	1N29	19N59	1N14	3N22	1N16	20S 1	1N48
2	23 5	4 37	4 52	2 8	24 19	1 4	21 28	1 30	19 49	1 13	3 19	1 16	20 1	1 48
3	23 0	0S22	4 19	2S50	24 18	1 11	21 13	1 31	19 39	1 13	3 16	1 15	20 0	1 48
4	22 56	5 15	3 30	7 35	24 15	1 19	20 57	1 32	19 30	1 13	3 13	1 15	20 0	1 48
5	22 50	9 47	2 30	11 50	24 9	1 25	20 41	1 32	19 20	1 13	3 10	1 15	19 60	1 48
6	22 45	13 43	1 22	15 23	24 1	1 31	20 23	1 33	19 10	1 13	3 7	1 15	19 59	1 48
7	22 39	16 51	0 12	18 4	23 49	1 36	20 6	1 34	18 59	1 13	3 4	1 15	19 59	1 47
8	22 32	19 3	0N59	19 45	23 36	1 40	19 48	1 34	18 49	1 13	3 0	1 14	19 59	1 47
9	22 25	20 12	2 4	20 23	23 19	1 44	19 29	1 35	18 39	1 12	2 57	1 14	19 59	1 47
10	22 18	20 18	3 3	19 58	23 1	1 46	19 10	1 35	18 28	1 12	2 54	1 14	19 58	1 47
11	22 11	19 23	3 51	18 34	22 40	1 48	18 50	1 36	18 17	1 12	2 50	1 14	19 58	1 47
12	22 3	17 33	4 28	16 19	22 17	1 50	18 30	1 36	18 7	1 12	2 47	1 14	19 58	1 46
13	21 54	14 56	4 52	13 24	21 52	1 50	18 9	1 36	17 56	1 12	2 44	1 14	19 58	1 46
14	21 46	11 43	5 2	9 57	21 26	1 50	17 47	1 36	17 44	1 12	2 40	1 13	19 57	1 46
15	21 37	8 4	4 59	6 8	20 58	1 49	17 26	1 36	17 33	1 11	2 37	1 13	19 57	1 46
16	21 27	4 8	4 43	2 6	20 28	1 48	17 3	1 36	17 22	1 11	2 33	1 13	19 57	1 46
17	21 17	0 4	4 15	1N60	19 57	1 46	16 41	1 36	17 11	1 11	2 29	1 13	19 57	1 45
18	21 7	4N 2	3 35	6 2	19 25	1 43	16 18	1 36	16 59	1 11	2 26	1 13	19 57	1 45
19	20 57	8 0	2 46	9 54	18 52	1 40	15 54	1 36	16 47	1 11	2 22	1 13	19 56	1 45
20	20 46	11 43	1 49	13 25	18 17	1 36	15 30	1 36	16 36	1 10	2 18	1 12	19 56	1 45
21	20 34	14 59	0 45	16 25	17 42	1 32	15 6	1 35	16 24	1 10	2 14	1 12	19 56	1 45
22	20 23	17 39	0S22	18 42	17 6	1 27	14 41	1 35	16 12	1 10	2 11	1 12	19 56	1 44
23	20 11	19 30	1 30	20 2	16 30	1 22	14 16	1 34	15 60	1 10	2 7	1 12	19 56	1 44
24	19 59	20 17	2 36	20 14	15 53	1 16	13 50	1 34	15 48	1 10	2 3	1 12	19 56	1 44
25	19 46	19 52	3 34	19 10	15 15	1 10	13 25	1 33	15 35	1 9	1 59	1 12	19 56	1 44
26	19 33	18 9	4 20	16 49	14 37	1 4	12 58	1 32	15 23	1 9	1 55	1 12	19 56	1 44
27	19 20	15 12	4 50	13 19	13 59	0 57	12 32	1 32	15 11	1 9	1 51	1 11	19 56	1 43
28	19 6	11 13	5 1	8 55	13 20	0 49	12 5	1 31	14 58	1 9	1 47	1 11	19 56	1 43
29	18 52	6 30	4 51	3 59	12 41	0 42	11 38	1 30	14 45	1 9	1 43	1 11	19 56	1 43
30	18 38	1 25	4 20	1S 8	12 2	0 34	11 10	1 29	14 33	1 8	1 39	1 11	19 56	1 43
31	18N24	3S39	3S33	6S 6	11N23	0N25	10N43	1N28	14N20	1N 8	1N34	1N11	19S56	1N43

Day	♅ Decl	♅ Lat	♆ Decl	♆ Lat	♇ Decl	♇ Lat
1	19N28	0N35	9S46	1N46	22N18	11N 2
5	19 25	0 35	9 46	1 46	22 15	11 2
9	19 21	0 35	9 46	1 46	22 12	11 1
13	19 18	0 35	9 46	1 46	22 9	11 0
17	19 14	0 35	9 46	1 45	22 7	10 60
21	19 10	0 35	9 47	1 45	22 4	10 59
25	19 7	0 35	9 48	1 45	22 1	10 59
29	19N 3	0N35	9S48	1N45	21N58	10N59

☽ PHENOMENA

d	h	m	
4	12	10	☽
11	22	50	○
20	2	18	☾
27	4	29	●

d	h	° '
2	22	0
9	14	20S23
17	0	0
24	4	20N18
30	7	0

d	h	° '
7	4	0
14	6	5N 3
21	16	0
28	0	5S 1

VOID OF COURSE ☽

Last Aspect		☽ Ingress		
1	1pm10	1	♍	1pm24
3	6am21	3	♎	3pm16
5	6pm53	5	♏	7pm10
7	11pm 0	8	♐	1am21
10	9am16	10	♑	9am35
12	7pm23	12	♒	7pm43
15	7am12	15	♓	7am33
17	1pm26	17	♈	8pm15
20	7am40	20	♉	7am58
22	3pm44	22	♊	4pm34
24	8pm52	24	♋	9pm 5
26	10pm 6	26	♌	10pm17
28	9pm51	28	♍	10pm 0
30	8pm16	30	♎	10pm20

d	h	
16	3	APOGEE
28	10	PERIGEE

DAILY ASPECTARIAN

Day	Aspect	Time
1 M	☉⚻♄	2am47
	☉∠☽	3 39
	☽⚺♃	4 21
	☿⚺♅	6 27
	♀□♆	7 51
	♀ ♌	10 43
	☽☌♇	11 3
	☽⚹♆	1pm10
	☽⚺♀	1 39
	☿⚺♂	3 41
	☽⚺♅	10 31
2 T	☽⚺♂	0am12
	☽⚹☿	1 16
	☽□♄	4 6
	☉⚹☽	5 59
	☽∥♃	6 22
	☽∠♆	1pm53
	☽∠♀	4 40
	☿⚻♄	7 44
	☽∠♅	11 29
3 W	☽∠♂	2am14
	☽☌♃	6 21
	☽⚺♇	12pm56
	☽#♃	1 58
	☽⚺♆	3 1
	☽⚹♀	8 14
4 Th	☽⚹♅	0am55
	☽⚹♂	4 49
	☉☌☿	5 37
	☽⚹♄	6 18
	♂∥♅	10 38
	☉□☽	12pm10
	☽□☿	12 50
	☽∠♇	2 36
	☽∥♆	11 54
5 F	☿∠♇	0am13
	☽∠♄	8 12
	☽⚺♃	10 19
	♂△♄	11 26
	☽⚹♇	4pm49
	☽☌♆	6 53
6 S	☉∠♇	0am32
	♀☌♅	5 1
	☽□♅	5 29
	☽□♀	5 31
	☽⚺♄	10 39
	☽□♂	11 54
	☽∠♃	1pm11
	☉△☽	9 4
7 Su	☽△☿	3am56
	♀#♄	9 4
	☽⚹♃	4pm38
	☽#♂	9 11
	♂∠♃	10 10
	☽□♇	11 0
8 M	☽⚺♆	1am 2
	☉⚼☽	2 34
	☽#♅	4 55
	☽#♀	10 9
	♀△♄	12pm 4
	☽△♅	12 19
	☽⚼☿	12 48
	☽∥♄	5 3
	☽☌♄	5 14
	☽△♀	5 48
	☽△♂	9 33
9 T	☽∠♆	4am54
	☉⚻☽	8 43
	♀∥♅	9 59
	☿⚼♄	3pm42
	☽⚼♅	4 32
	☽⚻☿	10 25
10 W	☽⚼♀	0am58
	☽□♃	1 10
	♀∠♃	3 14
	☽⚼♂	3 16
	☽△♇	7 17
	☽⚹♆	9 16
	☽∥♄	11 49
	☿⚹♃	4pm15
	☽⚻♅	9 13
	☉∥♇	11 39
11 Th	☽#♅	0am55
	☽⚺♄	1 49
	☽⚻♀	8 47
	☽⚻♂	9 32
	☽#♀	10 26
	☽⚼♇	12pm 8
	☽#♂	5 2
	♆SD	5 56
	☉☍☽	10 50
	♀☌♂	11 56
12 F	☿⚺♇	5am48
	☽∠♄	6 48
	☿∥♇	7 10
	☽△♃	11 40
	☽⚻♇	5pm28
	☿□♆	5 36
	☽□♆	7 23
	☿ ♌	7 42
	☽☍☿	7 44
	☉∥☿	9 5
13 S	☽☍♅	8am 0
	☽⚹♄	12pm14
	☽⚼♃	5 38
	☽☍♂	11 39
14 Su	☽☍♀	2am14
	♀∥♂	6 48
	☽∥♆	1pm 9
	☉⚻☽	3 14
15 M	☽⚻♃	0am 0
	☽☍♇	5 22
	☽△♆	7 12
	☽⚻☿	7pm19
	☽⚻♅	8 25
16 T	☉⚼☽	0am 6
	☽□♄	0 13
	☉⚼♄	1 30
	☿☌♅	2 23
	☽#♃	9 33
	☽⚼♆	1pm32
	☽⚻♂	3 26
	☽⚻♀	9 35
17 W	☿#♄	0am15
	☿△♄	1 31
	☽⚼♅	2 57
	☽⚼☿	7 27
	☉△☽	9 8
	☽☍♃	1pm26
	☽∥♃	2 41
	☽⚻♇	6 12
	☽⚻♆	7 55
	☽⚼♂	11 29
18 Th	☽⚼♀	7am22
	☿∥♅	8 41
	☽△♅	9 25
	☽△♄	12pm40
	☽△☿	7 13
19 F	☽⚼♇	0am26
	☿∠♃	0 58
	☽△♂	7 14
	☽#♆	11 13
	☽△♀	4pm39
	☽⚼♄	6 27
	☉⚹♃	11 39
20 S	☽⚻♃	2am 7
	☉□☽	2 18
	☽△♇	6 8
	☽☍♆	7 40
	☽□♅	8pm54
	☽⚻♄	11 34
21 Su	☽∥♀	0am45
	☽⚼♃	7 27
	☽∥♂	11 2
	☽□☿	3pm32
	☽∥☿	7 31
	☽□♂	8 21
22 M	☉⚺♇	5am 4
	☽□♀	8 10
	☽△♃	11 47
	☽□♇	2pm59
	☉⚹☽	3 44
	☽⚻♆	4 19
	☽∥♅	6 19
	☉□♆	11 43
23 T	☉ ♌	3am15
	☽⚹♅	4 52
	☽☍♄	6 57
	☽#♄	9 7
	☉∥☽	1pm 7
	☽⚼♆	7 6
	☉∠☽	8 32
	☿☌♂	10 23
24 W	♀⚺♃	4am32
	☿∥♂	4 38
	☽⚹♂	4 55
	☽⚹☿	5 28
	☉#♄	5 34
	☽∠♅	7 17
	☽□♃	5pm15
	☽⚹♀	6 17
	☽⚹♇	7 44
	☽△♆	8 52
	☽#♄	10 36
25 Th	☉⚺☽	0am 6
	☉∥☽	2 36
	☽∠♂	7 31
	☽⚺♅	8 44
	☽∠☿	10 8
	☽⚻♄	10 21
	♀☌♇	11 36
	☽∥♅	12pm53
	☽∠♇	8 44
	☽∠♀	9 32
26 F	♀⚹♆	0am48
	♀ ♍	3 11
	☽⚺♂	9 13
	☽⚼♄	10 51
	☽⚺☿	1pm39
	☽⚹♃	7 11
	☽⚺♇	9 5
	☽□♆	10 6
	☽⚺♀	11 58
27 S	☽∥♂	0am10
	☉☌☽	4 29
	☽∥☿	9 32
	☽☌♅	9 36
	☽△♄	10 52
	☽∥♀	6pm35
	☽∠♃	7 23
28 Su	☉∥♅	4am23
	☽#♆	7 28
	☽☌♂	11 12
	☽☌☿	6pm56
	☽⚺♃	7 27
	☽☌♇	8 54
	☽⚹♆	9 51
29 M	☿⚺♃	0am35
	☽☌♀	3 50
	☉⚺☽	7 23
	☽⚺♅	9 28
	☽□♄	10 28
	☿☌♇	3pm 4
	☽∠♆	9 50
	☽∥♃	10 57
30 T	☿⚹♆	0am22
	☿ ♍	1 44
	☉∠☽	9 10
	☽∠♅	9 43
	☽⚺♂	1pm23
	☽#♃	2 12
	☉☌♅	6 16
	☽☌♃	8 16
	☽⚺♇	9 19
	☽⚺♆	10 13
31 W	☽⚺☿	0am38
	☉△♄	6 51
	☽⚺♀	8 48
	☽⚹♅	10 28
	☽⚹♄	11 13
	☉⚹☽	11 32
	☽∠♂	3pm15
	☽∠♇	10 19

AUGUST 1957

LONGITUDE

Day	Sid. Time	☉	☽	☽ 12 Hour	Mean ☊	True ☊	☿	♀	♂	♃	♄	♅	♆	♇
	h m s	° ' "	° ' "	° ' "	° '	° '	° '	° '	° '	° '	° '	° '	° '	° '
1	20 37 21	8♌ 28 30	15♎ 24 26	22♎ 27 38	15♏ 29	15♏ 46R	2♍ 48	7♍ 6	25♌ 26	28♍ 56	7♐ 47R	7♌ 22	29♎ 56	29♌ 25
2	20 41 17	9 25 55	29 24 54	6♏ 16 21	15 26	15 44D	4 12	8 18	26 4	29 6	7 46	7 26	29 57	29 27
3	20 45 14	10 23 21	13♏ 2 9	19 42 38	15 23	15 44R	5 34	9 31	26 42	29 17	7 45	7 29	29 57	29 29
4	20 49 10	11 20 47	26 18 7	2♐ 49 0	15 20	15 44	6 54	10 43	27 20	29 27	7 44	7 33	29 58	29 30
5	20 53 7	12 18 14	9♐ 15 39	15 38 28	15 16	15 43	8 13	11 56	27 58	29 38	7 43	7 37	29 59	29 32
6	20 57 4	13 15 42	21 57 49	28 14 3	15 13	15 40	9 29	13 8	28 36	29 48	7 43	7 40	0♏ 0	29 34
7	21 1 0	14 13 11	4♑ 27 30	10♑ 38 25	15 10	15 33	10 43	14 20	29 13	29 59	7 42	7 44	0 1	29 36
8	21 4 57	15 10 40	16 47 4	22 53 40	15 7	15 24	11 56	15 33	29 51	0♎ 10	7 42	7 48	0 1	29 38
9	21 8 53	16 8 10	28 58 23	5♒ 1 24	15 4	15 12	13 5	16 45	0♍ 29	0 21	7 41	7 52	0 2	29 40
10	21 12 50	17 5 42	11♒ 2 52	17 2 54	15 0	14 59	14 13	17 57	1 7	0 32	7 41	7 55	0 3	29 42
11	21 16 46	18 3 15	23 1 41	28 59 20	14 57	14 44	15 18	19 9	1 45	0 42	7 41	7 59	0 4	29 44
12	21 20 43	19 0 48	4♓ 56 3	10♓ 52 0	14 54	14 31	16 21	20 22	2 23	0 54	7 41D	8 3	0 5	29 46
13	21 24 39	19 58 23	16 47 26	22 42 37	14 51	14 19	17 21	21 34	3 1	1 5	7 41	8 6	0 6	29 48
14	21 28 36	20 55 59	28 37 50	4♈ 33 28	14 48	14 10	18 18	22 46	3 39	1 16	7 41	8 10	0 7	29 50
15	21 32 33	21 53 37	10♈ 29 55	16 27 36	14 45	14 4	19 13	23 58	4 17	1 27	7 41	8 13	0 8	29 52
16	21 36 29	22 51 15	22 27 2	28 28 45	14 41	14 0	20 4	25 10	4 55	1 38	7 42	8 17	0 9	29 54
17	21 40 26	23 48 56	4♉ 33 19	10♉ 41 20	14 38	13 58D	20 52	26 22	5 33	1 50	7 42	8 21	0 10	29 56
18	21 44 22	24 46 38	16 53 25	23 10 13	14 35	13 58R	21 37	27 34	6 11	2 1	7 43	8 24	0 12	29 58
19	21 48 19	25 44 22	29 32 19	6♊ 0 18	14 32	13 58	22 18	28 46	6 49	2 13	7 43	8 28	0 13	0♍ 0
20	21 52 15	26 42 7	12♊ 34 44	19 16 4	14 29	13 57	22 56	29 58	7 28	2 24	7 44	8 31	0 14	0 1
21	21 56 12	27 39 54	26 4 37	3♋ 0 38	14 25	13 55	23 30	1♎ 10	8 6	2 36	7 45	8 35	0 15	0 3
22	22 0 8	28 37 43	10♋ 4 8	17 14 57	14 22	13 49	23 59	2 21	8 44	2 48	7 46	8 39	0 16	0 5
23	22 4 5	29 35 34	24 32 43	1♌ 56 48	14 19	13 42	24 24	3 33	9 22	2 59	7 47	8 42	0 18	0 7
24	22 8 2	0♍ 33 26	9♌ 26 22	17 0 20	14 16	13 33	24 44	4 45	10 0	3 11	7 48	8 46	0 19	0 9
25	22 11 58	1 31 19	24 37 28	2♍ 16 24	14 13	13 22	25 0	5 57	10 38	3 23	7 49	8 49	0 20	0 11
26	22 15 55	2 29 14	9♍ 55 40	17 33 52	14 10	13 13	25 10	7 8	11 17	3 35	7 50	8 53	0 22	0 13
27	22 19 51	3 27 11	25 9 36	2♎ 41 39	14 6	13 4	25 15R	8 20	11 55	3 47	7 52	8 56	0 23	0 15
28	22 23 48	4 25 9	10♎ 8 56	17 30 38	14 3	12 58	25 14	9 32	12 33	3 59	7 53	8 59	0 24	0 17
29	22 27 44	5 23 8	24 46 7	1♏ 54 58	14 0	12 55	25 7	10 43	13 11	4 11	7 55	9 3	0 26	0 19
30	22 31 41	6 21 9	8♏ 56 59	15 52 9	13 57	12 54D	24 54	11 55	13 50	4 23	7 57	9 6	0 27	0 21
31	22 35 37	7♍ 19 11	22♏ 40 37	29♏ 22 38	13♏ 54	12♏ 54	24♍ 35	13♎ 6	14♍ 28	4♎ 35	7♐ 58	9♌ 10	0♏ 29	0♍ 23

DECLINATION and LATITUDE

Day	☉	☽		☽ 12 Hr.	☿		♀		♂		♃		♄	
	Decl	Decl	Lat	Decl	Decl	Lat	Decl	Lat	Decl	Lat	Decl	Lat	Decl	Lat
1	18N 9	8S25	2S33	10S36	10N45	0N17	10N15	1N26	14N 7	1N 8	1N30	1N11	19S56	1N42
2	17 54	12 36	1 25	14 24	10 6	0 8	9 46	1 25	13 54	1 8	1 26	1 11	19 56	1 42
3	17 38	15 59	0 14	17 20	9 27	0S 1	9 18	1 24	13 41	1 8	1 22	1 10	19 56	1 42
4	17 23	18 26	0N56	19 16	8 49	0 10	8 49	1 22	13 27	1 7	1 18	1 10	19 56	1 42
5	17 7	19 51	2 1	20 10	8 11	0 20	8 20	1 21	13 14	1 7	1 13	1 10	19 56	1 41
6	16 51	20 14	2 59	20 2	7 33	0 30	7 51	1 19	13 1	1 7	1 9	1 10	19 56	1 41
7	16 34	19 35	3 47	18 55	6 56	0 40	7 21	1 18	12 47	1 7	1 5	1 10	19 56	1 41
8	16 17	18 2	4 24	16 56	6 19	0 50	6 52	1 16	12 34	1 6	1 0	1 10	19 56	1 41
9	16 0	15 40	4 48	14 14	5 43	1 0	6 22	1 14	12 20	1 6	0 56	1 10	19 57	1 41
10	15 43	12 40	4 59	10 58	5 8	1 11	5 52	1 12	12 6	1 6	0 51	1 10	19 57	1 40
11	15 25	9 10	4 57	7 17	4 33	1 21	5 22	1 10	11 53	1 6	0 47	1 9	19 57	1 40
12	15 8	5 20	4 41	3 21	3 59	1 32	4 52	1 8	11 39	1 5	0 42	1 9	19 57	1 40
13	14 50	1 19	4 14	0N43	3 25	1 43	4 22	1 6	11 25	1 5	0 38	1 9	19 57	1 40
14	14 31	2N45	3 35	4 45	2 53	1 53	3 51	1 4	11 11	1 5	0 33	1 9	19 58	1 39
15	14 13	6 43	2 47	8 38	2 22	2 4	3 21	1 2	10 57	1 5	0 29	1 9	19 58	1 39
16	13 54	10 28	1 51	12 12	1 52	2 15	2 50	0 60	10 42	1 4	0 24	1 9	19 58	1 39
17	13 35	13 49	0 50	15 19	1 23	2 26	2 19	0 57	10 28	1 4	0 19	1 9	19 58	1 39
18	13 16	16 38	0S15	17 47	0 56	2 36	1 48	0 55	10 14	1 4	0 15	1 9	19 59	1 39
19	12 57	18 44	1 22	19 27	0 30	2 47	1 18	0 52	9 60	1 4	0 10	1 9	19 59	1 38
20	12 37	19 54	2 25	20 6	0 5	2 57	0 47	0 50	9 45	1 3	0 5	1 8	19 59	1 38
21	12 17	19 60	3 24	19 36	0S17	3 8	0 16	0 47	9 31	1 3	0 1	1 8	19 60	1 38
22	11 57	18 53	4 12	17 52	0 38	3 17	0S15	0 45	9 16	1 3	0S 4	1 8	20 0	1 38
23	11 37	16 32	4 45	14 55	0 57	3 27	0 46	0 42	9 2	1 3	0 9	1 8	20 1	1 37
24	11 17	13 3	5 1	10 57	1 13	3 36	1 17	0 39	8 47	1 2	0 14	1 8	20 1	1 37
25	10 56	8 39	4 56	6 13	1 27	3 45	1 48	0 36	8 32	1 2	0 18	1 8	20 1	1 37
26	10 35	3 41	4 30	1 5	1 39	3 53	2 19	0 33	8 17	1 2	0 23	1 8	20 2	1 37
27	10 15	1S31	3 45	4S 4	1 48	4 1	2 50	0 30	8 3	1 1	0 28	1 8	20 2	1 37
28	9 54	6 33	2 45	8 53	1 54	4 8	3 21	0 27	7 48	1 1	0 33	1 8	20 3	1 36
29	9 32	11 4	1 35	13 3	1 56	4 14	3 52	0 24	7 33	1 1	0 38	1 8	20 3	1 36
30	9 11	14 49	0 21	16 20	1 56	4 19	4 23	0 21	7 18	1 1	0 43	1 8	20 4	1 36
31	8N49	17S36	0N52	18S37	1S52	4S22	4S54	0N18	7N 3	1N 0	0S47	1N 8	20S 4	1N36

Day	♅		♆		♇	
	Decl	Lat	Decl	Lat	Decl	Lat
1	19N 0	0N35	9S49	1N45	21N56	10N59
5	18 56	0 35	9 50	1 44	21 53	10 59
9	18 53	0 35	9 52	1 44	21 50	10 59
13	18 49	0 35	9 53	1 44	21 47	10 59
17	18 45	0 36	9 55	1 44	21 45	10 59
21	18 42	0 36	9 57	1 43	21 42	10 59
25	18 38	0 36	9 59	1 43	21 39	10 59
29	18N34	0N36	10S 1	1N43	21N37	10N59

☽ PHENOMENA

d	h	m	
2	18	56	☽
10	13	9	○
18	16	17	☾
25	11	33	●

d	h	°
5	21	20S14
13	8	0
20	14	20N 6
26	17	0

d	h	°
3	5	0
10	8	4N60
17	18	0
24	6	5S 2
30	7	0

VOID OF COURSE ☽

Last Aspect		☽ Ingress		
2	0am55	2	♏	1am 1
4	5am54	4	♐	6am48
6	3pm24	6	♑	3pm24
7	9pm19	9	♒	2am 2
11	1pm32	11	♓	2pm 2
13	10am46	14	♈	2am46
16	2pm51	16	♉	3pm 1
19	0am51	19	♊	0am52
21	2am58	21	♋	6am49
22	11pm46	23	♌	8am51
23	10pm55	25	♍	8am26
27	0am 8	27	♎	7am42
27	10pm54	29	♏	8am46
31	3am18	31	♐	1pm 8

d	h	
12	14	APOGEE
25	18	PERIGEE

DAILY ASPECTARIAN

Day	Aspect	Time
1 Th	☽∠☿	4am29
	♀⚺♅	5 36
	☽∥♆	7 38
	☽#♀	9 0
	☽#☿	11 8
	☽∠♀	12pm27
	☽∠♄	12 32
	♀□♄	1 18
	☽⚹♂	5 56
	♀#♆	9 19
	☽⚺♃	11 27
2 F	☽⚹♇	0am 3
	☽☌♆	0 55
	☽#♂	8 1
	☽⚹☿	9 17
	☿#♆	10 4
	☽□♅	2pm 6
	☽⚺♄	2 37
	☽⚹♀	5 7
	☉□☽	6 56
3 S	☽∠♃	2am15
	☉#☽	1pm38
	☿∥♀	11 47
4 Su	☽□♂	1am59
	☽⚹♃	5 52
	☽□♇	5 54
	☽⚺♆	6 45
	☽#♅	7 1
	♃⚺♇	9 0
	☿⚺♅	12pm19
	☿□♄	2 56
	☽△♅	8 54
	☽☌♄	9 7
	☽□☿	9 50
5 M	☽∥♄	2am19
	☽□♀	5 32
	☉△☽	6 10
	☽∠♆	10 46
6 T	☽⚼♅	1am22
	♆ ♏	7 47
	♄△♅	12pm11
	☉⚺♀	12 13
	☉⚼☽	1 3
	☽△♂	1 22
	☽△♇	2 36
	☽∥♄	3 8
	☽□♃	3 14
	☽⚹♆	3 24
7 W	♃ ♎	2am12
	♃⚺♆	3 45
	☽⚺♄	6 17
	☽⚻♅	6 23
	☽#♅	12pm13
	♀∠♆	1 28
	☽△☿	1 29
	♂☌♇	3 7
	☽⚼♇	7 47
	☽⚼♂	8 1
	☉⚻☽	8 35
	☽△♀	9 19
	☉∠♃	11 32
8 Th	♂ ♍	5am28
	♂⚹♆	6 30
	☽∠♄	11 36
	♂⚺♃	4pm18
	☉#☽	8 37
	☽⚼☿	10 4
9 F	☽⚻♇	1am23
	☽□♆	2 7
	☽△♃	2 45
	☽⚻♂	3 10
	☽⚼♀	6 7
	☽⚹♄	5pm18
	☽☍♅	5 44
10 S	☽#♂	4am21
	☽⚻☿	6 58
	☽⚼♃	9 5
	☉☍☽	1pm 9
	☽⚻♀	3 22
	☿∠♆	6 42
	☽∥♆	7 22
11 Su	☽☍♇	1pm32
	☽△♆	2 12
	☽⚻♃	3 43
	☽☍♂	6 34
12 M	☽#♀	3am16
	☽□♄	5 33
	☽⚻♅	6 19
	☽#☿	9 32
	☽⚼♆	8pm34
13 T	☽☍☿	1am14
	☽#♃	4 9
	☉⚻☽	7 1
	☽☍♀	10 46
	☽∥♃	11 17
	☽⚼♅	12pm52
14 W	☽∥☿	0am45
	☽⚻♇	2 26
	☽⚻♆	3 1
	☽☍♃	5 25
	☽∥♀	5 51
	♀∠♅	8 23
	☽⚻♂	10 45
	☉⚼☽	4pm 5
	☽△♄	6 20
	☽△♅	7 23
15 Th	☽⚼♇	8am49
	☽⚼♂	6pm39
	☽⚻☿	6 53
	☽#♆	8 19
16 F	☽⚼♄	0am29
	☉△☽	0 53
	☽∥♂	1 33
	☽⚻♀	6 1
	☽△♇	2pm51
	☽☍♆	3 21
	☽⚻♃	6 33
	☉∥☽	10 21
17 S	☽△♂	2am 4
	☽⚼☿	2 45
	☽⚻♄	6 11
	☽□♅	7 28
	☽⚼♀	2pm45
18 Su	☽⚼♃	0am15
	☽△☿	9 35
	☉□☽	4pm17
	☽△♀	10 24
	☽∥♅	11 55
19 M	☽□♇	0am51
	☽⚻♆	1 16
	☽△♃	5 4
	♇ ♍	5 46
	♂#♆	5 59
	☽□♂	2pm12
	☽☍♄	3 10
	☽⚹♅	4 35
	☿∥♃	11 59
20 T	♀ ♎	0am45
	♀⚺♇	1 17
	☽⚼♆	4 47
	♀⚺♆	5 28
	☿#♃	9 18
	♂□♄	10 35
	☽□☿	7pm17
	☽∠♅	7 37
	☿#♀	11 16
21 W	☉⚹☽	2am58
	☿∠♅	4 34
	☽⚹♇	6 56
	☽△♆	7 16
	☽□♀	9 39
	♀#♃	10 59
	☽□♃	11 27
	♀∥♃	1pm39
	☽⚻♄	8 6
	♂⚺♅	8 20
	☽⚺♅	9 35
	☽⚹♂	9 38
22 Th	☽∥♅	2am43
	☉∠☽	6 24
	☽∠♇	8 26
	♀☌♃	10 27
	☽⚼♄	9pm 7
	☽∠♂	11 42
	☽⚹☿	11 46
23 F	☉⚺☽	8am46
	☽⚺♇	9 5
	☽□♆	9 21
	☉ ♍	10 8
	☉☌♇	1pm41
	☽⚹♃	1 52
	☽⚹♀	3 51
	☿∥♀	5 29
	☉⚹♆	5 52
	☽△♄	9 23
	☽☌♅	10 55
24 S	☽∠☿	0am29
	☽⚺♂	0 56
	☉∥☽	11 4
	☽∠♃	2pm 3
	☽#♆	5 12
	☽∠♀	5 43
25 Su	☽⚺☿	0am36
	☽∥♂	0 39
	☽☌♇	8 45
	☽⚹♆	8 59
	☉☌☽	11 33
	☽⚺♃	1pm55
	☽⚺♀	7 16
	☽□♄	8 43
	☽⚺♅	10 21
26 M	☽☌♂	2am12
	☽#♀	5 42
	☽∠♆	8 33
	☽#☿	9 6
	♀⚹♄	2pm20
	☽#♃	2 59
	☽∥♃	7 3
	☽∠♅	10 3
27 T	☽☌☿	0am 8
	☽∥☿	1 19
	☽∥♀	6 52
	☽⚺♇	8 7
	☿SR	8 7
	☽⚺♆	8 19
	☉⚺♃	10 18
	♀⚹♅	12pm39
	☽☌♃	1 56
	☉⚺☽	2 8
	☉#♆	4 21
	☽⚹♄	8 20
	☽⚹♅	10 7
	☽☌♀	10 54
28 W	☽⚺♂	4am 4
	☽#♂	6 0
	☽∠♇	8 23
	☉#☽	4pm 8
	☉∠☽	4 13
	☽∥♆	6 5
	☽∠♄	8 55
29 Th	☽⚺☿	0am34
	☽∠♂	5 59
	☽⚹♇	9 20
	☽☌♆	9 31
	☽⚺♃	4pm 5
	☉⚹☽	7 13
	☽⚺♄	10 16
30 F	☽□♅	0am16
	☽∠☿	1 36
	☽⚺♀	5 36
	☽⚹♂	8 51
	☽∠♃	6pm27
31 S	☽⚹☿	3am18
	☽∠♀	10 39
	☽#♅	11 1
	☽□♇	1pm52
	☽⚺♆	2 1
	☉□♄	4 45
	☿∠♅	9 37
	☽⚹♃	9 48

SEPTEMBER 1957

LONGITUDE

Day	Sid. Time	☉	☽	☽ 12 Hour	Mean ☊	True ☊	☿	♀	♂	♃	♄	♅	♆	♇
	h m s	° ' "	° ' "	° ' "	° '	° '	° '	° '	° '	° '	° '	° '	° '	° '
1	22 39 34	8♍ 17 15	5♐ 58 35	12♐ 28 53	13♏ 51	12♏ 54R	24♍ 10R	14♎ 18	15♍ 6	4♎ 47	8♐ 0	9♌ 13	0♏ 30	0♍ 25
2	22 43 30	9 15 20	18 53 59	25 14 25	13 47	12 54	23 39	15 29	15 44	5 0	8 2	9 16	0 32	0 27
3	22 47 27	10 13 26	1♑ 30 40	7♑ 43 13	13 44	12 52	23 1	16 40	16 23	5 12	8 4	9 20	0 33	0 29
4	22 51 24	11 11 34	13 52 33	19 59 5	13 41	12 47	22 19	17 52	17 1	5 24	8 6	9 23	0 35	0 31
5	22 55 20	12 9 43	26 3 14	2♒ 5 23	13 38	12 40	21 31	19 3	17 40	5 37	8 9	9 26	0 37	0 33
6	22 59 17	13 7 54	8♒ 5 52	14 4 59	13 35	12 31	20 38	20 14	18 18	5 49	8 11	9 29	0 38	0 35
7	23 3 13	14 6 6	20 2 59	26 0 8	13 31	12 20	19 42	21 25	18 56	6 1	8 13	9 33	0 40	0 37
8	23 7 10	15 4 20	1♓ 56 38	7♓ 52 42	13 28	12 9	18 44	22 36	19 35	6 14	8 16	9 36	0 42	0 39
9	23 11 6	16 2 35	13 48 31	19 44 16	13 25	11 59	17 44	23 47	20 13	6 26	8 19	9 39	0 43	0 41
10	23 15 3	17 0 53	25 40 10	1♈ 36 25	13 22	11 49	16 44	24 58	20 52	6 39	8 21	9 42	0 45	0 43
11	23 18 59	17 59 12	7♈ 33 14	13 30 54	13 19	11 42	15 45	26 9	21 30	6 52	8 24	9 45	0 47	0 45
12	23 22 56	18 57 33	19 29 41	25 29 54	13 16	11 37	14 49	27 20	22 9	7 4	8 27	9 48	0 49	0 47
13	23 26 53	19 55 56	1♉ 31 56	7♉ 36 8	13 12	11 34D	13 56	28 31	22 47	7 17	8 30	9 51	0 50	0 48
14	23 30 49	20 54 21	13 42 58	19 52 52	13 9	11 34	13 9	29 41	23 26	7 29	8 33	9 54	0 52	0 50
15	23 34 46	21 52 49	26 6 21	2♊ 23 54	13 6	11 35	12 29	0♏ 52	24 4	7 42	8 36	9 57	0 54	0 52
16	23 38 42	22 51 18	8♊ 46 2	15 13 16	13 3	11 36	11 56	2 3	24 43	7 55	8 39	10 0	0 56	0 54
17	23 42 39	23 49 50	21 46 5	28 24 54	13 0	11 37R	11 31	3 13	25 22	8 8	8 43	10 3	0 58	0 56
18	23 46 35	24 48 24	5♋ 10 6	12♋ 1 57	12 57	11 36	11 15	4 24	26 0	8 20	8 46	10 6	1 0	0 58
19	23 50 32	25 47 0	19 0 35	26 6 1	12 53	11 34	11 9D	5 34	26 39	8 33	8 50	10 9	1 1	1 0
20	23 54 28	26 45 38	3♌ 18 4	10♌ 36 21	12 50	11 30	11 13	6 44	27 18	8 46	8 53	10 12	1 3	1 1
21	23 58 25	27 44 19	18 0 16	25 29 3	12 47	11 24	11 26	7 55	27 56	8 59	8 57	10 15	1 5	1 3
22	0 2 22	28 43 1	3♍ 1 42	10♍ 37 6	12 44	11 18	11 48	9 5	28 35	9 12	9 0	10 17	1 7	1 5
23	0 6 18	29 41 46	18 13 57	25 50 57	12 41	11 12	12 20	10 15	29 14	9 25	9 4	10 20	1 9	1 7
24	0 10 15	0♎ 40 33	3♎ 26 45	11♎ 0 5	12 37	11 7	13 2	11 25	29 53	9 37	9 8	10 23	1 11	1 9
25	0 14 11	1 39 21	18 29 45	25 54 45	12 34	11 3	13 51	12 35	0♎ 31	9 50	9 12	10 25	1 13	1 10
26	0 18 8	2 38 12	3♏ 14 13	10♏ 27 31	12 31	11 1D	14 48	13 45	1 10	10 3	9 16	10 28	1 15	1 12
27	0 22 4	3 37 4	17 34 11	24 33 59	12 28	11 1	15 53	14 55	1 49	10 16	9 20	10 31	1 17	1 14
28	0 26 1	4 35 59	1♐ 26 50	8♐ 12 50	12 25	11 2	17 4	16 5	2 28	10 29	9 25	10 33	1 19	1 16
29	0 29 57	5 34 55	14 52 11	21 25 14	12 22	11 4	18 21	17 15	3 7	10 42	9 29	10 36	1 21	1 17
30	0 33 54	6♎ 33 53	27♐ 52 23	4♑ 14 6	12♏ 18	11♏ 5R	19♍ 44	18♏ 25	3♎ 46	10♎ 55	9♐ 33	10♌ 38	1♏ 23	1♍ 19

DECLINATION and LATITUDE

Day	☉ Decl	☽ Decl	☽ Lat	☽ 12 Hr. Decl	☿ Decl	☿ Lat	♀ Decl	♀ Lat	♂ Decl	♂ Lat	♃ Decl	♃ Lat	♄ Decl	♄ Lat
1	8N28	19S21	1N60	19S48	1S44	4S25	5S24	0N15	6N48	1N 0	0S52	1N 7	20S 5	1N35
2	8 6	19 60	2 60	19 56	1 33	4 26	5 55	0 12	6 33	0 60	0 57	1 7	20 5	1 35
3	7 44	19 37	3 49	19 4	1 18	4 25	6 25	0 8	6 17	0 59	1 2	1 7	20 6	1 35
4	7 22	18 18	4 27	17 20	0 59	4 23	6 56	0 5	6 2	0 59	1 7	1 7	20 6	1 35
5	7 0	16 10	4 52	14 50	0 36	4 19	7 26	0 2	5 47	0 59	1 12	1 7	20 7	1 35
6	6 38	13 22	5 3	11 45	0 11	4 14	7 56	0S 2	5 32	0 59	1 17	1 7	20 7	1 34
7	6 15	10 2	5 1	8 13	0N18	4 6	8 26	0 5	5 16	0 58	1 22	1 7	20 8	1 34
8	5 53	6 19	4 46	4 22	0 50	3 56	8 56	0 9	5 1	0 58	1 27	1 7	20 9	1 34
9	5 30	2 23	4 19	0 22	1 24	3 44	9 25	0 12	4 46	0 58	1 32	1 7	20 9	1 34
10	5 8	1N39	3 41	3N40	1 60	3 31	9 55	0 16	4 30	0 57	1 37	1 7	20 10	1 34
11	4 45	5 38	2 52	7 34	2 36	3 16	10 24	0 19	4 15	0 57	1 42	1 7	20 11	1 33
12	4 22	9 25	1 56	11 11	3 13	2 59	10 53	0 23	3 59	0 57	1 47	1 7	20 11	1 33
13	3 59	12 51	0 54	14 23	3 50	2 42	11 22	0 26	3 44	0 56	1 52	1 7	20 12	1 33
14	3 36	15 47	0S12	16 60	4 25	2 23	11 50	0 30	3 28	0 56	1 57	1 7	20 13	1 33
15	3 13	18 2	1 18	18 51	4 58	2 4	12 18	0 34	3 12	0 56	2 2	1 7	20 13	1 32
16	2 50	19 26	2 21	19 47	5 29	1 44	12 46	0 37	2 57	0 55	2 7	1 7	20 14	1 32
17	2 27	19 52	3 20	19 40	5 57	1 24	13 14	0 41	2 41	0 55	2 12	1 7	20 15	1 32
18	2 4	19 12	4 9	18 26	6 21	1 4	13 42	0 45	2 26	0 55	2 17	1 7	20 15	1 32
19	1 41	17 23	4 46	16 3	6 41	0 45	14 9	0 49	2 10	0 54	2 22	1 7	20 16	1 32
20	1 17	14 28	5 6	12 37	6 57	0 27	14 36	0 52	1 54	0 54	2 27	1 6	20 17	1 31
21	0 54	10 34	5 7	8 19	7 9	0 9	15 2	0 56	1 39	0 54	2 33	1 6	20 18	1 31
22	0 31	5 55	4 47	3 25	7 15	0N 8	15 28	0 60	1 23	0 53	2 38	1 6	20 18	1 31
23	0 7	0 51	4 7	1S43	7 18	0 23	15 54	1 4	1 7	0 53	2 43	1 6	20 19	1 31
24	0S16	4S16	3 10	6 45	7 15	0 38	16 20	1 7	0 51	0 53	2 48	1 6	20 20	1 31
25	0 40	9 5	1 59	11 16	7 8	0 51	16 45	1 11	0 36	0 52	2 53	1 6	20 21	1 30
26	1 3	13 15	0 42	15 1	6 57	1 3	17 10	1 15	0 20	0 52	2 58	1 6	20 21	1 30
27	1 26	16 30	0N36	17 44	6 42	1 14	17 34	1 19	0 4	0 52	3 3	1 6	20 22	1 30
28	1 50	18 40	1 49	19 20	6 23	1 23	17 58	1 22	0S12	0 51	3 8	1 6	20 23	1 30
29	2 13	19 42	2 54	19 48	6 0	1 31	18 22	1 26	0 28	0 51	3 13	1 6	20 24	1 30
30	2S36	19S38	3N48	19S12	5N34	1N38	18S45	1S30	0S43	0N51	3S18	1N 6	20S25	1N30

Day	♅ Decl	♅ Lat	♆ Decl	♆ Lat	♇ Decl	♇ Lat
1	18N32	0N36	10S 3	1N43	21N35	10N60
5	18 28	0 36	10 5	1 43	21 32	11 0
9	18 25	0 36	10 7	1 43	21 30	11 1
13	18 22	0 36	10 10	1 43	21 28	11 1
17	18 19	0 36	10 13	1 42	21 26	11 2
21	18 16	0 36	10 15	1 42	21 24	11 3
25	18 13	0 36	10 18	1 42	21 22	11 4
29	18N10	0N37	10S21	1N42	21N20	11N 5

☽ PHENOMENA

d	h	m	
1	4	35	☽
9	4	56	○
17	4	2	☾
23	19	19	●
30	17	50	☽

d	h	° '
2	3	20S 0
9	14	0
16	22	19N52
23	4	0
29	10	19S48
6	9	5N 4
13	20	0
20	13	5S 9
26	13	0

VOID OF COURSE ☽

Last Aspect		☽ Ingress		
2	8am34	2	♑	9pm 6
4	3pm35	5	♒	7am50
7	3am 4	7	♓	8pm 4
9	1pm43	10	♈	8am45
12	5pm21	12	♉	8pm58
14	7pm53	15	♊	7am27
17	6am50	17	♋	2pm50
19	1pm32	19	♌	6pm31
20	11am22	21	♍	7pm12
23	6pm 6	23	♎	6pm33
24	11am 3	25	♏	6pm41
26	8pm54	27	♐	9pm28
29	7am 5	30	♑	4am 0

d	h	
8	17	APOGEE
23	5	PERIGEE

DAILY ASPECTARIAN

Day	Aspect	Time
1 Su	☽☌♄	3am44
	☉□☽	4 35
	☽△♅	5 59
	♂∠♆	3pm48
	☽⚹♀	4 56
	☽∠♆	5 40
	☽□♂	5 46
	♀∠♇	11 22
2 M	☉⚺♅	0am26
	☽□☿	8 34
	☽⚼♅	10 12
	♀⚺♂	11 15
	♀⋕♂	7pm44
	☽△♇	10 1
	☽⚹♆	10 10
3 T	☽□♃	7am14
	☽⚺♄	12pm43
	☽⚻♅	3 11
	☿∥♃	4 3
	☉△☽	6 19
	☽⋕♅	9 21
4 W	☽⚼♇	3am14
	☽△♂	6 30
	☽□♀	8 40
	☉⋕♀	12pm 5
	☽△☿	3 35
	☽∠♄	6 13
5 Th	☉⚼☽	2am23
	☽⚻♇	8 57
	☽□♆	9 4
	☽⚼♂	1pm52
	☽△♃	7 22
	☽⚼☿	7 26
6 F	☽⚹♄	0am10
	☽☍♅	2 48
	☿⚺♀	4 39
	☉⚻☽	10 59
	☽⚻♂	9pm38
	☽⚻☿	11 22
	☽∥♆	11 31
7 S	☽⚼♃	2am 0
	☽△♀	3 4
	☽∥♀	9 20
	☿☌♂	11 28
	☽☍♇	9pm22
	☽△♆	9 28
8 Su	☉⋕☽	3am 2
	☽⋕♂	8 38
	☽⚻♃	8 50
	☽⚼♀	12pm43
	☽□♄	12 50
	♀∠♄	1 59
	☽⚻♅	3 33
	☉∠♆	3 50
9 M	☽⚼♆	3am53
	☉☍☽	4 56
	☽∥♃	4 57
	☽⋕☿	5 5
	☿⋕♃	6 11
	☽☍☿	7 19
	☽☍♂	1pm43
	☉☌☿	8 33
	☽⚼♅	10 2
	☽⚻♀	10 26
	☽⋕♃	11 47
10 T	☽∥☿	2am25
	☽⚻♇	10 13
	☽⚻♆	10 18
	♀∥♆	11 16
	☽∥♂	4pm 3
	☉∥☽	7 4
	☽☍♃	10 34
	☿∠♆	11 17
11 W	☽△♄	1am43
	☽△♅	4 27
	☽⚻☿	3pm17
	☽⚼♇	4 31
	☉⚻☽	10 50
12 Th	☽⋕♆	4am56
	☽⚻♂	5 36
	☽⚼♄	7 57
	☽⋕♀	11 27
	☽☍♀	5pm21
	☽⚼☿	7 11
	☿∥♂	9 6
	☽△♇	10 33
	☽☍♆	10 37
13 F	☉∥☿	3am52
	☿∠♀	5 10
	☉⚼☽	7 19
	☽⚻♃	11 34
	☽⚼♂	1pm 3
	☽⚻♄	1 49
	☽□♅	4 30
	☽△☿	10 58
14 S	♀ ♏	6am20
	☉△☽	3pm11
	☽⚼♃	5 20
	☽△♂	7 53
15 Su	♀⚹♇	0am 4
	♀☌♆	0 40
	☉∥♂	2 34
	☽∥♅	4 9
	☽□♇	9 7
	☽⚻♆	9 11
	☽⚻♀	10 2
	☽△♃	10pm22
	☽☍♄	11 47
16 M	☽⚹♅	2am19
	☽□☿	5 42
	♂∠♅	11 41
	☽⚼♆	1pm20
	☽⚼♀	4 53
17 T	☉□☽	4am 2
	☽∠♅	5 59
	☽□♂	6 50
	☉⋕♃	12pm33
	☽⚹♇	4 32
	☽△♆	4 35
	☽△♀	10 30
18 W	☽□♃	5am39
	☽⚻♄	6 21
	☉∠♅	7 40
	☽⚺♅	8 41
	♂⋕♃	9 35
	☽⚹☿	10 32
	☽∥♅	1pm47
	☽∠♇	6 49
19 Th	☿SD	3am31
	☽⚼♄	8 12
	☽∠☿	12pm 6
	☉⚹☽	12 18
	☽⚹♂	1 32
	☽⚺♇	8 13
	☽□♆	8 16
	☽⋕♀	11 10
20 F	☽□♀	6am10
	☽⚹♃	9 7
	☽△♄	9 13
	☽☌♅	11 22
	☽⚺☿	1pm 9
	☉∠☽	2 52
	☽∠♂	3 25
	♃⚹♄	6 41
21 S	☽⋕♆	1am41
	☽∠♃	9 44
	☉☌♂	2pm29
	☽⚺♂	4 38
	☉⚺☽	4 41
	☽∥☿	5 31
	☽☌♇	8 55
	☽⚹♆	8 58
	♀⚺♄	10 22
22 Su	♀⚺♃	2am46
	☽□♄	9 30
	☽⚺♃	9 53
	☽⚹♀	10 23
	☽⚺♅	11 31
	☽☌☿	2pm21
	☽⋕♃	3 29
	☽∠♆	8 43
	☽∥♂	10 44
23 M	♀□♅	1am45
	☉∥☽	3 42
	☉⋕☽	4 14
	☉ ♎	7 27
	☽⋕♂	8 44
	☽∠♅	11 13
	☽∠♀	11 59
	☽∥♃	4pm55
	☽☌♂	6 6
	☉☌☽	7 19
	☽⚺♇	8 21
	☽⚺♆	8 25
24 T	♂ ♎	4am32
	☽⚹♄	9 4
	☽☌♃	9 57
	☽⚹♅	11 3
	☉⚺♇	11 48
	☉⚺♆	12pm56
	☽⚺♀	1 44
	☽⋕☿	2 16
	☽⚺☿	4 5
	☽∠♇	8 16
	☉⋕♂	9 35
25 W	☽∥♆	6am34
	☽∠♄	9 16
	☽∠☿	5pm57
	☽⚺♂	8 27
	☽⚹♇	8 39
	☽☌♆	8 44
	☉⚺☽	10 56
26 Th	♂⚺♇	1am 9
	♂⚺♆	3 9
	☽⚺♄	10 4
	☽⚺♃	11 30
	☽□♅	12pm 3
	☽☌♀	7 7
	☽⚹☿	8 54
	☽∠♂	10 40
27 F	☉∠☽	1am55
	☿∠♆	8 38
	☽∥♀	12pm33
	☽∠♃	1 26
	☽⋕♅	5 20
	☽□♇	11 40
	☽⚺♆	11 47
28 S	☽⚹♂	1am53
	☉⚹☽	6 0
	♃⚹♅	9 27
	♀⋕♅	12pm32
	☽☌♄	2 13
	☽△♅	4 15
	☽⚹♃	4 20
29 Su	☽∠♆	2am43
	☽⚺♀	4 45
	☽□☿	7 5
	☽⚼♅	7pm48
30 M	☽△♇	6am29
	☽⚹♆	6 38
	☽∠♀	11 29
	☽□♂	11 43
	☽∥♀	4pm10
	♀∠♂	4 43
	☉□☽	5 50
	☽⚺♄	10 17
30	☽□♅	0am16

OCTOBER 1957

LONGITUDE

Day	Sid. Time	☉	☽	☽ 12 Hour	Mean ☊	True ☊	☿	♀	♂	♃	♄	♅	♆	♇
	h m s	° ' "	° ' "	° ' "	° '	° '	° '	° '	° '	° '	° '	° '	° '	° '
1	0 37 51	7♎ 32 52	10♑ 30 54	16♑ 43 19	12♏ 15	11♏ 5R	21♍ 11	19♏ 34	4♎ 25	11♎ 8	9♐ 38	10♌ 41	1♏ 25	1♍ 21
2	0 41 47	8 31 54	22 51 54	28 57 11	12 12	11 4	22 41	20 44	5 4	11 21	9 42	10 43	1 28	1 22
3	0 45 44	9 30 57	4♒ 59 42	10♒ 59 58	12 9	11 1	24 16	21 53	5 43	11 34	9 47	10 45	1 30	1 24
4	0 49 40	10 30 1	16 58 28	22 55 38	12 6	10 57	25 52	23 2	6 22	11 47	9 51	10 48	1 32	1 26
5	0 53 37	11 29 8	28 51 54	4♓ 47 38	12 3	10 53	27 32	24 12	7 1	12 0	9 56	10 50	1 34	1 27
6	0 57 33	12 28 17	10♓ 43 12	16 38 55	11 59	10 48	29 13	25 21	7 40	12 13	10 1	10 52	1 36	1 29
7	1 1 30	13 27 27	22 35 5	28 31 56	11 56	10 43	0♎ 55	26 30	8 19	12 26	10 6	10 54	1 38	1 30
8	1 5 26	14 26 39	4♈ 29 44	10♈ 28 43	11 53	10 38	2 38	27 39	8 58	12 39	10 11	10 56	1 40	1 32
9	1 9 23	15 25 53	16 29 4	22 31 0	11 50	10 35	4 23	28 48	9 37	12 52	10 15	10 58	1 42	1 33
10	1 13 19	16 25 10	28 34 44	4♉ 40 28	11 47	10 33	6 7	29 56	10 17	13 5	10 21	11 0	1 45	1 35
11	1 17 16	17 24 28	10♉ 48 25	16 58 49	11 43	10 33D	7 52	1♐ 5	10 56	13 18	10 26	11 2	1 47	1 36
12	1 21 13	18 23 49	23 11 53	29 27 55	11 40	10 33	9 38	2 13	11 35	13 31	10 31	11 4	1 49	1 38
13	1 25 9	19 23 12	5♊ 47 10	12♊ 9 54	11 37	10 34	11 23	3 22	12 14	13 44	10 36	11 6	1 51	1 39
14	1 29 6	20 22 37	18 36 27	25 7 5	11 34	10 36	13 8	4 30	12 54	13 57	10 41	11 8	1 53	1 41
15	1 33 2	21 22 5	1♋ 42 5	8♋ 21 44	11 31	10 37	14 52	5 38	13 33	14 10	10 47	11 10	1 56	1 42
16	1 36 59	22 21 34	15 6 14	21 55 47	11 28	10 38R	16 37	6 46	14 12	14 23	10 52	11 12	1 58	1 44
17	1 40 55	23 21 7	28 50 30	5♌ 50 23	11 24	10 38	18 20	7 54	14 52	14 36	10 58	11 13	2 0	1 45
18	1 44 52	24 20 41	12♌ 55 21	20 5 14	11 21	10 37	20 4	9 2	15 31	14 48	11 3	11 15	2 2	1 46
19	1 48 48	25 20 18	27 19 39	4♍ 38 10	11 18	10 36	21 47	10 10	16 10	15 1	11 9	11 17	2 4	1 48
20	1 52 45	26 19 56	12♍ 0 9	19 24 50	11 15	10 34	23 29	11 17	16 50	15 14	11 14	11 18	2 7	1 49
21	1 56 42	27 19 38	26 51 24	4♎ 18 52	11 12	10 32	25 11	12 25	17 29	15 27	11 20	11 20	2 9	1 50
22	2 0 38	28 19 21	11♎ 46 15	19 12 30	11 9	10 31	26 52	13 32	18 9	15 40	11 26	11 21	2 11	1 51
23	2 4 35	29 19 6	26 36 37	3♏ 57 38	11 5	10 30D	28 33	14 39	18 48	15 53	11 32	11 22	2 13	1 53
24	2 8 31	0♏ 18 54	11♏ 14 40	18 27 0	11 2	10 30	0♏ 13	15 46	19 28	16 6	11 38	11 24	2 16	1 54
25	2 12 28	1 18 43	25 33 58	2♐ 35 8	10 59	10 30	1 53	16 53	20 8	16 18	11 43	11 25	2 18	1 55
26	2 16 24	2 18 35	9♐ 30 9	16 18 52	10 56	10 31	3 32	18 0	20 47	16 31	11 49	11 26	2 20	1 56
27	2 20 21	3 18 28	23 1 15	29 37 25	10 53	10 32	5 10	19 6	21 27	16 44	11 55	11 28	2 22	1 57
28	2 24 17	4 18 22	6♑ 7 34	12♑ 32 0	10 49	10 32	6 48	20 13	22 7	16 57	12 2	11 29	2 25	1 59
29	2 28 14	5 18 19	18 51 9	25 5 27	10 46	10 33	8 25	21 19	22 46	17 9	12 8	11 30	2 27	2 0
30	2 32 11	6 18 17	1♒ 15 25	7♒ 21 35	10 43	10 33R	10 2	22 25	23 26	17 22	12 14	11 31	2 29	2 1
31	2 36 7	7♏ 18 16	13♒ 24 32	19♒ 24 50	10♏ 40	10♏ 33	11♏ 39	23♐ 30	24♎ 6	17♎ 35	12♐ 20	11♌ 32	2♏ 31	2♍ 2

DECLINATION and LATITUDE

Day	☉ Decl	☽ Decl	☽ Lat	☽ 12 Hr. Decl	☿ Decl	☿ Lat	♀ Decl	♀ Lat	♂ Decl	♂ Lat	♃ Decl	♃ Lat	♄ Decl	♄ Lat
1	2S60	18S33	4N29	17S41	5N 5	1N43	19S 8	1S33	0S59	0N50	3S23	1N 6	20S26	1N29
2	3 23	16 37	4 57	15 23	4 33	1 48	19 30	1 37	1 15	0 50	3 28	1 6	20 26	1 29
3	3 46	13 60	5 11	12 28	3 59	1 51	19 52	1 41	1 31	0 50	3 34	1 6	20 27	1 29
4	4 9	10 49	5 11	9 3	3 23	1 54	20 13	1 44	1 46	0 49	3 39	1 6	20 28	1 29
5	4 33	7 13	4 57	5 19	2 45	1 55	20 34	1 48	2 2	0 49	3 44	1 6	20 29	1 29
6	4 56	3 22	4 31	1 22	2 5	1 56	20 55	1 52	2 18	0 48	3 49	1 6	20 30	1 28
7	5 19	0N38	3 53	2N38	1 24	1 55	21 15	1 55	2 34	0 48	3 54	1 6	20 31	1 28
8	5 42	4 37	3 5	6 34	0 42	1 54	21 34	1 59	2 50	0 48	3 59	1 6	20 32	1 28
9	6 5	8 28	2 9	10 16	0S 1	1 53	21 53	2 2	3 5	0 47	4 4	1 6	20 33	1 28
10	6 27	11 59	1 5	13 35	0 45	1 50	22 11	2 6	3 21	0 47	4 9	1 6	20 33	1 28
11	6 50	15 3	0S 1	16 21	1 29	1 48	22 29	2 9	3 37	0 47	4 14	1 6	20 34	1 28
12	7 13	17 28	1 9	18 22	2 13	1 44	22 46	2 12	3 52	0 46	4 19	1 6	20 35	1 27
13	7 35	19 4	2 15	19 31	2 58	1 40	23 3	2 16	4 8	0 46	4 24	1 6	20 36	1 27
14	7 58	19 43	3 15	19 40	3 42	1 36	23 19	2 19	4 24	0 45	4 29	1 6	20 37	1 27
15	8 20	19 20	4 6	18 44	4 27	1 32	23 35	2 22	4 39	0 45	4 34	1 6	20 38	1 27
16	8 42	17 52	4 45	16 44	5 12	1 27	23 50	2 25	4 55	0 45	4 39	1 6	20 39	1 27
17	9 4	15 21	5 10	13 43	5 56	1 21	24 4	2 28	5 11	0 44	4 44	1 6	20 40	1 27
18	9 26	11 53	5 16	9 51	6 40	1 16	24 18	2 31	5 26	0 44	4 49	1 6	20 41	1 26
19	9 48	7 39	5 3	5 20	7 24	1 10	24 31	2 34	5 42	0 43	4 54	1 6	20 42	1 26
20	10 10	2 54	4 30	0 25	8 8	1 4	24 44	2 37	5 57	0 43	4 59	1 6	20 43	1 26
21	10 31	2S 6	3 39	4S35	8 51	0 58	24 56	2 40	6 13	0 43	5 4	1 6	20 43	1 26
22	10 53	6 60	2 33	9 18	9 33	0 52	25 7	2 43	6 28	0 42	5 9	1 6	20 44	1 26
23	11 14	11 27	1 16	13 25	10 15	0 46	25 18	2 45	6 44	0 42	5 14	1 7	20 45	1 26
24	11 35	15 9	0N 4	16 37	10 56	0 39	25 28	2 48	6 59	0 41	5 19	1 7	20 46	1 26
25	11 56	17 49	1 23	18 44	11 37	0 33	25 38	2 50	7 14	0 41	5 23	1 7	20 47	1 25
26	12 17	19 21	2 34	19 40	12 17	0 26	25 46	2 53	7 30	0 40	5 28	1 7	20 48	1 25
27	12 37	19 41	3 35	19 26	12 57	0 19	25 54	2 55	7 45	0 40	5 33	1 7	20 49	1 25
28	12 58	18 56	4 22	18 12	13 35	0 13	26 2	2 57	7 60	0 40	5 38	1 7	20 50	1 25
29	13 18	17 15	4 55	16 6	14 13	0 6	26 9	2 60	8 15	0 39	5 43	1 7	20 51	1 25
30	13 38	14 47	5 13	13 19	14 51	0S 1	26 15	3 2	8 30	0 39	5 47	1 7	20 52	1 25
31	13S57	11S44	5N17	10S 2	15S27	0S 8	26S20	3S 4	8S45	0N38	5S52	1N 7	20S53	1N25

Day	♅ Decl	♅ Lat	♆ Decl	♆ Lat	♇ Decl	♇ Lat
1	18N 9	0N37	10S23	1N42	21N20	11N 5
5	18 7	0 37	10 26	1 42	21 18	11 6
9	18 4	0 37	10 29	1 42	21 17	11 8
13	18 2	0 37	10 32	1 42	21 16	11 9
17	18 1	0 37	10 35	1 42	21 15	11 10
21	17 59	0 37	10 38	1 42	21 14	11 11
25	17 58	0 37	10 41	1 42	21 14	11 13
29	17N56	0N38	10S44	1N42	21N13	11N14

☽ PHENOMENA

d	h	m	
8	21	43	○
16	13	44	☾
23	4	44	●
30	10	48	☽

d	h	° '
6	20	0
14	3	19N44
20	14	0
26	19	19S42

d	h	
3	12	5N12
11	0	0
17	20	5S16
23	23	0
30	18	5N17

VOID OF COURSE ☽

Last Aspect		☽ Ingress		
1	11pm37	2	♒	2pm 4
4	1pm33	5	♓	2am18
7	8am45	7	♈	2pm57
8	9pm43	10	♉	2am48
11	0am27	12	♊	1pm 1
14	3am33	14	♋	8pm55
16	1pm44	17	♌	2am 0
18	8pm28	19	♍	4am24
19	10pm45	21	♎	5am 4
23	4am44	23	♏	5am31
24	0am15	25	♐	7am34
26	9pm 1	27	♑	12pm41
29	7am56	29	♒	9pm33

d	h	
5	22	APOGEE
21	13	PERIGEE

DAILY ASPECTARIAN

Day	Aspect	Time
1 T	☽⚻♅	0am19
	☽□♃	1 13
	☽⋕♅	5 59
	☽⚼♇	11 17
	☽⚹♀	7pm23
	☽△☿	11 37
2 W	☽∠♄	3am38
	☉∥♃	7 12
	☽⚻♇	4pm50
	☽□♆	5 1
3 Th	☽△♂	1am31
	☉⋕☿	5 11
	☉⚹♄	6 55
	☽⚹♄	9 37
	☉△☽	9 50
	☽⚼☿	9 50
	☽☍♅	11 33
	☽△♃	1pm23
	☿⋕♃	2 52
	☿∠♅	10 47
4 F	☽∥♆	2am45
	☉⚹♅	7 24
	☽⚼♂	9 22
	☽□♀	1pm33
	♀∥♄	5 44
	☉⚼☽	6 45
	☽⚼♃	8 9
	☽⚻☿	8 51
5 S	☽☍♇	5am15
	☽△♆	5 29
	☉∥☽	3pm16
	☉☌♃	4 2
	☽⚻♂	5 27
	☿⋕♂	6 23
	☽∥♃	9 19
	☽□♄	10 33
6 Su	☽⚻♅	0am18
	☽⚻♃	3 5
	☉⚻☽	3 52
	☽∥♂	6 2
	☽⋕☿	9 19
	☿ ♎	11 9
	☽⚼♆	11 56
7 M	♀⋕♇	3am39
	☽∥☿	3 55
	☽⚼♅	6 43
	☿⚺♇	8 21
	☽△♀	8 45
	☿⚺♆	10 15
	☽⋕♂	12pm23
	☽⚻♇	6 2
	☽⚻♆	6 18
	☽☍☿	7 38
	☽⋕♃	8 2
8 T	♀∠♃	0am 2
	☉⋕☽	7 18
	☽☍♂	9 30
	☽△♄	11 28
	☽△♅	12pm57
	☽☍♃	4 38
	☽⚼♀	6 4
	☉☍☽	9 43
9 W	☽⚼♇	0am 9
	☽⋕♆	1pm25
	☽⚼♄	5 33
10 Th	♀ ♐	1am16
	♂⚹♄	2 49
	☽⚻♀	2 58
	☉∠♇	4 3
	☽△♇	5 56
	☽☍♆	6 15
	☽⚻☿	5pm19
	☽⚻♄	11 15
11 F	☽⚻♂	0am15
	☽□♅	0 27
	♂⚹♅	4 16
	☽⚻♃	4 56
	♀□♇	11 15
	☉⚻☽	1pm56
	♀⚺♆	3 8
12 S	☽⚼☿	3am11
	☽⚼♂	6 51
	☽∥♅	7 22
	☽⚼♃	10 22
	☿⚹♄	12pm48
	☽□♇	4 9
	☽⚻♆	4 31
	☽☍♀	6 58
	☿⚹♅	8 10
	☉⚼☽	9 8
13 Su	☽☍♄	9am 8
	☽⚹♅	10 2
	☽△☿	12pm11
	☽△♂	12 47
	☽△♃	3 11
	☿☌♂	6 51
	☽⚼♆	8 48
14 M	☉△☽	3am33
	♂∥♃	11 58
	☿☌♃	12pm51
	☽∠♅	1 54
15 T	☽⚹♇	0am 0
	☽△♆	0 25
	☿∥♃	4 8
	☽⚻♀	7 46
	☿∥♂	10 3
	☽⚻♄	4pm26
	☽⚺♅	5 3
	☽∥♅	10 6
	☽□♂	10 19
	☽□♃	10 42
16 W	☿∠♇	1am39
	☽∠♇	2 52
	☽□☿	3 3
	♂☌♃	9 30
	☽⚼♀	12pm47
	☉□☽	1 44
	☽⚼♄	6 59
17 Th	☽⚺♇	5am 1
	☽□♆	5 27
	☽△♀	4pm52
	☽△♄	8 49
	☽☌♅	9 10
18 F	☽⚹♃	3am13
	☽⚹♂	4 34
	☽⋕♆	7 43
	☉⋕☽	1pm11
	☽⚹☿	1 35
	☉⚹☽	8 28
19 S	☽⋕☿	1am 8
	☽∠♃	4 30
	☽∠♂	6 37
	☽☌♇	7 21
	☽⚹♆	7 50
	☽⋕♂	9 36
	☽⋕♃	1pm54
	☽∠☿	5 32
	☉∠♄	9 33
	☽□♄	10 45
	☽□♀	10 45
	♀☌♄	10 50
	☉∠☽	10 50
	☽⚺♅	10 52
	♂∠♇	11 26
20 Su	♀△♅	0am15
	☽⚺♃	5 19
	☉∠♀	7 48
	☽⚺♂	8 11
	☽∠♆	8 18
	☽⚺☿	8pm58
	♄△♅	9 4
	☽∠♅	11 9
21 M	☉⚺☽	0am49
	☉∥♆	7 22
	☽⚺♇	8 2
	☽⚺♆	8 32
	☽∥♃	2pm36
	☿∠♄	5 21
	☽∥♂	9 11
	☽⚹♅	11 19
	☽⚹♄	11 27
22 T	☽⚹♀	3am 4
	☽☌♃	6 22
	☽∠♇	8 13
	☽☌♂	10 46
	☽∥☿	3pm54
	☽∥♆	7 26
	☉∥☽	10 38
	☽∠♄	11 52
23 W	☽☌☿	3am34
	☉☌☽	4 44
	☽∠♀	5 22
	☽⚹♇	8 36
	☽☌♆	9 11
	☿∥♆	2pm17
	☉ ♏	4 25
	☿ ♏	8 51
24 Th	☽□♅	0am15
	☽⚺♄	0 38
	☉☌☿	3 29
	☽⚺♀	8 9
	☽⚺♃	8 11
	♀⚹♃	8 37
	☽⚺♂	2pm22
25 F	☿∠♀	0am18
	☿⚹♇	0 36
	☽⋕♅	1 38
	☿☌♆	6 15
	♀∠♆	9 15
	☽∠♃	9 57
	☉⚺☽	10 34
	☽□♇	10 52
	☽⚺♆	11 32
	☽⚺☿	12pm14
	☉⚹♇	2 53
	☽∠♂	5 13
	☉∥☿	11 12
26 S	☉☌♆	0am40
	☽△♅	3 24
	☽☌♄	4 6
	☽⚹♃	12pm34
	☽∠♆	1 51
	☉∠☽	2 52
	☽☌♀	4 20
	☽∠☿	6 10
	☽⚹♂	9 1
27 Su	☽⚼♅	6am14
	☽△♇	4pm19
	☽⚹♆	5 6
	☉⚹☽	8 21
28 M	☽⚹☿	1am26
	♃∠♇	3 44
	☽⚻♅	10 2
	☽⚺♄	11 8
	☽⋕♅	3pm30
	☽⚼♇	8 27
	☽□♃	8 43
29 T	☽⚺♀	5am10
	☽□♂	7 56
	☽∠♄	4pm 5
	☽∥☿	11 34
30 W	☽⚻♇	1am29
	☽□♆	2 25
	☉∥☽	8 39
	☉□☽	10 48
	☽∠♀	1pm18
	☽□☿	7 57
	☽☍♅	8 15
	☽⚹♄	9 51
	☿□♅	10 14
31 Th	☽∥♆	6am56
	☽△♃	8 28
	☿⚺♄	11 2
	☽∥♂	7pm16
	☽⚹♀	10 16
	☽△♂	10 40

NOVEMBER 1957

LONGITUDE

Day	Sid. Time h m s	☉ ° ' "	☽ ° ' "	☽ 12 Hour ° ' "	Mean ☊ ° '	True ☊ ° '	☿ ° '	♀ ° '	♂ ° '	♃ ° '	♄ ° '	♅ ° '	♆ ° '	♇ ° '
1	2 40 4	8♏ 18 18	25♒ 23 4	1♓ 19 47	10♏ 37	10♏ 33R	13♏ 15	24♐ 36	24♎ 46	17♎ 47	12♐ 26	11♌ 33	2♏ 34	2♍ 3
2	2 44 0	9 18 21	7♓ 15 33	13 10 55	10 34	10 33D	14 50	25 41	25 25	18 0	12 33	11 34	2 36	2 4
3	2 47 57	10 18 25	19 6 22	25 2 23	10 30	10 33	16 25	26 47	26 5	18 12	12 39	11 34	2 38	2 5
4	2 51 53	11 18 31	0♈ 59 25	6♈ 57 52	10 27	10 33	18 0	27 51	26 45	18 25	12 45	11 35	2 40	2 6
5	2 55 50	12 18 39	12 58 6	19 0 27	10 24	10 33	19 34	28 56	27 25	18 37	12 52	11 36	2 43	2 6
6	2 59 46	13 18 48	25 5 11	1♉ 12 34	10 21	10 33	21 8	0♑ 1	28 5	18 50	12 58	11 36	2 45	2 7
7	3 3 43	14 19 0	7♉ 22 48	13 36 2	10 18	10 33R	22 41	1 5	28 45	19 2	13 5	11 37	2 47	2 8
8	3 7 40	15 19 12	19 52 25	26 12 2	10 14	10 33	24 14	2 9	29 25	19 14	13 11	11 38	2 49	2 9
9	3 11 36	16 19 27	2♊ 34 58	9♊ 1 15	10 11	10 33	25 47	3 12	0♏ 5	19 27	13 18	11 38	2 51	2 10
10	3 15 33	17 19 44	15 30 54	22 3 55	10 8	10 32	27 19	4 16	0 45	19 39	13 24	11 39	2 54	2 10
11	3 19 29	18 20 2	28 40 18	5♋ 20 0	10 5	10 31	28 51	5 19	1 25	19 51	13 31	11 39	2 56	2 11
12	3 23 26	19 20 22	12♋ 3 1	18 49 17	10 2	10 30	0♐ 23	6 22	2 5	20 3	13 38	11 39	2 58	2 12
13	3 27 22	20 20 45	25 38 45	2♌ 31 21	9 59	10 29	1 54	7 24	2 45	20 15	13 44	11 40	3 0	2 13
14	3 31 19	21 21 9	9♌ 27 0	16 25 35	9 55	10 28D	3 25	8 26	3 25	20 27	13 51	11 40	3 2	2 13
15	3 35 15	22 21 35	23 26 59	0♍ 31 1	9 52	10 28	4 56	9 28	4 6	20 39	13 58	11 40	3 4	2 14
16	3 39 12	23 22 3	7♍ 37 29	14 46 7	9 49	10 28	6 26	10 30	4 46	20 51	14 5	11 40	3 7	2 14
17	3 43 9	24 22 32	21 56 35	29 8 31	9 46	10 29	7 57	11 31	5 26	21 3	14 11	11 40R	3 9	2 15
18	3 47 5	25 23 4	6♎ 21 29	13♎ 34 59	9 43	10 31	9 26	12 32	6 7	21 15	14 18	11 40	3 11	2 15
19	3 51 2	26 23 38	20 48 28	28 1 19	9 40	10 32	10 56	13 33	6 47	21 27	14 25	11 40	3 13	2 16
20	3 54 58	27 24 13	5♏ 12 56	12♏ 22 40	9 36	10 32R	12 25	14 33	7 27	21 39	14 32	11 40	3 15	2 16
21	3 58 55	28 24 49	19 29 53	26 33 58	9 33	10 32	13 53	15 32	8 8	21 50	14 39	11 40	3 17	2 17
22	4 2 51	29 25 28	3♐ 34 21	10♐ 30 32	9 30	10 31	15 21	16 32	8 48	22 2	14 46	11 39	3 19	2 17
23	4 6 48	0♐ 26 8	17 22 5	24 8 40	9 27	10 29	16 49	17 31	9 29	22 13	14 53	11 39	3 21	2 18
24	4 10 44	1 26 49	0♑ 50 5	7♑ 26 11	9 24	10 26	18 16	18 29	10 9	22 25	15 0	11 39	3 23	2 18
25	4 14 41	2 27 31	13 56 57	20 22 29	9 20	10 22	19 43	19 27	10 50	22 36	15 7	11 38	3 25	2 18
26	4 18 38	3 28 15	26 42 59	2♒ 58 43	9 17	10 19	21 9	20 24	11 30	22 48	15 14	11 38	3 27	2 19
27	4 22 34	4 28 59	9♒ 10 2	15 17 24	9 14	10 16	22 34	21 21	12 11	22 59	15 21	11 37	3 29	2 19
28	4 26 31	5 29 45	21 21 16	27 22 13	9 11	10 14	23 58	22 18	12 51	23 10	15 28	11 37	3 31	2 19
29	4 30 27	6 30 31	3♓ 20 47	9♓ 17 36	9 8	10 13D	25 21	23 14	13 32	23 21	15 35	11 36	3 33	2 19
30	4 34 24	7♐ 31 19	15♓ 13 16	21♓ 8 25	9♏ 5	10♏ 13	26♐ 43	24♑ 9	14♏ 13	23♎ 32	15♐ 42	11♌ 36	3♏ 35	2♍ 19

DECLINATION and LATITUDE

Day	☉ Decl	☽ Decl	☽ Lat	☽ 12 Hr. Decl	☿ Decl	☿ Lat	♀ Decl	♀ Lat	♂ Decl	♂ Lat	♃ Decl	♃ Lat	♄ Decl	♄ Lat
1	14S17	8S14	5N 7	6S22	16S 3	0S14	26S25	3S 5	9S 0	0N38	5S57	1N 7	20S54	1N24
2	14 36	4 27	4 44	2 29	16 38	0 21	26 30	3 7	9 15	0 37	6 2	1 7	20 55	1 24
3	14 55	0 30	4 9	1N30	17 12	0 28	26 33	3 9	9 30	0 37	6 6	1 7	20 56	1 24
4	15 14	3N29	3 23	5 28	17 45	0 34	26 36	3 10	9 45	0 37	6 11	1 7	20 57	1 24
5	15 32	7 23	2 27	9 15	18 17	0 41	26 38	3 12	9 60	0 36	6 16	1 7	20 57	1 24
6	15 50	11 2	1 25	12 42	18 48	0 47	26 40	3 13	10 14	0 36	6 20	1 7	20 58	1 24
7	16 8	14 15	0 18	15 39	19 19	0 54	26 40	3 14	10 29	0 35	6 25	1 7	20 59	1 24
8	16 26	16 53	0S51	17 55	19 48	1 0	26 41	3 15	10 44	0 35	6 30	1 7	21 0	1 24
9	16 43	18 44	1 59	19 19	20 17	1 6	26 40	3 16	10 58	0 34	6 34	1 7	21 1	1 23
10	17 1	19 38	3 2	19 42	20 44	1 12	26 39	3 17	11 13	0 34	6 39	1 8	21 2	1 23
11	17 17	19 30	3 56	19 1	21 11	1 18	26 37	3 17	11 27	0 33	6 43	1 8	21 3	1 23
12	17 34	18 16	4 39	17 16	21 36	1 24	26 35	3 18	11 41	0 33	6 48	1 8	21 4	1 23
13	17 50	15 60	5 6	14 30	22 0	1 29	26 32	3 18	11 55	0 32	6 52	1 8	21 5	1 23
14	18 6	12 48	5 17	10 54	22 24	1 35	26 28	3 18	12 10	0 32	6 57	1 8	21 6	1 23
15	18 22	8 50	5 9	6 39	22 46	1 40	26 24	3 18	12 24	0 31	7 1	1 8	21 7	1 23
16	18 37	4 21	4 42	1 58	23 7	1 45	26 19	3 18	12 38	0 31	7 6	1 8	21 8	1 23
17	18 52	0S27	3 58	2S52	23 27	1 50	26 14	3 18	12 52	0 30	7 10	1 8	21 8	1 23
18	19 7	5 15	2 58	7 34	23 46	1 55	26 8	3 17	13 5	0 30	7 14	1 8	21 9	1 23
19	19 21	9 47	1 47	11 51	24 3	1 59	26 1	3 17	13 19	0 29	7 19	1 8	21 10	1 22
20	19 35	13 44	0 29	15 24	24 19	2 3	25 54	3 16	13 33	0 29	7 23	1 8	21 11	1 22
21	19 49	16 49	0N49	17 58	24 34	2 7	25 46	3 15	13 46	0 28	7 27	1 8	21 12	1 22
22	20 2	18 51	2 4	19 25	24 48	2 11	25 38	3 14	13 60	0 28	7 31	1 9	21 13	1 22
23	20 15	19 42	3 9	19 41	25 1	2 14	25 29	3 13	14 13	0 27	7 36	1 9	21 14	1 22
24	20 27	19 24	4 3	18 50	25 12	2 17	25 19	3 11	14 26	0 27	7 40	1 9	21 15	1 22
25	20 39	18 2	4 42	17 1	25 22	2 19	25 9	3 9	14 40	0 26	7 44	1 9	21 15	1 22
26	20 51	15 49	5 6	14 26	25 30	2 21	24 59	3 7	14 53	0 26	7 48	1 9	21 16	1 22
27	21 3	12 54	5 14	11 16	25 37	2 23	24 48	3 5	15 6	0 25	7 52	1 9	21 17	1 22
28	21 13	9 31	5 9	7 41	25 43	2 24	24 37	3 3	15 18	0 25	7 56	1 9	21 18	1 22
29	21 24	5 47	4 49	3 50	25 47	2 25	24 25	3 1	15 31	0 24	8 0	1 9	21 19	1 22
30	21S34	1S52	4N18	0N 8	25S50	2S26	24S12	2S58	15S44	0N24	8S 4	1N 9	21S20	1N22

Day	♅ Decl	♅ Lat	♆ Decl	♆ Lat	♇ Decl	♇ Lat
1	17N56	0N38	10S46	1N42	21N13	11N15
5	17 55	0 38	10 49	1 42	21 13	11 17
9	17 55	0 38	10 52	1 42	21 14	11 18
13	17 54	0 38	10 55	1 42	21 14	11 20
17	17 54	0 38	10 58	1 42	21 15	11 22
21	17 55	0 39	11 1	1 42	21 15	11 23
25	17 55	0 39	11 3	1 42	21 16	11 25
29	17N56	0N39	11S 6	1N42	21N18	11N27

☽ PHENOMENA

d	h	m	
7	14	32	○
14	22	0	☾
21	16	20	●
29	6	58	☽

d	h	° '
3	3	0
10	9	19N43
16	22	0
23	5	19S44
30	11	0

d	h	° '
7	6	0
14	2	5S17
20	9	0
27	2	5N14

VOID OF COURSE ☽

Last Aspect		☽ Ingress		
31	10pm40	1	♓	9am19
3	5pm 3	3	♈	10pm 0
6	6am13	6	♉	9am38
8	9am26	8	♊	7pm 9
10	7am42	11	♋	2am24
12	2pm23	13	♌	7am36
14	10pm 0	15	♍	11am 7
17	4am22	17	♎	1pm26
19	1am 5	19	♏	3pm18
21	4pm20	21	♐	5pm52
23	8am42	23	♑	10pm30
25	4pm27	26	♒	6am16
28	5am53	28	♓	5pm16

d	h	
2	11	APOGEE
18	11	PERIGEE
30	7	APOGEE

DAILY ASPECTARIAN

Day	Aspect	Time
1 F	♀⚹♂	8am52
	☽☍♇	1pm28
	☽∥♃	2 23
	☽△♆	2 32
	☽⚼♃	3 13
2 S	☉△☽	4am32
	☽⚼♂	6 47
	☽⚻♅	8 43
	☽□♄	10 48
	☽△☿	5pm43
	♀⚼♅	7 27
	☽⚼♆	9 1
	☽⚻♃	10 9
3 Su	☉⚼☽	1pm42
	☽⚻♂	2 57
	☽⚼♅	3 7
	☽□♀	5 3
4 M	☽⚻♇	2am13
	☽⚻♆	3 24
	☽⚼☿	4 39
	☉□♅	6 43
	☿⚺♃	7 22
	☿#♅	7 36
	☽#♃	4pm50
	☽△♅	9 16
	☉⚻☽	10 34
	☽△♄	11 47
5 T	☽⚼♇	8am14
	☽☍♃	11 26
	☉⚺♄	2pm46
	☽⚻☿	3 3
	☽#♂	6 13
	♂∠♄	7 10
	☽#♆	10 38
	♀ ♑	11 46
6 W	☽⚼♄	5am43
	☽☍♂	6 13
	☽△♀	10 35
	☽△♇	1pm48
	☽☍♆	3 3
7 Th	☽□♅	8am12
	☽⚻♄	11 5
	☉☍☽	2pm32
	☽⚼♀	6 19
	☉#☽	6 44
	☽⚻♃	10 46
8 F	♀△♇	0am 5
	☽☍☿	9 26
	☽∥♅	11 55
	♂∥♆	1pm34
	♀⚹♆	3 47
	☽⚻♂	7 3
	♂ ♏	9 4
	☽□♇	11 13
9 S	☽⚻♆	0am31
	☽⚻♀	1 16
	☽⚼♃	3 32
	☽⚹♅	4pm51
	☽☍♄	8 5
10 Su	☽⚼♂	0am27
	☉⚻☽	3 37
	☽⚼♆	4 23
	☽△♃	7 42
	☿∥♄	4pm40
	☽∠♅	8 20
11 M	☽⚻☿	0am22
	☿#♇	2 54
	☽△♂	5 13
	☽⚹♇	6 21
	☽△♆	7 42
	☉⚼☽	9 6
	☽☍♀	12pm59
	☿ ♐	6 1
	☽⚺♅	11 18
12 T	☽⚻♄	2am50
	♂⚹♇	4 6
	☽∥♅	4 41
	☽⚼☿	6 40
	☉#☽	7 39
	☽∠♇	9 8
	☉△☽	1pm57
	☽□♃	2 23
	☉⚺♃	9 20
13 W	☿□♇	4am52
	☽⚼♄	5 27
	☉#♅	6 4
	♂☌♆	9 20
	☽⚺♇	11 28
	☽△☿	12pm16
	☽□♆	12 52
	☽□♂	1 2
	☿⚺♆	5 47
	☽⚻♀	10 7
14 Th	☿⚺♂	0am 6
	☽☌♅	3 49
	☽#♂	3 54
	☽△♄	7 38
	☽#♆	11 47
	☽⚹♃	7pm10
	☉□☽	10 0
15 F	☽⚼♀	1am53
	☽#♃	9 50
	☿∠♃	1pm16
	☽☌♇	2 54
	☽⚹♆	4 22
	☽⚹♂	6 57
	☽∠♃	8 59
	☽□☿	9 46
16 S	☽△♀	5am12
	☽⚺♅	6 48
	☽□♄	10 55
	☽∠♆	5pm38
	☽∠♂	9 22
	☽⚺♃	10 30
17 Su	♀⚻♅	3am29
	☉⚹☽	4 22
	♅SR	6 35
	☽∠♅	7 53
	☽⚺♇	5pm11
	☽⚺♆	6 42
	☽⚺♂	11 34
18 M	☽⚹☿	5am42
	☉∠☽	7 11
	☽⚹♅	8 49
	☽∥♃	10 25
	☽□♀	11 2
	☽⚹♄	1pm18
	☽∠♇	6 7
19 T	☽☌♃	1am 5
	☽∥♆	6 56
	☽∠☿	9 29
	☉⚺☽	9 59
	☿△♅	11 55
	☽∠♄	2pm26
	☽⚹♇	7 5
	☽☌♆	8 43
	☽∥♂	10 43
	♀⚺♄	11 40
20 W	☽☌♂	3am56
	☽□♅	10 48
	☽⚺☿	1pm27
	☽⚺♄	3 45
	☽⚹♀	4 49
21 Th	☽⚺♃	4am 1
	☽#♅	11 17
	☿☌♄	1pm25
	☉☌☽	4 20
	☽∠♀	8 13
	☽□♇	9 47
	☽⚺♆	11 34
22 F	☽∠♃	6am 3
	☽⚺♂	9 30
	☉ ♐	1pm40
	☽△♅	2 0
	♀⚼♇	6 40
	☽☌♄	7 35
	☽☌☿	10 55
23 S	☽⚺♀	0am16
	☽∠♆	1 44
	☽⚹♃	8 42
	☽∠♂	1pm16
	☽⚼♅	4 28
24 Su	☉⚺☽	1am12
	☿∠♆	1 58
	☽△♇	2 39
	☽⚹♆	4 38
	☿∥♀	9 8
	☿⚺♀	10 37
	☽⚹♂	5pm55
	☽⚻♅	7 44
	☉□♇	8 19
25 M	☽#♅	1am34
	☽⚺♄	2 11
	☽⚼♇	6 15
	☉∠☽	7 6
	☽☌♀	11 6
	☽⚺☿	12pm 7
	☽□♃	4 27
	☉⚺♆	11 37
26 T	♂□♅	4am30
	☽∠♄	6 46
	☽∥♂	7 41
	☽⚻♇	10 43
	☽□♆	12pm57
	☉⚹☽	2 6
	☽∠☿	8 29
	♄#♇	10 15
27 W	☽☍♅	4am48
	☽□♂	6 14
	☿⚹♃	8 11
	☽⚹♄	12pm13
	☽∥♆	1 15
28 Th	☽⚺♀	2am 2
	☽△♃	3 40
	☽⚹☿	5 53
	☉#♇	8 50
	☽∥♃	10 10
	☉∥♄	10 43
	☽☍♇	9pm56
29 F	☽△♆	0am25
	♀□♃	4 0
	☉□☽	6 58
	☽⚼♃	10 15
	☽∠♀	10 41
	☽⚻♅	4pm40
	☿⚼♅	9 44
	☽△♂	9 50
30 S	☽□♄	0am58
	☽⚼♆	6 50
	☽⚻♃	5pm 7
	☽⚹♀	7 37
	☽⚼♅	11 2

DECEMBER 1957

LONGITUDE

Day	Sid. Time	☉	☽	☽ 12 Hour	Mean ☊	True ☊	☿	♀	♂	♃	♄	♅	♆	♇
	h m s	° ' "	° ' "	° ' "	° '	° '	° '	° '	° '	° '	° '	° '	° '	° '
1	4 38 20	8♐ 32 8	27♓ 3 41	2♈ 59 41	9♏ 1	10♏ 15	28♐ 4	25♑ 4	14♏ 53	23♎ 43	15♐ 49	11♌ 35R	3♏ 37	2♍ 19
2	4 42 17	9 32 57	8♈ 57 0	14 56 13	8 58	10 16	29 23	25 58	15 34	23 54	15 56	11 34	3 39	2 20
3	4 46 13	10 33 47	20 57 53	27 2 28	8 55	10 18	0♑ 41	26 51	16 15	24 5	16 3	11 33	3 41	2 20
4	4 50 10	11 34 38	3♉ 10 27	9♉ 22 10	8 52	10 20R	1 56	27 44	16 56	24 15	16 10	11 32	3 43	2 20R
5	4 54 7	12 35 31	15 37 59	21 58 7	8 49	10 20	3 9	28 36	17 37	24 26	16 17	11 31	3 45	2 20
6	4 58 3	13 36 24	28 22 43	4♊ 51 54	8 46	10 18	4 19	29 27	18 17	24 37	16 24	11 30	3 46	2 20
7	5 2 0	14 37 18	11♊ 25 37	18 3 47	8 42	10 15	5 27	0♒ 18	18 58	24 47	16 31	11 29	3 48	2 20
8	5 5 56	15 38 13	24 46 13	1♋ 32 40	8 39	10 10	6 30	1 8	19 39	24 57	16 38	11 28	3 50	2 19
9	5 9 53	16 39 9	8♋ 22 47	15 16 12	8 36	10 4	7 30	1 57	20 20	25 8	16 45	11 27	3 52	2 19
10	5 13 49	17 40 6	22 12 30	29 11 13	8 33	9 58	8 24	2 45	21 1	25 18	16 52	11 26	3 54	2 19
11	5 17 46	18 41 4	6♌ 11 55	13♌ 14 9	8 30	9 52	9 14	3 32	21 42	25 28	17 0	11 25	3 55	2 19
12	5 21 42	19 42 3	20 17 30	27 21 35	8 26	9 47	9 57	4 18	22 23	25 38	17 7	11 23	3 57	2 19
13	5 25 39	20 43 4	4♍ 26 5	11♍ 30 41	8 23	9 44	10 33	5 3	23 5	25 48	17 14	11 22	3 59	2 19
14	5 29 36	21 44 5	18 35 8	25 39 15	8 20	9 43D	11 1	5 48	23 46	25 58	17 21	11 21	4 0	2 18
15	5 33 32	22 45 7	2♎ 42 50	9♎ 45 45	8 17	9 43	11 21	6 31	24 27	26 7	17 28	11 19	4 2	2 18
16	5 37 29	23 46 10	16 47 50	23 48 58	8 14	9 45	11 31R	7 13	25 8	26 17	17 35	11 18	4 4	2 18
17	5 41 25	24 47 15	0♏ 48 57	7♏ 47 38	8 11	9 46R	11 30	7 54	25 49	26 27	17 42	11 16	4 5	2 17
18	5 45 22	25 48 20	14 44 48	21 40 12	8 7	9 46	11 19	8 34	26 31	26 36	17 49	11 15	4 7	2 17
19	5 49 18	26 49 26	28 33 36	5♐ 24 40	8 4	9 44	10 56	9 13	27 12	26 45	17 56	11 13	4 8	2 16
20	5 53 15	27 50 33	12♐ 13 6	18 58 36	8 1	9 40	10 21	9 50	27 53	26 54	18 3	11 12	4 10	2 16
21	5 57 11	28 51 41	25 40 51	2♑ 19 33	7 58	9 33	9 35	10 26	28 35	27 3	18 10	11 10	4 11	2 15
22	6 1 8	29 52 49	8♑ 54 29	15 25 26	7 55	9 25	8 38	11 1	29 16	27 12	18 17	11 8	4 13	2 15
23	6 5 5	0♑ 53 57	21 52 16	28 14 56	7 52	9 15	7 31	11 34	29 57	27 21	18 24	11 6	4 14	2 14
24	6 9 1	1 55 6	4♒ 33 26	10♒ 47 52	7 48	9 5	6 17	12 6	0♐ 39	27 30	18 31	11 4	4 16	2 14
25	6 12 58	2 56 15	16 58 25	23 5 21	7 45	8 56	4 58	12 36	1 20	27 39	18 38	11 3	4 17	2 13
26	6 16 54	3 57 23	29 9 0	5♓ 9 47	7 42	8 49	3 36	13 5	2 2	27 47	18 45	11 1	4 18	2 13
27	6 20 51	4 58 32	11♓ 8 10	17 4 42	7 39	8 43	2 14	13 31	2 43	27 55	18 52	10 59	4 20	2 12
28	6 24 47	5 59 41	22 59 56	28 54 30	7 36	8 40	0 55	13 57	3 25	28 4	18 59	10 57	4 21	2 11
29	6 28 44	7 0 50	4♈ 49 2	10♈ 44 14	7 32	8 39D	29♐ 41	14 20	4 7	28 12	19 6	10 55	4 22	2 11
30	6 32 40	8 1 59	16 40 45	22 39 18	7 29	8 39	28 34	14 41	4 48	28 20	19 13	10 53	4 24	2 10
31	6 36 37	9♑ 3 8	28♈ 40 31	4♉ 45 6	7♏ 26	8♏ 40R	27♐ 35	15♒ 1	5♐ 30	28♎ 27	19♐ 20	10♌ 51	4♏ 25	2♍ 9

DECLINATION and LATITUDE

Day	☉	☽		☽ 12 Hr.	☿		♀		♂		♃		♄	
	Decl	Decl	Lat	Decl	Decl	Lat	Decl	Lat	Decl	Lat	Decl	Lat	Decl	Lat
1	21S44	2N 8	3N36	4N 6	25S51	2S25	23S60	2S55	15S56	0N23	8S 8	1N10	21S20	1N21
2	21 53	6 3	2 44	7 57	25 51	2 25	23 46	2 52	16 9	0 23	8 12	1 10	21 21	1 21
3	22 2	9 48	1 44	11 33	25 50	2 23	23 33	2 48	16 21	0 22	8 16	1 10	21 22	1 21
4	22 11	13 11	0 39	14 42	25 47	2 21	23 19	2 45	16 33	0 22	8 19	1 10	21 23	1 21
5	22 19	16 4	0S29	17 15	25 43	2 18	23 4	2 41	16 45	0 21	8 23	1 10	21 24	1 21
6	22 26	18 14	1 37	18 59	25 37	2 15	22 50	2 37	16 57	0 20	8 27	1 10	21 24	1 21
7	22 33	19 29	2 42	19 44	25 30	2 10	22 35	2 33	17 9	0 20	8 31	1 10	21 25	1 21
8	22 40	19 42	3 39	19 23	25 22	2 5	22 19	2 28	17 21	0 19	8 34	1 10	21 26	1 21
9	22 47	18 47	4 24	17 54	25 13	1 59	22 4	2 23	17 32	0 19	8 38	1 11	21 27	1 21
10	22 52	16 45	4 56	15 21	25 2	1 51	21 48	2 18	17 43	0 18	8 41	1 11	21 27	1 21
11	22 58	13 44	5 10	11 54	24 50	1 43	21 31	2 13	17 55	0 18	8 45	1 11	21 28	1 21
12	23 3	9 54	5 5	7 45	24 37	1 33	21 15	2 7	18 6	0 17	8 49	1 11	21 29	1 21
13	23 7	5 30	4 42	3 11	24 24	1 22	20 58	2 1	18 17	0 16	8 52	1 11	21 30	1 21
14	23 11	0 48	4 2	1S35	24 9	1 10	20 41	1 55	18 28	0 16	8 55	1 11	21 30	1 21
15	23 15	3S56	3 7	6 15	23 54	0 57	20 24	1 49	18 38	0 15	8 59	1 11	21 31	1 21
16	23 18	8 28	2 1	10 34	23 39	0 42	20 7	1 42	18 49	0 15	9 2	1 12	21 32	1 21
17	23 21	12 31	0 48	14 17	23 23	0 26	19 49	1 35	18 59	0 14	9 5	1 12	21 32	1 21
18	23 23	15 50	0N27	17 9	23 7	0 9	19 32	1 28	19 10	0 14	9 9	1 12	21 33	1 20
19	23 24	18 13	1 40	19 1	22 50	0N 9	19 14	1 20	19 20	0 13	9 12	1 12	21 34	1 20
20	23 26	19 31	2 46	19 45	22 34	0 29	18 57	1 12	19 30	0 12	9 15	1 12	21 34	1 20
21	23 26	19 41	3 42	19 21	22 18	0 48	18 39	1 4	19 39	0 12	9 18	1 12	21 35	1 20
22	23 27	18 45	4 24	17 55	22 2	1 8	18 21	0 55	19 49	0 11	9 21	1 13	21 36	1 20
23	23 26	16 52	4 52	15 37	21 46	1 28	18 3	0 46	19 58	0 10	9 24	1 13	21 36	1 20
24	23 26	14 11	5 5	12 37	21 31	1 47	17 46	0 37	20 8	0 10	9 27	1 13	21 37	1 20
25	23 25	10 56	5 3	9 9	21 16	2 5	17 28	0 27	20 17	0 9	9 30	1 13	21 38	1 20
26	23 23	7 17	4 47	5 22	21 3	2 21	17 10	0 17	20 26	0 9	9 33	1 13	21 38	1 20
27	23 21	3 24	4 19	1 25	20 50	2 35	16 53	0 7	20 35	0 8	9 36	1 13	21 39	1 20
28	23 19	0N35	3 40	2N34	20 39	2 47	16 35	0N 4	20 43	0 7	9 38	1 14	21 39	1 20
29	23 16	4 32	2 51	6 27	20 30	2 57	16 18	0 15	20 52	0 7	9 41	1 14	21 40	1 20
30	23 12	8 20	1 55	10 8	20 22	3 4	16 1	0 26	21 0	0 6	9 44	1 14	21 40	1 20
31	23S 8	11N50	0N53	13N26	20S17	3N 8	15S44	0N38	21S 8	0N 5	9S46	1N14	21S41	1N20

Day	♅		♆		♇	
	Decl	Lat	Decl	Lat	Decl	Lat
1	17N56	0N39	11S 7	1N42	21N18	11N27
5	17 57	0 39	11 10	1 43	21 20	11 29
9	17 59	0 39	11 12	1 43	21 21	11 31
13	18 0	0 39	11 14	1 43	21 23	11 32
17	18 2	0 40	11 16	1 43	21 25	11 34
21	18 4	0 40	11 18	1 43	21 27	11 35
25	18 6	0 40	11 20	1 44	21 29	11 37
29	18N 8	0N40	11S21	1N44	21N32	11N38

☽ PHENOMENA

d	h	m	
7	6	16	○
14	5	46	☾
21	6	12	●
29	4	53	☽

d	h	° '
7	17	19N45
14	4	0
20	15	19S45
27	20	0

d	h	° '
4	14	0
11	6	5S10
17	15	0
24	9	5N 6
31	20	0

VOID OF COURSE ☽

Last Aspect		☽ Ingress		
1	2am18	1	♈	5am57
3	12pm32	3	♉	5pm48
6	2am 9	6	♊	3am 1
8	0am20	8	♋	9am16
10	5am23	10	♌	1pm24
12	9am11	12	♍	4pm29
14	9am14	14	♎	7pm23
16	4pm25	16	♏	10pm36
18	9pm30	19	♐	2am31
21	6am12	21	♑	7am47
23	10am26	23	♒	3pm19
25	9pm15	26	♓	1am41
27	3pm47	28	♈	2pm13
30	11pm34	31	♉	2am38

d	h	
14	5	PERIGEE
28	4	APOGEE

DAILY ASPECTARIAN

Day	Aspect	Time
1 Su	☽□☿	2am18
	☉∠♃	5 17
	☽⚼♂	6 5
	☽⚻♇	10 39
	☽⚻♆	1pm18
2 M	☉△☽	1am19
	☽△♅	5 15
	☿ ♑	11 20
	☽#♃	1pm46
	☽⚻♂	2 4
	☽△♄	2 7
	♂⚺♄	3 22
	☽⚼♇	4 46
3 T	☽☍♃	6am15
	☽#♆	9 11
	☉⚼☽	9 55
	☽□♀	12pm32
	☽⚼♄	8 3
	☽△☿	9 19
	☽△♇	10 21
	☉△♅	11 7
	☿∠♂	11 50
4 W	☽☍♆	1am 3
	☿△♇	7 40
	♇SR	10 27
	☽□♅	4pm 9
	☉⚻☽	5 41
5 Th	☽⚻♄	1am15
	☽☍♂	3 58
	☽⚼☿	5 17
	☽#♂	7 24
	☿⚹♆	12pm20
	☽⚻♃	4 52
	☽∥♅	8 30
6 F	☽△♀	2am 9
	☽□♇	7 19
	☽⚻♆	10 1
	☽⚻☿	12pm 3
	♀ ♒	3 27
	☽⚼♃	8 58
7 S	☽⚹♅	0am 7
	☉∥♀	1 12
	☉☍☽	6 16
	☽⚼♀	7 29
	☽☍♄	9 18
	☽⚼♆	1pm22
	☽⚻♂	2 22
8 Su	☽△♃	0am20
	☽∠♅	3 1
	☽⚻♀	11 59
	☽⚹♇	1pm22
	☽△♆	4 4
	♀∠♄	5 30
	☽⚼♂	6 24
	☽☍☿	10 20
9 M	☉☌♄	2am47
	☽⚺♅	5 21
	☽∥♅	11 0
	♀⚻♇	11 14
	☽⚻♄	2pm42
	☽#♂	2 49
	☉⚻☽	3 32
	☽∠♇	3 33
	☽△♂	9 51
10 T	☽□♃	5am23
	☉∠♀	8 12
	☽⚼♄	4pm45
	☽⚺♇	5 22
	☽☍♀	7 10
	☉⚼☽	7 22
	☽□♆	8 6
11 W	♀∥♄	4am34
	☽⚻☿	5 28
	☉∠♆	5 47
	☽☌♅	8 53
	♂#♅	10 38
	♀□♆	12pm34
	♀#♇	12 56
	☽#♆	4 10
	☽△♄	6 33
	☉△☽	10 55
12 Th	☽□♂	3am45
	☽#♃	6 6
	☽⚼☿	8 17
	☽⚹♃	9 11
	☽☌♇	8pm24
	☽⚹♆	11 14
13 F	☽⚻♀	1am 7
	☽△☿	10 45
	☽∠♃	10 55
	☽⚺♅	11 44
	☽□♄	9pm53
14 S	☽∠♆	0am43
	☽⚼♀	3 57
	☉□☽	5 46
	☽⚹♂	9 14
	☽⚺♃	12pm40
	☽∠♅	1 9
	☿⚻♅	10 14
	☽⚺♇	11 18
15 Su	☽⚺♆	2am15
	☽△♀	6 49
	☽∠♂	12pm 3
	☽⚹♅	2 38
	☽□☿	2 54
16 M	☽∠♇	0am51
	☽⚹♄	1 21
	☽∥♃	3 13
	☿SR	10 55
	☉⚹☽	12pm51
	☽⚺♂	3 0
	☽∥♆	4 11
	☽☌♃	4 25
17 T	☽⚹♇	2am32
	☉∥☿	3 2
	☽∠♄	3 16
	☽☌♆	5 38
	☽□♀	12pm48
	☉∠☽	4 39
	☽□♅	5 58
	☽⚹☿	6 10
	☿∠♂	7 3
18 W	♂⚺♃	4am 3
	☿⚻♅	5 19
	☽⚺♄	5 22
	☉⚼♅	10 7
	♀∥♂	7pm23
	☽∠☿	7 33
	☉⚺☽	8 44
	☽⚺♃	8 49
	☽☌♂	9 30
	☽#♅	9 50
	☉⚹♃	10 4
19 Th	☽□♇	6am29
	☽⚺♆	9 47
	☽∥♀	1pm14
	☽⚹♀	7 36
	☽⚺☿	8 51
	☽△♅	10 11
	☽∥♂	10 51
	☽∠♃	11 27
20 F	☉⚺♂	3am13
	☿⚺♀	9 17
	☽☌♄	10 27
	☽∠♆	12pm21
	☽∠♀	11 32
21 S	☽⚼♅	0am52
	☽∥♂	1 5
	☽⚹♃	2 30
	☽⚺♂	5 30
	☉☌☽	6 12
	☽△♇	11 52
	☽⚹♆	3pm25
	☽☌☿	11 32
22 Su	☉ ♑	2am49
	☽⚺♀	4 2
	☽⚻♅	4 5
	♀☍♅	4 50
	☽∥♀	7 26
	☽#♅	9 54
	☽∠♂	10 25
	☽⚼♇	3pm22
	☽⚺♄	5 28
	♀#♅	9 48
23 M	♂ ♐	1am30
	☽□♃	10 26
	☿∥♄	2pm37
	☽⚹♂	4 7
	☉⚺☽	6 31
	☽⚻♇	7 34
	☽∠♄	10 0
	☽□♆	11 26
24 T	☿#♇	2am59
	☽⚺☿	3 0
	☉△♇	7 17
	☽☍♅	12pm30
	☽☌♀	3 8
	☽∥♆	9 17
25 W	☉∠☽	2am 3
	☽⚹♄	3 17
	☽∠☿	5 17
	☽∥♃	9 33
	☿⚹♆	11 50
	☉☌☿	8pm26
	☽△♃	9 15
26 Th	☽☍♇	6am 5
	☽□♂	6 5
	♂□♇	6 6
	☽⚹☿	7 58
	☉⚹♆	8 26
	☽△♆	10 18
	☉⚹☽	10 29
	☿⚺♂	6pm15
	☽⚻♅	11 41
27 F	☿△♇	0am37
	☽⚼♃	3 39
	☽⚺♀	5 0
	☽□♄	3pm47
	☽⚼♆	4 35
	☿∥♂	6 44
28 S	☽⚼♅	5am58
	☽⚻♃	10 24
	☽∠♀	12pm29
	☽□☿	2 32
	☿ ♐	5 55
	☽⚻♇	6 39
	☽△♂	10 29
	☽⚻♆	11 6
29 Su	☉□☽	4am53
	☿∠♀	5 24
	♂⚺♆	9 17
	☽△♅	12pm19
	☽⚹♀	7 52
30 M	☽⚼♇	0am58
	☿⚹♃	4 48
	☽△♄	5 9
	☽⚼♂	6 40
	☽#♃	9 26
	☽#♆	8pm37
	☽△☿	10 0
	☽☍♃	11 34
31 T	☽△♇	6am52
	☽⚼♄	11 16
	☽☍♆	11 21
	☽⚻♂	2pm17
	♄∠♆	10 4
	☉△☽	10 15
	☽□♅	11 50

JANUARY 1958

LONGITUDE

Day	Sid. Time	☉	☽	☽ 12 Hour	Mean ☊	True ☊	☿	♀	♂	♃	♄	♅	♆	♇
	h m s	° ' "	° ' "	° ' "	° '	° '	° '	° '	° '	° '	° '	° '	° '	° '
1	6 40 34	10♑ 4 17	10♉ 53 37	17♉ 6 40	7♏ 23	8♏ 40R	26♐ 47R	15♒ 18	6♐ 12	28♎ 35	19♐ 26	10♌ 49R	4♏ 26	2♍ 8R
2	6 44 30	11 5 26	23 24 45	29 48 17	7 20	8 39	26 8	15 33	6 53	28 43	19 33	10 46	4 27	2 7
3	6 48 27	12 6 34	6♊ 17 34	12♊ 52 51	7 17	8 35	25 40	15 47	7 35	28 50	19 40	10 44	4 28	2 7
4	6 52 23	13 7 42	19 34 10	26 21 28	7 13	8 29	25 23	15 58	8 17	28 58	19 47	10 42	4 29	2 6
5	6 56 20	14 8 50	3♋ 14 31	10♋ 12 58	7 10	8 21	25 15D	16 6	8 59	29 5	19 53	10 40	4 30	2 5
6	7 0 16	15 9 58	17 16 18	24 23 51	7 7	8 10	25 16	16 13	9 41	29 12	20 0	10 38	4 31	2 4
7	7 4 13	16 11 6	1♌ 34 53	8♌ 48 33	7 4	7 59	25 26	16 16	10 23	29 19	20 7	10 35	4 32	2 3
8	7 8 9	17 12 14	16 4 0	23 20 21	7 1	7 48	25 43	16 18R	11 5	29 25	20 13	10 33	4 33	2 2
9	7 12 6	18 13 22	0♍ 36 45	7♍ 52 27	6 58	7 39	26 8	16 17	11 47	29 32	20 20	10 31	4 34	2 1
10	7 16 3	19 14 30	15 6 45	22 19 5	6 54	7 32	26 39	16 14	12 29	29 38	20 26	10 28	4 35	2 0
11	7 19 59	20 15 37	29 29 2	6♎ 36 14	6 51	7 28	27 17	16 8	13 11	29 45	20 33	10 26	4 36	1 59
12	7 23 56	21 16 44	13♎ 40 31	20 41 43	6 48	7 26D	27 59	15 59	13 53	29 51	20 39	10 23	4 37	1 58
13	7 27 52	22 17 52	27 39 51	4♏ 34 55	6 45	7 26R	28 46	15 48	14 35	29 57	20 46	10 21	4 38	1 57
14	7 31 49	23 19 0	11♏ 27 0	18 16 12	6 42	7 26	29 37	15 35	15 17	0♏ 3	20 52	10 18	4 38	1 56
15	7 35 45	24 20 7	25 2 36	1♐ 46 18	6 38	7 25	0♑ 32	15 19	15 59	0 8	20 58	10 16	4 39	1 55
16	7 39 42	25 21 15	8♐ 27 22	15 5 50	6 35	7 22	1 31	15 1	16 41	0 14	21 5	10 13	4 40	1 54
17	7 43 38	26 22 22	21 41 42	28 14 58	6 32	7 16	2 33	14 40	17 24	0 19	21 11	10 11	4 41	1 52
18	7 47 35	27 23 29	4♑ 45 33	11♑ 13 23	6 29	7 6	3 37	14 17	18 6	0 25	21 17	10 8	4 41	1 51
19	7 51 32	28 24 35	17 38 23	24 0 28	6 26	6 54	4 44	13 52	18 48	0 30	21 23	10 6	4 42	1 50
20	7 55 28	29 25 40	0♒ 19 33	6♒ 35 35	6 23	6 40	5 53	13 25	19 30	0 34	21 29	10 3	4 42	1 49
21	7 59 25	0♒ 26 45	12 48 33	18 58 28	6 19	6 26	7 4	12 56	20 13	0 39	21 35	10 1	4 43	1 48
22	8 3 21	1 27 50	25 5 26	1♓ 9 35	6 16	6 12	8 17	12 25	20 55	0 44	21 42	9 58	4 43	1 46
23	8 7 18	2 28 53	7♓ 11 6	13 10 16	6 13	6 1	9 31	11 53	21 38	0 48	21 47	9 56	4 44	1 45
24	8 11 14	3 29 55	19 7 25	25 2 57	6 10	5 51	10 48	11 19	22 20	0 52	21 53	9 53	4 44	1 44
25	8 15 11	4 30 57	0♈ 57 19	6♈ 51 2	6 7	5 45	12 5	10 44	23 3	0 56	21 59	9 50	4 45	1 42
26	8 19 7	5 31 58	12 44 40	18 38 50	6 3	5 42	13 24	10 8	23 45	1 0	22 5	9 48	4 45	1 41
27	8 23 4	6 32 57	24 34 10	0♉ 31 22	6 0	5 40	14 44	9 32	24 28	1 4	22 11	9 45	4 45	1 40
28	8 27 1	7 33 55	6♉ 31 8	12 34 9	5 57	5 40	16 6	8 55	25 10	1 7	22 16	9 43	4 46	1 38
29	8 30 57	8 34 52	18 41 8	24 52 46	5 54	5 40	17 28	8 18	25 53	1 11	22 22	9 40	4 46	1 37
30	8 34 54	9 35 48	1♊ 9 41	7♊ 32 30	5 51	5 38	18 52	7 41	26 35	1 14	22 28	9 37	4 46	1 36
31	8 38 50	10♒ 36 43	14♊ 1 41	20♊ 37 40	5♏ 48	5♏ 35	20♑ 16	7♒ 4	27♐ 18	1♏ 17	22♐ 33	9♌ 35	4♏ 46	1♍ 34

DECLINATION and LATITUDE

Day	☉ Decl	☽ Decl	☽ Lat	☽ 12 Hr. Decl	☿ Decl	☿ Lat	♀ Decl	♀ Lat	♂ Decl	♂ Lat	♃ Decl	♃ Lat	♄ Decl	♄ Lat
1	23S 4	14N55	0S12	16N14	20S14	3N11	15S27	0N50	21S16	0N 5	9S49	1N14	21S42	1N20
2	22 59	17 22	1 18	18 19	20 12	3 11	15 11	1 2	21 24	0 4	9 51	1 15	21 42	1 20
3	22 54	19 2	2 22	19 31	20 13	3 9	14 55	1 15	21 31	0 3	9 54	1 15	21 43	1 20
4	22 48	19 43	3 20	19 38	20 16	3 6	14 39	1 28	21 39	0 3	9 56	1 15	21 43	1 20
5	22 42	19 16	4 8	18 37	20 20	3 2	14 24	1 41	21 46	0 2	9 59	1 15	21 44	1 20
6	22 35	17 39	4 43	16 25	20 26	2 56	14 9	1 55	21 53	0 1	10 1	1 15	21 44	1 20
7	22 28	14 56	5 0	13 12	20 33	2 49	13 55	2 9	21 60	0 1	10 3	1 15	21 45	1 20
8	22 20	11 16	4 59	9 9	20 41	2 42	13 41	2 23	22 6	0 0	10 5	1 16	21 45	1 20
9	22 12	6 55	4 39	4 34	20 50	2 34	13 27	2 38	22 13	0S 1	10 8	1 16	21 46	1 20
10	22 4	2 10	4 0	0S15	20 59	2 25	13 14	2 52	22 19	0 1	10 10	1 16	21 46	1 20
11	21 55	2S39	3 7	5 0	21 9	2 16	13 2	3 7	22 25	0 2	10 12	1 16	21 47	1 20
12	21 46	7 17	2 3	9 26	21 19	2 7	12 50	3 22	22 31	0 3	10 14	1 16	21 47	1 20
13	21 36	11 27	0 52	13 17	21 29	1 58	12 38	3 37	22 36	0 3	10 16	1 17	21 47	1 20
14	21 26	14 56	0N21	16 22	21 38	1 48	12 28	3 53	22 42	0 4	10 17	1 17	21 48	1 20
15	21 15	17 33	1 32	18 29	21 48	1 39	12 18	4 8	22 47	0 5	10 19	1 17	21 48	1 20
16	21 4	19 9	2 36	19 33	21 57	1 29	12 9	4 23	22 52	0 5	10 21	1 17	21 49	1 20
17	20 53	19 40	3 31	19 32	22 6	1 20	11 60	4 38	22 57	0 6	10 23	1 18	21 49	1 20
18	20 41	19 8	4 14	18 29	22 14	1 10	11 52	4 53	23 1	0 7	10 24	1 18	21 50	1 20
19	20 29	17 36	4 43	16 30	22 21	1 1	11 45	5 8	23 6	0 8	10 26	1 18	21 50	1 20
20	20 17	15 14	4 58	13 47	22 28	0 51	11 38	5 23	23 10	0 8	10 27	1 18	21 50	1 20
21	20 4	12 12	4 58	10 30	22 33	0 42	11 33	5 37	23 14	0 9	10 29	1 18	21 51	1 20
22	19 50	8 42	4 44	6 49	22 38	0 33	11 28	5 51	23 18	0 10	10 30	1 19	21 51	1 20
23	19 37	4 53	4 17	2 55	22 42	0 24	11 24	6 4	23 21	0 10	10 31	1 19	21 51	1 20
24	19 23	0 56	3 40	1N 3	22 45	0 15	11 20	6 17	23 25	0 11	10 33	1 19	21 52	1 20
25	19 8	3N 1	2 53	4 57	22 47	0 7	11 18	6 29	23 28	0 12	10 34	1 19	21 52	1 20
26	18 53	6 51	1 58	8 41	22 48	0S 1	11 16	6 41	23 30	0 13	10 35	1 19	21 52	1 20
27	18 38	10 26	0 58	12 5	22 47	0 10	11 15	6 52	23 33	0 13	10 36	1 20	21 53	1 20
28	18 23	13 37	0S 5	15 2	22 46	0 18	11 14	7 2	23 36	0 14	10 37	1 20	21 53	1 20
29	18 7	16 17	1 8	17 22	22 43	0 25	11 15	7 11	23 38	0 15	10 38	1 20	21 53	1 20
30	17 51	18 16	2 11	18 56	22 40	0 33	11 16	7 20	23 40	0 16	10 39	1 20	21 54	1 20
31	17S35	19N22	3S 8	19N33	22S35	0S40	11S17	7N27	23S41	0S16	10S40	1N21	21S54	1N20

Day	♅ Decl	♅ Lat	♆ Decl	♆ Lat	♇ Decl	♇ Lat
1	18N10	0N40	11S22	1N44	21N34	11N39
5	18 13	0 40	11 23	1 44	21 36	11 41
9	18 15	0 40	11 25	1 44	21 39	11 42
13	18 18	0 40	11 25	1 45	21 42	11 43
17	18 21	0 40	11 26	1 45	21 44	11 45
21	18 23	0 40	11 27	1 45	21 47	11 46
25	18 26	0 40	11 27	1 45	21 50	11 47
29	18N29	0N41	11S27	1N46	21N53	11N48

☽ PHENOMENA

d	h	m	
5	20	9	○
12	14	2	☾
19	22	8	●
28	2	17	☽

d	h	° '
4	3	19N43
10	11	0
17	0	19S40
24	6	0
31	14	19N33

d	h	° '
7	11	5S 2
13	17	0
20	12	4N60
27	22	0

VOID OF COURSE ☽

Last Aspect		☽ Ingress		
1	8am43	2	♊	12pm22
4	4pm42	4	♋	6pm22
6	8pm11	6	♌	9pm22
8	10pm12	8	♍	10pm59
10	8pm 7	11	♎	0am52
13	3am59	13	♏	4am 3
14	10pm38	15	♐	8am50
16	11pm 3	17	♑	3pm13
19	10pm 8	19	♒	11pm23
21	5pm16	22	♓	9am42
24	6am55	24	♈	10pm 3
26	11pm46	27	♉	10am57
28	9pm19	29	♊	9pm48

d	h	
9	0	PERIGEE
25	0	APOGEE

DAILY ASPECTARIAN

Day	Aspect	Time
1 W	☽⚼☿	1am37
	☽#♀	4 21
	☽□♀	8 43
	☽⊼♄	4pm36
	☉⊼♅	4 47
2 Th	☽⊼☿	4am56
	☉⚼☽	5 29
	☽⊼♃	10 4
	☽∥♅	10 8
	☽□♇	4pm18
	☿⚼♅	7 56
	☽⊼♆	8 38
3 F	☽☍♂	2am30
	☽⚹♅	8 5
	☉⊼☽	11 29
	♂#♇	12pm28
	☽⚼♃	1 51
	☽△♀	5 28
	☽⚼♆	11 51
4 S	☽☍♄	0am22
	☽☍☿	10 9
	☽∠♅	10 49
	♂∥♄	3pm54
	☽△♃	4 42
	☽⚼♀	8 15
	☽⚹♇	9 59
5 Su	☽△♆	2am11
	☿SD	8 33
	☽⊼♂	10 24
	☽⊻♅	12pm44
	☽∥♅	5 21
	☉☍☽	8 9
	☽⊼♀	10 11
	☽∠♇	11 39
6 M	☽⊼♄	4am39
	☽⚼♂	1pm 7
	☽⊼☿	1 35
	☽□♃	8 11
7 T	☽⊻♇	0am47
	☉⊻♀	2 11
	☽□♆	4 55
	☽⚼♄	5 55
	♂△♅	6 50
	☽#♀	7 45
	☿⚼♅	12pm32
	☽☌♅	2 54
	☽⚼☿	2 58
	☽△♂	3 20
	☉⚼♇	8 4
	☽#♆	11 9
8 W	☽☍♀	0am23
	☉⊼☽	2 1
	♀SR	2 57
	☽#♃	6 43
	☽△♄	6 54
	☽△☿	4pm23
	☽⚹♃	10 12
	☉∥♂	11 8
9 Th	☽☌♇	2am19
	☉⚼☽	4 38
	☽⚹♆	6 33
	☽⊻♅	4pm19
	☽□♂	7 24
	☽∠♃	11 13
10 F	☽⊼♀	1am50
	☉△☽	7 24
	☽∠♆	7 27
	☽□♄	8 56
	☽∠♅	5pm13
	☽□☿	8 7
11 S	☽⊻♃	0am26
	☽⚼♀	2 44
	☽⊻♇	4 12
	☉⊻♄	7 33
	☽⊻♆	8 37
	☽⚹♅	6pm26
	☉∥♄	8 38
12 Su	☽⚹♂	0am22
	☽△♀	3 54
	☽∠♇	5 37
	☉#♇	11 17
	☽⚹♄	12pm 1
	☉□☽	2 2
	☽∥♃	4 45
	☽∥♆	11 51
13 M	☽⚹☿	2am 2
	☽∠♂	3 29
	☽☌♃	3 59
	☽∥♀	7 16
	☽⚹♇	7 25
	☉∥☿	8 59
	☽☌♆	12pm 5
	♃ ♏	12 53
	☽∠♄	2 10
	♂∠♃	2 36
	☽□♅	10 0
14 T	☽∠☿	5am58
	☽⊻♂	7 6
	☽□♀	7 8
	♀⚹♂	7 30
	☿ ♑	10 3
	☿#♇	10 27
	☿⚹♃	12pm32
	☽⊻♄	4 43
	☿∠♀	7 35
	☉⚹☽	10 38
15 W	☿∥♄	1am24
	☽⊻♃	9 9
	☽#♅	9 47
	☽⊻☿	10 33
	☽□♇	12pm14
	☽⊻♆	5 11
16 Th	☽△♅	3am11
	☉∠☽	3 42
	☿△♇	8 47
	☽⚹♀	11 33
	☽∠♃	12pm20
	☽☌♂	3 43
	☽∠♆	8 19
	☽☌♄	11 3
17 F	☽⚼♅	6am21
	☉⊻☽	9 17
	☽∠♀	2pm12
	☽⚹♃	3 55
	☽△♇	6 39
	☽☌☿	9 41
	☽⚹♆	11 52
18 S	☽⊼♅	9am57
	☽#♅	1pm43
	☽⊻♀	5 10
	☽⚼♇	10 29
	☿⚹♆	11 19
19 Su	☽⊻♂	2am19
	☽⊻♄	7 7
	☉☌☽	10pm 8
20 M	☽□♃	0am29
	☽⊼♇	2 50
	♂∠♆	6 49
	☽□♆	8 23
	☽∠♂	8 28
	☽⊻☿	11 44
	☽∠♄	11 54
	☉ ♒	1pm29
	☽☍♅	6 37
21 T	☽☌♀	0am14
	☽∥♀	4 49
	☉□♃	5 17
	☽∥♆	5 25
	☽∥♃	12pm 3
	☽⚹♂	3 18
	☽⚹♄	5 16
	☽∠☿	8 2
22 W	♀∥♆	5am37
	☉⊼♇	7 8
	☽△♃	11 13
	☽☍♇	1pm12
	☉⊻☽	1 46
	☽△♆	7 6
23 Th	☽⚹☿	5am14
	☽⊼♅	5 28
	♂☌♄	6 29
	☿⊼♅	7 25
	☽⊻♀	8 59
	☽⚼♃	5pm24
	☉∠☽	10 37
24 F	☽⚼♆	1am15
	☽□♄	5 39
	☿⊻♀	6 45
	☽□♂	6 55
	☽⚼♅	11 37
	☽∠♀	1pm54
	☽⊼♃	11 58
25 S	☽⊼♇	1am32
	☉□♆	5 26
	☽⊼♆	7 43
	☉⚹☽	7 56
	☽△♅	6pm 1
	☽⚹♀	6 57
26 Su	☽□☿	1am31
	☽⚼♇	8 0
	♀☍♅	2pm35
	☽△♄	7 8
	☽△♂	11 46
27	☽#♃	1am14
M	♀∠♂	1 15
	☽#♀	5 50
	☽#♆	7 21
	♂⚼♅	9 18
	☽☍♃	1pm 9
	☽△♇	2 16
	☉#♅	3 59
	☉∠♄	4 27
	☽☍♆	8 29
28 T	☽⚼♄	1am31
	☉□☽	2 17
	☽□♀	4 32
	☽□♅	6 19
	☽⚼♂	7 42
	☿⚼♇	9 26
	☉☌♀	7pm48
	☽△☿	9 19
29 W	☽⊼♄	7am13
	☽⊼♂	2pm46
	☉#☽	6 53
30 Th	☽⊼♃	0am 8
	☉☍♅	0 33
	☽□♇	0 49
	☽∥♅	3 45
	☽⚼☿	5 44
	☽⊼♆	6 49
	♀∠♄	7 18
	♄#♇	8 21
	☽△♀	11 42
	☽⚹♅	3pm49
	☉△☽	5 10
31 F	☽⚼♃	4am 8
	☽⚼♆	10 27
	☽⊼☿	12pm42
	☽⚼♀	1 57
	☽☍♄	3 34
	☽∠♅	7 1
	☉⚼☽	10 37

FEBRUARY 1958

LONGITUDE

Day	Sid. Time	☉	☽	☽ 12 Hour	Mean ☊	True ☊	☿	♀	♂	♃	♄	♅	♆	♇
	h m s	° ' "	° ' "	° ' "	° '	° '	° '	° '	° '	° '	° '	° '	° '	° '
1	8 42 47	11♒ 37 36	27♊ 20 42	4♋ 10 55	5♏ 44	5♏ 29R	21♑ 42	6♒ 28R	28♐ 1	1♏ 20	22♐ 39	9♌ 32R	4♏ 47	1♍ 33R
2	8 46 43	12 38 29	11♋ 8 15	18 12 27	5 41	5 20	23 8	5 52	28 43	1 22	22 44	9 29	4 47	1 32
3	8 50 40	13 39 20	25 23 2	2♌ 39 22	5 38	5 9	24 35	5 18	29 26	1 25	22 49	9 27	4 47	1 30
4	8 54 36	14 40 9	10♌ 0 36	17 25 43	5 35	4 57	26 3	4 45	0♑ 9	1 27	22 55	9 24	4 47	1 29
5	8 58 33	15 40 58	24 53 35	2♍ 23 1	5 32	4 45	27 32	4 14	0 52	1 29	23 0	9 22	4 47R	1 27
6	9 2 30	16 41 45	9♍ 52 49	17 21 48	5 29	4 35	29 2	3 44	1 35	1 31	23 5	9 19	4 47	1 26
7	9 6 26	17 42 32	24 48 53	2♎ 13 9	5 25	4 27	0♒ 33	3 16	2 18	1 33	23 10	9 16	4 47	1 24
8	9 10 23	18 43 17	9♎ 33 47	16 50 12	5 22	4 22	2 4	2 50	3 0	1 34	23 15	9 14	4 47	1 23
9	9 14 19	19 44 1	24 1 57	1♏ 8 46	5 19	4 20D	3 36	2 27	3 43	1 36	23 20	9 11	4 47	1 21
10	9 18 16	20 44 44	8♏ 10 31	15 7 13	5 16	4 20	5 10	2 5	4 26	1 37	23 25	9 9	4 46	1 20
11	9 22 12	21 45 26	21 59 0	28 46 1	5 13	4 20R	6 43	1 46	5 9	1 38	23 30	9 6	4 46	1 18
12	9 26 9	22 46 8	5♐ 28 31	12♐ 6 46	5 9	4 19	8 18	1 29	5 52	1 39	23 35	9 4	4 46	1 17
13	9 30 5	23 46 48	18 41 3	25 11 39	5 6	4 17	9 54	1 15	6 35	1 39	23 39	9 1	4 46	1 15
14	9 34 2	24 47 27	1♑ 38 49	8♑ 2 47	5 3	4 12	11 30	1 3	7 18	1 40	23 44	8 59	4 45	1 14
15	9 37 59	25 48 5	14 23 46	20 41 57	5 0	4 4	13 8	0 54	8 2	1 40R	23 48	8 56	4 45	1 12
16	9 41 55	26 48 41	26 57 29	3♒ 10 29	4 57	3 54	14 46	0 47	8 45	1 40	23 53	8 54	4 45	1 11
17	9 45 52	27 49 16	9♒ 21 4	15 29 18	4 54	3 42	16 25	0 43	9 28	1 40	23 57	8 51	4 44	1 9
18	9 49 48	28 49 50	21 35 19	27 39 12	4 50	3 29	18 5	0 41D	10 11	1 39	24 1	8 49	4 44	1 8
19	9 53 45	29 50 22	3♓ 41 2	9♓ 40 58	4 47	3 16	19 45	0 42	10 54	1 39	24 6	8 46	4 44	1 6
20	9 57 41	0♓ 50 53	15 39 10	21 35 49	4 44	3 6	21 27	0 45	11 38	1 38	24 10	8 44	4 43	1 5
21	10 1 38	1 51 22	27 31 10	3♈ 25 30	4 41	2 57	23 10	0 50	12 21	1 37	24 14	8 42	4 43	1 3
22	10 5 34	2 51 49	9♈ 19 9	15 12 29	4 38	2 51	24 53	0 58	13 4	1 36	24 18	8 39	4 42	1 2
23	10 9 31	3 52 14	21 5 57	27 0 1	4 35	2 48	26 38	1 7	13 48	1 35	24 22	8 37	4 41	1 0
24	10 13 28	4 52 38	2♉ 55 13	8♉ 52 8	4 31	2 48D	28 24	1 19	14 31	1 33	24 25	8 35	4 41	0 59
25	10 17 24	5 53 0	14 51 21	20 53 30	4 28	2 48	0♓ 10	1 33	15 14	1 32	24 29	8 32	4 40	0 57
26	10 21 21	6 53 20	26 59 14	3♊ 9 14	4 25	2 49R	1 58	1 49	15 58	1 30	24 33	8 30	4 40	0 56
27	10 25 17	7 53 38	9♊ 24 8	15 44 33	4 22	2 50	3 46	2 8	16 41	1 28	24 36	8 28	4 39	0 54
28	10 29 14	8♓ 53 53	22♊ 11 5	28♊ 44 15	4♏ 19	2♏ 49	5♓ 36	2♒ 28	17♑ 24	1♏ 25	24♐ 40	8♌ 26	4♏ 38	0♍ 53

DECLINATION and LATITUDE

Day	☉ Decl	☽ Decl	☽ Lat	☽ 12 Hr. Decl	☿ Decl	☿ Lat	♀ Decl	♀ Lat	♂ Decl	♂ Lat	♃ Decl	♃ Lat	♄ Decl	♄ Lat
1	17S18	19N28	3S57	19N 5	22S28	0S47	11S19	7N34	23S43	0S17	10S41	1N21	21S54	1N20
2	17 1	18 25	4 35	17 27	22 21	0 54	11 22	7 40	23 44	0 18	10 41	1 21	21 54	1 20
3	16 44	16 12	4 56	14 41	22 12	1 1	11 25	7 45	23 45	0 19	10 42	1 21	21 55	1 21
4	16 26	12 56	4 60	10 57	22 2	1 7	11 29	7 49	23 46	0 20	10 42	1 22	21 55	1 21
5	16 8	8 47	4 43	6 28	21 51	1 13	11 33	7 52	23 47	0 20	10 43	1 22	21 55	1 21
6	15 50	4 4	4 6	1 36	21 38	1 19	11 37	7 55	23 47	0 21	10 43	1 22	21 55	1 21
7	15 32	0S54	3 13	3S21	21 24	1 24	11 42	7 56	23 47	0 22	10 44	1 22	21 56	1 21
8	15 13	5 44	2 7	8 1	21 9	1 29	11 47	7 57	23 47	0 23	10 44	1 22	21 56	1 21
9	14 54	10 10	0 54	12 8	20 53	1 34	11 53	7 56	23 47	0 24	10 44	1 23	21 56	1 21
10	14 35	13 55	0N20	15 28	20 35	1 39	11 58	7 55	23 47	0 24	10 45	1 23	21 56	1 21
11	14 15	16 47	1 32	17 51	20 15	1 43	12 4	7 54	23 46	0 25	10 45	1 23	21 56	1 21
12	13 56	18 38	2 37	19 10	19 55	1 47	12 10	7 51	23 45	0 26	10 45	1 23	21 57	1 21
13	13 36	19 26	3 32	19 26	19 33	1 51	12 16	7 48	23 44	0 27	10 45	1 24	21 57	1 21
14	13 16	19 11	4 16	18 40	19 10	1 54	12 22	7 45	23 42	0 28	10 45	1 24	21 57	1 21
15	12 55	17 57	4 45	16 60	18 45	1 57	12 28	7 40	23 40	0 28	10 44	1 24	21 57	1 21
16	12 35	15 52	5 0	14 33	18 19	1 59	12 34	7 36	23 39	0 29	10 44	1 24	21 57	1 21
17	12 14	13 5	5 1	11 29	17 51	2 2	12 40	7 31	23 36	0 30	10 44	1 24	21 57	1 21
18	11 53	9 46	4 48	7 58	17 22	2 4	12 46	7 25	23 34	0 31	10 44	1 25	21 57	1 21
19	11 32	6 6	4 22	4 10	16 52	2 5	12 51	7 19	23 31	0 32	10 43	1 25	21 58	1 21
20	11 11	2 13	3 44	0 15	16 21	2 6	12 57	7 13	23 29	0 33	10 43	1 25	21 58	1 21
21	10 49	1N43	2 57	3N40	15 48	2 7	13 2	7 6	23 25	0 33	10 42	1 25	21 58	1 21
22	10 27	5 34	2 2	7 25	15 13	2 7	13 8	6 59	23 22	0 34	10 42	1 26	21 58	1 21
23	10 5	9 12	1 2	10 53	14 38	2 7	13 13	6 52	23 19	0 35	10 41	1 26	21 58	1 22
24	9 43	12 29	0S 1	13 57	14 1	2 6	13 17	6 44	23 15	0 36	10 40	1 26	21 58	1 22
25	9 21	15 16	1 4	16 27	13 22	2 5	13 22	6 37	23 11	0 37	10 40	1 26	21 58	1 22
26	8 59	17 26	2 6	18 15	12 42	2 4	13 26	6 29	23 7	0 38	10 39	1 26	21 58	1 22
27	8 37	18 50	3 4	19 12	12 1	2 2	13 30	6 21	23 2	0 38	10 38	1 27	21 58	1 22
28	8S14	19N19	3S54	19N11	11S19	1S59	13S34	6N13	22S58	0S39	10S37	1N27	21S58	1N22

Day	♅ Decl	♅ Lat	♆ Decl	♆ Lat	♇ Decl	♇ Lat
1	18N31	0N41	11S27	1N46	21N55	11N48
5	18 34	0 41	11 27	1 46	21 58	11 49
9	18 37	0 41	11 27	1 46	22 0	11 50
13	18 39	0 41	11 26	1 46	22 3	11 50
17	18 42	0 41	11 26	1 47	22 6	11 51
21	18 45	0 40	11 25	1 47	22 8	11 51
25	18N47	0N40	11S24	1N47	22N11	11N51

☽ PHENOMENA

d	h	m	
4	8	6	○
10	23	34	☾
18	15	39	●
26	20	52	☽

d	h	° '
6	20	0
13	6	19S28
20	13	0
28	0	19N19

d	h	° '
3	16	5S 1
9	17	0
16	13	5N 2
24	0	0

VOID OF COURSE ☽

Last Aspect		☽ Ingress		
1	1am15	1	♋	4am41
2	10pm32	3	♌	7am38
4	8pm57	5	♍	8am11
6	9pm20	7	♎	8am24
8	10pm49	9	♏	10am 3
10	11pm34	11	♐	2pm12
13	10am11	13	♑	8pm56
14	11am15	16	♒	5am52
18	3pm39	18	♓	4pm40
20	5pm17	21	♈	5am 2
23	1pm13	23	♉	6pm 5
25	0am49	26	♊	5am53
28	4am35	28	♋	2pm17

d	h	
5	23	PERIGEE
21	15	APOGEE

DAILY ASPECTARIAN

Day	Aspect	Time
1 S	☽☍♂	1am15
	☽△♃	7 2
	☽✶♇	7 23
	☽△♆	1pm 2
	☽⚻♀	3 18
	☿⚺♄	4 57
	☽⚺♅	9 11
	☽∥♅	10 12
2 Su	☉⚻☽	2am46
	☽∠♇	9 9
	☉#☽	6pm39
	☽⚻♄	7 43
	☽☍☿	10 32
3 M	☽⚻♂	7am 3
	☽□♃	9 59
	☽⚺♇	10 5
	♀∥♆	1pm38
	☽□♆	3 29
	☽☍♀	3 44
	♂ ♑	6 57
	☽⚼♄	8 34
	♀□♆	10 51
	☽☌♅	11 1
4 T	☉☍☽	8am 6
	☽#♀	8 44
	☽⚼♂	8 45
	☽#♆	9 2
	♃✶♇	10 45
	☿#♇	10 57
	☽#♃	1pm20
	☿∥♄	3 38
	☽△♄	8 57
5 W	♆SR	3am19
	☽⚻☿	4 43
	☽△♂	10 3
	☽☌♇	10 30
	☽✶♃	10 35
	☽⚻♀	2pm28
	☉∠♂	2 29
	☽✶♆	3 50
	♂△♇	7 14
	♂✶♃	9 56
	☽⚺♅	11 6
6 Th	☽⚼☿	7am24
	☽∠♃	10 40
	☉⚻☽	11 43
	☽⚼♀	1pm46
	☿ ♒	3 22
	☽∠♆	3 53
	☽□♄	9 20
	☽∠♅	11 8
7 F	☽△☿	10am21
	☽⚺♇	10 40
	☽⚺♃	10 56
	☽□♂	12pm44
	☽△♀	1 19
	☿⚻♇	1 22
	☉⚼☽	1 45
	☿□♃	4 4
	☽⚺♆	4 10
	♀⚺♂	8 26
	☽✶♅	11 27
8 S	☿☌♀	9am31
	☽∠♇	11 14
	☉△☽	4pm16
	☽✶♄	10 49
9 Su	☿⚺♂	3am19
	☽∥♃	3 22
	☽∥♆	7 40
	☽∥♀	10 36
	☽✶♇	12pm20
	☽☌♃	12 47
	☽□♀	1 51
	☽✶♂	5 16
	☿□♆	6 3
	☽☌♆	6 11
	☽□☿	6 12
10 M	☽∠♄	0am25
	☽□♅	1 40
	☉∥☽	4 29
	♂✶♆	11 10
	☽∠♂	8pm37
	☉□☽	11 34
11 T	☽⚺♄	2am41
	♀□♃	10 49
	☽□♇	4pm30
	☽✶♀	5 0
	☽⚺♃	5 8
	☽⚺♆	10 44
12 W	☽#♅	0am 7
	☽⚺♂	0 45
	☿∠♄	4 19
	☽✶☿	5 48
	☽△♅	6 27
	☿☍♅	11 6
	☽∠♀	7pm37
	☽∠♃	8 17
	☉✶♄	8 45
	♀⚻♇	11 15
13 Th	☽∠♆	1am59
	☽☌♄	9 12
	☽⚼♅	9 47
	☉✶☽	10 11
	☽∠☿	1pm 4
	☽⚺♀	10 55
	☽△♇	11 14
	☽∥☿	13 6
14 F	☽✶♃	0am 2
	☽∥☿	1 5
	☽✶♆	5 49
	☽☌♂	11 15
	☽#♅	11 59
	☽⚻♅	1pm42
	☉∠☽	4 36
	☽⚺☿	9 14
15 S	☽⚼♇	3am26
	☿#♅	3 41
	♃SR	2pm57
	☽⚺♄	6 3
	☉⚺☽	11 42
16 Su	☉∥♀	0am52
	♄⚼♅	2 55
	♂⚻♅	4 38
	☽☌♀	7 20
	☽⚻♇	8 8
	☽□♃	9 5
	☽□♆	3pm 2
	☽☍♅	11 2
	☽∠♄	11 13
17 M	☽⚺♂	0am14
	☽∥♀	3 7
	☉∥☽	7 14
	☽∥♆	12pm22
	☽☌☿	3 59
	☽∥♃	5 21
18 T	☽✶♄	4am50
	♀SD	6 13
	☽∠♂	7 34
	☉☌☽	3pm39
	☽⚺♀	6 2
	☽☍♇	6 53
	☽△♃	7 57
19 W	☽△♆	2am 5
	☉ ♓	3 49
	☉∥♆	7 27
	☽⚻♅	10 8
	☽✶♂	3pm23
	☉⚺♀	9 22
20 Th	☽∠♀	0am11
	☽⚼♃	1 59
	☉☍♇	5 26
	☽⚼♆	8 12
	☽⚺☿	1pm41
	☽⚼♅	4 16
	☽□♄	5 17
	☉△♃	6 27
21 F	☽✶♀	6am48
	☽⚻♇	7 10
	☉∥♃	7 41
	☽⚻♃	8 19
	☉⚺☽	9 38
	☽⚻♆	2pm36
	☿✶♄	3 25
	☽△♅	10 39
22 S	☽∠☿	1am22
	☽□♂	8 9
	♀⚻♇	9 48
	☽⚼♇	1pm39
	☉∠☽	7 2
23 Su	☉#☽	5am39
	☽△♄	6 40
	☽#♃	10 28
	☽✶☿	1pm13
	☽#♆	3 48
	☉△♆	7 22
	☽△♇	8 5
	☽□♀	8 42
	☽☍♃	9 14
24 M	☽☍♆	3am33
	☉✶☽	4 19
	☽#♀	6 41
	☽#☿	10 15
	☽□♅	11 23
	☽⚼♄	1pm11
	♀□♃	9 22
	☿ ♓	9 44
25 T	☿∥♀	0am10
	☽△♂	0 49
	☿∠♂	1 34
	☿☍♇	10 26
	☿△♃	5pm54
	☽⚻♄	7 11
	☿⚺♀	9 53
	♂⚼♇	11 2
26 W	☽□♇	7am40
	☽⚼♂	8 14
	☽⚻♃	8 46
	☽△♀	9 39
	☽□☿	11 20
	☽⚻♆	2pm54
	☉□☽	8 52
	☽✶♅	10 13
	☽∥♅	11 7
27 Th	☿△♆	11am32
	☉⚻♅	1pm10
	☽⚼♃	1 18
	☽⚻♂	2 35
	☽⚼♀	2 59
	☽⚼♆	7 17
	☿∥♆	9 33
28 F	☽∠♅	2am17
	☽☍♄	4 35
	☽✶♇	3pm51
	☽△♃	4 48
	☽⚻♀	7 15
	☽△♆	10 36
	☽∥♅	11 9
	☿∥♃	11 30

LONGITUDE

Day	Sid. Time	☉	☽	☽ 12 Hour	Mean ☊	True ☊	☿	♀	♂	♃	♄	♅	♆	♇
	h m s	° ' "	° ' "	° ' "	° '	° '	° '	° '	° '	° '	° '	° '	° '	° '
1	10 33 10	9♓ 54 7	5♋ 24 28	12♋ 12 3	4♏ 15	2♏ 46R	7♓ 26	2♒ 50	18♑ 8	1♏ 23R	24♐ 43	8♌ 24R	4♏ 37R	0♍ 51R
2	10 37 7	10 54 19	19 7 7	26 9 40	4 12	2 41	9 17	3 13	18 51	1 20	24 46	8 22	4 37	0 50
3	10 41 3	11 54 29	3♌ 19 28	10♌ 36 5	4 9	2 34	11 10	3 39	19 35	1 18	24 50	8 19	4 36	0 48
4	10 45 0	12 54 36	17 58 51	25 26 55	4 6	2 26	13 3	4 6	20 19	1 15	24 53	8 17	4 35	0 47
5	10 48 57	13 54 42	2♍ 59 12	10♍ 34 30	4 3	2 18	14 57	4 34	21 2	1 11	24 56	8 15	4 34	0 45
6	10 52 53	14 54 46	18 11 32	25 48 57	4 0	2 11	16 52	5 5	21 46	1 8	24 59	8 13	4 33	0 44
7	10 56 50	15 54 48	3♎ 25 24	10♎ 59 39	3 56	2 6	18 48	5 37	22 29	1 5	25 2	8 12	4 32	0 42
8	11 0 46	16 54 48	18 30 35	25 57 14	3 53	2 3	20 44	6 10	23 13	1 1	25 4	8 10	4 31	0 41
9	11 4 43	17 54 47	3♏ 18 49	10♏ 34 44	3 50	2 2D	22 41	6 44	23 57	0 57	25 7	8 8	4 30	0 40
10	11 8 39	18 54 43	17 44 38	24 48 16	3 47	2 3	24 39	7 20	24 40	0 53	25 10	8 6	4 29	0 38
11	11 12 36	19 54 39	1♐ 45 36	8♐ 36 41	3 44	2 4	26 36	7 58	25 24	0 49	25 12	8 4	4 28	0 37
12	11 16 32	20 54 33	15 21 45	22 1 2	3 41	2 6R	28 34	8 36	26 8	0 45	25 14	8 2	4 27	0 35
13	11 20 29	21 54 24	28 34 53	5♑ 3 41	3 37	2 6	0♈ 32	9 16	26 52	0 40	25 17	8 1	4 26	0 34
14	11 24 26	22 54 15	11♑ 27 49	17 47 42	3 34	2 4	2 29	9 57	27 35	0 36	25 19	7 59	4 25	0 32
15	11 28 22	23 54 4	24 3 43	0♒ 16 16	3 31	2 1	4 25	10 38	28 19	0 31	25 21	7 58	4 24	0 31
16	11 32 19	24 53 51	6♒ 25 43	12 32 25	3 28	1 55	6 20	11 21	29 3	0 26	25 23	7 56	4 23	0 30
17	11 36 15	25 53 35	18 36 41	24 38 49	3 25	1 49	8 14	12 5	29 47	0 21	25 25	7 54	4 22	0 28
18	11 40 12	26 53 19	0♓ 39 5	6♓ 37 45	3 21	1 42	10 6	12 50	0♒ 31	0 15	25 27	7 53	4 20	0 27
19	11 44 8	27 53 0	12 35 2	18 31 11	3 18	1 36	11 56	13 36	1 15	0 10	25 28	7 52	4 19	0 26
20	11 48 5	28 52 40	24 26 25	0♈ 20 57	3 15	1 30	13 43	14 23	1 59	0 5	25 30	7 50	4 18	0 24
21	11 52 1	29 52 17	6♈ 15 2	12 8 55	3 12	1 26	15 26	15 10	2 42	29♎ 59	25 32	7 49	4 17	0 23
22	11 55 58	0♈ 51 53	18 2 51	23 57 7	3 9	1 23	17 7	15 58	3 26	29 53	25 33	7 48	4 15	0 22
23	11 59 54	1 51 26	29 52 3	5♉ 48 0	3 6	1 22D	18 43	16 47	4 10	29 47	25 34	7 46	4 14	0 21
24	12 3 51	2 50 57	11♉ 45 19	17 44 25	3 2	1 23	20 14	17 37	4 54	29 41	25 36	7 45	4 13	0 19
25	12 7 48	3 50 26	23 45 46	29 49 48	2 59	1 24	21 41	18 28	5 38	29 35	25 37	7 44	4 11	0 18
26	12 11 44	4 49 53	5♊ 57 2	12♊ 7 58	2 56	1 26	23 2	19 19	6 22	29 29	25 38	7 43	4 10	0 17
27	12 15 41	5 49 18	18 23 7	24 43 1	2 53	1 28	24 18	20 11	7 6	29 22	25 39	7 42	4 9	0 16
28	12 19 37	6 48 40	1♋ 8 11	7♋ 39 3	2 50	1 29R	25 27	21 4	7 50	29 16	25 39	7 41	4 7	0 15
29	12 23 34	7 48 0	14 16 4	20 59 34	2 47	1 29	26 31	21 57	8 34	29 9	25 40	7 40	4 6	0 13
30	12 27 30	8 47 17	27 49 48	4♌ 46 54	2 43	1 28	27 27	22 50	9 18	29 2	25 41	7 39	4 4	0 12
31	12 31 27	9♈ 46 33	11♌ 50 52	19♌ 1 29	2♏ 40	1♏ 26	28♈ 17	23♒ 45	10♒ 2	28♎ 55	25♐ 41	7♌ 38	4♏ 3	0♍ 11

DECLINATION and LATITUDE

Day	☉ Decl	☽ Decl	☽ Lat	☽ 12 Hr. Decl	☿ Decl	☿ Lat	♀ Decl	♀ Lat	♂ Decl	♂ Lat	♃ Decl	♃ Lat	♄ Decl	♄ Lat
1	7S51	18N47	4S33	18N 6	10S35	1S56	13S37	6N 4	22S53	0S40	10S36	1N27	21S59	1N22
2	7 29	17 9	4 59	15 55	9 50	1 53	13 40	5 56	22 48	0 41	10 35	1 27	21 59	1 22
3	7 6	14 26	5 7	12 42	9 3	1 49	13 42	5 48	22 42	0 42	10 34	1 27	21 59	1 22
4	6 43	10 44	4 56	8 36	8 16	1 44	13 44	5 39	22 37	0 43	10 32	1 28	21 59	1 22
5	6 20	6 17	4 25	3 52	7 27	1 39	13 46	5 31	22 31	0 44	10 31	1 28	21 59	1 22
6	5 57	1 23	3 34	1S 8	6 37	1 33	13 47	5 22	22 25	0 45	10 30	1 28	21 59	1 22
7	5 33	3S38	2 29	6 4	5 46	1 27	13 48	5 13	22 19	0 45	10 28	1 28	21 59	1 22
8	5 10	8 23	1 13	10 32	4 54	1 20	13 49	5 5	22 13	0 46	10 27	1 28	21 59	1 22
9	4 47	12 31	0N 7	14 16	4 1	1 13	13 49	4 56	22 6	0 47	10 25	1 29	21 59	1 22
10	4 23	15 47	1 24	17 2	3 7	1 5	13 48	4 47	21 59	0 48	10 24	1 29	21 59	1 23
11	3 60	18 0	2 34	18 42	2 12	0 56	13 47	4 39	21 52	0 49	10 22	1 29	21 59	1 23
12	3 36	19 6	3 33	19 15	1 17	0 47	13 46	4 30	21 45	0 50	10 21	1 29	21 59	1 23
13	3 13	19 7	4 19	18 44	0 22	0 37	13 44	4 22	21 37	0 51	10 19	1 29	21 59	1 23
14	2 49	18 7	4 51	17 17	0N34	0 27	13 42	4 13	21 30	0 52	10 17	1 29	21 59	1 23
15	2 25	16 15	5 8	15 2	1 30	0 16	13 39	4 4	21 22	0 53	10 15	1 30	21 59	1 23
16	2 2	13 40	5 10	12 9	2 26	0 5	13 36	3 56	21 14	0 54	10 13	1 30	21 59	1 23
17	1 38	10 32	4 58	8 48	3 22	0N 6	13 32	3 48	21 5	0 54	10 11	1 30	21 59	1 23
18	1 14	6 60	4 32	5 7	4 17	0 18	13 27	3 39	20 57	0 55	10 10	1 30	21 59	1 23
19	0 51	3 13	3 55	1 16	5 11	0 30	13 23	3 31	20 48	0 56	10 7	1 30	21 59	1 23
20	0 27	0N41	3 8	2N37	6 4	0 43	13 17	3 23	20 39	0 57	10 5	1 30	21 59	1 23
21	0 3	4 31	2 13	6 24	6 56	0 55	13 12	3 14	20 30	0 58	10 3	1 31	21 59	1 23
22	0N21	8 12	1 13	9 56	7 46	1 8	13 5	3 6	20 21	0 59	10 1	1 31	21 59	1 23
23	0 44	11 34	0 8	13 5	8 34	1 20	12 58	2 58	20 11	0 60	9 59	1 31	21 59	1 23
24	1 8	14 28	0S57	15 42	9 20	1 32	12 51	2 50	20 2	1 1	9 57	1 31	21 59	1 24
25	1 32	16 47	2 0	17 40	10 4	1 45	12 43	2 42	19 52	1 2	9 54	1 31	21 59	1 24
26	1 55	18 22	2 59	18 51	10 45	1 56	12 35	2 34	19 42	1 3	9 52	1 31	21 59	1 24
27	2 19	19 6	3 51	19 8	11 24	2 7	12 26	2 27	19 31	1 4	9 50	1 31	21 59	1 24
28	2 42	18 54	4 32	18 25	11 59	2 18	12 17	2 19	19 21	1 4	9 47	1 31	21 59	1 24
29	3 6	17 41	5 1	16 42	12 32	2 28	12 7	2 12	19 11	1 5	9 45	1 31	21 59	1 24
30	3 29	15 27	5 15	13 58	13 1	2 38	11 57	2 4	18 60	1 6	9 42	1 32	21 59	1 24
31	3N52	12N16	5S10	10N21	13N27	2N46	11S46	1N57	18S49	1S 7	9S40	1N32	21S58	1N24

Day	♅ Decl	♅ Lat	♆ Decl	♆ Lat	♇ Decl	♇ Lat
1	18N49	0N40	11S23	1N47	22N13	11N51
5	18 51	0 40	11 21	1 48	22 15	11 51
9	18 53	0 40	11 20	1 48	22 17	11 51
13	18 55	0 40	11 18	1 48	22 19	11 51
17	18 56	0 40	11 17	1 48	22 21	11 51
21	18 58	0 40	11 15	1 48	22 23	11 50
25	18 59	0 40	11 13	1 48	22 24	11 50
29	18N60	0N40	11S11	1N49	22N25	11N49

☽ PHENOMENA

d	h	m	
5	18	28	○
12	10	48	☾
20	9	50	●
28	11	19	☽

d	h	° '
6	7	0
12	12	19S14
19	20	0
27	7	19N 9

d	h	° '
2	23	5S 7
8	22	0
15	15	5N11
23	3	0
30	6	5S15

VOID OF COURSE ☽

Last Aspect	☽ Ingress
1 11pm32	2 ♌ 6pm27
4 11am 8	4 ♍ 7pm15
6 10am43	6 ♎ 6pm36
8 10am36	8 ♏ 6pm35
10 1pm38	10 ♐ 8pm57
12 5pm55	13 ♑ 2am37
15 8am44	15 ♒ 11am28
17 1pm34	17 ♓ 10pm42
20 9am50	20 ♈ 11am17
22 11pm50	23 ♉ 0am16
24 12pm39	25 ♊ 12pm20
27 8pm32	27 ♋ 9pm53
30 2am 5	30 ♌ 3am46

d	h	
6	9	PERIGEE
20	19	APOGEE

DAILY ASPECTARIAN

Day	Aspect	Time
1 S	☽△☿	4am10
	☽⚺♅	5 17
	☉△☽	8 36
	☿⚻♅	12pm12
	☽∠♇	6 20
	☽☍♂	11 32
2 Su	☽⚻♄	9am41
	☽⚼☿	10 10
	☉⚼☽	12pm27
	☽⚺♇	7 49
	☽□♃	8 38
3 M	☽☍♀	0am33
	☽□♆	2 6
	☽#♀	5 10
	☽☌♅	8 15
	☽⚼♄	10 46
	☽⚻☿	2pm49
	☉⚻☽	3 10
	☉☌☿	8 12
	☽#♆	8 18
4 T	☽#♃	1am11
	☽⚻♂	3 57
	☽△♄	11 8
	☽#☿	4pm45
	☽☌♇	8 28
	☽✶♃	9 10
	♀□♆	11 41
	☉#☽	11 47
5 W	☽✶♆	2am30
	☽⚻♀	2 36
	☽⚼♂	5 4
	☽⚺♅	8 19
	☿⚼♃	3pm 5
	☉☍☽	6 28
	☽∠♃	8 46
	☽☍☿	9 37
6 Th	☽∠♆	2am 8
	☽⚼♀	3 4
	☽△♂	5 54
	☽∠♅	7 54
	☽□♄	10 43
	☽⚺♇	7pm43
	☽⚺♃	8 19
7 F	☽⚺♆	1am46
	☽△♀	3 35
	☉⚼♃	3 44
	☽✶♅	7 32
	☉∥☽	8 46
	☽∥☿	8 55
	☿⚼♆	9 4
	♂#♇	9 24
	☉∥☿	10 35
	☽∠♇	7pm29
	☉⚻☽	9 16
8 S	☽⚻☿	4am 7
	☿∠♀	7 22
	☽□♂	7 58
	☽✶♄	10 36
	☽∥♃	11 25
	☽∥♆	4pm42
	☽✶♇	7 40
	☽☌♃	8 9
	☉⚼☽	11 18
9 Su	☽☌♆	1am57
	☿⚼♅	5 19
	☽□♀	5 53
	☽□♅	7 55
	☽⚼☿	8 20
	☽∥♀	8 43
	☽∠♄	11 16
10 M	☿✶♂	0am30
	♂∥♄	0 30
	☉△☽	2 7
	☿□♄	6 25
	☽✶♂	12pm25
	☽⚺♄	12 39
	☽△☿	1 38
	☉⚼♆	1 38
	♂⚺♄	5 1
	☽□♇	10 1
	☽⚺♃	10 22
11 T	♀☍♅	3am59
	☽⚺♆	4 43
	☽△♅	11 1
	☽✶♀	11 23
	☽∠♂	4pm 2
	☽#♅	5 16
12 W	☽∠♃	0am41
	☽∠♆	7 21
	☉□☽	10 48
	☽⚼♅	1pm50
	☽∠♀	3 40
	☿ ♈	5 32
	☽☌♄	5 55
	☽⚺♂	8 39
13 Th	☿⚻♇	0am27
	☿⚻♃	1 42
	☽△♇	3 39
	☽✶♃	3 50
	☽□☿	4 13
	☽#♅	7 5
	☽✶♆	10 49
	☽⚻♅	5pm29
	☽⚺♀	8 58
14 F	☉⚼♅	1am55
	☽⚼♇	7 42
	♀∠♄	1pm35
	♃✶♇	9 45
	☉✶☽	11 40
	☿⚻♆	11 47
15 S	☽⚺♄	2am29
	☽☌♂	8 44
	☽□♃	12pm23
	☽⚻♇	12 27
	☉#☿	4 36
	☽□♆	8 0
	☽✶☿	11 47
16 Su	☽∥♀	0am37
	☽☍♅	2 56
	☉∠☽	7 24
	☽∠♄	7 47
	☽☌♀	10 17
	☉□♄	12pm 6
	☽∥♆	6 33
	☿△♅	7 54
17 M	☽∥♃	2am25
	♂ ♒	7 12
	☽∠☿	10 53
	☽✶♄	1pm34
	☉⚺☽	3 48
	♂□♃	4 33
	♂⚻♇	10 3
	☽△♃	11 13
	☽☍♇	11 36
	☽⚺♂	11 42
18 T	☽△♆	7am23
	☽#☿	2pm 0
	☽⚻♅	2 30
	☽⚺☿	10 26
19 W	☽⚺♀	2am11
	☽⚼♃	5 11
	☽∠♂	7 53
	☽⚼♆	1pm36
	☉∥☽	4 18
	☽⚼♅	8 45
	☉#☽	10 43
20 Th	☽□♄	2am 9
	☉☌☽	9 50
	☽∠♀	10 44
	☽⚻♃	11 21
	☽⚻♇	12pm 6
	☽✶♂	4 19
	☿✶♀	4 49
	♃ ♎	7 4
	☽⚻♆	8 0
	☿⚼♇	11 14
21 F	☉⚻♃	2am25
	☉ ♈	3 6
	☽△♅	3 11
	☉⚻♇	12pm10
	☽⚼♇	6 33
	☽✶♀	7 28
	☽∥☿	8 12
	☽☌☿	9 47
22 S	☽#♃	12pm32
	☉∠♀	2 39
	☽△♄	3 16
	☽#♆	9 33
	☽☍♃	11 50
23 Su	☽△♇	0am58
	♂□♆	1 59
	☉⚺☽	4 24
	☽☍♆	8 49
	☽□♂	9 17
	☽#♀	10 43
	☽□♅	3pm57
	☽⚼♄	9 39
24 M	☽□♀	12pm39
	☉∠☽	1 19
	☿#♃	6 53
	☽⚺☿	7 19
25 T	☽⚻♄	3am40
	☉⚻♆	8 17
	☽⚻♃	11 25
	☽□♇	12pm55
	☽⚻♆	8 31
	☉✶☽	9 37
26 W	☽△♂	0am52
	☽✶♅	3 26
	☽∠☿	4 32
	☽⚼♃	4pm22
	☿#♆	4 35
	☽∥♅	5 14
27 Th	☽⚼♆	1am27
	☽△♀	3 41
	☽⚼♂	7 30
	☽∠♅	8 11
	☽✶☿	12pm21
	☽☍♄	1 45
	♂☍♅	6 58
	☽∥♅	8 22
	☽△♃	8 32
	☽✶♇	10 21
28 F	☿△♄	4am28
	☽△♆	5 31
	☽⚼♀	9 44
	☿#♀	9 51
	☉□☽	11 19
	☽⚺♅	12pm 2
	☽⚻♂	1 4
	☉△♅	8 48
29 S	☽∠♇	1am43
	☽⚻♀	2pm39
	☽⚻♄	8 15
	♂#♅	11 10
	☽□☿	11 18
30 Su	☽□♃	2am 5
	☽⚺♇	4 7
	☽□♆	10 46
	☽∥☿	4pm44
	☽☌♅	4 53
	☉△☽	8 14
	☽☍♂	8 47
	☽⚼♄	10 3
31 M	☽#♀	3am23
	☽#♆	7 3
	☽#♃	4pm12
	☿☍♃	6 4
	☽☍♀	9 7
	♂∠♄	9 21
	☽△♄	11 0
	☉⚼☽	11 3

APRIL 1958

LONGITUDE

Day	Sid. Time	☉	☽	☽ 12 Hour	Mean ☊	True ☊	☿	♀	♂	♃	♄	♅	♆	♇
	h m s	° ' "	° ' "	° ' "	° '	° '	° '	° '	° '	° '	° '	° '	° '	° '
1	12 35 23	10♈ 45 45	26♌ 18 25	3♍ 41 7	2♏ 37	1♏ 23R	29♈ 0	24♒ 40	10♒ 47	28♎ 49R	25♐ 42	7♌ 37R	4♏ 2R	0♍ 10R
2	12 39 20	11 44 56	11♍ 8 49	18 40 37	2 34	1 20	29 36	25 35	11 31	28 42	25 42	7 37	4 0	0 9
3	12 43 17	12 44 4	26 15 27	3♎ 52 8	2 31	1 18	0♉ 5	26 31	12 15	28 34	25 42	7 36	3 59	0 8
4	12 47 13	13 43 11	11♎ 29 25	19 6 2	2 27	1 17	0 27	27 27	12 59	28 27	25 42R	7 35	3 57	0 7
5	12 51 10	14 42 15	26 40 46	4♏ 12 26	2 24	1 16D	0 41	28 24	13 43	28 20	25 42	7 35	3 56	0 6
6	12 55 6	15 41 17	11♏ 40 1	19 2 38	2 21	1 16	0 49R	29 22	14 27	28 13	25 42	7 34	3 54	0 5
7	12 59 3	16 40 18	26 19 33	3♐ 30 16	2 18	1 17	0 50	0♓ 19	15 11	28 5	25 42	7 34	3 52	0 4
8	13 2 59	17 39 17	10♐ 34 24	17 31 46	2 15	1 18	0 44	1 18	15 55	27 58	25 42	7 33	3 51	0 3
9	13 6 56	18 38 13	24 22 23	1♑ 6 19	2 12	1 19	0 31	2 16	16 40	27 51	25 42	7 33	3 49	0 2
10	13 10 52	19 37 8	7♑ 43 48	14 15 10	2 8	1 20	0 13	3 15	17 24	27 43	25 41	7 33	3 48	0 1
11	13 14 49	20 36 2	20 40 48	27 1 8	2 5	1 20R	29♈ 49	4 15	18 8	27 36	25 41	7 32	3 46	0 0
12	13 18 46	21 34 54	3♒ 16 39	9♒ 27 52	2 2	1 20	29 21	5 14	18 52	27 28	25 40	7 32	3 45	0 0
13	13 22 42	22 33 43	15 35 16	21 39 22	1 59	1 19	28 48	6 15	19 36	27 20	25 39	7 32	3 43	29♌ 59
14	13 26 39	23 32 31	27 40 41	3♓ 39 40	1 56	1 18	28 11	7 15	20 21	27 13	25 38	7 32	3 41	29 58
15	13 30 35	24 31 18	9♓ 36 47	15 32 28	1 52	1 17	27 31	8 16	21 5	27 5	25 37	7 32D	3 40	29 57
16	13 34 32	25 30 3	21 27 8	27 21 10	1 49	1 16	26 49	9 17	21 49	26 57	25 36	7 32	3 38	29 56
17	13 38 28	26 28 45	3♈ 14 54	9♈ 8 42	1 46	1 15	26 6	10 19	22 33	26 50	25 35	7 32	3 37	29 56
18	13 42 25	27 27 26	15 2 51	20 57 40	1 43	1 15	25 23	11 20	23 18	26 42	25 34	7 32	3 35	29 55
19	13 46 21	28 26 5	26 53 24	2♉ 50 20	1 40	1 15D	24 40	12 22	24 2	26 34	25 33	7 32	3 33	29 54
20	13 50 18	29 24 42	8♉ 48 44	14 48 50	1 37	1 15	23 58	13 25	24 46	26 27	25 31	7 33	3 32	29 54
21	13 54 14	0♉ 23 17	20 50 54	26 55 11	1 33	1 15	23 18	14 27	25 30	26 19	25 30	7 33	3 30	29 53
22	13 58 11	1 21 50	3♊ 1 58	9♊ 11 31	1 30	1 15R	22 40	15 30	26 14	26 11	25 28	7 33	3 28	29 53
23	14 2 8	2 20 22	15 24 7	21 40 3	1 27	1 15	22 5	16 33	26 59	26 4	25 26	7 34	3 27	29 52
24	14 6 4	3 18 51	27 59 38	4♋ 23 11	1 24	1 15	21 34	17 37	27 43	25 56	25 25	7 34	3 25	29 51
25	14 10 1	4 17 18	10♋ 50 58	17 23 17	1 21	1 15	21 7	18 40	28 27	25 48	25 23	7 35	3 24	29 51
26	14 13 57	5 15 43	24 0 25	0♌ 42 36	1 18	1 15	20 44	19 44	29 11	25 41	25 21	7 35	3 22	29 50
27	14 17 54	6 14 6	7♌ 30 1	14 22 48	1 14	1 15D	20 26	20 48	29 55	25 33	25 19	7 36	3 20	29 50
28	14 21 50	7 12 26	21 20 59	28 24 33	1 11	1 15	20 13	21 52	0♓ 40	25 26	25 17	7 36	3 19	29 50
29	14 25 47	8 10 44	5♍ 33 20	12♍ 47 3	1 8	1 15	20 4	22 57	1 24	25 19	25 14	7 37	3 17	29 49
30	14 29 43	9♉ 9 1	20♍ 5 18	27♍ 27 32	1♏ 5	1♏ 15	20♈ 0D	24♓ 1	2♓ 8	25♎ 11	25♐ 12	7♌ 38	3♏ 15	29♌ 49

DECLINATION and LATITUDE

Day	☉ Decl	☽ Decl	☽ Lat	☽ 12 Hr. Decl	☿ Decl	☿ Lat	♀ Decl	♀ Lat	♂ Decl	♂ Lat	♃ Decl	♃ Lat	♄ Decl	♄ Lat
1	4N16	8N15	4S46	6N 0	13N49	2N53	11S35	1N49	18S38	1S 8	9S38	1N32	21S58	1N24
2	4 39	3 38	4 3	1 12	14 8	2 60	11 23	1 42	18 26	1 9	9 35	1 32	21 58	1 24
3	5 2	1S18	3 2	3S46	14 23	3 5	11 11	1 35	18 15	1 10	9 32	1 32	21 58	1 24
4	5 25	6 12	1 47	8 31	14 35	3 9	10 59	1 28	18 3	1 11	9 30	1 32	21 58	1 24
5	5 48	10 41	0 25	12 40	14 43	3 12	10 46	1 21	17 52	1 12	9 27	1 32	21 58	1 24
6	6 11	14 26	0N57	15 56	14 47	3 13	10 32	1 14	17 40	1 13	9 25	1 32	21 58	1 24
7	6 33	17 9	2 14	18 5	14 47	3 13	10 18	1 8	17 28	1 14	9 22	1 32	21 58	1 25
8	6 56	18 43	3 21	19 3	14 43	3 12	10 4	1 1	17 15	1 15	9 19	1 32	21 58	1 25
9	7 18	19 6	4 14	18 52	14 36	3 9	9 49	0 55	17 3	1 16	9 17	1 32	21 58	1 25
10	7 41	18 23	4 51	17 39	14 25	3 4	9 34	0 48	16 50	1 17	9 14	1 32	21 58	1 25
11	8 3	16 43	5 12	15 35	14 11	2 58	9 18	0 42	16 38	1 17	9 11	1 32	21 58	1 25
12	8 25	14 17	5 17	12 50	13 54	2 50	9 2	0 36	16 25	1 18	9 8	1 32	21 58	1 25
13	8 47	11 16	5 8	9 35	13 33	2 41	8 46	0 30	16 12	1 19	9 6	1 32	21 58	1 25
14	9 9	7 50	4 45	5 60	13 10	2 30	8 29	0 24	15 59	1 20	9 3	1 32	21 57	1 25
15	9 30	4 7	4 9	2 12	12 45	2 19	8 12	0 18	15 45	1 21	9 0	1 32	21 57	1 25
16	9 52	0 16	3 24	1N40	12 17	2 5	7 54	0 12	15 32	1 22	8 58	1 32	21 57	1 25
17	10 13	3N35	2 30	5 28	11 49	1 51	7 36	0 7	15 18	1 23	8 55	1 32	21 57	1 25
18	10 34	7 18	1 29	9 4	11 19	1 36	7 18	0 1	15 5	1 24	8 52	1 32	21 57	1 25
19	10 55	10 45	0 24	12 19	10 48	1 20	6 59	0S 4	14 51	1 25	8 49	1 32	21 57	1 25
20	11 16	13 47	0S42	15 6	10 17	1 4	6 40	0 10	14 37	1 26	8 47	1 32	21 57	1 25
21	11 37	16 15	1 47	17 14	9 47	0 47	6 21	0 15	14 23	1 27	8 44	1 32	21 57	1 25
22	11 57	18 2	2 48	18 37	9 17	0 30	6 1	0 20	14 9	1 28	8 41	1 32	21 57	1 25
23	12 17	18 58	3 42	19 6	8 49	0 13	5 41	0 25	13 55	1 28	8 38	1 32	21 56	1 26
24	12 37	18 60	4 26	18 39	8 21	0S 4	5 21	0 29	13 40	1 29	8 36	1 32	21 56	1 26
25	12 57	18 3	4 58	17 13	7 56	0 20	5 0	0 34	13 26	1 30	8 33	1 32	21 56	1 26
26	13 17	16 8	5 15	14 50	7 32	0 36	4 40	0 39	13 11	1 31	8 30	1 32	21 56	1 26
27	13 36	13 18	5 16	11 35	7 11	0 52	4 19	0 43	12 56	1 32	8 28	1 31	21 56	1 26
28	13 55	9 40	4 59	7 36	6 52	1 7	3 57	0 48	12 42	1 33	8 25	1 31	21 56	1 26
29	14 14	5 24	4 23	3 6	6 36	1 21	3 36	0 52	12 27	1 34	8 23	1 31	21 56	1 26
30	14N33	0N43	3S30	1S42	6N22	1S35	3S14	0S56	12S12	1S35	8S20	1N31	21S56	1N26

Day	♅ Decl	♅ Lat	♆ Decl	♆ Lat	♇ Decl	♇ Lat
1	19N 0	0N40	11S10	1N49	22N26	11N49
5	19 1	0 40	11 7	1 49	22 27	11 48
9	19 1	0 40	11 5	1 49	22 28	11 48
13	19 2	0 39	11 3	1 49	22 28	11 47
17	19 1	0 39	11 1	1 49	22 28	11 46
21	19 1	0 39	10 59	1 49	22 28	11 45
25	19 1	0 39	10 56	1 49	22 28	11 44
29	18N60	0N39	10S54	1N49	22N28	11N43

☽ PHENOMENA

d	h	m	
4	3	45	○
10	23	50	☾
19	3	24	●
26	21	36	☽

d	h	° '
2	18	0
8	20	19S 7
16	2	0
23	13	19N 6
30	4	0

d	h	° '
5	7	0
11	20	5N17
19	9	0
26	13	5S18

VOID OF COURSE ☽

Last Aspect		☽ Ingress		
1	4am36	1	♍	6am 1
2	11pm 8	3	♎	5am54
5	2am55	5	♏	5am17
6	4am45	7	♐	6am 7
9	6am 6	9	♑	10am 1
11	4pm44	11	♒	5pm42
14	4am35	14	♓	4am39
16	8am26	16	♈	5pm23
19	6am 5	19	♉	6am17
21	5pm49	21	♊	6pm 3
24	3am31	24	♋	3am47
26	2am59	26	♌	10am44
28	2pm23	28	♍	2pm41
30	8am19	30	♎	4pm 7

d	h	
3	21	PERIGEE
16	23	APOGEE

DAILY ASPECTARIAN

Day	Aspect	Time
1	☉⚹♂	1am17
T	☽⚹♃	4 3
	☽△☿	4 36
	☽☌♇	6 17
	☽⚹♆	12pm32
	☽⚺♅	6 20
	☉∥☽	7 20
2	☽⚻♂	0am37
W	☉⚻☽	1 2
	♀⚹♄	3 4
	☽∠♃	4 2
	☽⚼☿	5 43
	☽∠♆	12pm30
	☽∠♅	6 13
	☿ ♉	7 20
	☽□♄	11 8
3	☽⚻♀	0am26
Th	☽⚼♂	1 38
	☿△♇	2 38
	☽⚺♃	3 38
	♀∥♆	5 51
	☽⚺♇	6 6
	☽⚻☿	6 12
	☽⚺♆	12pm 9
	☽⚹♅	5 52
	☉#☽	7 46
4	☽⚼♀	1am37
F	☽△♂	2 28
	☉☍☽	3 45
	☽∠♇	5 42
	☽∥♃	5pm 9
	♄SR	7 40
	☽⚹♄	10 27
	♀△♃	10 28
5	☽∥♀	0am25
S	☽∥♆	2 33
	☽☌♃	2 37
	☽△♀	2 55
	☽⚹♇	5 26
	☽☍☿	6 27
	☉⚼♇	9 29
	☽☌♆	11 32
	☽□♅	5pm24
	☽∠♄	10 27
6	☽#☿	2am39
Su	☽□♂	4 45
	☉⚻☽	6 59
	☿SR	2pm23
	♀ ♓	4 0
	♀☍♇	5 46
	☽⚺♄	10 58
7	☽⚺♃	2am55
M	☽∥♂	3 12
	☽□♇	6 14
	☽□♀	7 8
	☽⚻☿	7 28
	☉⚼☽	9 35
	☿⚹♀	11 40
	☽⚺♆	12pm36
	☽△♅	6 52
8	☽#♅	1am42
T	☽∠♃	4 4
	☽⚼☿	8 46
	☽⚹♂	9 44
	☉△☽	1pm 9
	☽∠♆	2 16
	☽⚼♅	8 47
9	☽☌♄	2am20
W	☽#♅	5 35
	☽⚹♃	6 6
	☽△♇	10 4
	☽△☿	10 44
	☽∠♂	1pm46
	☽⚹♀	3 13
	☽⚹♆	4 52
	☽⚻♅	11 40
10	☿ ♈	12pm35
Th	♀△♆	12 50
	☿△♇	1 6
	☽⚼♇	1 25
	☽⚺♂	6 56
	☽∠♀	9 5
	☉□☽	11 50
11	☽∥♂	1am 6
F	☽⚺♄	9 26
	♇ ♌	11 25
	♀∥♃	12pm46
	☽□♃	12 58
	☽□☿	4 44
	☽⚻♇	5 41
12	☽□♆	0am54
S	☽#☿	3 45
	☽⚺♀	4 8
	☽☍♅	8 15
	☽∠♄	2pm20
	☉#♀	11 17
13	☽∥♆	1am34
Su	☽☌♂	8 27
	☉⚹☽	3pm 1
	☽∥♃	3 37
	☉#☽	3 55
	☉#♃	6 27
	☽∥♀	7 13
	☽⚹♄	7 56
	☽△♃	11 5
14	☽⚹☿	0am57
M	☽☍♇	4 35
	♀⚻♅	6 39
	☽△♆	12pm 2
	☽⚻♅	7 48
	☽☌♀	9 2
	☉∠☽	11 48
15	☽⚼♃	4am57
T	☽∠☿	5 33
	♅SD	8 22
	☽⚼♆	6pm18
	☿☍♃	6 34
16	☽⚺♂	0am48
W	☽⚼♅	2 12
	☉△♄	2 31
	☽□♄	8 26
	☉⚺☽	8 59
	☽⚺☿	10 18
	☽⚻♃	11 4
	☽⚻♇	5pm15
	☉☌☿	6 45
17	☽⚻♆	0am44
Th	☉☍♃	7 33
	☽△♅	8 43
	☽∠♂	9 21
	☿∠♀	10 55
	☽⚺♀	3pm45
	☿△♄	5 46
	☽⚼♇	11 44
18	☽#♀	0am 0
F	♀⚼♃	7 25
	☽#♃	10 31
	☿#♆	2pm41
	☽⚹♂	5 50
	☽☌☿	7 45
	☉∥☿	8 39
	☽△♄	9 17
	☽☍♃	11 22
19	☽∥☿	0am22
S	☽∠♀	1 4
	☉∥☽	1 28
	☽#♆	1 51
	☉☌☽	3 24
	☉#♆	5 2
	☽△♇	6 5
	☿⚹♂	10 33
	☽☍♆	1pm25
	☽□♅	9 27
20	☽⚼♄	3am25
Su	☽#♂	6 52
	☽⚹♀	10 5
	☉△♇	11 46
	☉ ♉	2pm27
	♂⚹♄	11 44
21	☽⚺☿	4am36
M	☽⚻♄	9 10
	☽□♂	9 48
	☽⚻♃	10 42
	☽□♇	5pm49
	☉⚺☽	8 27
	♂△♃	10 33
22	☽⚻♆	0am52
T	☽∠☿	8 37
	☽⚹♅	8 49
	☽⚼♃	3pm42
23	☽□♀	2am25
W	☉∠☽	4 2
	☽⚼♆	5 50
	☿#♃	9 39
	☽⚹☿	12pm17
	☽∠♅	1 42
	☽☍♄	7 7
	☽△♃	8 9
	☽△♂	11 26
24	☉☍♆	2am32
Th	☽⚹♇	3 31
	☽△♆	10 10
	☉⚹☽	10 49
	♀⚼♆	5pm53
	☽⚺♅	5 56
25	☽⚼♂	5am 5
F	☽∠♇	7 21
	☽△♀	3pm35
	☽□☿	6 15
	☉#♂	7 59
26	☽⚻♄	2am24
S	☽□♃	2 59
	☽⚻♂	9 49
	☽⚺♇	10 27
	☽□♆	4pm41
	☿⚺♀	5 29
	☽⚼♀	8 45
	♂☍♇	9 8
	☉□☽	9 36
	☉∥☽	9 59
27	☽☌♅	0am10
Su	♂ ♓	2 31
	☽#♂	2 52
	☽⚼♄	4 55
	☽#♆	4pm18
	☽△☿	10 4
28	☽⚻♀	0am58
M	☽△♄	6 40
	☽⚹♃	6 54
	☽#♃	7 25
	☉□♅	9 57
	☽☌♇	2pm23
	♀⚼♅	4 38
	☽☍♂	4 39
	☽∥☿	5 10
	☽⚹♆	8 12
	☽⚼☿	11 11
29	☽⚺♅	3am26
T	☉△☽	4 41
	☽∠♃	7 51
	☽#♀	10 13
	☽∠♆	9pm 0
	♃⚹♄	9 7
	☽⚻☿	11 51
30	☽∠♅	4am 9
W	☽☍♀	6 55
	☿SD	6 57
	☉⚼☽	7 5
	☽⚺♃	8 15
	☽□♄	8 19
	☽⚺♇	3pm49
	☽∥♀	6 14
	☽⚻♂	8 35
	☽⚺♆	9 20
	♀⚻♃	11 22

MAY 1958

LONGITUDE

Day	Sid. Time	☉	☽	☽ 12 Hour	Mean ☊	True ☊	☿	♀	♂	♃	♄	♅	♆	♇
	h m s	° ' "	° ' "	° ' "	° '	° '	° '	° '	° '	° '	° '	° '	° '	° '
1	14 33 40	10♉ 7 15	4♎ 53 4	12♎ 21 5	1♏ 2	1♏ 16	20♈ 1	25♓ 6	2♓ 52	25♎ 4R	25♐ 10R	7♌ 39	3♏ 14R	29♌ 49R
2	14 37 37	11 5 28	19 50 42	27 20 54	0 58	1 16R	20 7	26 11	3 36	24 57	25 7	7 39	3 12	29 48
3	14 41 33	12 3 38	4♏ 50 39	12♏ 18 54	0 55	1 16	20 17	27 16	4 20	24 50	25 5	7 40	3 11	29 48
4	14 45 30	13 1 47	19 44 38	27 6 52	0 52	1 16	20 33	28 22	5 4	24 43	25 2	7 41	3 9	29 48
5	14 49 26	13 59 54	4♐ 24 44	11♐ 37 29	0 49	1 15	20 53	29 27	5 48	24 36	24 59	7 42	3 7	29 48
6	14 53 23	14 58 0	18 44 30	25 45 21	0 46	1 14	21 17	0♈ 33	6 33	24 29	24 56	7 43	3 6	29 47
7	14 57 19	15 56 4	2♑ 39 44	9♑ 27 31	0 43	1 12	21 45	1 39	7 17	24 22	24 54	7 45	3 4	29 47
8	15 1 16	16 54 7	16 8 43	22 43 26	0 39	1 10	22 18	2 45	8 1	24 16	24 51	7 46	3 3	29 47
9	15 5 12	17 52 8	29 11 58	5♒ 34 39	0 36	1 9	22 55	3 51	8 45	24 9	24 48	7 47	3 1	29 47
10	15 9 9	18 50 8	11♒ 51 56	18 4 17	0 33	1 8D	23 35	4 57	9 29	24 3	24 45	7 48	2 59	29 47
11	15 13 6	19 48 6	24 12 16	0♓ 16 26	0 30	1 8	24 19	6 4	10 13	23 56	24 41	7 50	2 58	29 47D
12	15 17 2	20 46 3	6♓ 17 24	12 15 44	0 27	1 8	25 7	7 11	10 57	23 50	24 38	7 51	2 56	29 47
13	15 20 59	21 44 0	18 12 3	24 6 54	0 24	1 9	25 58	8 17	11 41	23 44	24 35	7 52	2 55	29 47
14	13 24 55	22 41 54	0♈ 0 52	5♈ 54 29	0 20	1 11	26 53	9 24	12 25	23 38	24 31	7 54	2 53	29 47
15	15 28 52	23 39 47	11 48 16	17 42 40	0 17	1 12	27 50	10 31	13 9	23 32	24 28	7 55	2 52	29 47
16	15 32 48	24 37 39	23 38 7	29 35 3	0 14	1 14R	28 51	11 39	13 53	23 26	24 25	7 57	2 50	29 47
17	15 36 45	25 35 30	5♉ 33 47	11♉ 34 40	0 11	1 14	29 55	12 46	14 36	23 21	24 21	7 59	2 49	29 47
18	15 40 41	26 33 20	17 37 58	23 43 55	0 8	1 13	1♉ 2	13 53	15 20	23 15	24 17	8 0	2 47	29 47
19	15 44 38	27 31 8	29 52 42	6♊ 4 30	0 4	1 11	2 11	15 1	16 4	23 10	24 14	8 2	2 46	29 48
20	15 48 35	28 28 54	12♊ 19 26	18 37 37	0 1	1 8	3 23	16 9	16 48	23 5	24 10	8 4	2 44	29 48
21	15 52 31	29 26 40	24 59 7	1♋ 24 0	29♎ 58	1 3	4 38	17 16	17 32	23 0	24 6	8 6	2 43	29 48
22	15 56 28	0♊ 24 24	7♋ 52 17	14 24 1	29 55	0 59	5 56	18 24	18 15	22 55	24 2	8 7	2 42	29 48
23	16 0 24	1 22 6	20 59 14	27 37 56	29 52	0 54	7 16	19 32	18 59	22 50	23 59	8 9	2 40	29 49
24	16 4 21	2 19 46	4♌ 20 9	11♌ 5 54	29 49	0 51	8 38	20 40	19 43	22 46	23 55	8 11	2 39	29 49
25	16 8 17	3 17 26	17 55 10	24 47 57	29 45	0 48	10 3	21 48	20 26	22 41	23 51	8 13	2 37	29 49
26	16 12 14	4 15 4	1♍ 44 13	8♍ 43 56	29 42	0 47D	11 31	22 57	21 10	22 37	23 47	8 15	2 36	29 50
27	16 16 10	5 12 40	15 47 0	22 53 16	29 39	0 47	13 1	24 5	21 53	22 33	23 43	8 17	2 35	29 50
28	16 20 7	6 10 14	0♎ 2 32	7♎ 14 32	29 36	0 48	14 34	25 14	22 37	22 29	23 39	8 20	2 33	29 51
29	16 24 4	7 7 48	14 28 55	21 45 14	29 33	0 50	16 9	26 22	23 20	22 25	23 34	8 22	2 32	29 51
30	16 28 0	8 5 19	29 2 58	6♏ 21 30	29 30	0 50R	17 46	27 31	24 3	22 21	23 30	8 24	2 31	29 52
31	16 31 57	9♊ 2 50	13♏ 40 9	20♏ 58 10	29♎ 26	0♏ 50	19♉ 26	28♈ 39	24♓ 47	22♎ 18	23♐ 26	8♌ 26	2♏ 30	29♌ 52

DECLINATION and LATITUDE

Day	☉ Decl	☽ Decl	☽ Lat	☽ 12 Hr. Decl	☿ Decl	☿ Lat	♀ Decl	♀ Lat	♂ Decl	♂ Lat	♃ Decl	♃ Lat	♄ Decl	♄ Lat
1	14N51	4S 6	2S22	6S28	6N10	1S47	2S52	0S60	11S57	1S36	8S18	1N31	21S56	1N26
2	15 10	8 44	1 3	10 52	6 1	1 59	2 30	1 4	11 41	1 37	8 15	1 31	21 55	1 26
3	15 27	12 50	0N20	14 34	5 55	2 10	2 7	1 8	11 26	1 37	8 13	1 31	21 55	1 26
4	15 45	16 4	1 41	17 16	5 52	2 20	1 44	1 11	11 11	1 38	8 10	1 31	21 55	1 26
5	16 3	18 11	2 54	18 47	5 50	2 30	1 22	1 15	10 55	1 39	8 8	1 30	21 55	1 26
6	16 20	19 5	3 54	19 5	5 52	2 38	0 59	1 18	10 40	1 40	8 5	1 30	21 55	1 26
7	16 37	18 47	4 38	18 13	5 55	2 46	0 35	1 21	10 24	1 41	8 3	1 30	21 55	1 26
8	16 53	17 24	5 6	16 23	6 1	2 52	0 12	1 25	10 8	1 42	8 1	1 30	21 55	1 26
9	17 10	15 10	5 16	13 47	6 9	2 58	0N11	1 28	9 53	1 43	7 59	1 30	21 54	1 26
10	17 26	12 15	5 11	10 36	6 19	3 3	0 35	1 31	9 37	1 44	7 56	1 30	21 54	1 26
11	17 41	8 52	4 51	7 4	6 31	3 7	0 59	1 33	9 21	1 44	7 54	1 30	21 54	1 26
12	17 57	5 11	4 19	3 17	6 46	3 11	1 23	1 36	9 5	1 45	7 52	1 29	21 54	1 26
13	18 12	1 21	3 36	0N35	7 2	3 13	1 47	1 39	8 49	1 46	7 50	1 29	21 54	1 26
14	18 27	2N31	2 44	4 25	7 19	3 15	2 11	1 41	8 33	1 47	7 48	1 29	21 54	1 26
15	18 42	6 17	1 45	8 6	7 39	3 16	2 35	1 44	8 17	1 48	7 46	1 29	21 54	1 26
16	18 56	9 50	0 42	11 28	7 60	3 17	2 59	1 46	8 1	1 49	7 44	1 29	21 53	1 26
17	19 10	13 0	0S24	14 25	8 22	3 17	3 23	1 48	7 45	1 49	7 42	1 28	21 53	1 26
18	19 23	15 40	1 29	16 46	8 46	3 16	3 47	1 50	7 28	1 50	7 40	1 28	21 53	1 26
19	19 37	17 40	2 31	18 22	9 12	3 14	4 12	1 52	7 12	1 51	7 39	1 28	21 53	1 26
20	19 50	18 51	3 27	19 7	9 38	3 12	4 36	1 54	6 56	1 52	7 37	1 28	21 53	1 26
21	20 2	19 8	4 13	18 54	10 6	3 9	5 0	1 56	6 40	1 53	7 35	1 28	21 53	1 26
22	20 14	18 25	4 48	17 42	10 35	3 5	5 25	1 57	6 23	1 54	7 34	1 27	21 53	1 26
23	20 26	16 44	5 8	15 32	11 5	3 1	5 49	1 59	6 7	1 54	7 32	1 27	21 52	1 26
24	20 38	14 7	5 12	12 30	11 36	2 56	6 13	1 60	5 50	1 55	7 30	1 27	21 52	1 26
25	20 49	10 43	4 59	8 46	12 8	2 51	6 38	2 1	5 34	1 56	7 29	1 27	21 52	1 26
26	20 60	6 40	4 29	4 29	12 40	2 45	7 2	2 2	5 17	1 57	7 28	1 27	21 52	1 26
27	21 10	2 12	3 42	0S 7	13 14	2 39	7 26	2 3	5 1	1 57	7 26	1 26	21 52	1 26
28	21 21	2S28	2 40	4 48	13 48	2 32	7 50	2 4	4 45	1 58	7 25	1 26	21 52	1 26
29	21 30	7 4	1 28	9 15	14 22	2 24	8 14	2 5	4 28	1 59	7 24	1 26	21 51	1 26
30	21 40	11 18	0 10	13 10	14 57	2 16	8 38	2 6	4 12	1 60	7 23	1 26	21 51	1 26
31	21N49	14S51	1N 9	16S16	15N32	2S 8	9N 2	2S 7	3S55	2S 0	7S22	1N25	21S51	1N26

Day	♅ Decl	♅ Lat	♆ Decl	♆ Lat	♇ Decl	♇ Lat
1	18N59	0N39	10S53	1N49	22N28	11N43
5	18 58	0 39	10 51	1 49	22 27	11 41
9	18 57	0 39	10 49	1 49	22 26	11 40
13	18 55	0 39	10 47	1 49	22 25	11 39
17	18 54	0 38	10 45	1 49	22 24	11 38
21	18 52	0 38	10 43	1 49	22 23	11 37
25	18 50	0 38	10 41	1 49	22 21	11 36
29	18N47	0N38	10S39	1N48	22N20	11N35

☽ PHENOMENA

d	h	m	
3	12	24	☍
10	14	38	☾
18	19	1	●
26	4	39	☽

d	h	° '
6	6	19S 7
13	8	0
20	19	19N 9
27	11	0

d	h	° '
2	18	0
9	4	5N17
16	15	0
23	18	5S13
30	3	0

VOID OF COURSE ☽

Last Aspect		☽ Ingress		
2	3pm55	2	♏	4pm15
4	4pm23	4	♐	4pm44
6	6pm59	6	♑	7pm21
8	2pm43	9	♒	1am30
11	11am 1	11	♓	11am27
13	12pm53	13	♈	11pm58
16	12pm24	16	♉	12pm50
18	11pm50	19	♊	0am14
21	9am 1	21	♋	9am23
23	3am20	23	♌	4pm15
25	8pm43	25	♍	9pm 0
27	1pm19	27	♎	11pm56
30	1am20	30	♏	1am34

d	h	
2	6	PERIGEE
14	11	APOGEE
30	7	PERIGEE

DAILY ASPECTARIAN

Day	Aspect	Time
1 Th	☉⚼♄	0am56
	♀□♄	1 16
	☉∠♀	4 17
	☽⚹♅	4 27
	☉⚻☽	9 0
	☽#☿	10 8
	♂△♆	11 25
	☽∠♇	3pm56
	☽∥♃	9 24
	☽⚼♂	9 55
2 F	☽☍☿	0am26
	☽☌♃	8 6
	☽⚹♄	8 25
	☽⚻♀	10 56
	☽∥♆	12pm 0
	☽∥♂	3 51
	☽⚹♇	3 55
	☽☌♆	9 20
	☽△♂	11 9
3 S	☽□♅	4am33
	☽∠♄	8 22
	☉☍☽	12pm24
	☽⚼♀	12 52
	☉#☽	9 3
4 Su	☽⚻☿	1am20
	☽⚺♃	8 1
	☽⚺♄	8 34
	☽△♀	3pm10
	☽□♇	4 23
	☽⚺♆	9 52
5 M	☽□♂	2am26
	☽⚼☿	2 29
	☿∠♂	4 29
	☽△♅	5 28
	♂∥♆	7 0
	♀⚻♇	7 25
	☽∠♃	8 33
	♀ ♈	12pm 0
	☉⚻☽	5 9
	☽#♅	5 48
	☽∠♆	10 54
6 T	☽△☿	4am28
	☽⚼♅	6 48
	☽⚹♃	9 44
	☽☌♄	10 34
	☽#♅	6pm 7
	☽△♇	6 59
	☉⚼☽	8 45
	☽□♀	10 4
7 W	☽⚹♆	0am43
	☽⚹♂	8 36
	☽⚻♅	8 58
	♂⚻♅	3pm38
	☽⚼♇	9 33
8 Th	☉△☽	1am29
	☉#☽	5 37
	♀⚻♆	6 16
	☽□☿	11 45
	☽∠♂	1pm17
	☽□♃	2 43
	☽⚺♄	3 51
9 F	☽⚻♇	1am 5
	☽□♆	7 9
	☽⚹♀	9 34
	♂⚼♃	11 36
	☽☍♅	4pm13
	☽⚺♂	7 9
	☽∠♄	7 57
10 S	☽∥♆	10am38
	☿☍♃	1pm20
	☉□☽	2 38
	☽∠♀	5 14
	☽∥♂	8 29
	☽△♃	11 29
11 Su	☽⚹☿	0am15
	☽⚹♄	0 57
	☽∥♃	6 32
	☿△♄	10 36
	☽☍♇	11 1
	☽#☿	2pm34
	☽△♆	5 19
	♇SD	9 57
12 M	☽⚺♀	1am58
	☽⚻♅	3 8
	☽⚼♃	5 4
	☽∠☿	8 16
	☽☌♂	9 58
	♀△♅	2pm49
	☽#♀	9 37
	☽⚼♆	11 25
13 T	☉⚹☽	7am48
	☽⚼♅	9 30
	☽⚻♃	11 8
	☽□♄	12pm53
	☽⚺☿	5 4
	☽∥♀	9 39
	☽⚻♇	11 32
14 W	☽⚻♆	5am50
	☽△♅	4pm 5
	☉∠☽	5 2
	☽☌♀	9 7
	☉⚻♃	9 8
15 Th	☽⚺♂	2am54
	☽⚼♇	6 3
	☿#♃	7 32
	☽#♃	9 43
	☽∥☿	9 58
	☽#♂	12pm22
	☉⚻♄	6 53
	☉∥♅	9 17
	☽☍♃	11 37
16 F	☿#♂	0am36
	☽△♄	1 33
	☿∠♂	1 57
	☉⚺☽	2 11
	☽#♆	6 40
	☽∠♂	11 16
	☽☌☿	11 32
	☽△♇	12pm24
	☽☍♆	6 30
	☿△♇	9 10
17 S	☿ ♉	1am53
	♂∥♃	4 18
	☽□♅	4 50
	☽⚼♄	7 32
	☽⚺♀	3pm50
	☽⚹♂	7 10
18 Su	☽⚻♃	10am59
	☽⚻♄	1pm 2
	☉☌☽	7 1
	♀⚼♇	7 14
	☽□♇	11 50
19 M	☽∠♀	0am18
	☽⚺☿	4 57
	☽⚻♆	5 35
	☿☍♆	11 28
	☽⚹♅	3pm49
	☽⚼♃	3 55
20 T	☽∥♅	0am27
	☽⚹♀	8 0
	☽□♂	9 3
	☽⚼♆	10 18
	☽∠☿	12pm48
	☽△♃	8 17
	☽∠♅	8 26
	☽☍♄	10 21
21 W	♂⚼♆	6am 1
	☉□♇	8 56
	☽⚹♇	9 1
	☉⚺☽	9 2
	☽∥♅	1pm14
	☉ ♊	1 51
	☽△♆	2 25
	♀⚺♂	3 9
	☽⚹☿	8 0
22 Th	☽⚺♅	0am28
	☿#♆	5 49
	☽∠♇	12pm45
	☉∠☽	2 56
	☽△♂	8 9
	☽□♀	9 7
23 F	☽□♃	3am20
	☽⚻♄	5 23
	♀#♂	10 31
	☽⚺♇	3pm55
	☿□♅	4 3
	☉⚹☽	8 9
	☽□♆	8 59
24 S	☽⚼♂	0am42
	☿⚼♄	4 27
	☽☌♅	6 52
	☉⚻♆	7 43
	☽⚼♄	8 5
	☽□☿	8 32
	☽∥☿	3pm52
25 Su	☽#♆	0am11
	☽⚻♂	4 39
	☽△♀	7 24
	☽⚹♃	8 17
	☽△♄	10 17
	♀☍♃	5pm26
	☽#♃	7 32
	☽☌♇	8 43
	☽∥♀	10 11
26 M	☽⚹♆	1am29
	☉□☽	4 39
	☽#♂	8 7
	☽∠♃	10 2
	☽⚺♅	11 13
	☽⚼♀	11 36
	♀△♄	4pm33
	☽△☿	6 44
27 T	♀#♃	0am29
	☽∠♆	3 2
	☽☍♂	10 52
	☽⚺♃	11 22
	☽∠♅	12pm43
	☽□♄	1 19
	☽⚻♀	3 14
	♂⚻♃	8 1
	☽⚼☿	11 6
	☽⚺♇	11 40
28 W	☽⚺♆	4am12
	☉△☽	10 57
	☽∥♂	11 4
	☽⚹♅	1pm50
29 Th	☽∠♇	0am37
	♂⚼♅	0 59
	☽∥♃	1 48
	☽⚻☿	3 5
	☉⚼♃	6 45
	☽#♀	7 0
	♂□♄	7 14
	☽☌♃	1pm 2
	☉⚼☽	1 30
	☽⚹♄	2 55
	☽⚻♂	3 22
	☽∥♆	8 9
	☽☍♀	9 15
30 F	☽⚹♇	1am20
	☽☌♆	5 41
	☉⚹♅	8 6
	☽□♅	3pm23
	☽∠♄	3 27
	☉⚻☽	3 53
	☽⚼♂	5 17
	♄⚼♅	11 18
31 S	☉#♄	6am12
	☽#☿	7 0
	☽☍☿	10 42
	☽⚺♃	2pm 8
	☽⚺♄	3 59
	☽△♂	7 14

JUNE 1958

LONGITUDE

Day	Sid. Time	☉	☽	☽ 12 Hour	Mean ☊	True ☊	☿	♀	♂	♃	♄	♅	♆	♇
	h m s	° ' "	° ' "	° ' "	° '	° '	° '	° '	° '	° '	° '	° '	° '	° '
1	16 35 53	10♊ 0 19	28♏ 14 46	5♐ 29 10	29♎ 23	0♏ 47R	21♉ 8	29♈ 48	25♓ 30	22♎ 15R	23♐ 22R	8♌ 29	2♏ 28R	29♌ 53
2	16 39 50	10 57 48	12♐ 40 35	19 48 17	29 20	0 43	22 52	0♉ 57	26 13	22 12	23 18	8 31	2 27	29 53
3	16 43 46	11 55 15	26 51 36	3♑ 49 58	29 17	0 38	24 39	2 6	26 56	22 9	23 13	8 33	2 26	29 54
4	16 47 43	12 52 42	10♑ 42 55	17 30 10	29 14	0 31	26 29	3 15	27 40	22 6	23 9	8 36	2 25	29 55
5	16 51 39	13 50 7	24 11 30	0♒ 46 53	29 10	0 24	28 20	4 24	28 23	22 3	23 5	8 38	2 24	29 55
6	16 55 36	14 47 32	7♒ 16 21	13 40 9	29 7	0 18	0♊ 14	5 33	29 6	22 1	23 0	8 41	2 23	29 56
7	16 59 33	15 44 56	19 58 33	26 11 57	29 4	0 14	2 11	6 43	29 49	21 59	22 56	8 43	2 21	29 57
8	17 3 29	16 42 20	2♓ 20 49	8♓ 25 43	29 1	0 10	4 9	7 52	0♈ 32	21 56	22 52	8 46	2 20	29 58
9	17 7 26	17 39 42	14 27 12	20 25 53	28 58	0 9D	6 10	9 1	1 14	21 55	22 47	8 48	2 19	29 58
10	17 11 22	18 37 5	26 22 27	2♈ 17 30	28 55	0 9	8 12	10 11	1 57	21 53	22 43	8 51	2 18	29 59
11	17 15 19	19 34 27	8♈ 11 44	14 5 46	28 51	0 10	10 17	11 21	2 40	21 51	22 38	8 54	2 17	0♍ 0
12	17 19 15	20 31 48	20 0 15	25 55 45	28 48	0 11R	12 23	12 30	3 23	21 50	22 34	8 56	2 16	0 1
13	17 23 12	21 29 8	1♉ 52 52	7♉ 52 8	28 45	0 12	14 30	13 40	4 5	21 49	22 30	8 59	2 15	0 2
14	17 27 8	22 26 29	13 54 0	19 58 55	28 42	0 11	16 39	14 50	4 48	21 48	22 25	9 2	2 15	0 3
15	17 31 5	23 23 49	26 7 13	2♊ 19 13	28 39	0 8	18 50	16 0	5 30	21 47	22 21	9 5	2 14	0 4
16	17 35 2	24 21 8	8♊ 35 8	14 55 6	28 36	0 3	21 0	17 10	6 12	21 46	22 16	9 8	2 13	0 5
17	17 38 58	25 18 27	21 19 12	27 47 25	28 32	29♎ 55	23 12	18 20	6 55	21 46	22 12	9 10	2 12	0 6
18	17 42 55	26 15 45	4♋ 19 40	10♋ 55 49	28 29	29 47	25 24	19 30	7 37	21 45	22 7	9 13	2 11	0 7
19	17 46 51	27 13 3	17 35 40	24 18 58	28 26	29 37	27 36	20 40	8 19	21 45D	22 3	9 16	2 10	0 8
20	17 50 48	28 10 20	1♌ 5 28	7♌ 54 50	28 23	29 28	29 47	21 50	9 1	21 45	21 59	9 19	2 10	0 9
21	17 54 44	29 7 36	14 46 48	21 41 5	28 20	29 20	1♋ 58	23 0	9 43	21 46	21 54	9 22	2 9	0 10
22	17 58 41	0♋ 4 52	28 37 24	5♍ 35 31	28 16	29 14	4 9	24 10	10 25	21 46	21 50	9 25	2 8	0 11
23	18 2 37	1 2 8	12♍ 35 12	19 36 17	28 13	29 10	6 18	25 21	11 7	21 47	21 45	9 28	2 7	0 12
24	18 6 34	1 59 22	26 38 37	3♎ 42 3	28 10	29 9D	8 26	26 31	11 48	21 48	21 41	9 32	2 7	0 13
25	18 10 31	2 56 35	10♎ 46 26	17 51 38	28 7	29 9	10 33	27 41	12 30	21 48	21 37	9 35	2 6	0 15
26	18 14 27	3 53 49	24 57 30	2♏ 3 49	28 4	29 10R	12 38	28 52	13 11	21 50	21 33	9 38	2 6	0 16
27	18 18 24	4 51 1	9♏ 10 23	16 16 53	28 1	29 9	14 41	0♊ 3	13 53	21 51	21 28	9 41	2 5	0 17
28	18 22 20	5 48 13	23 23 0	0♐ 28 18	27 57	29 7	16 43	1 13	14 34	21 52	21 24	9 44	2 5	0 18
29	18 26 17	6 45 25	7♐ 32 21	14 34 39	27 54	29 3	18 43	2 24	15 15	21 54	21 20	9 47	2 4	0 20
30	18 30 13	7♋ 42 36	21♐ 34 41	28♐ 31 56	27♎ 51	28♎ 55	20♋ 41	3♊ 34	15♈ 56	21♎ 56	21♐ 16	9♌ 51	2♏ 4	0♍ 21

DECLINATION and LATITUDE

Day	☉ Decl	☽ Decl	☽ Lat	☽ 12 Hr. Decl	☿ Decl	☿ Lat	♀ Decl	♀ Lat	♂ Decl	♂ Lat	♃ Decl	♃ Lat	♄ Decl	♄ Lat
1	21N57	17S26	2N24	18S19	16N 8	1S59	9N25	2S 7	3S38	2S 1	7S21	1N25	21S51	1N26
2	22 6	18 53	3 28	19 9	16 43	1 50	9 49	2 7	3 22	2 2	7 20	1 25	21 51	1 26
3	22 13	19 7	4 18	18 47	17 19	1 41	10 12	2 8	3 5	2 3	7 19	1 25	21 50	1 26
4	22 21	18 10	4 51	17 19	17 54	1 31	10 36	2 8	2 49	2 3	7 18	1 24	21 50	1 26
5	22 28	16 14	5 8	14 57	18 29	1 21	10 59	2 8	2 32	2 4	7 17	1 24	21 50	1 26
6	22 35	13 30	5 7	11 55	19 4	1 10	11 22	2 8	2 16	2 5	7 17	1 24	21 50	1 26
7	22 41	10 13	4 51	8 25	19 38	0 59	11 44	2 8	1 60	2 5	7 16	1 24	21 50	1 26
8	22 47	6 33	4 22	4 39	20 11	0 49	12 7	2 8	1 43	2 6	7 16	1 23	21 50	1 26
9	22 52	2 42	3 42	0 45	20 43	0 38	12 29	2 8	1 27	2 7	7 15	1 23	21 49	1 26
10	22 57	1N12	2 53	3N 8	21 14	0 27	12 52	2 7	1 10	2 7	7 15	1 23	21 49	1 26
11	23 2	5 2	1 56	6 53	21 44	0 16	13 13	2 7	0 54	2 8	7 14	1 22	21 49	1 25
12	23 6	8 40	0 55	10 23	22 12	0 5	13 35	2 6	0 37	2 9	7 14	1 22	21 49	1 25
13	23 10	11 59	0S 9	13 29	22 39	0N 6	13 57	2 6	0 21	2 9	7 14	1 22	21 49	1 25
14	23 14	14 51	1 13	16 4	23 3	0 17	14 18	2 5	0 5	2 10	7 14	1 22	21 49	1 25
15	23 17	17 6	2 15	17 57	23 25	0 27	14 39	2 4	0N11	2 10	7 14	1 21	21 48	1 25
16	23 19	18 36	3 11	19 0	23 45	0 37	14 59	2 3	0 28	2 11	7 14	1 21	21 48	1 25
17	23 22	19 11	3 59	19 7	24 3	0 47	15 19	2 3	0 44	2 12	7 14	1 21	21 48	1 25
18	23 24	18 47	4 36	18 12	24 18	0 56	15 39	2 2	0 60	2 12	7 14	1 21	21 48	1 25
19	23 25	17 21	4 58	16 16	24 30	1 4	15 59	2 0	1 16	2 13	7 14	1 20	21 48	1 25
20	23 26	14 58	5 5	13 26	24 39	1 12	16 18	1 59	1 32	2 13	7 15	1 20	21 47	1 25
21	23 26	11 43	4 54	9 49	24 46	1 20	16 37	1 58	1 48	2 14	7 15	1 20	21 47	1 25
22	23 27	7 48	4 26	5 39	24 49	1 27	16 56	1 57	2 4	2 14	7 15	1 20	21 47	1 25
23	23 26	3 25	3 42	1 8	24 50	1 33	17 14	1 55	2 20	2 15	7 16	1 19	21 47	1 24
24	23 26	1S11	2 45	3S29	24 48	1 38	17 32	1 54	2 35	2 15	7 16	1 19	21 47	1 24
25	23 25	5 45	1 37	7 56	24 44	1 42	17 50	1 52	2 51	2 16	7 17	1 19	21 47	1 24
26	23 23	10 1	0 22	11 57	24 36	1 46	18 7	1 51	3 7	2 16	7 18	1 18	21 46	1 24
27	23 21	13 43	0N53	15 16	24 27	1 49	18 23	1 49	3 22	2 17	7 18	1 18	21 46	1 24
28	23 19	16 36	2 5	17 40	24 15	1 52	18 39	1 47	3 38	2 17	7 19	1 18	21 46	1 24
29	23 16	18 28	3 9	18 58	24 0	1 53	18 55	1 45	3 53	2 18	7 20	1 18	21 46	1 24
30	23N13	19S10	4N 1	19S 5	23N44	1N54	19N11	1S44	4N 9	2S18	7S21	1N17	21S46	1N24

Day	♅ Decl	♅ Lat	♆ Decl	♆ Lat	♇ Decl	♇ Lat
1	18N46	0N38	10S38	1N48	22N18	11N34
5	18 43	0 38	10 37	1 48	22 17	11 33
9	18 40	0 38	10 35	1 48	22 15	11 32
13	18 37	0 38	10 34	1 48	22 12	11 31
17	18 34	0 38	10 33	1 48	22 10	11 30
21	18 31	0 38	10 32	1 47	22 8	11 29
25	18 28	0 38	10 32	1 47	22 5	11 28
29	18N24	0N37	10S31	1N47	22N 2	11N27

☽ PHENOMENA

d	h	m	
1	20	56	○
9	6	59	☾
17	8	0	●
24	9	45	☽

d	h	° '
2	16	19S10
9	17	0
17	3	19N11
23	18	0
30	2	19S10

5	11	5N 9
12	21	0
19	21	5S 5
26	7	0

VOID OF COURSE ☽

Last Aspect		☽ Ingress		
1	2am42	1	♐	2am54
3	5am13	3	♑	5am23
5	8am48	5	♒	10am34
7	7pm19	7	♓	7pm24
9	4pm39	10	♈	7am21
12	5am10	12	♉	8pm13
14	2am 2	15	♊	7am31
17	8am 0	17	♋	4pm 4
19	7am26	19	♌	10pm 4
21	3pm36	22	♍	2am22
23	11pm46	24	♎	5am43
25	6pm42	26	♏	8am31
27	10am52	28	♐	11am12
30	0am37	30	♑	2pm33

d	h	
11	5	APOGEE
26	9	PERIGEE

DAILY ASPECTARIAN

Day	Aspect	Time
1 Su	♀△♇	1am38
	☽□♇	2 42
	☽⚻♀	2 48
	♀ ♉	4 8
	☽⚺♆	6 59
	☽∠♃	2pm52
	☿⚻♃	2 56
	☽△♅	5 1
	☽#♅	8 30
	☉☍☽	8 56
2 M	☿⚻♄	5am28
	☽⚼♀	5 59
	☽∠♆	8 1
	☽✱♃	3pm59
	☽☌♄	5 50
	☽⚼♅	6 21
	☽⚻☿	7 41
3 T	☽□♂	0am 9
	☽△♇	5 13
	♀☍♆	6 51
	☽✱♆	9 34
	☽△♀	9 49
	☉∥♇	12pm23
	☽#♅	1 5
	☽⚻♅	8 16
4 W	☽⚼☿	1am33
	♀#♆	1 33
	☽#☿	3 3
	☉⚻☽	4 6
	☽⚼♇	7 24
	☽□♃	8pm 9
	☽⚺♄	10 0
5 Th	☿✱♂	0am45
	☽✱♂	8 2
	☽△☿	8 48
	☉⚼☽	9 6
	☿∥♅	9 22
	☽⚻♇	10 26
	☽□♆	2pm57
	☿□♇	8 9
	☽□♀	8 30
	☿ ♊	8 59
6 F	☽∠♄	1am22
	☽☍♅	2 38
	☽∠♂	1pm34
	☽#♀	2 21
	☉△☽	3 17
	☽∥♆	9 18
7 S	☿⚻♆	2am11
	☽△♃	3 50
	♂⚻♇	4 40
	☽✱♄	5 39
	♂ ♈	6 21
	☽☍♇	7pm19
	☽∥♃	7 29
	☽⚺♂	8 13
	♀⚼♄	11 51
	☽△♆	11 59
8 Su	☽□☿	4am15
	☽⚼♃	9 2
	☽✱♀	12pm 2
	☽⚻♅	12 42
	☉⚼♆	3 39
	♀□♅	7 17
9 M	☽⚼♆	5am45
	☉□☽	6 59
	☽∥♂	8 20
	☿⚼♃	8 42
	☽⚻♃	2pm56
	☽□♄	4 39
	☽⚼♅	6 53
	☽∠♀	9 20
	☽#♂	11 50
10 T	☽⚻♇	7am20
	☿✱♅	7 41
	♂⚻♆	11 38
	☽⚻♆	12pm 1
	☽☌♂	12 2
	♇ ♍	10 16
11 W	☽△♅	1am26
	☿#♄	4 2
	☽✱☿	5 9
	☽⚺♀	7 6
	☽⚼♇	1pm51
	☽#♃	2 21
12 Th	☿∥♇	0am28
	☉✱☽	1 10
	☿⚺♀	3 8
	☽☍♃	3 42
	☽△♄	5 10
	☽#♆	1pm25
	☽∠☿	6 11
	☽△♇	8 16
13 F	☽☍♆	0am45
	☽⚺♂	4 42
	☉△♃	8 1
	☉∠☽	10 2
	☽⚼♄	11 11
	☽□♅	2pm17
	☽∥♀	6 13
	☉☍♄	11 28
14 S	☽☌♀	2am 2
	☿⚼♆	6 27
	☽⚺☿	6 38
	☽∠♂	12pm21
	☉∥☿	12 56
	☽⚻♃	3 32
	☽⚻♄	4 41
	☉⚺☽	6 14
15 Su	☽□♇	7am39
	☽⚻♆	11 48
	☉∠♅	6pm 2
	☽✱♂	7 11
	☽⚼♃	8 32
	☽∥♅	11 49
16 M	☽✱♅	1am 2
	☿△♃	8 19
	☿☍♄	1pm23
	☽⚼♆	4 18
	☽⚺♀	5 50
17 T	☽△♃	0am49
	☽☍♄	1 37
	☽☌☿	4 13
	☽∠♅	5 20
	☉☌☽	8 0
	☿∠♅	10 54
	☽✱♇	4pm16
	☽△♆	8 5
18 W	☽∠♀	0am20
	☽∥♅	5 15
	☽□♂	6 19
	☽⚺♅	8 56
	☉☌☿	4pm44
	☽∠♇	7 34
19 Th	♃SD	1am42
	☽✱♀	6 1
	☽□♃	7 26
	☽⚻♄	7 55
	☽∥♀	1pm 6
	☉⚺☽	6 27
	☽⚺☿	9 15
	☽⚺♇	10 20
	♀⚻♃	10 29
20 F	☽□♆	1am53
	☿ ♋	2 21
	♀⚻♄	2 49
	☿✱♇	4 0
	☽⚼♄	10 18
	♂△♅	11 18
	☽☌♅	2pm31
	☽△♂	2 41
	☉∠☽	10 47
21 S	☿△♆	1am57
	☽∠☿	4 32
	☽#♆	7 34
	☽✱♃	12pm 8
	☽△♄	12 19
	☽□♀	3 36
	☽⚼♂	6 10
	☉ ♋	9 57
22 Su	☉✱♇	2am41
	☽☌♇	2 42
	☉✱☽	2 42
	☽#♃	3 3
	☽✱♆	6 3
	☽✱☿	11 15
	☽∠♃	2pm 2
	♃✱♄	6 9
	☽⚺♅	6 39
	☽⚻♂	9 20
23 M	☽∥♂	5am26
	☽∠♆	7 45
	☽□♄	3pm36
	☽⚺♃	3 43
	☽∠♅	8 23
	☽△♀	11 46
24 T	☉△♆	3am 6
	☽⚺♇	6 6
	☽#♂	7 46
	☽⚺♆	9 18
	☉□☽	9 45
	☿⚺♅	12pm43
	♀∠♂	2 15
	☽✱♅	9 58
	☽□☿	11 33
25 W	☽☍♂	3am 4
	☽⚼♀	3 33
	☽∠♇	7 35
	☽∥♃	8 24
	☽✱♄	6pm15
	☽☌♃	6 42
26 Th	☽∥♆	3am 5
	☽⚻♀	7 12
	☽✱♇	8 59
	☿□♂	9 41
	☽☌♆	12pm 3
	☉△☽	4 11
	☽∠♄	7 28
	♀ ♊	11 9
27 F	☽□♅	0am52
	♀∥♅	3 42
	♀□♇	5 5
	☿∠♇	7 6
	☽⚻♂	8 20
	☿∠♀	9 49
	☽△☿	10 52
	☉⚼☽	7pm19
	☽⚺♄	8 40
	☽⚺♃	9 27
28 S	☽⚼♂	11am 0
	☽□♇	11 44
	☽☍♀	2pm28
	☽⚺♆	2 43
	☽⚼☿	4 27
	♀⚻♆	5 22
	☉⚻☽	10 34
	☽∠♃	10 55
	☽#♅	11 0
29 Su	♂⚼♇	2am55
	☽△♅	3 51
	☽△♂	1pm49
	☽∠♆	4 15
	☽⚻☿	10 13
	☽☌♄	11 28
30 M	☽✱♃	0am37
	☽⚼♅	5 39
	☿⚻♄	6 54
	☽△♇	3pm11
	☿□♃	3 45
	☽✱♆	6 7
	☽⚻♀	10 42

LONGITUDE

Day	Sid. Time	☉	☽	☽ 12 Hour	Mean ☊	True ☊	☿	♀	♂	♃	♄	♅	♆	♇
	h m s	° ' "	° ' "	° ' "	° '	° '	° '	° '	° '	° '	° '	° '	° '	° '
1	18 34 10	8♋ 39 48	5♑ 25 52	12♑ 16 0	27♎ 48	28♎ 46R	22♋ 37	4♊ 45	16♈ 37	21♎ 58	21♐ 12R	9♌ 54	2♏ 3R	0♍ 22
2	18 38 7	9 36 59	19 1 57	25 43 20	27 45	28 35	24 31	5 56	17 18	22 0	21 8	9 57	2 3	0 24
3	18 42 3	10 34 9	2♒ 19 56	8♒ 51 33	27 41	28 23	26 23	7 7	17 58	22 3	21 3	10 1	2 2	0 25
4	18 46 0	11 31 20	15 18 11	21 39 52	27 38	28 13	28 13	8 18	18 39	22 5	20 59	10 4	2 2	0 27
5	18 49 56	12 28 32	27 56 45	4♓ 9 8	27 35	28 4	0♌ 1	9 29	19 20	22 8	20 55	10 7	2 2	0 28
6	18 53 53	13 25 43	10♓ 17 21	16 21 50	27 32	27 57	1 47	10 40	20 0	22 11	20 52	10 11	2 1	0 29
7	18 57 49	14 22 54	22 23 6	28 21 41	27 29	27 53	3 31	11 51	20 40	22 14	20 48	10 14	2 1	0 31
8	19 1 46	15 20 6	4♈ 18 12	10♈ 13 17	27 26	27 51	5 12	13 2	21 20	22 17	20 44	10 18	2 1	0 32
9	19 5 42	16 17 18	16 7 38	22 1 53	27 22	27 51	6 52	14 13	22 0	22 20	20 40	10 21	2 1	0 34
10	19 9 39	17 14 31	27 56 45	3♉ 52 55	27 19	27 51	8 30	15 25	22 40	22 24	20 36	10 25	2 1	0 35
11	19 13 35	18 11 44	9♉ 51 2	15 51 44	27 16	27 50	10 5	16 36	23 20	22 28	20 33	10 28	2 1	0 37
12	19 17 32	19 8 57	21 55 37	28 3 14	27 13	27 48	11 39	17 47	24 0	22 32	20 29	10 32	2 0	0 39
13	19 21 29	20 6 11	4♊ 15 4	10♊ 31 31	27 10	27 44	13 10	18 59	24 39	22 36	20 26	10 35	2 0	0 40
14	19 25 25	21 3 26	16 52 55	23 19 27	27 7	27 37	14 40	20 10	25 18	22 40	20 22	10 39	2 0D	0 42
15	19 29 22	22 0 40	29 51 16	6♋ 28 20	27 3	27 28	16 7	21 22	25 57	22 44	20 19	10 42	2 0	0 43
16	19 33 18	22 57 56	13♋ 10 31	19 57 35	27 0	27 17	17 32	22 33	26 36	22 49	20 15	10 46	2 0	0 45
17	19 37 15	23 55 12	26 49 12	3♌ 44 52	26 57	27 5	18 55	23 45	27 15	22 53	20 12	10 49	2 1	0 47
18	19 41 11	24 52 28	10♌ 44 6	17 46 17	26 54	26 53	20 16	24 57	27 54	22 58	20 9	10 53	2 1	0 48
19	19 45 8	25 49 44	24 50 50	1♍ 57 7	26 51	26 43	21 34	26 8	28 32	23 3	20 5	10 57	2 1	0 50
20	19 49 5	26 47 1	9♍ 4 33	16 12 34	26 47	26 35	22 50	27 20	29 11	23 8	20 2	11 0	2 1	0 52
21	19 53 1	27 44 18	23 20 42	0♎ 28 31	26 44	26 30	24 4	28 32	29 49	23 14	19 59	11 4	2 1	0 53
22	19 56 58	28 41 35	7♎ 35 40	14 41 54	26 41	26 28D	25 15	29 44	0♉ 27	23 19	19 56	11 7	2 1	0 55
23	20 0 54	29 38 52	21 47 0	28 50 49	26 38	26 27	26 24	0♋ 56	1 5	23 25	19 53	11 11	2 2	0 57
24	20 4 51	0♌ 36 10	5♏ 53 15	12♏ 54 13	26 35	26 27R	27 31	2 8	1 42	23 30	19 51	11 15	2 2	0 59
25	20 8 47	1 33 28	19 53 38	26 51 25	26 32	26 27	28 34	3 20	2 20	23 36	19 48	11 18	2 2	1 0
26	20 12 44	2 30 46	3♐ 47 29	10♐ 41 42	26 28	26 24	29 35	4 32	2 57	23 42	19 45	11 22	2 3	1 2
27	20 16 40	3 28 5	17 33 55	24 23 56	26 25	26 19	0♍ 33	5 44	3 34	23 49	19 43	11 26	2 3	1 4
28	20 20 37	4 25 25	1♑ 11 33	7♑ 56 30	26 22	26 11	1 28	6 56	4 11	23 55	19 40	11 29	2 3	1 6
29	20 24 34	5 22 45	14 38 34	21 17 27	26 19	26 1	2 20	8 8	4 47	24 1	19 38	11 33	2 4	1 8
30	20 28 30	6 20 5	27 52 57	4♒ 24 51	26 16	25 49	3 9	9 20	5 24	24 8	19 35	11 37	2 4	1 9
31	20 32 27	7♌ 17 27	10♒ 52 57	17♒ 17 10	26♎ 13	25♎ 36	3♍ 54	10♋ 32	6♉ 0	24♎ 15	19♐ 33	11♌ 41	2♏ 5	1♍ 11

DECLINATION and LATITUDE

Day	☉ Decl	☽ Decl	☽ Lat	☽ 12 Hr. Decl	☿ Decl	☿ Lat	♀ Decl	♀ Lat	♂ Decl	♂ Lat	♃ Decl	♃ Lat	♄ Decl	♄ Lat
1	23N10	18S42	4N38	18S 4	23N26	1N54	19N25	1S42	4N24	2S19	7S22	1N17	21S46	1N24
2	23 6	17 10	4 58	16 3	23 5	1 54	19 40	1 40	4 39	2 19	7 23	1 17	21 46	1 23
3	23 1	14 45	5 2	13 16	22 43	1 53	19 54	1 38	4 54	2 20	7 24	1 17	21 45	1 23
4	22 57	11 38	4 49	9 54	22 20	1 51	20 7	1 36	5 9	2 20	7 25	1 16	21 45	1 23
5	22 52	8 5	4 23	6 11	21 55	1 48	20 20	1 33	5 24	2 20	7 27	1 16	21 45	1 23
6	22 46	4 15	3 44	2 17	21 28	1 45	20 33	1 31	5 39	2 21	7 28	1 16	21 45	1 23
7	22 40	0 19	2 57	1N38	21 1	1 41	20 45	1 29	5 54	2 21	7 29	1 15	21 45	1 23
8	22 34	3N34	2 2	5 28	20 32	1 37	20 56	1 27	6 8	2 21	7 31	1 15	21 45	1 23
9	22 27	7 18	1 2	9 4	20 3	1 32	21 7	1 24	6 23	2 22	7 32	1 15	21 45	1 23
10	22 20	10 44	0S 0	12 19	19 32	1 27	21 17	1 22	6 37	2 22	7 34	1 15	21 44	1 22
11	22 12	13 46	1 3	15 5	19 1	1 21	21 27	1 20	6 52	2 22	7 36	1 14	21 44	1 22
12	22 5	16 15	2 4	17 15	18 29	1 14	21 36	1 17	7 6	2 23	7 37	1 14	21 44	1 22
13	21 56	18 3	3 0	18 38	17 57	1 8	21 45	1 15	7 20	2 23	7 39	1 14	21 44	1 22
14	21 48	19 0	3 49	19 7	17 24	1 0	21 53	1 12	7 34	2 23	7 41	1 14	21 44	1 22
15	21 39	18 60	4 27	18 36	16 51	0 52	22 0	1 10	7 48	2 23	7 43	1 13	21 44	1 22
16	21 29	17 57	4 52	17 2	16 17	0 44	22 7	1 7	8 2	2 24	7 44	1 13	21 44	1 22
17	21 20	15 53	5 1	14 29	15 43	0 36	22 13	1 5	8 16	2 24	7 46	1 13	21 44	1 21
18	21 10	12 51	4 52	11 3	15 9	0 27	22 19	1 2	8 29	2 24	7 48	1 13	21 44	1 21
19	20 59	9 4	4 26	6 57	14 36	0 17	22 24	0 59	8 43	2 24	7 51	1 12	21 44	1 21
20	20 48	4 44	3 43	2 26	14 2	0 8	22 28	0 57	8 56	2 24	7 53	1 12	21 44	1 21
21	20 37	0 6	2 46	2S13	13 28	0S 2	22 32	0 54	9 9	2 25	7 55	1 12	21 43	1 21
22	20 26	4S31	1 38	6 45	12 54	0 13	22 36	0 51	9 22	2 25	7 57	1 12	21 43	1 21
23	20 14	8 52	0 25	10 52	12 21	0 24	22 38	0 48	9 35	2 25	7 59	1 11	21 43	1 20
24	20 2	12 42	0N50	14 21	11 48	0 34	22 40	0 46	9 48	2 25	8 2	1 11	21 43	1 20
25	19 49	15 47	2 1	16 58	11 16	0 46	22 41	0 43	10 1	2 25	8 4	1 11	21 43	1 20
26	19 36	17 54	3 4	18 34	10 44	0 57	22 42	0 40	10 13	2 25	8 7	1 11	21 43	1 20
27	19 23	18 57	3 56	19 3	10 12	1 9	22 42	0 37	10 26	2 25	8 9	1 10	21 43	1 20
28	19 10	18 53	4 33	18 27	9 42	1 21	22 41	0 35	10 38	2 25	8 12	1 10	21 43	1 20
29	18 56	17 45	4 55	16 49	9 12	1 33	22 40	0 32	10 50	2 25	8 14	1 10	21 43	1 19
30	18 42	15 40	5 1	14 20	8 43	1 45	22 38	0 29	11 2	2 25	8 17	1 10	21 43	1 19
31	18N27	12S51	4N51	11S12	8N16	1S57	22N36	0S26	11N14	2S25	8S20	1N 9	21S43	1N19

Day	♅ Decl	♅ Lat	♆ Decl	♆ Lat	♇ Decl	♇ Lat
1	18N22	0N37	10S31	1N47	22N 1	11N27
5	18 19	0 37	10 31	1 47	21 58	11 26
9	18 15	0 37	10 31	1 47	21 56	11 26
13	18 11	0 37	10 31	1 46	21 53	11 25
17	18 7	0 37	10 31	1 46	21 50	11 24
21	18 3	0 37	10 31	1 46	21 47	11 24
25	17 59	0 37	10 32	1 46	21 44	11 24
29	17N55	0N37	10S33	1N45	21N41	11N23

☽ PHENOMENA

d	h	m	
1	6	5	○
9	0	21	☾
16	18	34	●
23	14	20	☽
30	16	47	○

d	h	°	'
7	2	0	
14	12	19N	7
21	1	0	
27	10	19S	3

d	h	°	'
2	17	5N	2
10	0	0	
17	0	5S	1
23	8	0	
29	20	5N	1

VOID OF COURSE ☽

Last Aspect		☽ Ingress		
2	11am27	2	♒	7pm45
4	12pm51	5	♓	3am57
6	8pm50	7	♈	3pm18
9	12pm41	10	♉	4am 9
11	6pm 3	12	♊	3pm47
14	4pm29	15	♋	0am16
17	0am47	17	♌	5am31
19	6am32	19	♍	8am42
21	9am32	21	♎	11am12
23	8am31	23	♏	1pm58
25	4pm 9	25	♐	5pm26
27	11am 3	27	♑	9pm53
29	5pm 6	30	♒	3am53

d	h	
8	23	APOGEE
21	11	PERIGEE

DAILY ASPECTARIAN

Day	Aspect	Time
1 T	☉☍☽	6am 5
	☽#♅	6 51
	☽⚻♅	7 52
	☽⚼♇	5pm31
	☽□♂	8 45
	☉∥☿	11 19
2 W	☽⚺♄	3am43
	☽⚼♀	3 44
	☽□♃	5 20
	☉⚺♅	9 5
	☽☍☿	11 27
	☽⚻♇	8pm30
	♀⚼♃	10 30
	☽□♆	11 28
3 Th	☽∠♄	6am48
	☽△♀	9 39
	☽☍♅	2pm12
	☉⚻☽	4 23
4 F	☽⚹♂	6am39
	☽∥♆	7 53
	☽⚹♄	10 40
	☽△♃	12pm51
	☿∥♇	8 31
	☉⚼☽	11 1
	☿ ♌	11 47
5 S	☽∥♃	4am 2
	☽⚻☿	4 39
	☽☍♇	4 52
	☿⚺♇	6 10
	☽△♆	7 53
	☿#♄	8 59
	☽∠♂	1pm 3
	♀⚹♅	1 41
	☽#♂	3 52
	☽⚼♃	5 53
	☽⚻♅	11 47
6 Su	☽□♀	0am49
	☿□♆	3 20
	☉△☽	6 43
	☽⚼♆	1pm18
	☽⚼☿	2 59
	☽⚺♂	8 22
	☽□♄	8 50
	☽⚻♃	11 41
7 M	♂△♄	4am 4
	☽⚼♅	5 45
	☿∥♀	9 52
	☽⚻♇	4pm23
	☽⚻♆	7 23
8 T	☽△☿	2am 8
	☉∠♇	5 18
	☿⚼♄	7 14
	☽△♅	12pm12
	☽∥♂	5 32
	☽⚹♀	7 42
	☽⚼♇	10 51
9 W	☉□☽	0am21
	☽#♃	1 37
	☽△♄	9 11
	☽☌♂	12pm40
	☽☍♃	12 41
	♂☍♃	1 16
	☽#♆	10 19
10 Th	☽△♇	5am22
	☽∠♀	5 33
	☽☍♆	8 13
	☽⚼♄	3pm24
11 F	☽□☿	0am33
	☽□♅	1 15
	☿☌♅	6 0
	♀⚼♆	8 16
	☽⚺♀	2pm56
	☉⚹☽	6 3
	☽⚻♄	9 10
12 S	☽⚻♃	1am11
	☽⚺♂	4 17
	☿∥♅	1pm 8
	☽□♇	5 4
	☽⚻♆	7 40
	♀#♄	10 30
	☽∥☿	10 47
13 Su	☉∠☽	1am46
	☽∥♅	2 27
	☽⚼♃	6 27
	☉⚻♄	7 38
	☽∠♂	10 54
	☉∥♇	11 8
	☽⚹♅	12pm10
	☉∥♀	4 46
	☽⚹☿	7 17
	♀∥♇	9 58
14 M	☽⚼♆	0am14
	♀☍♄	3 47
	♆SD	6 0
	☽☍♄	6 29
	☽☌♀	6 46
	☉⚺☽	8 25
	☉#♄	10 1
	☽△♃	10 50
	♂#♃	1pm10
	☽∠♅	4 21
	☽⚹♂	4 29
15 T	☽⚹♇	1am35
	☽∠☿	2 34
	☽△♆	3 55
	☽⚺♅	7pm41
	☉□♃	7 48
	☽∥♅	8 59
16 W	☽∠♇	4am35
	♀△♃	5 32
	☽⚺☿	8 36
	☽⚻♄	12pm28
	☽□♃	5 6
	☽⚺♀	6 8
	☉☌☽	6 34
17 Th	☽□♂	0am47
	☽∥☿	1 48
	☽⚺♇	6 53
	☽□♆	9 0
	☽⚼♄	2pm27
	☉⚺♀	5 10
	☿△♄	10 1
	☽∠♀	10 31
18 F	☽☌♅	0am15
	☽#♆	3pm17
	☽△♄	3 58
	☽☌☿	5 53
	♀∠♅	7 52
	☽⚹♃	8 57
19 S	☉⚺☽	1am47
	☽∥♂	1 58
	☽⚹♀	2 23
	☽△♂	6 32
	☽#♃	6 57
	☽☌♇	10 8
	☽⚹♆	12pm 6
	☽∠♃	10 25
20 Su	☽⚺♅	3am15
	☉∠☽	4 53
	☿⚹♃	6 19
	☽⚼♂	8 59
	☽∠♆	1pm22
	☽□♄	6 23
	☽⚺♃	11 48
21 M	☽⚺☿	1am19
	☽∠♅	4 36
	♂ ♉	7 4
	☉⚹☽	7 55
	☽□♀	9 32
	☽⚻♂	11 24
	☽⚺♇	12pm43
	☽⚺♆	2 36
22 T	☽∠☿	4am54
	♀ ♋	5 27
	☽⚹♅	5 59
	☽∠♇	2pm 6
	♂△♇	6 52
	☽∥♃	6 54
	☽⚹♄	8 48
23 W	♀⚹♇	0am26
	☽☌♃	2 47
	☽#♂	4 25
	♀⚹♂	6 17
	☽⚹☿	8 31
	☉ ♌	8 51
	☽∥♆	9 53
	☉□☽	2pm20
	☽⚹♇	3 36
	☽☍♂	4 32
	☽△♀	4 59
	☽☌♆	5 25
	☽#☿	6 44
	♀△♆	10 7
	☽∠♄	10 13
24 Th	☽□♅	9am12
	☉⚺♇	9 42
	♂☍♆	12pm46
	☽⚼♀	9 3
	☽⚺♄	11 50
25 F	☽⚺♃	6am26
	☉□♆	12pm 8
	☽□☿	4 9
	☽□♇	7 13
	☽⚺♆	8 58
	☉△☽	9 37
	♄#♇	10 11
	☽⚻♂	10 28
26 S	☽#♅	1am 1
	☽⚻♀	1 24
	☽∠♃	8 36
	☿#♆	8 50
	☿ ♍	10 8
	☽△♅	1pm14
	☿∥♂	4 40
	☽∠♆	11 6
27 Su	☉⚼☽	1am42
	☽⚼♂	1 50
	☽☌♄	3 45
	☉□♂	6 45
	☽⚹♃	11 3
	♂#♆	12pm55
	☿☌♇	1 43
	☽⚼♅	3 39
	☽△♇	11 50
28 M	☽△☿	0am32
	☽⚹♆	1 32
	☽△♂	5 33
	☉⚼♄	5 55
	☉⚻☽	6 10
	☽☍♀	11 12
	☿⚹♆	4pm15
	♂⚼♄	6 6
	☽⚻♅	6 26
	☽#♅	9 22
29 T	☽⚼♇	2am41
	☽⚼☿	5 10
	☽⚺♄	8 58
	☽□♃	5pm 6
30 W	☽⚻♇	6am 1
	☽□♆	7 41
	☽⚻☿	10 16
	☽∠♄	12pm17
	☽□♂	2 29
	☉☍☽	4 47
	☿#♃	8 56
	☽⚻♀	11 18
31 Th	☽☍♅	1am29
	☽#♂	11 9
	☽⚹♄	4pm14
	☽∥♆	4 34
	♀⚺♅	11 50

AUGUST 1958

LONGITUDE

Day	Sid. Time	☉	☽	☽ 12 Hour	Mean ☊	True ☊	☿	♀	♂	♃	♄	♅	♆	♇
	h m s	° ' "	° ' "	° ' "	° '	° '	° '	° '	° '	° '	° '	° '	° '	° '
1	20 36 23	8♌ 14 49	23♒ 37 27	29♒ 53 47	26♎ 9	25♎ 25R	4♍ 36	11♋ 45	6♉ 36	24♎ 21	19♐ 31R	11♌ 44	2♏ 5	1♍ 13
2	20 40 20	9 12 12	6♓ 6 18	12♓ 15 9	26 6	25 15	5 14	12 57	7 12	24 28	19 29	11 48	2 6	1 15
3	20 44 16	10 9 36	18 20 35	24 22 55	26 3	25 7	5 48	14 10	7 47	24 36	19 27	11 52	2 7	1 17
4	20 48 13	11 7 1	0♈ 22 33	6♈ 19 55	26 0	25 2	6 18	15 22	8 23	24 43	19 25	11 55	2 7	1 19
5	20 52 9	12 4 27	12 15 33	18 9 59	25 57	25 0	6 44	16 35	8 58	24 50	19 23	11 59	2 8	1 21
6	20 56 6	13 1 55	24 3 50	29 57 44	25 53	24 59D	7 5	17 47	9 33	24 58	19 21	12 3	2 9	1 23
7	21 0 2	13 59 24	5♉ 52 21	11♉ 48 21	25 50	24 59R	7 22	19 0	10 7	25 5	19 20	12 7	2 9	1 24
8	21 3 59	14 56 53	17 46 25	23 47 14	25 47	24 59	7 33	20 12	10 42	25 13	19 18	12 10	2 10	1 26
9	21 7 56	15 54 25	29 51 28	5♊ 59 45	25 44	24 58	7 40R	21 25	11 16	25 21	19 17	12 14	2 11	1 28
10	21 11 52	16 51 58	12♊ 12 40	18 30 44	25 41	24 55	7 41	22 38	11 50	25 29	19 15	12 18	2 12	1 30
11	21 15 49	17 49 32	24 54 25	1♋ 24 3	25 38	24 50	7 38	23 51	12 23	25 37	19 14	12 21	2 13	1 32
12	21 19 45	18 47 7	7♋ 59 53	14 42 1	25 34	24 43	7 28	25 4	12 57	25 45	19 13	12 25	2 14	1 34
13	21 23 42	19 44 44	21 30 23	28 24 49	25 31	24 34	7 14	26 16	13 30	25 54	19 12	12 29	2 15	1 36
14	21 27 38	20 42 23	5♌ 24 58	12♌ 30 18	25 28	24 24	6 53	27 29	14 3	26 2	19 11	12 32	2 15	1 38
15	21 31 35	21 40 2	19 40 12	26 53 54	25 25	24 14	6 28	28 42	14 35	26 11	19 10	12 36	2 16	1 40
16	21 35 31	22 37 42	4♍ 10 34	11♍ 29 18	25 22	24 6	5 57	29 55	15 7	26 19	19 9	12 40	2 17	1 42
17	21 39 28	23 35 24	18 49 13	26 9 25	25 19	23 59	5 21	1♌ 9	15 39	26 28	19 8	12 43	2 19	1 44
18	21 43 25	24 33 7	3♎ 29 6	10♎ 47 31	25 15	23 55	4 41	2 22	16 10	26 37	19 7	12 47	2 20	1 46
19	21 47 21	25 30 51	18 4 2	25 18 7	25 12	23 53D	3 56	3 35	16 42	26 46	19 7	12 51	2 21	1 48
20	21 51 18	26 28 36	2♏ 29 22	9♏ 37 29	25 9	23 53	3 8	4 48	17 12	26 55	19 7	12 54	2 22	1 50
21	21 55 14	27 26 23	16 42 16	23 43 35	25 6	23 54R	2 18	6 1	17 43	27 4	19 6	12 58	2 23	1 52
22	21 59 11	28 24 11	0♐ 41 24	7♐ 35 42	25 3	23 55	1 25	7 15	18 13	27 14	19 6	13 2	2 24	1 54
23	22 3 7	29 21 59	14 26 31	21 13 55	24 59	23 54	0 32	8 28	18 43	27 23	19 6	13 5	2 25	1 56
24	22 7 4	0♍ 19 49	27 57 57	4♑ 38 41	24 56	23 50	29♌ 39	9 41	19 13	27 33	19 6D	13 9	2 27	1 58
25	22 11 0	1 17 40	11♑ 16 9	17 50 23	24 53	23 45	28 47	10 55	19 42	27 42	19 6	13 13	2 28	2 0
26	22 14 57	2 15 32	24 21 27	0♒ 49 19	24 50	23 38	27 58	12 8	20 10	27 52	19 6	13 16	2 29	2 2
27	22 18 54	3 13 26	7♒ 14 2	13 35 36	24 47	23 29	27 12	13 22	20 39	28 2	19 6	13 20	2 31	2 4
28	22 22 50	4 11 21	19 54 2	26 9 21	24 44	23 20	26 31	14 35	21 7	28 12	19 7	13 23	2 32	2 6
29	22 26 47	5 9 17	2♓ 21 38	8♓ 30 57	24 40	23 12	25 55	15 49	21 34	28 22	19 7	13 27	2 33	2 8
30	22 30 43	6 7 15	14 37 25	20 41 12	24 37	23 5	25 25	17 3	22 2	28 32	19 7	13 30	2 35	2 10
31	22 34 40	7♍ 5 15	26♓ 42 29	2♈ 41 33	24♎ 34	23♎ 0	25♌ 3	18♌ 16	22♉ 28	28♎ 42	19♐ 8	13♌ 34	2♏ 36	2♍ 12

DECLINATION and LATITUDE

Day	☉ Decl	☽ Decl	☽ Lat	☽ 12 Hr. Decl	☿ Decl	☿ Lat	♀ Decl	♀ Lat	♂ Decl	♂ Lat	♃ Decl	♃ Lat	♄ Decl	♄ Lat
1	18N12	9S28	4N26	7S38	7N49	2S 9	22N32	0S23	11N26	2S25	8S22	1N 9	21S43	1N19
2	17 57	5 44	3 49	3 47	7 24	2 22	22 28	0 20	11 38	2 25	8 25	1 9	21 43	1 19
3	17 42	1 49	3 2	0N 8	6 60	2 34	22 24	0 18	11 49	2 25	8 28	1 9	21 43	1 19
4	17 27	2N 5	2 7	4 1	6 38	2 46	22 19	0 15	12 0	2 25	8 31	1 9	21 43	1 18
5	17 11	5 53	1 7	7 41	6 17	2 58	22 13	0 12	12 12	2 25	8 34	1 8	21 43	1 18
6	16 54	9 25	0 5	11 3	5 58	3 10	22 7	0 9	12 23	2 25	8 37	1 8	21 43	1 18
7	16 38	12 34	0S58	13 59	5 41	3 22	21 59	0 6	12 34	2 25	8 40	1 8	21 43	1 18
8	16 21	15 14	1 58	16 21	5 26	3 33	21 52	0 4	12 44	2 25	8 43	1 8	21 43	1 18
9	16 4	17 17	2 55	18 1	5 13	3 44	21 43	0 1	12 55	2 25	8 46	1 7	21 44	1 17
10	15 47	18 34	3 44	18 52	5 3	3 55	21 34	0N 2	13 6	2 25	8 49	1 7	21 44	1 17
11	15 30	18 57	4 24	18 47	4 55	4 5	21 25	0 4	13 16	2 24	8 52	1 7	21 44	1 17
12	15 12	18 21	4 51	17 40	4 51	4 14	21 15	0 7	13 26	2 24	8 55	1 7	21 44	1 17
13	14 54	16 44	5 3	15 32	4 48	4 22	21 4	0 10	13 36	2 24	8 58	1 7	21 44	1 17
14	14 36	14 6	4 58	12 26	4 49	4 29	20 52	0 13	13 46	2 24	9 2	1 6	21 44	1 16
15	14 17	10 34	4 35	8 32	4 53	4 35	20 40	0 15	13 56	2 23	9 5	1 6	21 44	1 16
16	13 58	6 21	3 53	4 4	4 60	4 40	20 28	0 18	14 6	2 23	9 8	1 6	21 44	1 16
17	13 40	1 43	2 56	0S39	5 10	4 43	20 14	0 20	14 15	2 23	9 12	1 6	21 44	1 16
18	13 20	3S 1	1 47	5 20	5 23	4 45	20 1	0 23	14 24	2 22	9 15	1 6	21 44	1 16
19	13 1	7 34	0 31	9 40	5 39	4 45	19 46	0 25	14 33	2 22	9 18	1 5	21 45	1 16
20	12 42	11 37	0N46	13 23	5 57	4 43	19 31	0 28	14 42	2 22	9 22	1 5	21 45	1 15
21	12 22	14 56	1 59	16 14	6 19	4 39	19 16	0 30	14 51	2 21	9 25	1 5	21 45	1 15
22	12 2	17 18	3 4	18 5	6 42	4 34	18 60	0 33	15 0	2 21	9 29	1 5	21 45	1 15
23	11 42	18 36	3 57	18 51	7 8	4 26	18 43	0 35	15 9	2 21	9 32	1 5	21 45	1 15
24	11 21	18 49	4 36	18 32	7 35	4 17	18 26	0 37	15 17	2 20	9 36	1 4	21 45	1 15
25	11 1	17 59	4 60	17 13	8 3	4 6	18 8	0 40	15 25	2 20	9 40	1 4	21 46	1 14
26	10 40	16 13	5 7	15 1	8 32	3 53	17 50	0 42	15 33	2 19	9 43	1 4	21 46	1 14
27	10 20	13 39	4 58	12 8	9 1	3 39	17 31	0 44	15 41	2 19	9 47	1 4	21 46	1 14
28	9 59	10 30	4 35	8 45	9 30	3 23	17 12	0 46	15 49	2 18	9 51	1 4	21 46	1 14
29	9 37	6 55	3 59	5 2	9 58	3 6	16 52	0 49	15 57	2 17	9 54	1 4	21 47	1 14
30	9 16	3 6	3 12	1 9	10 24	2 49	16 32	0 51	16 4	2 17	9 58	1 3	21 47	1 13
31	8N55	0N47	2N17	2N43	10N49	2S30	16N11	0N53	16N12	2S16	10S 2	1N 3	21S47	1N13

Day	♅ Decl	♅ Lat	♆ Decl	♆ Lat	♇ Decl	♇ Lat
1	17N52	0N37	10S33	1N45	21N39	11N23
5	17 48	0 37	10 34	1 45	21 36	11 23
9	17 44	0 37	10 36	1 45	21 33	11 23
13	17 40	0 37	10 37	1 45	21 30	11 23
17	17 36	0 37	10 39	1 44	21 27	11 23
21	17 32	0 38	10 40	1 44	21 24	11 23
25	17 27	0 38	10 42	1 44	21 22	11 23
29	17N23	0N38	10S44	1N44	21N19	11N23

☽ PHENOMENA

d	h	m	
7	17	50	☾
15	3	34	●
21	19	45	☽
29	5	54	○

d	h	° '
3	11	0
10	22	18N57
17	9	0
23	17	18S52
30	19	0

d	h	° '
6	2	0
13	5	5S 4
19	10	0
25	23	5N 7

VOID OF COURSE ☽

Last Aspect		☽ Ingress		
1	1am25	1	♓	12pm12
3	2am11	3	♈	11pm15
6	1am51	6	♉	12pm 5
8	5am25	9	♊	0am17
11	1am20	11	♋	9am26
13	9am 6	13	♌	2pm44
15	10am55	15	♍	5pm 7
17	0am31	17	♎	6pm17
19	2pm36	19	♏	7pm50
21	7pm45	21	♐	10pm48
24	2am50	24	♑	3am39
26	6am35	26	♒	10am28
28	4pm 9	28	♓	7pm25
30	3pm14	31	♈	6am36

d	h	
5	18	APOGEE
17	15	PERIGEE

DAILY ASPECTARIAN

Day	Aspect	Time
1	☽△♃	1am25
F	☽⚼♀	6 35
	☽∥♃	7 6
	☽#☿	12pm 9
	☽☍♇	2 35
	☽△♆	4 14
	☽☍☿	10 13
2	☽⚹♂	2am14
S	☉⚻☽	6 33
	☽⚼♃	6 38
	☉∥♅	10 44
	☽⚻♅	11 10
	☽△♀	2pm50
	☽⚼♆	9 34
3	☽□♄	2am11
Su	☽∠♂	9 17
	☽⚻♃	12pm33
	☉⚼☽	2 44
	☽⚼♅	5 3
4	☽⚻♇	1am53
M	☽⚻♆	3 31
	☽⚻☿	12pm24
	☽⚺♂	4 59
	♀∠♇	7 17
	☉☌♅	9 36
	☽△♅	11 26
	☉△☽	11 36
5	☽∥☿	2am25
T	☽⚼♇	8 19
	☽□♀	9 46
	☽△♄	2pm27
	☽#♃	6 16
	☽⚼☿	7 51
6	☽☍♃	1am51
W	☽#♆	8 29
	☽△♇	2pm55
	☽☍♆	4 27
	☽⚼♄	8 52
	☽∥♂	11 53
7	☽△☿	3am 4
Th	♀⚻♄	6 27
	☽☌♂	9 2
	☽□♅	12pm41
	☉□☽	5 50
8	☽⚻♄	3am 3
F	☽⚹♀	5 25
	☉∥☽	10 39
	☽⚻♃	3pm 0
	♀#♄	11 41
9	☽□♇	3am11
S	☽⚻♆	4 34
	☽∥♅	6 50
	☽∠♀	2pm13
	☽□☿	3 17
	☿SR	6 47
	☽⚼♃	8 38
	☽⚺♂	11 14
10	☽⚹♅	0am10
Su	☿∠♀	1 9
	♀∥♇	6 23
	☽⚼♆	9 31
	☉⚹☽	9 37
	☽☍♄	1pm23
	☽⚺♀	9 49
	♂□♅	10 22
11	☽△♃	1am20
M	☽∠♅	4 34
	☽∠♂	4 49
	☽⚹♇	12pm17
	☽△♆	1 30
	☉∠☽	3 45
	☽⚹☿	11 4
12	☽⚺♅	7am58
T	☽⚹♂	9 15
	☉△♄	10 28
	☽∥♅	12pm 0
	☽∠♇	3 21
	♀□♃	3 30
	☽⚻♄	7 57
	☉⚺☽	8 41
13	☽∠☿	1am14
W	☽□♃	7 43
	☽☌♀	9 6
	☽⚺♇	5pm31
	☽□♆	6 36
	☉∥☽	7 34
	☽⚼♄	9 53
14	☽∥♂	2am20
Th	☽⚺☿	2 26
	☽☌♅	12pm 7
	☽□♂	3 9
	☽△♄	11 9
	☽#♆	11 37
15	☉☌☽	3am34
F	☽#♃	8 44
	☽⚹♃	10 55
	☽⚺♀	4pm22
	☉∥♂	6 1
	☽☌♇	7 55
	☽⚹♆	8 54
16	♀ ♌	1am29
S	☽☌☿	2 48
	☽∥☿	6 58
	☽∠♃	11 51
	☽⚺♅	1pm59
	☽△♂	6 37
	☽∠♀	7 13
	☽∠♆	9 31
17	☽□♄	0am31
Su	☉⚺☽	8 21
	♀⚺♇	11 57
	☽⚺♃	12pm38
	☽∠♅	2 38
	☽⚼♂	8 4
	☽⚺♇	9 11
	☽⚹♀	9 59
	☽⚺♆	10 6
	♀□♆	11 18
18	☽⚺☿	1am52
M	☉∠☽	10 40
	☽#☿	12pm56
	☽⚹♅	3 21
	☽⚻♂	9 39
	☽∠♇	9 54
19	☽∠☿	1am22
T	☽⚹♄	1 44
	☿⚺♀	4 16
	☽∥♃	10 0
	♀⚼♄	10 27
	☉⚹☽	1pm14
	☽☌♃	2 36
	☽∥♆	5 59
	☽⚹♇	10 54
	☽☌♆	11 47
20	☽⚹☿	1am 2
W	☽∠♄	2 43
	☽□♀	4 14
	☉#☽	6 33
	☉⚹♃	1pm10
	☽□♅	5 38
	☿⚹♆	9 38
	☽#♂	11 23
21	☽☍♂	1am47
Th	☽⚺♄	4 5
	☿☌♇	11 28
	☽⚺♃	5pm57
	☉□☽	7 45
22	☽□☿	1am12
F	☽□♇	2 6
	☽#♅	2 52
	☽⚺♆	2 58
	☽△♀	12pm30
	☽∠♃	8 21
	☽△♅	9 37
23	☽#♀	2am43
S	☽∠♆	5 16
	☽⚻♂	7 50
	☽☌♄	8 13
	☿ ♌	2pm37
	☉☌☿	3 11
	☉ ♍	3 47
	☽⚼♀	5 34
	♂⚻♄	6 28
	☽⚹♃	11 14
24	☽⚼♅	0am20
Su	♄SD	0 35
	☽△☿	2 50
	☉△☽	4 34
	☽△♇	7 12
	☽⚹♆	8 3
	☽⚼♂	11 38
	☽#♀	8pm18
	☽⚻♀	11 17
25	☽⚻♅	3am33
M	☽⚼☿	4 19
	☽#♅	8 37
	☉⚼☽	9 54
	☽⚼♇	10 29
	☽⚺♄	2pm18
	☽△♂	4 0
	☉☌♇	6 10
	☉#♆	9 21
26	☿⚹♃	2am29
T	☉⚹♆	5 47
	☽⚻☿	6 18
	☽#♂	6 29
	☽□♃	6 35
	☽⚻♇	2pm18
	☽□♆	3 8
	☉⚻☽	3 52
	☽∠♄	6 8
	♀☌♅	11 16
27	♀∥♅	7am40
W	☽☍♅	11 33
	☽☍♀	12pm48
	☽∥♆	10 21
	☽⚹♄	10 29
28	☽□♂	2am24
Th	☉#☽	4 2
	☽∥♃	4 28
	☽#☿	6 7
	☉#♃	7 40
	☽☍☿	12pm 5
	☉∥☿	2 3
	☽△♃	4 9
	☿#♃	8 44
	☽☍♇	11 33
29	☽△♆	0am23
F	☉☍☽	5 54
	☽⚻♅	9pm47
	☽⚼♃	9 49
30	☽⚻♀	5am19
S	☽⚼♆	5 51
	☽□♄	8 54
	☽⚹♂	3pm14
	☿#♆	8 28
	☽⚻☿	8 46
	♀∥♂	11 41
31	☽⚼♅	3am44
Su	☽⚻♃	4 3
	☽⚻♇	11 2
	☽⚻♆	11 50
	☽⚼♀	2pm40
	♀△♄	5 4
	☽∠♂	10 28
	☉⚻☽	10 42

LONGITUDE

Day	Sid. Time	☉	☽	☽ 12 Hour	Mean ☊	True ☊	☿	♀	♂	♃	♄	♅	♆	♇
	h m s	° ' "	° ' "	° ' "	° '	° '	° '	° '	° '	° '	° '	° '	° '	° '
1	22 38 36	8♍ 3 16	8♈ 38 39	14♈ 34 10	24♎ 31	22♎ 57R	24♌ 48R	19♌ 30	22♉ 55	28♎ 53	19♐ 9	13♌ 37	2♏ 38	2♍ 14
2	22 42 33	9 1 19	20 28 29	26 22 1	24 28	22 55D	24 41D	20 44	23 21	29 3	19 10	13 41	2 39	2 16
3	22 46 29	9 59 24	2♉ 15 17	8♉ 8 48	24 25	22 56	24 43	21 57	23 46	29 13	19 11	13 44	2 40	2 18
4	22 50 26	10 57 31	14 3 6	19 58 49	24 21	22 57	24 53	23 11	24 11	29 24	19 12	13 47	2 42	2 20
5	22 54 23	11 55 40	25 56 31	1♊ 56 53	24 18	22 59	25 12	24 25	24 36	29 34	19 13	13 51	2 44	2 22
6	22 58 19	12 53 51	8♊ 0 31	14 8 3	24 15	23 0R	25 39	25 39	25 0	29 45	19 14	13 54	2 45	2 24
7	23 2 16	13 52 4	20 20 8	26 37 19	24 12	22 59	26 15	26 53	25 24	29 56	19 15	13 58	2 47	2 26
8	23 6 12	14 50 18	3♋ 0 9	9♋ 29 7	24 9	22 58	26 59	28 7	25 47	0♏ 7	19 17	14 1	2 48	2 28
9	23 10 9	15 48 35	16 4 34	22 46 46	24 5	22 54	27 51	29 21	26 9	0 18	19 18	14 4	2 50	2 30
10	23 14 5	16 46 54	29 35 52	6♌ 31 51	24 2	22 50	28 50	0♍ 35	26 31	0 29	19 20	14 7	2 52	2 32
11	23 18 2	17 45 15	13♌ 34 32	20 43 32	23 59	22 45	29 57	1 49	26 53	0 40	19 21	14 11	2 53	2 34
12	23 21 58	18 43 38	27 58 20	5♍ 18 14	23 56	22 40	1♍ 10	3 3	27 14	0 51	19 23	14 14	2 55	2 36
13	23 25 55	19 42 3	12♍ 42 22	20 9 45	23 53	22 36	2 29	4 18	27 34	1 2	19 25	14 17	2 57	2 38
14	23 29 52	20 40 30	27 39 20	5♎ 10 1	23 50	22 32	3 53	5 32	27 54	1 14	19 27	14 20	2 59	2 39
15	23 33 48	21 38 58	12♎ 40 40	20 10 14	23 46	22 31D	5 22	6 46	28 14	1 25	19 29	14 24	3 0	2 41
16	23 37 45	22 37 28	27 37 44	5♏ 2 19	23 43	22 30	6 56	8 0	28 32	1 36	19 31	14 27	3 2	2 43
17	23 41 41	23 36 0	12♏ 23 13	19 39 50	23 40	22 31	8 33	9 15	28 50	1 48	19 33	14 30	3 4	2 45
18	23 45 38	24 34 34	26 51 44	3♐ 58 36	23 37	22 32	10 14	10 29	29 8	2 0	19 36	14 33	3 6	2 47
19	23 49 34	25 33 10	11♐ 0 15	17 56 36	23 34	22 33	11 57	11 44	29 25	2 11	19 38	14 36	3 8	2 49
20	23 53 31	26 31 47	24 47 42	1♑ 33 38	23 30	22 34R	13 42	12 58	29 41	2 23	19 41	14 39	3 9	2 51
21	23 57 27	27 30 25	8♑ 14 35	14 50 46	23 27	22 34	15 29	14 12	29 57	2 35	19 43	14 42	3 11	2 53
22	0 1 24	28 29 6	21 22 25	27 49 49	23 24	22 32	17 17	15 27	0♊ 11	2 47	19 46	14 45	3 13	2 54
23	0 5 21	29 27 48	4♒ 13 12	10♒ 32 51	23 21	22 29	19 6	16 41	0 26	2 58	19 49	14 48	3 15	2 56
24	0 9 17	0♎ 26 32	16 49 3	23 2 3	23 18	22 26	20 56	17 56	0 39	3 10	19 52	14 51	3 17	2 58
25	0 13 14	1 25 17	29 12 6	5♓ 19 26	23 15	22 23	22 46	19 10	0 52	3 22	19 55	14 53	3 19	3 0
26	0 17 10	2 24 5	11♓ 24 17	17 26 53	23 11	22 20	24 36	20 25	1 4	3 34	19 58	14 56	3 21	3 2
27	0 21 7	3 22 54	23 27 28	29 26 14	23 8	22 17	26 26	21 40	1 16	3 46	20 1	14 59	3 23	3 4
28	0 25 3	4 21 45	5♈ 23 27	11♈ 19 21	23 5	22 15	28 16	22 54	1 26	3 59	20 4	15 2	3 25	3 5
29	0 29 0	5 20 38	17 14 12	23 8 16	23 2	22 15D	0♎ 6	24 9	1 36	4 11	20 7	15 4	3 27	3 7
30	0 32 56	6♎ 19 33	29♈ 1 51	4♉ 55 18	22♎ 59	22♎ 15	1♎ 55	25♍ 24	1♊ 45	4♏ 23	20♐ 11	15♌ 7	3♏ 29	3♍ 9

DECLINATION and LATITUDE

Day	☉	☽		☽ 12 Hr.	☿		♀		♂		♃		♄	
	Decl	Decl	Lat	Decl	Decl	Lat	Decl	Lat	Decl	Lat	Decl	Lat	Decl	Lat
1	8N33	4N36	1N17	6N26	11N11	2S12	15N50	0N55	16N19	2S16	10S 6	1N 3	21S47	1N13
2	8 11	8 12	0 13	9 53	11 31	1 53	15 29	0 57	16 26	2 15	10 9	1 3	21 48	1 13
3	7 49	11 28	0S51	12 56	11 49	1 34	15 7	0 58	16 33	2 14	10 13	1 3	21 48	1 13
4	7 27	14 16	1 52	15 28	12 3	1 15	14 44	1 0	16 40	2 13	10 17	1 3	21 48	1 12
5	7 5	16 29	2 50	17 21	12 14	0 57	14 22	1 2	16 47	2 13	10 21	1 2	21 48	1 12
6	6 43	18 1	3 41	18 28	12 21	0 39	13 58	1 4	16 53	2 12	10 25	1 2	21 49	1 12
7	6 21	18 43	4 23	18 44	12 25	0 22	13 35	1 5	16 60	2 11	10 29	1 2	21 49	1 12
8	5 58	18 31	4 53	18 4	12 25	0 6	13 11	1 7	17 6	2 10	10 33	1 2	21 49	1 12
9	5 36	17 21	5 10	16 23	12 22	0N 9	12 46	1 9	17 12	2 9	10 37	1 2	21 50	1 12
10	5 13	15 11	5 10	13 45	12 15	0 23	12 22	1 10	17 18	2 8	10 41	1 2	21 50	1 11
11	4 50	12 5	4 52	10 14	12 4	0 37	11 57	1 12	17 24	2 8	10 45	1 1	21 50	1 11
12	4 28	8 11	4 15	5 60	11 50	0 49	11 31	1 13	17 29	2 7	10 49	1 1	21 50	1 11
13	4 5	3 42	3 21	1 19	11 32	0 60	11 5	1 14	17 35	2 6	10 53	1 1	21 51	1 11
14	3 42	1S 5	2 12	3S29	11 10	1 10	10 39	1 15	17 41	2 5	10 57	1 1	21 51	1 11
15	3 19	5 50	0 54	8 5	10 46	1 19	10 13	1 17	17 46	2 3	11 1	1 1	21 52	1 10
16	2 56	10 12	0N28	12 8	10 18	1 26	9 46	1 18	17 51	2 2	11 5	1 1	21 52	1 10
17	2 33	13 51	1 47	15 21	9 48	1 33	9 19	1 19	17 56	2 1	11 9	1 1	21 52	1 10
18	2 9	16 35	2 58	17 32	9 15	1 38	8 52	1 20	18 1	2 0	11 13	1 0	21 53	1 10
19	1 46	18 12	3 56	18 36	8 40	1 43	8 25	1 21	18 6	1 59	11 18	1 0	21 53	1 10
20	1 23	18 42	4 39	18 32	8 3	1 46	7 57	1 22	18 10	1 58	11 22	1 0	21 53	1 9
21	0 59	18 7	5 5	17 27	7 24	1 49	7 29	1 23	18 15	1 56	11 26	1 0	21 54	1 9
22	0 36	16 34	5 15	15 29	6 43	1 50	7 1	1 23	18 19	1 55	11 30	0 60	21 54	1 9
23	0 13	14 13	5 8	12 47	6 1	1 51	6 33	1 24	18 24	1 54	11 34	0 60	21 54	1 9
24	0S11	11 14	4 47	9 34	5 18	1 51	6 4	1 25	18 28	1 52	11 38	0 60	21 55	1 9
25	0 34	7 48	4 13	5 59	4 34	1 50	5 35	1 25	18 32	1 51	11 42	0 60	21 55	1 9
26	0 57	4 6	3 27	2 11	3 49	1 49	5 7	1 26	18 36	1 49	11 47	0 59	21 56	1 8
27	1 21	0 16	2 33	1N39	3 3	1 47	4 38	1 26	18 39	1 48	11 51	0 59	21 56	1 8
28	1 44	3N33	1 32	5 24	2 17	1 44	4 8	1 26	18 43	1 46	11 55	0 59	21 57	1 8
29	2 7	7 12	0 28	8 55	1 31	1 41	3 39	1 27	13 47	1 45	11 59	0 59	21 57	1 8
30	2S31	10N33	0S38	12N 4	0N44	1N38	3N10	1N27	18N50	1S43	12S 4	0N59	21S57	1N 8

Day	♅		♆		♇	
	Decl	Lat	Decl	Lat	Decl	Lat
1	17N21	0N38	10S46	1N44	21N17	11N24
5	17 17	0 38	10 48	1 43	21 14	11 24
9	17 13	0 38	10 50	1 43	21 12	11 25
13	17 9	0 38	10 53	1 43	21 10	11 25
17	17 6	0 38	10 55	1 43	21 7	11 26
21	17 2	0 38	10 58	1 43	21 5	11 27
25	16 59	0 38	11 1	1 43	21 3	11 28
29	16N56	0N38	11S 4	1N43	21N 2	11N29

☽ PHENOMENA			
d	h	m	
6	10	25	☾
13	12	3	●
20	3	18	☽
27	21	44	○
d	h	° '	
7	7	18N46	
13	19	0	
19	23	18S42	
27	2	0	
2	5	0	
9	12	5S12	
15	16	0	
22	2	5N15	
29	10	0	

VOID OF COURSE ☽ Last Aspect		☽ Ingress		
2	5pm44	2	♉	7pm24
4	10pm27	5	♊	8am 7
7	1pm51	7	♋	6pm23
9	6pm28	10	♌	0am42
11	10pm45	12	♍	3am20
14	0am25	14	♎	3am45
15	10am56	16	♏	3am50
18	3am54	18	♐	5am16
20	3am18	20	♑	9am13
22	2pm19	22	♒	4pm 4
24	5am53	25	♓	1am34
27	7am 3	27	♈	1pm 8
29	5am54	30	♉	1am58

d	h	
2	11	APOGEE
14	17	PERIGEE
29	22	APOGEE

DAILY ASPECTARIAN

Day	Aspect	Time
1 M	☽⚼☿	2am18
	☽△♅	10 7
	☽⚼♇	5pm27
	☽△♄	9 19
	☉∥☽	11 54
2 T	☽△♀	0am34
	☽⚺♂	6 4
	☿SD	7 40
	☉⚼☽	7 52
	☽△☿	8 34
	☽⋕♃	2pm17
	☽☍♃	5 44
	☽⋕♆	6 40
3 W	☽△♇	0am 5
	☽☍♆	0 51
	☽∥☿	2 58
	☽⚼♄	3 55
	☉△☽	5pm 9
	☽□♅	11 28
4 Th	☽∥♀	3am57
	☽⚻♄	10 26
	☽□♀	8pm36
	☽☌♂	9 12
	☽□☿	10 27
5 F	☽∥♂	4am 0
	♀□♂	5 10
	☽⚻♃	7 23
	☽∥♅	10 50
	☽□♇	12pm52
	☽⚻♆	1 35
	☿☌♀	11 53
6 S	☉□☽	10am25
	☽⚹♅	11 36
	☽⚼♃	1pm24
	☽⚼♆	7 4
	☽☍♄	9 55
7 Su	☉⚺♅	2am25
	♃ ♏	8 52
	☽⚺♂	9 58
	☽⚹☿	11 57
	☽⚹♀	1pm51
	☽∠♅	4 29
	☽△♃	6 31
	☽⚹♇	10 59
	☽△♆	11 38
8 M	☉∠♃	8am23
	☽∠♂	2pm48
	☽∠☿	5 42
	☽⚺♅	8 21
	☽∠♀	8 34
	☉⚹☽	11 29
9 T	☽∥♅	1am55
	☽∥♂	1 59
	☽∠♇	2 34
	♂∥♅	3 2
	☽⚻♄	5 49
	♀ ♍	12pm36
	☽⚹♂	6 28
	♀⚹♃	9 34
	☽⚺☿	10 33
10 W	☽□♃	1am34
	☽⚺♀	1 54
	☉∠☽	4 5
	☽⚺♇	5 6
	☽□♆	5 41
	☽⚼♄	8 13
	☿∥♀	10 47
11 Th	☽∥☿	0am10
	☽☌♅	1 1
	☽∥♀	1 7
	☿ ♍	1 9
	☉∠♆	3 26
	☉⚺☽	7 33
	☽⋕♆	8 1
	☽⋕♃	8 36
	☽△♄	9 44
	♀☌♇	2pm44
	☿⚹♃	5 3
	♀⚹♆	9 13
	☽□♂	10 45
12 F	☽⚹♃	4am47
	☽☌☿	5 44
	☽☌♇	7 36
	☽⚹♆	8 7
	☽☌♀	9 6
	☉□♄	4pm46
	☉∥☽	9 52
	♃∥♆	11 15
13 S	☽⚺♅	2am34
	☿☌♇	2 38
	☽∠♃	5 26
	☿⚹♆	8 19
	☽∠♆	8 27
	♀⋕♃	9 56
	☽□♄	10 50
	♀⋕♆	11 18
	☉☌☽	12pm 3
14 Su	☽△♂	0am25
	☽∠♅	2 42
	☽⚺♃	5 47
	☽⚺♇	8 1
	☽⚺♆	8 31
	☽⚺☿	11 2
	☿⋕♃	11 25
	☉⋕☽	12pm 5
	☽⚺♀	1 43
	☿⋕♆	4 18
15 M	☽⚼♂	0am54
	☽⚹♅	2 45
	☽∠♇	8 2
	☽⚹♄	10 56
	☽∠☿	1pm45
	☉⚺☽	3 23
	☽∠♀	3 53
	☽⋕♀	9 46
16 T	☽⋕☿	0am34
	☽⚻♂	1 30
	☽∥♆	4 20
	☽∥♃	5 29
	☽☌♃	6 31
	☽⚹♇	8 15
	☽☌♆	8 46
	☽∠♄	11 11
	☽⚹☿	4pm57
	☉∠☽	5 22
	☽⚹♀	6 23
17 W	☽□♅	3am29
	☽⚺♄	11 51
	☉⚹☽	7pm54
18 Th	☽☍♂	3am54
	☽⋕♅	5 52
	☽⚺♃	8 46
	☽□♇	10 0
	☽⚺♆	10 32
	☿☌♀	1pm11
	☽⋕♂	9 30
19 F	☽□♀	1am22
	☽□☿	1 51
	☽△♅	6 13
	☽∠♃	10 50
	☽∠♆	12pm21
	☽☌♄	3 0
20 S	☉□☽	3am18
	☽⚼♅	8 37
	☽⚻♂	8 50
	☿∥♀	12pm32
	☿⚺♅	1 13
	☽⚹♃	1 40
	☽△♇	2 20
	☽⚹♆	2 53
	☽⋕♂	9 2
21 Su	♂ ♊	5am26
	♀⚺♅	9 53
	☽⚻♅	11 46
	☽△♀	11 58
	☽⚼♂	12pm25
	☽△☿	3 15
	☽⚼♇	5 36
	☽⋕♅	6 3
	☽⚺♄	9 1
22 M	☿∠♃	7am20
	☿∠♆	12pm39
	☉△☽	2 19
	☽△♂	4 44
	☽⚼♀	6 43
	♃⚹♇	7 4
	☽⚻♇	9 35
	☽□♃	9 37
	☽□♆	10 10
	☽⚼☿	11 44
23 T	☽∠♄	1am 8
	☉∠♅	8 32
	☿□♄	9 39
	☉ ♎	1pm 9
	☽☍♅	8 12
	☽∥♃	9 1
	☉⚼☽	9 8
24 W	☽∥♆	1am42
	☽⚻♀	2 23
	♀∠♃	5 33
	☽⚹♄	5 53
	☉△♂	6 41
	♀∠♆	7 2
	☽⚻☿	9 18
	♃☌♆	4pm15
25 Th	☽□♂	3am19
	☉⚻☽	4 43
	☽☍♇	7 27
	☽△♆	8 5
	☽△♃	8 18
	♀□♄	2pm52
	☽⋕♀	4 37
26 F	☽⋕☿	2am14
	☽⚻♅	7 2
	☽⚼♆	1pm50
	☽⚼♃	2 29
	☉⚺♇	3 51
	☽□♄	5 5
	☉∥☽	5 52
	☽☍♀	7 59
27 S	☉⚺♆	0am 4
	☽☍☿	7 3
	☉⋕☽	11 11
	☉⚺♃	12pm 7
	☽⚼♅	1 9
	☽⚹♂	3 55
	☽∥☿	5 19
	☽⚻♇	7 21
	☽⚻♆	8 0
	☽⚻♃	9 6
	☉☍☽	9 44
28 Su	☽∥♀	3am21
	☉⋕☿	11 23
	☽△♅	7pm35
	☽∠♂	10 42
	☿ ♎	10 46
	☿∠♅	11 43
29 M	☽⚼♇	1am48
	☽△♄	5 54
	☽⚻♀	3pm43
	☿△♂	9 46
30 T	☽⋕♆	4am 3
	☽⚺♂	5 37
	☽⚻☿	6 56
	☽△♇	8 24
	☽☍♆	9 6
	☽☍♃	11 6
	☽⋕♃	12pm12
	☽⚼♄	12 35
	☉⚻☽	4 13
	☿⚺♇	4 38
	☉⋕♀	5 37
	☿⚺♆	9 16

OCTOBER 1958

LONGITUDE

Day	Sid. Time	☉	☽	☽ 12 Hour	Mean ☊	True ☊	☿	♀	♂	♃	♄	♅	♆	♇
	h m s	° ' "	° ' "	° ' "	° '	° '	° '	° '	° '	° '	° '	° '	° '	° '
1	0 36 53	7♎ 18 31	10♉ 48 56	16♉ 43 11	22♎ 56	22♎ 15	3♎ 43	26♍ 38	1♊ 54	4♏ 35	20♐ 14	15♌ 10	3♏ 31	3♍ 11
2	0 40 49	8 17 30	22 38 25	28 35 6	22 52	22 17	5 31	27 53	2 1	4 48	20 18	15 12	3 33	3 12
3	0 44 46	9 16 32	4♊ 33 42	10♊ 34 42	22 49	22 18	7 18	29 8	2 8	5 0	20 22	15 15	3 35	3 14
4	0 48 43	10 15 36	16 38 38	22 46 1	22 46	22 19	9 5	0♎ 23	2 14	5 13	20 25	15 17	3 37	3 16
5	0 52 39	11 14 43	28 57 23	5♋ 13 17	22 43	22 19	10 51	1 37	2 19	5 25	20 29	15 20	3 39	3 17
6	0 56 36	12 13 52	11♋ 34 13	18 0 41	22 40	22 20R	12 36	2 52	2 24	5 38	20 33	15 22	3 42	3 19
7	1 0 32	13 13 3	24 33 7	1♌ 11 53	22 36	22 19	14 20	4 7	2 27	5 50	20 37	15 25	3 44	3 21
8	1 4 29	14 12 16	7♌ 57 17	14 49 29	22 33	22 19	16 3	5 22	2 30	6 3	20 41	15 27	3 46	3 22
9	1 8 25	15 11 32	21 48 33	28 54 22	22 30	22 18	17 46	6 37	2 31	6 15	20 45	15 29	3 48	3 24
10	1 12 22	16 10 50	6♍ 6 40	13♍ 25 2	22 27	22 18	19 28	7 52	2 32R	6 28	20 49	15 31	3 50	3 25
11	1 16 18	17 10 10	20 48 48	28 17 13	22 24	22 17	21 9	9 7	2 32	6 41	20 54	15 34	3 52	3 27
12	1 20 15	18 9 32	5♎ 49 18	13♎ 23 59	22 21	22 17	22 50	10 22	2 31	6 54	20 58	15 36	3 54	3 28
13	1 24 12	19 8 57	21 0 6	28 36 27	22 17	22 17D	24 29	11 37	2 29	7 6	21 2	15 38	3 57	3 30
14	1 28 8	20 8 23	6♏ 11 47	13♏ 44 56	22 14	22 17	26 8	12 52	2 26	7 19	21 7	15 40	3 59	3 31
15	1 32 5	21 7 52	21 14 50	28 40 30	22 11	22 17R	27 47	14 7	2 23	7 32	21 11	15 42	4 1	3 33
16	1 36 1	22 7 22	6♐ 1 7	13♐ 16 5	22 8	22 17	29 24	15 22	2 18	7 45	21 16	15 44	4 3	3 34
17	1 39 58	23 6 55	20 24 53	27 27 15	22 5	22 17	1♏ 1	16 37	2 13	7 58	21 21	15 46	4 5	3 36
18	1 43 54	24 6 28	4♑ 23 2	11♑ 12 15	22 2	22 17	2 37	17 52	2 6	8 11	21 26	15 48	4 8	3 37
19	1 47 51	25 6 4	17 55 3	24 31 38	21 58	22 17D	4 13	19 7	1 59	8 24	21 30	15 50	4 10	3 39
20	1 51 47	26 5 42	1♒ 2 21	7♒ 27 35	21 55	22 17	5 48	20 22	1 51	8 37	21 35	15 52	4 12	3 40
21	1 55 44	27 5 21	13 47 46	20 3 21	21 52	22 17	7 22	21 37	1 42	8 50	21 40	15 53	4 14	3 41
22	1 59 41	28 5 2	26 14 49	2♓ 22 38	21 49	22 17	8 56	22 53	1 32	9 3	21 45	15 55	4 17	3 43
23	2 3 37	29 4 44	8♓ 27 17	14 29 12	21 46	22 18	10 29	24 8	1 21	9 16	21 51	15 57	4 19	3 44
24	2 7 34	0♏ 4 29	20 28 51	26 26 37	21 42	22 19	12 2	25 23	1 10	9 29	21 56	15 58	4 21	3 45
25	2 11 30	1 4 15	2♈ 22 54	8♈ 18 4	21 39	22 20	13 34	26 38	0 57	9 42	22 1	16 0	4 23	3 46
26	2 15 27	2 4 3	14 12 27	20 6 24	21 36	22 20R	15 5	27 53	0 44	9 55	22 6	16 1	4 26	3 48
27	2 19 23	3 3 52	26 0 10	1♉ 54 5	21 33	22 21	16 36	29 8	0 30	10 8	22 12	16 3	4 28	3 49
28	2 23 20	4 3 44	7♉ 48 23	13 43 21	21 30	22 20	18 7	0♏ 24	0 15	10 21	22 17	16 4	4 30	3 50
29	2 27 16	5 3 38	19 39 13	25 36 17	21 27	22 19	19 37	1 39	0 0	10 34	22 23	16 6	4 32	3 51
30	2 31 13	6 3 34	1♊ 34 47	7♊ 35 0	21 23	22 17	21 6	2 54	29♉ 44	10 47	22 28	16 7	4 34	3 52
31	2 35 9	7♏ 3 32	13♊ 37 13	19♊ 41 45	21♎ 20	22♎ 15	22♏ 35	4♏ 9	29♉ 27	11♏ 0	22♐ 34	16♌ 8	4♏ 37	3♍ 53

DECLINATION and LATITUDE

Day	☉ Decl	☽ Decl	☽ Lat	☽ 12 Hr. Decl	☿ Decl	☿ Lat	♀ Decl	♀ Lat	♂ Decl	♂ Lat	♃ Decl	♃ Lat	♄ Decl	♄ Lat
1	2S54	13N28	1S41	14N44	0S 3	1N34	2N40	1N27	18N53	1S41	12S 8	0N59	21S58	1N 8
2	3 17	15 51	2 41	16 47	0 49	1 29	2 10	1 27	18 57	1 40	12 12	0 59	21 58	1 7
3	3 41	17 33	3 34	18 7	1 36	1 25	1 41	1 27	18 60	1 38	12 16	0 59	21 59	1 7
4	4 4	18 29	4 18	18 39	2 23	1 20	1 11	1 27	19 3	1 36	12 20	0 59	21 59	1 7
5	4 27	18 35	4 52	18 17	3 9	1 14	0 41	1 27	19 6	1 34	12 25	0 58	21 60	1 7
6	4 50	17 45	5 12	16 60	3 55	1 9	0 11	1 27	19 8	1 32	12 29	0 58	21 60	1 7
7	5 13	16 0	5 18	14 47	4 41	1 3	0S19	1 26	19 11	1 30	12 33	0 58	22 0	1 7
8	5 36	13 21	5 6	11 42	5 26	0 57	0 49	1 26	19 13	1 28	12 37	0 58	22• 1	1 6
9	5 59	9 52	4 37	7 52	6 11	0 51	1 19	1 26	19 16	1 26	12 42	0 58	22 1	1 6
10	6 22	5 43	3 50	3 27	6 56	0 45	1 49	1 25	19 18	1 24	12 46	0 58	22 2	1 6
11	6 45	1 6	2 46	1S18	7 40	0 38	2 19	1 25	19 20	1 22	12 50	0 58	22 2	1 6
12	7 7	3S42	1 30	6 3	8 23	0 32	2 49	1 24	19 22	1 19	12 54	0 58	22 3	1 6
13	7 30	8 18	0 7	10 26	9 6	0 25	3 19	1 24	19 24	1 17	12 59	0 58	22 3	1 6
14	7 52	12 23	1N17	14 7	9 48	0 19	3 49	1 23	19 26	1 15	13 3	0 58	22 4	1 5
15	8 15	15 35	2 34	16 48	10 30	0 12	4 18	1 22	19 28	1 12	13 7	0 58	22 4	1 5
16	8 37	17 42	3 40	18 18	11 11	0 5	4 48	1 21	19 29	1 10	13 11	0 57	22 4	1 5
17	8 59	18 36	4 30	18 36	11 52	0S 2	5 18	1 20	19 30	1 7	13 16	0 57	22 5	1 5
18	9 21	18 20	5 3	17 47	12 31	0 9	5 47	1 19	19 32	1 5	13 20	0 57	22 5	1 5
19	9 43	17 0	5 17	16 0	13 10	0 16	6 17	1 18	19 33	1 2	13 24	0 57	22 6	1 5
20	10 5	14 49	5 14	13 27	13 49	0 22	6 46	1 17	19 34	0 60	13 28	0 57	22 6	1 4
21	10 26	11 57	4 56	10 20	14 26	0 29	7 15	1 16	19 35	0 57	13 33	0 57	22 7	1 4
22	10 48	8 38	4 24	6 50	15 3	0 36	7 44	1 15	19 35	0 54	13 37	0 57	22 7	1 4
23	11 9	4 59	3 41	3 6	15 39	0 43	8 13	1 14	19 36	0 51	13 41	0 57	22 8	1 4
24	11 30	1 12	2 48	0N43	16 14	0 49	8 42	1 12	19 36	0 48	13 45	0 57	22 8	1 4
25	11 51	2N37	1 49	4 29	16 48	0 56	9 10	1 11	19 37	0 46	13 49	0 57	22 9	1 4
26	12 12	6 18	0 45	8 3	17 22	1 3	9 38	1 10	19 37	0 43	13 54	0 57	22 9	1 4
27	12 32	9 44	0S20	11 19	17 54	1 9	10 6	1 8	19 37	0 40	13 58	0 57	22 10	1 3
28	12 53	12 47	1 25	14 7	18 26	1 15	10 34	1 7	19 37	0 37	14 2	0 57	22 10	1 3
29	13 13	15 19	2 26	16 21	18 57	1 22	11 2	1 5	19 36	0 34	14 6	0 57	22 10	1 3
30	13 33	17 12	3 21	17 52	19 27	1 28	11 29	1 4	19 36	0 31	14 10	0 56	22 11	1 3
31	13S52	18N21	4S 7	18N37	19S56	1S34	11S56	1N 2	19N35	0S27	14S14	0N56	22S11	1N 3

Day	♅ Decl	♅ Lat	♆ Decl	♆ Lat	♇ Decl	♇ Lat
1	16N54	0N38	11S 5	1N43	21N 1	11N29
5	16 51	0 39	11 8	1 43	20 59	11 30
9	16 49	0 39	11 11	1 42	20 58	11 31
13	16 46	0 39	11 14	1 42	20 57	11 32
17	16 44	0 39	11 17	1 42	20 56	11 34
21	16 42	0 39	11 20	1 42	20 55	11 35
25	16 40	0 39	11 23	1 42	20 54	11 36
29	16N39	0N40	11S26	1N42	20N54	11N38

☽ PHENOMENA				VOID OF COURSE ☽ Last Aspect		☽ Ingress	
d	h	m		2	11am50	2 ♊	2pm51
6	1	20	☾	4	7am27	5 ♋	2am 1
12	20	52	●	6	2am13	7 ♌	9am51
19	14	7	☽	8	10pm11	9 ♍	1pm50
27	15	41	○	11	0am 8	11 ♎	2pm44
				13	6am10	13 ♏	2pm12
				14	3pm 6	15 ♐	2pm 9
d	h	° '		17	4am56	17 ♑	4pm23
4	14	18N39		19	2pm 7	19 ♒	10pm 4
11	5	0		22	3am54	22 ♓	7am20
17	6	18S38		24	2am56	24 ♈	7pm11
24	8	0		27	7am 9	27 ♉	8am 8
31	21	18N40		29	8pm23	29 ♊	8pm50
6	20	5S18		d	h		
13	2	0		13	3	PERIGEE	
19	8	5N18		27	0	APOGEE	
26	17	0					

DAILY ASPECTARIAN

Day	Aspect	Time
1 W	☽⚼♀	1am52
	☽□♅	8 52
	☿⚺♃	1pm 5
	☽⚼☿	6 56
	☽⚻♄	7 14
2 Th	☉⚼☽	1am26
	☽△♀	11 50
	☽∥♅	1pm26
	☽☌♂	7 6
	☽□♇	9 20
	☽⚻♆	10 3
3 F	☽⚻♃	0am54
	☿#♀	1 25
	☽△☿	6 26
	☉△☽	10 15
	♀ ♎	4pm45
	☽✶♅	9 19
	♀∠♅	10 14
4 S	☽⚼♆	3am54
	☽⚼♃	7 7
	☽☍♄	7 27
5 Su	☽∠♅	2am39
	☽□♀	5 42
	☽⚺♂	6 30
	☽✶♇	8 20
	☽△♆	9 3
	♃∠♄	11 9
	☉☌☿	12pm31
	☽△♃	12 35
	♀△♂	2 15
6 M	☉□☽	1am20
	☽□☿	2 13
	☽⚺♅	7 7
	♀⚺♇	8 44
	☽∠♂	10 54
	☽∠♇	12pm35
	☽∥♅	2 5
	♀⚺♆	4 16
	☽⚻♄	4 46
7 T	☽✶♂	2pm17
	☿✶♅	3 19
	☽⚺♇	3 52
	☽□♆	4 34
	☽✶♀	6 58
	☽⚼♄	7 58
	☽□♃	8 35
8 W	☽#♃	5am21
	☉∥☿	10 46
	☉✶☽	11 46
	☽☌♅	1pm 7
	☽#♆	3 34
	♀⚺♃	3 40
	☽✶☿	4 7
	☿⚼♂	8 28
	☽△♄	10 11
	☽∠♀	11 38
9 Th	☉✶♅	7am26
	☿∠♇	8 59
	☉∠☽	3pm12
	☽□♂	6 4
	☽#☿	6 17
	☽☌♇	7 32
	☽✶♆	8 13
	☉#☽	8 42
	☽∠☿	8 55
10 F	☽✶♃	0am36
	☽⚺♀	3 10
	♂SR	9 50
	☽⚺♅	3pm28
	☉⚺☽	5 41
	☽#♀	6 23
	☿✶♄	8 7
	☽∠♆	8 51
11 S	☽□♄	0am 8
	☽⚺☿	0 37
	☽∠♃	1 25
	☉⚼♂	8 43
	☽∠♅	3pm40
	☽△♂	6 45
	☽∥♀	7 3
	☽⚺♇	8 16
	☽⚺♆	8 57
12 Su	☽⚺♃	1am43
	☉∠♇	7 49
	☽☌♀	7 51
	☽✶♅	3pm30
	☽⚼♂	6 28
	☉∥☽	7 14
	☽∠♇	8 3
	☉☌☽	8 52
13 M	☽✶♄	0am 4
	☽∥☿	5 15
	☽☌☿	6 10
	☽∥♆	4pm49
	☽⚻♂	6 4
	☽✶♇	7 46
	☽☌♆	8 29
	☽∠♄	11 52
14 T	☽☌♃	1am48
	☽∥♃	4 33
	☽⚺♀	11 33
	☽□♅	3pm 6
	☉⚺☽	11 48
	☽⚺♄	11 55
15 W	☉✶♄	1am34
	☽#♅	11 32
	☽⚺☿	11 51
	☽∠♀	1pm54
	☽☍♂	5 57
	☽□♇	7 59
	☽⚺♆	8 46
16 Th	☉∠☽	1am57
	☽⚺♃	2 53
	☿∥♆	2 56
	♀✶♅	7 15
	☿ ♏	8 52
	☽∠☿	3pm39
	☽△♅	4 10
	☽✶♀	5 0
	☽∠♆	9 46
17 F	☽☌♄	1am35
	☽∠♃	4 23
	☉✶☽	4 56
	♀⚼♂	10 29
	☿⚻♂	4pm45
	☽⚼♅	5 45
	☽⚻♂	8 4
	☽✶☿	8 32
	☽△♇	10 40
	☽✶♆	11 33
18 S	☽✶♃	6am46
	♀∠♇	2pm40
	☿✶♇	3 15
	☽⚻♅	8 14
	☽⚼♂	10 20
	☿☌♆	11 14
19 Su	☽⚼♇	1am19
	☽□♀	2 24
	☽#♅	3 42
	☽⚺♄	6 32
	☿∥♃	9 44
	☉□☽	2pm 7
20 M	☽△♂	1am29
	☽⚻♇	4 54
	☽□♆	5 54
	☽∥☿	7 20
	☽□☿	10 7
	☽∠♄	10 26
	☽∥♃	11 34
	☿∠♄	12pm45
	☽□♃	2 25
21 T	♀✶♄	0am59
	☽☍♅	4 0
	☽∥♆	4 44
	☉∥☽	10 12
	☽✶♄	3pm14
	☽△♀	4 43
22 W	☿☌♃	1am59
	☉△☽	3 54
	☽∥♀	5 18
	☽□♂	10 12
	☽☍♇	2pm39
	☽△♆	3 47
23 Th	☽⚼♀	1am30
	☽△♃	1 38
	☽△☿	4 37
	☉⚼☽	12pm12
	☉∥♆	2 31
	☽⚻♅	2 57
	☽⚼♆	9 44
	☉ ♏	10 12
24 F	☽□♄	2am56
	☽⚼♃	8 11
	☽⚻♀	11 1
	☽⚼☿	3pm 8
	☿#♅	6 23
	☉⚻☽	9 6
	☽✶♂	9 10
	☽⚼♅	9 12
	☉⚻♂	9 41
25 S	☽⚻♇	2am49
	☽⚻♆	4 5
	☽⚻♃	3pm 7
26 Su	☽⚻☿	2am 4
	☽∠♂	3 3
	☽△♅	3 42
	☽⚼♇	9 21
	☿□♅	2pm59
	☽△♄	4 11
27 M	☽#♀	3am16
	☽☍♀	7 9
	☽⚺♂	8 58
	☽#♆	12pm48
	☉☍☽	3 41
	☽△♇	3 55
	♀ ♏	4 27
	☽☍♆	5 16
	☉✶♇	6 23
	♀⚻♂	9 49
	☽⚼♄	10 56
28 T	☉#☽	0am57
	☽☍♃	5 16
	☉☌♆	10 56
	☽#♃	11 31
	☽□♅	4pm47
	☽☍☿	11 54
29 W	♂ ♉	0am 1
	☽⚻♄	5 32
	☽∥♅	3pm54
	☽☌♂	8 23
	♀∥♆	9 42
30 Th	☽⚻♀	2am57
	☽□♇	4 36
	☽⚻♆	6 1
	☿#♂	7 25
	☉⚻☽	9 46
	☽⚻♃	6pm43
	♀✶♇	6 50
	☿⚺♄	11 38
31 F	☽✶♅	4am59
	♀☌♆	9 0
	☽⚼♆	11 52
	☽⚼♀	12pm12
	☉∠♄	1 21
	☽☍♄	5 46
	☉⚼☽	6 8
	☽⚻☿	8 5

Diurnal Motion Logarithms, 0 to 24 Hours/Degrees

HOURS OR DEGREES

MINUTES OF TIME OR ARC	0	1	2	3	4	5	6	7	8	9	10	11	12	13	14	15	16	17	18	19	20	21	22	23	MINUTES OF TIME OR ARC
0	INFINITE	1.38021	1.07918	.90309	.77815	.68124	.60206	.53511	.47712	.42597	.38021	.33882	.30103	.26627	.23408	.20412	.17609	.14976	.12494	.10146	.07918	.05799	.03779	.01848	0
1	3.15836	1.37303	1.07558	.90068	.77635	.67980	.60086	.53408	.47622	.42517	.37949	.33816	.30043	.26571	.23357	.20364	.17564	.14934	.12454	.10108	.07882	.05765	.03746	.01817	1
2	2.85733	1.36597	1.07200	.89829	.77455	.67836	.59965	.53305	.47532	.42436	.37877	.33750	.29983	.26516	.23305	.20316	.17519	.14891	.12414	.10070	.07846	.05730	.03713	.01785	2
3	2.68124	1.35902	1.06846	.89591	.77276	.67692	.59846	.53202	.47442	.42356	.37805	.33685	.29922	.26460	.23253	.20267	.17474	.14849	.12373	.10032	.07810	.05696	.03680	.01754	3
4	2.55630	1.35218	1.06494	.89354	.77097	.67549	.59726	.53100	.47352	.42276	.37733	.33619	.29862	.26405	.23202	.20219	.17429	.14806	.12333	.09994	.07774	.05662	.03647	.01723	4
5	2.45939	1.34545	1.06145	.89119	.76920	.67406	.59607	.52997	.47262	.42197	.37661	.33554	.29802	.26349	.23151	.20171	.17384	.14764	.12293	.09956	.07738	.05627	.03615	.01691	5
6	2.38021	1.33882	1.05799	.88885	.76743	.67264	.59488	.52895	.47173	.42117	.37589	.33489	.29743	.26294	.23099	.20123	.17339	.14722	.12253	.09918	.07702	.05593	.03582	.01660	6
7	2.31326	1.33229	1.05456	.88652	.76567	.67122	.59370	.52793	.47083	.42038	.37517	.33424	.29683	.26239	.23048	.20076	.17294	.14679	.12213	.09880	.07666	.05559	.03549	.01629	7
8	2.25527	1.32585	1.05115	.88420	.76391	.66981	.59251	.52692	.46994	.41958	.37446	.33359	.29623	.26184	.22997	.20028	.17249	.14637	.12173	.09842	.07630	.05524	.03516	.01597	8
9	2.20412	1.31951	1.04777	.88190	.76216	.66840	.59134	.52591	.46905	.41879	.37375	.33294	.29563	.26129	.22945	.19980	.17204	.14595	.12133	.09804	.07594	.05490	.03484	.01566	9
10	2.15836	1.31326	1.04442	.87961	.76042	.66700	.59016	.52489	.46817	.41800	.37303	.33229	.29504	.26074	.22894	.19932	.17159	.14553	.12094	.09766	.07558	.05456	.03451	.01535	10
11	2.11697	1.30710	1.04109	.87733	.75869	.66560	.58899	.52389	.46728	.41721	.37232	.33164	.29445	.26019	.22843	.19884	.17114	.14510	.12054	.09729	.07522	.05422	.03418	.01504	11
12	2.07918	1.30103	1.03779	.87506	.75696	.66421	.58782	.52288	.46640	.41642	.37161	.33099	.29385	.25964	.22792	.19837	.17070	.14468	.12014	.09691	.07486	.05388	.03386	.01472	12
13	2.04442	1.29504	1.03451	.87281	.75524	.66282	.58665	.52187	.46552	.41564	.37090	.33035	.29326	.25909	.22741	.19789	.17025	.14426	.11974	.09653	.07450	.05353	.03353	.01441	13
14	2.01223	1.28913	1.03126	.87056	.75353	.66143	.58549	.52087	.46464	.41485	.37019	.32970	.29267	.25854	.22690	.19742	.16980	.14384	.11935	.09616	.07414	.05319	.03321	.01410	14
15	1.98227	1.28330	1.02803	.86833	.75182	.66005	.58433	.51987	.46376	.41407	.36949	.32906	.29208	.25800	.22640	.19694	.16936	.14342	.11895	.09578	.07379	.05285	.03288	.01379	15
16	1.95424	1.27755	1.02482	.86611	.75012	.65868	.58317	.51888	.46288	.41329	.36878	.32842	.29148	.25745	.22589	.19647	.16891	.14300	.11855	.09540	.07343	.05251	.03256	.01348	16
17	1.92791	1.27187	1.02164	.86390	.74843	.65730	.58202	.51788	.46201	.41251	.36808	.32777	.29090	.25690	.22538	.19599	.16847	.14258	.11816	.09503	.07307	.05217	.03223	.01317	17
18	1.90309	1.26627	1.01848	.86170	.74674	.65594	.58087	.51689	.46113	.41173	.36737	.32713	.29031	.25636	.22488	.19552	.16802	.14217	.11776	.09465	.07272	.05183	.03191	.01286	18
19	1.87961	1.26074	1.01535	.85951	.74506	.65457	.57972	.51590	.46026	.41095	.36667	.32649	.28972	.25582	.22437	.19505	.16758	.14175	.11736	.09428	.07236	.05149	.03158	.01254	19
20	1.85733	1.25527	1.01223	.85733	.74339	.65321	.57858	.51491	.45939	.41017	.36597	.32585	.28913	.25527	.22386	.19457	.16714	.14133	.11697	.09390	.07200	.05115	.03126	.01223	20
21	1.83614	1.24988	1.00914	.85517	.74172	.65186	.57744	.51392	.45852	.40940	.36527	.32522	.28854	.25473	.22336	.19410	.16669	.14091	.11658	.09353	.07165	.05081	.03093	.01192	21
22	1.81594	1.24455	1.00607	.85301	.74006	.65051	.57630	.51294	.45766	.40863	.36457	.32458	.28796	.25419	.22286	.19363	.16625	.14049	.11618	.09316	.07129	.05047	.03061	.01161	22
23	1.79663	1.23928	1.00303	.85087	.73841	.64916	.57516	.51196	.45679	.40785	.36387	.32394	.28737	.25365	.22235	.19316	.16581	.14008	.11579	.09278	.07094	.05014	.03029	.01130	23
24	1.77815	1.23408	1.00000	.84873	.73676	.64782	.57403	.51098	.45593	.40708	.36318	.32331	.28679	.25311	.22185	.19269	.16537	.13966	.11539	.09241	.07058	.04980	.02996	.01100	24
25	1.76042	1.22894	0.99699	.84661	.73512	.64648	.57290	.51000	.45507	.40631	.36248	.32267	.28621	.25257	.22135	.19222	.16493	.13925	.11500	.09204	.07023	.04946	.02964	.01069	25
26	1.74339	1.22386	0.99401	.84450	.73348	.64514	.57178	.50903	.45421	.40555	.36179	.32204	.28562	.25203	.22084	.19175	.16449	.13883	.11461	.09166	.06987	.04912	.02932	.01038	26
27	1.72700	1.21884	0.99105	.84239	.73185	.64381	.57065	.50805	.45335	.40478	.36109	.32141	.28504	.25149	.22034	.19128	.16405	.13842	.11421	.09129	.06952	.04878	.02899	.01007	27
28	1.71120	1.21388	0.98810	.84030	.73023	.64249	.56953	.50708	.45250	.40401	.36040	.32077	.28446	.25095	.21984	.19081	.16361	.13800	.11382	.09092	.06916	.04845	.02867	.00976	28
29	1.69596	1.20897	0.98518	.83822	.72861	.64117	.56841	.50612	.45164	.40325	.35971	.32014	.28388	.25041	.21934	.19035	.16317	.13759	.11343	.09055	.06881	.04811	.02835	.00945	29
30	1.68124	1.20412	0.98227	.83614	.72700	.63985	.56730	.50515	.45079	.40249	.35902	.31951	.28330	.24988	.21884	.18988	.16273	.13717	.11304	.09018	.06846	.04777	.02803	.00914	30
31	1.66700	1.19932	0.97939	.83408	.72539	.63853	.56619	.50419	.44994	.40173	.35833	.31888	.28272	.24934	.21834	.18941	.16229	.13676	.11265	.08981	.06810	.04744	.02771	.00884	31
32	1.65321	1.19457	0.97652	.83203	.72379	.63722	.56508	.50322	.44909	.40097	.35765	.31826	.28214	.24881	.21785	.18895	.16185	.13635	.11226	.08943	.06775	.04710	.02739	.00853	32
33	1.63985	1.18988	0.97367	.82998	.72220	.63592	.56397	.50226	.44825	.40021	.35696	.31763	.28157	.24827	.21735	.18848	.16141	.13593	.11187	.08906	.06740	.04676	.02706	.00822	33
34	1.62688	1.18523	0.97084	.82795	.72061	.63462	.56287	.50131	.44740	.39945	.35627	.31700	.28099	.24774	.21685	.18802	.16098	.13552	.11148	.08869	.06705	.04643	.02674	.00791	34
35	1.61429	1.18064	0.96803	.82592	.71903	.63332	.56177	.50035	.44656	.39869	.35559	.31638	.28042	.24720	.21635	.18755	.16054	.13511	.11109	.08832	.06670	.04609	.02642	.00761	35
36	1.60206	1.17609	0.96524	.82391	.71745	.63202	.56067	.49940	.44571	.39794	.35491	.31575	.27984	.24667	.21586	.18709	.16010	.13470	.11070	.08796	.06634	.04576	.02610	.00730	36
37	1.59016	1.17159	0.96246	.82190	.71588	.63073	.55957	.49845	.44487	.39719	.35422	.31513	.27927	.24614	.21536	.18662	.15967	.13429	.11031	.08759	.06599	.04542	.02578	.00699	37
38	1.57858	1.16714	0.95971	.81991	.71432	.62945	.55848	.49750	.44403	.39643	.35354	.31451	.27869	.24561	.21487	.18616	.15923	.13388	.10992	.08722	.06564	.04509	.02546	.00669	38
39	1.56730	1.16273	0.95697	.81792	.71276	.62816	.55739	.49655	.44320	.39568	.35286	.31389	.27812	.24508	.21437	.18570	.15880	.13347	.10953	.08685	.06529	.04475	.02514	.00638	39
40	1.55630	1.15836	0.95424	.81594	.71120	.62688	.55630	.49560	.44236	.39493	.35218	.31326	.27755	.24455	.21388	.18523	.15836	.13306	.10914	.08648	.06494	.04442	.02482	.00607	40
41	1.54558	1.15404	0.95154	.81397	.70966	.62561	.55522	.49466	.44152	.39419	.35150	.31264	.27698	.24402	.21339	.18477	.15793	.13265	.10876	.08611	.06459	.04409	.02450	.00577	41
42	1.53511	1.14976	0.94885	.81201	.70811	.62434	.55414	.49372	.44069	.39344	.35083	.31203	.27641	.24349	.21289	.18431	.15749	.13224	.10837	.08575	.06424	.04375	.02419	.00546	42
43	1.52489	1.14553	0.94617	.81006	.70658	.62307	.55306	.49278	.43986	.39269	.35015	.31141	.27584	.24296	.21240	.18385	.15706	.13183	.10798	.08538	.06389	.04342	.02387	.00516	43
44	1.51491	1.14133	0.94352	.80811	.70504	.62180	.55198	.49184	.43903	.39195	.34948	.31079	.27527	.24244	.21191	.18339	.15663	.13142	.10760	.08501	.06354	.04308	.02355	.00485	44
45	1.50515	1.13717	0.94088	.80618	.70352	.62054	.55091	.49091	.43820	.39121	.34880	.31017	.27470	.24191	.21142	.18293	.15620	.13101	.10721	.08464	.06319	.04275	.02323	.00455	45
46	1.49560	1.13306	0.93825	.80425	.70200	.61929	.54984	.48998	.43738	.39046	.34813	.30956	.27413	.24138	.21093	.18247	.15576	.13061	.10682	.08428	.06284	.04242	.02291	.00424	46
47	1.48626	1.12898	0.93565	.80234	.70048	.61803	.54877	.48905	.43655	.38972	.34746	.30894	.27357	.24086	.21044	.18201	.15533	.13020	.10644	.08391	.06250	.04209	.02259	.00394	47
48	1.47712	1.12494	0.93305	.80043	.69897	.61678	.54770	.48812	.43573	.38899	.34679	.30833	.27300	.24033	.20995	.18155	.15490	.12979	.10605	.08355	.06215	.04175	.02228	.00363	48
49	1.46817	1.12094	0.93048	.79853	.69746	.61554	.54664	.48719	.43491	.38825	.34612	.30772	.27244	.23981	.20946	.18110	.15447	.12938	.10567	.08318	.06180	.04142	.02196	.00333	49
50	1.45939	1.11697	0.92791	.79663	.69596	.61429	.54558	.48626	.43409	.38751	.34545	.30710	.27187	.23928	.20897	.18064	.15404	.12898	.10528	.08282	.06145	.04109	.02164	.00303	50
51	1.45079	1.11304	0.92537	.79475	.69447	.61306	.54452	.48534	.43327	.38678	.34478	.30649	.27131	.23876	.20848	.18018	.15361	.12857	.10490	.08245	.06111	.04076	.02133	.00272	51
52	1.44236	1.10914	0.92283	.79287	.69298	.61182	.54347	.48442	.43245	.38604	.34411	.30588	.27075	.23824	.20800	.17973	.15318	.12817	.10452	.08209	.06076	.04043	.02101	.00242	52
53	1.43409	1.10528	0.92032	.79101	.69149	.61059	.54241	.48350	.43164	.38531	.34345	.30527	.27018	.23772	.20751	.17927	.15275	.12776	.10413	.08172	.06041	.04010	.02069	.00212	53
54	1.42597	1.10146	0.91781	.78915	.69002	.60936	.54136	.48258	.43082	.38458	.34278	.30466	.26962	.23720	.20702	.17881	.15232	.12736	.10375	.08136	.06006	.03977	.02038	.00181	54
55	1.41800	1.09766	0.91532	.78729	.68854	.60813	.54031	.48167	.43001	.38385	.34212	.30406	.26906	.23668	.20654	.17836	.15190	.12695	.10337	.08099	.05972	.03944	.02006	.00151	55
56	1.41017	1.09390	0.91285	.78545	.68707	.60691	.53927	.48076	.42920	.38312	.34146	.30345	.26850	.23616	.20605	.17790	.15147	.12655	.10298	.08063	.05937	.03911	.01974	.00121	56
57	1.40249	1.09018	0.91039	.78361	.68561	.60569	.53823	.47984	.42839	.38239	.34080	.30284	.26794	.23564	.20557	.17745	.15104	.12615	.10260	.08027	.05903	.03878	.01943	.00091	57
58	1.39493	1.08648	0.90794	.78179	.68415	.60448	.53719	.47893	.42758	.38166	.34014	.30224	.26738	.23512	.20509	.17700	.15061	.12574	.10222	.07991	.05868	.03845	.01911	.00060	58
59	1.38751	1.08282	0.90551	.77996	.68269	.60327	.53615	.47803	.42677	.38094	.33948	.30163	.26683	.23460	.20460	.17654	.15019	.12534	.10184	.07954	.05834	.03812	.01880	.00030	59
60	1.38021	1.07918	0.90309	.77815	.68124	.60206	.53511	.47712	.42597	.38021	.33882	.30103	.26627	.23408	.20412	.17609	.14976	.12494	.10146	.07918	.05799	.03779	.01848	.00000	60